First Edition
Blue Book of
AR-15s & Variations

by S.P. Fjestad
Edited by John B. Allen & Thomas A. Toupin

$29.95 - Standard Softcover Edition

$19.95 - Online Subscription
(includes complete and searchable AR-15 database with digital images – updated monthly)

PUBLISHER'S NOTE, COPYRIGHT

First Edition *Blue Book of AR-15s & Variations*

Publisher's Note:

This book is the result of nonstop and continuous firearms research obtained by attending and/or participating in trade shows, gun shows, auctions, and also communicating with contributing editors, gun dealers, collectors, company historians, and other knowledgeable industry professionals worldwide each year. This book represents an analysis of information and prices for which AR-15 style carbines, rifles, pistols, and shotguns have actually been selling for during this time period at an average retail level. Although every reasonable effort has been made to compile an accurate and reliable guide, gun prices may vary significantly (especially auction prices) depending on such factors as the locality of the sale, the number of sales we were able to consider, and economic conditions. Accordingly, no representation can be made that the guns listed may be bought or sold at prices indicated, nor shall the author or publisher be responsible for any error made in compiling and recording such prices and related information.

Content Disclaimer:

This book does not contain information or values on machine guns, NFA classified firearms, or AR-15 style firearms accessories (i.e., scopes, optics, furniture, suppressor/silencers, etc.).

All Rights Reserved
Copyright 2018
Blue Book Publications, Inc.
8009 34th Avenue South, Suite 250
Minneapolis, MN 55425 U.S.A.
GPS Coordinates: N44° 51 28.44, W93° 13.1709

Customer Service: 800-877-4867, ext. 3 (domestic only)
Phone No.: 952-854-5229
Fax No.: 952-853-1486
General Email: support@bluebookinc.com
Website: BlueBookOfGunValues.com

Published and printed in the United States of America

ISBN 10: 1-947314-08-4
ISBN 13: 978-1-947314-08-5

Library of Congress ISSN number – 2639-5894

No part of this publication may be reproduced in any form whatsoever, by photograph, mimeograph, fax transmission or any other mechanical or electronic means. Nor can it be broadcast or transmitted, by translation into any language, nor by electronic recording or otherwise, without the express written permission from the publisher – except by a reviewer, who may quote brief passages for critical articles and/or reviews.

The percentage breakdown by firearms condition factor with respective values per condition and the *Photo Percentage Grading System*™ (PPGS) are copyrighted by Blue Book Publications, Inc. Any unauthorized usage of these systems for the evaluation of firearms values and color photo percentage breakdown is expressly forbidden by the publisher.

TABLE OF CONTENTS

Title Page 1

Publisher's Note, Copyright 2

Table of Contents 3

General Information 4

Meet the Staff 5

Acknowledgements, Credits, About the Cover 6

Foreword by S.P. Fjestad 7

AMERICA'S RIFLE - THE AR-15 & VARIATIONS
   Its Turbulent History & Unpredictable Future by S.P. Fjestad 8-13

How to Use This Book 14-15

Anatomy of an AR-15 Rifle/Carbine 16

Anatomy of an AR-15 Pistol & Shotgun 17

AR-15 Terminology Pictured & Described 18-28
   AR-15 Gas Operating Systems & Components 18-19
   AR-15 Handguard Styles & Mounting Platforms 20
   AR-15 Popular Accessory Mounting Options 20-21
   AR-15 Muzzle Devices 22
   AR-15 Stocks, Braces & Buffer Tubes 23-24
   AR-15 Triggers 25
   AR-15 Sights & Optics 26-28
   AR-15 Parts Diagrams 29-31

Glossary 32-43

Abbreviations 44-45

AR-15 Calibers and Dangerous Combinations 46

AR-15 Grading Criteria - 47

PPGS Conversion Guidelines/NRA Condition Standards 48

NRA Membership 148

A-Z Sections 49-378

AR-15 Current Manufacturers/Trademark Index 379-381

Index 382-384

GENERAL INFORMATION

While many of you have probably dealt with our company for years, it may be helpful for you to know a little bit more about our operation, including information on how to contact us regarding our various titles and other informational services.

Blue Book Publications, Inc.
8009 34th Avenue South, Suite 250
Minneapolis, MN 55425 USA
GPS Coordinates: N44° 51 28.44, W93° 13.1709

Phone: 952-854-5229 • Customer Service (domestic and Canada): 800-877-4867
Fax: 952-853-1486 (available 24 hours a day)
Website: BlueBookOfGunValues.com

General Email: support@bluebookinc.com - we check our email at 9am, 12pm, and 4pm M - F (excluding major U.S. holidays). Please refer to individual email addresses listed below with phone extension numbers.

To find out the latest information on our products, including availability and pricing, consumer related services, and up-to-date industry information (blogs, trade show recaps with photos/captions, upcoming events, feature articles, etc.), please check our website, as it is updated on a regular basis. Surf us - you'll have fun!

Since our phone system is equipped with voice mail, you may also wish to know extension numbers, which have been provided below:

Ext. 1000 - Beth Schreiber	(beths@bluebookinc.com)	Ext. 1800 - Tom Stock	(toms@bluebookinc.com)
Ext. 1200 – John Andraschko	(johnand@bluebookinc.com)	Ext. 1900 – Sarah Peterson	(sarahs@bluebookinc.com)
Ext. 1300 - S.P. Fjestad	(stevef@bluebookinc.com)	Ext. 2000 – Tom Toupin	(tomt@bluebookinc.com)
Ext. 1400 – Kayla McCarthy	(kaylam@bluebookinc.com)	Ext. 2200 – Alexandra Sitzman	(alexs@bluebookinc.com)
Ext. 1500 - Clint Schmidt	(clints@bluebookinc.com)	Lisa Beuning	(lisab@bluebookinc.com)
Ext. 1600 - John Allen	(johna@bluebookinc.com)		

Office hours are: 8:30am - 5:00pm CST, Monday - Friday.

Additionally, an after-hours message service is available for ordering. All orders are processed within 24 hours of receiving them, assuming payment and order information is correct. Depending on the product, we typically ship UPS, Media Mail, or Priority Mail. Expedited shipping services are also available domestically for an additional charge. Please contact us directly for an expedited shipping quotation.

All correspondence regarding technical information/values on guns or guitars is answered in a FIFO (first in, first out) system. That means that letters, faxes, and emails are answered in the order in which they are received.

Online subscriptions and informational services are available for the following titles: *Blue Book of AR-15s & Variations, Blue Book of Gun Values, Blue Book of Antique American Firearms & Values, Blue Book of Modern Black Powder Arms, Ammo Encyclopedia, American Gunsmiths, Blue Book of Airguns, Blue Book of Electric Guitars, Blue Book of Acoustic Guitars,* and the *Blue Book of Guitar Amplifiers.*

As this edition goes to press, the following titles/products are currently available, unless otherwise specified:

Blue Book of Gun Values by S.P. Fjestad

Ammo Encyclopedia by Michael Bussard

Blue Book Pocket Guide for Beretta Firearms & Values by S.P. Fjestad

Blue Book Pocket Guide for Browning/FN Firearms & Values by S.P. Fjestad

Blue Book Pocket Guide for Colt Dates of Manufacture by R.L. Wilson

Blue Book Pocket Guide for Colt Firearms & Values by S.P. Fjestad

Blue Book Pocket Guide for Remington Firearms & Values by S.P. Fjestad

Blue Book Pocket Guide for Smith & Wesson Firearms & Values by S.P. Fjestad

Blue Book Pocket Guide for Sturm Ruger Firearms & Values by S.P. Fjestad

Blue Book Pocket Guide for Winchester Firearms & Values by S.P. Fjestad

Blue Book of Airguns by Dr. Robert D. Beeman & John B. Allen

Blue Book of Modern Black Powder Arms by John B. Allen

Seven Serpents – The History of Colt's Snake Guns by Gurney Brown

Colt's Python – King of the Seven Serpents by Gurney Brown

The Book of Colt Firearms, 3rd Edition by R.L. Wilson

The Book of Colt Memorabilia by John Ogle

The Book of Colt Memorabilia Pricing Guide by John Ogle

Book of Colt Paper 1834-2011 by John Ogle

L.C. Smith Production Records by Jim Stubbendieck

American Engravers III– Masterpieces in Metal by America's Engraving Artisans by C. Roger Bleile

American Gunsmiths, 2nd Edition by Frank Sellers

Parker Gun Identification & Serialization, compiled by Charlie Price and edited by S.P. Fjestad

Blue Book of Electric Guitars by Zachary R. Fjestad

Blue Book of Acoustic Guitars by Zachary R. Fjestad

Blue Book of Guitar Amplifiers Edited by Ryan Triggs

Blue Book of Guitars DVD-ROM

Blue Book of Guitar Amplifiers CD-ROM

Gibson Flying V by Larry Meiners & Zachary R. Fjestad

Gibson Amplifiers 1933-2008 – 75 Years of the Gold Tone by Wallace Marx Jr.

The Marshall Bluesbreaker – The Story of Marshall's First Combo by John R. Wiley

If you would like to get more information about any of the above publications/products, simply check our websites: bluebookofgunvalues.com and bluebookofguitarvalues.com

We would like to thank all of you for your business in the past – you are the reason we are successful. Our goal remains the same – to give you the best products, the most accurate and up-to-date information for the money, plus the highest level of customer service available in today's marketplace. If something's right, tell the world over time. If something's wrong, please tell us immediately – we'll make it right.

MEET THE STAFF

S.P. Fjestad
Author/Publisher

John B. Allen
Author & Associate Editor Arms Division

Tom Toupin
Sales Manager

Lisa Beuning
Modern Gun Manuscript Supervisor

These are the folks that put this 1st Edition *Blue Book of AR-15s & Variations* together and made it work in various levels. As far as the content team is concerned, never have so few suffered for so long!

Tom Stock
CFO

John Andraschko
Technology Director

Clint H. Schmidt
Art Director

Kayla McCarthy
Antique Manuscript Supervisor

Beth Schreiber
Operations Manager

Alexandra Sitzman
Operations

Sarah Peterson
Web Media Manager/Proofreader

Cassandra Faulkner
Research Coordinator/Proofreader

ACKNOWLEDGEMENTS

The publisher would like to express his thanks to the following people and companies for their contributions in this 1st Edition *Blue Book of AR-15s & Variations*:

Tim Bailey – Bailey & Associates

Pete Brownell – Brownells

Shane Cuperus – FNH USA

Mark Eliason – Windham Weaponry

Dustin Emholtz – Luth-AR, LLC

Tom Gresham – Gun Talk Radio

Steve Hernandez

Michael Kassner

Kane Kennedy – *Davidson's*

Tom Spithaler – Olympic Arms

G. Brad Sullivan

Jim Supica – Director of NRA Museums

CREDITS

Cover Design – Clint H. Schmidt, Thomas A. Toupin, and S.P. Fjestad

Art Director – Clint H. Schmidt

Content Supervisor – Lisa Beuning

Specialized Editorial Content – Thomas A. Toupin

Proofing – Lisa Beuning, Sarah Peterson, Cassandra Faulkner, and John B. Allen

Printing – Bang Printing, located in Brainerd, MN

ABOUT THE FRONT COVER

The front cover features the following: the top gun is a BCM (Bravo Company Manufacturing) Model RECCE-16 KMR-A carbine featuring a 16 in. barrel, Mod 0 buttstock, Mod 3 pistol grip, and KMR Alpha handguard in Dark Bronze finish.

Photo Courtesy of BCM

The gun on the bottom is a Daniel Defense Model DDM4V1 with 16 in. M4 barrel, flash suppressor, DDM4 rail, and DD buttstock with Soft Touch overmolding.

Photo Courtesy of Daniel Defense

ABOUT THE BACK COVER

The back cover highlights an Aero Precision AR-15 pistol based on the M4E1 upper and lower receiver set with the following features: Aero Precision Quantum M-LOK Handguard, SureFire X3000U-B weapon mounted light, Magpul MOE grip, Magpul PMAG 30 Gen M3, Trijicon MRO 1x25MM red dot sight, and Maxim Defense PDW Brace.

Photo courtesy of Maxim Defense

FOREWORD BY S.P. FJESTAD

Never have so few suffered for so long on one project! The main content team (left to right): John B. Allen - Associate Editor, Lisa Beuning - Content Supervisor, S.P. Fjestad - Author/Publisher, and Thomas A. Toupin - Sales Manager/Co-Editor, shown examining one of Tom's custom builds.

Dateline/Deadline: Oct. 9, 2018

Location: BBP HQ, Suite 250, One Appletree Square, Minneapolis, MN

Assignment/Mission: Write up an engaging/edgy Foreword in 45 minutes

You can't make this stuff up – Lisa happened to mention earlier that 17 years ago today she delivered her son, Logan, via a planned C-section, which kind of reminds me of how this whole project went down, especially towards the end.

While it was a planned pregnancy, a lot of unwanted complications happened along the way and at the end, a publishing C-section was also needed to give birth to this 1st Edition *Blue Book of AR-15s & Variations*. In the end, we couldn't even decide on a name!! Hopefully, you'll agree that our new "baby" was worth all the pre-delivery drama.

Throughout the past six months, I've asked a lot of people within the firearms industry to guess at how many current AR-15 trademarks/manufacturers there are. Most answers varied from 30 to 50. When the smoke cleared, and the word processing finally stopped on this 1st Edition, the total was 232 – twenty years ago there were less than 30! This also explains why this A-Z database was so difficult and time-consuming to complete, while making sure that all values were also up-to-date. It also proves why AR-15s have become an industry onto themselves.

Make no mistake about it – the AR-15 had a very rocky start. Between 1957-1963, the nomenclature actually referred to a select-fire machine gun manufactured by both ArmaLite and Colt for military use only. Interest was low and sales were minimal. The U.S. Military completely bungled the testing, and if it hadn't been for Air Force General Curtis LeMay, there might not be an AR-15 civilian model today. It certainly didn't help that the AR-15 civilian sporter was finally released in 1964 at the start of an extremely unpopular Vietnam War. Very few shooters/hunters at the time wanted a dangerous looking military style firearm in their gun cabinets. It became a little more popular in the '70s and finally started taking off in the '80s. And we all know what happened during the past three decades once federal and state legislation started impacting consumer sales. Only today, the U.S. Army announced that it had selected the 6.8 SPC (?) cartridge for its next order of M4A1 carbines! Currently, there are over 10 million AR-15s in circulation in the U.S. alone.

So, here's what you need to know about this book:

- This is the most complete and thorough database ever assembled on AR-15 pistols, rifles, and shotguns.

- It provides the most up-to-date values on all makes/models, including the recent drop on many AR-15 values.

- Remains the only database where proprietary terms and terminology are included within the model descriptions.

- Has morphed more into an encyclopedia than a normal Blue Book because of all the additional color sections up front, including AR-15 anatomies and illustrations with descriptions (see pages 16-31).

- Features the most condensed and complete 8-page editorial ever published on the history and future of the AR-15 and variations.

- This database is also available online, which gives the user a tremendous advantage in searchability by make/model.

Time's almost up! At the end, this project really turned into a team effort, and I would really like to thank John B. Allen, Tom Toupin, Lisa Beuning, Cassandra Faulkner, Sarah Peterson, and our long-suffering art director, Clint Schmidt, for making this book much better during the last two weeks of its pregnancy.

Also, the contributing editors and firearms industry personnel also deserve kudos for the help and support they have provided over the years. We hope you think this new "toddler" was worth all our efforts, and hopefully you can follow its development in future editions.

Sincerely,

S.P. Fjestad
S.P. Fjestad
Author & Publisher

AMERICA'S RIFLE
THE AR-15 & VARIATIONS
ITS TURBULENT HISTORY & UNPREDICTABLE FUTURE
BY S.P. FJESTAD

Marketplace Hurricanes & Storm Surges

Even in the darkest and oftentimes destructive annals of both U.S. military and commercial U.S. small arms history, there can be no greater or more twisted story than what happened initially with the development of the AR-15 and its many variations. It wouldn't surprise me if there have been more words written about the AR-15 than the 10+ million carbines/rifles that have been manufactured and sold in America alone since 1964!

For the rest of this paragraph, think of the AR-15 industry as the Atlantic Ocean. During the 1960s and '70s, this was a very tranquil body of water, and living along the coastline was slow paced and uneventful, almost boring. However, an offshore storm started brewing in approximately 1984, and by 1990, a small hurricane finally reached land. During these turbulent six years, AR-15 MSRs went from $599 to $860 – an increase of over 30%. However, in retrospect, this initial storm seemed to pale in comparison to the major hurricane that hit on Sept. 24, 1994. Looking back, it could have been called Hurricane Crime Bill in weather parlance. A major tidal surge occurred almost immediately, creating unpredictable and high AR-15 prices with market chaos – the Colt AR-15 Sporter Target went from $898 to $1,019 in 12 months. The next devastating storm didn't occur until the Obama Administration took office in 2008, and this category 5 hurricane would prove to be the longest and largest catastrophic weather event ever to hit the east coast. Mother Nature battered and bruised AR-15 values non-stop for eight years. After the storm finally ended, weather experts blamed either new anti-gun legislation or the fear created by potential anti-gun legislation for the runaway demand that created the artificially high prices.

Off to a Rocky Start

The year was 1956. It might be remembered best by Elvis Presley's hip shaking performance on the Ed Sullivan show while grinding out "Hound Dog" and IBM's release of the first computer with an internal hard drive. Tinseltown also released its mega-hit "The Ten Commandments" starring Charleton Heston, who, 42 years later, would become the NRA's first five term president.

On the other side of Hollywood, a small company called ArmaLite was developing some interesting and unique rifle designs. Its chief engineer, Eugene Stoner, was an up and coming small arms inventor, who, along with the other eight ArmaLite employees, were fervently working after hours, trying to develop a working prototype of their newest design, the AR-10 (ArmaLite Rifle). This new lightweight, modular design featured a unique gas operating system, rotating bolt, straight line composite stock, hinged aluminum upper and lower receiver, and non-detachable carry handle that protected the charging lever on the top of the receiver.

The hurry was to get a rifle to Springfield Armory for testing, as the U.S. Army was already well underway evaluating a replacement for the aging M1 Garand.

ArmaLite was a subdivision of Fairchild Engine & Airplane Corporation that worked closely with Lockheed, developing new airplane patents. Working with new aircraft designs manufactured on state-of-the-art CNC machinery, it also had access to the exotic metals and synthetic materials of the time, including titanium, high strength aluminum alloys, and synthetic composites. Having these advanced technological resources at its disposal was extremely beneficial in developing fresh, lightweight firearms designs, which the company then sold to gun companies with large manufacturing capabilities.

In early 1957, the fourth prototype of the AR-10, chambered for the 7.62 NATO cal., finally made a late appearance for testing at the Springfield Armory. Unfortunately, its steel sleeved aluminum barrel, specified by ArmaLite's president, George Sullivan, despite Stoner's staunch objections, burst in the middle of a shooting torture test. While it was immediately replaced by a steel barrel, its reputation was so damaged that the Springfield Armory report concluded not to adopt this unproven design. Instead, the Springfield M14 was chosen as the next U.S. military small arms rifle, and production got underway immediately.

A year later, a deflated ArmaLite completed approximately fifty

Original ArmaLite AR-10 select fire machine gun in 7.62 NATO cal. A hallmark feature of this model is the charging handle that protrudes from the top of the receiver, thus explaining the protective carry handle with built-in rear sight. It's marked "Hollywood, Calif. U.S.A." Note large perforated muzzle brake.

AR-10s in its small workshop, as demonstrators for sales agents, including the famous international arms dealer, Sam Cummings. These are referred to as the "Hollywood" models, and some of them had improperly machined barrel extensions that created testing problems later. Unfortunately, this small batch of AR-10s still in development did not generate any military interest or sales. With no potential military contracts in sight, ArmaLite sold an exclusive five-year manufacturing licensing agreement to the large Dutch arms company, Artillery Inrichtingen.

Later in 1957, Fairchild decided to scale down its final AR-10 prototype in response to the U.S. Army's request to develop a new lightweight select fire rifle, based on a smaller .223 caliber. This was mostly due to the Army no longer being satisfied with the performance of the M1/M2 carbines in .30 Carbine cal. Early

AMERICA'S RIFLE - THE AR-15 & VARIATIONS BY S.P. FJESTAD, CONT.

Scanned image taken from the Remington Center Fire Rifle Cartridges section of its 1966 catalog. Originally designed as a military cartridge, the .223 Rem. cal. was not popular during the 1960s as a commercial caliber since the Colt AR-15 was the only semi-auto rifle chambered for it until 1969.

battlefield reports from the jungles of Vietnam indicated the Russian AK-47 was outperforming the much heavier M14, which was not controllable in full auto, plus it limited the amount of additional ammo soldiers needed for extended firefights. A year later, ArmaLite delivered ten select fire AR-15s with one hundred 25 shot mags. for testing. Even though the extensive testing proved the AR-15 was more reliable than the M14, the stubborn Army Chief of Staff stood by the M14 as the Army's choice.

Now more than disappointed and frustrated by the lack of acceptance, with still no forthcoming military contracts, the strapped for cash ArmaLite sold its manufacturing rights trademarks for both the AR-10 and the AR-15 to Colt's Patent Fire Arms Manufacturing Company in late 1959.

1960 – A New Beginning

Colt's engineers immediately started to modify ArmaLite's existing AR-15 design, most notably moving the vertical charging handle from the top of the receiver to a more convenient pull type handle located on the back of the receiver. Utilizing these design improvements, Colt rebranded the rifle as the Colt-ArmaLite AR-15 and offered it in select fire operation only for potential military contracts. Malaysia became the first country to give Colt a contract and later that year, Colt manufactured its first batch of 300 branded Colt-ArmaLite AR-15s. Surprisingly, Colt did not offer its new rifle in a semi-auto version to civilians because it didn't think there would be much consumer interest in such a radical looking modern sporting rifle the press would later refer to as an "assault rifle".

Eugene Stoner, after overseeing ArmaLite's survival rifle project, the AR-7, saw a much better career opportunity with Colt, and left ArmaLite in 1961 to help with continued AR-15 development. During the early '60s, the U.S. military's botched testing and evaluation procedures easily resulted in the most bungled testing of a small arms design in U.S. history. Between U.S. Ordnance Corp.'s corruption and ineptitude, military infighting, Congressional bureaucracy and inquiries, plus almost legendary political foot dragging, years went by before major decisions were made on whether or not to adopt the AR-15. Politicians on Capitol Hill were also worried and concerned about the large amount of money needed to fund these potentially large and lucrative AR-15 contracts. Especially since at the time, there was an enormous surplus of M2 carbines and ammunition left over from World War II and Korea, accounting for millions in unwanted ordnance.

With elections coming up, no senators or congressmen wanted to be on the record as having wasted money because of military pressure for a new, questionable rifle to be used in an already unpopular Vietnam War. Mostly through the persistent efforts of Air Force General Curtis LeMay, who was the military's staunchest supporter of the AR-15 at the time, an Air Force contract was finally awarded to Colt for 8,500 ArmaLite AR-15s in 1961. The Army brass remained indecisive, but eventually other small Air Force and Army contracts followed. Maybe the best story from this entire period was when the president of Fairchild celebrated his birthday with his good friend LeMay and let him shoot the select fire ArmaLite AR-15 at some watermelons at around 100 yards. LeMay was immediately impressed with the smooth functioning of this new lightweight design and wondered why he hadn't been able to evaluate one earlier.

Colt Hits the Jackpot!

Finally, in 1963, the Air Force standardized the select fire AR-15 for the newly designated M16 rifle in 5.56 cal. This would be the end of the ArmaLite AR-15 model designation available in select fire.

Now that Colt was flush with military contract money, maintaining the substantially increased M16 production to Mil-Spec standards became a major problem, and it took years for the bugs and quality control to finally make the M16 a reliable military rifle in the harsh battle conditions in Vietnam.

While the M16 took off rapidly with additional contracts totaling over $45 million by 1964, the potential consumer segment had not been addressed until late 1963. Originally designed as a military caliber, the .223 Rem./5.56mm cal. hadn't been offered as a commercial cartridge. That finally changed when Colt introduced the first semi-auto version of the AR-15 in late 1963 and named it the Comanche. It was short-lived however, since another rival company had already trademarked that name on one of its bolt action rifles. The name was changed to the Model AR-15 Sporter and it had an original retail price of $189.50 – serialization started at SP00001. As a comparison, Colt's Python and the SAA revolver each had an MSR of $125. Sales for this new AR-15 Sporter chambered in the new .223 Rem. cal. were very sluggish.

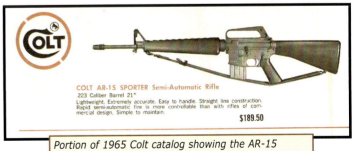

Portion of 1965 Colt catalog showing the AR-15 Sporter with an MSR of $189.50!

Despite Colt's advertising that its Washington D.C. representative shot a polar bear, Dahl sheep, and several species of East African plains game with his AR-15, the public didn't buy this hunting hype. It certainly didn't help that the rifle was released at the start of an extremely unpopular Vietnam War where the almost identical, sinister looking M16 was just being introduced. The AR-15 sporting rifle had become so unpopular it was removed from Colt's catalog during 1968. Very few shooters/hunters at the time wanted a "dangerous" looking military style firearm in their gun cabinets, which resulted in only 16,000 rifles being sold by the end of 1970. As a comparison, Remington measured its sales of sporting rifles in the hundreds of thousands during the same time period. Interestingly, the AR-15 was the only semi-auto sporting rifle chambered for the .223 Rem. cartridge during the 1960s, until ArmaLite released the AR-180 in 1969. Maybe part of the gun's stigma is that this caliber was originally developed for military application, and many hunters thought it wasn't adequate for hunting.

Getting Through the Sluggish '70s

Throughout the early 1970s, sales of the AR-15 did not improve, but Colt really didn't care at the time, because it was still desperately trying to fulfill military contracts. By 1975, the retail had gone up to $234.95. During 1977, Colt's patent rights had expired on the AR-15 design originally purchased from ArmaLite 18 years earlier, but nobody seemed to care because this tactical looking modern sporting rifle was still not very popular with consumers. Between 1970 and 1975, Colt sold approximately 40,000 AR-15s and the second half of the decade, sales had increased to almost 60,000 units. This was partially due to many U.S. soldiers coming home after Vietnam and wanting the same type of rifle they had carried in the Asian jungles. Most American shooters still didn't agree.

AR-15 ad clipped out of a 1977 issue of Shotgun News. As a comparison, the Colt MSR on a Python was $290, and the SAA listed for $255. Note the 500 rounds of ammo for $97.50!

Feast or Famine – The Crazy 1980s

The 1980s were mostly good years for Colt, but the coming end of the Cold War would change things quickly. During 1980, Colt sold 23,400 AR-15s – this was the highest annual total since the rifle was introduced. Sales continued to increase through 1982, then fell off to 6,800 by 1984. Colt now had some competition in the .223 Rem. cal. semi-auto configuration, including the Ruger Ranch Rifle, which partly explains the decline in sales.

Colt's business strategy at the time was to leave civilian firearms innovation to their competitors, assuming that its handgun business would survive on their traditional revolver and M1911 designs. Instead, Colt focused on their existing military contracts. This strategy proved to be an epic failure for Colt through a series of catastrophic events. In 1984, the U.S. military announced the Beretta 92F in 9mm Para. cal. would replace Colt's venerable M1911. This was not much of a loss for Colt's business, as the M1911A1 military production had stopped in 1945. However, the military side of Colt's business was still booming because new U.S. military contracts created a major demand for more upgraded M16s, plus the M16A2 model had just been adopted.

Unfortunately during 1985, Colt's work force, members of the United Auto Workers, went on strike for higher wages. The strike would ultimately last for five years and was one of the longest-running and most bitter labor strikes in American history. With replacement workers now taking over the manufacturing process, the quality of Colt's firearms began to decline rapidly. Things began to spiral downward in a hurry, and during the height of the strike, Colt's production of AR-15s plummeted from approximately 18,400 to only 432 one year later!

Maybe the biggest news of the decade regarding the AR-15 and variations was that in 1988, dissatisfied with Colt's production quality, the U.S. military awarded the contract for future M16 production to Fabrique Nationale (FN). Commercial sales now became very important to help Colt through this major drop in military revenue. The company quickly found out that the transition from military to commercial sales couldn't be reversed overnight.

During 1989, ending this roller coaster decade, George H.W. Bush enacted the "Assault Weapons Ban," which banned the importation of semi-auto rifles made overseas, particularly in China. This included ARs, SKSs, AK47s, and any semi-auto rifle that had a 30-shot mag. The bill did not affect domestic manufacturing or previous private ownership but did effectively ban over 700,000 guns scheduled to be imported into the U.S. during 1990.

The 1990s – The Clinton Years, Crime, & The Crime Bill

During the 1990s, sales of AR-15 rifles had increased dramatically, partly as a result of the flat-top upper receiver, which allowed scopes and other sighting devices to be easily mounted, as well as new features such as free floating handguards that increased accuracy.

Unfortunately, during the early 1990s, there were a number of shootings and standoffs, some of which involved the AR-15. Maybe two of the biggest and the most publicized were the siege of the Branch Davidian compound in Waco, TX and the Ruby Ridge standoff in Idaho. Bill Clinton had been elected President in 1992 and was not known as a supporter of the 2nd Amendment. The same year, Colt's Manufacturing Company entered Chapter 11 bankruptcy hearings followed by a period of extended litigation.

Largely due to Clinton's and other Democrat anti-gun efforts, on September 24, 1994, what is now known as the Crime Bill was enacted. It immediately affected many popular AR-15 features such as flash hiders, bayonet lugs, folding/collapsible stocks, pistol grips, and high capacity (over 10 shots) magazines were banned. This law created a "high tide" on not just AR-15s, but other popular tactical style carbines/rifles as well, including AK-47 semi-autos. While the Crime Bill did not prevent previous private ownership (non-retroactive) of

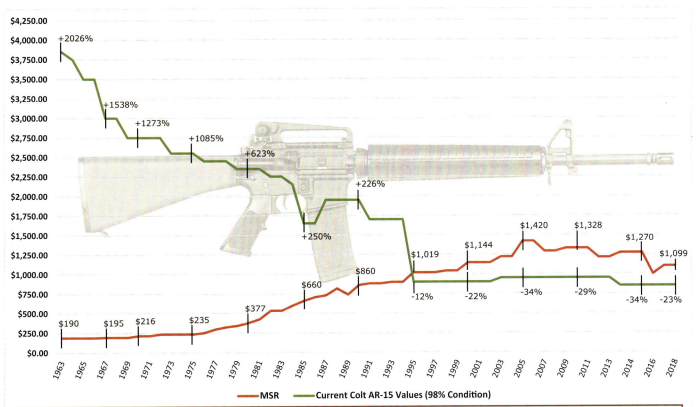

The two colored lines on this graph show a comparison of Colt's Manufacturer's Suggested Retail prices (MSR) for their commercially sold AR-15s and their current retail values in the secondary market from 1963-2018. Also shown are some percentages of value increase or decrease throughout the same time frame. Since no one variation/model was produced from the beginning to date, standard entry-level production models were selected with similar configurations and features.

rifles with these features, it did effectively ban any future manufacture of rifles domestically for ten years. One company's answer to this new law was Olympic Arms, which released the PCR, or "Politically Correct Rifle", with features that complied with the Crime Bill.

By the end of the '90s, 32 companies were making AR-15 clones and sales were improving annually. Of note is that Colt, now out of bankruptcy, received another military contract to supply 19,000 M16s (M4 carbine variant) to the U.S. Army and Special Forces Command.

The New Millennium - A Superstar Emerges

Early in the new millennium, dramatic increases in AR-15 sales really began to change the landscape of the firearms marketplace – the tail now started wagging the dog. Domestic sales were as follows by years: 2000 – approx. 85,000 units, 2001 – approx. 58,500 units, 2002 – approx. 86,000 units, 2003 – 103,000 units (the first time AR production had broken 100,000), 2004 – 95,000 units, 2005 – 125,000 units, 2006 – 173,500 units, 2007 – 220,000 units, 2008 (Obama gets elected) – 321,000 units, 2009 – 433,000 units, 2010 – 248,000 units, 2011 – 458,000 units, 2012 (Obama re-elected) – 992,000 units, 2013 – 1,280,000 units, 2014 – 841,000.

On September 24, 2004, the 10-year Crime Bill sunsetted, and will be remembered in the history books as doing very little to prevent or stop crime.

One of the biggest reasons for the huge increase in sales was because many new millennial shooters were embracing the AR-15's modular weapons system design. Back in the 1960s and '70s, the AR-15 Sporters were almost impossible to accessorize and owners had to accept the guns for what they were in their factory configuration, with almost no modifications being possible. Once the flat-top upper receivers were introduced with Picatinny rails, followed by rail assemblies on the forearm, adjustable stocks, and an ever-increasing variety of finishes, including many camo options, these new consumers could basically custom build a gun to the specifications and features they wanted.

However, everything changed directly after the Sandy Hook elementary school shooting in Newtown, CT on December 14, 2012. By the following Monday, gun speculators were already panic buying virtually any AR-15 on a dealer's rack, gladly paying 15%-30% above retail, and then putting it on their credit cards, convinced that the value could only go up. This "herd of buffalo" was already charging hard, but it quickly became a full-blown stampede that kept running non-stop for another four years. The AR-15 configuration suddenly became the gun industry's superstar, and became so popular, the NSSF (National Shooting Sports Foundation) gave it a new, softer title – the MSR (Modern Sporting Rifle) to replace older terms like "paramilitary", "black", and the press' favorite, "assault rifle".

During this turbulent period, an AR-15's real value wasn't the primary consideration when purchasing – only the perceived urgency, increasing prices (not values), and a tight/mostly backordered supply. While many of us thought Bill Clinton would go down in American history as being the best gun selling president, he's going to look like an understudy compared to what happened during Obama's two terms.

During the 2013 SHOT Show in Las Vegas, one well-known AR-15 manufacturer went into the show with 127,000 units on back order. Four days later, frenzied dealer orders had increased this to 157,000 units! This market chaos resulted in almost no predictability for AR-15 values. The only thing consumers cared about was whether or not they could get one – cost was no object.

Timeline: Nov. 9, 2016 - The Party's Over
How/Why AR-15s Lost Over $3 Billion in Value in Less Than a Year!

Q: What did AR-15s and Hillary Clinton have in common after election night?

A: Both were big losers in the last presidential election!

After nearly a decade of unprecedented demand when spooked buyers bought over 7 million AR-15s, this craze finally collapsed the day after Trump was elected. While it never officially flat-lined, it was the medical equivalent of an unexpected, major heart attack and this patient is still recovering. Yet, this previous red-hot marketplace hasn't gone away – it's just adjusting to substantially reduced sales plus trying to reinvent itself to a changing customer base. Never in the history of American modern commercial firearms has one configuration so totally controlled and dominated the marketplace for this length of time.

When Fear, Greed, and Speculation Controlled the Marketplace

So, what are the biggest factors in drastically changing the buying dynamics of today's AR-15 consumers compared to the buyers from the Obama era? Yesteryear's sales were primarily leveraged as a result of three politically driven components – fear, greed, and speculation. Fear was created by potential anti-gun legislation stemming from a Democratic President and Congress. Consumers bought en masse because they were convinced the AR-15 configuration and its high-cap magazines might become illegal to own with little or no warning – this triggered the perfect storm which started the fast and furious feeding frenzy. Greed compounded the problem when buyers purchased two guns or more (and don't forget the expensive cases/bricks of ammo), and finally, rampant speculation ratcheted prices up quickly.

Things settled down for a little bit during 2014, when AR-15 sales were 500,000 units less than 2013. Two years later, once gun owners sensed that Clinton could win the presidential election, the restless herd was off and thundering again. It all abruptly ended in the wee hours of November 9, 2016, when this AR party finally came to a screeching halt. What's important to focus on is that most of these buyers did not purchase their AR-15s to shoot. It was all centered around a "buy it today before it's too late tomorrow" attitude.

From 26 AR-15 Manufacturers/Trademarks to over 230 in 16 Years!

After the AR crash following the last presidential election, hundreds of thousands of AR-15s surfaced in the secondary marketplace, including countless tables like this at gun shows.

Maybe the best way to comprehend the seismic change in this volatile portion of the firearms industry is to consider 16 years ago in the 23rd Edition of the *Blue Book of Gun Values*, there were only 26 AR-15 manufacturers/trademarks listed. Six years later, the number had increased to 76 entries. In the most recent 39th Edition, there are a staggering 291 current and discontinued listings! Obviously, something's going to have to give – soon, as demand is now considerably down from its peak years. Expect to see quite a few fresh headstones in this relatively new AR-15 cemetery for deceased manufacturers during the next 36 months. Many will have passed after less than ten years in business!

The Race to the Bottom Was On!

Now that the race to the bottom was on, prices finally cratered last summer after nearly a decade where demand always exceeded supply. One long-term industry professional volunteered "it's the

biggest glut of unsalable inventory" he'd ever seen in over 30 years in the business. Backordered AR-15s, which peaked during the 2009 SHOT Show, are now nonexistent, with almost all makes/models in plentiful supply. Even worse – if today's savvy buyers can purchase a new basic AR-15 for around $450, used/previously sold rifles/carbines are now worth even less, since most of them are 98% or like new condition. Prices can't get any lower because most manufacturers can't make these entry level guns for less than current selling prices of used mint guns.

Now that the smoke has settled, most common AR-15s in .223 Rem./5.56 NATO cal. bought during the Obama era have lost anywhere from 35%-60% of their purchase price! These jittery consumers who overpaid for their AR-15s between 2008-2016 have now lost over $3 billion in value since the election! Not exactly a gun investment Cinderella story.

Quality and Manufacturer/Trademark Notoriety Never Lose Value

It should be noted however, that previously established AR-15 manufacturers that produce high quality carbines/rifles in relatively small quantities such as H&K, JP Enterprises, Knight's Armament, LaRue Tactical, Les Baer, STI, Stoner Rifle, etc. have not been subject to these lower price points. This non-speculative customer base who wants the best is solid, stable, and well-heeled, and as a result, these customers are not dumping their guns into the secondary marketplace today because money (or lack of it) is not an issue. It should also be pointed out that Colt AR-15s, which have been around since 1963, are more collectible (and valuable) than offerings from the other short-term mass manufacturers.

A New AR-15 Customer Emerges

So, what's radically changed in today's AR-15 marketplace? A lot. Sources polled for this article indicated that a different AR-15 consumer has emerged within the past several years. There are now basically two different segments of buyers that need to be recognized. The first group is focused on the price and value of complete guns. Consumers no longer feel the pressure to buy an AR-15 because a better deal might surface tomorrow. These younger, potential buyers are now accustomed to seeing $400-$500 advertised prices, and some makes/models even have $100-$150 factory rebates.

Custom Builds – AR-15s Hope for the Future

The second and fastest growing segment of this changed AR-15 market comes from buyers who concentrate on getting a gun custom built and accessorized to his/her shooting requirements. This typically means buying a forged lower receiver for $50-$125+, possibly upgrading with titanium parts/kits for another $75-$150, picking out the right barrel ($200-$400), then adding furniture to suit their specific needs ($175-$350), followed by optics ($150 on up) to complete the build. What's interesting about this scenario is that even though these consumers will end up with an AR-15 platform that may cost $800+, they would rather spend more for a custom built-to-spec gun than buying a complete entry level carbine/rifle for $400-$500 without optics. Since today's consumers are now more focused on shooting and there is almost no chance of any federal anti-gun legislation passing in Washington in the near future – the fear and speculation factors are finally over, at least for now……

This custom build Aero Precision AR-15 pistol with an arm brace is an example of one of the hottest areas in the AR marketplace currently, mostly because they are not regulated by the National Firearms Act and do not require a $200 tax stamp. Photo courtesy of Maxim Defense.

Why All the Dominoes Went Down in 2017

Another big issue is how the AR-15 configuration impacted the entire firearms industry during most of 2017. New, non-returnable AR-15 inventory had become a serious problem for most dealers and distributors, since it greatly reduced their cash flow. Even worse, this negatively impacted dealers by not ordering new products for the fall hunting season like usual, since all their money was tied up in unsalable AR-15s. So, what happened? As cash flow became critically low, most dealers and distributors had no choice other than to slash prices and dump inventory at a significant loss, quickly turning the previous seller's spree into a buyer's bonanza.

Rubbing the Dimly Lit AR-15 Crystal Ball – What's the Future?

So, what are AR-15 manufacturers/trademarks doing today to create new demand in this sluggish marketplace? They're trying to figure out how to entice new buyers into the marketplace by offering them new/different finishes, features, and options. Over 50 (no typo) caliber offerings manufactured to date ranging from .17 Rem.-.50 Beowulf have certainly also helped. Enterprising dealers are now taking standard makes/models and customizing them in-shop to offer their customers something new/different. Recently relaxed BATFE interpretations on arm braces are also making the AR-15 pistol marketplace more viable. And if silencers are de-regulated, gunsmiths will be busy for years threading and modifying AR-15 barrels.

Is anything major going to change in the near future? More importantly, is the AR-15 platform finally starting to run out of ways to reinvent itself? Make no mistake about it – this marketplace is now concentrating its efforts on first-time buyers and custom builders. The hundreds of thousands of consumers who purchased their AR-15s during 2008-2016 either don't want any more or are trying to sell what they have.

Looking ahead, the only thing that could significantly change this surplus situation around in the foreseeable future is an anti-gun Democrat winning the 2020 presidential election and/or the continuing threat of what can happen virtually overnight after a mass shooting. Let's hope the worn-out and tired buffalo herd gets to rest for a while – it deserves a little R&R. ∎

HOW TO USE THIS BOOK

The values listed in this First Edition *Blue Book of AR-15s & Variations* are based on the national average retail prices gathered from gun shows, dealers, and auction sites. Do not expect to walk into a gun/pawn shop or trade/gun show and think that the proprietor/dealer will pay you the retail value listed within this text for your gun(s). Resale offers on most models could be anywhere from close to retail to up to 50% less than the values listed, depending on condition, availability, and overall supply/demand economics. Prices paid by dealers will be dependent upon locality, desirability, dealer inventory, and potential profitability. In other words, if you want to receive 100% of the price (retail value), then you have to do 100% of the work (become the retailer, which also includes assuming 100% of the risk).

Included in this First Edition is the most extensive Glossary ever compiled for AR firearms, sights, and optics. Combined with the Anatomy illustrations, this will help you immensely in determining correct terminology on the wide variety of AR firearms available in today's marketplace. Also see Abbreviations for more detailed information about both nomenclature and terminology abbreviations.

This book also includes a Trademark Index of current AR firearms manufacturers, importers, and distributors, which is actually a source book unto itself. It includes the most websites and information.

The Index might be the fastest way to find the make/model you are looking for. To find a model in this text, first look under the name of the manufacturer, trademark, brand name, and in some cases, the importer. Next, find the correct category name (if any), which are typically PISTOLS: SEMI-AUTO, RIFLES: SEMI-AUTO, and SHOTGUNS: SEMI-AUTO. In some cases, models will appear with MSRs only after the heading/category description.

Once you find the correct model or sub-model, and determine the specimen's percentage of original condition, refer to the corresponding percentage column showing the value of a currently manufactured or discontinued model. **Editor/Publisher's note: Law enforcement and military models, full auto machine guns and other Class III variations, in addition to NFA items (with the exception of factory silencers on currently manufactured guns) are NOT included in this text/database.**

For the sake of simplicity, the following organizational framework has been adopted throughout this publication.

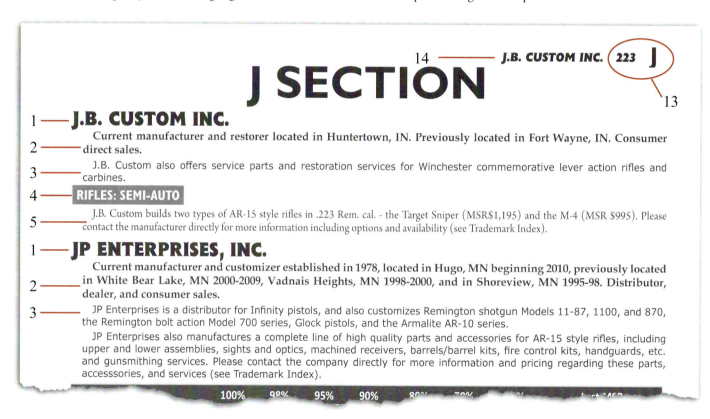

1. Manufacturer Name or Trademark – brand name, importer, trademark or manufacturer is listed alphabetically in uppercase bold face type.

2. Manufacturer Status – This information is listed directly beneath the manufacturer/trademark heading, providing current status and location along with importer information for foreign trademarks.

3. Manufacturer Description – These notes may appear next under individual heading descriptions and can be differentiated by the typeface. This will be specific information relating to the trademark or models.

4. Category Name – (normally, in alphabetical sequence) in upper case (inside a screened gray box), referring to various tactical configurations, including Pistols, Rifles, and Shotguns.

5. Category Note – May follow a category name to help explain the category, and/or provide limited information on models and current MSRs.

6. Value Additions/Subtractions – Value add ons or subtractions may be encountered directly under individual price lines or in some cases, category names, and are typically listed in either dollar amounts or percentages. These individual lines appear bolder than other descriptive typeface. On many guns less than 15 years old, these add/subtract adjustments will reflect the last factory MSRs (manufacturer's suggested retail price) for that option, and need to be either added or subtracted to ascertain the original MSR.

7. Model Name and Description – Model Name appears flush left, is bold faced in all upper-case letters, either in chronological order (normally) or alphabetical order (sometimes, the previous model name and/or close sub

HOW TO USE THIS BOOK, CONT.

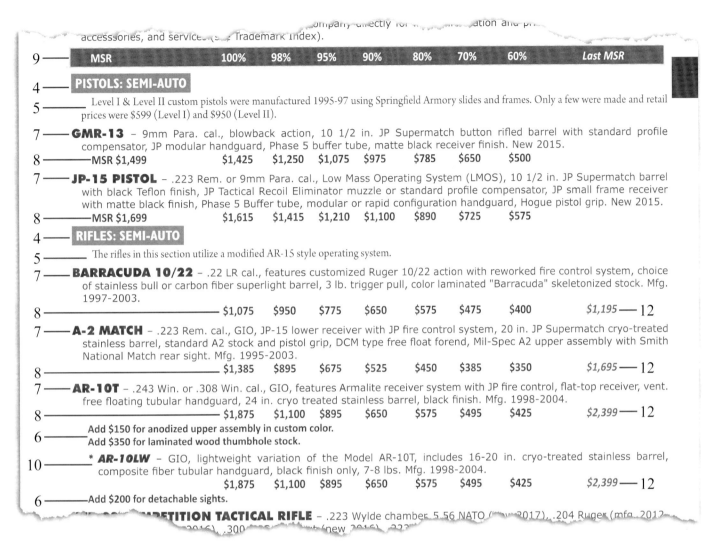

8. Value line – This pricing information will follow directly below the model name and description. The information appears in descending order from left to right with the values corresponding to a condition factor shown in the Grading Line near the top of the page. A pricing line with an MSR automatically indicates the gun is currently manufactured, and the MSR (Manufacturer's Suggested Retail) is shown left of the 100% column. 100% price on a currently manufactured gun also assumes not previously sold at retail. In some cases, N/As (Not Applicable) are listed and indicate that either there is no MSR on this particular model or the condition factor is not frequently encountered, and the value is not predictable. On a currently manufactured gun, the lower condition specimens will bottom out at a value, and a lesser condition gun value will approximate the lowest value listed. Recently manufactured 100% specimens without boxes, warranties, etc., that are currently manufactured must be discounted slightly (5%-20%, depending on the desirability of make and model).

9. Grading Line – The 100%-60% grading line will normally appear at or near the top of each page.
Percentages of original finish, (condition factors with corresponding prices/values, if applicable) are listed between 60% and 100%. Please consult the Photo Percentage Grading System (PPGS), available at no charge online at BlueBookOfGunValues.com and also included in the *Blue Book of Gun Values*.

10. Sub-model Name and Description – Variations within a model appear as sub-models, and they are differentiated from model names because they are preceded by a bullet, indented, and are in upper and lower case type, and are usually followed by a short description.

11. Model Note (not shown) – Model notes and other pertinent information may follow price lines and value additions/subtractions. These appear in different type, and should be read since they contain both important and other critical, up-to-date information.

12. On many discontinued models and sub-models, an italicized value may appear at the end of the price line, indicating the last manufacturer's suggested retail price (LAST MSR).

13. Alphabetical Designator/Page Number – Capital letter indicating which alphabetical section you are in and the page number you are on.

14. Manufacturer Heading/Continued Heading – Continued Headings may appear at the top of the page, indicating a continuation of information for the manufacturer/trademarks from the previous page.

ANATOMY OF AN AR-15 RIFLE/CARBINE

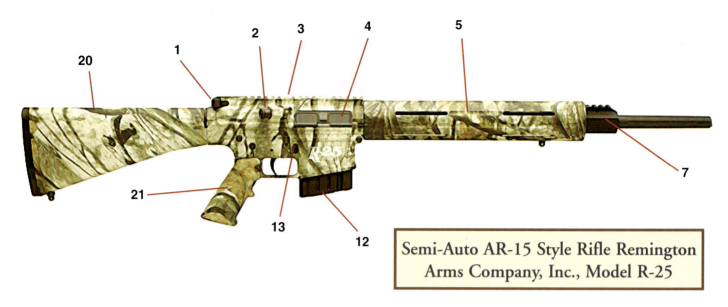

Semi-Auto AR-15 Style Rifle Remington Arms Company, Inc., Model R-25

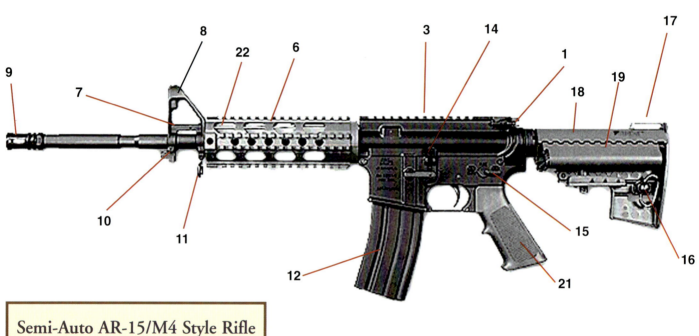

Semi-Auto AR-15/M4 Style Rifle DSA Inc., ZM-4 Carbine

1.	Charging handle	9.	Flash suppressor	17.	Single point sling attachment
2.	Forward bolt assist	10.	Bayonet mounting lug	18.	Collapsible stock
3.	Flat-top upper w/Picatinny rail	11.	Front sling swivel	19.	Cheekpiece
4.	Ejection port dust cover	12.	Detachable box magazine	20.	Fixed buttstock
5.	Free floating forearm	13.	Magazine release button	21.	Pistol grip
6.	Quad rail forearm	14.	Bolt release lever	22.	Gas tube
7.	Gas block w/Picatinny rail	15.	Safety lever		
8.	A2 style front sight	16.	Rear sling swivel		

ANATOMY OF AN AR-15 PISTOL & SHOTGUN

17

AR-15 Pistol
Springfield Armory SAINT™ AR-15

AR-15 Shotgun
Iver Johnson Arms, Inc. STRYKER-12 Shotgun

1. Charging handle	10. A2 type front sight	19. Pistol grip
2. Forward bolt assist	11. Forearm	20. Trigger
3. Flat-top upper receiver w/Picatinny rail	12. Front sling swivel	21. Trigger Guard
4. Ejection port	13. A4 type detachable carry handle	22. Detachable box magazine
5. Dust cover	14. Adj. rear sight	23. Bolt release lever
6. Free floating forearm with M-LOK system	15. Fixed buttstock	24. Magazine release button
7. Forward Hand Stop	16. Rubber Buttpad	25. Safety button
8. Flash suppressor	17. Pistol Forearm Brace	26. Lower Receiver
9. Muzzle brake	18. Buffer Assembly	27. Picatinny Rails

AR-15 TERMINOLOGY PICTURED & DESCRIBED
AR-15 GAS OPERATING SYSTEMS & COMPONENTS

DIRECT/GAS IMPINGEMENT OPERATION (GIO):

Direct Impingement/Gas Impingement AR-15 operating systems are the original and most common systems used for the AR-15 platform of pistols, carbines, and rifles. When the gun is fired, high pressure gas is generated in the barrel, then directed through a small port in the barrel up through the gas block. The gas then travels rearward through a gas tube (these vary in length) into the gas key on the bolt carrier group to cycle the action. Extended shooting without cleaning of this type of operating system can result in a gas related residue build-up within the upper receiver, because it is forcing dirty gas back into the gun's action as it is fired.

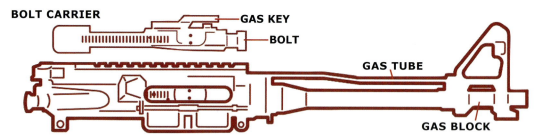

This illustration depicts an AR-15 upper receiver and barrel using the direct impingement gas system. Image courtesy of Springfield Armory

GAS PISTON OPERATION (GPO):

Unlike the gas impingement high pressure gas to operate the bolt carrier group, the gas piston operating system differs in that the high pressure gas is used to force a mechanical operating rod/spring assembly attached to the bolt carrier group which then cycles the action. The benefit of this system is that no gas ever enters the upper receiver, so it remains almost as clean as before firing.

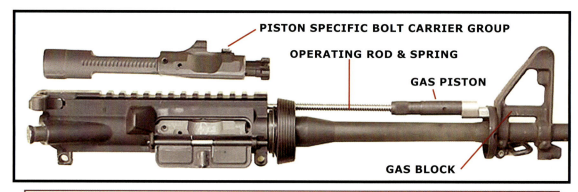

AR-15 upper receiver and barrel assembly showing the various components of a gas piston operating system

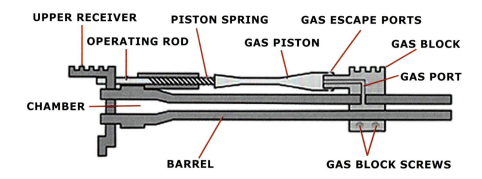

This cross-sectional diagram illustrates the AR-15 gas piston operating system. Image courtesy of Guns Magazine

AR-15 GAS OPERATING SYSTEMS & COMPONENTS

GAS BLOCKS

Front Sight Block (FSB):
FSB gas blocks have a fixed front sight built into the gas block as a one-piece unit.

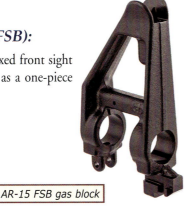

AR-15 FSB gas block

Railed Gas Block:
Railed gas blocks contain a Picatinny rail on top to allow the attachment of a flip-up front sight.

Railed gas block for AR-15 with sling swivel.

Low Profile Gas Block:
A low profile gas block is designed to be small enough to fit under a free float handguard.

AR-15 low profile gas block

Adjustable Gas Block:
Adjustable gas blocks allow the user to adjust the amount of high pressure gas that passes through the gas block to the piston, which allows gas adjustments for various reasons and helps with fine tuning the cycling of the pistol, carbine, or rifle. These adjustments take into consideration varying size buffer weights, buffer springs, lightweight bolt carrier groups, and can also be fine-tuned for use with suppressors. The adjustment is usually done by an Allen screw.

Radical Firearms low profile adjustable AR-15 gas block. Note Allen screw gas adjustment on upper portion of this block

GAS SYSTEM LENGTHS

There are different length gas systems which are associated with different length barrels. The Port Distance signifies the distance between the upper receiver and the gas port on the gas block.

SYSTEM	BARREL LENGTH	PORT DISTANCE
Pistol Length	UNDER 10"	4"
Carbine Length	10"-18"	7"
Mid-Length	14"-20"	9"
Dissipator Length	16"	12"
Rifle Length	20"+	12"

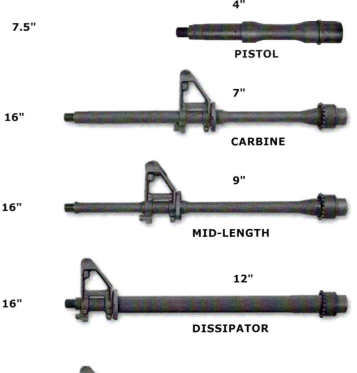

AR-15 HANDGUARD STYLES & MOUNTING PLATFORMS

DROP-IN HANDGUARD:

This style of handguard utilizes a delta ring and handguard cap to provide tension from the delta ring to hold the handguard in place. These handguards are two-piece, consisting of an upper and lower section. This type of handguard is the easiest to replace even if limited tools are available and are usually lighter weight than other handguard options.

Example of a two-piece carbine length drop-in or standard AR-15 handguard

STANDARD HANDGUARD:

This is the original drop-in handguard that has evolved over time from original AR-15 style variations. The accessory mounting options are limited on these handguards, but the holes on the upper and lower side can accept Picatinny rail sections for accessory mounting. Mounting in other areas would require drilling and modification of the handguard.

FREE FLOAT HANDGUARD/FOREARM:

Free float handguards are popular because they are not mounted/attached to the barrel. Rather, they are installed securely by the barrel nut to the receiver and support their own weight plus possible accessories. The advantage of free float handguards/forearms is improved accuracy, but they typically are a little heavier than drop-in/standard handguards.

Midwest Industries 10" Gen2 SS-Series one-piece free float vented handguard with integral top Picatinny rail

AR-15 POPULAR ACCESSORY MOUNTING OPTIONS

Standard handguards present challenges when the user wants to add the wide variety of accessories available today to their guns, especially when many are now custom builds. These accessories and options have significantly evolved over the past five years providing AR users an almost endless variety of choices and options.

PICATINNY RAIL:

The Picatinny rail is also known as Mil-Std 1913 rail or STANAG 2324 rail. Picatinny is named after the Picatinny Arsenal which originally developed the standardized mounting system for the U.S. Army in 1992. This rail system was originally designed for mounting a scope on top of large caliber rifles and evolved over time into a general accessory mounting system. Picatinny rails can be found built into upper receivers, many handguards, and as attachment parts for handguard systems. The Picatinny rail is a strip which is undercut to form the shape of a flattened "T". This provides a secure base, utilizing slots and flats that allow various accessories to be attached easily and quickly. Most Picatinny rails are machined out of aluminum. The Picatinny system replaced the Weaver rail mount system in popularity during the mid-90s.

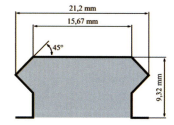
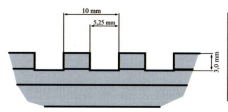

Picatinny front/end cross section with dimensions (L), and side view (R) showing spacing and dimensions of slots and flats.
Diagram and dimensions by Johan Fredriksson, CC BY-SA 3.0, https://commons.wikimedia.org/w/index.php?curid=14686720

PICATINNY QUAD RAIL:

This design allows a user to mount accessories anywhere on the 4 rail sections (top, bottom, and both sides) of the handguard. The disadvantage is added weight since they are significantly heavier than many other handguard systems. This quad rail handguard configuration dominated the AR-15 marketplace (both factory-installed and after market sales) until the introduction of the KeyMod handguard system.

Daniel Defense DDM4 10" free float Picatinny quad rail handguard

AR-15 POPULAR ACCESSORY MOUNTING OPTIONS

KeyMod Handguard System:

KeyMod was originally developed by VLTOR Weapon Systems and was eventually available as a non-proprietary design which quickly allowed widespread manufacture and was soon adopted by the entire firearms industry. The design is called KeyMod because the mounting area resembles a vintage keyhole. The advantage of a KeyMod design allows a very lightweight handguard by removing all of the heavy Picatinny rail mounts which cover the traditional Picatinny quad rail. The unique design allows the user to mount individual Picatinny rail sections only to the section(s) of the handguard where the accessory is mounted, allowing substantial weight saving by removing the unused rail areas. Many of these rails incorporate an integral Picatinny rail on the top of the handguard.

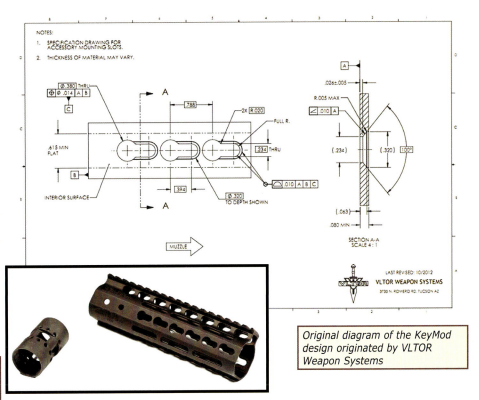

Original diagram of the KeyMod design originated by VLTOR Weapon Systems

Noveske NSR-10 free float KeyMod – includes handguard with upper integral Picatinny rail and barrel nut, various lengths available

M-LOK Handguard System:

M-LOK (Modular Lock) is a handguard rail interface system patented by Magpul Industries. Magpul freely licenses the M-LOK design to manufacturers that want to use this handguard system, as long as they agree to adhere to specific manufacturing standards. M-LOK allows the use of individual rail sections, and in some cases accessories can be directly mounted to the handguard. In a 2017 USSOCOM (The United States Special Operations Command) sponsored test of the M-LOK and KeyMod system, the findings showed that M-LOK outperformed KeyMod in drop testing, load testing, and repeatability of point of aim when re-installing laser sight accessories. These results led to many consumers preferring the M-LOK system over KeyMod.

VTAC (Viking Tactics) M-LOK free float handguard – note M-LOK specific hardware with Allen screw/wrench for fast and easy installation or removal (T). Magpul MOE M-LOK drop-in handguard (B).

M-LOK allows the user to mount rail sections or accessories without removing the handguard using a specialized "cammed T-nut design".

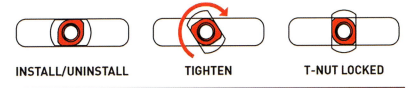

Cammed T-nut diagram depicting attachment of T-nut hardware to M-LOK handguard section

AR-15 MUZZLE DEVICES

Muzzle devices are available in an almost endless amount of designs and variations, but they fit into specific categories based on their design features and what they have to offer the shooter in terms of results and performance.

There are four main categories of muzzle devices – muzzle brakes, flash hiders/flash suppressors, compensators, and silencers/suppressors. The first three categories usually share some similar characteristics and design elements, but silencers/suppressors do not and require BATF approval and a $200 tax stamp per suppressor to legally own.

MUZZLE BRAKE:

Free float handguards are popular because they are not mounted/attached to the barrel. Rather, they are installed securely by the barrel nut to the receiver and support their own weight plus possible accessories. The advantage of free float handguards/forearms is improved accuracy, but they typically are a little heavier than drop-in/standard handguards.

ATI (Advanced Technology International) Steel Shark AR-15 muzzle brake

FLASH HIDER/FLASH SUPPRESSOR:

Flash hiders reduce the visible flash and/or flames that escape the muzzle while firing. The intent of this muzzle device is to help the shooter avoid a blinding effect when shooting, in low light or no light conditions. It is often believed they are meant to remove a telltale shooting flash to the enemy of an opposing fighting force. This, however is a secondary benefit to the device as it only reduces the flash and does not eliminate it totally. Flash hiders and suppressors do not reduce muzzle blast or felt recoil.

Noveske KX-5 Flaming Pig flash suppressor (L) and SureFire flash hider with suppressor adaptor SF3P-556-1/2-28 (R)

COMPENSATOR:

A compensator, working on a similar concept as a ported muzzle brake, redirects the gas upwards after helping to prevent muzzle rise or muzzle climb when firing. They also allow the operator to shoot faster while still maintaining consistent target groupings. The downside is also similar to the muzzle brake - they can be very loud in a range environment and do not offer additional flash suppression.

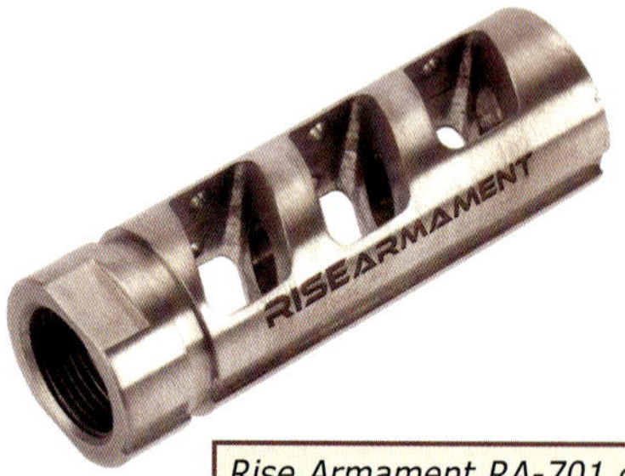

Rise Armament RA-701 compensator

SILENCER/SUPPRESSOR:

Silencers/suppressors reduce the noise of gunfire by giving the escaping gasses a larger yet contained space to allow expansion. Internal baffles (flow directing or obstructing vanes or panels) inside divide the silencer into various chambers for the gas expansion. Sound levels are reduced anywhere from 14.3-43 decibels depending on the design and various other factors, including caliber, ammunition type, barrel length, plus other features of a specific firearm. Most common suppressors will attach via a specific muzzle adaptor. Suppressors can also thread directly onto a barrel if the thread pitch matches. This is the only category of muzzle devices that requires a BATF tax stamp ($200) to legally own in most states.

Knights Armament 5.56QDC suppressor

AR-15 STOCKS, BRACES, & BUFFER TUBES

FIXED STOCK:

The synthetic stock and forearm from Eugene Stoner's original AR-10 design remained relatively unchanged with only minor changes in the length for many years. A fixed stock is a static position stock that does not have an adjustment feature. They may also contain a space for storage at the end of the buttstock. Fixed stocks will mount to a rifle length buffer tube, which is smooth and cylindrical in design. Modern manufacturing has also created fixed stocks that feature adjustable cheek welds.

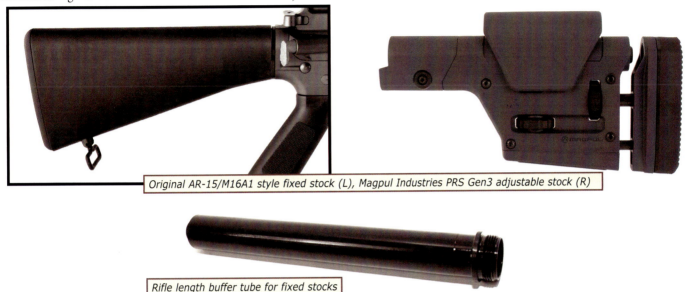

Original AR-15/M16A1 style fixed stock (L), Magpul Industries PRS Gen3 adjustable stock (R)

Rifle length buffer tube for fixed stocks

TELESCOPING/ADJUSTABLE STOCK:

The first telescoping stocks for the Stoner design were introduced circa 1966 with the release of the CAR-15 (Colt Automatic Rifle) sub-machine gun and the Colt Commando, both which featured adjustable stocks in an effort to provide specialized units with shorter, more maneuverable weaponry. The stock locks into holes within a channel on the buffer tube, and the length of pull is adjusted by depressing a lever or button and sliding the stock into a hole corresponding with the desired length. The corresponding buffer tubes come in two common variations, Mil-Spec and Commercial-Spec.

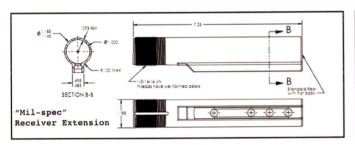 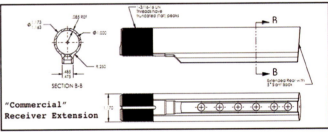

Comparison diagrams showing the specific differences of a Mil-Spec buffer tube and a Commercial-Spec buffer tube.

Original Colt M4 stock (shown with spring and buffer weight) (L), Magpul Industries MOE stock, and Mission First Tactical Battlelink Minimalist stock (R)

AR-15 STOCKS, BRACES, & BUFFER TUBES

PISTOL BRACES AND BUFFER TUBES:

The AR-15 pistol has been growing in popularity since the early 1990s. It is a short barrel alternative AR-15 to a National Firearms Act restricted short barrel rifle. Instead of using a stock, an AR-15 pistol will feature a short, cylindrical buffer tube that is not specifically designed to accept the attachment of a stock. With the advent of pistol braces, a device that is designed to aid a shooter in the practice of firing a pistol with a single hand, there has been much controversy surrounding the common use of braces on AR-15 pistols. As this edition went to press, it is commonly accepted that the addition of a pistol brace does not constitute a 'redesign' of the firearm from a pistol to a short barrel rifle. However, laws vary from state to state, and rulings can change quickly. Pistol braces have allowed shooters more flexibility of use with their AR-15 pistol over a plain pistol buffer tube.

Since its first appearance in 2013, the pistol brace has expanded to various manufacturers and is available in many different forms.

Phase 5 Gen 2 pistol buffer tube (L), KAK Industry pistol buffer tube (R) - designed to accept pistol braces.

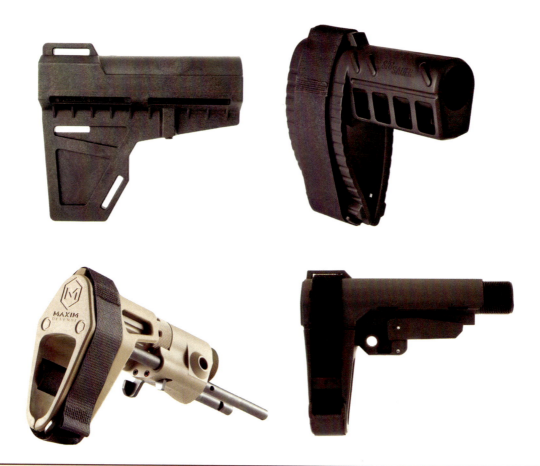

KAK Industry Shockwave (top left), Sig Sauer SBX, Maxim Defense Pistol CQB PDW Brace, and SB Tactical SBA3 (bottom right)

AR-15 TRIGGERS

STANDARD TRIGGER ASSEMBLY VS. DROP-IN:

A standard AR-15 trigger assembly breaks down into multiple pieces (hammer, hammer spring, disconnector, disconnector spring, trigger, trigger spring, and hammer & trigger pins), whereas the drop-in style trigger is a self-contained single unit. Custom triggers come in both variants and offer improvement over the standard or Mil-Spec trigger, allowing the shooter a smoother and lightened trigger pull. The benefits of a drop-in trigger offer the shooter the advantage of utilizing the original hammer and trigger pins to install without having to line up additional pieces.

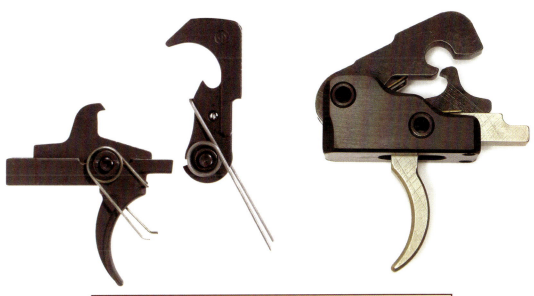

Standard AR-15 trigger assembly (L), one-piece AR-15 drop-in trigger (R)

SINGLE STAGE VS. TWO-STAGE TRIGGER:

Single stage triggers are the most common and straight forward AR-15 trigger design. The shooter simply places his/her finger on the trigger, applies pressure, and the trigger does its job. Two-stage triggers are exactly what the name implies - there is an extra stage in the trigger pull. The first stage is usually heavier than the second stage. Once shooters reach the second stage, they can pull through this stage to finish firing the gun. If the shooter is in the second stage of the trigger pull, and releases the trigger without firing, the trigger spring will push it forward and return the trigger back to the first stage.

AR-15 SIGHTS & OPTICS

IRON SIGHTS:

The basic concept of proper iron sight usage is the shooter lining his/her eye up with the rear and front sights in tandem over their intended target. Iron sights are available in many different designs from different manufacturers, but most share similar primary characteristics. Popular AR-15 style iron sight choices include a ghost ring rear sight that can transition into an aperture/peep sight. Also available are folding/flip-up iron sights that are often used as a backup to an electronic sight which can flip up and co-witness (front and back sights can be viewed in line with the optic). Additionally, iron sights can also be mounted at a 45 degree angle on the firearm and can be utilized by the shooter quickly by slightly turning the gun to view them.

Troy Industries HK style folding front (L) and rear battle sights

Front Sights:

Front sights can be fixed as a built in feature to the gas block, fixed as an attachment to handguard or gas block, or they can be flipped up and attached to the handguard rail or gas block rail.

Anderson Manufacturing 16" carbine length M4 upper with fixed front gas block sight (L), Diamondhead Diamond gas block with front combat flip-up sight, Magpul MBUS Pro flip-up front sight (R).

Rear Sights:

Rear sights can be fixed to the receiver, charging handle, or able to flip up and down with user interaction.

APERTURE/PEEP SIGHT:

The aperture sight or peep sight mode on the rear sight is typically used for more precise shooting, and many times for longer distances.

Magpul MBUS rear sight in aperture/peep sight mode

GHOST RING:

The ghost ring mode on AR-15 rear sights is the larger bore sight versus the aperture/peep sight. It is the standard issue on USGI carry handles. Often the ghost ring and the peep sight will have different zeros, unless specified by the manufacturer. The ghost ring is better for quick target acquisition and closer shooting (0-200 yards) compared to the peep sight.

Magpul MBUS rear sight, ghost ring sight mode

A1/A2/A3/A4 REAR SIGHTS:

These are military designations specifically for rear sight styles. Specifically the A1 type sights are considered "Field Sights". These sights have adjustments on the rear sight for windage only and are usually fixed, although they can be purchased without the carry handle - only windage adjustments are possible.

The A2/A3 sights are adjustable for windage, elevation, and also provide a bullet drop compensator wheel. These sights are fixed in the carry handle as part of the upper receiver.

The A4 variation will function the same with windage and elevation but is attached to a removable carry handle. The A4 variation features a bullet drop compensator adjustment wheel as well.

A1 style rear sight adjustable for windage only.

A2 rear sight has adjustments for both windage and elevations. Carry handle is non-detachable.

A4 rear sight on removable carry handle that is adjustable for both windage and elevation.

AR-15 SIGHTS & OPTICS

RED DOT STYLE SIGHTS:

The following illustration of a red dot sight reticle represents the most common example. Commonly encountered types of red dot style sights include: Reflex, Holographic, and Prismatic. They are also available in a wide variety of reticle styles and colors.

Examples of Reflex red dot sights - Vortex Sparc AR (L) and Trijicon MRO

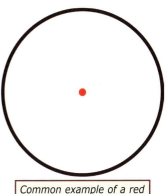

Common example of a red dot sight reticle

Red dot sights are available in many different shapes and sizes – they can also have various magnifications. Most are mounted on a Picatinny rail or the various types of newer handguard systems.

HOLOGRAPHIC SIGHTS:

Holographic sights project a reticle seen only by the shooter using laser technology that transmits a hologram of a reticle recorded in 3-D onto a special holographic film controlled by specialized digital electronics. This allows the user to control functions such as brightness to adjust for ambient light levels, battery power indicators, and auto shutdown features. This reticle imaging has similar technology to what is used by fighter pilots for target acquisition. These units are almost completely free of the problem of parallax distortion (the line from the eye to the reticle not being parallel with the barrel) compared to red dots which increase this problem because of longer shooting distances. The holographic sight accounts for these problems using its on-board technology.

EOTech is the most widely known manufacturer of holographic sights for rifles. This model is an EOTech HHSIII 518-2 holographic sight with EOTech G33 3x fast transition magnifier.

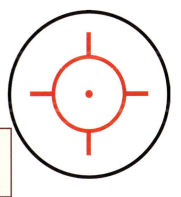

This illustration represents a common EOTech reticle style, but many more are available, depending on the shooter's needs and requirements.

REFLEX SIGHTS:

Reflex sights are arguably the most common electronic sighting system in use for AR-15 style rifles. They are among the most affordable and easy to use. These sights use an LED (light-emitting diode) to project a small aiming point (usually a red dot, but also available in many other colors) onto the lens inside the sight. Some of the higher end models use a compound called Tritium, a radioactive form of hydrogen that emits fluorescent light. Tritium is also well-known for its use on night sights for handguns. Unlike iron sights, in which the shooter lines up the front and rear sight with his/her eye, reflex sights allow the user to look through the sight from different positions even if not lined up with the sight tube and not compromise their point of aim. These sights are very popular for fast target acquisition and transition.

Aimpoint Micro H-1 reflex sight

AR-15 SIGHTS & OPTICS

PRISMATIC SIGHTS:

Prismatic sights share characteristics of reflex sights and rifle scopes. Instead of a projected dot reticle using an LED and lens, Prismatic sights flip the reticle image using a prism. The reticle is often etched into the glass and then illuminated. Prismatic sights allow for manufacturers to offer built in magnification, but a downside is they have shorter eye relief versus a reflex sight.

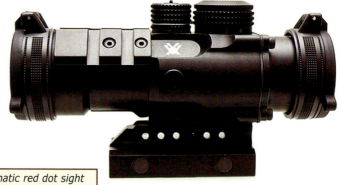

Vortex Spitfire 3x Prismatic red dot sight

RIFLE SCOPES:

Rifle scopes offer the user a wide variety of glass optics and have a lot of variations, reticles, and magnifications. Rifle scopes are identified by their magnification factor(s) as well as the size of the objective lens. For example: the designation 3-9x40 refers to the scope magnification which varies from 3x up to 9x magnification, and the objective lens size is 40 millimeters. Rifle scopes also come in various tube sizes, the most common being 1 in. (25.4mm) tube or a 30 millimeter. These tube sizes are critical when selecting the correct ring sizes for pistol, carbine, or rifle mounting. A wide variety of scope mounts are available to fit each shooter's particular need and requirements. Most reticles and crosshairs used in rifle scopes are fixed (although a few are adjustable), and in some cases can also be illuminated by built in electronics. Typically, horizontal and vertical scope sighting adjustments can be made using calibrated dials on the scope's exterior.

Leupold Mark AR 1.5-4x20, FireDot SPR, matte 1 in. scope mounted on a Wilson Combat .300 AAC Blackout AR-15 with a Wilson Combat 1 in. Accu-Rizer AR-15 specific scope mount.

AR-15 PARTS DIAGRAMS

AR-15 LOWER PARTS KIT

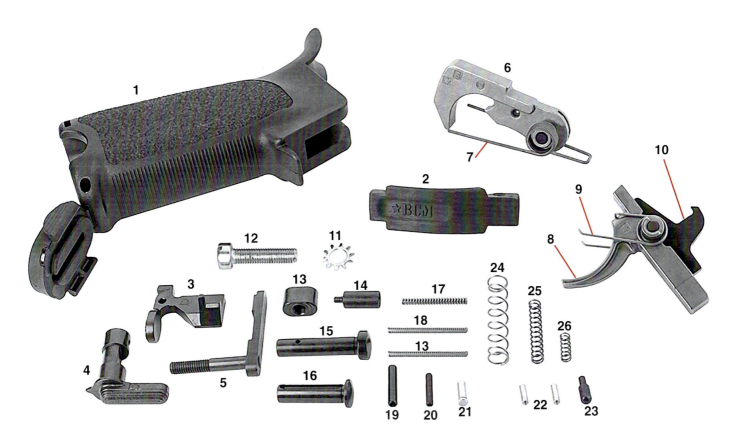

1.	Pistol Grip	10.	Disconnector	19.	Trigger Guard Roll Pin
2.	Trigger Guard	11.	Lock Washer	20.	Bolt Catch Roll Pin
3.	Bolt Catch	12.	Pistol Grip Screw	21.	Safety Detent Pin
4.	Safety Selector Switch	13.	Magazine Release Button	22.	Takedown Pin & Pivot Pin
5.	Magazine Catch	14.	Buffer Retainer	23.	Bolt Catch Plunger
6.	Hammer	15.	Pivot Pin	24.	Magazine Catch Spring
7.	Hammer Spring	16.	Takedown Pin	25.	Buffer Retainer Spring
8.	Trigger	17.	Safety Detent Spring	26.	Bolt Catch Plunger Spring
9.	Trigger Spring	18.	Takedown & Pivot Pin Springs		

AR-15 PARTS DIAGRAMS

AR-15 BOLT CARRIER GROUP

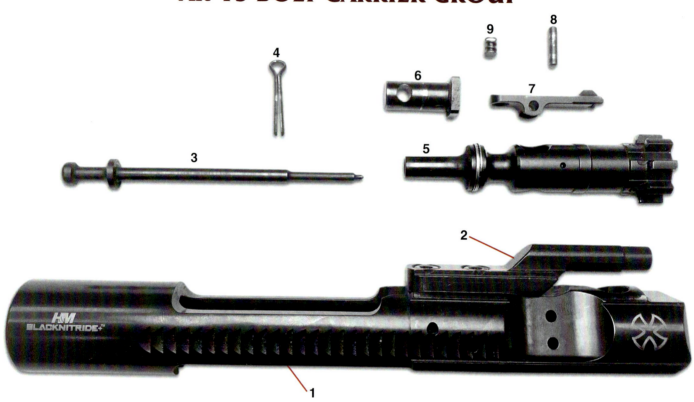

1.	Bolt Carrier	6.	Bolt Cam Pin
2.	Gas Key	7.	Extractor
3.	Firing Pin	8.	Extractor Pin
4.	Firing Pin Retaining Pin	9.	Extractor Spring
5.	Bolt		

AR-15 PARTS DIAGRAMS

AR-15 RIFLE EXPANDED VIEW DIAGRAM

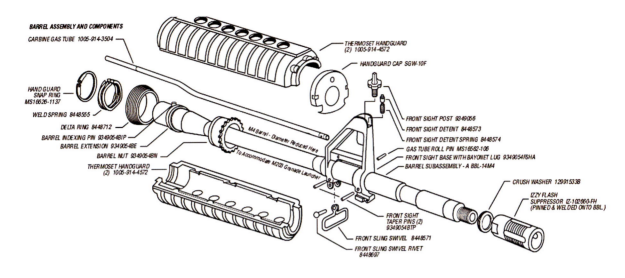
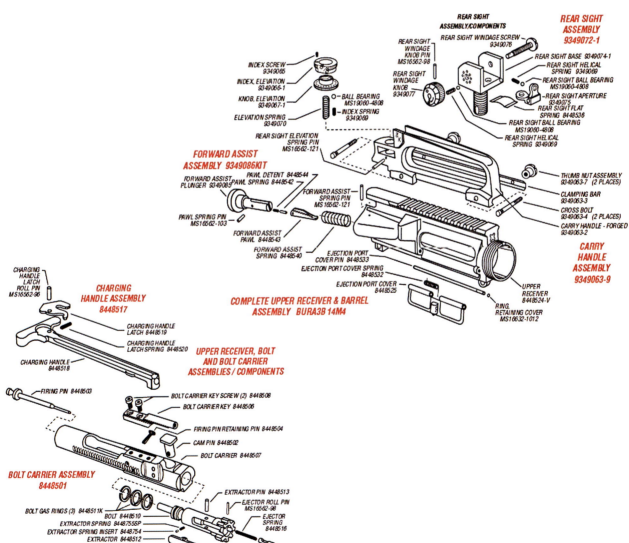

GLOSSARY

AR TYPE SEMI-AUTO SPORTING RIFLES VS. ASSAULT RIFLES

Jim Supica, Director of NRA Museums

WHAT IS AN ASSAULT RIFLE?

A true **military assault rifle** is a military rifle with the following **three features**:

1. **Capable of full-auto fire** – i.e. one pull of the trigger can fire multiple rounds, like a machine gun. This may be either:
   a. **Full auto** – The gun continues to fire as long as the trigger is held back until the magazine is empty, or
   b. **Burst fire** – The gun fires a certain number of rounds, usually 3, with each pull of the trigger.

Most true military assault rifles are "**select-fire.**" The shooter can choose to set the rifle for semi-auto or full-auto operation.

2. **Fires an intermediate-power cartridge** – A military assault rifle takes ammunition that is less powerful than a "high-power" rifle cartridge such as the .30-06, but more powerful than a pistol-class cartridge such as the 9mm or .45 ACP. Example, comparing muzzle energy in foot/pounds for the three types of cartridges:
   a. High-power rifle cartridges - .30-06, 8mm Mauser, etc. *Approx. 2,200 to 2,900 ft-lbs.*
   b. Pistol-class cartridges. – 9mm, .45 ACP, etc. *Approx. 300 to 450 ft-lbs.*
   c. Intermediate-power cartridges. – 5.56x45 NATO & 7.62x39. *Approx. 1,200 to 1,500 ft-lbs.*

3. **Uses a detachable box magazine** – Typical capacity is 20 to 30 rounds.

WHAT IS A MODERN SPORTING RIFLE?

"Modern sporting rifle" is a fairly recent term sometimes used to describe semi-automatic rifles that are cosmetically similar to true military assault rifles. They have the following features:

1. **Capable of semi-auto fire only.** One pull of the trigger fires one round only.

2. **Different models fire different cartridges.** Most are chambered for the intermediate power cartridges .223 Win. (5.56x45 NATO) and 7.62x39mm. Some models are chambered for more powerful cartridges, and others for less powerful cartridges.

3. **Uses a detachable box magazine.** Capacity varies. These have been used on semi-auto sporting rifles since 1905.

Note: Expansion of the term "Assault Rifle" to include modern semi-auto sporting rifles

In the 1980's, the term "assault rifle" began to be inaccurately applied to semi-automatic sporting rifles that bore a cosmetic resemblance to true military assault rifles. This incorrect appropriation of the term was used both by anti-gun politicians and by firearms media writers. The term "assault weapon" is sometimes used to include handguns and shotguns in addition to rifles.

WHAT IS AN AR RIFLE?

"AR-style rifle" or "AR-type rifle" refers to a rifle that cosmetically resembles the military M16 pattern, but which can be fired only in semi-auto mode – i.e., one pull of the trigger fires one round only. The term originated with the semi-auto Colt sporting rifle Model AR-15.

1. **Origin of the term** – "AR" stands for "**ArmaLite Rifle.**" ArmaLite is the name of the company that first developed AR pattern rifles. It does not stand for "assault rifle."

2. **Earliest examples** – Both the full-automatic military assault rifle Model M16 and the semi-automatic sporting rifle Model AR-15 were introduced by Colt in 1963. The sporting semi-auto model was initially named the SP-1 (for Sporting), with the AR-15 designation introduced a bit later.

3. **Broader use of the term** – Although only rifles with Stoner/ArmaLite type actions are correctly called "AR style rifles," the term is sometimes used to include other rifles that have different types of semi-auto actions, but which share other features of the AR.

A-Z Listings

1989 BUSH BAN

Refers to the U.S. Federal executive branch study and resulting regulations which banned the importation of firearms that did not meet sporting criteria, i.e. certain paramilitary semi-auto only rifles and shotguns. The study was undertaken in response to the Stockton, CA tragedy in which an AK-47 type rifle was criminally used by a so-called mass murderer. The Federal regulation, U.S.C. Title 18, Section 922r, applies to imported firearms and to firearms assembled in the U.S. using imported components. It is important to note that even though the Assault Weapon Ban (which applied to U.S. manufactured firearms, not imports) has expired, Section 922r remains in effect, and has the force of U.S. Federal law, regardless of its executive branch origin as opposed to U.S. Senate and House of Representatives legislation. Also see Section 922r.

5R

Five groove rifling developed in Russia. Instead of conventional six groove rifling with opposing lands and sharp edged transitions between lands and grooves, 5R lands oppose grooves and the sides of lands are cut at a sixty-five degree angle. Claimed benefits are: decreased bullet deformation, less jacket fouling, increased velocity, and greater accuracy.

A1 STYLE

Refers to an AR style rifle in A1 configuration, or A1 specific components (triangular handguard, short fixed buttstock, receiver with integral carry handle, four slot bird cage flash hider, smooth pistol grip, rear flip sight with short and long range apertures, lighter weight 1:14 twist barrel).

A2 STYLE

Refers to an AR style rifle in A2 configuration, or A2 specific components (circular bi-lateral handguard, longer fixed buttstock, receiver with integral carry handle and spent case deflector, five slot bird cage flash hider, finger rib pistol grip, windage and elevation adjustable rear flip sight with small day and large low light apertures, heavier weight 1:7 twist barrel).

A3 STYLE

Refers to an AR style rifle in A3 configuration, or A3 specific components (circular bi-lateral handguard, collapsible buttstock, receiver with integral carry handle and spent case deflector, A2 flash hider/pistol grip/rear sight/barrel).

GLOSSARY, CONT.

A4 STYLE

Refers to an AR style rifle in A4 configuration, or A4 specific components (similar to A2 except for flat-top receiver with Picatinny rail, detachable carry handle, and Modular Weapons System handguard).

ACTION

An assembly consisting of the receiver or frame and the mechanism by which a firearm is loaded, fired, and unloaded. See ACTION TYPES for the various kinds of actions.

ACTION TYPES

Actions are broadly classified as either manual or self-loading. Manual actions may be single shot or repeater. Single shot actions include dropping block (tilting, falling, and rolling), break, hinged, and bolt. Repeater actions include revolver, bolt, lever, pump, and dropping block. Self-loading actions may be semi-automatic or automatic. Semi-auto and automatic actions by sub-type are:

    a. blowback: simple, lever delayed, roller delayed, gas delayed, toggle delayed, hesitation locked, and chamber-ring delayed.

    b. blow-forward.

    c. recoil: short, long, and inertia.

    d. gas: short stroke piston, long stroke piston, direct impingement, and gas trap.

ADJUSTABLE FRONT SIGHT

A front sight which can be moved, relative to the barrel's axis, vertically for elevation and/or horizontally for windage adjustments.

ADJUSTABLE REAR SIGHT

A rear sight which can be moved, relative to the barrel's axis, vertically for elevation and/or horizontally for windage adjustments.

ADJUSTABLE SIGHT

A firearm sight which can be adjusted so that the shooter's point of aim and the projectile's point of impact coincide at a desired target distance. On a majority of firearms only the rear sight is adjustable, but front sights may also be adjustable.

ADJUSTABLE (COLLAPSIBLE, TELESCOPING) AND FOLDING STOCKS

An adjustable stock allows the stock to be lengthened or shortened to accommodate shooters of various statures. Also see AR-15 TERMINOLOGY section.

AK/AKM STYLE ACTION

A gas operated rifle action with a long-stroke gas piston, a tilting breechblock locking design, and a heavy milled (early versions) or lighter sheet metal (later versions) receiver. No regulator is used; the overall design, machining, tolerances, ease of maintenance, and component durability assure reliable function in all circumstances.

ANY OTHER WEAPON

Any other firearm which is not an NFA defined machine gun, short barrel rifle, short barrel shotgun, modern shoulder stocked pistol, suppressor (BATFE uses the term "silencer"), or destructive device. An AOW is: a device capable of being concealed on a person from which a shot can be discharged through the energy of an explosive; a smooth bore barrel pistol or revolver designed or redesigned to fire a fixed shotgun shell; a weapon with combination shotgun and rifle barrels twelve inches or more but less than eighteen inches in length, from which only a single discharge can be made from either barrel without manual reloading; and any such weapon which may be readily restored to fire. AOW examples: H&R Handyguns, Ithaca Auto-Burglar guns, cane guns, and guns modified/disguised so as to be unrecognizable as firearms.

APERTURE SIGHT

An iron rear sight which has a hole or aperture in a disc or semi-circular blade instead of a rectangular or "vee" notch of an open sight. May also be a front sight, or adjustable for windage/elevation, or have adjustable/interchangeable apertures.

AR-15 STYLE ACTION

A gas operated rifle action with a direct gas impingement system (i.e. no gas piston, no regulator, no moving parts), a bolt carrier enclosing a multi-lugged rotating bolt locking design, and a two-part light-weight receiver. Propellant gas flows through a gas tube, acts directly upon the bolt carrier to cycle the action, and vents into the receiver. AR-15 style actions have fewer parts, are more adaptable/modifiable, and are significantly lighter than AK, FAL, or HK91 style actions. However, more maintenance, cleaning, and lubrication are absolutely required for reliability, in contrast to other gas operated actions.

ASSAULT RIFLE

Definition usually depends on if you're pro-gun or anti-gun. If you're pro-gun, it generally refers to a military styled, short to immediate range battle rifle capable of selective fire (semi-auto or full auto). If you're anti-gun, it can include almost anything, including sporter rifles from the turn of the 20th century.

ASSAULT WEAPONS BAN

Popular title for the Violent Crime Control and Law Enforcement Act of 1994, Public Law 103-322. See VIOLENT CRIME...LAW 103-322.

AUTO LOADING/LOADER

See SEMI-AUTO ACTION.

AUTOMATIC ACTION

An action design which continuously fires and performs all steps in the operating cycle if the trigger remains fully depressed and ammunition is present in the firearm's magazine or feeding system. Also known as full auto or fully automatic. Machine guns utilize automatic actions, which may be recoil, gas, or externally powered.

BACK UP IRON SIGHTS

Flip-up or fixed iron sights which are not the primary sight system. They are used if the primary optical sight system fails and usually co-witness (optic sight picture and back up sight picture share the same zero).

BARREL

The steel tube (may be wrapped in a sleeve of synthetic material) which a projectile travels through. May or may not be rifled.

BARREL THROAT

At the breech end of a barrel, the segment of the bore which tapers from a non-rifled projectile diameter to a fully rifled dimension. Also known as a forcing cone, leade, lede, or throat.

BATFE 922r COMPLIANT

A semi-auto paramilitary rifle (assembled with U.S. and foreign manufactured parts) which meets the statutory requirements of Section 922r of the United States code. Also refers to U.S. made parts which bring the rifle into compliance.

GLOSSARY, CONT.

BILLET RECEIVER (LOWER/UPPER)
A billet is a length (usually with square or round profile) of material that has been extruded into shape, either by continuous casting or hot rolling. Manufacturing a final product from a billet usually requires increased machining time.

BLOWBACK ACTION
A semi-automatic or automatic firearm operating design which uses expanding propellant gasses to push a heavy unlocked breech bolt open, and which relies upon the inertia of its moving parts to keep the action closed until the bullet has exited the muzzle and pressure has decreased to a safe level.

BLUING
The chemical process of artificial oxidation (rusting) applied to gun parts so that the metal attains a dark blue or nearly black appearance.

BOLT
An assembly which reciprocates along the axis of a firearm's bore; it supports the cartridge case head and locks the action. Also see BOLT ACTION.

BORE
Internal dimensions of a barrel (smooth or rifled) that can be measured using the Metric system (i.e. millimeters), English system (i.e. inches), or by the Gauge system (see GAUGE). On a rifled barrel, the bore is measured across the lands. Also, it is a traditional English term used when referring to the diameter of a shotgun muzzle (gauge in U.S. measure).

BOX MAGAZINE
A boxlike feed device for a firearm, which allows cartridges to be stacked one on top of the other. Most box magazines are removable for reloading.

BRACE
A device that is designed to aid a shooter in the practice of firing a pistol with a single hand. Since AR-15 pistols feature a short, cylindrical buffer tube that is not specifically designed to accept the attachment of a stock, pistol braces were developed. Also see AR-15 TERMINOLOGY section.

BRADY ACT/BILL
See Brady Handgun Violence Prevention Act.

BRADY HANDGUN VIOLENCE PREVENTION ACT
1998 Federal legislation which established the National Instant Criminal Background Check System (NICS). Also commonly known as the Brady Bill, or the Brady Act. See NATIONAL INSTANT CRIMINAL BACKGROUND CHECK SYSTEM.

BREECH
The rear end of a barrel where a cartridge is chambered. Also commonly used in reference to the entire chamber, breech, and receiver of long guns.

BULL BARREL
A heavier, thicker than normal barrel with little or no taper.

BULLET BUTTON
A magazine locking device for AR-15 style rifles. It transforms a rifle with a standard manually operable magazine release and detachable magazine functionality into a fixed magazine rifle in order to comply with the State of California's firearm statutes. Depressing the "button" with a tool, e.g. bullet tip, small screwdriver, etc., is the only way to remove the magazine (which cannot hold more than ten rounds).

BUTT SPIKE
A fixed or adjustable monopod mounted near the rear on the bottom of a rifle's buttstock that, when used with forearm support of the rifle, enables the user to observe the target area for extended periods with minimal fatigue.

BUTTPAD
A rubber or synthetic composition part attached to the buttstock's end; intended to absorb recoil energy, prevent damage to the buttstock, and vary length of pull. May be fixed, solid, ventilated, or adjustable (horizontally, vertically, cant).

BUTTPLATE
A protective plate, usually steel, attached to the back of the buttstock.

BUTTSTOCK
The portion of a stock which is positioned against the user's shoulder; also known as the butt. On AR-15/M16 style or similar long guns, the separate component which is attached to the rear of the receiver. Also see STOCK.

CALIBER
The diameter of the bore (measured from land to land), usually measured in either inches or millimeters/centimeters. It does not designate bullet diameter.

CAMO (CAMOUFLAGE) FINISH
Refers to a patterned treatment using a variety of different colors/patterns that enables a gun to blend into a particular outdoors environment. In most cases, this involves a film or additional finish applied on top of a gun's wood and/or metal parts (i.e. Mossy Oak Break-Up, Mossy Oak Brush, Advantage Timber, Realtree Hardwoods, Realtree Max-4, Muddy Girl, etc.). Mossberg introduced camo finishes on its shotguns in the mid-1980s.

CARTOUCHE
Generally refers to a manufacturer's inspector marking impressed into the wood of a military gun, usually in the form of initials inside a circle or oval.

CASE COLORS
See COLOR CASE HARDENING.

CENTERFIRE
Refers to ammunition with primers centrally positioned in the cartridge case head; or to a firearm which is chambered for centerfire ammunition.

CERAKOTE
A ceramic based firearms coating with improved performance and reliability compared to traditional firearms finishes. Offers abrasion, corrosion, and solvent protection, in many colors and designs.

CHAMBER
Rear part of the barrel which has been reamed out so that it will contain a cartridge. When the breech is closed, the cartridge is supported in the chamber, and the chamber must align the primer with the firing pin, and the bullet with the bore.

CHAMBER THROAT
See BARREL THROAT.

CHARGING HANDLE
A semi-auto firearm component which is manipulated to cycle the action, but which does not fire the cartridge. Also called cocking handle, cocking knob, or operating handle.

GLOSSARY, CONT.

CHECKERING

A functional decoration consisting of pointed pyramids cut into the wood or metal surfaces of a firearm. Generally applied to the pistol grip and forend/forearm areas, affording better handling and control.

CHEEKPIECE

An elevated section of the upper buttstock on which the shooter's cheek rests when holding a rifle or shotgun in firing position. It may be integral to the buttstock, or a separate component. Adjustable cheekpieces may be moved in one or more ways: up, down, fore, aft, or side-to-side.

CHOKE

The muzzle constriction on a shotgun which controls the spread of the shot.

CHOKE TUBES

Interchangeable screw-in devices allowing different choke configurations (i.e., cylinder, improved cylinder, improved modified, modified, or full). While most choke tubes fit flush with the end of the barrel, some choke tubes now also protrude from the end of the barrel. Most recently made shotguns usually include three to five choke tubes with the shotgun.

CLIP

A metal or synthetic material formed/shaped to hold cartridges in readiness to be loaded into a magazine or chamber. A clip is NOT a magazine (i.e., stripper clips for most variations of the Mauser Broomhandle). Also known as a stripper or cartridge clip.

COIN FINISH

Older definition referring to a metal finish, typically on a rifle or shotgun, which resembles the finish of an old silver coin. Most coin finishes are based on nickel plating (not chrome) and are generally high polish.

COLLAPSIBLE STOCK

Mostly used in reference to a buttstock which can be shortened or lengthened along its fore to aft axis. Also applies in theory to top-folding, under-folding, and side folding buttstocks; all of which when folded reduce the weapon's length.

COLOR CASE HARDENING

A method of hardening steel and iron while imparting colorful swirls as well as surface figure. Traditional color case hardening using charcoal and bone meal is achieved by putting the desired metal parts in a crucible packed with a mixture of charcoal and finely ground animal bone to temperatures in the 800°C – 900°C range, after which they are slowly cooled. Then they are submerged into cold water, leaving a thin, colorful protective finish. Can also be achieved by treating the necessary metal parts with a cyanide liquid, which helps harden the metal surface, and can be denoted from charcoal color case hardening by a more layered color appearance.

COMB

The portion of the stock on which the shooter's cheek rests.

COMPENSATOR

Slots, vents, or ports machined into a firearm's barrel near its muzzle, or a muzzle device, which allow propellant gasses to escape upwards and partially reduce muzzle jump. Also see AR-15 TERMINOLOGY section.

CRIME BILL

Popular title for the Violent Crime Control and Law Enforcement Act of 1994, Public Law 103-322. See VIOLENT CRIME...LAW 103-322.

CRIMP

A turning in of the case mouth to affect a closure or to prevent the projectile(s) from slipping out of the case mouth. Various crimps include: roll, pie, star or folded, rose, stab, and taper.

CROSSBOLT

A transverse locking rod/bar used in many SxS boxlock shotguns and a few rifles, which locks the standing breech and barrels to each other. Originally designed by W.W. Greener, this term is also referred to as the Greener crossbolt. Also a transverse metal bolt which reinforces and prevents damage to the stock from recoil or abusive handling.

CROWNING

The rounding or chamfering normally done to a barrel muzzle to ensure that the mouth of the bore is square with the bore axis and that its edges are countersunk below the surface to protect it from impact damage. Traditionally, crowning was accomplished by spinning an abrasive-coated brass ball against the muzzle while moving it in a figure-eight pattern, until the abrasive had cut away any irregularities and produced a uniform and square mouth.

CRYOGENIC TEMPERING

Computer controlled cooling process that relieves barrel stress by subjecting the barrel to a temperature of -310° Fahrenheit for 22 hours.

CURIO/RELIC

Firearms which are of special interest to collectors by reason of some quality other than that which is normally associated with firearms intended for sporting use or as offensive or defensive weapons. Must be older than 50 years.

DA/SA

A semi-auto pistol fire control design which allows an initial shot to be fired in double action mode, and subsequent shots in single action mode until the magazine is empty or the user decocks the pistol. For most modern semi-auto pistols, the cocking is either manual or automatic; and in both instances the trigger and hammer/striker are returned to their respective double action states. See also DOUBLE ACTION and SINGLE ACTION.

DE-HORNING

The removal of all sharp edges from a firearm that would cut or pinch the shooter, the shooter's clothing, and/or holster, but still maintains the nice clean lines of the firearm.

DELAYED IMPINGEMENT GAS SYSTEM

A trademarked gas operating system for AR-15 style carbines, designed by Allan Zitta. Similar to a gas piston action in concept, it has instead an operating rod and recoil spring which run through the receiver, over the barrel, and sleeve the gas tube at the gas block. The gas tube does not enter the receiver, and the recoil spring replaces the buffer and spring in the AR-15 buttstock.

DETACHABLE MILITARY STYLE BIPOD

A bipod designed for severe/heavy use and greater durability, with a Picatinny rail or other type of quick attach/detach mounting system.

GLOSSARY, CONT.

DETACHABLE MAGAZINE

On any gun a detachable magazine permits relatively quick and easy reloading. However, stripper clips, first used on rifles in the late 19th century, may offer as quick a reload as a magazine change (or quicker).

DIRECT IMPINGEMENT GAS SYSTEM

A gas operating system in which high pressure and temperature propellant gas is routed into the firearm receiver to make contact with and move action components. There are no "moving parts" (e.g. piston, return spring, operating rod, tappet) in a direct impingement gas system. A typical direct impingement gas system has a gas block surrounding the barrel and covering the gas port, and a gas tube.

DOUBLE-BARREL(ED)

A gun which has two barrels joined either side-by-side or one over the other.

DOVETAIL

A flaring machined or hand-cut slot that is also slightly tapered toward one end. Cut into the upper surface of barrels and sometimes actions, the dovetail accepts a corresponding part on which a sight is mounted. Dovetail slot blanks are used to cover the dovetail when the original sight has been removed or lost; this gives the barrel a more pleasing appearance and configuration.

DRILLED & TAPPED

Refers to holes drilled into the top of a receiver/frame and threaded, which allow scope bases, blocks, rings, or other sighting devices to be rigidly attached to the gun.

EJECTOR

A firearm component which propels an extracted cartridge or fired case out of the receiver or chamber. Ejectors may be fixed or movable, spring loaded or manually activated. Also see SELECTIVE AUTOMATIC EJECTOR.

ELASTOMER

A synthetic elastic polymer, soft and compressible like natural rubber, used for seals, grip and stock inlays, and other molded firearm components.

ELECTRO-OPTICAL SIGHT

An optical sight (see definition) with the addition of electronic battery powered components which illuminate a reticle (least complex), or which generate a reticle/optional reticles. Electro-optical sights may be: magnifying, non-magnifying, full-tube traditional optical design, or reflex types (see REFLEX SIGHT).

ELEVATION

A firearm sight's vertical distance above the barrel's bore axis; also the adjustment of a sight to compensate for the effect of gravity on a projectile's exterior ballistic path.

ENGINE TURNING

Machined circular polishing on metal, creating a unique overlapping pattern.

ENGRAVING

The art of engraving metal in decorative patterns. Scroll engraving is the most common type of hand engraving encountered. Much of today's factory engraving is rolled on which is done mechanically. Hand engraving requires artistry and knowledge of metals and related materials.

ERGO SUREGRIP

A Falcon Industries Inc. right-hand or ambidextrous replacement pistol grip for AR-15/M-16 style rifles. The grip has finger grooves, upper rear extension to support the web of the shooter's hand, is oil and solvent resistant, and a non-slip textured overmolded rubber surface.

ETCHING

A method of decorating metal gun parts, usually done by acid etching or photo engraving.

EXTRACTOR

A device which partially pulls a cartridge or fired hull/case/casing(s) from the chamber, allowing it to be removed manually.

FIBER OPTIC SIGHT

An iron sight with fiber optic light gathering rods or cylinders; the rod ends are perceived as glowing dots and enhance sight visibility and contrast.

FIT AND FINISH

Terms used to describe over-all firearm workmanship.

FIRE CONTROL GROUP

All components necessary to cause a cartridge to be fired; may be a self-contained assembly, easily disassembled or not user-serviceable, detachable, modular/interchangeable, and may or may not include a safety, bolt release, or other parts.

FIRING PIN

That part of a firearm which strikes the cartridge primer, causing detonation.

FIXED STOCK

A fixed stock is a static position stock that does not have an adjustment feature. They may also contain a space for storage at the end of the stock. Fixed stocks will mount to a rifle length buffer tube, which is smooth and cylindrical in feature. Modern manufacturing has also created fixed stocks that feature adjustable cheek welds. Also see AR-15 TERMINOLOGY section.

FLASH SUPPRESSOR/HIDER

A muzzle attachment which mechanically disrupts and reduces muzzle flash. It does not reduce muzzle blast or recoil. Also see AR-15 TERMINOLOGY section.

FLAT-TOP UPPER

An AR-15/M16 style or other tactical semi-auto rifle with a literally flat receiver top. The majority of flat-top uppers have an extended Picatinny rail for mounting iron sights, optical sights, and other accessories, which provides much more versatility than the original "carry handle" receiver design.

FLOATING BARREL

A barrel bedded to avoid contact with any point on the stock.

FN FAL STYLE ACTION

A gas operated rifle action with a short-stroke spring-loaded gas piston, a tilting breechblock locking design, and a heavy receiver. A regulator valve allows the user to increase the volume of gas entering the system in order to ensure reliable operation in adverse conditions. Unlike direct gas impingement or delayed blowback operating systems, propellant gas does not vent into the receiver and fire control components.

GLOSSARY, CONT. 37

FOLDING STOCK
Usually a buttstock hinged at or near the receiver so that it can be "folded" towards the muzzle, reducing the firearm's overall length. Not an adjustable stock as defined above, and usually does not prevent operating/firing when in its folded position.

FOREARM
In this text, a separate piece of wood in front of the receiver and under the barrel used for hand placement when shooting.

FORGED RECEIVER (LOWER/UPPER)
Forging is the manufacturing process of applying thermal and mechanical energy to pieces of metal to cause the material to change shape while in a solid state to reduce the amount of machining time needed to produce a final product.

FORWARD BOLT ASSIST
A button, usually found on AR-15 type rifles, which may be pushed or struck to move the bolt carrier fully forward so that the extractor has completely engaged the cartridge rim and the bolt has locked. Mainly used to close/lock the bolt when the rifle's chamber and receiver are excessively fouled or dirty.

FREE FLOATING FOREARM
A forearm which does not contact the barrel at any point, as it attaches and places mechanical stress only on the receiver. An accuracy enhancement for AR-15/M16 style rifles, which by their modular design, are not able to have a conventionally free floated barrel in a one-piece stock.

FULL AUTO
See AUTOMATIC ACTION

GAS BLOCK (FIXED OR ADJUSTABLE)
On an AR-15 specifically, there is a small "gas port" in the barrel that vents gas when fired. A gas block is mounted over the gas port and directs the gas to the gas tube which then travels through the gas tube into the receiver, where it powers the bolt carrier group and auto-cycles the next round. This is known as a "direct impingement" gas system. A gas block can be fixed or adjustable. A fixed gas block needs to be matched with the correct length gas tube and an adjustable gas block can regulate the amount of gas allowed to the action. Also see AR-15 TERMINOLOGY section.

GAS IMPINGEMENT OPERATING SYSTEM
An action in which high pressure propellant gas is diverted from the barrel to supply the energy required to unlock the breech, extract/eject the fired case, load a cartridge, and lock the breech. This type of system generates a large amount of heat and also a considerable amount of fouling directly back into the action.

GAS PISTON OPERATING SYSTEM
A gas operation design in which a piston is used to transfer propellant gas energy to the action components. No gas enters the receiver or makes contact with other action components. Consequently, less heat is absorbed by, and less fouling accumulates in the receiver. This system also has a much different recoil pulse or "feel".

GAS PORT
A small opening in the barrel of a gas operated firearm which allows high pressure gas to flow into the gas system's components. Also an escape vent in a firearm's receiver, a safety feature.

GAS TUBE
On an AR-15 specifically the gas tube is the small tube above the barrel attached to the gas block. When the firearm is fired, it directs the gas into the receiver. Since the amount of gas in the system directly affects felt recoil and function, reliability, and performance of the action, the length of the gas tube needs to be matched proportionately to the length of the barrel. The following are standard recommendations for gas system lengths (distance from receiver to gas port) compared to barrel length. Also see AR-15 TERMINOLOGY section.

SYSTEM	BARREL LENGTH	PORT DISTANCE
Pistol Length	UNDER 10"	4"
Carbine Length	10"-18"	7"
Mid-Length	14"-20"	9"
Dissipator Length	16"	12"
Rifle Length	20"+	12"

GAUGE/GA.
A unit of measure used to determine a shotgun's bore. Determined by the amount of pure lead balls equaling the bore diameter needed to equal one pound (i.e., a 12 ga. means that 12 lead balls exactly the diameter of the bore weigh one pound). In this text, .410 is referenced as a bore (if it was a gauge, it would be a 68 ga.).

GAUGE VS. BORE DIAMETER
10-Gauge = Bore Diameter of .775 inches or 19.3mm
12-Gauge = Bore Diameter of .729 inches or 18.2mm
16-Gauge = Bore Diameter of .662 inches or 16.8mm
20-Gauge = Bore Diameter of .615 inches or 15.7mm
28-Gauge = Bore Diameter of .550 inches or 13.8mm
68-Gauge = Bore Diameter of .410 inches or 12.6mm

GCA
The Gun Control Act of 1968, 18 USC Chapter 44.

GLACIERGUARDS
AR 15/M 16 carbine length replacement handguard (two-piece) which has fifteen internal heat dispersing fins rather than the standard heat shield. The fins provide greater strength and rigidity; fiber-reinforced polymer shells resist heat and reduce weight. A DPMS product.

GRIP
The handle used to hold a handgun, or the area of a stock directly behind and attached to the frame/receiver of a long gun.

GRIPS
Can be part of the frame or components attached to the frame used to assist in accuracy, handling, control, and safety of a handgun. Many currently manufactured semi-auto handguns have grips that are molded w/checkering as part of the synthetic frame.

GROOVES
The spiral depressions of the rifling in a barrel bore; created by cutting, swaging, broaching, hammering, cation action, or other methods. Also see LANDS and RIFLING.

HAMMER
A part of a gun's mechanism which applies force to the firing pin or other components, which in turn fires the gun.

GLOSSARY, CONT.

HAMMERLESS
Some "hammerless" firearms do in fact have hidden hammers, which are located in the action housing. Truly hammerless guns, such as the Savage M99, have a firing mechanism based on a spring-powered striker.

HANDGUARD
A wooden, synthetic, or ventilated metal part attached above the barrel and ahead of the receiver to protect the shooter's hand from the heat generated during semi-auto rapid firing. Also see AR-15 TERMINOLOGY section.

HEEL
Back end of the upper edge of the butt stock at the upper edge of the buttplate or recoil pad.

HK91/G3 STYLE ACTION
A roller locked delayed blowback rifle action. There is no gas system per se; gas pressure in the cartridge case pushes the case against the bolt and bolt carrier. Spring-loaded rollers in the bolt resist unlocking and carrier/bolt movement until chamber pressure has dropped to a safe level. Components are heavier, recoil (actual and perceived) is greater, chambers must be fluted to assure extraction, and cocking effort is much greater than direct gas or gas piston weapons.

ILAFLON
Industrielack AG trademarked ceramic reinforced enamel firearms finish coating; highly resistant to abrasion, corrosion, and chemicals/solvent.

INTERCHANGEABLE BARRELS
The AR design includes a detachable "upper" – the portion of the gun that includes the barrel. This means that a single AR may be quickly and easily changed for a variety of different uses simply by switching the upper.

INTRAFUSE
A trademarked system of synthetic stocks and accessories designed for tactical firearms.

IN-THE-WHITE
Refers to a gun's finish w/o bluing, nickel, case colors, gold, etc. Since all metal surfaces are normally polished, the steel appears white, hence, "in-the-white" terminology.

IRON SIGHTS
A generic term for metallic front or rear sights which do not use optical lens (magnifying or non-magnifying) components. Also see AR-15 TERMINOLOGY section.

KEYMOD
KeyMod is an accessory mounting system developed through a partnership between Noveske Rifleworks LLC and VLTOR Weapons Systems circa 2012. This mounting system has been integrated with firearms handguards for the attachment of KeyMod compatible accessories. To attach a KeyMod compatible accessory, line up the lugs on the accessory with the round part of the keyhole, push it in, slide it forward, and tighten the set screws. Also see AR-15 TERMINOLOGY section.

KRYPTEK
A proprietary camo finish utilizing a multi-directional design to effectively conceal in a multitude of terrains that have either a lateral or vertical flow. The bi-level layering of the patterns incorporate background transitional shading and sharp random geometrical foregrounds to create a three dimensional effect that ensures the utmost in concealment at both close and long ranges. Patterns include Highlander, Typhon, and Raid.

LAMINATED STOCK
A gunstock made of many layers of wood glued together under pressure. The laminations become very strong, preventing damage from moisture or heat, and warping.

LANDS
Portions of the bore left between the grooves of the rifling in the bore of a firearm. In rifling, the grooves are usually twice the width of the land. Land diameter is measured across the bore, from land to land.

LASER SIGHT
An aiming system which projects a beam of laser light onto the target. Usually mounted so the beam is parallel to the barrel bore but not a "traditional" front or rear sight as the shooter does not look through the laser apparatus.

LENS COATINGS
Metallic coatings on optic surfaces which increase light transmission, image brightness, and color rendition. Also used to improve abrasion resistance and filter out unwanted or harmful light.

M1913 PICATINNY RAIL
Original designation for a Picatinny rail. Also see PICATINNY RAIL.

M4 STYLE
Refers to an AR style rifle in M4 carbine configuration (A2 configuration but with short handguard, short barrel, and relocated gas block).

MACHINE GUN
National Firearms Act and Gun Control Act of 1968 definition:

Any weapon which shoots, is designed to shoot, or can be readily restored to shoot, automatically more than one shot, without manual reloading, by a single function of the trigger. The term shall also include the frame or receiver of any such weapon, any part designed and intended solely and exclusively, or combination of parts designed and intended, for use in converting a weapon into a machine gun, and any combination of parts from which a machine gun can be assembled if such parts are in the possession or control of a person.

MAGAZINE (MAG.)
The container (may be detachable) which holds cartridges under spring pressure to be fed into the gun's chamber. A clip is NOT a magazine. May be a single or double or multiple column, rotary, helical, drum, or other design. The term "high capacity" denotes a magazine capable of holding more than ten rounds.

MAGNUM (MAG.)/MAGNUM AMMUNITION
A term first used by Holland & Holland in 1912 for their .375 H&H Magnum cartridge. The term has now been applied to rimfire, centerfire, or shotshell cartridges having a larger cartridge case, heavier shot charge, or higher muzzle velocity than standard cartridges or shotshells of a given caliber or gauge. Most Magnum rifle cartridges are belted designs.

MAINSPRING
The spring that delivers energy to the hammer or striker.

MELONITE
A trademarked name for a metal case hardening and surface finishing process which provides exceptional wear, abrasion, and corrosion resistance; and very high surface hardness. The generic name for this process is ferritic nitrocarburizing.

GLOSSARY, CONT. 39

MICROMETER SIGHT
A windage and elevation adjustable sight with very precise and small increments of adjustment.

MICRO SLICK
A firearms finish coating which creates a permanently lubricated surface; it impedes galling and seizing of firearm components.

MIL
See MILRADIAN

MIL-DOT
A reticle with dots spaced center-to-center one milradian apart; the distance to an object of known dimension may be calculated based upon the number of milradians which are subtended by the target's known dimension.

MIL-SPEC / MIL-STD
A series of quality control standards used by manufacturers to guarantee machine tolerances ensuring the consistency and interchangeability of parts.

MILRADIAN
The horizontal angle subtended by one unit of measurement at 1,000 units distance. Also called a "mil".

MINUTE OF ANGLE (MOA)
1/60 of a degree of circular angle; at 100 yards it subtends 1.047 inches. Also commonly used to describe a firearm's accuracy and precision capability, i.e. a rifle which shoots under one minute of angle. Abbreviated MOA.

M-LOK
M-LOK is an accessory mounting system developed by Magpul Industries Corp. circa 2014. This mounting system has been integrated with firearms handguards for the attachment of M-LOL compatible accessories. The M-LOK rail utilizes a T-slot nut capable of only 90-degree rotation, reinforced by thread-locking fluid, making it suited for applications on free float handguards. It was designed to work with both metal and polymer parts. Also see AR-15 TERMINOLOGY section.

MODERN SPORTING RIFLE
A National Shooting Sports Foundation term for civilian legal semi-automatic AR-15 style rifles. The NSSF promotes its usage to counter the negative anti-gun connotations, confusion, and misunderstandings which have become associated with the term "AR-15". A modern sporting rifle is not an automatic or assault rifle, not a regulated NFA weapon, not a military/law enforcement M16 despite its similar cosmetic appearance, and no more powerful than other traditional configuration sporting/hunting/competition rifles of the same caliber. Sometimes called Sport Utility Rifle or SUR. Note: the letters "AR" stand for ArmaLite Rifle.

MODULAR WEAPONS SYSTEM
A generic term of military origin for quick attach/detach components/systems which allow flexibility and adaptability for using various sighting, illumination, and other accessories, etc. on a weapon. Also see PICATINNY RAIL.

MONTE CARLO STOCK
A stock with an elevated comb used primarily for scoped rifles.

MUZZLE
The forward end of the barrel where the projectile exits.

MUZZLE BRAKE
A muzzle device (permanent or removable) or barrel modification which reduces muzzle jump and recoil by diverting propellant gasses sideways or to the rear. Not to be confused with a flash hider or a flash suppressor. Also see COMPENSATOR and The AR-15 TERMINOLOGY section.

NATIONAL INSTANT CRIMINAL BACKGROUND CHECK SYSTEM (NICS)
A U. S. federal government system which an FFL must, with limited exceptions, contact for information on whether receipt of a firearm by a person who is not licensed under 18 U.S.C. 923 would violate Federal or state law.

NFA
The National Firearms Act, 26 USC Chapter 53.

NFA FIREARM
A firearm which must be registered in the National Firearm Registration and Transfer Record, as defined in the NFA and 27 CFR, Part 479. Included are: machine guns, frames or receivers of machine guns, any combination of parts designed and intended for use in converting weapons into machine guns, any combination of parts from which a machine gun can be assembled if the parts are in the possession or under control of a person, silencers and any part designed or intended for fabricating a silencer, short-barreled rifles, short-barreled shotguns, destructive devices, and "any other weapon". NFA semi-auto carbines with less than 16 in. barrels are not listed in this book.

NICS CHECK
See NATIONAL INSTANT CRIMINAL BACKGROUND CHECK SYSTEM.

NIGHT SIGHTS
Iron sights with radioactive Tritium gas capsules; the capsules are inserted into recesses in the sight body with their ends facing the shooter. The Tritium glow provides sight alignment and aiming references in lowlight/no-light conditions.

NP3/NP3 PLUS
An electroless plated nickel-phosphorus alloy firearms finish which offers uniform thickness, lubricity, and hardness equivalent to hard chromium plating.

OBJECTIVE LENS
A telescopic sight's front, usually larger lens which may be adjustable to reduce parallax error.

OCULAR LENS
The rear lens of a telescopic sight, normally adjustable by rotation to focus the sight image.

OPEN SIGHT
A simple rear iron sight with a notch – the shooter aims by looking through the notch at the front sight and the target.

OPTICAL SIGHT
A generic term for a sight which has one or more optical lenses through which the weapon is aimed. Optical sights usually magnify the target image, but there are many non-magnifying optical sights.

PARALLAX
Occurs in telescopic sights when the primary image of the objective lens does not coincide with the reticle. In practice, parallax is detected in the scope when, as the viewing eye is moved laterally, the image and the reticle appear to move in relation to each other.

GLOSSARY, CONT.

PARAMILITARY

Typically refers to a firearm configured or styled to resemble a military weapon with one or more of the military weapon's configurations or features, EXCEPT FOR automatic or selective fire capability. Paramilitary firearms may be slide action (primarily shotguns), bolt action, or semi-automatic (most handguns and rifles).

PARKERIZING

Matte rust-resistant oxide finish, usually dull gray or black in color, found on military guns.

PEEP SIGHT

A rear sight consisting of a disc or blade with a hole or aperture through which the front sight and target are aligned. Also see AR-15 TERMINOLOGY section.

PICATINNY RAIL

A serrated flat rail typically located on the top of a frame/slide/receiver, but may also be located on the sides and bottom, allowing different optics/sights/accessories to be on the gun. Developed at the U.S. Army's Picatinny Arsenal. Also see AR-15 TERMINOLOGY section.

PISTOL FOREARM BRACE

See BRACE

POLYGONAL

Rifling w/o sharp edged lands and grooves. Advantages include a slight increase in muzzle velocity, less bullet deformation, and reduced lead fouling since there are no traditional lands and grooves. See RIFLING.

PORTED BARREL

A barrel with multiple holes or slots drilled near the muzzle. See PORTING.

PORTING

Multiple holes or slots drilled into a firearm barrel near the muzzle. Porting reduces felt/perceived recoil, and if located on the upper half of the barrel reduces muzzle jump. Disadvantages are increased muzzle blast and noise.

POST-BAN

See 1989 BUSH BAN, and SECTION 922r.

PRE-BAN

See 1989 BUSH BAN, and SECTION 922r.

PRIMER

A percussion device designed to ignite the propellant charge of a centerfire cartridge or shotshell by generating flame and high temperature expanding gasses.

PRIMER RING

Refers to a visible dark ring around the firing pin hole in a breech or bolt face, created by the impact of centerfire ammunition primer cups when a cartridge is fired.

PROOF MARK

Proof marks are usually applied to all parts actually tested, but normally appear on the barrel (and possibly frame), usually indicating the country of origin and time-frame of proof (especially on European firearms). In the U.S., there is no federalized or government proof house, only the manufacturer's in-house proof mark indicating that a firearm has passed its manufacturer's quality control standards per government specifications.

QUAD RAIL FOREARM

A rifle forearm with upper, lower, and lateral Picatinny rails which allow attachment of multiple accessories.

RATE OF TWIST

The distance in which rifling makes one complete revolution; normally expressed as one turn in a specific number of inches or millimeters. Also called rifling pitch, or merely twist.

RECEIVER

That part of a rifle or shotgun (excluding hinged frame guns) which houses the bolt, firing pin, mainspring, trigger group, and magazine or ammunition feed system. The barrel is threaded or pressed into the somewhat enlarged forward part of the receiver, called the receiver ring. At the rear of the receiver, the butt or stock is fastened. In semiautomatic pistols, the frame or housing is sometimes referred to as the receiver. On AR firearms there are an upper and a lower receiver. The upper receiver contains bolt carrier group and barrel. The lower contains the buffer tube assembly and fire control assembly and is considered the firearm by the ATF. An 80% lower is a lower receiver with 80% or less of the machining that is needed to assemble it into a firearm completed and is not considered a firearm by the ATF.

RECOIL

The rearward motion of a firearm when a shot is fired (i.e. the gun recoiled); the term for the energy or force transferred into the firearm as it discharges a projectile.

RECOIL ACTION/OPERATION

A self-loading or automatic action which uses recoil energy to unlock, extract, eject, cock the firing mechanism, and reload the chamber.

RECOIL SPRING GUIDE ROD

A metal or synthetic rod which positions the recoil spring within the firearm's receiver or slide, and prevents binding/dislocation of the spring during its compression or expansion.

RED DOT SIGHT

See REFLEX SIGHT.

REFLEX SIGHT

An optical sight which generates reticle image upon a partially curved objective lens; the reticle appears superimposed in the field of view and focused at infinity. Most reflex sights are non-magnifying and battery powered. Fiber optic light collectors or tritium may also be used to generate the reticle. Reflex sights are adjustable and virtually parallax free. Popularly known as "red dot" sights; they are NOT laser sights.

RELIC

See CURIO/RELIC.

REPEATER/REPEATING ACTION

A manual action with a magazine or cylinder loaded with more than one cartridge; all cartridges may be fired without reloading.

RETICLE

The shapes, lines, marks, etc. which provide an aiming reference when using an optical sight. Reticles may be illuminated electronically, with Tritium, or with fiber optics, and are available in a multitude of designs for many differing requirements.

GLOSSARY, CONT.

RIFLING

The spirally cut grooves in the bore of a rifle or handgun barrel. The rifling causes the bullet to spin, stabilizing the bullet in flight. Rifling may rotate to the left or the right, the higher parts of the bore being called lands, the cuts or lower parts being called the grooves. Many types exist, such as oval, polygonal, button, Newton, Newton-Pope gain twist, parabolic, Haddan, Enfield, segmental rifling, etc. Most U.S.-made barrels have a right-hand twist, while British gun makers prefer a left-hand twist. In practice, there seems to be little difference in accuracy or barrel longevity.

RIMFIRE

Self contained metallic cartridge where the priming compound is evenly distributed within the cartridge head, but only on the outer circumference of the rim. Detonated by the firing pin(s) striking the outer edge of the case head.

RINGS

See SCOPE RINGS.

SAFETY

A mechanism(s) in/on a gun which prevents it from firing. There are many different types and variations.

SAAMI

The Sporting Arms and Ammunition Manufacturers' Institute; a branch of the National Shooting Sports Foundation.

SCOPE RINGS (BLOCKS/BASES)

Metal mounts used to attach a scope to the top of a gun's frame/receiver.

SEAR

The pivoting part in the firing or lock mechanism of a gun. The sear is linked to the trigger, and may engage the cocking piece, striker, or the firing pin.

SECTION 922r

A 1989 Federal regulation which established sporting criteria for centerfire weapons, either imported, or assembled from imported and domestic components. Firearms which do not meet the criteria are "banned", i.e. non-importable as of the regulation's effective date. Also the source of the popular terms "pre-ban" and post-ban". Due to the complexity of this regulation readers are advised to refer to the actual text of the regulation and contact the BATFE. Also see 1989 BUSH BAN.

SELECTIVE FIRE

Describes a firearm which has more than one firing mode; which is controlled, or "selected", by the user. Most often used in reference to firearms which can fire in semi-auto, burst, or full auto mode.

SEMI-AUTO ACTION/SEMI-AUTOMATIC/SELFLOADING/ AUTOLOADING

A pistol, rifle, or shotgun that is loaded manually for the first round. Upon pulling the trigger, the gun fires, ejects the fired round, cocks the firing mechanism, and feeds a fresh round from the magazine. The trigger must be released after each shot and pulled again to fire the next round. The semi-auto action fires one shot and one shot only with each pull of the trigger allowing the shooter to focus on aim between shots instead of having to manipulate the action to load a fresh round.

SHELL DEFLECTOR

A protrusion of the receiver near the ejection port which is positioned and shaped to deflect an ejected case away from the shooter's body. Especially appreciated by left-handed shooters when firing a semi-auto with right side ejection.

SHORT ACTION

A rifle action designed for short overall length cartridges.

SHORT BARREL RIFLE

Any rifle having one or more barrels less than sixteen inches in length and any weapon made from a rifle (whether by alteration, modification, or otherwise) if such weapon, as modified, has an overall length of less than twenty-six inches.

SHORT BARREL SHOTGUN

Any shotgun, which was originally equipped with a shoulder stock, with a barrel or barrels less than eighteen inches long and any weapon made from a shotgun (whether by alteration, modification, or otherwise) if such weapon as modified has an overall length of less than twenty-six inches.

SHOTSHELL

An assembly consisting of a rimmed metal head, paper or plastic base wad, 209 battery cup primer, and paper or plastic body. A shotshell cartridge is a shotshell loaded with propellant, wad column, and shot charge or a single large diameter slug.

SIDE FOLDING STOCK

A folding stock variation which has its buttstock rotate horizontally, usually to the right side of the firearm's receiver. See FOLDING STOCK.

SIDE LEVER

Refers to opening mechanism lever on either left or right side of receiver/frame.

SIGHT(S)

Any part or device which allows a firearm to be aimed, versus merely pointed, at a target. There are two main systems: "iron" and optical. Iron sights, also known as "open" sights, are now made of other substances than metal and in many variations. Optical sights have a lens, or lenses, which may or may not magnify the target image. Also see AR-15 TERMINOLOGY section.

SILENCER

See SUPPRESSOR.

SINGLE SHOT ACTION

An action which limits storing or loading only a single cartridge, and is manually operated.

SLING SWIVELS

Metal loops affixed to the gun to which a carrying strap is attached.

SOUND SUPPRESSOR

See SUPPRESSOR.

SPECIAL IMPACT MUNITIONS

A class or type of firearm ammunition loaded with one or more projectiles; when fired at a human target the projectiles have a low probability of causing serious injury or death. For example: bean bag, baton, tear gas, and rubber ball rounds. A sub-class of SIMs is known as SPLLAT, or special purpose less lethal anti terrorist munitions.

SPORT UTILITY RIFLE

See MODERN SPORTING RIFLE.

GLOSSARY, CONT.

SQUIB LOAD

A cartridge with no propellant, or so little propellant, that when fired in a semi-auto the action does not cycle; and in any type of firearm a squib load most likely results in the projectile remaining in and completely obstructing the barrel's bore.

STANDOFF/BREACHING BARREL

Refers to a barrel that has a jagged muzzle to assist in the physical entry of a door and allows no slipping.

STATE COMPLIANT

Firearms whose features have been changed to comply with state laws/regulations such as CA, MA, MD, NJ, NY, HI, etc. are not listed in this text, as there are almost endless variations. Values of state compliant guns in the secondary marketplace will not be as high as the standard non-compliant models from which they are derived.

STOCK

Usually refers to the buttstock of a long gun, or that portion of a rifle or shotgun that comes in contact with the shooter's shoulder, and is attached to the frame/receiver.

STRIKER

An elongated firing pin, or a separate component which imparts energy to a firing pin. Most commonly found in hammerless semi-auto pistols.

SUPPRESSOR

A mechanical device, usually cylindrical and detachable, which alters and decreases muzzle blast and noise. Commonly referred to, in error, as a silencer, it acts only on the sound of the firearms discharge. It does not have any effect on the sounds generated by: the firearm's moving parts, a supersonic bullet in flight, or the bullet's impact. Legality varies per state. Also see AR-15 TERMINOLOGY section.

TACTICAL

An imprecise term referring to certain features on handguns, rifles, and shotguns. Before 2000, a tactical gun generally referred to a rifle or carbine designed for military or law enforcement. In today's marketplace, tactical refers to certain features of both handguns and long arms.

TACTICAL RIFLES

Semi-auto, bolt action, or slide action rifles which have at least two of the following factory/manufacturer options or features: magazine capacity over ten rounds, non-glare finish (generally but there may be exceptions), Mil-Std 1913 Picatinny or equivalent rail(s), mostly synthetic stocks which may be fixed, folding, collapsible, adjustable, or with/ without pistol grip, most have sling attachments for single, traditional two, or three point slings, Tritium night sights, and some Assault Weapon Ban characteristics, such as flash suppressors, detachable magazines, bayonet lugs, etc.

TACTICAL SHOTGUNS

Semi-auto or slide action shotguns which have at least two of the following factory/manufacturer options or features: higher capacity (than sporting/hunting shotguns) magazines, or magazine extensions, non-glare finish (generally but there may be exceptions), Mil-Std 1913 Picatinny or equivalent rail(s), mostly synthetic stocks which may be fixed, folding, collapsible, adjustable, or with/without pistol grip, most have sling attachments for single, traditional two, or three point slings, some Assault Weapon Ban characteristics, such as bayonet lugs, or detachable high capacity magazines, rifle or night or ghost ring sights (usually adjustable), and short (18-20 inches) barrels with fixed cylinder choke.

TAKEDOWN

A gun which can be easily disassembled into two sections for carrying or shipping.

TARGET STOCK

A stock optimized for accuracy, consistency, ergonomics, and reliability; for firearms used primarily in formal known-distance competition shooting. Rifle versions may have many adjustment options (e.g. length of pull, cast, comb/cheek piece, buttplate, palm rest, hand stop, accessory attachment); handgun versions may have thumb or palm rests, spacers, inserts, etc.

TENIFER

A trademarked name for a metal case hardening and surface finishing process which provides exceptional wear, abrasion, and corrosion resistance; and very high surface hardness. The generic name for this process is ferritic nitrocarburizing.

THUMBHOLE STOCK (CRIME BILL)

An adaptation of the sporter thumbhole stock design which removed a weapon from semi-auto assault weapon legal status. The thumbhole was/is very large and provides the functionality of a true pistol grip stock.

THUMBHOLE STOCK (SPORTER)

A sporter/hunting stock with an ergonomic hole in the grip; the thumb of the shooter's trigger hand fits into the hole which provides for a steadier hold.

TORQUE

The force which causes a rifled firearm to counter-rotate when a projectile travels down its bore.

TRACER

A type of military bullet that emits a colored flame from its base when fired allowing the gunner to adjust his fire onto a target.

TRAJECTORY

The curved flight path of a bullet from muzzle to target; resembling but not a true parabolic arc.

TRAJECTORY TABLE

A numerical table of computed data summarizing the down range trajectory of a projectile.

TRIGGER

Refers to a release device (mechanical or electrical) in the firing system that starts the ignition process. Usually a curved, grooved, or serrated piece of metal which is pulled rearward by the shooter's finger, and which releases the sear or hammer.

TRIGGER GUARD

Usually a circular or oval band of metal, horn, or plastic that goes around the trigger to provide both protection and safety in shooting circumstances.

TRIGGER SAFETY

A trigger assembly component which must be depressed or otherwise moved before the trigger can be pulled completely through to fire the weapon. Most often a pivoting blade in the center of a trigger which protrudes from the face of the trigger when it is engaged/"on" and automatically resets itself.

TURRETS

Cylinders on an optical sight's main tube which hold adjustment knobs or screws. A turret is dedicated to one of several functions: windage, elevation, parallax, reticle type, reticle illumination, or ranging.

GLOSSARY, CONT.

TWIST RATE

Refers to the distance required for one complete turn of rifling, usually expressed as a ratio such as 1:12 in. twist, which refers to one complete twist of rifling within 12 inches of barrel. Typically, the heavier the bullet, the faster the twist rate needs to be.

UNDER FOLDING STOCK

A folding stock variation; the buttstock rotates downwards and underneath the frame/receiver. See FOLDING STOCK.

UNLOAD

To remove all ammunition/cartridges from a firearm or magazine.

UNSERVICEABLE FIREARM

A firearm that is damaged and cannot be made functional in a minimal amount of time.

UPPER ASSEMBLY

For a semi-auto pistol this includes the barrel and slide assembly, for AR style rifles it includes the barrel, bolt and receiver housing.

VARIABLE POWER OPTICAL SIGHT

An optical sight with multiple magnification levels, most common are 3-9 power general purpose scopes.

VENTILATED

Denotes a component with holes, slots, gaps, or other voids which reduce weight, promote cooling, have a structural purpose, or are decorative.

VERNIER

Typically used in reference to a rear aperture (peep) sight. Usually upper tang mounted, and is adj. for elevation by means of a highly accurate finely threaded screw.

VIOLENT CRIME CONTROL AND LAW ENFORCEMENT ACT OF 1994, PUBLIC LAW 103-322

On September 13, 1994, Congress passed the Violent Crime Control and Law Enforcement Act of 1994, Public Law 103-322. Title IX, Subtitle A, Section 110105 of this Act generally made it unlawful to manufacture, transfer, and possess semiautomatic assault weapons (SAWs) and to transfer and possess large capacity ammunition feeding devices (LCAFDs). The law also required importers and manufacturers to place certain markings on SAWs and LCAFDs, designating they were for export or law enforcement/government use. Significantly, the law provided that it would expire 10 years from the date of enactment. Accordingly, effective 12:01 am on September 13, 2004, the provisions of the law ceased to apply and the following provisions of the regulations in Part 478 no longer apply:

- Section 478.11- Definitions of the terms "semiautomatic assault weapon" and "large capacity ammunition feeding device"
- Section 478.40- Entire section
- Section 478.40a- Entire section
- Section 478.57- Paragraphs (b) and (c)
- Section 478.92- Paragraph (a)(3) – [NOTE: Renumbered from paragraph (a)(2) to paragraph (a)(3) by TD ATF – 461 (66 FR 40596) on August 3, 2001]
- Section 478.92- Paragraph (c)
- Section 478.119- Entire section- [NOTE: An import permit is still needed pursuant to the Arms Export Control Act- see 27 CFR 447.41(a)]

- Section 478.132- Entire section
- Section 478.153- Entire section

NOTE: The references to "ammunition feeding device" in section 478.116 are not applicable on or after September 13, 2004.

NOTE: The references to "semiautomatic assault weapons" in section 478.171 are not applicable on or after September 13, 2004.

Information from BATFE Online - Bureau of Alcohol, Tobacco and Firearms, and Explosives an official site of the U.S. Department of Justice.

WAD

A shotshell component in front of the powder charge and has a cup or flat surface that the shot charge rests on. Various types of wads exist with the most common being a column of plastic.

WEAVER-STYLE RAIL

A mounting rail system similar in dimensions and use as the Picatinny Rail. Weaver-style grooves are .180 wide and do not always have consistent center-to-center widths. Most Weaver-style accessories will fit the Picatinny system, however Picatinny accessories will not fit the Weaver-style system. Also see PICATINNY RAIL.

WILDCAT CARTRIDGE

An experimental or non-standard cartridge, not commercially manufactured, often using a standard cartridge case which has been significantly modified.

WINDAGE

The deflection of a projectile from its trajectory due to wind. Also, adjustment of a firearm's sight(s) to compensate for the deflection.

WUNDHAMMER GRIP/SWELL

Originally attributed to custom gunsmith Louis Wundhammer, it consists of a bulge on the right side of the pistol grip that ergonomically fills the palm of a right-handed shooter.

YOUTH DIMENSIONS

Usually refers to shorter stock dimensions and/or lighter weight enabling youth/women to shoot and carry a firearm.

ZERO

The procedure of adjusting a firearm's sight(s) so that the point of aim coincides with the bullet's point of impact at a selected range.

ABBREVIATIONS

*	Banned due to 1994-2004 Crime Bill (may be current again)
5R	Five (groove) Rifling
A	Standard Grade Walnut
A.R.M.S.	Atlantic Research Marketing Systems
A2	AR-15 Style/Configuration w/fixed carry handle
A3	AR-15 Style/Configuration w/ detachable carry handle
ACB	Advanced Combat Bolt (LWRC)
ACR	Adaptive Combat Rifle
ACS	MAGPUL Adaptable Carbine/Storage (stock)
ACT	Advanced Combat Trigger (ALG Defense)
adj.	Adjustable
AECA	Arms Export Control Act
AFG	MAGPUL Angled Fore Grip
Ambi	Ambidextrous
AMU	Army Marksman Unit
AOW	Any Other Weapon (NFA)
AR	ArmaLite Rifle
ASAP	MAGPUL Ambi Sling Attachment Point
ATACS	Advanced Tactical Concealment System (camo pattern)
ATR	All Terrain Rifle (Mossberg)
ATS	All Terrain Shotgun (Mossberg)
AWB	Assault Weapons Ban
B	Blue
BAD	MAGPUL Battery Assist Device (bolt catch lever)
BAD-ASS	Battle Arms Development Ambi Safety Selector
BAN/CRIME	
BILL ERA	Mfg. between Nov. 1989 - Sept. 12, 2004
BBL	Barrel
BCG	Bolt Carrier Group
BMG	Browning Machine Gun
BUIS	Back-Up Iron Sight(s)
c.	Circa
C/B 1994	Introduced Because of 1994 Crime Bill
CAD	Computer Assisted Design
cal.	Caliber
CAR	Colt Automatic Rifle or Carbine
CAWS	Close Assault Weapons System
CC	Case Colors
CCA	Colt Collectors Association
CF	Centerfire
CFR	Code of Federal Regulations
CH	Cross Hair
CHF	Cold Hammer Forged
CMV	Chrome Moly Vanadium Steel
CNC	Computer Numeric Controlled (machining/machinery)
COMM.	Commemorative
COMP	Compensated/Competition
C.O.P.	Continuous Optics Platform (Aero Precision USA)

CQB	Close Quarter Battle
CQC	Close Quarter Combat
C-R	Curio-Relic
CSAT	Combat Shooting & Tactics (accessories)
CTF	Copper/Tin Frangible (bullet)
CTG/CTGE	Cartridge
CTR	MAGPUL Compact/Type Restricted (stock)
DAK	Double Action Kellerman Trigger (SIG)
DBM	Detachable Box Magazine
DCM	Director of Civilian Marksmanship
DI	Direct Impingement Gas System, see Glossary
DIGS	Delayed Impingement Gas System, see Glossary
DISC or disc.	Discontinued
DMR	Designated Marksman Rifle (U.S Army, LWRC)
DPMS	Defense Procurement Manufacturing Services
EGLM	Enhanced Grenade Launcher Module (FNH)
EMAG	MAGPUL Export MAGazine
EXC	Excellent
F	Full Choke
FA	Forearm
FDE	Flat Dark Earth (finish color)
FFL	Federal Firearms License
FGS	Forward Guard Shield (Radical Firearms)
FHR	First-Gen Hybrid Rail (Radical Firearms)
FIRSH	Free Floating Integrated Rail System Handguard
FMJ	Full Metal Jacket
FN	Fabrique Nationale
FNC	Fabrique Nationale Carabine
FNH USA	Fabrique Nationale Herstal (U.S. sales and marketing)
FNH	Fabrique Nationale Herstal
FPS	Feet Per Second
FQR	First-Gen Quad Rail (Radical Firearms)
ga.	Gauge
GCA	Gun Control Act
GIO	Gas Impingement Operation
G-LAD	Green Laser Aiming Device
GOVT	Government
GPO	Gas Piston Operation
gr.	Grain
HAMR	High accuracy multi-range rifle scope
HB	Heavy Barrel
H-BAR	H(eavy)-BARrel, AR-15/M16
HC	Hard Case
HK	Heckler und Koch
HMR	Hornady Magnum Rimfire
HP	High Power (FN/Browning pistol)
HPJ	High Performance Jacket
IAR	Infantry Automatic Rifle (LWRC)
ILS	Integral Locking System (North American Arms)

in.	Inch
intro.	Introduced
ITAR	International Traffic (in) Arms Regulation
KAC	Knight's Armament Co.
KMC	Knight's Manufacturing Co.
L	Long
LBC	Les Baer Custom (Inc.)
lbs.	Pounds
LCW	Lauer Custom Weaponry
LEM	Law Enforcement Model or Modification
LEO	Law Enforcement Only
LMT	Lewis Machine and Tool (Company)
LOP	Length of Pull
LPI	Lines Per Inch
LR	Long Rifle
LT	Long Tang or Light
LTR	Light Tactical Rifle (Rem.)
LWRC	Land Warfare Resources Corporation
LWRC	Leitner-Wise Rifle Company, Inc.
M&P	Military & Police
M-4	Newer AR-15/M16 Carbine Style/ Configuration
Mag.	Magnum Caliber
mag.	Magazine
MARS	Modular Accessory Rail System
MBUS	MAGPUL Back-Up Sight
MC	Monte Carlo
MCS	Modular Combat System (Rem.)
MFG or Mfg.	Manufactured/manufacture
MFT	Mission First Tactical
MIAD	MAGPUL Mission Adaptable (grip, other)
mil	see Glossary
mil-dot	See Glossary
Mil-Spec	Mfg. to Military Specifications
Mil-Std	Mfg. to Military Standards
MK	Mark
mm	Millimeter
MOA	Minute of Angle
MOE	MAGPUL Original Equipment
MOUT	Military Operations (on) Urbanized Terrain
MR	Matted Rib
MRP	Monolithic Rail Platform (lewis Machine & Tool)
MRR	Modular Railed Receiver (Patriot Ordnance Factory)
MS2	MAGPUL Multi Mission Sling System
MSR	Manufacturer's Suggested Retail
MVG	MAGPUL MOE Vertical Grip
MWS	Modular Weapons System
N	Nickel
N/A	Not Applicable or Not Available
NATO	North Atlantic Treaty Organization
NFA	National Firearms Act (U.S. 1934)
NIB	New in Box
NM	National Match
no.	Number
NP3/NP3 Plus	Nickel-Phosphorus (firearm coating)

ABBREVIATIONS, CONT. 45

NVD/E	Night Vision Device/Equipment
OA	Overall
OAL	Overall Length
OBO	Or Best Offer
ODG	Olive Drab Green (finish color)
ORB	Oil-Rubbed Bronze (finish from Sig Sauer)
ORC	Optics Ready Carbine
oz.	Ounce
PAD	Personal Anti-recoil Device (Savage)
Para.	Parabellum
PBR	Patrol Bolt Rifle (FNH)
PDA	Personal Defense Assistant (PARA USA INC.)
PFFR	Percantage of factory finish remaining
PG	Pistol Grip
PGF	Precision Guided Firearm
PMAG	MAGPUL Polymer MAGazine
POR/P.O.R.	Price on Request
POST-'89	Paramilitary mfg. after Federal legislation in Nov. 1989
POST-BAN	Refers to production after Sept. 12, 2004
PPD	Post Paid
PRE-'89	Paramilitary mfg. before Federal legislation in Nov. 1989
PRE-BAN	Mfg. before September 13, 1994 per C/B or before Nov. 1989.
PRS/PRS2	MAGPUL Precision Rifle/Sniper (stock)
PSD	Personal Security Detail rifle (LWRC)
PSR	Precision Shooting Rifle (FNH)
PST	Port Selector Technology
PXT	Power Extractor Technology (PARA USA INC.)
QD	Quick Detachable
Q.D.S.	Quick Deploy Sight (YHM)
RACS	Remington Arms Chassis System
RAS	Rail Adapter System
RB	Round Barrel/Round Butt
RDS	Rapid Deployment Stock
REC	Receiver
REM.	Remington
REM. MAG.	Remington Magnum
REPR	Rapid Engagement Precision Rifle (LWRC)
RF	Rimfire
RFM	Rim Fire Magnum
RIS	Rail Interface system
RSA	MAGPUL Rail Sling Attachment
RVG	MAGPUL Rail Vertical Grip
S&W	Smith & Wesson
S/N	Serial Number
SAAMI	Sporting Arms and Ammunition Manufacturers' Institute
SABR	Sniper/Assaulter Battle Rifle (LWRC)

SASS	Single Action Shooting Society or (U.S. Army) Semi Automatic Sniper System
SAW	Semiautomatic Assault Weapon
SAW	Squad Automatic Weapon
SBR	Short Barrel Rifle
SCAR	Special (Operations Forces) Combat Assault Rifle (FNH)
ser.	serial
SIG	Schweizerische Industriegesellschaft
SIM	Special Impact Munition
SMG	Submachine Gun
SNT	Single Non-Selective Trigger
SOCOM	Special Operations Command
SOPMOD	Special Operations Peculiar Modification
SP	Special Purpose
SPC	Special Purpose Cartridge
SPEC	Special
SPEC-OPS	Special Operations
Spl.	Special
SPLLAT	Special Purpose Low Lethality Anti Terrorist (Munition)
SPR	Special Police Rifle (FNH), Special Purpose Rifle
SPS	Special Purpose Synthetic (Remington)
SPS	Superalloy Piston System (LWRC)
sq.	Square
SS	Single Shot or Stainless Steel
SSA	Super Short Action
SSR	Sniper Support Rifle (FNH)
SUR	Sport Utility Rifle - see Glossary
SWAT	Special Weapons Assault Team
SWAT	Special Weapons and Tactics
TAS	Tactical adjustable sight
TB	Threaded Barrel
TBA	To be Announced
TBM	Tactical Box Magazine
TD	Take Down
TDR	Target Deployment Rifle (Rem.)
TGT	Target
TiN	TiN coating (STI International)
TIR	Target Interdiction Rifle (Rem.)
TPS	Tactical Police Shotgun (FNH)
TRPAFD	Take Red Pen Away From Dave!
TSOB	Scope Mount Rail Weaver Type
TSR XP USA	Tactical Sport Rifle - Extreme Performance Ultra Short Action (FNH)
TSR XP	Tactical Sport Rifle - Extreme Performance (FNH)
TT	Target Trigger
TTR	Tactical Target Rifle (PARA USA INC.)
TTU	Tactical Trigger Unit (Wilson Combat)
TWS	Tactical Weapons System (Rem.)

UBR	MAGPUL Utility/Battle Rifle (stock)
UCIW	Ultra Compact Individual Weapon (LWRC)
UIT	Union Internationale de Tir
UMC	Union Metallic Cartridge Co.
URX	Upper Receiver Extending (free floating barrel system, Knight's Armament)
USA	Ultra Safety Assurance (Springfield Inc.)
USAMU	U.S. Army Marksmanship Unit
USC	Universal Self-Loading Carbine (H&K)
USG	United States Government (FNH model suffix)
USPSA	United States Practical Shooting Association
USR	Urban Sniper Rifle (Rem.)
USSOCOM	U.S. Special Operations Command
VAT	Value Added Tax
vent.	Ventilated
VG	Very Good
VTAC	Viking Tactics, Inc. (accessories)
w/	With
w/o	Without
WCF	Winchester Center Fire
WFF	Watch For Fakes
WO	White Outline
WRF	Winchester Rim Fire
WRM	Winchester Rimfire Magnum
WSL	Winchester Self-Loading
WSM	Winchester Short Magnum
WSSM	Winchester Super Short Magnum
WW	World War
YHM	Yankee Hill Machine

AR-15 CALIBERS & DANGEROUS COMBINATIONS

While most people associate the centerfire calibers .223 Rem., 5.56 NATO (5.56x45mm), .308 Win., and 7.62 NATO (7.62x51mm), plus .22 LR for the rimfire variations with AR type rifles, there are actually over 50 calibers currently available on the AR-15 platform. As this edition went to press, they are:

.17 HMR	.260 Rem.	.300 WSM
.17 Rem.	6.5 Creedmoor	.300 Fireball
.204 Ruger	6.5 Grendel	.300 ACC Blackout
.22 LR	.270 Win.	.338 Federal
5.56 NATO	6.8x43mm Rem. SPC	.338 Lapua
.222 Rem.	6.8 SPC	.338 Norma
.222 Special	7mm Rem. Mag.	9mm Para.
.223 Rem.	7.62x39mm	.375 Raptor
.223 Wylde chamber (5.56 NATO or .223 Rem.)	7.62mm NATO	.40 S&W
	7.62x51mm	10mm
.22-250 Rem.	.30 Carbine	.408 CheyTac
.223 WSSM	.30 Rem. AR	.45 ACP
.243 Win.	.308 Win.	.450 Bushmaster
.243 WSSM	.30-06	.450 Thumper
6 Creedmoor	.300 Win. Mag.	.458 SOCOM
.25-45 Sharps	.300 RSUM	.50 Beowulf
.25 WSSM	.300 WSSM	
.25-06 Rem.	.300 OSSM	

DANGEROUS CALIBER INTERCHANGEABILITY CONSIDERATIONS

The discharge of ammunition in a firearm that is not designed to shoot that ammunition can be dangerous, resulting in serious injury or even worse to the user and/or bystanders, as well as damage to the firearm. This unsafe condition is caused by an excessive buildup and/or release of high-pressure gas in a firearm's chamber, barrel, and/or action beyond which the firearm is designed to withstand. In the interest of safety, you should use only ammunition of the caliber or gauge designated by the firearm manufacturer for use in that firearm. Markings indicating the correct caliber or gauge of ammunition to be used in a firearm are usually found on the firearm's barrel, frame, or receiver. If the caliber or gauge is not clearly marked on the firearm, or if it appears the original markings have been altered or modified in any way, do not use the firearm.

Before World War I (1914-1918), each American ammunition manufacturer used dimensional, pressure, and ballistic performance standards based on individual company practices and procedures. When the U.S. entered World War I in 1917, these multiple standards caused serious difficulties. As a result, after the War, the American firearms and ammunition industry formed the Sporting Arms and Ammunition Manufacturers' Institute (SAAMI) to serve as a clearing house for standardized dimensions, practices, and procedures. Today, SAAMI continues this work under the National Shooting Sports Foundation (NSSF). In addition to developing standardized cartridge and chamber dimensions, interior ballistics, and exterior ballistics, SAAMI operates in the fields of metallurgy, chemistry, and engineering to help solve industry-wide problems. SAAMI also distributes safety brochures dealing with proper handling and storage of ammunition and components.

It is important to note that the commercial .223 Rem. cartridge is NOT the same as the 5.56x45mm NATO cartridge and they are NOT interchangeable. If the caliber designation marked on a barrel is marked .223 Rem./.223 Remington, do not attempt to shoot 5.56 NATO cal. ammunition in it. However, barrels that are marked .223 Wylde or 5.56 NATO can safely shoot .223 Rem. ammunition. The .223 Wylde is not a caliber, but rather a term for a chamber boring and is capable of safely firing both the 5.56 NATO and .223 Rem. calibers.

For more information on ammunition including an expanded SAAMI approved list of Dangerous Combinations, please refer to SAAMI at www.saami.org/index.cfm and the Ammo Encyclopedia available at BlueBookOfGunValues.com.

AR-15 GRADING CRITERIA

The older NRA modern condition descriptions that relied upon conditions such as "Excellent", "Very Good", or "Fair" have served the firearms community for many years. However, many of today's dealers/collectors, especially those who deal in modern guns, have turned away from this older, subjective system. There is too much variance within some of these older NRA subjective grades which can make accurate grading difficult.

Most dealers and collectors are now utilizing what is essentially an objective method for deciding the condition of a gun: THE PERCENTAGE OF ORIGINAL FACTORY FINISH(ES) REMAINING ON THE GUN. This is an acquired skill, so please visit BlueBookOfGunValues.com and click on Photo Percentage Grading System listed under CONTENT INFORMATION (then click on pistols, rifles, shotguns, etc.). The images graphically depict condition factors, such as 98%, 90%, 70% or less original finish remaining. Remember, sometimes an older unfired AR-15 described as NIB can actually be 98% or less condition, simply because of the wear accumulated by taking it in and out of the box and excessive handling. Of course, factors such as quality of finish(es), special orders/features, historical significance and/or provenance, etc. can and do affect prices immensely. Also, it seems that every year bore condition becomes more important in the overall grading factor and price. Never pay a premium for condition that isn't there. Remember, original condition still beats everything else to the bank.

Every gun's unique condition factor – and therefore the price – is best determined by the percentage of original finish(es) remaining, with the key consideration being the overall frame/receiver finish. The key word here is "original", for if anyone other than the factory has refinished the gun, its value as a collector's item has been diminished. Finish wear typically accumulates first on those areas which get the most usage from either shooting, storage, or gun case wear.

There are several very important factors in determining AR-15 wear on carbines/rifles, pistols, and shotguns. Since most AR finishes utilize either a dull or matte black exterior type of finish, they are extremely resistant. These wear-resistant finishes/coatings are unlike blue or nickel finishes, and become much more difficult to accurately ascertain how much an AR-15 has been used.

These critical tell-tale signs are typically dents/scratches/scuffing on the metal receiver edges and stock/forearm, a noticeable primer ring on the bolt face (indicating a lot of usage), plus excessive wear on and around the safety lever and magazine release levers. Also check for any excessive wear in or around the receiver takedown and pivot pins. Remember to look at the top of the charging handle when it's fully extended for noticeable wear, in addition to any metal on metal contact points on the bolt carrier group. Since the bolt carrier group is the main moving part on an AR-15, this will accumulate wear (and shooting residue build-up) the fastest.

For your convenience, NRA Condition Standards are listed (see Table of Contents). Converting from this grading system to percentages can now be done accurately. Remember the price is wrong if the condition factor isn't right!

PHOTO PERCENTAGE GRADING SYSTEM (PPGS) CONVERSION GUIDELINES

The following NRA to PPGS conversion factors have been provided to assist the reader to accurately ascertain correct condition factors.

New/Perfect – 100% condition with or without box. 100% on currently manufactured firearms assumes NIB (New In Box) condition and not sold previously at retail.

Mint – no less than 99% condition with almost no observable wear. Can also include guns sold previously at retail, that may have, only been shot occasionally.

Excellent – 95%+ - 98% condition.

Very Good – 80% - 95% condition (all parts/finish should be original).

Good - 60% – 80% condition (all parts/finish should be original).

Fair – 20% - 60% condition (all parts/finish may or may not be original but must function properly and shoot).

Poor – under 20% condition (shooting not a factor).

NRA CONDITION STANDARDS

The NRA modern condition factors listed below have been provided as guidelines to assist the reader in converting and comparing condition factors to the Photo Percentage Grading System™ - please visit BlueBookOfGunValues.com and click on Photo Percentage Grading System listed under CONTENT INFORMATION (then click on pistols, rifles, shotguns, etc.). NRA antique and modern condition standards are now represented in the PPGS. In order to use this book correctly, the reader is urged to examine these images carefully. Once the gun's condition has been accurately assessed, only then can values be correctly ascertained.

NRA MODERN CONDITION DESCRIPTIONS

New – not previously sold at retail, in same condition as current factory production.

Perfect – in new condition in every respect, may have previously been sold at retail.

Excellent – near new condition, shows little use, no noticeable marring of wood or metal, bluing near perfect (except at muzzle or sharp edges).

Very Good – in perfect working condition, no appreciable wear on working surfaces, no corrosion or pitting, only minor surface dents or scratches.

Good – in safe working condition, minor wear on working surfaces, no broken parts, no corrosion or pitting that will interfere with proper functioning.

Fair – in safe working condition, but well worn, perhaps requiring replacement of minor parts or adjustments which should be indicated in advertisement, no rust, but may have corrosion pits which do not render firearm unsafe or inoperable.

A SECTION

2 VETS ARMS CO., LLC

Previous custom AR-15 style rifle manufacturer located in Eufaula, OK circa 2014-2017.

MSR	100%	98%	95%	90%	80%	70%	60%	Last MSR

RIFLES: SEMI-AUTO

2 Vets Arms Co., LLC was a female Service-connected Disabled Veteran Owned Business (SDVOB) that specialized in building high performance custom rifles for American patriots with an emphasis on serving the U.S. Military Veteran and those actively serving in the U.S. Armed Forces. A portion of the proceeds from each sale went to support honored military veterans and veteran support organizations.

.300 BLACKOUT – .300 AAC Blackout cal., GIO, AR-15 style, low profile gas block, 16 in. free floating stainless steel barrel, CTR Mil-Spec (standard or five optional style) buttstock, Magpul MOE grip and trigger guard, carbine length free float quad rail, optional lightweight free float tube, or PRI carbon fiber free float forend, side charging upper receiver, 2VA lower receiver and parts kit. Disc.

	$1,385	$895	$675	$525	$450	$385	$350	$1,675

5.56mm RIFLE – 5.56 NATO cal., GIO, 16 in. free floating M4 profile stainless barrel, option of A2 front sight or low profile gas block, CTR Mil-Spec buttstock, Magpul MOE grip and trigger guard, side charging upper receiver, 2VA lower receiver and parts kit. Disc.

	$995	$625	$495	$450	$395	$350	$325	$1,199

6.8 SPC II – 6.8 SPC II cal., GIO, low profile gas block, match grade 16, 18, or 20 in. free floating stainless steel barrel, Magpul CTR Mil-Spec (standard or five optional) buttstock, Magpul MOE grip and trigger guard, standard rifle length free float quad rail or optional lightweight quad rail, free float tube or PRI carbon fiber tube, side charging upper receiver, 2VA lower receiver and parts kit. Disc.

	$1,350	$875	$650	$525	$450	$385	$350	$1,650

2VA 5.56 ALPHA – 5.56 NATO cal., GIO, AR-15 style, mid-length gas system, 16 in. stainless steel match barrel with full flutes, billet side charged upper receiver, forged lower receiver, B5 SOPMOD Alpha stock, BCM Gunfighter grip, KNS anti-rotation pins, Geissele SAA fire controls, Battle Arms Development ambi selector, Phase 5 enhanced side charged compatible BAD lever, 13 in. KeyMod compatible free float rail. Mfg. 2014-2017.

	$1,575	$995	$775	$575	$495	$425	$395	$1,875

2VA 5.56 BRAVO – 5.56 NATO cal., GIO, AR-15 style, 16 in. chrome moly barrel, billet side charged upper receiver, forged lower receiver, A2 front sight base, B5 Bravo stock and forend, Umbrella Corp. grip, G.I. fire controls, Phase 5 enhanced side charged compatible BAD lever. Mfg. 2014-2017.

	$1,075	$675	$500	$450	$400	$350	$325	$1,300

2VA 6.8 DMR – 6.8 SPC cal., GIO, AR-15 style, intermediate-length gas system, 20 in. stainless steel match barrel, Battle Comp BABC compensator, billet side charged upper receiver, forged lower receiver, adj. two-stage trigger, B5 SOPMOD Alpha stock, BCM Gunfighter grip, 15 in. tactical Evo rail. Mfg. 2014-2015.

	$1,525	$975	$750	$575	$495	$425	$375	$1,849

2VA LRRP – 5.56 NATO or .300 AAC Blackout cal., GIO, mid-length gas system, 16 in. stainless steel barrel, B5 Systems SOPMOD Alpha buttstock, BCM Gunfighter grip, 10 in. tactical lightweight Evolution rail and Texas Custom Guns micro gas block, LAR side charged upper receiver, 2VA forged lower receiver. Disc. 2015.

	$1,350	$875	$650	$525	$450	$385	$350	$1,650

2VA SOPMOD – 5.56 NATO or .300 AAC Blackout cal., GIO, mid-length gas system, 16 in. stainless steel barrel, B5 SOPMOD Alpha buttstock, BCM Gunfighter grip, 10 in. Spectre quad rail covering Texas Custom Guns micro gas block, LAR side charged upper receiver, 2VA lower receiver. Disc. 2017.

	$1,250	$825	$575	$475	$425	$375	$350	$1,499

2VA 308 SPECIAL PURPOSE RIFLE – .308 Win. cal., 18 in. fluted stainless steel match grade barrel with black Nitride finish, two-stage Geissele trigger, B5 Systems Bravo collapsible buttstock, 15 in. lightweight free float tube, ambidextrous side charging system and safety selector, 7 lbs. 13 oz. Mfg. 2015-2017.

	$1,575	$995	$775	$575	$495	$425	$395	$1,875

2A ARMAMENT LLC

Current ultra-lightweight AR-15 style carbine/rifle manufacturer located in Boise, ID beginning 2009.

PISTOLS: SEMI-AUTO

BALIOS LITE AR PISTOL – 5.56 NATO cal., refreshed aesthetics, carbine length gas system, 7 1/2, 10 1/2, or 12 1/2 in. barrel, Magpul PMAG, ALG ACT trigger group, Magpul MIAD grip, Gen 2 billet upper and lower receiver, 7, 10, or 12 in. extruded M-LOK or KeyMod rail, titanium T3 compensator, KAK Industry pistol blade stabilizer, Type III hardcoat anodized black finish.

MSR $2,299		$1,955	$1,710	$1,465	$1,330	$1,075	$880	$685

A 50 2A ARMAMENT LLC, cont.

MSR	100%	98%	95%	90%	80%	70%	60%	Last MSR

BALIOS LITE .300 BLK AR – .300 AAC Blackout cal., refreshed aesthetics, carbine length gas system, 8 in. barrel, Magpul PMAG, ALG ACT trigger group, Gen 2 billet upper and lower receiver, 7 in. extruded M-LOK or KeyMod rail, titanium X3 compensator, Type III hardcoat anodized black finish.

	100%	98%	95%	90%	80%	70%	60%	
MSR $2,299	$1,955	$1,710	$1,465	$1,330	$1,075	$880	$685	

RIFLES: SEMI-AUTO

ALR-16 – 5.56 NATO cal., mid-length gas system, forward assist, 2A 16 in. lightweight barrel, Magpul PMAG, ALG ACT trigger group, billet upper and lower receiver, titanium T3 compensator, 15 in. extruded Aethon rail M-LOK, built-in QD mounts, Type III hardcoat anodized black finish, 5 lbs. 4 oz. New 2017.

	100%	98%	95%	90%	80%	70%	60%	
MSR $2,459	$1,975	$1,150	$925	$650	$575	$495	$425	

BALIOS LITE AR – .22 LR cal., 2A 16 1/2 in. lightweight fluted barrel, Grade 5 6AL-4V titanium bolt stainless steel collar, ejector, extractor, ALG ACT trigger, Mission First Minimalist stock, Magpul MIAD grip, Balios-Lite Gen 2 billet upper and lower receiver, titanium T3 compensator, 15 in. extruded BL-RAIL, M-LOK, or KeyMod handguard, firing pin, synthetic polymer buffer, Type III hardcoat anodized black finish, 3 lbs. 11 oz. New 2017.

	100%	98%	95%	90%	80%	70%	60%	
MSR $1,399	$1,150	$750	$550	$465	$415	$375	$350	

BLR-16 GEN 2 – 5.56 NATO cal., mid-length gas system, Magpul PMAG, ALG ACT trigger group, Mission First Minimalist stock, Magpul MIAD grip, billet upper and lower receiver, refreshed aesthetics, 15 in. extruded BL-RAIL, M-LOK, or KeyMod handguard, Type III hardcoat anodized black finish, 5 lbs. New late 2017.

	100%	98%	95%	90%	80%	70%	60%	
MSR $2,459	$1,975	$1,150	$925	$650	$575	$495	$425	

BLR-16 RIFLE – 5.56 NATO cal., mid-length gas system, 16 in. pencil profile stainless steel barrel, titanium T3 compensator, Magpul PMAG, ALG ACT trigger group, Mission First Minimalist stock, Magpul MIAD grip, 15 in. extruded BL-RAIL, M-LOK, or KeyMod handguard, billet upper and lower receiver, Type III hardcoat anodized black (disc. 2017) or Hydro dipped KUIU Vias 2.0 pattern finish, 5 lbs. New 2016.

	100%	98%	95%	90%	80%	70%	60%	
MSR $2,779	$2,225	$1,395	$1,050	$675	$595	$525	$475	

Subtract $600 for Type III hardcoat anodized black finish (disc. 2017).

BLR-CARBON RIFLE – 5.56 NATO cal., mid-length gas system, 16 in. Proof Research carbon fiber barrel, titanium T3 compensator, flared magwell, Magpul PMAG, CMC two-stage trigger, Magpul CTR stock, Magpul MIAD grip, 15 in. extruded BL-RAIL, M-LOK, or KeyMod handguard, billet upper and lower receivers, 2A-Gray Cerakote finish, 5 1/2 lbs. New 2016.

	100%	98%	95%	90%	80%	70%	60%	
MSR $3,699	$2,950	$1,925	$1,400	$825	$675	$625	$575	

XLR-18 RIFLE – .308 Win. cal., rifle length gas system, 18 in. 2A contour lightweight barrel, CMC two-stage flat trigger, Mission First Tactical stock, Magpul MIAD grip, 15 in. Xanthos-lite rail in M-LOK format, Mil-Spec receiver, BCM Gunfighter charging handle, 6.75 lbs.

	100%	98%	95%	90%	80%	70%	60%	
MSR $3,199	$2,550	$1,650	$1,250	$700	$625	$575	$525	

XLR-20 RIFLE – 6.5mm Creedmoor cal., 20 in. lightweight barrel, two-stage flat trigger, Mission First Tactical stock, Magpul MIAD grip, 15 in. Xanthos-lite rail in M-LOK format, Mil-Spec billet AR10 receiver, BCM Gunfighter charging handle, hardcoat anodized black or KUIU camo finish, 6.85 lbs. New 2018.

	100%	98%	95%	90%	80%	70%	60%	
MSR $3,209	$2,625	$1,725	$1,300	$725	$650	$595	$525	

Add $320 for KUIU camo finish.

5TC (5 TOES CUSTOM)

Current manufacturer of hand-crafted custom pistols and rifles located in Carrollton, TX.

Sergeant First Class John Wayne Walding and David Feherty started 5 Toes Custom circa 2014. SFC Walding is a Green Beret and recipient of the Silver Star who served combat tours in Afghanistan and Iraq. David Feherty is a former professional golfer turned writer and broadcaster. SFC Walding's personal sacrifice - losing his right leg in combat - led to his unlikely meeting and subsequent friendship with David Feherty. 5TC is unique in that it provides hand-crafted custom rifles, built by great Americans, while giving back to charities.

RIFLES: SEMI-AUTO

For models listed below, please contact the company directly for additional options, upgrades, availability, and pricing (see Trademark Index).

5TC-10 – .308 Win., 6.5mm Creedmoor, or .260 Rem. cal., Proof Research 416 SS carbon fiber barrel, Magpul furniture, AR gold trigger, ambidextrous controls, Lantac BCG and brake, SLR handguard, JP Silent captured spring.

5TC-15 – .223 Wylde chamber, 6.8 SPC, 6.5 Grendel, .22 Nosler, or .300 AAC Blackout cal., Proof Research 416 SS carbon fiber barrel, Magpul furniture, AR gold trigger, ambidextrous controls, Lantac BCG and brake, SLR handguard, JP Silent captured spring.

A06 ARMS

Current AR-15 style carbine/rifle manufacturer located in Fairplay, CO beginning 2013.

A06 ARMS, cont. 51 A

MSR	100%	98%	95%	90%	80%	70%	60%	Last MSR

RIFLES: SEMI-AUTO

A06 ALPHA18 – various cals., 18 in. black Nitride barrel, ambi bolt release, DLC bolt carrier group, made with 7075 aluminum, built to customer specifications.

| MSR $2,390 | $1,875 | $1,100 | $895 | $650 | $575 | $495 | $425 | |

A06 ALPHA24 – various cals., AR-15 style, 24 in. stainless steel barrel, no brake, ambi bolt release, DLC bolt carrier group, SLR rail, made with 7075 aluminum, built to customer specifications.

| MSR $2,490 | $1,975 | $1,150 | $925 | $650 | $575 | $495 | $425 | |

A06 HOG – various cals., AR-15 style, 18, 20, or 22 in. stainless steel barrel, ambi bolt release, DLC bolt carrier group, SLR rail, made with 7075 aluminum, built to customer specifications.

| MSR $2,810 | $2,295 | $1,450 | $1,075 | $675 | $595 | $525 | $475 | |

Add $98 for 20 or 22 in. barrel.

A06 MIL16 – various cals., AR-15 style, 16 in. stainless steel barrel, DLC bolt carrier group, SLR rail, made with 6061 aluminum, built to customer specifications.

| MSR $1,490 | $1,250 | $825 | $575 | $475 | $425 | $375 | $350 | |

A06 ONE16 – 5.56 NATO or .300 AAC Blackout cal., AR-15 style, 16 in. stainless steel barrel, ambi bolt release, DLC bolt carrier group, SLR rail, made with 7075 aluminum, built to customer specifications.

| MSR $2,155 | $1,725 | $1,050 | $850 | $625 | $550 | $475 | $425 | |

AR 57 LLC

Current AR-15 style rifle manufacturer located in Woodinville, WA. AR 57 LLC's former name was 57 Center LLC and was previously located in Bellevue and Redmond, WA.

CARBINES: SEMI-AUTO

AR57A1 - PDW – 5.7x28mm cal., 16 in. barrel with flash suppressor, 50 shot box magazine runs horizontally over barrel and can be inserted from top or side of weapon, M4 carbine 6-pos. stock with forged aluminum stock tube, ergonomic design custom grip with battery and accessory compartment, Mil-Spec fire control group, front and rear upper Picatinny rails between mag., lower accessory rails, includes four 50 shot mags., black matte finish. Mfg. 2010-2013.

| | $915 | $575 | $475 | $415 | $350 | $325 | $300 | *$1,099* |

AR57 GEN II/LEM – 5.7x28mm cal., 16 in. fluted barrel with flash hider, two 50 shot mags., ambidextrous mag. release and charging handle, carbine buffer, semi-auto bolt, ergonomic design custom grip with battery and accessory compartment, extended rear quad rail. Mfg. 2013-2016.

| | $915 | $575 | $475 | $415 | $350 | $325 | $300 | *$1,099* |

AR57-SLC – 5.7x28mm cal., 16 in. lightweight barrel, flash hider, two 50 shot mags., carbine buffer, ambidextrous charging handle, M-LOK rail, multi-cal. SLC receiver, 10 lbs. New 2018.

| MSR $1,099 | $915 | $575 | $475 | $415 | $350 | $325 | $300 | |

ACCURATE TOOL & MFG. CO.

Current custom pistol and rifle manufacturer located in Lexington, KY.

PISTOLS: SEMI-AUTO

Accurate Tool & Mfg. Co. also offers custom built 1911 pistols styled like Government, Commander, and Officer models. The following listings reflect base MSR only. Please contact the company directly for additional options, upgrades, availability, and pricing (see Trademark Index).

AR PISTOL – 5.56 NATO or .300 AAC Blackout cal., pistol length gas system, 7 1/2 or 8 1/2 in. cold hammer forged barrel, 20 shot mag., extended feed ramps, flat-top upper receiver, forged lower receiver with extension, H buffer, and flip-up rear sight, Samson Evo handguard, Thordsen cheek riser, Mil-Spec phosphate finish.

| MSR $1,345 | $1,125 | $1,000 | $875 | $750 | $675 | $575 | $475 | |

RIFLES: SEMI-AUTO

The following models reflect base MSR only. Please contact the company directly for more information including pricing, options, and availability (see Trademark Index).

AR-10 – .308 Win. cal., match grade stainless steel barrel with Lantac flash suppressor or silencer mount of choice, 20 shot mag., extended feed ramp, mid-length gas system, forged flat-top upper and forged lower receiver with H buffer and flip-up rear sight, CMR rail system (one-piece free float handguard), in-house Cerakote finish of choice.

| MSR $2,995 | $2,550 | $2,225 | $1,825 | $1,575 | $1,300 | $1,100 | $950 | |

A 52 ACCURATE TOOL & MFG. CO., cont.

MSR	100%	98%	95%	90%	80%	70%	60%	Last MSR

CLASSIC CARBINE – 5.56 NATO cal., carbine length gas system, 16 in. M4 profile barrel, M4 feed ramp barrel extension, enhanced flared magwell, M4 stock, aluminum forged upper and lower receivers, Type III hardcoat anodized finish.

	100%	98%	95%	90%	80%	70%	60%	Last MSR
MSR $1,020	$865	$550	$465	$395	$350	$325	$300	

LE CARBINE – 5.56 NATO cal., carbine length gas system, 16 in. cold hammer forged barrel, A2 flash suppressor, 30 shot mag., fixed front sight base, flip-up rear sight (on lower only), extended feed ramp, flat-top upper and forged lower with Mil-Spec rec. extension and H buffer, standard M4 type handguard, Mil-Spec phosphate finish.

	100%	98%	95%	90%	80%	70%	60%	Last MSR
MSR $1,290	$1,075	$675	$500	$450	$400	$350	$325	

LE MIDDY – 5.56 NATO cal., 16 in. cold hammer forged barrel with A2 flash suppressor, 30 shot mag., F marked front sight base, mid-length gas system, extended feed ramps, flat-top upper rec., forged lower receiver with extension, H buffer, and flip-up rear sight, Mil-Spec phosphate finish.

	100%	98%	95%	90%	80%	70%	60%	Last MSR
MSR $1,590	$1,315	$850	$625	$500	$435	$375	$350	

ADAMS ARMS

Current rifle manufacturer established circa 2007, located in Palm Harbor, FL. Adams Arms also manufactures a complete line of accessories for the AR-15 platform, in addition to barrels, upper assemblies, and free floating rails.

PISTOLS: SEMI-AUTO

P2 – 5.56 NATO cal., GPO, 7 1/2 or 11 1/2 in. heavy or Govt. contour barrel with QPQ Melonite/black Nitride finish, Manimal Extended A2 flash hider, Hiperfire EDT trigger, Defiance flip-up sights, SBA3 pistol brace, angled pistol grip, ambidextrous safety selector and charging handle, forged A4 flat-top upper receiver, M4 feed ramps, Adams Arms M-LOK rail system, 5.86-5.98 lbs. New mid-2017.

	100%	98%	95%	90%	80%	70%	60%	Last MSR
MSR $1,500	$1,275	$1,125	$1,025	$875	$750	$625	$525	

P2 SMALL FRAME – .308 Win. cal., mid-length gas system, GPO, 12 1/2 in. Govt. contour barrel with QPQ Melonite/black Nitride finish, Manimal flash hider, Hiperfire EDT trigger, Defiance flip-up sights, SBA3 pistol brace, angled pistol grip, ambidextrous safety selector and charging handle, forged A4 flat-top upper receiver, M4 feed ramps, Adams Arms M-LOK rail system, 8.14 lbs.

	100%	98%	95%	90%	80%	70%	60%	Last MSR
MSR $2,000	$1,700	$1,500	$1,250	$1,100	$950	$825	$675	

TACTICAL EVO BASE PISTOL – 5.56 NATO cal., GPO, 7 1/2 in. Government contour heavy barrel with A2 flash hider, 30 shot GI aluminum mag., Samson free float lightweight modular rail system, no sights, adj. gas block, forged lower receiver with beveled magwell, forged A4 flat-top upper receiver with M4 feed ramps and Picatinny rail, pistol buffer tube, A2 grip, hardcoat anodized black finish. Mfg. 2015-2017.

	100%	98%	95%	90%	80%	70%	60%	Last MSR
	$925	$850	$725	$625	$550	$475	$425	$1,098

TACTICAL EVO UPGRADED PISTOL – 5.56 NATO cal., GPO, 7 1/2 in. heavy contour pistol length or 11 1/2 in. carbine length Voodoo barrel with A2 flash hider, 30 shot GI aluminum mag., flat-top Picatinny rail, three adj. gas settings, extended Samson Evolution rail, pistol buffer tube, ambidextrous safety, beveled magwell, Samson fixed front and rear sights, upgraded JP fire control group, Ergo grip, hardcoat anodized black finish, approx. 6 lbs. Mfg. 2015-2017.

	100%	98%	95%	90%	80%	70%	60%	Last MSR
	$925	$850	$725	$625	$550	$475	$425	$1,099

XLP EVO UPGRADED PISTOL – .300 AAC Blackout cal., GPO, 12 1/2 in. medium contour barrel with VDI .30 cal. Jet compensator and black Nitride finish, 30 shot GI aluminum mag., Samson free float lightweight modular rail system, XLP low profile gas block, upgraded JP Fire Control group, Mil-Spec forged upper and lower receiver, M4 feed ramps, beveled magwell, flat-top Picatinny rail, pistol buffer tube, 12 in. Evolution handguard, no sights, Magpul MOE grip, JP trigger, 5.95 lbs. Mfg. 2015-2017.

	100%	98%	95%	90%	80%	70%	60%	Last MSR
	$1,350	$1,200	$1,075	$950	$815	$700	$575	$1,605

RIFLES: SEMI-AUTO

Adams Arms manufactures a complete line of AR-15 platform rifles. For more information on options, availability, and delivery time, please contact the company directly (see Trademark Index).

Adams Arms manufactured the Huldra line of AR-15 style rifles/carbines exclusively for Fleet Farm until mid-2016 and also manufactures the Korstog AR-15s. Please refer to the H and K sections for a recent listing.

MID BASE – 5.56 NATO cal., GPO, 16 in. Govt. contour Melonite barrel with A2 flash hider, Mil-Spec 6-position retractable stock, 30 shot GI aluminum magazine, Mil-Spec forged upper and lower receiver with Picatinny rail, ribbed mid-length M4 style molded polymer handguards with lower heat shield, black hardcoat anodized, Kryptek Highlander, Kryptek Nomad, or Kryptek Typhon camo (new 2015) finish, 6.4 lbs. Disc. 2017.

	100%	98%	95%	90%	80%	70%	60%	Last MSR
	$865	$550	$465	$395	$350	$325	$300	$1,016

Add $139 for Kryptek Highlander, Nomad, or Typhon (new 2015) finish.

ADAMS ARMS, cont. 53 A

MSR	100%	98%	95%	90%	80%	70%	60%	Last MSR

CARBINE BASE – .223 Rem. cal., GPO, similar to Mid Base model, except has 16 in. M4 profile barrel and short forearm. Disc.

| | $850 | $550 | $465 | $395 | $350 | $325 | $295 | $994 |

Add $515 for Carbine MOE model with Magpul handguards, stock, grip, and PMAG (disc.).

* ***Limited Edition Carbine Base Model*** – .223 Rem./5.56 NATO cal., 16 in. Melonite barrel, A2 flash hider, no sights, Mil-Spec 6-pos. retractable stock, A2 grip, forged A4 flat-top upper with Picatinny rail, forged lower receiver, M4 feed ramps, two-piece polymer carbine length handguard with lower heat shield, FDE finish, 6.2 lbs. Limited mfg. 2016-2017.

| | $800 | $525 | $450 | $385 | $340 | $325 | $295 | $930 |

MID TACTICAL EVO – 5.56 NATO cal., GPO, 16 in. Govt. contour Melonite barrel with A2 flash hider, 30 shot GI aluminum mag., Picatinny flat-top rail with dry lube internal finish and laser engraved, Samson free float lightweight modular rail system, Mil-Spec forged upper and lower receiver, beveled magwell, M4 feed ramps, enhanced 6-pos. buttstock, hardcoat black anodized, Kryptek Highlander, Kryptek Nomad, or Kryptek Typhon camo (new 2015) finish, 7 lbs. Disc. 2017.

| | $1,125 | $700 | $525 | $450 | $400 | $350 | $325 | $1,349 |

Add $139 for Kryptek Highlander, Nomad, or Typhon camo (new 2015) finish.

* ***Mid Tactical Evo XLP*** – 5.56 NATO cal., 16 in. Govt. contour Melonite barrel with A2 flash hider, 30 shot GI aluminum mag., XLP multi-adj. low profile gas block, forged lower receiver with beveled magwell, forged M4 upper with M4 feed ramps and Picatinny rail, Samson free float lightweight modular rail system, VLTOR IMOD collapsible stock, hardcoat anodized black finish, 7 lbs. Disc. 2015.

| | $1,150 | $750 | $550 | $465 | $415 | $375 | $350 | $1,389 |

CARBINE TACTICAL EVO – 5.56 NATO cal., GPO, 16 in. M4 profile Melonite barrel with A2 flash hider, 30 shot GI aluminum mag., Samson free float lightweight modular rail system, no sights, forged lower with beveled magwell and A4 flat-top upper receiver with M4 feed ramps and Picatinny rail, Ergo grip, enhanced 6-position buttstock, hardcoat anodized black finish, 7 lbs. Disc.

| | $1,125 | $700 | $525 | $450 | $400 | $350 | $325 | $1,327 |

MID TACTICAL ELITE – 5.56 NATO cal., GPO, 16 in. Govt. contour Melonite barrel with A2 flash hider, VLTOR IMOD collapsible stock, Ergo grip, 30 shot GI aluminum magazine, Samson free float lightweight modular quad rail system, Mil-Spec forged upper and lower receiver, hardcoat anodized finish, Picatinny flat-top rail with dry lube internal finish and laser engraved. Disc. 2015.

| | $1,125 | $700 | $525 | $450 | $400 | $350 | $325 | $1,349 |

CARBINE TACTICAL ELITE – 5.56 NATO cal., GPO, 16 in. M4 contour Melonite barrel, A2 flash hider, 30 shot GI aluminum mag., Picatinny flat-top rail with dry lube internal finish and laser engraved, Samson free float lightweight modular rail system, Mil-Spec forged upper and lower receiver, beveled magwell, M4 feed ramps, enhanced 6-pos. buttstock, hardcoat anodized black finish, 7 lbs. Disc. 2015.

| | $1,125 | $700 | $525 | $450 | $400 | $350 | $325 | $1,327 |

C.O.R. ULTRA LITE RIFLE – 5.56 NATO cal., 16 1/2 in. Ultra Lite contour Melonite barrel with VDI Jet Compensator, Hiperfire HiperTouch 24 Competition Fire Control, 30 shot GI aluminum mag., no sights, Samson free float lightweight modular rail system, forged lower with beveled magwell, forged M4 upper with M4 feed ramps and flat-top Picatinny rail, Evolution Rail handguard, hand stop, 2 in. rails, QD mount, Magpul MOE stock, Magpul K2 grip, hardcoat anodized black finish. Mfg. 2015-2017.

| | $1,475 | $950 | $725 | $550 | $475 | $395 | $350 | $1,800 |

MID EVO ULTRA LITE – 5.56 NATO cal., GPO, 16 in. Ultra Lite barrel with Jet Compensator and black Nitride finish, 30 shot GI aluminum mag., Samson free float lightweight modular rail system, forged A4 flat-top upper receiver with Picatinny rail, M4 feed ramps, forged lower with beveled magwell, Evolution Rail handguard, no sights, enhanced 6-pos. buttstock, Ergo grip, hardcoat anodized black finish, 6.7 lbs. Mfg. 2015-2017.

| | $1,425 | $925 | $700 | $550 | $475 | $395 | $350 | $1,743 |

P1 – 5.56 NATO cal., GPO, mid-length gas system, 16 in. Govt. contour barrel with QPQ Melonite/black Nitride finish, A2 flash hider, standard GI trigger, enhanced trigger guard, no sights, 6-pos. collapsible stock with QD mounts, ergonomic grips, forged A4 flat-top upper receiver, Magpul MOE handguard, Picatinny Adjustable Block piston system, M4 feed ramps, 7 lbs. New mid-2017.

| MSR $1,000 | $850 | $550 | $465 | $395 | $350 | $325 | $295 | |

P1 SMALL FRAME .308 – .308 Win. cal., GPO, mid-length gas system, 16 in. Govt. contour barrel with QPQ Melonite/black Nitride finish, A2 flash hider, Hiperfire EDT trigger, enhanced trigger guard, 6-pos. collapsible stock with QD mounts, ergonomic grip, Picatinny Adjustable Block piston system, forged flat-top upper receiver, M4 feed ramps, Magpul MOE handguard, 34 in. OAL, 7.97 lbs. New mid-2017.

| MSR $1,500 | $1,250 | $825 | $575 | $475 | $425 | $375 | $350 | |

A 54 ADAMS ARMS, cont.

MSR	100%	98%	95%	90%	80%	70%	60%	Last MSR

P2 – 5.56 NATO cal., GPO, mid-lengfth gas system, 16 in. Govt. contour barrel with QPQ Melonite/black Nitride finish, Manimal extended A2 flash hider, Defiance flip-up sights, Hiperfire EDT trigger, enhanced trigger guard, ergonomic grip, 6-pos. collabsible stock with QD mounts, forged A4 flat-top upper receiver, Adams Arms M-LOK rail system, M4 feed ramps, ambidextrous safety selector and charging handle, 33 in. OAL, 7.16 lbs. New mid-2017.

MSR $1,500	$1,250	$825	$575	$475	$425	$375	$350	

P2 SMALL FRAME .308 – .308 Win. cal., GPO, mid-length gas system, 16 in. Govt. contour barrel with QPQ Melonite/black Nitride finish, Manimal A2 flash hider, Hiperfire EDT trigger, Defiance flip-up sights, 6-pos. collapsible stock with QD mounts, ergonomic grip, ambidextrous safety selector and charging handle, forged A4 flat-top upper receiver, M4 feed ramps, Adams Arms M-LOK rail system, 34 in. OAL, 8.14 lbs. New mid-2017.

MSR $2,000	$1,675	$1,000	$825	$625	$550	$475	$425	

P3 – 5.56 NATO cal., GPO, rifle length gas system, 16 1/2 in. Competition barrel with QPQ Melonite/black Nitride finish, Jet Comp muzzle device, flat-faced AR gold trigger, enhanced trigger guard, no sights, adj. Luth-AR stock with cheek riser, rubber ergonomic grip, ambidextrous safety selector and charging handle, Micro Block piston system, forged A4 flat-top upper receiver, M4 feed ramps, Adams Arms M-LOK rail system, 7.6 lbs. New mid-2017.

MSR $2,000	$1,675	$1,000	$825	$625	$550	$475	$425	

P3 SMALL FRAME .308 – .308 Win. cal., GPO, mid-length gas system, 16 in. Govt. or 18 in. fluted barrel with QPQ Melonite/black Nitride finish, Jet Comp muzzle device, flat-faced AR gold trigger, enhanced trigger guard, no sights, adj. Luth-AR stock with cheek riser, rubber ergonomic grip, ambidextrous safety selector and charging handle, Micro Block piston system, forged flat-top upper receiver, M4 feed ramps, Adams Arms M-LOK rail system, 34-39 in. OAL, 8.14-8.53 lbs. New mid-2017.

MSR $2,500	$2,050	$1,250	$950	$650	$575	$495	$475	

P3+ SMALL FRAME 6.5 CREEDMOOR – 6.5mm Creedmoor cal., short stroke GPO, rifle+2 in. length gas system, 24 in. heavy Proof Research carbon fiber wrapped barrel, American Precision Arms Little Bastard muzzle device, flat-faced AR gold trigger, enhanced trigger guard, adj. Luth-AR stock with cheek riser, rubber ergonomic grip, ambidextrous safety selector and charging handle, Micro Adjustable Piston System, ergonomic free float rail, forged flat-top upper receiver, Adams Arms M-LOK rail system handguard, 46 in. OAL, 8.8 lbs. New 2018.

MSR $4,000	$3,275	$2,225	$1,550	$925	$725	$675	$650	

SMALL FRAME .308 ALPHA-S RIFLE – .308 Win. cal., XLP low profile block, 18 in. barrel, VDI Jet compensator, 20 shot mag., AR gold trigger, Luth-AR adj. buttstock, Magpul K2 grip, Samson 15 in. evolution rail, hardcoat anodized black finish, 8.85 lbs. Mfg. 2015-2017.

	$1,795	$1,050	$875	$625	$550	$475	$425	$2,266

SMALL FRAME .308 PATROL BATTLE RIFLE – .308 Win. cal., 16 in. barrel, VDI Jet compensator, 20 shot mag., enhanced SOPMOD buttstock, Magpul K2 grip, Samson extended evolution rail, hardcoat anodized black finish, 8.15 lbs. Mfg. 2015-2017.

	$1,475	$950	$725	$550	$475	$395	$350	$1,776

SMALL FRAME .308 PATROL ENHANCED – .308 Win. cal., 16 in. barrel, 20 shot mag., enhanced SOPMOD buttstock, Magpul K2 grip, Magpul MOE handguard, hardcoat anodized black finish, 7.8 lbs. Mfg. 2015-2017.

	$1,250	$825	$575	$475	$425	$375	$350	$1,489

ULTRA LITE ADVANCED DISSIPATOR RIFLE – 5.56 NATO cal., GPO, 16 1/2 in. match grade Ultra Lite Voodoo barrel, 30 shot Magpul PMAG, Diamondhead D45 Swing Sights, low mass bolt carrier, forged lower receiver with beveled magwell, forged M4 upper with M4 feed ramps and flat-top Picatinny rail, Magpul MOE handguard and trigger guard, Magpul MOE stock and grip, hardcoat anodized black finish. Mfg. 2015-2017.

	$1,125	$700	$525	$450	$400	$350	$325	$1,326

ADCOR DEFENSE

Current AR-15 style carbine/rifle manufacturer located in Baltimore, MD.

RIFLES/CARBINES

A-556 ELITE – 5.56 NATO, 7.62x39mm, or .300 AAC Blackout cal., GPO, 16, 18, or 20 in. chrome-lined free floating barrel, forward placed reversible/ambidextrous charging handle, multi-purpose regulator, optics ready, ejection port dust wiper, two-piece keyed quad rail system, tool-less field strip design, custom rifle stock, custom ergonomic rifle grip with aggressive texturing, black, FDE, ODG, or Patriot Brown finish. New 2013.

MSR $2,295	$1,795	$1,050	$875	$625	$550	$475	$425	

Add $100 for 7.62x39mm or .300 AAC Blackout cal.

A-556 ELITE GI – 5.56 NATO cal., GIO, 16, 18, or 20 in. chrome-lined barrel with or without ambidextrous forward charging handle, multi-position gas regulator with removable gas tube, ejection port dust wiper, key-locked, highly rigid rail system mounts to upper receiver, upper and lower rails separate with push of a button, no tools needed, custom rifle stock, custom ergonomic rifle grip with aggressive texturing, black, FDE, ODG, or Patriot Brown finish, 6.9 lbs. New 2013.

MSR $1,995	$1,650	$1,000	$795	$595	$495	$425	$395	

Add $100 for 18 or 20 in. barrel.

ADCOR DEFENSE, cont. **55** **A**

MSR		100%	98%	95%	90%	80%	70%	60%	Last MSR

B.E.A.R. – 5.56 NATO cal., GPO with multi-position regulator, 16 or 18 in. free floating chrome-lined barrel, forward placed reversible/ambidextrous charging handle, ejection port dust wiper, two-piece keyed quad rail system, aluminum alloy receivers and rail systems, configured with sights or optics ready, 6.45-7.6 lbs. Disc. 2013.

| | | $1,675 | $1,000 | $825 | $625 | $550 | $475 | $425 | $2,092 |

* B.E.A.R. Elite – 5.56 NATO cal., GPO, similar to B.E.A.R., except has hammer forged chrome-lined barrel, comes with sights or optics ready, also features Magpul MOE rifle stock, Magpul MOE ergonomic rifle grip with aggressive texturing, 6.45-7.6 lbs. Disc. 2015.

Retail pricing was not available for this model.

B.E.A.R. GI – 5.56 NATO cal., GIO with multi-position gas regulator and removable gas tube, 16 or 18 in. chrome-lined barrel, with or w/o ambidextrous forward placed charging handle, ejection port dust wiper, key-locked, highly rigid rail system mounts to upper receiver, upper and lower rails separate with the push of a button, no special tools needed, approx. 6.8 lbs. Disc. 2014.

| | | $1,795 | $1,050 | $875 | $625 | $550 | $475 | $425 | |

* B.E.A.R. GI Elite – 5.56 NATO cal., GIO, similar to B.E.A.R. GI, except also features hammer forged chrome-lined barrels, Magpul MOE rifle stock, Magpul MOE ergonomic rifle grip with aggressive texturing, approx. 6.8 lbs. Disc. 2015.

Retail pricing was not available for this model.

B.E.A.R. LIMITED EDITION SIGNATURE SERIES – 5.56 NATO cal., 18 or 20 in. hammer forged, chrome-lined barrel, full billet upper and lower receiver, Magpul pistol grip and buttstock, AMBI Products ambidextrous fire selector switch, matte black finish, hand-built and signed by Michael Brown. Mfg. mid-2013.

| | | $1,875 | $1,100 | $895 | $650 | $575 | $495 | $425 | $2,399 |

ADEQ FIREARMS COMPANY

Current manufacturer established in 2010 by A.M. de Quesada, located in Tampa, FL.

Manufacturer of custom and standard production AR-15 style firearms, sniper rifles, 1911 pistols, and firearm suppression systems. Along with the civilian sales, the company handles custom built firearms for law enforcement and government agencies as well as security contract operating companies. In addition, the company makes a limited number of custom arsenal rebuilds of classic vintage military weapons based on parts availability.

PISTOLS: SEMI-AUTO

PALADIN DAGGER – .22 LR (special order by request) or 5.56 NATO cal., AR style pistol, custom built from Paladin lower receiver. Mfg. 2012-2016.

| | | $1,025 | $925 | $800 | $685 | $595 | $515 | $440 | $1,200 |

RIFLES: SEMI-AUTO

PALADIN PATROL CARBINE – 5.56 NATO, 6.8 SPC (disc.), 7.62x39mm (disc.), or .300 AAC Blackout cal., rotary bolt GIO, available in semi-auto, M4 configuration, or 3-round bursts (NFA rules apply), 16 or 18 in. chrome-lined (disc.) or Nitride finished (new 2016) barrel, A2 front and quick detach A2 rear sights, Mil-Spec forged aluminum upper and lower receivers with anodized finish, manganese phosphate barrel finish, standard A2 round mid-length handguards, GI pistol grip, Rogers 6-position adj. commercial tube buttstock, SST, includes cable lock, sling, and owner's manual, 5.8 lbs. Mfg. 2011-2017.

| | | $765 | $515 | $440 | $375 | $335 | $315 | $295 | $900 |

Add $99 for Magpul MOE stock (Carbine 02).

Add $318 for Troy free float forearm, Magpul stock, and BUIS (Carbine 03).

PALADIN ULTRALIGHT – 5.56 NATO cal., 16 in. Voodoo Tactical barrel, Magpul stock, pistol grip, Magtech magnesium infused lower receiver. Mfg. 2013-2014.

| | | $1,475 | $950 | $725 | $550 | $475 | $395 | $350 | $1,776 |

PRECISION LONG RANGE RIFLE – 7.62 NATO cal., GIO, 18 in. fluted bull barrel with GoGun flash hider, anodized receiver and manganese phosphate barrel finish, PRi Gen3 carbon fiber forearm handguards, Magpul PRS buttstock, SST, includes Leupold Mark IV ER/T optics, pelican case, sniper data book, and cleaning kit, 11.6 lbs. Mfg. 2011-2013.

| | | $1,875 | $1,100 | $895 | $650 | $575 | $495 | $425 | $2,300 |

RECON – 5.56 or 7.62 NATO cal., 16 (5.56 NATO cal., disc.) in. Nitride or 18 (7.62 NATO cal.) in. SASS fluted barrel, Lantac flash hider, Dueck offset sights (18 in. barrel only), Magpul ACS stock, Troy MRF handguard, Ergo pistol grip. Mfg. 2014-2016.

| | | $1,795 | $1,050 | $875 | $625 | $550 | $475 | $425 | $2,200 |

VENATOR BATTLE RIFLE – 7.62 NATO cal., rotary bolt GIO, AR-15 style, 16, 18, or 20 in. chrome-lined barrel with GoGun Talon muzzle brake, 20 shot detachable box mag., A2 front and quick detach A2 rear sights, Mil-Spec anodized receiver finish and manganese phosphate barrel finish, free float aluminum handguard with Troy Alpha rail system, 6-position adj. commercial tube buttstock, SST, 8.1 lbs. Mfg. 2011-2014.

| | | $1,475 | $950 | $725 | $550 | $475 | $395 | $350 | $1,800 |

A 56 ADVANCED ARMAMENT CORP.

MSR		100%	98%	95%	90%	80%	70%	60%	Last MSR

ADVANCED ARMAMENT CORP.

Previous manufacturer of AR-15 style rifles located in Lawrenceville, GA. Advanced Armament Corp. is part of the Remington Outdoor Group. Previously part of the Freedom Group. AAC currently manufactures silencers and accessories.

RIFLES: SEMI-AUTO

MPW – 5.56 NATO or .300 AAC Blackout cal., GIO, 16 in. barrel with AAC 51T Blackout flash hider, Geissele two-stage trigger, 6-position Magpul CTR stock, Magpul MOE grip, nickel boron coated bolt carrier and cam pin, free floating quad rail sized to match length of barrel. Disc.

		$1,350	$875	$650	$525	$450	$385	$350	$1,600

AERO PRECISION USA

Current semi-auto rifle manufacturer located in Tacoma, WA.

RIFLES/CARBINES: SEMI-AUTO

Aero Precision USA offers a complete line of AR-15 upper and lower receivers, as well as parts. Guns can be built per individual customer specifications. Please contact the company directly for more information including pricing, options, and availability (see Trademark Index).

AC-15 RIFLE – 5.56 NATO cal., carbine length gas system, 16 in. M4 profile barrel with A2 flash hider, Magpul 30 shot PMAG, Magpul MBUS rear and A2 front sights, M4 collapsible stock, A2 pistol grip, M4 carbine handguard with double heat shield, hardcoat anodized black finish, 6.24 lbs. New 2016.

MSR $729		$640	$500	$415	$370	$325	$300	$275	

AC-15M MID-LENGTH RIFLE – 5.56 NATO cal., mid-length gas system, 16 in. barrel with A2 flash hider, 30 shot Magpul PMAG, Magpul MBUS rear and A2 front sights, M4 collapsible stock, A2 pistol grip, M4 upper and Gen 2 lower receiver with flared magwell, M4 mid-length handguard with heat shield, hardcoat anodized black finish. New 2016.

MSR $739		$640	$500	$415	$370	$325	$300	$275	

AR15 BLACKHAWK – 5.56 NATO cal., 16 in. barrel with A2 flash hider, mid-length upper receiver with C.O.P. (Continuous Optics Platform), low profile gas block, standard charging handle, forged aluminum upper and lower receiver, marked "Cal Multi", works with standard AR-15 components and magazines, threaded rear takedown pin detent hole, Magpul MOE pistol grip stock, Aero Precision billet trigger guard, configured rail system, matte black, FDE/Desert, OD/Olive, Titanium, Tungsten, or Burnt Bronze finish. Disc. 2015.

		$1,100	$675	$525	$450	$400	$350	$325	$1,300

Add $150 for FDE/Desert, OD/Olive, Titanium, Tungsten, or Burnt Bronze finish.

AR15 BLACKHAWK ELITE – 5.56 NATO cal., carbine length gas system, forged aluminum construction, 16 in. barrel with A2 flash hider, mid-length upper receiver with Continuous Optics Platform, M4 feed ramps, free float handguard rail system, fully enclosed dust cover pin, works with standard AR-15 components and magazines, threaded rear takedown pin detent hole, adj. tactical stock, hardcoat anodized matte black finish. Disc. 2015.

		$1,175	$775	$550	$465	$415	$375	$350	$1,400

AR15 RIFLE W/QUANTUM HANDGUARD – 5.56 NATO cal., 16 in. CMV mid-length barrel, A2 flash hider, 30 shot PMAG, 15 in. Quantum handguard (KeyMod or M-LOK), M4 sliding stock. Mfg. 2017 only.

		$740	$500	$435	$375	$335	$315	$295	$875

AR15 M4E1 RIFLE – .300 AAC Blackout or 5.56 NATO/.223 Wylde chamber, 16 in. mid-length barrel with A2 flash hider, Gen 2 enhanced series handguard of choice, M4E1 upper, billet trigger guard, Magpul MOE grip, Magpul STR stock, black or FDE finish.

MSR $970		$825	$535	$450	$385	$340	$325	$295	

Add $9 for .223 Wylde chamber.

AR15 M4E1 RIFLE (RIFLE-LENGTH) – 5.56 NATO/.223 Wylde chamber, low profile gas block, 18 in. rifle length barrel with A2 flash hider, 30 shot PMAG, M4E1 Enhanced upper receiver, Gen 2 lower receiver with flared magwell, AR-15/M4 buffer kit, Gen 2 Enhanced Series handguard of choice, billet trigger guard, Magpul MOE grip, Magpul STR stock, black or FDE finish.

MSR $970		$825	$535	$450	$385	$340	$325	$295	

Add $30 for .223 Wylde chamber.

C.O.P. (CONTINUOUS OPTICS PLATFORM) – 5.56 NATO cal., 16 in. M4 barrel, billet trigger guard, MOE grip, mid-length C.O.P. receiver, integrated upper receiver and handguard system, black or FDE finish. Disc. 2015.

		$1,100	$675	$525	$450	$400	$350	$325	$1,299

Add $150 for FDE finish.

AERO PRECISION USA, cont. 57 A

MSR	100%	98%	95%	90%	80%	70%	60%	Last MSR

C.O.P. M4 RIFLE – 5.56 NATO cal., carbine length gas system, low profile gas block, 16 in. M4 profile barrel, M4 collapsible stock, A2 pistol grip, C.O.P. M4 upper receiver with rail panels, Gen 2 lower with flared magwell, black anodized finish. New 2016.

| MSR $1,050 | $875 | $550 | $465 | $395 | $350 | $325 | $300 | |

M5 .308 RIFLE 16 IN. – .308 Win. cal., 16 in. chrome moly barrel with A2 flash hider, low profile gas block, forged aluminum construction, custom integrated upper receiver and free floated handguard system, standard charging handle, works with standard DPMS .308 components and magazines, threaded rear takedown pin detent hole, integrated trigger guard, standard Mil-Spec receiver extension, Magpul STR stock, Magpul MOE pistol grip, EK12 handguard, continuous top rail, matte black hardcoat anodized or FDE/Desert finish. Disc. 2016.

| | $1,100 | $675 | $525 | $450 | $400 | $350 | $325 | $1,325 |

Add $75 for FDE/Desert finish.

* **M5 .308 Rifle 18 or 20 In.** – .308 Win. cal., 18 or 20 in. chrome moly barrel with A2 flash hider, low profile gas block, forged aluminum construction, custom integrated upper receiver and free floating handguard system, standard charging handle, works with standard DPMS .308 components and magazines, threaded rear takedown pin detent hole, integrated trigger guard, standard Mil-Spec receiver extension, Magpul PRS stock, Magpul MOE pistol grip, EK12 handguard, continuous top rail, matte black hardcoat anodized or FDE/Desert finish. Disc. 2017.

| | $1,275 | $850 | $600 | $495 | $425 | $375 | $350 | $1,550 |

Add $10 for 20 in. barrel.

Add $75 for FDE/Desert finish on 18 in. barrel, or $85 for FDE/Desert finish on 20 in. barrel.

M5E1 RIFLE – .308 Win. cal., low profile gas block, 16, 18, or 20 in. chrome moly or stainless steel barrel, A2 birdcage flash hider, 20 shot PMAG, custom integrated M5E1 Enhanced Series upper receiver, Gen 2 lower with flared magwell, Gen 2 Enhanced Series handguard of choice, Magpul STR (16 in. barrel only) or Magpul PRS (18 or 20 in. barrel only) stock, Magpul MOE grip, black or FDE finish.

| MSR $1,490 | $1,250 | $825 | $575 | $475 | $425 | $375 | $350 | |

Add $50 for stainless steel barrel.

Add $210 for 18 or 20 in. barrel with Magpul PRS stock.

* **M5E1 Rifle 6.5 Creedmoor** – 6.5mm Creedmoor cal., 18, 20, or 22 in. stainless steel mid-length barrel, A2 birdcage flash hider, 20 shot PMAG, custom integrated M5E1 Enhanced Series upper receiver, Gen 2 lower with flared magwell, Gen 2 Enhanced Series handguard of choice, low profile gas block, Magpul PRS Gen 3 stock, Magpul MOE grip, black or FDE finish.

| MSR $1,755 | $1,425 | $925 | $700 | $550 | $475 | $395 | $350 | |

Add $10 for 20 in. barrel or $20 for 22 in. barrel.

M16A4 SPECIAL EDITION RIFLE – 5.56 NATO cal., GIO, 20 in. barrel with A2 flash hider, Magpul 30 shot PMAG, A2 front sight block with bayonet lug, A2 stock and grip, M4 upper receiver, A2 detachable carry handle, rifle length A2 style handguard, Special Edition M16A4 lower receiver with custom engraving, M16A4 sling, black anodized finish, 8 lbs. Mfg. 2016 only.

| | $875 | $550 | $465 | $395 | $350 | $325 | $300 | $1,050 |

AKLYS DEFENSE LLC

Current rifle manufacturer founded in 2014, located in Baton Rouge, LA.

Aklys Defense also manufactures parts, accessories, and firearms-related gear. Please contact the company directly for more information including pricing, options, and availability (see Trademark Index).

RIFLES: SEMI-AUTO

FALCATA MOE – 5.56 NATO or .300 AAC Blackout cal., 16 in. M4 profile barrel with A2 flash hider, Magpul MBUS rear sight, 6-pos. collapsible Magpul stock, Magpul high temperature polymer forearm, Magpul grip, M4 feed ramps, forged aluminum upper and lower receivers, Type III hardcoat anodized black receivers and choice of black, Dark Desert Brown (disc. 2016), OD Green (disc. 2016), pink (disc. 2016), tan (disc. 2016), or custom Cerakote (disc. 2016) finish, 6.6 lbs. New 2014.

| MSR $985 | $850 | $550 | $465 | $395 | $350 | $325 | $295 | |

Add $10 for Dark Desert Brown or pink finish (disc. 2016). Add $145 for custom Cerakote finish (disc. 2016).

FALCATA ELITE – 5.56 NATO or .300 AAC Blackout cal., 16 or 18 in. Melonite finished chrome moly barrel with competition muzzle brake, 12.3 (16 in. model) or 15 in. (18 in. model) Samson rail, TI-7 stock with battery compartments, black, dark brown, FDE, ODG, or pink finish. New 2014.

| MSR $1,285 | $1,075 | $675 | $500 | $450 | $400 | $350 | $325 | |

FALCATA HEAVY RIFLE – .308 Win. cal., 16 or 18 in. stainless carbon fiber barrel with MOJO magnum muzzle brake, 12 in. rail, collapsible or Magpul PRS stock, black, FDE, or ODG finish. New 2014.

| MSR $1,750 | $1,425 | $925 | $700 | $550 | $475 | $395 | $350 | |

A 58 AKSA ARMS

MSR		100%	98%	95%	90%	80%	70%	60%	Last MSR

AKSA ARMS

Current trademark of AR-15 style shotguns, conversions, O/U, SXS, single shot, lever-action, semi-auto, and slide-action shotguns. Currently manufactured by Silah Insaat Metal SAN. Tic. LTD. STI, located in Konya, Turkey. No current importation.

ALAN & WILLIAM ARMS, INC.

Current semi-auto rifle manufacturer established in 2012, located in Cheyenne Wells, CO.

RIFLES: SEMI-AUTO

Many options and upgrades are available, and each rifle can be customized per individual specifications. Please contact the company directly for more information including pricing, options, and availability (see Trademark Index).

AR-15 – 5.56 NATO cal., cold hammer forged barrel, chrome-lined bore and chamber, M4 feed ramp barrel extension and flat-top receiver, CNC machined aircraft grade aluminum lower receiver, Geissele SSA two-stage trigger, BCM Gunfighter charging handle and bolt, manganese phosphate barrel finish, hardcoat anodized matte black finish.

MSR $2,100	$1,725	$1,050	$850	$625	$550	$475	$425

ALASKA MAGNUM AR'S

Current manufacturer located in Fairbanks, AK.

Alaska Magnum AR's manufactures AR-15 style rifles designed as true big game rifles.

RIFLES: SEMI-AUTO

GRIZZLY – 6.9 AR Short or .460 GrizzinatAR cal., adj. rifle length gas system, 18 in. match grade stainless steel barrel with muzzle brake, aluminum lower and flat-top upper with Picatinny rail handguard, synthetic stock, non-slip ergonomic ambidextrous grip, free float forend, nickel bolt carrier group, stainless steel firing pin, Cerakote finish.

MSR $3,999	$3,400	$2,975	$2,475	$2,075	$1,725	$1,450	$1,250

KODIAK – 6.9 AR Long, .300 RCM, .338 RCM, or .375 GrizzinatAR cal., adj. rifle length gas system, 20 in. match grade stainless steel barrel with muzzle brake, aluminum lower and flat-top upper receiver with Picatinny rail handguard, nickel bolt carrier group, synthetic buttstock, non-slip ergonomic ambidextrous grip, free float forend, Cerakote finish.

MSR $3,999	$3,400	$2,975	$2,475	$2,075	$1,725	$1,450	$1,250

WOLVERINE – .450 Bushmaster cal., adj. rifle length gas system, 18 in. match grade stainless steel barrel with muzzle brake, flat-top upper with Picatinny rail handguard, synthetic buttstock, free float forend, non-slip ergonomic ambidextrous grip, Cerakote finish.

MSR $2,999	$2,550	$2,225	$1,825	$1,575	$1,300	$1,100	$950

ALBERTA TACTICAL RIFLE SUPPLY

Current manufacturer located in Calgary, Alberta, Canada.

Each gun is built per customer's specifications.

RIFLES: SEMI-AUTO

MODERN HUNTER – .223 Wylde, 6.5mm Creedmoor, .260 Rem., or .308 Win. cal., integrated ambi bolt release, 18 1/2 in. stainless steel match grade barrel with light, medium, heavy contour, or Proof Research carbon fiber, hinged dust cover over ejection port, SST, A2 fixed or 6-pos. collapsible AR stock, AR style grip, ambi safety, free float tube, non-reciprocating folding charge handle, billet upper and lower receivers, hard anodized black finish.

MSR $3,650	$3,085	$2,700	$2,200	$1,895	$1,575	$1,325	$1,140

MODERN VARMINT – .223 Wylde or 6.5 Grendel cal., integrated ambi bolt release, GIO, 18 1/2 in. stainless threaded barrel with light, medium, heavy contour, or Proof Research carbon fiber, hinged dust cover over ejection port, SST, A2 fixed or 6-pos. collapsible AR stock, AR style grip, free float tube, non-reciprocating folding charge handle.

MSR $3,350	$2,865	$2,495	$2,025	$1,725	$1,425	$1,215	$1,040

* ***Modern Varmint Factory Model*** – .223 Wylde chamber, GIO, 18 1/2 in. chrome-lined threaded barrel with light contour only, hinged dust cover over ejection port, SST, A2 fixed or 6-pos. collapsible AR stock, AR style grip, free float tube, non-reciprocating folding charge handle, integrated ambi bolt release.

MSR $2,750	$2,335	$2,040	$1,750	$1,590	$1,285	$1,050	$815

ALEXANDER ARMS LLC

Current manufacturer of AR-15 style rifles located in Radford, VA. Law enforcement, military, dealer, and consumer sales.

ALEXANDER ARMS LLC, cont. 59 A

MSR	100%	98%	95%	90%	80%	70%	60%	Last MSR

RIFLES: SEMI-AUTO

.50 BEOWULF – .50 Beowulf cal., AR-15 style, GIO, shoots 300-400 grain bullet at approx. 1,800 feet per second, forged upper and lower receiver, 7 shot mag., rotary locking bolt and gas delay mechanism, various configurations include Entry, Over Match kit, Over Match Plus kit, Over Match Tactical kit, Precision Entry, Precision kit, AWS, and Law Enforcement (POR). New 2002.

* ***Beowulf AWS 16 (Advanced Weapons System)*** – .50 Beowulf cal., GIO, low profile gas block, 16 1/2 in. chrome moly barrel, 7 shot mag., military style trigger, black A2 stock, forged flat-top receiver with Picatinny rail, free float Midwest Industries four rail handguard system, black A2 stock, includes soft carry bag, black, FDE, or OD Green finish.

MSR $1,570		$1,315	$850	$625	$500	$435	$375	$350

Add $330 for FDE or OD Green finish.

* ***Beowulf Entry 16.5*** – .50 Beowulf cal., GIO, 16 1/2 in. chrome moly barrel, mid-length A2 handguard, Picatinny rail, 7 shot mag., forged flat-top receiver, black or coyote brown (disc.) A2 stock.

MSR $1,155		$975	$595	$495	$425	$365	$335	$300

* ***Beowulf Hunter*** – .50 Beowulf cal., 16 in. chrome moly barrel, forged flat-top receiver, G10 rifle handguard, tactical trigger, B5 Systems SOPMOD collapsible stock, Ergo grip, Kryptek Highlander camo finish. New 2015.

MSR $1,750		$1,425	$925	$700	$550	$475	$395	$350

* ***Beowulf Overmatch Plus*** – .50 Beowulf cal., GIO, 16 in. chrome moly barrel, forged flat-top receiver, detachable iron sights and rear carry handle, mid-length A2 handguard, Picatinny rail, 7 shot mag., black A2 stock.

MSR $1,260		$1,065	$650	$500	$450	$395	$350	$325

* ***Beowulf Overwatch .50*** – .50 Beowulf cal., extended range model, rotary locking bolt and gas delay mechanism, 24 in. stainless steel barrel, 7 shot mag., shoots 334 grain bullet at approx. 2,000 feet per second, forged upper and lower receiver, 9 1/4 lbs. Mfg. 2004-2005.

		$1,475	$950	$725	$550	$475	$395	$350	*$1,789*

* ***Beowulf 24 Overwatch*** – .50 Beowulf cal., GIO, 24 in. barrel, full-length free float handguard, standard trigger and buttstock, Picatinny rail. Disc. 2009.

		$1,475	$950	$725	$550	$475	$395	$350	*$1,789*

* ***Beowulf Piston Rifle*** – .50 Beowulf cal., GPO, 10 shot mag., 16 1/2 in. threaded barrel with no standard muzzle device, Picatinny rail receiver, M4 stock, Samson EX handguard, includes soft carry bag. Mfg. 2012-2013.

		$1,675	$1,000	$825	$625	$550	$475	$425	*$2,000*

* ***Beowulf Precision 16*** – .50 Beowulf cal., GIO, 16 in. chrome moly barrel, composite free float G10 handguards, Picatinny rail, low profile gas block, 7 shot mag., forged flat-top receiver, black furniture standard or optional camo upgrades available.

MSR $1,413		$1,175	$775	$550	$465	$415	$375	$350

Add $330 for camo upgrades.

* ***Beowulf Tactical*** – .50 Beowulf cal., 16 1/2 in. chrome moly threaded barrel, 7 shot mag., Geissele SSA or Alexander Arms tactical trigger, B5 Systems SOPMOD Bravo collapsible stock, flat-top receiver, low profile gas block, Manticore Arms Transformer Rail handguard, includes soft carry bag, FDE, ODG, or black finish. New 2017.

MSR $1,750		$1,425	$925	$700	$550	$475	$395	$350

GENGHIS – 5.45x39mm cal., GIO, M4 styling with 16 in. stainless steel barrel, forged upper and lower receiver, 10 shot mag., various configurations included Entry ($1,066 last MSR), Over Match kit ($1,158 last MSR), Over Match Plus kit ($1,267 last MSR), and Over Match Tactical kit ($1,372 last MSR). Mfg. 2002-2005.

6.5 GRENDEL – 6.5 Grendel cal., GIO, M4 styling with 16, 18 1/2, 19, 20, or 24 in. stainless steel barrel, 10 shot mag. New 2004.

* ***Grendel AWS*** – 6.5 Grendel cal., GIO, 20 or 24 in. stainless steel fully lapped threaded barrel with A2 flash hider, free float Midwest Industries railed handguard, Picatinny rail, 10 shot mag., A2 stock, black furniture.

MSR $1,292		$1,075	$675	$500	$450	$400	$350	$325

Add $105 for 24 in. barrel.

* ***Grendel 20 (19.5) Entry*** – 6.5 Grendel cal., GIO, 19 1/2 (disc.) or 20 in. stainless steel fully lapped threaded barrel with A2 flash hider, 10 shot mag., A2 black buttstock, Ergo grip, composite free float handguard, Picatinny rail, includes soft carry case, black furniture standard or optional camo upgrades available, 7 1/2 lbs.

MSR $1,208		$1,025	$625	$495	$450	$395	$350	$325

Add $330 for camo upgrades.

A 60 ALEXANDER ARMS LLC, cont.

MSR	100%	98%	95%	90%	80%	70%	60%	Last MSR

* Grendel GDMR – 6.5 Grendel cal., GIO, 16 (disc.), 20, or 24 in. barrel, A2 flash hider, 10 shot mag., full tactical model, tactical single stage trigger, Troy fold up front and rear backup iron sights, Magpul PRS OD Green or black (disc.) stock, Ergo grip, LaRue four rail handguard, sight base, bipod mount, Magpul rail covers, removable top Picatinny rail, 9.2 lbs. Disc. 2013, reintroduced 2015.

| MSR $2,890 | $2,295 | $1,450 | $1,075 | $675 | $595 | $525 | $475 | |

* Grendel Hunter – 6.5 Grendel cal., GIO, 19 1/2 in. stainless steel fully lapped threaded barrel, 10 shot mag., flat-top receiver, full-length military handguard, Picatinny rail, black or coyote brown stock, standard trigger. Disc. 2012.

| | $1,135 | $725 | $525 | $465 | $415 | $375 | $350 | *$1,370* |

* Grendel Hunter 18 – 6.5 Grendel cal., GIO, 18 in. fluted stainless steel barrel, 10 shot mag., tactical trigger, B5 Systems SOPMOD collapsible stock, Ergo grip, G10 rifle handguard, MK10 3 in. Picatinny rail installed on top of handguard, ships in soft carry bag, Kryptek Highlander camo finish. New 2015.

| MSR $1,750 | $1,425 | $925 | $700 | $550 | $475 | $395 | $350 | |

* Grendel SC Hunter – 6.5 Grendel cal., 18 in. stainless steel fluted barrel, 10 shot mag., tactical trigger, B5 Systems SOPMOD collapsible stock, forged receiver, titanium side charging handle, G10 rifle handguard, Kryptek Highlander camo dip finish. New 2015.

| MSR $1,920 | $1,600 | $1,000 | $775 | $575 | $495 | $425 | $395 | |

* Grendel Incursion Complete Rifle – 6.5 Grendel cal., 16 in. lightweight Melonite button rifled barrel, 10 shot mag., military trigger, M4 stock, flat-top receiver, MK10 free float handguard, ships in soft cover bag, black furniture standard or optional camo upgrades available, 5.9 lbs. New 2015.

| MSR $1,100 | $915 | $575 | $475 | $415 | $350 | $325 | $300 | |

Add $330 for optional camo upgrades.

* Lite 16/Lite 18 (Grendel Lightweight Rifle) – 6.5 Grendel cal., GIO, lightweight 16, 18, 20 (disc. 2014), or 24 (mfg. 2014 only) in. button rifled fluted stainless steel barrel with A2 flash hider, 10 shot mag., military-style trigger, M4 collapsible stock, composite free floating handguard, includes soft carry bag, black furniture standard or optional camo upgrades available, 6.4 lbs. New 2012.

| MSR $1,449 | $1,195 | $795 | $550 | $465 | $415 | $375 | $350 | |

Add $105 for 18 in. barrel.
Add $88 for 24 in. barrel (mfg. 2014 only).
Add $330 for optional camo upgrades.

* Grendel MK3 Gas Piston – 6.5 Grendel cal., GPO, 16, 18, or 24 in. button rifled and fluted Lite series barrel with AAC flash hider, 10 shot mag., black or tactical dark earth furniture, includes soft carry bag. Mfg. 2012-2013.

| | $1,050 | $650 | $495 | $450 | $395 | $350 | $325 | *$2,150* |

* Grendel Overwatch 6.5 – 6.5 Grendel cal., GIO, 24 in. stainless steel barrel with match chamber, extremely accurate, forged and hard anodized upper and lower receiver. Mfg. 2004-disc.

| | $1,250 | $825 | $575 | $475 | $425 | $375 | $350 | *$1,499* |

* Grendel 24 Overwatch – 6.5 Grendel cal., GIO, 24 in. stainless steel fully lapped threaded barrel with A2 flash hider, A2 buttstock, Ergo grip, composite free float G10 handguard, flat-top receiver with Picatinny rail, low profile gas block, black furniture standard or optional camo upgrades available, 9 lbs.

| MSR $1,313 | $1,100 | $675 | $525 | $450 | $400 | $350 | $325 | |

Add $330 for camo upgrades.

* Grendel Sniper Rifle (GSR Series) – 6.5 Grendel cal., GIO, 16 (disc. 2014), 20 (new 2015), 24 (new 2015), or 28 (disc.) in. fluted barrel, A2 flash hider, 10 shot mag., blade style single stage tactical trigger, Magpul PRS stock, LaRue SPR mount and Ergo deluxe grip, side charging handle, billet receiver, MK10 vented composite handguard, includes soft carry bag, black or FDE finish, 10 lbs. New 2012.

| MSR $3,190 | $2,550 | $1,650 | $1,250 | $700 | $625 | $575 | $525 | |

* Grendel Tactical 16 – 6.5 Grendel cal., GIO, 16 in. threaded barrel with or w/o flutes, A2 flash hider, M4 style or folding stock, with or w/o rail, mid-length handguard, 10 shot mag., fixed or folding sights, includes soft carry bag. Disc. 2015, reintroduced 2017.

| MSR $1,750 | $1,425 | $925 | $700 | $550 | $475 | $395 | $350 | |

* Grendel Ultralight – 6.5 Grendel cal., GIO, 16, 18, or 20 in. unthreaded free floating 5R cut rifled barrel with six straight flutes, integral three prong flash hider (16 or 18 in. barrel only), vented composite handguard, M4 collapsible stock, Enedine buffer. Disc. 2012.

| | $1,725 | $1,050 | $850 | $625 | $550 | $475 | $425 | *$2,100* |

ALEXANDER ARMS LLC, cont. 61 A

MSR	100%	98%	95%	90%	80%	70%	60%	Last MSR

.17 HMR – .17 HMR cal., blowback operating system, 18 in. stainless steel button rifled barrel with spiral flutes, muzzle brake, six vent A1 flash hider, two 10 shot mags., 6-pos. adj. stock, M4-style buttstock, flat-top receiver with Picatinny rail, G10 composite handguard, non-vented mid-length free float tube, black furniture standard or optional camo upgrades available, 7 1/2 lbs. New 2011.

| MSR $1,045 | $875 | $550 | $465 | $395 | $350 | $325 | $300 | |

Add $330 for camo upgrades.

* **.17 HMR Tactical Complete Rifle** – .17 HMR cal., blowback operating system, 18 in. stainless steel button-rifled barrel with straight flutes, two 10 shot mags., tactical trigger (choice of Geissele SSA or Alexander Arms Tactical Trigger), B5 Systems SOPMOD Bravo collapsible stock, Manticore Arms Transformers rail handguard, choice of two sets of panels, Graphite Black, FDE, or OD Green Cerakote finish, 7.5 lbs. New late 2017.

| MSR $1,750 | $1,425 | $925 | $700 | $550 | $475 | $395 | $350 | |

5.56 NATO – 5.56 NATO cal., GIO, mid-length gas system, 16 or 20 (disc. 2014) in. fluted barrel, A2 flash hider, M4 stock, 30 shot mag.

* **5.56 NATO Rifle (Incursion Complete Rifle)** – 5.56 NATO cal., GIO, mid-length gas system, 16 or 20 (disc. 2014) in. fluted barrel with A2 flash hider, 30 shot mag., military-style trigger, M4 stock, A2 grip, flat-top receiver with Picatinny rail, free floated G10 (disc.) or MK10 composite handguard, includes soft carry bag, black furniture standard or optional camo upgrades available, 6.1 lbs. New 2012.

| MSR $1,100 | $915 | $575 | $475 | $415 | $350 | $325 | $300 | |

Add $330 for camo upgrades.
Add $88 for 20 in. barrel (disc. 2014).

* **5.56 NATO Tactical Complete Rifle** – 5.56 NATO cal., GIO, 16 in. chrome moly lightweight barrel with Melonite finish, 30 shot mag., tactical trigger, B5 Systems SOPMOD Bravo collapsible stock, Ergo grip, Manticore Arms Transformer handguard with choice of two sets of panels, Graphite Black, FDE, or OD Green Cerakote finish.

| MSR $1,750 | $1,425 | $925 | $700 | $550 | $475 | $395 | $350 | |

.300 AAC BLACKOUT – .300 AAC Blackout cal., GIO, M4 styling with 16 in. stainless steel barrel, 30 shot mag.

* **.300 AAC Blackout Complete Rifle** – .300 AAC Blackout cal., GIO, 16 in. fluted stainless steel barrel with AAC Blackout flash hider, 30 shot mag., G10 free floated composite handguard, M4 stock, A2 grip, black furniture, includes soft carry bag. New 2012.

| MSR $1,155 | $975 | $595 | $495 | $425 | $365 | $335 | $300 | |

* **.300 AAC Tactical Complete Rifle** – .300 AAC Blackout cal., GIO, 16 in. fluted barrel with AAC Blackout flash hider, 30 shot mag., tactical trigger, B5 Systems SOPMOD Bravo collapsible stock, flat-top receiver, Manticore Arms Transformer rail handguard with choice of two sets of panels, includes soft carry bag, Graphite Black, FDE, or OD Green Cerakote finish. New 2012.

| MSR $1,750 | $1,425 | $925 | $700 | $550 | $475 | $395 | $350 | |

ALEX PRO FIREARMS

Current AR-15 style rifle and accessories manufacturer located in Alexandria, MN since 2014.

PISTOLS: SEMI-AUTO

223 PISTOL – 5.56 NATO cal., carbine length gas system, 10 1/2 in. medium contour barrel with black Cerakote finish, A2 birdcage muzzle device, single stage Mil-Spec trigger, SB Tactical SBM4 pistol brace, Mil-Spec A2 grip, M16 Nitride BCG, APF 9 in. M-LOK rail, black finish, 6.4 lbs. Disc. 2017.

| | $925 | $850 | $725 | $625 | $550 | $475 | $425 | $1,100 |

300 BLACKOUT / 5.56 NATO PISTOL – .300 AAC Blackout or 5.56 NATO (new 2018) cal., pistol (.300 BO) or carbine (5.56 NATO) length gas system, 10 1/2 in. medium contour stainless steel barrel with Cerakote finish, A2 birdcage muzzle device, single stage Mil-Spec trigger, SB Tactical SBM4 pistol brace, Mil-Spec A2 grip, M16 Nitride BCG, APF 9 in. M-LOK rail, hardcoat anodized black finish, 6.4 lbs.

| MSR $1,100 | $925 | $850 | $725 | $625 | $550 | $475 | $425 | |

308 PISTOL – .308 Win. cal., mid-length gas system, 12 1/2 in. stainless steel medium contour barrel with black Cerakote finish, A2 birdcage muzzle device, single stage Mil-Spec trigger, SB Tactical SBM4 pistol brace, Mil-Spec A2 grip, LR-308 Nitride BCG, APF 12 1/2 in. M-LOK rail, black finish, 8.2 lbs.

| MSR $1,440 | $1,215 | $1,085 | $950 | $815 | $715 | $600 | $500 | |

6.5 GRENDEL PISTOL – 6.5 Grendel cal., mid-length gas system, 15 1/2 in. stainless steel, A2 birdcage muzzle brake, SST, SB Tactical SBM4 pistol brace, Mil-Spec A2 grip, Nitride BCG, 12 1/2 in. M-LOK rail, hardcoat anodized black finish, 7.2 lbs. New 2018.

| MSR $1,175 | $975 | $885 | $765 | $650 | $575 | $495 | $435 | |

A 62 ALEX PRO FIREARMS, cont.

MSR	100%	98%	95%	90%	80%	70%	60%	Last MSR

APF PISTOL – 9mm Para., .40 S&W, 10mm, or .45 ACP cal., 10 1/2 in. stainless steel barrel, PCC-FH muzzle brake, SST, SB Tactical SBM4 pistol brace, Mil-Spec A2 grip, 9 in. M-LOK rail, hardcoat anodized black finish, 5.8 lbs. New 2018.

| MSR $1,500 | $1,275 | $1,125 | $1,025 | $875 | $750 | $625 | $525 | |

RIFLES/CARBINES: SEMI-AUTO

22-250 FIELD – .22-250 Rem. cal., rifle length gas system, 20 in. stainless steel medium light contour fluted barrel, A2 birdcage muzzle device, SST, Luth-AR MBA-2 stock, Magpul MOE grip, LR-308 nickel boron BCG, APF 15 1/2 in. M-LOK rail, black Cerakote finish, 9 lbs.

| MSR $1,570 | $1,315 | $850 | $625 | $500 | $435 | $375 | $350 | |

243 FIELD – .243 Win. cal., rifle length gas system, 20 in. medium light contour stainless steel barrel, SST, Magpul MOE 6-pos. Mil-Spec stock, Magpul MOE grip, LR-308 nickel boron BCG, APF 15 1/2 in. M-LOK rail, black Cerakote finish, 9 lbs.

| MSR $1,250 | $1,050 | $650 | $495 | $450 | $395 | $350 | $325 | |

22-250 TARGET – .243 Win. cal., rifle length gas system, 24 in. stainless steel medium heavy contour fluted barrel, CMC 3.5 lb. single stage flat blade trigger, Magpul PRS Gen 3 stock, Ergo SureGrip, LR-308 nickel boron BCG, APF 15 1/2 in. M-LOK rail, black or FDE Cerakote finish, 11.6 lbs.

| MSR $1,875 | $1,575 | $995 | $775 | $575 | $495 | $425 | $395 | |

Add $125 for FDE Cerakote finish.

308 CARBINE – .308 Win. cal., rifle length gas system, 16 in. stainless steel medium contour barrel with black Cerakote finish, A2 birdcage muzzle device, single stage Mil-Spec trigger, Magpul MOE 6-pos. Mil-Spec stock, Magpul MOE grip, LR-308 Nitride BCG, APF 15 1/2 in. M-LOK rail, black finish, 9 lbs.

| MSR $1,200 | $995 | $625 | $495 | $450 | $395 | $350 | $325 | |

308 HUNTER – .308 Win. cal., 18 in. stainless steel medium contour barrel with black Cerakote finish, A2 birdcage muzzle device, single stage Mil-Spec trigger, Luth-AR MBA-2 stock, Magpul MOE grip, nickel boron BCG, APF 15 1/2 in. M-LOK rail, black Cerakote finish, 9 lbs.

| MSR $1,375 | $1,135 | $725 | $525 | $465 | $415 | $375 | $350 | |

308 MATCH CARBINE – .308 Win. cal., rifle length gas system, 16 in. stainless steel medium contour barrel with black Cerakote finish, APF Butcher 16 muzzle device, single stage flat blade trigger, Magpul ACS 6-pos. Mil-Spec stock, Ergo SureGrip, nickel boron BCG, APF 15 1/2 in. M-LOK rail, black, Burnt Bronze, Tungsten, or FDE Cerakote finish, 9.2 lbs.

| MSR $1,500 | $1,250 | $825 | $575 | $475 | $425 | $375 | $350 | |

Add $125 for Burnt Bronze, Tungsten, or FDE Cerakote finish.

308 TARGET – .308 Win. cal., rifle length gas system, 20 in. stainless steel medium contour barrel with black Cerakote finish, APF Butcher 16 muzzle device, single stage flat blade trigger, Magpul PRS stock, Ergo SureGrip, nickel boron BCG, APF 15 1/2 in. M-LOK rail, black or FDE Cerakote finish, 10.4 lbs.

| MSR $1,875 | $1,575 | $995 | $775 | $575 | $495 | $425 | $395 | |

Add $125 for FDE Cerakote finish.

450 BUSHMASTER HUNTER – .450 Bushmaster cal., mid-length gas system, 18 in. stainless steel barrel, 450 muzzle brake, SST, Luth-AR MBA-2 stock, Magpul MOE grip, Nitride BCG, 15 1/2 in. M-LOK rail, hardcoat anodized black finish, 7.6 lbs. New 2018.

| MSR $1,315 | $1,100 | $675 | $525 | $450 | $400 | $350 | $325 | |

6.5 HUNTER – 6.5mm Creedmoor cal., rifle length gas system, 22 in. stainless steel fluted barrel, A2 birdcage muzzle device, single stage Mil-Spec trigger, Luth-AR MBA-2 stock, Magpul MOE grip, APF 15 1/2 in. M-LOK rail, black Cerakote finish, 9.4 lbs.

| MSR $1,440 | $1,195 | $795 | $550 | $465 | $415 | $375 | $350 | |

6.5 TARGET – 6.5mm Creedmoor cal., rifle length gas system, 24 in. stainless steel medium heavy contour fluted barrel, APF Butcher 16 muzzle device, single stage flat blade trigger, Magpul PRS stock, Ergo SureGrip, nickel boron BCG, APF 15 1/2 in. M-LOK rail, black or FDE Cerakote finish, 11.6 lbs.

| MSR $1,875 | $1,575 | $995 | $775 | $575 | $495 | $425 | $395 | |

Add $125 for FDE Cerakote finish.

ALPHA – .223 Wylde chamber, 16 in. barrel, A2 birdcage muzzle device, SST, Mil-Spec 6-pos. stock, A2 grip, with or w/o optics, 9 in. M-LOK rail, Nitride BCG, hardcoat anodized black finish, 6.2 lbs. New 2018.

| MSR $750 | $645 | $500 | $415 | $370 | $325 | $300 | $275 | |

Add $150 for optics.

ALEX PRO FIREARMS, cont. 63 A

MSR	100%	98%	95%	90%	80%	70%	60%	Last MSR

CARBINE – 9mm Para., .40 S&W, 10mm, or .45 ACP cal., 16 in. stainless steel barrel, PCC-FH muzzle device, Magpul MOE 6-pos. Mil-Spec stock, Magpul MOE grip, 12 1/2 in. M-LOK rail, hardcoat anodized black finish, 6.4 lbs. New 2018.

	100%	98%	95%	90%	80%	70%	60%	Last MSR
MSR $1,500	$1,250	$825	$575	$475	$425	$375	$350	

CARBINE 5.56 NATO – 5.56 NATO cal., mid-length gas system, 16 in. SOCOM contour barrel, A2 birdcage muzzle device, single stage Mil-Spec trigger, Magpul MOE 6-pos. Mil-Spec stock, Magpul MOE grip, M16 nickel boron BCG, APF 12 1/2 in. M-LOK rail, black finish, 6.6 lbs.

	100%	98%	95%	90%	80%	70%	60%	Last MSR
MSR $1,125	$935	$575	$475	$415	$350	$325	$300	

CARBINE 300 BLACKOUT – .300 AAC Blackout cal., carbine gas system, 16 in. stainless steel medium contour fluted barrel with black Cerakote finish, A2 birdcage muzzle device, single stage Mil-Spec trigger, Magpul MOE 6-pos. Mil-Spec stock, Magpul MOE grip, M16 nickel boron BCG, APF 12 1/2 in. M-LOK rail, black finish, 6.6 lbs.

	100%	98%	95%	90%	80%	70%	60%	Last MSR
MSR $1,125	$935	$575	$475	$415	$350	$325	$300	

CARBINE .450 BUSHMASTER – .450 Bushmaster cal., mid-length gas system, 16 in. stainless steel barrel, 450 muzzle brake, single stage Mil-Spec trigger, Magpul MOE 6-pos. Mil-Spec stock, Magpul MOE grip, Nitride BCG, 12 1/2 in. M-LOK rail, hardcoat anodized black finish, 7.3 lbs. New 2018.

	100%	98%	95%	90%	80%	70%	60%	Last MSR
MSR $1,125	$935	$575	$475	$415	$350	$325	$300	

DMR (DESIGNATED MARKSMAN RIFLE) – .223 Wylde, .224 Valkyrie (new 2018), 6.5 Grendel, or .22 Nosler cal., rifle or mid-length gas system, 18 in. medium contour stainless steel barrel, APF Butcher 16 muzzle device, single stage flat blade trigger, Magpul ACS 6-pos. Mil-Spec stock, Ergo SureGrip, nickel boron BCG, APF 15 1/2 in. M-LOK rail, black finish, 6.8 lbs.

	100%	98%	95%	90%	80%	70%	60%	Last MSR
MSR $1,440	$1,195	$795	$550	$465	$415	$375	$350	

Add $60 for 6.5 Grendel or .224 Valkyrie (new 2018) cal.

ECONO CARBINE – .223 Wylde chamber, carbine gas system, 16 in. M4 contour barrel with phosphate finish, A2 birdcage muzzle device, single stage Mil-Spec trigger, no sights, Mil-Spec 6-pos. stock, Mil-Spec A2 grip, M16 Nitride BCG, Magpul M-LOK rail, black finish, 6.2 lbs. Disc. 2017.

	100%	98%	95%	90%	80%	70%	60%	Last MSR
	$645	$500	$415	$370	$325	$300	$275	$750

Add $100 for Vortex Strikefire red dot sights.

Add $150 for Nikon scope.

ECONO CARBINE 300 BLACKOUT – .300 AAC Blackout cal., carbine gas system, 16 in. medium contour fluted barrel with black Cerakote finish, A2 birdcage muzzle device, single stage Mil-Spec trigger, no sights, Mil-Spec 6-pos. stock, Mil-Spec A2 grip, M16 Nitride BCG, Magpul M-LOK rail, black finish, 6.2 lbs.

	100%	98%	95%	90%	80%	70%	60%	Last MSR
	$725	$500	$435	$375	$335	$315	$295	$836

Add $115 for Vortex Strikefire sights.

Add $199 for Nikon scope.

MATCH CARBINE – .223 Wylde chamber, mid-length gas system, 16 in. stainless steel SOCOM contour barrel, APF Butcher 16 muzzle device, CMC 3 1/2 lb. single stage flat blade trigger, Magpul ACS 6-pos. Mil-Spec stock, Ergo SureGrip, M16 Nickel boron BCG, APF 15 1/2 in. M-LOK rail, hardcoat anodized black or Cerakote finish in Burnt Bronze, Tungsten, or FDE, 6.8 lbs.

	100%	98%	95%	90%	80%	70%	60%	Last MSR
MSR $1,250	$1,050	$650	$495	$450	$395	$350	$325	

Add $125 for Burnt Bronze, Tungsten, or FDE finish.

MLR (MAGNUM LONG RIFLE) – .26 Nosler, .28 Nosler, .30 Nosler, .33 Nosler, 7mm Rem. Mag., or .300 Win. Mag. cal., rifle length gas system, 22 in. stainless steel barrel with Cerakote finish, MLR muzzle brake, CMC 3.5 lb. flat blade trigger, Luth-AR MBA 2 stock, Ergo SureGrip, 15 1/2 in. M-LOK handguard, Nitride BCG, black, FDE, or Sniper Green Cerakote finish, 9.8 lbs. New 2018.

	100%	98%	95%	90%	80%	70%	60%	Last MSR
MSR $3,850	$3,125	$2,100	$1,475	$875	$695	$650	$575	

TARGET – 5.56 NATO (disc. 2017), .223 Wylde, or .204 Ruger cal., rifle length gas system, 24 in. stainless steel heavy contour fluted barrel, SST, Luth-AR MBA-2 stock, Magpul MOE grip, M16 nickel boron BCG, APF 15 1/2 in. M-LOK rail, hardcoat anodized black or Snow Camo Cerakote (.204 Ruger only) finish, 9.2 lbs.

	100%	98%	95%	90%	80%	70%	60%	Last MSR
MSR $1,500	$1,250	$825	$575	$475	$425	$375	$350	

Add $250 for Snow Camo Cerakote finish (.204 Ruger cal. only).

VARMINT – .223 Wylde, .22 Nosler (new mid-2017), or .224 Valkyrie (new 2018) cal., rifle length gas system, 20 or 22 (new 2018, .224 Valkyrie or .22 Nosler only) in. stainless steel medium contour barrel, A2 birdcage muzzle device, SST, Luth-AR MBA-2 stock, Magpul MOE grip, M16 nickel boron BCG, APF 15 1/2 in. M-LOK rail, hardcoat anodized black or Snow Camo Cerakote finish, 7.9 lbs.

	100%	98%	95%	90%	80%	70%	60%	Last MSR
MSR $1,315	$1,100	$675	$525	$450	$400	$350	$325	

Add $250 for Snow Camo Cerakote finish.

MSR	100%	98%	95%	90%	80%	70%	60%	Last MSR

ALPHA FOXTROT

Current pistol and rifle manufacturer located in Duluth, GA.

PISTOLS: SEMI-AUTO

Alpha Foxtrot manufactures an AF-C (aluminum aftermarket pistol frame) and MF-C (modular aftermarket pistol frame) in 9mm Para. or .40 S&W cal. The frame comes with a choice of hardcoat anodized custom colors and finishes, weighs 9.3 oz., extended bite-proof beavertail, includes rail kit w/locking block and pins, stainless steel rail, and is 6.95 in. OAL. MSR is $299.

AF15 PISTOL – 5.56 NATO cal., GIO, 7 in. barrel, 7076 T-6 forged aluminum receiver, Picatinny rail, hardcoat anodized black finish.

MSR $999	$850	$550	$465	$395	$350	$325	$295	

RIFLES: SEMI-AUTO

AF15 RIFLE – 5.56 NATO cal., GIO, 16 in. barrel, forged aluminum receiver, Picatinny rail, hardcoat anodized black finish.

MSR $749	$645	$500	$415	$370	$325	$300	$275	

AMBUSH FIREARMS

Current trademark of semi-auto rifles manufactured by Daniel Defense located in Black Creek, GA beginning 2010. An additional manufacturing facility is located in Ridgeland, SC.

RIFLES/CARBINES: SEMI-AUTO

All Ambush rifles come with a lifetime guarantee.

AMBUSH A11 6.8/5.56 – 5.56 NATO (new 2012) or 6.8 SPC cal., AR-15 style, 18 in. barrel, free floating full-length Picatinny modular rail with two smaller rails on bottom and front, 5 shot mag., Geissele super semi-auto trigger, Magpul MOE adj. stock, pistol grip, black (standard, disc. 2013), pink (mfg. 2013), Mossy Oak Break-Up Infinity (mfg. 2012-2013), or Realtree AP camo coverage, 6 lbs. Mfg. 2011-2016.

	$1,475	$950	$725	$550	$475	$395	$350	*$1,799*

AMBUSH 300 AAC BLACKOUT – .300 AAC Blackout (7.62x35mm) cal., AR-15 style, 18 in. barrel, 5 shot mag., Geissele super semi-auto trigger, Magpul MOE adj. stock, free floating full-length Picatinny modular rail with two smaller rails on bottom and front, pistol grip, black, Mossy Oak Break-Up Infinity (disc. 2013), or Realtree AP camo coverage, 6 1/2 lbs. Mfg. 2012-2016.

	$1,475	$950	$725	$550	$475	$395	$350	*$1,799*

Subtract $40 for Mossy Oak Blaze Pink finish (disc.).

DD5 AMBUSH – .308 Win. cal., rifle length gas system, 18 in. chrome-lined, free floating, cold hammer forged, heavy phosphate coated barrel with S2W profile and DD superior suppression device, 5 shot Magpul PMAG, flared magwell, integral oversized trigger guard, Geissele SSA two-stage trigger, ambidextrous controls, full-length Picatinny top rail and KeyMod forearm, Soft Touch rubber overmolding on DD pistol grip and adj. buttstock, interchangeable buttpads, DD full-latch impact plastic case, Kryptek Highlander or Realtree Xtra (new 2017) finish, 8.6 lbs., 35 3/8-39 in. OAL. New 2016.

MSR $3,096	$2,450	$1,595	$1,200	$700	$675	$575	$525	

DDM4 AMBUSH – 5.56 NATO, 6.8 SPC, or .300 AAC Blackout (7.62x35mm) cal., 16 (.300 AAC Blackout only) or 18 in. chrome-lined, free floating, cold hammer forged, heavy phosphate coated barrel with S2W profile and knurled thread protector, 5 shot Magpul PMAG, flared magwell, integral oversized trigger guard, Geissele SSA two-stage trigger, ambidextrous safety, full-length Picatinny top rail and M-LOK forearm, Soft Touch rubber overmolding on DD pistol grip and adj. buttstock, interchangeable buttpads, DD full-latch impact plastic case, Kryptek Highlander or Realtree Xtra finish, 32 1/4-37 in. OAL, 6.55-7 lbs. New 2018.

MSR $1,899	$1,575	$995	$775	$575	$495	$425	$395	

AMERICAN DEFENSE MFG. LLC

Current AR-15 style rifle manufacturer located in New Berlin, WI.

RIFLES: SEMI-AUTO

All American Defense Manufacturing products are 100% designed by shooters and built in the USA. In addition to AR-15 rifles, American Defense Manufacturing also manufactures the patented Auto Lock System, as well as mounts, rings, bases, and other AR-15 accessories.

AMERICAN DEFENSE MFG. LLC, cont. 65 A

MSR	100%	98%	95%	90%	80%	70%	60%	Last MSR

UIC (UNIVERSAL IMPROVED CARBINE) MOD 1 – .223 Wylde chamber or .300 AAC Blackout (disc. 2016) cal., 16 in. lightweight contour chrome-lined barrel with Griffin Armament Tactical (disc. 2016) or A2 compensator, Mil-Spec bolt carrier group, fully ambidextrous lower billet receiver, forged Mil-Spec upper receiver, ADM HD buffer, Type III Teflon hardcoat black finish. Mfg. 2015-2017.

	100%	98%	95%	90%	80%	70%	60%	Last MSR
	$1,250	$825	$575	$475	$425	$375	$350	*$1,500*

UIC (UNIVERSAL IMPROVED CARBINE) MOD 2 – .223 Wylde chamber or .300 AAC Blackout cal., 16 in. lightweight contour chrome-lined barrel with Griffin Armament Flash compensator, billet upper receiver, ADM heavy duty gas tube, two-stage adj. trigger, fully ambidextrous lower billet receiver and charging handle, ADM buffer, choice of Low Light, KeyMod, or M-LOK rail system, steel endplate, Type III Teflon hardcoat black, FDE, ADM Grey, ADM Bronze, or ADM Green finish. New 2015.

MSR $1,850	$1,525	$975	$750	$575	$495	$425	$375

Add $150 for FDE, ADM Grey, Bronze, or Green finish.

* **UIC MOD 2 .224 Valkyrie** – .224 Valkyrie cal., rifle length gas system, 18 or 22 in. Hybrid contour stainless steel barrel with Nitride finish, Battlecomp muzzle device, competition-style magwell, two-stage match trigger, enlarged trigger guard, Magpul PRO BUIS, Magpul PRS Gen3 stock, HD buffer, billet aluminum fully ambidextrous upper and lower receiver set, 15 in. M-LOK handguard, Type III hardcoat anodized black finish. New 2018.

MSR $2,300	$1,875	$1,100	$895	$650	$575	$495	$425

* **UIC MOD 2 Special Edition** – .223 Wylde chamber, 16 in. Criterion barrel with Melonite finish, 13 1/2 in. low light handguard, Red Distressed or White Distressed Cerakote finish. New 2018.

MSR $2,600	$2,125	$1,325	$995	$675	$595	$525	$475

* **UIC MOD 2 Special Edition Package** – .223 Wylde chamber, 16 in. Criterion barrel with Melonite finish, Trijicon MRO sights with special edition Pink AD-MRO-CO mount, 15 in. low light handguard, includes Gear Sector Offset light mount in pink for 1 in. flashlight, Gear Sector GS-1240 2-point sling in pink, Pink Cerakote finish. New 2018.

MSR $2,500	$2,050	$1,250	$950	$650	$575	$495	$475

* **UIC MOD 2 SPR** – .223 Wylde chamber, Mil-Spec rifle length gas system, 18 in. Hybrid contour stainless steel Criterion barrel with Nitride finish, Battlecomp 1.0 muzzle device, competition-style magwell, enlarged trigger guard, two-stage match trigger, Magpul PRO BUIS, Magpul PRS Gen3 stock, HD buffer, billet aluminum fully ambidextrous upper and lower receiver set, Mil-Spec enhanced BCG with Nitride QPQ finish, ambi charging handle, 15 in. low light handguard, Type III hardcoat anodized black finish, 8.6 lbs. New 2018.

MSR $2,150	$1,725	$1,050	$850	$625	$550	$475	$425

UIC (UNIVERSAL IMPROVED CARBINE) MOD 3 – 5.56 NATO or .300 AAC Blackout cal., 16 in. lightweight contour chrome-lined barrel with Griffin Armament Flash compensator, low profile adj. gas block (features 3 settings), billet upper receiver, ADM heavy duty gas tube, two-stage adj. trigger, fully ambidextrous lower billet receiver and charging handle, ADM buffer, choice of Low Light, KeyMod, or M-LOK rail system, steel endplate, Type III Teflon hardcoat black, FDE (disc. 2017), ADM Grey (disc. 2017), ADM Bronze (disc. 2017), or ADM Green (disc. 2017) finish. New 2015.

MSR $2,000	$1,675	$1,000	$825	$625	$550	$475	$425

Add $150 for FDE, ADM Grey, ADM Bronze, or ADM Green finish (disc. 2017).

UIC 10A – 6.5mm Creedmoor cal., Mil-Spec rifle length gas system, 18 or 22 in. stainless steel Criterion barrel, Battlecomp 51T muzzle device, competition-style magwell, enlarged trigger guard, two-stage trigger, Magpul PRO BUIS, Magpul PRS Gen 3 stock, QD endplate, Lantac .308 enhanced bolt carrier group, ambi charging handle, 15 in. M-LOK handguard, HD buffer, billet aluminum fully ambidextrous upper and lower receiver set, Type III hardcoat anodized black finish, 9 lbs. 4 oz. New 2018.

MSR $2,600	$2,125	$1,325	$995	$675	$595	$525	$475

Add $100 for 22 in. barrel.

UIC 10A CSASS – .308 Win. cal., rifle length gas system, 18 in. stainless steel barrel, Battlecomp 51T muzzle device, competition style magwell, enlarged trigger guard, two-stage match trigger, Magpul PRO BUIS, Magpul PRS Gen 3 stock, QD endplate, ambidextrous safety selector and charging handle, fully ambidextrous controls featuring a right side bolt catch and release lever and left side magazine release, billet aluminum upper and lower receiver, 15 in. M-LOK handguard, ADM HD buffer, Type III hardcoat anodized finish, 9 lbs. 4 oz.

MSR $2,400	$1,975	$1,150	$925	$650	$575	$495	$425

UIC 10A DMR – .308 Win. cal., rifle length gas system, 16 in. stainless steel heavy barrel, Battlecomp 51T muzzle device, competition style magwell, enlarged trigger guard, two-stage match trigger, Magpul PRO BUIS, Magpul PRS Gen 3 stock, QD endplate, ambidextrous safety selector and charging handle, ADM HD buffer, billet aluminum upper and lower receivers, fully ambidextrous controls featuring a right side bolt catch and release lever and left side magazine release, 15 in. M-LOK handguard, Type III hardcoat anodized finish, 9 lbs. 4 oz.

MSR $2,400	$1,975	$1,150	$925	$650	$575	$495	$425

A 66 AMERICAN DEFENSE MFG. LLC, cont.

MSR	100%	98%	95%	90%	80%	70%	60%	Last MSR

UIC 10A HEAVY RECON – .308 Win. cal., rifle length gas system, 16 in. stainless steel barrel, Battlecomp 51T muzzle device, competition style magwell, enlarged trigger guard, two-stage match trigger, Magpul PRO BUIS, Magpul SL stock, QD endplate, ambidextrous safety selector and charging handle, ADM HD buffer, billet aluminum upper and lower receivers, fully ambidextrous controls featuring a right side bolt catch and release lever and left side magazine release, 13 1/2 in. M-LOK handguard, Type III hardcoat anodized finish, 8 lbs. 4 oz.

| MSR $2,300 | $1,875 | $1,100 | $895 | $650 | $575 | $495 | $425 | |

AMERICAN PRECISION ARMS

Current manufacturer established in 2001, located in Jefferson, GA.

RIFLES: SEMI-AUTO

LYCAN – .223 Rem. cal., 16 or 18 in. Broughton threaded barrel, McCormick match trigger, dual spring extractor, Hogue grip, SOPMOD adj. stock, LaRue or Knight (disc.) forend, black or nickel boron (disc.) finish. Disc. 2011.

| | $2,775 | $1,825 | $1,350 | $750 | $650 | $595 | $525 | $3,450 |

URBAN SNIPER .223 – .223 Rem. cal., 20 in. Broughton 5C stainless barrel, 20 shot mag., JP match grade trigger, standard carrier assembly, LMT SOPMOD adj. stock, Badger Ordnance forend, DPMS PSG-1 style grip. Disc. 2011.

| | $1,975 | $1,150 | $925 | $650 | $575 | $495 | $425 | $2,450 |

URBAN SNIPER .308 – .308 Win. cal., 20 in. Rock Creek 5R stainless barrel, 10 shot mag., DPMS upper and lower receiver, standard carrier assembly, JP match grade trigger, Magpul PRS adj. stock, Badger Ordnance forend. Disc. 2011.

| | $2,450 | $1,595 | $1,200 | $700 | $675 | $575 | $525 | $3,098 |

AMERICAN SPIRIT ARMS

Current manufacturer established circa 1995, located in Scottsdale, AZ. In April 2015, American Spirit Arms announced its sale to American Spirit Investments, LLC, and emphasized focus on their patented AR-15 side charger technology. They confirmed that the American Spirit Arms brand will be retained.

PISTOLS: SEMI-AUTO

American Spirit Arms previously offered a 5.56 NATO cal. AR-15 style pistol with A2 fixed carry handle (last MSR was $1,199, disc. 2012).

9MM PISTOL A2 – 9mm Para. cal., 7 1/2 in. chrome moly barrel, 25 shot mag., forged lower and forged A2 upper receiver with fixed carry handle, fixed front iron sight base, includes hard carry case. Disc. 2016.

| | $1,100 | $995 | $875 | $735 | $650 | $550 | $465 | $1,300 |

A2 PISTOL – 5.56 NATO cal., 7 1/2 in. chrome moly barrel, 30 shot mag., forged lower receiver and forged A2 upper with fixed carry handle, includes hard case. Disc. 2014.

| | $1,200 | $1,075 | $950 | $800 | $700 | $600 | $495 | $1,390 |

AR-15 PISTOL WITH HANDGUARD – 5.56 NATO cal., 7 1/2 in. chrome moly barrel, 30 shot mag., forged A3 flat-top upper receiver, Picatinny rail, carbine length free float handguard, includes hard carry case. Disc. 2014.

| | $1,135 | $1,015 | $885 | $740 | $675 | $575 | $475 | $1,350 |

AR-15 PISTOL WITH QUAD RAIL – 5.56 NATO cal., 7 1/2 in. chrome moly barrel, 30 shot mag., forged A3 (disc. 2014) or side charging flat-top upper receiver, forged lower, Picatinny rail, quad rail with gas block, includes hard carry case. Disc. 2016.

| | $1,200 | $1,075 | $950 | $800 | $700 | $600 | $495 | $1,400 |

SIDE CHARGING 9MM PISTOL (FLAT TOP 9MM PISTOL) – 9mm Para. cal., 7 1/2 in. chrome moly barrel, 25 shot mag., forged lower and forged A3 (disc. 2015) or side charging (new 2015) flat-top upper receiver, Picatinny rail, fixed front iron sight base, includes hard carry case. Disc. 2016.

| | $1,350 | $1,200 | $1,075 | $950 | $815 | $700 | $575 | $1,600 |

RIFLES/CARBINES: SEMI-AUTO

ASA-A2 RIFLE – 5.56 NATO cal., GIO, 20 in. Govt. profile barrel, 30 shot mag., fixed (A2) buttstock, fixed carry handle, M4 feed ramps, includes hard carrying case. Disc. 2014.

| | $1,075 | $675 | $500 | $450 | $400 | $350 | $325 | $1,296 |

ASA-A320(G) SIDE CHARGING RIFLE – 5.56 NATO cal., GIO, 20 in. chrome moly barrel, 30 shot mag., choice of flat-top or fixed carry handle, side charging upper with Picatinny rail (became standard 2015), forged lower, gas block with Picatinny rail, rifle length handguard, M4 feed ramps, A2 fixed stock, includes hard carrying case. Disc. 2016.

| | $1,075 | $675 | $500 | $450 | $400 | $350 | $325 | $1,300 |

AMERICAN SPIRIT ARMS, cont. 67 A

MSR	100%	98%	95%	90%	80%	70%	60%	Last MSR

ASA-DISSIPATOR A2 CARBINE – 5.56 NATO cal., GIO, 16 in. M4 barrel, 30 shot mag., adj. open rear sights, A2 fixed buttstock, M4 feed ramps, Dissipator CAR length gas system, front and rear sling swivels, includes hard carrying case. Disc. 2014.

	$1,150	$750	$550	$465	$415	$375	$350	$1,386

ASA-M4A2 CARBINE – 5.56 NATO cal., GIO, 16 in. barrel, 30 shot mag., fixed carry handle, 6-pos. M4 collapsible stock, includes hard carrying case. Disc. 2014.

	$1,075	$675	$500	$450	$400	$350	$325	$1,296

ASA-M4A3 SIDE CHARGING CARBINE – 5.56 NATO cal., GIO, carbine length gas system, 16 in. M4 barrel with Nitride finish, 30 shot PMAG, A2 fixed front sight or gas block, flat side charging upper with Picatinny rail (became standard 2015), M4 feed ramps, 6-position collapsible stock, front and rear sling swivels, includes hard carrying case. Disc. 2016.

	$1,075	$675	$500	$450	$400	$350	$325	$1,300

ASA-M4CS1 SIDE CHARGING CARBINE – 5.56 NATO cal., GIO, carbine length gas system, 16 in. M4 profile barrel with A2 flash hider, 30 shot PMAG, low profile gas block, M4 feed ramps, flat-top receiver (side charging upper became standard 2015) with Picatinny rail, 10 in. Samson Evo quad rail, tactical trigger guard, Ergo grip, Magpul MOE collapsible buttstock, black or FDE finish, includes hard carrying case. Mfg. 2013-2016.

	$1,250	$825	$575	$475	$425	$375	$350	$1,476

ASA-M4CS2 SIDE CHARGING CARBINE – 5.56 NATO cal., GIO, carbine length gas system, 16 in. M4 profile barrel with A2 flash hider, 30 shot PMAG, flat-top upper receiver (side charging upper became standard 2015) with Picatinny rail, M4 feed ramps, Midwest Industries Gen 2 drop-in quad rail, tactical trigger guard, A2 fixed front sight or gas block, Magpul MOE collapsible buttstock, FDE or ODG furniture, includes hard carrying case. Mfg. 2013-2016.

	$1,250	$825	$575	$475	$425	$375	$350	$1,476

ASA-MID-LENGTH SIDE CHARGING RIFLE (A3 M16 RIFLE) – 5.56 NATO cal., carbine length gas system, 16 in. Nitride mid-length barrel, 30 shot mag., M4 feed ramps, forged lower and flat-top upper (side charging upper became standard 2015) receiver with Picatinny rail, gas block with 1913 rail, front and rear sling swivels, 6-pos. buttstock, includes hard carrying case. Disc. 2016.

	$1,075	$675	$500	$450	$400	$350	$325	$1,300

ASA-SIDE CHARGING DISSIPATOR (A3G CARBINE) – 5.56 NATO cal., GIO, 16 in. chrome moly barrel, 30 shot mag., M4 feed ramps, gas block with Picatinny rail, Magpul MOE rifle length handguard with dissipator CAR-length gas system underneath, flat-top upper receiver (side charging upper became standard 2015) with Picatinny rail, forged lower, front and rear sling swivels, Magpul 6-pos. stock, includes hard carrying case.

MSR $1,400	$1,150	$750	$550	$465	$415	$375	$350	

ASA-SPR SIDE CHARGING RIFLE (ASA-SPR) – 5.56 NATO (disc.) or .308 Win. (new 2015) cal., GIO, mid-length gas system, 18 in. stainless steel heavy profile barrel with A2 flash hider, 30 shot PMAG, flat-top upper (side charging upper became standard in 2015) receiver, low profile gas block, 12 in. Samson Evo quad rail, two-stage trigger, M4 feed ramps, Ergo grip, MOE trigger guard, VLTOR EMOD stock, includes hard carrying case. Mfg. 2013-2016.

	$2,295	$1,450	$1,075	$675	$595	$525	$475	$2,800

ASA-9mm AR-15 RIFLE M4/A2 CARBINE – 9mm Para. cal., GIO, 16 in. lightweight barrel, 25 shot mag., forged upper with fixed carrying handle, forged lower, fixed front sight base, adj. open rear sights, drop-in magwell adapter, 4-pos. collapsible CAR stock, front and rear sling swivels, includes hard carrying case. Disc. 2016.

	$995	$625	$495	$450	$395	$350	$325	$1,200

ASA-9mm SIDE CHARGING RIFLE M4 CARBINE (A3G CARBINE) – 9mm Para. cal., GIO, 16 in. chrome moly barrel, 25 shot mag., flat-top receiver (side charging upper became standard 2015) with Picatinny rail, forged lower receiver, gas block with Picatinny rail, drop-in magwell adapter, front and rear sling swivels, 4-pos. collapsible CAR stock, includes hard carrying case. Disc. 2016.

	$1,075	$675	$500	$450	$400	$350	$325	$1,300

ASA SIDE CHARGING BULL BARREL CARBINE (ASA-BULL A3 CARBINE) – 5.56 NATO cal., GIO, carbine length gas system, 16 in. stainless steel bull barrel, flat-top upper (side charging upper option became available 2015) with Picatinny rail, forged lower receiver, M4 feed ramps, free float handguard with gas block, choice of 6-pos. collapsible or fixed A2 stock, includes 30 shot PMAG and hard carrying case. Disc. 2016.

	$1,315	$850	$625	$500	$435	$375	$350	$1,600

ASA-BULL A3 RIFLE – 5.56 NATO cal., GIO, 24 in. bull barrel, fixed buttstock. Disc. 2012.

	$1,225	$825	$575	$475	$425	$375	$350	$1,475

A 68 AMERICAN SPIRIT ARMS, cont.

MSR	100%	98%	95%	90%	80%	70%	60%	Last MSR

ASA-BULL BARREL FLAT TOP RIFLE – .223 Rem. cal., 24 in. stainless steel bull barrel, forged A3 flat-top upper receiver with Picatinny rail, free float handguard with gas block, 30 shot mag., M4 feed ramps, A2 buttstock, includes hard carrying case. Disc. 2014.

	$1,475	$950	$725	$550	$475	$395	$350	$1,800

ASA-BULL SIDE CHARGER CARBINE – 5.56 NATO cal., 24 in. stainless steel bull barrel, 30 shot mag., aluminum flat-top side charging upper receiver, Picatinny rail, forged lower receiver, front and rear sling swivels, M4 feed ramps, standard A2 buttstock, includes hard carrying case. Disc. 2014.

	$1,675	$1,000	$825	$625	$550	$475	$425	$2,000

ASA-BULL SIDE CHARGER CARBINE/RIFLE – .223 Rem. cal., GIO, 16 (carbine) or 24 (rifle) in. stainless steel bull barrel, left side charger, Magpul PRS stock with circular free floating handguard and gas block. Disc. 2014.

	$1,425	$925	$700	$550	$475	$395	$350	$1,725

ASA-308 SIDE CHARGER CARBINE/RIFLE – .308 Win. cal., GIO, 16 (standard-disc. 2012 or bull - new 2013), 20 (bull) or 24 (disc. 2011) in. bull barrel, flat-top receiver with Picatinny rail, full-length quad rail became standard 2012, Hogue grip, two-stage trigger, Magpul CTR stock, includes two 20 shot AR-10 mags. Disc. 2014.

	$2,125	$1,325	$995	$675	$595	$525	$475	$2,600

Add $450 for 20 in. bull barrel.

Subtract approx. $600 if without full-length quad rail.

ASA 20 INCH 308 SIDE CHARGER RIFLE – .308 Win. cal., 20 in. stainless steel bull barrel, JP compensator, rifle length gas system, ASA aerospace aluminum lower and flat-top side charging upper receiver with Picatinny rail, low profile gas block, Nitride carrier, Hogue grip, Harris bipod, Magpul PRS stock, includes 20 shot Armalite Gen2 mag. and hard carrying case. Mfg. 2015-2016.

	$2,585	$2,250	$1,840	$1,575	$1,300	$1,100	$950	$3,050

9mm G9 GLOCK MAG COMPATIBLE AR15 – 9mm Para. cal., closed bolt blowback system, 16 in. chrome moly barrel, uses standard Glock 9mm mags., ASA side charging upper receiver with Mil-Std 1913 rail, dedicated 9mm Glock magazine lower, 13.6 in. M-LOK rail, 6-pos. collapsible Magpul MOE stock, includes one Glock 17 mag. and hard carrying case, black finish. New 2017.

MSR $1,350	$1,125	$700	$525	$450	$400	$350	$325	

CS1 SIDE CHARGING CARBINE – 5.56 NATO cal., mid-length gas system, 16 in. Nitride barrel, A2 flash hider, 30 shot PMAG, upgraded tactical trigger guard, Magpul MOE collapsible buttstock, Ergo grip, 13.6 in. M-LOK rail, low profile gas block, M4 feed ramps, side charging flat-top upper receiver with Mil-Std 1913 rail, includes hard carrying case, black, FDE, or Olive Drab Green finish. New 2017.

MSR $1,200	$995	$625	$495	$450	$395	$350	$325	

M4ML SIDE CHARGING MID-LENGTH RIFLE – 5.56 NATO cal., 16 in. Nitride mid-length heavy barrel, 30 shot mag., 6-pos. buttstock, M4 feed ramps, ASA side charging upper receiver with Mil-Std 1913 rail, ASA forged lower receiver, mid-length handguard with gas system underneath, includes hard carrying case, black finish. New 2017.

MSR $1,100	$915	$575	$475	$415	$350	$325	$300	

M4 OEM SIDE CHARGING CARBINE – 5.56 NATO cal., carbine length gas system, 16 in. Nitride M4 barrel, 30 shot PMAG, 6-pos. stock, M4 feed ramps, ASA flat side charging upper receiver with Mil-Std 1913 rail, ASA lower receiver, gas block, Mil-Spec receiver extension, includes hard carrying case, black finish.

MSR $900	$765	$515	$440	$375	$335	$315	$295	

SPR 18 IN. SIDE CHARGING RIFLE – 5.56 NATO cal., mid-length gas system, 18 in. stainless steel barrel, 30 shot PMAG, two-stage trigger, optional flip-up rear sights, Magpul STR stock, Ergo grip, M4 feed ramps, 13 1/2 in. M-LOK rail, ASA side charging flat-top upper and lower receiver, low profile gas block, includes hard carrying case, black finish. New 2017.

MSR $1,500	$1,250	$825	$575	$475	$425	$375	$350	

AMERICAN SPIRIT ARMS CORP.

Previous rifle and components manufacturer 1998-2005, located in Tempe, AZ. Previously located in Scottsdale, AZ.

RIFLES: SEMI-AUTO

The following listings are for AR-15 style rifles/carbines using GIO operation.

Add $25 for green furniture, $65 for black barrel finish, $75 for fluted barrel, $125 for porting, $119 for two-stage match trigger, and $55 for National Match sights on .223 cal. models listed below.

ASA 24 IN. BULL BARREL FLAT-TOP RIFLE – .223 Rem. cal., AR-15 style, GIO, forged steel lower receiver, forged aluminum flat-top upper receiver, 24 in. stainless steel bull barrel, free floating aluminum handguard, includes Harris bipod. Mfg. 1999-2005.

	$850	$700	$625	$550	$500	$450	$400	$950

AMERICAN TACTICAL INC. (AMERICAN TACTICAL IMPORTS - ATI)

MSR	100%	98%	95%	90%	80%	70%	60%	Last MSR

Current importer located in Summerville, SC, beginning late 2013. Previously located in Rochester, NY.

American Tactical Inc. imports a wide variety of firearms and products, including pistols, AR-15 style and AK-47 design semi-auto rifles, and shotguns. Trademarks, imports, and private labels include Alpha shotguns, American Tactical Imports (ATI), Cavalry O/Us (new 2013), FMK (disc. 2013), Firepower Xtreme, German Sport Guns (GSG), Head Down Products (mfg. 2012-2013), ISSC (mfg. 2015-2016), Masterpiece Arms (MPA, disc. 2011), Omni, Ottoman Shotguns (disc. 2011), Tisas (imported 2008-2011), and Xtreme Rifles (disc. 2012). Please see individual listings for current or most recent model information and pricing.

PISTOLS: SEMI-AUTO

MILSPORT AR-15 PISTOL – 9mm Para. cal., 5 1/2 in. barrel, 2 in. flash can, 17 shot mag., 7 in. KeyMod handguard, billet lower and forged upper receiver, black finish. New 2012.

| MSR $870 | $735 | $650 | $580 | $515 | $450 | $385 | $340 | |

MILSPORT PISTOL – 5.56 NATO cal., forged aluminum frame, 7 1/2 in. barrel, 30 shot mag., KeyMod rail, anodized black finish.

| MSR $660 | $565 | $485 | $415 | $350 | $310 | $270 | $255 | |

OMNI HYBRID – 5.56 NATO cal., 7 1/2 in. barrel, 30 shot PMAG, Omni Hybrid lower and aluminum upper receiver, 7 in. free float quad rail, black finish, 4 3/4 lbs. Mfg. 2015 only.

| | $525 | $465 | $400 | $340 | $300 | $265 | $250 | $600 |

OMNI HYBRID 300 – .300 AAC Blackout cal., 8 1/2 in. barrel, 30 shot PMAG, complete Omni Hybrid lower and aluminum upper receiver, 7 in. free float rail, black finish. Mfg. 2015 only.

| | $585 | $500 | $435 | $365 | $325 | $280 | $265 | $670 |

OMNI HYBRID MAXX – 5.56 NATO cal., 7 1/2 or 10 1/2 (new 2017) in. barrel, 30 shot PMAG, 7 or 10 (new 2017) in. free floating KeyMod quad rail, complete Omni Hybrid polymer upper and lower receiver, black finish, 4 3/4 lbs. New 2015.

| MSR $670 | $585 | $500 | $435 | $365 | $325 | $280 | $265 | |

OMNI HYBRID MAXX 300 – .300 AAC Blackout cal., 8 1/2 or 10 1/2 (new 2017) in. barrel, 30 shot PMAG, complete Omni Hybrid polymer upper and lower receiver, 7 or 10 (new 2017) in. free floating KeyMod rail, optics ready, black finish, 4.95 lbs. New 2015.

| MSR $670 | $585 | $500 | $435 | $365 | $325 | $280 | $265 | |

OMNI HYBRID AR-15 – 5.56 NATO or .300 AAC Blackout cal., 7 1/2 or 8 1/2 in. barrel, two 30 shot PMAGs, complete Omni Hybrid polymer lower receiver, 7 in. buffer tube, 7 in. free float quad rail, flip-up iron or red dot sights, black Nitride finish, 4 3/4-5.2 lbs. Mfg. 2015-2016.

| | $550 | $480 | $415 | $350 | $310 | $270 | $255 | $620 |

Add $50 for flip-up iron sights or $60 for red dot sights.

RIFLES/CARBINES: SEMI-AUTO

.300 AAC CARBINE – .300 AAC Blackout cal., GIO, 10 or 30 shot mag., 16 in. heavy barrel with muzzle brake, 6-position stock, flat-top receiver with Picatinny rail, 9 in. quad rail handguard, black hardware and finish. Mfg. 2012-2013.

| | $850 | $550 | $465 | $395 | $350 | $325 | $295 | $999 |

AT-15 – 5.56 NATO cal., AR-15 style, GIO, 16 in. barrel with muzzle brake, flat-top receiver with mid-length quad rail handguard, post front sight, collapsible stock, 30 shot mag. Limited importation 2011 only.

| | $615 | $495 | $415 | $360 | $325 | $300 | $275 | $719 |

HDH16 CARBINE – 5.56 NATO cal., GIO, 10 or 30 shot mag., 16 in. heavy barrel, A3 flat-top receiver with Picatinny rail, 6-position stock, black hardware and finish, includes hard case. Mfg. 2012-2013.

| | $645 | $500 | $415 | $370 | $325 | $300 | $275 | $750 |

MILSPORT CARBINE – 5.56 NATO or .300 AAC Blackout cal., 16 in. barrel, 30 shot mag., 6-pos. stock, low profile gas block, 13 in. KeyMod handguard, Picatinny rail, includes Nano Composite Parts Kit. New 2018.

| MSR $530 | $475 | $415 | $375 | $335 | $310 | $295 | $275 | |

MILSPORT M4 CARBINE – 5.56 NATO cal., GIO, 30 shot PMAG, 16 in. barrel, A3 flat-top receiver with Picatinny rail, tubular ribbed handguard, forged aluminum upper and billet aluminum lower, 7 in. drop-in quad rail, 6-position stock, black hardware and finish, includes hard case. Mfg. 2012-2017.

| MSR $770 | $665 | $500 | $415 | $375 | $335 | $315 | $295 | |

A 70 AMERICAN TACTICAL INC. (AMERICAN TACTICAL IMPORTS - ATI), cont.

MSR	100%	98%	95%	90%	80%	70%	60%	Last MSR

MILSPORT .223 WYLDE – .223 Wylde chamber, 18 in. SOCOM profile stainless steel barrel, muzzle covered with thread protector, Extreme Target trigger, optics ready, 6-pos. collapsible Rogers Super-Stoc, 15 in. free float KeyMod rail handguard, forged aluminum upper and lower receiver, carbine buffer. New 2017.

| MSR $700 | $595 | $485 | $415 | $350 | $315 | $295 | $275 | |

MILSPORT 9MM AR-15 CARBINE – 9mm Para. cal., 16 in. barrel, A2 flash hider, 30 shot mag., 10 in. free float KeyMod rail handguard, forged upper and billet lower receiver, 6-position Rogers Super-Stoc, black finish. New 2012.

| MSR $900 | $765 | $515 | $440 | $375 | $335 | $315 | $295 | |

MILSPORT 5.56 AR-15 CARBINE – 5.56 NATO cal., .223 Wylde chamber, 18 in. match grade barrel, A2 flash hider, 30 shot mag., Rogers Super-Stoc, low profile Nitride steel gas block, 15 in. free floating KeyMod rail handguard, forged upper receiver, Mil-Spec internal parts, black finish. Disc. 2017.

| | $725 | $500 | $435 | $375 | $335 | $315 | $295 | $840 |

MILSPORT AR-15 RIA – 5.56 NATO cal., 16 in. mid-length barrel, A2 flash hider, 13 in. KeyMod rail handguard, anodized black finish. Disc. 2017.

| | $675 | $500 | $425 | $375 | $335 | $315 | $295 | $800 |

MILSPORT AR-15 RIA ALUMINUM – 5.56 NATO, .300 AAC Blackout, or 6.5 Grendel cal., 16 in. barrel, 30 shot mag., 6-pos. M4 stock, aluminum receivers, 10 (6.5mm Grendel only) or 13 in. KeyMod rail handguard. New 2018.

| MSR $580 | $515 | $450 | $395 | $350 | $315 | $295 | $275 | |

MILSPORT AR-15 RIA (CURRENT MFG.) – 9mm Para. cal., blowback operation, 16 in. barrel with black Nitride finish, A2 compensator, 6-pos. adj. Rogers Super-Stoc, billet 9mm lower and forged aluminum upper receiver, 10 in. KeyMod rail handguard, Cerakote Burnt Bronze finish. New 2017.

| MSR $959 | $825 | $535 | $450 | $385 | $340 | $325 | $295 | |

MILSPORT 3 GUN – 5.56 NATO cal., .223 Wylde chamber, 16 in. barrel, Rifenbark S.O.M. brake, single stage trigger, Luth-AR MB4 stock with cheekpiece, Ergo grip, aluminum Milsport receivers, 13 in. free float KeyMod rail handguard, 6.65 lbs. New 2018.

| MSR $950 | $800 | $525 | $450 | $385 | $340 | $325 | $295 | |

V916/VX916 CARBINE – 5.56 NATO cal., GIO, 10 or 30 shot mag., 16 in. heavy barrel, flat-top receiver with Picatinny rail, 9 or 13 in. quad rail handguard, 6-position stock, black hardware and finish, includes hard case. Mfg. 2012-2013.

| | $765 | $515 | $440 | $375 | $335 | $315 | $295 | $889 |

Add $20 for 13 in. quad rail (Model VX916).

OMNI 22 (VK22 STANDARD) – .22 LR cal., AR-15 style, GIO, 16 in. barrel, fixed or telestock, black finish, flat-top receiver with Picatinny rail, 10 or 28 shot mag. Disc. 2013.

| | $400 | $350 | $300 | $265 | $235 | $220 | $210 | $470 |

OMNI 22 OPS (VK22 TACTICAL) – .22 LR cal., AR-15 style, GIO, 16 in. barrel, fixed or telestock, black finish, flat-top receiver, 10 or 28 shot mag., quad rail, vertical foregrip, tactical rear sight. Disc. 2013.

| | $460 | $385 | $330 | $285 | $250 | $230 | $220 | $520 |

OMNI 556 – 5.56 NATO cal., GIO, 16 in. M4 style barrel, 10 or 30 shot mag., fixed or telescoping stock, 7 in. quad rail, flat-top receiver with Picatinny rail, Omni polymer lower receiver, black furniture. Mfg. 2013-2015.

| | $550 | $475 | $400 | $350 | $315 | $295 | $275 | $650 |

OMNI HYBRID M4 – 5.56 NATO cal., GPO, 16 in. barrel, 10 or 30 shot mag., flat-top polymer lower receiver, interlock hammer and trigger pin retainment system, enhanced trigger guard, beveled magwell, 6-position adj. stock, matte black finish, includes AR-15 parts kit, 7 lbs. Mfg. 2014-2015.

| | $535 | $460 | $395 | $350 | $315 | $295 | $275 | $620 |

OMNI HYBRID 22 COMBO – .22 LR cal. with complete 5.56 aluminum upper and Hybrid lower receiver, 16 in. barrel, 28 (.22 LR) or 30 (5.56) shot PMAG, 10 in. quad rail, 6-position stock, black finish. Mfg. 2015-2016.

| | $425 | $375 | $350 | $325 | $300 | $290 | $275 | $495 |

OMNI HYBRID 300 AAC BLACKOUT – .300 AAC Blackout cal., 16 in. barrel, 30 shot PMAG, complete Hybrid lower and aluminum upper receiver, 7 in. quad rail, 6-pos. stock, black finish, 6 1/2 lbs. Mfg. 2015-2016.

| | $550 | $475 | $400 | $350 | $315 | $295 | $275 | $650 |

OMNI HYBRID MAXX – 5.56 NATO cal., 16 in. M4 black Nitride coated barrel, flat-top, optics ready, 10 or 30 shot PMAG, complete Omni Hybrid upper and lower polymer receiver, 6-pos. stock, black or FDE (new 2016) finish, 6 1/4 lbs. Mfg. 2015-2017.

| | $575 | $485 | $415 | $350 | $315 | $295 | $275 | $670 |

Subtract $60 for no furniture (stripped model ATIGOMX556S).
Add $60 for 13 in. KeyMod rail (ATIGOMX556KM13).

AMERICAN TACTICAL INC. (AMERICAN TACTICAL IMPORTS - ATI), cont. 71 A

MSR	100%	98%	95%	90%	80%	70%	60%	Last MSR

OMNI HYBRID MAXX 5.56 – 5.56 NATO cal., 16 in. barrel, 30 shot PMAG, 7 in. quad rail handguard, complete Omni Hybrid polymer upper and lower receiver, 6-pos. stock, black or FDE (new 2016) finish, 6 1/2 lbs. Mfg. 2015-2017.

| | $595 | $485 | $415 | $350 | $315 | $295 | $275 | $695 |

OMNI HYBRID MAXX 22 COMBO – .22 LR cal. with complete Omni Hybrid 5.56 upper and lower receiver, 16 in. barrel, 10 in. free float quad rail handguard, 28 (.22 LR) or 30 (5.56) shot PMAG, black or FDE (new 2016) finish. Mfg. 2015-2016.

| | $665 | $500 | $415 | $375 | $335 | $315 | $295 | $770 |

OMNI HYBRID MAXX 300 – .300 AAC Blackout cal., 16 in. barrel, 30 shot PMAG, 6-pos. stock, 10 in. free float quad rail handguard, complete Omni Hybrid polymer upper and lower receiver, black or FDE (mfg. 2016 only) finish, 6 1/2 lbs. New 2015.

| MSR $700 | $595 | $485 | $415 | $350 | $315 | $295 | $275 | |

OMNI HYBRID P3 – .300 AAC Blackout cal., 16 in. barrel, 30 shot mag., 6-pos. M4 stock, low profile gas block, 10 in. KeyMod rail handguard, Omni Hybrid polymer upper and metal lower receiver with front and rear metal inserts, features a Nano Composite Parts Kit. New 2018.

| MSR $450 | $395 | $335 | $285 | $250 | $225 | $215 | $200 | |

OMNI HYBRID TRANSLUCENT MAXX – 5.56 NATO cal., 16 in. black Nitride coated barrel, two 30 shot PMAGs, 10 in. free float quad rail handguard, low profile gas block, metal reinforced polymer upper and lower receivers, 6-pos. Rogers Super-Stoc, black finish. Mfg. 2015 only.

| | $595 | $485 | $415 | $350 | $315 | $295 | $275 | $700 |

SHOTGUNS: SEMI-AUTO

OMNI HYBRID MAXX – .410 bore, 2 1/2 in. chamber, GPO, 18 1/2 in. threaded barrel, Remington style chokes, 5 shot mag., 6-pos. adj. Super-Stoc, 10 in. free floating quad rail, ambidextrous sling plate, Omni Hybrid lower receiver, black finish, 6 1/2 lbs. Mfg. 2016 only.

| | $790 | $685 | $615 | $550 | $485 | $415 | $370 | $930 |

OMNI HYBRID MAXX LIMITED .410 SHOTGUN – .410 bore, GPO, 18 1/2 in. barrel, 5 shot mag., 6-pos. adj. Super-Stoc, 13 in. free floating KeyMod rail, Omni Hybrid lower receiver, black finish, 6 1/2 lbs. New 2017.

| MSR $600 | $525 | $465 | $400 | $350 | $300 | $250 | $200 | |

AM-TAC PRECISION

Previous manufacturer of AR-15 style carbines/rifles located in Garden City, ID from 2009-2015.

RIFLES: SEMI-AUTO

AM-TAC Precision produced firearms, components, and tactical products for the professional and recreational user.

LTC RIFLE – 5.56 NATO or .300 AAC Blackout cal., GIO, 16 in. stainless steel match grade barrel, "Jake Brake" muzzle device, KeyMod Rail System V2 handguard with Qik System, 30 shot mag., forged receivers, MBUS front and flip-up rear sights, ALG ACT trigger, BCM Mod 4 charging handle, QD endplate, enhanced trigger guard, Magpul MOE grip, MOE Mil-Spec 6-position stock, black finish, 6.28-6.6 lbs. Disc. 2015.

| | $1,650 | $1,000 | $795 | $595 | $495 | $425 | $395 | $1,969 |

PREDITOR ELITE RIFLE – 5.56 NATO or .300 AAC Blackout cal., GIO, 16 in. stainless steel match grade barrel, thread protector, 10 or 20 shot mag., 13 in. KeyMod rail system handguard, forged receivers, Magpul MOE grip, fixed A2 rifle stock, ALG ACT trigger, BCM Mod 4 charging handle, QD endplate, enhanced trigger guard, two-color Cerakote camo finish. Disc. 2015.

| | $1,675 | $1,000 | $825 | $625 | $550 | $475 | $425 | $2,049 |

ANATOLIA MANUFACTURING COMPANY LLC

Current shotgun manufacturer located in Orlando, FL.

SHOTGUNS: SEMI-AUTO

ARMAGON G12 – 12 ga., 2 3/4 or 3 in. chamber, GPO, steel chrome-lined barrel in various lengths, includes 3 chokes, 5 shot mag., collapsible stock and pistol grip can be interchanged with the AR-15, high grade aluminum upper receiver, 30% glass filled nylon lower receiver, black finish.

| MSR $625 | $550 | $480 | $415 | $350 | $310 | $270 | $255 | |

A 72 ANDERSON MANUFACTURING

MSR	100%	98%	95%	90%	80%	70%	60%	Last MSR

ANDERSON MANUFACTURING

Current rifle manufacturer established during 2010, located in Hebron, KY. Distributor and dealer sales.

PISTOLS: SEMI-AUTO

AM15 7.5 PISTOL – 5.56 NATO cal., 7 1/2 in. barrel with Knight Stalker flash hider, low profile gas block, 30 shot mag., forged receiver, Anderson's EXT free float forearm, Magpul grip, black finish, 4.9 lbs. New 2015.

MSR $759	$650	$575	$515	$445	$385	$335	$300

Add $200 for RF85 No Lube treatment.

AM15 .300 BLACKOUT PISTOL – .300 AAC Blackout cal., 10 1/2 in. heavy barrel, Knight Stalker flash hider, 30 shot mag., forged receivers, low profile steel gas block, 9 in. KeyMod forearm, no sights, Magpul MOE grip, black anodized finish.

MSR $732	$635	$550	$500	$425	$375	$325	$285

RIFLES/CARBINES: SEMI-AUTO

Anderson Manufacturing utilizes a proprietary metal treatment for all its rifles and carbines called RF-85. This metal treatment reduces friction on steel surfaces by 85%, and RF-85 treated weapons do not require any wet lubricants, which also result in less dirt and carbon fouling in the action.

AM10-BD – .308 Win. cal., GIO, 18 in. heavy barrel with flash hider, free float forearm, Magpul MOE buttstock and pistol grip, Picatinny rail and elevated modular rail, black furniture, 8.5 lbs. Disc. 2014.

	$1,135	$725	$525	$465	$415	$375	$350	$1,365

AM10-HUNTER (.308 HUNTER) – .308 Win. cal., 16, 18, or 20 in. chrome moly barrel with Anderson Knight Stalker flash hider, 20 shot mag., optic ready, forged receiver, stainless steel trigger and hammer, EXT free float forearm, low profile gas block, Magpul grip, Ti7 buttstock, black furniture, 8.9 lbs. New 2015.

MSR $1,259	$1,065	$650	$500	$450	$395	$350	$325

Add $17 for 18 in. barrel or $27 for 20 in. barrel.
Add $200 for No Lube RF85 treatment.

AM10-MSR – .308 Win. cal., GIO, 22 in. fluted barrel with crowned muzzle, low profile gas block, 14 1/4 in. free float forearm, A2 buttstock and pistol grip, black furniture, 9 lbs. Disc. 2014.

	$1,100	$675	$525	$450	$400	$350	$325	$1,319

AM10-SNIPER 24 – .308 Win. cal., 24 in. straight fluted barrel, 20 shot mag., Timney trigger, Luth-AR stock, Ergo pistol grip, forged receivers, AM-10 charging handle, low profile gas block, EXT 15 in. forearm, no sights, black anodized finish.

MSR $2,122	$1,725	$1,050	$850	$625	$550	$475	$425

Add $200 for No Lube RF85 treatment.

AM15-300 BLACKOUT (300 BLACKOUT) – .300 AAC Blackout cal., 16 in. barrel with Anderson Knight Stalker flash hider, low profile gas block, forged receiver, 30 shot mag., EXT free float forearm, stainless steel trigger and hammer, Magpul buttstock and grip, Picatinny rail, ambi sling mount, 6.2 lbs. New 2015.

MSR $784	$675	$500	$425	$375	$335	$315	$295

Add $200 for No Lube RF85 treatment.

AM15-6.5 GRENDEL – 6.5 Grendel cal., 16 in. M4 contour barrel, A2 flash hider, 30 shot mag., 6-pos. buttstock, A2 pistol grip, forged receivers, A2 handguard, black anodized finish, 6.2 lbs. New 2018.

MSR $689	$595	$485	$415	$350	$315	$295	$275

Add $200 for No Lube RF85 treatment.

AM15-7.62x39 – 7.62x39mm cal., 16 in. heavy barrel, A2 flash hider, 30 shot mag., M4 Anderson buttstock, A2 pistol grip, forged receivers, A2 plastic handguard, standard gas block with rail, black anodized finish.

MSR $689	$595	$485	$415	$350	$315	$295	$275

Add $200 for No Lube RF85 treatment.

AM15-HBOR16/AM15-HBOR20 – .223 Rem. cal., GIO, 16 or 20 in. heavy barrel with target crown and flash suppressor, Wilson target trigger, Magpul PRS adj. stock, Magpul MIAD grip, front mounted low profile gas block, free floated handguard with upper and lower Picatinny rails, tactical charging handle, hard anodized finish, aluminum flat-top receiver, includes two-30 shot magazines and black hard case, 9.44 lbs. Disc. 2014.

	$1,175	$775	$550	$465	$415	$375	$350	$1,411

Add $50 for 20 in. barrel.
Add $210 for AM-15HBOR16-Billet or AM-15HBOR20-Billet models (disc. 2012).

ANDERSON MANUFACTURING, cont. 73 A

MSR	100%	98%	95%	90%	80%	70%	60%	Last MSR

AM15-3 GUN ELITE – 5.56 NATO cal., 18 in. heavy (disc.) or Nordic barrel, Lantac Dragon .223/5.56 (disc.) or DR20 No Rise muzzle brake, 30 shot mag., forged receivers, AM-15 tactical charging handle, steel adj. gas block, 15 in. EXT free float forearm, Magpul PRS buttstock, Magpul MOE pistol grip, black anodized finish, 8 1/2 lbs.

	100%	98%	95%	90%	80%	70%	60%	
MSR $2,234	$1,795	$1,050	$875	$625	$550	$475	$425	

AM15-CARBINE 300 BLACKOUT KEYMOD – .300 AAC Blackout cal., 16 in. M4 contour barrel, A2 flash hider, carbine gas set up, forged receivers, Magpul 6-pos. buttstock and pistol grip, Anderson 12 in. KeyMod handguard, low profile steel gas block, standard charging handle, ambi sling mount. New 2017.

	100%	98%	95%	90%	80%	70%	60%	
MSR $829	$695	$500	$425	$375	$335	$315	$295	

Add $200 for No Lube RF85 treatment.

AM15-CARBINE KEYMOD – 5.56 NATO/.223 Rem. cal., 16 in. chrome moly steel M4 contour barrel, Knight Stalker brake, carbine gas set up, forged receivers, 6-pos. buttstock, A2 pistol grip, Anderson 12 in. KeyMod handguard, low profile steel gas block, standard charging handle, ambi sling mount. New 2017.

	100%	98%	95%	90%	80%	70%	60%	
MSR $821	$695	$500	$425	$375	$335	$315	$295	

Add $200 for No Lube RF85 treatment.

AM15-KEYMOD RIFLE – 5.56 NATO/.223 Rem. cal., 16 in. chrome moly steel M4 barrel, DR20 muzzle brake, Magpul 6-pos. buttstock and pistol grip, carbine gas set up, forged receivers, Anderson 15 in. KeyMod handguard, low profile steel gas block, standard charging handle, ambi sling mount. New 2017.

	100%	98%	95%	90%	80%	70%	60%	
MSR $821	$695	$500	$425	$375	$335	$315	$295	

Add $200 for No Lube RF85 treatment.

AM15-M4-15 – 5.56 NATO/.223 Rem. cal., 16 in. M4 contour barrel, Knight Stalker flash hider, 30 shot mag., optic ready, Magpul buttstock and grip, forged receivers, low profile gas block, no rail, EXT 15 in. free float forearm, 8 lbs. New 2017.

	100%	98%	95%	90%	80%	70%	60%	
MSR $737	$645	$500	$415	$370	$325	$300	$275	

Add $200 for No Lube RF85 treatment.

AM15-M416 (M4 CARBINE) – .223 Rem. or 6.8 SPC cal., GIO, 16 in. M4 heavy barrel with Phantom flash hider, front mounted low profile gas block, Magpul MOE 6-position adj. pistol grip stock, quad rail forend with upper and lower Picatinny rails, 8 in. free float modular forearm, hard anodized finish, aluminum flat-top receiver, includes two 30 shot Magpul magazines and black hard case, 6.3 lbs. Disc. 2014.

	100%	98%	95%	90%	80%	70%	60%	Last MSR
	$875	$550	$465	$395	$350	$325	$300	$1,038

Add $210 for AM15M416-Billet model in .223 Rem. cal. (disc. 2012), or $337 for AM15M416-Billet model in 6.8 SPC cal. (disc. 2012).

* **AM15-M416 Camo** – .223 Rem. cal., similar to AM15-M416, except features 8 in. free float CAMO forearm, A2 pistol grip, tactical intent buttstock, and digital camo coverage. Mfg. 2013-2014.

	100%	98%	95%	90%	80%	70%	60%	Last MSR
	$975	$595	$495	$425	$365	$335	$300	$1,152

* **AM15-M4 LE (AM15-M416 LE)** – 5.56 NATO/.223 Rem. cal., 16 in. M4 contour barrel with flash hider, A2 front sight, 30 shot mag., 6 in. free float modular forearm, A2 buttstock and grip, 6.4 lbs.

	100%	98%	95%	90%	80%	70%	60%	
MSR $1,104	$935	$575	$475	$415	$350	$325	$300	

Add $306 for No Lube RF85 treatment.

* **M4 Tiger (AM15-M416 Tiger)** – 5.56 NATO cal., 16 in. chrome moly M4 contour barrel with Knight Stalker flash hider, 30 shot mag., low profile gas block, EXT free float forearm, Magpul buttstock and pistol grip, Tiger striped finish on upper and lower receivers, stainless steel trigger and hammer, ambi sling mount, 6.3 lbs. Mfg. 2013-2016.

	100%	98%	95%	90%	80%	70%	60%	Last MSR
	$950	$595	$495	$425	$365	$335	$300	$1,127

* **AM15-M416 ZE** – .223 Rem. cal., similar to AM15-M416, except features 8 in. free float ZOMBIE forearm. Disc. 2014.

	100%	98%	95%	90%	80%	70%	60%	Last MSR
	$915	$575	$475	$415	$350	$325	$300	$1,078

AM15-M4 (CURRENT MFG.) – 5.56 NATO cal., 16 in. M4 barrel with Anderson Knight Stalker flash hider, 30 shot mag., low profile gas block, forged receiver, Picatinny rail, EXT free float forearm, Magpul buttstock and pistol grip, stainless steel match grade trigger and hammer, standard charging handle, ambi sling mount, black furniture, 6.3 lbs.

	100%	98%	95%	90%	80%	70%	60%	
MSR $741	$645	$500	$415	$370	$325	$300	$275	

Add $200 for No Lube RF85 treatment.

AM15-M4-TAC – 5.56 NATO cal., 16 in. M4 contour barrel, DR20 muzzle brake, 30 shot mag., front and rear Magpul MBUS sights, Magpul MOE buttstock, Magpul MOE grip, forged receivers, ambi charging handle, low profile steel gas block, EXT 15 in. forearm with angled fore grip, black anodized finish, 9 lbs. New 2018.

	100%	98%	95%	90%	80%	70%	60%	
MSR $1,590	$1,315	$850	$625	$500	$435	$375	$350	

AM15-PATRIOT RIFLE – 5.56 NATO/.223 Rem. (chambered in .223 Wylde) cal., 16 in. stainless steel spiral fluted heavy barrel, DR20 flash hider, 30 shot mag., match grade trigger and hammer, optic ready, Magpul 6-pos. buttstock, Magpul MOE pistol grip, forged receivers, Anderson EXT 15 in. free float handguard, low profile gas block, tactical charging handle assembly with "PULL FOR FREEDOM" engraved on stem of handle, no rail, upper, lower, ejection port cover and 15 in. handguard have American Flag Battle Worn Cerakote red/white/blue finish. New 2017.

	100%	98%	95%	90%	80%	70%	60%	
MSR $1,228	$1,050	$650	$495	$450	$395	$350	$325	

A 74 ANDERSON MANUFACTURING, cont.

MSR	100%	98%	95%	90%	80%	70%	60%	Last MSR

AM-15 OPTIC READY (AM15-AOR/HEAVY BARREL CARBINE) – 5.56 NATO cal., GIO, 16 in. M4 contour heavy barrel with A2 flash hider and Picatinny rail, 30 shot mag., front mounted low profile gas block, forged aluminum flat-top receiver, ribbed oval M4 handguard, optic ready front sight, 6-position collapsible buttstock, A2 pistol grip, black anodized finish, includes hard case, 6.4 lbs.

MSR $617	$535	$460	$395	$350	$315	$295	$275	

Add $200 for No Lube RF85 treatment.

Add $210 for AM15-AOR16 Billet model (disc. 2012).

AM15-SNIPER – 5.56 NATO cal., 24 in. stainless steel fluted barrel, 30 shot mag., Timney trigger, EXT free float forearm, Magpul PRS buttstock, Ergo pistol grip, tactical charging handle, forged receivers, Harris LMS bipod, black furniture, 12 1/4 lbs. New 2015.

MSR $1,735	$1,425	$925	$700	$550	$475	$395	$350	

Add $200 for No Lube RF85 treatment.

AM15-VS24 (HEAVY BARREL VARMINTER) – .223 Rem. cal., GIO, 24 in. stainless steel fluted bull barrel with target crown, flat-top receiver, 14 in. free float modular forearm tube, Magpul PRS buttstock, Ergo tactical deluxe palm shelf pistol grip, two 30 shot mags., low profile gas block, tactical charging handle, Timney trigger, black furniture, includes Harris bipod and black hard case, 9.44 lbs. Disc. 2014.

	$1,385	$895	$675	$525	$450	$385	$350	$1,681

Add $210 for AM-15VS24-Billet model (disc. 2012).

ANGSTADT ARMS

Current manufacturer located in Charlotte, NC.

Angstadt Arms specializes in lightweight personal defense weapons for civilian and law enforcement use.

PISTOLS: SEMI-AUTO

JACK9 PISTOL w/SBA3 BRACE – 9mm Para. cal., GIO, 6 in. chrome moly threaded barrel with black Melonite finish, A2 flash suppressor, 15 shot Glock mag., last round bolt hold open, flared magwell, integrated oversized trigger guard, SB Tactical SBA3 pistol stabilizing brace with 5-pos. adj. LOP settings and integral ambi QD sling socket, Magpul K2 pistol grip, Angstad Arms 5 1/2 in. free float M-LOK handguard, top Picatinny rail, billet aluminum lower receiver with iconic skull design by Sharps Bros. and slick side upper receiver with ejection port, hardcoat anodized matte black finish, 5 lbs. New 2018.

MSR $1,495	$1,275	$1,125	$1,025	$875	$750	$625	$525

UDP-9 – 9mm Para. cal., GIO, 6 in. chrome moly barrel with A2 flash suppressor, accepts Glock magazines, standard pistol buffer tube, aluminum upper and lower receiver with matte black hardcoat anodized finish, flared magwell, integrated oversized trigger guard, Odin Works 5 1/2 in. free float KeyMod handguard with continuous top Picatinny rail, B5 Systems pistol grip, 5 lbs. Mfg. 2015-2017.

	$1,050	$950	$815	$715	$625	$535	$450	$1,249

Add $76 for Shockwave stabilizing brace.

* **UDP-9 with SBA3 Brace** – 9mm Para. cal., GIO, 6 in. chrome moly threaded barrel with black Melonite finish, A2 flash suppressor, 15 shot Glock mag., last round bolt hold open, flared magwell, integrated oversized trigger guard, SB Tactical SBA3 pistol stabilizing brace with 5-pos. adj. LOP settings and integral ambi QD sling socket, Magpul K2 pistol grip, Angstadt Arms 5 1/2 in. free float M-LOK handguard, top Picatinny rail, billet aluminum lower and slick side upper with ejection port, hardcoat anodized matte black finish, 5 lbs. New 2018.

MSR $1,395	$1,200	$1,075	$950	$800	$700	$600	$495

UDP-9 PDW (PERSONAL DEFENSE WEAPON) – 9mm Para. cal., 16 in. chrome moly barrel, A2 style flash suppressor, flared magwell, integrated oversized trigger guard, Magpul MOE stock, K2 pistol grip, billet aluminum lower and slick side upper receiver, Odin Works 12 1/2 in. free float KeyMod handguard with continuous top Picatinny rail, matte black hardcoat anodized finish, 5 lbs. Disc. 2017.

	$1,350	$1,200	$1,075	$950	$815	$700	$575	$1,599

RIFLES: SEMI-AUTO

UDP-9 RIFLE – 9mm Para. cal., GIO, AR-15 style, 16 in. chrome moly barrel with A2 flash suppressor and black phosphate finish, accepts Glock mags., billet aluminum lower with flared magwell, integrated oversized trigger guard, Odin Works 12 1/2 in. free float KeyMod handguard with continuous top Picatinny rail, Magpul MOE stock, K2 pistol grip, matte black hardcoat anodized finish, 5 lbs. New 2015.

MSR $1,499	$1,250	$825	$575	$475	$425	$375	$350

MSR	100%	98%	95%	90%	80%	70%	60%	Last MSR

ARCHER MANUFACTURING

Current AR-15 style pistol and rifle manufacturer established during 2015, located in Hutto, TX.

PISTOLS: SEMI-AUTO

AM-15 PISTOL – 5.56 NATO or .300 AAC Blackout cal., Geissele low profile gas block, 7 or 9 in. Shilen match grade barrel, Geissele MK4 M-LOK handguard, Magpul Gen2 MBUS sights, Phase 5 Hex 2 pistol buffer assembly, SIG pistol stabilizing brace, Type III hardcoat anodized black finish. Mfg. 2015-2016.

	100%	98%	95%	90%	80%	70%	60%	Last MSR
	$1,350	$1,200	$1,075	$950	$815	$700	$575	*$1,595*

RIFLES: SEMI-AUTO

AM-10 – .243 Win., 6.5mm Creedmoor, .260 Rem., 7mm-08 Rem., or .308 Win. cal., 16, 18, 21, or 23 in. Shilen match grade barrel, Magpul MBUS ProL sights, ALG Defense quality Mil-Spec trigger, Magpul CTR buttstock, billet DPMS compatible matched receiver set, Midwest Industries 308 SS M-LOK handguard, Geissele low profile gas block, BCM Gunfighter Mod 4 charging handle, Type III hardcoat anodized black finish. Mfg. 2015-2016.

	100%	98%	95%	90%	80%	70%	60%	Last MSR
	$1,675	$1,000	$825	$625	$550	$475	$425	*$2,095*

AM-10 PREMIUM – .243 Win., 6.5mm Creedmoor, .260 Rem., 7mm-08 Rem., or .308 Win. cal., 16, 18, 21, or 23 in. Shilen match grade barrel, Magpul MBUS ProL sights, Geissele SSA trigger, Magpul UBR stock, MIAD grip, billet DPMS compatible matched receiver set, Midwest Industries 308 SS M-LOK handguard, Geissele low profile gas block, BCM Gunfighter Mod 4 charging handle, BattleComp BABC, H Series Cerakote finish in ODG, FDE, grey, or two-tone (ODG or FDE w/black furniture). Mfg. 2015-2016.

	100%	98%	95%	90%	80%	70%	60%	Last MSR
	$1,975	$1,150	$925	$650	$575	$495	$425	*$2,495*

AM-15/AM-15F – 5.56 NATO or .300 AAC Blackout cal., Geissele low profile gas block, 16 in. Shilen match grade barrel, ALG Defense quality Mil-Spec trigger, Magpul Gen2 MBUS sights, Magpul CTR buttstock, BCM Gunfighter Mod 4 charging handle, ALG Defense 15 in. EMR V2 or V3 handguard, ALG Defense True Mil-Spec polished buffer tube and buffer system, forged receiver set with forward assist (AM-15F), or billet matched receiver set (AM-15), Armor Black, Magpul FDE, or Mil-Spec ODG finish or Hill Country or Urban Jungle Cerakote camo finish. Mfg. 2015-2016.

	100%	98%	95%	90%	80%	70%	60%	Last MSR
	$1,315	$850	$625	$500	$435	$375	$350	*$1,595*

Add $100 for billet matched receiver set (AM-15).

Add $150 for Hill Country or Urban Jungle Cerakote camo finish.

ARCHER MOUNTAIN CARBINE – 5.56 NATO or .300 AAC Blackout cal., Geissele low profile gas block, 16 in. Shilen match grade barrel, ALG Defense quality Mil-Spec trigger, Magpul Gen2 MBUS sights, Magpul CTR buttstock, BCM Gunfighter Mod 4 charging handle, ALG Defense 15 in. EMR V2 or V3 handguard, ALG Defense True Mil-Spec polished buffer tube and buffer system, Robar PolymAR polymer receiver set, Armor Black, Magpul FDE, or Mil-Spec ODG finish or Hill Country or Urban Jungle Cerakote camo finish. Mfg. 2015-2016.

	100%	98%	95%	90%	80%	70%	60%	Last MSR
	$1,385	$895	$675	$525	$450	$385	$350	*$1,695*

Add $150 for Hill Country or Urban Jungle Cerakote camo finish.

CLOSE QUARTERS COMBAT – 5.56 NATO cal., 16 in. Shilen match grade barrel, BattleComp BC1.0 muzzle device, 30 shot Magpul Gen3 PMAG, BCM Gunfighter charging handle, Geissele Super gas block, Geissele MK4 9 1/2 in. handguard, AMFG matched and forged upper and lower receivers, Geissele SSA trigger, SOPMOD extractor upgrade, Magpul SL stock, MIAD 1.1 grip, includes Patriot hard case. New 2017.

	100%	98%	95%	90%	80%	70%	60%	
MSR $2,295	$1,795	$1,050	$875	$625	$550	$475	$425	

DESIGNATED MARKSMAN RIFLE (DMR) – 5.56 NATO cal., 16 or 18 in. heavy DMR contour Shilen match grade barrel, BattleComp BC1.0 muzzle device, 30 shot Magpul Gen3 PMAG, Geissele SSA trigger, BCM Gunfighter charging handle, SOPMOD extractor upgrade, Geissele super gas block, Geissele 15 in. MK8 handguard, AMFG matched and forged upper and lower receivers, AMFG polished buffer tube assembly, Magpul SL stock, MIAD 1.1 grip, includes Patriot hard case. New 2017.

	100%	98%	95%	90%	80%	70%	60%	
MSR $2,295	$1,795	$1,050	$875	$625	$550	$475	$425	

ENHANCED PATROL RIFLE – 5.56 NATO cal., 16 in. Shilen match grade barrel with A2 flash hider, 30 shot Magpul Gen3 PMAG, Geissele super gas block, AMFG matched and forged upper and lower receiver, ALG Defense QMS trigger, SOPMOD extractor upgrade, BCM Gunfighter charging handle, ALG Defense EMR V2 13 in. black rail, Magpul CTR stock, A2 grip, AMFG polished buffer tube assembly, includes Patriot hard case. New 2017.

	100%	98%	95%	90%	80%	70%	60%	
MSR $1,695	$1,385	$895	$675	$525	$450	$385	$350	

LIGHT TRUCK GUN – 5.56 NATO cal., 16 in. Shilen match grade barrel with A2 flash hider, 30 shot Magpul Gen3 PMAG, ALG Defense QMS trigger, A2 front sight base and sight kit, AMFG matched and forged upper and lower receivers, SOPMOD extractor upgrade, MOE handguard, grip, and stock, includes Patriot hard case. New 2017.

	100%	98%	95%	90%	80%	70%	60%	
MSR $1,395	$1,150	$750	$550	$465	$415	$375	$350	

A 76 ARCHER MANUFACTURING, cont.

MSR		100%	98%	95%	90%	80%	70%	60%	Last MSR

RECCE – .300 AAC Blackout cal., 16 in. Recce contoured Shilen match grade barrel, Daniel Defense superior suppression device flash hider, 30 shot Magpul Gen3 PMAG, Magpul MBUS Gen2 flip-up front and rear sight, ALG Defense QMS trigger, Geissele super gas block, ALG Defense EMR V2 black rail, SOPMOD extractor upgrade, Magpul CTR stock, A2 grip, includes Patriot hard case. New 2017.

| MSR $1,695 | | $1,385 | $895 | $675 | $525 | $450 | $385 | $350 | |

ARIZONA ARMORY

Current AR-15 style rifle manufacturer located in Phoenix, AZ since 2007.

RIFLES: SEMI-AUTO

All rifles can be customized per individual specifications with a wide variety of upgrades and options. Conversion kits, Magpul, Midwest Industries, and Yankee Hill Machine upgrade packages are also available.

AA-15 CARBINE – 5.56 NATO cal., GIO, 16 in. M4 chrome moly barrel, 30 shot mag., CAR 4-position stock, CAR handguard, AZA billet lower, AZA billet A3 flat-top slick side upper.

| MSR $775 | | $665 | $500 | $415 | $375 | $335 | $315 | $295 | |

AA-15 M4A3 BASIC – 5.56 NATO cal., GIO, 16 in. M4 chrome moly barrel, AZA billet lower and A3 flat-top upper with forward assist, M4 handguards, M4 6-position stock, 30 shot mag.

| MSR $875 | | $745 | $500 | $435 | $375 | $335 | $315 | $295 | |

AA-15 M4A3 OPERATOR – 5.56 NATO cal., GIO, 16 in. M4 chrome-lined barrel with M4 feed ramp, A2 flash suppressor, 30 shot mag., M4 double heat shield handguard, two-stage National Match trigger, M4 6-pos. stock, AZA billet lower and A3 flat-top upper receiver with forward assist.

| MSR $985 | | $850 | $550 | $465 | $395 | $350 | $325 | $295 | |

AA-15 18 SPR – .223 Rem. cal., GIO, 18 in. stainless steel 1x8 SPR barrel, 20 shot mag., A2 stock, rifle length YHM lightweight railed free float handguard, low profile gas block, AZA billet lower and slick side A3 upper, two-stage match trigger, YHM QDS folding backup iron sights.

| MSR $1,075 | | $895 | $575 | $475 | $395 | $350 | $325 | $300 | |

AA-15 20V/T – .223 Rem./5.56 NATO (.223 Wylde chamber) cal., GIO, Walther 20 in. stainless steel target crown barrel, aluminum free float tube, AZA billet lower and A3 billet slick side upper, adj. JP trigger, A2 stock, single Picatinny rail gas block, optic ready no sights, 5 shot mag.

| MSR $1,025 | | $865 | $550 | $465 | $395 | $350 | $325 | $300 | |

AA-15 20M – 5.56 NATO cal., GIO, 20 in. stainless steel match barrel with A2 flash suppressor, 30 shot mag., adj. trigger, National Match A2 rear sight assembly, National Match front sight, AZA billet lower, A2 forged upper, anti-rotation trigger/hammer pins, A2 free float handguards. Disc. 2014.

This model was available as a special order and was POR.

AA-15 9MM – 9mm Para. cal., GIO, 16 in. chrome moly barrel with A2 flash suppressor, AZA billet lower, A3 billet smooth side upper with 9mm door kit, standard trigger group, CAR 4-position stock with 9mm buffer, CAR handguards, 9mm mag. block adapter with last round bolt hold open, 32 shot mag.

| MSR $975 | | $850 | $550 | $465 | $395 | $350 | $325 | $295 | |

ARMALITE

Previous manufacturer located in Costa Mesa, CA, approx. 1954-circa 1980s.

RIFLES: SEMI-AUTO

AR-10 – 7.62 NATO cal., GIO, select-fire machine gun, originally designed by Eugene Stoner, 20.8 in. barrel, rotating bolt locks into barrel extension (not receiver), 20 shot detachable mag., hinged aluminum upper and lower receiver, non-detachable carry handle designed to protect top of receiver charge lever, approx. 7 1/2 lbs. Approx. 50 were mfg. circa 1957 by ArmaLite in California (aka Hollywood Model). Approx. 9,900 mfg. for military contracts under ArmaLite licensing agreement to Artillerie Inrichtingen, Holland. Mfg. 1957-1960.

Values for these select-fire rifles depend on originality, condition, and desirability of features and military contract.

AR-15 – .223 Rem. (prototype cals. were also mfg.), GIO, scaled down version of the AR-10, select-fire machine gun, 20 in. barrel, bolt locks into barrel extension, 20 shot detachable mag., hinged aluminum upper and lower receiver, charging handle on top of receiver (early ArmaLite mfg.) or pull handle in back of receiver (Colt mfg.), with or w/o forward bolt assist on military contracts, approx. 6 1/2 lbs. Less than 20,000 mfg. circa 1958-1963.

Values for these select-fire rifles depend on year of manufacture, originality, and condition.

This model was the final predecessor of the M16 select-fire machine gun introduced during 1964.

ARMALITE, cont. **77 A**

MSR	100%	98%	95%	90%	80%	70%	60%	Last MSR

AR-180 – .223 Rem. cal., GPO, 18 1/4 in. barrel, folding stock. Manufactured by Armalite in Costa Mesa, CA, 1969-1972, Howa Machinery Ltd., Nagoya, Japan, 1972 and 1973, and by Sterling Armament Co. Ltd., Dagenham, Essex, England.

	100%	98%	95%	90%	80%	70%	60%	Last MSR
Sterling Mfg.	$1,795	$1,050	$875	$625	$550	$475	$425	
Howa Mfg.	$2,125	$1,325	$995	$675	$595	$525	$475	
Costa Mesa Mfg.	$2,125	$1,325	$995	$675	$595	$525	$475	

ARMALITE, INC.

Current manufacturer located in Geneseo, IL. New manufacture began in 1995 after Eagle Arms, Inc. purchased the ArmaLite trademarks. In July of 2013, Armalite was purchased by Strategic Amory Corps. The ArmaLite trademark was originally used by Armalite (no relation to ArmaLite, Inc.) during manufacture in Costa Mesa, CA, approx. 1959-1973 (see Armalite listing). Dealer and distributor sales.

For Eagle Arms branded/manufactured carbines/rifles, please refer to the Eagle Arms listings in the E section.

PISTOLS: SEMI-AUTO

AR-10 PISTOL – 7.62x51mm/.308 Win. cal., carbine length gas system, 13.9 in. black Cerakote stainless steel barrel, threaded with flash suppressing compensator, 20 shot Magpul PMAG, folding receiver extension, arm brace, 12 in. aluminum tactical KeyMod handguard, Raptor ambidextrous charging handle, Mil-Std 1913 rail, two-stage precision trigger, Magpul K2 pistol grip, 8.8 lbs. Mfg. 2015-2017.

	100%	98%	95%	90%	80%	70%	60%	Last MSR
	$2,285	$1,995	$1,650	$1,425	$1,160	$1,000	$875	$2,699

EAGLE-15 PISTOL – .223 Rem./5.56x45mm cal., 6 or 11 in. chrome moly/chrome-lined barrel with flash suppressor, 20 shot Magpul PMAG, single stage trigger, front sight base, Sig pistol brace, Magpul K2 grip, carbine length gas system, 5 or 10 in. tactical KeyMod handguard, forged aluminum lower and flat-top upper with full-length Mil-Std 1913 rail, black hard anodized aluminum finish, 6 lbs. New 2018.

	100%	98%	95%	90%	80%	70%	60%	Last MSR
MSR $996	$850	$750	$650	$575	$475	$385	$300	

M-15 PISTOL – 5.56x45mm/.223 Rem. cal., 6 or 11 1/2 in. double lapped chrome-lined barrel with flash suppressing compensator, 20 shot Magpul PMAG, folding receiver extension, arm brace, 5 in. light contour aluminum KeyMod handguard, Raptor ambidextrous charging handle, Mil-Std 1913 rail, two-stage precision trigger, 6 lbs. Mfg. 2015-2017.

	100%	98%	95%	90%	80%	70%	60%	Last MSR
	$1,795	$1,575	$1,325	$1,150	$995	$850	$700	$2,099

Add $150 for 11 1/2 in. barrel.

RIFLES: SEMI-AUTO

All ArmaLite AR-15 style semi-auto rifles have a limited lifetime warranty. Some previously manufactured models had stainless steel barrels and NM triggers at an additional charge. Descriptions and pricing are for currently manufactured models.

Beginning 2009, a forward bolt assist became standard on all AR-10A4 upper receivers.

Add $99-$228 for A4 carry handle assembly.

Add $150 for 100% Realtree Hardwoods or Advantage Classic camo finish (disc.).

AR-10 SERIES – various configurations, GIO, with or w/o sights and carry handle, choice of standard green, black (new 1999), or camo (disc.) finish, supplied with two 10 shot mags. (until 2004), current mfg. typically ships with one 10 round and one 20 round mag., during 2014, several variations of the AR-10 Series now accept third party polymer mags., two-stage NM trigger became standard during 2008. New late 1995.

* **AR-10A2 Rifle (Infantry)** – .243 Win. (disc. 2003) or 7.62 NATO cal., GIO, 20 in. chrome-lined threaded barrel with flash suppressor, forged A2 upper with forward assist and A2 front sight, forged lower with tactical two-stage trigger, carry handle, Hi-Cap stock, Black or Green finish, includes one 10 shot mag., one 20 shot mag., sling, and hard case, 9.2 lbs. Disc. 2013.

	100%	98%	95%	90%	80%	70%	60%	Last MSR
	$1,315	$850	$625	$500	$435	$375	$350	$1,583

* **AR-10A2 Carbine** – 7.62 NATO cal., GIO, 16 in. threaded barrel with flash suppressor, forged A2 upper with forward assist and A2 front sight, forged lower receiver, tactical two-stage trigger, 6-pos. collapsible stock with extended tube, Black or Green finish, includes one 10 shot mag., one 20 shot mag., sling, and hard case, 9 lbs. Disc. 2013.

	100%	98%	95%	90%	80%	70%	60%	Last MSR
	$1,315	$850	$625	$500	$435	$375	$350	$1,583

Add $74 for 4-way quad rail on front of forearm (mfg. 2004-2008).

* **AR-10A4 Rifle SPR - Special Purpose Rifle** – .243 Win. (disc. 2003, reintroduced 2011-2013, black only) or 7.62 NATO cal., GIO, 20 in. chrome-lined barrel with flash suppressor, forged flat-top upper receiver with Picatinny rail and gas block, forward assist, forged lower with tactical two-stage trigger, removable front sight, A2 stock, black (BF) or Green (F, disc. 2013) finish, includes one 10 shot mag., one 20 shot mag. (disc. 2014), sling, and hard case, 8.9 lbs. Disc. 2016.

	100%	98%	95%	90%	80%	70%	60%	Last MSR
	$1,315	$850	$625	$500	$435	$375	$350	$1,571

Add $35 for permanently affixed muzzle brake (10A4BF-2, new 2013).

A 78 ARMALITE, INC., cont.

MSR		100%	98%	95%	90%	80%	70%	60%	Last MSR

* **AR-10A4 Carbine** – 7.62 NATO cal., similar to AR-10A4 SPR Rifle, except has 16 in. barrel, mid-length handguard, and 6-position collapsible stock with G.I. diameter extension tube, 7.8 lbs. Disc. 2014.

		$1,315	$850	$625	$500	$435	$375	$350	$1,571

Add $414 for SIR System (Selective Integrated Rail System, mfg. 2004-2006).

* **AR-10A4 Mod 1** – .308 Win. cal., GIO, 16 in. barrel with flash suppressor, forged one-piece upper receiver/rail system with detachable side and bottom rails, two-stage tactical trigger, collapsible tube stock with pistol grip, black finish and furniture.

While this model was advertised during 2012, it never went into production.

* **AR-10A2 Carbine (AR-10A4 Tactical Carbine)** – 7.62 NATO/.308 Win. cal., GIO, 16 in. double lapped chrome-lined chrome moly barrel with flash suppressor, 20 shot Magpul PMAG, two-stage tactical trigger, forged aluminum A4 flat-top upper receiver with Picatinny rail and detachable carry handle, A2 front sight, aluminum handguard tube, 6-pos. collapsible stock, 9 lbs. Mfg. 2014-2017.

		$1,315	$850	$625	$500	$435	$375	$350	$1,571

* **AR-10A4243BF** – .243 Win. cal., 20 in. match grade chrome moly barrel, two-stage tactical trigger, anodized aluminum lower receiver, forged flat-top upper receiver with Picatinny gas block, forward assist, fixed polymer stock, includes one 5 shot and one 10 shot mag., sling, 9 lbs. Disc. 2013.

		$1,315	$850	$625	$500	$435	$375	$350	$1,571

* **AR-10B Rifle** – .308 Win. cal., patterned after the early Armalite AR-10 rifle, GIO, featuring tapered M16 handguards, pistol grip, distinctive charging lever on top inside of carry handle (cannot be used to mount sighting devices), original brown color, 20 in. barrel, 9 1/2 lbs. Mfg. 1999-2008.

		$1,385	$895	$675	$525	$450	$385	$350	$1,698

* **AR-10A Carbine (A10A4CBF/CF)** – 7.62 NATO/.308 Win. cal., 16 in. double lapped chrome-lined chrome moly threaded barrel with flash suppressor, two-stage tactical trigger, anodized aluminum lower receiver, forged flat-top upper receiver with Picatinny rail and forward assist, 6-pos. collapsible stock, 20 shot Magpul PMAG, standard 8 in. handguard, Picatinny rail gas block, matte black (CBF) or green (CF, disc. 2014) finish, 7 3/4 lbs. Mfg. 2013-2017.

		$1,315	$850	$625	$500	$435	$375	$350	$1,571

* **AR-10 B Series Carbine** – 7.62 NATO/.308 Win. cal., mid-length gas system, 16 in. double lapped chrome moly threaded barrel, flash suppressor, 20 shot mag., front sight base, tactical two-stage trigger, 8 in. handguard, forged aluminum lower and flat-top upper with Picatinny rail, charging handle, 6-pos. collapsible stock, black anodized finish, 7.6 lbs. Disc. 2017.

		$1,315	$850	$625	$500	$435	$375	$350	$1,571

* **AR-10 National Match** – 7.62 NATO cal., GIO, 20 in. stainless steel match barrel with stainless A2 flash suppressor, forged flat-top receiver with Picatinny rail and forward assist, NM quad rail free float handguard, detachable carry handle, forged lower with two-stage NM trigger, 10 shot mag., Mil-Std 1913 rail handguard, extended elevation NM sights, includes two 20 shot mags., USMC sling, black hard case, 11 1/2 lbs. Mfg. 2009-2013.

		$1,875	$1,100	$895	$650	$575	$495	$425	$2,365

AR-10SOF (SPECIAL OPERATION FORCES) CARBINE – .308 Win. cal., GIO, available in either A2 or A4 configurations, fixed tube stock, 16 in. barrel, black finish only. Mfg. 2003-2004.

		$1,275	$850	$600	$495	$425	$375	$350	$1,503

Add $52 for A2 configuration (includes Picatinny rail).

* **AR-10T Carbine (10TCBNF, Navy Model)** – 7.62 NATO cal., 16 in. triple lapped stainless barrel with A2 flash suppressor, forged flat-top upper with Picatinny rail and forward assist, Picatinny gas block, round mid-length free floating handguard, forged lower with two-stage NM trigger, Hi-Cap stock, Black finish, includes two 10 shot mags. and hard case, 8 1/2 lbs. Mfg. 2004-2012.

		$1,600	$1,000	$775	$575	$495	$425	$395	$1,914

* **AR-10T Rifle** – .243 Win. (mfg. 1995-2003 and 2009-2010), .260 Rem. (mfg. 2009-2013), .300 RSUM (mfg. 2004-2008, Ultra Mag. Model), 7mm-08 Rem. (mfg. 2009-2010), .338 Federal (mfg. 2009-2013), or 7.62 NATO cal., GIO, features 20 (7.62 NATO), 22 (.338 Federal or .260 Rem., disc. 2013), or 24 (disc. 2008) in. stainless steel heavy match barrel, two-stage NM trigger, black fiberglass (disc. 2008) or aluminum handguard tube, fixed A2 buttstock, flat-top receiver with Picatinny rail, w/o sights or carry handle, forward bolt assist became standard in 2009, Green (disc. 2013) or Black finish, includes one (new 2014) or two (disc. 2013) 10 shot mags. and hard case, 9 1/2-10 1/2 lbs. Disc. 2017.

		$1,350	$875	$650	$525	$450	$385	$350	$1,649

Add $80 for .338 Federal cal. (disc. 2013).
Add $214 for .300 RSUM cal. (disc. 2008).
Add $250 for Lothar Walther barrel (disc.).

ARMALITE, INC., cont. 79 A

MSR	100%	98%	95%	90%	80%	70%	60%	Last MSR

* AR-10B Target (10TBNF/NF) – .308 Win. cal., 20 in. triple lapped stainless steel match grade barrel, forged flat-top receiver, NM two-stage trigger, Picatinny gas block, fixed polymer stock, free float handguard, pistol grip, 10 shot mag., hard anodized matte black (BNF) or green (NF, disc. 2013) finish, 10.3 lbs. Disc. 2015.

	$1,600	$1,000	$775	$575	$495	$425	$395	$1,914

AR-10 SASS – .260 Rem. or .308 Win. cal., 20 in. barrel, 25 shot mag., black or brown finish. Mfg. 2017 only.

	$2,775	$1,825	$1,350	$750	$650	$595	$525	$3,499

AR-10 SASS MKII – .260 Rem., .308 Win., or 7.62x51mm cal., 18 in. stainless steel barrel, AWC PSR thread-over suppressor ready muzzle, 20 shot Magpul PMAG, Timney trigger, Magpul PSR stock, 15 in. enhanced receiver M-LOK handguard, Raptor ambi charging handle, two-pos. selectable gas block, 9.4 lbs. New mid-2018.

Please contact the company directly for pricing and availability for this model.

AR-10 SUPER SASS RIFLE (10SBF) – 7.62 NATO cal., GIO, mock AAC (disc.) or A2 flash suppressor, 20 in. triple lapped ceramic coated stainless steel threaded barrel with A2 flash suppressor, forged flat-top upper receiver with Picatinny rail, forward assist, adj. gas block, SuperSASS quad rail free floating handguard with rail covers, forged lower receiver, 20 shot mag., fully adj. Sniper stock, black finish, two-stage NM trigger, available with various accessories, includes one 10 shot mag., one 20 shot mag., USMC quick adjust sling, sling swivel mount, and hard case, 9.4-11.8 lbs. Disc. 2017.

	$2,550	$1,650	$1,250	$700	$625	$575	$525	$3,100

* AR-10A Super SASS Rifle (A10SBF) – 7.62 NATO/.308 Win. cal., 20 in. Cerakote stainless steel match threaded barrel with flash suppressor, 20 shot Mapgul PMAG, National Match two-stage trigger, Armalite floating rail systems handguard, Gas Buster charging handle, quad Mil-Std 1913 rail, Magpul PRS stock, 11.8 lbs. Mfg. 2012-2017.

	$2,450	$1,595	$1,200	$700	$675	$575	$525	$3,099

This model has magazine interchangeability with the AR-10B.

»AR-10 CSASS (AR-10A Super SASS Carbine - A10SCBF) – 7.62 NATO/.308 Win. cal., 16 in. Cerakote stainless steel match threaded barrel with flash suppressor, 20 shot Magpul PMAG, Armalite floating rail systems handguard, Gas Buster charging handle, National Match two-stage trigger, quad Mil-Std 1913 rail, B5 buttstock, 9.1 lbs. Mfg. 2014-2017.

	$2,450	$1,595	$1,200	$700	$675	$575	$525	$3,099

This model has magazine interchangeability with the AR-10B.

AR-10 DEFENSIVE SPORTING RIFLE (DSR10) – 7.62x51mm/.308 Win. cal., 16 in. double lapped chrome-lined barrel with flash suppressor, 20 shot Magpul PMAG, 8 in. handguard, Mil-Std 1913 rail gas block, single-stage trigger, 6-position collapsible buttstock, 7.9 lbs. New 2015.

MSR $1,049	$875	$550	$465	$395	$350	$325	$300	

AR-10 QUAD-RAIL (AR-10A4 LOW PROFILE CARBINE) – 7.62x51mm/.308 Win. cal., 16 in. double lapped chrome-lined chrome moly threaded barrel with flash suppressor, anodized aluminum receiver, forged aluminum upper receiver with free float quad rail handguards, low profile gas block, 20 shot Magpul PMAG, two-stage tactical trigger, B5 adjustable stock, 8.8 lbs. Mfg. 2014-2016.

	$1,525	$975	$750	$575	$495	$425	$375	$1,850

AR-10 TACTICAL – 7.62x51mm/.308 Win. cal., 16, 18, or 20 in. black Cerakote stainless steel threaded barrel with flash hiding compensator, 25 shot Magpul PMAG, 15 in. KeyMod handguard, full-length Picatinny rail, Magpul MBUS flip-up sights, Raptor ambidextrous charging handle, two-stage precision trigger, MOE+ pistol grip, Magpul STR Multi-position collapsible (16 or 18 in.) or MBA-1 (20 in.) buttstock, 8.8 lbs. New 2015.

MSR $1,999	$1,650	$1,000	$795	$595	$495	$425	$395	

Add $100 for 18 or 20 in. barrel.

AR-10 A SERIES TACTICAL CARBINE – 7.62 NATO/.308 Win. cal., mid-length gas system, 16 in. double lapped chrome moly barrel, flash suppressor, 20 shot Magpul PMAG, A2 front sight base, tactical two-stage trigger, 8 in. handguard, charging handle, 6-pos. collapsible stock, forged aluminum lower and flat-top upper receiver with Picatinny rail and forward assist, black anodized finish, 7.8 lbs. Disc. 2017.

	$1,315	$850	$625	$500	$435	$375	$350	$1,571

AR-10 VSR (VERSATILE SPORTING RIFLE) – 7.62x51mm/.308 Win. cal., 18 in. black Cerakote stainless steel threaded barrel with knurled thread protector, 20 shot Magpul PMAG, top Picatinny rail, 15 in. free floating VSR handguard, Raptor ambidextrous charging handle, two-stage trigger, MBA-1 lightweight precision buttstock adjustable for LOP and comb height, 8.8 lbs. Mfg. 2015-2017.

	$1,575	$995	$775	$575	$495	$425	$395	$1,899

AR-10 3-GUN COMPETITION RIFLE – 7.62x51mm/.308 Win. cal., 18 in. stainless steel barrel, 25 shot Magpul PMAG, 15 in. free floating 3-Gun handguard, ambidextrous safety and Raptor charging handle, two inch Mil-Std rail section, Timney 3 lb. single stage trigger, Ergo wide grip, lightweight MBA-1 buttstock is adjustable for cheekpiece and LOP, 8.9 lbs. New 2015.

MSR $2,199	$1,725	$1,050	$850	$625	$550	$475	$425	

A 80 ARMALITE, INC., cont.

MSR		100%	98%	95%	90%	80%	70%	60%	Last MSR

AR-180B – .223 Rem. cal., GPO, polymer lower receiver with formed sheet metal upper, standard AR-15 trigger group/ magazine, incorporates the best features of the M15 (lower group with trigger and magwell) and early AR-180 (gas system, which keeps propellant gas outside of the receiver) rifles, 19.8 in. barrel with integral muzzle brake, 6 lbs. Mfg. 2003-2007.

		$1,250	$825	$575	$475	$425	$375	$350	$750

For more information on the original ArmaLite AR-180 and variations, please refer to the previous ArmaLite listing.

M4A1C CARBINE – features GIO, 16 in. chrome-lined 1:9 twist heavy barrel with National Match sights and detachable carrying handle, grooved barrel shroud, 7 lbs. Disc. 1997.

		$800	$525	$450	$385	$340	$325	$295	$935

M4C CARBINE – similar to M4A1C Carbine, except has non-removable carrying handle and fixed sights, 7 lbs. Disc. 1997.

		$745	$500	$435	$375	$335	$315	$295	$870

M-15 RIFLE/CARBINE VARIATIONS – .223 Rem. cal. standard unless otherwise noted, GIO, various configurations, barrel lengths, sights, and other features.

* **M-15A4 SPR Mod 1 (15SPR1CB)** – 5.56 NATO, 6.8 SPC (mfg. 2012-2013, reintroduced 2016), or 7.62x39mm (mfg. 2012-2013) cal., GIO, 16 in. chrome-lined threaded barrel with flash hider, gas block with rail, forged flat-top receiver with Picatinny rail and laser engraved rail numbering, three extra detachable rails, collapsible stock, tactical two-stage trigger, aluminum lower receiver, ARMS polymer (disc. 2013) or flip-up front and rear sights, black furniture, includes one 30 shot mag., sling, and hard case, 6 1/2 lbs. Mfg. mid-2010-2016.

		$1,315	$850	$625	$500	$435	$375	$350	$1,589

Add $35 for mid-length free floating quad rail (disc. 2013).
Add $160 for 7.62x39mm cal. (disc. 2013).
Add $155 for 6.8 SPC cal.

* **M-15A2/A4 National Match Rifle** – .223 Rem. cal., features GIO, 20 in. stainless steel NM sleeved 1:8 twist barrel with flash suppressor, forged A2 receiver with NM hooded rear sights and A2 NM clamp on front sight, forged lower with NM two-stage trigger, grooved barrel shroud, black or green furniture, with or w/o detachable carrying handle, includes one 30 shot mag., USMC quick adjust sling, and hard case, 9 lbs. Disc. 2013.

		$1,175	$775	$550	$465	$415	$375	$350	$1,422

* **M-15A2 Golden Eagle** – .223 Rem. cal., similiar to M15A2 National Match Rifle, except has 20 in. heavy barrel, 9.4 lbs. Limited mfg. 1998 only.

		$1,125	$700	$525	$450	$400	$350	$325	$1,350

* **M-15A2 Service Rifle** – 5.56 NATO cal., GIO, includes 20 in. chrome-lined 1:9 twist barrel, green or black furniture, forged A2 receiver, fixed stock, A2 front sight, tactical two-stage trigger, flash suppressor, carrying handle, includes one 30 shot mag., sling, and hard case, 8.2 lbs. Disc. 2013.

		$975	$595	$495	$425	$365	$335	$300	$1,174

* **M-15A2 Carbine** – 5.56 NATO cal., similar to M15A2 Service Rifle, except has 16 in. barrel, 6-position collapsible stock with G.I. diameter extension tube, includes one 30 shot mag., sling, and hard case, 7 lbs. Disc. 2013.

		$975	$595	$495	$425	$365	$335	$300	$1,174

* **M-15A4 National Match SPR** – .223 Rem. cal., similar to M15A2 National Match, except has forged flat-top receiver with Picatinny rail and NM detachable carry handle, includes one 30 shot mag., USMC quick adjust sling, and hard case, 9.8 lbs. Disc. 2013.

		$1,195	$795	$550	$465	$415	$375	$350	$1,435

* **M-15A4 SPR (Special Purpose Rifle, 15A4/15A4B)** – 5.56 NATO cal., GIO, 20 in. chrome-lined HBAR threaded barrel, gas block with rail, forged flat-top upper with Picatinny rail, forged lower with tactical two-stage trigger, Hi-Cap stock, Green (15A4) or Black (15A4B) finish, includes one 30 shot mag., sling, and hard case, 7.8 lbs. Disc. 2013.

		$895	$575	$475	$395	$350	$325	$300	$1,073

* **M-15A4 SPR II National Match (Special Purpose Rifle)** – 5.56 NATO cal., similar to M-15A4 SPR, except has triple lapped rifled barrel, strengthened free floating barrel sleeve and two-stage match trigger, green or black furniture. Mfg. 2003-2005.

		$1,225	$825	$575	$475	$425	$375	$350	$1,472

* **M-15A4 Carbine** – 5.56 NATO, 6.8 SPC (mfg. 2009-2013, reintroduced 2016), or 7.62x39mm (mfg. 2009-2013) cal., 16 in. chrome moly threaded barrel, forged flat-top upper with Picatinny rail, gas block with rail, forged lower with tactical two-stage trigger, 6-pos. collapsible stock with G.I. diameter extension tube, green (15A4C) or black (15A4CB) furniture, includes one 30 shot mag., sling, and hard case, 6 1/2-7 lbs. Disc. 2015.

		$895	$575	$475	$395	$350	$325	$300	$1,073

Add $42 for 6.8 SPC cal.
Add $42 for 7.62x39mm cal. (disc. 2013).
Subtract $60 for fixed front sight w/detachable carry handle (disc.).

ARMALITE, INC., cont. 81 A

MSR	100%	98%	95%	90%	80%	70%	60%	Last MSR

* **M-15A4 CBA2K** – 5.56 NATO cal., GIO, 16 in. double lapped chrome-lined barrel, flash suppressor, two-stage tactical trigger, forged flat-top receiver with Picatinny rail, A2 front sight, 8 in. mid-length handguard, forged lower receiver, 6-position collapsible stock with G.I. diameter extension tube, includes one 30 shot mag., sling, and hard case, 6 1/2 lbs. Mfg. 2008-2013.

	$875	$550	$465	$395	$350	$325	$300	*$1,031*

* **M-15ARTN** – .223 Rem. cal., GIO, 20 in. stainless steel barrel, National Match trigger, green or black finish. Mfg. 2004-2007.

	$1,100	$675	$525	$450	$400	$350	$325	*$1,322*

* **M-15T Target (15A4TBN Rifle Eagle Eye)** – 5.56 NATO/.223 Wylde chamber, GIO, 20 or 24 (disc. 2009) in. stainless steel heavy barrel, two-stage NM trigger, smooth green or black fiberglass (disc. 2008) or lightweight aluminum round floating handguard, Picatinny front sight rail but w/o sights and carrying handle, A2 stock, black or green furniture, includes one 10 shot mag. and hard case, 8.6 lbs. Disc. 2005, reintroduced 2007-2016, reintroduced 2018.

MSR $1,318	$1,100	$675	$525	$450	$400	$350	$325	

* **M-15 Target (15TBN)** – .223 Rem. cal., GIO, 18 in. triple lapped stainless steel match threaded barrel with flash suppressor, forged flat-top upper receiver with Picatinny rail, free float quad rail handguards, includes one 10 shot mag., collapsible stock, two-stage NM trigger, pistol grip, matte black finish, 7.9 lbs. Mfg. 2014-2016.

	$1,195	$795	$550	$465	$415	$375	$350	*$1,449*

* **M-15A4T Carbine (Eagle Eye)** – features GIO, 16 in. stainless steel 1:9 twist heavy barrel, Picatinny rail, smooth fiberglass handguard tube, two-stage trigger, 7.1 lbs. Mfg. 1997-2004.

	$1,150	$750	$550	$465	$415	$375	$350	*$1,383*

* **M-15A4 Predator** – similar to M-15A4T Eagle Eye, except has 1:12 twist barrel. Disc. 1996.

	$1,125	$700	$525	$450	$400	$350	$325	*$1,350*

* **M-15A4 Action Master** – GIO, includes 20 in. stainless steel 1:9 twist barrel, two-stage trigger, muzzle brake, Picatinny flat-top design w/o sights or carrying handle, 9 lbs. Disc. 1997.

	$975	$595	$495	$425	$365	$335	$300	*$1,175*

* **M-15SOF (Special Operation Forces) Carbine** – .223 Rem. cal., GIO, available in either A2 or A4 configurations, fixed tube stock, 16 in. barrel, black finish only. Mfg. 2003-2004.

	$915	$575	$475	$415	$350	$325	$300	*$1,084*

Add $69 for A2 configuration (includes Picatinny rail).

M-15 DEFENSIVE SPORTING RIFLE (DSR15/DSR15F) – 5.56x45mm/.223 Wylde chamber, 16 in. double
lapped chrome-lined barrel with flash suppressor, 30 shot Magpul PMAG, 8 in. handguard, Mil-Std 1913 rail gas block or A2 front sight base (DSR15F), single-stage trigger, 6-position collapsible buttstock, 6.1 lbs. New 2015.

MSR $799	$675	$500	$425	$375	$335	$315	$295	

M-15 LIGHT TACTICAL CARBINE – 5.56 NATO, 6.8 SPC (disc. 2017), or 7.62x39mm (disc. 2017) cal., mid-
length GIO, 16 in. chrome-lined threaded barrel, flash suppressor, 30 shot mag., single stage trigger, forged aluminum receivers, top Picatinny rail, 10 in. aluminum tactical KeyMod handguard, anodized black finish, 6 lbs. New 2016.

MSR $999	$850	$550	$465	$395	$350	$325	$295	

M-15 PISTON – 5.56 NATO cal., GPO, 16 in. chrome moly barrel, 30 shot Magpul PMAG, 15 in. piston KeyMod
handguard, Raptor ambidextrous charging handle, Mil-Std 1913 rail, two-stage precision trigger, Magpul STR buttstock adjustable for LOP and comb height, 7.3 lbs. Mfg. 2015-2016.

	$1,795	$1,050	$875	$625	$550	$475	$425	*$2,249*

M-15 TACTICAL – 5.56x45mm/.223 Wylde chamber, GIO, 16 or 18 in. black Cerakote stainless steel threaded barrel
with flash hiding compensator, 30 shot Magpul PMAG, two-stage precision trigger, full-length Picatinny rail, 15 in. aluminum tactical KeyMod handguard, Magpul STR multi-position collapsible stock, 7.2 lbs. New 2015.

MSR $1,599	$1,315	$850	$625	$500	$435	$375	$350	

Add $100 for 18 in. barrel.

M-15 VSR (VERSATILE SPORTING RIFLE) – 5.56x45mm/.223 Wylde chamber, GIO, 18 in. black Cerakote
stainless steel threaded barrel with knurled thread protector, 20 shot Magpul PMAG, 15 in. free floating VSR handguard, Raptor ambidextrous charging handle, top Picatinny rail, two-stage precision trigger, MBA-1 lightweight buttstock adj. for LOP and comb height, 7 1/2 lbs. Mfg. 2015-2017.

	$1,125	$700	$525	$450	$400	$350	$325	*$1,349*

M-15 3-GUN COMPETITION RIFLE – 5.56x45mm/.223 Wylde chamber, GIO, 18 in. free floating stainless steel
barrel, adj. gas block, 30 shot Magpul PMAG, 12 in. free floating 3-Gun handguard, two inch Mil-Std rail section, Timney 3 lb. single stage trigger, MBA-1 lightweight precision buttstock adjustable for LOP and comb height, 6.6 lbs. New 2015.

MSR $1,699	$1,385	$895	$675	$525	$450	$385	$350	

A 82 ARMALITE, INC., cont.

MSR	100%	98%	95%	90%	80%	70%	60%	Last MSR

LEC15A4CBK (LAW ENFORCEMENT CARBINE) – 5.56 NATO cal., GIO, 16 in. double lapped chrome-lined threaded barrel, forged flat-top receiver with Picatinny rail, flash suppressor, A2 front sight, 8 in. handguard, tactical two-stage trigger, 6-position collapsible stock with G.I. diameter extension tube, includes one 30 shot mag., sling, and hard case, 6 1/2 lbs. Mfg. 2009-2016.

	$850	$550	$465	$395	$350	$325	$295	$989

ARMS LLC

Previous manufacturer located in Aurora, Oregon 2008-2016.

PISTOLS: SEMI-AUTO

Arms LLC manufactured the ARMS-5 and ARMS-15 AR-15 style pistols. Each model was built to customer specifications.

RIFLES: SEMI-AUTO

Arms LLC manufactured the following AR-15 style models: ARMS-15 Classic, ARMS-15 Elite Custom, ARMS-15 Quadrail, ARMS-15 Long Range, ARMS-5 SBR, and the ARMS-5 rifle. Each model was built to customer specifications.

THE ARMS ROOM (ARMS ROOM LLC)

Current manufacturer of pistols and AR-15 style carbines/rifles located in Orlando, FL until 2017.

RIFLES: SEMI-AUTO

MARK WALTERS SIGNATURE RIFLE – 5.56 NATO cal., mid-length gas system, 16 in. stainless steel barrel, GT Micro Predator flash hider, 30 shot PMAG, GT extended mag. release, stainless steel low profile gas block, integral trigger guard, MBUS Pro front and rear sights, Rogers Super-Stoc, MOE pistol grip, GT ambi selector, custom Mark Walters Edition laser engraving, GT Ultra slimline octagonal 5-sided KeyMod free floating handguard with monolithic top rail, Type III hardcoat anodized black finish. Disc. 2016.

	$1,250	$825	$575	$475	$425	$375	$350	$1,495

TAR-15 BOOT RIFLE PACKAGE – 5.56 NATO cal., carbine length GIO, 16 in. chrome moly M4 profile barrel, A2 flash hider, fixed front sight base, Magpul Gen 2 rear flip-up sight, M4 stock and buffer tube, double heat shield handguards, M16 bolt carrier group, flat-top upper with M4 cuts, Mil-Spec upper and lower parts, black anodized finish. Disc. 2017.

	$550	$475	$400	$350	$315	$295	$275	$845

TAR-15 GRUNT RIFLE PACKAGE – 5.56 NATO cal., GIO, 16 in. chrome moly barrel, M4 barrel profile, fixed front sight base, black anodized finish, A2 flash hider, two-piece drop-in quad rail, M16 bolt carrier group, flat-top upper with M4 cuts, Magpul Gen 2 rear flip-up sight, Arms Room lower receiver, Mil-Spec upper and lower parts, Rogers Super-Stoc and buffer tube, Magpul MOE Plus grip. Disc. 2017.

	$875	$550	$465	$395	$350	$325	$300	$1,035

TAR-15 SAPPER RIFLE PACKAGE – 5.56 NATO cal., GIO, 16 in. chrome moly M4 profile barrel, Phantom flash hider, Magpul MBUS folding front and rear sights, front sight adj. tool, M4 stock and buffer tube, M4 grip, free float quad rail, M16 bolt carrier group, flat-top upper with M4 cuts, Arms Room lower receiver, Mil-Spec upper and lower parts, black anodized finish. Disc. 2017.

	$915	$575	$475	$415	$350	$325	$300	$1,085

TAR-15 SCOUT RIFLE PACKAGE – 5.56 NATO cal., GIO, 16 in. chrome moly M4 profile barrel, twisted Phantom flash hider, Magpul MBUS folding front and rear sights, front sight adj. tool, Rogers Super-Stoc, Mil-Spec buffer tube, Ergo or Magpul MOE grip, free float quad rail, M16 bolt carrier group, flat-top upper with M4 cuts, Arms Room lower receiver, Mil-Spec upper and lower parts, black anodized finish.

	$935	$575	$475	$415	$350	$325	$300	$1,115

ZMB-02 ZOMBIE KILLER CARBINE – 5.56 NATO cal., GIO, 16 in. chrome moly barrel, Phantom flash hider, front and rear sights, Rogers Super-Stoc and Mil-Spec buffer tube, pistol grip, OD or black quad rail, M16 bolt carrier group, M4 cut, Mil-Spec upper and lower parts, laser etched ejection port door, Zombie engraved logo with color fill, "LIVE - DEAD - UNDEAD" selector designations, includes soft case, black and green two-tone finish. Disc. 2014.

	$1,100	$675	$525	$450	$400	$350	$325	$1,324

ARMS TECH LTD.

Previous manufacturer located in Phoenix, AZ 1987-2012.

RIFLES: SEMI-AUTO

Previously, the company also offered the Urban Support Rifle for the civilian marketplace.

SUPER MATCH INTERDICTION POLICE MODEL – .243 Win., .300 Win. Mag., or .308 Win. (standard) cal., AR-15 style, GIO, features 22 in. free floating Schnieder or Douglas air gauged stainless steel barrel, McMillan stock, updated trigger group, detachable box mag., 13 1/4 lbs. Limited mfg. 1996-98.

	$3,950	$3,650	$3,300	$3,000	$2,750	$2,350	$2,000	$4,800

ARMSCOR 83 A

MSR	100%	98%	95%	90%	80%	70%	60%	Last MSR

ARMSCOR

Current trademark of firearms manufactured by Arms Corporation of the Philippines (manufacturing began 1952) established in 1985 (Armscor Precision - API). The Armscor trademark is not being imported into the U.S. currently, but still exists in some foreign marketplaces. Previously imported and distributed 1999-2014 by Armscor Precision International (full line), located in Pahrump, NV. Previously imported 1995-1999 by K.B.I., Inc. located in Harrisburg, PA, by Ruko located in Buffalo, NY until 1995 and by Armscorp Precision Inc. located in San Mateo, CA until 1991.

In 1991, the importation of Arms Corporation of the Philippines firearms was changed to Ruko Products, Inc., located in Buffalo, NY. Barrel markings on firearms imported by Ruko Products, Inc. state "Ruko-Armscor" instead of the older "Armscorp Precision" barrel markings. All Armscorp Precision, Inc. models were discontinued in 1991.

The models listed also provide cross-referencing for older Armscorp Precision and Ruko imported models.

RIFLES: SEMI-AUTO

M-1600 – .22 LR cal., GIO blowback action, 10 or 15 (disc.) shot mag., 18 in. barrel, copy of the Armalite M16, ebony stock, 5 1/4 lbs. Importation disc. 2014.

| | $180 | $150 | $130 | $110 | $100 | $80 | $70 | |

* M-1600R – .22 LR cal., similar to M-1600, except has stainless steel retractable buttstock and vent. barrel hood, 7 1/4 lbs. Importation disc. 1995, reintroduced 2008-2011.

| | $155 | $135 | $115 | $105 | $85 | $70 | $55 | |

ASTRA ARMS S.A.

Current manufacturer established in 2007 and located in Sion, Switzerland. No current U.S. importation.

Astra manufactures a line of AR-15 style tactical rifles called the Sturmgewher 4 Series. Current models include the Carbine, Commando, and Pistol. Astra also manufactures machine guns MG556 (5.56x5 NATO), MG762 (7.62x51 NATO) and MG127 (12.7x99 NATO-.50 BMB) and launchers GL203 (40x46mm) and SL203 (12/70). These models are not currently imported into the U.S. Please contact the company directly for more information, including availability and pricing (see Trademark Index).

AUSTRALIAN AUTOMATIC ARMS PTY. LTD.

Previous manufacturer located in Tasmania, Australia. Previously imported and distributed by California Armory, Inc. located in San Bruno, CA.

PISTOLS: SEMI-AUTO

SAP – .223 Rem. cal., GIO, 10 1/2 in. barrel, SA, 20 shot mag., fiberglass stock and forearm, 5.9 lbs. Imported 1986-1993.

| | $795 | $700 | $600 | $550 | $500 | $475 | $450 | $799 |

RIFLES: SEMI-AUTO

SAR – .223 Rem. cal., GIO, AR-15 style, 16 1/4 or 20 in. (new 1989) barrel, 5 or 20 shot M16 style mag., fiberglass stock and forearm, 7 1/2 lbs. Imported 1986-89.

| | $1,250 | $1,000 | $900 | $800 | $775 | $750 | $700 | $663 |

Add $25 for 20 in. barrel.

This model was also available in a fully automatic version (AR).

SP – .223 Rem. cal., GIO, AR-15 style, sporting configuration, 16 1/4 or 20 in. barrel, wood stock and forearm, 5 or 20 shot M16 style mag., 7 1/4 lbs. Imported late 1991-93.

| | $850 | $750 | $650 | $600 | $550 | $500 | $475 | $879 |

Add $40 for wood stock.

AXELSON TACTICAL

Current manufacturer and dealer located in Minden, NV.

PISTOLS: SEMI-AUTO

COMBAT 5.56 PISTOL – 5.56 NATO cal., carbine length gas tube, 12 1/2 in. Faxon barrel, Talon muzzle brake, BCM low profile gas block and buffer system, forged aluminum upper and lower receivers, 9 in. GunRec slim profile M-LOK rail system, ALG combat trigger, CMMG lower parts kit, BCM Gunfighter Mod 4 charging handle, B5 Systems Bravo buttstock, BCM Gunfighter Mod 1 grip, Type III hardcoat anodized black finish. Mfg. 2016-2017.

| | $1,350 | $1,200 | $1,075 | $950 | $815 | $700 | $575 | $1,629 |

COMBAT 300 BLK PISTOL – .300 AAC Blackout cal., Type III hardcoat anodized finish. Mfg. 2016-2017.

| | $1,465 | $1,275 | $1,125 | $1,000 | $850 | $735 | $595 | $1,729 |

A 84 AXELSON TACTICAL, cont.

MSR	100%	98%	95%	90%	80%	70%	60%	Last MSR

RIFLES: SEMI-AUTO

AXE-10 PRECISION 6.5 – 6.5mm Creedmoor or .260 Rem. cal., 20, 22, or 24 in. Proof Research carbon fiber barrel, Axelson ROC Competition 762 brake, Geissele SSA-E trigger, Magpul PRS stock, Proof Research Cam gas system, Superlative Arms bleed off gas block, 18 in. carbon fiber M-LOK rail system, JP enhanced bolt, comes in black Pelican case. New 2018.

	100%	98%	95%	90%	80%	70%	60%
MSR $4,845	$3,925	$2,800	$1,750	$1,150	$875	$775	$700

AXE AR15 – 5.56 NATO cal., 16 in. barrel, Talon muzzle brake, 12 in. slim profile M-LOK rail system, "Arch Angel" charging handle, M4 style billet aluminum lower receiver, ALG combat trigger group, B5 Systems enhanced SOPMOD buttstock, BCM Gunfighter Mod 0 pistol grip, FDE finish. Mfg. 2016 only.

	100%	98%	95%	90%	80%	70%	60%	Last MSR
	$1,875	$1,100	$895	$650	$575	$495	$425	$2,299

Add $50 for Battle Axe, Desert Axe, Freedom Axe, Night Axe, Na Koa Ke Kai, Reaper, and Spartan models featuring different finishes.

AXE AR15 PRECISION ELITE – 5.56 NATO cal., 16 in. Proof Research barrel (chambered in .223 Wylde), BattleComp muzzle brake, Seekins adj. gas block, 14 in. Centurion Arms rail system, AXTS ambidextrous Raptor charging handle, M4 style billet aluminum lower receiver, Geissele SSA-E trigger, B5 Systems enhanced SOPMOD buttstock, BCM pistol grip, FDE finish. Mfg. 2016 only.

	100%	98%	95%	90%	80%	70%	60%	Last MSR
	$1,875	$1,100	$895	$650	$575	$495	$425	$2,299

Add $50 for Battle Axe, Desert Axe, Freedom Axe, Night Axe, Na Koa Ke Kai, Reaper, and Spartan models featuring different finishes.

AXE CAR 556 – 5.56 NATO cal., GIO, carbine length gas system, 10 1/2 in. QPQ Nitride barrel with pinned and welded 5 1/2 in. flash hider, ALG combat trigger, B5 Systems Bravo stock, BCM Gunfighter MOD 1 grip, forged aluminum upper and lower receiver, fixed carry handle on A2 upper, Axelson combat extended charging handle, CAR handguard with heat shield. New 2017.

	100%	98%	95%	90%	80%	70%	60%
MSR $1,295	$1,075	$675	$500	$450	$400	$350	$325

AXE M4C – 5.56 NATO cal., GIO, carbine length gas system, 10 1/2 in. QPQ Nitride barrel with pinned and welded 5 1/2 in. flash hider, ALG combat trigger, B5 Systems Bravo stock, Bravo Company Gunfighter MOD 1 grip, forged aluminum upper and lower receivers, Axelson combat extended charging handle, CAR handguard with heat shield. New 2017.

	100%	98%	95%	90%	80%	70%	60%
MSR $1,295	$1,075	$675	$500	$450	$400	$350	$325

AXE PATROL RIFLE – 5.56 NATO cal., GIO, 16 in. Nitride barrel with A2 flash hider, Mil-Spec trigger, Magpul MOE stock, Magpul MOE grip, forged aluminum upper and lower receiver, Magpul MOE mid-length handguard, mid-length gas system, QPQ Nitride BCG, Axelson Combat extended charging handle, black finish.

	100%	98%	95%	90%	80%	70%	60%
MSR $1,095	$915	$575	$475	$415	$350	$325	$300

"AXE" SPECIAL PURPOSE RIFLE – 5.56 NATO cal. chambered for .223 Wylde, GIO, stainless steel 18 in. barrel with muzzle brake, 15 shot mag., Magpul MBUS PRO sights, enhanced SOPMOD stock, 15 in. free floating rail system, 3 color camouflage finish with Cerakote. Limited mfg. 2015.

	100%	98%	95%	90%	80%	70%	60%	Last MSR
	$3,695	$3,235	$2,770	$2,515	$2,030	$1,665	$1,295	$3,695

This model was designed to honor Matt Axelson as well as the other SEAL team members of Operation Red Wings who lost their lives in 2005 while fighting the Taliban in Afghanistan.

BLACK PEARL 556 COMPETITION RIFLE – 5.56 NATO cal., GIO, 16 in. ultra lightweight Nitride barrel, Axelson ROC Competition 10 port tunable brake, drop-in adj. SST, ultra-lightweight carbon fiber fixed stock, BCM Gunfighter Mod 1 grip, forged aluminum upper and lower receivers, Axelson carbon fiber 15 in. M-LOK compatible rail system, mid-length gas system, DLC BCG, Axelson Combat extended charging handle, hardcoat anodized black finish, 4.9 lbs.

	100%	98%	95%	90%	80%	70%	60%
MSR $2,495	$1,975	$1,150	$925	$650	$575	$495	$425

Add $500 for 16 in. Proof Research carbon fiber barrel (.223 Wylde chamber).

CHARLIE MIKE PRECISION SIGNATURE AR-10 – 6.5mm Creedmoor or .260 Rem. cal., 24 in. Proof Research carbon fiber barrel, Axelson .30 cal. ROC competition brake, Proof Research Cam gas system, Superlative Arms bleed off gas block, 18 in. carbon fiber M-LOK rail system, Geissele SSA-E trigger, JP Enhanced BCG, Magpul PRS stock, comes in Pelican rifle case. New 2018.

	100%	98%	95%	90%	80%	70%	60%
MSR $5,500	$4,675	$4,100	$3,525	$2,950	$2,500	$2,050	$1,775

This model is a limited edition custom precision rifle designed by Charlie Melton (SEAL Sniper Instructor), and includes one spot in a Charlie Mike Precision Long Range Rifle Course ($1,000 value).

COMBAT 300 – .300 AAC Blackout cal., GIO, 16 in. Faxon chrome-lined (mfg. 2016) or Axelson QPQ Nitride (new 2017) barrel, Talon (mfg. 2016) or Axelson ROC (new 2017) muzzle brake, BCM carbine length gas tube, low profile gas block and buffer system, forged aluminum upper and lower receivers, 15 in. Centurion Arms slim profile lightweight M-LOK rail system, Geissele SSA-E enhanced (mfg. 2016) or ALG combat (new 2017) trigger, CMMG lower parts kit, BCM Gunfighter Mod 4 charging handle (mfg. 2016) or Axelson combat charging handle (new 2017), B5 Systems Bravo buttstock, BCM Gunfighter MOD 1 grip, Type III hardcoat anodized black or Cerakote finish in Battle Worn Bronze (new 2017) or Battle Worn Gray (new 2017). New 2016.

	100%	98%	95%	90%	80%	70%	60%
MSR $1,895	$1,575	$995	$775	$575	$495	$425	$395

Add $300 for Battle Worn Gray or Battle Worn Bronze Cerakote finish (new 2017).

AXELSON TACTICAL, cont. 85 A

MSR	100%	98%	95%	90%	80%	70%	60%	Last MSR

COMBAT 308 – .308 Win. cal., 16 in. Faxon barrel, Battlecomp BABC muzzle brake, forged aluminum upper and lower receivers, BCM mid-length gas tube, low profile gas block, and buffer system, BCM Gunfighter 762 charging handle, Centurion Arms CMR rail system, Geissele SSAE trigger, CMMG lower parts kit, B5 Systems enhanced SOPMOD buttstock, BCM Gunfighter grip, Type III hardcoat anodized finish. Mfg. 2016 only.

	$2,295	$1,450	$1,075	$675	$595	$525	$475	$2,849

COMBAT 5.56 SPR – 5.56 NATO cal., 18 in. Faxon chrome-lined barrel, Talon muzzle brake, BCM carbine length gas tube, low profile gas block, and buffer system, forged aluminum upper and lower receivers, 14 in. slim profile lightweight M-LOK rail system, ALG combat trigger, Strike Industries charging handle with extended latch, B5 Systems Bravo buttstock, BCM Gunfighter Mod 1 grip, Type III hardcoat anodized black finish. Mfg. 2016 only.

	$1,575	$995	$775	$575	$495	$425	$395	$1,899

COMBAT 5.56 – 5.56 NATO cal., GIO, 16 in. Faxon chrome-lined barrel, Talon muzzle brake, BCM gas tube, low profile gas block, and buffer system, Strike Industries charging handle with extended latch (mfg. 2016) or Axelson combat charging handle (new 2017), forged aluminum upper and lower receivers, 15 in. Centurion Arms slim profile lightweight M-LOK rail, ALG combat trigger, B5 Systems Bravo buttstock, BCM Gunfighter Mod 1 grip, Type III hardcoat anodized black or Cerakote finish in Battle Worn Gray (new 2017) or Battle Worn Bronze (new 2017). New 2016.

MSR $1,795	$1,475	$950	$725	$550	$475	$395	$350	

Add $400 for Battle Worn Gray or Battle Worn Bronze Cerakote finish (new 2017).

"DIETZ" SPECIAL PURPOSE RIFLE – 5.56 NATO cal., 16 in. Faxon chrome-lined barrel, Talon muzzle brake, Bravo Company carbine length gas tube, gas block, and buffer system, BCM Gunfighter Mod 1 charging handle, Axelson Tactical forged aluminum upper and lower receivers with hardcoat anodized finish, 12 in. slim profile M-LOK rail system, ALG combat trigger, B5 Systems SOPMOD stock, BCM Gunfighter Mod 1 grip, serial numbers Dietz01-Dietz99. Only 99 rifles mfg. beginning 2016.

MSR $3,595	$3,050	$2,675	$2,175	$1,875	$1,550	$1,300	$1,125	

FREEDOM TRIBUTE RIFLE – 5.56 NATO cal., 16 in. barrel with Nitride finish, Freedom Flag Spiked Star muzzle brake, Cerakote Magpul mag., ALG ACT trigger, B5 SOPMOD stock, BCM Mod 1 grip, billet receiver set with custom Cerakote finish, 15 in. Centurion Arms rail, BCM Gunfighter charging handle, includes walnut custom wood collectors box with engraving. Limited mfg. of 100 units beginning 2018.

MSR $3,499	$2,965	$2,585	$2,100	$1,800	$1,495	$1,265	$1,085	

GEN2 WARRIOR SERIES 556 – 5.56 NATO cal., 16 in. barrel with Nitride finish, Talon muzzle brake, ALG combat trigger, B5 SOPMOD stock, Bravo Company Gunfighter Mod 1 grip, Axelson Tactical extended charging handle, billet aluminum upper and lower receivers, 15 in. Centurion Arms slim profile lightweight M-LOK rail system, hardcoat anodized black finish. New 2018.

MSR $1,795	$1,475	$950	$725	$550	$475	$395	$350	

REAPER01 AR10 – .308 Win. cal., 16 in. Proof Research barrel, "Talon" muzzle brake, low profile gas block, Centurion Arms 14 in. slim profile rail system, AXTS ambidextrous Raptor charging handle, forged aluminum M4 lower receiver, Geissele SSA-E trigger, Battle Arms Development ambidextrous selector lever, Seekins Precision mag. release button, Magpul PRS buttstock, B5 Systems pistol grip. Mfg. 2016-2017.

	$3,275	$2,875	$2,365	$2,000	$1,675	$1,425	$1,200	$3,849

SUPERHERO COMBAT RIFLE – 5.56 NATO cal., GIO, available in "Axe Man", "Captain Axe", or "Super Axe" configuration, 16 in. barrel, Axelson Tactical Talon brake, ALG combat trigger, Bravo B5 Systems buttstock, BCM Gunfighter Mod 1 grip, hardcoat anodized aluminum upper and lower receivers, 12 in. Guntec slim profile lightweight M-LOK rail, BCM Gunfighter Mod 4 charging handle. Mfg. mid-2016-2017.

	$1,675	$1,000	$825	$625	$550	$475	$425	$2,049

TEXAS TRIBUTE RIFLE – 5.56 NATO cal., 16 in. barrel with Nitride finish, Freedom Flag Spiked Star muzzle brake, Cerakote Magpul mag., ALG ACT trigger, B5 SOPMOD stock, BCM Mod 1 grip, custom receiver set with custom Cerakote finish, 15 in. Centurion Arms rail, BCM Gunfighter charging handle, includes hard plastic gun case with backpack. New 2017.

MSR $2,999	$2,550	2,225	$1,825	$1,575	$1,300	$1,100	$950	

VIETNAM SPECIAL PURPOSE LIMITED EDITION – 5.56 NATO cal., GIO, 11 1/2 in. chrome moly steel barrel with 5 1/2 in. permanently attached flash suppressor, ALG combat trigger, fixed forged front sight, LWRCI UCIW ultra compact stock, BCM Gunfighter Mod 1 grip, hardcoat anodized aluminum forged upper and lower receivers, carbine handguards, BCM Gunfighter Mod 4 charging handle, includes three mags., custom box, and challenge coins, Vietnam Tiger Stripe custom Cerakote finish by Nevada Cerakote. Limited mfg. 2016 only.

	$2,125	$1,875	$1,550	$1,325	$1,100	$950	$825	$2,499

This gun was made to capture the spirit of the heroes of the Vietnam era by being a rifle that could be taken into battle today carrying the spirit of all the warriors past - honoring and remembering those who made it home and those who didn't.

A 86 AXELSON TACTICAL, cont.

MSR	100%	98%	95%	90%	80%	70%	60%	Last MSR

VIETNAM VETERANS TRIBUTE RIFLE – 16 in. barrel with Nitride finish, Freedom Flag Spiked Star muzzle brake, Cerakote Magpul mag., ALG ACT trigger, B5 SOPMOD stock, BCM Mod 1 grip, BCM Gunfighter charging handle, Axelson Tactical DLC bolt carrier group, 15 in. Centurion Arms rail, billet receivers with custom Cerakote finish, includes walnut custom wood collectors box with engraving. Limited mfg. of 100 units only beginning 2018.

MSR $2,995	$2,550	2,225	$1,825	$1,575	$1,300	$1,100	$950

UKKO'S HAMMER DMR – 6.5mm Creedmoor, 6.5x47 LM, or .260 Rem. cal., 16 in. Lilja match grade stainless steel barrel, Axelson ROC Competition 762 brake, Geissele SSA-E trigger, JP enhanced BCG, AR10 billet or forged aluminum upper and lower receiver, B5 Systems SOPMOD and Magpul PRS stock, Superlative Arms bleed off gas block, 15 in. Centurion Arms handguard, black anodized or Camo Cerakote finish, 9 1/4 lbs.

MSR $3,245	$2,625	$1,725	$1,300	$725	$650	$595	$525

Add $455 for Camo Cerakote finish.

This model was a special project done in collaboration with Monte Gould of IMTT USA and IMTT Finland.

AZTEK ARMS

Previous rifle manufacturer located in Mapleton, UT until 2015.

RIFLES: SEMI-AUTO

Aztek Arms manufactured AR-15 style rifles in various configurations until 2015.

NOTES

B SECTION

87 B

BCI DEFENSE LLC

Current manufacturer of AR-15 style rifles and accessories, established in 2012 and located in Bremen, IN.

MSR	100%	98%	95%	90%	80%	70%	60%	Last MSR

PISTOLS: SEMI-AUTO

BCI DEFENSE PISTOL – 5.56 NATO or .300 AAC Blackout cal., GIO, 10 1/2 in. barrel, QMS trigger, All Season trigger guard, KAK stabilizer, A2 pistol grip, Mil-Spec safety, forged aluminum upper and lower receiver, 9 in. free float handguard, Type III Class 2 hardcoat anodized black finish, 5.38-5.42 lbs.

| MSR $965 | $825 | $700 | $625 | $575 | $5000 | $425 | $385 | |

Add $20 for .300 AAC Blackout cal.

LIL' DAGGER – 5.56 NATO or .300 AAC Blackout cal., GIO, 10 1/2 in. Faxon Firearms barrel, Envoy 3-prong (5.56 NATO) or Aurora Rainmaker (.300 AAC Blackout) flash hider, ALG Defense combat trigger, All Season trigger guard, SPARC AR red dot sight, SB Tactical stabilizer, Hogue overmolded rubber grip, ambidextrous safety, forged aluminum upper and lower receiver with Battle Worn Cerakote finish, Azimuth Technologies enhanced BCG, 9 in. free float M-LOK handguard, Cerakote finish in blue, Battleship Gray, Burnt Bronze, OD Green, or red, 5.38 lbs. New 2018.

| MSR $1,300 | $1,100 | $995 | $875 | $735 | $650 | $550 | $465 | |

Add $50 for .300 AAC Blackout cal.

PROFESSIONAL SERIES PISTOL – 5.56 NATO or .300 AAC Blackout cal., GIO, 10 1/2 in. Faxon Firearms barrel, 3-prong (5.56 NATO) or Aurora (.300 AAC Blackout) flash hider, 30 shot mag., ALG Defense combat trigger, SB Tactical stabilizer, Ergo grip, ambidextrous safety selector, Azimuth Technologies enhanced BCG, 9 in. free float M-LOK handguard, mid (5.56 NATO) or carbine (.300 AAC Blackout) length gas tube, Hydro Dip or Cerakote finish, 5.38 lbs. New 2018.

| MSR $999 | $850 | $725 | $650 | $585 | $515 | $450 | $395 | |

Add $21 for .300 AAC Blackout cal.

RIFLES: SEMI-AUTO

DAGGER SERIES – 5.56 NATO or .300 AAC Blackout cal., 16 in. Faxon Firearms barrel, Envoy 3-prong (5.56 NATO) or Aurora Rainmaker (.300 AAC Blackout) flash hider, 30 shot mag., ALG Defense combat trigger, All Season trigger guard, Vortex Sparc II (disc.) or SPARC AR red dot sights, Hogue overmolded collapsible buttstock, Mission First Tactical react ergonomic foregrip, Hogue overmolded rubber grips, ambi safety, forged aluminum upper and lower receiver with Battle Worn Cerakote finish, enhanced BCG from Azimuth Technologies, 15 in. free float handguard w/QD sockets (M-LOK compatible), mid (5.56 NATO) or carbine (.300 AAC Blackout) length gas tube, Battleship Grey, blue, Burnt Bronze, OD Green, or red Cerakote finish, 7.13-7.3 lbs.

| MSR $1,425 | $1,175 | $775 | $550 | $465 | $415 | $375 | $350 | |

Add $120 for .300 AAC Blackout cal.

DOMESTIC DEFENSE – 5.56 NATO cal., GIO, 16 in. barrel, A2 flash hider, 30 shot mag., QMS ALG Defense trigger, standard buttstock w/QD socket, A2 pistol grip, forged aluminum upper and lower receiver, plastic M4 handguard with heat shields, Type III Class 2 hardcoat anodized black finish, 6.11 lbs.

| MSR $599 | $515 | $450 | $395 | $350 | $315 | $295 | $275 | |

PROFESSIONAL SERIES – 5.56 NATO, .300 AAC Blackout, or 6.5 Grendel (new 2018) cal., GIO, 16 in. Faxon Firearms barrel, 3-pronged flash hider, 30 shot mag., ALG Defense combat trigger, All Season trigger guard, B5 Systems enhanced SOPMOD stock, Ergo grip, ambidextrous safety, mid (5.56 NATO or 6.5 Grendel) or carbine (.300 AAC Blackout) length gas tube, forged aluminum upper and lower receiver with Cerakote or Hydro Dip finish, Azimuth Technologies BCG, 15 in. free float handguard w/QD sockets (M-LOK compatible), Cerakote finish in Armor Black, FDE, Sniper Grey, or OD Green, Hydro Dip finish in Multicam Black or Vista Camo, 6.48-6.69 lbs.

| MSR $1,140 | $950 | $595 | $495 | $425 | $365 | $335 | $300 | |

Add $120 for .300 AAC Blackout cal.

Add $310 for 6.5 Grendel cal. (new 2018).

Add $60 for Multicam Black or Vista Camo (Hydro Dip) finish.

SENTRY – 5.56 NATO cal., GIO, 16 in. Mossberg barrel, A2 compensator-flash hider, 30 shot mag., QMS trigger from ALG Defense, standard buttstock w/QD sockets, A2 pistol grip, Mil-Spec safety selector, forged aluminum upper and lower receiver, Mil-Spec BCG from Azimuth Technologies, 9 in. free float quad rail handguard, Type III Class 2 hardcoat anodized finish, 6.21 lbs.

| MSR $900 | $765 | $515 | $440 | $375 | $335 | $315 | $295 | |

THE AMERICAN – 5.56 NATO cal., GIO, 16 in. barrel, A2 compensator-flash hider, 30 shot mag., QMS trigger from ALG Defense, standard buttstock w/QD socket, A2 pistol grip, forged aluminum upper and lower receiver, 9, 12, or 15 in. free float handguard (M-LOK compatible), Type III Class 2 hardcoat anodized black finish, 6.04-6.30 lbs.

| MSR $825 | $695 | $500 | $425 | $375 | $335 | $315 | $295 | |

Add $20 for 12 in. or $40 for 15 in. handguard.

B 88 BNTI ARMS

MSR	100%	98%	95%	90%	80%	70%	60%	Last MSR

BNTI ARMS

Current manufacturer of AR-15 style carbines/rifles with headquarters in Jacksonville, FL.

RIFLES/CARBINES: SEMI-AUTO

BNTI Arms also manufactures short-barrel NFA carbines that are not included in this text.

.308 BATTLE RIFLE – .308 Win. cal., GIO, 16 1/2 in. match grade stainless steel barrel, A2 flash hider, Magpul ACS polymer stock, Mil-Spec forged aluminum upper and lower receiver, 13 1/2 in. KeyMod rail. New 2017.

Please contact the company directly for current pricing and availability on this model.

WARRIOR SERIES – 5.56 NATO or 7.62x39mm cal., GIO, 16 in. barrel, A2 flash hider, 28 shot stainless steel mag., Magpul ACS-L polymer stock, Mil-Spec forged aluminum upper and lower receiver, full-length Picatinny rail. New 2017.

Please contact the company directly for current pricing and availability on this model.

BARNES PRECISION MACHINE, INC.

Current semi-auto pistol and rifle manufacturer located in Apex, NC. Dealer and consumer direct sales.

PISTOLS: SEMI-AUTO

CQB PISTOL – 5.56 NATO or .300 AAC Blackout cal., 7 1/2 in. stainless steel barrel with A2 flash hider, breaching tip, BPM bolt carrier group with nickel boron coating, Magpul MBUS sights with front sight adjustment tool, SIG SB15 stabilizing blade, Magpul MOE grip, forged upper and lower receivers, PSFFRS Ultralite Extreme 7 in. handguard with quick detach sling swivel inserts, black or FDE finish. New 2015.

MSR $1,308	$1,100	$995	$875	$735	$650	$550	$465

Add $34 for FDE finish.

RIFLES: SEMI-AUTO

Barnes also manufactures AR-15 parts and accessories. Many options are available for each rifle. Please contact the company directly for a complete list and pricing (see Trademark Index). All rifles include a plastic hard case and one Magpul PMAG.

Add $272 for Basic Robar NP3 coating rifle upgrade.

Add $433 for Maritime Robar NP3 coating rifle upgrade.

BPM BASIC PATROL CARBINE – 5.56 NATO/.223 Rem. cal., mid-length gas system, 16 in. barrel (.223 Wylde chambered), A2 flash hider with breaching tip, M4 stock, A2 grip, PSFFRS Ultralite Extreme 12 1/2 in. handguard in black or FDE finish with quick detach sling swivel inserts, nickel boron BCG, forged upper and lower receiver, Type III hardcoat anodized black finish.

MSR $750	$645	$500	$415	$370	$325	$300	$275

BPM CQB .308 RIFLE – .308 Win. cal., 16 in. stainless steel match grade barrel, flash hider, 20 shot mag., Geissele G2S trigger or HYPERFIRE 24e, MBUS, Magpul MOE stock, Magpul grip, 14 in. ULE handguard, billet upper and lower receivers, includes standard enhanced battle rifle package (EBR), black or FDE finish. Mfg. 2016-2017.

	$2,050	$1,250	$950	$650	$575	$495	$475	$2,550

BPM LONG RANGE .308 RIFLE – 7.62 NATO/.308 Win., or 6.5mm Creedmoor cal., 20 or 24 in. stainless steel match grade barrel, flash hider, 20 shot mag., Geissele G2S trigger or HYPERFIRE 24e, MBUS, Magpul MOE rifle stock, Magpul grip, 14 in. ULE handguard, billet upper and lower receivers, includes standard enhanced battle rifle package (EBR), black or FDE finish. Mfg. 2016-2017.

	$2,225	$1,395	$1,050	$675	$595	$525	$475	$2,700

Add $150 for 6.5mm Creedmoor cal.

BPM LR-10 – 7.62 NATO or 6.5mm Creedmoor cal., 20 or 24 in. stainless steel match grade barrel with flash hider, 20 shot mag., Geissele G2S or HYPERFIRE 24e trigger, MBUS sights, Magpul MOE stock, Magpul grip, BPM 14 in. ULE handguard, billet upper and lower receivers, FDE finish.

MSR $2,700	$2,225	$1,395	$1,050	$675	$595	$525	$475

Add $150 for 6.5mm Creedmoor cal.

CQB MODERN BATTLE RIFLE – .223/5.56 NATO cal., mid-length gas system, 16 in. barrel, A2 flash hider with breaching tip, 30 shot PMAG, Magpul extended mag. release, Magpul trigger guard, Geissele G2S trigger, Magpul MBUS flip-up sights, Magpul K2 grip, Magpul CTR stock, Badger Ordnance G3 ambi charging handle, three Magpul M-LOK handrail covers, Cerakote upper and lower receivers, BPM endplate QD mount, 14 1/2 in. PSFFRS M-LOK handguard in FDE finish with quick detach sling swivel inserts, Forbus Tactical ambi mag. release, includes Patriot hard case.

MSR $2,179	$1,725	$1,050	$850	$625	$550	$475	$425

CQB MOE 16 – .300 AAC Blackout cal., carbine length adj. gas system, 16 in. stainless steel match brade barrel, A2 style flash hider with breaching tip, Magpul MBUS sights with front sight adjustment tool, Magpul MOE stock and grip, 12 1/2 in. PSFFRS Ultralite Extreme handguard in black or FDE finish with quick detach sling swivel inserts and removable bipod stud, nickel boron BCG, forged upper and lower receivers, Type III hardcoat anodized finish.

MSR $1,458	$1,225	$825	$575	$475	$425	$375	$350

BARNES PRECISION MACHINE, INC., cont. 89 B

MSR	100%	98%	95%	90%	80%	70%	60%	Last MSR

CQB PATROLMAN'S CARBINE – 5.56 NATO cal., .223 Wylde chambered, GPO, 16 or 18 (new 2014) in. BPM stainless steel match barrel, low profile gas block, A2 style flash hider, 12 in. Ultralite XT modular free float rail system, optional sling swivels, Magpul MBUS Gen2 sights, 6-position MOE adj. stock, Picatinny rail, breaching tip, black or FDE finish, includes hard plastic Patriot AR case. Disc. 2014.

	$1,100	$675	$525	$450	$400	$350	$325	$1,308

Add $11 for 18 in. barrel (new 2014).
Add $28 for FDE finish.

* ***CQB Patrolman's Carbine .300 Blackout*** – .300 AAC Blackout cal., GIO, carbine length adj. gas system, 16 in. stainless steel barrel with BPM A2 style flash hider, breaching tip, Magpul MOE stock and pistol grip, Magpul MBUS sights, flat-top Picatinny rail receiver with 12 in. quad rail, includes plastic hard case, black finish. Mfg. 2013-2016.

	$1,350	$875	$650	$525	$450	$385	$350	$1,636

* ***CQB Patrolman's Carbine MOE Package*** – 5.56 NATO cal., .223 Wylde chambered, GPO, 16 or 18 (new 2014) in. BPM stainless steel match barrel, stainless steel low profile gas block, A2 style flash hider, 12 in. Ultralite Extreme handguard w/quick detach sling swivel inserts and removable bipod stud, Magpul MBUS Gen2 sights, 6-position Magpul MOE adj. stock, Magpul grip, Picatinny rail, breaching tip, black finish, includes hard plastic Patriot AR case.

MSR $1,458	$1,225	$825	$575	$475	$425	$375	$350	

Add $33 for 18 in. barrel.

DESIGNATED MARKSMAN RIFLE – 5.56 NATO cal., GIO, 18 in. BPM stainless steel match barrel, 2 in. Ultralite XT modular free float rail system, optional sling swivels, A2 fixed (disc. 2013), Magpul PRS, or MOE stock, Picatinny rail, Miculek muzzle brake, Hiperfire match trigger, black finish.

MSR $1,637	$1,350	$875	$650	$525	$450	$385	$350	

Add $157 for Magpul PRS stock.

MARITIME CQB PATROLMAN'S CARBINE – 5.56 NATO cal., .223 Wylde chambered, GPO, 16 in. stainless steel match barrel with A2 flash hider, 12 in. Ultralite Extreme handguard w/quick detach sling swivel inserts and removable bipod stud, Magpul MBUS sights with front sight adjustment tool, Magpul MOE stock and grip, Picatinny rail, breaching tip, Robar NP3 coating on upper, lower, and parts kit, includes hard plastic Patriot AR case. New 2015.

MSR $1,974	$1,650	$1,000	$795	$595	$495	$425	$395	

THREE GUN MATCH CARBINE – .223 Rem./5.56 NATO cal., .223 Wylde chambered, GIO, mid-length gas system, 16 or 18 in. BPM stainless steel match barrel, Miculek compensator, Magpul PMAG, HIPERFIRE match trigger, Magpul MOE (disc.) or ACE SOCOM stock, Magpul MIAD grip, forged upper and lower receiver, MGI style adj. gas tube, 12 1/2 or 14 1/2 in. PSFFRS Ultralite Extreme handguard with quick detach sling swivel inserts and removable bipod stud, includes Patriot AR case, Robar NP3 electroless nickel or black finish.

MSR $1,721	$1,425	$925	$700	$550	$475	$395	$350	

Add $11 for 18 in. barrel.
Add $25 for 14 1/2 in. handguard.

BARRETT FIREARMS MANUFACTURING, INC.

Current manufacturer and shotgun importer established in 1982, located in Murfreesboro, TN. Dealer direct sales.

PISTOLS: SEMI-AUTO

REC7 DI PISTOL – 5.56 NATO, 6.8 SPC, or .300 AAC Blackout cal., GIO, 11 1/2 in. match grade stainless steel barrel, muzzle brake, ALG Defense ACT trigger, black finish. Limited mfg. beginning mid-2017.

MSR $2,499	$2,125	$1,875	$1,550	$1,325	$1,100	$950	$825	

This model is available through participating Barrett R.E.D. partners and distributors. Please contact Barrett Customer Service at 615-896-2938 for more information and availability.

RIFLES: SEMI-AUTO

MODEL M468 – 6.8 SPC cal., 16 in. barrel with muzzle brake, 5, 10, or 30 shot mag., dual spring extractor system, folding front and rear sight, two-stage trigger, aluminum upper and lower receiver, gas block, integrated rail system, choice of full or telescoping 4-position stock, 8 lbs. Mfg. 2005-2008.

	$2,225	$1,395	$1,050	$675	$595	$525	$475	$2,700

Add $1,590 for Model M468 upper conversion kit.

MODEL REC7 – 5.56 NATO or 6.8 SPC cal., AR-15 style, GPO, 16 in. chrome-lined barrel with A2 flash hider, 30 shot mag., aluminum upper and lower receiver, SST, folding front and ARMS rear sight, 6-position MOE stock, ARMS selective integrated rail system (disc.) or Omega X rail (current mfg.), tactical soft case and two mags., 7.62 lbs. Mfg. 2008-2013.

	$1,600	$1,000	$775	$575	$495	$425	$395	$1,950

Add $1,650 per individual upper conversion kit.
Add $676 for Aimpoint Micro T-1 optics (mfg. 2011-2012).

B 90 BARRETT FIREARMS MANUFACTURING, INC., cont.

MSR	100%	98%	95%	90%	80%	70%	60%	Last MSR

MODEL REC7 DI – 5.56 NATO, 6.8 SPC, or .300 AAC Blackout cal., GIO, 16 or 18 in. match grade stainless steel barrel, muzzle brake, 20 (18 in.) or 30 (16 in.) shot mag., ALG Defense ACT trigger, Barrett 15 in. KeyMod handguard, BCM Gunfighter charging handle, black, Tungsten Grey, OD Green, FDE, Multi-Role Brown, or Burnt Bronze receiver finish. New 2016.

| MSR $1,899 | $1,575 | $995 | $775 | $575 | $495 | $425 | $395 | |

MODEL REC7 GEN II – 5.56 NATO or 6.8 SPC cal., GPO, 16 in. barrel with PWS Triad flash suppressor, 30 shot mag., beveled magwell, Geissele SSA trigger, PRI flip-up iron sights, Magpul MOE pistol grip stock, BCM charging handle, Barrett handguard with KeyMod, includes one KeyMod rail attachment and soft carrying case, available in black, Tungsten Grey, FDE, OD Green, Multi-Role Brown (new 2017), or Burnt Bronze (new 2017) finish. New 2014.

| MSR $2,499 | $1,975 | $1,150 | $925 | $650 | $575 | $495 | $425 | |

* ***Model REC7 Gen II DMR*** – 5.56 NATO or 6.8 SPC cal., GPO, 18 in. barrel, Barrett muzzle brake, 10 shot mag., Magpul MBUS Pro sights, Magpul MOE pistol grip stock, Geissele trigger, Barrett handguard with KeyMod rail attachment, available in black, grey, FDE, OD Green, Multi-Role Brown (new 2017), or Burnt Bronze (new 2017) finish, includes soft carrying case. New 2016.

| MSR $2,799 | $2,225 | $1,395 | $1,050 | $675 | $595 | $525 | $475 | |

* ***Model REC7 Gen II Flyweight*** – 5.56 NATO or 6.8 SPC (new 2017) cal., GPO, 16 in. lightweight barrel, thread protector, PWS Triad flash suppressor, 20 shot mag., Geissele trigger, Magpul MOE pistol grip stock, Barrett handguard with KeyMod rail attachment, black, grey, FDE, OD Green, Multi-Role Brown (new 2017), or Burnt Bronze (new 2017) finish, includes soft carrying case. New 2016.

| MSR $2,199 | $1,725 | $1,050 | $850 | $625 | $550 | $475 | $425 | |

BATTLE ARMS DEVELOPMENT, INC. (B.A.D., INC.)

Current manufacturer located in Henderson, NV since 2009.

Battle Arms Development, Inc. (B.A.D. Inc.) is a design, research, and development firm focusing on small arms design including firearm components, tools, gauges, accessories, and complete weapon systems. All Battle Arms Development products are 100% made in the U.S.A.

PISTOLS: SEMI-AUTO

BAD556-LW 300BLK PISTOL – .300 AAC Blackout cal., 7 1/2 in. barrel, 6.7 in. M-LOK handguard, ambi. charging handle, MAGPUL Gen M3 PMAG, lightweight upper and lower receiver, .750 in. dia. titanium gas block, pistol length gas tube, AR-15 semi-auto FCG polished 4 1/2 - 51/2 lbs. pull trigger, carbine buffer spring, Sabertube - Tail Hook Brace combo, 3-pos. ATG grip, ambi safety selector, includes hard polymer rifle case. New 2018.

| MSR $2,110 | $1,795 | $1,575 | $1,325 | $1,150 | $995 | $850 | $700 | |

RIFLES: SEMI-AUTO

BAD556-LW RIFLE – .300 AAC Blackout cal., 16 in. barrel, A2 compensator, Magpul Gen M2 PMAG, enhanced mag. release, Mil-Spec mag. catch, SST, lightweight buttstock combo, 3-pos. ATG grip, carbine buffer spring, lightweight upper and lower receiver, titanium gas block, carbine length gas tube, M16 BCG, Strike Industries Arch charging handle, 15 in. M-LOK handguard, Mil-Spec dust cover assembly, ambi safety selector, includes hard polymer rifle case.

| MSR $2,400 | $1,975 | $1,150 | $925 | $650 | $575 | $495 | $425 | |

BAD556-LW THE 300 SPARTAN RIFLE – 5.56 NATO cal., 16 in. Ultramatch Lightrigid stainless steel fluted barrel (.223 Wylde chamber), VG6 Epsilon compensator or BattleComp, Magpul Gen 2 PMAG with MAGPOD floorplate, MFT Battlelink Minimalist stock, MFT G27 tactical pistol grip, low profile Grade 5 titanium gas block, stainless steel mid-length gas tube, lightweight billet aluminum upper and lower receivers, Fortis Shift short angled foregrip, BCM Gunfighter charging handle, 14 in. Fortis Switch 556 rail system, Mil-Spec ejection port cover, ambi safety selector, CMC trigger, Mil-Spec carbine buffer tube, 300 Spartan inspired custom theme Cerakote paint job, includes hard rifle case, 5.7 lbs.

| MSR $3,100 | $2,550 | $1,650 | $1,250 | $700 | $625 | $575 | $525 | |

BAD556-LW VADER RIFLE – 5.56 NATO cal., 16 in. Ultramatch Lightrigid stainless steel fluted barrel (.223 Wylde chamber), VG6 Epsilon compensator or BattleComp, Magpul Gen 2 PMAG with MAGPOD floorplate, low profile Grade 5 titanium gas block, stainless steel mid-length gas tube, lightweight billet aluminum upper and lower receivers, Fortis Shift short angled foregrip, BCM Gunfighter charging handle, 14 in. Fortis Switch 556 rail system, Mil-Spec ejection port cover, ambi safety selector, CMC trigger, Sabertube buffer tube with lightweight stock, 3-position adj. tactical grip, Darth Vader inspired custom theme Cerakote paint job, includes hard rifle case, 5.4 lbs.

| MSR $3,350 | $2,700 | $1,775 | $1,325 | $750 | $650 | $595 | $525 | |

BATTLE RIFLE COMPANY

Current manufacturer of AR-15 style pistols and rifles established in 2010, located in Houston, TX. Previously located in Seabrook, TX.

BATTLE RIFLE COMPANY, cont. 91 B

MSR	100%	98%	95%	90%	80%	70%	60%	Last MSR

PISTOLS: SEMI-AUTO

BR4 ATTACHE 5.56 – 5.56 NATO cal., 7 1/2 (disc. 2016), 10 1/2, or 11 1/2 (disc. 2016) in. barrel with A2 flash suppressor, Picatinny/M-LOK hybrid rail, black finish, 5 lbs. 6 oz.

MSR $1,195	$1,025	$925	$800	$685	$595	$500	$435	

Add $100 for optional SIG Brace.

BR4 ATTACHE 9MM – 9mm Para. cal., blowback action, Colt SMG configuration with 32 shot straight mag., pistol buffer tube with Nomex cover, single point sling adapter, Ergo pistol grip, black finish. Mfg. 2015-2016.

	$1,200	$1,075	$950	$800	$700	$600	$495	*$1,395*

Add $100 for optional SIG Brace.

RIFLES: SEMI-AUTO

In addition to Cerakote and Duracoat fiinishes, Battle Rifle Company also added custom painting to their rifles beginning in 2016. Colors include: Afghanatan, Artic Jungle, Concrete Jungle, Deep Jungle, Desert Jungle, Norway, Scorched Earth, Sedona, Tundra, Pinko, Battle Royale, and NWU Type 3.

BR4 CUTLASS – 5.56 NATO cal., 16 in. barrel w/muzzle brake, iron sights, collapsible stock, designed for maritime use, vent quad rails, Custom Battle Rifle Ocean Blue finish, 7 lbs. 3 oz. New 2017.

MSR $1,595	$1,315	$850	$625	$500	$435	$375	$350	

BR4 DMR – 5.56 NATO cal., flash suppressor, standard, ECS, or Magpul PRS stock, Ergo pistol grip, black finish. Mfg. 2016-2017.

	$1,475	$950	$725	$550	$475	$395	$350	*$1,795*

BR4 LIT-CARBINE – 5.56 NATO or .300 AAC Blackout cal., 16 or 20 (new 2015) in. SOCOM profile barrel with flash suppressor, 12 or 15 in. free float Gen. 2 SS rail, SST, sling adaptor, enhanced combat stock with Battle Rifle logo, black furniture, available with KeyMod rail. Disc. 2015.

	$1,385	$895	$675	$525	$450	$385	$350	*$1,695*

Add $100 for 20 in. barrel (new 2015).
Add $100 for KeyMod option with 12 in. rail. or $100 for 15 in. rail (disc. 2014).
Add $200 for KeyMod option with 15 in. rail (disc. 2014).

BR4 ODIN – 5.56 NATO cal., 16 in. cryogenically treated barrel with Battle Rifle flash suppressor, mid-length gas port, 12 1/2 in. KeyMod handguard, BAD lever, custom ALG trigger, MFT Minimalist stock, Ergo pistol grip, black furniture, 6.1 lbs. Mfg. 2015-2016.

	$1,475	$950	$725	$550	$475	$395	$350	*$1,795*

BR4 SPARTAN – 5.56 NATO, 6.8 SPC, 7.62x39mm, 7.62x6mm (mfg. 2014-2015), or .300 AAC Blackout (disc. 2017) cal., GIO, choice of 16 in. HBAR profile or SOCOM profile barrel with flash suppressor, gas block with A2 front sight tower, collapsible stock, forged aluminum flat-top upper receiver with Picatinny rall and laser engraved, lower receiver with matching two-piece quad rail, polished trigger, black furniture, Ergo pistol grip, buttstock pad, includes one 30 shot mag. and black case, 6 1/2 lbs.

MSR $1,195	$995	$625	$495	$450	$395	$350	$325	

Add $100 for .300 AAC Blackout cal. (disc. 2017).

BR4 SPECTRE – 5.56 NATO, 6.8 SPC, or .300 AAC Blackout cal., 16 in. HBAR or SOCOM profile barrel with BRC Disintegrator flash suppressor, custom ALG trigger, 11 in. free float quad rail, FAB Defense folding sights, Ergo pistol grip, buttstock pad, micro gas block under quad rail, SST, Hogue buttstock with QD points (disc.) or custom stock from Choate, black or FDE (new 2015) furniture.

MSR $1,195	$995	$625	$495	$450	$395	$350	$325	

Add $100 for FDE finish (new 2015).

BR4 SPR (SPECIAL PURPOSE RIFLE) – .223 Wylde chamber, 18 in. stainless steel barrel, muzzle brake, Geissele SSA trigger, Magpul flip-up sights, Magpul ACS stock, Ergo pistol grip, nickel boron BCG, 15 in. battle rifle HEXrail, single point endplate, black finish. New 2016.

MSR $1,895	$1,575	$995	$775	$575	$495	$425	$395	

BR4 STRYKER – 5.56 NATO cal., 16 in. M4 or SOCOM profile barrel with flash suppressor, flip-up front sight, quad rail with continuous top rail, Ergo pistol grip, buttstock pad, SST, single point sling adapter. Disc. 2014.

	$1,150	$750	$550	$465	$415	$375	$350	*$1,395*

BR4 TRIDENT – 5.56 NATO cal., 16 in. stainless steel barrel, muzzle brake, stainless steel springs, fire control group, pins, and lower parts, "F" type front sight base, Magpul flip-up rear sight, specially designed for MARSEC (Maritime Security), bayonet lug, sling swivel, high temp Cerakote finished upper and lower receivers, buffer tube, 7 in. free float slim quad rail, M4 buttstock, M4 pistol grip. New 2016.

MSR $1,595	$1,315	$850	$625	$500	$435	$375	$350	

B 92 BATTLE RIFLE COMPANY, cont.

MSR	100%	98%	95%	90%	80%	70%	60%	Last MSR

BR4 TROOPER – 5.56 NATO cal., 16 in. M4 profile barrel with A2 flash hider, 30 shot mag., carbine or mid-length, optional quad rail, carry handle with sights, collapsible or MOE stock, black furniture.

MSR $995	$850	$550	$465	$395	$350	$325	$295	

Add $100 for mid-length, quad rail, or MOE stock (disc. 2014).

Add $154 for mid-length MOE Trooper model (disc. 2014).

BR4 WOLVERINE – 5.56 NATO or .300 AAC Blackout cal., 16 in. M4 profile barrel, 5 1/2 in. simulated suppressor, 15 1/2 in. KeyMod rail, front and rear flip-up sights, Ergo pistol grip, Mission First Tactical stock, single point sling adaptor, black furniture. Mfg. 2014 only.

	$1,315	$850	$625	$500	$435	$375	$350	$1,595

BR10 – 7.62 NATO cal., 16 or 18 in. stainless steel cryogenically treated barrel w/polygonal rifling, compact muzzle brake, Geissele SSA two-stage trigger, Magpul Pro sights, Magpul ACS adj. stock, AXTS Raptor charging handle, BAD ambidextrous selector switch, QD single point sling back plate, ODIN Works T6 rail with 5 slot accessory rail, black Nitride finish, 8 lbs. 11 oz. New 2017.

MSR $2,895	$2,295	$1,450	$1,075	$675	$595	$525	$475	

BR15 DMR – 5.56 NATO cal., 20 in. heavy barrel with flash suppressor, rifle length quad rail, Harris style bipod, SST or two-stage trigger, Ergo pistol grip, standard, ECS, or Magpul PRS stock, black furniture.

MSR $1,695	$1,385	$895	$675	$525	$450	$385	$350	

Add $200 for Magpul PRS stock (disc. 2014).

BR15 LIT-RIFLE – 5.56 NATO or .300 AAC Blackout cal., GIO, light infantry tactical rifle, 16 (disc. 2013) or 20 in. threaded, chrome-lined barrel with flash suppressor, 30 shot mag., Magpul MBUS front and rear sights, M16 bolt carrier with nickel finish, forged flat-top upper receiver with Picatinny rail, laser, and free float 12 (16 in. barrel, disc. 2013) or 15 (20 in. barrel) in. rail, forged aluminum lower receiver, polished trigger, ECS stock, single point sling endplate, includes black case, 6.7-7.9 lbs. Disc. 2014.

	$1,385	$895	$675	$525	$450	$385	$350	$1,695

Add $100 for two-stage trigger option.

BR15 STANDARD – 5.56 NATO cal., 20 in. barrel with A2 flash suppressor, 30 shot mag., rifle length polymer handguards, carry handle rear sight, standard A2 fixed stock and pistol grip, SST, black furniture. Disc. 2015.

	$1,075	$675	$500	$450	$400	$350	$325	$1,295

BR15 PATROLMAN – 5.56 NATO cal., GIO, 16 in. steel straight profile barrel with flash suppressor, 30 shot mag., collapsible stock, carbine or mid-length forearm, black furniture, 7 1/2 lbs. Disc. 2013.

	$1,195	$795	$550	$465	$415	$375	$350	$1,449

BR15 VARMITEER – 5.56 NATO cal., 18 or 20 in. heavy barrel, low profile gas block, 10 shot mag., rifle length forend tube, optics ready, Ergo pistol grip, Magpul stock, available in black, Desert Tan pattern, or Woodland pattern finish. Disc. 2014.

	$1,075	$675	$500	$450	$400	$350	$325	$1,295

BR15 6mmx45 – 6mmx45 cal., AR-15 style, 18 or 20 in. barrel, mid (18 in.) or rifle (20 in.) length gas sytem, KeyMod 15 1/2 in. rail, ECS stock, black furniture, includes bipod. Disc. 2014.

	$1,315	$850	$625	$500	$435	$375	$350	$1,595

Add $100 for 20 in. barrel.

BR16 PRECISION TACTICAL RIFLE – 5.56 NATO cal., GIO, 20 in. heavy threaded barrel with flash suppressor, 30 shot mag., gas block with A2 front sight tower, forged aluminum lower and flat-top upper with Picatinny rail and laser engraved, two-piece quad rail, polished trigger, black furniture, fixed or adj. stock, includes bipod match 600 meter sights and black case. Disc. 2013.

	$1,385	$895	$675	$525	$450	$385	$350	$1,695

Add $100 for Magpul PRS or CAA Ansl adj. stock.

BR308 (WARHAMMER) – .308 Win. cal., GIO, 16, 18, or 20 in. barrel with Disintegrator flash suppressor, Geissele SSA trigger system, enhanced combat stock system w/sling swivel attachment and easy grip adjustments, cheek weld designed finish w/Battle Rifle logo, Harris style bipod (18 or 20 in. only), forearm grip (16 in. only), 6-position buffer tube, ambi charging handle, Magpul front and rear MBUS sights, custom ambi pistol grip, heavy buffer, low profile gas block, additional rails for lights/optics, ambi fire control selector switch (option), includes one mag. and tactical bag. Disc. 2016.

	$2,125	$1,325	$995	$675	$595	$525	$475	$2,695

Add $100 for 18 in. barrel or $200 for 20 in. barrel.

DEFENDER – 5.56 NATO cal., 16 in. barrel, A2 flash suppressor, M4 buttstock, Mil-Spec pistol grip, rail height front gas block, M4 handguards. New 2016.

MSR $795	$675	$500	$425	$375	$335	$315	$295	

MSR	100%	98%	95%	90%	80%	70%	60%	Last MSR

BAZOOKA BROTHERS MFG.

Current manufacturer of AR-15 style carbines/rifles, pistols, and components established circa 2002, located in Russiaville, IN.

PISTOLS: SEMI-AUTO

MODEL B-AR45 PISTOL – 8 or 10 in. barrel, M4 or quad rail handguard, buffer tube, RMW extreme upper receiver, black finish.

Please contact the company directly for more information including price, options, and availability (see Trademark Index).

RIFLES/CARBINES: SEMI-AUTO

MODEL B-AR45 CARBINE – .45 ACP cal., AR-15 style, 16 in. Melonite barrel, A2 flash hider, A2 front sight, 6-pos. CAR stock, quad rail handguard, black finish.

MSR $1,235	$1,050	$650	$495	$450	$395	$350	$325

BLACK CREEK PRECISION

Current manufacturer of AR-15 style pistols, rifles, and shotguns located in Jacksonville, FL.

PISTOLS: SEMI-AUTO

BCP 6.75 – 9mm Para. cal., 6 3/4 in. threaded barrel, A2 flash hider, two 20 shot Colt-style mags., Ergo grip, aluminum alloy upper receiver, Picatinny rail, 5 1/2 in. ODIN Works KeyMod handguard, bolt carrier assembly, stainless steel firing pin, SB15 pistol brace, bullet pictogram safety markings, aluminum trigger guard, Type III Class 2 hardcoat anodized black finish, 7 1/2 lbs.

MSR $1,459	$1,235	$1,100	$985	$835	$725	$615	$515

BCP 10 – 9mm Para. cal., 10 in. threaded barrel, A2 flash hider, two 20 shot Colt-style mags., Ergo grip, aluminum alloy upper receiver, Picatinny rail, 9 1/2 in. ODIN WorksKeyMod handguard, bolt carrier assembly, stainless steel firing pin, SB15 pistol brace, bullet pictogram safety markings, aluminum trigger guard, Type III Class 2 hardcoat anodized black finish, 7 1/2 lbs.

MSR $1,559	$1,315	$1,165	$1,050	$915	$785	$665	$550

RIFLES: SEMI-AUTO

AR15 PATROL/PATROL SERIES RIFLE – 5.56 NATO or 7.62 NATO cal., carbine length gas tube, 16 1/2 in. steel barrel, A2 flash hider, one 30 shot Magpul PMAG (5.56 NATO) or one 28 shot anti-tilt stainless steel mag. (7.62 NATO), A2 front sight or flip-up front sight, Rogers Super-Stoc, BCP QD endplate, standard M4 grip, aluminum buffer tube, charging handle, Type III Class 2 hardcoat anodized black finish, 7 lbs.

MSR $899	$765	$515	$440	$375	$335	$315	$295

Add $330 for 7.62 NATO cal.

BCP .308 BATTLE RIFLE – .308 Win. cal., 16 1/2 in. match grade barrel, Magpul ACS stock, 90 degree ambidextrous safety selector, BCP or ODIN Works 13 1/2 in. KeyMod handguard, matched forged upper and lower receiver, Type III Class 2 hardcoat anodized black finish, Cerakote colors optional, 8 lbs.

MSR $2,299	$1,795	$1,050	$875	$625	$550	$475	$425

ENHANCED ENTRY LEVEL CARBINE – 5.56 NATO cal., 16 1/2 in. stainless steel barrel, A2 flash hider, A2 front sight, Magpul MOE stock, forged upper and lower receiver w/M4 feed ramp, Picatinny rail, Type III Class 2 hardcoat anodized black, carbon fiber, FDE, OD Green, Highlander Camo, ATACS Foliage Green, Bounty Hunter, Inglorious Ingot, Zack Green Jelly Bean, Pink Muddy Girl or High Desert finish, 7 lbs.

MSR $1,029	$875	$550	$465	$395	$350	$325	$300

Add $39 for FDE finish.
Add $149 for carbon fiber, Highlander Camo, ATACS Foliage Green, Bounty Hunter, Inglorious Ingot, Zack Green Jelly Bean, Pink Muddy Girl or High Desert finish.

STANDARD 9MM WITH ODIN RAIL – 9mm Para. cal., 16 in. steel threaded barrel, A2 flash hider, two 20 shot Colt-style mags., aluminum frame, Rogers Super-Stoc, BCP QD endplate, Ergo grip, 15 1/2 in. ODIN Works KeyMod handguard, aluminum forged upper receiver, M4 feed ramps, 1913 Picatinny rail, aluminum charging handle, bullet pictogram safety markings, Type III Class 2 hardcoat anodized black finish, 7 1/2 lbs.

MSR $1,299	$1,075	$675	$500	$450	$400	$350	$325

BLACK DAWN ARMORY (BLACK DAWN INDUSTRIES)

Current manufacturer of semi-auto pistols and rifles located in Sedalia, MO since 2010.

Black Dawn Armory currently manufactures a complete line of AR-15 style rifles as well as designing their own parts. Their Pro-Shop offers accessories geared toward the AR market, and they also have their own in-house Custom Shop that offers a wide range of services and finish options.

B 94 BLACK DAWN ARMORY (BLACK DAWN INDUSTRIES), cont.

MSR	100%	98%	95%	90%	80%	70%	60%	Last MSR

PISTOLS: SEMI-AUTO

BDP-556-10DMM – 5.56 NATO cal., 10 1/2 in. barrel, Magpul PMAG, enhanced trigger guard, ALG Defense QMS trigger, Ergo grip, T6 aluminum upper and lower receivers, laser engraved T-marks, M4 feed ramps, 9 in. MMR free float forend, ODIN Works pistol buffer tube, ambi sling mount, Type III hardcoat anodized finish in black, FDE, or OD Green. Mfg. 2016-2017.
Retail pricing was not available for this model.

BDP-300-8SFC – .300 AAC Blackout cal., 8 1/2 in. barrel, Magpul PMAG, ALG Defense QMS trigger, enhanced trigger guard, Ergo grip, 7 in. MFRC free float forend, T6 aluminum upper and lower receivers, laser engraved T-marks, M4 feed ramps, ODIN Works pistol buffer tube, ambi sling mount, Type III hardcoat anodized black finish. Mfg. 2016-2017.
Retail pricing was not available for this model.

RIFLES: SEMI-AUTO

BDR-10 – .308 Win. cal., GIO, 16 or 20 in. M4 profile barrel, Magpul MOE collapsible stock, Magpul MOE grip, flared magwell, free floating handguard, Magpul 20 shot PMAG, black anodized finish, includes hard case. Mfg. 2012-2014.
Retail pricing was not available for this model.

BDR-15A – 5.56 NATO/.223 Rem. cal., GIO, 16 in. M4 profile barrel with A2 flash hider, 30 shot PMAG, A2 front sight, MBUS rear sight, Magpul MOE collapsible stock, Magpul MOE grip, enhanced trigger guard, flared magwell, ambi sling mount, M4 feed ramp, carbine length MFR rail, black, FDE, or OD Green finish, includes hard case, 6 lbs. 10 oz. Mfg. 2012-2014.

	100%	98%	95%	90%	80%	70%	60%	Last MSR
	$1,050	$650	$495	$450	$395	$350	$325	*$1,249*

BDR-15B – 5.56 NATO/.223 Rem. cal., GIO, 16 in. M4 profile barrel with A2 flash hider, 30 shot PMAG, MBUS front and rear sights, Magpul MOE collapsible stock, Magpul MOE grip, enhanced trigger guard, flared magwell, ambi sling mount, M4 feed ramp, mid-length MFR rail, black, FDE, or OD Green finish, includes hard case, 6 lbs. 15 oz. Disc. 2017.

	100%	98%	95%	90%	80%	70%	60%	Last MSR
	$1,075	$675	$500	$450	$400	$350	$325	*$1,279*

BDR-50B-16LMR – .50 BMG cal., 16 in. barrel, Magpul PMAG, Black Dawn enhanced trigger guard, ALG Defense QMS trigger, 6-pos. collapsible MOE stock, Ergo grip, ambi sling mount, 12.6 or 15.1 in. free float MFR handguard, CNC machined T6 aluminum upper and lower receivers, laser engraved T-Marks, M4 feed ramps, IonBonded BCG, black, FDE, or OD Green finish.

MSR $1,500	$1,250	$825	$575	$475	$425	$375	$350	

BDR-243 22W – .308 Win., .243 Rem., .260 Rem., or 6.5mm Creedmoor cal., 22 in. stainless steel barrel, ALG Defense QMS trigger, enhanced trigger guard, Magpul fixed MOE stock, Ergo grip, 15 in. free float KeyMod handguard, nickel boron BCG, billet charging handle with badger latch, adj. gas block, includes Patriot case with foam cutouts, black finish. New 2018.

MSR $2,000	$1,675	$1,000	$825	$625	$550	$475	$425	

BDR-556 3GLW (3 GUN LIGHTWEIGHT) – 5.56 NATO cal., 16 in. barrel, Lantac brake, Mission First Minimalist stock, X-Tech tactical grip, Black Dawn receiver set, 15 in. MMR BD rail, IonBond BCG, SST, black finish, 6.2 lbs. New 2018.

MSR $1,400	$1,150	$750	$550	$465	$415	$375	$350	

BDR-556-16AFC – 5.56 NATO cal., GIO or GPO, 16 in. barrel, Magpul PMAG, enhanced trigger guard, ALG Defense QMS trigger, 6-pos. collapsible MOE stock, Ergo grip, ambi sling mount, CNC machined T6 aluminum upper and lower receivers, laser engraved T-Marks, M4 feed ramps, IonBonded BCG, Black Dawn free float forend, black, FDE, or OD Green finish.

MSR $1,250	$1,050	$650	$495	$450	$395	$350	$325	

Add $230 for gas piston operation (GPO).

BDR-556-16APFC-BLK (BDR-15AP) – 5.56 NATO/.223 Rem. cal., GPO, 16 in. M4 profile barrel with A2 flash hider, A2 front sight, MBUS rear sight, 30 shot mag., Magpul MOE collapsible stock, Magpul MOE grip, enhanced trigger guard, flared magwell, ambi sling mount, M4 feed ramp, carbine length MFR rail, black, FDE (disc. 2014), or OD Green (disc. 2014) finish, includes hard case and one 30 shot PMAG, 6 lbs. 10 oz. Mfg. 2012-2017.

	100%	98%	95%	90%	80%	70%	60%	Last MSR
	$1,275	$850	$600	$495	$425	$375	$350	*$1,549*

BDR-556-16BMR – 5.56 NATO cal., GIO or GPO, 16 in. barrel, Magpul PMAG, Black Dawn enhanced trigger guard, ALG Defense QMS trigger, 6-pos. collapsible MOE stock, Ergo grip, ambi sling mount, CNC machined T6 aluminum upper and lower receivers, laser engraved T-Marks, M4 feed ramps, IonBonded BCG, 9.3, 12.6, or 15.1 in. MFR free float handguard, black, FDE, or OD Green finish.

MSR $1,280	$1,075	$675	$500	$450	$400	$350	$325	

Add $240 for gas piston operation (GPO).

BDR-556-16BPFM (BDR-15BP) – 5.56 NATO/.223 Rem. cal., GPO, 16 in. M4 profile barrel with A2 flash hider, MBUS front and rear sights, 30 shot mag., Magpul MOE collapsible stock, Magpul MOE grip, enhanced trigger guard, flared magwell, ambi sling mount, M4 feed ramp, mid-length MFR rail, available in black, FDE (disc. 2014), or OD Green (disc. 2014) finish, includes hard case and one 30 shot PMAG, 6 lbs. 15 oz. Disc. 2017.

	100%	98%	95%	90%	80%	70%	60%	Last MSR
	$1,275	$850	$600	$495	$425	$375	$350	*$1,549*

BLACK DAWN ARMORY (BLACK DAWN INDUSTRIES), cont. 95 B

MSR	100%	98%	95%	90%	80%	70%	60%	Last MSR

BDR-556-16M (BDR-15M) – 5.56 NATO/.223 Rem. cal., GIO or GPO, 16 in. M4 profile barrel with A2 flash hider, A2 front sight, MBUS rear sight, 30 shot mag., Magpul 6-pos. collapsible stock, Magpul MOE grip, enhanced trigger guard, flared magwell, ambi sling mount, M4 feed ramp, carbine length MFR rail, available in black, FDE, or OD Green finish, includes hard case and one 30 shot PMAG, 7 lbs.

| MSR $1,200 | $995 | $625 | $495 | $450 | $395 | $350 | $325 | |

Add $230 for gas piston operation (GPO).

BDR-556-16MP (BDR-15MP) – 5.56 NATO/.223 Rem. cal., GPO, 16 in. M4 profile barrel with A2 flash hider, A2 front sight, MBUS rear sight, 30 shot mag., Magpul MOE collapsible stock, Magpul MOE grip, enhanced trigger guard, flared magwell, ambi sling mount, M4 feed ramp, carbine length MFR rail, available in black, FDE (disc. 2015), or OD Green (disc. 2015) finish, includes hard case and one 30 shot PMAG, 7 lbs. Mfg. 2012-2017.

| | $1,275 | $850 | $600 | $495 | $425 | $375 | $350 | *$1,549* |

BDR-556-20EML (BDR-15E) – 5.56 NATO/.223 Rem. cal., AR-15 style, GIO or GPO, 20 in. M4 profile heavy barrel, target crown, 30 shot mag., enhanced trigger guard, ALG Defense QMS trigger, no sights, Magpul MOE fixed A2 stock, Ergo grip, 15 in. free floating handguard, M4 feed ramps, black anodized finish, 8 lbs. 9 oz.

| MST $1,250 | $1,050 | $650 | $495 | $450 | $395 | $350 | $325 | |

Add $230 for gas piston operation (GPO).

BDR-300-16FFM (BDR-15BLK) – .300 AAC Blackout cal., GIO, 16 in. M4 profile barrel with A2 flash hider, no sights, 30 shot mag., Magpul MOE collapsible stock, Magpul MOE grip, enhanced trigger guard, flared magwell, ambi sling mount, M4 feed ramp, mid-length MFR rail, available in black, FDE, or OD Green finish, includes hard case and one 30 shot PMAG, 6 lbs. 11 oz. Mfg. 2012-2017.

| | $1,075 | $675 | $500 | $450 | $400 | $350 | $325 | *$1,299* |

BDR-16A – 5.56 NATO/.223 Rem. cal., GIO, 16 in. barrel, A2 front sight, MBUS rear sight, Magpul MOE collapsible stock, Magpul MOE grip, available in black, Flat Dark Earth, or OD Green finish. Mfg. 2015-2017.

| | $1,050 | $650 | $495 | $450 | $395 | $350 | $325 | *$1,249* |

* **BDR-16AP** – 5.56 NATO cal., similar to BDR-16A, except features GPO. Mfg. 2015-2017.

| | $1,225 | $825 | $575 | $475 | $425 | $375 | $350 | *$1,475* |

BDR-16 BLK – .300 AAC Blackout cal., 16 in. barrel, free float MFR handguard, IonBonded heavy bolt carrier group, forged aluminum upper and lower receivers, Magpul pistol grip, MOE collapsible stock, black, FDE, or ODG finish, 6 lbs. 7 oz. Mfg. 2015-2017.

| | $1,050 | $650 | $495 | $450 | $395 | $350 | $325 | *$1,250* |

BDR-16M – 5.56 NATO cal., GIO, 16 in. barrel, Magpul PMAG, ALG Defense QMS trigger, MBUS rear sight, A2 front sight, MOE 6-pos. collapsible stock, Magpul MOE pistol grip, IonBonded heavy bolt carrier group, forged aluminum upper and lower receivers, Magpul MOE handguard, black, FDE, or ODG finish, 7 lbs. New 2015.

| MSR $2,000 | $995 | $625 | $495 | $450 | $395 | $350 | $325 | |

* **BDR-16MP** – 5.56 NATO cal., similar to BDR-16M, except features GPO. Mfg. 2015-2017.

| | $1,150 | $750 | $550 | $465 | $415 | $375 | $350 | *$1,399* |

300 AAC BLACKOUT – .300 AAC Blackout cal., 16 in. barrel, Magpul PMAG, Black Dawn enhanced trigger guard, ALG Defense QMS trigger, 6-pos. collapsible MOE stock, Ergo grip, ambi sling mount, 9.3, 12.6, or 15.1 in. MFR Black Dawn free float forend, CNC machined T6 aluminum upper and lower receivers, laser engraved T-Marks, M4 feed ramps, IonBonded BCG, black, OD Green, or FDE finish. New 2018.

| MSR $1,300 | $1,075 | $675 | $500 | $450 | $400 | $350 | $325 | |

ALPHA – 5.56 NATO cal., GIO, custom built model featuring 16 in. M4 profile barrel with A2 muzzle brake and M4 extensions, fixed A2 front sight, forged aluminum upper and lower receivers, flat-top upper receiver w/M4 feed ramp, enhanced flared magwell, standard A2 grip, 6-position collapsible stock, black anodized finish, accessories include Black Dawn rear flip sight, two 30 shot mags., and a case, 9 lbs. Disc. 2014.

Retail pricing was not available for this model.

BRAVO – 5.56 NATO cal., GIO, custom built model similar to Alpha, except accessories include extended Black Dawn MFR free float rail enclosing a low profile gas block, Black Dawn front and rear flip-up sights, two 30 shot mags., and hard case. Disc. 2014.

Retail pricing was not available for this model.

CHARLIE EDITION – 5.56 NATO cal., GPO, custom built model, 16 in. M4 profile barrel with A2 muzzle brake and M4 extensions, two 30 shot mags., Black Dawn rear flip-up sight, includes hard case. Disc. 2014.

Retail pricing was not available for this model.

B 96 BLACK DAWN ARMORY (BLACK DAWN INDUSTRIES), cont.

MSR	100%	98%	95%	90%	80%	70%	60%	Last MSR

DELTA EDITION – 5.56 NATO cal., custom built model featuring GPO, 16 in. M4 profile barrel and M4 extensions, two 30 shot mags., forged aluminum lower and flat-top upper receiver with M4 feed ramps, enhanced flared magwell, standard A2 grip, 6-position collapsible stock, Black Dawn MFR free float rail enclosing a Black Dawn low profile gas block, front and rear flip-up sights, includes hard case, black anodized finish, 9 lbs. Disc. 2014.

Retail pricing was not available for this model.

ECHO EDITION – 5.56 NATO cal., GIO, custom built model featuring 20 in. HBAR profile barrel, M4 extensions, 11 in. target crown, fluted and vented free float tube forend with sling swivel stud, 4-rail Picatinny gas block, flat-top upper receiver with M4 feed ramp, enhanced flared magwell, A2 fixed stock, Hogue overmolded pistol grip, black anodized finish, accessories include two 20 shot mags. and hard case. Disc. 2014.

Retail pricing was not available for this model.

MOE EDITION – 5.56 NATO cal., GIO, custom built model featuring 16 in. M4 profile barrel with A2 muzzle brake and M4 extensions, fixed A2 front and Magpul MBUS rear sights, forged aluminum lower and flat-top upper receiver w/M4 feed ramps, enhanced flared magwell, Magpul MOE carbine length handguard, Magpul MOE pistol grip and Magpul MOE 6-position collapsible stock, black anodized finish, includes one 30 shot mag. and hard case, 9 lbs. Disc. 2014.

Retail pricing was not available for this model.

ZOMBIE SLAYER – 5.56 NATO cal., GIO, custom built model similar to Alpha, except accessories included are one 30 shot Zombie magazine and hard case. Disc. 2014.

Retail pricing was not available for this model.

BLACK FORGE LLC

The assets of Black Forge were acquired by Invincible Arms, LLC located in Willoughby, OH, beginning 2015. Invincible Arms operates that brand exclusively as the parts and components arm of the company. Black Forge previously manufactured semi-auto pistols and rifles until 2014, and was located in Orlando, FL.

PISTOLS: SEMI-AUTO

TIER 1 PISTOL – 5.56 NATO cal., AR-15 style, GIO, 10 1/2 in. carbine length barrel with Carlson Comps TAC brake, aluminum flat-top A3 upper receiver, aluminum forged lower receiver, 10 1/2 in. modular rail system with full-length top Picatinny rail, two 3 in. and one 5 in. rail sections, M4 feed ramps, 30 shot detachable mag., Black Forge winter trigger guard, single stage trigger, Magpul industries or U.S. Palm Battle grip, investment cast fire controls, Carpenter M16 LEO bolt carrier group with Black Forge Niphos coating, hardcoat anodized matte black finish. Mfg. 2014-2015.

	100%	98%	95%	90%	80%	70%	60%	Last MSR
	$1,125	$995	$850	$775	$625	$500	$425	$1,250

* **Tier 1 Pistol SIG PSB** – 5.56 NATO cal., similar to Tier 1 pistol, except has fully adj. SIG PSB tactical style stock. Mfg. 2014-2015.

	100%	98%	95%	90%	80%	70%	60%	Last MSR
	$1,250	$1,095	$950	$850	$695	$575	$450	$1,385

RIFLES: SEMI-AUTO

All Black Forge rifles and carbines came with a limited lifetime warranty.

A3 FLAT-TOP CARBINE – 5.45x39mm (disc. 2014) or 5.56 NATO cal., GIO, 16 1/2 in. chrome moly steel barrel with A2 birdcage flash hider, A3 flat-top removable carry handle, A2 front sight post gas block, adj. rear sights, 6-position collapsible stock and poly grip with Mil-Spec size buffer tube, double shield M4 handguard, black furniture. Disc. 2015.

	100%	98%	95%	90%	80%	70%	60%	Last MSR
	$800	$525	$450	$385	$340	$325	$295	$949

Add $100 for 5.45x39mm cal. (disc. 2014).

BF15 M4 TIER 1 – 5.56 NATO cal., AR-15 style, GIO, 16 1/2 in. M4 barrel with A2 birdcage flash suppressor, F-Marked A2 front sight post gas block, 30 shot mag., aluminum flat-top A3 upper receiver w/Picatinny rail, Magpul MBUS Gen2 or A.R.M.S. rear flip-up sight, double shield M4 handguard, Magpul (disc. 2013) or Black Forge winter (new 2014) trigger guard, aluminum forged lower receiver w/Black Forge logo, SST, Rogers Super-Stoc with Cam-Lock System, 6-position collapsible stock w/buffer tube, Magpul MOE or U.S. Palm Battle (new 2014) grip, black furniture, Black Forge Niphos coating (new 2014). Disc. 2015.

	100%	98%	95%	90%	80%	70%	60%	Last MSR
	$915	$575	$475	$415	$350	$325	$300	$1,099

BF15 M4 TIER 2 – 5.56 NATO or 5.45x39mm (disc. 2014) cal., AR-15 style, GIO, 16 1/2 in. M4 barrel with A2 birdcage flash hider, F-Marked A2 front sight post gas block, aluminum flat-top A3 upper receiver with Mil-Spec 1913 Picatinny rail system featuring M4 feed ramps, aluminum forged lower receiver with Black Forge logo, SST, Magpul Industries MBUS Gen 2 or A.R.M.S. rear flip-up sight, double heat shield M4 handguard, 6-pos. collapsible stock with Mil-Spec size buffer tube, standard M4 furniture and manganese phosphate BCG finish, black, Kryptek Typhon or Urban Red camo (new 2014) finish. Disc. 2015.

	100%	98%	95%	90%	80%	70%	60%	Last MSR
	$850	$550	$465	$395	$350	$325	$295	$999

Add $100 for Urban Red camo (new 2014) or Kryptek Typhon finish.

BLACK FORGE LLC, cont. 97 B

MSR	100%	98%	95%	90%	80%	70%	60%	Last MSR

BF15 M4 TIER 3 – 5.56 NATO cal., GIO, 16 1/2 in. M4 barrel with A2 birdcage flash hider, F-Marked A2 front sight post gas block, aluminum flat-top A3 upper receiver with Mil-Spec Picatinny rail system featuring M4 feed ramps, double shield M4 handguard, forged aluminum lower, SST, 6-pos. collapsible stock with Mil-Spec size buffer tube, black furniture. Mfg. 2014-2015.

	$765	$515	$440	$375	$335	$315	$295	*$899*

BF15 TIER 1R – .300 AAC Blackout cal., 16 1/2 in. M4 barrel with Carlson Impact muzzle brake, 6-pos. collapsible stock with Mil-Spec size buffer tube, low profile gas block, 13 1/2 in. modular rail system with full-length top Picatinny rail, two 3 in. and one 5 in. rail sections, aluminum flat-top A3 upper receiver, M4 feed ramps, aluminum forged lower with Black Forge logo and safety designations, Black Forge winter trigger guard, Rogers Super-Stoc with innovative Cam-Lock System, stainless springs, Magpul Industries or U.S. Palm Battle grip, Black Forge Niphos BCG coating. Disc. 2015.

	$1,175	$775	$550	$465	$415	$375	$350	*$1,425*

BF15 YOUTH M4 – 5.56 NATO cal., GIO, 16 1/2 in. threaded barrel with F-marked A2 front sight post gas block, aluminum flat-top A3 upper with Mil-Spec Picatinny rail system featuring M4 feed ramps, SST, forged lower receiver, 6-pos. Roger's Super-Stoc with buffer tube, slim carbine handguards, M4 accessories, black furniture, anodized type 2 color DiamondDyze finish in orange, violet, green, blue, or red. Disc. 2015.

	$850	$550	$465	$395	$350	$325	$295	*$979*

MID-PISTON DRIVEN CARBINE – 5.56 NATO cal., Adams Arms mid-length piston driven operating system, 16 1/2 in. Voodoo Innovations Government Contour barrel with VG6 Epsilon muzzle brake, 30 shot detachable mag., aluminum flat-top A3 upper receiver with Mil-Spec 1913 Picatinny rail system and M4 feed ramps, aluminum forged lower receiver, Black Forge winter trigger guard, B5 SOPMOD stock with Damage Industries QD stock endplate, Damage Industries vertical grip, Magpul MOE grip, sling swivels, billet charging handle with V3 extended latch, ODIN Works 9 in. KeyMod handguard, custom Cerakote finish in Blue Titanium, Foliage Green, or FDE. Mfg. 2014-2015.

	$1,315	$850	$625	$500	$435	$375	$350	*$1,599*

Add $50 for Blue Titanium finish.

CAR PISTON DRIVEN CARBINE – 5.56 NATO cal., similar to Mid-Piston Driven Carbine, except has Roger's Super-Stoc and PWS enhanced buffer tube, available in Sniper Green, Sniper Gray, and Burnt Bronze finish. Mfg. 2014-2015.

	$1,275	$850	$600	$495	$425	$375	$350	*$1,549*

Subtract $150 for Burnt Bronze finish.

BLACKHEART FIREARMS (BLACKHEART INTERNATIONAL LLC)

Current firearms manufacturer located in Clarksburg, WV. Previously located in Fairmont and Philippi, WV. The company also manufactures separate components for AK-47 and AR-15 style carbines/rifles, in addition to custom bolt actions and barreled actions.

PISTOLS: SEMI-AUTO

BHI-15 S2 AR57 PISTOL – 5.7x28mm cal., 12 in. free float barrel, aluminum upper and lower receiver, Geissele Super Dynamic Combat trigger, Wolff trigger springs, Stark SE-1 pistol grip, black anodized finish. Disc 2014.

	$1,100	$995	$875	$735	$650	$550	$465	*$1,304*

RIFLES: SEMI-AUTO

Blackheart International also makes a variety of NFA carbines for military and law enforcement.

3g PRO – 5.56 NATO cal., AR-15 style, mid-length gas system, 16 in. Wilson Combat match grade stainless steel barrel with Rolling Thunder compensator, 30 shot mag., BHI aluminum free float modular handguard with full-length top rail, Geissele Super Dynamic Combat two-stage trigger group, Mil-Spec A3 flat-top aluminum upper and BHI-15 Multi caliber aluminum lower receiver, MBUS Pro Offset sights, BHI-Stark pistol grip, Magpul CTR collapsible stock, hardcoat anodized black finish. New 2015.

MSR $2,395		$1,875	$1,100	$895	$650	$575	$495	$425

BHI-15 (A) – 5.56 NATO cal., AR-15 style, GIO, 16 in. chrome-lined barrel, 30 shot mag., manganese phosphate barrel finish, A2 flash hider, standard collapsible stock, polycarbonate handguard, A3 flat-top upper and aluminum lower receiver, standard charging handle, front post sight, rear aperture sight, Mil-Spec trigger group, Wolff springs, detachable carry handle, hardcoat anodized black finish. Disc. 2014.

	$1,050	$650	$495	$450	$395	$350	$325	*$1,245*

BHI-15 MIL-SPEC2 AR57 RIFLE – 5.7x28mm cal., 16 in. free float fluted barrel and Gen 2 receiver, aluminum upper and lower receivers, Mil-Spec trigger group, A2 pistol grip, hardcoat anodized black finish, 5.91 lbs. Disc. 2014.

	$1,200	$1,075	$950	$800	$700	$600	$495	*$1,411*

B 98 BLACKHEART FIREARMS (BLACKHEART INTERNATIONAL LLC), cont.

MSR	100%	98%	95%	90%	80%	70%	60%	Last MSR

BHI-15 S2 – 5.56 NATO cal., AR-15 style, GIO, 16 in. chrome-lined barrel with SureFire flash hider/suppressor adapator, 30 shot mag., flat-top receiver with Picatinny rail, manganese phosphate barrel finish, Magpul CTR collapsible stock, aluminum free float tube, mid-length handguard, PRI Gasbuster charging handle, Geissele SSA two-stage trigger, Wolff springs, Stark SE-1 pistol grip, titanium firing pin, hardcoat anodized black finish. Disc. 2014.

	$1,675	$1,000	$825	$625	$550	$475	$425	*$2,095*

Add $1,800 for BHI-15 S Executive Package - a complete tactical support system for your rifle including Harris bipod and adapter, Magpul flip-up front and rear sights, Aimpoint Micro-H1 with QD mount and lens covers, Insight M3X tactical illuminator light, J. Dewey field cleaning kit, and hard travel case with padded nylon.

BHI-15 S2 AR57 RIFLE – 5.7x28mm cal., 16 in. free float fluted barrel, milled aluminum lightweight AR57 upper receiver, BHI-15 S2 lower receiver, Geissele Super Dynamic Combat trigger, Wolff trigger springs, Stark SE-1 pistol grip, hardcoat anodized black finish, 6.15 lbs. Disc. 2014.

	$1,425	$925	$700	$550	$475	$395	$350	*$1,721*

BHI-15 SPR2 (SPECIAL PURPOSE RIFLE) – 5.56 NATO cal., AR-15 style, GIO, 20 in. chrome-lined barrel with SureFire flash hider/suppressor adaptor, manganese phosphate barrel finish, 20 shot mag., flat-top receiver with Picatinny rail, aluminum free float tube, rifle length handguard, PRI Gasbuster charging handle, Geissele SSA two-stage trigger, Mil-Spec A3 flat-top upper, aluminum lower, hard-chromed titanium firing pin, Magpul PRS adj. stock, adj. DPMS Panther Tactical grip, oversized magwell, hardcoat anodized black finish. Disc. 2014.

	$1,975	$1,150	$925	$650	$575	$495	$425	*$2,475*

Add $1,600 for BHI-15 SPR Executive Package - a complete tactical support system for your rifle including Leupold Mark-AR 3x9 scope, Harris bipod and adapter, Magpul flip-up front and rear sights, Freedom Reaper Scope mount, J. Dewey field cleaning kit, and hard travel case with padded nylon.

SAAR.308R AR-10 CARBINE – .308 Win. cal., 16 in. stainless steel barrel with SureFire SOCOM muzzle brake adapter, 20 shot mag., BHI free float modular handguard with full-length top rail, Geissele Super Dynamic Combat trigger, BHI .308/7.62 flat-top aluminum upper and lower receivers, BHI-Stark pistol grip, Magpul CTR collapsible stock, hardcoat anodized black finish. New 2015.

MSR $3,100	$2,550	$1,650	$1,250	$700	$625	$575	$525	

SAAR.308R AR-10 SPECIAL PURPOSE RIFLE – .308 Win. cal., 20 in. stainless steel barrel with black phosphate finish and Surefire muzzle brake/suppressor adapter or A2 compensator, 20 shot mag., BHI rifle length modular handguard with top rail, BHI .308/7.62 flat-top aluminum upper and lower receivers, Geissele Super Dynamic Combat trigger, DMPS grip, Magpul PRS stock, hardcoat anodized black finish. New 2015.

MSR $3,500	$2,875	$1,875	$1,375	$795	$675	$625	$575	

SAAR.556BLK – .300 AAC Blackout cal., AR-15 style, 16 in. barrel with black phosphate finish and A2 muzzle, 30 shot mag., BHI free float modular handguard with full-length top rail, Geissele Super Dynamic Combat trigger, Mil-Spec A3 flat-top aluminum upper and BHI-15 multi caliber aluminum lower receiver, BHI-Stark pistol grip, Magpul CTR collapsible stock, hardcoat anodized black finish. New 2015.

MSR $2,049	$1,675	$1,000	$825	$625	$550	$475	$425	

SAAR.556R – 5.56 NATO cal., AR-15 style, 16 in. barrel with black Nitride finish and A2 compensator, 30 shot mag., BHI free float modular handguard, Mil-Spec A3 flat-top aluminum upper and BHI-15 multi-caliber lower receivers, Mil-Spec trigger, BHI-Stark pistol grip, 6-position collapsible stock, hardcoat anodized black finish. New 2015.

MSR $1,149	$950	$595	$495	$425	$365	$335	$300	

SAAR.556RE – 5.56 NATO cal., 16 in. stainless steel barrel with A2 compensator, carbine length gas system, 30 shot mag., BHI free float modular handguard, ALG Defense Advanced Combat trigger, Mil-Spec A3 flat-top aluminum and BHI-15 multi-caliber lower receivers, BHI-Stark pistol grip, Magpul CTR collapsible stock, hardcoat anodized black finish. New 2015.

MSR $1,295	$1,075	$675	$500	$450	$400	$350	$325	

SAAR.556RSE – 5.56 NATO cal., AR-15 style, carbine length gas system, 16 in. barrel with black Nitride finish and SureFire muzzle brake/suppressor adapter, 30 shot mag., PRI Gasbuster charging handle, BHI free float modular handguard with full-length top rail, Geissele Super Dynamic Combat two-stage trigger, BHI-Stark pistol grip, Mil-Spec A3 flat-top aluminum upper and BHI-15 multi-caliber aluminum lower receiver, Magpul CTR collapsible stock, hardcoat anodized black finish. New 2015.

MSR $1,995	$1,650	$1,000	$795	$595	$495	$425	$395	

SAAR.556SPR – 5.56 NATO cal., AR-15 style, rifle length gas system, 20 in. barrel with black Nitride finish and SureFire suppressor adapter or A2 muzzle brake, 20 shot mag., PRI Gasbuster charging handle, BHI free float modular handguard with full-length top rail, Geissele Super Dynamic Combat trigger, Mil-Spec A3 flat-top upper and BHI-15 multi caliber lower receiver, Magpul PRS stock, hardcoat anodized black finish. New 2015.

MSR $2,495	$1,975	$1,150	$925	$650	$575	$495	$425	

BLACK RAIN ORDNANCE, INC.

MSR	100%	98%	95%	90%	80%	70%	60%	Last MSR

Current rifle and pistol manufacturer established in 2008, located in Neosho, MO. Dealer and distributor sales.

PISTOLS: SEMI-AUTO

BRO SPEC15 PISTOL – 5.56 NATO or .300 AAC Blackout cal., GIO, low profile gas block, 10 1/2 in. chrome moly barrel with A2 flash hider, Mil-Spec GI trigger, MOE grip, black Nitride bolt and carrier groups, forged upper/lower receivers, forged charging handle, 10 in. M-LOK Hybrid handguard, black finish, 5.6 lbs. New 2016.

| MSR $899 | $775 | $685 | $615 | $550 | $485 | $415 | $375 | |

PG5 – .223 Rem. cal., GPO, 7 1/2 in. stainless fluted black barrel with HCC flash hider, 30 shot PMAG, 7 in. quad rail, adj. low profile gas block, milled billet aluminum receiver, black MOE grip, black anodized finish, 5 lbs. 4 oz. Mfg. 2015 only.

| | $1,625 | $1,425 | $1,200 | $1,075 | $925 | $795 | $650 | *$1,889* |

PG9 – .223 Rem. cal., GPO, 7 1/2 in. stainless steel fluted barrel, 30 shot PMAG, black 7 in. quad rail, milled billet aluminum receiver, adj. low profile gas block, black MOE grip, Norguard finish, 5 lbs. 4 oz. Mfg. 2015 only.

| | $1,625 | $1,425 | $1,200 | $1,075 | $925 | $795 | $650 | *$1,889* |

RIFLES: SEMI-AUTO

COMPETITION SERIES - BRO COMP3G – 5.56 NATO or .308 Win. cal., rifle length gas system, adj. gas block, 16 or 18 in. fluted stainless steel barrel, Competition compensator, BRO-DIT trigger with KNS, Luth-AR MBA-1 stock, MOE grip, billet receivers, 17 3/4 in. SLM M-LOK handguard, black, Blue Titanium, Smith's Grey, or Norguard (new 2017) finish. New 2016.

| MSR $2,249 | $1,795 | $1,050 | $875 | $625 | $550 | $475 | $425 | |

Add $500 for .308 Win. cal.

HUNTING SERIES - BRO PREDATOR .308 – .308 Win. or 6.5mm Creedmoor (new 2017) cal., GIO, 18, 20, 22 (new 2017), or 24 (disc. 2017) in. fluted stainless steel barrel, round competition compensator, DIT trigger, Magpul MIAD grip, Magpul Precision Rifle stock, rifle length low profile adj. gas block, Fallout 10 billet aluminum upper and lower receiver, 15 in. M-LOK Hybrid handguard, nickel boron BCG, anodized black or Cerakote finish in FDE, OD Green, or Norguard (2017 only), 10.4-11 lbs. New 2016.

| MSR $2,649 | $2,125 | $1,325 | $995 | $675 | $595 | $525 | $475 | |

Add $50 for 6.5mm Creedmoor cal. (new 2017).

HUNTING SERIES - BRO PREDATOR 5.56 – 5.56 NATO cal., adj. gas block, rifle length gas system, 18, 20, or 24 in. fluted stainless steel barrel, BRO-DIT trigger with KNS, Magpul PRS stock, MOE grip, billet receivers, 15 in. M-LOK handguard, black, FDE, ODG, or Norguard (new 2017) finish. New 2016.

| MSR $2,149 | $1,725 | $1,050 | $850 | $625 | $550 | $475 | $425 | |

RECON SERIES - BRO FORCE – 5.56 NATO, .300 AAC Blackout, or .308 Win. cal., adj. gas block, 16 in. Divot mid-length gas stainless barrel, milled flash suppressor, nickel boron bolt carrier, aluminum billet receivers, BRO-DIT trigger with KNS, UBR stock, MOE grip, 15 in. M-LOK handguard, Skulls, Norguard (new 2017), or FDE finish. New 2016.

| MSR $2,199 | $1,725 | $1,050 | $850 | $625 | $550 | $475 | $425 | |

Add $500 for .308 Win. cal.

RECON SERIES - BRO SCOUT – 5.56 NATO, .300 AAC Blackout, or .308 Win. cal., mid-length gas system, adj. gas block, 16 in. lightweight profile barrel, slim milled flash suppressor, BRO-DIT trigger with KNS, MFT Minimalist stock, MOE grip, billet receivers, 15 in. SLM M-LOK handguard, black, Smith's Grey, FDE, ODG, or Norguard Cerakote finish. New 2016.

| MSR $1,949 | $1,600 | $1,000 | $775 | $575 | $495 | $425 | $395 | |

Add $500 for .308 Win. cal.

RECON SERIES - BRO URBAN – 5.56 NATO, .300 AAC Blackout, or .308 Win. cal., adj. gas block, 16 in. double flute stainless barrel, milled flash suppressor, mid-length gas system, aluminum billet receivers, BRO-DIT trigger with KNS, MOE SL stock, MOE grip, 12 in. M-LOK handguard, black or Norguard finish. New 2016.

| MSR $1,849 | $1,525 | $975 | $750 | $575 | $495 | $425 | $375 | |

Add $500 for .308 Win. cal.

BRO SPEC15 6.5 GRENDEL – 6.5 Grendel cal., GIO, 20 in. non-fluted machined finish stainless steel barrel, multi-ported compensator, GI trigger, Magpul ACS-L buttstock, Magpul MOE grip, low profile non-adj. gas block, forged aluminum upper and lower receiver, Nitride coated BCG, 15 in. M-LOK Slim handguard, 8 lbs. 1 oz. New mid-2018.

| MSR $1,499 | $1,250 | $825 | $575 | $475 | $425 | $375 | $350 | |

BRO SPEC15 .224 VALKYRIE – .224 Valkyrie cal., GIO, 18 or 22 in. non-fluted machined finish stainless steel barrel, multi-ported compensator, GI trigger, Magpul ACS-L buttstock, Magpul MOE grip, low profile non-adj. gas block, forged aluminum upper and lower receiver, Nitride coated BCG, M-LOK Slim handguard, 7 lbs. 6.4 oz.-8 lbs. 3.2 oz. New 2018.

| MSR $1,449 | $1,195 | $795 | $550 | $465 | $415 | $375 | $350 | |

Add $50 for 22 in. barrel.

B 100 BLACK RAIN ORDNANCE, INC., cont.

MSR	100%	98%	95%	90%	80%	70%	60%	Last MSR

BRO SPEC15 .450 BUSHMASTER – .450 Bushmaster cal., GIO, 16 in. SOCOM profile chrome moly barrel, .450 BRO Tank compensator, GI trigger, Magpul MOE buttstock, GI grip, carbine length low profile non-adj. gas block, forged aluminum upper and lower receiver, M-LOK Hybrid handguard, 7 lbs. 1 oz. New mid-2018.

MSR $1,399	$1,150	$750	$550	$465	$415	$375	$350	

BRO SPEC15 .458 SOCOM – .458 SOCOM cal., GIO, 16 in. vanadium steel barrel, BRO .458 compensator, GI trigger, Magpul MOE buttstock, GI grip, carbine length low profile non-adj. gas block, forged aluminum upper and lower receiver, Nitride coated BCG, 15 in. M-LOK Hybrid handguard, 8 lbs. New 2018.

MSR $1,399	$1,150	$750	$550	$465	$415	$375	$350	

BRO SPEC15 AMERICAN FLAG RIFLE – 5.56 NATO cal., GIO, 16 in. M4 profile chrome moly barrel, A2 flash hider, Mil-Spec trigger, enhanced GI stock, A2 grip, carbine length low profile adj. gas block, forged aluminum upper and lower receiver, 10 in. BRO Slim handguard (M-LOK compatible), American flag artwork Cerakote high temp paint. Limited mfg. beginning 2018.

MSR $1,199	$995	$625	$495	$450	$395	$350	$325	

BRO SPEC15 BLT CARBINE – 5.56 NATO or .300 AAC Blackout cal., GIO, 16 in. M4 profile chrome moly barrel, A2 flash hider, GI trigger, Magpul MOE buttstock, Magpul MOE grip, carbine length low profile non-adj. gas block, forged aluminum upper and billet lower receiver, Nitride coated BCG, BRO M-LOK Hybrid handguard, 7 lbs. 4 oz.

MSR $999	$850	$550	$465	$395	$350	$325	$295	

BRO SPEC15 CARBINE – 5.56 NATO or .300 AAC Blackout cal., GIO, 16 in. M4 profile chrome moly barrel, A2 flash hider, GI trigger, enhanced GI buttstock, GI grip, carbine length low profile non-adj. gas block, forged aluminum upper and lower receiver, Nitride coated BCG, BRO M-LOK Hybrid handguard, right or left-hand configuration, 7 lbs. 4 oz. New 2016.

MSR $899	$765	$515	$440	$375	$335	$315	$295	

Add $300 for left-hand configuration.

BRO SPEC15 SOCOM PLUS – 5.56 NATO or .300 AAC Blackout cal., GIO, 16 in. SOCOM profile chrome moly barrel, A2 flash hider, DIT trigger, Magpul MOE-SL buttstock, Magpul MOE grip, mid-length low profile non-adj. gas block, forged aluminum upper and lower receiver, nickel boron BCG, 15 in. BRO SLM handguard, 7 lbs. 4 oz.

MSR $1,299	$1,075	$675	$500	$450	$400	$350	$325	

BRO SPEC15-SSP – 5.56 NATO or .300 AAC Blackout cal., 16 in. chrome moly SOCOM barrel with A2 flash hider, BRO-DIT trigger with KNS, MOE SL stock, MOE grip, forged upper and lower receivers, forged charging handle with billet tac latch, nickel boron bolt and carrier group, SLM M-LOK handguard, low profile gas block, black finish. Disc. 2017.

	$1,075	$675	$500	$450	$400	$350	$325	*$1,299*

SPEC15 BLACK & TAN CARBINE – 5.56 NATO or .300 AAC Blackout cal., GIO, 16 in. M4 profile chrome moly barrel, A2 flash hider, GI trigger, Magpul MOE buttstock with FDE finish, FDE Magpul MOE grip, carbine length low profile non-adj. gas block, forged aluminum upper and lower receiver, Nitride coated BCG, BRO M-LOK Hybrid handguard with FDE finish, black metal finish, 7 lbs. 4 oz.

MSR $999	$850	$550	$465	$395	$350	$325	$295	

LIMITED EDITION NRA RIFLE – .223 Rem. cal., GPO, 16 in. custom stainless two-tone barrel with straight flute and round competition compensator, 30 shot PMAG, adj. low profile gas block, milled billet aluminum receiver, MOE stock and grip, black anodized finish, officially licensed by the NRA, 6 lbs. 7 oz. Limited mfg. 2015 only.

	$1,875	$1,650	$1,400	$1,200	$1,025	$875	$725	*$2,209*

PG1 – .223 Rem. cal., GPO or GIO, 20 shot mag., 16 in. slim blast stainless steel barrel with flash suppressor, detachable folding sights, flat-top Picatinny rail with 7 in. black barrel quad rail, black pistol grip and collapsible MOE stock, Pink Splash receiver finish. Disc. 2015.

	$1,675	$1,000	$825	$625	$550	$475	$425	*$2,039*

Add $350 for PG1 with gas piston operation (GPO).

PG2 – .223 Rem. cal., GIO or GPO, 20 shot mag., 16 in. partially fluted black barrel with flash suppressor, flat-top Picatinny rail with 7 in. FDE quad rail, FDE UBR stock, Digital Tan receiver finish, detachable folding sights. Disc. 2015.

	$1,975	$1,150	$925	$650	$575	$495	$425	*$2,439*

Add $360 for PG2 with gas piston operation (GPO).

PG3 – .223 Rem. cal., GIO or GPO, 20 shot mag., 16 in. black/white finished partially spiral fluted barrel with flash suppressor, flat-top Picatinny rail with 7 in. black quad rail, black UBR stock, Silver Skulls receiver finish, detachable folding sights, 7 lbs. 4 oz. Disc. 2015.

	$1,875	$1,100	$895	$650	$575	$495	$425	*$2,379*

Add $400 for PG3 with gas piston operation (GPO).

PG4 – .223 Rem. cal., GIO, 20 shot mag., 24 in. partially fluted black bull barrel, flat-top Picatinny rail with 12 in. black or FDE (disc. 2012, reintroduced 2015) quad rail, black PRS stock, black or FDE (disc. 2012, reintroduced 2015) finish. Disc. 2015.

	$1,795	$1,050	$875	$625	$550	$475	$425	*$2,239*

Add $30 for FDE finish (disc. 2012, reintroduced 2015).

BLACK RAIN ORDNANCE, INC., cont. 101 B

MSR		100%	98%	95%	90%	80%	70%	60%	Last MSR

PG5 – .223 Rem. cal., GIO or GPO, 20 shot mag., 16 in. partially fluted stainless black barrel with flash suppressor, flat-top Picatinny rail with 7 in. black quad rail, black MOE stock, black finish, detachable folding sights, 6 lbs. 7 oz. Disc. 2015.
| | | $1,725 | $1,050 | $850 | $625 | $550 | $475 | $425 | $2,109 |

Add $330 for PG5 with gas piston operation (GPO).

PG6 – .223 Rem. cal., GIO or GPO, adjustable low profile gas block, 16 in. partially fluted black barrel with flash suppressor, milled billet aluminum receiver, flat-top Picatinny rail with 9 in. FDE quad rail, FDE MOE stock, detachable folding sights, 30 shot PMAG, black anodized receiver finish, 6 lbs., 7 oz. Disc. 2015.
| | | $1,725 | $1,050 | $850 | $625 | $550 | $475 | $425 | $2,109 |

Add $360 for PG6 with gas piston operation (GPO).

PG7 – Disc. 2011.
| | | $1,650 | $1,000 | $795 | $595 | $495 | $425 | $395 | $1,989 |

PG8 – Disc. 2011.
| | | $1,650 | $1,000 | $795 | $595 | $495 | $425 | $395 | $1,989 |

PG9 – .223 Rem. cal., GIO or GPO, 20 shot mag., 16 in. M4 partially fluted MACH barrel with flash suppressor, flat-top Norguard finished receiver with 7 in. black quad rail, black pistol grip and MOE stock, detachable folding sights, 6 lbs. 7 oz. Disc. 2015.
| | | $1,725 | $1,050 | $850 | $625 | $550 | $475 | $425 | $2,109 |

Add $350 for PG9 with gas piston operation (GPO).

PG11 – .223 Rem. cal., GIO, 20 shot mag., 18 or 20 (disc. 2014) in. partially fluted black barrel with compensator, no sights, flat-top Picatinny rail with 12 in. black or Flat Dark Earth modular rail, black or FDE UBR stock, black, Digital Tan, Flat Dark Earth, Norguard, Pink Splash, or Silver Skulls receiver finish, 7 lbs. 10 oz. Disc. 2015.
| | | $2,125 | $1,325 | $995 | $675 | $595 | $525 | $475 | $2,689 |

Add $40 for Digital Tan, Flat Dark Earth, Norguard, Pink Splash, or Silver Skulls finish.

PG12 – .308 Win. cal., GIO, 20 shot mag., 18 (disc. 2014) or 20 in. partially fluted black or stainless finished barrel with compensator, flat-top Picatinny rail with 12 in. black or FDE modular rail, black or FDE PRS stock, black, Digital Tan, FDE, Norguard, Pink Splash, or Silver Skulls finish, 9 lbs. 8 oz. Disc. 2015.
| | | $2,550 | $1,650 | $1,250 | $700 | $625 | $575 | $525 | $3,189 |

Add $40 for Digital Tan, FDE, Norguard, Pink Splash, or Silver Skulls finish.

PG13 – .308 Win. cal., GIO, 20 shot mag., 18 in. partially spiral fluted black/white finished barrel with flash suppressor, no sights, Silver Skull finished receiver with flat-top Picatinny rail and 9 in. black modular rail, black pistol grip and UBR stock, 9 lbs. 8 oz. Disc. 2015.
| | | $2,450 | $1,595 | $1,200 | $700 | $675 | $575 | $525 | $3,049 |

PG14 – .308 Win. cal., GIO, 20 shot mag., 18 in. partially fluted stainless barrel with flash suppressor, Norguard finished receiver with Picatinny rail and 9 in. black modular rail, black pistol grip and MOE stock, no sights, 8 lbs. 13 oz. Disc. 2015.
| | | $2,125 | $1,325 | $995 | $675 | $595 | $525 | $475 | $2,699 |

PG15 – .308 Win. cal., GIO, 18 or 20 in. partially fluted black barrel with compensator, milled billet aluminum receiver, adj. low profile gas block, flat-top Picatinny rail with 12 in. black modular rail, 20 shot mag., black MOE stock, MIAD grip, black or FDE receiver finish, 8 lbs. 1 oz. Mfg. 2013-2015.
| | | $2,295 | $1,450 | $1,075 | $675 | $595 | $525 | $475 | $2,809 |

Add $50 for FDE finish.

PG16 – .308 Win. cal., GIO, 20 shot mag., 24 in. partially fluted black bull barrel, flat-top Picatinny rail with 12 in. black or FDE modular rail, black or FDE pistol grip and PRS stock, black or FDE finish, no sights, 11 lbs. Disc. 2015.
| | | $2,295 | $1,450 | $1,075 | $675 | $595 | $525 | $475 | $2,869 |

Add $30 for FDE finish.

PG17 – .223 Rem. cal., GIO, 20 shot mag., 18 or 24 in. partially fluted black bull barrel, no sights, flat-top Picatinny rail with 9 or 12 in. modular rail, pistol grip and UBR stock, black or FDE finish. Disc. 2013.
| | | $1,875 | $1,100 | $895 | $650 | $575 | $495 | $425 | $2,359 |

Add $30 for FDE finish.

BLACK RIFLE COMPANY LLC

Previous rifle and accessories manufacturer located in Clackamas, OR until 2014.

RIFLES/CARBINES: SEMI-AUTO

BRC FORGED RECEIVER MOE CARBINE – AR-15 style, GIO, stainless steel low profile gas block, 16 in. M4 Isonite barrel with Victory compensator/flash hider, Magpul MOE stock and grip, tactical trigger, forged upper and lower receiver, CNC machined quad rail, hardcoat anodized Cerakote ceramic coating, black or Flat Dark Earth finish. Disc. 2014.
| | | $1,525 | $975 | $750 | $575 | $495 | $425 | $375 | $1,849 |

B 102 BLACK RIFLE COMPANY LLC, cont.

MSR	100%	98%	95%	90%	80%	70%	60%	Last MSR

BRC FORGED RECEIVER MID-LENGTH CARBINE – AR-15 style, GIO, similar to BRC Forged Receiver MOE Carbine, except has 16 in. mid-length gas medium contour Isonite barrel, Black, Dark Earth, Olive Drab, Sniper Gray, or White finish. Disc. 2014.

	$1,525	$975	$750	$575	$495	$425	$375	$1,849

BRC BILLET MID-LENGTH CARBINE – AR-15 style, GIO, similar to BRC Forged MOE Carbine, except has 16 in. gas medium contour barrel, billet mid-length receiver, Magpul MOE stock and grip standard, other stock options are available, choice of Black, Dark Earth, Olive Drab, Sniper Gray, or White finish. Disc. 2014.

	$1,525	$975	$750	$575	$495	$425	$375	$1,849

Add $50 for 14 1/2 in. pinned compensator.

BRC SASS RIFLE – 6.8 SPC cal., AR-15 style, GIO, 18 in. match barrel with Victory compensator, stainless steel polished carrier with MP tested bolt, Magpul PRS stock, Ergo grip, billet receivers, 13 in. MQR rail, tactical latch. Disc. 2014.

	$1,795	$1,050	$875	$625	$550	$475	$425	$2,200

BLACK WEAPONS ARMORY

Previous custom manufacturer located in Tucson, AZ until 2014.

RIFLES: SEMI-AUTO

Black Weapons Armory manufactured custom AR-15 rifles built to customer specifications and gunsmithing as well as AR-15 parts and accessories. Previous models included the PUG (Practical Ugly Gun) - last MSR in 2014 was $2,050.

BOHICA

Previous manufacturer and customizer located in Sedalia, CO circa 1993-1994.

RIFLES: SEMI-AUTO

M16-SA – .223 Rem., .50 AE, or various custom cals., AR-15 style, GIO, 16 or 20 in. barrel, A2 sights, standard handguard, approx. 950 were mfg. through September 1994.

	$1,385	$895	$675	$525	$450	$385	$350	

Add $100 for flat-top receiver with scope rail.

Add $65 for two-piece, free floating handguard.

In addition to the rifles listed, Bohica also manufactured a M16-SA Match variation (retail was $2,295, approx. 10 mfg.), a pistol version of the M16-SA in both 7 and 10 in. barrel (retail was $1,995, approx. 50 mfg.), and a limited run of M16-SA in .50 AE cal. (retail was $1,695, approx. 25 mfg.).

BRAVO COMPANY MFG., INC.

Current rifle manufacturer located in Hartland, WI.

PISTOLS: SEMI-AUTO

RECCE-9 KMR-A PISTOL – .300 AAC Blackout cal., GIO, 9 in. BCM enhanced profile barrel, Mod 1 7.62 compensator, Mod 3 pistol grip, KMR Alpha 8 handguard, Mod 4 charging handle, forged aluminum flat-top upper and lower receivers, M4 feed ramp extension, Type III hardcoat anodized black finish, 4.9 lbs. New 2016.

MSR $1,500	$1,275	$1,125	$1,025	$875	$750	$625	$525	

RECCE-9 MCMR PISTOL – .300 AAC Blackout cal., pistol length gas system, 9 in. BCM enhanced taper barrel with fluting profile and manganese phosphate finish, Mod 1 7.62 compensator, BCM PNT trigger and trigger guard, Mod 3 pistol grip, BCM MCMR-8 free float handguard, BCM Gunfighter charging handle, forged aluminum flat-top upper and lower receiver, M4 feed ramp extension, Type III hardcoat anodized black finish, approx. 25 in. OAL, 4.9 lbs. New 2018.

MSR $1,500	$1,275	$1,125	$1,025	$875	$750	$625	$525	

RECCE-11 KMR-A / RECCE-11 KMR-A ELW PISTOL – 5.56 NATO cal., carbine length gas system, 11 1/2 in. Govt. profile or enhanced lightweight barrel, Mod 0 compensator, Mod 3 pistol grip, KMR Alpha-10 handguard, Mod 4 charging handle, forged aluminum flat-top upper and lower receivers, black finish, 5-5.1 lbs., approx. 27 in. OAL. New 2016.

MSR $1,400	$1,200	$1,075	$950	$800	$700	$600	$495	

RECCE-11 MCMR / RECCE-11 MCMR ELW PISTOL – 5.56 NATO cal., carbine length gas system, 11 in. enhanced lightweight or 11 1/2 in. USGI profile barrel, Mod 0 compensator, BCM PNT™ trigger and trigger guard, Mod 3 pistol grip, BCM MCMR-10 free float handguard, BCM Gunfighter charging handle, forged aluminum flat-top upper and lower receivers, hardcoat anodized black finish, 5-5.1 lbs., approx. 27 in. OAL. New 2018.

MSR $1,400	$1,200	$1,075	$950	$800	$700	$600	$495	

BRAVO COMPANY MFG., INC., cont. 103 B

MSR	100%	98%	95%	90%	80%	70%	60%	Last MSR

RECCE-12 KMR-A PISTOL – .300 AAC Blackout cal., GIO, 12 1/2 in. BCM enhanced profile barrel, Mod 1 7.62 compensator, Mod 3 pistol grip, KMR-10 handguard, Mod 4 charging handle, forged aluminum flat-top upper and lower receivers, M4 feed ramp extension, Type III hardcoat anodized black finish, 5.2 lbs. New 2016.

| MSR $1,500 | $1,275 | $1,125 | $1,025 | $875 | $750 | $625 | $525 | |

RECCE-12 MCMR PISTOL – .300 AAC Blackout cal., pistol length gas system, 12 1/2 in. BCM enhanced taper barrel with fluting profile and manganese phosphate finish, Mod 1 7.62 compensator, BCM PNT™ trigger and trigger guard, Mod 3 pistol grip, MCMR-10 free float handguard, BCM Gunfighter charging handle, forged aluminum flat-top upper and lower receiver, M4 feed ramp extension, Type III hardcoat anodized black finish, 5.2 lbs., 28.5 in. OAL. New 2018.

| MSR $1,500 | $1,275 | $1,125 | $1,025 | $875 | $750 | $625 | $525 | |

RIFLES/CARBINES: SEMI-AUTO

Bravo Company Mfg., Inc. manufactures a line of AR-15 style rifles with many available options and accessories. The company is also a dealer/distributor for other companies that specialize in tactical gear.

A4 RIFLE – 5.56 NATO cal., GIO, chrome-lined bore and chamber, polymer handguards, detachable carry handle with windage and elevation adj. 600m rear sight, fixed buttstock, Mil-Spec F-marked forged front sights, M4 flat-top receiver, Mod 4 charging handle, MOE enhanced trigger guard, M4 feed ramp barrel extension, hardcoat anodized black finish. Disc. 2014.

| | $1,025 | $625 | $495 | $450 | $395 | $350 | $325 | $1,219 |

BCM PRECISION 18 RIFLE – 5.56 NATO cal., GIO, 18 in. steel barrel, M4 feed ramp barrel extension, forged aluminum lower and flat-top upper receivers, BCM Mod 4 charging handle, tactical handguard, Magpul MOE enhanced trigger guard, M4 stock, hardcoat anodized finish, 6 lbs. 10 oz. Mfg. 2015 only.

Retail pricing was not available for this model.

BCM SAM-RIFLE – 5.56 NATO cal., GIO, 20 in. heavy profile stainless steel barrel, M4 feed ramp barrel extension, forged aluminum lower and flat-top upper receivers, BCM Mod 4 charging handle, Magpul MOE enhanced trigger guard, KAC free float handguard, taper pinned KAC folding front sight, A2 fixed stock, hardcoat anodized finish. Mfg. 2015 only.

| | $915 | $575 | $475 | $415 | $350 | $325 | $300 | $1,099 |

CAR-16LW MOD 0 CARBINE – 5.56 NATO cal., GIO, 16 in. lightweight barrel, basic rifle with double heat shield handguards, no rear sight, hardcoat anodized black finish, adj. Magpul stock, Mil-Spec F-marked forged front sight, M4 flat-top receiver, upper Picatinny rail, Mod 4 charging handle, chrome-lined bore and chamber. Disc. 2014.

| | $915 | $575 | $475 | $415 | $350 | $325 | $300 | $1,099 |

CAR-16LW MOD 1 CARBINE – 5.56 NATO cal., similar to CAR-16LW, except has detachable carry handle with windage and elevation adj. 600m rear sight. Disc. 2014.

| | $1,025 | $625 | $495 | $450 | $395 | $350 | $325 | $1,219 |

EAG TACTICAL CARBINE – 5.56 NATO cal., GIO, 14 1/2 in. Government profile barrel with permanently attached A2X flash hider for a civilian legal 16 in. barrel, M4 feed ramp barrel extension, F-marked forged front sight and pinned front sight base, BCM Mod 3 charging handle, forged aluminum lower and flat-top upper receivers, LaRue Tactical 9 in. Stealth free float handguard, Troy Industries/BCM folding battle sight, three TangoDown SCAR rail covers, TangoDown QD vertical Grip-K, Battle Grip, and PR#4 sling mount, Magpul MOE enhanced trigger guard, Magpul MOE stock, also includes SureFire G2 LED illuminator and VTAC light mount, black or FDE finish. New 2015.

| MSR $2,263 | $1,795 | $1,050 | $875 | $625 | $550 | $475 | $425 | |

HALEY STRATEGIC JACK CARBINE – 5.56 NATO cal., GIO, 14 1/2 in. Govt. profile barrel with permanently attached BCM Gunfighter compensator for a civilian legal 16 in. barrel, M4 feed ramp barrel extension, forged aluminum lower and flat-top upper receiver, Geissele super modular rail, BCM Mod 4 charging handle, ALG Defense ACT trigger, enhanced trigger guard, diopter front folding battle sight and rear battle sight, B5 Systems SOPMOD Bravo stock, Haley Strategic Thorntail offset light mount, hardcoat anodized finish, 6 lbs. 11 oz. Mfg. 2015-2017.

| | $1,795 | $1,050 | $875 | $625 | $550 | $475 | $425 | $2,263 |

M4 MOD 0 CARBINE – 5.56 NATO cal., GIO, 16 in. barrel, chrome-lined bore and chamber, basic rifle with double heat shield handguards, no rear sight, adj. Magpul stock, Mil-Spec F-marked forged front sight, M4 flat-top receiver, upper Picatinny rail, Mod 4 charging handle, MOE enhanced trigger guard, M4 feed ramp barrel extension, hardcoat anodized black finish.

| MSR $1,202 | $1,025 | $625 | $495 | $450 | $395 | $350 | $325 | |

M4 MOD 1 CARBINE – 5.56 NATO cal., GIO, 16 in. barrel, chrome-lined bore and chamber, double heat shield handguards, detachable carry handle with windage and elevation adj. 600m rear sight, adj. Magpul stock, Mil-Spec F-marked forged front sight, M4 flat-top receiver, Mod 4 charging handle, MOE enhanced trigger guard, M4 feed ramp barrel extension, hardcoat anodized black finish, 6.9 lbs.

| MSR $1,334 | $1,125 | $700 | $525 | $450 | $400 | $350 | $325 | |

B 104 BRAVO COMPANY MFG., INC., cont.

MSR	100%	98%	95%	90%	80%	70%	60%	Last MSR

M4 MOD 2 CARBINE – 5.56 NATO cal., GIO, 16 in. barrel, chrome-lined bore and chamber, drop-in tactical handguard, folding rear battle sight, adj. Magpul stock, Mil-Spec F-marked forged front sight, M4 flat-top receiver, quad rail, Mod 4 charging handle, MOE enhanced trigger guard, M4 feed ramp barrel extension, hardcoat anodized black finish.

MSR $1,509	$1,275	$850	$600	$495	$425	$375	$350	

M4 MOD 3 CARBINE – 5.56 NATO cal., GIO, 16 in. M4 barrel, F-marked forged front sight, pinned front sight base, folding rear iron sight, M4 feed ramp barrel extension, BCM Mod 4 charging handle, forged aluminum upper and lower receivers, tactical handguard with double heat shield, Magpul MOE enhanced trigger guard, M4 stock, hardcoat anodized finish, 6 lbs. 8 oz. Disc. 2015.

Retail pricing was not available for this model.

MID-16 MOD 0 CARBINE – 5.56 NATO cal., GIO, 16 in. barrel, chrome-lined bore and chamber, basic rifle with Magpul MOE handguards, no rear sight, adj. Magpul stock, Mil-Spec F-marked forged front sight, M4 flat-top receiver, upper Picatinny rail, Mod 4 charging handle, M4 feed ramp barrel extension, hardcoat anodized black finish.

MSR $1,218	$1,025	$625	$495	$450	$395	$350	$325	

MID-16 MOD 2 CARBINE – 5.56 NATO cal., GIO, 16 in. barrel, chrome-lined bore and chamber, drop-in tactical handguard, folding rear battle sight, adj. Magpul stock, Mil-Spec F-marked forged front sight, M4 flat-top receiver, quad rail, Mod 4 charging handle, MOE enhanced trigger guard, M4 feed ramp barrel extension, hardcoat anodized black finish.

MSR $1,534	$1,275	$850	$600	$495	$425	$375	$350	

MID-16 MOD 3 CARBINE – 5.56 NATO cal., GIO, 16 in. Government profile steel barrel, M4 feed ramp, F-marked forged front sight, pinned front sight base, folding rear iron sight, BCM Mod 4 charging handle, forged aluminum upper and lower receivers, modular tactical handguard, Magpul MOE enhanced trigger guard, M4 stock, hardcoat anodized finish, 6 lbs. 11 oz. Mfg. 2015 only.

Retail pricing was not available for this model.

MID-16LW MOD 0 CARBINE – 5.56 NATO cal., GIO, 16 in. lightweight barrel, chrome-lined bore and chamber, M4 flat-top receiver, adj. Magpul stock, Mil-Spec F-marked forged front sights, Mod 4 charging handle, Magpul MOE enhanced trigger guard, hardcoat anodized black finish. Mfg. 2011-2015.

	$935	$575	$475	$415	$350	$325	$300	*$1,119*

MK12 MOD 0 / MK12 MOD 0-A5 PRECISION RIFLE – 5.56 NATO cal., 18 in. MK12 profile stainless steel barrel with flash hider or compensator, Magpul MOE enhanced trigger guard, PRI folding front sight base, A2 fixed or A5 adj. (MK12 MOD 0-A5) stock, PRI Gen III 12 in. carbon fiber handguard, optics ready railed upper receiver, forged aluminum lower, BCM Mod 4 charging handle, hardcoat anodized black or FDE finish. New 2015.

MSR $2,550	$2,050	$1,250	$950	$650	$575	$495	$475	

Add $150 for FDE finish.

RECCE-14 CARBINE – 5.56 NATO cal., M4 feed ramp barrel extension, USGI profile 14 1/2 in. plus permanent BCM Mod 1 compensator for total 16.1 in. manganese phosphate finished barrel, chrome-lined bore and chamber, BCM PNT™ trigger and trigger guard, adj. BCM Mod 0 SOPMOD stock, quad rail, free float 12 in. handguard, BCM Mod 3 pistol grip, M4 flat-top receiver, BCM Gunfighter charging handle, hardcoat anodized black finish, 6.3 lbs., 31 1/2-34 1/2 in. OAL. New 2018.

MSR $1,500	$1,250	$825	$575	$475	$425	$375	$350	

RECCE-14 KMR-A CARBINE – 5.56 NATO cal., USGI profile 14 1/2 in. plus permanent BCM Mod 1 compensator for total 16.1 in. manganese phosphate finished barrel, M4 feed ramp barrel extension, chrome-lined bore and chamber, BCM PNT™ trigger and trigger guard, adj. BCM Mod 0 SOPMOD stock, KMR-A13 free float handguard, BCM Mod 3 pistol grip, M4 flat-top receiver, BCM Gunfighter charging handle, hardcoat anodized black finish, 31 1/2-34 1/2 in. OAL, 6 lbs. New 2018.

MSR $1,500	$1,250	$825	$575	$475	$425	$375	$350	

RECCE-14 KMR-LW CARBINE – 5.56 NATO cal., enhanced lightweight profile 14 1/2 in. plus permanent BCM Mod 1 compensator for total 16.1 in. manganese phosphate finished barrel, M4 feed ramp barrel extension, chrome-lined bore and chamber, BCM PNT™ trigger and trigger guard, adj. BCM Mod 0 SOPMOD stock, KMR-ALPHA10 free float handguard, BCM Mod 3 pistol grip, M4 flat-top receiver, BCM Gunfighter charging handle, hardcoat anodized black finish, 31.5-34.5 in. OAL, 6 lbs. New 2018.

MSR $1,500	$1,250	$825	$575	$475	$425	$375	$350	

RECCE-14 MCMR CARBINE – 5.56 NATO or .300 AAC Blackout cal., AR-15 style, mid-length gas system, 16 in. USGI profile, manganese phosphate finish barrel, Mod 0 compensator, Mod 0 buttstock, Mod 3 pistol grip, BCM MCMR-15 free float handguard, Gunfighter charging handle, QD endplate, M4 feed ramp, flat-top with laser T markings, aluminum forged upper and lower receivers, hardcoat anodized black finish, 32.5-35.5 in. OAL, 6.1 lbs. New 2018.

MSR $1,500	$1,250	$825	$575	$475	$425	$375	$350	

BRAVO COMPANY MFG., INC., cont. 105 B

MSR	100%	98%	95%	90%	80%	70%	60%	Last MSR

RECCE-14 MCMR-LW CARBINE – 5.56 NATO cal., enhanced lightweight profile 14 1/2 in. plus permanent BCM Mod 1 compensator for total 16.1 in. manganese phosphate finished barrel, chrome-lined bore and chamber, BCM PNT™ trigger and trigger guard, adj. BCM Mod 0 SOPMOD stock, MCMR-10 free float handguard, BCM Mod 3 pistol grip, M4 feed ramp barrel extension, M4 flat-top receiver, BCM Gunfighter charging handle, hardcoat anodized black finish, 31.5-34.5 in. OAL, 5.7 lbs. New 2018.

MSR $1,500	$1,250	$825	$575	$475	$425	$375	$350	

RECCE-16 CARBINE – 5.56 NATO cal., 16 in. barrel, chrome-lined bore and chamber, MOE enhanced trigger guard, adj. Magpul stock, Magpul MOE handguards, M4 feed ramp barrel extension, full-length quad rail, M4 flat-top receiver, Mod 4 charging handle, hardcoat anodized black, Cerakote Dark Bronze, FDE, OD Green, or Tactical Gray finish, Precision model configuration, 32 1/2-35 1/2 in. OAL, approx. 6 lbs.

MSR $1,400	$1,150	$750	$550	$465	$415	$375	$350	

Add $100 for Cerakote Dark Bronze, FDE, OD Green, or Tactical Gray finish.

RECCE-16 PRECISION CARBINE – 5.56 NATO cal., GIO, 16 in. medium profile stainless steel barrel, A2 flash hider, free float rail system, mid-length gas system, tactical handguard, M4 feed ramp barrel extension, BCM Mod 4 charging handle, forged aluminum flat-top upper and lower receivers, Magpul MOE enhanced trigger guard, M4 stock, black hardcoat anodized finish. Disc. 2015.

	$1,150	$750	$550	$465	$415	$375	$350	*$1,399*

RECCE-16 KMR-A .300 BLACKOUT – .300 AAC Blackout cal., AR-15 style, carbine length gas system, 16 in. BCM enhanced taper with fluting and manganese phosphate finished barrel, Mod 1 compensator, Mod 0 buttstock, Mod 3 pistol grip, KMR Alpha-13 handguard, Mod 4 charging handle, QD endplate, M4 feed ramp flat-top with laser T markings, aluminum forged upper and lower receivers, hardcoat anodized black finish, 32.5-35.5 in. OAL., 6 lbs. New 2016.

MSR $1,500	$1,250	$825	$575	$475	$425	$375	$350	

RECCE-16 KMR-A CARBINE – 5.56 NATO cal., GIO, 16 in. Govt. profile barrel, Mod 0 compensator, Mod 0 buttstock, Mod 3 pistol grip, KMR Alpha-15 handguard, Mod 4 charging handle, QD endplate, M4 feed ramp flat-top with laser T markings, aluminum forged upper and lower receivers, black or Dark Bronze finish, 6 lbs. New 2016.

MSR $1,400	$1,150	$750	$550	$465	$415	$375	$350	

Add $100 for Dark Bronze finish.

RECCE-16 KMR-A PRECISION RIFLE – 5.56 NATO cal., GIO, 16 in. Govt. profile stainless steel barrel, Mod 0 compensator, Mod 0 buttstock, Mod 3 pistol grip, aluminum forged flat-top upper and lower receivers, KMR Alpha-15 handguard, Mod 4 charging handle, M4 feed ramp extension, black finish, 6 1/2 lbs. New 2016.

MSR $1,630	$1,350	$875	$650	$525	$450	$385	$350	

RECCE-16 KMR-LW (LIGHTWEIGHT) CARBINE – 5.56 NATO cal., GIO, 16 in. standard enhanced lightweight profile barrel, Mod 0 compensator, Mod 0 buttstock, Mod 3 pistol grip, KMR Alpha-15 handguard, Mod 4 charging handle, QD endplate, M4 feed ramp flat-top with laser T markings, aluminum forged upper and lower receivers, black finish, 6 lbs. New 2016.

MSR $1,490	$1,250	$825	$575	$475	$425	$375	$350	

RECCE-16 MCMR CARBINE – 5.56 NATO or .300 AAC Blackout cal., AR-15 style, mid-length gas system, 16 in. USGI profile, manganese phosphate finished barrel, Mod 0 compensator, Mod 0 buttstock, Mod 3 pistol grip, BCM MCMR-15 free float handguard, Gunfighter charging handle, QD endplate, M4 feed ramp, flat-top with laser T markings, aluminum forged upper and lower receivers, hardcoat anodized black finish, 32.5-35.5 in. OAL, 6.1 lbs. New 2018.

MSR $1,400	$1,150	$750	$550	$465	$415	$375	$350	

Add $100 for .300 AAC Blackout cal.

RECCE-16 MCMR-LW CARBINE – 5.56 NATO cal., AR-15 style, mid-length gas system, 16 in. enhanced lightweight profile, manganese phosphate finished barrel, Mod 0 compensator, BCM PNT trigger and trigger guard, Mod 0 buttstock, Mod 3 pistol grip, BCM MCMR-13 free float handguard, Gunfighter charging handle, QD endplate, M4 feed ramp, flat-top with laser T markings, aluminum forged upper and lower receivers, hardcoat anodized black finish, 32.5-35.5 in. OAL, 5.8 lbs. New 2018.

MSR $1,400	$1,150	$750	$550	$465	$415	$375	$350	

RECCE-16 MCMR PRECISION RIFLE – 5.56 NATO cal., AR-15 style, GIO, 16 in. medium profile stainless steel barrel, Mod 0 compensator, BCM PNT trigger, BCM trigger guard, BCM buttstock, Mod 3 pistol grip, aluminum forged flat-top upper and lower receiver, BCM MCMR-15 free float handguard, Mod 4 charging handle, M4 feed ramp extension, black finish, 32 1/2-35 1/2 in. OAL, 6 1/2 lbs. New 2018.

MSR $1,630	$1,350	$875	$650	$525	$450	$385	$350	

RECCE-18 KMR-A PRECISION RIFLE – 5.56 NATO cal., rifle length gas system, 18 in. Govt. profile stainless steel barrel, Mod 0 compensator, Mod 0 buttstock, Mod 3 pistol grip, aluminum forged flat-top upper and lower receivers, KMR Alpha-15 handguard, Mod 4 charging handle, M4 feed ramp extension, black finish, 6 1/2 lbs. New 2016.

MSR $1,650	$1,350	$875	$650	$525	$450	$385	$350	

B 106 BRAVO COMPANY MFG., INC., cont.

MSR	100%	98%	95%	90%	80%	70%	60%	Last MSR

RECCE-18 MCMR PRECISION RIFLE – 5.56 NATO cal., AR-15 style, rifle length gas system, 18 in. MK12 profile stainless steel barrel, Mod 0 compensator, Mod 0 buttstock, Mod 3 pistol grip, aluminum forged flat-top upper and lower receiver, BCM MCMR-15 free float handguard, Mod 4 charging handle, M4 feed ramp extension, hardcoat anodized black finish, 34-37 in. OAL, 6 1/2 lbs. New 2018.

| MSR $1,650 | $1,350 | $875 | $650 | $525 | $450 | $385 | $350 | |

BUSHMASTER FIREARMS INTERNATIONAL

Current trademark of carbines, rifles, and pistols established in 1978, currently manufactured in Huntsville, AL, and company headquarters located in Madison, NC. Previously located in Windham, ME until 2011. On March 31, 2011, Freedom Group Inc. announced that Bushmaster's manufacturing facility in Windham, ME would be closing, and new Bushmaster products would be produced in other Freedom Group facilities. The previous company name was Bushmaster Firearms, and the name changed after the company was sold on April 13, 2006 to Cerberus, and became part of the Freedom Group Inc. Older mfg. was by Gwinn Arms Co. located in Winston-Salem, NC 1972-1974. The Quality Parts Co. gained control in 1986. Distributor, dealer, or consumer direct sales.

During 2003, Bushmaster purchased Professional Ordnance, previous maker of the Carbon 15 Series of semi-auto pistols and rifles/carbines. For pre-2003 Carbon 15 manufacture, please refer to the Professional Ordnance section in this text.

Bushmaster formed a custom shop during 2009, and many configurations are now available by special order only. Please contact Bushmaster directly for more information and availability on these special order guns.

PISTOLS: SEMI-AUTO

CARBON-15 TYPE P21S/TYPE 21 – 5.56 NATO cal., GIO, ultra lightweight carbon fiber upper and lower receivers, 7 1/4 in. "Profile" stainless steel barrel, quick detachable muzzle compensator, ghost ring sights, 10 or 30 (new late 2004) shot mag., A2 pistol grip, also accepts AR-15 type mags., Stoner type operating sytem, tool steel bolt, extractor and carrier, 40 oz. Mfg. 2003-2012 (Bushmaster mfg.).

| | | $725 | $625 | $550 | $475 | $400 | $325 | $295 | $871 |

Subtract approx. $200 if without full-length barrel shroud and Picatinny rail (Type 21, disc. 2005).

CARBON-15 TYPE 97/TYPE P97S – GIO, similar to Professional Ordnance Carbon 15 Type 20, except has fluted barrel, Hogue overmolded pistol grip and chrome plated bolt carrier, Type 97S has full-length barrel shroud, upper and lower Picatinny rail, 46 oz. Mfg. 2003-2012 (Bushmaster mfg.).

| | | $695 | $600 | $525 | $450 | $375 | $300 | $285 | $825 |

Add $78 for Model P97S with full-length barrel shroud and lower Picatinny rail.

Subtract approx. $100 if w/o full-length barrel shroud and lower Picatinny rail (disc.)

CARBON-15 9MM – 9mm Para. cal., blowback operation, carbon fiber composite receivers, 7 1/2 in. steel barrel with A1 birdcage flash hider, A2 front sight, full-length Picatinny optics rail, Neoprene foam sleeve over buffer tube, 10 or 30 shot mag, 4.6 lbs. Mfg. 2006-2012.

| | | $785 | $710 | $625 | $550 | $475 | $400 | $325 | $871 |

PIT VIPER AP-21 – 5.56 NATO cal., GIO, 7 1/4 in. barrel with birdcage flash suppressor, visible upper gas transfer tube, receiver Picatinny rail, approx. 3 1/2 lbs. Limited mfg. 2011 only.

| | | $725 | $625 | $550 | $475 | $400 | $325 | $295 | $873 |

SQUAREDROP PISTOL – 5.56 NATO or .300 AAC Blackout cal., 7, 9, or 10 in. chrome moly steel barrel, AAC SquareDrop and Blackout flash hider, 30 shot mag., Mil-Std upper and lower receiver, SquareDrop rail, SB tactical arm brace, ALG defense fire control group. New 2018.

| MSR $1,399 | $1,175 | $1,000 | $850 | $725 | $600 | $500 | $400 | |

XM-15 PATROLMAN'S AR PISTOL – 5.56 NATO cal., GIO, 7 or 10 1/2 in. stainless steel barrel with A2 flash hider, knurled free float tubular handguard, flat-top receiver with Picatinny rail, Phase 5 ambi single point sling attachment, A2 pistol grip and standard trigger guard, aluminum pistol buffer tube with foam featuring laser engraved Bushmaster logo, 30 shot mag., approx. 5 1/2 lbs. Mfg. 2013-2015.

| | | $825 | $700 | $600 | $525 | $450 | $375 | $325 | $973 |

XM-15 ENHANCED PATROLMAN'S AR PISTOL – 5.56 NATO cal., GIO, 7 or 10 1/2 in. stainless steel barrel with AAC 3-prong flash hider, 30 shot mag., free float lightweight quad rail handguard, Phase 5 ambi single point sling attachment, Magpul MOE pistol grip and trigger guard, aluminum pistol buffer tube with foam featuring laser engraved Bushmaster logo. Mfg. 2013-2015.

| | | $995 | $875 | $750 | $675 | $550 | $450 | $350 | $1,229 |

RIFLES: SEMI-AUTO

All current AR-15 style Bushmaster rifles are shipped with a hard plastic lockable case. Most Bushmaster barrels are marked "5.56 NATO", and can be used safely with either 5.56 NATO (higher velocity/pressure) or .223 Rem. cal. ammo.

Information and values for state compliant variations are not listed.

BUSHMASTER FIREARMS INTERNATIONAL, cont. 107 B

MSR	100%	98%	95%	90%	80%	70%	60%	Last MSR

During 2006, Bushmaster began offering a complete gas piston upper receiver/barrel assembly. Last MSRs ranged from $580-$990, depending on caliber and configuration.

The XM-10 typically refers to 7.62 NATO cal., and XM-15 refers to 5.56 NATO cal. on the current models listed.

.300 AAC BLACKOUT – .300 AAC Blackout cal., GIO, 16 in. M4 contour barrel with AAC Blackout muzzle brake, Magpul ACS stock and MOE grip, free floating quad rail, 30 shot mag. (AR compatible), flat-top receiver with Picatinny rail, 6 1/2 lbs. Mfg. 2012-2015.

	$1,275	$850	$600	$495	$425	$375	$350	$1,508

.450 CARBINE/RIFLE – .450 Bushmaster cal., GIO, 16 (carbine) or 20 in. chrome moly steel barrel, 5 shot mag., solid A2 buttstock with trapdoor, A2 pistol grip, forged aluminum A3 flat-top upper receiver with Picatinny rail, free floating vented aluminum forend, 8 1/2 lbs. New 2008.

MSR $1,299	$1,075	$675	$500	$450	$400	$350	$325	

450 BM SD CARBINE – .450 Bushmaster cal., 16 or 20 in. chrome moly steel barrel with muzzle brake, 5 shot mag., ALG advanced combat trigger, B5 SOPMOD stock (16 in. barrel) or Remington R25 stock with recoil pad (20 in. barrel), Hogue grip, Mil-Std upper and lower receiver, rifle length AAC Squaredrop handguard, 6 lbs. New 2018.

Please contact the company directly for pricing and availability for this model.

6.8mm SPC/7.62x39mm CARBINE – 6.8mm SPC or 7.62x39mm (new 2010) cal., GIO, 16 in. M4 profile barrel with Izzy muzzle brake, 6-position telescoping stock, available in A2 (disc. 2012) or A3 configuration, 26 shot mag., includes black web sling, extra mag. and lockable carrying case, approx. 7 lbs. Mfg. late 2006-late 2013.

	$1,175	$775	$550	$465	$415	$375	$350	$1,402

Add $100 for A3 configuration (disc. 2010).

BUSHMASTER RIFLE – 5.56 NATO cal., GPO, top (older models with aluminum receivers) or side mounted charging handle (recent mfg.), steel receiver (current mfg.), 18 1/2 in. barrel, parkerized finish, adj. sights, wood stock, 6 1/4 lbs., base values are for folding stock model.

	$645	$500	$415	$370	$325	$300	$275	$350

Add $40 for electroless nickel finish (disc. 1988).

Add $65 for fixed rock maple wood stock.

This model uses a 30 shot M-16 mag. and the AK-47 gas piston system.

* ***Bushmaster Rifle Combination System*** – GPO, includes rifle with both metal folding stock and wood stock with pistol grip.

	$745	$500	$435	$375	$335	$315	$295	$450

TARGET/COMPETITION A-2/A-3 RIFLE (XM15-E2S) – 5.56 NATO cal., GIO, patterned after the Colt AR-15, 20, 24 (disc. 2012), or 26 (disc. 2002) in. Govt. spec. match grade chrome-lined or stainless steel (new 2002) barrel with A2 flash hider, 10 or 30 shot mag., manganese phosphate or Realtree Camo (20 in. barrel only, mfg. 2004-late 2006) finish, rear sight adj. for windage and elevation, cage flash suppressor (disc. 1994), approx. 8.3 lbs. Mfg. began 1989 in U.S.

MSR $969	$825	$535	$450	$385	$340	$325	$295	

Add $30 for A3 configuration with removable carry handle.

Add $88 for stainless steel barrel with A3 removable carry handle (disc. 2015).

Add $194 for heavy 1 in. diameter competition barrel (disc. 2011).

Add $50 for fluted barrel or $40 for stainless steel barrel (mfg. 2002-2009).

Add $10 for 24 in. (disc. 2012) or $25 for 26 in. (disc. 2002) barrel.

Add $60 for Realtree Camo finish (disc.).

HEAVY BARREL CARBINE A-2/A-3 (XM15-E2S, SHORTY CARBINE) – 5.56 NATO cal., GIO, 11 1/2 (LE only, disc. 1995), 14 (LE only, disc. 1994), or 16 in. heavy barrel with birdcage flash suppressor, 30 shot mag., choice of A2 or A3 configuration, fixed (disc.) or telescoping buttstock, approx. 7.4 lbs. Mfg. began 1989.

MSR $895	$765	$515	$440	$375	$335	$315	$295	

Add $52 for A3 configuration with removable carry handle.

This model does not have the target rear sight system of the XM15-E2S rifle.

* ***M4 Post-Ban Carbine (XM15-E2S)*** – 5.56 NATO cal., GIO, 16 in. barrel, fixed or telestock (new late 2004) tubular stock, pistol grip, black, Flat Dark Earth, OD Green, phosphate (disc.), A-TACS camo, or Desert Camo (stock, pistol grip, and forearm only, disc. 2005) finish, M4 carbine configuration with permanently attached Izzy muzzle brake, 30 shot mag. became standard in late 2004. Mfg. 2003-2015.

	$1,125	$700	$525	$450	$400	$350	$325	$1,331

Add $107 for A-TACS camo.

Add $35 for desert camo finish (disc. 2005).

Add $85 for A3 removable carrying handle (disc. 2012).

B 108 BUSHMASTER FIREARMS INTERNATIONAL, cont.

MSR	100%	98%	95%	90%	80%	70%	60%	Last MSR

* XM-15 Limited Edition 20th Anniversary Rifle – GIO, 20 in. barrel, features 20th Anniversary engraving on upper and lower receiver, special medallion in buttstock, includes hardwood presentation case. Limited mfg. 1998-99.

| | $1,385 | $895 | $675 | $525 | $450 | $385 | $350 | |

* XM-15 Limited Edition 25th Anniversary Carbine – GIO, skeletonized tubular stock, pistol grip, A3 type flat-top with flip-up sights, laser engraved 25th Anniversary crest on lower magwell, nickel plated ejection port cover. Limited mfg. of 1,500 during 2003.

| | $1,385 | $895 | $675 | $525 | $450 | $385 | $350 | $1,695 |

* E2 Carbine – 5.56 NATO cal., GIO, 16 in. match chrome-lined barrel with new M16A2 handguard and short suppressor, choice of A1 or E2 sights. Mfg. 1994-1995.

| | $765 | $515 | $440 | $375 | $335 | $315 | $295 | |

Add approx. $50 for E2 sighting system.

AK CARBINE – 5.56 NATO cal., 17 in. barrel featuring AK-47 style muzzle brake, telestock standard, choice of A2 or A3 configuration, ribbed oval forearm, approx. 7 1/2 lbs. Mfg. 2008-2010.

| | $1,025 | $625 | $495 | $450 | $395 | $350 | $325 | $1,215 |

Add $85 for A3 removable carry handle.

DISSIPATOR CARBINE – 5.56 NATO cal., GIO, 16 in. heavy barrel with full-length forearm and special gas block placement (gas block system is located behind the front sight base and under the rifle length handguard), 30 shot mag., A2 or A3 style with choice of solid buttstock or 6-position telestock, lockable carrying case. Mfg. 2004-2010.

| | $1,050 | $650 | $495 | $450 | $395 | $350 | $325 | $1,246 |

Add $25 for telestock.
Add $50 for fluted barrel (disc. 2005).
Add $115 for A3 removable carrying handle.

MOE DISSIPATOR CARBINE – 5.56 NATO cal., GIO, 16 in. barrel with chrome-lined bore and chamber, mid-length gas system, flat-top Picatinny rail, features Magpul Original Equipment (MOE) accessories such as 30 shot PMAG, rifle length handguard, MBUS rear flip sight, Magpul MOE adj. stock with rubber buttpad, MOE grip, black finish, 6.42 lbs. New 2011.

| MSR $1,099 | $915 | $575 | $475 | $415 | $350 | $325 | $300 | |

MOE .223 MID-LENGTH – 5.56 NATO cal., GIO, 16 in. barrel with chrome-lined bore and chamber, 30 shot Magpul PMAG, MBUS rear flip sight, Magpul MOE stock, Magpul MOE pistol grip, mid-length handguard, black or Flat Dark Earth (disc. 2014) finish, 6 1/2 lbs. New 2011.

| MSR $1,099 | $915 | $575 | $475 | $415 | $350 | $325 | $300 | |

MOE .308 MID-LENGTH – .308 Win. cal., GIO, otherwise similar to MOE .223 Mid-length, except has 20 shot mag., Black, OD Green, or FDE finish, 6.1 lbs. Mfg. 2011-2015.

| | $1,275 | $850 | $600 | $495 | $425 | $375 | $350 | $1,546 |

MOE M4-TYPE CARBINE/A-TACS CARBINE – 5.56 NATO cal., GIO, 16 in. heavy profile M4 barrel, 30 shot PMAG, Magpul adj. A-frame buttstock, Magpul MOE handguard, grip, enhanced trigger guard, and Magpul MBUS rear flip sight, Black, OD Green (disc. 2014), FDE (disc. 2014), or A-TACS camo (disc. 2014) finish, 6.42 lbs. Mfg. 2011-2016.

| | $915 | $575 | $475 | $415 | $350 | $325 | $300 | $1,099 |

Add $106 for A-TACS camo (disc. 2014).

M4 A.R.M.S. CARBINE – 5.56 NATO cal., GIO, 16 in. chrome moly vanadium steel barrel with chrome-lined bore and chamber, 30 shot mag., A3 removable carry handle, black, Foliage Green (new 2010), or Flat Dark Earth (new 2010) anodized finish, Magpul adj. buttstock with optional MOE (new 2010), Hogue pistol grip, optional Troy four rail handguard and front sights or A.R.M.S. 41-B front and rear flip-up sights (new 2010, became standard 2011), 6.2 lbs. Mfg. 2009-2011.

| | $1,050 | $650 | $495 | $450 | $395 | $350 | $325 | $1,247 |

Subtract approx. 10% if without A.R.M.S. front and rear flip-up sights.

PATROLMAN'S CARBINE – 5.56 NATO, 6.8 SPC, or 7.62x39mm NATO cal., GIO, 16 in. standard barrel, choice of A2 (bullet button) or A3 configuration, two-piece tubular handguard, 6-position adj. stock, black finish only, approx. 6 1/2 lbs. Disc. 2013.

| | $1,065 | $650 | $500 | $450 | $395 | $350 | $325 | $1,275 |

M4 PATROLMAN'S CARBINE – 5.56 NATO cal., GIO, choice of A2 or A3 configuration, 16 in. chrome-lined M4 barrel with A2 flash hider, 30 shot mag., 6-position telestock, detachable carry handle (A3 only), black anodized finish, approx. 6 1/2 lbs. New 2009.

| MSR $895 | $765 | $515 | $440 | $375 | $335 | $315 | $295 | |

Add $52 for A3 detachable carry handle.

BUSHMASTER FIREARMS INTERNATIONAL, cont. 109 B

MSR	100%	98%	95%	90%	80%	70%	60%	Last MSR

M4 A3 PATROLMAN'S CARBINE CERAKOTE – 5.56 NATO cal., GIO, 16 in. M4 barrel with A2 flash hider, A3 upper with removable carry handle, A2 carbine two-piece handguard, 6-position M4 stock, 30 shot mag., choice of OD Green or FDE Cerakote finished receiver, 6.7 lbs. Mfg. 2013-2014.

	$1,100	$675	$525	$450	$400	$350	$325	$1,321

M4 A3 PATROLMAN'S CARBINE W/QUAD RAIL – 5.56 NATO cal., 16 in. M4 chrome-lined barrel with A2 flash hider, 30 shot mag., aluminum free float quad rail handguard, forged A3 flat-top upper with detachable carry handle, forged lower with 6-position lightweight M4 stock. New 2011.

MSR $1,099	$915	$575	$475	$415	$350	$325	$300	

M17S BULLPUP – 5.56 NATO cal., GIO, semi-auto bullpup configuration featuring gas operated rotating bolt, 10 (C/B 1994) or 30* shot mag., 21 1/2 plain or 22 (disc.) in. barrel with flash suppressor (disc.), glass composites and aluminum construction, phosphate coating, 8 1/4 lbs. Mfg. 1992-2005.

	$750	$650	$525	$475	$425	$400	$385	$765

MINIMALIST-SD – 5.56 NATO/.223 Rem. or .300 AAC Blackout cal., 16 in. lightweight or heavy (.300 AAC Blackout) barrel, AAC 51T flash hider, ACT trigger, Mission First Tactical Minimalist stock and grip, QD cup, rounded rubber buttpad, rifle length AAC SquareDrop handguard, A3 flat-top upper receiver, 6-6.3 lbs. New late 2016.

MSR $1,169	$975	$595	$495	$425	$365	$335	$300	

MODULAR CARBINE – 5.56 NATO cal., GIO, 16 in. barrel with flash suppressor, includes many Bushmaster modular accessories, such as skeleton telestock and four-rail free floating tubular forearm, detachable folding front and rear sights, 10 or 30 (new late 2004) shot mag., 6.3 lbs. Mfg. 2004-2014.

	$1,475	$950	$725	$550	$475	$395	$350	$1,793

SUPERLIGHT CARBINE – 5.56 NATO cal., GIO, 16 in. lightweight barrel, choice of fixed (disc.), 6-position telestock, or stub (disc.) stock with finger groove pistol grip, A2 or A3 type configuration, 30 shot mag., black finish, 5.8-6 1/4 lbs. Mfg. 2004-2013.

	$1,075	$675	$500	$450	$400	$350	$325	$1,291

Subtract 5% if without telestock.

Subtract approx. $75 if without A3 removable carry handle.

ACR BASIC A-TACS CARBINE – 5.56 NATO cal., GPO, 16 1/2 in. barrel with A2 flash hider, 30 shot PMAG, fixed A-frame composite stock with rubber buttpad and sling mounts, black (disc. 2013), Coyote Brown (disc. 2010), or A-TACS camo finish, 8.2 lbs. Disc. 2014.

	$2,125	$1,325	$995	$675	$595	$525	$475	$2,604

ACR BASIC FOLDER – .223 Rem. or 6.8 SPC (mfg. 2013-2015) cal., GPO, 16 1/2 in. barrel with A2 flash hider, 30 shot PMAG, Magpul MBUS front/rear flip-up sights, composite handguard with heat shield, folding and 6-position polymer stock with rubber buttpad and sling mount, black or Coyote Brown finish, 8.2 lbs. New mid-2011.

MSR $2,149	$1,725	$1,050	$850	$625	$550	$475	$425	

ACR BASIC ORC CARBINE – 5.56 NATO cal., GPO, 16 1/2 in. barrel with muzzle brake, full-length top Picatinny rail w/o sights and fixed stock, 30 shot mag., Black or Coyote Brown finish, 8.2 lbs. Mfg. 2011-2013.

	$1,875	$1,100	$895	$650	$575	$495	$425	$2,343

ACR BASIC FOLDER ORC – 5.56 NATO cal., GPO, 16 1/2 in. barrel with muzzle brake, similar to ACR Enhanced Carbine, except does not have 3-sided aluminum handguard with Picatinny rails, Black or Coyote Brown finish, 8.2 lbs. Mfg. 2011 only.

	$1,975	$1,150	$925	$650	$575	$495	$425	$2,490

ACR DMR – 5.56 NATO cal., 18 1/2 in. stainless steel Melonite-treated barrel, AAC 51T Blackout flash hider, Geissele trigger, ACR railed handguard, Magpul PRS style stock, 8 3/4 lbs. Mfg. 2014-2015.

	$2,225	$1,395	$1,050	$675	$595	$525	$475	$2,799

ACR DMR (CURRENT MFG.) – 5.56 NATO/.223 Rem. cal., GPO, 18 1/2 in. hammer forged stainless, Melonite-treated barrel with 51T AAC flash hider, Geissele trigger, modular system for changing barrels and calibers instantly, Magpul PRS2 stock with LOP and cheek weld adjustments, three-rail aluminum handguard, 10.4 lbs. New 2017.

MSR $2,569	$2,050	$1,250	$950	$650	$575	$495	$475	

ACR ENHANCED – 5.56 NATO or 6.8 SPC (while advertised in 2010, this caliber hasn't been mfg. to date) cal., Bushmaster proprietary GPO, modular design allows caliber interchangeability by changing the barrel, magazine, and bolt head, 16 1/2 in. chrome moly steel barrel with Melonite coating, AAC Blackout NSM flash hider, ambidextrous controls, adj. two-position gas piston, 30 shot mag., folding or 6-position telestock, black or Coyote Brown finish, three sided aluminum handguard, Magpul MBUS front/rear flip-up sights, upper and lower accessory rails, includes sling, hard case, and extra mag., 8.2 lbs. New 2010.

MSR $2,249	$1,795	$1,050	$875	$625	$550	$475	$425	

B 110 BUSHMASTER FIREARMS INTERNATIONAL, cont.

MSR	100%	98%	95%	90%	80%	70%	60%	Last MSR

ACR ORC BULLET BUTTON – .223 Rem. cal., 16 in. M4 contour barrel with A2 flash hider, 10 shot mag., Bullet Button lower receiver. Mfg. 2015-2016.

| | $1,795 | $1,050 | $875 | $625 | $550 | $475 | $425 | $2,249 |

ACR PATROL CARBINE – 5.56 NATO or 6.8 SPC cal., GPO, 16 1/2 in. chrome moly steel barrel with Melonite coating, AAC Blackout flash hider, ratchet-style suppressor mounting, 30 shot mag., fixed stock, adj. cheekpiece, Picatinny rail, includes sling and three mags, 8.2 lbs. Mfg. 2010-2014.

| | $2,050 | $1,250 | $950 | $650 | $575 | $495 | $475 | $2,552 |

ACR SPECIAL PURPOSE CARBINE – 5.56 NATO cal., GPO, 16 1/2 in. cold hammer forged barrel, folding and 6-position telescoping polymer stock with rubber buttpad and sling mounts, quad Picatinny rails, and includes three 30 shot PMAG magazines and soft nylon case, black finish only, 8.3 lbs. Mfg. 2011-2014.

| | $2,225 | $1,395 | $1,050 | $675 | $595 | $525 | $475 | $2,799 |

ORC (OPTICS READY CARBINE) – 5.56 NATO or .308 Win. (mfg. 2010-2012) cal., GIO, 16 in. barrel with A2 birdcage flash suppressor, receiver length Picatinny rail with risers ready for optical sights, 6-position telestock, 30 shot mag., oval M4 type forearm, 6 lbs. Mfg. 2008-2013.

| | $935 | $575 | $475 | $415 | $350 | $325 | $300 | $1,112 |

Add $239 for .308 Win. cal. (mfg. 2010-2012).

ORC 5.56 – 5.56 NATO cal., GPO, 16 or 18 (disc.) in. heavy profile barrel with flash suppressor, full-length receiver Picatinny rail, heavy oval handguard, 6-position telescoping stock, 10 or 30 shot mag., black finish, 7 3/4 lbs. Mfg. 2011-2014.

| | $915 | $575 | $475 | $415 | $350 | $325 | $300 | $1,083 |

MOE/ORC GAS PISTON CARBINE – 5.56 NATO cal., GPO, 16 in. barrel, MOE carbine features many Magpul accessories, is available in black, OD Green, or FDE finish, ORC model does not have MOE features, but 6-position tactical stock and receiver length Picatinny rail with risers for optics, approx. 6.3 lbs. Mfg. 2011-2012.

| | $1,050 | $650 | $495 | $450 | $395 | $350 | $325 | $1,247 |

Add $89 for ORC model.

Add $100-$149 for extra Magpul features on MOE model.

GAS PISTON CARBINE – 5.56 NATO cal., GPO, 16 in. M4 profile barrel with flash suppressor, telestock, ribbed oval forearm with flip-up sight. Mfg. 2008-2010.

| | $1,525 | $975 | $750 | $575 | $495 | $425 | $375 | $1,850 |

HUNTER – .308 Win. cal., GIO, 20 in. fluted barrel, vented free floating aluminum forearm tube, 10 shot mag., Hogue rubberized pistol grip (Hunter) or A2 grip (Vista, disc. late 2011), Grey/Green or camo finish, 8.2 lbs. Mfg. 2011-2013.

| | $1,385 | $895 | $675 | $525 | $450 | $385 | $350 | $1,685 |

Add $100 for Vista Hunter model (disc. late 2011).

PREDATOR – 5.56 NATO/.223 Rem. cal., GIO, includes DCM (disc.) 20 in. extra fluted, or stainless steel (disc. 2006) predator barrel, two-stage competition trigger, rubberized pistol grip, flat-top receiver with mini-risers (adds 1/2 in. height for scope mounting), free floating vented tube forearm, 5 or 10 (disc.) shot mag., controlled ejection path, choice of black or A-TACS Digital Camo (mfg. 2011-2013, compliant configuration only) finish, 8 lbs. Mfg. 2006-2013, reintroduced 2017.

| MSR $1,159 | $975 | $595 | $495 | $425 | $365 | $335 | $300 | |

Last MSR in 2013 was $1,415.

Add $104 for A-TACS Digital Camo finish (compliant configuration only, disc. 2013).

The stainless variation included an adj. ergonomic pistol grip.

DCM COMPETITION RIFLE – 5.56 NATO cal., GIO, includes DCM competition features such as modified A2 rear sight, 20 in. extra heavy 1 in. diameter competition barrel, custom trigger job, and free floating handguard. Mfg. 1998-2005.

| | $1,250 | $825 | $575 | $475 | $425 | $375 | $350 | $1,495 |

DCM-XR COMPETITION RIFLE – 5.56 NATO cal., GIO, 20 in. extra heavy competition barrel, dual aperture rear sight and competition ground for clarity front sight, free floating ribbed forearm, competition trigger, choice of A2 solid or A3 removable carry handle, 13 1/2 lbs. Mfg. 2008-2010.

| | $950 | $595 | $495 | $425 | $365 | $335 | $300 | $1,150 |

Add $100 for A3 removable carry handle.

CARBINE-15 COMPETITION – 5.56 NATO cal., GIO, various configurations, choice of extra heavy or heavy barrel in 20 or 24 in. with or w/o muzzle brake, A2 or A3 configuration, various type of sights, 8.5-13.85 lbs. Mfg. 2011 only.

| | $935 | $575 | $475 | $415 | $350 | $325 | $300 | $1,112 |

Add approx. $75 for A3 removable carry handle.

Add $194 for heavy 1 in. diameter competition barrel.

BUSHMASTER FIREARMS INTERNATIONAL, cont. 111 B

MSR	100%	98%	95%	90%	80%	70%	60%	Last MSR

CARBON-15 R21 – 5.56 NATO cal., GIO, Stoner type operating system, 16 in. "Profile" stainless steel barrel, quick detachable muzzle compensator, ultra lightweight carbon fiber upper and lower receivers, tool steel bolt, extractor and carrier, optics mounting base, fixed tube stock, 10 or 30 (new late 2004) shot mag., also accepts AR-15 type mags., 3.9 lbs. Mfg. 2003-2009 (Bushmaster mfg.).

	$850	$550	$465	$395	$350	$325	$295	$990

* Carbon-15 Lady – 5.56 NATO cal., GIO, 16 in. barrel, includes overall tan finish (except for barrel) and webbed tube stock with recoil pad, chrome/nickel plating on small parts, supplied with soft case, 4 lbs. Mfg. 2004-2006.

	$850	$550	$465	$395	$350	$325	$295	$989

CARBON-15 (R97/97S) – 5.56 NATO cal., AR-15 style, GIO, 16 in. fluted stainless steel barrel, quick detachable muzzle compensator, ultra lightweight carbon fiber upper and lower receivers, hard chromed tool steel bolt, extractor and carrier, optics mounting base, 10 or 30 (new late 2004) shot mag., quick detachable stock, also accepts AR-15 type mags., 3.9 or 4.3 (Model 97S) lbs. Mfg. 2003-2010.

	$1,075	$675	$500	$450	$400	$350	$325	$1,300

Subtract approx. $175 without Picatinny rail and "Scout" extension, double walled heat shield foregrip, ambidextrous safety, and multi-carry silent sling (Model Type 97, disc. 2005).

CARBON-15 .22 LR – .22 LR cal., GIO, similar to Carbon-15 R21, 16 in. barrel, Picatinny rail, 10 shot mag., fixed stock, approx. 4.4 lbs. Disc. 2009.

	$675	$500	$425	$375	$335	$315	$295	$790

Bushmaster also made a Carbon-15 .22 rimfire upper receiver/barrel assembly, which is exclusively designed for Bushmaster lower receivers - last MSR was $387 (new 2005).

CARBON-15 9MM – 9mm Para. cal., blowback operation, carbon fiber composite receiver, 16 in. steel barrel with A1 birdcage flash suppressor, A2 front sight and dual aperture rear sight, Picatinny optics rail, collapsible stock, 10 or 30 shot mag., 5.7 lbs. Mfg. 2006-2012.

	$800	$525	$450	$385	$340	$325	$295	$933

CARBON-15 TOP LOADING RIFLE – 5.56 NATO cal., GIO, carbon fiber composite receiver, 16 in. M4 profile barrel with Izzy suppressor, A2 front sight and dual aperture rear sight, Picatinny optics rail, collapsible stock, 10 shot top-loading internal mag., 5.8 lbs. Mfg. 2006-2010.

	$915	$575	$475	$415	$350	$325	$300	$1,100

CARBON-15 MODEL 4 CARBINE – 5.56 NATO cal., GIO, carbon composite receiver, collapsible tube stock, 14 1/2 (LE only), or 16 (disc. 2012) in. barrel with compensator, 30 shot mag., semi-auto design styled after the military M4, 5 1/2 lbs. Mfg. 2005-2013.

	$825	$535	$450	$385	$340	$325	$295	$956

CARBON-15 FLAT-TOP CARBINE – 5.56 NATO cal., GIO, 16 in. M4 barrel, muzzle fitted with Izzy flash hider, 30 shot mag., receiver length Picatinny rail with dual aperture flip-up rear sight, 6-position stock, black finish, 5 1/2 lbs. Mfg. 2006-2015.

	$825	$535	$450	$385	$340	$325	$295	$956

CARBON-15 SUPERLIGHT ORC W/RED DOT – 5.56 NATO cal., GIO, 16 in. super light contour barrel with A2 flash hider, 10 (disc. 2013) or 30 shot mag., red dot optical sight with rings and riser blocks, 6-position stock, black finish. Mfg. 2012-2015.

	$745	$500	$435	$375	$335	$315	$295	$866

CARBON-15 M4 QUAD RAIL – 5.56 NATO cal., GIO, 16 in. M4 barrel with A2 flash hider, 30 shot mag., fixed front sight base and bayonet lug, Mission First Tactical polymer quad rail with rail covers, 6-position stock, black finish, 6 1/4 lbs. Mfg. 2014-2015.

	$745	$500	$435	$375	$335	$315	$295	$866

CARBON-15 C22 COMBO – .22 LR and 5.56 NATO cals., GIO, includes two barrels chambered for .22 LR and 5.56 NATO cals., flat-top receiver with Picatinny rail, 16 in. M4 style barrels with A2 flash hiders, fixed front sight base, Mission First Tactical polymer quad rail with rail covers, 6-position stock, supplied with 25 shot (.22 LR cal.) and 30 shot (5.56 NATO) magazines. Mfg. 2013-2015.

	$1,025	$625	$495	$450	$395	$350	$325	$1,222

CARBON 22 – .22 LR cal., 16 in. M4 contour barrel with A2 flash hider, 25 shot mag., 6-position stock assembly, Mission First Tactical polymer quad rail with rail covers. Mfg. 2014-2015.

	$425	$375	$350	$325	$300	$290	$275	$499

B 112 BUSHMASTER FIREARMS INTERNATIONAL, cont.

MSR	100%	98%	95%	90%	80%	70%	60%	Last MSR

V-MATCH COMPETITION RIFLE – 5.56 NATO cal., GIO, top-of-the line match/competition rifle, flat-top receiver with extended aluminum barrel shroud, choice of 20, 24, or 26 (disc. 2002) in. barrel, 8.3 lbs. Mfg. 1994-2010.

| | $935 | $575 | $475 | $415 | $350 | $325 | $300 | $1,115 |

Add $50 for fluted barrel.

Add $10 for 24 in. or $25 for 26 in. (disc. 2002) barrel.

Add $117 for A3 removable carry handle.

* ***V-Match Commando Carbine*** – 5.56 NATO cal., GIO, 16 in. barrel, flat-top receiver with extended aluminum barrel shroud. Mfg. 1997-2010.

| | $935 | $575 | $475 | $415 | $350 | $325 | $300 | $1,105 |

Add $50 for fluted barrel. Add $117 for A3 removable carry handle.

VARMINTER – 5.56 NATO/.223 Rem. cal., GIO, includes DCM (disc.) 24 in. extra heavy fluted or stainless steel (disc. 2013) varmint barrel, competition trigger, rubberized pistol grip, flat-top receiver with mini-risers (adds 1/2 in. height for scope mounting), free floating vented tube forearm, 5 shot mag., controlled ejection path, choice of Black or A-TACS Digital camo (mfg. 2011-2013, compliant configuration only) finish. Mfg. 2002-2013, reintroduced 2017.

| MSR $1,159 | $975 | $595 | $495 | $425 | $365 | $335 | $300 | |

Add $71 for stainless steel barrel (compliant variation only, disc. 2013).

Add $105 for A-TACS Digital camo coverage (compliant configuration only, disc. 2013).

The stainless variation included an adj. ergonomic pistol grip.

VARMINTER W/2020 OPTICS – 5.56 NATO cal., GIO, 24 in. fluted barrel, features Remington's new 2020 Digital Optic System, Magpul stock, includes wheeled hard case with custom fitted foam insert. Mfg. 2014 only.

| | $4,000 | $2,850 | $1,775 | $1,200 | $875 | $775 | $700 | $5,000 |

BUSHMASTER .308 SERIES – .308 Win. cal., GIO, 16 or 20 in. phosphate coated heavy alloy steel barrel with Izzy compensator, 20 shot mag., solid buttstock or skeletonized stock, available in A2 or A3 style with a variety of configurations, including muzzle brakes, flash suppressors, and sighting options. Mfg. late 2004-2005.

| | $1,425 | $925 | $700 | $550 | $475 | $395 | $350 | $1,750 |

Add $10 for 20 in. barrel.

Add $25 for A3 removable carry handle.

Add $50 (16 in. barrel) or $60 (20 in. barrel) for skeletonized stock.

Add approx. $100 for free floating foream.

XM-10 .308 ENHANCED ORC – .308 Win. cal., GIO, 16 in. chrome-lined barrel, Troy modular free floating handguard, Magpul PRS stock and MIAD grip, two-stage trigger, 9 lbs. Mfg. 2014-2016.

| | $1,315 | $850 | $625 | $500 | $435 | $375 | $350 | $1,599 |

XM-10 DMR – 7.62 NATO cal., 18 1/2 in. stainless Cerakote bull barrel, Troy free floating handguard, Magpul PRS stock, MIAD grip and trigger guard, AAC 51T Blackout muzzle brake, Geissele trigger, 10 1/2 lbs. Mfg. 2014 only.

| | $1,650 | $1,000 | $795 | $595 | $495 | $425 | $395 | $1,999 |

XM-10 ORC GEN 1 (ORC .308) – 7.62 NATO cal., GPO, 16 or 18 (disc.) in. heavy profile barrel with A2 birdcage flash suppressor, full-length receiver Picatinny rail, heavy oval handguard, 6-position telescoping stock, 20 shot mag., black finish, 7 3/4 lbs. Mfg. 2011-2015, reintroduced 2017.

| MSR $1,249 | $1,050 | $650 | $495 | $450 | $395 | $350 | $325 | |

XM-15 ORC – .300 AAC Blackout cal., AR-15 style, FNC barrel, A2 flash hider, 30 shot PMAG, collapsible stock, vented and knurled free float tube, forged Teflon coated upper and lower receiver. New 2018.

| MSR $929 | $800 | $525 | $450 | $385 | $340 | $325 | $295 | |

XM-15 TACTICAL ORC (BASIC TACTICAL CARBINE) – 5.56 NATO cal., GIO, 16 in. mid-length stainless steel barrel with AAC 51T Blackout flash hider, 15 in. Barnes Precision modular free float handguard, Magpul MOE grip, Magpul MOE stock, two-stage match trigger, enhanced trigger guard, 7 3/4 lbs. Mfg. 2014-2015.

| | $1,125 | $700 | $525 | $450 | $400 | $350 | $325 | $1,350 |

XM-15 QRC (QUICK RESPONSE CARBINE) – 5.56 NATO cal., GIO, 16 in. superlight contour chrome moly barrel with A2 birdcage flash hider, 10 shot mag., quick detach mini red dot sight, forged lower and A3 flat-top upper receiver, 6-position collapsible M4 stock, Melonite coated barrel. New 2016.

| MSR $769 | $665 | $500 | $415 | $375 | $335 | $315 | $295 | |

Subtract $30 if without mini red dot sight (Optics Ready model).

XM-15 3-GUN ENHANCED CARBINE – 5.56 NATO cal., GIO, 16 in. mid-length stainless steel barrel, Rolling Thunder compensator, 15 in. AP Custom carbon fiber handguard, Timney trigger, Magpul MIAD grip, Magpul MOE stock, PVD bolt carrier group, crimson anodized receiver, Bravo Company charging handle, ambi selector switch, Arrendondo mag. release, black finish, 7 3/4 lbs. Mfg. 2014-2015.

| | $1,425 | $925 | $700 | $550 | $475 | $395 | $350 | $1,750 |

C SECTION

113 C

C3 DEFENSE, INC.

Previous manufacturer of AR-15 style rifles, upper/lower receivers, and related components located in Hiram, GA until 2013.

MSR	100%	98%	95%	90%	80%	70%	60%	Last MSR

RIFLES: SEMI-AUTO

C3 Defense discontinued all manufacture of complete firearms in 2013. C3 Defense also offered the short barrel C315 Clandestine Series for military/law enforcement.

C315 RANGER – .223 Rem. cal., GIO, 16 in. barrel, matte black finish, forged upper and lower receiver, flared magwell, M4 feed ramps, Mil-Spec trigger group, A2 front post sight, 30 shot mag., 6-position retractable stock, A2 grip, M16 bolt carrier group, Magpul rear MBUS.

	$850	$550	$465	$395	$350	$325	$295	*$995*

C315 RECON – .223 Rem. cal., GIO, 16 in. barrel, matte black finish, forged upper and lower receiver, flared magwell, M4 feed ramps, Mil-Spec trigger group, A2 front sight, 30 shot mag., Magpul MOE stock and grip, M16 bolt carrier group, Magpul MBUS and polymer extended trigger guard.

	$935	$575	$475	$415	$350	$325	$300	*$1,112*

C315 SFR (STANDARD FULL RIFLE) – .223 Rem. cal., GIO, 16 in. barrel, 30 shot mag., flared magwell, Mil-Spec trigger group, Magpul extended trigger guard, A2 front sight, Magpul MOE stock, front textured A2 grip, billet upper and lower receiver, tension screw, M4 feed ramps, carbine length handguard with rail, matte black finish.

	$1,125	$700	$525	$450	$400	$350	$325	*$1,349*

C315 EFR (ENHANCED FULL RIFLE) – .223 Rem. or .300 AAC Blackout cal., GIO, 16 in. barrel, Triad flash suppressor, 30 shot mag., enhanced billet upper and lower, flared magwell, tension screw, M4 feed ramps, Mil-Spec trigger group, 13 in. free float handguard with rail, Magpul MOE stock and grip, Magpul front and rear MBUS, M16 bolt carrier group, matte black finish.

	$1,315	$850	$625	$500	$435	$375	$350	*$1,579*

C315 EFR OW (OVERWATCH) – .223 Rem. or 6.8 SPC cal., GIO, 18 in. stainless steel barrel with fitted bolt, Triad flash suppressor, 20 shot mag., enhanced billet upper and lower, flared magwell, tension screw, front textured grip, M4 feed ramps, two-stage match trigger, 13 in. free float handguard with rail, chromed NM bolt carrier, Magpul UBR stock and MIAD grip, Magpul front and rear MBUS, matte black finish.

	$2,050	$1,250	$950	$650	$575	$495	$475	*$2,539*

CMMG, INC.

Current manufacturer of AR-15 style carbines/rifles and related components and accessories established in 2002, located in Fayette, MO.

PISTOLS: SEMI-AUTO

MK3 K – .308 Win. cal., 12 1/2 in. medium taper stainless steel barrel with A2 muzzle compensator, 20 shot PMAG, billet receivers, single stage trigger, Magpul MOE pistol grip, RKM11 KeyMod free floating handguard, with or without KAK Shockwave brace and tube, 7 1/2 lbs. New 2015.

MSR $1,600	$1,350	$1,200	$1,075	$950	$815	$700	$575

Add $50 for KAK Shockwave brace and tube.

MK4 K – 5.56 NATO cal., 12 1/2 in. barrel with A2 muzzle compensator, 30 shot PMAG, Magpul MOE pistol grip and trigger guard, with or without KAK Shockwave brace, 6 lbs. New 2015.

MSR $1,000	$850	$725	$650	$585	$515	$450	$395

Add $50 for KAK Shockwave brace.

MK4 PDW – .300 AAC Blackout cal., 8 in. medium taper barrel with A2 muzzle compensator, 30 shot Magpul PMAG, single stage trigger, free floating KeyMod handguard, Magpul MOE pistol grip, ambidextrous rear sling mount, 5.3 lbs. New mid-2014.

MSR $1,000	$850	$725	$650	$585	$515	$450	$395

Add $50 for pistol stabilizing brace.

MK9 PDW – 9mm Para. cal., 8 1/2 in. barrel with A2 muzzle compensator, 32 shot mag., free floating KeyMod handguard, Magpul MOE pistol grip and MOE trigger guard, single stage trigger, with or without KAK Shockwave arm brace (new 2018), ambidextrous rear sling mount, 5.3 lbs. New mid-2014.

MSR $1,100	$925	$850	$725	$625	$550	$475	$425

Add $50 for KAK Shockwave arm brace and tube (new 2018).

C 114 CMMG, INC., cont.

MSR	100%	98%	95%	90%	80%	70%	60%	Last MSR

MK47 MUTANT AKS8 – 7.62x39mm cal., 8 in. medium taper barrel, KRINK muzzle device, 30 shot Magpul AK/AKM MOE mag., SST, Magpul MOE pistol grip, billet receivers, RKM9 KeyMod handguard, with or w/o KAK Shockwave arm brace, black finish. New 2016.

| MSR $1,550 | $1,315 | $1,165 | $1,050 | $915 | $785 | $665 | $550 | |

Add $50 for KAK Shockwave arm brace.

MK47 MUTANT K – 7.62x39mm cal., 10 in. medium taper barrel, SV muzzle brake, accepts all standard AK mags., Magpul MOE pistol grip, billet aluminum receivers, RKM9 KeyMod handguard, with or w/o KAK Shockwave brace, black finish, 6 lbs. New 2016.

| MSR $1,500 | $1,275 | $1,125 | $1,025 | $875 | $750 | $625 | $525 | |

Add $50 for KAK Shockwave brace.

MKG PDW GUARD – .45 ACP cal., 8 in. medium taper barrel, 13 shot mag., Magpul MOE pistol grip, with or w/o KAK Shockwave arm brace and tube, black finish. New 2018.

| MSR $1,300 | $1,100 | $995 | $875 | $735 | $650 | $550 | $465 | |

Add $50 for KAK Shockwave arm brace and tube.

MKGs PDW GUARD – 9mm Para. cal., 8 1/2 in. medium taper barrel, 33 shot mag., with or w/o KAK Shockwave brace, black finish. New 2018.

| MSR $1,300 | $1,100 | $995 | $875 | $735 | $650 | $550 | $465 | |

Add $50 for KAK Shockwave arm brace.

MKW ANVIL K – 6.5 Grendel or .458 SOCOM cal., 12 1/2 in. medium taper chrome moly or stainless steel barrel, A2 compensator (6.5 Grendel) or SV muzzle brake (.458 SOCOM), 10 shot mag. (.458 cal. utilizes Lancer L5), Magpul MOE pistol grip, RKM11 handguard, with or w/o KAK Shockwave arm brace and tube, black finish. New 2018.

| MSR $1,700 | $1,450 | $1,275 | $1,125 | $1,000 | $850 | $735 | $595 | |

Add $50 for KAK Shockwave arm brace and tube.
Add $150 for .458 SOCOM cal.

RIFLES: SEMI-AUTO

.22 LR SERIES

* **M4 Profile Model 22A7C3D** – .22 LR cal., AR-15 style, GIO, 16 in. WASP treated chrome moly steel M4 barrel, phosphated bolt group, 6-position stock, 25 shot grey mag., optics ready with railed gas block or low profile railed gas block, black finish. Disc. 2013.

| | $650 | $575 | $510 | $440 | $385 | $340 | $325 | $750 |

* **Lightweight Model 22A1CF6** – .22 LR cal., AR-15 style, GIO, 16 in. WASP treated chrome moly steel M4 lightweight barrel, stainless steel bolt group with BHOA and forward assist adapter, M4 handguard, 6-position stock, 25 shot Evolution mag., "F" marked front sight base and Magpul MBUS rear sight, black finish. Disc. 2013.

| | $725 | $500 | $435 | $375 | $335 | $315 | $295 | $830 |

.300 AAC BLACKOUT SERIES

* **Model 30AF8A6** – .300 AAC Blackout cal., GIO, 16 in. M300 profile WASP treated chrome moly steel barrel, 30 shot PMAG, optics ready with low profile gas block, K9 quad rail, mid-length free float tube, 6-position stock, black finish. Disc. 2013.

| | $850 | $550 | $465 | $395 | $350 | $325 | $295 | $1,000 |

* **Model 30A77E1 Stainless** – .300 AAC Blackout cal., GIO, 16 in. M300 profile stainless steel barrel, 30 shot PMAG, mid-length handguard, carbine low profile gas block, 6-position stock, "F" marked front sight base and Magpul MBUS rear sight, black finish. Disc. 2013.

| | $850 | $550 | $465 | $395 | $350 | $325 | $295 | $1,050 |

* **Model 30AF8DF** – .300 AAC Blackout cal., GIO, 16 in. M300 profile WASP treated chrome moly barrel, 30 shot PMAG, Revolution handguard with 5 slot rails and Revolution modular handguard panels, "F" marked front sight base and Magpul MBUS rear sight, 6-position stock, black finish. Disc. 2013.

| | $875 | $550 | $465 | $395 | $350 | $325 | $300 | $1,050 |

.308 MK3 SERIES

– .308 Win./7.62 NATO cal., GIO, standard barrel options include 16 or 18 in. stainless steel medium contour or a hammer forged chrome-lined barrel, aluminum upper and lower receivers, uses SR25 or LR308 mags., and can be configured with Magpul MOE stocks, MOE pistol grips, and CMMG two-stage triggers. Disc. 2013.

* **Model 38A20FB** – .308 Win. cal., GIO, 18 in. medium contour stainless steel threaded barrel, 20 shot PMAG, low profile gas block, 10 in. modular free float tube, 4-slot rail, Mil-Spec 6-position stock, standard trigger, black finish. Disc. 2013.

| | $1,195 | $795 | $550 | $465 | $415 | $375 | $350 | $1,450 |

CMMG, INC., cont. 115 C

MSR	100%	98%	95%	90%	80%	70%	60%	Last MSR

* **Model 38AB136** – .308 Win. cal., GIO, 16 in. medium contour cold hammer forged stainless steel barrel, 20 shot PMAG, low profile gas block, 10 in. modular free float tube, three 4-slot rails, Mil-Spec 6-position Magpul MOE stock and grip, two-stage trigger, black finish. Disc. 2013.

	$1,315	$850	$625	$500	$435	$375	$350	$1,600

* **Model 38A6DFO** – .308 Win. cal., GIO, 16 in. hammer forged barrel, 20 shot PMAG, low profile gas block, modular free float tube, 4-slot rail, Magpul MOE stock and grip, two-stage trigger, black finish. Disc. 2013.

	$1,525	$975	$750	$575	$495	$425	$375	$1,850

* **Model 38AF432** – .308 Win. cal., GIO, 18 in. threaded hammer forged barrel, 20 shot PMAG, low profile gas block, 10 in. modular free float tube, 4-slot rail, 6-position stock, black finish. Disc. 2013.

	$1,385	$895	$675	$525	$450	$385	$350	$1,700

5.56 HAMMER FORGED SERIES – 5.56 NATO cal., GIO, 16 in. hammer forged chrome-lined M4, M10, or Government profile barrel, 30 shot Magpul PMAG, "F" marked front sight base, with or w/o Magpul MBUS rear sight, black or FDE finish, other options available. Disc. 2013.

* **Model 55AD33B** – 5.56 NATO cal., GIO, 16 in. hammer forged chrome-lined barrel, 30 shot Magpul PMAG, mid-length low profile gas block, "F" marked front sight base and Magpul MBUS rear sight, Magpul MOE rifle length handguard, Mil-Spec 6-position Magpul MOE stock and grip, black finish. Disc. 2013.

	$1,050	$650	$495	$450	$395	$350	$325	$1,250

* **Model 55AD3A1** – 5.56 NATO cal., GIO, 16 in. M10 profile cold hammer forged chrome-lined barrel, 30 shot PMAG, mid-length handguard, "F" marked front sight base and Magpul MBUS rear sight, 6-position stock, black finish. Disc. 2013.

	$995	$625	$495	$450	$395	$350	$325	$1,180

* **Model 55AD37C** – 5.56 NATO cal., GIO, 16 in. M10 profile hammer forged chrome-lined barrel, 30 shot Magpul PMAG, "F" marked front sight base and Magpul MBUS rear sight, mid-length low pro gas block, Magpul MOE rifle length handguard, Mil-Spec 6-position Magpul MOE stock and grip, FDE finish. Disc. 2013.

	$1,050	$650	$495	$450	$395	$350	$325	$1,250

* **Model 55AD3B2** – 5.56 NATO cal., GIO, 16 in. M10 profile hammer forged chrome-lined barrel, 30 shot Magpul PMAG, "F" marked front sight base and rear sight, mid-length low profile gas block, Mil-Spec 6-position stock, black finish. Disc. 2013.

	$995	$625	$495	$450	$395	$350	$325	$1,200

* **Model 55A8433** – 5.56 NATO cal., GIO, 16 in. M4 profile hammer forged chrome-lined barrel, 30 shot Magpul PMAG, "F" marked front sight base and rear sight, Mil-Spec 6-position stock, black finish. Disc. 2013.

	$950	$595	$495	$425	$365	$335	$300	$1,150

* **Model 55A5252** – 5.56 NATO cal., GIO, 16 in. Government profile hammer forged chrome-lined barrel, 30 shot Magpul PMAG, "F" marked front sight base and Magpul MBUS rear sight, Magpul MOE mid-length handguard, Mil-Spec 6-position Magpul MOE stock and grip, black finish. Disc. 2013.

	$1,050	$650	$495	$450	$395	$350	$325	$1,250

* **Model 55A5244** – 5.56 NATO cal., GIO, 16 in. Government profile hammer forged chrome-lined barrel, 30 shot Magpul PMAG, "F" marked front sight base and Magpul MBUS rear sight, Magpul MOE mid-length handguard, Mil-Spec 6-position Magpul MOE stock and grip, FDE furniture. Disc. 2013.

	$1,050	$650	$495	$450	$395	$350	$325	$1,250

* **Model 55A526D** – 5.56 NATO cal., GIO, 16 in. Government profile hammer forged chrome-lined barrel, 30 shot Magpul PMAG, "F" marked front sight base and rear sight, Mil-Spec 6-position stock, black finish. Disc. 2013.

	$995	$625	$495	$450	$395	$350	$325	$1,200

5.56 LE SERIES – 5.56 NATO cal., GIO or GPO, 16 in. chrome moly M4 or bull barrel, 30 shot Magpul PMAG, WASP (Weapon Armament Surface Protection) finish, the Nitriding conversion is applied to the barrel inside and out, along with the front sight base and uppers, LE rifles use "T" marked upper receivers with M4 feed ramps and forged lower receivers with Mil-Spec components, black or FDE finish. Disc. 2013.

* **Model 55AE1AD** – 5.56 NATO cal., GIO or GPO, 16 in. WASP treated M4 profile chrome moly steel barrel, 30 shot Magpul PMAG, "T" marked front sight base, rear sight, M4 handguard, Mil-Spec 6-position stock, A2 pistol grip, FDE furniture. Disc. 2013.

	$800	$525	$450	$385	$340	$325	$295	$950

* **Model 55AE1BB** – 5.56 NATO cal., GPO or GIO, 16 in. WASP treated M4 profile chrome moly steel barrel, optics ready with piston system, Mil-Spec 6-position stock, 30 shot Magpul PMAG, black finish. Disc. 2013.

	$875	$550	$465	$395	$350	$325	$300	$1,050

C 116 CMMG, INC., cont.

MSR	100%	98%	95%	90%	80%	70%	60%	Last MSR

* **Model 55AED49** – 5.56 NATO cal., GIO or GPO, 16 in. WASP treated chrome moly steel bull barrel, 30 shot Magpul PMAG, optics ready with low profile gas block, carbine length round free float tube, Mil-Spec 6-position stock, black finish. Disc. 2013.

	$725	$500	$435	$375	$335	$315	$295	$850

* **Model 55AEDA5** – 5.56 NATO cal., GIO or GPO, 16 in. WASP treated chrome moly steel bull barrel, 30 shot Magpul PMAG, optics ready with piston system, Revolution handguard with 5 slot rails, Mil-Spec 6-position stock, black finish. Disc. 2013.

	$995	$625	$495	$450	$395	$350	$325	$1,200

5.56 STAINLESS STEEL SERIES – 5.56 NATO cal., GIO, 16, 18, 22, or 24 in. stainless steel M4 profile or bull barrel, with or w/o fluting, 30 shot Magpul PMAG, low profile gas block, A1 or 6-position stock, free float tube, black finish. Disc. 2013.

* **Model 55ABB89** – 5.56 NATO cal., GIO, 16 in. stainless steel bull barrel, 30 shot Magpul PMAG, carbine length round free float handguard tube, low profile gas block, 6-position stock, black finish. Disc. 2013.

	$765	$515	$440	$375	$335	$315	$295	$900

* **Model 55A3C9E** – 5.56 NATO cal., GIO, 18 in. stainless steel bull barrel, 30 shot Magpul PMAG, optics ready with low profile gas block, mid-length round free float tube, Mil-Spec 6-position stock, black finish. Disc. 2013.

	$800	$525	$450	$385	$340	$325	$295	$930

* **Model 55A8EDC** – 5.56 NATO cal., GIO, 22 in. stainless steel bull barrel, 30 shot Magpul PMAG, optics ready low profile gas block, rifle length round free float tube, A1 stock, black finish. Disc. 2013.

	$850	$550	$465	$395	$350	$325	$295	$980

* **Model 55AE392** – 5.56 NATO cal., GIO, 25 in. stainless steel fluted barrel, 30 shot Magpul PMAG, optics ready with low profile gas block, rifle length round free float tube, A1 stock, black finish. Disc. 2013.

	$915	$575	$475	$415	$350	$325	$300	$1,100

* **Model 55A3866** – 5.56 NATO cal., GIO, 16 in. stainless steel M4 profile barrel, 30 shot Magpul PMAG, optics ready with railed gas block, Mil-Spec 6-position stock, black finish. Disc. 2013.

	$800	$525	$450	$385	$340	$325	$295	$950

MK3 – .308 Win. or 6.5mm Creedmoor (new 2018) cal., 18 in. stainless steel heavy taper barrel with A2 compensator, 20 shot PMAG, RKM15 KeyMod free float handguard, billet aluminum receiver, SST, A2 pistol grip, A1 buttstock, 9.3 lbs. New 2014.

MSR $1,650	$1,350	$875	$650	$525	$450	$385	$350	

Add $150 for 6.5mm Creedmoor cal. (new 2018).

MK3 3GR – .308 Win. cal., 18 in. stainless steel heavy taper barrel with CMMG SV muzzle brake, RKM15 KeyMod free float handguard, billet aluminum receiver, Geissele SSA trigger, Magpul MOE pistol grip, trigger guard, and buttstock, 9.4 lbs. New 2014.

MSR $1,900	$1,575	$995	$775	$575	$495	$425	$395	

MK3 CBR (CARBINE BATTLE RIFLE) – .308 Win. cal., GIO, 16 in. Nitride stainless steel match barrel, SureFire SOCOM suppressor adapter muzzle brake, 5, 10, or 20 shot PMAG, full-length free float Revolution KeyMod handguard and KeyMod accessory attachment system, one 5-slot rail, Magpul MOE pistol grip and ACS-L buttstock, Geissele SSA two-stage trigger, two-position selector safety, black or FDE (mfg. 2016-2017) finish, 8.7 lbs.

MSR $2,000	$1,675	$1,000	$825	$625	$550	$475	$425	

Add $150 for FDE finish (mfg. 2016-2017).

MK3 D – .308 Win. cal., GIO, 16 in. chrome-lined hammer forged barrel with A2 compensator, 20 shot PMAG, RKM15 KeyMod free float handguard, billet aluminum receiver, SST, Magpul MOE pistol grip and stock, black furniture, 8.2 lbs. Mfg. 2014 only.

	$1,675	$1,000	$825	$625	$550	$475	$425	$2,000

MK3 DTR /DTR2 – 6.5mm Creedmoor cal., 24 in. heavy taper stainless steel barrel with SV muzzle brake, 20 shot Magpul PMAG, single stage (DTR) or Geissele SSA two-stage (DTR2) trigger, Magpul PRS adj. stock, Magpul MOE pistol grip, RML15 M-LOK handguard, billet aluminum receivers, black finish, 11.3 lbs. New 2018.

MSR $2,100	$1,725	$1,050	$850	$625	$550	$475	$425	

Add $175 for MK3 DTR2 with Geissele SSA two-stage trigger.

MK3 P – 6.5mm Creedmoor cal., 24 in. stainless steel heavy taper barrel, SV muzzle brake, 20 shot Magpul PMAG, SST, Magpul MOE rifle buttstock, Magpul MOE grip, RKM15 KeyMod handguard, billet aluminum receivers, black finish, 10.4 lbs. New 2018.

MSR $1,900	$1,575	$995	$775	$575	$495	$425	$395	

CMMG, INC., cont. 117 C

MSR	100%	98%	95%	90%	80%	70%	60%	Last MSR

MK3 T – .308 Win. cal., 16.1 in. medium taper stainless steel barrel with A2 compensator, 20 shot Magpul PMAG, RKM15 KeyMod free float handguard, billet aluminum receiver, SST, A2 pistol grip, M4 buttstock, black furniture, 8.1 lbs. New 2014.

| MSR $1,700 | $1,385 | $895 | $675 | $525 | $450 | $385 | $350 | |

MK4 – 5.56 NATO cal., 14 1/2 in. chrome-lined barrel with permanently attached A2 compensator (to meet minimum requirements), 30 shot PMAG, single stage trigger, MBUS rear sight, M4 buttstock, A2 pistol grip, forged aluminum receivers, M4 two-piece handguard, black finish, 6 1/2 lbs. Disc. 2016.

| | $950 | $595 | $495 | $425 | $365 | $335 | $300 | *$1,150* |

MK4 3GR – 5.56 NATO cal., 18 in. stainless steel medium taper profile barrel with CMMG SV muzzle brake, RKM14 KeyMod free float handguard, Geissele SSA two-stage trigger, Magpul MOE pistol grip, trigger guard, rifle buttstock, black furniture, 7 lbs. New 2014.

| MSR $1,400 | $1,150 | $750 | $550 | $465 | $415 | $375 | $350 | |

MK4 A4 (GOVERNMENT PROFILE MODEL 22A6A1F) – .22 LR or 5.56 NATO (new 2014) cal., AR-15 style, GIO, 20 in. WASP treated chrome moly steel Government profile barrel with A2 compensator, stainless steel bolt group with BHOA and forward assist adapter, "F" marked front sight base and Magpul MBUS rear sight, A2 two-piece handguard, A1 (disc.) or M4 buttstock with A2 pistol grip, 25 shot Evolution mag., black finish, 6 1/2 lbs. Disc. 2016.

| | $785 | $525 | $450 | $385 | $340 | $325 | $295 | *$925* |

Add $225 for 5.56 NATO cal.

MK4 B16/B18 – 5.56 NATO cal., 16 or 18 in. bull barrel, 30 shot PMAG, single-stage trigger, Mil-Spec buttstock extension, Mil-Spec pistol grip, forged 7075 -T6 receiver, target crown muzzle, CMMG RKM KeyMod handguard, 7.2-7.6 lbs.

| MSR $1,000 | $850 | $550 | $465 | $395 | $350 | $325 | $295 | |

Add $50 for 18 in. barrel (B18).

MK4 D – 5.56 NATO cal., 16.1 in. medium taper hammer forged barrel with A2 compensator, RKM14 KeyMod free float handguard, forged aluminum receiver, SST, Magpul MOE pistol grip, trigger guard, and buttstock, 6.4 lbs. Disc. 2016.

| | $1,150 | $750 | $550 | $465 | $415 | $375 | $350 | *$1,400* |

MK4 DTR2 – .224 Valkyrie cal., long range AR-15, 24 in. medium taper stainless steel barrel, SV brake, 10 shot 6.8 SPC mag., Geissele SSA trigger, Magpul PRS stock, Magpul MOE pistol grip, forged aluminum upper and lower receiver, RML14 handguard, ambidextrous charging handle, black or Cerakote finish in FDE, Burnt Bronze, Midnight Bronze, Sniper Grey, or Titanium, 9.2 lbs. New 2018.

| MSR $1,700 | $1,385 | $895 | $675 | $525 | $450 | $385 | $350 | |

Add $150 for Cerakote finish in FDE, Burnt Bronze, Midnight Bronze, Sniper Grey, or Titanium.

MK4 HT – .22 LR, 5.56 NATO, or .300 AAC Blackout (disc. 2016) cal., GIO or GPO (5.56 NATO only, disc. 2016), 16.1 in. heavy taper chrome moly or stainless steel (disc. 2016) barrel with castellated thread protector, 30 shot Magpul PMAG, SST, M4 buttstock, A2 pistol grip, RKM KeyMod free float handguard, forged aluminum receiver, black finish, 7 lbs. New 2014.

| MSR $925 | $785 | $525 | $450 | $385 | $340 | $325 | $295 | |

Add $125 for 5.56 NATO cal.
Add $125 for stainless steel barrel (disc. 2016).
Add $175 for .300 AAC Blackout cal. (disc. 2016).
Add $425 for GPO (gas piston operation) disc. 2016.

MK4LE – .22 LR, 5.56 NATO, or .300 AAC Blackout cal., AR-15-style, GIO, 16 in. WASP treated chrome moly steel M4 profile barrel or M300 multi-role profile barrel (.300 AAC Blackout only) with A2 compensator, 30 shot PMAG, M4 two-piece handguard, M4 buttstock with A2 pistol grip, forged aluminum receiver, SST, black furniture, "F" marked front sight base and MBUS rear sight, 6.2 lbs.

| MSR $850 | $725 | $500 | $435 | $375 | $335 | $315 | $295 | |

Add $130 for 5.56 NATO cal. or $150 for .300 AAC Blackout cal.

* **MK4LE Optics Ready** – 5.56 NATO or .300 AAC Blackout cal., 16 in. barrel, A2 compensator, 30 shot PMAG, forged 7075-T6 aluminum receivers, SST, M4 two-piece handguard, railed gas block, no sights, M4 buttstock, A2 pistol grip, black finish, 6.7 lbs.

| MSR $950 | $800 | $525 | $450 | $385 | $340 | $325 | $295 | |

MK4LEM – 5.56 NATO cal., GIO, 16 in. chrome moly steel medium taper profile barrel with A2 compensator, mid-length two-piece handguard, forged aluminum receiver, SST, M4 buttstock with A2 pistol grip, black furniture, 6 1/2 lbs. Mfg. 2014-2016.

| | $800 | $525 | $450 | $385 | $340 | $325 | $295 | *$950* |

C 118 CMMG, INC., cont.

MSR	100%	98%	95%	90%	80%	70%	60%	Last MSR

MK4 MSR – 5.56 NATO cal., 16 in. medium taper barrel with SV muzzle brake, 30 shot Magpul PMAG, SST, Magpul MOE pistol grip, trigger guard, and stock, RKM14 KeyMod handguard, black finish, 6.7 lbs. New 2018.

| | MSR $1,150 | $950 | $595 | $495 | $425 | $365 | $335 | $300 | |

MK4 P – .22 Nosler cal., 22 in. medium taper stainless steel barrel, SV muzzle brake, 10 shot mag., SST, Magpul MOE rifle stock, Magpul MOE pistol grip, forged 7075-T6 aluminum receiver, RKM14 KeyMod handguard, black finish, 7.3 lbs. New 2018.

| | MSR $1,200 | $995 | $625 | $495 | $450 | $395 | $350 | $325 | |

MK4 RCE – 5.56 NATO, .300 AAC Blackout, or .22 Nosler (new 2018) cal., gas operated, 16 (5.56 NATO or .300 AAC Blackout only) or 18 (.22 Nosler cal. only) in. Nitride (16 in. barrel only) or stainless steel medium taper profile barrel with CMMG SV brake, 30 shot mag., M4 flat-top upper receiver, aluminum lower, RKM14 KeyMod free float handguard, Geissele two-stage trigger, Magpul MOE pistol grip, MOE trigger guard, CTR buttstock, black or FDE (mfg. 2015-2017) finish, 6.7 lbs. New 2014.

| | MSR $1,350 | $1,125 | $700 | $525 | $450 | $400 | $350 | $325 | |

Add $50 for stainless steel barrel.
Add $50 for .22 Nosler cal. (new 2018).
Add $100 for FDE finish (mfg. 2015-2017).

MK4 S – 5.56 NATO or .22 Nosler (new 2018) cal., 16 (5.56 NATO only, new 2018) or 18 in. stainless steel medium taper barrel with A2 compensator, 10 (.22 Nosler) or 30 shot PMAG (5.56 NATO), SST, 6-pos. M4 buttstock, A2 pistol grip, RKM14 KeyMod free float handguard, forged aluminum receiver, black finish, 6.7 lbs.

| | MSR $1,100 | $915 | $575 | $475 | $415 | $350 | $325 | $300 | |

MK4 T – 9mm Para. (disc. 2014), .22 LR, .300 AAC Blackout, or 5.56 NATO cal., 16.1 in. medium taper chrome moly or stainless steel barrel with A2 compensator, 30 shot PMAG, RKM11 KeyMod free float handguard, forged aluminum receiver, SST, A2 pistol grip, M4 buttstock, 6.3 lbs. New 2014.

| | MSR $1,000 | $850 | $550 | $465 | $395 | $350 | $325 | $295 | |

Add $100 for stainless steel barrel.
Add $150 for 5.56 NATO or .300 AAC Blackout cal. or $250 for 9mm Para. cal. (disc. 2014).

MK4 V – 5.56 NATO cal., 24 in. fluted medium contour stainless steel barrel with target crown, RKM14 KeyMod free float handguard, forged aluminum receiver, SST, A2 pistol grip, A1 fixed buttstock, 7 1/2 lbs. Mfg. 2014-2016.

| | | $1,050 | $650 | $495 | $450 | $395 | $350 | $325 | $1,250 |

MK4 V2 – 5.56 NATO (disc. 2017) or .22 Nosler (new 2018) cal., 24 in. fluted stainless steel barrel, recessed target crown, 10 (.22 Nosler, new 2018) or 30 shot PMAG (disc. 2017), Geissele SSA two-stage trigger, forged 7075-T6 aluminum receivers, RKM14 KeyMod handguard, Magpul MOE pistol grip, stock, and trigger guard, 7 1/2 lbs. New 2015.

| | MSR $1,450 | $1,195 | $795 | $550 | $465 | $415 | $375 | $350 | |

MK9LE – 9mm Para. cal., 16.1 in. barrel with A2 compensator, utilizing Colt pattern magazines, 32 shot mag., "F" marked front sight base and MBUS rear sight, M4 type 2-piece handguard, forged receivers, single stage trigger, A2 pistol grip, M4 buttstock with 6-position receiver extension, black finish, 6.2 lbs. New 2015.

| | MSR $1,100 | $915 | $575 | $475 | $415 | $350 | $325 | $300 | |

* **MK9LE OR** – 9mm Para. cal., similar to MK9LE, except has no sights, comes ready to accept your favorite optic or iron sights, 7.2 lbs. Mfg. 2015-2017.

| | | $895 | $575 | $475 | $395 | $350 | $325 | $300 | |

MK9 T – 9mm Para. cal., 16.1 in. M4 barrel with A2 compensator, 32 shot mag., free floating RKM11 handguard, forged receivers, A2 pistol grip, M4 buttstock with 6-pos. receiver extension, single stage trigger, 6.3 lbs. New 2015.

| | MSR $1,150 | $950 | $595 | $495 | $425 | $365 | $335 | $300 | |

MK47 MUTANT SERIES – 7.62 NATO cal., GIO, 16.1 in. free floated barrel, fully modular, interchangable trigger assembly, rail, grip, buffer tube assembly, buttstock, muzzle brake, and gas system, billet aluminum upper and lower receivers, the lower receiver is designed to accept standard AK magazines, full-length Picatinny rail, optics ready, only 7.2 lbs. New 2015.

* **MK47 Mutant AKM** – 7.62 NATO cal., 16.1 in. barrel with SV muzzle brake, 30 shot AKM PMAG, RKM15 handguard, mid-sized billet receivers, single stage trigger, MOE pistol grip, CTR buttstock, 7.2 lbs. New 2015.

| | MSR $1,650 | $1,350 | $875 | $650 | $525 | $450 | $385 | $350 | |

* **MK47 Mutant AKM2** – 7.62 NATO cal., 16.1 in. barrel with SV muzzle brake, 30 shot AKM PMAG, RKM15 handguard, mid-sized billet aluminum receiver based on MK3 platform, Geissele SSA trigger, Magpul MOE pistol grip, CTR buttstock, top of the line Mutant rifle offering the most features, 7.2 lbs. New 2015.

| | MSR $1,850 | $1,525 | $975 | $750 | $575 | $495 | $425 | $375 | |

MSR		100%	98%	95%	90%	80%	70%	60%	Last MSR

CMMG, INC., cont. 119

* **MK47 Mutant AKS13** – 7.62 NATO cal., pinned gas block, 13 in. medium taper barrel with KRINK muzzle device pinned and welded to meet the 16 in. legal requirement, 30 shot AK PMAG (accepts standard AK mags.), single stage Mil-Spec trigger, Magpul CTR stock, MOE pistol grip, billet aluminum receivers, RKM15 KeyMod handguard, black furniture, 7.4 lbs. New 2016.

MSR $1,750 $1,425 $925 $700 $550 $475 $395 $350

* **MK47 Mutant T** – 7.62 NATO cal., GIO, 16.1 in. barrel with A2 compensator, 30 shot AKM PMAG, RKM15 handguard, billet receivers, single stage trigger, A2 pistol grip stock, this is the entry-level Mutant designed to give the user the opportunity to upgrade as they see fit, 7.2 lbs. New 2015.

MSR $1,500 $1,250 $825 $575 $475 $425 $375 $350

GUARD DRB – 9mm Para. or .45 ACP cal., radial delayed blowback operating system, 16 in. medium taper barrel, SV muzzle brake, 13 (.45 ACP) or 33 (9mm) shot mag., Magpul CTR buttstock, Magpul MOE pistol grip, black finish. New 2018.

MSR $1,400 $1,150 $750 $550 $465 $415 $375 $350

GUARD DRB2 – 9mm Para. or .45 ACP cal., radial delayed blowback operating system, 16 in. medium taper barrel, SV muzzle brake, 13 (.45 ACP) or 33 (9mm Para.) shot mag., Geissele SSA two-stage trigger, Magpul CTR buttstock, Magpul MOE pistol grip, black finish. New 2018.

MSR $1,600 $1,315 $850 $625 $500 $435 $375 $350

GUARD T – 9mm Para. or .45 ACP (new 2018) cal., radial delayed blowback action, 16 in. medium taper barrel, A2 compensator (9mm Para.) or SV muzzle brake (.45 ACP, new 2018), 13 (.45 ACP) or 33 (9mm Para.) shot mag., SST, M4 buttstock w/6-pos. Mil-Spec receiver extension, A2 pistol grip, forged upper and lower receiver, 6 lbs. New 2017.

MSR $1,300 $1,075 $675 $500 $450 $400 $350 $325

MKW ANVIL T – .458 SOCOM or 6.5 Grendel (new 2018) cal., 16 in. medium taper stainless steel barrel with SV muzzle brake (.458 SOCOM) or A2 compensator (6.5 Grendel), 10 shot Lancer L5 mag., single stage Mil-Spec trigger, Mil-Spec buttstock, Mil-Spec pistol grip, low profile (6.5 Grendel) or adj. (.458 SOCOM) gas block, billet 7075-T6 receiver, KeyMod handguard, 7.5 lbs. New 2016.

MSR $1,700 $1,425 $925 $700 $550 $475 $395 $350

Add $150 for .458 SOCOM cal.

MKW ANVIL XBE – .458 SOCOM cal., GIO, 16 in. stainless steel barrel, SV muzzle brake, Lancer L5 10 shot mag., SST Mil-Spec trigger, no sights, Magpul CTR carbine stock, Magpul MOE pistol grip, adj. gas block, billet 7075-T6 receivers, Type III hardcoat anodized finish, 7 lbs. 8 oz. New 2016.

MSR $1,950 $1,600 $1,000 $775 $575 $495 $425 $395

MKW ANVIL XBE2 – .458 SOCOM cal., 16 in. medium taper stainless steel barrel, SV muzzle brake, 10 shot Lancer L5 mag., Geissele SSA two-stage trigger, CTR carbine stock with 6-position receiver extension, Magpul MOE pistol grip, CMMG RKM15 KeyMod handguard, adj. gas block, mid-sized billet 7075 receiver, 7.4 lbs. New 2016.

MSR $2,150 $1,725 $1,050 $850 $625 $550 $475 $425

MKW ANVIL XFT – 6.5 Grendel cal., GIO, 16 in. stainless steel barrel, SV muzzle brake, 10 shot mag., SST Mil-Spec trigger, no sights, Magpul CTR carbine stock with 6-pos. receiver extension, Magpul MOE pistol grip, low profile gas block, billet 7075-T6 receivers, Type III hardcoat anodized finish. New 2018.

MSR $1,800 $1,525 $975 $750 $575 $495 $425 $375

MKW ANVIL XFT2 – 6.5 Grendel cal., GIO, 16 in. medium taper stainless steel barrel with SV muzzle brake, 10 shot mag., Geissele SSA two-stage trigger, Magpul CTR carbine stock with 6-pos. receiver extension, Magpul MOE pistol grip, low profile gas block, hardcoat anodized black finish. New 2018.

MSR $2,000 $1,675 $1,000 $825 $625 $550 $475 $425

CARACAL

Current manufacturer of semi-auto pistols and rifles established in 2006, located in the Abu Dhabi, United Arab Emirates. Currently imported beginning 2011 by Caracal USA, located in Newinton, NH. Previously located in Trussville, AL and Knoxville, TN. Currently distributed in Italy exclusively by Fratelli Tanfoglio Snc, located in Brescia, Italy.

In 2016, Caracal joined forces with Wilcox Industries Corp. located in Newington, NH.

RIFLES: SEMI-AUTO

CAR814 A2 – 5.56 NATO cal., GIO, 16 in. modified M4 barrel, A2 flash hider, Lancer Systems L5 AWM 30 shot mag., Mil-Spec trigger, rear flip-up sight, Magpul CTR carbine stock, Caracal pistol grip, 12 in. free float handguard with M-LOK, 2-point quick detach sling, black or tan finish, 7 lbs.

MSR $999 $850 $550 $465 $395 $350 $325 $295

C 120 CARACAL, cont.

MSR		100%	98%	95%	90%	80%	70%	60%	Last MSR

CAR814 A2 COMP – .223 Wylde chamber, GIO, 18 in. Proof Research carbon fiber barrel with 2-port self-timing muzzle brake, Lancer Systems L5 AWM 30 shot mag., XMR extended mag. release, Geissele S3G single stage trigger, no sights, 6-pos. Minimalist buttstock, Caracal grip, 15 in. free float handguard with M-LOK, 6.4 lbs. New 2018.

| MSR $1,799 | | $1,475 | $950 | $725 | $550 | $475 | $395 | $350 | |

CAR814 A2 PATROL – 5.56 NATO cal., GIO, 16 in. modified M4 barrel, A2 flash hider, 30 shot steel mag., flip-up rear sight, Magpul CTR carbine stock, Caracal grip, Magpul MOE handguard, 2-point QD sling, black or FDE finish, 7 lbs. New 2018.

| MSR $1,249 | | $1,050 | $650 | $495 | $450 | $395 | $350 | $325 | |

Add $50 for FDE finish.

CAR816 A2 – 5.56 NATO cal., GPO, 16 in. modified M4 barrel, A2 flash hider, 30 shot stainless steel/polymer mag., Mil-Spec trigger, front and rear flip-up sights, Magpul STR carbine stock, Caracal pistol grip, quick detach sling, Caracal 9.1 in. handguard with M-LOK, Picatinny rail mount for optics, 3-position adj. gas valve, black or FDE finish, 7.4 lbs. New late 2016.

| MSR $1,849 | | $1,525 | $975 | $750 | $575 | $495 | $425 | $375 | |

Add $50 for FDE finish.

CAVALRY ARMS CORPORATION

Previous manufacturer located in Gilbert, AZ until 2010. Previously located in Mesa, AZ.

RIFLES/CARBINES: SEMI-AUTO

Cavalry Arms Corporation manufactured the CAV-15 Series, patterned after the AR-15 style carbine/rifle. Cavalry Arms also made conversions for select slide action shotguns.

CAV-15 SCOUT CARBINE – .223 Rem. cal., GIO, 16 in. chrome-lined barrel, A2 flash hider, A3 flat-top upper receiver, C6 handguards, longer sight radius, stand alone rear sight, black, green, or Coyote Brown finish. Disc. 2010.

| | | $725 | $500 | $435 | $375 | $335 | $315 | $295 | *$850* |

Add $92 for YHM flip-up front or rear sight.
Add $199 for drop-in rail system.
Add $259 for free float system.

CAV-15 RIFLEMAN – .223 Rem. cal., GIO, 20 in. chrome-lined Govt. profile barrel, A2 flash hider, A3 flat-top upper receiver, A2 handguard, stand alone rear sight, black, green, or Coyote Brown finish. Disc. 2010.

| | | $725 | $500 | $435 | $375 | $335 | $315 | $295 | *$850* |

Add $92 for YHM flip-up front or rear sight.
Add $279 mid-length free float system.
Add $310 for rifle length free float system.

CENTURY ARMS (CENTURY INTERNATIONAL ARMS, INC.)

Current importer and distributor founded in 1961 with current corporate offices located in Delray Beach, FL. Century International Arms, Inc. was previously headquartered in St. Albans, VT until 1997, and Boca Raton, FL from 1997-2004. The company rebranded in late 2014 and is now known as Century Arms.

Century Arms imports a large variety of used military rifles, shotguns, and pistols. Because inventory changes daily, especially on tactical style rifles, carbines and pistols, please contact the company directly for the most recent offerings and pricing (see Trademark Index).

Additionally, Century Arms imports a wide range of accessories, including bayonets, holsters, stocks, magazines, grips, mounts, scopes, misc. parts, new and surplus ammunition, etc., and should be contacted directly (see Trademark Index) for a copy of their most recent catalog, or check their web site for current offerings.

RIFLES/CARBINES: SEMI-AUTO

C15A1 SPORTER – 5.56 NATO cal., AR-15 style, based on M16A1, GIO, triangular "Vietnam era" style handguard, 16 in. barrel with muzzle brake, fixed stock, includes two original Colt 30 shot mags. (disc. 2011) or fixed 10 shot mag. (current mfg.), choice of green polymer or walnut wood furniture, A3 carry handle and sights. Importation began mid-2010.

This model is POR.
Add 15% for High Cap Mag. model.

C15 M4 – 5.56 NATO cal., AR-15 style, 16 in. barrel with birdcage muzzle brake, flat-top receiver with detachable carry handle, adj. T6 stock, one 30 shot mag. Importation began 2014.

| No MSR | | $725 | $500 | $435 | $375 | $335 | $315 | $295 | |

CENTURY ARMS (CENTURY INTERNATIONAL ARMS, INC.), cont. 121 C

MSR	100%	98%	95%	90%	80%	70%	60%	Last MSR

SHOTGUNS

MKA 1919 – 12 ga., AR-15 style, gas operation, aluminum alloy upper, one piece polymer lower receiver, pistol grip fixed stock, matte black or 100% camo finish, right side magwell mag. release, bolt stop, 5 shot detachable mag., A2 removable carry handle and front sight, three internal chokes, integral Picatinny rail, approx. 6 1/2 lbs. Imported from Turkey beginning mid-2012.

No MSR	$850	$750	$640	$575	$475	$385	$300	

CHARLES DALY: 1976-2010

Previous manufactured trademark imported late 1996-early 2010 by KBI, Inc. located in Harrisburg, PA. Previously imported by Outdoor Sports Headquarters, Inc. located in Dayton, OH until 1995.

In 1976, Sloan's Sporting Goods sold the Daly division to Outdoor Sports Headquarters, Inc., a sporting goods wholesaler located in Dayton, OH. OSHI continued the importation of high-grade Daly shotguns, primarily from Italy and Spain. By the mid-1980s, the Charles Daly brand was transformed into a broad consumer line of excellent firearms and hunting accessories.

In 1996, OSHI was sold to Jerry's Sports Center, Inc. of Forest City, PA, a major wholesaler of firearms and hunting supplies. Within a few months of Jerry's acquisition of OSHI, K.B.I., Inc. of Harrisburg, PA, purchased the Charles Daly trademark from JSC. As it turned out, Michael Kassnar, president of K.B.I., Inc., had produced almost all of the Charles Daly products for OSHI from 1976-1985 in his capacity of president of Kassnar Imports, Inc. K.B.I., Inc. resurrected the complete line of O/U and SxS shotguns in early 1997.

In 1998, the line expanded to include rimfire rifles and the first pistol produced under the Daly name, a Model 1911-A1 in .45 ACP cal. In 1999, semi-auto and slide action shotguns were also reintroduced. In 2000, the additions included 3 1/2 in. slide actions and semi-autos, Country Squire .410 bore shotguns, bolt action centerfire rifles, and the DDA 10-45, the first double action pistol produced under the Charles Daly name.

During 2004, Charles Daly began importing Bul Transmark pistols from Israel. In 2007, the Little Sharps single shot rifles were introduced.

In 2008, a Charles Daly Defense line was established, which included AR-15 style semi-auto rifles.

On Jan. 29, 2010, K.B.I. announced it was shutting its doors and discontinued importation of all models.

RIFLES/CARBINES: SEMI-AUTO

All recently manufactured semi-auto rifles have forged aluminum alloy receivers that are hardcoat Mil-Spec anodized and Teflon coated, manganese phosphate barrel (except stainless), radiused aluminum magazine release button, aluminum trigger guard, safety selector position on right side of receiver, dust cover, brass deflector, forward assist, and include one magazine and hard plastic carrying case. All recently manufactured rifles were covered by a lifetime repair policy.

D-M4/D-M4P CARBINE – 5.56 NATO cal., GIO, 16 in. chrome moly match barrel with M-203 mounting groove, A2 birdcage flash hider, 10, 20, or 30 shot mag., forged "F" front sight base with bayonet lug and rubber coated sling swivel, A3 detachable carry handle, T-marked flat-top upper, 6-position telestock, oval double heat shield M4 forend. Mfg. 2008-2009.

	$950	$595	$495	$425	$365	$335	$300	*$1,143*

Add $90 for M4 feed ramps (Model DM-4).

D-M4LE CARBINE – 5.56 NATO cal., GIO, similar to D-M4 carbine, except has Mil-Spec diameter receiver extension with "H" buffer. Mfg. 2008-2009.

	$1,135	$725	$525	$465	$415	$375	$350	*$1,373*

D-M4S CARBINE – 5.56 NATO cal., GIO, similar to D-M4 carbine, except has two Picatinny riser blocks, oval double heat shield M4 forend with QD sling swivel and swivel/bipod stud installed, Magpul enhanced trigger guard. Mfg. 2008-2009.

	$995	$625	$495	$450	$395	$350	$325	*$1,189*

D-M4LT CARBINE – 5.56 NATO cal., GIO, chrome-lined lightweight A1 barrel, permanently attached Phantom suppressor, 30 shot Magpul PMAG, Mil-Spec diameter receiver extension with "H" buffer, slim carbine type forend. Limited mfg. 2009.

	$1,135	$725	$525	$465	$415	$375	$350	*$1,373*

Add $890 for permanently attached Smith Vortex flash suppressor, Magpul CTR stock with buttpad, and Daniel Defense light rail (Model D-M4LTD, mfg. 2009 only).

Add $1,050 for VLTOR Modstock, mid-length gas system, Smith Vortex suppressor, Daniel Defense light rail, and Magpul grip (Model D-M4MG, mfg. 2009 only).

Add $150 for A2 birdcage flash hider, full-length handguard, Troy flip-up BUIS (Model D-M4MLL, mfg. 2009 only).

D-M4LX CARBINE – 5.56 NATO cal., GIO, 16 in. chrome moly HBAR fluted match barrel, Phantom flash suppressor, M4 feed ramps, T-marked flat-top upper, flip-up rear sight, folding front gas block with bayonet lug, aluminum free floating quad rail forend with swiveling sling stud, nine 5-slot low profile ladder style quad rail covers, Ace M4 SOCOM standard length telestock with half buttpad, Ergo Ambi AR grip. Mfg. 2008-2009.

	$1,475	$950	$725	$550	$475	$395	$350	*$1,783*

122 CHARLES DALY: 1976-2010, cont.

MSR	100%	98%	95%	90%	80%	70%	60%	Last MSR

D-MCA4 RIFLE – .223 Rem. cal., 20 in. chrome-lined Govt. profile barrel with A2 birdcage flash hider, 30 shot Mil-Spec mag., A3 detachable carry handle, forged front sight base, A2 handguard, A2 buttstock. Limited mfg. 2009.

	$1,100	$675	$525	$450	$400	$350	$325	$1,317

Add $622 for KAC M5 quad rail with KAC panels (Model D-MCA4-M5).

D-M4LED CARBINE – 5.56 NATO cal., GIO, 16 in. chrome-lined Govt. profile barrel, A2 birdcage flash hider, Magpul CTR Mil-Spec buttstock, M4 feed ramps, Daniel Defense light rail, Magpul MIAD grip, Troy rear BUIS, FDE finish. Limited mfg. 2009.

	$1,795	$1,050	$875	$625	$550	$475	$425	$2,209

D-MR20 RIFLE – 5.56 NATO cal., GIO, 20 in. Wilson Arms stainless steel fluted bull barrel, Magpul PRS II stock, three slot riser blocks, Daniel Defense light rail forearm with Picatinny rail gas block, two-stage match trigger, Phantom suppressor, 20 shot mag. Mfg. 2009.

	$1,650	$1,000	$795	$595	$495	$425	$395	$1,979

DR-15 TARGET – 5.56 NATO cal., GIO, 20 in. chrome moly match HBAR barrel, A2 upper with carry handle, fixed A2 buttstock, A2 birdcage flash hider, forged front sight tower with bayonet lug and rubber coated sling swivel. Limited mfg. 2008.

	$915	$575	$475	$415	$350	$325	$295	$1,089

DV-24 MATCH TARGET/VARMINT – 5.56 NATO cal., GIO, 24 in. free float match stainless steel bull barrel, T-marked flat-top upper, two Picatinny riser blocks, ported aluminum tube forend with swivel/bipod stud installed, Ace skeletonized buttstock, Picatinny rail milled gas block, two-stage match trigger. Mfg. 2008-2009.

	$1,150	$750	$550	$465	$415	$375	$350	$1,389

JR CARBINE – 9mm Para. (JR9), .40 S&W (JR40), or .45 ACP (JR45) cal., GIO, 16 1/4 in. triangular contoured barrel, 13 (.45 ACP), 15 (.40 S&W), or 17 (9mm) shot mag., features unique magwell interchangability, allowing the owner to use handgun magazine of choice, matte black synthetic 6-position telescoping AR stock, anodized aluminum receiver, Picatinny rail, free float quad rail forearm, ergonomic AR grip, includes two mags., approx. 6 1/2 lbs. Disc. 2009.

	$850	$550	$465	$395	$350	$325	$295	$987

CHATTAHOOCHEE GUN WORKS, LLC

Current custom manufacturer located in Phenix City, AL.

RIFLES: SEMI-AUTO

CGW-15 B 16 M1 – .223/5.56 Wylde chamber, GIO, 16 in. chrome moly barrel, low profile gas block, solid billet lower receiver and forged T-marked upper, Midwest Industries free float rail system, Gunfighter charging handle, Magpul CTR stock, A2 grip, black finish.

MSR $1,550		$1,275	$850	$600	$495	$425	$375	$350

CGW-15 B 16-R1V – 5.56 NATO cal., GIO, 16 in. stainless steel barrel, A2 flash hider, A4 barrel extension, extended feed ramps, low profile gas block, solid billet upper and lower receiver, CGW Gunfighter charging handle, H-buffer, 13 1/2 or 15 in. KeyMod free float handguard, Magpul MOE pistol grip carbine stock, Magpul MOE or Ergo grip, hardcoat anodized finish, nickel Teflon, Magpul Gray, FDE, or OD Green finish upgrades also available.

MSR $1,999		$1,650	$1,000	$795	$595	$495	$425	$395

CGW-15 R16B-KAC-1 – .223/5.56 Wylde chamber, GIO, 16 in. stainless steel barrel, A2 flash hider, A4 barrel extension, low profile gas block, H-buffer, extended feed ramps, billet lower, forged T-marked upper, Knights Armament with front sight 12 1/2 in. free float handguard w/1913 rails, CGW Gunfighter charging handle, Magpul CTR stock, Magpul MOE+ grip, hardcoat anodized finish.

MSR $1,700		$1,385	$895	$675	$525	$450	$385	$350

CGW-15 SM-16 – 5.56 NATO cal., GIO, 16 in. cold hammer forged lightweight profile barrel, A2 flash suppressor, 30 shot mag., F-marked fixed front sight base, Magpul MBUS rear sight, flat-top upper and forged Mil-Spec lower receiver, Magpul MOE mid-length handguards, forged charging handle, Magpul MOE carbine stock, Mil-Spec trigger group, Mil-Spec heavy phosphate finish.

MSR $1,225		$1,025	$625	$495	$450	$395	$350	$325

CGW-15 16 IN. NICKEL TEFLON – 5.56 NATO or .300 AAC Blackout cal., GIO, 16 in. stainless steel barrel, A2 or Blackout 51 T flash suppressor, 30 shot mag., CGW low profile gas block, solid billet upper and lower receivers with Nickel Teflon finish, Mil-Spec receiver extension, CGW KeyMod rail, free float handguard w/Picatinny rail, Magpul MOE+ grip, staked endplate, H-Buffer, CGW Gunfighter charging handle, engraved Chattahoochee Gun Works logo, Magpul CTR stock.

MSR $1,950		$1,600	$1,000	$775	$575	$495	$425	$395

CHATTAHOOCHEE GUN WORKS, LLC, cont. 123 C

MSR	100%	98%	95%	90%	80%	70%	60%	Last MSR

CGW 7.62 – 7.62 NATO cal., GIO, 20 in. Kreiger barrel, SureFire muzzle brake or AAC BrakeOut adaptor muzzle device, 20 shot PMAG, solid billet upper and lower receiver, Superior Weapons Systems E1 free float tube, Geissele SSA trigger, Magpul CTR stock, Magpul+ grip.

	100%	98%	95%	90%	80%	70%	60%	Last MSR
MSR $2,499	$1,975	$1,150	$925	$650	$575	$495	$425	

CGW 7.62 16 IN. – 7.62 NATO cal., GIO, 16 or 18 in. match grade stainless steel barrel, black or bead blasted finish, A2 muzzle brake, 20 shot PMAG, solid billet upper and lower receiver, Superior Weapons Systems E1 free float tube or 15 in. KeyMod rail, VLTOR IMOD or Magpul CTR stock, Magpul+ or Ergo grip.

	100%	98%	95%	90%	80%	70%	60%	Last MSR
MSR $2,100	$1,725	$1,050	$850	$625	$550	$475	$425	

CHRISTENSEN ARMS

Current rifle manufacturer established in 1995, currently located in Gunnison, UT. Previously located in Fayette, UT during 2000-2010, and in St. George, UT during 1995-99. Direct sales only.

RIFLES: SEMI-AUTO

Christensen Arms also offered a Carbon One Challenge drop-in barrel (16 oz.) for the Ruger Model 10/22. Last MSR was $499 (disc. 2010).

CA-10 DMR – .243 Win. (new 2016), .260 Rem. (new 2016), 6.5mm Creedmoor (new 2016), or .308 Win. cal., GIO, 18, 20, 22, or 24 in. match grade carbon wrapped stainless steel barrel, threaded with titanium side baffle brake, Christensen LTM trigger, Magpul adj. STR buttstock, Hogue overmolded grip, carbon fiber handguard with integrated carbon Picatinny rails in KeyMod or M-LOK, ambidextrous mag. release, extended charging handle, oversized bolt release, Type III hardcoat anodized black or Cerakote finish in Burnt Bronze or Tungsten, 7.1 lbs. New 2014.

	100%	98%	95%	90%	80%	70%	60%	Last MSR
MSR $3,245	$2,625	$1,725	$1,300	$725	$650	$595	$525	

CA-10 G2 – 6.5mm Creedmoor or .308 Win. cal., GIO, 18 or 20 in. stainless steel or carbon fiber wrapped barrel, threaded muzzle, stainless steel or titanium flash hider, flared magwell, integrated undercut trigger guard, match grade trigger, BCM Gunfighter stock, 15 in. KeyMod or M-LOK handguard, Christensen Arms G2 Edition aluminum lower receiver, hardcoat anodized black finish, 7.2-7.7 lbs. New 2016.

	100%	98%	95%	90%	80%	70%	60%	Last MSR
MSR $2,595	$2,050	$1,250	$950	$650	$575	$495	$475	

Add $400 for carbon fiber wrapped barrel.

CA-10 RECON – .243 Win., 6.8 Creedmoor, .308 Win., or .338 Federal cal., GIO, 16-24 in. carbon fiber match grade barrel, various stock configurations, flat-top receiver with Picatinny rail, adj. Timney trigger, carbon fiber handguard, 20 shot mag., black carbon fiber or camo forearm finish, 6-8 lbs. Mfg. 2011-2013.

	100%	98%	95%	90%	80%	70%	60%	Last MSR
	$2,875	$1,875	$1,375	$795	$675	$625	$575	*$3,575*

Subtract $200 for steel barrel.

CARBON ONE CA-15 SERIES (AR-15) – .223 Rem. cal., GIO, forged aluminum upper and lower receiver, choice of round shroud with quad rails or integrated forearm with full Picatinny rail on top, adj. stock, carbon fiber wrapped stainless steel barrel, ambidextrous charging handle, Timney adj. drop-in trigger, 30 shot detachable AR-15 style mag., 5.5-7 lbs. Mfg. 2009-2010.

	100%	98%	95%	90%	80%	70%	60%	Last MSR
	$2,375	$1,525	$1,150	$700	$625	$550	$475	*$2,950*

CA-15 C2 – .204 Ruger, .223 Wylde chamber, or .300 AAC Blackout cal., GIO, fixed gas block, 16-24 in. threaded barrel with stainless steel flash suppressor, match grade trigger, Magpul adj. CTR stock, Magpul MOE grip, carbine, rifle, or mid-length gas tube, CA carbon fiber Slim-Line profile KeyMod or M-LOK 15 in. handguard, billet upper and lower receivers, Type III hardcoat anodized black finish, 5.65 lbs. Mfg. 2016 only.

	100%	98%	95%	90%	80%	70%	60%	Last MSR
	$1,650	$1,000	$795	$595	$495	$425	$395	*$1,999*

CA-15 G2 – .223/5.56 Wylde chamber, GIO, 16 in. stainless steel or carbon fiber wrapped barrel, threaded muzzle, stainless steel or titanium flash hider, flared magwell, match grade trigger, BCM Gunfighter stock, Christensen Arms G2 Edition upper and lower aluminum receivers, 14 3/4 in. slim-line carbon fiber KeyMod or M-LOK handguard, hard anodized black finish, 5.8-5.9 lbs. New 2016.

	100%	98%	95%	90%	80%	70%	60%	Last MSR
MSR $1,749	$1,425	$925	$700	$550	$475	$395	$350	

Add $546 for carbon fiber wrapped barrel and titanium flash hider.

CA-15 3G – .223 Wylde chamber, GIO, 16 or 18 in. stainless steel carbon fiber wrapped barrel, titanium side baffle brake, flared magwell, Hiperfire trigger, integrated undercut trigger guard, BCM Gunfighter stock, Christensen Arms G2 Edition upper and lower receivers, 14 3/4 in. slim-line carbon fiber M-LOK handguard, hard anodized black finish, 5.9 lbs. Mfg. 2016-2017.

	100%	98%	95%	90%	80%	70%	60%	Last MSR
	$2,450	$1,595	$1,200	$700	$675	$575	$525	*$3,045*

CA-15 PREDATOR – .223 Rem., .204 Ruger, 6.8 SPC, or 6.5 Grendel cal., GIO, 20 or 24 in. carbon fiber match grade barrel, collapsible stock, flat-top receiver with Picatinny rail, ambidextrous controls, adj. Timney trigger, 20 shot mag., Hogue pistol grip, black, King's Desert Shadow, or King's Snow Shadow finish, 5.5-7 lbs. Mfg. 2011-2012.

	100%	98%	95%	90%	80%	70%	60%	Last MSR
	$2,375	$1,525	$1,150	$700	$625	$550	$475	*$2,995*

124 CHRISTENSEN ARMS, cont.

MSR	100%	98%	95%	90%	80%	70%	60%	Last MSR

CA-15 RECON – .204 Ruger, .223 Wylde chamber, 6.5 Grendel, 6.8 SPC, or .300 AAC Blackout cal., GPO, 16 or 20 in. match grade carbon fiber barrel, titanium birdcage flash suppressor, 30 shot mag., carbon fiber handguard with built-in Picatinny rails, adj. stock, adj. Timney trigger, Hogue pistol grip, factory black synthetic, Digital Desert Brown, King's Desert Shadow, or King's Snow Shadow finish, 5.5-7 lbs. Mfg. 2011-2015.

| | $2,700 | $1,775 | $1,325 | $750 | $650 | $595 | $525 | *$3,395* |

CA-15 VTAC – .223 Wylde chamber or .300 AAC Blackout (disc. 2016) cal., GIO, 16 in. straight fluted stainless steel black Nitride finished barrel or carbon fiber wrapped barrel, titanium (became standard 2017) flash hider, flared magwell, VTAC self-contained trigger, BCM Gunfighter stock, Magpul MOE pistol grip, 15 in. free float KeyMod or M-LOK handguard with integral rails, machined billet upper and lower receivers, Picatinny rail, Type III hardcoat anodized black finish, 5 1/2 lbs. Mfg. mid-2015-2017.

| | $2,295 | $1,450 | $1,075 | $675 | $595 | $525 | $475 | *$2,845* |

Subtract approx. $150 if with Nitride finished barrel and standard flash hider.

* CA-15 VTAC 3G – .243 Win., .260 Rem., 6.5mm Creedmoor, or .308 Win. cal., 16 in. threaded stainless steel or carbon fiber wrapped barrel with titanium flash suppressor, BCM Gunfighter buttstock, Magpul MOE grip, low mass bolt carrier, adj. gas block, billet receivers with top Picatinny rail, mid-length gas tube, 15 in. KeyMod or M-LOK handguard, Type III hardcoat anodized black finish, 5 1/2 lbs. Mfg. 2016 only.

| | $2,375 | $1,525 | $1,150 | $700 | $625 | $550 | $475 | *$2,999* |

Add $200 for carbon fiber wrapped barrel.

CD-15 RECON – .223 Wylde or 5.56 NATO cal., GIO, 16-24 in. match grade carbon fiber wrapped barrel, OSS suppressor, Christensen LTM trigger, aluminum receiver, carbon fiber handguard with integrated carbon Picatinny rails, nickel boron coated bolt carrier, ambidextrous magazine release, oversized bolt release, extended charging handle, Hogue overmolded grip, Type III hardcoat anodized black or Cerakote receiver colors, numerous finish options available, 7.3 lbs. Mfg. 2014-2015.

| | $3,925 | $2,800 | $1,750 | $1,150 | $875 | $775 | $700 | *$4,890* |

CHRISTIAN ARMORY WORKS

Current custom rifle manufacturer located in Rock Spring, GA.

RIFLES: SEMI-AUTO

A2 STANDARD – various cals., M4 profile barrel with A2 flash hider, Daniel Defense chrome bore, SST, A2 sight base (no rear sight), Magpul MOE stock, forearm, and grip, billet receiver set, Mil-Spec BCG and charging handle assembly.
This model is built per customer specifications and base MSR starts at $1,289.

PRECISION TARGET SYSTEMS – various cals., 18 in. target barrel with polygonal rifling, two-stage trigger, Magpul PRS precision stock, YHM rifle length forearm.
This model is built per customer specifications and base MSR starts at $1,649.

STANDARD NP3 TACTICAL – various cals., Daniel Defense 16 in. mid-length barrel, Troy flash hider, Mil-Spec trigger, Magpul flip-up sights, Magpul STR stock, Ergo grip, YHM Black Diamond rifle length forearm, NP3 coating on all parts.
This model is built per customer specifications and base MSR starts at $1,897.

STANDARD TACTICAL DEFENSE – various cals., chrome-lined Daniel Defense or Target BHW barrel, Magpul mag., Magpul MOE stock, free float forearm, available with no sights, Troy Industries, or Magpul sights.
This model is built per customer specifications and base MSR starts at $1,399.

CIMARRON F.A. CO.

Current importer, distributor, and retailer located in Fredricksburg, TX. Cimarron is currently importing A. Uberti, D. Pedersoli, Chiappa Firearms, Pietta, and Armi-Sport firearms and black powder reproductions and replicas. Previous company name was Old-West Co. of Texas. Dealer sales only.

Please refer to the *Blue Book of Modern Black Powder Arms* by John Allen (also online) for more information and prices on Cimarron's lineup of modern black powder models.

PISTOLS: SEMI-AUTO

M4-22 – .22 LR cal., AR-15 style, blowback action, 6 in. barrel with muzzle brake, quad rail, includes A2 carry handle, black finish, 5, 10, or 28 shot Atchison style conversion mag., cased with cleaning kit, 3.9 lbs. Mfg. by Armi Chiappa in Italy. Imported 2011-2012.

| | $450 | $375 | $325 | $275 | $250 | $225 | $195 | *$587* |

CIVILIAN FORCE ARMS

Current 1911 style pistol and AR-15 style pistol, rifle, and parts and accessories manufacturer located in Yorkville, IL beginning late 2014.

Civilian Force Arms was founded by former Army soldier and Purple Heart recipient Yonas Hagos. Yonas prides himself on producing weapons that are American Made, Built To Survive™.

CIVILIAN FORCE ARMS, cont. 125 C

MSR	100%	98%	95%	90%	80%	70%	60%	Last MSR

PISTOLS: SEMI-AUTO

All CFA firearms carry a lifetime warranty for any mechanical or manufacturer defects. Each model comes with a hard case, two magazines, gun lock, and manual.

KATY-15 – .223 Rem./5.56 NATO cal., GIO, 10 1/2 in. M4 profile chrome moly threaded barrel, Phantom muzzle brake, two 30 shot mags., aluminum trigger guard with 3-4 lb. Velocity drop-in trigger, A.R.M.S. flip-up front and rear sights, Blade Brace, MFT Engage EPG 16V2 black pistol grip, manual safety, M4 feed ramps, forged aluminum M4A4 flat-top upper w/Picatinny rail, 9 in. black Midwest Industries G2 T-Series rail, BCM Mod 4 charging handle, hardcoat anodized black finish, 6.2 lbs., 23.25 in. OAL. New 2018.

	100%	98%	95%	90%	80%	70%	60%	Last MSR
MSR $1,199	$1,075	$950	$800	$750	$600	$475	$375	

SWEEPER-15 – .223 Rem./5.56 NATO cal., GIO, 7 1/2 in. M4 profile chrome moly barrel, Phantom muzzle brake, 30 shot mag., aluminum trigger guard, A.R.M.S. flip-up front and rear sights, SIG brace, MFT Engage black pistol grip, manual safety, low profile gas block, forged aluminum M4A4 flat-top upper w/Picatinny rail, 9 in. Midwest Industries G2 T-Series rail, BCM Mod 4 charging handle, hardcoat anodized black finish, 6.2 lbs.

	100%	98%	95%	90%	80%	70%	60%	Last MSR
MSR $1,699	$1,450	$1,275	$1,125	$1,000	$850	$735	$595	

SWEEPER-15 GEN2 – .223 Rem./5.56 NATO cal., GPO, 10 1/2 in. M4 profile chrome moly threaded barrel, Phantom muzzle brake, 30 shot mag., aluminum trigger guard, A.R.M.S. flip-up front and rear sights, SIG brace, Gen2 MFT black pistol grip, manual safety, M4 feed ramps, forged aluminum M4A4 flat-top upper w/Picatinny rail, Adams Arms .740 piston, 9.2 in. black Fortis Rev carbine cutout rail, BCM Mod 4 charging handle, hardcoat anodized black finish, 6.4 lbs.

	100%	98%	95%	90%	80%	70%	60%	Last MSR
MSR $1,849	$1,575	$1,385	$1,185	$1,065	$915	$785	$635	

SWEEPER-15 ZOMBIE EDITION – .223 Rem./5.56 NATO cal., GIO, 10 1/2 in. M4 profile chrome moly threaded barrel, Phantom muzzle brake, two 30 shot mags., aluminum trigger guard with 3-4 lb. Velocity drop-in trigger, A.R.M.S. flip-up front and rear sights, Blade Brace, MFT black pistol grip, manual safety, M4 feed ramps, forged aluminum M4A4 flat-top upper with Picatinny rail, 9 in. black Midwest Industries G2 T-Series rail, BCM Mod 4 charging handle, hardcoat anodized white and black finish, 6.2 lbs., 23.25 in. OAL.

	100%	98%	95%	90%	80%	70%	60%	Last MSR
MSR $1,899	$1,600	$1,385	$1,185	$1,065	$915	$785	$635	

WARRIOR-15 – .223 Rem./5.56 NATO cal., GIO, 10 1/2 in. M4 profile chrome moly threaded barrel, KAK Flash Can muzzle brake, two 30 shot mags., aluminum trigger guard with 3-4 lb. Velocity drop-in trigger, A.R.M.S. flip-up front and rear sights, KAK Blade brace, MFT Engage EPG 16V2 black pistol grip, manual safety, M4 feed ramps, forged aluminum M4A4 flat-top upper with Picatinny rail, 9 in. black Midwest Industries G2 T-Series rail, BCM Mod 4 charging handle, hardcoat anodized black finish, 6.2 lbs., 23.25 in. OAL. New 2018.

	100%	98%	95%	90%	80%	70%	60%	Last MSR
MSR $1,350	$1,200	$1,050	$900	$800	$650	$550	$425	

XENA-15 GEN3 – .223 Rem./5.56 NATO cal., GIO, 10 1/2 in. M4 profile chrome moly barrel, A2 flash hider, aluminum trigger guard, MFT black pistol grip, manual safety, M4 feed ramps, forged aluminum M4A4 flat-top upper w/Picatinny rail, carbine plastic handguard, AR-15 pistol buffer tube kit, standard Mil-Spec charging handle, hardcoat anodized black finish, 6.2 lbs. Disc. 2017.

	100%	98%	95%	90%	80%	70%	60%	Last MSR
	$725	$500	$435	$375	$335	$315	$295	*$829*

XENA-15 GEN4 – .223 Rem./5.56 NATO cal., GIO, 10 1/2 in. M4 profile chrome moly barrel, A2 flash hider, 30 shot mag., aluminum trigger guard, A.R.M.S. flip-up front and rear sights, Magpul MOE black plastic grip, manual safety, M4 feed ramps, Mil-Spec charging handle, carbine quad rail, AR-15 pistol buffer tube kit, forged aluminum M4A4 flat-top upper w/Picatinny rail. Disc. 2017.

	100%	98%	95%	90%	80%	70%	60%	Last MSR
	$725	$500	$435	$375	$335	$315	$295	*$849*

RIFLES: SEMI-AUTO

All CFA firearms carry a lifetime warranty for any mechanical or manufacturer defects. Each model comes with a hard case, two magazines, gun lock, and manual, unless otherwise noted.

DAKOTA-15 – .223 Rem./5.56 NATO cal., GIO, 18 in. straight flute heavy chrome moly barrel, Phantom 3102 flash hider, 30 shot mag., low profile gas block, manual safety, M4A4 forged aluminum flat-top upper w/Picatinny rail, nickel boron bolt carrier group, M4 feed ramps, 6-position Mil-Spec Mission First Tactical BMS-Battlelink stock, MFT Engage black pistol grip, aluminum trigger guard, 15 in. Fortis Rev2 rail, BCM Mod 4 charging handle, CAA bipod, hardcoat anodized black finish, 8.2 lbs.

	100%	98%	95%	90%	80%	70%	60%	Last MSR
	$1,575	$995	$775	$575	$495	$425	$395	*$1,899*

DAKOTA-15 DMR – .223 Rem./5.56 NATO cal., GIO, mid-length gas system, 18 in. straight flute heavy chrome moly barrel, Phantom 3102 QD muzzle brake, 3 or 4 lb. Velocity drop-in trigger, Magpul PRS sniper stock, MFT Engage black pistol grip, manual safety, M4A4 type flat-top upper receiver with Picatinny rail, low profile gas block, nickel boron bolt carrier group, M4 feed ramps, BCM Mod 4 charging handle, 15 in. Fortis Rev2 rail, ATLAS B10 bipod, hardcoat anodized black finish, 36.125 in. OAL, 8.2 lbs. New 2018.

	100%	98%	95%	90%	80%	70%	60%	Last MSR
MSR $2,099	$1,675	$1,000	$825	$625	$550	$475	$425	

126 CIVILIAN FORCE ARMS, cont.

MSR	100%	98%	95%	90%	80%	70%	60%	Last MSR

DAKOTA-15 HUNTER EDITION – .223 Rem./5.56 NATO cal., GIO, 18 in. straight flute heavy chrome moly barrel, Phantom 3102 flash hider, 30 shot mag., low profile gas block, manual safety, M4A4 forged aluminum flat-top upper receiver with Picatinny rail, M4 feed ramps, 6-position Mil-Spec Mission First Tactical BMS-Battlelink stock, MFT Engage black pistol grip, aluminum trigger guard, 15 in. Fortis Rev2 rail with Multi-Cam finish, BCM Mod 4 charging handle, CAA bipod, 8.2 lbs.

	100%	98%	95%	90%	80%	70%	60%	Last MSR
	$1,675	$1,000	$825	$625	$550	$475	$425	*$2,099*

HAGOS-15 – .223 Rem./5.56 NATO or .300 AAC Blackout cal., GIO, 16 in. M4 profile chrome moly barrel, Phantom muzzle brake, low profile gas block, 30 shot mag., manual safety, A.R.M.S. flip-up front and rear sights, M4 feed ramps, 15 in. Midwest Industries SS Series Gen2 rail, forged aluminum M4A4 flat-top upper w/Picatinny rail, BCM Mod 4 charging handle, 6-position Mil-Spec Mission First Tactical BMS-Battlelink Minimalist stock, MFT Engage black pistol grip, hardcoat anodized black finish, 6 1/2 lbs.

	100%	98%	95%	90%	80%	70%	60%	
MSR $1,499	$1,250	$825	$575	$475	$425	$375	$350	

Add $100 for .300 AAC Blackout cal.

KATY-15 – .223 Rem./5.56 NATO or .300 AAC Blackout cal., GIO, 16 in. M4 profile chrome moly barrel, Phantom muzzle brake, low profile gas block, 30 shot mag., manual safety, A.R.M.S. flip-up front and rear sights, M4 feed ramps, 12 in. Midwest Industries T-Series rail, forged aluminum M4A4 flat-top upper w/Picatinny rail, BCM Mod 4 charging handle, 6-position Mil-Spec Mission First Tactical BMS-Battlelink Minimalist stock, MFT Engage black pistol grip, hardcoat anodized black finish, 7 lbs.

	100%	98%	95%	90%	80%	70%	60%	
MSR $1,149	$950	$595	$495	$425	$365	$335	$300	

Add $50 for .300 AAC Blackout cal.

NATALIA-15 – .223 Rem./5.56 NATO cal., GPO, 16 in. M4 profile chrome-lined barrel, Lantac Dragon threaded muzzle brake, low profile gas block, 30 shot mag., A.R.M.S. flip-up front and rear sight, manual safety, forged aluminum M4A4 flat-top upper w/Picatinny rail, M4 feed ramps, machined aluminum trigger guard, 9 in. Fortis Rev carbine cutout rail, BCM Mod 4 charging handle, 6-position Mil-Spec Mission First Tactical BMS (Battlelink Minimalist Stock), MFT Engage black pistol grip, hardcoat anodized black finish, 6.8 lbs.

	100%	98%	95%	90%	80%	70%	60%	Last MSR
	$1,725	$1,050	$850	$625	$550	$475	$425	*$2,199*

NATASHA – .223 Rem./5.56 NATO or .300 AAC Blackout cal., GIO, 16 in. M4 profile chrome moly barrel, threaded Phantom muzzle brake, 30 shot mag., manual safety, A.R.M.S. flip-up front and rear sights, forged aluminum M4A4 flat-top upper w/Picatinny rail, M4 feed ramps, BCM Mod 4 charging handle, 15 in. Midwest Industries T-Series Gen2 rail, 6-position Mil-Spec MFT Battlelink Minimalist stock, MFT Engage black pistol grip, machined aluminum trigger guard, hardcoat anodized black finish, 7.1 lbs.

	100%	98%	95%	90%	80%	70%	60%	Last MSR
	$1,315	$850	$625	$500	$435	$375	$350	*$1,599*

Add $100 for .300 AAC Blackout cal.

OPERATOR-15 – .223 Rem./5.56 NATO cal., GIO, 16 in. M4 profile chrome moly barrel, threaded Phantom muzzle brake, 30 shot mag., low profile gas block, manual safety, forged aluminum M4A4 flat-top upper w/Picatinny rail, M4 feed ramps, 15 in. CFA free float quad rail, machined aluminum enhanced trigger guard, A.R.M.S. front and rear flip-up sights, BCM Mod 4 charging handle, 6-position Mil-Spec MFT Battlelink Minimalist stock, MFT Engage black pistol grip, hardcoat anodized black finish, 7 1/2 lbs.

	100%	98%	95%	90%	80%	70%	60%	Last MSR
	$1,315	$850	$625	$500	$435	$375	$350	*$1,599*

PATRIOT-15 – .223 Rem./5.56 NATO cal., GIO, 16 in. M4 profile chrome moly barrel, threaded Lantac Dragon muzzle brake, low profile gas block, 30 shot mag., A.R.M.S. front and rear flip-up sights, forged aluminum M4A4 flat-top upper w/Picatinny rail, M4 feed ramps, BCM Mod 4 charging handle, manual ambidextrous safety, 14.8 in. Fortis Rev rail, drop-in trigger, 6-position Mil-Spec MFT Battlelink Minimalist stock, MFT EPGI16 Engage pistol grip, hardcoat anodized black finish, 7.2 lbs.

	100%	98%	95%	90%	80%	70%	60%	Last MSR
	$1,795	$1,050	$875	$625	$550	$475	$425	*$2,299*

PHANTOM-15 – .223 Rem./5.56 NATO cal., GIO, 16 in. M4 profile chrome moly barrel, CFA muzzle brake, low profile gas block, 30 shot mag., manual safety, A.R.M.S. flip-up front and rear sights, M4 feed ramps, CFA 12 in. Phantom rail, forged aluminum M4A4 flat-top upper w/Picatinny rail, BCM Mod 4 charging handle, 6-position Mil-Spec Mission First Tactical BMS-Battlelink Minimalist stock, MFT Engage black pistol grip, hardcoat black anodized finish, 7 lbs.

	100%	98%	95%	90%	80%	70%	60%	Last MSR
	$1,075	$675	$500	$450	$400	$350	$325	*$1,299*

REACHER-308 – .308 Win./7.62 NATO cal., GIO, 18 in. stainless steel barrel, threaded low profile CFA muzzle brake, 20 shot mag., manual ambidextrous safety, billet aluminum AR10 type flat-top upper w/Picatinny rail, VLTOR BCM Mod 4 charging handle, 12 in. CFA 308 rail, 6-position Mil-Spec MFT Battlelink Minimalist stock, MFT Engage black pistol grip, hardcoat anodized black finish, 9 1/2 lbs.

	100%	98%	95%	90%	80%	70%	60%	Last MSR
	$1,795	$1,050	$875	$625	$550	$475	$425	*$2,299*

CIVILIAN FORCE ARMS, cont. 127 C

MSR	100%	98%	95%	90%	80%	70%	60%	Last MSR

REACHER-308 GEN2 – .308 Win./7.62 NATO cal., GIO, 20 in. stainless steel barrel, threaded low profile Fortis muzzle brake, 20 shot mag., manual ambidextrous safety, machined aluminum trigger guard, billet aluminum AR10 type flat-top upper w/Picatinny rail, VLTOR BCM Mod 4 charging handle, 15 in. Fortis Switch 308 rail, Mako SSR25 Sniper buttstock w/adj. cheek well, MFT Engage pistol grip, CAA bipod, hardcoat anodized black finish, 12 lbs.

	$2,125	$1,325	$995	$675	$595	$525	$475	$2,699

REACHER-308 WARRIOR – .308 Win./7.62 NATO cal., GIO, 16 in. salt bath Nitride finished stainless steel barrel, CFA Shark muzzle brake, two 20 shot mags., 3 or 4 lb. Velocity drop-in trigger, machined aluminum trigger guard, 6-pos. Mil-Spec MFT Battlelink Minimalist stock, 15 in. CFA Super Slim KeyMod LR308 rail, MFT Engage EPG16 V2 black pistol grip, manual ambidextrous safety, AR10 type flat-top upper w/Picatinny rail, 308 bolt carrier group with Nitride finish, VLTOR BCM Mod 4 charging handle, low profile gas block, hardcoat anodized black finish, 33.375-37.125 in. OAL, 9 1/2 lbs. New 2018.

MSR $1,899	$1,575	$995	$775	$575	$495	$425	$395	

REACHER EVO-308 – .308 Win./7.62 NATO cal., GIO, 18 in. stainless steel barrel, 20 shot mag., manual ambidextrous safety, billet aluminum AR10 type flat-top upper w/Picatinny rail, 9 in. UTG two-piece rail, machined aluminum trigger guard, 6-position Mil-Spec MFT Battlelink Minimalist stock, MFT Engage black pistol grip, hardcoat anodized black or FDE finish, 9 1/2 lbs.

	$1,475	$950	$725	$550	$475	$395	$350	$1,799

REACHER EVO-308 SCORPION – .308 Win./7.62 NATO cal., GIO, 18 in. stainless steel barrel, threaded low profile CFA Shark muzzle brake, 20 shot mag., manual ambidextrous safety, billet aluminum AR10 type flat-top upper w/Picatinny rail, 13 in. UTG Super Slip LR308 rail, VLTOR BCM Mod 4 charging handle, machined aluminum trigger guard, 6-position Mil-Spec MFT Battlelink Minimalist stock, MFT Engage black pistol grip, hardcoat anodized black finish, 9 1/2 lbs.

	$1,575	$995	$775	$575	$495	$425	$395	$1,899

REACHER-308 SNIPER EDITION – .308 Win./7.62 NATO cal., GIO, 18 in. stainless steel barrel, threaded low profile muzzle brake, 20 shot mag., manual ambidextrous safety, VLTOR BCM Mod 4 charging handle, billet aluminum AR10 type flat-top upper w/Picatinny rail, 12 in. Phantom 308 rail, Mako SSR25 Sniper buttstock w/adj. cheek well, MFT Engage pistol grip, hardcoat anodized black finish, CAA bipod, 11 lbs.

	$2,050	$1,250	$950	$650	$575	$495	$475	$2,599

SALLY-15 – .223 Rem./5.56 NATO or .300 AAC Blackout cal., GIO, 16 in. M4 profile chrome moly barrel, Phantom muzzle brake, low profile gas block, 30 shot mag., manual safety, A.R.M.S. flip-up front and rear sights, M4 feed ramps, 12 in. Midwest Industries S-Series rail, forged aluminum M4A4 flat-top upper w/Picatinny rail, BCM Mod 4 charging handle, 6-position Mil-Spec Mission First Tactical BMS-Battlelink Minimalist stock, MFT Engage black pistol grip, hardcoat black anodized finish, 6.8 lbs.

	$915	$575	$475	$415	$350	$325	$300	$1,099

Add $100 for .300 AAC Blackout cal.

SCORPION-15 – .223/5.56 Wylde chamber, GIO, 16 in. M4 profile chrome moly barrel, Shark threaded muzzle brake, low profile gas block, 30 shot mag., manual safety, A.R.M.S. front and rear flip-up sights, BCM Mod 4 charging handle, forged aluminum M4A4 flat-top upper w/Picatinny rail, M4 feed ramps, 15 in. Leaper Slim rail, machined aluminum enhanced trigger guard, 6-position Mil-Spec MFT Battlelink Minimalist stock, MFT Engage black pistol grip, hardcoat anodized black finish, 6 1/2 lbs.

	$995	$625	$495	$450	$395	$350	$325	$1,199

WARRIOR-15 – .223 Rem./5.56 NATO cal., GIO, 16 in. M4 profile stainless steel barrel, Knight muzzle brake, two 30 shot mags., 3 or 4 lb. Velocity drop-in trigger, A.R.M.S #71L-R flip-up rear and A.R.M.S #71L-F flip-up front sights, 6-position Mil-Spec Mission First Tactical Battlelink Minimalist stock, 15 in. CFA Slim M-LOK rail handguard, MFT Engage black pistol grip, manual safety, forged aluminum M4A4 flat-top upper with Picatinny rail, M16 Mil-Spec with manganese phosphate BCG, M4 feed ramps, low profile gas block, hardcoat anodized black finish, 32.375-36.125 in. OAL, 6 1/2 lbs. New 2018.

MSR $1,299	$1,075	$675	$500	$450	$400	$350	$325	

WARRIOR-15XL – .223 Rem./5.56 NATO cal., GIO, 16 in. M4 mid-length pencil profile chrome moly vanadium steel barrel, KAK Flash Can muzzle brake 1/2 x 28 in. threaded, two 30 shot mags., 3 or 4 lb. Velocity drop-in trigger, A.R.M.S #71L-R flip-up rear and A.R.M.S #71L-F flip-up front sights, 6-position Mil-Spec Mission First Tactical Battlelink Minimalist stock, 15 in. CFA Slim M-LOK rail handgaurd, MFT Engage EPG16 V2 black pistol grip, manual safety, forged aluminum M4A4 flat-top upper with Picatinny rail, M16 Mil-Spec with manganese phosphate BCG, BCM Mod 4 charging handle, M4 feed ramps, low profile gas block, hardcoat anodized black finish, 6 lbs. New 2018.

MSR $1,399	$1,150	$750	$550	$465	$415	$375	$350	

XENA-15 – .223 Rem./5.56 NATO cal., GIO, 16 in. M4 profile chrome moly barrel, A2 flash hider, 30 shot mag., manual safety, M4 feed ramps, forged aluminum M4A4 flat-top upper receiver with Picatinny rail, aluminum trigger guard, buffer tube, carbine handguard, front sight post and rear MFT backup sight, standard charging handle, 6-position Mil-Spec MFT stock, MFT Engage black pistol grip, hardcoat anodized black finish, 6.3 lbs.

	$675	$500	$425	$375	$335	$315	$295	$799

C 128 CIVILIAN FORCE ARMS, cont.

MSR	100%	98%	95%	90%	80%	70%	60%	Last MSR

XENA-15 A2 – .223 Rem./5.56 NATO cal., GIO, 20 in. M4 profile chrome moly barrel, A2 flash hider, 30 shot mag., manual safety, front iron sight post, rear carry handle fixed sight, standard charging handle, M4A4 forged aluminum flat-top upper with Picatinny rail, M4 feed ramps, rifle length handguard, fixed A2 buttstock, A2 pistol grip, hardcoat anodized black finish, 8 1/2 lbs.

	$915	$575	$475	$415	$350	$325	$300	*$1,099*

XENA-15 GEN2 MOE – .223/5.56 Wylde chamber, GIO, 16 in. M4 profile chrome moly barrel, threaded A2 flash hider, 30 shot mag., manual safety, front iron sight post, A.R.M.S. flip-up or Magpul rear sight, CFA True Mil-Spec Gen3 charging handle, forged aluminum M4A4 flat-top upper w/Picatinny rail, M4 feed ramps, Magpul carbine plastic handguard, 6-position Mil-Spec Magpul MOE stock, Magpul MOE black pistol grip, hardcoat anodized black finish, 6 1/2 lbs.

	$725	$500	$435	$375	$335	$315	$295	*$829*

XENA-15 GEN3 – .223 Rem./5.56 NATO cal., GIO, 16 in. M4 profile chrome moly barrel, A2 flash hider, 30 shot mag., manual safety, A.R.M.S. flip-up front and rear sights, Mil-Spec standard charging handle, M4 feed ramps, M4A4 forged aluminum flat-top upper w/Picatinny rail, carbine plastic handguard, 6-position Mil-Spec MFT stock, MFT Engage black pistol grip, hardcoat anodized black finish, 6 1/2 lbs.

	$725	$500	$435	$375	$335	$315	$295	*$829*

* ***XENA-16 GEN3 Sport*** – .223 Rem./5.56 NATO cal., GIO, 16 in. M4 profile chrome moly barrel, A2 flash hider, 30 shot mag., manual safety, M4 feed ramps, M4A4 forged aluminum flat-top upper w/Picatinny rail, Mil-Spec charging handle, carbine plastic handguard, 6-position Mil-Spec MFT stock, MFT Engage black pistol grip, hardcoat anodized black finish, 6.4 lbs.

	$675	$500	$425	$375	$335	$315	$295	*$789*

XENA-15 GEN4 – .223 Rem./5.56 NATO cal., GIO, 16 in. M4 profile chrome moly barrel, A2 flash hider, 30 shot mag., manual safety, A.R.M.S. flip-up front and rear sights, M4 feed ramps, carbine UTG aluminum handguard, M4A4 forged aluminum flat-top upper w/Picatinny rail, CFA Mil-Spec Gen3 charging handle, 6-position Mil-Spec MFT stock, MFT Engage black pistol grip, hardcoat anodized black finish, 6.7 lbs.

MSR $899	$765	$515	$440	$375	$335	$315	$295	

* ***XENA-15 GEN4 Sport*** – .223 Rem./5.56 NATO cal., GIO, 16 in. M4 profile chrome moly barrel, A2 flash hider, 30 shot mag., manual safety, M4 feed ramps, carbine UTG handguard, M4A4 forged aluminum flat-top upper w/Picatinny rail, 6-position Mil-Spec MFT stock, MFT Engage black pistol grip, hardcoat anodized black finish, 6.4 lbs.

	$695	$500	$425	$375	$335	$315	$295	*$809*

XENA-15 GEN4.1 – .223 Rem./5.56 NATO cal., GIO, 16 in. M4 profile chrome moly barrel, A2 flash hider, 30 shot mag., manual safety, A.R.M.S. flip-up front and rear sights, Mil-Spec charging handle, M4 feed ramps, M4A4 forged aluminum flat-top upper w/Picatinny rail, carbine UTG aluminum slim handguard, 6-position Mil-Spec MFT stock, MFT Engage black pistol grip, hardcoat anodized black finish, 6.6 lbs.

MSR $899	$765	$515	$440	$375	$335	$315	$295	

XENA-15 GEN4 HUNTER EDITION – .223 Rem./5.56 NATO cal., GIO, 18 in. M4 profile fluted chrome moly barrel, A2 flash hider, 30 shot mag., manual safety, front iron sight post, flip-up rear sight, aluminum trigger guard, Mil-Spec charging handle, M4 feed ramps, carbine UTG aluminum handguard, M4A4 forged aluminum flat-top upper receiver w/Picatinny rail, 6-position Mil-Spec MFT stock, MFT Engage black pistol grip, Multi-Cam finish, 9 lbs.

MSR $1,149	$950	$595	$495	$425	$365	$335	$300	

XENA-15 2.0 – .223 Rem./5.56 NATO cal., GIO, 16 in. M4 profile chrome moly barrel, A2 flash hider, 30 shot mag., manual safety, M4 feed ramps, forged aluminum M4A4 flat-top upper receiver w/Picatinny rail, aluminum trigger guard, buffer tube, carbine two-piece quad rail, front sight post and rear MFT backup sight, standard Mil-Spec charging handle, 6-position Mil-Spec MFT stock, MFT Engage black pistol grip, hardcoat anodized black finish, 6.5 lbs.

	$725	$500	$435	$375	$335	$315	$295	*$849*

XENA-15 MOE 2.1 – .223 Rem./5.56 NATO cal., GIO, 16 in. M4 profile chrome moly parkerized barrel, A2 flash hider, two 30 shot mags., 6-position Mil-Spec Magpul MOE stock, two-piece Magpul MOE M-LOK handguard, black Magpul MOE forward grip, MFT Engage black pistol grip, manual safety, forged aluminum M4A4 flat-top upper w/Picatinny rail, M16 Mil-Spec with manganese phosphate BCG, M4 feed ramps, hardcoat anodized black finish, 32.3-36.1 in. OAL, 6.5 lbs. New 2018.

MSR $929	$800	$525	$450	$385	$340	$325	$295	

XENA-47 GEN4 – 7.62x39mm cal., GIO, 16 in. M4 profile chrome moly barrel, A2 flash hider, two 30 shot AR Stoner mags., A.R.M.S. #71L-F&R flip-up front and rear sights, 6-position Mil-Spec MFT stock, CFA aluminum handguard, MFT Engage black pistol grip, manual safety, M4A4 forged aluminum flat-top upper w/Picatinny rail, AK47 Mil-Spec bolt carrier group with manganese phosphate, M4 feed ramps, standard Mil-Spec charging handle, hardcoat anodized black finish, 7.2 lbs. New 2018.

MSR $999	$850	$550	$465	$395	$350	$325	$295	

CIVILIAN FORCE ARMS, cont. 129 C

MSR	100%	98%	95%	90%	80%	70%	60%	Last MSR

XENA-47 GEN4.1 – 7.62x39mm cal., GIO, 16 in. M4 profile chrome moly barrel, A2 flash hider, two 30 shot AR Stoner mags., A.R.M.S. #71L-F&R flip-up front and rear sights, 6-position Mil-Spec MFT stock, CFA Slim aluminum handguard, MFT Engage black pistol grip, manual safety, M4A4 forged aluminum flat-top upper with Picatinny rail, AK47 Mil-Spec bolt carrier group with manganese phosphate, M4 feed ramps, standard Mil-Spec charging handle, hardcoat anodized black finish, 6.9 lbs. New 2018.

| | MSR $999 | | $850 | $550 | $465 | $395 | $350 | $325 | $295 |

COBALT KINETICS

Current AR-15 style manufacturer located in Washington, UT.

PISTOLS: SEMI-AUTO

STEALTH PISTOL – 5.56 NATO or .300 AAC Blackout cal., dual-drop operating system, 9 in. chrome moly steel barrel, adj. trigger, billet aluminum grip, Shockwave Blade arm brace, linear compensator serves as flash hider, striking devices, Armor Black, OD Green, Cobalt, or FDE finish.

| | MSR $1,950 | | $1,600 | $1,000 | $775 | $575 | $495 | $425 | $395 |

RIFLES/CARBINES: SEMI-AUTO

27 EXPERT STAGE I – .223 Wylde chamber, adj. gas block, 16 or 18 in. CMV chrome moly barrel, 5R rifling, Pro muzzle brake, AR gold trigger, flat blade, push button safety selector, dual drop bolt release, 16 in. Cobalt Pro billet M-LOK handguard, fully ambidextrous controls, billet dust cover, Pro buffer system, available in Armor Black, CK Slate, Cobalt Gray, or stainless steel finish, 8.22 lbs.

| | MSR $3,495 | | $2,775 | $1,825 | $1,350 | $750 | $650 | $595 | $525 |

* **27 Expert Stage II** – .223 Wylde chamber, adj. gas block, 16 or 18 in. fluted stainless steel barrel, 6 groove rifling, Pro muzzle brake, AR gold trigger, flat blade, push button safety selector, dual drop bolt release, 16 in. Cobalt Pro billet M-LOK handguard, fully ambidextrous controls, billet dust cover, Pro buffer system, available in Armor Black, CK Slate, Cobalt Gray, or stainless steel finish, 8.22 lbs.

| | MSR $3,760 | | $3,050 | $1,975 | $1,425 | $850 | $675 | $625 | $575 |

27 SENTRY STAGE I – 5.56 NATO cal., light contour chrome moly barrel with Nitride finish, slick-side upper receiver, Mil-Spec controls, 15 in. M-LOK handguard, Picatinny rail, available in Armor Black, Cobalt, FDE, or OD Green finish.

| | MSR $1,765 | | $1,475 | $950 | $725 | $550 | $475 | $395 | $350 |

* **27 Sentry Stage II** – 5.56 NATO cal., lightweight contour chrome moly barrel with Nitride finish, Edge muzzle brake, adj. SST, slick-side upper receiver, ambidextrous controls, billet dust cover, 15 in. M-LOK handguard, Picatinny rail, available in Armor Black, Cobalt, FDE, or OD Green finish.

| | MSR $1,940 | | $1,600 | $1,000 | $775 | $575 | $495 | $425 | $395 |

EDGE STAGE I – 5.56 NATO cal., fixed gas block, 16 in. Govt. contour barrel, A2 birdcage flash hider, Mil-Spec mag. release, CK serialized billet fixed stock, Hogue OMFG grip, mated serialized billet receiver set, short-throw safety selector, dual-drop bolt release, 16 in. Cobalt serialized EDGE billet M-LOK handguard, Mil-Spec dust cover and fire control, single side charging handle, available in Armor Black, Cobalt, FDE, or stainless steel finish.

| | MSR $2,175 | | $1,725 | $1,050 | $850 | $625 | $550 | $475 | $425 |

* **Edge Stage II** – .223 Wylde chamber, adj. gas block, 16 in. CMV steel barrel, 5R rifling, Edge muzzle brake, adj. SST, Cobalt serialized billet stock, Hogue OMFG grip, short-throw safety selector, dual-drop bolt release, 16 in. Cobalt billet M-LOK handguard, ambidextrous charge handle, billet dust cover and fire control, fully ambidextrous controls, extended mag. release, available in Armor Black, Cobalt, FDE, or stainless steel finish.

| | MSR $2,615 | | $2,125 | $1,325 | $995 | $675 | $595 | $525 | $475 |

* **Edge Stage III** – .223 Wylde chamber, adj. gas block, 16 in. fluted stainless steel barrel, 6 grooves, Edge muzzle brake, adj. SST, Cobalt serialized billet stock, Hogue OMFG grip, short-throw safety selector, dual-drop bolt release, 16 in. Cobalt billet M-LOK handguard, ambidextrous charge handle, billet dust cover and fire control, fully ambidextrous controls, extended mag. release, available in Armor Black, Cobalt, FDE, or stainless steel finish.

| | MSR $2,750 | | $2,225 | $1,395 | $1,050 | $675 | $595 | $525 | $475 |

EDGE XL STAGE I – .308 Win. cal., fixed mid-length gas system, 16 or 18 in. medium profile barrel, A2 birdcage flash hider, Mil-Spec trigger, Cobalt Edge billet fixed stock, rubber overmolded grip, short-throw safety selector, Mil-Spec single side controls, dual-drop bolt release, Standard 308 buffer system, Second Gen upper and handguard design, micro-polished QPQ finished bolt group, available in Armor Black, Cobalt, FDE, or stainless steel finish.

| | MSR $2,740 | | $2,225 | $1,395 | $1,050 | $675 | $595 | $525 | $475 |

* **Edge XL Stage II** – .308 Win. cal., fixed mid-length gas system, 16 or 18 in. medium profile barrel, Cobalt Pro-30 muzzle brake, adj. SST, Cobalt Edge billet fixed stock, Cobalt billet grip, short-throw safety selector, ambidextrous controls, dual-drop bolt release, Cobalt PRO buffer system, Second Gen upper and handguard design, micro-polished QPQ finished bolt group, available in Armor Black, Cobalt, FDE, or stainless steel finish.

| | MSR $3,185 | | $2,550 | $1,650 | $1,250 | $700 | $625 | $575 | $525 |

C 130 COBALT KINETICS, cont.

MSR	100%	98%	95%	90%	80%	70%	60%	Last MSR

EDGE CARBINE STAGE I – 5.56 NATO cal., fixed gas block, 16 in. Govt. contour barrel, A2 flash hider, Mil-Spec fire control, 6-position collapsible stock, Hogue OMFG grip, short-throw safety selector, dual-drop bolt release, 16 in. Serialized EDGE M-LOK billet handguard, single-side charge handle, Mil-Spec dust cover, available in Armor Black, Cobalt, FDE, or stainless steel finish.

MSR $1,995	$1,650	$1,000	$795	$595	$495	$425	$395	

* **Edge Carbine Stage II** – .223 Wylde chamber, adj. gas block, 16 in. CMV steel barrel, 5R rifling, Edge muzzle brake, adj. SST, 6-position collapsible stock, Hogue OMFG grip, short-throw safety selector, dual-drop bolt release, 16 in. Cobalt billet M-LOK handguard, ambidextrous charge handle, billet dust cover and fire control, fully ambidextrous controls, extended mag. release, available in Armor Black, Cobalt, FDE, or stainless steel finish.

MSR $2,440	$1,975	$1,150	$925	$650	$575	$495	$425	

EDGE CARBINE XL STAGE I – .308 Win. cal., fixed mid-length gas system, 16 in. CMV steel medium profile barrel, A2 birdcage flash hider, Mil-Spec trigger, rubber overmolded collapsible stock, rubber overmolded grip, dual-drop bolt control, Mil-Spec single side controls, Second Gen upper handguard design, standard 308 pattern buffer system, billet machined chassis, micro-polished QPQ finished bolt group, available in stainless steel, Armor Black, Cobalt, or FDE finish.

MSR $2,575	$2,050	$1,250	$950	$650	$575	$495	$475	

* **Edge Carbine XL Stage II** – .308 Win. cal., fixed mid-length gas system, 16 in. CMV steel medium profile barrel, Cobalt linear comp. muzzle brake, adj. SST, rubber overmolded collapsible stock, Cobalt billet grip, dual-drop bolt control, ambidextrous controls, Second Gen upper handguard design, Cobalt Pro buffer system, billet machined chassis, micro-polished QPQ finished bolt group, available in stainless steel, Armor Black, Cobalt, or FDE finish.

MSR $2,995	$2,375	$1,525	$1,150	$700	$625	$550	$475	

EVOLVE – .223 Wylde chamber, adj. gas block, 16 in. Proof Research carbon fiber wrapped barrel w/Cobalt Pro muzzle brake, AR gold trigger, adj. stock, billet pistol grip, short-throw safety selector, dual-drop bolt release, fully ambidextrous controls, 16 in. Cobalt Pro billet M-LOK handguard, billet dust cover, Pro buffer system, available in Armor Black, CK Slate, Cobalt, FDE, or stainless steel finish.

MSR $5,395	$4,500	$3,950	$3,400	$3,050	$2,500	$2,000	$1,600	

OVERWATCH LE – .223 Wylde chamber, 6.8 SPC II, or 6.5 Grendel cal., fixed gas block, 18 in. CMV steel, medium weight barrel, Vortex A4 flash hider, Timney Targa two-stage trigger, adj. stock, Cobalt billet pistol grip, short-throw safety selector, dual drop bolt release, bag rider, Mil-Spec dust cover, 16 in. Pro billet M-LOK handguard, fully ambidextrous controls, extended mag. release, available in Armor Black, Cobalt, FDE, OD Green, or stainless steel finish.

MSR $3,700	$3,050	$1,975	$1,425	$850	$675	$625	$575	

Add $175 for 6.8 SPC II or 6.5. Grendel cal.

* **Overwatch XL LE** – .308 Win., 6.8 SPC II, or 6.5 Grendel cal., fixed gas block, 20 in. CMV steel medium weight barrel, Vortex A4 flash hider, two-stage trigger, adj. billet stock w/bag rider, rubber overmolded pistol grip, short-throw safety selector, dual drop bolt release, Mil-Spec dust cover, Second Gen upper and lower handguard, premium ambidextrous controls, Standard AR 308 buffer system, available in Armor Black, Cobalt, FDE, OD Green, or stainless steel finish.

MSR $3,700	$3,050	$1,975	$1,425	$850	$675	$625	$575	

Add $175 for 6.8 SPC II or 6.5. Grendel cal.

OVERWATCH P.R.S. – .223 Wylde chamber, 6.8 SPC II, or 6.5 Grendel cal., fixed gas block, 18 in. stainless steel medium weight barrel, Pro muzzle brake, ATC gold trigger, adj. stock, Cobalt billet pistol grip, short-throw safety selector, dual drop bolt release, bag rider, billet flat dust cover, 16 in. Pro billet M-LOK handguard, fully ambidextrous controls, available in Armor Black, Cobalt, FDE, or stainless steel finish.

MSR $3,870	$3,125	$2,100	$1,475	$875	$695	$650	$575	

* **Overwatch XL P.R.S.** – .308 Win. or 6.5mm Creedmoor cal., fixed rifle length gas system, 20 (.308 Win.) or 24 (6.5mm Creedmoor) in. stainless steel, medium weight barrel, Pro-30 or Pro-65 muzzle brake, ATC gold trigger, adj. billet stock w/bag rider, Cobalt billet pistol grip, short-throw safety selector, dual drop bolt release, billet flat dust cover, Second Gen upper and handguard design, premium ambidextrous controls, micro-polished QPQ finished bolt group, available in Armor Black, Cobalt, FDE, or stainless steel finish.

MSR $5,495	$4,550	$4,000	$3,400	$3,100	$2,500	$2,050	$1,600	

TEAM STAGE I – .223 Wylde chamber, adj. gas block, 16 in. CMV steel barrel w/Cobalt Pro muzzle brake, 5R rifling, AR gold trigger, flat blade, mated serialized billet fixed stock, billet pistol grip, short-throw safety selector, dual-drop bolt release, fully ambidextrous controls, 16 in. Cobalt Pro billet M-LOK handguard, billet dust cover, Cobalt PRO buffer kit, available in Armor Black, CK Slate, Cobalt, FDE, or stainless steel finish.

MSR $3,500	$2,875	$1,875	$1,375	$795	$675	$625	$575	

* **Team Stage II** – .223 Wylde chamber, adj. gas block, 16 in. fluted stainless steel barrel w/Cobalt Pro muzzle brake, 6 grooves, AR gold trigger, flat blade, mated serialized billet fixed stock, billet pistol grip, short-throw safety selector, dual-drop bolt release, extended mag. release, fully ambidextrous controls, 16 in. Cobalt Pro billet M-LOK handguard, billet dust cover, full Cobalt Pro buffer kit, available in Armor Black, CK Slate, Cobalt, FDE, or stainless steel finish.

MSR $3,760	$3,050	$1,975	$1,425	$850	$675	$625	$575	

COBALT KINETICS, cont. 131 C

MSR	100%	98%	95%	90%	80%	70%	60%	Last MSR

* ***Team Stage III*** – .223 Wylde chamber, adj. gas block, 16 in. Proof Research carbon fiber wrapped barrel w/Cobalt Pro muzzle brake, 6 grooves, AR gold trigger, flat blade, mated serialized billet fixed stock, billet pistol grip, short-throw safety selector, dual-drop bolt release, extended mag. release, fully ambidextrous controls, 16 in. Cobalt Pro billet M-LOK handguard, billet dust cover, full Cobalt Pro buffer kit, available in Armor Black, CK Slate, Cobalt, FDE, or stainless steel finish.

MSR $4,595	$3,695	$2,650	$1,675	$1,050	$795	$725	$700	

COBB MANUFACTURING, INC.

Previous rifle manufacturer located in Dallas, GA until 2007.

On Aug. 20, 2007, Cobb Manufacturing was purchased by Bushmaster, and manufacture was moved to Bushmaster's Maine facility. Please refer to the Bushmaster section for current information.

RIFLES: SEMI-AUTO

MCR (MULTI-CALIBER RIFLE) SERIES – available in a variety of calibers from 9mm Para. to .338 Lapua, offered in MCR 100, MCR 200, MCR 300, and MCR 400 configurations, variety of stock, barrel and finish options. Mfg. 2005-2007. **Prices on this series started at $3,000, and went up according to options chosen by customer.**

COLT'S MANUFACTURING COMPANY, LLC

Current manufacturer with headquarters located in West Hartford, CT.

Manufactured from 1836-1842 in Paterson, NJ; 1847-1848 in Whitneyville, CT; 1854-1864 in London, England; and from 1848-date in Hartford, CT. Colt Firearms became a division of Colt Industries in 1964. In March 1990, the Colt Firearms Division was sold to C.F. Holding Corp. located in Hartford, CT, and the new company was called Colt's Manufacturing Company, Inc. The original Hartford plant was closed during 1994, the same year the company was sold again to a new investor group headed by Zilkha Co., located in New York, NY. During 1999, Colt Archive Properties LLC, the historical research division, became its own entity.

In late 1999, Colt discontinued many of their consumer revolvers, but reintroduced both the Anaconda and Python Elite through the Custom Shop. Production on both models is now suspended. The semi-auto pistols remaining in production are now referred to as Model "O" Series.

In November 2003, Colt was divided into two separate companies, Colt Defense LLC (military/law enforcement) and Colt's Manufacturing Company LLC (handguns and match target rifles). The largest portion of Colt Defense's business is now in sporting rifles, a line of business the company got back into during 2011. Military orders have been on the decline since 2009.

During 2013, Colt Defense LLC acquired Colt's Manufacturing LLC for $60.5 million and reunited Colt's military and civilian handgun businesses. By combining the two companies after a decade long split, Colt Defense has eliminated the risk that its contract with Colt's Manufacturing to sell commercial firearms to civilian sportsmen and hunters under its namesake brand wouldn't be extended beyond March 2014. The company plans to remain in West Hartford.

For more information and current pricing on both new and used Colt airguns, please refer to the *Blue Book of Airguns* by Dr. Robert Beeman & John Allen (also available online). For more information and current pricing on both new and used Colt black powder reproductions and replicas, please refer to the *Blue Book of Modern Black Powder Arms* by John Allen (also available online).

RIFLES: SEMI-AUTO, CENTERFIRE, AR-15 & VARIATIONS

The AR-15 rifle and variations are the civilian versions of the U.S. armed forces M-16 model, which was initially ordered by the U.S. Army in 1963. Colt's obtained the exclusive manufacturing and marketing rights to the AR-15 from the Armalite division of the Fairchild Engine and Airplane Corporation in 1961.

Factory Colt AR-15 receivers are stamped with the model names only (Sporter II, Government Model, Colt Carbine, Sporter Match H-Bar, Match Target), but are not stamped with the model numbers (R6500, R6550, R6521, MT6430, CR6724). Because of this, if an AR-15 rifle/carbine does not have its original box, the only way to determine whether the gun is pre-ban or not is to look at the serial number and see if the configuration matches the features listed below within the two pre-ban subcategories.

AR-15 production included transition models, which were made up of obsolete and old stock parts. These transition models include: blue label box models having large front takedown pins, no internal sear block, 20 in. barrel models having bayonet lugs, misstamped nomenclature on receivers, or green label bolt assemblies.

Rifling twists on the Colt AR-15 have changed throughout the years, and barrel twists are stamped at the end of the barrel on top. They started with a 1:12 in. twist, changed to a 1:7 in. twist (to match with the new, longer .223 Rem./5.56mm SS109-type bullet), and finally changed to a 1:9 in. twist in combination with 1:7 in. twist models as a compromise for bullets in the 50-68 grain range. Current mfg. AR-15s/Match Targets have rifling twists/turns incorporated into the model descriptions.

Colt's never sold pre-ban lower receivers individually. It only sold completely assembled rifles.

A Colt letter of provenance for the following AR-15 models is $100 per gun.

C 132 COLT'S MANUFACTURING COMPANY, LLC, cont.

MSR	100%	98%	95%	90%	80%	70%	60%	Last MSR

AR-15, Pre-Ban, 1963-1989 Mfg. w/Green Label Box

Common features of 1963-1989 mfg. AR-15s are bayonet lug, flash hider, large front takedown pin, no internal sear block, and no reinforcement around the magazine release button.

AR-15 boxes during this period of mfg. had a green label with serial number affixed on a white sticker. Box is taped in two places with brown masking tape. NIB consists of the rifle with barrel stick down the barrel, plastic muzzle cap on flash hider, factory tag hanging from front sight post, rifle in plastic bag with ser. no. on white sticker attached to bag, cardboard insert, accessory bag with two 20 round mags., manual, sling, and cleaning brushes. Cleaning rods are in separate bag.

Pre-ban parts rifles are rifles which are not assembled in their proper factory configuration. Counterfeit pre-ban rifles are rifles using post-ban receivers and assembled into a pre-ban configuration (it is a felony to assemble or alter a post-ban rifle into a pre-ban configuration).

Add $100 for NIB condition.

Add $300 for early green label box models with reinforced lower receiver.

SP-1 (R6000) – .223 Rem. cal., GIO, original Colt tactical configuration without forward bolt assist, 20 in. barrel with 1:12 in. twist, identifiable by the triangular shaped handguards/forearm, no case deflector, A1 sights, finishes included parkerizing and electroless nickel, approx. 6 3/4 lbs. Ser. no. range SP0001-SP16000 through 1976. Mfg. 1963-1984.

	$2,450	$2,150	$1,850	$1,650	$1,500	$1,350	$1,200	

Add 40%-60% for mint original models with early two and three digit serial numbers.

Pre-ban serialization is ser. no. SP360,200 and lower.

Early SP-1s were packaged differently than later standard green box label guns.

* SP-1 Carbine (R6001) – .223 Rem. cal., similar to SP-1, except has 16 in. barrel, ribbed handguards, collapsible buttstock, high gloss finish.

	$3,000	$2,600	$2,250	$1,950	$1,800	$1,500	$1,350	

Mint original condition models with early two and three digit serial numbers are selling in the $3,250 - $3,500 range.

Pre-ban serialization is ser. no. SP360200 and lower.

Early SP-1s were packaged differently than later standard green box label guns.

SPORTER II (R6500) – .223 Rem. cal., GIO, various configurations, receiver stamped "Sporter II", 20 in. barrel, 1:7 twist, A1 sights and forward assist, disc.

	$1,850	$1,650	$1,450	$1,250	$1,100	$950	$850	

Serial numbers SP360200 and below are pre-ban.

* Sporter II Carbine (R6420) – .223 Rem. cal., similar to Sporter II, except has 16 in. barrel, A1 sights and collapsible buttstock.

	$2,500	$2,200	$1,900	$1,750	$1,600	$1,400	$1,250	

Serial numbers SP360200 and below are pre-ban.

GOVERNMENT MODEL (R6550) – .223 Rem. cal., GIO, receiver is stamped Government Model, 20 in. barrel with 1:7 in. twist and bayonet lug, A2 sights, forward assist and brass deflector, very desirable because this model has the closest configurations to what the U.S. military is currently using.

	$2,250	$1,950	$1,800	$1,650	$1,400	$1,200	$950	

In 1987, Colt replaced the AR-15A2 Sporter II Rifle with the AR-15A2 Govt. Model. This new model has the 800 meter rear sighting system housed in the receiver's carrying handle (similar to the M-16 A2).

Serial numbers GS008000 and below with GS prefix are pre-ban.

* Government Model (6550K) – .223 Rem. cal., similar to R6550, except does not have bayonet lug, originally supplied with .22 L.R. cal. conversion kit.

	$2,100	$1,900	$1,750	$1,600	$1,450	$1,250	$1,000	

Subtract $300 w/o conversion kit.

Serial numbers GS008000 and below with GS prefix are pre-ban.

* Government Model (R6550CC) – .223 Rem. cal., similar to R6550, except has Z-Cote tiger striped camo finish, very scarce (watch for cheap imitation paint jobs).

	$3,500	$3,350	$3,100	$2,800	$2,600	$2,400	$2,000	

Serial numbers GS008000 and below with GS prefix are pre-ban.

H-BAR MODEL (R6600) – GIO, HBAR model with 20 in. heavy barrel, 1:7 twist, forward assist, A2 sights, brass deflector, 8 lbs. New 1986.

	$2,100	$1,900	$1,750	$1,600	$1,450	$1,250	$1,000	

Serial numbers SP360200 and below are pre-ban.

COLT'S MANUFACTURING COMPANY, LLC, cont. 133 C

MSR	100%	98%	95%	90%	80%	70%	60%	Last MSR

* **H-Bar (R6600K)** – similar to R6600, except has no bayonet lug, supplied with .22 LR cal. conversion kit.

| | $1,850 | $1,650 | $1,450 | $1,250 | $1,100 | $950 | $850 | |

Subtract $300 if w/o conversion kit.

Serial numbers SP360200 and below are pre-ban.

* **Delta H-Bar (R6600DH)** – similar to R6600, except has 3-9x rubber armored scope, removable cheekpiece, adj. scope mount, and black leather sling, test range selected for its accuracy, aluminum transport case. Mfg. 1987-1991.

| | $2,500 | $2,200 | $1,900 | $1,750 | $1,600 | $1,400 | $1,250 | $1,460 |

Serial numbers SP360200 and below are pre-ban.

AR-15, Pre-Ban, 1989-Sept. 11, 1994 Mfg. w/Blue Label Box

Common features of 1989-1994 AR-15 production include a small front takedown pin, internal sear block, reinforcement around the mag. release button, flash hider, no bayonet lug on 20 in. models, A2 sights, brass deflector, and forward bolt assist. Models R6430 and 6450 do not have A2 sights, brass deflector, or forward bolt assist.

Blue label boxed AR-15s were mfg. between 1989-Sept. 11, 1994. Please refer to box description under Pre-1989 AR-15 mfg.

Pre-ban parts rifles are rifles which are not assembled in their proper factory configuration. Counterfeit pre-ban rifles are rifles using post-ban receivers and assembled into a pre-ban configuration.

Add $100 for NIB condition.

AR-15A3 TACTICAL CARBINE (R-6721) – .223 Rem. cal., GIO, M4 flat-top with 16 in. heavy barrel, 1:9 twist, A2 sights, pre-ban configuration with flash hider, bayonet lug, and 4-position, collapsible stock, removable carry handle, 134 were sold commercially in the U.S., most collectible AR-15. Mfg. 1994 only.

| S/N 134 and lower | $3,000 | $2,500 | $2,275 | $2,050 | $1,900 | $1,775 | $1,600 | |
| S/N 135 and higher | $2,000 | $1,850 | $1,700 | $1,450 | $1,225 | $1,050 | $900 | |

On the R-6721, serial numbers BD000134 and below are pre-ban.

Please note the serial number cutoff on this model, as Colt shipped out a lot of unstamped post-ban law enforcement only "LEO" rifles before finally stamping them as a restricted rifle.

GOVERNMENT CARBINE (R6520) – .223 Rem cal., GIO, receiver is stamped Government Carbine, two-position collapsible buttstock, 800 meter adj. rear sight, 16 in. barrel with bayonet lug, 1:7 twist, shortened forearm, 5 lbs. 13 oz. Mfg. 1988-94.

| | $2,275 | $2,125 | $2,000 | $1,850 | $1,650 | $1,500 | $1,250 | $880 |

Add $200 for green label box.

On the R6520, serial numbers GC018500 and below are pre-ban.

Please note the serial number cutoff on this model, as Colt shipped out a lot of unstamped post-ban law enforcement only "LEO" rifles before finally stamping them as a restricted rifle.

This model was manufactured in both green and blue label configurations.

COLT CARBINE (R6521) – receiver is stamped Colt Carbine, similar to R6520, except has no bayonet lug, 16 in. barrel, 1:7 twist. Disc. 1988.

| | $2,275 | $2,125 | $2,000 | $1,850 | $1,650 | $1,500 | $1,250 | $770 |

Serial numbers CC001616 and below are pre-ban.

SPORTER LIGHTWEIGHT (R6530) – .223 Rem. cal., GIO, receiver is stamped Sporter Lightweight, 16 in. barrel, 1:7 twist, similar to R6520, except does not have bayonet lug or collapsible stock.

| | $2,000 | $1,850 | $1,700 | $1,450 | $1,225 | $1,050 | $900 | $740 |

Serial numbers SI027246 and below are pre-ban.

9mm CARBINE (R6430) – 9mm Para. cal., similar to R6450 Carbine, except does not have bayonet lug or collapsible stock. Mfg. 1992-1994.

| | $2,150 | $2,050 | $1,950 | $1,800 | $1,600 | $1,450 | $1,150 | |

Serial numbers NL004800 are pre-ban.

9mm CARBINE (R6450) – 9mm Para. cal., GIO, carbine model with 16 in. barrel, 1:10 twist, bayonet lug, w/o forward bolt assist or brass deflector, two-position collapsible stock, 20 shot mag., 6 lbs. 5 oz.

| | $2,250 | $2,100 | $2,000 | $1,800 | $1,600 | $1,500 | $1,250 | $696 |

On the R6450, serial numbers TA010100 are pre-ban.

Please note the serial number cutoff on this model, as Colt shipped out a lot of unstamped post-ban law enforcement only "LEO" rifles before finally stamping them as a restricted rifle.

This model was manufactured with either a green or blue label.

134 COLT'S MANUFACTURING COMPANY, LLC, cont.

MSR	100%	98%	95%	90%	80%	70%	60%	Last MSR

7.62x39mm CARBINE (R6830) – 7.62x39mm cal., GIO, 16 in. barrel w/o bayonet lug, 1:12 twist, fixed buttstock. Mfg. 1992-1994.

| | $1,850 | $1,700 | $1,550 | $1,400 | $1,200 | $1,025 | $875 | |

Serial numbers LH011326 are pre-ban.

TARGET COMPETITION H-BAR RIFLE (R6700) – .223 Rem. cal., GIO, flat-top upper receiver for scope mounting, 20 in. H-Bar barrel (1:9 in. twist), quick detachable carry handle with a 600-meter rear sighting system, dovetailed upper receiver grooved to accept Weaver style scope rings, 8 1/2 lbs.

| | $1,850 | $1,700 | $1,550 | $1,400 | $1,200 | $1,025 | $875 | |

Serial numbers CH019500 and below are pre-ban.

COMPETITION H-BAR CUSTOM SHOP (R6701) – .223 Rem. cal., similar to the R6700, but with detachable scope mount, custom shop enhancements added to trigger and barrel, 2,000 mfg. from Colt Custom Shop.

| | $1,950 | $1,800 | $1,650 | $1,500 | $1,350 | $1,200 | $1,000 | |

MATCH H-BAR (R6601) – GIO, heavy 20 in. HBAR barrel with 1:7 twist, fixed buttstock. 8 lbs.

| | $1,850 | $1,700 | $1,550 | $1,400 | $1,200 | $1,025 | $875 | |

* **Delta H-Bar (R6601DH)** – similar to R6601, except has 3-9x rubber armored variable scope, removable cheekpiece, adj. scope mount, black leather sling, test range selected for its accuracy, aluminum transport case. Mfg. 1987-91.

| | $2,500 | $2,300 | $2,150 | $2,000 | $1,800 | $1,600 | $1,450 | *$1,460* |

Serial numbers MH086020 and below are pre-ban.

SPORTER TARGET (R6551) – similar to R6601, except had 20 in. barrel with reduced diameter underneath handguard, 7 1/2 lbs.

| | $1,850 | $1,700 | $1,550 | $1,400 | $1,200 | $1,025 | $875 | |

On the R6551, serial numbers ST038100 and below are pre-ban.

AR-15, Post-Ban, Mfg. Sept. 12, 1994-Present

During 2007, Colt released the M-5 Military Carbine and the LE 10-20, with 11 1/2, 14 1/2, or 16 in. barrel. These guns were only available for military and law enforcement.

During 2013, Colt released a line of competition rifles, manufactured under license by Bold Ideas, located in Breckenridge, TX. Every rifle/carbine comes with a 100 yard target.

State compliant variations are not listed in this text. Values are typically similar to the models from which they were derived.

Add $368 for Colt Scout C-More Sight (disc.).
Add $444 for Colt Tactical C-More Sight (disc.).

COMPETITION CRP-18 WITH GUNGODDESS TOUCH – .223 Rem. cal., GIO, 18 in. match grade stainless steel fluted barrel with triple port muzzle brake, 30 shot Magpul mag., enlarged trigger guard, Geissele two-stage match trigger, Magpul CTR 6-pos. adj. stock with locking adjustments, Magpul MOE grip, matched bolt and carrier with H-buffer, GunGoddess 15 in. free float handguard, one 2 in. accessory rail, Colt Competition charging handle with extended tactical latch, black finish, 7.22 lbs. New 2015.

| MSR $1,995 | $1,800 | $1,550 | $1,350 | $1,200 | $1,000 | $800 | $650 | |

Add $130 for Robin Egg Blue, Pink, Bright Purple, Snow White, Crimson, Zombie Green, Brushed Nickel, or Crushed Silver furniture.

COMPETITION PRO – .223/5.56 Wylde chamber, GIO, 18 in. match grade stainless steel fluted barrel, fully adj. gas block, triple chamber or SureFire muzzle brake, forged upper and lower receiver, flat-top with Picatinny rail, 30 shot mag., matte black finish, Geissele two-stage match trigger, Magpul adj. stock, grip, and forend, approx. 7 lbs. Mfg. 2013.

| | $1,850 | $1,600 | $1,400 | $1,250 | $1,000 | $850 | $650 | *$2,029* |

EXPERT CRE-16 – 5.56 NATO cal., similar to Expert CRE-18, except has 16 in. barrel. Mfg. 2014-2015.

| | $1,400 | $1,200 | $1,050 | $950 | $750 | $650 | $500 | *$1,599* |

EXPERT CRE-16T GEN2 – .223 Rem. cal., mid-length gas system, 16 in. stainless steel HBAR contour match grade barrel, steel muzzle brake, Magpul 30 shot PMAG, Magpul enlarged trigger guard, no sights, Hogue overmolded collapsible stock, Hogue rubber beavertail grip, low profile fixed gas block, extended charging handle, M-LOK 12 in. aluminum-alloy float tube handguard, matte black finish, 6.66 lbs.

| MSR $1,599 | $1,400 | $1,200 | $1,050 | $950 | $750 | $650 | $500 | |

EXPERT CRE-16T GEN3 PRECISION CARBINE – .223/5.56 Wylde chamber, fixed gas block, 16 in. stainless steel HBAR mid-weight barrel, 3-chamber muzzle brake, 30 shot mag., Hogue stock with buttpad, Hogue grip, 15 in. M-LOK float-tube handguard with sling swivel mount. New 2017.

| MSR $1,699 | $1,500 | $1,350 | $1,150 | $1,050 | $850 | $700 | $550 | |

COLT'S MANUFACTURING COMPANY, LLC, cont. 135 C

MSR	100%	98%	95%	90%	80%	70%	60%	Last MSR

EXPERT CRE-18/CRE-18 RR – 5.56 NATO cal., GIO, low profile gas block, forged and precision fitted upper and lower receivers, matte black finish, 18 in. midweight match grade air gauged polish stainless steel barrel, 10 or 30 shot Magpul mag., competition nickel Teflon coated match target trigger, enlarged Magpul trigger guard, Magpul MOE four position adj. stock or CTR adj. stock (Model CRE-18 RR, new 2014), Expert Brake (CRE-18) or ProBrake (CRE-18 RR, mfg. 2014-2015), 15 in. vented modular float tube handguard, 5 1/2 in. top mounted Picatinny handguard rail with 11 slots, two 3 in. accessory rails with five slots each or quad rails (CRE-18 RR, disc. 2015), Hogue rubber finger groove grip, competition charging handle with extended tactical latch, matched bolt and bolt carrier with H-buffer, 13 slot Picatinny rail on flat-top upper receiver. New 2013.

| MSR $1,599 | $1,400 | $1,200 | $1,050 | $950 | $750 | $650 | $500 | |

Add $100 for CRE-18 RR model with quad rails and ProBrake (mfg. 2014-2015).

EXPERT CRE-18T GEN2 – .223 Rem. cal., rifle length gas system, 18 in. stainless steel HBAR contour match grade barrel, steel muzzle brake, Magpul 30 shot PMAG, Magpul enlarged trigger guard, no sights, Hogue overmolded collapsible stock, Hogue rubber beavertail grip, low profile fixed gas block, extended charging handle, M-LOK 15 in. aluminum-alloy float tube handguard, matte black finish, 7 lbs.

| MSR $1,599 | $1,400 | $1,200 | $1,050 | $950 | $750 | $650 | $500 | |

EXPERT CRE-18T GEN3 LONG RANGE RIFLE – .223/5.56 Wylde chamber, fixed gas block, 18 in. stainless steel HBAR mid-weight barrel, 3-chamber muzzle brake, 30 shot mag., Hogue stock with buttpad, Hogue grip, 15 in. M-LOK float-tube handguard with sling swivel mount. New 2017.

| MSR $1,699 | $1,500 | $1,350 | $1,150 | $1,050 | $850 | $700 | $550 | |

MARKSMAN CRX-16/CRX-16E – .223 Rem. cal., GIO, low profile gas block, 16 in. midweight match grade manganese phosphate chrome moly steel barrel, Expert brake, 10 or 30 shot Magpul mag., competition match target nickel Teflon coated trigger, enlargd Magpul trigger guard, carbine style four position adj. buttstock or Magpul MOE fixed rifle stock (CRX-16E), checkered A2 style finger groove grip, forged and precision fitted upper and lower receivers, 12 in. vented modular float tube handguard, 5 1/2 in. top mounted Picatinny handguard rail with 11 slots, two 3 in. accessory rails with five slots each, matched bolt and bolt carrier with H-buffer, 13 slot Picatinny rail on flat-top upper receiver, matte black finish. Mfg. 2013-2015.

| | $1,250 | $1,100 | $950 | $850 | $700 | $550 | $450 | *$1,399* |

MARKSMAN CRX-16 GEN2 – 5.56 NATO cal., carbine length fixed gas system, blackened 16 in. HBAR contour barrel, triple chamber steel muzzle brake, Magpul 30 shot PMAG, Magpul enlarged trigger guard, no sights, Hogue overmolded collapsible stock, Hogue beavertail grip, extended charging handle, M-LOK 12 in. aluminum alloy float tube handguard, matte black finish, 6.65 lbs. New 2016.

| MSR $1,199 | $1,075 | $950 | $800 | $750 | $600 | $475 | $375 | |

MARKSMAN CRX-16 GEN3 LIGHT CARBINE – 5.56 NATO cal., fixed gas block, 16 in. chrome moly, mid-weight barrel, 3-chamber muzzle brake, 30 shot mag., Hogue stock with buttpad, Hogue grip, 15 in. M-LOK float-tube handguard with sling swivel mount. New 2017.

| MSR $1,249 | $1,125 | $1,000 | $850 | $750 | $600 | $500 | $400 | |

MARKSMAN CRZ-16 GEN2 – 5.56 NATO cal., low profile fixed gas block, blackened 16 in. HBAR contour barrel, twin chamber steel muzzle brake, Magpul 30 shot PMAG, Magpul enlarged trigger guard, no sights, M4 collapsible stock, A2 grip, extended charging handle, M-LOK 10 in. aluminum-alloy float tube handguard, matte black finish, 6 lbs. New 2016.

| MSR $999 | $900 | $800 | $700 | $600 | $500 | $400 | $325 | |

PRO CRB-16 – .300 AAC Blackout or .300 Whisper (new 2014) cal., GIO, patented low profile adj. gas block, forged and precision fitted upper and lower receivers, matte black finish, 16 in. match grade air gauged stainless steel barrel with Colt competition triple port muzzle brake, 10 or 30 shot aluminum mag., Geissele two-stage match trigger, Magpul enlarged trigger guard, Magpul STR six position adj. stock with locking adjustments, Magpul MOE grip with extended backstrap, Hogue 12 in. multi-piece slotted free floated tubular handguard, Competition charging handle with extended tactical latch, matched bolt and bolt carrier with H-buffer, 13 slot Picatinny rail on flat-top upper receiver, 6.7 lbs. Mfg. 2013-2015.

| | $1,600 | $1,400 | $1,200 | $1,100 | $900 | $700 | $550 | *$1,799* |

PRO CRC-22 – 6.5mm Creedmoor cal., 22 in. fluted stainless steel HBAR+ match barrel, ProBrake, 20 shot Magpul mag., PRS adj. stock, 3 rails, 15 in. float tube modular handguard. Mfg. 2014-2015.

| | $2,675 | $2,350 | $2,000 | $1,800 | $1,450 | $1,200 | $950 | *$2,979* |

PRO CRC-22 GEN2 – 6.5mm Creedmoor cal., rifle length adj. gas system, 22 in. polished HBAR contour heavy fluted stainless steel barrel, triple chamber steel muzzle brake, Magpul 20 shot PMAG, enlarged integral trigger guard, no sights, Luth-AR stock, Ergo tactical beavertail grip, extended charging handle, M-LOK 15 in. aluminum alloy float tube handguard, matte black finish, 11.2 lbs. New 2016.

| MSR $2,899 | $2,600 | $2,300 | $1,950 | $1,750 | $1,450 | $1,150 | $900 | |

MSR	100%	98%	95%	90%	80%	70%	60%	Last MSR

PRO CRG-20 – 6.5mm Grendel cal., GIO, patented low profile adj. gas block, forged and precision fitted upper and lower receivers, matte black finish, 20 in. match grade air gauged chrome moly steel custom barrel with black Nitride finish, 10 or 25 shot aluminum mag., Colt competition match target trigger, nickel Teflon coated, 15 in. vented modular free floated tubular handguard, 10 in. top mounted Picatinny handguard rail with 23 slots and 2-3 accessory rails, oversized trigger guard, Magpul CTR 6-position adj. buttstock with locking adjustments, Magpul MOE pistol grip with extended backstrap, competition charging handle with extended tactical latch, matched bolt and bolt carrier with H-buffer, 13 slot Picatinny rail on flat-top upper receiver. Limited mfg. 2013 only.

	$1,450	$1,300	$1,100	$1,000	$800	$650	$500	*$1,649*

PRO CRL-16 – .308 Win. cal., GIO, low profile adj. gas block, CNC machined and precision fitted upper and lower receivers, matte black finish, 16 in. tapered midweight match grade air gauged polished stainless steel custom barrel with triple port muzzle brake, 10 or 20 shot Magpul mag., integral enlarged trigger guard, Geissele two-stage SSA-E match trigger, Magpul CTR six position adj. stock with locking adjustments, Magpul MOE pistol grip with extended backstrap, 12 1/2 in. free floated tubular handguard, top mounted Picatinny handguard rail, two 3 in. accessory rails, competition charging handle with extended tactical latch, matched bolt and bolt carrier, 18 slot Picatinny rail on flat-top upper receiver. Mfg. 2013-2015.

	$2,100	$1,850	$1,600	$1,450	$1,150	$950	$750	*$2,339*

PRO CRL-16 GEN2 – .308 Win. cal., adj. mid-length gas system, 16 in. polished HBAR contour heavy tapered stainless steel barrel, triple chamber vented muzzle brake, Magpul 20 shot PMAG, SST, enlarged integral trigger guard, no sights, Hogue overmolded 6-pos. collapsible stock, Hogue rubber beavertail grip, M-LOK 12 in. aluminum-alloy float tube handguard, extended charging handle, matte black finish, 8.67 lbs. New 2016.

	$2,050	$1,800	$1,550	$1,400	$1,150	$900	$700	

PRO CRL-20 – .308 Win. cal., adj. rifle length gas system, 20 in. match barrel with six flutes, 3-chamber muzzle brake, 20 shot Magpul mag., Geissele match trigger, Magpul PRS stock, 15 in. float tube handguard, 3 rails. Mfg. 2013-2015.

	$2,675	$2,350	$2,000	$1,800	$1,450	$1,200	$950	*$2,979*

PRO CRL-20 GEN2 – .308 Win. cal., rifle length adj. gas system, 20 in. polished HBAR contour heavy fluted stainless steel barrel, triple chamber steel muzzle brake, Magpul 20 shot PMAG, enlarged trigger guard, no sights, Luth-AR stock, Ergo tactical beavertail grip, extended charging handle, M-LOK 15 in. aluminum alloy float tube handguard, matte black finish, 10.8 lbs. New 2016.

MSR $2,899	$2,600	$2,300	$1,950	$1,750	$1,450	$1,150	$900	

PRO CRP-16 – 5.56 NATO cal., GIO, low profile adj. gas block, forged and precision fitted upper and lower receivers, matte black finish, 16 in. two-diameter heavy weight match grade air gauged polished stainless steel barrel, triple port muzzle brake, 10 or 30 shot Magpul mag., Geissele two-stage match trigger, Magpul enlarged trigger guard, Magpul CTR 6-position adj. stock with locking adjustments, Magpul MOE grip with extended backstrap, competition 12 in. vented modular float tube handguard, 5 1/2 in. top mounted Picatinny handguard rail with 11 slots, two 3 in. accessory rails, competition charging handle with extended tactical latch matched bolt and bolt carrier with H-buffer, 13 slot Picatinny rail on flat-top upper receiver. New 2013.

MSR $1,899	$1,700	$1,500	$1,300	$1,150	$950	$750	$600	

PRO CRP-18 THREE-GUN MATCH RIFLE – 5.56 NATO cal., similar to CRP-16, except has 18 in. custom fluted mid-weight barrel, 15 in. vented modular float tube handguard, and full length Picatinny top handguard rail with one 2 in. accessory rail. Mfg. 2013-2015.

	$1,850	$1,600	$1,400	$1,250	$1,000	$850	$650	*$2,019*

PRO CRP-18LV (LIGHT VARMINT RIFLE) – .223 Rem. cal., adj. rifle length gas system, 18 in. stainless steel HBAR match barrel, 3-chamber muzzle brake, 30 shot Magpul mag., Geissele match trigger, Magpul CTR 6-pos. stock, 15 in. float tube modular handguard, 4 rails. Disc. 2015.

	$1,700	$1,500	$1,300	$1,150	$950	$750	$600	*$1,899*

PRO CRP-18 GEN2 – .223 Rem. cal., rifle length adj. gas system, 18 in. polished HBAR stainless steel barrel, triple chamber muzzle brake, Magpul 30 shot PMAG, Magpul enlarged trigger guard, no sights, Luth-AR stock, Ergo tactical beavertail grip, extended charging handle, M-LOK 15 in. aluminum alloy float tube handguard, matte black finish, 7 lbs. New 2016.

MSR $1,999	$1,800	$1,550	$1,350	$1,200	$1,000	$800	$650	

PRO CRP-18 GEN3 3-GUN COMPETITION – .223/5.56 Wylde chamber, fully adj. gas block, 18 in. stainless steel HBAR mid-weight barrel, 3-chamber fluted muzzle brake, 30 shot mag., Hogue stock with buttpad, Hogue grip, 15 in. M-LOK float-tube handguard with sling swivel mount. New 2017.

MSR $1,999	$1,800	$1,550	$1,350	$1,200	$1,000	$800	$650	

COLT'S MANUFACTURING COMPANY, LLC, cont. 137 C

MSR	100%	98%	95%	90%	80%	70%	60%	Last MSR

PRO CRP-20/20L/22RR – .223 Rem. cal., adj. rifle length gas system, 20 in. stainless steel extra heavy match barrel, 3-chamber vented muzzle brake, 30 shot Magpul mag., Geissele match trigger, Magpul CTR 6-position (CRP-20) or Magpul PRS adj. sniper (CRP-20L or CRP-20RR) stock, forged receivers, 15 in. float tube modular handguard with 3 rails, polished barrel (CRP-20 or CRP-20L) or blackened barrel (CRP-20RR) finish. Mfg. 2013-2015.

| | $1,700 | $1,500 | $1,300 | $1,150 | $950 | $750 | $600 | *$1,899* |

Add $100 for CRP-20L or CRP-20SS model.

PRO CRP-20VR (VARMINT RIFLE) – .223 Rem. cal., adj. rifle length gas system, 20 in. stainless steel HBAR match barrel, 3-chamber muzzle brake, 30 shot Magpul mag., Geissele match trigger, Magpul MOE fixed stock, forged receivers, 15 in. float tube modular handguard, 4 rails. New 2013.

| MSR $1,899 | $1,700 | $1,500 | $1,300 | $1,150 | $950 | $750 | $600 | |

SPORTING RIFLE CSR-1516/CSR-1518 – .223 Rem. or 5.56 NATO cal., GIO, 16 (CSR-1516) or 18 (CSR-18) in. midweight match grade chrome moly black manganese phosphate threaded steel barrel with standard flash suppressor, 10 or 30 shot mag., nickel Teflon coated match target trigger, adj. 6-position carbine (CSR-16) or rifle stock with wide cheekpiece (CSR-18), rubber over-molded finger groove grip with integral beavertail, solid steel machined low profile gas block, forged alloy upper and lower receivers, 12 in. float tube handguard, standard charging handle, bolt, and bolt carrier, top mounted seven slot accessory rail, matte black finish. Mfg. 2013-2015.

| | $900 | $800 | $700 | $600 | $500 | $400 | $325 | *$990* |

Add $59 for CSR-18.

TACTICAL PATROL CARBINE CRX-16 RR – 5.56 NATO cal., low pro gas system, 16 in. chrome moly M4 contour barrel, ProBrake, quad rails, CTR stock, 6 lb. trigger, 30 shot mag. Mfg. 2014-2015.

| | $1,250 | $1,100 | $950 | $850 | $700 | $550 | $450 | *$1,379* |

COLT ACCURIZED RIFLE (CR6720/CR6724) – .223 Rem. cal., GIO, 20 (CR6720) or 24 (CR6724, disc. 2012, reintroduced 2014) in. stainless match barrel, matte finish, accurized AR-15, 8 (disc. 1998) or 9 (new 1999) shot mag., 9.41 lbs. New 1997.

| MSR $1,374 | $1,250 | $1,100 | $950 | $850 | $700 | $550 | $450 | |

MATCH TARGET COMPETITION H-BAR RIFLE (MT6700/MT6700C) – .223 Rem. cal., GIO, features flat-top upper receiver for scope mounting, 20 in. barrel (1:9 in. twist), quick detachable carry handle which incorporates a 600-meter rear sighting system, counterbored muzzle, dovetailed upper receiver is grooved to accept Weaver style scope rings, supplied with two 5 (disc.), 8 (disc.), or 9 (new 1999) shot mags., cleaning kit, and sling, matte black finish, 8 1/2 lbs. Mfg. 1992-2013.

| | $1,125 | $1,000 | $850 | $750 | $600 | $500 | $400 | *$1,230* |

Add $57 for compensator (MT6700C, mfg. 1999-disc).

MATCH TARGET COMPETITION H-BAR II (MT6731) – .223 Rem. cal., GIO, flat-top, 16.1 in. barrel (1:9 in.), 9 shot mag., matte finish, 7.1 lbs. Mfg. 1995-2012.

| | $1,050 | $900 | $800 | $700 | $600 | $475 | $375 | *$1,173* |

MATCH TARGET LIGHTWEIGHT (MT6430, MT6530, or MT6830) – .223 Rem. (MT6530, 1:7 in. twist), 7.62x39mm (MT6830, disc. 1996, 1:12 in. twist), or 9mm Para. (MT6430, disc. 1996, 1:10 in. twist) cal., GIO, features 16 in. barrel (non-threaded per C/B 1994), initially shorter stock and handguard, rear sight adjustable for windage and elevation, includes two detachable 5, 8, or 9 (new 1999) shot mags., approx. 7 lbs. Mfg. 1991-2002.

| | $1,000 | $850 | $750 | $700 | $550 | $450 | $350 | *$1,111* |

Add $200 for .22 LR conversion kit (disc. 1994).

MATCH TARGET M4 CARBINE (MT6400/MT6400R) – .223 Rem. cal., GIO, similar to current U.S. armed forces M4 model, except semi-auto, 9 or 10 shot mag., 16.1 in. barrel, 1:7 in. twist, matte black finish, fixed tube buttstock, A3 detachable carrying handle, 7.3 lbs. Mfg. 2002-2013.

| | $1,100 | $950 | $800 | $750 | $600 | $500 | $375 | *$1,211* |

Add $341 for quad accessory rail (MT6400R).

MATCH TARGET 6400001 – 5.56 NATO cal., GIO, 16.1 in. M4 barrel with flash suppressor, 10 shot mag., flat-top receiver, fixed tube stock, Magpul Gen. II rear backup sight, two-piece ribbed handguard with post front sight, black finish, 7 lbs. Mfg. 2013 only.

| | $1,325 | $1,150 | $1,000 | $900 | $750 | $600 | $475 | *$1,461* |

MATCH TARGET 6400R001 – 5.56 NATO cal., 16.1 in. M4 barrel with flash suppressor, 10 shot mag., flat-top receiver with Picatinny rail integrated with quad rail handguard, Magpul Gen. II rear sight and flip-up adj. post front sight, black finish, 7.2 lbs. Mfg. 2013 only.

| | $1,650 | $1,450 | $1,250 | $1,100 | $900 | $750 | $600 | *$1,825* |

138 COLT'S MANUFACTURING COMPANY, LLC, cont.

MSR	100%	98%	95%	90%	80%	70%	60%	Last MSR

MATCH TARGET H-BAR RIFLE (MT6601/MT6601C) – .223 Rem. cal., GI, heavy 20 in. HBAR barrel, 1:7 in. twist, A2 sights, 8 lbs. Mfg. 1986-2010.

| | $1,100 | $950 | $800 | $750 | $600 | $500 | $375 | $1,218 |

Add $200 for .22 LR conversion kit (mfg. 1990-94).

Add $1 for compensator (MT6601C, new 1999).

TACTICAL ELITE MODEL (TE6700) – .223 Rem. cal., GIO, 20 in. heavy barrel, 1:8 in. twist, Hogue finger groove pistol grip, Choate buttstock, fine tuned for accuracy, scope and mount included, approx. 1,000 rifles made by the Custom Shop circa 1996-97.

| | $2,450 | $2,150 | $1,850 | $1,650 | $1,350 | $1,100 | $850 | |

TARGET GOVT. MODEL RIFLE (MT6551) – .223 Rem. cal., GIO, semi-auto version of the M16 rifle with forward bolt assist, 20 in. barrel (1:7 in.), straight line black nylon stock, aperture rear and post front sight, 5, 8, or 9 (new 1999) shot mags., 7 1/2 lbs. Disc. 2002.

| | $1,050 | $900 | $800 | $700 | $600 | $475 | $375 | $1,144 |

Add $200 for .22 LR conversion kit (mfg. 1990-94).

SPORTER CARBINE (SP6920) – .223 Rem. cal., GIO, has M-4 features including flat-top receiver with A3 removable carry handle, 16.1 in. barrel with flash hider, 4-position collapsible buttstock, ribbed oval handguard, matte black finish, 5.95 lbs. Mfg. 2011 only.

| | $1,050 | $900 | $800 | $700 | $600 | $475 | $375 | $1,155 |

Add 15% for the legal LE6920 variation that were sold to civilians.

The last 100 carbines of the Model LE6920 marked "Law Enforcement Carbine" and "Restricted" were sold as commercial guns to FFL dealers. Each of these has a factory letter stating as such.

COLT SPORTER (SP6940) – .223 Rem. cal., GIO, 16.1 in. fully floated barrel, 20 shot mag., flip-up adj. sights, 4-position collapsible stock, one-piece monolithic upper receiver, flat-top receiver with full-length quad Picatinny rails, matte black metal finish, 6.1 lbs. Mfg. 2011 only.

| | $1,350 | $1,200 | $1,000 | $900 | $750 | $600 | $475 | $1,500 |

Add 15% for the legal LE6940 variation that were sold to civilians.

The last 100 carbines of the Model LE6940 marked "Law Enforcement Carbine" and "Restricted" were sold as commercial guns to FFL dealers. Each of these has a factory letter stating as such.

SP901 RIFLE – .308 Win. cal., GIO, 16 in. full floated heavy chrome-lined barrel, direct gas system, locking bolt, matte black finish, one-piece monolithic upper receiver with rail, upper receiver can be swapped out for .223, ambidextrous operating controls, flip-up post sights, bayonet lug and flash hider. Mfg. mid-2011.

While advertised in 2011, this model never went into production (see LE901-16S).

COLT CARBINE AR6450 – 9mm Para. cal., GIO, 16.1 in. barrel with flash suppressor, A3 detachable carrying handle, 32 shot mag., grooved aluminum handguard, A2 post front sight, adj. Rogers Super-Stoc, matte finish, 6.35 lbs. Mfg. 2012 only.

| | $1,050 | $900 | $800 | $700 | $600 | $475 | $375 | $1,176 |

COLT CARBINE AR6520TRI – 5.56 NATO cal., GIO, 16.1 in. barrel, matte black finish, 30 shot mag., adj. sights. Mfg. 2013 only.

| | $1,125 | $1,000 | $850 | $750 | $600 | $500 | $400 | $1,223 |

LIGHTWEIGHT CARBINE (AR6720) – 5.56 NATO cal., GIO, 16.1 in. light barrel with flash hider and A2 front sight, 30 shot PMAG, ribbed aluminum forearm, A3 detachable carrying handle, MBUS Gen 2 rear sight, matte black finish, adj. stock, 6.2 lbs. New 2012.

| MSR $999 | $900 | $800 | $700 | $600 | $500 | $400 | $325 | |

COLT CARBINE AR6720LECAR – 5.56 NATO cal., GIO, 16.1 in. barrel, Magpul Gen. II rear sight with adj. post front sight, 30 shot mag., matte black finish, 6 lbs. Mfg. 2013 only.

| | $1,325 | $1,150 | $1,000 | $900 | $750 | $600 | $475 | $1,468 |

TACTICAL CARBINE (AR6721) – 5.56 NATO cal., GIO, 16.1 in. heavy barrel with flash hider and A2 front sight, 30 shot PMAG, MBUS Gen 2 rear sight, ribbed aluminum forearm, A3 detachable carrying handle, matte black finish, adj. stock, 7.3 lbs. Mfg. 2012 - 2017.

| | $825 | $700 | $600 | $550 | $450 | $375 | $300 | $929 |

9MM CARBINE (AR6951) – 9mm Para. cal., GIO, 16.1 in. barrel with flash suppressor, 32 shot mag., folding rear sight, adj. Rogers Super-Stoc, flat-top receiver, A3 detachable carrying handle, grooved aluminum handguard, choice of matte black or Muddy Girl (AR6951MPMG, limited mfg. 2015 only) finish, 6.4 lbs. New 2012.

| MSR $1,099 | $975 | $850 | $750 | $650 | $550 | $450 | $350 | |

Last MSR for Muddy Girl finish was $1,567 in 2015.

Add $319 for Muddy Girl camo finish (limited mfg. 2015 only).

COLT'S MANUFACTURING COMPANY, LLC, cont. 139 C

MSR	100%	98%	95%	90%	80%	70%	60%	Last MSR

AR15 A4 RIFLE – 5.56 NATO cal., GIO, 20 in. barrel with flash suppressor, 30 shot mag., flat-top receiver with removable carry handle, A2 style buttstock and front sight, ribbed handguard, black finish, 7.7 lbs. New 2013.

| MSR $1,099 | $975 | $850 | $750 | $650 | $550 | $450 | $350 | |

AR15 A4MP-FDE – 5.56 NATO cal., GIO, 20 in. barrel with flash suppressor, Flat Dark Earth (FDE) furniture, 30 shot mag., 2/3 quad rail with cover, A2 front sight with Magpul Gen. II rear sight, fixed stock, matte black barrel, matte black or FDE (new 2014) receiver finish, 7 1/2 lbs. Mfg. 2013-2014.

| | $1,175 | $1,050 | $900 | $800 | $650 | $550 | $400 | $1,304 |

Add $35 for FDE receiver finish.

COLT CARBINE AR-6821/AR-6821MP-R – .300 AAC Blackout cal., AR-6821 is similar to AR-6720, AR-6821MP-R has Magpul furniture and accessory rail. Mfg. 2015 only.

| | $1,050 | $900 | $800 | $700 | $600 | $475 | $375 | $1,155 |

Add $113 for Magpul furniture and accessory rail.

COLT CARBINE CR6724001 – 5.56 NATO cal., GIO, 24 in. stainless barrel without sights, one-piece flat-top upper receiver with integrated 2/3 length quad Picatinny rail, fixed non-adj. stock, 10 shot mag., black finish, 8.8 lbs. Mfg. 2013-2015.

| | $1,500 | $1,350 | $1,150 | $1,050 | $850 | $700 | $550 | $1,653 |

AR-15 SCOPE (3X/4X) AND MOUNT – initially offered with 3x magnification scope, then switched to 4x. Disc.

| | $395 | $300 | $240 | $185 | $160 | $130 | $115 | $344 |

LE901-16S (SP901) – .308 Win. cal., GIO, 16.1 in. heavy full floated barrel with bayonet lug and flash hider, flat-top with Picatinny rail, one-piece upper receiver with BUIS, ambidextrous controls, flip-up adj. front sight post, flip-up adj. rear sight, 20 shot mag., fixed stock, matte black finish, 9.4 lbs. Mfg. 2012-2015.

| | $2,350 | $2,050 | $1,750 | $1,600 | $1,300 | $1,050 | $800 | $2,544 |

M.A.R.C.901 MONOLITHIC – .308 Win. cal., GIO, 16.1 or 18 (LE901-18SE, mfg. 2015 only) in. heavy full floated barrel with bayonet lug and flash hider, 20 shot mag., one-piece monolithic flat-top upper receiver with Picatinny rail, BUIS, ambidextrous controls, adj. VLTOR buttstock, matte black or FDE (LE901FDE-16SE) finish, 9.4 lbs. Mfg. 2015-17.

| | $1,800 | $1,550 | $1,350 | $1,200 | $1,000 | $800 | $650 | $1,999 |

Add $100 for FDE finish (model LE901FDE-16SE), disc. 2015.

M.A.R.C.901 CARBINE (AR901-16S) – .308 Win. cal., 16.1 in. heavy free floating barrel with muzzle brake, 20 shot mag., retractable B5 Bravo buttstock, flat-top receiver with full length Picatinny rail, vent tubular handguard with 3 Picatinny rails. Mfg. 2015 -2016.

| | $1,250 | $1,100 | $950 | $850 | $700 | $550 | $450 | $1,399 |

LE6900 – 5.56 NATO cal., GIO, 16.1 in. barrel, no sights, 30 shot mag., matte black finish, 6 lbs. Mfg. 2012-mid-2013.

| | $800 | $700 | $600 | $550 | $450 | $350 | $275 | $899 |

LE6920 M4 CARBINE – 5.56 NATO cal., GIO, 16.1 in. barrel with bayonet lug and flash hider, 30 shot mag., adj. front sight post, ribbed handguard, Magpul Gen2 backup rear sight, flat-top receiver with Picatinny rail, collapsible stock, matte black finish, 6.9 lbs. New 2012.

| MSR $999 | $900 | $800 | $700 | $600 | $500 | $400 | $325 | |

LE6920AE – 5.56 NATO cal., 16.1 in. barrel, ambidextrous mag. release, bolt catch and fire selector, 30 shot PMAG, MBUS rear Gen. 2 sights, collapsible stock, matte black finish, 6.38 lbs. Mfg. 2014-2016.

| | $1,250 | $1,100 | $950 | $850 | $700 | $550 | $450 | $1,374 |

LE6920-OEM1/OEM2 M4 – 5.56 NATO cal., 16.1 in. barrel with muzzle brake, includes pistol grip and rear buffer tube, flat-top receiver with Picatinny rail, no furniture, OEM1 (disc. 2016) includes A2 style front sight. New 2015.

| MSR $849 | $765 | $650 | $600 | $500 | $425 | $350 | $275 | |

LE6920 SOCOM – 5.56 NATO cal., GIO, 16.1 in. barrel with bayonet lug and flash hider, 30 shot mag., flat-top receiver with BUIS, Knights Armament rail system, adj. front sight post, flip-up adj. rear sight, non-adj. tube stock, matte black finish, 7.2 lbs. Mfg. 2012-2014.

| | $1,450 | $1,300 | $1,100 | $1,000 | $800 | $650 | $500 | $1,602 |

LE6920MP-R – 5.56 NATO cal., 16.1 in. barrel, 30 shot PMAG, MBUS rear Gen. 2 sight, Troy rail, Magpul MOE furniture, black finish, 7.11 lbs. Mfg. 2014-2015.

| | $1,150 | $1,000 | $850 | $800 | $650 | $500 | $400 | $1,268 |

LE6920MP & VARIATIONS – 5.56 NATO cal., GIO, 16.1 in. barrel with bayonet lug and flash hider, 30 shot PMAG, adj. front sight post, MBUS Gen2 backup rear sight, Magpul MOE carbine collapsible stock with MOE handguard and pistol grip, flat-top receiver with Picatinny rail, MOE trigger guard, Magpul MOE furniture in black (LE6920MP-B), A-TACS Foliage/Green (LE6920MPFG, new 2013), Olive Drab (LE6920MP-OD), USA One Nation Hydro-dipped (LE6920MP-USA,

C 140 COLT'S MANUFACTURING COMPANY, LLC, cont.

MSR	100%	98%	95%	90%	80%	70%	60%	Last MSR

new 2014), ATAC camo hydro-dipped (LE6920MPATAC, new 2014), or Steel Gray (LE6920MP-STG, new 2015), 6.9 lbs. Mfg. 2012-mid-2015.

	$1,125	$1,000	$850	$750	$600	$500	$400	$1,229

Add $87 for USA One Nation Hydro-Dipped Magpul furniture (LE6920-USA, new 2014).

Add $166 for ATACS Foliage/Green finish (LE6920MPFG).

Add $247 for ATAC camo Hydro-Dipped Magpul furniture (LE6920MPATAC, new 2014).

* **LE6920MPG** – 5.56 NATO cal., similar to LE6920MP, except features Olive Drab Green upper and lower receivers, OD Green Magpul furniture (LE6920MPG-OD) or Black Magpul furniture (LE6920MPG-B, new 2014), vertical grip. Mfg. 2012-mid-2015.

	$1,225	$1,050	$900	$850	$700	$550	$425	$1,361

* **LE6920MPFDE** – 5.56 NATO cal., similar to LE6920MP, except features Flat Dark Earth Magpul MOE furniture with vertical grip, Flat Dark Earth finish. Mfg. 2012-mid-2015.

	$1,225	$1,050	$900	$850	$700	$550	$425	$1,361

* **LE6920MPFDE-R** – 5.56 NATO cal., similar to LE6920MP, except features Flat Dark Earth coated upper and lower receivers, FDE Troy Rail, FDE Magpul furniture. Mfg. 2014-mid-2015.

	$1,400	$1,200	$1,050	$950	$750	$650	$500	$1,572

LE6920MPS-B/FDE – 5.56 NATO cal., 16.1 in. barrel, 30 shot round PMAG, MBUS Gen 2 rear sight, Magpul MOE SL carbine vertical pistol grip stock, Magpul MOE SL handguard, Black or FDE furniture.

MSR $1,099	$975	$850	$750	$650	$550	$450	$350	

LE6920-R TROOPER – 5.56 NATO cal., GIO, 16.1 in. barrel, 30 shot mag., single stage trigger, milled aluminum receiver, full-length top Picatinny rail, anodized black finish, 6 1/2 lbs. New 2018.

MSR $1,049	$925	$800	$700	$650	$500	$425	$325	

LE6940 M4 MONOLITHIC – 5.56 NATO cal., GIO, 16.1 in. full floated barrel with bayonet lug and flash hider, 1-piece upper receiver, 30 shot mag., flip-up adj. front sight post, Magpul Gen2 backup rear sight, collapsible stock, matte black finish, 6.9 lbs. New 2012.

MSR $1,399	$1,250	$1,100	$950	$850	$700	$550	$450	

LE6940P – 5.56 NATO cal., GPO, 16.1 in. full floated barrel with bayonet lug and flash hider, one-piece upper receiver, 30 shot mag., flip-up adj. front sight post, Magpul Gen2 backup rear sight, collapsible stock, matte black finish, 6.9 lbs. Mfg. 2012-mid-2015.

	$1,950	$1,700	$1,450	$1,300	$1,100	$900	$700	$2,105

* **LE6940MPFG** – 5.56 NATO cal., similar to LE6940P, except features A-TACS Forest Green Camo. Mfg. 2012-2013.

	$1,250	$1,100	$950	$850	$700	$550	$450	$1,395

LE6940AE-3G – 5.56 NATO cal., 16.1 in. barrel, 30 shot PMAG, Colt articulating piston system, lower receiver features ambidextrous operating controls and 3 operating controls on both sides, monolithic upper is fully modular with smooth handguard allowing for different rail locations, A2 grip, M4 buttstock, MBUS rear Gen. 2 sight, black furniture, 7.2 lbs. Mfg. 2014-2015.

	$1,750	$1,550	$1,300	$1,200	$950	$800	$600	$1,945

LE6960-CCU (COMBAT UNIT CARBINE) – 5.56 NATO cal., GIO, 16 in. chrome-lined barrel, 30 shot mag., SST, optic ready, Magpul MOE SL buttstock, Magpul MOE SL pistol grip, ambidextrous safety, aluminum receiver, mid-length gas system, hardcoat anodized black finish, 6.47 lbs. New late 2016.

MSR $1,299	$1,150	$1,000	$850	$800	$650	$500	$400	

LT6720-R – 5.56 NATO cal., 16.1 in. barrel, 30 shot PMAG, MBUS front and rear Gen 2 sights, Troy rail, Magpul ACS telescoping stock, black Magpul furniture, matte black finish, 6.48 lbs. Mfg. 2014 - 2016.

	$1,175	$1,050	$900	$800	$650	$550	$400	$1,321

* **LT6720MPMG** – 5.56 NATO cal., 16.1 in. light contour barrel with birdcage flash hider, 30 shot mag., Magpul MBUS sights, Magpul ACS Muddy Girl camo telescoping stock, trigger guard, and pistol grip, Muddy Girl camo finish, 6.2 lbs. Mfg. 2014-mid-2015.

	$1,300	$1,150	$1,000	$900	$700	$600	$450	$1,448

EXPANSE M4 – 5.56 NATO cal., GIO, 16.1 in. barrel, 30 shot round aluminum mag., adj. front sight post, flat-top Picatinny rail, matte black finish, 6.44 lbs. New 2016.

MSR $799	$700	$650	$550	$500	$400	$325	$275	

CRM 16A1 CLASSIC SERIES – 5.56 NATO cal., 20 in. barrel, 20 shot mag., single stage trigger, A1 style fixed sights, gray furniture (including triangular forearm), A1 style buttstock, A1 style grips, semi-auto reproduction of the Vietnam era M16A1, left side of mag. well marked "COLT AR-15/PROPERTY OF U.S. GOVT./M16A1/CAL. 5.56 MM", 6.37 lbs. New mid-2016.

MSR $2,499	$2,250	$1,950	$1,700	$1,550	$1,250	$1,000	$800	

COLT'S MANUFACTURING COMPANY, LLC, cont. 141 C

MSR	100%	98%	95%	90%	80%	70%	60%	Last MSR

RIFLES: SEMI-AUTO, RIMFIRE, AR-15 & VARIATIONS

The following models are manufactured by Carl Walther, located in Ulm, Germany, under license from New Colt Holding Corp., and imported/distributed by Walther Arms.

M4 CARBINE – .22 LR cal., GIO, 16.2 in. shrouded barrel, flat-top receiver, 10 or 30 shot mag., detachable carry handle, single left-side safety lever, four position retractable stock, ribbed aluminum handguard, black finish, approx. 6 lbs. Mfg. by Umarex under license from Colt and imported by Walther Arms. Imported 2009-2016.

	$475	$400	$350	$315	$285	$250	$225	*$569*

* **M4 Ops** – .22 LR cal., GIO, 16.2 in. barrel, 10 or 30 shot mag., aluminum upper and lower receiver, black finish, quad tactical rail interface system with elongated Picatinny rail on top of barrel and frame, inline barrel/stock design, cartridge case deflector, muzzle compensator, detachable rear sight, four position collapsible stock, ejection port cover, approx. 6 1/2 lbs. Mfg. by Umarex under license from Colt and imported by Walther Arms. Imported 2009-2016.

	$515	$435	$375	$340	$310	$285	$250	*$599*

M16 – .22 LR cal., GIO, 21.2 in. barrel, 10 or 30 shot mag., flat-top receiver with detachable carry handle, fixed stock, elongated ribbed aluminum handguard, removable rear sight, ejection port cover, single left-side safety lever, black finish, approx. 6 1/4 lbs. Mfg. 2009-2010.

	$575	$525	$475	$425	$395	$375	$350	*$599*

* **M16 SPR (Special Purpose Rifle)** – .22 LR cal., GIO, 21.2 in. barrel, 30 shot mag., black finish, fixed stock, aluminum upper and lower receiver, quad tactical rail interface system with Picatinny rail, flip-up front and rear sights, inline barrel/stock design, cartridge case deflector, muzzle compensator. Mfg. 2009-2010.

	$625	$575	$525	$475	$450	$415	$395	*$670*

FACTORY COMMEMORATIVES & SPECIAL/LIMITED EDITIONS

During the course of a year, we receive many phone calls and letters on Colt non-factory special editions and limited editions that do not appear in this section. It should be noted that Colt factory commemoratives and special/limited editions are guns that has been manufactured, marketed, and sold through the auspices of the specific trademark (in this case Colt). There have literally been hundreds of non-factory special and limited editions which, although mostly made by Colt (some were subcontracted), were not marketed or retailed by Colt. These guns are NOT factory Colt commemoratives or special/limited editions and for the most part, do not have the desirability factor that the factory commemoratives and special/limited editions have. Your best alternative to find out more information about the multitude of these special/limited editions is to write: COLT ARCHIVE PROPERTIES, LLC, P.O. Box 1868, Hartford, CT, 06144. If anyone could have any information, it will be the factory. Their research fee is $100 per gun, with a premium charge for factory engraving. If they cannot obtain additional information on the variation you request, they will refund $50. Unfortunately, in some cases, a special/limited edition may not be researchable. In situations like this, do not confuse rarity with desirability.

Typically, non-factory special and limited editions are made for distributors. These sub-contracts seem to be mostly made to signify/commemorate an organization, state, special event or occasion, personality, etc. These are typically marketed and sold through a distributor to dealers, or a company/individual to those people who want to purchase them. These non-factory special/limited editions may or may not have a retail price and often times, since demand is regional, values may decrease rapidly in other areas of the country. In some cases, if the distributor/wholesaler who ordered the initial non-factory special/limited edition is known (and still in business), you may be able to find more information by contacting them directly (i.e. Lew Horton, Davidson's, etc.). Overall desirability is the key to determining values on these non-factory special/limited editions.

The word commemorative as it applies to firearms is almost an obsolete term - kind of like calling a flight attendant a stewardess these days. The last factory gun Colt designated a "Colt Commemorative" was manufactured back in the mid-1980s. One of the biggest reasons Colt dropped its commemorative program was because during this time period, it became more advantageous for Colt to sell large domestic distributors special order guns with the features these distributors wanted. This way Colt did not have to inventory, market, and sell these guns through the company. In today's marketplace, Colt is now producing factory special/limited editions which are marketed and sold through the auspices of Colt, so a line in the sand has now been drawn between factory Colt commemoratives and special/limited editions versus non-factory special/limited editions. The word commemorative has never applied to non-factory guns. In this text, recent Colt factory special/limited editions will appear as listings in those sections where their standard models are listed. Older factory special/limited editions will appear in this section.

Because the commemorative consumer is now more in charge (consumers now own most of the guns since distributor/dealer inventories are depleted) than during the 1980s, commemorative firearms are possibly as strong as they have ever been. When the supply side of commemorative economics has to be purchased from knowledgable collectors or savvy dealers and demand stays the same or increases slightly, prices have no choice but to go up. If and when the manufacturers crank up the commemorative production runs again (and it won't be like the good old days), the old marketplace characteristics may reappear. Until then, however, the commemorative marketplace remains steady, with values having become more predictable.

As a reminder on commemoratives, I would like to repeat a few facts, especially for the beginning collector, but applicable to all manufacturers of commemoratives. Commemoratives are current production guns designed as a reproduction of an historically famous gun model, or as a tie-in with historically famous persons or events. They are generally of very excellent quality and often embellished with select woods and finishes such as silver, nickel, or gold plating. Obviously, they are manufactured to be instant collectibles and to be pleasing to the eye. As with firearms

C 142 COLT'S MANUFACTURING COMPANY, LLC, cont.

	100%	Issue Price	Qty. Made

in general, not all commemorative models have achieved collector status, although most enjoy an active market. Consecutive-numbered pairs as well as collections based on the same serial number may bring a premium. Remember that handguns usually are in some type of wood presentation case, and that rifles may be cased or in packaging with graphics styled to the particular theme of the collectible. The original factory packaging and papers should always accompany the firearm, as they are necessary to realize full value at the time of sale, and get more important every year.

NIB commemorative firearms should be absolutely new, unfired, and as issued, since any obvious use or wear removes it from collector status and lowers its value significantly. Many owners have allowed their commemoratives to sit in their boxes while encased in plastic wrappers for years without inspecting them for corrosion or oxidation damage. This is risky, especially if stored inside a plastic wrapper for long periods of time, since any accumulated moisture cannot escape. Periodic inspection should be implemented to ensure no damage occurs - this is important, since even light "freckling" created from touching the metal surfaces can reduce values significantly. A mint or unfired gun without its original packaging can lose as much as 50% of its normal value - many used commemoratives get sold as "fancy shooters" with little, if any, premiums being asked.

A final note on commemoratives: One of the characteristics of commemoratives/special editions is that over the years of ownership, most of them stay in the same NIB condition. Thus, if supply always is constant and in one condition, demand has to increase before price appreciation can occur. After 47 years of commemorative/special edition production, many model's performance records can be accurately analyzed and the appreciation (or depreciation) can be compared against other purchases of equal vintage. You be the judge.

DELTA MATCH H-BAR RIFLE – AR-15 A2 H-Bar rifle selectively chosen and equipped with 3-9x variable power rubber armored scope, leather sling, shoulder stock cheekpiece, cased. Mfg. 1987, ser. no. range N/A.

	100%	Issue Price	Qty. Made
	$1,500	$1,425	open

CONTROLLED CHAOS ARMS

Current custom AR-15 style manufacturer located in Baxter, IA.

Controlled Chaos Arms builds and manufactures AR rifles and carbines, and offers other firearm industry products such as suppressors and gunsmithing services, provides finishes and weapon maintenance, as well as gun and rifle training. Please contact the company directly for more information on all their products and services including current models, options, pricing, and availability (see Trademark Index).

MSR	100%	98%	95%	90%	80%	70%	60%	Last MSR

RIFLES: SEMI-AUTO

AR-15 CARBINE PACKAGE – 5.56 NATO cal., GIO, 16 in. M4 profile barrel with A2 birdcage flash hider, tactical charging handle assembly, removable rear sight, Gen2 six-position stock, standard trigger, Ergo pistol grip, M4 polished feed ramp, includes soft case, takedown tool, and two Extreme Duty 30 shot mags.

MSR $1,300	$1,075	$675	$500	$450	$400	$350	$325

CORE RIFLE SYSTEMS

Current trademark of carbines, rifles, and pistols manufactured by Good Time Outdoors, Inc. (GTO), located in Ocala, FL.

PISTOLS: SEMI-AUTO

CORE15 ROSCOE R1 PISTOL – 5.56 NATO cal., 10 1/2 in. carbine length gas system barrel with Midwest Industries flash hider and black Nitride finish, Magpul 30 shot mag., Core15 KeyMod 9 1/2 in. rail, KAK Industries pistol buffer tube, forged M4 upper and T6 lower receivers, beveled magwell, M4 feed ramps, Picatinny flat-top rail, stainless steel gas tube, Hardcore V.2 charging handle, oversized trigger guard, Ergo Swift grip, 5.6 lbs. New 2015.

MSR $880	$800	$700	$600	$550	$450	$350	$275

* **CORE15 Roscoe RB1 Pistol** – 5.56 NATO cal., carbine length gas system, 10 1/2 in. barrel with Midwest Industries flash hider, Magpul 30 shot mag., oversized trigger guard, Ergo Swift grip, SIG Sauer SB15 pistol stabilizing brace, KAK Industries pistol buffer tube, forged M4 upper and T6 lower receivers, beveled magwell, M4 feed ramps, Picatinny flat-top rail, stainless steel gas tube, Hardcore V.2 charging handle, black Nitride finish, 6.7 lbs. New 2015.

MSR $900	$825	$700	$600	$550	$450	$375	$300

CORE15 300BO ROSCOE R2 PISTOL – .300 AAC Blackout cal., 9 1/2 in. pistol length gas system barrel with Midwest Industries flash hider and black Nitride finish, Magpul 30 shot mag., Core15 KeyMod 9 1/2 in. rail, KAK Industries pistol buffer tube, forged M4 upper and T6 lower receivers, beveled magwell, M4 feed ramps, Picatinny flat-top rail, stainless steel gas tube, Hardcore V.2 charging handle, oversized trigger guard, Ergo Swift grip, 5.6 lbs. New 2015.

MSR $880	$800	$700	$600	$550	$450	$350	$275

* **CORE15 300BO Roscoe RB2 Pistol** – .300 AAC Blackout cal., similar to 300 BO Roscoe R2, except includes SIG Sauer SB15 pistol stabilizing brace, 6.7 lbs. New 2015.

MSR $900	$825	$700	$600	$550	$450	$375	$300

CORE RIFLE SYSTEMS, cont. 143 C

MSR	100%	98%	95%	90%	80%	70%	60%	Last MSR

CORE15 ROSCOE RSW1 PISTOL – .223/5.56 NATO cal., GIO, 10 1/2 in. barrel with black Nitride finish, Midwest Industries flash hider, 30 shot PMAG, Magpul MOE grip, bullet pictogram safety and laser engraved T-markings, M4 feed ramps, Mil-Spec forged upper and lower receiver, beveled magwell, M16 bolt carrier group, 9 1/2 in. KeyMod rail, V2 charging handle, Type III Class 2 hardcoat anodized black finish, 5.6 lbs. New 2017.

| MSR $900 | $825 | $700 | $600 | $550 | $450 | $375 | $300 | |

CORE15 300BO ROSCOE RSW2 PISTOL – .300 AAC Blackout cal., GIO, pistol length gas system, 10 1/2 in. barrel with black Nitride finish, Midwest Industries flash hider, 30 shot PMAG, oversized trigger guard, Magpul MOE grip, M4 feed ramps, Mil-Spec forged upper and lower receiver, beveled magwell, M16 bolt carrier group, 9 1/2 in. KeyMod rail, V2 charging handle, KAK Industries pistol buffer tube and shockwave blade, Type III Class 2 hardcoat anodized black finish, 5.6 lbs. New 2017.

| MSR $900 | $825 | $700 | $600 | $550 | $450 | $375 | $300 | |

RIFLES: SEMI-AUTO

GTO Guns manufactures a complete line of AR-15 style carbines and rifles, in addition to uppers in various cals., lower receivers, and related accessories.

CORE15 HOGUE KEYMOD RIFLE – 5.56 NATO or .300 AAC Blackout cal., GIO, 16 in. Govt. profile barrel with black Nitride or black phosphate finish, 30 shot PMAG, oversized trigger guard, Hogue 6-position retractable stock, Hogue pistol grip, KeyMod 12 1/2 in. rail, Hardcore V.2 billet charging handle, stainless steel gas tube, Mil-Spec buffer tube, forged upper and lower receivers, beveled magwell, M4 feed ramps, flat-top Picatinny rail, Type III hardcoat anodized finish, 6 1/2 lbs. New 2016.

| MSR $1,000 | $850 | $550 | $465 | $395 | $350 | $325 | $295 | |

Add $100 for .300 AAC Blackout cal.

CORE15 KEYMOD LW – 5.56 NATO cal., low pro gas block, 14 1/2 in. pencil profile barrel with pinned and welded Yankee Hill Phantom flash hider, black Nitride finish, Mission First Tactical 30 shot mag., oversized trigger guard, Mission First Tactical Minimalist stock, Ergo black SureGrip, Core15 KeyMod 12 1/2 in. rail, Mil-Spec buffer tube, Hardcore V.2 billet charging handle, Mil-Spec forged upper and lower receivers, flat-top Picatinny rail, Type III hardcoat anodized finish, 5 lbs. 14 oz.

| MSR $1,000 | $850 | $550 | $465 | $395 | $350 | $325 | $295 | |

CORE15 KEYMOD SCOUT – 5.56 NATO or .300 AAC Blackout (new 2016) cal., GIO, carbine length gas system, 16 in. mid-length profile barrel, A2 flash hider, 30 shot mag., low profile gas block, forged lower and flat-top upper with Picatinny rail, 12 1/2 or 15 in. Core15 KeyMod rail system, 6-pos. retractable stock, A2 pistol grip, black Nitride finish, 6 1/2 lbs. New 2015.

| MSR $900 | $765 | $515 | $440 | $375 | $335 | $315 | $295 | |

Add $30 for 15 in. KeyMod rail.

Add $100 for .300 AAC Blackout cal. (new 2016).

CORE15 M4 PISTON RIFLE – 5.56 NATO cal., AR-15 style, utilizes Core15/Adams Arms GPO, 16 in. M4 chrome-lined barrel with A2 flash hider, M1913 Picatinny optics rails, Magpul 20 shot PMAG, Tapco 6-position adj. stock, M4 style thermoset molded polymer handguards with dual heat shields, A2 pistol grip, flat-top receiver, matte black finish or custom colors also available, marked GTO near gas block, 6.2 lbs. New 2011.

| MSR $1,290 | $1,075 | $675 | $500 | $450 | $400 | $350 | $325 | |

CORE15 M4 RIFLE – 5.56 NATO cal., utilizes standard GIO, A2 elevated front sight, with one Picatinny rail, otherwise similar to Core15 M4 Piston Rifle, 5.9 lbs. New 2011.

| MSR $930 | $800 | $525 | $450 | $385 | $340 | $325 | $295 | |

CORE15 MFT KEYMOD RIFLE – 5.56 NATO or .300 AAC Blackout cal., GIO, 16 in. Govt. profile barrel with black Nitride or black phosphate finish, MFT 30 shot mag., oversized trigger guard, Mission First Tactical Minimalist stock, MFT G27 grip, low profile gas block, KeyMod 12 1/2 in. rail, Hardcore V.2 billet charging handle, stainless steel gas tube, Mil-Spec buffer tube, forged upper and lower receivers, beveled magwell, flat-top Picatinny rail, Type III hardcoat anodized finish, 6 1/2 lbs. New 2016.

| MSR $980 | $850 | $550 | $465 | $395 | $350 | $325 | $295 | |

Add $80 for .300 AAC Blackout cal.

CORE15 MOE .300 BLACKOUT RIFLE – .300 AAC Blackout cal., GIO, 16 in. stainless steel barrel with SureFire 3-prong flash hider, Magpul 30 shot PMAG, forged T6 M4 flat-top upper with internal dry lube and laser T-markings, V.2 charging handle, forged lower receiver with hardcoat anodized finish, M4 feed ramps, and beveled magwell, Magpul MOE 6-position stock and pistol grip, Magpul MOE handguard, black furniture, 5.8 lbs. New 2013.

| MSR $1,280 | $1,075 | $675 | $500 | $450 | $400 | $350 | $325 | |

C 144 CORE RIFLE SYSTEMS, cont.

MSR	100%	98%	95%	90%	80%	70%	60%	Last MSR

CORE15 MOE M4 RIFLE – 5.56 NATO cal., 16 in. M4 profile barrel with A2 flash hider, choice of GIO or GPO, 30 shot Magpul mag., forged upper and lower receivers, M4 feed ramps, Magpul MOE handguard, MBUS rear sight, Magpul MOE 6-position stock and pistol grip, oversized trigger guard, black furniture, low profile or Picatinny gas block, 5.9-6.2 lbs. Mfg. 2012-2016.

	$950	$595	$495	$425	$365	$335	$300	$1,140

Add $450 for Core15 MOE M4 Piston rifle with gas piston assembly.

CORE15 MOE MID-LENGTH RIFLE – 5.56 NATO cal., GIO, 18 in. heavy stainless steel barrel with polygonal rifling and A2 flash hider, Magpul MOE 6-position pistol grip stock, Magpul 30 shot PMAG, oversized trigger guard, forged upper receiver with flat-top Picatinny rail, forged lower with M4 feed ramps and beveled magwell, enclosed vent. forearm, black furniture, 6.2 lbs. Mfg. 2012-2014.

	$1,175	$775	$550	$465	$415	$375	$350	$1,420

* **Core15 MOE Mid-Length Piston Rifle** – 5.56 NATO cal., similar to Core15 MOE Mid-Length rifle, except has GPO, Magpul MOE handguard, MOE Black or Desert Tan (mfg. 2012 only) hardware, 6.9 lbs. Mfg. 2012-2014.

	$1,425	$925	$700	$550	$475	$395	$350	$1,730

CORE15 MOE M-LOK RIFLE – 5.56 NATO or .300 AAC Blackout cal., GIO, 16 in. Govt. profile barrel with black Nitride or black phosphate finish, A2 flash hider, 30 shot PMAG, oversized trigger guard, Core15 A Frame front sight, Magpul MOE 6-position retractable stock, Magpul MOE M-LOK carbine length forearm, Magpul MOE grip, Hardcore V.2 charging handle, stainless steel gas tube, Mil-Spec buffer tube, forged T6 lower with beveled magwell, forged T6 M4 upper receiver with M4 feed ramps, flat-top Picatinny rail, laser engraved T-markings, Type III hardcoat anodized finish, 6 lbs. New 2016.

MSR $1,140	$950	$595	$495	$425	$365	$335	$300	

Add $280 for .300 AAC Blackout cal.

* **CORE15 MOE M-LOK Piston Rifle** – 5.56 NATO cal., GPO, 16 in. Govt. profile barrel with black Nitride finish, 30 shot PMAG, oversized trigger guard, Magpul MOE 6-position retractable stock, Magpul MOE M-LOK carbine length forearm, Magpul MOE grip, Hardcore V.2 charging handle, stainless steel gas tube, Mil-Spec buffer tube, forged T6 lower with beveled magwell, forged T6 M4 upper receiver with M4 feed ramps, flat-top Picatinny rail, laser engraved T-markings, Type III hardcoat anodized finish, 6 lbs. New 2016.

MSR $1,590	$1,315	$850	$625	$500	$435	$375	$350	

CORE15 SCOUT UL II RIFLE – 5.56 NATO or .300 AAC Blackout cal., carbine length gas system, 16 in. Govt. profile barrel with A2 flash hider and black Nitride or black phosphate finish, Hexmag 30 shot mag., oversized trigger guard, A frame front sight base, Core15 6-position retractable stock, A2 pistol grip, beveled magwell, Midwest Industries SS Series drop-in modular rail, Mil-Spec forged T6 lower and M4 upper receiver with M4 feed ramps, flat-top Picatinny rail, Mil-Spec buffer tube, Hardcore V.2 billet charging handle, Type III hardcoat anodized finish, 6 lbs. 5 oz.

MSR $950	$800	$525	$450	$385	$340	$325	$295	

Add $140 for .300 AAC Blackout cal.

CORE15 SCOUT RIFLE – 5.56 NATO cal., GIO, 16 in. M4 profile barrel with A2 flash hider, Mil-Spec forged upper and lower receiver, stainless steel gas tube, chrome-lined stainless steel bolt carrier, 30 shot mag., 6-position retractable stock, M4 style thermoset molded polymer handguards, A2 pistol grip, Hardcore billet charging handle, Type III Class II hardcoat anodized finish in black, OD Green, or FDE, 6 lbs. New 2014.

MSR $830	$725	$500	$435	$375	$335	$315	$295	

CORE15 TAC M4 RIFLE – 5.56 NATO cal., GIO, 16 in. M4 profile barrel with A2 flash hider, 30 shot Magpul mag., forged T6 lower receiver with beveled magwell, forged M4 upper receiver with flat-top Picatinny rail, Hardcore V.2 charging handle, free floating quad rail, oversized trigger guard, forged "F" marked A frame front sight base and Magpul MBUS rear sight, Magpul MOE 6-position pistol grip stock, 5.9 lbs. Mfg. 2012-2016.

	$1,075	$675	$500	$450	$400	$350	$325	$1,280

* **CORE15 Tac M4 Piston Rifle** – 5.56 NATO cal., GPO, similar to Core15 Tac M4 Rifle, except has monolithic Melonite coated bolt carrier group, Picatinny flat-top gas block, and Magpul MOE MBUS front and rear sights, 6.2 lbs. Mfg. 2012-2016.

	$1,425	$925	$700	$550	$475	$395	$350	$1,730

CORE15 TAC M4 UL RIFLE – 5.56 NATO cal., GIO, 16 in. chrome moly M4 profile barrel with A2 flash hider, stainless steel gas tube, A frame front sight base (forged), optional low profile or Picatinny gas block, Magpul MBUS rear sight, 6-position retractable stock with A2 pistol grip, Magpul 30 shot PMAG, forged upper receiver with flat-top Picatinny rail and M4 feed ramps, forged lower with beveled magwell, black furniture, 5.2 lbs. New 2013.

MSR $1,170	$975	$595	$495	$425	$365	$335	$300	

CORE RIFLE SYSTEMS, cont. 145 C

MSR	100%	98%	95%	90%	80%	70%	60%	Last MSR

CORE15 TAC M4 V.2 RIFLE – 5.56 NATO cal., 16 in. M4 profile barrel with A2 flash hider, choice of GIO or GPO, flat-top model with full-length Picatinny rail on top of receiver and quad rail, Magpul ACS 6-position pistol grip stock, 30 shot Magpul mag., approx. 6 lbs. Mfg. 2012-2013.

| | $1,075 | $675 | $500 | $450 | $400 | $350 | $325 | *$1,299* |

CORE15 TAC 6.5 GRENDEL RIFLE – 6.5mm Grendel cal., GIO, 18 or 20 in. fluted barrel with black Nitride finish or stainless steel, Lantac Dragon muzzle brake, ASC 25 shot stainless steel mag., oversized trigger guard, Hogue 6-position retractable stock, Hogue pistol grip, KeyMod 15 in. rail, Hardcore V.2 billet charging handle, stainless steel gas tube, low profile gas block, forged upper and lower receivers, M4 feed ramps, flat-top Picatinny rail, beveled magwell, 6 1/2 lbs. New 2016.

| MSR $1,490 | $1,250 | $825 | $575 | $475 | $425 | $375 | $350 | |

Add $50 for stainless steel barrel.

CORE15 TAC II .300 BLACKOUT RIFLE – .300 AAC Blackout cal., carbine length GIO, 16 in. stainless steel barrel, forged T6 M4 flat-top upper with internal dry lube and laser T-markings, V.2 charging handle, Gen 2 free float mid-length quad rail, forged lower receiver with anodized finish, M4 feed ramps, beveled magwell, Magpul ACS 6-position stock, Magpul MOE pistol grip, Magpul 30 shot PMAG, low profile gas block, black furniture, 5.9 lbs. New 2013.

| MSR $1,390 | $1,150 | $750 | $550 | $465 | $415 | $375 | $350 | |

CORE15 TAC II M4 RIFLE – 5.56 NATO cal., GIO, 16 in. M4 profile barrel with A2 flash hider, forged lower receiver with M4 feed ramps and beveled magwell, forged upper receiver with full-length flat-top Picatinny rail, Gen 2 mid-length two-piece quad rail, Magpul ACS 6-position pistol grip stock, 30 shot Magpul mag., V.2 charging handle, oversized trigger, 5.9 lbs. Mfg. 2012-2014.

| | $1,075 | $675 | $500 | $450 | $400 | $350 | $325 | *$1,300* |

CORE15 TAC II.V RIFLE – .223/5.56 NATO cal., GIO, 16 in. Govt. profile barrel with black Nitride finish, A2 flash hider, 30 shot PMAG, oversized trigger guard, Magpul MOE 6-pos. stock, A2 pistol grip, M16 bolt carrier group, 10 in. Samson Evolution rail, forged lower and upper receiver, top Picatinny rail, beveled magwell, M4 style polymer handguard with dual heat shields, Type III Class II hardcoat anodized black finish, 6.2 lbs.

| MSR $1,200 | $995 | $625 | $495 | $450 | $395 | $350 | $325 | |

CORE15 TAC III RIFLE – 5.56 NATO cal., GIO, 16 in. chrome moly barrel with A2 flash hider, low profile gas block, forged lower receiver with beveled magwell, forged upper with M4 feed ramps, flat-top Picatinny rail, Gen 2 SS Series free float forearm, stainless steel gas tube, V.2 charging handle, Magpul MOE MBUS front and rear sights, Magpul MOE 6-position pistol grip stock, Magpul 30 shot PMAG, oversized trigger guard, black, Burnt Bronze (new 2016), or Sniper Gray (new 2016) finish, 5.9 lbs. New 2013.

| MSR $1,390 | $1,150 | $750 | $550 | $465 | $415 | $375 | $350 | |

Add $110 for Burnt Bronze or Sniper Grey finish (new 2016).

CORE 15 TAC IV RIFLE – .223 Rem./5.56 NATO cal.,16 in. mid-length barrel, muzzle brake, 30 shot Magpul mag., 15 in. Manticore Arms Transformer rail (KeyMod or M-LOK), forged M4 upper receiver, Type III hardcoat anodized finish, M4 feed ramps, 1913 Picatinny rail flat-top, forged lower receiver with beveled magwell, oversized trigger guard, ambi safety selector, Hardcore V.2 charging handle, standard Mil-Spec buffing tube, mid-length gas tube, low profile gas block, Ergo black SureGrip, MFT Minimalist stock, ambi sling adapter, includes hardshell case, 7 lbs. New 2017.

| MSR $1,470 | $1,225 | $825 | $575 | $475 | $425 | $375 | $350 | |

CORE15 TAC MID-LENGTH RIFLE – 5.56 NATO cal., GIO, 18 in. heavy stainless steel match grade barrel with polygonal rifling and A2 flash hider, forged upper and lower receivers, flat-top receiver with Gen 2 mid-length two-piece quad rail system, V.2 charging handle, Magpul UBR buttstock, Magpul MIAD grip, Magpul 30 shot PMAG, black finish, 8 lbs. Mfg. 2012-2014.

| | $1,135 | $725 | $525 | $465 | $415 | $375 | $350 | *$1,630* |

* **Core15 TAC Mid-Length Piston Rifle** – 5.56 NATO cal., GPO, similar to Core15 TAC Mid-Length rifle, adjustable gas settings, Picatinny flat-top gas block, 8 1/2 lbs. Mfg. 2012-2014.

| | $1,525 | $975 | $750 | $575 | $495 | $425 | $375 | *$1,850* |

CORE15 HARDCORE SYSTEM X RIFLES – 5.56 NATO cal., GIO, 16 or 18 in. barrel, Magpul Gen3 20 or 30 shot mag., 15 in. aluminum KeyMod rail, H2 buffer, angled groove low pro gas block, Magpul MBUS Pro front and rear sights, integral oversized trigger guard, ambidextrous safety, Core15 Hardcore billet solid aluminum alloy upper and lower receivers, nickel boron bolt carrier group, stainless steel gas tube, Hardcore scalloped billet charging handle. New 2015.

All X System rifles also include a Boyt HM 44 hardshell case, Magpul 20 and 30 shot magazines, range log, Otis Technologies MSR/AR cleaning system and a Frog Lube Tube.

* **Core15 Hardcore System X1** – 5.56 NATO or 6.5mm Grendel (new 2016) cal., GIO, 16 or 18 (new 2016) in. mid-length fluted barrel with Lantac Dragon muzzle brake, black Nitride finish or stainless steel (new 2016, 18 in. barrel only), Magpul Gen3 20 or 30 shot mag., Magpul MBUS Pro front and rear sights, Magpul ACS 6-pos. collapsible stock, black Hogue rubber grip, in-house Sniper Grey Cerakote finish. New 2015.

| MSR $2,500 | $2,050 | $1,250 | $950 | $650 | $575 | $495 | $475 | |

Add $50 for left-hand.

C 146 CORE RIFLE SYSTEMS, cont.

MSR	100%	98%	95%	90%	80%	70%	60%	Last MSR

* Core15 Hardcore System X2 – 5.56 NATO or 6.5 Grendel (new 2016) cal., GIO, 16 or 18 (new 2016) in. mid-length fluted barrel with Lantac Dragon muzzle brake and black Nitride or stainless steel (new 2016, 18 in. barrel only) finish, Magpul Gen3 20 or 30 shot mag., Magpul MBUS Pro front and rear sights, Magpul UBR collapsible stock, black Hogue rubber grip, in-house Sniper Grey Cerakote finish, includes Leupold MK6 1x16x20 scope with mount and adj. Atlas BT10 bipod 1913 Picatinny rail mount. New 2015.

| MSR $5,500 | $4,600 | $4,100 | $3,525 | $2,950 | $2,500 | $2,050 | $1,775 | |

* Core15 Hardcore System X3 – 5.56 NATO or 6.5mm Grendel (new 2016) cal., GIO, 18 or 20 (new 2016) in. fluted rifle length barrel with black Nitride or stainless steel (new 2016, 20 in. barrel only) finish, Magpul Gen3 20 or 30 shot mag., Magpul MBUS Pro front and rear sights, Magpul ACS stock, black Hogue rubber grip, in-house Sniper Grey Cerakote finish. New 2015.

| MSR $2,600 | $2,125 | $1,325 | $995 | $675 | $595 | $525 | $475 | |

* Core15 Hardcore System X4 – 5.56 NATO or 6.5mm Grendel (new 2016) cal., GIO, 18 or 20 (new 2016) in. fluted rifle length barrel with black Nitride or stainless steel (new 2016, 20 in. barrel only) finish, Magpul Gen3 20 or 30 shot mag., Magpul MBUS Pro front and rear sights, Magpul UBR collapsible stock, black Hogue rubber grip, includes Leupold MK6 3x18x44 scope with mount, adj. Atlas BT10 bipod 1913 Picatinny rail mount. New 2015.

| MSR $5,600 | $4,675 | $4,150 | $3,525 | $2,950 | $2,500 | $2,050 | $1,775 | |

CORE30 MOE RIFLE – .308 Win. cal., GIO, 16 in. CMV mid-length barrel with SureFire SOCOM 3-prong flash hider, low profile gas block, Magpul MOE 6-position stock and grip, Magpul 20 shot PMAG, Magpul MOE mid-length forearm, aluminum alloy lower and upper with Picatinny rail and laser engraved T-markings, integral oversized trigger guard, V3 billet charging handle, hardcoat anodized finish, 8 lbs. New 2013.

| MSR $1,950 | $1,600 | $1,000 | $775 | $575 | $495 | $425 | $395 | |

CORE30 MOE LR RIFLE – .308 Win. cal., GIO, 18 in. CMV mid-length barrel with SureFire SOCOM muzzle brake, low profile gas block, aluminum alloy upper receiver with Picatinny rail, Geissele SSA-E two-stage match trigger, integral oversized trigger guard, MOE mid-length forearm, Magpul MOE 6-position stock and grip, V3 billet charging handle, anodized finish, Magpul 20 LR PMAG, 8 1/2 lbs. Mfg. 2013-2016.

| | $1,875 | $1,100 | $895 | $650 | $575 | $495 | $425 | *$2,350* |

CORE30 MOE M-LOK – .308 Win. or 6.5mm Creedmoor cal., low profile gas block, 16, 18, 20, or 22 in. barrel with black Nitride finish, SureFire SOCOM 3-prong flash hider, Magpul 20 shot PMAG, integral oversized trigger guard, Magpul MOE 6-position stock, Magpul MOE mid-length forearm, Magpul MOE grip, V.3 billet charging handle, Mil-Spec buffer tube, aluminum alloy upper with Picatinny rail and laser engraved T-markings, Type III hardcoat anodized finish, 8 lbs. New 2016.

| MSR $1,950 | $1,600 | $1,000 | $775 | $575 | $495 | $425 | $395 | |

Add $50 for 20 in. barrel (6.5mm Creedmoor only).

Add $400 for 18 in. barrel (.308 Win. only).

Add $450 for 22 in. barrel (6.5mm Creedmoor only).

* CORE30 MOE M-LOK Stainless – 6.5mm Creedmoor cal., similar to Core30 MOE M-LOK, except has 20 or 22 in. fluted stainless steel barrel with bead blasted finish. New 2016.

| MSR $2,400 | $1,975 | $1,150 | $925 | $650 | $575 | $495 | $425 | |

CORE30 TAC RIFLE – .308 Win. cal., GIO, 16 in. CMV mid-length barrel with SureFire SOCOM muzzle brake, low profile gas block, Magpul 20 shot LR PMAG, Magpul ACS 6-position stock, Magpul MOE grip, Samson STAR 13.2 in. quad rail, V3 billet charging handle, integral oversized trigger guard, hardcoat anodized finish, Geissele SSA-E two-stage match trigger, aluminum alloy lower and upper receiver with Picatinny rail and laser engraved T-markings, black furniture, 9 lbs. Mfg. 2013-2014, reintroduced 2016.

| MSR $2,470 | $1,975 | $1,150 | $925 | $650 | $575 | $495 | $425 | |

CORE30 TAC LR RIFLE – .308 Win. cal., GIO, 18 in. stainless steel match grade mid-length barrel with SureFire SOCOM muzzle brake, low profile gas block, Magpul 20 LR PMAG, aluminum alloy upper receiver with Picatinny rail, Geissele SSA-E two-stage match trigger, integral oversized trigger guard, Magpul UBR stock, Magpul MIAD grip, APEX Gator grip, 15 in. free float modular forearm, V3 billet charging handle, anodized finish, 9 1/2 lbs. New 2013.

| MSR $2,880 | $2,295 | $1,450 | $1,075 | $675 | $595 | $525 | $475 | |

CORE30 TAC II RIFLE – .308 Win. or 6.5mm Creedmoor cal., GIO, 16, 18, 20, or 22 in. fluted (6.5mm Creedmoor only) or non-fluted barrel with black Nitride finish or stainless steel, SureFire SOCOM muzzle brake, 20 shot Magpul PMAG, single stage trigger, integral oversized trigger guard, Magpul ACS 6-position stock, Magpul MOE grip, 15 in. KeyMod rail, V.3 billet charging handle, low profile gas block, Mil-Spec buffer tube, aluminum alloy upper and lower receivers, Picatinny rail, Type III hardcoat anodized finish, 9 lbs. New 2016.

| MSR $2,400 | $1,975 | $1,150 | $925 | $650 | $575 | $495 | $425 | |

Add $70 for 6.5mm Creedmoor cal.

MSR	100%	98%	95%	90%	80%	70%	60%	Last MSR

CORONADO ARMS

Current rifle manufacturer located in Dixon, CA.

RIFLES/CARBINES: SEMI-AUTO

CA-15 CARBINE – 5.56 NATO or 6.8 SPC cal., AR-15 style, GIO, Lothar Walther button rifled barrel, 10 shot mag., Geissele trigger, extended upper and lower receivers, flared and broached magwell, Magpul MOE grip, Magpul STR stock, black hardcoat anodized finish, 7 1/4 lbs.

MSR $1,650	$1,350	$875	$650	$525	$450	$385	$350	

CA-15 COMPETITION CARBINE – .223/5.56 Wylde chamber, GIO, 16 in. stainless steel barrel with Crosshill Technologies X-Comp Compensator or muzzle brake, 10 shot mag., Gunfighter Industries Mod 4 charging handle, Geissele 3-gun trigger, KeyMod rifle length handguard, extended upper receiver, adj. gas block, Magpul STR stock, Magpul MOE grip, approx. 8 lbs. New 2015.

MSR $1,995	$1,650	$1,000	$795	$595	$495	$425	$395	

CA-15 RIFLE – 5.56 NATO or 6.8 SPC cal., AR-15 style, GIO, Lothar Walther button rifled and fluted bull barrel, 10 shot mag., mid-length gas system, Geissele two-stage trigger, extended upper and lower receivers, flared and broached magwell, Magpul MOE grip, Magpul PRS stock, black hardcoat anodized finish. New 2014.

MSR $2,450	$1,975	$1,150	$925	$650	$575	$495	$425	

CA-15 COMPETITION RIFLE – .223/5.56 Wylde chamber, GIO, 18 in. button rifled barrel, competition muzzle brake, adj. gas block, 10 shot mag., Gunfighter Industries Mod 4 charging handle, Geissele two-stage trigger, KeyMod rifle length handguard, Magpul MOE+ grip, Magpul PRS stock, 9 1/2 lbs. New 2016.

MSR $2,550	$2,050	$1,250	$950	$650	$575	$495	$475	

CRUSADER WEAPONRY

Previous manufacturer located in Murray, UT until 2015.

RIFLES: SEMI-AUTO

BROADSWORD – 7.62 NATO cal., AR-10 patterned rifle, 16, 18, 20, or 24 in. polygonal rifled barrel with BattleComp compensator, billet receiver, Apex free floating handguard, accepts Magpul PMAGs, treated with Slipstream weapon lubricant, includes Plano tactical hard case. Disc. 2015.

	$2,375	$1,525	$1,150	$700	$625	$550	$475	$2,950

GUARDIAN – 5.56 NATO or 6.8 SPC cal., mid-length gas system, 16 in. polygonal rifled barrel with Vortex flash hider, free float handguard, Magpul CTR buttstock, Magpul MIAD grip, Magpul MBUS backup sights, ambi single point sling attachment, quad rail forend with end cap, Slipstream basic rifle treatment, includes Bulldog hard sided rifle case. Disc. 2015.

	$1,675	$1,000	$825	$625	$550	$475	$425	$2,000

LONGBOW – 7.62 NATO cal., 24 in. polygonal rifled barrel with BattleComp muzzle brake, Magpul PRS stock, DPMS Panther target grip, JP adj. trigger, Apex handguard, Slipstream basic rifle treatment (Cerakote finishes and airburshed camo are optional), rifle gas system with low profile gas block. Disc. 2015.

	$2,815	$2,465	$1,995	$1,700	$1,400	$1,200	$1,035	$3,297

PALADIN – 5.56 NATO cal., 20 or 24 in. match grade polygonal rifled heavy barrel with target crown, rifle length gas system, low profile gas block, APEX free float tube forearm, target grip, JP trigger, Magpul PRS stock, Slipstream treatment, includes hard case. Disc. 2015.

	$1,725	$1,050	$850	$625	$550	$475	$425	$2,100

TEMPLAR – 5.56 NATO cal., AR-15 style, mid-length gas system, 18 in. polygonal rifled barrel with BattleComp compensator, Magpul UBR buttstock, Magpul MIAD grip, Magpul MBUS sights, Apex handguard with top rail, Slipstream basic rifle treatment, Plano tactical hard rifle case. Disc. 2015.

	$1,795	$1,050	$875	$625	$550	$475	$425	$2,200

D SECTION

D&L SPORTS, INC.

Current manufacturer located in Chino Valley, AZ.

Gunsmith Dave Lauck manufactures a complete line of 1911 style custom pistols, AR-15 style semi-auto carbines, and precision bolt action rifles. A wide variety of options and accessories are available. Additionally, D&L offers custom gunsmithing services. Please contact the company directly for more information, including pricing, options, and delivery time (see Trademark Index).

D.A.R. GmbH (DYNAMICS ARMS RESEARCH)

Current AR-15 style rifle and carbine manufacturer located in Fraureuth, Germany (previously located in Lichentanne, Germany). No current U.S. importation.

RIFLES: SEMI-AUTO

D.A.R. currently manufactures a variety of good quality AR-15 style carbines and rifles in various configurations. Additionally, the company also manufactures a variety of AR-15 style components and mounts. Please contact the company directly for U.S. availability and pricing (see Trademark Index).

DPMS FIREARMS (LLC)

Current trademark manufactured in St. Cloud, MN and by Remington Arms Co. in Huntsville, AL beginning late 2014. Previous manufacturer established in 1986 and located in St. Cloud and Becker, MN. Previous company name was DPMS, Inc. (Defense Procurement Manufacturing Services, Inc.) DPMS Firearms assembles high quality AR-15 style rifles, in addition to related parts and components. Distributor and dealer sales.

In December 2007, Cerberus Capital Management acquired the assets of DPMS. The new company name became DPMS Firearms, LLC, and currently is DPMS Firearms.

MSR	100%	98%	95%	90%	80%	70%	60%	Last MSR

PISTOLS: SEMI-AUTO

PANTHER .22 LR PISTOL – .22 LR cal., blowback action, 8 1/2 in. heavy chrome moly steel barrel, 10 shot mag., black aircraft aluminum flat-top upper receiver, black forged aircraft aluminum lower receiver, phosphate and hard chrome finished bolt and carrier, aluminum trigger guard, ribbed aluminum tubular handguard, no sights, 4 1/4 lbs. Limited mfg. 2006-2007.

	100%	98%	95%	90%	80%	70%	60%	Last MSR
	$700	$625	$550	$475	$425	$375	$325	$850

RIFLES: SEMI-AUTO

Each new DPMS rifle/carbine comes equipped with two mags. (high cap where legal), a nylon web sling, and a cleaning kit. Post-crime bill manufactured DPMS rifles may have pre-ban features, including collapsible stocks, high capacity mags, and a flash hider/compensator. Models with these features are not available in certain states.

The Panther AR-15 Series was introduced in 1993 in various configurations, including semi-auto GIO and slide action, and feature a tactical design in various barrel lengths and configurations, with a 10 or 30 shot mag.

300 AAC BLACKOUT – .300 AAC Blackout cal., 16 in. heavy chrome-lined barrel, Blackout suppressor adapter or an inert slipover mock suppressor, AP4 stock, A2 pistol grip, choice of carbine or mid-length handguard (disc. 2016) or DPMS M111 modular free float tube (new 2017), 7-7 1/2 lbs. New 2012.

MSR $1,149	$875	$550	$465	$395	$350	$325	$300	

COMPACT HUNTER – .308 Win. cal., 16 in. Teflon coated stainless steel barrel, B5 Systems SOPMOD stock, two-stage match trigger, carbon fiber free float handguard, Hogue rubber pistol grip, 7 3/4 lbs. Mfg. 2012-2014.

	$1,250	$825	$575	$475	$425	$375	$350	$1,499

LITE HUNTER (PANTHER LITE 308/338) – .243 Win., .260 Rem., .308 Win. ,or .338 Federal cal., 18 (disc. 2012) or 20 (new 2012) in. free floating barrel, no sights, carbon fiber free floating handguard, bipod stud, A3 style flat-top, Picatinny rail, A2 stock (new 2012), Hogue rubber grips, various accessories and options available. Mfg. 2009-2014.

	$1,250	$825	$575	$475	$425	$375	$350	$1,499

LONG RANGE LITE – .308 Win. cal., 24 in. stainless steel barrel, A2 fixed stock, two-stage match trigger, carbon fiber free float handguard, Hogue rubber pistol grip, 10 1/4 lbs. Mfg. 2012-2014.

	$1,250	$825	$575	$475	$425	$375	$350	$1,499

MOE SL CARBINE – 5.56 NATO cal., 16 in. chrome-lined barrel with AAC Blackout flash hider, enhanced trigger guard, backup sights, Magpul MOE SL furniture, Picatinny rail, matte black or FDE finish, approx. 6.5 lbs. New 2018.

MSR $1,099	$915	$575	$475	$415	$350	$325	$300	

D 150 DPMS FIREARMS (LLC), cont.

MSR	100%	98%	95%	90%	80%	70%	60%	Last MSR

MOE WARRIOR – 5.56 NATO cal., 16 in. heavy barrel, supressor adapter, enhanced trigger guard, backup sights, Magpul MOE stock, MOE handguard and pistol grip, sling adapter, black or Dark Earth finish, 7.3 lbs. Mfg. 2012-2014.

| | $975 | $595 | $495 | $425 | $365 | $335 | $300 | $1,159 |

TAC2 – 5.56 NATO cal., 16 in. barrel with Panther flash hider, Magpul ACS stock, MOE pistol grip, new M111 modular handguard system, utilizes a full rifle length gas system, A2 front and Magpul rear sights, 8 1/2 lbs. New 2012.

| MSR $1,249 | $1,050 | $650 | $495 | $450 | $395 | $350 | $325 | |

TAC20 – .308 Win. cal., 20 in. heavy chrome moly barrel, A2 fixed stock, detachable carry handle, Panther flash hider, 11 1/2 lbs. Mfg. 2012-2015.

| | $1,075 | $675 | $500 | $450 | $400 | $350 | $325 | $1,299 |

TPR (TACTICAL PRECISION RIFLE) – 5.56 NATO cal., AR-15 style, 20 in. heavy stainless steel barrel with AAC flash hider, two-stage trigger, B5 Systems SOPMOD (disc. 2017) or Magpul MOE (new 2018) stock, Magpul MOE pistol grip, M111 modular handguard, 7 3/4 lbs. New 2012.

| MSR $1,249 | $1,050 | $650 | $495 | $450 | $395 | $350 | $325 | |

PANTHER A2/A3 CLASSIC – 5.56 NATO cal., 16 (disc.) or 20 in. heavy barrel, ribbed barrel shroud, A3 stock with detachable carrying handle with sights, or A2 fixed stock, 9 lbs. Disc. 2015.

| | $850 | $550 | $465 | $395 | $350 | $325 | $295 | $980 |

Add $76 for left-hand variation (Southpaw Panther, disc.).

* Panther Classic Bulldog – 5.56 NATO cal., 20 in. stainless fluted bull barrel, flat-top, adj. buttstock, vented free float handguard, 11 lbs. Disc. 1999.

| | $1,025 | $625 | $495 | $450 | $395 | $350 | $325 | $1,219 |

PANTHER CARBINE 16 – 5.56 NATO cal., 16 in. heavy barrel with A2 birdcage flash hider, A3 flat-top upper, Pardus 6-position collapsible stock, GlacierGuard handguard, A2 pistol grip, 7.1 lbs. Disc. 2015.

| | $850 | $550 | $465 | $395 | $350 | $325 | $295 | $979 |

PANTHER 7.62x39mm CARBINE/RIFLE – 7.62x39mm Russian cal., 16 or 20 in. heavy barrel, black Zytel buttstock with trapdoor assembly, A2 flash hider, A2 pistol grip, 7-9 lbs. Mfg. 2000-2011.

| | $725 | $500 | $435 | $375 | $335 | $315 | $295 | $850 |

Add $10 for 20 in. barrel.

PANTHER DCM – .223 Rem. cal., 20 in. stainless steel heavy barrel, National Match sights, two-stage trigger, black Zytel composition buttstock, 9 lbs. Mfg. 1998-2003, reintroduced 2006-2012.

| | $875 | $550 | $465 | $395 | $350 | $325 | $300 | $1,129 |

PANTHER CLASSIC SIXTEEN – 5.56 NATO cal., 16 in. lightweight chrome moly (new 2012) or heavy (disc. 2011) barrel with A2 birdcage flash hider, adj. sights, black Zytel composition buttstock (disc.) or A2 fixed pistol grip stock, 7.1 lbs. Mfg. 1998-2014.

| | $745 | $500 | $435 | $375 | $335 | $315 | $295 | $859 |

Add $55 for Panther Free Float Sixteen with free floating barrel and vent. handguard (disc. 2008).

A1 LITE 20 (PANTHER LITE A1/A3) – 5.56 NATO cal., 16 (disc.) or 20 (new 2007) in. post-ban chrome moly barrel with A2 birdcage flash hider (new 2007), 1:9 in. twist, non-collapsible fiberite CAR (disc.) or A2 fixed pistol grip stock, choice of forged A1 upper with forward bolt assist or A3 (disc.) carry handle, black Teflon finish, 6-7.3 lbs. Mfg. 2002-2014.

| | $725 | $500 | $435 | $375 | $335 | $315 | $295 | $829 |

LITE 16 A2 – 5.56 NATO cal., 16 in. lightweight barrel with A2 birdcage flash hider, forged upper and lower receivers, GlacierGuard handguard, Pardus stock, A2 sights, 6 lbs.

| MSR $829 | $725 | $500 | $435 | $375 | $335 | $315 | $295 | |

LITE 16M A2 – 5.56 NATO cal., 16 in. lightweight barrel with A2 birdcage flash hider, A2 sights, Pardus stock, forged upper and lower receivers, M-111 modular free floating handguard, 6 lbs. New 2018.

| MSR $869 | $745 | $500 | $435 | $375 | $335 | $315 | $295 | |

PANTHER LO-PRO CLASSIC – 5.56 NATO cal., 16 in. bull barrel, A2 fixed stock, flat-top lo-pro upper receiver with push pin, 7 3/4 lbs. Mfg. 2002-2012.

| | $665 | $500 | $415 | $375 | $335 | $315 | $295 | $769 |

PANTHER TUBER – 5.56 NATO cal., 16 in. post-ban heavy free float barrel with full-length 2 in. diameter aluminum free float handguard, adj. A2 rear sights. Mfg. 2002-2008.

| | $665 | $500 | $415 | $375 | $335 | $315 | $295 | $754 |

DPMS FIREARMS (LLC), cont. 151 D

MSR	100%	98%	95%	90%	80%	70%	60%	Last MSR

PANTHER A2 TACTICAL – 5.56 NATO cal., 16 in. heavy manganese phosphate barrel, standard A2 handguard, 9 3/4 lbs. Mfg. 2004-2013.

	$745	$500	$435	$375	$335	$315	$295	$859

PANTHER AP4 CARBINE – 5.56 NATO cal., 16 in. M4 contour barrel with A2 flash hider, with or w/o attached Miculek compensator, fixed fiberglass reinforced polymer M4 stock, 7 1/4 lbs. Mfg. 2004-2012.

	$825	$535	$450	$385	$340	$325	$295	$959

Add $54 for Miculek compensator.

* ***Panther AP4 Carbine (Disc.)*** – 6.8x43mm SPC or 5.56x45mm cal., 16 in. barrel, collapsible stock, includes carrying handle, 6 1/2 lbs. Disc.

	$785	$525	$450	$385	$340	$325	$295	$904

PANTHER AP4 A2 CARBINE – 5.56 NATO cal., 16 in. chrome moly steel heavy barrel with A2 flash hider, standard A2 front sight assembly, A2 fixed carry handle and adj. rear sight, forged aircraft aluminum upper and lower receiver, hardcoat anodized Teflon coated black finish, AP4 6-position telescoping fiber reinforced polymer stock, GlacierGuard handguard, 7.1 lbs. New 2006.

MSR $945	$800	$525	$450	$385	$340	$325	$295	

PANTHER A2 CARBINE "THE AGENCY" – 5.56 NATO cal., 16 in. chrome moly steel barrel with A2 flash hider, two 30 shot mags., A3 flat-top forged receiver, two-stage trigger, EoTech and "Mangonel" rear sights, Ergo SureGrip forearm and collapsible stock, A3 flat-top forged receiver, two-stage trigger, tactical charging handle, package includes SureFire quad rail and flashlight, 7 lbs. Mfg. 2007-2012.

	$1,675	$1,000	$825	$625	$550	$475	$425	$2,069

LR-6.5 (PANTHER 6.5) – 6.5mm Creedmoor cal., 24 in. stainless steel free float bull barrel, single rail gas block, no sights, ribbed aluminum free float tube handguard, bipod stud, A3 style flat-top, black Teflon coated, standard A2 black Zytel Mil-Spec stock, A2 pistol grip, 11.3 lbs. Mfg. 2009-2014.

	$1,050	$650	$495	$450	$395	$350	$325	$1,239

PANTHER 6.8mm CARBINE/RIFLE – 6.8x43mm Rem. SPC cal., 16 (new 2007) or 20 in. chrome moly manganese phosphate steel barrel with A2 flash hider, two 25 shot mags., standard A2 front sight assembly, A3 flat-top upper receiver with detachable carry handle and adj. rear sight, aluminum aircraft alloy lower receiver, black standard A2 Zytel Mil-Spec stock with trap door assembly, A2 handguard, approx. 9 lbs. Mfg. 2006-2011.

	$865	$550	$465	$395	$350	$325	$300	$1,019

Add $10 for 20 in. barrel.

PANTHER 6.8 SPCII HUNTER – 6.8x43mm Rem. SPC cal., 18 in. steel barrel with Miculek compensator, aluminum A3 flat-top with forward assist, black Zytel skeletonized A2 stock, mid-length carbine fiber free floating forearm tube, 7.65 lbs. Mfg. 2011-2012.

	$1,065	$650	$500	$450	$395	$350	$325	$1,269

PANTHER RECON MID-LENGTH CARBINE – 5.56 NATO or 7.62 NATO (mfg. 2012-2014) cal., 16 in. stainless steel heavy barrel with AAC blackout flash hider, flat-top aluminum upper receiver with Magpul BUIS front and rear sights, mid-length quad rail free floating forearm tube, Magpul MOE stock and pistol grip, 7.7 lbs. New 2011.

MSR $1,197	$995	$625	$495	$450	$395	$350	$325	

PANTHER LBR CARBINE – 5.56 NATO cal., 16 in. lightweight stainless barrel with A2 flash hider, muzzle brake, flat-top receiver with integral Picatinny rail, Magpul MOE stock with A2 pistol grip, vent. free floating handguard with front upper Picatinny rail, choice of matte black or Muddy Girl camo (new 2018) finish, 7 1/4 lbs. New 2011.

MSR $979	$850	$550	$465	$395	$350	$325	$295	

* ***Panther LBR DIVA Edition*** – 5.56 NATO cal., similar to Panther LBR, except has 16 in. chrome moly barrel and Leopard print especially for women. Mfg. 2012-2014.

	$850	$550	$465	$395	$350	$325	$295	$979

PRAIRIE PANTHER – 5.56 NATO cal., 20 in. heavy fluted free float barrel, flat-top, vented handguard, 8 3/4 lbs. Disc. 1999.

	$825	$535	$450	$385	$340	$325	$295	$959

PRAIRIE PANTHER (CURRENT MFG.) – .223 Rem. or 6.8 SPC (black finish only, disc. 2014) cal., 20 in. stainless steel fluted heavy barrel, target crown, carbon fiber free float tube, no sights, hard anodized finish, choice of black with carbon fiber handguard (mfg. 2011-2015), King's Desert Shadow (Desert), King's Snow Shadow (mfg. 2011-2015) or Mossy Oak Brush (Brush) camo coverage, A3 Picatinny rail flat-top, tactical charging handle assembly, Magpul winter trigger guard, skeletonized black Zytel Mil-Spec stock with trapdoor assembly, A2 pistol grip stock, two-stage trigger, approx. 7.1 lbs. New 2010.

MSR $1,289	$1,075	$675	$500	$450	$400	$350	$325	

Subtract approx. $60 for black finish (disc. 2015).

D 152 DPMS FIREARMS (LLC), cont.

MSR	100%	98%	95%	90%	80%	70%	60%	Last MSR

ARCTIC PANTHER – .223 Rem. cal., 20 in. barrel, similar to Prairie Panther, except has white powder coat finish on receiver and aluminum handguard, railed gas block, 9 lbs. Mfg. 1997-2015.

| | $995 | $625 | $495 | $450 | $395 | $350 | $325 | $1,197 |

PANTHER BULL/SWEET 16 – .223 Rem. cal., features 16 (Sweet 16), 20, or 24 in. stainless free float bull barrel, flat-top, aluminum forearm, A2 fixed stock, aluminum pistol grip, A2 handguard, railed gas block/optics ready, 7 3/4-9 1/2 lbs.

| MSR $979 | $850 | $550 | $465 | $395 | $350 | $325 | $295 | |

Add $10 for 20 in. barrel (Panther Bull 20).
Add $20 for 24 in. barrel (Panther Bull 24).

* ***Panther Bull Classic*** – .223 Rem. cal., 20 in. long 1 in. bull barrel, adj. sights, 10 lbs. Mfg. 1998-2008.

| | $785 | $525 | $450 | $385 | $340 | $325 | $295 | $910 |

Add $200 for SST lower.

* ***Panther Bull Twenty-Four Special*** – 5.56 NATO cal., 24 in. stainless fluted barrel, adj. A2 buttstock with sniper pistol grip, JP trigger, 10 1/4 lbs. Mfg. 1998-2015.

| | $1,125 | $700 | $525 | $450 | $400 | $350 | $325 | $1,348 |

* ***Panther Super Bull*** – .223 Rem. cal., 16, 20, or 24 in. extra heavy free float bull barrel, flat-top receiver, handguard, approx. 11 lbs. Mfg. 1997-98, 24 in. model reintroduced during late 2004, disc. 2006.

| | $995 | $625 | $495 | $450 | $395 | $350 | $325 | $1,199 |

* ***Panther Super Bull 24*** – .223 Rem. cal., 24 in. extra heavy stainless steel bull barrel (1 1/8 in. diameter barrel), flat-top, hi-rider upper receiver, skeletonized A2 buttstock, 11 3/4 lbs. Mfg. 1999-2004.

| | $995 | $625 | $495 | $450 | $395 | $350 | $325 | $1,199 |

PANTHER PARDUS – .223 Rem. cal., 16 in. stainless steel free float bull barrel, integrated compensator, titanium Nitride plated steel bolt and carrier, three rail extruded upper receiver, aluminum alloy upper and lower receiver, Teflon coated tan or black 6-position telescoping fiber reinforced polymer stock, curved and serrated buttplate, four-rail aluminum handguard, no sights, includes two 30 shot mags., 8.1 lbs. Mfg. 2006-2008.

| | $1,315 | $850 | $625 | $500 | $435 | $375 | $350 | $1,600 |

PANTHER MK-12 5.56 NATO – 5.56 NATO cal., 18 in. stainless heavy free float barrel with flash hider, one-piece four rail tube and six long rail covers, A3 flat-top receiver, 5-position SOPMOD collapsible stock with tactical pistol grip, two-stage trigger, two 30 round mags., Midwest Industry flip-up sights, 8 3/4 lbs. Mfg. 2007-2014.

| | $1,350 | $875 | $650 | $525 | $450 | $385 | $350 | $1,649 |

PANTHER MK-12 7.62 NATO – 7.62 NATO cal., 18 in. stainless steel heavy barrel, flash hider, Midwest Industries flip-up rear sight, gas block with flip-up front sight, A3 Picatinny rail flat-top, aluminum lower receiver, integral trigger guard, Magpul CTR adj. stock, Hogue rubber grip with finger grooves, two-stage match trigger, hardcoat anodized black finish, four rail free float tube, six rail covers, approx. 9.6 lbs. Mfg. 2010-2014.

| | $1,475 | $950 | $725 | $550 | $475 | $395 | $350 | $1,799 |

PANTHER SDM-R – .223 Rem. cal., 20 in. heavy stainless free float barrel with A2 flash hider, four rail aluminum tube, pistol grip stock, National Match front sight, Harris bipod with rail adapter, two 30 shot mags., 8.85 lbs. Mfg. 2007-2008.

| | $1,175 | $775 | $550 | $465 | $415 | $375 | $350 | $1,404 |

PANTHER 20TH ANNIVERSARY – .223 Rem. cal., 20 in. stainless steel fluted bull barrel, phosphated steel bolt and carrier, hi-rider forged high polished chrome upper and lower receiver with commemorative engraving, chrome plated charging handle, semi-auto trigger group, aluminum trigger guard and mag. release button, A2 black Zytel Mil-Spec stock with trap door assembly and engraved DPMS logo, no sights, vented aluminum handguard, includes two 30 shot mags., approx. 9 1/2 lbs. Limited mfg. of 100 rifles in 2006.

| | $1,650 | $1,000 | $795 | $595 | $495 | $425 | $395 | $1,995 |

PANTHER RACE GUN – .223 Rem. cal., 24 in. stainless steel barrel with Hot Rod handguard, IronStone steel and aluminum stock with rubber buttplate and brass weights, 16 lbs. Mfg. 2001-2008.

| | $1,425 | $925 | $700 | $550 | $475 | $395 | $350 | $1,724 |

PANTHER SINGLE SHOT – 5.56 NATO cal., 20 in. barrel, A2 black Zytel stock and handguard, single shot only w/o magazine, 9 lbs. Disc. 2008.

| | $695 | $500 | $425 | $375 | $335 | $315 | $295 | $819 |

AP4 CARBINE .22 LR – .22 LR cal., 16 in. barrel, GlacierGuard M4 handguard, A2 pistol grip and flash hider, AP4 stock with detachable carry handle, 6 1/2 lbs. Disc. 2014.

| | $800 | $700 | $600 | $545 | $445 | $345 | $275 | $935 |

DPMS FIREARMS (LLC), cont. 153 D

MSR	100%	98%	95%	90%	80%	70%	60%	Last MSR

BULL CARBINE .22 LR – .22 LR cal., 16 in. bull barrel, aluminum handguard, A2 pistol grip and flash hider, fixed A2 stock, no sights, 7.3 lbs. Disc. 2015.

	$800	$700	$600	$545	$445	$345	$275	$935

PANTHER .22 LR RIFLE – .22 LR cal., AR-15 style receiver, 16 in. bull barrel, black Teflon metal finish, Picatinny rail, black Zytel A2 buttstock, 7.8 lbs. Mfg. 2003-2008.

	$695	$615	$525	$475	$375	$315	$245	$804

PANTHER DCM .22 LR RIFLE – .22 LR cal., 20 in. fluted stainless steel HBAR barrel with 1:16 in. twist, A2 upper receiver with National Match sights, black Teflon finish, A2 stock and handguards, also available with optional DCM handguard system. Mfg. 2004-2008.

	$850	$745	$645	$575	$475	$385	$300	$994

PANTHER AP4 .22 LR RIFLE – .22 LR cal., 16 in. M4 contoured barrel, M4 handguards and pinned carstock, A3 flat-top upper receiver, detachable carry handle with A2 sights and black Teflon finish, 6 1/2 lbs. Mfg. 2004-2008.

	$765	$675	$575	$525	$425	$345	$275	$894

PANTHER LR-.308 – .308 Win. cal., 24 in. free float bull barrel with 1:10 in. twist, ribbed aluminum forearm tube, aircraft alloy upper/lower, A2 fixed pistol grip stock, black Teflon finish, 11 1/4 lbs. Mfg. mid-2003-2014.

	$995	$625	$495	$450	$395	$350	$325	$1,199

* **Panther LR-.308B** – .308 Win. cal., similar to Long Range Rifle, except has 18 in. chrome moly bull barrel and carbine length aluminum handguard. Mfg. late 2003-2012.

	$995	$625	$495	$450	$395	$350	$325	$1,189

* **Panther LR-.308T** – 7.62 NATO cal., similar to .308B, except has 16 in. HBAR. Mfg. 2004-2012.

	$995	$625	$495	$450	$395	$350	$325	$1,189

* **Panther LR-.308 AP4** – 7.62 NATO cal., similar to Panther .308 Long Range, except has AP4 6-position telescoping fiber reinforced polymer stock. Disc. 2012.

	$1,075	$675	$500	$450	$400	$350	$325	$1,299

* **Panther LR-.308 Classic** – 7.62 NATO cal., similar to Panther LR-.308, except has 20 in. barrel, A3 style flat-top receiver and removable carry handle. Mfg. mid-2008-2014.

	$995	$625	$495	$450	$395	$350	$325	$1,199

PANTHER LR-308C – .308 Win. cal., 20 in. heavy steel free float barrel, features A3 flat-top receiver with detachable carrying handle, standard A2 front sight assembly, four rail standard length tube, two 19 shot mags., 11.1 lbs. Mfg. 2007-2008.

	$1,065	$650	$500	$450	$395	$350	$325	$1,254

PANTHER LRT-SASS – 7.62 NATO cal., 18 in. stainless steel contoured barrel with Panther flash hider, A3 style flat-top upper receiver solid aluminum lower receiver, AR-15 trigger group, ambi-selector, JP adj. trigger, black waterproof VLTOR Clubfoot carbine 5-position (disc.) or Magpul stock, vented handguard and Panther tactical pistol grip, Magpul sights, approx. 11 1/2 lbs. Mfg. 2006-2014.

	$1,725	$1,050	$850	$625	$550	$475	$425	$2,179

PANTHER MINI-SASS – 5.56 NATO cal., 18 in. stainless steel fluted barrel with Panther flash hider, forged A3 flat-top upper receiver, aircraft aluminum alloy lower receiver, aluminum trigger guard, Magpul PRS stock, tactical pistol grip, Magpul sights, includes Harris bipod, 10 1/4 lbs. New 2008.

MSR $1,599	$1,315	$850	$625	$500	$435	$375	$350	

PANTHER LR-30S – .300 RSUM cal., 20 in. stainless steel free float fluted bull barrel, aluminum upper and lower receiver, hardcoat anodized Teflon coated black skeletonized synthetic stock, integral trigger guard, ribbed aluminum tube handguard, includes two 4 shot mags., nylon web sling and cleaning kit. Mfg. 2004-2008.

	$1,065	$650	$500	$450	$395	$350	$325	$1,255

PANTHER LR-204 – .204 Ruger cal., 24 in. fluted stainless steel bull barrel, no sights, A3 flat-top forged upper and lower receiver, semi-auto trigger group, standard A2 black Zytel Mil-Spec stock with trapdoor assembly, includes two 30 shot mags., 9 3/4 lbs. Mfg. 2006-2015.

	$1,025	$625	$495	$450	$395	$350	$325	$1,213

PANTHER LR-243 – .243 Win. cal., 20 in. chrome moly steel heavy (disc. 2012) or lightweight (Lite Hunter) free float barrel, no sights, raised Picatinny rail, aluminum upper and lower receiver, standard AR-15 trigger group, skeletonized black Zytel Mil-Spec stock with trapdoor assembly, ribbed aluminum free float handguard, includes two 19 shot mags., 10 3/4 lbs. Mfg. 2006-2013.

	$1,250	$825	$575	$475	$425	$375	$350	$1,499

D 154 DPMS FIREARMS (LLC), cont.

MSR	100%	98%	95%	90%	80%	70%	60%	Last MSR

PANTHER LR-260 SERIES – .260 Rem. cal., 18 (mfg. 2007-2012, LR-260L), 20 (LR-260H, Lite Hunter) or 24 (LR-260) in. stainless steel fluted bull barrel, no sights, raised Picatinny rail, thick walled aluminum upper receiver, solid lower receiver, standard AR-15 trigger group, integral trigger guard, A2 black Zytel stock with trapdoor assembly, includes two 19 shot mags., 11.3 lbs. Mfg. 2006-2014.

	$1,050	$650	$495	$450	$395	$350	$325	$1,239

Add $260 for 18 in. barrel (LR-260L) with skeletonized stock, Miculek compensator and JRD trigger (disc. 2012).

PANTHER ORACLE – 5.56 NATO or 7.62 NATO (disc. 2015) cal., 16 in. chrome moly heavy barrel, A2 flash hider, gas block with single rail, no sights, GlacierGuards oval carbine length handguard, A3 Picatinny flat-top, hardcoat anodized black finish, integral trigger guard, Pardus 6-position telescoping stock with cheekpiece, A2 pistol grip, curved and serrated buttplate, multiple sling slots, approx. 8.3 lbs. New 2010.

* *Panther Oracle 5.56 NATO cal.*

MSR $611	$535	$460	$395	$350	$315	$295	$275	

Add $30 for stainless steel barrel (disc. 2014).

Add $80 for quad rail handguard (disc. 2014).

Add $110 for ATACS Oracle Carbine (includes ATACS camo coverage), mfg. 2011-2014.

* *Panther Oracle 7.62 NATO cal.* – Disc. 2015, reintroduced 2017.

MSR $969	$825	$535	$450	$385	$340	$325	$295	

Add $90 for ATACS Oracle Carbine (includes ATACS camo coverage) mfg. 2011-2015.

PANTHER SPORTICAL – 5.56 NATO or 7.62 NATO cal., 16 in. chrome moly heavy or light contour barrel, single rail gas block, A2 flash hider, various rails and accessories. Mfg. mid-2008-2015.

	$645	$500	$415	$370	$325	$300	$275	$746

PANTHER REPR – 7.62 NATO cal., 18 in. chrome moly (disc.) or 20 in. fluted stainless steel free float barrel, Gem Tech flash hider/suppressor, micro gas block, A3 style flat-top upper receiver, milled aluminum lower receiver, hardcoat anodized coyote brown finish, removable hinged trigger guard, Picatinny rail, four rail tube handguard, Magpul PRS stock, Hogue rubber grip with finger grooves, 9 1/2 lbs. Mfg. 2009-2014.

	$2,050	$1,250	$950	$650	$575	$495	$475	$2,589

PANTHER RAPTR CARBINE – 5.56 NATO cal., 16 in. chrome moly steel contoured barrel, 30 shot mag., flash hider, A2 front sight, Mangonel flip-up rear sight, Ergo Z-Rail two-piece four rail handguard, Crimson Trace vertical grip with integrated light and laser combination, A3 Picatinny rail flat-top, dust cover, aluminum trigger guard, AP4 6-position telescoping polymer stock, Ergo Ambi SureGrip, hardcoat anodized black finish, 8.2 lbs. Mfg. 2010-2011.

	$1,350	$875	$650	$525	$450	$385	$350	$1,649

PANTHER CSAT TACTICAL – 5.56 NATO cal., 16 in. chrome moly steel contoured barrel, 30 shot mag., A2 front sight assembly with A2 front sight post, detachable rear sight, four rail free float tube, A3 Picatinny rail flat-top, aluminum lower receiver, Magpul CTR adj. stock, Magpul MIAD pistol grip, 7.8 lbs. Mfg. 2010-2012.

	$1,475	$950	$725	$550	$475	$395	$350	$1,799

PANTHER CSAT PERIMETER – 5.56 NATO cal., similar to Tactical, except has 16 in. heavy barrel, approx. 8 lbs. Mfg. 2010-2011.

	$1,475	$950	$725	$550	$475	$395	$350	$1,799

PANTHER 3G1 – 5.56 NATO or 7.62 NATO (mfg. 2012-2014) cal., 18 in. stainless standard or heavy barrel, 30 shot mag., Miculek compensator, no sights, VTAC modular handguard, bipod stud, A3 Picatinny rail flat-top, black anodized finish, aluminum trigger guard, JP adj. trigger group, Magpul CTR adj. stock, Hogue rubber pistol grip, 7 3/4 lbs. New 2010.

MSR $1,399	$1,150	$750	$550	$465	$415	$375	$350	

PANTHER 3G2 – 5.56 NATO cal., 16 in. stainless lightweight barrel with Miculek compensator, Magpul STR buttstock, M111 modular handguard, Ergo rubber pistol grip, Magpul Gen. 2 BUIS sights, enhanced charging handle, two-stage trigger, 7 lbs. 2 oz. Mfg. 2013-2015.

	$1,175	$775	$550	$465	$415	$375	$350	$1,420

GII AP4 – .308 Win./7.62 NATO cal., 16 in. lightweight chrome-lined barrel with Cancellation Brake flash hider, forged anodized Teflon coated upper and lower receiver, F marked front sight base, Magpul BUIS rear sight, 6-position M4 collapsible stock, carbine length GlacierGuard handguard, A2 pistol grip, matte black finish, 7 1/4 lbs. New 2014.

MSR $1,399	$1,150	$750	$550	$465	$415	$375	$350	

GII APR-OR – .308 Win./7.62 NATO cal., 16 in. lightweight barrel, A2 birdcage flash hider, railed gas block optics ready, AP4 stock, A2 pistol grip, DPMS carbine length GlacierGuard handguard, Teflon coated upper and lower receivers, 7 lbs. New 2017.

MSR $1,139	$875	$550	$465	$395	$350	$325	$300	

DPMS FIREARMS (LLC), cont. 155 D

MSR	100%	98%	95%	90%	80%	70%	60%	Last MSR

GII BULL 24 – .308 Win. cal., 24 in. stainless steel bull barrel, A2 stock, aluminum free float handguard, and no flash hider, 10 lbs. New 2014.

| MSR $1,299 | $1,075 | $675 | $500 | $450 | $400 | $350 | $325 | |

GII HUNTER – .243 Rem. (mfg. 2015, reintroduced 2018), .260 Rem. (mfg. 2015, reintroduced 2018), .308 Win., or .338 Federal (mfg. 2015 only) cal., 20 in. stainless steel barrel with target crown, no sights, Hogue pistol grip, carbon fiber free float tube handguard, Magpul MOE stock, 7.76 lbs. New 2014.

| MSR $1,599 | $1,315 | $850 | $625 | $500 | $435 | $375 | $350 | |

GII COMPACT HUNTER – .243 Win. (disc. 2016, reintroduced 2018), .260 Rem. (disc. 2016, reintroduced 2018), .308 Win., or .338 Federal (disc. 2016) cal., 16 (new 2017) or 18 (disc. 2016) in. stainless Teflon coated barrel, carbon fiber free float tube handguard, Magpul MOE (disc. 2016) or B5 SOPMOD (new 2017) stock, Hogue pistol grip, black finish, 6.9 lbs. New 2015.

| MSR $1,599 | $1,315 | $850 | $625 | $500 | $435 | $375 | $350 | |

GII MOE – .308 Win./7.62 NATO cal., 16 in. lightweight chrome-lined barrel, Magpul BUIS sights, MOE carbine stock, Magpul MOE pistol grip, and carbine length MOE handguard, 7 1/4 lbs. New 2014.

| MSR $1,499 | $1,250 | $825 | $575 | $475 | $425 | $375 | $350 | |

GII RECON – .308 Win./7.62 NATO cal., 16 in. stainless steel bead blasted mid-length barrel with Advanced Armament Blackout silencer adapter, mid-length gas system, forged anodized Teflon coated A3 type upper and lower receiver, Magpul front and rear BUIS sight, Magpul MOE 6-position collapsible stock, Magpul MOE pistol grip, four rail free float tube handguard, matte black finish, 8 1/2 lbs. New 2014.

| MSR $1,699 | $1,385 | $895 | $675 | $525 | $450 | $385 | $350 | |

GII SASS – .308 Win./7.62 NATO cal., mid-length gas system, 18 in. Teflon coated stainless steel fluted bull barrel with Panther flash hider, forged anodized Teflon coated A3 type upper and lower receiver, Magpul front sight and rear BUIS sight, Magpul PRS rifle stock, Harris bipod and adapter, Panther tactical grip, four rail free float tube handguard, matte black finish, 10 1/2 lbs. New 2014.

| MSR $2,279 | $1,795 | $1,050 | $875 | $625 | $550 | $475 | $425 | |

GEN I ORACLE – 7.62 NATO cal., compact, 16 in. heavy barrel, optics ready, GlacierGuard handguard, black finish. Mfg. 2016 only.

| | $825 | $535 | $450 | $385 | $340 | $325 | $295 | *$954* |

DRD TACTICAL

Current semi-auto pistol and rifle manufacturer. Dealer and distributor sales.

PISTOLS: SEMI-AUTO

CDR15 10.5 – .223 Rem./5.56 NATO cal., GIO, 10 1/2 in. melanite coated steel barrel with flash hider, 30 shot Magpul PMAG, billet aluminum receivers, DRD QD 7 in. 1913 rail with Magpul L-4 rail panels, hardcoat anodized black finish, 5.2 lbs. Mfg. 2015 only.

| | $850 | $725 | $650 | $585 | $515 | $450 | $395 | *$995* |

CDR15 11.5 – 5.56 NATO cal., GIO, 11 1/2 in. hammer forged barrel, 30 shot Magpul PMAG, DRD quick takedown 7 in. rail with Magpul L-4 rail panels, billet aluminum receivers, hardcoat anodized black finish, 5.4 lbs. Mfg. 2015 only.

| | $975 | $885 | $765 | $655 | $575 | $495 | $435 | *$1,150* |

M762 – 7.62x51mm NATO/.308 cal., GIO, 12 in. Lothar-Walther stainless steel barrel with Noveske KX3 flash suppressor, 20 shot mag., AR-15 style safety selector, Magpul MOE grips, SIG SB15 pistol stabilizing brace, DRD QD 13 in. 1913 rail with Magpul L-4 rail panels, hardcoat anodized black finish, includes custom cut foam hard case with pistol tray, 8.8 lbs. Mfg. 2015 only.

| | $2,550 | $2,225 | $1,825 | $1,575 | $1,300 | $1,100 | $950 | *$2,995* |

M762 12 IN. – 7.62 NATO cal., GIO, 12 in. stainless steel barrel, two 20 shot Magpul PMAGs, billet aluminum receivers, DRD quick takedown 9 in. rail with Magpul L4 rail panels, hardcoat anodized black finish, 8 1/2 lbs. Mfg. 2015 only.

| | $1,575 | $1,385 | $1,185 | $1,065 | $915 | $785 | $635 | *$1,850* |

APTUS PISTOL – 5.56 NATO or .300 AAC Blackout cal., GIO, 7 1/2 in. barrel, 30 shot mag., standard AR trigger, billet aluminum lower/upper receiver, non-reciprocating left-side charging handle, DRD tactical patented QD 7 M-LOK rail, Type III hardcoat black anodized or NiB Battle Worn finish, 5.6 lbs.

| MSR $1,495 | $1,275 | $1,125 | $1,025 | $875 | $750 | $625 | $525 | |

Add $450 for NiB Battle Worn finish.

D 156 DRD TACTICAL, cont.

MSR	100%	98%	95%	90%	80%	70%	60%	Last MSR

APTUS W/PISTOL BRACE – 5.56 NATO or .300 AAC Blackout cal., GIO, 7 1/2 in. barrel, 30 shot mag., standard AR trigger, billet aluminum lower/upper receiver, non-reciprocating left-side charging handle, DRD tactical patented QD 7 M-LOK rail, folding SBT pistol brace, Type III hardcoat black anodized or NiB Battle Worn finish, 5.6 lbs.

	100%	98%	95%	90%	80%	70%	60%
MSR $1,775	$1,485	$1,315	$1,150	$1,025	$875	$750	$615

Add $550 for NiB Battle Worn finish.

RIFLES/CARBINES: SEMI-AUTO

APTUS – 5.56 NATO or .300 AAC Blackout cal., GIO, 16 in. barrel, 30 shot mag., AR type trigger, Magpul adj. folding stock, forged upper and lower aluminum receiver, non-reciprocating left-side charging handle, DRD Tactical Patented QD 15 M-LOK rail, hardcoat black anodized or NIB Battle Worn finish, 7.5 lbs. New late 2017.

MSR $1,695	$1,450	$1,275	$1,095	$985	$800	$650	$525

CDR-15 – 5.56 NATO or .300 AAC Blackout cal., AR-15 style, carbine or mid-length gas block, GIO, 16 in. chrome-lined or Melonite coated (.300 Blackout only) hammer forged barrel, two 30 shot mags., Magpul CTR stock, MOE grip, Ergo rubberized grip, billet receiver, 13 in. QD tactical rail, custom cut foam hard case, parkerized, matte black, or NiB Battle Worn finish, 6.9 lbs.

MSR $1,900	$1,625	$1,425	$1,225	$1,100	$895	$725	$575

Add $550 for NiB Battle Worn finish.

G762 – 7.62x51mm NATO cal., GIO, hammer forged chrome-lined 16 or 18 in. barrel, 20 shot mag., accepts standard G3/HK 91 magazines, billet upper and lower receiver, 1913 mounting rail accepts Magpul L4 panels at 3, 6, and 9 o'clock positions, tactical buttstock, black hardcoat anodized finish, includes hard case, 8.7 lbs. Disc. 2015.

	$2,765	$2,425	$2,075	$1,875	$1,525	$1,250	$975	*$3,250*

KIVAARI 338 – .338 Lapua or .300 Norma (new 2017) Mag. cal., GIO, 24 in. quick takedown barrel with Silencer Co. QD muzzle brake, two 10 shot mags., two-stage match trigger, Magpul PRS fully adj. stock, ambidextrous safety, billet aluminum receiver, bolt catch, and mag. release, non-reciprocating left side charging handle, 17 in. Magpul M-LOK rail, includes Atlas adj. bipod and choice of Tactical Tailor backpack or hard case, black anodized, Cerakote FDE, or NiB Battle Worn finish, 13.6 lbs. New mid-2015.

MSR $5,000	$4,250	$3,725	$3,195	$2,895	$2,350	$1,925	$1,500

Add $650 for NiB Battle Worn finish.

Add $3,995 for NiB Battle Worn finish w/Tracking Point.

M762 – 7.62x51mm NATO or 6.5mm Creedmoor cal., GIO, hammer forged chrome-lined 16 or 18 (disc.) in. barrel with flash suppressor, two 20 shot round PMAGs, standard AR type trigger, Magpul MOE stock/grip, billet upper and lower receiver, quick takedown 13 in. rail, includes hard case with pistol tray, black hardcoat anodized or NiB Battle Worn finish, 8.7 lbs.

MSR $2,400	$2,050	$1,800	$1,550	$1,400	$1,125	$925	$725

Add $550 for NiB Battle Worn finish.

PARATUS P762 GEN 2 – 7.62x51mm NATO cal., GIO, designed for quick takedown, hammer forged chrome-lined 16 or 18 (disc.) in. barrel, 20 shot mag., Geissele two-stage trigger, Magpul adj. folding stock and grips, billet upper and lower receiver, 1913 mounting rail, includes small hard case, backpack, or diplomatic attaché case, black hardcoat anodized or NiB Battle Worn finish, 9.2 lbs.

MSR $3,300	$2,800	$2,450	$2,100	$1,900	$1,550	$1,260	$985

Add $550 for NiB Battle Worn finish.

DSA INC.

Current manufacturer, importer, and distributor of semi-auto rifles and related components established during 1987 and currently located in Barrington, IL. Previously located in Round Lake and Grayslake, IL.

DSA Inc. is a manufacturer of FAL design and SA58 style rifles for both civilian and law enforcement purposes (L.E. certificates must be filled out for L.E. purchases). Until recently, DSA, Inc. also imported a sporterized SIG 550 rifle.

RIFLES: SEMI-AUTO

The SA-58 and ZM-4 rifles listed are available in a standard DuraCoat solid or camo pattern finishes. Patterns include: ACU, Advanced Tiger Stripe, Afghan, AmStripe, Belgian, Belgian Digital, Belgian Advanced Tiger Stripe, Black Forest MirageFlage, Desert MirageFlage, MultiColor, OD MirageFlage, Mossy Oak Breakup (disc.), Rhodesian, Thailand Marine, Tiger Stripe (disc.), Underbrush (disc.), Urban MirageFlage, Urban Tiger Stripe, Vietnam Tiger stripe (disc.), Wilderness MirageFlage, Winter Twig (disc.), or Woodland Prestige. DSA Inc. makes three types of forged steel receivers, and they are distinguished by the machining cuts on Types I and II, and no cuts on Type III.

Add $50 for MK16 fluted M4 barrel.

Add $65 for stainless steel M4 barrel.

Add $90 for Magpul MOE furniture.

DSA INC., cont. 157 D

MSR		100%	98%	95%	90%	80%	70%	60%	Last MSR

DS-AR SERIES – .223 Rem cal., GIO, available in a variety of configurations including carbine and rifle, standard or bull barrels, various options, stock colors, and features. Mfg. 2006-2008.

		$850	$550	$465	$395	$350	$325	$295	$1,000

Add $243 for SOPMOD Carbine. Add $30 for 1R Carbine. Add $150 for 1V Carbine. Add $130 for S1 Bull rifle. Add $500 for DCM rifle. Add $30 for XM Carbine.

Add $1,395 - $1,515 for monolithic rail platform. Add $675 for Z4 GTC Carbine with corrosion resistant operating system.

DS-CV1 CARBINE – 5.56 NATO cal., GIO, 16 in. chrome moly D4 barrel with press on mock flash hider, fixed Shorty buttstock, D4 handguard and heat shield, forged front sight base, forged lower receiver, forged flat-top upper receiver, variety of Duracoat solid or camo finishes available, 6 1/4 lbs. Mfg. 2004-2005.

		$725	$500	$435	$375	$335	$315	$295	$850

DS-LE4 CARBINE – 5.56 NATO cal., GIO, 16 in. chrome moly D4 barrel with threaded A2 flash hider, collapsible CAR buttstock, D4 handguard with heat shield, forged lower receiver, forged front sight base with bayonet lug, forged flat-top upper receiver, Duracoat solid or camo finish, 6.15 or 6 1/4 lbs. Mfg. 2004-2012.

Retail pricing was not available for this model.

DSA CUSTOM MANCOW EDITION RIFLE – 5.56 NATO cal., 16 in. HBAR barrel, A2 flash hider, Magpul PMAG, steel low profile gas block, 13 1/2 in. Diamondhead USA VRS-T handguard, forged aluminum charging handle, Mil-Spec 6-pos. buffer tube, B5 Systems SOPMOD stock, CCA pistol grip, cow camo finish. New 2017.

Please contact the company directly for pricing and availability for this model.

WARZ M-4 RIFLE – 5.56 NATO cal., GIO, 16 in. lightweight stainless steel barrel, SureFire ProComp muzzle device, Magpul PMAG, steel micro gas block, A.R.M.S. front and rear sights, 15 in. Midwest Industries Gen III stainless steel handguard, forged lightweight enhanced upper receiver, BCM Ambi Gunfighter charging handle, Mil-Spec 6-position buffer tube, enhanced trigger guard, B5 Systems SOPMOD stock, Magpul MIAD pistol grip, Seekins Precision ambi selector switch. New 2016.

MSR $1,495		$1,250	$825	$575	$475	$425	$375	$350	

WARZ M-4 GM EDITION – 5.56 NATO cal., 16 in. fluted mid-length barrel, titanium birdcage flash hider, Magpul PMAG, nickel Teflon coated ejection port door, enhanced alloy trigger guard, ALG Defense Advanced Combat Trigger, Magpul SL Series buttstock, Magpul SL pistol grip, M4 feed ramps, Geissele 13 in. Super MK4 modular M-LOK handguard, Magpul M-LOK rail panel set, or Magpul M-LOK rail hand stop, forged A3M4 upper receiver, forged enhanced lower, Bravo Company Mod4 Gunfighter charging handle, ambi sling mount endplate, 6-pos. buffer tube, Seekins Precision ambi selector. New 2017.

MSR $1,365		$1,135	$725	$525	$465	$415	$375	$350	

WARZ M-4 TITANIUM EDITION – 5.56 NATO cal., 16 in. lightweight mid-length stainless steel barrel, Griffin Armament titanium Minimalist muzzle brake, M4 feed ramps, Magpul 30 shot PMAG, FDE enhanced alloy trigger guard, Geissele SSA-E trigger, A.R.M.S. front and rear folding sight set, FDE Seekins Precision ambi selector, stainless steel mid-length gas tube, Midwest Industries SS G3 15 in. free float handguard and two-tone handguard panel set, forged lightweight enhanced receivers, Bravo Company ambi Gunfighter charging handle, nickel Teflon coated bolt carrier group and 6-pos. buffer tube, black B5 Systems SOPMOD stock, two-tone Magpul MIAD modular pistol grip, HGTi titanium metal parts, includes plastic hard case. New 2017.

MSR $1,695		$1,385	$895	$675	$525	$450	$385	$350	

* **WarZ M-4 Titanium V2 Edition** – 5.56 NATO cal., 16 in. lightweight mid-length stainless steel barrel, titanium enhanced birdcage flash hider, M4 feed ramps, Magpul 30 shot PMAG, enhanced alloy trigger guard, Geissele Super Dynamic Combat trigger, Seekins Precision ambi selector, stainless steel mid-length gas tube, Midwest Industries 12 1/2 in. free float M-LOK lightweight handguard, Magpul rubber M-LOK rail, forged lightweight enhanced receivers, Bravo Company Mod4 Gunfighter charging handle, nickel Teflon coated BCG and 6-pos. buffer tube, B5 Systems Bravo stock with HGTi titanium buttstock metal, Magpul SL pistol grip, HGTi titanium metal parts, includes plastic hard case. New 2017.

MSR $1,695		$1,385	$895	$675	$525	$450	$385	$350	

* **WarZ M-4 Titanium X Edition** – 5.56 NATO cal., 16 in. chrome-lined M4 profile barrel, HGTi titanium birdcage flash hider, X Products X-15 skeletonized 50 round drum mag., enhanced alloy trigger guard, Geissele Automatics SSA-E trigger, A.R.M.S. front and rear backup sights, Noveske short throw ambi selector, M4 feed ramps, steel micro gas block, stainless steel carbine gas tube, X Products 14 1/2 in. Cobra free float M-LOK handguard and G10 M-LOK handguard panels, forged lightweight enhanced upper and forged lower receiver, Bravo Company ambi Gunfighter charging handle, nickel Teflon coated BCG and 6-pos. buffer tube, BufferLoc System, B5 Systems Bravo stock, X Products modular pistol grip, HGTi titanium metal parts, includes plastic hard case. New 2017.

MSR $1,895		$1,575	$995	$775	$575	$495	$425	$395	

ZM-4 SERIES – .223 Rem./5.56 NATO or .300 AAC Blackout (disc. 2015) cal., GIO, 16 or 20 in. barrel, forged upper and lower receiver, various configurations, black finish, detachable magazine, hard case. New 2004.

D 158 DSA INC., cont.

MSR	100%	98%	95%	90%	80%	70%	60%	Last MSR

* **ZM-4 .300 Blackout** – .300 AAC Blackout cal., GIO, 16 in. blue or stainless steel barrel with Trident flash hider, A3 flat-top alloy receiver, forged front sight base with bayonet lug, M4 handguard with heat shield, Hogue pistol grip, 6-position collapsible M4 stock, matte black finish. Mfg. 2013-2015.

| | $745 | $500 | $435 | $375 | $335 | $315 | $295 | $853 |

Add $20 for stainless steel barrel.

* **ZM-4 A2 Carbine** – 5.56 NATO cal., 16 in. M4 barrel with A2 flash hider, alloy upper and lower receiver, A2 carry handle receiver, forged front sight base with bayonet lug, M4 handguard with heat shield, 6-position collapsible M4 stock. Disc. 2015.

| | $725 | $500 | $435 | $375 | $335 | $315 | $295 | $831 |

* **ZM-4 A2 Rifle** – 5.56 NATO cal., 20 in. M4 barrel with A2 flash hider, alloy upper and lower receiver, A2 carry handle receiver, forged front sight base with bayonet lug, rifle length handguard with heat shield, fixed A2 stock, Hogue pistol grip. Disc. 2015.

| | $725 | $500 | $435 | $375 | $335 | $315 | $295 | $844 |

* **ZM-4 Flat-Top Carbine With Rail** – 5.56 NATO cal., 16 in. M4 barrel with A2 flash hider, alloy lower and A3 flat-top upper receiver, forged front sight base with bayonet lug, folding detachable rear sight, carbine length quad rail handguard, 6-pos. collapsible M4 stock, Hogue pistol grip. Mfg. 2015 only.

| | $875 | $550 | $465 | $395 | $350 | $325 | $300 | $1,050 |

* **ZM-4 Gas Piston CQB** – .223 Rem. cal., GPO, 16 in. chrome-lined free floating barrel, A2 flash hider, 30 shot mag., Mil-Spec forged lower receiver, CQB forged upper receiver, one-piece bolt carrier, quick change barrel system, collapsible CAR stock. Disc. 2010.

| | $2,295 | $1,450 | $1,075 | $675 | $595 | $525 | $475 | $2,870 |

* **ZM-4 MIDFAL** – 5.56 NATO cal., 16 in. chrome moly barrel with FAL Belgian style flash hider, detachable mag., forged alloy lower and flat-top upper receiver, forged front sight base with bayonet lug, enhanced steel charging handle and Delta ring, ambi selector switch, folding rear iron sight, Magpul enhanced trigger guard, Magpul MOE mid-length handguard, Magpul MOE pistol grip, Magpul or ACE fixed skeleton stock, includes hard gun case. Mfg. 2013-2015.

| | $800 | $525 | $450 | $385 | $340 | $325 | $295 | $936 |

* **ZM-4 Mid-Length Carbine** – 5.56 NATO cal., 16 in. fluted or non-fluted mid-length barrel with A2 flash hider, M4 A3 flat-top receiver, forged front sight base with bayonet lug, mid-length handguards with heat shield, alloy upper and lower receiver, 6-pos. collapsible M4 stock, Hogue pistol grip.

| MSR $834 | $725 | $500 | $435 | $375 | $335 | $315 | $295 | |

Add $13 for fluted barrel.

* **ZM-4 MK16 (Enhanced Carbine)** – 5.56 NATO cal., GIO, 16 in. enhanced MK16 fluted M4 barrel with YHM muzzle brake, alloy lower and A3 flat-top upper receiver, forged front sight base with bayonet lug, ambidextrous selector switch, enhanced Delta ring, Magpul MOE handguard, 6-position MOE stock, Magpul MOE pistol grip, matte black finish. Mfg. 2013-2015.

| | $800 | $525 | $450 | $385 | $340 | $325 | $295 | $929 |

* **ZM-4 M.R.C. (MULTI-ROLE CARBINE)** – 5.56 NATO cal., GIO, 16 in. chrome-lined heavy barrel, 3-prong Trident flash hider, steel low profile gas block, Magpul PMAG, Magpul MBUS front and rear sights, 13 1/2 in. Diamondhead USA VRS-T handguard, BCM Ambi Gunfighter charging handle, Mil-Spec 6-position buffer tube, B5 Systems SOPMOD stock, Hogue pistol grip. New 2016.

| MSR $1,275 | $1,065 | $650 | $500 | $450 | $395 | $350 | $325 | |

* **ZM-4 Spartan** – .223 Rem. cal., GIO, 16 in. fluted chrome moly barrel, Yankee Hill Machine Phantom flash hider, Mil-Spec forged lower and flat-top upper receiver, forged front sight base with lug, Magpul trigger guard, Robar NP3 bolt, carrier, and charging handle, Hogue pistol grip, SOPMOD collapsible stock, and two-piece rail system became standard 2013, 6.65 lbs. Disc. 2014.

| | $1,225 | $825 | $575 | $475 | $425 | $375 | $350 | $1,455 |

» **ZM-4 Spartan Leo** – 5.56 NATO cal., 16 in. fluted chrome moly barrel with Yankee Hill Machine Phantom flash hider, detachable mag., forged lower with Spartan Series logo, forged flat-top upper with mid-length gas system and forged front sight base, Rock River Arms competition trigger, Magpul trigger guard, Yankee Hill Machine two-piece rail system and plastic handguard, LMT SOPMOD collapsible stock, Hogue pistol grip, includes hard gun case, 7 lbs. Disc. 2015.

| | $1,225 | $825 | $575 | $475 | $425 | $375 | $350 | $1,455 |

* **ZM-4 Standard Flat-Top Carbine** – .223 Rem./5.56 NATO cal., GIO, 16 in. chrome moly M4 barrel with A2 flash hider, detachable mag., Mil-Spec forged lower and A3 flat-top upper receiver, forged front sight base with bayonet lug, M4 handguard with heat shield, 6-pos. collapsible M4 stock, Hogue pistol grip, includes hard gun case, 6 1/4 lbs.

| MSR $845 | $725 | $500 | $435 | $375 | $335 | $315 | $295 | |

Subtract $11 if without chrome-lined barrel.

DSA INC., cont. 159 D

MSR	100%	98%	95%	90%	80%	70%	60%	Last MSR

* **ZM-4 Standard Flat-Top Rifle** – 5.56 NATO cal., 20 in. M4 barrel with A2 flash hider, alloy lower and A3 flat-top upper receiver, forged front sight base with bayonet lug, rifle length handguard with heat shield, fixed A2 stock, Hogue pistol grip.

MSR $820		$695	$500	$425	$375	$335	$315	$295

* **ZM-4 Standard MRP** – .223 Rem. cal., GIO, 16 or 18 in. chrome-lined (16 in.) or stainless steel free float barrel, Mil-Spec forged lower receiver, LMT MRP forged upper receiver with 20 1/2 in. full-length quad rail, LMT enhanced bolt, dual extractor springs, collapsible CAR stock, detachable 30 shot mag., A2 flash hider. Disc. 2010.

		$2,125	$1,325	$995	$675	$595	$525	$475	$2,695

Add $100 for stainless steel barrel.

* **ZM-4 WerkerZ V1 Rifle** – 5.56 NATO cal., GIO, 16 in. fluted steel barrel, 3-prong Trident flash hider, Magpul PMAG, Magpul MOE M-LOK handguard, enhanced contour Delta ring, Picatinny gas block, forged lightweight enhanced upper receiver, Mil-Spec forged alloy charging handle, enhanced trigger guard, B5 Systems SOPMOD stock, Magpul MOE pistol grip. New 2016.

MSR $965		$825	$535	$450	$385	$340	$325	$295

* **ZM-4 WerkerZ V2 Rifle** – 5.56 NATO cal., GIO, 16 in. fluted heavy chrome-lined barrel, 3-prong Trident flash hider, Magpul PMAG, Magpul SL Series M-LOK handguard, enhanced contour Delta ring, Picatinny gas block, forged lightweight enhanced upper receiver, forged steel charging handle, Mil-Spec 6-position buffer tube, enhanced trigger guard, B5 Systems SOPMOD stock, Magpul MOE pistol grip. New 2016.

MSR $1,065		$895	$575	$475	$395	$350	$325	$300

Z-IAR RIFLE – 5.56 NATO cal., GIO, 16 in. chrome moly fluted barrel with A2 flash hider, detachable mag., VLTOR collapsible stock, forged lower with ambi safety switch, forged flat-top upper with steel charging handle, VLTOR rail interface handguard system with customizable rails, VLTOR collapsible stock, incorporates new features such as Bufferloc and Keyloc technologies, includes hard gun case, 8.4 lbs. Mfg. 2015 only.

Retail pricing was not available for this model.

DANE ARMORY LLC

Previous AR-15 style rifle manufacturer located in Mesa, AZ until 2013.

RIFLES: SEMI-AUTO

All rifles included a case and manual.

DCM SERVICE AR-15 – .223 Rem. cal., National Match barrel, F-marked front sight base, fixed synthetic pistol grip stock, free float forend tube, chromed bolt carrier, A4 configuration with carry handle, matte black finish.

	$1,525	$975	$750	$575	$495	$425	$375	$1,850

HIGH POWER MATCH AR – .223 Rem. or .308 Win. cal., heavy barrel, Dane Armory exclusive free float handguard, Sinclair or Centra sight options, wide variety of stocks, handguard, and accessories. Disc. 2013.

Base price on this model was $1,950.

PISTOL CALIBER AR – .223 Rem. or .308 Win. cal., heavy barrel, Dane Armory exclusive free float handguard, Sinclair or Centra sight options, wide variety of stocks, handguard, and accessories. Disc. 2013.

Base price on this model was $2,150.

DANIEL DEFENSE

Current manufacturer located in Black Creek, GA, with facilities also located in Ridgeland, SC.

PISTOLS: SEMI-AUTO

DDMK18 – 5.56 NATO cal., GIO, 10.3 in. cold hammer forged Govt. profile barrel with DD improved flash suppressor, pistol receiver extension, MK18 RIS II rail system, black or FDE hardcoat anodized finish, 5.4 lbs. New 2015.

MSR $1,836		$1,575	$1,385	$1,185	$1,065	$915	$785	$635

Add $263 for Law Tactical Gen III adaptor (new 2016).

DDM4300 – .300 AAC Blackout cal., GIO, 10.3 in. cold hammer forged S2W barrel with DD improved flash suppressor, pistol length gas system, pinned low profile gas block, 30 shot Magpul PMAG, pistol receiver extension, 9 in. M4 rail, polymer pistol grip with Soft Touch overmolding, black finish, 5.3 lbs. New 2015.

MSR $1,836		$1,575	$1,385	$1,185	$1,065	$915	$785	$635

DDM4V7p – 5.56 NATO or .300 AAC Blackout cal., GIO, 10.3 in. cold hammer forged Govt. profile barrel with DD improved flash suppressor, carbine length low profile gas block, Daniel Defense pistol grip with integral trigger guard and Soft Touch overmolding, M-LOK attachment technology, AR pistol receiver extension, SOB pistol stabilizing brace, Type III hardcoat anodized black finish, 5.4 lbs. New 2018.

MSR $1,679		$1,425	$1,250	$1,115	$985	$850	$725	$585

Add $263 for Law Tactical Gen III adaptor.

D 160 DANIEL DEFENSE, cont.

MSR	100%	98%	95%	90%	80%	70%	60%	Last MSR

RIFLES/CARBINES: SEMI-AUTO

In addition to the models listed below, Daniel Defense can build a custom rifle based on customer specifications. Please contact the company directly for this service (see Trademark Index). Daniel Defense also offers a complete line of tactical accessories and parts. All carbines and rifles come with a limited lifetime warranty. For information on Daniel Defense's Ambush line of hunting rifles please refer to Ambush Firearms in the "A" section.

DDM4 CARBINE SERIES – 5.56 NATO cal., GIO, 16 in. chrome-lined barrel, A2 birdcage flash hider, 10, 20, or 30 shot mag., Mil-Spec enhanced magwell, A4 feed ramp, A1.5 BUIS sight, pinned "F" marked front sight base, Omega X rails, Magpul 5-position collapsible buttstock (disc.) or Daniel Defense pistol grip buttstock with Soft Touch overmolding, A2 vertical grip, includes plastic case.

* **DDM4V1** – 5.56 NATO cal., GIO, 16 in. chrome-lined M4 standard or lightweight (new 2012) barrel, DD improved flash suppressor, curved and serrated front sight, DDM4 rail, QD swivel attachment points, original Daniel Defense rifle, DD buttstock with Soft Touch overmolding, black finish, 6.7 lbs.

MSR $1,889	$1,575	$995	$775	$575	$495	$425	$395	

* **DDM4V2** – 5.56 NATO cal., GIO, 16 in. chrome-lined barrel, similar to DDM4V1, except lightweight configuration with Omega X 7.0 rail system, also available with lightweight carbine barrel (DDM4V2LW). Mfg. 2011-2013.

$1,475	$950	$725	$550	$475	$395	$350	*$1,759*

* **DDM4V3** – 5.56 NATO or 6.8 SPC (mfg. 2012-2015) cal., GIO, 16 in. chrome-lined Government profile barrel or lightweight carbine barrel (DDM4V3LW, disc. 2015) with flash suppressor, curved and serrated front sight, 9 in. free float Omega quad rail, black finish, 6 1/2 lbs. Disc. 2016.

$1,475	$950	$725	$550	$475	$395	$350	*$1,799*

* **DDM4V4** – 5.56 NATO cal., GIO, 16 in. hammer forged carbine barrel, pinned low profile gas block, Omega X 9.0 rail system, available in lightweight profile (disc. 2011), no sights, fixed sights, or flip-up sights. Disc. 2013.

$1,350	$875	$650	$525	$450	$385	$350	*$1,639*

Add $120 for fixed sights.

Add $299 for flip-up sights (disc. 2011).

* **DDM4V5** – 5.56 NATO or .300 AAC Blackout (mfg. mid-2012-2014) cal., GIO, 16 in. hammer forged Govt. or lightweight barrel, DD improved flash suppressor, 30 shot mag., no sights, fixed sights, or flip-up sights (disc. 2011), pinned low profile gas block, Omega X (disc.) or DD M4 12.0 rail system, DD pistol grip buttstock with Soft Touch overmolding, Type III hardcoat anodized black, Daniel Defense Tornado or Mil-Spec+ Cerakote (disc. 2016) finish, 6.4 or 6.15 (lightweight) lbs.

MSR $1,773	$1,475	$950	$725	$550	$475	$395	$350

Add $168 for Daniel Defense Tornado or Mil-Spec+ Cerakote (disc. 2016) finish.

Add $299 for flip-up sights (disc. 2011).

»**DDM4V5S** – 5.56 NATO cal., AR-15 style, GIO, 14 1/2 in. (16.1 w/muzzle) Govt. profile chrome moly barrel with extended DD improved flash suppressor (pinned and welded to reach the NFA required barrel length), Daniel Defense buttstock, vertical grip and pistol grip, DDM4 Rail 12.0 with Mil-Std Picatinny rail with QD swivel attachment points, Type III hardcoat anodized black or Mil-Spec+ Cerakote finish, 6.23 lbs. New 2016.

MSR $1,857	$1,575	$995	$775	$575	$495	$425	$395

Add $67 for Mil-Spec+ Cerakote finish.

* **DDM4V7 / DDM4V7 LW** – 5.56 NATO or 6.8 SPC (disc. 2014) cal., GIO, 16 (5.56 NATO) or 18 (6.8 SPC, disc. 2014) in. Govt. or lightweight barrel with flash hider (disc.) or DD improved flash suppressor (new 2017), 30 shot mag., with or w/o sights, DD pistol grip buttstock with Soft Touch overmolding, flat-top receiver, full-length top Picatinny rail, forearm features three modular Picatinny rails that are moveable (disc.) or free floating MFR XS 15.0 handguard with M-LOK attachment technology (new 2017), Type III hardcoat anodized black, Mil-Spec+, Tornado (new 2017), or Deep Woods (new mid-2017) Cerakote finish, 6 1/2 lbs. New 2012.

MSR $1,679	$1,385	$895	$675	$525	$450	$385	$350

Add $110 for fixed sights.

Add $168 for Mil-Spec+, Tornado (new 2017), or Deep Woods (new mid-2017) Cerakote finish.

* **DDM4V7 PRO** – 5.56 NATO cal., GIO, low profile gas block, 18 in. S2W profile cold hammer forged steel barrel, Daniel Defense Muzzle Climb Mitigator, 30 shot Magpul PMAG, flared magwell, Geissele Automatics Super Dynamic 3 Gun trigger, Daniel Defense polymer buttstock and pistol grip with Soft Touch overmolding, Mil-Spec upper and lower receivers, M4 feed ramps, M16 profile bolt carrier group, 15 in. MFR XS M-LOK rail, full-length top Picatinny rail, VLTOR Gunfighter Mod 4 charging handle, 6-position Mil-Spec aluminum receiver extension, includes full latch impact plastic case, Type III hardcoat anodized black finish, 7.4 lbs. New mid-2016.

MSR $1,941	$1,600	$1,000	$775	$575	$495	$425	$395

* **DDM4V9** – 5.56 NATO cal., GIO, low profile gas block, mid-length gas system, 16 in. Govt. profile chrome moly barrel, Daniel Defense flash suppressor, 30 shot PMAG, CNC machined aluminum upper and lower receiver, glass

DANIEL DEFENSE, cont. 161 D

MSR	100%	98%	95%	90%	80%	70%	60%	Last MSR

filled polymer adj. buttstock with Soft Touch overmolding, flared magwell, vertical grip and pistol grip, 15 in. quad rail aluminum handguard, 3 low profile rail ladders, 6-position receiver extension, no sights, M16 chrome-lined bolt carrier group, H buffer, hardcoat anodized finish, 6.6 lbs. New 2014.

| MSR $1,773 | $1,475 | $950 | $725 | $550 | $475 | $395 | $350 | |

»**DDM4V9 S2W (Strength to Weight)** – 5.56 NATO cal., similar to DDM4V9, except has 18 in. S2W cold hammer forged profile barrel, black finish, 7 1/2 lbs. Mfg. 2014-2015.

| | $1,385 | $895 | $675 | $525 | $450 | $385 | $350 | $1,689 |

»**DDM4V9 Lightweight** – 5.56 NATO cal., similar to DDM4V9, except has 16 in. lightweight profile barrel and Daniel Defense Tornado Cerakote finish, 6.34 lbs. Mfg. 2014-2016.

| | $1,525 | $975 | $750 | $575 | $495 | $425 | $375 | $1,840 |

* **DDM4V11 / DDM4V11 LW** – 5.56 NATO cal., GIO, 16 in. cold hammer forged Govt. or lightweight barrel, iron sights, DD improved flash suppressor, 15 in. SLiM rail with KeyMod attachments, top Picatinny rail, iron sights, DD pistol grip buttstock with Soft Touch overmolding, Type III hardcoat anodized black, Cerakote finish in Mil-Spec+, Tornado, Deep Woods (new mid-2017), or Kryptek Typhon (new 2016), 6.28 lbs. New 2015.

| MSR $1,679 | $1,385 | $895 | $675 | $525 | $450 | $385 | $350 | |

Add $52 for Kryptek Typhon finish (new 2016).

Add $168 for Mil-Spec+, Tornado, or Deep Woods (new mid-2017) Cerakote finish.

* **DDM4V11 Pro** – 5.56 NATO cal., GIO, 18 in. cold hammer forged S2W barrel with DD Muzzle Climb Mitigator Gen II muzzle, 30 shot Magpul PMAG, Geissele Super Dynamic 3-Gun trigger, machined aluminum upper and lower receivers with M4 feed ramps and enhanced flared magwell, 15 in. SLiM rail, VLTOR BCM Gunfighter Mod 4 charging handle, top Picatinny rail with KeyMod attachment, 6-pos. aluminum receiver extension, polymer pistol grip buttstock with Soft Touch overmolding, black hardcoat anodized or Daniel Defense Tornado Cerakote (2016-2017) finish, 7 1/2 lbs. New 2015.

| MSR $1,941 | $1,600 | $1,000 | $775 | $575 | $495 | $425 | $395 | |

Add $158 for Daniel Defense Tornado Cerakote finish (mfg. 2016-2017).

* **DDM4V11 SLW** – 5.56 NATO cal., AR-15 style, GIO, 14 1/2 in. (16 in. with muzzle) cold hammer forged lightweight profile barrel, pinned and welded extended flash suppressor (to reach NFA requirements), polymer pistol grip buttstock with Soft Touch overmolding, free floating Slim Rail 12.0 handguard, KeyMod attachments, full-length top Picatinny rail, Type III hardcoat anodized black, Cerakote finishes in Mil-Spec+, Daniel Defense Tornado (mfg. 2016-2017) or Deep Woods (new 2018), 6.09 lbs. New 2016.

| MSR $1,752 | $1,475 | $950 | $725 | $550 | $475 | $395 | $350 | |

Add $168 for Mil-Spec+, Daniel Defense Tornado (disc. 2017), or Deep Woods Cerakote finish.

* **DDM4V11 300** – .300 AAC Blackout cal., GIO, free floating 16 in. cold hammer forged chrome moly S2W profile barrel, DD improved flash suppressor, carbine length gas system, polymer pistol grip buttstock with Soft Touch overmolding, 15 in. Picatinny free float SLiM rail with KeyMod attachment, forged aluminum upper and lower receivers, M16 bolt carrier group, Mil-Spec+ Cerakote finish, 6 3/4 lbs. New 2016.

| MSR $1,847 | $1,525 | $975 | $750 | $575 | $495 | $425 | $375 | |

DDM4 ISR (INTEGRALLY SUPPRESSED RIFLE) – .300 AAC Blackout cal., GIO, 16.1 in. S2W barrel (9 in. barrel with permanently attached suppressor), integral suppressor, 30 shot Magpul PMAG, pistol length gas system, 12 in. modular float rail with three modular Picatinny rail sections, 6-pos. aluminum receiver extension, enhanced flared magwell, rear receiver QD swivel, M4 feed ramps, polymer pistol grip buttstock with Soft Touch overmolding, black anodized or Mil-Spec+ (new 2017) or Deep Woods (new 2018) Cerakote finish, 7 1/2 lbs. Mfg. 2015, reintroduced 2017.

| MSR $3,044 | $2,450 | $1,595 | $1,200 | $700 | $675 | $575 | $525 | |

Add $154 for Mil-Spec+ (new 2017) or Deep Woods (new 2018) finish.

DD5V1 – .308 Win. cal., AR-15 style, mid-length gas system, 16 in. cold hammer forged S2W profile barrel, extended DD Superior suppression device, flared magwell, integral oversized trigger guard, Geissele SSA two-stage trigger, DD pistol grip buttstock with Soft Touch overmolding and two buttpads, ambidextrous safety selector, 15 in. Picatinny top rail, KeyMod handguard, configurable modular charging handle, Type III hardcoat anodized black, Mil-Spec+, Deep Woods (new mid-2017), Kryptek Typhon (disc.), or Tornado (new 2017) Cerakote finish, 8.3 lbs. New 2016.

| MSR $3,044 | $2,450 | $1,595 | $1,200 | $700 | $675 | $575 | $525 | |

Add $154 for Mil-Spec+, Deep Woods (new mid-2017) or Tornado (new 2017) Cerakote finish.

Add $150 for Kryptek Typhon finish (mfg. 2016 only).

* **DD5V1m** – .308 Win. cal., AR-15 style, mid-length gas system, 16 in. cold hammer forged S2W profile barrel with integral DD improved flash suppressor, flared magwell, integral oversized trigger guard, Geissele SSA two-stage trigger, DD pistol grip buttstock with Soft Touch overmolding and two buttpads, ambidextrous safety selector, 15 in. Picatinny top rail, M-LOK handguard, configurable modular charging handle, Type III hardcoat anodized black or Deep Woods Cerakote finish, 8.3 lbs. New 2018.

| MSR $3,044 | $2,450 | $1,595 | $1,200 | $700 | $675 | $575 | $525 | |

Add $154 for Deep Woods Cerakote finish.

D 162 DANIEL DEFENSE, cont.

MSR	100%	98%	95%	90%	80%	70%	60%	Last MSR

DD5V2 – .308 Win. cal., free floating 18 in. cold hammer forged S2W profile barrel, extended DD superior suppression device, rifle length gas system, DD pistol grip buttstock with Soft Touch overmolding and two buttpads, 15 in. top Picatinny rail, KeyMod handguard, ambi safety selector, mag. catch. bolt release, and configurable modular charging handle, black or Daniel Defense Deep Woods (new 2018) finish, 8.6 lbs. New 2016.

| MSR $3,044 | $2,450 | $1,595 | $1,200 | $700 | $675 | $575 | $525 | |

Add $154 for Daniel Defense Deep Woods finish (new 2018).

* **DD5V2m** – .308 Win. cal., free floating 18 in. cold hammer forged S2W profile barrel, extended DD superior suppression device, rifle length gas system, DD pistol grip buttstock with Soft Touch overmolding and two buttpads, 15 in. top Picatinny rail, M-LOK handguard, ambi safety selector, mag. catch bolt release, and configurable modular charging handle, black finish, 8.6 lbs. New 2018.

| MSR $3,044 | $2,450 | $1,595 | $1,200 | $700 | $675 | $575 | $525 | |

DD CARBINE SERIES – 5.56 NATO or 6.8 SPC cal., GIO, 16 in. chrome-lined barrel, similar to DDM4 Series, except Mil-Spec buttstock. New 2010.

* **DDXV/XV EZ** – GIO, 16 in. cold hammer forged barrel, "F" marked fixed front sight base, flared magwell on lower receiver, Magpul enhanced trigger guard, M16 bolt carrier group, rear receiver QD sling swivel attachment, with (XV EZ) or w/o (XV, disc. 2011) EZ CAR 7.0 rail system and A1 fixed rear sight. Disc. 2013.

| | $1,175 | $775 | $550 | $465 | $415 | $375 | $350 | $1,419 |

Add $68 for EZ CAR 7.0 rail system.

Add $129 for XVM model with mid-length barrel.

* **DDV6.8** – 6.8 SPC cal., GIO, 16 in. cold hammer forged mid-length barrel, Omega X 9.0 VFG and A1.5 fixed rear sight. Disc. 2011.

| | $1,275 | $850 | $600 | $495 | $425 | $375 | $350 | $1,537 |

M4A1 – 5.56 NATO cal., AR-15 style, GIO, pinned low profile gas block, 14 1/2 in. (16 in. w/muzzle) cold hammer forged M4 profile barrel with pinned and welded (to reach NFA requirements) DD improved flash suppressor, M4A1 RIS II rail system, Type III hardcoat anodized FDE or Mil-Spec+ or Deep Woods (new mid-2017) Cerakote finish, 6 3/4 lbs. New 2016.

| MSR $1,910 | $1,600 | $1,000 | $775 | $575 | $495 | $425 | $395 | |

Add $168 for Mil-Spec+ or Deep Woods (new mid-2017) Cerakote finish.

MK12 – 5.56 NATO cal., GIO, 18 in. cold hammer forged stainless steel MK12 barrel, DD improved flash suppressor, rifle length gas system, 20 shot Magpul PMAG, upper receiver with 12 in. M4 free floating rail, Geissele SSA two-stage trigger, 6-pos. aluminum receiver extension, VLTOR Mod 4 charging handle, polymer pistol grip buttstock with Soft Touch overmolding, Type III hardcoat anodized black, DD Tornado Cerakote, DD Deep Woods (new 2018), or Kryptek Typhon (2016-2017) finish, 7.41 lbs. New mid-2014.

| MSR $2,099 | $1,675 | $1,000 | $825 | $625 | $550 | $475 | $425 | |

Add $50 for Kryptek Typhon finish (new 2016).

Add $168 for Daniel Defense Tornado or DD Deep Woods Cerakote finish.

DARK STORM INDUSTRIES, LLC (DSI)

Current AR-15 style rifle manufacturer as well as AR-15 parts and accessories manufacturer/distributor established in late 2012, located in Oakdale, NY.

PISTOLS: SEMI-AUTO

DS-9 HAILSTORM – 9mm Para. cal., 7 1/2 in. threaded barrel, cone flash hider, 17 shot detachable mag., ultralight narrow profile KeyMod 10 in. barrel shroud, billet aluminum lower and upper receiver with last round bolt hold open, ambi safety selector, saddle cheek riser, Thordsen enhanced buffer tube cover with QD sling sockets, Hogue pistol grip, black or FDE (disc. 2017) finish, 3 lbs. 14 oz.

| MSR $1,095 | $925 | $850 | $725 | $625 | $550 | $475 | $425 | |

Add $100 for FDE finish (disc. 2017).

DS-15 HAILSTORM – 5.56 NATO cal., 7 1/2 in. threaded barrel, conical muzzle blast deflector, 30 shot detachable mag., billet aluminum lower receiver, forged upper receiver with forward assist and ejection port cover, M16 bolt carrier group, ambi safety selector, ultralight narrow profile KeyMod 9 in. barrel shroud, saddle cheek riser, Thordsen enhanced buffer tube cover with QD sling sockets, Hogue pistol grip, black or FDE (disc. 2017) finish, 5 lbs. 13 oz.

| MSR $995 | $850 | $725 | $650 | $585 | $515 | $450 | $395 | |

Add $100 for FDE finish (disc. 2017).

RIFLES: SEMI-AUTO

DS-9 LIGHTNING – 9mm Para. cal., GIO, 16 in. SOCOM profile threaded stainless steel barrel with Competition compensator, Glock 17 shot mag., billet aluminum lower and forged upper receiver with forward assist and ejection port

DARK STORM INDUSTRIES, LLC (DSI), cont. 163 D

MSR	100%	98%	95%	90%	80%	70%	60%	Last MSR

cover, 9mm nickel boron coated bolt carrier group, ambidextrous safety selector, 11 in. forearm Troy Battle Alpha rail, trigger lock, Magpul CTR adj. stock, Hogue pistol grip, black or FDE (disc. 2017) finish.

| MSR $1,295 | $1,075 | $675 | $500 | $450 | $400 | $350 | $325 | |

Add $100 for FDE finish (disc. 2017).

* **DS-9 Lightning Featureless** – 9mm Para. cal., GIO, 16 in. SOCOM profile stainless steel barrel, Glock 10 shot mag., billet aluminum lower and forged upper receiver with forward assist and ejection port cover, nickel boron coated 9mm bolt carrier group, Spec Ops Gen 2 charging handle, DSI billet ambidextrous safety selector, 11 in. forearm Troy Battle Alpha rail, Thordsen FRS-15 Gen. 2 rifle stock with rubber buttpad, Thordsen enhanced buffer tube cover with QD sling sockets, ambidextrous sling plate, black or FDE (disc. 2017) finish.

| MSR $1,295 | $1,075 | $675 | $500 | $450 | $400 | $350 | $325 | |

Add $100 for FDE finish (disc. 2017).

DS-9 MOE – 9mm Para. cal., GIO, 16 in. M4 profile threaded Nitride barrel with A2 style birdcage flash hider, Glock 17 shot mag., billet aluminum lower and forged upper receiver with forward assist and ejection port cover, trigger lock, 7 in. Magpul MOE drop-in (disc. 2016) or M-LOK (new 2017) forearm, rail front sight block, Magpul MOE adj. stock and pistol grip, black, pink, grey, FDE, or ODG finish.

| MSR $995 | $850 | $550 | $465 | $395 | $350 | $325 | $295 | |

* **DS-9 MOE Featureless** – 9mm Para. cal., GIO, 16 in. M4 profile barrel, Glock 10 shot mag., billet aluminum lower and forged upper receiver with forward assist and ejection port cover, Magpul MOE 7 in. drop-in (disc. 2016) or M-LOK (new 2017) forearm, rail front sight block, Thordsen FRS-15 rifle stock, Thordsen standard buffer tube cover, trigger lock, black, pink (disc. 2017), grey, FDE, or ODG finish.

| MSR $995 | $850 | $550 | $465 | $395 | $350 | $325 | $295 | |

DS-9 TYPHOON – 9mm Para. cal., GIO, 16 in. M4 profile threaded Nitride barrel with CQB compensator, Glock 17 shot mag., trigger lock, billet aluminum lower, forged upper rec. with forward assist and ejection port cover, ambidextrous safety selector, DSI Ultralight narrow profile KeyMod 12 in. (disc. 2016) or M-LOK (new 2017) forearm, Magpul CTR adj. stock, Hogue pistol grip, ambidextrous sling plate, black, FDE, or ODG finish, 6 lbs. 4 oz.

| MSR $1,195 | $995 | $625 | $495 | $450 | $395 | $350 | $325 | |

Add $100 for FDE or ODG finish.

* **DS-9 Typhoon Featureless** – 9mm Para. cal., GIO, 16 in. M4 profile Nitride barrel, Glock 10 shot mag., billet aluminum lower and forged upper receiver with forward assist and ejection port cover, Spec Ops Gen 2 charging handle, ambidextrous safety selector, DSI Ultralight narrow profile KeyMod 12 in. (disc. 2016) or M-LOK (new 2017) forearm, trigger lock, Thordsen FRS-15 Gen 2 rifle stock with rubber buttpad, Thordsen enhanced buffer tube cover with QD sling sockets, ambidextrous sling plate, black, FDE, or ODG finish.

| MSR $1,195 | $995 | $625 | $495 | $450 | $395 | $350 | $325 | |

Add $100 for FDE or ODG finish.

DS-10 HUNTER – .308 Win. or 6.5mm Creedmoor cal., 18 in. threaded barrel, steel thread protector, Lancer L7 10 shot fixed or Magpul 20 shot PMAG, Magpul MOE stock, Hogue overmolded rubber pistol grip, billet aluminum upper and lower receivers, forward assist, ejection port cover, charging handle, safety selector, Ultralight narrow profile M-LOK 15 in. forearm, steel micro gas block, mid-length gas system, Next G2 camo finish. New 2018.

| MSR $1,395 | $1,150 | $750 | $550 | $465 | $415 | $375 | $350 | |

Add $50 for 6.5mm Creedmoor cal.

DS-10 LIGHTNING – .308 Win. or 6.5mm Creedmoor cal., mid-length gas system, 18 in. threaded barrel, stainless steel compensator, 10 (fixed) or 20 (detachable) shot Magpul PMAG, Troy Battle rail Alpha 15 in. forearm, steel micro gas block, nickel boron bolt carrier group, billet aluminum upper and lower receiver, no sights, trigger lock, Spec Ops Gen 2 charging handle, ambi safety selector, Magpul CTR adj. stock, ambi sling plate, Hogue overmolded rubber pistol grip, black finish. New 2017.

| MSR $1,595 | $1,315 | $850 | $625 | $500 | $435 | $375 | $350 | |

Add $50 for 6.5mm Creedmoor cal.

* **DS-10 Lightning Featureless** – .308 Win. or 6.5mm Creedmoor cal., mid-length gas system, 18 in. stainless steel barrel, 10 shot detachable Magpul PMAG, billet aluminum upper and lower receiver, Spec Ops Gen 2 charging handle, ambi safety selector, no sights, trigger lock, Thordsen standard buffer tube cover, nickel boron bolt carrier group, Troy Battle Rail Alpha 15 in. forearm, steel micro gas block, Thordsen FRS-15 rifle stock, black finish. New 2017.

| MSR $1,595 | $1,315 | $850 | $625 | $500 | $435 | $375 | $350 | |

Add $50 for 6.5mm Creedmoor cal.

DS-10 MOE – .308 Win. or 6.5mm Creedmoor cal., mid-length gas system, 18 in. threaded barrel with A2 style birdcage flash hider, 10 (fixed) or 20 (detachable) shot Magpul PMAG, no sights, Magpul MOE 11 in. drop-in or M-LOK forearm, Magpul MOE adj. stock, Magpul MOE pistol grip, black upper and lower receiver, black, FDE, or ODG (mfg. 2017 only) stock, grip, and forearm finish. New 2017.

| MSR $1,195 | $995 | $625 | $495 | $450 | $395 | $350 | $325 | |

Add $50 for 6.5mm Creedmoor cal.

D 164 DARK STORM INDUSTRIES, LLC (DSI), cont.

MSR	100%	98%	95%	90%	80%	70%	60%	Last MSR

* DS-10 MOE Featureless – .308 Win. or 6.5mm Creedmoor cal., mid-length gas system, 18 in. barrel, 10 shot Magpul PMAG, trigger lock, no sights, Magpul MOE 11 in. drop-in or M-LOK forearm, Thordsen FRS-15 rifle stock, Thordsen standard buffer tube cover, aluminum top and bottom rail gas block, billet aluminum upper and lower receiver, black, FDE, or ODG (mfg. 2017 only) finish. New 2017.

| MSR $1,195 | $995 | $625 | $495 | $450 | $395 | $350 | $325 | |

Add $50 for 6.5mm Creedmoor cal.

DS-10 TYPHOON – .308 Win. or 6.5mm Creedmoor cal., mid-length gas system, 18 in. threaded barrel, CQB compensator, 20 shot Magpul PMAG, billet aluminum upper and lower receiver, forward assist, ejection port cover, Spec Ops Gen 2 charging handle, no sights, trigger lock, ultralight narrow profile M-LOK 15 in. forearm, Magpul CTR adj. stock, ambi sling plate, Hogue overmolded rubber pistol grip, black, FDE, or ODG finish. New 2017.

| MSR $1,395 | $1,150 | $750 | $550 | $465 | $415 | $375 | $350 | |

Add $50 for 6.5mm Creedmoor cal.

Add $100 for FDE or ODG finish.

* DS-10 Typhoon Featureless – .308 Win. or 6.5mm Creedmoor cal., mid-length gas system, 18 in. barrel, Magpul 10 shot PMAG, steel micro gas block, no sights, Spec Ops Gen 2 charging handle, trigger lock, billet aluminum upper and lower receiver, ambi safety selector, Thordsen standard buffer tube cover, ultralight narrow profile M-LOK 15 in. forearm, Thordsen FRS-15 rifle stock, black, FDE, or ODG finish. New 2017.

| MSR $1,395 | $1,150 | $750 | $550 | $465 | $415 | $375 | $350 | |

Add $50 for 6.5mm Creedmoor cal.

Add $100 for FDE or ODG finish.

DS-15 HUNTER – .300 AAC Blackout cal., carbine gas system, 16 in. DSI Nitride barrel, 10 shot mag., trigger lock, 90 degree safety selector, forged upper receiver w/forward assist and ejection port cover, M16 bolt carrier group, extended takedown and pivot pins, charging handle, Custom Hydro-Dipped Next Gen Camo finish, 6 lbs. 15 oz. New 2018.

| MSR $1,095 | $915 | $575 | $475 | $415 | $350 | $325 | $300 | |

DS-15 JULY 4th 2018 FEATURELESS – 5.56 NATO cal., 16 in. barrel, 10 shot mag., M4 style fixed stock, spur grip, Mil-Spec buffer tube, carbine gas system, forged aluminum open trigger lower receiver, forged aluminum upper with forward assist and ejection port cover, M16 BCG, 10 in. free float quad rail forearm, black finish. New 2018.

| MSR $695 | $595 | $485 | $415 | $350 | $315 | $295 | $275 | |

DS-15 LIGHTNING – 5.56 NATO, .300 AAC Blackout (disc. 2017), or .458 SOCOM (disc. 2017) cal., GIO, micro gas block, 16 in. stainless steel threaded barrel with Competition compensator, fixed or detachable 10 shot Magpul PMAG, no sights, trigger lock, FX billet lower receiver, forged upper w/forward assist and ejection port cover, 11 in. Troy Battle rail Alpha forearm, Magpul CTR adj. stock, Hogue pistol grip, black or FDE (disc. 2017) finish.

| MSR $1,295 | $1,075 | $675 | $500 | $450 | $400 | $350 | $325 | |

Add $100 for .458 SOCOM cal. (disc. 2017).

* DS-15 Lightning Featureless – 5.56 NATO, .300 AAC Blackout (disc. 2017), or .458 SOCOM (disc. 2017) cal., GIO, micro gas block, 16 in. stainless steel barrel, 10 shot Magpul PMAG, no sights, trigger lock, billet lower receiver, forged upper w/forward assist and ejection port cover, NiB M16 bolt carrier group, Spec Ops Gen 2 charging handle, ambidextrous safety selector, 11 in. Troy Battle Alpha rail forearm, Thordsen FRS-15 Gen 2 rifle stock with rubber buttpad, Thordsen enhanced buffer tube w/QD sling sockets, black or FDE (disc. 2017) finish.

| MSR $1,295 | $1,075 | $675 | $500 | $450 | $400 | $350 | $325 | |

Add $100 for .458 SOCOM cal. (disc. 2017).

DS-15 M4S – 5.56 NATO cal., 16 in. threaded barrel, A2 birdcage flash hider, 30 shot mag., carbine gas system, A2 front sight base with bayonet lug and sling swivel, dual diopter rear sight, forged aluminum closed trigger lower receiver, forged upper with forward assist and ejection port cover, M16 bolt carrier group, 7 in. drop-in forearm, M4 style adj. stock, Mil-Spec buffer tube, A2 pistol grip, black finish. New 2017.

| MSR $845 | $725 | $500 | $435 | $375 | $335 | $315 | $295 | |

* DS-15 M4S Featureless – 5.56 NATO cal., 16 in. barrel, 10 shot mag., A2 front sight base and sling swivel, Magpul MBUS rear sight, Thordsen fixed rifle stock, Thordsen standard buffer tube cover, buffer tube, carbine gas system, forged aluminum lower and upper receiver with forward assist and ejection port cover, M16 BCG, CAR15 7 in. drop-in forearm, black finish. New 2018.

| MSR $845 | $725 | $500 | $435 | $375 | $335 | $315 | $295 | |

DS-15 MOE – 5.56 NATO or .300 AAC Blackout cal., GIO, rail gas block, 16 in. M4 profile threaded barrel with A2 style birdcage flash hider, 20 shot fixed or detachable Magpul PMAG, trigger lock, no sights, Magpul MOE 7 in. drop-in (disc. 2016) or M-LOK (new 2017) forearm, Magpul MOE adj. pistol grip stock, billet lower receiver and forged upper with forward assist and ejection port cover, black, grey, pink, FDE, or ODG finish.

| MSR $895 | $765 | $515 | $440 | $375 | $335 | $315 | $295 | |

Add $50 for .300 AAC Blackout cal.

DARK STORM INDUSTRIES, LLC (DSI), cont. 165 D

MSR	100%	98%	95%	90%	80%	70%	60%	Last MSR

* **DS-15 MOE Featureless** – 5.56 NATO or .300 AAC Blackout cal., GIO, rail gas block, 16 in. SOCOM profile blued barrel, 10 shot Magpul PMAG, no sights, trigger lock, billet lower receiver and forged upper with forward assist and ejection port cover, M16 bolt carrier group, Magpul MOE 7 in. drop-in (disc. 2016) or M-LOK (new 2017) forearm, Thordsen FRS-15 rifle stock, Thordsen standard buffer tube cover, black, grey, pink, FDE, or ODG finish.

| MSR $895 | $765 | $515 | $440 | $375 | $335 | $315 | $295 | |

Add $50 for .300 AAC Blackout cal.

DS-15 SIGNATURE WILDFIRE – 5.56 NATO cal., carbine gas system, 16 in. threaded barrel, CQB compensator, 30 shot Amend mag., steel micro gas block, Ultralight narrow profile M-LOK 12 in. forearm, Signature Series red anodized billet safety selector levers, billet mag. release button, and Mil-Spec buffer tube, Signature Series drop-in trigger and matching Oakley Fuel Cell sunglasses, trigger lock, billet aluminum lower and forged upper receiver with forward assist and ejection port cover, Spec Ops Gen 2 charging handle, no sights, Magpul CTR adj. stock, ambi sling plate, Hogue pistol grip, matte black & gray Cerakote finish, 6 lbs. 5 oz. Mfg. 2017 only.

| | $1,475 | $950 | $725 | $550 | $475 | $395 | $350 | $1,795 |

* **DS-15 Signature Wildfire Featureless** – 5.56 NATO cal., carbine gas system, 16 in. M4 profile barrel, 10 shot Magpul PMAG, steel micro gas block, billet aluminum lower receiver and forged upper with forward assist and ejection port cover, Spec Ops Gen 2 charging handle, no sights, trigger lock, billet ambi safety selector, Ultralight narrow profile M-LOK 12 in. forearm, Signature Series red anodized billet safety selector levers, red anodized billet mag. release button, drop-in trigger, and matching Oakley fuel cell sunglasses, Thordsen FRS-15 Gen 2 rifle stock with rubber buttpad, Thordsen enhanced buffer tube cover with QD sling sockets, ambi sling plate, matte black and gray Cerakote finish, 6 lbs. 12 oz. Mfg. 2017 only.

| | $1,475 | $950 | $725 | $550 | $475 | $395 | $350 | $1,795 |

* **DS-15 Signature Wildfire Fixed** – 5.56 NATO cal., carbine gas system, 16 in. threaded barrel, CQB compensator, fixed 10 shot Magpul PMAG, steel micro gas block, Signature Series red anodized billet safety selector levers, red anodized extended takedown and pivot pins, red anodized Mil-Spec buffer tube, Signature Series drop-in trigger and matching Oakley fuel cell sunglasses, trigger lock, no sights, FX billet aluminum lower receiver, forged upper receiver with forward assist and ejection port cover, Spec Ops Gen 2 charging handle, Ultralight narrow profile M-LOK 12 in. forearm, Magpul CTR adj. stock, ambi sling plate, Hogue pistol grip, matte black and gray Cerakote finish, 6 lbs. 15 oz. Mfg. 2017 only.

| | $1,475 | $950 | $725 | $550 | $475 | $395 | $350 | $1,795 |

DS-15 2018 SIGNATURE SERIES FREEDOM FLAG – 5.56 NATO cal., 16 in. threaded stainless steel barrel, stainless steel CQB compensator, fixed 10 shot Magpul PMAG or 30 shot detachable mag., Magpul CTR adj. stock, ambi sling plate, Hogue pistol grip, optic ready, carbine gas system, forged upper receiver with forward assist and ejection port cover, billet aluminum lower, Spec Ops Gen 2 charging handle, 15 in. extended length M-LOK forearm, billet ambidextrous 90 degree safety selector, M16 (10 shot) or nickel Teflon (20 shot) BCG, steel micro gas block, Signature Series Brush finish on barrel and compensator, Signature Series Battle Worn American Flag Cerakote finish, 6 lbs. 12 oz. New 2018.

| MSR $1,776 | $1,475 | $950 | $725 | $550 | $475 | $395 | $350 | |

* **DS-15 2018 Signature Series Freedom Flag Featureless** – 5.56 NATO cal., 16 in. stainless steel barrel, 10 shot Magpul PMAG, Thordsen FRS-15 Gen 2 rifle stock with rubber buttpad, Thordsen enhanced buffer tube cover with QD sling sockets, optic ready, carbine gas system, forged upper receiver with forward assist and ejection port cover, billet aluminum lower, billet ambidextrous charging handle, 15 in. extended length M-LOK forearm, billet ambidextrous 90 degree safety selector, NiB BCG, steel micro gas block, Signature Series Brush finish on barrel and compensator, Signature Series Battle Worn American Flag Cerakote finish, 6 lbs. 12 oz. New 2018.

| MSR $1,776 | $1,475 | $950 | $725 | $550 | $475 | $395 | $350 | |

DS-15 SPORT – 5.56 NATO cal., GIO, rail gas block, 16 in. SOCOM profile barrel, 30 shot fixed or detachable Magpul PMAG, billet lower and forged sport upper receiver, trigger lock, M16 bolt carrier group, DSI 7 in. drop-in quad rail forearm, M4 style adj. pistol grip stock, black finish. Disc. 2017.

| | $675 | $500 | $425 | $375 | $335 | $315 | $295 | $795 |

* **DS-15 Sport Featureless** – 5.56 NATO cal., GIO, rail gas block, 16 in. SOCOM profile barrel, 10 shot Magpul PMAG, trigger lock, no sights, FX billet lower receiver and forged Sport side upper, M16 bolt carrier group, DSI 7 in. quad rail forearm, M4 style pinned stock, Spur Gen 2 grip, black finish. Disc. 2017.

| | $675 | $500 | $425 | $375 | $335 | $315 | $295 | $795 |

DS-15 THUNDER – 5.56 NATO or .300 AAC Blackout cal., GIO, micro gas block, 16 in. threaded barrel with Competition compensator, fixed or detachable 10 shot Magpul PMAG, no sights, trigger lock, FX billet lower receiver, forged upper w/forward assist and ejection port cover, 10 1/4 in. Diamondhead VRS-T (disc. 2016) or KeyMod (new 2017) forearm, Magpul STR adj. stock, Hogue pistol grip, black finish. Disc. 2017.

| | $1,150 | $750 | $550 | $465 | $415 | $375 | $350 | $1,395 |

D 166 DARK STORM INDUSTRIES, LLC (DSI), cont.

MSR	100%	98%	95%	90%	80%	70%	60%	Last MSR

* **DS-15 Thunder Featureless** – 5.56 NATO or .300 AAC Blackout cal., GIO, micro gas block, 16 in. barrel, 10 shot detachable Magpul PMAG, no sights, trigger lock, KeyMod forearm (new 2017), Thordsen FRS-15 rifle stock with rubber buttpad, black finish. Disc. 2017.

	$1,150	$750	$550	$465	$415	$375	$350	$1,395

DS-15 TYPHOON – 5.56 NATO or .300 AAC Blackout cal., GIO, micro gas block, 16 in. M4 profile threaded barrel with CQB compensator, fixed or detachable 10 shot PMAG, trigger lock, no sights, FX billet lower receiver, forged upper with forward assist and ejection port cover, M16 bolt carrier group, ambidextrous safety selector, DSI Ultralight narrow profile KeyMod 12 in. forearm (disc. 2016) or upgraded to M-LOK (new 2017) forearm, Magpul CTR adj. stock, Hogue pistol grip, ambidextrous sling plate, black, FDE, or ODG finish, 6 lbs. 15 oz.

MSR $1,095	$915	$575	$475	$415	$350	$325	$300	

Add $100 for FDE or ODG finish.

* **DS-15 Typhoon .22 LR** – .22 LR cal., blowback operation, 16 in. threaded barrel, CQB compensator, fixed 10 shot extended style mag., Magpul CTR adj. stock, ambi sling plate, Hogue pistol grip, optic ready, trigger lock, 12 in. ultralight narrow profile M-LOK forearm, billet aluminum lower and forged upper receiver with forward assist and ejection port cover, ambi charging handle, ambi 90 degree safety selector, stainless steel .22 LR BCG, black finish, 6 lbs. New 2018.

MSR $1,095	$915	$575	$475	$415	$350	$325	$300	

* **DS-15 Typhoon Featureless** – 5.56 NATO or .300 AAC Blackout cal., micro gas block and carbine gas system, 16 in. SOCOM profile barrel, 10 shot Magpul PMAG, trigger lock, no sights, billet lower receiver, forged upper w/forward assist and ejection port cover, Spec Ops Gen 2 charging handle, ambidextrous safety selector, DSI Ultralight narrow profile KeyMod 12 in. (disc. 2016) or M-LOK (new 2017) forearm, Thordsen FRS-15 Gen 2 rifle stock with rubber buttpad, Thordsen enhanced buffer tube cover w/QD sling sockets, ambidextrous sling plate, black, FDE, or OD Green finish, 6 lbs. 12 oz.

MSR $1,095	$915	$575	$475	$415	$350	$325	$300	

Add $100 for FDE or OD Green finish.

DEL-TON INCORPORATED

Current rifle and pistol manufacturer located in Elizabethtown, NC. Dealer sales. Previously distributed until 2011 by American Tactical Imports, located in Rochester, NY.

PISTOLS: SEMI-AUTO

LIMA KEYMOD PISTOL – 5.56 NATO cal., AR-15 style, 7 1/2 in. barrel with A2 flash hider, 30 shot mag., aluminum trigger guard, M4 feed ramps, pistol length handguard, Samson Evolution KeyMod 6 1/2 in. free float rail, forged aluminum lower and flat-top upper receivers, pistol buffer tube, hardcoat anodized black finish, 4.8 lbs. New 2016.

	$775	$685	$615	$550	$485	$415	$375	

RIFLES/CARBINES: SEMI-AUTO

Del-Ton manufactures a wide variety of AR-15 style carbines/rifles, as well as a full line of rifle kits. Many options, accessories, and parts are also available. Please contact the company for more information, including current availability and options (see Trademark Index). All rifles include a hard case, two mags., and buttstock cleaning kit.

A2 CARBINE – .223 Rem. cal., GIO, 16 in. heavy chrome moly barrel, fixed A2 stock, CAR handguard with single heat shield, A2 flash hider, black furniture, carry handle, includes sling. Disc. 2012.

	$645	$500	$415	$370	$325	$300	$275	$750

A2 DT-4 CARBINE – .223 Rem. cal., GIO, 16 in. chrome moly barrel, 6-position M4 stock, 30 shot mag., CAR handguard with single heat shield, A2 flash hider, black furniture, includes sling. Disc. 2012.

	$645	$500	$415	$370	$325	$300	$275	$750

ALPHA 220H – 5.56 NATO cal., GIO, 20 in. chrome moly heavy profile barrel with threaded muzzle and A2 flash hider, forged aluminum T6 upper and lower receiver, 30 shot mag., A2 configuration with rear sight, rifle length handguard with single heat shield, standard A2 Black Zytel buttstock with trapdoor assembly, A2 grip, black furniture, 8.2 lbs.

MSR $918	$785	$525	$450	$385	$340	$325	$295	

ALPHA 308 MLOK – .308 Win. cal., 18 in. heavy profile barrel, threaded muzzle, A2 flash hider, 20 shot Magpul PMAG, right-hand ejection, SST, integral enhanced trigger guard, Magpul MOE buttstock, Mil-Spec buffer tube, Ergo Ambi grip, M4 feed ramps, forged aluminum upper and lower receivers, Picatinny rail, Magpul MOE M-LOK rifle length handguard, hardcoat anodized black finish, 9 lbs. New 2018.

MSR $1,100	$915	$575	$475	$415	$350	$325	$300	

ALPHA 308 SS MLOK – .308 Win. cal., 18 in. stainless steel heavy profile barrel, threaded muzzle, A2 flash hider, 20 shot Magpul PMAG, right-hand ejection, SST, integral enhanced trigger guard, Magpul MOE buttstock, Mil-Spec buffer

DEL-TON INCORPORATED, cont. 167 D

MSR	100%	98%	95%	90%	80%	70%	60%	Last MSR

tube, Ergo Ambi grip, M4 feed ramps, forged aluminum upper and lower receivers, Picatinny rail, Magpul MOE M-LOK rifle length handguard, hardcoat anodized black finish, 9 lbs. New 2018.

| MSR $1,114 | $915 | $575 | $475 | $415 | $350 | $325 | $300 | |

ALPHA 320H – 5.56 NATO cal., GIO, similar to Alpha 220H, except features M4 feed ramps, no sights, and A3 flat-top receiver, 8 lbs.

| MSR $822 | $695 | $500 | $425 | $375 | $335 | $315 | $295 | |

ALPHA 320G (STANDARD GOVERNMENT PROFILE RIFLE) – 5.56 NATO cal., GIO, 20 in. chrome moly standard or heavy profile barrel with threaded muzzle and A2 flash hider, Government profile, M4 feed ramps, A2 reinforced Zytel buttstock, A2 grip, 30 shot mag., standard length handguard with single heat shield, black furniture, forged aluminum upper and lower receivers, A3 flat-top or A2 upper with carry handle, includes sling, 7.4 lbs.

| MSR $822 | $695 | $500 | $425 | $375 | $335 | $315 | $295 | |

ALPHA 320P – 5.56 NATO cal., GIO, post-ban rifle, 20 in. heavy chrome moly barrel with crowned muzzle, M4 feed ramps, 10 shot mag., fixed A2 reinforced Zytel buttstock with trapdoor assembly, A2 grip, black furniture, rifle length handguard with single heat shield, flat-top A3 or A2 upper with carry handle, includes sling, 7.8 lbs. Disc. 2013.

| | $675 | $500 | $425 | $375 | $335 | $315 | $295 | $780 |

DTI-4 CARBINE – .223 Rem. cal., GIO, 16 in. chrome moly M4 profile barrel, 6-position M4 stock, 30 shot mag., CAR handguard with single heat shield, A2 flash hider, black furniture, A3 flat-top or A2 upper with carry handle, includes sling. Disc. 2012.

| | $645 | $500 | $415 | $370 | $325 | $300 | $275 | $750 |

DTI-15 CARBINE – .223 Rem. cal., GIO, 16.1 in. barrel, 30 shot mag., hard anodized black oxide finish, adj. 6-position collapsible stock with M249-style pistol grip, fixed front sights, approx. 7 3/4 lbs. Mfg. mid-2011-2012.

| | $745 | $500 | $435 | $375 | $335 | $315 | $295 | $859 |

DTI EVOLUTION – 5.56 NATO cal., GIO, lightweight profile 16 in. chrome-lined barrel with threaded muzzle and A2 flash hider, low profile gas block, M4 feed ramps, Samson Evolution free float forend with accessory rails, Samson quick flip dual aperture rear sight, Samson folding front sight, forged aluminum upper and lower receiver, A3 flat-top with white T marks, hardcoat anodized metal finish, two-stage trigger, Magpul CTR stock, buffer tube, Magpul MOE+ grip, black or Dark Earth furniture, 6 1/2 lbs. New 2013.

| MSR $1,319 | $1,100 | $675 | $525 | $450 | $400 | $350 | $325 | |

DTI EXTREME DUTY – 5.56 NATO cal., GIO, 16 in. hammer forged chrome-lined barrel with threaded muzzle/A2 flash hider, T6 aluminum upper and lower receiver, M4 carbine handguard with double heat shield, M4 5-position reinforced fiber buttstock with Mil-Spec buffer tube, A2 grip, Samson quick flip dual aperture rear sight, black finish, 6.4 lbs. New 2012.

| MSR $1,119 | $915 | $575 | $475 | $415 | $350 | $325 | $300 | |

DTI TRX MID-LENGTH RIFLE/CARBINE – 5.56 NATO cal., GIO, 16 in. barrel, A2 flash hider, threaded muzzle, Troy TRX battlerail handguard, 30 shot mag., and BattleAx CQB adj. stock, black or tan finish, 7.2 lbs. Mfg. 2012 only.

| | $1,050 | $650 | $495 | $450 | $395 | $350 | $325 | $1,250 |

DT SPORT CARBINE – 5.56 NATO cal., GIO, lightweight profile 16 in. barrel with threaded muzzle/A2 flash hider, 10 or 30 shot mag., forged aluminum A3 flat-top upper receiver with forward assist, forged aluminum lower with A2 grip, M4 6-position buttstock with commercial buffer tube, oval ribbed handguard with A2 front sight and single heat shield, manganese phosphate under front sight base, 5.8 lbs. Mfg. 2011-2015, reintroduced 2017.

| MSR $697 | $595 | $485 | $415 | $350 | $315 | $295 | $275 | |

* **DT Sport Lite** – 5.56 NATO cal., GIO, 16 in. lightweight profile barrel, threaded muzzle, A2 flash hider, aluminum trigger guard, M4 6-pos. buttstock, A2 grip, forged aluminum A3 flat-top upper and lower receivers, H buffer, aluminum Delta ring carbine length handguard with single heat shield, black finish, 5.8 lbs. New 2016.

| MSR $649 | $550 | $475 | $400 | $350 | $315 | $295 | $275 | |

* **DT Sport-Mod 2** – 5.56 NATO cal., GIO, lightweight profile 16 in. barrel with threaded muzzle, A2 flash hider, 30 shot mag., Mako rear backup polymer sight, M4 6-position buttstock with commercial buffer tube, forged aluminum A3 flat-top upper receiver with forward assist, forged aluminum lower with A2 grip, manganese phosphate under front sight base, aluminum delta ring assembly single heat shield handguard, 5.8 lbs. Mfg. 2011-2015, reintroduced 2017.

| MSR $697 | $595 | $485 | $415 | $350 | $315 | $295 | $275 | |

* **DT Sport OR** – 5.56 NATO cal., GIO, similar to DT Sport Carbine, except is Optics Ready, so does not include the A2 front sight tower, manganese phosphate under low profile gas block, 5.6 lbs. New 2013.

| MSR $705 | $615 | $495 | $415 | $360 | $325 | $300 | $275 | |

D 168 DEL-TON INCORPORATED, cont.

MSR	100%	98%	95%	90%	80%	70%	60%	Last MSR

ECHO 216 (A2 LIGHTWEIGHT) – 5.56 NATO cal., GIO, 16 in. chrome moly M4 barrel with threaded muzzle and A2 flash hider, forged T6 aluminum upper and lower receiver, carry handle, 30 shot mag., carbine length handguard with single heat shield, A2 configuration with rear sight, M4 5-position stock with buffer tube, A2 grip, black furniture, 6.6 lbs. New 2012.

| MSR $890 | $765 | $515 | $440 | $375 | $335 | $315 | $295 | |

    * *Echo 216F* – 5.56 NATO cal., GIO, similar to Echo 216, except features A2 reinforced Zytel buttstock with trap door assembly, 6.8 lbs. Mfg. 2012-2013.

| | $675 | $500 | $425 | $375 | $335 | $315 | $295 | $788 |

    * *Echo 216H* – 5.56 NATO cal., GIO, similar to Echo 216, except features 16 in. chrome moly heavy barrel, A2 reinforced Zytel buttstock and A2 grip, trap door assembly, 7 lbs. Disc. 2014.

| | $675 | $500 | $425 | $375 | $335 | $315 | $295 | $793 |

ECHO 300 BLK – .300 AAC Blackout cal., GIO, 16 in. heavy profile barrel with A2 flash hider, F-marked front sight base, M4 Mil-Spec buttstock, H-buffer, forged aluminum upper with Picatinny rail, M4 feed ramps, carbine length aluminum Delta ring single heat shield handguard, black finish, 6.6 lbs. Disc. 2017.

| | $765 | $515 | $440 | $375 | $335 | $315 | $295 | $890 |

ECHO 308 – .308 Win. cal., GIO, 16 in. heavy profile barrel with A2 style flash hider, Magpul 20 shot PMAG, integral trigger guard, knurled aluminum forend, M4 buttstock, H-buffer, A2 grip, M4 feed ramps, forged aluminum receiver, carbine length knurled free float handguard tube, black finish, 8.2 lbs.

| MSR $948 | $800 | $525 | $450 | $385 | $340 | $325 | $295 | |

ECHO 316 – 5.56 NATO cal., GIO, 16 in. barrel with threaded muzzle and manganese phosphate finish, A2 flash hider, forged aluminum lower and A3 flat-top upper receiver, aluminum trigger guard, M4 front sight base, M4 five-position reinforced fiber buttstock with Mil-Spec buffer tube, carbine length aluminum delta ring single heat shield handguards, A2 grip, hardcoat anodized Mil-Spec matte black finish. New 2014.

| MSR $753 | $665 | $500 | $415 | $375 | $335 | $315 | $295 | |

ECHO 316H – 5.56 NATO cal., GIO, 16 in. chrome moly heavy barrel with threaded muzzle and A2 flash hider, M4 feed ramps, carbine length handguard with single heat shield, front sight base, T6 aluminum upper and lower, A3 flat-top with white T marks, M4 5-position reinforced carbon buttstock with buffer tube, A2 grip, black furniture, 6.6 lbs. New 2012.

| MSR $753 | $665 | $500 | $415 | $375 | $335 | $315 | $295 | |

    * *Echo 316H OR* – 5.56 NATO cal., GIO, similar to Echo 316H, except has single rail gas block and is optics ready, 6.4 lbs. Mfg. 2013-2015.

| | $695 | $500 | $425 | $375 | $335 | $315 | $295 | $816 |

ECHO 316L KEYMOD – 5.56 NATO cal., GIO, 16 in. lightweight profile barrel, threaded muzzle, A2 flash hider, aluminum trigger guard and mag. catch button, front sight base, M4 5-pos. buttstock, A2 grip, M4 feed ramps, forged aluminum lower and A3 upper with Picatinny rail, round forward assist, right-hand ejection, H buffer, Samson Evolution KeyMod carbine length handguard, 7.2 in. free float rail, hardcoat anodized black finish, 5.8 lbs. New 2016.

| MSR $921 | $785 | $525 | $450 | $385 | $340 | $325 | $295 | |

ECHO 316L LIGHTWEIGHT CARBINE – 5.56 NATO cal., GIO, 16 in. chrome moly barrel with A2 flash hider and threaded muzzle, forged T6 aluminum upper and lower receiver, carbine length handguard with single heat shield, 6-position M4 reinforced carbon fiber buttstock, 5.8 lbs. Mfg. 2012 only.

| | $645 | $500 | $415 | $370 | $325 | $300 | $275 | $750 |

ECHO 316L OR – 5.56 NATO cal., 16 in. barrel, threaded muzzle, A2 flash hider, 30 shot mag., right-hand ejection, enhanced trigger guard, optics ready, M4 6-pos. buttstock, Mil-Spec buffer tube, A2 grip, low profile gas block, forged aluminum lower and A3 flat-top upper receiver, CAR handguard with single heat shield and aluminum Delta Ring assembly, hardcoat anodized black finish, 5.6 lbs.

| MSR $816 | $695 | $500 | $425 | $375 | $335 | $315 | $295 | |

ECHO 316M – 5.56 NATO cal., GIO, 16 in. barrel with threaded muzzle and A2 flash hider, 30 shot mag., aluminum trigger guard, F-marked front sight base, Samson dual aperture rear sight, M4 5-position buttstock, Mil-Spec buffer tube, A2 grip, M4 feed ramps, carbine length aluminum Delta ring single heat shield handguard, forged lower and flat-top upper receivers, hardcoat anodized black finish, 6.6 lbs. New 2016.

| MSR $822 | $695 | $500 | $425 | $375 | $335 | $315 | $295 | |

ECHO 316 MLOK – 5.56 NATO cal., GIO, 16 in. heavy profile barrel, threaded muzzle, A2 flash hider, front sight base, Magpul MOE 5-pos. stock, forged aluminum lower and A3 flat-top upper with Picatinny rail, M4 feed ramps, Magpul MOE H buffer, Magpul M-LOK carbine length aluminum delta ring handguard, black or FDE finish, 6.8 lbs. New 2016.

| MSR $863 | $745 | $500 | $435 | $375 | $335 | $315 | $295 | |

DEL-TON INCORPORATED, cont. 169 D

MSR	100%	98%	95%	90%	80%	70%	60%	Last MSR

ECHO 316 MOE – 5.56 NATO cal., GIO, 16 in. chrome moly heavy profile barrel, threaded muzzle, A2 flash hider, A3 flat-top, Magpul MOE polymer stock with buffer tube and Magpul MOE grip, 30 shot PMAG, forged T6 aluminum upper and lower receiver, Magpul MOE carbine length handguard with heat resistant construction, ODG, black, or tan finish, 6.8 lbs. Mfg. 2012-2015.

	$765	$515	$440	$375	$335	$315	$295	$877

ECHO 316 OR – 5.56 NATO cal., 16 in. heavy profile barrel, threaded muzzle, A2 flash hider, M4 5-pos. buttstock, Mil-Spec buffer tube, A2 grip, M4 feed ramps, forged aluminum lower and A3 flat-top upper receiver, CAR handguard, single heat shield, aluminum Delta ring assembly, 6 1/2 lbs.

MSR $816	$695	$500	$425	$375	$335	$315	$295	

ECHO 316P – 5.56 NATO cal., GIO, M4 post-ban rifle, 16 in. chrome moly barrel with pinned YHM muzzle brake, 10 shot mag., M4 feed ramps, forged aluminum T6 upper and lower receivers, A3 flat-top upper, pinned M4 reinforced carbon fiber buttstock with commercial buffer tube, black furniture, carbine length handguard with single heat shield, 6.9 lbs.

MSR $822	$695	$500	$425	$375	$335	$315	$295	

ECHO 316PF (POST-BAN CARBINE) – 5.56 NATO cal., GIO, A3 post-ban rifle, 16 in. heavy profile chrome moly barrel with target crowned muzzle, no flash hider, 10 shot mag., M4 feed ramps, fixed A2 reinforced Zytel buttstock with trap door assembly, A2 grip, black furniture, carbine length handguard with single heat shield, forged aluminum T6 upper and lower receivers, A3 upper, 6.9 lbs. Disc. 2013.

	$675	$500	$425	$375	$335	$315	$295	$780

ECHO 7.62x39 – 7.62x39mm cal., GIO, 16 in. heavy profile barrel, threaded muzzle, A2 flash hider, aluminum trigger guard and mag. catch button, front sight base, M4 buttstock, A2 grip, forged aluminum lower and A3 flat-top upper with Picatinny rail, M4 feed ramps, right-hand ejection, aluminum Delta ring carbine length handguard with single heat shield, H buffer, 6.6 lbs. New 2016.

MSR $753	$665	$500	$415	$375	$335	$315	$295	

M4 CARBINE – .223 Rem. cal., GIO, 16 in. chrome moly barrel, 30 shot mag., black furniture, 6-position M4 stock, CAR handguard with single heat shield, A2 flash hider, includes sling. Disc. 2012.

	$645	$500	$415	$370	$325	$300	$275	$750

Add $9 for Tapco Model with Tapco buttstock, SAW grip, polymer mags., and short vertical grip (new 2012).

SIERRA 3G – .223 Wylde chamber, GIO, mid-length gas system, 16 in. lightweight profile barrel, DTI brake, Magpul 30 shot PMAG, right-hand ejection, Magpul CTR stock, Mil-Spec buffer tube, Magpul Ergo grip, Samson Evolution KeyMod free float forend, forged aluminum A3 flat-top upper receiver, M4 feed ramps, hardcoat anodized black finish. New late 2015.

MSR $1,319	$1,100	$675	$525	$450	$400	$350	$325	

SIERRA 216H (A2 MID-LENGTH CARBINE) – 5.56 NATO cal., GIO, 16 in. chrome moly barrel with threaded muzzle and A2 flash hider, heavy profile, forged aluminum T6 upper and lower receiver, carry handle, 30 shot mag., A2 configuration with rear sight, A2 reinforced Zytel buttstock with trap door assembly, A2 grip, mid-length handguard with single heat shield, Black furniture, 7.4 lbs. Disc. 2014.

	$675	$500	$425	$375	$335	$315	$295	$793

SIERRA 316H (MID-LENGTH CARBINE) – 5.56 NATO cal., GIO, 16 in. mid-length chrome moly barrel with A2 flash hider, heavy profile, 30 shot mag., black furniture, M4 5-position buttstock, A2 grip, Mil-Spec buffer tube, forged aluminum T6 upper and lower receiver, A3 flat-top, mid-length handguard with single heat shield, M4 feed ramps, 7 lbs.

MSR $753	$665	$500	$415	$375	$335	$315	$295	

SIERRA 316 MLOK – 5.56 NATO cal., GIO, 16 in. heavy profile barrel, threaded muzzle/A2 flash hider, 30 shot mag., Magpul MOE trigger guard, front sight base, Magpul MOE polymer stock, Magpul MOE grip, M4 feed ramps, forged aluminum lower and A3 flat-top upper with Picatinny rail, round forward assist, H buffer, Magpul MOE mid-length aluminum Delta ring handguard, black, Dark Earth, or ODG finish, 7 lbs. New 2016.

MSR $877	$765	$515	$440	$375	$335	$315	$295	

SIERRA 316 MOE – 5.56 NATO cal., GIO, 16 in. chrome moly barrel, threaded muzzle, A2 flash hider, A3 flat-top, Magpul MOE polymer stock and Magpul MOE grip and trigger guard, 30 shot PMAG, forged T6 aluminum upper and lower receiver, Magpul MOE mid-length handguard with heat resistant polymer construction, ODG (disc. 2015), black, or dark earth (disc. 2015) finish, 7.1 lbs. Mfg. 2012-2015.

	$765	$515	$440	$375	$335	$315	$295	$877

SIERRA 316P – 5.56 NATO cal., GIO, A3 mid-length post-ban rifle, 16 in. chrome moly barrel with pinned YHM muzzle brake, 10 shot mag., M4 feed ramps, pinned M4 reinforced carbon fiber buttstock with commercial buffer tube, black furniture, mid-length handguard with single heat shield, forged aluminum lower and A3 flat-top upper receiver, 6.9 lbs. Disc. 2013.

	$695	$500	$425	$375	$335	$315	$295	$806

DESERT ORDNANCE

MSR		100%	98%	95%	90%	80%	70%	60%	Last MSR

DESERT ORDNANCE

Current rifle manufacturer located in McCarren, NV. Current distributor for U.S. Ordnance.

RIFLES: SEMI-AUTO

Desert Ordnance offers a complete line of AR-15 style tactical and hunting rifles, mostly in 5.56 NATO cal. Many options and configurations are available, as well as a wide variety of parts and accessories. Please contact the company directly for more information, including pricing and availability (see Trademark Index).

DEVIL DOG ARMS LLC

Current pistol and rifle manufacturer located in Geneva, IL since 2016.

RIFLES: SEMI-AUTO

DDA-10 DMR – .308 Win. or 6.5mm Creedmoor cal., 20 or 22 (6.5mm Creedmoor only) in. barrel, black or black CF finish. New 2018.

MSR $2,899	$2,295	$1,450	$1,075	$675	$595	$525	$475

Add $500 for black CF finish.

DDA-10 HUNTER – .308 Win. or 6.5mm Creedmoor cal., 18 or 20 (6.5mm Creedmoor only) in. barrel, Type III hardcoat anodized black or black CF finish. New 2018.

MSR $2,499	$1,975	$1,150	$925	$650	$575	$495	$425

Add $750 for black CF finish.

DDA-10 .308 TACTICAL – .308 Win. cal., 16 in. barrel, black finish. New 2018.

MSR $2,399	$1,875	$1,100	$895	$650	$575	$495	$425

MRP-10 – .308 Win./7.62 NATO cal., GIO, 18 in. LM profile barrel, DDA tactical flash suppressor, ALG QMS trigger, Magpul MOE buttstock, Magpul MOE+ pistol grip, aluminum free float 15 in. Hex handguard, billet lower and M4A4 flat-top upper receiver, includes DDA Patriot hard case, Otis .308 cleaning kit, Type III hardcoat anodized black, FDE, or NibX finish. New 2017.

MSR $1,499	$1,250	$825	$575	$475	$425	$375	$350

Add $100 for FDE finish.
Add $200 for NibX finish.

DDA-15 COMPETITION – .223 Rem. cal., 16 in. barrel. New 2018.

MSR $2,249	$1,795	$1,050	$875	$625	$550	$475	$425

DDA-15 DMR – .223 Rem. cal., 20 in. barrel. New 2018.

MSR $2,649	$2,125	$1,325	$995	$675	$595	$525	$475

Add $650 for CF finish.

DDA-15 PRO COMPETITION – .223 Rem. cal., 16 in. barrel. New 2018.

MSR $3,499	$2,775	$1,825	$1,350	$750	$650	$595	$525

DDA-15 TACTICAL – .223 Rem. cal., 16 in. barrel. New 2018.

MSR $2,149	$1,725	$1,050	$850	$625	$550	$475	$425

HPR-15 – New 2018.

MSR $1,199	$995	$625	$495	$450	$395	$350	$325

KRP-15 (KEYMOD RIFLE PACKAGE) – .223 Rem./5.56 NATO cal., GIO, 16 in. Nitride finished barrel, DDA tactical muzzle brake, ALG QMS trigger, Magpul MOE 6-pos. buttstock, Magpul MOE+ pistol grip, DDA aluminum free float 15 in. KeyMod handguard, billet machined lower and M4A4 flat-top upper receiver, Type III hardcoat anodized black finish, 36 in. OAL, 7 lbs.

MSR $1,199	$995	$625	$495	$450	$395	$350	$325

RIS-15 (RAIL INTEGRATED SIGHT) – 5.56 NATO cal., GIO, 16 in. Nitride finished barrel, DDA tactical muzzle brake, 30 shot PMAG, Geissele ALG QMS trigger, DDA RIS front sight, Magpul MBUS rear sight, Magpul MOE 6-pos. buttstock, M4A4 flat-top upper receiver, aluminum free float 13 in. RIS handguard, includes DDA Bulldog soft case, Micro Otis cleaning kit, Type III hardcoat anodized black or FDE Cerakote finish, 36 in. OAL, 7 lbs.

MSR $1,199	$995	$625	$495	$450	$395	$350	$325

Add $100 for FDE Cerakote finish.

DEVIL DOG ARMS INC.

Previous handgun and AR-15 style rifle, parts, and accessories manufacturer located in Lake Zurich, IL until 2015.

DEVIL DOG ARMS INC., cont. 171 D

MSR	100%	98%	95%	90%	80%	70%	60%	Last MSR

HANDGUNS: SEMI-AUTO

DDA-15B-EPP – 5.56 NATO cal., GIO, 10 1/2 in. M4 profile barrel with DDA Tri-Comp tactical muzzle brake, 3D billet machined lower and A4 flat-top upper receiver, M4 feed ramp, DDA billet charging handle, Geissele ALG Defense trigger, DDA 9 in. aluminum free float octagon KeyMod handguard, Magpul MBUS polymer flip-up sights, Magpul MOE rubberized pistol grip, hardcoat anodized finish in black or FDE, 7 lbs. Disc. 2015.

	$1,315	$1,165	$1,050	$915	$785	$665	$550	$1,549

Add $100 for arm brace.

DDA-15B-MPP – 5.56 NATO cal., GIO, 7 1/2 in. M4 profile barrel with DDA tactical muzzle brake and Nitride finish, 3D billet machined lower and A4 flat-top upper receiver, M4 feed ramp, DDA billet charging handle, Geissele ALG Defense trigger, DDA 6 1/2 in. aluminum free float octagon KeyMod handguard, Magpul MBUS polymer flip-up sights, Magpul MOE rubberized pistol grip, hardcoat anodized finish in black or FDE, 6 lbs. 3 oz. Disc. 2015.

	$1,175	$1,050	$950	$850	$750	$650	$525	$1,399

Add $100 for arm brace.

RIFLES: SEMI-AUTO

DDA-10B-CERBERUS – 7.62 NATO cal., GIO, 18 in. match grade competition profile stainless steel barrel with DDA Tri-Comp Precision muzzle brake, 3D billet machined lower and flat-top upper receiver, DDA tactical mag. release, ambi selector and billet ambi-charging handle, Dueck Defense Rapid Transition Offset sights, CMC single stage competition trigger, 15 in. aluminum free float octagon Hex or KeyMod handguard, Magpul PRS Sniper adj. buttstock, Accu-Grip Adj. Competition pistol grip, NiB-X coated, 10 lbs. Mfg. 2015 only.

	$2,295	$1,450	$1,075	$675	$595	$525	$475	$2,899

DDA-10B-MRP – 7.62 NATO cal., GIO, 18 in. LM profile stainless steel barrel with DDA Tri-Comp precision muzzle brake, 3D billet machined lower and flat-top upper receiver, DDA tactical mag. release, ambi-selector, and billet charging handle, Geissele ALG Defense Combat trigger, DDA 15 in. aluminum free float octagon HEX or KeyMod handguard, Magpul MBUS polymer flip-up sights, Magpul MOE rifle buttstock, Magpul MOE rubberized pistol grip, hardcoat anodized finish in black or FDE, 9 lbs. 4 oz. Disc. 2015.

	$1,650	$1,000	$795	$595	$495	$425	$395	$1,999

DDA-10B-PRP – 7.62 NATO cal., GIO, 20 in. match grade precision bull stainless steel barrel with DDA Tri-Comp Precision muzzle brake, 3D billet machined lower and flat-top upper receiver, DDA tactical mag. release, ambi selector and billet charging handle, HiperFire 24C trigger, no sights, 15 in. aluminum free float octagon Hex or KeyMod handguard, Ergo Tactical Palm SureGrip pistol grip, Magpul PRS Sniper adj. buttstock, hardcoat anodized finish in black or FDE, 11 lbs. 9 oz. Mfg. 2015 only.

	$2,225	$1,395	$1,050	$675	$595	$525	$475	$2,799

DDA-10B-TRP – 7.62 NATO cal., GIO, 16 in. tactical grade stainless steel barrel with DDA tactical flash suppressor, 3D billet machined lower and flat-top upper receiver, DDA tactical mag. release, ambi selector, and billet ambi-charging handle, HiperFire 24 trigger, 15 in. aluminum free float octagon Hex or KeyMod handguard, Magpul MBUS polymer flip-up sights, Magpul MIAD adj. pistol grip, Falcon F93 8-pos. tactical entry buttstock, hardcoat anodized finish in black or FDE, 9 lbs. 8 oz. Mfg. 2015 only.

	$1,975	$1,150	$925	$650	$575	$495	$425	$2,499

DDA-15B-BRP – .300 AAC Blackout cal., GIO, 16 in. LM profile stainless steel barrel with DDA Tri-Comp Precision muzzle brake, 3D billet machined lower and A4 flat-top upper receiver, M4 feed ramp, tactical mag. release, ambi selector, and billet charging handle, Magpul MBUS polymer flip-up sights, DDA 15 in. aluminum free float octagon HEX or KeyMod handguard, HiperFire 24 trigger, Magpul CTR 6-pos. buttstock, Magpul MOE rubberized pistol grip, hardcoat anodized finish in black or FDE, 7 lbs. 3 oz. Disc. 2015.

	$1,575	$995	$775	$575	$495	$425	$395	$1,899

DDA-15B-CRP – 5.56 NATO cal., GIO, 18 in. match grade competition profile stainless steel barrel with DDA 3Gun Competition muzzle brake, 3D billet machined lower and A4 flat-top upper receiver, M4 feed ramp, DDA tactical mag. release, ambi selector, and billet ambi charging handle, DDA 15 in. aluminum free float octagon HEX or KeyMod handguard, HiperFire 24 3G or 24C trigger, Magpul STR 6-pos. buttstock, Magpul MIAD adj. pistol grip, hardcoat anodized finish in black or FDE, 8 lbs. Disc. 2015.

	$1,650	$1,000	$795	$595	$495	$425	$395	$1,999

DDA-15B-DMRP – 5.56 NATO cal., GIO, 18 in. match grade competition profile stainless steel barrel with DDA 3Gun Competition muzzle brake, 3D billet machined lower and A4 flat-top upper receiver, M4 feed ramp, DDA tactical mag. release, ambi selector, and billet charging handle, HiperFire 24E trigger, DDA aluminum free float 15 in. octagon HEX or KeyMod handguard, Magpul MIAD adj. pistol grip, Magpul PRS Sniper adj. buttstock, hardcoat anodized finish in black or FDE, 8 lbs. Disc. 2015.

	$1,675	$1,000	$825	$625	$550	$475	$425	$2,099

D 172 DEVIL DOG ARMS INC., cont.

MSR	100%	98%	95%	90%	80%	70%	60%	Last MSR

DDA-15B-ERP – 5.56 NATO cal., GIO, 16 in. HP profile barrel with black Nitride finish and DDA Tri-Comp tactical muzzle brake, 3D billet lower and A4 flat-top upper receiver, M4 feed ramp, Geissele ALG defense trigger, DDA 13 in. aluminum free float octagon HEX or KeyMod handguard, Magpul MBUS polymer flip-up sights, Magpul CTR 6-pos. buttstock, Magpul MOE rubberized pistol grip, hardcoat anodized finish in black or FDE, 7 lbs. 9 oz. Disc. 2015.

	100%	98%	95%	90%	80%	70%	60%	Last MSR
	$1,275	$850	$600	$495	$425	$375	$350	*$1,549*

DDA-15B-MRP – 5.56 NATO cal., GIO, 16 in. M4 profile barrel with black Nitride finish and DDA tactical muzzle brake, Geissele ALG defense trigger, Magpul MOE polymer ergonomic handguard, Magpul MBUS polymer flip-up sights, 3D billet lower and A4 flat-top upper receiver, M4 feed ramp, Magpul MOE rubberized pistol grip, Magpul MOE 6-pos. buttstock, hardcoat anodized finish in black or FDE, 6 lbs. 13 oz. Disc. 2015.

	$1,150	$750	$550	$465	$415	$375	$350	*$1,399*

DDA-15B-ORTHROS – 5.56 NATO cal., GIO, 18 in. match grade competition profile stainless steel barrel with DDA 3Gun Competition muzzle brake, 3D billet machined lower and A4 flat-top upper receiver, M4 feed ramp, DDA tactical mag. release, ambi selector and billet ambi charging handle, Dueck Defense Rapid Transition Offset sights, CMC single stage competition trigger, 15 in. aluminum free float octagon Hex or KeyMod handguard, Falcon F93 8-pos. Tactical Entry buttstock, Accu-Grip Adj. Competition pistol grip, NiB-X coated, 7 lbs. 8 oz. Mfg. 2015 only.

	$1,975	$1,150	$925	$650	$575	$495	$425	*$2,459*

DDA-15B-TRP – 5.56 NATO cal., GIO, 16 in. M4 profile barrel with black Nitride finish and DDA tactical flash suppressor, 3D billet machined lower and A4 flat-top upper receiver, M4 feed ramp, DDA 15 in. aluminum free float octagon HEX or KeyMod handguard, Magpul MBUS polymer flip-up sights, tactical mag. release, ambi selector, and billet charging handle, Magpul ACS 6-pos. buttstock, Magpul MIAD adj. pistol grip, HiperFire 24 trigger, hardcoat anodized finish in black or FDE, 7 lbs. 9 oz. Disc. 2015.

	$1,575	$995	$775	$575	$495	$425	$395	*$1,899*

GG2G (GIRL'S GUIDE TO GUNS) SERIES – This series was done in collaboration with Natalie Foster, creator of Girl's Guide to Guns to bring color and design to her Devil Dog Arms custom rifles to suit the style and wardrobe of the most discerning female shooters. DuraCoat Signature colors available are Fast as Lightning, Audrey's Arsenal, Gunning For You, Blushing Bullet, UnderCover, Bullet Breeze, Silver Bullet, Kiss My AK, and Champagne & Lead. Mfg. 2015 only.

* **GG2G-15 Classic** – 5.56 NATO cal., GIO, 16 in. M4 profile chrome moly barrel with DDA Tri-Comp tactical muzzle brake and Nitride finish, 3D billet lower and A4 flat-top upper receiver, M4 feed ramp, Geissele ALG Mil-Spec Combat trigger, 13 in. aluminum free float octagon Hex handguard, Magpul MBUS polymer flip-up sights, Magpul MOE 6-pos. buttstock, Magpul MOE+ rubberized pistol grip, DuraCoat Signature color finish, 6 lbs. 8 oz. Mfg. 2015 only.

	$1,250	$825	$575	$475	$425	$375	$350	*$1,499*

* **GG2G-15 Natalie Signature** – 5.56 NATO cal., GIO, 18 in. match grade competition stainless steel barrel with 3-Gun Competition muzzle brake, 3D billet lower and A4 flat-top upper receiver, M4 feed ramp, HiperFire 24 trigger, Magpul MBUS polymer flip-up sights, 15 in. aluminum free float octagon Hex handguard, Magpul STR 6-pos. buttstock, Magpul MOE+ rubberized pistol grip, NiB-X coating on metal parts, DuraCoat Signature color finish, 7 lbs. Mfg. 2015 only.

	$1,475	$950	$725	$550	$475	$395	$350	*$1,799*

DEZ TACTICAL ARMS, INC.

Current AR-15 style rifle manufacturer located in south central WI since 2012.

RIFLES/CARBINES: SEMI-AUTO

BR4-15 CARBINE MIL-SPEC – 5.56 NATO cal., GIO, 16 in. CMV steel barrel with black Nitride finish, 30 shot mag., A2 front sight base with carbine length gas tube, forged receivers, M4 feed ramps, charging handle, M4 military style forearm, stainless steel trigger, tactical 6-position buttstock, Mil-Spec grip, includes Plano hard plastic case, 6 lbs. 10 oz. New 2015.

MSR $899	$765	$515	$440	$375	$335	$315	$295	

COMPETITION RIFLE – 5.56 NATO cal., GIO, 18 in. fluted heavy contour stainless steel barrel, 3 port compensator or YHM Phantom muzzle brake, 30 shot E-Lander mag., adj. low profile gas system, forged aluminum A4 upper and lower receiver, M4 feed ramps, charging handle, nickel boron bolt carrier group, DEZ Arms 15 in. Competition KeyMod free float handguard, Magpul extended trigger guard, Hiperfire Hipertouch trigger, Mil-Spec carbine assembly with FAB Defense 6-position buttstock, adj. cheek riser, ambi Ergo grip, includes Plano hard plastic case, 8 lbs. New 2015.

MSR $1,849	$1,525	$975	$750	$575	$495	$425	$375	

COVERT OPS CARBINE V2 – .223 Rem. cal., GIO, 16 in. HBAR chrome moly button rifled barrel, YHM Phantom muzzle brake, 30 shot Magpul PMAG with transparent round count window, stainless steel military grade trigger, YHM smooth profile mid-length free floating forearm with end cap, FAB Defense 6-position adj. stock with adj. cheekpiece, Ambi Ergo grip or UTG combat sniper grip with FAB Defense magwell grip, forged upper receiver with M4 grooved

DEZ TACTICAL ARMS, INC., cont. 173 D

MSR	100%	98%	95%	90%	80%	70%	60%	Last MSR

feed ramps, charging handle with extended tactical latch, forged aluminum lower receiver, Mil-Spec bolt carrier group, carbine length gas tube, 7.1 lbs.

| MSR $1,399 | $1,150 | $750 | $550 | $465 | $415 | $375 | $350 | |

COVERT OPS CARBINE V3 – 5.56 NATO cal., 16 in. match grade rifle. New 2015.

| MSR $1,399 | $1,150 | $750 | $550 | $465 | $415 | $375 | $350 | |

DTA-4 CARBINE – .223 Rem. cal., GIO, 16 in. chrome moly button rifled barrel, 30 shot aluminum mag., forged upper receiver with M4 grooved feed ramps and charging handle, A2 front sight base with carbine length gas tube, military handguard, M4 military style carbine length forearm, forged aluminum lower receiver, A2 flash hider, stainless steel military grade trigger, tactical 6-position collapsible adj. stock, military style grip, approx. 6 1/2 lbs.

| MSR $1,099 | $915 | $575 | $475 | $415 | $350 | $325 | $300 | |

    * DTA-4 Carbine Optic Ready – .223 Rem. cal., GIO, similar to DTA-4, except has top rail gas block instead of A2 front sight base. New 2015.

| MSR $1,099 | $915 | $575 | $475 | $415 | $350 | $325 | $300 | |

DTA-4 ENHANCED CARBINE – .223 Rem. or .300 AAC Blackout cal., GIO, 16 in. chrome moly button rifled barrel, 30 shot Magpul PMAG, forged upper receiver with M4 grooved feed ramps, A2 front sight base with carbine length gas tube, Magpul MOE handguard, carbine length forearm, forged aluminum lower receiver, A2 flash hider, stainless steel military grade trigger, Magpul MOE 6-position adj. stock, Israeli grip, approx. 6 lbs. 13 oz.

| MSR $1,219 | $1,025 | $625 | $495 | $450 | $395 | $350 | $325 | |

Add $15 for .300 AAC Blackout cal.

DARK ASSAULT CARBINE – 7.62 NATO cal., GIO, 16 in. HBAR match grade barrel with flash suppressor, 30 shot mag., low profile gas block with carbine length gas tube, YHM Diamond profile free floating mid-length handguard with end cap, forged receivers, ALG Defense trigger, M4 feed ramps, charging handle, 6-pos. shock absorbing buttstock with adj. cheek riser, Ambi Ergo grip and FAB Defense magwell grip, black finish, includes Plano hard plastic case, 8 lbs. 6 oz. New 2015.

| MSR $1,499 | $1,250 | $825 | $575 | $475 | $425 | $375 | $350 | |

FLAWLESS RIFLE – .223 Rem. cal., GIO, 20 or 24 in. chrome moly HBAR button rifled diamond fluted barrel, 30 shot Magpul PMAG with transparent round count window, forged upper receiver with M4 grooved feed ramps and charging handle with extended tactical latch, forged aluminum lower receiver, Mil-Spec bolt carrier group, quad rail with rifle length gas tube, YHM diamond profle free floating rifle length forearm with end cap, stainless steel military grade trigger, .50 cal. style flash enhancer, FAB Defense 6-position adj. stock with adj. cheekpiece, Ergo Suregrip, 9 lbs. Disc. 2014.

| | $1,315 | $850 | $625 | $500 | $435 | $375 | $350 | *$1,600* |

Add $10 for 24 in. barrel.

HUNTER RIFLE – 6.8 SPC cal., GIO, match grade 16 in. heavy contour barrel, enhanced flash hider, 25 shot mag., adj. low profile carbine length gas tube, YHM TJ Competition mid-length free float handguard, continuous top Picatinny rail, nickel Teflon coated ALG ACT trigger system, nickel boron bolt carrier group, Mil-Spec A4 forged aluminum upper and lower receiver, Magpul extended trigger guard, M4 grooved feed ramps, extended charging handle, Magpul MOE fixed rifle stock, ambi Ergo grip, includes hard plastic Plano case, 7 lbs. 15 oz. New 2016.

| MSR $1,459 | $1,225 | $825 | $575 | $475 | $425 | $375 | $350 | |

TRU-FLIGHT CARBINE – .223 Rem. cal., GIO, 16 in. chrome moly button rifled barrel, 30 shot Magpul PMAG with transparent round count window, forged upper receiver with M4 grooved feed ramps and extended charging handle, forged aluminum lower receiver, Mil-Spec bolt carrier group, single rail Picatinny gas block with carbine length gas tube, YHM carbine length free floating forearm, stainless steel military grade trigger, three port compensator, FAB Defense 6-position adj. stock with adj. cheekpiece, Israeli grip with FAB Defense magwell grip, 6.8 lbs. Disc. 2014.

| | $1,135 | $725 | $525 | $465 | $415 | $375 | $350 | *$1,370* |

TWISTED ELITE CARBINE – .223 Rem. cal., GIO, 16 in. chrome moly HBAR button rifled twist fluted barrel, 30 shot Magpul PMAG with transparent round count window, forged upper receiver with M4 grooved feed ramps and extended charging handle, forged aluminum lower receiver, Mil-Spec bolt carrier group, low profile gas block with carbine length gas tube, YHM carbine length free floating "Todd Jarrett Competition" forearm, stainless steel military grade trigger, YHM Phantom muzzle brake, FAB Defense 6-position adj. stock with adj. cheekpiece, Ergo SureGrip with FAB Defense magwell grip, black or FDE (new 2015) finish, 7.2 lbs.

| MSR $1,419 | $1,175 | $775 | $550 | $465 | $415 | $375 | $350 | |

Add $150 for FDE finish (new 2015).

ULTRA LIGHT RIFLE – 5.56 NATO cal., GIO, 16 in. match grade chrome moly barrel, YHM Phantom Comp/flash hider, 30 shot Magpul PMAG, low profile gas block with carbine length gas tube, Mil-Spec A4 forged aluminum upper and lower receiver, M4 feed ramps, charging handle, Nitride coated bolt carrier group, DEZ Arms KeyMod carbine length free float handguard, ALG Defense Q.M.S. trigger, Mil-Spec carbine assembly with 6-position stock, A2 pistol grip, 6.2 lbs. New 2015.

| MSAR $1,299 | $1,075 | $675 | $500 | $450 | $400 | $350 | $325 | |

D 174 DEZ TACTICAL ARMS, INC., cont.

MSR	100%	98%	95%	90%	80%	70%	60%	Last MSR

USAR10-16E ULTRAMATCH RIFLE – 7.62x51 cal., 16 in. HBAR fluted contour barrel with enhanced flash hider, 20 shot Magpul PMAG, HiperFire HiperTouch 24E trigger, enhanced rifle buffer assembly with Magpul MOE fixed rifle stock, ambi Ergo grip, billet aluminum upper and lower receivers, M4 feed ramps, extended charging handle, DEZ Arms mid-length KeyMod free float handguard, adj. low profile gas tube, includes Plano hard plastic case, black finish, 9 lbs. Disc. 2017.

	$2,125	$1,325	$995	$675	$595	$525	$475	*$2,649*

USAR10-18 ULTRAMATCH RIFLE – 7.62x51 cal., 18 in. HBAR fluted contour barrel with A2 flash hider, ALG Defense QMS trigger, enhanced rifle buffer assembly with A2 fixed rifle stock, A2 pistol grip, billet aluminum upper and lower receivers, M4 feed ramps, charging handle, DEZ Arms quad rail free float handguard, rubber ladder rail covers, top Picatinny gas block with mid-length gas tube, includes Plano hard plastic case, 9 lbs. 9 oz. Disc. 2017.

	$1,725	$1,050	$850	$625	$550	$475	$425	*$2,189*

USAR10-18P ULTRAMATCH PATRIOT RIFLE – 7.62x51 cal., 18 in. fluted HBAR contour barrel with A2 flash hider, 20 shot Magpul PMAG, HiperFire HiperTouch 24E trigger, enhanced rifle buffer assembly with Magpul MOE fixed rifle stock, Israeli style pistol grip, billet aluminum upper and lower receivers, M4 feed ramps, charging handle, adj. low profile gas block, rifle length free floated quad rail handguard with rubber ladder rail covers, includes Plano hard plastic case, 9 lbs. 15 oz.

MSR $2,649	$2,125	$1,325	$995	$675	$595	$525	$475	

USAR10-20SS-BB ULTRAMATCH RIFLE – 7.62x51 cal., 16 in. stainless steel or Nitride coated bull fluted contour match grade barrel with enhanced flash hider, low profile gas block, 20 shot PMAG, HiperFire HiperTouch 24E trigger, enhanced rifle buffer assembly with Luth-AR MBA rifle stock, Ergo Deluxe grip, billet aluminum upper and lower receivers, M4 feed ramps, extended charging handle, DEZ Arms rifle length KeyMod free float handguard with one 5-slot modular rail segment, includes Plano hard plastic case, Burnt Bronze Cerakote finish, 14 lbs. 1 oz.

MSR $2,839	$2,295	$1,450	$1,075	$675	$595	$525	$475	

USAR10-20SS-SG ULTRAMATCH RIFLE – 7.62x51 cal., 20 in. stainless steel or Nitride coated bull fluted contour barrel with enhanced flash hider, 20 shot PMAG, HiperFire HiperTouch 24E trigger, enhanced rifle buffer assembly with Magpul MOE fixed rifle stock, Ergo deluxe grip, low profile gas block, billet aluminum upper and lower receivers, M4 feed ramps, extended charging handle, DEZ Arms 15 in. free float KeyMod handguard with one 5-slot modular rail segment, includes Plano hard plastic case, Sniper Grey Cerakote finish, 11 lbs. 1 oz.

MSR $2,800	$2,295	$1,450	$1,075	$675	$595	$525	$475	

USAR10-24-BLK ULTRAMATCH RIFLE – 7.62x51 cal., 24 in. match grade steel fluted bull barrel with enhanced flash hider, low profile gas block, 20 shot PMAG, HiperFire HiperTouch 24E trigger, enhanced rifle buffer assembly with Magpul PRS stock, Ergo Deluxe grip, billet aluminum upper and lower receivers, M4 feed ramps, extended charging handle, DEZ Arms 19 in. free float KeyMod handguard, SS extended, includes one 5-slot modular rail segment, Magpul BAD lever, includes Plano hard plastic case, black finish, 12 lbs. 9 oz.

MSR $2,999	$2,375	$1,525	$1,150	$700	$625	$550	$475	

DIAMONDBACK FIREARMS

Current pistol and AR-15 style rifle manufacturer established during 2009 and located in Cocoa, FL. Distributor and dealer sales.

During late 2012, Taurus Holdings purchased an exclusive global distribution agreement with Diamondback Firearms, LLC. Taurus assumed all sales and marketing efforts of the Diamondback branded products from its Miami office.

PISTOLS: SEMI-AUTO

DB9RPB10 – 9mm Para. cal., 10 in. free float Melonite barrel, A2 flash hider, 33 shot plastic mag., pistol buffer tube, forged aluminum lower and 9mm upper receiver, 9 in. KeyMod rail handguard, hardcoat anodized black finish, Magpul MOE pistol grip. New 2017.

MSR $890	$775	$685	$615	$550	$485	$415	$370	

DB9RPBB10 – 9mm Para. cal., 10 in. free float black Nitride barrel, A2 flash hider, Magpul MOE 31 shot plastic mag., pistol buffer tube, forged aluminum lower and 9mm upper receiver, 9 in. KeyMod rail handguard, Burnt Bronze Cerakote finish, Magpul MOE pistol grip. New 2018.

MSR $919	$795	$695	$625	$550	$485	$415	$370	

DB15 – 5.56 NATO or .300 AAC Blackout cal., GIO, 7 1/2 or 10 1/2 in. chrome moly barrel, forged aluminum lower and A3 flat-top forged aluminum upper receiver, SST, no sights, Diamondback aluminum modified four rail handguard, A2 style pistol grip, black, Flat Dark Earth, OD Green, or Tactical Gray (new 2017) finish. New 2014.

MSR $860	$725	$650	$580	$515	$450	$385	$340	

Add $10 for Flat Dark Earth or $54 for OD Green or Tactical Gray (new 2017) finish.

DIAMONDBACK FIREARMS, cont. 175 D

MSR	100%	98%	95%	90%	80%	70%	60%	Last MSR

RIFLES: SEMI-AUTO

DB9RB – 9mm Para. cal., 16 in. free float Melonite barrel, A2 flash hider, 33 shot plastic mag., Roger's pistol grip buttstock, forged aluminum lower and 9mm upper receiver, 9 in. KeyMod handguard rail, Mil-Spec buffer tube, hardcoat anodized black finish. New 2017.

MSR $919	$785	$525	$450	$385	$340	$325	$295	

DB9RBB – 9mm Para. cal., 16 in. free float black Nitride barrel, A2 flash hider, 31 shot plastic mag., Roger's pistol grip buttstock, forged aluminum lower and 9mm upper receiver, 15 in. KeyMod handguard rail, Mil-Spec buffer tube, Burnt Bronze Cerakote finish. New 2018.

MSR $939	$795	$535	$450	$385	$340	$325	$295	

DB10 – .308 Win. cal., GIO, 18 in. HBAR barrel with A2 flash hider and black Nitride finish, 20 shot mag., low profile gas block, no sights, CNC machined billet aluminum lower with custom trigger guard and T-marked upper receiver, Odin KeyMod rail, Magpul ACS stock, Magpul MOE+ pistol grip, black anodized or Flat Dark Earth finish, 8.5 lbs. Mfg. 2015-2018.

	100%	98%	95%	90%	80%	70%	60%	Last MSR
	$1,675	$1,000	$825	$625	$550	$475	$425	*$2,049*

Add $33 for Flat Dark Earth finish.

DB10CKMB / DB10CKMFDE – .308 Win. cal., mid-length gas system, 16 in. barrel, A2 flash hider, 20 shot Magpul PMAG, Rogers AR Mil-Spec Super-Stoc, A2 style pistol grip, Melonite coated AR10 bolt carrier w/multi-cal. bolt, DPMS style barrel extension, high-pressure firing pin, 10 in. KeyMod rail handguard, black or FDE (new-late 2016) finish, 7 lbs. 15 oz.-8 lbs. 1 oz. New 2016.

MSR $960	$825	$535	$450	$385	$340	$325	$295	

Add $40 for FDE finish (new-late 2016).

DB10CMLB – .308 Win. cal., mid-length gas system, 16 in. barrel, A2 flash hider, 20 shot Magpul PMAG, Rogers AR Mil-Spec Super-Stoc, A2 style pistol grip, Azimuth Melonite coated AR 10 bolt carrier w/multi-cal. bolt, DPMS style barrel extension, high-pressure firing pin, 10 in. KeyMod rail handguard, black Nitride finish, 7 lbs. 15 oz., 34.12-37.31 in. OAL. New 2018.

MSR $960	$825	$535	$450	$385	$340	$325	$295	

DB10ELB / DB10ELFDE – .308 Win. cal., mid-length gas system, 18 in. SS fluted barrel, A2 flash hider, 20 shot Magpul PMAG, Magpul CTR Mil-Spec stock, Magpul MOE grip, Melonite coated AR10 style carrier w/multi-cal. bolt, DPMS style barrel, 15 in. KeyMod rail handguard, black or FDE finish (mfg. 2016-2017), 7.5 oz. New 2016.

MSR $1,100	$915	$575	$475	$415	$350	$325	$300	

Add $40 for FDE finish (DB10ELFDE mfg. 2016-2017).

DB10ELBB – .308 Win. cal., mid-length gas system, 18 in. SS fluted barrel, A2 flash hider, one 20 shot Magpul PMAG or two 20 round aluminum mags., adaptive tactical adj. stock (Ex Performance), Hexmag pistol grip, Azimuth Melonite coated AR10 style carrier w/multi-cal. bolt, DPMS style barrel extension, Diamondback aluminum 15 in. KeyMod rail handguard, black Oxide finish, 8 lb. 7.5 oz., 35 3/4-38 in. OAL. New 2018.

MSR $1,121	$935	$575	$475	$415	$350	$325	$300	

DB10 ELITE – .308 Win. cal., 18 in. heavy barrel with JP compensator, 20 shot Magpul mag., CNC machined billet lower with custom trigger guard and T marked upper receiver, CMC trigger, 15 in. LW KeyMod rail, no sights, Magpul PRS stock, Ergo SureGrip, black anodized or Flat Dark Earth finish, 10 1/2 lbs. Mfg. 2015-2016.

	100%	98%	95%	90%	80%	70%	60%	Last MSR
	$2,125	$1,325	$995	$675	$595	$525	$475	*$2,619*

Add $34 for Flat Dark Earth finish.

DB10EMLB – .308 Win. cal., mid-length gas system, 18 in. SS fluted barrel, A2 flash hider, one 20 shot Magpul PMAG or two 20 round aluminum mags., adaptive tactical adj. stock (Ex Performance), Hexmag pistol grip, Azimuth Melonite coated AR10 style carrier w/multi-cal. bolt, DPMS style barrel extension, Diamondback aluminum 15 in. M-LOK rail handguard, black Oxide finish, 8 lb. 7.5 oz., 35 3/4-38 in. OAL. New 2018.

MSR $1,100	$915	$575	$475	$415	$350	$325	$300	

DB1065CB / DB1065CFDE – 6.5mm Creedmoor cal., 20 in. stainless steel fluted barrel w/double side port muzzle brake, multi-textured rubber pistol grip, black or FDE finish, 15 in. Victor M-LOK rail. New mid-2017.

MSR $1,229	$1,050	$650	$495	$450	$395	$350	$325	

Add $30 for FDE finish (DB1065CFDE).

DB15 5.56 NATO – 5.56 NATO cal., GIO, 16 in. chrome moly M4 contour free floating barrel with A2 flash hider, A3 flat-top upper receiver, Diamondback aluminum modified four rail or standard two-piece handguard, 4-position M4 stock, black or Flat Dark Earth finish, available with no sights, A2 front sights, or Magpul sights, 6.65 lbs. Mfg. 2013-2017.

		98%	95%	90%	80%	70%	60%	Last MSR
	$575	$485	$415	$350	$315	$295	$275	*$756*

Add $141 for Magpul sights.
Add $143 for A2 front sights.
Add $263 for four rail handguard or $296 for four rail handguard and Magpul sights.
Add $285 for Flat Dark Earth finish and four rail handguard.

D 176 DIAMONDBACK FIREARMS, cont.

MSR	100%	98%	95%	90%	80%	70%	60%	Last MSR

* **DB15 Camo** – 5.56 NATO cal., 16 in. chrome moly M4 contour free floating barrel with A2 flash hider, M4 stock, A2 style pistol grip, forged lower and A3 flat-top upper receiver, Diamondback aluminum modified four rail handguard, no sights or Magpul sights, Digital Green Camo or Digital Tan Camo finish, 6.65 lbs. Mfg. 2013-2017.

| | $1,050 | $650 | $495 | $450 | $395 | $350 | $325 | $1,221 |

Add $33 for Magpul sights.

* **DB15 Fluted** – 5.56 NATO cal., GIO, 16 or 18 in. fluted barrel, 13 1/2 in. fluted Underside KeyMod rail or 15 in. Elite KeyMod rail, forged upper and lower receivers, A2 style pistol grip, ATI Strikeforce stock with aluminum civilian buffer tube assembly, no sights, black anodized or Stone Grey finish, 6.65 lbs. Mfg. 2013-2017.

| | $1,315 | $850 | $625 | $500 | $435 | $375 | $350 | $1,589 |

Add $360 for 15 in. Elite KeyMod rail and Stone Grey finish.

* **DB15 Nickel** – 5.56 NATO cal., GIO, 30 shot mag., 16 in. M4 contour free floating barrel with A2 flash hider, A3 flat-top upper receiver, aluminum four rail handguard, nickel boron coating, 6-position Magpul CTR stock, Magpul MIAD grip, no sights, 6.65 lbs. Mfg. 2013-2017.

| | $995 | $625 | $495 | $450 | $395 | $350 | $325 | $1,199 |

Add $28 for Magpul sights.

DB15 .300 BLACKOUT – .300 AAC Blackout cal., GIO, 16 in. chrome moly M4 contour free float barrel with A2 flash hider, forged lower and A3 flat-top upper receiver, no sights, A2 front sights, or Magpul sights, Diamondback aluminum modified four rail or standard two-piece handguard, A2 style pistol grip, ATI Strikeforce stock with aluminum civilian buffer tube assembly, black or Flat Dark Earth finish, 6.65 lbs. Disc. 2016.

| | $865 | $550 | $465 | $395 | $350 | $325 | $300 | $1,010 |

Add $10 for A2 front sight only.
Add $130 for four rail handguard, no sights.
Add $160 for Flat Dark Earth finish or $198 for FDE finish with Magpul sights.
Add $231 for four rail handguard with Magpul sights.

* **DB15 .300 Blackout Camo** – .300 AAC Blackout cal., 16 in. chrome moly M4 contour free floating barrel with A2 flash hider, M4 stock, A2 style pistol grip, forged lower and A3 flat-top upper receiver, Diamondback aluminum modified four rail handguard, no sights or Magpul sights, Digital Green Camo or ATAC Camo finish, 6.65 lbs. Disc. 2016.

| | $1,065 | $650 | $500 | $450 | $395 | $350 | $325 | $1,264 |

Add $104 for Magpul sights.
Add $104 for ATAC camo finish with Magpul sights.

* **DB15 .300 Blackout Nickel** – .300 AAC Blackout cal., GIO, 16 in. M4 contour free floating barrel with A2 flash hider, forged lower and A3 flat-top upper receiver, aluminum four rail handguard, nickel boron coating, 6-position Magpul CTR stock, Magpul MIAD grip, no sights or Magpul sights, 6.65 lbs. Mfg. 2013-2016.

| | $1,050 | $650 | $495 | $450 | $395 | $350 | $325 | $1,244 |

Add $99 for Magpul sights.

DB15E300B / DB15E300FDE / DB15EML300B – .300 AAC Blackout cal., pistol length GIO, 16 in. chrome moly free float, M4 contour, Melonite coated barrel, A2 flash hider, Magpul 30 shot PMAG with window, enhanced trigger guard, Magpul CTR (disc. 2017) or Adaptive Tactical adj. (Ex Performance, new 2018) stock with Mil-Spec buffer tube, Magpul MOE (disc. 2017) or Hexmag (new 2018) pistol grip, forged aluminum lower and A3 flat-top upper receiver, 15 in. KeyMod or M-LOK (new 2018) handguard, black anodized hardcoat, ODG (disc. 2017), Tactical Gray (disc. 2017), or FDE (disc. 2017) finish, 32 1/2-36 1/4 in. OAL, 6 lbs. 9 oz.

| MSR $850 | | $725 | $500 | $435 | $375 | $335 | $315 | $295 |

Add $10 for FDE, ODG, or Tactical Gray finish.

DB15US300B – .300 AAC Blackout cal., carbine gas system, 16 in. chrome moly barrel, aluminum Mil-Spec 30 shot mag., A2 front sight only, 6-pos. ATI Mil-Spec buttstock and buffer tube, A2 style pistol grip, forged aluminum lower and A3 flat-top upper receiver, standard two-piece handguard, hardcoat anodized black finish, 5 lbs. 5 oz. Mfg. 2017 only.

| | $595 | $485 | $415 | $350 | $315 | $295 | $275 | $690 |

DB1547EMLB (ELITE BLACK) – 7.62x39mm cal., carbine gas system, 16 in. chrome moly black Nitride barrel, aluminum 28 shot mag., adaptive tactical EX buttstock, Hexmag pistol grip, forged aluminum lower and A3 flat-top upper receiver, 15 in. M-LOK rail handguard, hardcoat anodized black finish, 32 1/2-36 1/4 in. OAL, approx. 8 lbs. New 2018.

| MSR $844 | | $725 | $500 | $435 | $375 | $335 | $315 | $295 |

DB1565GEMLB (ELITE BLACK) – 6.5 Grendel cal., mid-length gas system, 18 in. chrome moly free float black Nitride barrel, aluminum 6.5 Grendel mag., adaptive tactical EX buttstock, Hexmag pistol grip w/enhanced trigger guard, forged aluminum lower and A3 flat-top upper receiver, 15 in. M-LOK rail handguard, hardcoat anodized black finish. New 2018.

| MSR $865 | | $745 | $500 | $435 | $375 | $335 | $315 | $295 |

DIAMONDBACK FIREARMS, cont. 177 D

MSR	100%	98%	95%	90%	80%	70%	60%	Last MSR

DB1565GEMLFDE (ELITE FLAT DARK EARTH) – 6.5 Grendel cal., mid-length gas system, 18 in. chrome moly free float black Nitride barrel, aluminum 6.5 Grendel mag., adaptive tactical EX buttstock, Hexmag pistol grip w/ enhanced trigger guard, forged aluminum lower and A3 flat-top upper receiver, 15 in. M-LOK rail handguard, hardcoat anodized black finish. New 2018.

| MSR $898 | $765 | $515 | $440 | $375 | $335 | $315 | $295 | |

DB15CB / DB15CCB / DB15CCBB – 5.56 NATO/.223 Rem. cal., GIO, carbine length gas system, 16 in. chrome moly Melonite coated free floating barrel with A2 flash hider, 30 shot aluminum mag., 6-position ATI Mil-Spec stock, A2 type pistol grip, A3 flat-top upper receiver, 9 or 10 (DB15CCB and DB15CCBB) in. Diamondback aluminum T-marked 4-rail, hardcoat anodized black or Burnt Bronze Cerakote (DB15CCBB) finish, 32 1/2-36 1/4 in. OAL. New 2018.

| MSR $690 | $595 | $485 | $415 | $350 | $315 | $295 | $275 | |

Add $19 for Burnt Bronze Cerakote (DB15CCBB) finish.

DB15CCMLB – 5.56 NATO/.223 Rem. cal., GIO, 16 in. chrome moly black Nitride free floating barrel with A2 flash hider, 30 shot metal mag., Roger's Super-Stoc, A2 type pistol grip, A3 flat-top upper receiver, 12 in. M-LOK aluminum rail, hardcoat anodized black or Burnt Bronze Cerakote finish, 32-36 in. OAL, 6.65 lbs. New 2018.

| MSR $642 | $550 | $475 | $400 | $350 | $315 | $295 | $275 | |

Add $19 for Burnt Bronze Cerakote (DB15CCBB) finish.

DB15CCRFDE – 5.56 NATO/.223 Rem. cal., GIO, 16 in. chrome moly black Nitride free floating barrel with A2 flash hider, 30 shot metal mag., Roger's AR Super-Stoc, A2 type pistol grip, A3 flat-top upper receiver, 10 in. Diamondback aluminum four-rail handguard, Flat Dark Earth or Burnt Bronze Cerakote finish. New 2018.

| MSR $710 | $615 | $495 | $415 | $360 | $325 | $300 | $275 | |

Add $19 for Burnt Bronze Cerakote (DB15CCBB) finish.

DB15CMLB / DB15CMLXB – 5.56 NATO/.223 Rem. cal., carbine length stainless steel GIO, 16 in. chrome moly free floating barrel with A2 flash hider, 30 shot metal mag., Roger's AR Super-Stoc, A2 type pistol grip, A3 flat-top upper receiver, 9 1/2 or 11 (DB15CMLXB) in. M-LOK aluminum four rail handguard, hardcoat anodized black finish. New 2018.

| MSR $720 | $615 | $495 | $415 | $360 | $325 | $300 | $275 | |

Add $20 for DB15CMLXB with 11 in. M-LOK aluminum four rail.

DB15EB / DB15EMLB / DB15EODG / DB15ETG – 5.56 NATO/.223 Rem. cal., carbine length gas system, 16 in. chrome moly free floating Melonite coated barrel, DB muzzle brake, Magpul 30 shot PMAG, Adaptive Tactical adj. stock (Ex Performance), Hexmag pistol grip, enhanced trigger guard, forged 7075 T6 aluminum lower and A3 flat-top upper receiver, Diamondback aluminum 15 in. KeyMod or M-LOK (DB15EMLB) rail handguard, hardcoat anodized black, Olive Drab Green (DB15EODG), or Tactical Gray (DB15ETG) finish, 32 1/2-36 1/4 in. OAL, approx. 7 lbs. New 2018.

| MSR $850 | $725 | $500 | $435 | $375 | $335 | $315 | $295 | |

Add $9 for Olive Drab Green (DB15EODG), or Tactical Gray (DB15ETG) finish.

DB15USB – 5.56 NATO/.223 Rem. cal., carbine length GIO, 16 in. chrome moly, M4 contour free floating Melonite coated barrel with A2 flash hider, A2 front sight only, ATI Strikeforce stock with aluminum buffer tube, A2 pistol grip, A3 flat-top upper receiver, standard two-piece handguard, hardcoat anodized black finish, 32 1/2-36 1/4 in. OAL, 6.65 lbs. New 2018.

| MSR $680 | $595 | $485 | $415 | $350 | $315 | $295 | $275 | |

DB308G2B – .308 Win. cal., mid-length gas system, 16 in. barrel, A2 flash hider, 20 shot aluminum mag., Roger's Super-Stoc, A2 style pistol grip, Melonite coated AR10 bolt carrier w/multi-cal. bolt, DPMS style barrel extension, high-pressure firing pin, 15 in. M-LOK QD rail handguard, hardcoat anodized black finish, 33 3/4-37 in. OAL, 7 lbs. 15 oz. New 2018.

| MSR $1,059 | $895 | $575 | $475 | $395 | $350 | $325 | $300 | |

DB15CCKM300B / DB15CCKM300FDE / DB15CCML300B / DB15CCML300BB – .300 AAC Blackout cal., GIO, mid-length gas system, 16 in. chrome moly free floating, black Nitride barrel, A2 flash hider, 30 shot metal mag., Rogers Super-Stoc, A2 type pistol grip, forged 7075 T6 aluminium lower, A3 flat-top, 12 in. KeyMod or M-LOK (DB15CCML300B) rail handguard, hardcoat anodized black, Burnt Bronze (DB15CCML300BB) or FDE (DB15CCKM300FDE) Cerakote finish, 32-36 in. OAL, 6.65 lbs. New 2018.

| MSR $668 | $575 | $485 | $415 | $350 | $315 | $295 | $275 | |

Add $35 for DB15CCKM300FDE with FDE or DB15CCML300BB with Burnt Bronze Cerakote finish.

DLASK ARMS CORP.

Current manufacturer and distributor located in British Columbia, Canada. Direct sales.

RIFLES: SEMI-AUTO

DAR-701 TARGET – AR-15 style, GIO, 22, 24, or 26 in. stainless steel or blue barrel, aluminum alloy construction, two front sling swivels on the tube. Disc. 2013.

| | $1,795 | $1,050 | $875 | $625 | $550 | $475 | $425 | $2,200 |

D 178 DOUBLE D ARMORY, LTD

MSR	100%	98%	95%	90%	80%	70%	60%	Last MSR

DOUBLE D ARMORY, LTD

Current AR-15 style rifle manufacturer located in Greenwood Village, CO since 2012. Dealer and distributor sales.

RIFLES: SEMI-AUTO

Double D Armory also manufactures AR-15 parts as well as their own hardcoat anodized proprietary camo patterns called COVERCEAL™.

SST 5.56 NATO – 5.56 NATO cal., GIO, 16 in. Lothar Walther match grade stainless steel barrel with polygonal rifling and black Nitride finish, A2 flash suppressor, 30 shot mag., mid-length gas system, nickel boron bolt carrier group, aluminum billet upper and lower receiver, M4 feed ramps, Bravo Co. Gunfighter Mod 4 charging handle, 15 in. enhanced free floating handguard, ALG Defense combat trigger, oversized trigger guard, flared magwell, B5 Systems 6-pos. collapsible stock, Magpul MOE+ or B5 Systems grip, full-length top Picatinny rail, choice of hardcoat anodized proprietary camo pattern finish, 6.2 lbs. Mfg. 2015-2017.

	100%	98%	95%	90%	80%	70%	60%	Last MSR
	$1,600	$1,000	$775	$575	$495	$425	$395	*$1,949*

SST .300 BLACKOUT – .300 AAC Blackout cal., 16 in. standard Lothar Walther barrel, carbine length gas system, otherwise similar to Model SST 5.56, 6.2 lbs. Mfg. 2015-2017.

	100%	98%	95%	90%	80%	70%	60%	Last MSR
	$1,600	$1,000	$775	$575	$495	$425	$395	*$1,949*

SSTF-V1 – 5.56 NATO cal., GIO, 16 in. mid-Government or light profile chrome moly barrel with black Nitride finish, A2 flash suppressor, 30 shot mag., Mil-Spec trigger, Magpul MBUS or Diamondhead Poly pop-up sights, Magpul SL stock, Magpul MOE or K2 grip, mid-length gas system, Mil-Spec charging handle, 15 in. M-LOK free float handguard, 6.4 lbs.

MSR $1,399	$1,150	$750	$550	$465	$415	$375	$350

SSTF-V2 – 5.56 NATO cal., GIO, 16 in. mid-Government or lightweight profile chrome moly barrel with black Nitride finish, A2 flash suppressor, 30 shot mag., Mil-Spec trigger, Magpul SL buttstock, Magpul MOE or K2 grip, Magpul MBUS or Diamondhead Poly pop-up sights, 15 in. free float M-LOK handguard, mid-length gas system, BCM Gunfighter Mod 4 charging handle, forged upper and lower receivers, nickel boron M16 BCG, choice of camo anodize pattern finish, 6.4 lbs. New 2018.

MSR $1,545	$1,275	$850	$600	$495	$425	$375	$350

DOUBLESTAR CORP.

Current manufacturer located in Winchester, KY. Distributed by J&T Distributing. Dealer sales only.

Doublestar Corp. also currently manufactures AR-15 accessories and uppers.

PISTOLS: SEMI-AUTO

ARP7 – 5.56 NATO cal., GIO, 7 1/2 in. heavy free floating barrel, Big Timber brake, 30 shot mag., low profile gas block, M4 feed ramps, Billet Backbone charging handle, Ergo pistol grip, Doublestar 7 in. Cloak M-LOK, forged aluminum flat-top upper and lower receiver, 24.5 in. OAL, 5.4 lbs.

MSR $1,300	$1,100	$995	$875	$735	$650	$550	$465

DSC .300 BLACKOUT AR PISTOL – .300 AAC Blackout cal., 7 1/2 or 9 in. rifled barrel, pistol length free float aluminum handguard, pistol tube, 4 3/4 lbs. New 2014.

MSR $1,407	$1,250	$1,075	$950	$800	$700	$600	$495

MINI DRAGON DSC 7.5 AR PISTOL – 5.56 NATO, .300 AAC Blackout, or 9mm Para. cal., AR-15 style, GIO, 7 1/2 in. chrome moly steel heavy barrel, 30 shot mag., pistol length free float aluminum handguard, Picatinny rail gas block, forged lower and A3 flat-top upper receiver with M4 feed ramps, forward assist, dust cover, DSC pistol tube, A2 grip, hardcoat anodized finish, 4.7 lbs.

MSR $920	$780	$685	$585	$530	$430	$350	$275

MINI DRAGON DSC 10.5 AR PISTOL – 5.56 NATO or 9mm Para. cal., AR-15 style, GIO, 10 1/2 in. chrome moly steel heavy barrel with A2 muzzle, single heat shield CAR handguard, A2 upper receiver, front sight tower, DSC pistol tube, A2 pistol grip, 5 1/2 lbs.

MSR $1,284	$1,075	$965	$820	$715	$625	$535	$450

Add $220 for 9mm Para. cal.

MINI DRAGON DSC 11.5 AR PISTOL – 5.56 NATO or 9mm Para. (disc.) cal., AR-15 style, GIO, 11 1/2 in. chrome moly steel heavy barrel with A2 muzzle, 30 shot mag., front sight tower, CAR length polymer handguard, T6 aluminum A3 flat-top upper receiver with M4 feed ramps, forward assist, dust cover, A2 pistol grip, hardcoat anodized finish, 5.7 lbs.

MSR $1,284	$1,075	$965	$820	$715	$625	$535	$450

Add $220 for 9mm Para. cal. (disc.).

DOUBLESTAR CORP., cont. 179 D

MSR	100%	98%	95%	90%	80%	70%	60%	Last MSR

DSC STAR-15 PISTOL – .223 Rem. cal., AR-15 style, GIO, 7 1/2, 10 1/5, or 11 1/2 in. chrome moly match barrel, A2 flash hider, front sight assembly or rail gas block. Disc. 2010.

	$875	$750	$675	$600	$525	$450	$395	$950

RIFLES/CARBINES: SEMI-AUTO

Double Star Corp. makes a complete line of AR-15 style carbines/rifles, as well as a line of SBRs (Short Barreled Rifles) for military/law enforcement.

ARC (ALWAYS READY CARBINE) – 5.56 NATO or .300 AAC Blackout (new 2017) cal., GIO, low profile gas block, 16 in. lightweight barrel, A2 flash hider, 30 shot mag., Samson folding front and rear sights, Ace SOCOM stock, Ergo SureGrip, 15 in. Samson Evolution free floating handguard, aluminum Mil-Spec flat-top upper, M4 feed ramps, forward assist, dust cover, DSC TAC latch charging handle, hardcoat anodized black finish, 6.8 lbs. New 2016.

MSR $1,370	$1,135	$725	$525	$465	$415	$375	$350	

BUMP DRAGON – while this model was advertised in 2016, no further information is available.

Last advertised MSR was $1,284.

MDM (MODERN DESIGNATED MARKSMAN) – 5.56 NATO cal., GIO, 16 in. stainless steel Wilson air gauged barrel, A2 flash hider, 30 shot mag., no sights, Magpul ACS buttstock, Hogue pistol grip, low profile gas block, 15 in. Samson Evolution free floating handguard, aluminum Mil-Spec flat-top upper receiver, M4 feed ramps, forward assist, dust cover, standard charging handle, 8.35 lbs. New 2016.

MSR $1,570	$1,315	$850	$625	$500	$435	$375	$350	

DSC .204 RUGER – .204 Ruger cal., GIO, 20 or 24 in. stainless steel fluted or non-fluted bull barrel, Picatinny rail gas block, Mil-Spec flat-top, free float aluminum tube handguard, A2 pistol grip and buttstock. Mfg. 2013 only.

	$935	$575	$475	$415	$350	$325	$300	$1,125

DSC .300 BLACKOUT – .300 AAC Blackout cal., GIO, 16 in. HBAR barrel, black Nitride coating, Picatinny rail gas block, CAR handguard, Mil-Spec flat-top with M4 feed ramp, A2 pistol grip, 6-position commercial spec DS-4 stock, 6.7 lbs. New 2013.

MSR $970	$825	$535	$450	$385	$340	$325	$295	

DSC 3 GUN RIFLE – 5.56 NATO cal., AR-15 style, GIO, 30 shot mag., 18 in. fluted stainless heavy barrel with Carlson Comp muzzle brake, DSC enhanced trigger guard, Timney trigger, Samson 15 in. Evolution handguard, Ace ARFX buttstock, Hogue or Ergo Ambi SureGrip, 7 1/2 lbs. New 2012.

MSR $1,550	$1,315	$850	$625	$500	$435	$375	$350	

DSC COMMANDO – 5.56 NATO cal., GIO, 16 in. chrome moly HBAR lightweight barrel, permanently attached flash hider, Picatinny rail gas block or "F" marked FSB, two-piece CAR length polymer handguard, Mil-Spec flat-top or A2 upper receiver, A2 pistol grip, 6-position DS-4 buttstock, front sight base, 6.45 lbs. Mfg. 2013-2017.

	$1,150	$750	$550	$465	$415	$375	$350	$1,400

DSC C3 CONSTANT CARRY CARBINE – 5.56 NATO cal., GIO, 16 in. lightweight A-1 profile barrel, comes with Magpul MBUS front and rear sights or w/o sights, Ace Ltd. AR-UL-E buttstock, A2 pistol grip, steel low profile gas block, Samson Evolution 9 in. handguard, Mil-Spec flat-top upper with M4 feed ramp, 5 1/2 lbs. New 2013.

MSR $1,065	$895	$575	$475	$395	$350	$325	$300	

Add $135 for Magpul MBUS front and rear sights.

DSC COVERT DRAGON – 5.56 NATO cal., low profile gas block, GIO, 16 in. chrome moly heavy barrel, A2 flash hider, 30 shot mag., A2 pistol grip, forged aluminum upper and lower receiver, M4 feed ramps, charging handle, 13 in. DRD Tactical QD rail, standard trigger group, DS4 6-pos. adj. buttstock, 7.05 lbs. New 2017.

MSR $1,316	$1,100	$675	$525	$450	$400	$350	$325	

DSC CRITTERSLAYER – .223 Rem. cal., AR-15 style, GIO, 24 in. fluted Shaw barrel, full-length Picatinny rail on receiver and Badger handguard, two-stage match trigger, palm rest, ergonomic pistol grip with finger grooves, includes Harris LMS swivel bipod, flat-top or high rise upper receiver, 11 1/2 lbs. Disc. 2010.

	$1,195	$795	$550	$465	$415	$375	$350	$1,430

Add $40 for ported barrel.

* DSC CritterSlayer Jr. – .223 Rem. cal., GIO, similar to CritterSlayer, except has 16 in. barrel and fully adj. A2 style buttstock, DSC flat-top or high rise upper receiver. Disc. 2010.

	$950	$595	$495	$425	$365	$335	$300	$1,150

Add $65 for detachable carrying handle or $35 for removable front sight.

Add $200 for Enhanced CritterSlayer Jr. with 16 in. Expedition barrel, CAR handguard, and adj. buttstock.

DSC DEER RIFLE – 6.8 SPC cal., AR-15 style, GIO, 20 in. chrome moly heavy barrel with A2 phantom flash hider, 5 shot mag., Ace ARFX skeleton stock, Next Camo water transfer finish, winter trigger guard, 7 3/4 lbs. Mfg. 2012-2014.

	$1,195	$795	$550	$465	$415	$375	$350	$1,450

D 180 DOUBLESTAR CORP., cont.

MSR	100%	98%	95%	90%	80%	70%	60%	Last MSR

DSC DS-4 – 5.56 NATO, 6.5 Grendel, 6.8 SPC, or 7.62x39mm (disc.) cal., GIO, AR-15 style, patterned after the Military M4, GIO, 16 in. chrome moly barrel with Phantom A2 flash hider, 30 shot mag., double heat shield handguard, A2 or flat-top upper receiver with M4 feed ramps, forward assist, dust cover, A2 pistol grip, 6-position buttstock, matte black, tactical pink (disc.), or OD Green (disc.) finish, 6.3 lbs.

	100%	98%	95%	90%	80%	70%	60%	
MSR $940	$800	$525	$450	$385	$340	$325	$295	

DSC DS-4 FDE – 5.56 NATO cal., GIO, 16 in. chrome moly M4 barrel, Flat Dark Earth Teflon coated finish, Picatinny rail gas block or "F" marked FSB, double heat shield two-piece polymer handguard, flat-top upper receiver, A2 pistol grip, 6-position buttstock, Magpul rear BUIS, FDE finish. Mfg. mid-2012-2017.

	$1,150	$750	$550	$465	$415	$375	$350	$1,390

* DSC DS-4 OD – 5.56 NATO cal., similar to DS-4 FDE, except features OD Green finish. Mfg. mid-2012-2017.

	$1,150	$750	$550	$465	$415	$375	$350	$1,390

DSC DS-4 MOE – 5.56 NATO cal., AR-15 style, GIO, 16 in. chrome moly barrel, Magpul MOE features include handguard, upper receiver, pistol grip, enhanced trigger guard, rear BUIS, 6-position commercial spec Magpul MOE stock, 30 shot mag., FDE finish, 6.3 lbs. Disc. 2017.

	$1,250	$825	$575	$475	$425	$375	$350	$1,476

DSC EXPEDITION CARBINE/RIFLE – 5.56 NATO cal., AR-15 style, GIO, 16 or 20 (disc.) in. lightweight contour barrel with integrated muzzle brake, single heat shield CAR handguard, A2 or flat-top upper receiver, A2 pistol grip, A2 or 6-position commercial spec stock, 6.35 lbs. Disc. 2014.

	$875	$550	$465	$395	$350	$325	$300	$1,030

Add $65 for detachable carry handle (disc.).

DSC LIGHTWEIGHT TACTICAL – 5.56 NATO cal., GIO, fluted 16 in. chrome moly HBAR barrel, Picatinny rail gas block or "F" marked FSB, single heat shield two-piece CAR length polymer handguard, Mil-Spec flat-top or A2 upper receiver, D-4 six position buttstock, 6.9 lbs. Mfg. mid-2012-2017.

	$1,150	$750	$550	$465	$415	$375	$350	$1,400

DSC MARKSMAN RIFLE – 5.56 NATO cal., AR-15 style, GIO, 20 in. Wilson Arms stainless steel barrel, Daniel Defense free float handguard, Picatinny rail gas block, A2 Phantom flash hider, Magpul PRS buttstock, adj. LOP, Magpul MIAD pistol grip, two-stage trigger, front and rear flip sight, approx. 9 lbs. Disc. 2017.

	$1,525	$975	$750	$575	$495	$425	$375	$1,804

Add $185 for bipod.

DSC MIDLENGTH CARBINE – 5.56 NATO cal., 16 in. heavy barrel with A2 flash hider, 30 shot aluminum mag., front sight tower, mid-length polymer handguard, DS-4 stock, A2 pistol grip, 6.7 lbs. Mfg. 2014-2017.

	$1,125	$700	$525	$450	$400	$350	$325	$1,350

DSC MIDNIGHT DRAGON – 5.56 NATO cal., AR-15 style, GIO, 24 in. stainless steel bull barrel with spiral fluting and black Nitride coating, aluminum free float handguard with bipod stud, A3 flat-top upper receiver, Ace ARFX buttstock, Ergo tactical pistol grip, DSC two-stage trigger, Badger TAC latch, DSC enhanced trigger guard, 9 1/4 lbs. New 2012.

	100%	98%	95%	90%	80%	70%	60%	
MSR $1,116	$935	$575	$475	$415	$350	$325	$300	

DSC MSD MIL-SPEC DRAGON – 5.56 NATO cal., 16 in. barrel, "F" marked front sight tower, DS-4 Mil-Spec stock, 6.1 lbs. Mfg. 2014-2017.

	$915	$575	$475	$415	$350	$325	$300	$1,088

DSC PATROL RIFLE – 5.56 NATO cal., AR-15 style, GIO, 16 in. chrome moly lightweight barrel with A2 phantom flash hider, Slimline quad rail handguard with three low profile rail covers, flip-up rear sight, 6-position DS-4 buttstock, Hogue overmolded pistol grip, 6 1/2 lbs. Disc. 2017.

	$915	$575	$475	$415	$350	$325	$300	$1,089

DSC STAR-CAR CARBINE – 5.56 NATO, 6.5 Grendel, 6.8 SPC, or 9mm Para. cal., AR-15 style, GIO, 16 in. chrome moly steel heavy barrel with Phantom A2 flash hider, 30 shot mag., single heat shield CAR handguard, A2 or flat-top upper receiver, standard A2 pistol grip, fixed post-ban CAR type stock, 6.7 lbs.

	100%	98%	95%	90%	80%	70%	60%	
MSR $930	$800	$525	$450	$385	$340	$325	$295	

Add $75 for 6.8 SPC, $125 for 6.5 Grendel, or $220 for 9mm Para. cal.

DSC STAR M4 CARBINE – .223 Rem. cal., AR-15 M4 carbine design, GIO, fixed M4 style post-ban buttstock, 16 in. barrel, M4 handguard, 6.76 lbs. Disc. 2012.

	$785	$525	$450	$385	$340	$325	$295	$910

Add $85 for detachable carrying handle.

DSC STAR DISSIPATOR – 5.56 NATO cal., AR-15 style, GIO, 16 in. dissipator chrome moly steel barrel with full-length handguard, A2 or 6-position CAR buttstock, A2 or flat-top upper receiver, 6.9 lbs. Disc. 2014.

	$875	$550	$465	$395	$350	$325	$300	$1,030

DOUBLESTAR CORP., cont. 181 D

MSR	100%	98%	95%	90%	80%	70%	60%	Last MSR

DSC STAR 10-B RIFLE – .308 Win. cal., GIO, 18 in. stainless steel fluted and free floating barrel with Bullseye muzzle brake, ACE Hammer stock, Hogue pistol grip, Samson Evo Evolution handguard, billet aluminum flat-top upper and lower receivers, BCM Gunfighter charging handle, Type III hardcoat anodized black finish, approx. 10 lbs. New 2015.

| MSR $2,550 | $2,050 | $1,250 | $950 | $650 | $575 | $495 | $475 | |

DSC STAR 10-BX RIFLE – 6.5mm Creedmoor or .260 Rem. cal., GIO, 22 in. stainless steel free floating heavy barrel, Bullseye muzzle brake, 20 shot mag., ACE Hammer buttstock, Hogue pistol grip, low profile gas block, 15 in. Samson Evolution handguard, BCM Gunfighter charging handle, billet aluminum flat-top upper with brass deflector and dust cover, lower receiver with integrated trigger guard and enhanced magwell, 45.5 in. OAL. New 2018.

| MSR $2,550 | $2,050 | $1,250 | $950 | $650 | $575 | $495 | $475 | |

DSC STAR-15 LIGHTWEIGHT TACTICAL – .223 Rem. cal., AR-15 style, GIO, 16 in. fluted HBAR barrel with attached muzzle brake, shorty A2 buttstock, A2 or flat-top upper receiver, 6 1/4 lbs. Disc. 2004, reintroduced 2009-2010.

| | $800 | $525 | $450 | $385 | $340 | $325 | $295 | $930 |

Add $65 for detachable carrying handle.

DSC STAR-15 RIFLE/CARBINE – 5.56 NATO, 6.5 Grendel, 6.8 SPC, or 7.62x39mm (disc. 2013) cal., AR-15 style, GIO, 16 (disc.) or 20 in. match barrel with A2 flash hider, ribbed forearm, two-piece rifle handguard, standard A2 buttstock and pistol grip, A2 or flat-top upper receiver, 8 lbs. Disc. 2017.

| | $1,125 | $700 | $525 | $450 | $400 | $350 | $325 | $1,326 |

Add $65 for flat-top with detachable carrying handle.
Add $75 for 6.8 SPC or 7.62x39mm (disc. 2013) cal. or $125 for 6.5 Grendel cal.

DSC STAR-15 9MM CARBINE – 9mm Para. cal., AR-15 style, GIO, 16 in. barrel, ribbed forearm, A2 or flat-top upper receiver, 7 1/2 lbs. Mfg. 2004, reintroduced 2009-2010.

| | $915 | $575 | $475 | $415 | $350 | $325 | $300 | $1,080 |

Add $65 for detachable carry handle.

DSC STAR-15 6.8 SPC RIFLE/CARBINE – 6.8 SPC cal., GIO, 16 or 20 in. chrome moly barrel, A2 upper or flat-top, A2 (rifle) or 6-position DS-4 buttstock, 7-8 lbs. Disc. 2010.

| | $800 | $525 | $450 | $385 | $340 | $325 | $295 | $935 |

Add $65 for detachable carry handle.

DSC STAR-15 6.8 SPC SUPER MATCH RIFLE – 6.8 SPC cal., GIO, 20, 22, or 24 in. free float super match stainless steel bull barrel, Picatinny rail gas block, two-piece NM free floating handguard. Disc. 2010.

| | $895 | $575 | $475 | $395 | $350 | $325 | $300 | $1,075 |

DSC STAR-15 .204 RUGER RIFLE – .204 Ruger cal., GIO, 24 in. chrome moly barrel, A2 buttstock, A2 flash hider. Disc. 2010.

| | $875 | $550 | $465 | $395 | $350 | $325 | $300 | $1,050 |

DSC STAR-15 6.5 GRENDEL CARBINE/RIFLE – 6.5 Grendel cal., GIO, 16 or 20 in. chrome moly barrel, A2 or 6-position (Carbine) buttstock. Disc. 2010.

| | $850 | $550 | $465 | $395 | $350 | $325 | $295 | $985 |

Add $65 for detachable carry handle.

DSC STAR-15 6.5 GRENDEL SUPER MATCH RIFLE – 6.5 Grendel cal., GIO, 20, 22, or 24 in. free floating match bull barrel, A2 buttstock, Picatinny rail gas block, two-piece NM free floating handguard. Disc. 2010.

| | $935 | $575 | $475 | $415 | $350 | $325 | $300 | $1,125 |

DSC STAR-15 DCM SERVICE RIFLE – 5.56 NATO cal., AR-15 style, GIO, 20 in. free float match barrel, National Match front and rear sights, two-stage match trigger, DCM handguard, 8 lbs. Disc.

| | $850 | $550 | $465 | $395 | $350 | $325 | $295 | $1,000 |

DSC SUPERMATCH RIFLE – 5.56 NATO, 6.5 Grendel, or 6.8 SPC cal., AR-15 style, GIO, 16, 20, 22 (disc. 2013), or 24 in. free float stainless steel Super Match barrel, 10 shot aluminum mag., flat-top or high rise upper receiver, includes Picatinny rail and one-piece National Match handguard, A2 stock, 7.8-9 3/4 lbs. Disc. 2017.

| | $865 | $550 | $465 | $395 | $350 | $325 | $300 | $1,020 |

Add $65 for 6.8 SPC or $115 for 6.5 Grendel cal.

DSC TARGET CARBINE – .223 Rem. cal., AR-15 style, GIO, 16 in. dissipator barrel with full-length round one-piece National Match handguard, flip-up sights, Picatinny rail, flat-top upper receiver. Disc.

| | $975 | $595 | $495 | $425 | $365 | $335 | $300 | $1,175 |

DSC ZOMBIE SLAYER – 5.56 NATO cal., AR-15 style, GIO, 14 1/2 in. DS4 barrel (16 in. with permanently attached A2 phantom flash hider), flat-top upper receiver with detachable GI carry handle, two 30 shot magazines, 6-position D4 stock, double heat shield handguards, USMC multi-purpose bayonet, "Zombie Slayer" lasered lower, 6.1 lbs. Mfg. 2012-2014.

| | $1,050 | $650 | $495 | $450 | $395 | $350 | $325 | $1,245 |

MAYBE THE ONLY THING BETTER THAN THIS BOOK IS THE ONLINE SUBSCRIPTION!

Only $19.95/year!

- **Includes monthly updates** keeping you informed of all the new AR-15 makes/models.
- **Features thousands of images** allowing for fast and easy identification.
- **Manufacturer/Model searchable database** allowing you to find the model you need.
- Historical pricing with dynamic interactive graphs keeps you up-to-date on your AR-15 purchases as investments.
- Your own personal online inventory solution - keep track of your collection and track the change in value.
- Includes access to BBP's industry standard Photo Percentage Grading System – why guess a gun's condition when you can be sure?

Visit BLUEBOOKOFGUNVALUES.COM
to view sample pages and ordering

Good Information Never Sleeps!

E SECTION

E.M.F. CO., INC.

Current importer and distributor established 1956, located in Santa Ana, CA. Distributor and dealer sales. E.M.F. stands for Early & Modern Firearms Inc.

For information on Great Western, Dakota Single Action and Hartford revolvers, rifles, and carbines imported by E.M.F., please refer to these individual sections. EMF previously imported Accu-Tech, Citadel, Excel, Howa, and ISSC pistols, rifles and shotguns from 2014-2015. Please refer to their individual sections for these listings. Please refer to the *Blue Book of Modern Black Powder Arms* by John Allen (also online) for more information and prices on E.M.F.'s lineup of modern black powder models.

MSR	100%	98%	95%	90%	80%	70%	60%	*Last MSR*

RIFLES: SEMI-AUTO

J R CARBINE – 9mm Para., .40 S&W, or .45 ACP cal., blowback operation, utilizes standard M4/AR-15 furniture and trigger components, right or left-hand action, Glock magazine, can be converted to other popular pistol mags., flat-top receiver, quad rail forend, black adj. stock, extended pistol grip, tri-flatted barrel design, patented ejection and extraction features, compatible with AR-15 accessories. Mfg. in U.S.A. by J R Carbines, LLC mid-2010-2013.

	$675	$600	$525	$475	$425	$400	$350	*$750*

Please refer to Just Right Carbines listing for current manufacture.

J R CARBINE 12 – 9mm Para., .40 S&W, or .45 ACP cal., blowback operation, utilizes standard M4/AR-15 furniture and trigger components, right or left-hand action, Glock magazine, can be converted to other popular pistol mags., flat-top receiver, quad rail forend, black adj. stock, extended pistol grip, tri-flatted barrel design, patented ejection and extraction features, compatible with AR-15 accessories. Mfg. in U.S.A. by J R Carbines, LLC mid-2010-2013.

	$675	$600	$525	$475	$425	$400	$350	*$750*

Please refer to Just Right Carbines listing for current manufacture.

EAGLE ARMS, INC.

Current trademark of AR-15 style pistols and carbines/rifles manufactured by ArmaLite, Inc. beginning 2017. Eagle Arms, Inc. was a previous manufacturer located in Geneseo, IL until they became a division of ArmaLite, Inc. 1995-2002. In 2003, Eagle Arms became a separate company, and no longer a division of ArmaLite. Manufacture of pre-1995 Eagle Arms rifles was in Coal Valley, IL.

PISTOLS: SEMI-AUTO

EAGLE-15 – 5.56 NATO cal., 6 or 11 in. chrome moly barrel with flash suppressor, 20 shot mag., single stage trigger, Magpul K2 grip and SIG brace, standard safety, aluminum forged flat-top receiver, full-length Picatinny rail, 5 or 10 in. tactical handguard, hardcoat anodized black finish, 5.4-6 lbs. New 2018.

MSR $996	$850	$700	$600	$500	$425	$350	$290

RIFLES: SEMI-AUTO, CURRENT

EAGLE-15 – .223 Rem./5.56x45mm cal., 16 in. chrome moly straight taper barrel with flash suppressor, 30 shot Magpul PMAG, single stage trigger, A2 front sight base or gas block with Picatinny rail (ORC model), 6-pos. collapsible stock, carbine length gas system, 6 in. standard handguard, forged aluminum lower and flat-top upper with Picatinny rail, hard anodized finish, 6 1/2 lbs. New 2017.

MSR $599	$515	$450	$395	$350	$315	$295	$275

EAGLE-15 MISSION FIRST TACTICAL – .223 Wylde chamber, GIO, gas block rail, 16 in. straight taper heavy barrel, flash suppressor, 30 shot MFT mag., A2 front sight, polymer backup sight, 6 in. standard handguard, 6-pos. MFT BMS stock, forged aluminum lower and flat-top upper receiver, Picatinny rail, SST, charging handle, black anodized finish, 6 1/2 lbs. New 2017.

MSR $650	$550	$475	$400	$350	$315	$295	$275

EAGLE-15 OPTICS READY CARBINE – .223 Wylde chamber, GIO, gas block rail, 16 in. straight taper heavy barrel with Cerakote finish, flash suppressor, 30 shot Magpul PMAG, SST, 6 in. standard handguard, forged aluminum lower and flat-top upper receiver with Picatinny rail, charging handle, 6-pos. collapsible stock, 6 1/2 lbs. New 2017.

MSR $599	$515	$450	$395	$350	$315	$295	$275

EAGLE-15 VERSATILE SPORTING RIFLE (VSR) – .223 Rem./5.56x45mm cal. (.223 Wylde chamber), 16 in. chrome moly barrel with flash suppressor and knurled thread protector, 30 shot Magpul PMAG, SST, 6-pos. collapsible stock, rubberized Ergo grip, free float rail system, carbine length gas system, 15 in. VSR handguard with KeyMod attachments, forged aluminum lower and flat-top upper with Picatinny rail, hard anodized aluminum finish, 6.6 lbs. New 2018.

MSR $818	$695	$500	$425	$375	$335	$315	$295

E 184 EAGLE ARMS, INC., cont.

MSR	100%	98%	95%	90%	80%	70%	60%	Last MSR

RIFLES: SEMI-AUTO, RECENT

On the following M-15 models manufactured 1995 and earlier, A2 accessories included a collapsible carbine type buttstock (disc. per 1994 C/B) and forward bolt assist mechanism. Accessories are similar, with the addition of National Match sights. The A2 suffix indicates the rifle is supplied with carrying handle, A4 designates a flat-top receiver, some are equipped with a detachable carrying handle.

AR-10 MATCH RIFLE – .308 Win. cal., AR-15 style, GIO, very similar to the Armalite AR-10 A4 rifle, 20 or 24 (Match rifle) in. chrome moly barrel, 10 shot mag., no sights, black stock with pistol grip and forearm, A2 (Service rifle) or A4 style flat-top upper receiver, 9.6 lbs. Mfg. 2001-2005.

	$850	$550	$465	$395	$350	$325	$295	$1,000

Add $65 for Service rifle with A2 front/rear sights.

Add $480 for 24 in. barrel and aluminum free floating handguard.

MODEL M15 A2/A4 RIFLE (EA-15 E-1) – .223 Rem. or .308 Win. cal., GIO, patterned after the Colt AR-15A, 20 in. barrel, A2 sights or A4 flat-top, with (pre 1993) or w/o forward bolt assist, 7 lbs. Mfg. 1990-1993, reintroduced 2002-2005.

	$675	$500	$425	$375	$335	$315	$295	$795

Add $40 for .223 cal. flat-top (Model E15A4B).

Add $205 for .308 Win. cal. flat-top.

* ***Model M15 A2/A4 Rifle Carbine (EA9025C/EA9027C)*** – .223 Rem. or .308 Win. cal., GIO, 16 in. barrel, collapsible (disc. per C/B 1994) or fixed (new 1994) buttstock, 5 lbs. 14 oz. Mfg. 1990-1995, reintroduced 2002-2005.

	$675	$500	$425	$375	$335	$315	$295	$795

Add $40 for flat-top (Model E15A4CB).

1997 retail for the pre-ban models was $1,100 (EA9396).

Beginning 1993, the A2 accessory kit became standard on this model.

* ***Model M15 A2 H-BAR Rifle (EA9040C)*** – .223 Rem. or .308 Win. cal., GIO, heavy target barrel, includes E-2 accessories, 8 lbs. 14 oz. Mfg. 1990-1995.

	$765	$515	$440	$375	$335	$315	$295	$895

1997 retail for this pre-ban model was $1,100 (EA9200).

* ***Model M15 A4 Rifle Eagle Spirit (EA9055S)*** – .223 Rem. or .308 Win. cal., GIO, designed for IPSC shooting, 16 in. premium air gauged National Match barrel, fixed stock, full-length tubular aluminum handguard, includes match grade accessories, 8 lbs. 6 oz. Mfg. 1993-1995, reintroduced 2002 only.

	$725	$500	$435	$375	$335	$315	$295	$850

The 1995 pre-ban variation of this model retailed at $1,475 (EA9603).

* ***Model M15 A2 Rifle Golden Eagle (EA9049S)*** – .223 Rem. or .308 Win. cal., GIO, 20 in. extra heavy barrel, two-stage trigger, National Match accessories, 12 lbs. 12 oz. Mfg. 1991-1995, reintroduced 2002 only.

	$935	$575	$475	$415	$350	$325	$300	$1,125

The 1997 pre-ban variation of this model retailed at $1,300 (EA9500).

* ***Model M15 A4 Rifle Eagle Eye (EA9901)*** – .223 Rem. or .308 Win. cal., GIO, designed for silhouette matches, 24 in. free floating barrel, weighted buttstock, tubular aluminum handguard, 14 lbs. Mfg. 1993-1995.

	$1,250	$825	$575	$475	$425	$375	$350	$1,495

* ***Model M15 Rifle Action Master (EA9052S)*** – .223 Rem. or .308 Win. cal., GIO, match rifle, free floating 20 in. barrel with compensator, fixed stock, flat-top, solid aluminum handguard tube, National Match accessories, 8 lbs. 5 oz. Mfg. 1992-1995, reintroduced 2002 only.

	$725	$500	$435	$375	$335	$315	$295	$850

The 1995 pre-ban variation of this model retailed at $1,475 (EA5600).

* ***Model M15 A4 Rifle Special Purpose (EA9042C)*** – .223 Rem. or .308 Win. cal., GIO, 20 in. barrel, flat-top (A4) or detachable handle receiver. Disc. 1995.

	$825	$535	$450	$385	$340	$325	$295	$955

The 1995 pre-ban variation of this model retailed at $1,165 (EA9204).

* ***Model M15 A4 Rifle Predator (EA9902)*** – .223 Rem. or .308 Win. cal., GIO, post-ban only, 18 in. barrel, National Match trigger, flat-top (A4) or detachable handle receiver. Mfg. 1995 only.

	$1,125	$700	$525	$450	$400	$350	$325	$1,350

MSR	100%	98%	95%	90%	80%	70%	60%	Last MSR

EDWARD ARMS COMPANY

Current manufacturer located in Phoenix, AZ.

Edward Arms Company manufactures precision weapon systems from the AR-15 platform to custom 1911 handguns.

RIFLES: SEMI-AUTO

MSRs reflect base pricing only. Please contact the company directly for more information including options, availability, and delivery time (see Trademark Index).

15V2L RIFLE – 5.56 NATO cal., AR-15 style, 16 in. chrome-lined barrel, Magpul CTR buttstock, Ergo grip, YHM lightweight rifle length quad rail, 6-position Mil-Spec tube, Tungsten buffer, black receivers and rail, four grip/stock colors available. Disc. 2017.

	$1,575	$995	$775	$575	$495	$425	$395	$1,860

B.A.R. RIFLE – 5.56 NATO cal., AR-15 style, 16 in. chrome-lined barrel, Magpul CTR buttstock, Ergo grip, 12 1/2 or 15 in. Samson Evolution rifle length rail, 6-pos. Mil-Spec tube, Tungsten buffer, black receiver and rail, four grip/stock colors available. Disc.

	$1,425	$925	$700	$550	$475	$395	$350	$1,750

EA10 L.R.T. (LONG RANGE TACTICAL) – .308 Win. cal., AR-15 style, mid-length gas system, 18 in. stainless steel threaded barrel, Timney trigger, integral trigger guard, Magpul PRS AR10 stock, Ergo grip, 13.8 in. Troy Battle rail, Battle Arms Development ambi-lever, AR10 billet charging handle, billet machined lower and flat-top upper receiver with laser T-marks, includes U.S. Peace Keeper case, Type III hardcoat anodized finish (optional colors available). Disc. 2017.

	$2,450	$1,595	$1,200	$700	$675	$575	$525	$3,000

SLR COMBAT RIFLE – 5.56 NATO cal., AR-15 style, 16 in. chrome-lined barrel, Magpul CTR buttstock, YHM SLR rifle length forearm, Ergo grip, 6-pos. Mil-Spec tube, Tungsten buffer, black receivers and rail, four grip/stock colors available. Disc. 2017.

	$1,675	$1,000	$825	$625	$550	$475	$425	$2,000

EVOLUTION USA

Current rifle manufacturer located in White Bird, ID since 1984. Distributor and dealer sales.

RIFLES: SEMI-AUTO

GRENADA – .223 Rem. cal., GIO, design based on the AR-15 with flat-top upper receiver, 17 in. stainless steel match barrel with integral muzzle brake, NM trigger. Disc. 2000.

	$995	$625	$495	$450	$395	$350	$325	$1,195

DESERT STORM – .223 Rem. cal., paramilitary design based on the AR-15, GIO, 21 in. stainless steel match barrel with integral muzzle brake, NM trigger, flat-top upper receiver. Disc. 2003.

	$995	$625	$495	$450	$395	$350	$325	$1,189

IWO JIMA – GIO, carrying handle incorporating iron sights, 20 in. stainless steel match barrel, A2 HBAR action, tubular handguard. Limited mfg.

	$1,350	$875	$650	$525	$450	$385	$350	

MAYBE THE ONLY THING BETTER THAN THIS BOOK IS THE ONLINE SUBSCRIPTION!

Only $19.95/year!

- **Includes monthly updates** keeping you informed of all the new AR-15 makes/models.
- **Features thousands of images** allowing for fast and easy identification.
- **Manufacturer/Model searchable database** allowing you to find the model you need.
- Historical pricing with dynamic interactive graphs keeps you up-to-date on your AR-15 purchases as investments.
- Your own personal online inventory solution - keep track of your collection and track the change in value.
- Includes access to BBP's industry standard Photo Percentage Grading System – why guess a gun's condition when you can be sure?

Visit BLUEBOOKOFGUNVALUES.COM
to view sample pages and ordering

Good Information Never Sleeps!

F SECTION

187 **F**

F-1 FIREARMS

Current AR-10 and AR-15 style pistol and rifle manufacturer located in Texas since 2012.

MSR	100%	98%	95%	90%	80%	70%	60%	Last MSR

PISTOLS: SEMI-AUTO

BDR-15 BILLET PISTOL – 5.56 NATO cal., chambered in .223 Wylde or .300 AAC Blackout, 6 1/2, 8 1/2, or 10 1/2 in. barrel, Noveske KX3 or KX5 flash suppressor, beveled magwell, oversized trigger guard, Hyperfire EDT2 trigger, Magpul MOE adj. buttstock and grip, aluminum receiver set and handguard, S7M Super Lite (M-LOK) rail, Type III hardcoat anodized black (standard) or several color options available.

MSR $2,005	$1,700	$1,500	$1,250	$1,100	$950	$825	$675	

BDR-15-3G BILLET PISTOL – 5.56 NATO cal., chambered in .223 Wylde or .300 AAC Blackout, 6 1/2, 8 1/2, or 10 1/2 in. barrel, Noveske KX3 or KX5 flash suppressor, beveled magwell, oversized trigger guard, Hyperfire EDT2 trigger, Magpul MOE adj. buttstock and grip, aluminum skeletonized upper and lower receiver set, S7M Super Lite (M-LOK) rail, Type III hardcoat anodized black (standard) or several color options available, 5 lbs.

MSR $2,060	$1,775	$1,525	$1,275	$1,125	$975	$850	$685	

DEATH WISH EDITION PISTOL – .223 Wylde chamber, 7 in. barrel, Noveske KX3 suppressor, Hiperfire EDT2 trigger, Magpul MOE grip, black ambidextrous safety selector, 7075-T6 aircraft aluminum receiver set and handguard, C7K 9 in. handguard, Phase 5 hex tube, YHM non-adj. gas block, Type III Class 2 hardcoat anodized black finish, 5.36 lbs. Limited mfg. beginning 2018.

MSR $2,310	$1,950	$1,725	$1,450	$1,250	$1,050	$900	$750	

DYNAMIS CARBINE PISTOL – 5.56 NATO cal. chambered in .223 Wylde or .300 AAC Blackout, 8 1/2 or 10 1/2 in. medium contour match grade stainless steel barrel, Slay-AR compensator, extended mag. release, beveled magwell, Hiperfire EDT heavy gunner trigger, oversized trigger guard, 7075-T6 aluminum Dynamis receiver set and Dynamis rail system, M-LOK mounting points integrated into the Dynamis logo, six QD sling mount attachment points, DLC coated BCG, ambi safety selector, includes tactical case, Type III Class 2 hardcoat anodized black finish, 6.84 lbs. Mfg. in collaboration with Dynamis Alliance beginning 2018.

MSR $2,450	$2,095	$1,825	$1,525	$1,315	$1,085	$950	$815	

UDP-9 PCC (PISTOL CALIBER CARBINE) – 9mm Para. cal., 5 1/2 to 16 in. barrel, Slay-AR compensator, M-LOK compatible handguard, UDP-9-45 3G upper receiver, 4 3/4, 7, or 10 in. handguard, Raptor charging handle, 3G skeletonizing, black finish. New 2018.

MSR $1,750	$1,485	$1,315	$1,150	$1,025	$875	$750	$615	

UDR-15 STYLE 2 PISTOL – chambered in .223 Wylde or .300 AAC Blackout, 7, 8 1/2, or 10 1/2 in. barrel, Noveske KX3 or KX5 flash suppressor, beveled magwell, oversized trigger guard, Magpul MOE adj. buttstock and grip, 7.7 in. S7M Super Lite (M-LOK) rail, low profile gas block, aircraft aluminum chasis, 3G skeletonizing, NiB BCG, Type III Class 2 hard anodized black finish, 5 lbs. New 2018.

MSR $2,060	$1,775	$1,525	$1,275	$1,125	$975	$850	$685	

RIFLES: SEMI-AUTO

BADASSARY SPECIAL EDITION RIFLE – 5.56 NATO cal., 16 in. light contour barrel with black Nitride finish, DS muzzle brake, 30 shot Magpul mag., Magpul front and rear flip-up sights, Magpul CTR stock, Style 2 grip with paracord and blue finger attachments, silver safety selector paddles, Raptor charging handle, DLC BCG, BDR-15-3G skeletonized receiver set, C7K 14 3/4 in. handguard, includes tactical case, custom patriot fade splash polish anodizing finish, 7 lbs. Limited mfg. beginning 2018.

MSR $3,130	$2,550	$1,650	$1,250	$700	$625	$575	$525	

BDR-10 BILLET FULL BUILD RIFLE – .308 Win. or 6.5mm Creedmoor cal., 16, 18, or 20 in. medium contour match grade stainless steel barrel, beveled magwell, Hyperfire EDT2 trigger, oversized trigger guard, Magpul MOE adj. buttstock and grip, 14 3/4 in. C7K lightweight KeyMod free float rail system, Raptor ambidextrous charging handle, low profile gas block, BDR-10 large frame receiver set, Type III hardcoat anodized black finish or several color options available, 8.63 lbs.

MSR $2,800	$2,295	$1,450	$1,075	$675	$595	$525	$475	

Add $10 for 18 in. barrel or $20 for 20 in. barrel.

BDR-10 3G SKELETONIZED COMPLETE RIFLE – .308 Win. or 6.5mm Creedmoor cal., 16, 18, or 20 in. medium contour match grade stainless steel barrel, beveled magwell, Hyperfire EDT2 trigger, oversized trigger guard, Magpul MOE adj. buttstock and grip, BDR-10 large frame receiver set, low profile gas block, 14 3/4 in. C7K 308 contoured KeyMod rail, Raptor ambidextrous charging handle, Type III hardcoat anodized black finish or several color options available, 8.63 lbs.

MSR $2,850	$2,295	$1,450	$1,075	$675	$595	$525	$475	

Add $10 for 18 in. barrel or $20 for 20 in. barrel.

F 188 F-1 FIREARMS, cont.

MSR	100%	98%	95%	90%	80%	70%	60%	Last MSR

BDR-15 3G SKELETONIZED COMPLETE RIFLE – 5.56 NATO cal. chambered in .223 Wylde, .300 AAC Blackout, or 7.62x39mm, 16 in. match grade stainless steel barrel, CMB flat faced compensator, beveled magwell, Hyperfire EDT heavy gunner trigger, oversized trigger guard, Magpul MOE adj. buttstock and grip, aircraft aluminum BDR-15 3G receiver set and handguard, Raptor ambidextrous charging handle, NiB BCG, 12 3/4 in. C7K contoured KeyMod rail, low profile gas block, 3G skeletonizing, Type III Class 2 hardcoat anodized black finish or several other color options available, 6.84 lbs. New 2018.

| MSR $2,060 | $1,675 | $1,000 | $825 | $625 | $550 | $475 | $425 | |

BDR-15 BILLET COMPLETE RIFLE – 5.56 NATO cal., chambered in .223 Wylde, .300 AAC Blackout, or 7.62x39, low profile gas block, 16 in. stainless steel match grade barrel, flat faced compensator, beveled magwell, oversized trigger guard, Hyperfire EDT2 trigger, Magpul MOE adj. buttstock and grip, aluminum BDR-15 receiver set and handguard, C7K contoured KeyMod rail, NiB bolt carrier group, Type III hardcoat anodized black (standard) or several color options available, 7.15 lbs.

| MSR $1,995 | $1,650 | $1,000 | $795 | $595 | $495 | $425 | $395 | |

DEMOLITION RANCH LIMITED EDITION FULL BUILD RIFLE – 5.56 NATO cal., 16 in. light contour barrel with black Nitride finish, Dragon Slay-AR suppressor, 30 shot Magpul mag., beveled magwell, Hiperfire EDT2 trigger, oversized trigger guard, Vortex Sparc AR red dot sight, CTR buttstock, MOE black grip, ambidextrous black safety selector, UDR-15 3G Gen 2 upper and lower receiver with H7M 14.3 in. handguard, scalloped upper receiver Picatinny rail, black Raptor charging handle, custom laser Demolition Ranch on handguard and charging handle, includes tactical case, Type II hardcoat anodized black finish, 6.86 lbs. Limited mfg. beginning 2018.

| MSR $2,411 | $1,975 | $1,150 | $925 | $650 | $575 | $495 | $425 | |

* **Demolition Ranch Pro Limited Edition Full Build Rifle** – .223 Wylde chamber, 16 in. light contour barrel with black Nitride finish, Dragon Slay-AR compensator, 30 shot Magpul mag., beveled magwell, CMC flat trigger, oversized trigger guard, Vortex Sparc AR red dot sight, black Minimalist buttstock, black skeleton grip with paracord, black ambidextrous safety selectors, scalloped upper receiver Picatinny rail, F1 Firearms Durabolt DLC carrier group, UDR-15 3G Gen 2 upper and lower receiver with 14.3 in. H7M handguard with Multicam finish, black Raptor charging handle, custom laser Demolition Ranch on handguard and charging handle, Type II hardcoat anodized black finish, 6.69 lbs. Limited mfg. beginning 2018.

| MSR $2,795 | $2,225 | $1,395 | $1,050 | $675 | $595 | $525 | $475 | |

DYNAMIS CARBINE – 5.56 NATO cal. chambered in .223 Wylde or .300 AAC Blackout, 16 in. medium contour match grade stainless steel barrel, Slay-AR compensator, extended mag. release, beveled magwell, Hiperfire EDT heavy gunner trigger, oversized trigger guard, 7075-T6 aluminum Dynamis receiver set and Dynamis rail system, M-LOK mounting points integrated into the Dynamis logo, six QD sling mount attachment points, DLC coated BCG, ambi safety selector, includes tactical case, Type III Class 2 hardcoat anodized black finish, 6.84 lbs. Mfg. in collaboration with Dynamis Alliance beginning 2018.

| MSR $2,450 | $1,975 | $1,150 | $925 | $650 | $575 | $495 | $425 | |

* **Dynamis Carbine Custom** – 5.56 NATO cal. chambered in .223 Wylde or .300 AAC Blackout, 16 in. medium contour match grade stainless steel barrel, Slay-AR compensator, extended mag. release, beveled magwell, Hiperfire EDT heavy gunner trigger, oversized trigger guard, 7075-T6 aluminum Dynamis receiver set and Dynamis rail system, 10 1/4 in. D7M handguard, M-LOK mounting points integrated into the Dynamis logo, six QD sling mount attachment points, DLC coated BCG, ambi safety selector, includes tactical case, Type III Class 2 hardcoat anodized black finish, 6.84 lbs. Mfg. in collaboration with Dynamis Alliance beginning 2018.

| MSR $2,450 | $1,975 | $1,150 | $925 | $650 | $575 | $495 | $425 | |

* **Dynamis Carbine Scout Upgrade** – 5.56 NATO cal. chambered in .223 Wylde or .300 AAC Blackout, 16 in. Proof Research carbon fiber wrapped barrel, Slay-AR compensator, extended mag. release, beveled magwell, Geissele SSA-E trigger, oversized trigger guard, 7075-T6 aluminum Dynamis receiver set and Dynamis rail system, M-LOK mounting points integrated into the Dynamis logo, six QD sling mount attachment points, DLC coated BCG, ambi safety selector, includes tactical case, Type III Class 2 hardcoat anodized black finish, 6.84 lbs. Mfg. in collaboration with Dynamis Alliance beginning 2018.

| MSR $3,050 | $2,450 | $1,595 | $1,200 | $700 | $675 | $575 | $525 | |

FDR-15 FORGED MOD 1 FULL BUILD RIFLE – 5.56 NATO cal., low profile gas block, 16 in. match grade barrel, A2 flash hider, Mil-Spec trigger, Magpul BUIS front and rear flip-up sights, Magpul MOE grip, choice of C7K, S7M, or H7M handguard, Mil-Spec charging handle and Synth kit, includes Flambeau 6500 AR tactical gun case, black Nitride finish, approx. 7 lbs.

| MSR $1,200 | $995 | $625 | $495 | $450 | $395 | $350 | $325 | |

FDR-15 FORGED MOD 2 FULL BUILD RIFLE – 5.56 NATO cal., low profile gas block, 16 in. medium contour match grade barrel, CMB flat faced compensator, Hyperfire EDT2 trigger, Troy BUIS front and rear sights, Magpul MOE grip, choice of C7K, S7M, or H7M handguard, Mil-Spec charging handle and Synth kit, includes Flambeau 6500AR tactical gun case, nickel boron coated, 7.06 lbs.

| MSR $1,400 | $1,150 | $750 | $550 | $465 | $415 | $375 | $350 | |

F-1 FIREARMS, cont. **189** **F**

MSR	100%	98%	95%	90%	80%	70%	60%	Last MSR

FDR-15 FORGED MOD 3 FULL BUILD RIFLE – 5.56 NATO cal., low profile gas block, 16 in. fluted match grade barrel, CMB flat faced compensator, Hyperfire EDT2 trigger, Magpul MOE stock and grip, choice of C7K, S7M, or H7M handguard, AXTS Raptor ambidextrous charging handle, Mil-Spec Synth kit, includes Vortex Optics StrikerFire II red/ green dot scope and Flambeau 6500AR tactical gun case, nickel boron coated, 7 1/2 lbs.

| MSR $1,600 | $1,315 | $850 | $625 | $500 | $435 | $375 | $350 | |

OLD GLORY LIMITED EDITION FULL BUILD RIFLE – .223 Wylde chambered, 16 in. brick fluted barrel, flat faced compensating brake, beveled magwell, high grade billet aluminum construction, Hiperfire EDT2 performance trigger, oversized trigger guard, Vortex StrikerFire II red dot sight, Magpul MOE stock, ambi charging handle, Durabolt Silver BCG, M-LOK side and bottom rail mounts, scalloped top rail, front and rear Picatinny rails, one-piece free float design, 14.3 in. H7M ultra lite handguard, BDR-15-3G receiver set, Old Glory red, white, and blue finish, 7.46 lbs. Limited mfg. beginning 2018.

| MSR $3,022 | $2,450 | $1,595 | $1,200 | $700 | $675 | $575 | $525 | |

PATRIOT RIFLE – 5.56 NATO cal., light contour barrel, angle face muzzle brake, Mil-Spec trigger, MOE stock and grip, Raptor charging handle, 15 in. M7M Miculek handguard, black Nitride BCG, skeletonized FDR set, Proudly American Cerakote finish, 6.44 lbs. Limited mfg. beginning 2018.

| MSR $2,285 | $1,795 | $1,050 | $875 | $625 | $550 | $475 | $425 | |

UDR-15-3G STYLE 2 SKELETONIZED COMPLETE RIFLE – 5.56 NATO cal. chambered in .223 Wylde, .300 AAC Blackout, or 7.62x39mm, 16 in. match grade stainless steel barrel, beveled magwell, oversized trigger guard, Magpul MOE adj. buttstock and grip, scalloped Mil-Spec 1913 Picatinny rail, aluminum upper receiver, 3G skeletonizing, NiB BCG, C7K contoured KeyMod rail, low profile gas block, Type III Class 2 hardcoat anodized black finish or several color options available. New 2018.

| MSR $2,050 | $1,675 | $1,000 | $825 | $625 | $550 | $475 | $425 | |

Add $135 for left-hand configuration.

FN AMERICA LLC (FNH USA)

Current manufacturer and importer established in 1998, located in McLean, VA. Dealer and distributor sales.

In the U.S., FN (Fabrique Nationale) is represented by two entities - FNH USA, which is responsible for sales, marketing, and business development, and FNM, which stands for FN Manufacturing, which handles manufacturing. FNH USA has two separate divisions - commercial/law enforcement, and military operations. FN Manufacturing is located in Columbia, SC. Design, research and development are conducted under the authority of FN Herstal S.A. In mid-2014, it was announced that the consolidation of FN Manufacturing LLC and FNH USA LLC would be called FN America LLC, and headquarters would remain in McLean.

Some of the firearms that FNM currently produces for the U.S. government are M16 rifles, M249 light machine guns, and M240 medium machine guns. FNM also produces the FNP line of handguns for the commercial, military, and law enforcement marketplaces. FNM is one of only three small arms manufacturers designated by the U.S. government as an industry base for small arms production. In November 2004, the FN model was chosen by the U.S. Special Operations Command (USSOCOM) for the new SCAR military rifle.

PISTOLS: SEMI-AUTO

In addition to the models listed, FNH USA also imported the HP-SA ($800 last MSR), and the HP-SFS until 2006.

All FNP guns come standard with three magazines and a lockable hard case.

FN15 PISTOL 5.56 – 5.56x45mm cal., GIO, 10 1/2 in. cold hammer forged chrome-lined free floating barrel, stainless steel pinned gas block, A2 flash hider, 30 shot Magpul PMAG, SBX-K pistol stabilizing brace, Magpul MOE grip, ergonomic safety lever and mag. release, hard anodized aluminum flat-top receiver, Mil-Std 1913 rail, 9 in. Midwest Industries rail with M-LOK, carbine length gas system, forward assist, pistol buffer kit, 5.2 lbs. New 2018.

| MSR $1,599 | $1,350 | $1,200 | $1,075 | $950 | $815 | $700 | $575 | |

FN 15 PISTOL .300 BLACKOUT – .300 AAC Blackout cal., GIO, 12 in. cold hammer forged chrome-lined free floating barrel, stainless steel pinned gas block, SureFire ProComp 762 muzzle brake, 30 shot Magpul PMAG, SBX-K pistol stabilizing brace, Magpul MOE grip, ergonomic safety lever and mag. release, hard anodized aluminum flat-top receiver, Mil-Std 1913 rail, 10 in. Midwest Industries rail with M-LOK, pistol length gas system, forward assist, pistol buffer kit, 5.56 lbs. New 2018.

| MSR $1,599 | $1,350 | $1,200 | $1,075 | $950 | $815 | $700 | $575 | |

RIFLES/CARBINES: SEMI-AUTO

FN 15 1776 – 5.56x45mm cal., GIO, 16 in. alloy steel button-broached barrel, A2 style compensator, 30 shot Magpul PMAG Gen 3, optics ready Mil-Std 1913 flat-top rail, 6-pos. collapsible stock, two-piece single heat shield, oval handguard, sling attachments, matte black finish, 6.6 lbs. Mfg. 2015-2016.

| | $765 | $515 | $440 | $375 | $335 | $315 | $295 | *$899* |

190 FN AMERICA LLC (FNH USA), cont.

MSR	100%	98%	95%	90%	80%	70%	60%	Last MSR

FN 15 CARBINE – 5.56x45mm cal., GIO, 16 in. barrel with A2 style compensator, 30 shot aluminum mag., A2 style front sights, removable M4 style rear carrying handle, flat-top upper receiver with rail, two-piece oval handguard, 6-pos. collapsible stock, matte black finish, 6.94 lbs. Mfg. 2014-2016.

	$950	$595	$495	$425	$365	$335	$300	*$1,149*

FN 15 COMPETITION – 5.56x45mm cal., GIO, 18 in. cold hammer forged barrel, SureFire ProComp 556 muzzle brake, steel low profile gas block, 30 shot mag., Timney trigger, Magpul MOE-SL collapsible buttstock, Magpul MOE black pistol grip, rifle length gas system, H2 buffer, nickel boron bolt carrier group, extended rifle length M-LOK 16 in. handguard, ambidextrous bolt release, billet aluminum upper and lower receiver with anodized blue finish, 8.1 lbs. New 2016.

MSR $2,249	$1,795	$1,050	$875	$625	$550	$475	$425	

FN 15 DMR – 5.56x45mm cal., GIO, 18 in. chrome-lined free floating barrel with SureFire ProComp 556 muzzle brake, 30 shot Magpul PMAG, Magpul MBUS Pro sights, Timney competition trigger, Midwest Industries SSM M-LOK 15 in. handguard, flat-top receiver with rail, Magpul STR buttstock, Magpul MOE grip, matte black finish, 7.2 lbs. Mfg. 2015-2016.

	$1,575	$995	$775	$575	$495	$425	$395	*$1,899*

FN 15 DMR II – 5.56x45mm cal., GIO, 18 in. cold hammer forged chrome-lined free floating barrel with pinned gas block, SureFire ProComp 556 muzzle device, 30 shot Magpul PMAG, 3.5 lb. Timney match trigger, Magpul MOE STR buttstock, Magpul MOE grip, ergonomic safety lever and mag. release, FN Rail System with M-LOK technology, hard anodized aluminum flat-top upper receiver with 1913 Mil-Spec rail, upgraded Mil-Spec lower receiver, forward assist, 7.03 lbs. New 2017.

MSR $1,999	$1,650	$1,000	$795	$595	$495	$425	$395	

FN 15 MD HEAVY BARREL CARBINE – 5.56x45mm cal., GIO, 16 in. cold hammer forged chrome-lined free floating heavy profile barrel, pinned gas block, PWS muzzle brake, 10 shot Magpul PMAG, FN combat trigger, collapsible 6-pos. stock with sling mount, A2 pistol grip, ergonomic safety lever and mag. release, 12 in. free float Midwest Industry rail with M-LOK, hard anodized aluminum flat-top receiver with Mil-Spec rail, 7.1 lbs. New 2018.

MSR $1,399	$1,150	$750	$550	$465	$415	$375	$350	

FN 15 MD HEAVY BARREL RIFLE – 5.56x45mm cal., GIO, 20 in. cold hammer forged chrome-lined free floating heavy barrel with pinned gas block and muzzle thread protector, 15 in. free float Samson evolution rail, 10 shot Magpul PMAG, hard anodized aluminum flat-top receiver, Mil-Spec rail, FN combat trigger, fixed A2 buttstock, A2 pistol grip, ergonomic safety lever and mag. release, forward assist, 8.7 lbs. New 2018.

MSR $1,399	$1,150	$750	$550	$465	$415	$375	$350	

FN 15 MILITARY COLLECTOR M4 – 5.56x45mm cal., GIO, 16 in. button-broached barrel, 30 shot AR style mag., A2 style front and adj. rear sights, 6-pos. stock with sling mount, M4 pistol grip, ambi safety lever, Knights Armament M4 RAS adapter rail with rail covers, hard anodized aluminum flat-top receiver with Picatinny rail, matte black finish, 6.6 lbs. New 2015.

MSR $1,749	$1,425	$925	$700	$550	$475	$395	$350	

FN 15 MILITARY COLLECTOR M16 – 5.56x45mm cal., GIO, 20 in. button-broached barrel, A2 compensator, 30 shot aluminum AR style mag., A2 style front and adj. rear sights, fixed A2 buttstock, M16 pistol grip, ambi selector, Knights Armament M5 RAS adaptor rail with rail covers, hard anodized aluminum flat-top receiver with Picatinny rail, matte black finish, 8.2 lbs. New 2015.

MSR $1,749	$1,425	$925	$700	$550	$475	$395	$350	

FN 15 MOE SLG – 5.56x45mm cal., GIO, 16 in. alloy steel button-broached barrel, A2 compensator, 30 shot Magpul PMAG, Magpul MBUS rear and A2 style front sights, Magpul MOE SL gray buttstock and grip, hard anodized aluminum receiver, Magpul MOE SL gray M-LOK carbine handguard, forward assist, matte black/gray finish, 6.8 lbs. Mfg. 2015-2016.

	$995	$625	$495	$450	$395	$350	$325	*$1,199*

FN 15 RIFLE – 5.56x45mm cal., GIO, 20 in. barrel with A2 compensator, 30 shot mag., flat-top receiver with rail, A2-style front sights, removable carrying handle, two-piece ribbed round handguard with heat shields, fixed stock with sling mount and storage compartment, matte black finish, 7.97 lbs. Mfg. 2014-2016.

	$950	$595	$495	$425	$365	$335	$300	*$1,149*

FN 15 SPORTING – .223 Rem. cal., GIO, 18 in. match grade cold hammer forged free floating barrel with SureFire ProComp 556 muzzle brake, 30 shot mag., Timney competition trigger, flat-top receiver with rail, Samson Evolution 15 in. handguard, Magpul CTR buttstock, Magpul MOE grip, matte black finish, 7.7 lbs. New 2015.

MSR $1,749	$1,425	$925	$700	$550	$475	$395	$350	

FN 15 SRP TACTICAL – 5.56x45mm cal., GIO, 16 in. button-broached barrel with pinned and welded A2 style flash hider, 30 shot mag., FN combat trigger, A2 style grip, 6-pos. buttstock, hard anodized aluminum flat-top receiver, Mil-Std 1913 rail, Midwest Rail System with M-LOK technology, mid-length gas system, Precision Reflex low profile gas block with magnesium phosphate finish, Mil-Spec buffer tube, ergonomic safety lever and mag. release, forward assist, 6 lbs. New 2017.

MSR $1,199	$995	$625	$495	$450	$395	$350	$325	

FN AMERICA LLC (FNH USA), cont. 191 F

MSR	100%	98%	95%	90%	80%	70%	60%	Last MSR

FN 15 TACTICAL – 5.56x45mm cal., GIO, 16 in. match grade free floating barrel with FNH USA 3-prong flash hider, 30 shot Magpul PMAG, aluminum flat-top receiver with rail, Magpul MBUS sights, Midwest Industries LWM 12 in. handguard with M-LOK accessory mounting system, Magpul MOE grip, enhanced combat trigger, Magpul MOE SL buttstock, matte black finish, 6.6 lbs. Mfg. 2015-2016.

	$1,250	$825	$575	$475	$425	$375	$350	$1,479

FN 15 TACTICAL II – 5.56x45mm cal., GIO, 16 in. cold hammer forged chrome-lined free floating barrel with pinned gas block, FN 3-prong flash hider, 30 shot Magpul PMAG, FN combat trigger, Magpul MOE SL buttstock, Magpul MOE grip, ergonomic safety lever and mag. release, hard anodized aluminum flat-top upper receiver with 1913 Mil-Spec rail, enhanced Mil-Spec lower receiver, FN Rail System with M-LOK technology, forward assist, 6.7 lbs. New 2017.

MSR $1,599	$1,315	$850	$625	$500	$435	$375	$350	

FN 15 TACTICAL .300 BLK – .300 AAC Blackout cal., GIO, 16 in. match grade hammer forged, free floating barrel, SureFire ProComp 762 muzzle brake, low profile gas block, 30 shot mag., Magpul front and rear sight assembly, Magpul MOE-SL buttstock and MOE pistol grip, carbine length gas system, H buffer, lightweight 12 in. M-LOK rail, 6 3/4 lbs. Mfg. 2016 only.

	$1,250	$825	$575	$475	$425	$375	$350	$1,479

FN 15 TACTICAL .300 BLK II – .300 AAC Blackout cal., GIO, 16 in. cold hammer forged chrome-lined free floating barrel with pinned gas block, SureFire ProComp 762 muzzle device, 30 shot Magpul PMAG, FN combat trigger, Magpul MOE SL buttstock, Magpul MOE grip, ergonomic safety lever and magazine release, hard anodized aluminum flat-top receiver with 1913 Mil-Spec rail, FN Rail System with M-LOK technology, forward assist, carbine length gas system, 6.91 lbs. New 2017.

MSR $1,599	$1,315	$850	$625	$500	$435	$375	$350	

FN 15 TACTICAL CARBINE FDE P-LOK – 5.56x45mm cal., 16 in. cold hammer forged chrome-lined barrel, FN 3-prong flash hider, 30 shot Magpul PMAG, 16 in. cold hammer forged chrome-lined barrel, FN combat trigger, B5 Systems buttstock and grip, ergonomic safety lever and mag. release, mid-length gas block, P-LOK handguard with M-LOK technology, hard anodized aluminum flat-top receiver with Picatinny rail, forward assist, FDE finish, 7.2 lbs. New 2018.

MSR $1,499	$1,250	$825	$575	$475	$425	$375	$350	

FALKOR DEFENSE

Current AR-15 style rifle manufacturer located in Kalispell, MT beginning 2016.

PISTOLS: SEMI-AUTO

BLITZ – .223 Wylde chamber, AR-15 style, 10 1/2 in. steel barrel, Falkor "Blast Cap" muzzle brake, 30 shot Lancer L5AWM mag., flared magwell with magwell grip, Geissele Super Dynamic 3-Gun trigger, Hogue rubber overmold grip, short throw safety selector, Falkor "Fatty" free float 11 1/2 in. M-LOK handguard, anti-tilt Nitride BCG, pistol buffer system, ambidextrous controls, ambi matched billet upper and lower receiver with hard anodized finish, charging handle, QuickSnap dust cover. New 2017.

MSR $2,600	$2,200	$1,925	$1,600	$1,375	$1,125	$975	$850	

RIFLES: SEMI-AUTO

ALPHA DMR – .308 Win. cal., 18 in. carbon fiber (disc.) or DRACOS Straightjacket barrel, VG6 Gamma muzzle brake, 20 shot Lancer mag., flared magwell with magwell grip, Geissele SSA-E two-stage trigger (disc.) or Trigger Tech straight two-stage adj. trigger, Luth-AR MBA-1 stock, Hogue rubber overmold or VZ grip, hard anodized billet upper and lower receiver, QuickSnap dust cover, FALKOR "Tranny" free float 15.4 in. M-LOK handguard, FALKOR MACH 10 ambi charging handle, ambidextrous mirrored controls, grey or shadow finish, 9 lbs.

MSR $4,010	$3,275	$2,225	$1,550	$925	$725	$675	$650	

Add $200 for shadow finish.

BREACHER – .308 Win. cal., 16 in. steel barrel, "King" muzzle device, 20 shot Lancer mag., Geissele Super Dynamic 3-Gun trigger, flared magwell, Mission First Tactical Battlelink stock, Hogue rubber overmold grip, ambi matched billet hard anodized upper and lower receivers, ambidextrous mirrored controls, QuickSnap dust cover, 5 Barrier handguard, MACH 10 ambi charging handle, grey or shadow finish, 8.1 lbs. Disc. 2017.

	$2,375	$1,525	$1,150	$700	$625	$550	$475	$2,900

Add $200 for shadow finish.

CAITLYN – .223 Wylde chamber, 16 in. Proof Research carbon fiber barrel, VG6 Epsilon high performance muzzle brake, 30 shot Hex mag., mid-length gas system, flared magwell w/magwell grip, Geissele SSA-E two-stage trigger, Mission First Tactical Battlelink stock, Hogue rubber overmold grip, Falkor Mach 15 ambi charging handle, ambi short throw safety selector, Falkor "Tranny" free float 14.6 in. M-LOK handguard, ambi matched billet upper and lower hard anodized receivers, QuickSnap dust cover, grey or shadow finish, 6.3 lbs.

MSR $3,299	$2,625	$1,725	$1,300	$725	$650	$595	$525	

F 192 FALKOR DEFENSE, cont.

MSR	100%	98%	95%	90%	80%	70%	60%	Last MSR

OMEGA – 6.5mm Creedmoor cal., 22 in. DRACOS StraightJacket barrel, VG6 GAMMA muzzle brake, 20 shot Lancer mag., no sights, flared magwell with magwell grip, TriggerTech adaptable AR primary trigger, VZ grip, Luth-AR MBA-1 stock, Falkor MACH 10 ambi charging handle, Falkor "Tranny" free float 19.13 in. M-LOK handguard, anti-tilt Nitride BCG, ambi matched billet upper and lower receiver with hard anodized finish, ambi takedown pins, ambidextrous mirrored controls, QuickSnap dust cover, gray or shadow finish, 10 1/4 lbs. New 2017.

MSR $3,995	$3,200	$2,150	$1,525	$895	$695	$650	$575

Add $200 for shadow finish or $450 for custom Cerakote finish.

PETRA – .300 Norma cal., 24 in. DRACOS composite barrel, DS-300 muzzle brake, 10 shot mag., flared magwell with magwell grip, TriggerTech two-stage adj. trigger, Magpul PRS stock, Hogue rubber overmold grip, Falkor Mach 300 ambi charging handle, short throw safety selector, Falkor "Tranny" free float 19 in. M-LOK handguard, ambi matched billet upper and lower hard anodized receivers, QuickSnap dust cover, grey or shadow finish, 11.8 lbs. Disc. 2017

	$5,350	$4,750	$4,100	$3,450	$3,000	$2,550	$2,050	$6,499

Add $200 for shadow finish.

PETRA CARBON FIBER – .300 Win. Mag. cal., 20 in. Proof Research carbon fiber (disc. 2017) or 22 in. DRACOS Straightjacket barrel, DS-300 muzzle brake, 10 shot mag., flared magwell w/magwell grip, Geissele SSA-E two-stage trigger (disc. 2017) or TriggerTech two-stage adj. trigger, Luth-AR MBA-1 stock, Hogue rubber overmold grip, Falkor Mach 300 ambi charging handle, short throw safety selector, Falkor "Tranny" free float 19 in. M-LOK handguard, ambi matched billet upper and lower hard anodized receivers, QuickSnap dust cover, grey, shadow, or limited edition Woodland Cerakote (disc. 2017) finish, 10.3 lbs.

MSR $5,800	$4,850	$4,250	$3,675	$3,100	$2,650	$2,200	$1,875

Add $200 for shadow finish.

Add $300 for limited edition Woodland Cerakote finish (new 2017).

RECCE – .223 Wylde chamber, 16 in. Proof Research steel barrel, VG6 Epsilon high performance muzzle brake, 30 shot Hex mag., mid-length gas system, flared magwell with magwell grip, Geissele Super Dynamic 3-Gun trigger, Mission First Battlelink Minimalist stock, Hogue rubber overmold grip, Falkor Mach 15 ambi charging handle, ambi short throw safety selector, Falkor "Tranny" free float 14.6 in. M-LOK handguard, ambi matched billet upper and lower hard anodized receivers, QuickSnap dust cover, grey or shadow finish, 6.6 lbs.

MSR $2,350	$1,875	$1,100	$895	$650	$575	$495	$425

FAXON FIREARMS

Current rifle and parts/components manufacturer located in Cincinnati, OH since 2012.

RIFLES: SEMI-AUTO

FX 5510 - 3 GUN READY RIFLE – .223 Wylde chamber, GIO, 18 in. Match Series 5R Gunner barrel, Hiperfire trigger, ambidextrous safety, 15 in. carbon fiber handguard, adj. gas block, 5.96 lbs. New 2018.

MSR $2,199	$1,725	$1,050	$850	$625	$550	$475	$425

FX 6500 – 6.5 Grendel cal., 18 in. Match Series 5R Gunner barrel, Hiperfire trigger, ambidextrous safety, 15 in. carbon fiber handguard, 6.05 lbs. New 2018.

MSR $1,899	$1,575	$995	$775	$575	$495	$425	$395

FIGHTLITE INDUSTRIES (ARES DEFENSE SYSTEMS INC.)

Current semi-auto rifle and accessories manufacturer established in 1997, located in Melbourne, FL.

In mid-2016, the company changed its name from ARES Defense Systems Inc. to FightLite Industries. FightLite plans to maintain the ARES, ARES Defense, and related logos and product names as sub-brands of FightLite Industries.

PISTOLS: SEMI-AUTO

SCR PISTOL – 5.56 NATO or .300 AAC Blackout cal., GIO, 7 1/4 in. free floating threaded barrel, 10 shot detachable mag., Shockwave Technologies grip, 12 in. Picatinny top rail, KeyMod or M-LOK handguard, hardcoat anodized black finish, 3.9 lbs. New 2018.

MSR $865	$735	$650	$580	$515	$450	$385	$340

RIFLES: SEMI-AUTO

FightLite Industries manufactures quality firearms and firearm accessories for military, law enforcement, and the sporting market. Previous mission configurable weapons available for military and law enforcement only included: ARES-16 MCR, ARES-16 AMG-1, and the ARES-16 AMG-2.

ARES-15 MCR (MISSION CONFIGURABLE RIFLE) – 5.56 NATO cal., AR-15 style, GPO, 16 1/4 in. barrel, patented upper receiver system allows multiple configurations, including a 3-second barrel change, 6-pos. telescoping stock, Mil-Spec handguard with rail interface system, optional belt feed module, approx. 7 1/2 lbs. Mfg. 2014-2016.

	$2,050	$1,250	$950	$650	$575	$495	$475	$2,566

Add $1,984 for belt feed module.

FIGHTLITE INDUSTRIES (ARES DEFENSE SYSTEMS INC.), cont. 193 F

MSR	100%	98%	95%	90%	80%	70%	60%	Last MSR

ARES-15 MCR SUB CARBINE – 5.56 NATO cal., GPO, 16 1/4 in. quick change barrel, 30 shot mag., patented upper receiver system, left-side folding buttstock assembly, Mil-Spec co-planar handguard with rail interface system, includes SKB briefcase system, 7 1/2 lbs. Mfg. 2014-2016.

	$3,050	$1,975	$1,425	$850	$675	$625	$575	$3,789

ARES SCR (SPORT CONFIGURABLE RIFLE) – 5.56 NATO or 7.62x39mm cal., GIO, 16 1/4 or 18 in. light barrel, sporterized configuration with standard flat-top upper receiver or flat-top with dust cover, Magpul MOE handguard, modular design permits changing calibers, supplied with 5 shot mag., Sporter, Sporter Short, or Monte Carlo stock, 5.7 lbs. New 2014.

	$745	$500	$435	$375	$335	$315	$295	

Add $30 for flat-top upper receiver with dust cover.

MCR-013 – 5.56 NATO cal., GPO, dual feed, 16 1/4 in. quick change barrel, 30 shot mag., front and rear adj. sight, billet upper receiver, feed cover, and charging handle, KeyMod or Mil-Std 1913 rail, black 6-pos. synthetic telescoping stock with Mil-Spec receiver extension tube, Type III hardcoat anodized black finish, 7 1/2 lbs. Mfg. 2017 only.

	$3,600	$2,500	$1,650	$1,025	$775	$695	$650	$4,450

MCR-014 – 5.56 NATO cal., GPO, 16 1/4 in. quick change barrel, 30 shot mag., front and rear adj. sights, 6-position black synthetic telescoping stock with Mil-Spec receiver extension tube, precision machined billet upper receiver with feed cover and charging handle, KeyMod or Mil-Std 1913 rail, manganese phosphate, Nitride, or Type III hardcoat anodized black finish, 7 1/2 lbs. Mfg. mid-2016-2017.

	$3,695	$2,650	$1,675	$1,050	$795	$725	$700	$4,559

MCR-100 – 5.56 NATO cal., GPO, 16 1/4 in. quick change barrel with RipBrake, 30 shot mag., 6-pos. synthetic telescoping stock with Mil-Spec receiver extension tube, dual feed, Mil-Std 1913 handguard with rail interface system, billet upper receiver, MCR extended bolt catch, Manganese Phosphate and hardcoat anodized black finish, 9.45 lbs.

MSR $5,260	$4,450	$3,900	$3,350	$3,000	$2,450	$2,000	$1,550	

SCR-010 – 5.56 NATO/.223 Rem. cal., 16 1/4 in. chrome moly barrel, Mil-Spec barrel extension, 5 shot mag., high-impact synthetic polymer stock, sporter style profile and handguard, carbine length Magpul MOE, captive push-pin takedown aerospace grade receiver, hardcoat anodized black finish, 5.7 lbs.

MSR $999	$850	$550	$465	$395	$350	$325	$295	

SCR-002 / SCR-002T – 5.56 NATO/.223 Rem. cal., 16 1/4 in. chrome moly threaded or non-threaded barrel, Mil-Spec barrel extension, 5 shot mag., high-impact synthetic polymer stock, sporter style profile and handguard, carbine length Magpul MOE, captive push-pin takedown aerospace grade upper receiver with ejection port dust cover, hardcoat anodized black finish, 5.7 lbs.

MSR $999	$850	$550	$465	$395	$350	$325	$295	

Add $24 for threaded barrel.

FIREBIRD PRECISION

Current manufacturer located in Mountainair, NM.

Firebird Precision builds custom made AR-15 style rifles and shotguns in a variety of configurations and calibers. Each gun is built to individual customer specifications, and a wide variety of options and features are available. Please contact the company directly for available options, delivery time, and an individualized price quotation (see Trademark Index).

FLINT RIVER ARMORY LLC

Current AR-15 style pistol and rifle manufacturer located in Huntsville, AL.

PISTOLS: SEMI-AUTO

CSA45-P – .45 ACP cal., AR-15 style, 10 in. stainless steel chrome moly barrel, 25 shot mag., KeyMod forearm, one-piece bolt carrier, forged aluminum receiver, black finish, 9 lbs. Disc. 2017.

	$1,275	$1,125	$1,025	$875	$750	$625	$525	$1,495

RIFLES: SEMI-AUTO

CSA45 – .45 ACP cal., GPO, 16 in. chrome moly barrel, 25 shot stainless steel mag., polymer stock, KeyMod forearm, one-piece bolt carrier, billet aluminum receivers, one-piece buffer/lower receiver, black finish, 6.1 lbs.

MSR $995	$850	$550	$465	$395	$350	$325	$295	

FORT DISCOVERY, INC.

Current AR-15 style manufacturer located in Sequim, WA.

F 194 FORT DISCOVERY, INC., cont.

MSR	100%	98%	95%	90%	80%	70%	60%	Last MSR

RIFLES: SEMI-AUTO

EXPEDITION RIFLE – 5.56 NATO cal., 16 in. chrome-lined heavy barrel, custom magwell, integral trigger guard, rear folding backup sight, Magpul MOE stock, M4 feed ramps, commercial size buffer tube, Magpul furniture, hardcoat anodized upper and lower receiver, includes custom Fort Discovery Challenge coin (with matching serial number of the rifle), handcrafted pine box, two Magpul mags., single point CQD sling attachment, LOKSAK bag.

| MSR $1,792 | $1,475 | $950 | $725 | $550 | $475 | $395 | $350 |

FOSTECH MFG.

Current semi-auto shotgun and accessories manufacturer located in Seymour, IN.

SHOTGUNS: SEMI-AUTO

ORIGIN 12 TACTICAL SHOTGUN – 12 ga., GIO, 18 1/2 in. quick change barrel, 8 shot standard detachable box mag., 20 or 30 shot drum mags. are optional, 3 point operational trigger, last shot bolt hold-open, includes all-weather tactical hard case, choice of hard black, hard nickel, or hard black with nickel internals, 9 lbs. 3 oz. New 2015.

| MSR $2,600 | $2,400 | $2,250 | $2,000 | $1,750 | $1,500 | $1,300 | $1,100 |

Add $100 for hard black finish with nickel internals or $200 for hard nickel finish.

FRANKLIN ARMORY

Current manufacturer of AR-15 style semi-auto pistols and rifles/carbines located in Morgan Hill, CA and Minden, NV.

Franklin Armory specializes in producing legal firearms for restrictive jurisdictions such as California (O7/FFL and Class II SOT manufacturer) as well as for the non-restrictive states.

PISTOLS: SEMI-AUTO

SALUS PISTOL – 5.56 NATO, 7.62x39mm (disc. 2015) or .450 BM (new 2015) cal., GIO, 7 1/2 in. barrel with threaded barrel, crowned muzzle and Triad flash hider, 30 shot mag., knurled free float handguard tube, aluminum upper and lower receiver with full Picatinny rail, forward assist, flared magwell, padded receiver extension/buffer tube, Ergo Ambi SureGrip, black finish, includes tactical soft side case.

| MSR $1,495 | $1,275 | $1,125 | $1,025 | $875 | $750 | $625 | $525 |

Add $145 for .450 BM (new 2015).
Add $155 for 7.62x39mm cal. (disc. 2015).

SE-SSP 7 1/2 IN. PISTOL – 5.56 NATO, 7.62x39mm (disc. 2015), or .450 BM (new 2015) cal., GIO, 7 1/2 in. barrel with A2 flash hider (compensator on .450 BM), single rail Picatinny gas block, optional forged front sight gas block with integral bayonet lug and front sling swivel, knurled free float handguard tube, forged aluminum lower and A4 upper receiver with full Picatinny rail, forward assist, ambi sling mount, padded receiver extension/buffer tube, A2 pistol grip, 30 shot mag., black finish, includes tactical soft side case.

| MSR $1,040 | $870 | $740 | $650 | $585 | $515 | $450 | $395 |

Add $15 for forged front sight gas block.
Add $135 for 7.62x39mm cal. (disc. 2015).
Add $315 for .450 BM cal. (new 2015).

SE-SSP 11 1/2 IN. PISTOL – 5.56 NATO, 6.8 SPC, 7.62x39mm, .300 AAC Blackout (disc. 2015) or .450 Bushmaster cal., GIO, 11 1/2 in. threaded barrel, crowned muzzle, hider or compensator (on .450 Bushmaster only), CAR handguards with aluminum liners, A4 forged aluminum flat-top upper receiver, otherwise similar to SE-SSP 7 1/2 in. pistol.

| MSR $1,020 | $860 | $725 | $650 | $585 | $515 | $450 | $395 |

Add $20 for forged front sight gas block.
Add $50 for .300 AAC Blackout cal. (disc. 2015).
Add $155 for 7.62x39mm cal.
Add $180 for .450 Bushmaster cal.
Add $215 for 6.8 SPC cal.

XO-26S SALUS PISTOL – 5.56 NATO, 6.8 SPC, 7.62x39mm, .300 AAC Blackout, or .450 Bushmaster cal., GIO, 11 1/2 in. threaded barrel, crowned muzzle, Phantom toothed flash hider, 9 (450 Bushmaster), 25 (6.8 SPC), or 30 shot mag., low profile gas block, carbine length gas system, full Picatinny rail, forward assist, 9 in. KeyMod rail handguard, pop up front and rear MBUS sights, billet aluminum upper and lower receivers, flared magwell, integral cold weather trigger guard, EPG16 grip, Black, Desert Smoke, or Olive Drab Green finish.

| MSR $1,875 | $1,575 | $1,385 | $1,200 | $1,065 | $900 | $775 | $625 |

Add $25 for .300 AAC Blackout cal.
Add $125 for .450 BM cal.
Add $140 for 7.62x39mm cal., or $225 for 6.8 SPC cal.

FRANKLIN ARMORY, cont. 195 F

MSR	100%	98%	95%	90%	80%	70%	60%	Last MSR

XO-26 R2 (XO-26) – 5.56 NATO, 6.8 SPC, .300 AAC Blackout, 7.62x39mm (disc. 2015), or .450 Bushmaster cal., GIO, 11 1/2 in. barrel with Phantom toothed flash hider or Ross Schuler Compensator (on .450 Bushmaster only), Specter length free float forearm quad rail, low profile gas block, forged aluminum lower and A4 flat-top upper with full Picatinny rail, pop-up front and rear sights, forward assist, ambi sling mount, custom tuned trigger, padded receiver extension/buffer tube, Magpul MIAD grip, 9 (.450 Bushmaster), 25 (6.8 SPC), or 30 shot mag., black finish, includes tactical soft side case.

| | MSR $1,470 | | $1,245 | $1,100 | $985 | $835 | $725 | $615 | $515 | |

Add $20 for .300 AAC Blackout cal.

Add $130 for .450 Bushmaster or $160 for 6.8 SPC cal.

Add $140 for 7.62x39mm cal. (disc. 2015).

* **XO-26b** – 5.56 NATO, 6.8 SPC, .300 AAC Blackout (disc. 2015), or 7.62x39mm (disc. 2015) cal., 11 1/2 in. barrel with A2 or Toothed flash hider, carbine length gas system, forged aluminum A4 flat-top upper with full Picatinny rail, 25 (6.8 SPC) or 30 shot mag., Magpul MOE handguard, forward assist, forged aluminum lower with ambi sling mount, padded receiver/extension buffer tube, Magpul MIAD grip, hardcoat anodized black finish.

| | MSR $1,130 | | $940 | $850 | $725 | $625 | $550 | $475 | $425 | |

Add $225 for 6.8 SPC cal.

Add $45 for .300 AAC Blackout (disc. 2015) or $170 for 7.62x39mm cal. (disc.2015).

XOW – 5.56 NATO, 7.62x39mm, or .450 Bushmaster (new 2015) cal., GIO, 7 1/2 in. barrel with PWS CQB flash hider, A4 forged aluminum flat-top upper receiver with carbine length forearm quad rail, rail covers, Magpul RVG forward vertical grip, Magpul MBUS pop-up front and rear sights, forward assist, full Picatinny rail, forged aluminum lower receiver with ambi sling mount, padded receiver extension/buffer tube, Magpul MIAD grip, Magpul enhanced trigger guard, PWS enhanced padded buffer tube, 30 shot mag., black, FDE, or ODG furniture, includes tactical soft side case. Disc. 2015.

| | MSR $1,850 | | $1,560 | $1,375 | $1,190 | $1,050 | $900 | $775 | $625 | |

Add $100 for 7.62x39mm or $200 for .450 Bushmaster (new 2015) cal.

RIFLES: SEMI-AUTO

3GR – 5.56 NATO cal., GIO, 18 in. barrel with threaded muzzle crown, EGW compensator, A4 forged aluminum upper receiver with Desert Smoke finish, full Picatinny rail, ambi tac latch, forward assist, forged aluminum lower receiver with black finish, Ergo Ambi SureGrip and Magpul MOE trigger guard, 10 or 20 shot mag., Ace ARFX stock with bottom Picatinny rail, adj. comb and LOP, sling mountable. Disc. 2013.

| | | | $1,475 | $1,300 | $1,100 | $1,000 | $825 | $675 | $525 | *$1,650* |

* **3GR-L** – 5.56 NATO cal., GIO, 18 in. fluted barrel with threaded muzzle crown and compensator, low profile adj. gas block, mid-length gas system, FSR 13 in. rail system, 10 or 20 shot mag., integral cold weather trigger guard, Magpul PRS stock with bottom Picatinny rail, Ergo Ambi SureGrip, flared magwell, push button QD sling mounts, ambi tac latch, forward assist, forged aluminum lower receiver with black finish, adj. comb and LOP, aluminum upper and lower receivers with Desert Smoke finish.

| | MSR $2,310 | | $1,950 | $1,725 | $1,450 | $1,250 | $1,050 | $900 | $750 | |

Add $390 for the Franklin Armory Binary Firing System (3-position selectable trigger system), new 2016.

10-8 R2 (10-8 CARBINE) – 5.56 NATO, 6.8 SPC, 7.62x39mm (disc. 2015), or .300 AAC Blackout (new 2016) cal., GIO, 16 in. medium contour barrel with Triad flash suppressor, forged front sight, free float forearm quad rail, A4 forged aluminum upper receiver with full Picatinny rail, Magpul MBUS rear sight, forward assist, forged aluminum lower receiver with custom tuned trigger, Ergo Gapper, Ergo Ambi SureGrip, M4 6-position adj. stock with rear sling mount positions, 10, 20, 25 (6.8 SPC only), or 30 shot mag., black furniture.

| | MSR $1,335 | | $1,115 | $1,000 | $875 | $735 | $650 | $550 | $465 | |

Add $20 for .300 AAC Blackout cal. (new 2016).

Add $150 for 6.8 SPC cal.

Add $155 for 7.62x39mm cal. (disc. 2015).

F17-L – .17 WSM cal., GPO, 20 in. stainless steel bull barrel, target crown, free float fluted and vented handguard, forward assist, aluminum upper and lower receivers, anodized Olive Drab Green finish, flared magwell, integral cold weather trigger guard, 10 shot mag., Magpul MOE rifle stock, Magpul MIAD adj. grip, ambidextrous push button QD sling mounts. New mid-2014.

| | MSR $2,000 | | $1,700 | $1,500 | $1,250 | $1,100 | $950 | $825 | $675 | |

F17-M4 – .17 WSM cal., GPO, 16 in. medium contour barrel, threaded muzzle crown, A2 flash hider, 10 shot mag., M4 6-position stock, A2 grip, forged aluminum upper and lower, TML-7 free float and knurled handguard, M-LOK compatible forward slots, forward assist, Type III hardcoat anodized black finish.

| | MSR $1,500 | | $1,275 | $1,125 | $1,025 | $875 | $750 | $625 | $525 | |

F17-SPR – .17 WSM cal., GPO, 18 in. chrome moly barrel, 10 shot mag., MFT Battlelink Minimalist stock, rubber buttpad, Mission First Tactical EPG16 grip, forged aluminum upper and lower receivers, free float knurled handguard, M-LOK compatible forward slots, forward assist, Type III hardcoat anodized black finish. New 2016.

| | MSR $1,800 | | $1,525 | $1,350 | $1,175 | $1,050 | $900 | $775 | $625 | |

F 196 FRANKLIN ARMORY, cont.

MSR	100%	98%	95%	90%	80%	70%	60%	Last MSR

F17-V4 – .17 WSM cal., GPO, 20 in. bull barrel, target crown with recessed muzzle crown, 10 shot mag., forged aluminum upper and lower receivers, TML-12 free float knurled handguard, integral tripod adapter, forward assist, A2 grip, A2 stock with storage compartment, black finish. New 2015.

MSR $1,500	$1,275	$1,125	$1,025	$875	$750	$625	$525	

FEATURELESS RIFLE – 5.56 NATO cal., GIO, 16 in. HBAR contour barrel with threaded muzzle crown and Phantom brake, Magpul MOE handguard, A4 forged aluminum upper receiver with full Picatinny rail and forward assist, forged aluminum lower receiver with Hammerhead grip, 10 or 20 shot mag., ACE ARUL stock with rubber buttpad, aluminum receiver extension, black, FDE, or ODG furniture. Disc. 2013.

	$1,025	$925	$800	$685	$595	$515	$440	*$1,200*

HBAR 16 IN. – 5.56 NATO, 6.8 SPC, or 7.62x39mm cal., GIO, 16 in. HBAR contour barrel, threaded muzzle crown with A2 flash hider, CAR handguards, Picatinny rail gas block with carbine length gas system, or optional forged front sight gas block with integral bayonet lug and front sling swivel, A4 forged aluminum upper receiver with full Picatinny rail and forward assist, forged aluminum lower receiver with A2 pistol grip, 10, 20, 25 (6.8 SPC only), or 30 shot mag., M4 6-position collapsible stock with rear sling mounts and aluminum receiver extension, black furniture.

MSR $1,080	$910	$775	$675	$595	$515	$450	$395	

Add $20 for forged front sight gas block.
Add $95 for 6.8 SPC cal.
Add $140 for 7.62x39mm cal.

* **HBAR 20 IN.** – 5.56 NATO, 6.8 SPC, 7.62x39mm, or .450 Bushmaster cal., GIO, similar to HBAR 16 in., except has 20 in. HBAR contour barrel, threaded muzzle crown with flash hider or compensator (.450 Bushmaster only), A2 handguard, forged front sight gas block with integral bayonet lug and front sling swivel, or optional Picatinny rail gas block with carbine length gas system, A2 stock with storage compartment.

MSR $1,095	$925	$850	$725	$625	$550	$475	$425	

Add $20 for forged front sight gas block.
Add $90 for 6.8 SPC cal.
Add $130 for 7.62x39mm cal.
Add $165 for .450 Bushmaster cal.

LTW – 5.56 NATO cal., GIO, 16 in. lightweight contour barrel with A2 flash hider, 30 shot mag., Picatinny rail gas block with carbine length gas system, optional forged front sight gas block with integral bayonet lug and front sling swivel, CAR handguard, A4 forged aluminum upper receiver with full Picatinny rail and forward assist, forged aluminum lower receiver with A2 pistol grip, M4 6-position collapsible stock with rear sling mounts and aluminum receiver extension, black furniture. Disc. 2015.

	$925	$850	$725	$625	$550	$475	$425	*$1,100*

Add $25 for forged front sight gas block.

M4 – 5.56 NATO or .300 AAC Blackout cal., GIO, 16 in. M4 contour barrel with threaded muzzle crown A2 flash hider, M4 double heat shield handguard with aluminum liners, forged front sight gas block with integral bayonet lug and front sling swivel or optional Picatinny rail gas block, A4 forged aluminum upper receiver with full Picatinny rail and forward assist, forged aluminum lower receiver, 10, 20, or 30 shot mag., M4 6-position collapsible stock with aluminum CAR receiver extension, A2 pistol grip, black furniture.

MSR $1,100	$925	$850	$725	$625	$550	$475	$425	

Add $25 for forged front sight gas block.
Add $45 for .300 AAC Blackout cal.
Add $425 for the Franklin Armory Binary Firing System (3-position selectable trigger system), new 2016.

* **M4-HTF** – 5.56 NATO cal., GIO, 16 in. M4 contour fluted barrel, steel construction, low profile gas block, EGW compensator, forged aluminum A4 upper receiver with Specter length free float forearm quad rail, pop up front and rear sights, forward assist, forged aluminum lower receiver with Ergo Gapper, Ergo Ambi SureGrip, ACE ARFX stock with rubber buttpad and foam padded receiver extension, 10, 20, or 30 shot mag., black furniture. Disc. 2015.

	$1,475	$1,290	$1,125	$1,000	$850	$735	$595	*$1,735*

* **M4-L** – 5.56 NATO or .300 AAC Blackout cal., GIO, 16 in. M4 contour barrel, threaded muzzle crown with A2 flash hider, forged front sight with carbine length gas system, Magpul MOE carbine length handguard, 10 or 20 shot mag., Magpul ACS stock with integral storage compartment, aluminum upper and lower receivers, Black, Desert Smoke, or Olive Drab Green finish, full Picatinny rail with MBUS rear sight, Magpul MIAD adj. grip.

MSR $1,770	$1,500	$1,310	$1,140	$1,000	$850	$735	$595	

Add $65 for .300 AAC Blackout cal.

* **M4-OPL** – 5.56 NATO or .300 AAC Blackout cal., GPO, similar to M4-L, except utilizes the Osprey Defense Piston System.

MSR $2,200	$1,875	$1,650	$1,400	$1,200	$1,025	$875	$725	

Add $70 for .300 AAC Blackout cal.

FRANKLIN ARMORY, cont. 197 F

MSR		100%	98%	95%	90%	80%	70%	60%	Last MSR

* M4-MOE – 5.56 NATO or .300 AAC Blackout cal., GIO, 16 in. M4 contour barrel with threaded muzzle crown A2 flash hider, Magpul MOE handguard, forged front sight gas block with integral bayonet lug and front sling swivel or optional Picatinny rail gas block, A4 forged aluminum upper receiver with full Picatinny rail and forward assist, forged aluminum lower receiver with Magpul MOE grip and trigger guard, 10 or 20 shot mag., Magpul MOE 6-position collapsible stock with rubber buttpad, aluminum carbine length receiver extension, black furniture.

| | MSR $1,200 | $1,025 | $925 | $800 | $685 | $595 | $515 | $440 | |

Add $25 for forged front sight gas block.

Add $60 for .300 AAC Blackout cal.

PRAEFECTOR – 5.56 NATO, 6.8 SPC, or .450 BM cal., 20 in. medium contour barrel with Revere compensator, 9 (disc. 2016),10 (new 2017) 25, or 30 shot mag., Magpul MOE rifle stock, Ergo Ambi SureGrip, low profile gas block, forged aluminum lower and A4 upper receivers, full Picatinny rail, forward assist, FSR 15 in. handguard, black anodized finish. New 2015.

| | MSR $1,420 | $1,210 | $1,075 | $950 | $800 | $700 | $600 | $495 | |

Add $135 for 6.8 SPC or $150 for .450 BM cal.

SLT-M MILITIA MODEL – 7.62 NATO cal., 20 in. barrel, rifle length gas system, 10 or 20 shot mag., Libertas billet machined upper receiver with Smoke Composites 15 in. carbon fiber handguard, forward assist, Osprey Defense gas piston, Diamondhead front and rear sights, aluminum lower with ambidextrous controls, flared magwell, integral Cold Weather trigger guard, Ergo Ambi SureGrip, Smoke Composites A2 carbon fiber stock, black, Desert Smoke, or Olive Drab Green finish. New 2015.

Please contact the company directly for pricing and availability on this model.

TMR-L – 5.56 NATO or 6.8 SPC cal., GIO, 20 in. full heavy contour barrel with recessed muzzle crown, low profile gas block with rifle length gas system, aluminum upper and lower receiver with Black, Desert Smoke, or Olive Drab Green finish, full Picatinny rail, Gen. 1 tac latch, flared magwell, 10 or 20 shot mag., Magpul PRS stock with bottom Picatinny rail, adj. comb and LOP, Ergo Ambi SureGrip.

| | MSR $2,035 | $1,715 | $1,500 | $1,250 | $1,100 | $950 | $825 | $675 | |

Add $45 for 6.8 SPC cal.

V1 – 5.56 NATO cal., GIO, 24 in. full heavy contour stainless steel fluted barrel with recessed muzzle crown, single rail Picatinny rail gas block, free float fluted and vented handguard with bipod stud, A4 forged aluminum upper receiver with full picatinny rail, Gen 1 tac latch, forward assist, forged aluminum lower receiver with Magpul MIAD adj. grip, Magpul MOE trigger guard, 10 shot mag., Magpul PRS stock, adj. comb and LOP, bottom Picatinny rail, black furniture.

| | MSR $1,700 | $1,450 | $1,275 | $1,125 | $1,000 | $850 | $735 | $595 | |

* V1-L – 5.56 NATO cal., GIO, 24 in. full heavy contour stainless steel fluted barrel with recessed muzzle crown, Picatinny rail gas block with rifle length gas system, fluted and vented free float rail with sling/bipod stud, aluminum upper receiver with free float fluted and vented handguard, Gen 1 tac latch, forward assist, aluminum lower receiver with flared magwell, push button QD sling mounts, Magpul MIAD adj. grip, 10 or 20 shot mag., Magpul PRS stock, adj. comb and LOP, bottom Picatinny rail, black furniture.

| | MSR $2,090 | $1,795 | $1,575 | $1,325 | $1,150 | $995 | $850 | $700 | |

V2 – 5.56 NATO or 6.5mm Grendel (disc. 2015) cal., similar to V1, except does not have fluted barrel.

| | MSR $1,560 | $1,310 | $1,150 | $1,040 | $875 | $750 | $625 | $525 | |

Add $100 for 6.5mm Grendel cal. (disc. 2015).

* V2-L – 5.56 NATO or 6.5mm Grendel (disc. 2015) cal., similar to V1-L, except does not have fluted barrel.

| | MSR $2,000 | $1,700 | $1,500 | $1,250 | $1,100 | $950 | $825 | $675 | |

Add $115 for 6.5mm Grendel cal. (disc. 2015).

V3 – 5.56 NATO or 6.5mm Grendel cal., GIO, 24 in. full heavy contour stainless steel barrel with recessed muzzle crown, single rail Picatinny rail gas block with rifle length gas system, free float fluted and vented handguard, A4 forged aluminum upper receiver with full Picatinny rail, forward assist, forged aluminum lower receiver with A2 grip, 10 shot mag, A2 stock with storage compartment and rear sling mount, black furniture. Disc. 2015.

| | | $935 | $850 | $725 | $625 | $550 | $475 | $425 | *$1,125* |

Add $85 for 6.5mm Grendel cal.

V4 – 5.56 NATO or 6.8 SPC cal., 20 in. full heavy contour barrel, recessed muzzle crown, rifle length gas system, 10 shot mag., single rail Picatinny gas block, forged aluminum upper and lower receivers, full Picatinny rail, forward assist, TML-12 free float handguard with M-LOK slots and integral tripod adapter, A2 stock with storage compartment for cleaning kit, A2 grip, Type III hardcoat anodized black finish.

| | MSR $1,135 | $950 | $850 | $725 | $625 | $550 | $475 | $425 | |

Add $50 for 6.8 SPC cal.

F 198 FULTON ARMORY

MSR	100%	98%	95%	90%	80%	70%	60%	Last MSR

FULTON ARMORY

Current rifle manufacturer and parts supplier located in Savage, MD. Dealer sales.

RIFLES/CARBINES: SEMI-AUTO

Fulton Armory makes a comprehensive array of the four U.S. Gas Operated Service Rifles: M1 Garand, M1 Carbine, M14 and AR-15-style, including corresponding commercial versions and upper receiver assemblies and related parts and components.

ACCUTRON NRA MATCH RIFLE

Last MSR range was $1,300-$2,200.

FAR-15 A2 SERVICE RIFLE – .223 Rem./5.56 NATO cal., 20 in. HBAR profile chrome-lined barrel with A2 flash suppressor, A2 upper receiver, FA lower with Accu-Wedge, single stage trigger, M16 bolt carrier group, 12 in. round A2 handguard with heat shields, GI front sight with bayonet lug, fixed A2 buttstock with A2 buttplate and aluminum door assembly, carry handle, A2 pistol grip, includes 10 shot mag. and black nylon "Silent" sling, 8.05 lbs.

	100%	98%	95%	90%	80%	70%	60%
MSR $1,210	$1,025	$625	$495	$450	$395	$350	$325

FAR-15 A4 SERVICE RIFLE – .223 Rem./5.56 NATO cal., 20 in. HBAR profile chrome-lined barrel with A2 flash suppressor, A3/A4 numbered upper receiver, FA lower with Accu-Wedge, GI front sight with bayonet lug, fixed A2 buttstock with buttplate and aluminum door assembly, A2 pistol grip, 12 in. round A2 handguard with heat shields, single stage trigger, includes one 10 shot mag. and black nylon "Silent" sling.

	100%	98%	95%	90%	80%	70%	60%
MSR $1,130	$950	$595	$495	$425	$365	$335	$300

FAR-15 GUARDIAN – .223 Rem./5.56 NATO cal., 20 in. HBAR (Guardian-H) or pencil (Guardian-L) profile chrome-lined barrel with A2 flash suppressor, A3/A4 flat-top numbered upper receiver and FA lower with Accu-Wedge, 13 1/2 in. Diamondhead VRS-X handguard float tube, modular rail system, low profile steel gas block, two-stage non-adj. trigger, fixed A2 buttstock with A2 buttplate and aluminum door assembly, right-handed Ergo SureGrip, includes one 10 shot mag. and black nylon "Silent" sling, 6.85-7.95 lbs.

	100%	98%	95%	90%	80%	70%	60%
MSR $1,450	$1,195	$795	$550	$465	$415	$375	$350

FAR-15 LEGACY RIFLE – .223 Rem./5.56 NATO cal., 20 in. "Pencil" profile chrome-lined barrel with M16 3-prong muzzle brake, M16 Slick Side upper receiver with A1 rear sight, Slick-Side chrome bolt carrier with forward assist notches, USGI M16 triangular handguard, GI gas block with bayonet lug, A1 round front sight post, FA lower receiver with Accu-Wedge, USGI M16 grip, single stage trigger, A1 fixed buttstock, includes one 10 shot mag. and black nylon "Silent" sling, 6 3/4 lbs.

	100%	98%	95%	90%	80%	70%	60%
MSR $1,270	$1,065	$650	$500	$450	$395	$350	$325

FAR-15 LIBERATOR – .223 Rem./5.56 NATO cal., 20 in. HBAR (Liberator-H) or pencil (Liberator-L) profile chrome-lined barrel with A2 flash suppressor, A3/A4 flat-top numbered upper and FA lower receiver with Accu-Wedge, 12 in. Daniel Defense Lite rail with rail covers, low profile steel gas block, two-stage non-adj. trigger, fixed A2 buttstock with A2 buttplate and aluminum door assembly, right-handed Ergo SureGrip, includes one 10 shot mag. and black nylon "Silent" sling, 7-8.1 lbs.

	100%	98%	95%	90%	80%	70%	60%
MSR $1,700	$1,385	$895	$675	$525	$450	$385	$350

FAR-15 PEERLESS NM A2 SERVICE RIFLE – .223 Rem./5.56 NATO cal., 20 in. HBAR profile stainless steel barrel with A2 flash suppressor, National Match two-stage trigger, 12 in. round floated and modified A2 handguard, steel float tube, Northern Competition NM rear sight with hooded aperture, custom pillared rear sight base and power wedge front sight base with NM front sight post, A2 upper with fixed carry handle, FA lower with Accu-Wedge, A2 buttstock with A2 buttplate, A2 pistol grip, includes one 10 shot mag. and black nylon "Silent" sling, 9.85 lbs.

	100%	98%	95%	90%	80%	70%	60%
MSR $1,600	$1,315	$850	$625	$500	$435	$375	$350

FAR-15 PEERLESS NM A4 SERVICE RIFLE – .223 Rem./5.56 NATO cal., 20 in. HBAR profile stainless steel barrel with A2 flash suppressor, A3/A4 flat-top numbered upper receiver with detachable carry handle and rear sight base, FA lower with Accu-Wedge and marked "US Rifle", Northern Competition National Match hooded aperture rear sight, NM front sight post and drilled and tapped front sight base, 12 in. round A2 handguard modified for steel float tube, GI gas block with bayonet lug, A2 buttstock with A2 buttplate, A2 pistol grip, non-adj. two-stage NM trigger, includes one 10 shot mag. and black nylon "Silent" sling, 11 1/4 lbs.

	100%	98%	95%	90%	80%	70%	60%
MSR $1,750	$1,425	$925	$700	$550	$475	$395	$350

FAR-15 PHANTOM – .223 Rem./5.56 NATO cal., 20 in. HBAR (Phantom-H) or pencil (Phantom-L) profile chrome-lined barrel with A2 flash suppressor, A3/A4 flat-top numbered upper, FA lower with Accu-Wedge, 13 1/2 in. Diamondhead VRS-T handguard float tube, modular rail system, low profile steel gas block, two-stage non-adj. trigger, fixed A2 buttstock with A2 buttplate and aluminum door assembly, right-handed Ergo SureGrip, includes one 10 shot mag. and black nylon "Silent" sling, 7-8.10 lbs.

	100%	98%	95%	90%	80%	70%	60%
MSR $1,450	$1,195	$795	$550	$465	$415	$375	$350

FAR-15 PREDATOR VARMINT RIFLE – .223 Rem./5.56 NATO cal., GIO, 24 in. stainless steel bull barrel with plain muzzle, compression fit gas block, flat-top upper, bolt carrier drilled and tapped for side cocking handle, forged lower receiver with Accu-Wedge, fixed A2 buttstock with A2 buttplate and aluminum door assembly, Ergo SureGrip, single stage trigger, includes one 10 shot mag. and Nylon "Silent" sling.

	100%	98%	95%	90%	80%	70%	60%
MSR $1,250	$1,050	$650	$495	$450	$395	$350	$325

FULTON ARMORY, cont. 199 F

MSR	100%	98%	95%	90%	80%	70%	60%	Last MSR

* FAR-15 Predator Varmint Lite – .223 Rem./5.56 NATO cal., 20 in. HBAR profile stainless steel barrel with threaded muzzle and A2 flash suppressor, A3/A4 flat-top numbered upper and FA lower receiver with Accu-Wedge, two-stage non-adj. match trigger, 12 in. PVR round knurled handguard float tube with bipod stud, compression fit gas block, fixed A2 buttstock with A2 buttplate and aluminum door assembly, right-handed Ergo SureGrip, includes one 10 shot mag., nylon "Silent" sling, 8.05 lbs.

MSR $1,200	$995	$625	$495	$450	$395	$350	$325	

FAR-15 STOWAWAY – .223 Rem./5.56 NATO cal., 16 in. pencil profile chrome-lined barrel with A2 flash suppressor, GI M16 bolt carrier, barrel extension, and extractor, A1 C7 forged upper receiver, 7 in. triangular handguard with heat shields, front sight gas block with bayonet lug, FA lower receiver with Accu-Wedge, Shorty fixed buttstock, A2 pistol grip, single stage trigger, includes one 10 shot mag., black nylon "Silent" sling, 5 3/4 lbs.

MSR $800	$675	$500	$425	$375	$335	$315	$295	

FAR-308 LIBERATOR – .308 Win./7.62 NATO cal., 18 1/2 in. lightweight chrome moly (Liberator-L) or medium weight stainless steel (Liberator-H) barrel with A2 flash suppressor, compression fit gas block, A3/A4 flat-top upper and FA lower with modified Accu-Wedge, DPMS pattern parts, nickel boron bolt carrier group, 12 in. Liberator .308 handguard float tube, lightweight 4-rail with rail covers, two-stage non-adj. trigger, fixed A1 buttstock with A2 buttplate and aluminum door assembly, right-handed Ergo SureGrip, includes one 10 shot mag. and black nylon "Silent" sling, 9 1/4-9 3/4 lbs.

MSR $1,800	$1,475	$950	$725	$550	$475	$395	$350	

FAR-308 M110 SERVICE RIFLE – .308 Win./7.62 NATO cal., 20 in. M110 stainless steel barrel with A2 flash suppressor, compression fit gas block with top rail, A3/A4 flat-top upper and FA lower with modified Accu-Wedge, DPMS Pattern parts, nickel boron bolt carrier group with staked key, extended bolt stop, 12 in. Liberator handguard float tube, lightweight 4-rail with rail covers, two-stage non-adj. trigger, fixed A1 buttstock with A2 buttplate and aluminum door assembly, A2 pistol grip, includes one 10 shot mag. and black nylon "Silent" sling, 10.85 lbs.

MSR $1,800	$1,475	$950	$725	$550	$475	$395	$350	

FAR-308 PVR-H – .308 Win./7.62 NATO cal., 24 in. match quality stainless steel heavy bull barrel with A2 flash suppressor, compression fit gas block, high rise side-cocking upper receiver with nickel boron bolt carrier group, FA lower with modified Accu-Wedge, DPMS pattern parts, two-stage match trigger, 12 in. round knurled PVR handguard float tube, fixed A1 buttstock with A2 buttplate and aluminum door assembly, right-handed Ergo SureGrip, includes one 10 shot mag. and black nylon "Silent" sling, 10.6 lbs.

MSR $1,600	$1,315	$850	$625	$500	$435	$375	$350	

FAR-308 PVR-L – .308 Win./7.62 NATO cal., 20 in. M110 match grade stainless steel barrel with A2 flash suppressor, compression fit gas block, A3/A4 flat-top upper receiver and FA lower with modified Accu-Wedge, DPMS pattern parts, nickel boron bolt carrier group, 12 in. round knurled handguard float tube, two-stage non-adj. trigger, fixed A1 buttstock with A2 buttplate and aluminum door assembly, right-handed Ergo SureGrip, includes one 10 shot mag. and black nylon "Silent" sling, 9.8 lbs.

MSR $1,600	$1,315	$850	$625	$500	$435	$375	$350	

FAR-6.5 PVR – 6.5mm Creedmoor cal., 24 in. match quality stainless steel heavy bull barrel with A2 flash suppressor, compression fit gas block, high rise side-cocking upper receiver with nickel boron bolt carrier group, FA lower with modified Accu-Wedge, DPMS pattern parts, two-stage match trigger, 12 in. round knurled PVR handguard float tube, fixed A1 buttstock with A2 buttplate and aluminum door assembly, right-handed Ergo SureGrip, includes one 10 shot mag. and black nylon "Silent" sling, 10.85 lbs.

MSR $1,600	$1,315	$850	$625	$500	$435	$375	$350	

HORNET LIGHTWEIGHT RIFLE
Last MSR in 2003 was $750.

MILLENNIAL LIGHTWEIGHT CARBINE
Last MSR in 2002 was $850.

MILLENNIAL LIGHTWEIGHT RIFLE
Last MSR in 2002 was $750.

TITAN UPR
Last MSR was $3,370.

UBR (UNIVERSAL BATTLE RIFLE)
Last MSR was $1,100.

UPR (UNIVERSAL PRECISION RIFLE))
Last MSR was $1,798.

MAYBE THE ONLY THING BETTER THAN THIS BOOK IS THE ONLINE SUBSCRIPTION!

Only $19.95/year!

- **Includes monthly updates** keeping you informed of all the new AR-15 makes/models.
- **Features thousands of images** allowing for fast and easy identification.
- **Manufacturer/Model searchable database** allowing you to find the model you need.
- Historical pricing with dynamic interactive graphs keeps you up-to-date on your AR-15 purchases as investments.
- Your own personal online inventory solution - keep track of your collection and track the change in value.
- Includes access to BBP's industry standard Photo Percentage Grading System – why guess a gun's condition when you can be sure?

Visit BLUEBOOKOFGUNVALUES.COM
to view sample pages and ordering

Good Information Never Sleeps!

G SECTION

G2 PRECISION, LLC

Current AR-15 style manufacturer located in Porter, TX.

MSR	100%	98%	95%	90%	80%	70%	60%	Last MSR

RIFLES: SEMI-AUTO

G215CF – .300 AAC Blackout cal., GIO, carbine length gas system, 16 in. Proof Research carbon fiber reinforced stainless steel match grade barrel, titanium compensator brake, CMC curved two-stage trigger, Magpul CTR buttstock, G2 grip, G2 with nickel boron coated BCG, 15 in. Recce M-LOK handguard, forged aluminum receivers, G2 ambi selector and forward assist, Raptor Ambi by AXTS charging handle, hardcoat anodized Type III finish, 6.6 lbs. New 2017.

	100%	98%	95%	90%	80%	70%	60%
MSR $2,499	$1,975	$1,150	$925	$650	$575	$495	$425

G215SS – .300 AAC Blackout or cal. or .223 Wylde chamber, G2 Precision 16 in. medium profile stainless steel match grade barrel, compensator brake, carbine length gas system, CMC curved two-stage trigger, Magpul CTR buttstock, G2 grip, G2 with nickel boron coated BCG, 15 in. Recce M-LOK handguard, Raptor Ambi by AXTS charging handle, forged aluminum receivers, G2 ambi selector, forward assist, hardcoat anodized Type III finish, 7 lbs. 6 oz. Mfg. 2017 only.

	100%	98%	95%	90%	80%	70%	60%	Last MSR
	$1,650	$1,000	$795	$595	$495	$425	$395	*$1,999*

TEAM NEVER QUIT MK12CF SPR – .223 Wylde chamber, GIO, 18 in. Proof Research carbon fiber reinforced stainless steel barrel, titanium compensator brake, CMC curved two-stage trigger, Magpul Mil-Spec SPR buttstock, Ergo grip, Raptor Ambi by AXTS charging handle, G2 BCG with nickel boron coating, G2 Precision 15 in. Recce M-LOK handguard, forged aluminum upper and lower receivers, G2 forward assist and ambi selector, hardcoat anodized Type III finish. Disc. 2017.

	100%	98%	95%	90%	80%	70%	60%	Last MSR
	$2,295	$1,450	$1,075	$675	$595	$525	$475	*$2,899*

TEAM NEVER QUIT MK12SS SPR – .223 Wylde chamber, GIO, 18 in. G2 Precision stainless steel barrel, stainless steel compensator brake, 20 shot mag., CMC curved two-stage trigger, Magpul Mil-Spec SPR buttstock, Ergo SureGrip original, Raptor Ambi by AXTS charging handle, G2 BCG with nickel boron coating, G2 Precision 15 in. Recce M-LOK handguard, forged aluminum upper and lower receivers, G2 forward assist and ambi selector, hardcoat anodized Type III finish, 7 lbs. 11 oz.

	100%	98%	95%	90%	80%	70%	60%
MSR $2,299	$1,795	$1,050	$875	$625	$550	$475	$425

GA PRECISION

Current manufacturer established in 1999, located in N. Kansas City, MO.

RIFLES: SEMI-AUTO

GAP-10 G2 – 6mm Creedmoor, 6.5mm Creedmoor, .243 Win., .260 Rem., .338 Federal, or .308 Win. cal., 16 1/2-22 in. stainless steel barrel, 20 shot mag., Geissele SSΛ-E two-stage trigger, 13 1/2 in. SP3R V3 rail, BCM Mod 3 charging handle, GAP-10 G2 upper and lower receivers by Seekins Precision, Magpul MOE A2 stock standard (Magpul PRS optional), ambi safety and bolt release, matte black hardcoat anodized finish, matte Cerakote on barrel and gas block. New 2016.

	100%	98%	95%	90%	80%	70%	60%
MSR $3,060	$2,450	$1,595	$1,200	$700	$675	$575	$525

G.A.R. ARMS

Current AR-15 style manufacturer located in Fairacres, NM.

RIFLES/CARBINES: SEMI-AUTO

GR-15 MTCSS – .223 Wylde chamber, GIO, 16 in. LW50 stainless steel barrel, Phantom flash hider, two 30 shot mags., YHM quad rail gas block, Daniel Defense 9 in. modular free float rail, Magpul bolt catch BAD lever (battery assist device), two-stage match trigger, Hogue grip, Magpul PRS black sniper stock, charging handle with tactical latch, A3 flat-top upper, Magpul aluminum trigger guard, includes hard rifle case.

	100%	98%	95%	90%	80%	70%	60%
MSR $1,800	$1,475	$950	$725	$550	$475	$395	$350

GR-15 ORHS (OPTICS READY HUNTER STANDARD) – 5.56 NATO cal., GIO, 16 or 20 in. E.R. Shaw chrome moly heavy weight barrel, M4 feed ramps, charging handle, free float aluminum forend, Mil-Spec trigger, 5 (20 in.) or 10 (16 in.) shot mag., A3 flat-top upper, high riser block for optics, A2 fixed stock, hard rifle case.

	100%	98%	95%	90%	80%	70%	60%
MSR $1,270	$1,065	$650	$500	$450	$395	$350	$325

Add $10 for 20 in. barrel.

GR-15 STAINLESS 16 IN. – .223 Rem. cal., GIO, 16 in. stainless steel bison barrel, two 20 shot mags., carbine length free floating handguard, charging handle, forged aluminum lower and A3 flat-top upper receiver, right-hand ejection, A2 buttstock.

	100%	98%	95%	90%	80%	70%	60%
MSR $1,205	$1,025	$625	$495	$450	$395	$350	$325

G 202 G.A.R. ARMS, cont.

MSR	100%	98%	95%	90%	80%	70%	60%	Last MSR

* GR-15 Stainless 20 In. – .223 Rem. cal., GIO, 20 in. stainless steel barrel, two 20 shot mags., right-hand ejection, A2 buttstock, rifle length handguard, charging handle, forged aluminum A3 flat-top upper receiver, forged aluminum lower.

| MSR $1,217 | $1,025 | $625 | $495 | $450 | $395 | $350 | $325 | |

GR-15 STANDARD CARBINE – 5.56 NATO cal., GIO, 16 in. Government contour M4 barrel with A2 flash hider, threaded muzzle, M4 feed ramps, parkerized finish, charging handle, carbine length handguard with single heat shield, forged aluminum lower and A3 flat-top upper receiver, right hand ejection, 6-position collapsible buttstock, single rail gas block, 30 shot mag., standard sling, includes hard rifle case.

| MSR $910 | $785 | $525 | $450 | $385 | $340 | $325 | $295 | |

* GR-15 Standard Rifle – 5.56 NATO cal., similar to GR-15 A3 Standard Carbine, except features 20 in. barrel, rifle length handguard, and A2 fixed buttstock.

| MSR $950 | $800 | $525 | $450 | $385 | $340 | $325 | $295 | |

GR-15 TAC DEFENDER – 5.56 NATO cal., GIO, 16 in. Government contour barrel with A2 flash hider, Troy Industries 7, 10, or 13.8 in. free float quad rails, M4 feed ramps, charging handle, forged aluminum lower receiver and A3 flat-top upper, ejection port cover and round forward assist, right hand ejection, 6-position collapsible buttstock, carbine length handguard and single heat shield (13.8 in. model only), black or FDE parkerized finish.

| MSR $1,060 | $895 | $575 | $475 | $395 | $350 | $325 | $300 | |

Add $100 for 7 in. Troy Industries free float quad rail.

Add $131 for 13.8 in. Troy Industries free float quad rail.

GR-15 TACDE7 – 5.56 NATO cal., GIO, elite version of Tac Defender model, 16 in. M4 barrel, parkerized finish, M4 feed ramps, Troy 7 in. free float quad rail in FDE, Troy rail covers in FDE, single rail gas block, YHM (disc.) or Troy gas block mounted flip-up front sight, YHM (disc.) or Troy flip-up rear sight, Vortex (disc.) or Troy Medieval flash suppressor, Magpul trigger guard in FDE, Troy BattleAx pistol grip in FDE, Troy BattleAx CQB lightweight stock in FDE, Troy 30 shot Battlemag, Troy rifle sling, charging handle with tactical latch, two-stage match trigger.

| MSR $1,884 | $1,575 | $995 | $775 | $575 | $495 | $425 | $395 | |

* GR-15 TACDE10 – 5.56 NATO cal., similar to GR-15 TACDE7, except features Troy 10 in. free float quad rail, black finish.

| MSR $1,917 | $1,600 | $1,000 | $775 | $575 | $495 | $425 | $395 | |

GR-15 TAC EVO (EVOLUTION) – 5.56 NATO cal., GIO, 16 in. Government contour barrel with A2 flash hider, threaded muzzle, parkerized finish, M4 feed ramps, charging handle, Samson 7 in. free float with add-on rails, forged aluminum lower receiver and forged A3 flat-top upper, M4 collapsible buttstock, two 30 shot mags., right hand ejection, includes hard rifle case.

| MSR $1,158 | $975 | $595 | $495 | $425 | $365 | $335 | $300 | |

GR-15 TACE CARBINE – 5.56 NATO cal., GIO, 16 in. fluted barrel, parkerized finish, M4 feed ramps, two-stage match trigger, A3 flat-top upper, Midwest Industries flash hider/impact device, Midwest Industries free float quad rail, gas block with flip-up front and rear sights, Magpul ACS stock, Magpul OD Green 30 shot mag., Magpul enhanced aluminum trigger guard, Hogue OD Green pistol grip.

| MSR $1,760 | $1,475 | $950 | $725 | $550 | $475 | $395 | $350 | |

GR-15 TACPB CARBINE – 5.56 NATO cal., GIO, 16 in. barrel, 30 shot mag., M4 feed ramps, Mil-Spec trigger, Troy Industries free float 7.2 in. Alpha BattleRail, YHM single rail gas block, Troy Industries rear flip-up Tritium BattleSight, Troy Industries front gas block mounted flip-up BattleSight, Magpul MOE fixed stock, standard A2 pistol grip, charging handle with tactical latch, includes hard rifle case, parkerized finish.

| MSR $1,600 | $1,315 | $850 | $625 | $500 | $435 | $375 | $350 | |

GR-15 TACTC – 5.56 NATO cal., GIO, 16 in. M4 barrel with A2 flash hider, charging handle, Tapco M4 6-position commercial stock, Tapco saw cut pistol grip, Tapco vertical foregrip and Tapco Intrafuse handguard with quad rails for mounting lights/lasers, Tapco bipod, two Tapco 30 shot mags., Tapco sling system, includes hard rifle case.

| MSR $1,223 | $1,025 | $625 | $495 | $450 | $395 | $350 | $325 | |

GR-15 TACTICAL CARBINE – 5.56 NATO cal., GIO, 16 in. Govt. contour M4 barrel with A2 flash hider, parkerized finish, two 30 shot mags., M4 feed ramps, charging handle, carbine length handguard, single heat shield, drop-in quad rails, A3 flat-top forged aluminum upper and lower receiver, right-hand ejection, M4 6-position collapsible buttstock, includes hard rifle case.

| MSR $1,000 | $850 | $550 | $465 | $395 | $350 | $325 | $295 | |

GR-15 VTAC DEFENDER – 5.56 NATO cal., GIO, 16 in. Govt. contour barrel with A2 flash hider, two 30 shot mags., Troy Industries 9 in. VTAC free float rails, charging handle, forged aluminum A3 flat-top upper receiver, forged lower, right-hand ejection, M4 collapsible buttstock, parkerized finish, includes hard rifle case.

| MSR $1,090 | $915 | $575 | $475 | $415 | $350 | $325 | $300 | |

G.A.R. ARMS, cont. 203 G

MSR	100%	98%	95%	90%	80%	70%	60%	Last MSR

GR-15 ZTAC ZOMBIE TACTICAL CARBINE – 5.56 NATO cal., GIO, 16 in. M4 Govt. contour barrel with A2 flash hider, parkerized finish, M4 feed ramps, Ergo Z free float rail, Ergo vertical forward grip, Ergo ambidextrous pistol grip in Zombie Green, Ergo Zombie Green magwell cover, Ergo Zombie Green rail covers and ladder rail covers, Zombie Hunter dust cover, Zombie Hunter magazine catch, Zombie Hunter charging handle, front and rear flip-up sights, Ergo F93 eight position stock, BullDog Zombie coffin soft rifle case.

| MSR $1,620 | $1,350 | $875 | $650 | $525 | $450 | $385 | $350 | |

GWACS ARMORY

Current manufacturer of AR-15 style carbines/rifles, receivers, and accessories, located in Tulsa, OK.

RIFLES: SEMI-AUTO

CAV-15 – 5.56 NATO cal., gas operated, 16 in. chrome moly Nitride M4 Wilson barrel with A2 flash suppressor, flat-top receiver with tactical A4 quad rail, Magpul MOE stock, Magpul MOE handguard, Magpul Gen2 backup rear sight, standard charging handle, Mil-Spec trigger assembly, M16 bolt carrier group, optics ready, black, Coyote Tan, Flat Dark Earth, OD Green, or Zombie Green finish, approx. 6 lbs. Disc. 2016.

| | $725 | $500 | $435 | $375 | $335 | $315 | $295 | $839 |

CAV-15 MKII AR15 RL – 5.56 NATO cal., 18 in. stainless steel barrel, A2 flash hider, Leepers detachable front and rear sights, Mil-Spec M16 bolt carrier assembly, aluminum M4 flat-top upper with standard charging handle integrated on the CAV-15 MKII polymer lower with Mil-Spec trigger assembly, MOE rifle length handguard, low profile gas block, carbine buffer and spring, includes case and one mag., custom Cerakote pink finish. New 2017.

| MSR $1,285 | $1,075 | $675 | $500 | $450 | $400 | $350 | $325 | |

CAV-15 MKII LWT – 5.56 NATO cal., AR-15 style, 16 in. chrome moly matte light contour "pencil" barrel with A2 flash hider, heat resistant GlacierGuard polymer handguard, single rail gas block, ejection port door, forward assist, charging handle, bolt and carrier assembly, black finish, 5 lbs. 12 oz. Disc. 2016.

| | $515 | $450 | $395 | $350 | $315 | $295 | $275 | $600 |

CAV-15 TAC15 KM – 5.56 NATO cal., 16 in. chrome moly Nitride M4 barrel, A2 flash hider, Mil-Spec M16 bolt carrier assembly, aluminum M4 flat-top upper with standard charging handle integrated on the CAV-15 MKII polymer lower with Mil-Spec trigger assembly, carbine buffer and spring, 15 in. KeyMod handguard, low profile gas block, 6 lbs. 3 oz. Disc. 2017.

| | $665 | $500 | $415 | $375 | $335 | $315 | $295 | $769 |

CAV-15 TACTICAL A4 MOE – 5.56 NATO cal., 16 in. chrome moly Nitride M4 Wilson barrel with A2 flash hider, MKII lower with carbine buffer and Mil-Spec trigger assembly, aluminum flat-top upper with charging handle, MOE handguard, gas block, black finish, 6 lbs. 2 oz. Disc. 2017.

| | $515 | $450 | $395 | $350 | $315 | $295 | $275 | $599 |

CAV-15 TACTICAL A4 QUAD – 5.56 NATO cal., 16 In. chrome moly Nitride M4 Wilson barrel, A2 flash hider, fixed front sight, Mil-Spec M16 bolt carrier assembly, aluminum M4 flat-top upper with standard charging handle integrated on the CAV-15 MKII polymer lower with Mil-Spec trigger assembly, Field Sport quad rail handguard, black or FDE finish, 6 lbs. 2 oz.

| MSR $670 | $575 | $485 | $415 | $350 | $315 | $295 | $275 | |

LTAC AR-15 RIFLE – .223 Wylde chambered, 16 in. lightweight contour barrel, mid-length gas system, fully populated CAV-15 lower receiver, carbine buffer and spring, aluminum mid-length forearm kit, parkerized finish, 6 lbs. 3oz. Disc. 2017.

| | $615 | $495 | $415 | $360 | $325 | $300 | $275 | $710 |

GILBOA

Current trademark manufactured by Silver Shadow Advanced Security Systems Ltd., located in Kiryat Ono, Israel. Currently imported and distributed by LDB Supply, located in Dayton, OH.

CARBINES: SEMI-AUTO

Silver Shadow manufactures the Gilboa line of AR-15 semi-auto carbines in calibers ranging from .223 Rem., 9mm Para., 7.62x35mm, 7.62x39mm, and .300 AAC Blackout in various tactical configurations. Please contact the distributor directly for more information regarding pricing, availability, and the wide variety of options (see Trademark Index).

GREY GHOST PRECISION

Current AR-15 style rifle manufacturer located in Lakewood, WA.

RIFLES: SEMI-AUTO

6.5 CREEDMOOR – 6.5mm Creedmoor cal., 22 in. Proof Research stainless steel barrel, CMC or Geissele SSA-E trigger, Magpul Gen 3 PRS stock, rifle length gas system, Superlative Arms adj. gas block, 16 in. KeyMod or M-LOK handguard, billet upper and lower receivers, Type III True Black hardcoat anodized finish.

MSR	100%	98%	95%	90%	80%	70%	60%	Last MSR
MSR $3,099	$2,450	$1,595	$1,200	$700	$675	$575	$525	

Add $160 for Geissele SSA-E trigger.

GREY GHOST PRECISION DARK .300 BLACKOUT – .300 AAC Blackout cal., 16 in. barrel with black Nitride coating, target crown, threaded muzzle with Lantac Dragon muzzle brake, single stage trigger, Magpul CTR stock, Magpul pistol grip, billet upper receiver with M4 feed ramps and billet ambi lower receiver, 14 in. KeyMod or M-LOK handguard, slide lock charging handle, Battle Arms Development BAD-CASS safety selector, Type III True Black hardcoat anodized finish.

MSR	100%	98%	95%	90%	80%	70%	60%
MSR $2,250	$1,795	$1,050	$875	$625	$550	$475	$425

GREY GHOST PRECISION HEAVY .308 – .308 Win. cal., 16 in. match grade barrel with black Nitride coating, target crown, threaded muzzle with Lantac Dragon muzzle brake, mid-length gas system, single stage trigger, Magpul ACS-L stock, Magpul pistol grip, billet upper receiver and ambi lower receiver, 14 in. KeyMod handguard, carbine buffer set, Battle Arms Development BAD-CASS safety selector, Type III True Black hardcoat anodized finish.

MSR	100%	98%	95%	90%	80%	70%	60%
MSR $2,500	$2,050	$1,250	$950	$650	$575	$495	$475

GREY GHOST PRECISION LIGHT 5.56 – 5.56 NATO cal., 16 in. barrel with black Nitride coating, target crown, threaded muzzle, mid-length gas system, single stage trigger, Magpul CTR stock, Magpul pistol grip, billet upper receiver with M4 feed ramps and billet ambi lower receiver, 14 in. KeyMod or M-LOK handguard, Battle Arms Development BAD-CASS safety selector, Type III True Black hardcoat anodized finish.

MSR	100%	98%	95%	90%	80%	70%	60%
MSR $2,000	$1,675	$1,000	$825	$625	$550	$475	$425

GUN ROOM CO., LLC

Please refer to the Noreen Firearms LLC listing in the N section.

NOTES

H SECTION

205 H

HM DEFENSE & TECHNOLOGY

Current AR-15 style pistol and rifle manufacturer, located in Mount Orab, OH.

MSR	100%	98%	95%	90%	80%	70%	60%	Last MSR

PISTOLS: SEMI-AUTO

HMP15 – 5.56 NATO/.223 Rem. cal., 9 1/2 in. chrome moly barrel with threaded muzzle, 30 shot mag., Shockwave Blade adj. pistol stabilizer, pistol length gas system, custom HM disconnect endplate, Mil-Spec components, forged aluminum lower and M4 upper receiver, M4 feed ramps, 8 in. free float Picatinny rail, Type III hardcoat anodized black finish. New 2018.

MSR $895	$775	$685	$615	$550	$485	$415	$375	

HMP15F-556 – 5.56 NATO/.223 Rem. cal., 9 1/2 in. straight fluted stainless steel barrel with flash hider, Magpul PMAG, MOE Magpul black grip, steel gas block, 9 1/4 in. free floated Picatinny rail, buffer tube with foam pad, full forged receiver, Type III hardcoat anodized black finish. Disc. 2017.

	$725	$650	$575	$515	$450	$385	$345	$845

HMP15F-300 – .300 AAC Blackout cal., 10 1/2 in. straight fluted stainless steel barrel with flash hider, Magpul PMAG, MOE Magpul black grip, 9 1/4 in. free floated Picatinny rail, full forged receiver, steel gas block, buffer tube with foam pad, Type III hardcoat anodized black finish. Disc. 2017.

	$725	$650	$575	$515	$450	$385	$345	$845

RAIDER M5 – 5.56 NATO/.223 Rem. cal., 12 1/2 in. chrome moly barrel with threaded muzzle, 30 shot mag., Shockwave Blade adj. pistol stabilizer, mid-length gas system, custom HM disconnect endplate, M16 BCG, forged aluminum lower receiver and M4 upper with flat-top Picatinny rail, Type III Class II hardcoat anodized black finish. New 2018.

MSR $1,145	$975	$885	$765	$650	$575	$495	$435	

RIFLES: SEMI-AUTO

DEFENDER M5 / DEFENDER M5L – 5.56 NATO/.223 Rem. cal., 16 in. match grade HM monobloc barrel with integrally machined gas block, CNC machined muzzle brake, 30 shot mag., custom trigger guard, HM Mil-Spec black stock, Magpul MOE grip, mid-length gas system, 12 (M5) or 15 (M5L) in. free float Picatinny rail (M-LOK compatible), forged lower and M4 upper receiver, M4 feed ramps, monobloc dust cover, QD endplate, Type III hardcoat anodized black finish. New 2018.

MSR $1,145	$950	$595	$495	$425	$365	$335	$300	

Add $100 for 15 in. free float Picatinny rail.

GUARDIAN F5 ELITE – 5.56 NATO/.223 Rem. cal., 16 in. chrome moly match grade spiral fluted barrel with black Cerakote finish, 30 shot mag., custom trigger guard, black Mil-Spec HM stock and grip, carbine length gas system, custom 12 in. free float Picatinny rail (M-LOK compatible), forged lower and M4 upper receiver, M4 feed ramps, M16 BCG, Mil-Spec components, QD endplate, Type III hardcoat anodized black finish. New 2018.

MSR $895	$765	$515	$440	$375	$335	$315	$295	

HM15F-300 – .300 AAC Blackout cal., 16 in. spiral fluted stainless barrel, HM flash hider, Magpul PMAG, MOE Magpul stock, MOE Magpul grip, 12 in. Picatinny rail, QD endplate, hardcoat anodized black finish. Disc. 2017.

	$765	$515	$440	$375	$335	$315	$295	$895

HM15-SPFSS-300 – .300 AAC Blackout cal., 16 in. spiral fluted stainless barrel, Mil-Spec flash hider, Magpul PMAG, full billet upper and lower receiver, MOE Magpul stock, MOE Magpul grip, carbine length or 14 in. Picatinny rail, hardcoat anodized black finish. Disc. 2017.

	$1,250	$825	$575	$475	$425	$375	$350	$1,495

Add $50 for 14 in. Picatinny rail (HM15-SPFSS-300-LR).

HM15F-556 – 5.56 NATO/.223 Rem. cal., 16 in. spiral fluted chrome moly black barrel, VI-556 black flash hider, Magpul PMAG, Magpul MOE stock, Magpul MOE grip, 12 in. Picatinny rail, carbine gas system, steel gas block, QD endplate, full forged receiver, Type III hardcoat anodized black finish. Disc. 2017.

	$800	$525	$450	$385	$340	$325	$295	$945

HM15-MB-556 – 5.56 NATO cal., 16 in. HM monobloc barrel, V1-556 black flash hider, 30 shot mag., mid-length gas system, integral gas block, billet lower, 12 in. Picatinny HM Defense rail (accepts Magpul MOE 1913 style rail sections), Magpul MOE black buttstock, Magpul MOE black grip, QD endplate, Type III hardcoat anodized black finish, includes special serial number. New 2016.

MSR $1,495	$1,250	$825	$575	$475	$425	$375	$350	

HM15 RANGER V224 – .224 Valkyrie cal., 20 in. match grade barrel, 10 shot mag., custom Mil-Spec HM stock, Magpul MOE grip, rifle length gas system, forged aluminum lower and forged upper receiver with M4 feed ramps, forward assist, 15 in. free float Picatinny flat-top rail, black finish. New 2018.

MSR $1,395	$1,150	$750	$550	$465	$415	$375	$350	

H 206 HM DEFENSE & TECHNOLOGY, cont.

MSR	100%	98%	95%	90%	80%	70%	60%	Last MSR

HM15-SPFCR-556 – 5.56 NATO/.223 Rem. cal., 16 in. spiral fluted chrome moly black barrel, VI-556 black flash hider, 30 shot mag., Magpul MOE stock, Magpul MOE grip, full billet upper and lower receiver, 12 (HM15-SPFCR-556-F) or 14 in. Picatinny rail, QD endplate, steel gas block, carbine gas system, Type III hardcoat adonized black finish. Disc. 2017.

	$995	$625	$495	$450	$395	$350	$325	$1,195

Add $50 for 14 in. Picatinny rail (HM15-SPFCR-556-LR).

HM15-SPFCR-556-FDE – 5.56 NATO/.223 Rem. cal., 16 in. spiral fluted chrome moly black barrel, V1-556 black flash hider, 30 shot mag., carbine gas system, steel gas block, 12 in. Picatinny rail, billet lower receiver with FDE Cerakote finish, Magpul MOE stock, Magpul MOE grip, QD endplate. Mfg. 2016-2017.

	$1,075	$675	$500	$450	$400	$350	$325	$1,295

HM15F-556-S – 5.56 NATO/.223 Rem. cal., 16 in. chrome moly black barrel, V1-556 flash hider, 30 shot mag., steel gas block, carbine gas system, 9 in. Picatinny rail (accepts Magpul MOE 1913 style rail sections), Mil-Spec adj. stock, Type III hardcoat anodized black finish. Mfg. 2016-2017.

	$645	$500	$415	$370	$325	$300	$275	$745

HAHN TACTICAL

Current AR-15 style rifle and parts manufacturer, located in Winchester, VA, since 2015.

PISTOLS: SEMI-AUTO

REAPER PISTOL – 5.56 NATO, .223 Wylde, or .300 AAC Blackout cal., 10 in. black Nitride barrel, Black Rain Ordnance flash hider, Spikes JACK billet lower with a Hahn Tactical upper, 9 in. custom skeleton-themed handguard, SIG stabilizing brace, Magpul MOE backup sights, Mil-Spec trigger with Hahn Tactical adjuster, Magpul MOE grip, custom Cerakote finish. New 2015.

	$1,385	$895	$675	$525	$450	$385	$350	

RIFLES: SEMI-AUTO

FREEDOM-15 TACTICAL RIFLE – 5.56 NATO, .223 Wylde, or .300 AAC Blackout cal., 16 in. lightweight fluted black Nitride barrel, Yankee Hill Machine Phantom flash hider/compensator, Hahn Tactical forged aluminum upper and lower with flared magwell, 13 in. handguard, Mil-Spec trigger with Hahn Tactical adjuster, Magpul MOE backup sights, Magpul MOE grip, Magpul CTR stock. New 2015.

MSR $1,500	$1,250	$825	$575	$475	$425	$375	$350	

PRECISION 15 – 5.56 NATO, .223 Wylde, or .300 AAC Blackout cal., 16 in. lightweight fluted black Nitride barrel, Yankee Hill Machine Phantom flash hider/compensator, 15 in. handguard, Mil-Spec trigger with Hahn Tactical adjustor, T6 aluminum billet upper and lower, Magpul MOE backup sights, Magpul CTR stock, Magpul MOE grip. New 2015.

MSR $2,000	$1,675	$1,000	$825	$625	$550	$475	$425	

HAILEY ORDNANCE CO.

Current AR-15 style rifle manufacturer located in Oklahoma City, OK.

RIFLES: SEMI-AUTO

HOC-4 – 5.56 NATO cal., fluted barrel with Nitride finish, Hailey Ordnance A2 flash hider, carbine gas system, Magpul PMAG, Magpul MOE furniture, billet aluminum upper and lower receivers, Teflon coated fire control group, Bravo Company buffer tube and charging handle, ambi controls and markings, ships in a hard case, Cerakote finish.

MSR $1,050	$875	$550	$465	$395	$350	$325	$300	

HOC-15 – 5.56 NATO cal., mid-length gas system, Lothar Walther fluted stainless steel barrel or FN medium profile chrome-lined barrel, includes two Magpul PMAGs, Magpul STR or CTR stock, billet aluminum upper and lower receiver, match grade fire control group, Bravo Company buffer tube and charging handle, KNS anti-rotation pins, ambi controls and markings, ships in a hard case, black or Desert Tan Nitride or Cerakote finish.

MSR $1,850	$1,525	$975	$750	$575	$495	$425	$375	

HARDENED ARMS

Current manufacturer of custom AR-15 firearms, parts, and accessories, located in Friday Harbor, WA.

PISTOLS: SEMI-AUTO

COMPLETE PISTOL w/SDX RAIL – 5.56 NATO, 7.62x39, or .300 AAC Blackout cal., 10 1/2 in. chrome moly barrel with black Mag-Phos (.300 AAC Blackout only) or black Melonite finish, threaded muzzle, A2 flash hider, low profile gas block, pistol length gas system, forged flat-top upper and lower receiver, M4 feed ramp, AR-15 pistol buffer tube, SDX skinny rail (.300 AAC Blackout only) or SDX rail free float 10 in. handguard, single point sling attachment, black anodized finish.

MSR $550	$475	$415	$375	$335	$310	$295	$275	

Add $200 for 7.62x39 or .300 AAC Blackout cal.

HARDENED ARMS, cont. 207 H

MSR	100%	98%	95%	90%	80%	70%	60%	Last MSR

HD QUAD RAIL PISTOL – 5.56 NATO, .300 AAC Blackout, or 7.62x39mm cal., 7 1/2 (5.56 NATO), 8 1/2 (.300 AAC Blackout), or 10 1/2 (7.62x39mm or .300 AAC Blackout) in. chrome moly high-end barrel with black Melonite finish, threaded muzzle, A2 flash hider, low profile gas block, pistol length gas system, Mil-Spec parts, AR-15 pistol buffer tube, single point sling attachment, M4 feed ramp flat-top upper receiver, HD quad rail free float 7 or 10 in. handguard without end cap, with or w/o Shockwave stabilizer, black anodized finish.

| MSR $690 | $595 | $485 | $415 | $350 | $315 | $295 | $275 | |

Add $10 for 8 1/2 or 10 1/2 in. barrel.
Add $50-$70 for Shockwave stabilizer.

* **Quad Rail w/Sig Kit** – 5.56 NATO or .300 AAC Blackout cal., pistol length gas system, 7 1/2 (5.56 NATO) or 10 1/2 (.300 AAC Blackout) in. chrome moly high-end barrel, A2 flash hider, laser etched M4 feed ramp flat-top T-marked upper receiver, forged lower receiver, AR-15 pistol buffer tube, free float quad rail with 7 (5.56 NATO) or 10 (.300 AAC Blackout) in. handguard w/o end cap, low profile gas block, full auto chrome-lined bolt carrier group Mil-Spec charging handle, pistol buffer kit, SB-15 SIG arm brace (5.56 NATO) or SIG arm brace only (.300 AAC Blackout), black Mag-Phos barrel finish, black anodized receiver. Disc. 2017.

| | $765 | $515 | $440 | $375 | $335 | $315 | $295 | *$899* |

TALON RAIL PISTOL – 5.56 NATO, 7.62x39, or .300 AAC Blackout cal., 7 1/2 (5.56 NATO or 7.62x39), 8 1/2 (.300 AAC Blackout), or 10 1/2 in. chrome moly high-end barrel with black Mag-Phos or black Melonite finish, threaded muzzle, A2 flash hider, low profile gas block, pistol length gas system, M4 feed ramp flat-top upper receiver with black anodized finish, forged lower receiver with AR-15 pistol buffer tube and single point sling attachment, Talon free float 7 or 10 in. handguard without end cap, full auto chrome-lined BCG, Mil-Spec charging handle.

| MSR $800 | $675 | $500 | $425 | $375 | $335 | $315 | $295 | |

Add $80 for Talon Rail Complete with Citadel (5.56 NATO cal., 10 1/2 in. barrel).

RIFLES: SEMI-AUTO

.223 WYLDE SPECIAL EDITION SS – .223 Wylde chamber, 16 in. stainless steel barrel, stainless tactical muzzle brake, low profile gas block, mid-length gas system, 12 in. featherweight skeletonized free float quad rail, nickel boron BCG, Fortis extended charging handle, Magpul RVG vertical foregrip, Magpul ACS-L carbine stock, Mil-Spec billet lower, M4 feed ramp flat-top upper receiver, black anodized finish. New 2018.

| MSR $900 | $765 | $515 | $440 | $375 | $335 | $315 | $295 | |

16 IN. BLACK WIDOW SUPPRESSED RIFLE – .300 AAC Blackout cal., pistol length gas system, 10 1/2 in. Melonite barrel (with pin suppressor bringing the barrel length past 16 in. which qualifies it as a rifle), threaded muzzle, 30 shot Magpul mag., Magpul CTR stock, collapsible carbine buffer tube, M4 feed ramp flat-top upper receiver with black anodized finish, forged lower receiver, 10 or 15 in. tactical quad rail.

| MSR $1,350 | $1,125 | $700 | $525 | $450 | $400 | $350 | $325 | |

Add $100 for 15 in. tactical quad rail.

* **Black Widow Gen II Suppressed Rifle** – .300 AAC Blackout cal., 10 1/2 in. barrel with Melonite finish (pinned suppressor brings barrel length past 16 in. which qualifies it as a rifle), threaded muzzle, pistol length gas system, M4 feed ramp flat-top upper receiver with black anodized finish, forged lower, 10 in. HD quad rail, Mil-Spec parts, collapsible carbine buffer tube, Mil-Spec stock, Black Widow Gen II suppressor can.

| MSR $800 | $675 | $500 | $425 | $375 | $335 | $315 | $295 | |

16 IN. .300 BLACKOUT MELONITED CAMO – .300 AAC Blackout cal., 16 in. HBAR profile Melonite barrel with M4 extension, threaded muzzle, A2 flash hider, M4 collapsible stock, pistol length gas system, low profile gas block, M4 feed ramp flat-top upper receiver, Mil-Spec lower, free floating 10 in. Scorpion rail, Camo, Camo Jungle, Camo Desert, or Camo Snow Cerakote finish. New 2018.

| MSR $1,200 | $1,025 | $625 | $495 | $450 | $395 | $350 | $325 | |

16 IN. GRENDEL RIFLE – 6.5 Grendel cal., SOCOM gas system, 16 in. barrel w/M4 extension, A2 flash hider, 12 in. Scorpion free floating rail w/FDE Cerakote finish, low profile gas block, forged upper and lower receiver, black Melonite or QPQ finish. Disc. 2017.

| | $1,075 | $675 | $500 | $450 | $400 | $350 | $325 | *$1,300* |

16 IN. M4 MELONITED QUAD RAIL RIFLE – 5.56 NATO cal., carbine length gas system, 16 in. M4 profile barrel with black Melonite finish and M4 extension, threaded muzzle, A2 flash hider, M4 collapsible stock, M4 feed ramp flat-top upper receiver, Mil-Spec forged lower receiver, low profile gas block, HD Tactical quad rail free float 10 in. handguard without end cap, Mil-Spec, BCM Gunfighter, or Rapid Ambidextrous charging handle, black anodized or Cerakote finish in Camo, Desert, Jungle, or Snow Camo.

| MSR $530 | $475 | $415 | $375 | $335 | $310 | $295 | $275 | |

Add $470 for Camo, Desert, Jungle, or Snow Camo Cerakote finish.
Add $31 for BCM Gunfighter charging handle.
Add $67 for Rapid Ambidextrous charging handle.

H 208 HARDENED ARMS, cont.

MSR		100%	98%	95%	90%	80%	70%	60%	Last MSR

16 IN. MELONITED HBAR HD QUAD RAIL RIFLE – .300 AAC Blackout or 7.62x39mm cal., 16 in. barrel with black Melonite/QPQ finish and M4 extension, threaded muzzle, A2 flash hider, M4 collapsible stock, low profile gas block, pistol length gas system, M4 feed ramp flat-top upper receiver, 10 in. HD Tactical quad rail free float handguard, Mil-Spec forged lower receiver, Mil-Spec, BCM Gunfighter, or Rapid Ambidextrous charging handle, black anodized, Camo, Snow Camo, or Jungle Camo Cerakote (Cerakote in 7.62x39mm only) finish.

| MSR $800 | | $675 | $500 | $425 | $375 | $335 | $315 | $295 | |

Add $350 for Camo, Snow Camo, or Jungle Camo Cerakote finishes in 7.62x39mm cal.
Add $31 for BCM Gunfighter charging handle.
Add $67 for Rapid Ambidextrous charging handle.

16 IN. SS SPIRAL FLUTED SOCOM – 5.56 NATO cal., carbine length gas system, 16 in. stainless steel, spiral fluted barrel with SOCOM profile and M4 extension, 1:9 barrel twist, short comb muzzle brake, laser etched T-marked upper receiver, low profile gas block, SDX rail with free float 10 in. handguard, M4 feed ramps, black anodized Mil-Spec finished upper receiver, available in black/pink, black/blue, black/purple, black/red, black/green, or black/silver two-tone Cerakote finish, 6.3 lbs. Disc. 2017.

| | | $850 | $550 | $465 | $395 | $350 | $325 | $295 | $999 |

* ***16 in. SS Straight Bull Barreled Rifle*** – 5.56 NATO cal., carbine length gas system, 16 in. stainless steel fluted bull barrel w/ith SOCOM profile and M4 extension, 1:9 barrel twist, short comb muzzle brake, laser etched T-marked upper receiver, low profile gas block, Scorpion rail with free float 10 in. handguard, M4 feed ramps, black anodized Mil-Spec finished upper receiver, available in black/pink, black/blue, black/purple, black/red, black/green, or black/silver two-tone Cerakote finish, 7.2 lbs. Disc. 2017.

| | | $850 | $550 | $465 | $395 | $350 | $325 | $295 | $999 |

16 IN. SOCOM MELONITED HD QUAD RAIL RIFLE – 5.56 NATO cal., 16 in. SOCOM profile barrel with black Melonite finish and M4 extension, threaded muzzle, A2 flash hider, M4 collapsible stock, low profile gas block, carbine length gas system, M4 feed ramp flat-top upper receiver, HD quad rail free float 10 in. handguard without end cap, Mil-Spec forged lower receiver, black anodized finish.

| MSR $700 | | $595 | $485 | $415 | $350 | $315 | $295 | $275 | |

16 IN. M4 MELONITED TALON RAIL RIFLE – 5.56 NATO cal., carbine length gas system, 16 in. M4 profile barrel with M4 extension, A2 flash hider, M4 collapsible stock, low profile gas block, 12 in. Talon tactical free float rail, M4 feed ramp flat-top receiver and Mil-Spec forged lower receiver, black Melonite finish.

| MSR $830 | | $725 | $500 | $435 | $375 | $335 | $315 | $295 | |

16 IN. TALON RAIL RIFLE – 7.62x39mm cal., carbine length gas system, 16 in. SOCOM profile barrel with black Melonite finish and M4 extension, threaded muzzle, A2 flash hider, M4 collapsible stock, adj. gas piston system pinned to barrel for duty grade install, one-piece bolt carrier, M4 feed ramp flat-top upper receiver, 12 in. tactical TLN rail, Mil-Spec forged lower receiver, black anodized finish.

| MSR $830 | | $725 | $500 | $435 | $375 | $335 | $315 | $295 | |

* ***16 In. Talon Rail Rifle .300 Blackout*** – .300 AAC Blackout cal., carbine length gas system, 16 in. HBAR profile barrel with black Melonite finish and M4 extension, threaded muzzle, A2 flash hider, M4 collapsible stock, low profile gas block, M4 feed ramp flat-top upper receiver, 12 in. Talon rail, Mil-Spec forged lower receiver, black anodized finish.

| MSR $900 | | $765 | $515 | $440 | $375 | $335 | $315 | $295 | |

18 IN. HBAR MELONITED HD QUAD RAIL RIFLE – 7.62x39mm cal., carbine length gas system, 18 in. barrel with HBAR extension and black Melonite/QPQ finish, threaded muzzle, A2 flash hider, 10 shot mag., low profile gas block, M4 feed ramp flat-top upper receiver, HD quad rail free float 12 in. handguard without end cap, Mil-Spec forged lower, M4 collapsible stock, black anodized finish.

| MSR $570 | | $495 | $435 | $385 | $340 | $315 | $295 | $275 | |

18 IN. MELONITED QUAD RAIL – 5.56 NATO (disc. 2017) or 6.5 Grendel (new 2018) cal., 18 in. SOCOM (disc. 2017) barrel with black Melonite finish and M4 extension, threaded muzzle, A2 flash hider, M4 collapsible stock, mid-length gas system, low profile gas block, M4 feed ramp flat-top upper receiver, HD quad rail free float 12 in. handguard without end cap, Mil-Spec forged lower, black anodized finish.

| MSR $750 | | $645 | $500 | $415 | $370 | $325 | $300 | $275 | |

18 IN. SDX RAIL LIGHTWEIGHT RIFLE – 5.56 NATO cal., 18 in. SOCOM barrel with M4 extension, threaded muzzle, fixed skeleton stock, mid-length adj. gas system, adj. gas block, 15 in. SDX M-LOK rail, M4 feed ramp flat-top upper receiver, Mil-Spec forged lower, 7.2 lbs. New 2018.

| MSR $1,000 | | $850 | $550 | $465 | $395 | $350 | $325 | $295 | |

19.5 IN. .224 VALKYRIE SDX RAIL LIGHTWEIGHT RIFLE – .224 Valkyrie cal., 19.5 in. SOCOM mid-length barrel with M4 extension, threaded muzzle, 10 shot mag., rifle length adj. gas system, 15 in. SDX M-LOK slim rail, fixed skeleton rifle length stock, M4 feed ramp flat-top upper receiver, Mil-Spec forged lower. New 2018.

| MSR $800 | | $675 | $500 | $425 | $375 | $335 | $315 | $295 | |

HARDENED ARMS, cont. 209 H

MSR	100%	98%	95%	90%	80%	70%	60%	Last MSR

20 IN. GRENDEL RIFLE – 6.5 Grendal cal., rifle length gas sytem, 20 in. HBAR barrel with M4 extension, collapsible stock, 15 in. tactical quad rail w/o end cap, thread protector, laser etched T-marked upper and Mil-Spec forged lower receiver, low profile gas block, black Melonite finish, includes bolt carrier group package and charging handle.

| MSR $880 | $765 | $515 | $440 | $375 | $335 | $315 | $295 | |

24 IN. BULL BARREL RIFLE – 5.56 NATO cal., rifle length gas system, 24 in. HBAR profile barrel w/M4 extension, A2 flash hider, collapsible M4 stock, laser-etched T-marked upper receiver and Mil-Spec forged lower receiver, 15 in. handguard w/o end cap, low profile gas block, black Melonite finish. Disc. 2017.

| | $800 | $525 | $450 | $385 | $340 | $325 | $295 | *$950* |

"GUNS AND LACE" EDITION RIFLE – 5.56 NATO cal., mid-length gas system, 16 in. mid-length SOCOM barrel with M4 extension, A2 flash hider, fully adj. rifle length buttstock, 13 in. CMX KeyMod handguard, M4 feed ramp flat-top receiver and forged Mil-Spec lower receiver, low profile gas block, red Cerakote finish.

| MSR $1,250 | $1,050 | $650 | $495 | $450 | $395 | $350 | $325 | |

HATCHER GUN COMPANY

Current custom pistol, rifle, and shotgun manufacturer located in Elsie, NE and established in 1983.

Hatcher Gun Company manufactures custom pistols, rifles, and shotguns for both the civilian and law enforcement marketplaces. Rifles include a series of AR-15 models in various barrel lengths and configurations, pistols include a bolt action model based on the Remington XP-100, and shotguns include modified Saiga semi-autos. NFA items include short barreled Saigas and SxS shotguns. Please contact the company directly for more information, availability, and pricing (see Trademark Index).

RIFLES: SEMI-AUTO

Hatcher Gun Company also manufactures custom AR-15 style rifles per customer specifications. Please contact the company directly for options, pricing, and availability.

HGC AR08 RAPTR GEN 2 – .308 Win. cal., 18 in. stainless steel fluted bull barrel, M2-72 muzzle brake, 25 shot Magpul PMAG, Elftmann match trigger, flip-up sights, Magpul PRS stock, Hogue grip, billet lower and A3 billet left side charging upper, checkering on magwell, low profile gas block, 12 1/2 in. KeyMod handguard, adj. bipod, includes black nylon sling and tactical soft case, Coyote Tan or black Cerakote finish, 10 lbs. New 2016.

| MSR $2,500 | $2,050 | $1,250 | $950 | $650 | $575 | $495 | $475 | |

* **HGC AR08 RAPTR Gen 2 Carbon Fiber** – .308 Win. cal., 18 in. Christensen carbon fiber barrel, M2-72 muzzle brake, 25 shot Magpul PMAG, Elftmann match trigger, flip sights, Luthar adj. stock, Hogue grip, ODIN 15 1/2 in. KeyMod handguard, billet lower and A3 billet left side charging upper, low profile gas block, checkering on front of magwell, includes adj. bipod, sling swivel, one 3 in. KeyMod rail section, black nylon sling and tactical soft case, Cerakote Coyote tan and black finish, 8.4 lbs. New 2016.

| MSR $2,895 | $2,295 | $1,450 | $1,075 | $675 | $595 | $525 | $475 | |

HGC AR08 RECON – .308 Win. cal., 16 in. HBAR threaded barrel, flash suppressor, 25 shot Magpul PMAG, standard Mil-Spec trigger, flip sights, 6-pos. collapsible stock, 12 1/2 in. KeyMod handguard, billet lower and A3 billet upper receiver, low profile gas block, checkering on front magwell, steel bolt carrier, includes sling swivel, one 3 in. KeyMod rail section, black nylon sling and tactical soft case, Coyote Tan or black Cerakote finish, 8.5 lbs.

| MSR $1,675 | $1,385 | $895 | $675 | $525 | $450 | $385 | $350 | |

HGC AR15HB .204 LEFT HAND – .204 Ruger cal., 20 in. Lilja stainless steel fluted bull barrel, target crown muzzle, Gemtech QD flash suppressor, 30 shot mag., checkering on front of magwell, Jewell two-stage AR trigger, Magpul PRS buttstock, ambi mag. release and safety selelctor, Gen 4 billet lower and A3 left-hand upper receiver, DPMS free float vented handguard, drilled and tapped for swivel stud and bipod, engraved pictograph of SAFE and FIRE on each side of receiver, single rail gas block, tactical latch, includes sling swivel, black nylon sling and tactical soft case, custom Leupold VX-3 SF 30mm 6.5x20x50 scope, and TPS TSR 30mm low rings, Cerakote Magpul Dark Earth finish, 10.75 lbs.

| MSR $3,675 | $2,950 | $1,925 | $1,400 | $825 | $675 | $625 | $575 | |

HGC AR15HB BULL – 5.56 NATO/.223 Rem. cal., 24 in. SS bull barrel, 30 shot mag., standard semi-auto trigger group, flip-up sight set, A2 standard stock, single rail gas block drilled and tapped with swivel stud, checkering on front of magwell, round free float handguard, engraved pictograph of "SAFE" and "FIRE" on each side of receiver, round forward assist, solid machined trigger guard, includes black nylon sling and tactical case, black hardcoat anodized finish, 9.75 lbs.

| MSR $1,240 | $1,050 | $650 | $495 | $450 | $395 | $350 | $325 | |

HGC AR15HB CAR HBAR – 5.56 NATO/.223 Rem. cal., 16 in. HBAR barrel, 30 shot mag., standard semi-auto trigger group, flip-up sight set, M4 6-pos. collapsible stock, single rail gas block drilled and tapped with swivel stud, checkering on front of magwell, custom Gen 4 billet lower and A3 octagon upper receiver, CAR quad rail handguard, engraved pictograph of "SAFE" and "FIRE" on each side of receiver, includes black nylon sling and tactical case, hardcoat anodized black finish, 6 1/2 lbs.

| MSR $1,070 | $895 | $575 | $475 | $395 | $350 | $325 | $300 | |

H 210 HATCHER GUN COMPANY, cont.

MSR	100%	98%	95%	90%	80%	70%	60%	Last MSR

HGC AR15HB HBAR – 5.56 NATO/.223 Rem. cal., 20 in. HBAR barrel, 30 shot mag., standard semi-auto trigger group, flip-up sight set, A2 standard stock, single rail gas block drilled and tapped with swivel stud, checkering on front of magwell, rifle length quad rail handguard, engraved pictograph of "SAFE" and "FIRE" on each side of receiver, includes black nylon sling and case, black hardcoat anodized finish, 8 lbs.

| MSR $1,070 | $895 | $575 | $475 | $395 | $350 | $325 | $300 | |

HGC AR15HB CAR M4 – 5.56 NATO/.223 Rem. cal., AR-15 style, 16 in. M4 barrel, 30 shot mag., standard semi-auto trigger group, flip-up sight set, M4 6-pos. collapsible stock, single rail gas block, CAR quad rail handguard, Gen 4 billet lower and A3 upper receiver, sling swivel, checkering on front of magwell, engraved pictograph marked "SAFE" and "FIRE" on each side, black Type III hardcoat anodized finish, 6 1/2 lbs.

| MSR $1,070 | $895 | $575 | $475 | $395 | $350 | $325 | $300 | |

HGC AR15HB SIDEWINDER GEN 2 – 5.56 NATO/.223 Rem. cal., 16 in. stainless steel fluted HBAR barrel, A2 flash suppressor, 30 shot aluminum mag., flip sight set, standard grip, 6-pos. collapsible stock, Gen 4 billet lower and A3 billet left side charging upper receiver, 12 1/2 in. KeyMod handguard, low profile gas block, checkering on front of magwell, includes one 3 in. KeyMod rail section, QD sling swivel, black nylon sling, and tactical soft case, black or Magpul Dark Earth/black finish, 7 1/2 lbs.

| MSR $1,450 | $1,195 | $795 | $550 | $465 | $415 | $375 | $350 | |

Add $200 for Magpul Dark Earth/black finish.

HEAD DOWN PRODUCTS, LLC

Current AR-15 style semi-auto rifle manufacturer located in Dallas, GA. Previously distributed until 2013 by American Tactical Imports, located in Rochester, NY.

PISTOLS: SEMI-AUTO

HD15 SLICK SIDE PISTOL – 5.56 NATO cal., 10.3 or 12 1/2 in. barrel, carbine or mid-length gas system, 9 in. M-LOK handguard, SBN carrier and Gearhead Tailhook Gen 1, Cerakote finish available in several different colors.

| MSR $1,949 | $1,650 | $1,450 | $1,225 | $1,085 | $935 | $800 | $650 | |

PROVECTUS PV9 BILLET PISTOL – 5.56 NATO cal., 7 1/2 in. HDP profile barrel with A2 flash hider, 30 shot Lancer mag., HD Provectus 9 in. rail system, single stage drop-in trigger, integral trigger guard, Head Down skull engraved on ambi Raptor charging handle, milled billet upper and lower receivers, flared magwell, SIG brace, Ergo rubber ambi grip, hardcoat anodized finish, includes hard rifle case. Mfg. 2015-2017.

| | $1,400 | $1,235 | $1,100 | $975 | $850 | $725 | $585 | *$1,650* |

TRITON BILLET PISTOL – 5.56 NATO cal., 7 1/2 in. HDP profile barrel with A2 flash hider, 30 shot Lancer mag., 7 in. CAR length quad rail, integral trigger guard, flared magwell, SIG stock, plastic grip, Type III hardcoat anodized finish. Mfg. 2015-2017.

| | $1,025 | $925 | $800 | $685 | $595 | $515 | $435 | *$1,199* |

RIFLES/CARBINES: SEMI-AUTO

ARCADIUS-DMR .308 BILLET RIFLE – .308 Win. cal., 22 in. stainless steel HDP profile barrel with PVX muzzle device, rifle length gas system, 20 shot PMAG 15 in. HD Gen II Mod II rail, single stage drop-in trigger, Head Down skull engraved on ambi Raptor charging handle, billet upper and lower receivers, integral trigger guard, flared magwell, Magpul PRS stock, Ergo Ambi pistol grip, Type III hardcoat anodized finish. Mfg. 2015-2017.

| | $1,725 | $1,050 | $850 | $625 | $550 | $475 | $425 | *$2,199* |

ARCADIUS-MR .308 BILLET RIFLE – .308 Win. cal., 18 in. stainless steel HDP profile barrel with PVX muzzle device, 20 shot PMAG, mid-length gas system, 15 in. HD Gen II MOD II rail, single stage drop-in trigger, Head Down skull engraved on ambi Raptor charging handle, billet upper and lower receivers, integral trigger guard, flared magwell, Magpul PRS stock, Ergo Ambi pistol grip, Type III hardcoat anodized finish. Mfg. 2015-2017.

| | $1,675 | $1,000 | $825 | $625 | $550 | $475 | $425 | *$2,099* |

ARCADIUS-PR .308 BILLET RIFLE – .308 Win. cal., 16 in. stainless steel HDP profile barrel with PVX muzzle device, 20 shot PMAG, mid-length gas system, 13 in. HD Gen II Mod II rail, single stage drop-in trigger, Head Down skull engraved on ambi Raptor charging handle, billet upper and lower receivers, integral trigger guard, flared magwell, HDF stock, Ergo Ambi grip, Type III hardcoat anodized finish. Mfg. 2015-2017.

| | $1,575 | $995 | $775 | $575 | $495 | $425 | $395 | *$1,899* |

ARCADIUS-S .308 BILLET RIFLE – .308 Win. cal., 16 in. stainless steel HDP profile barrel with A2 flash hider, 20 shot PMAG, carbine length gas system, 10 in. HD Gen II MOD II rail, billet upper and lower receivers, integral trigger guard, flared magwell, 6-pos. stock, Mil-Spec plastic pistol grip, Type III hardcoat anodized finish. Mfg. 2015-2017.

| | $1,385 | $895 | $675 | $525 | $450 | $385 | $350 | *$1,659* |

HEAD DOWN PRODUCTS, LLC, cont. 211 H

MSR	100%	98%	95%	90%	80%	70%	60%	Last MSR

HD15 SLICK SIDE RIFLE – 5.56 NATO cal., 16 or 18 (heavy barrel only) in. standard or heavy barrel, rifle or mid-length gas system, 15 in. M-LOK handguard, SBN carrier, Mission First Minimalist stock, Cerakote finish in black, FDE, Battleship Grey, Burnt Bronze, Cobalt, and several other colors.

| MSR $1,849 | $1,525 | $975 | $750 | $575 | $495 | $425 | $375 | |

HDX TAC7 – 5.56 NATO cal., GIO, 16 in. profile Melonite coated barrel, 7 in. free floating rail system handguard, matte black hardcoat anodized finish, 6-position collapsible stock with standard pistol grip, two 30 shot mags., A2 flash hider, forged upper and lower receiver, flared magwell, vertical bipod grip, two rail covers. Disc. 2013.

| | $915 | $575 | $475 | $415 | $350 | $325 | $300 | *$1,099* |

MK12 BILLET RIFLE – 5.56 NATO cal., GIO, 18 in. HDP profile barrel with A2 flash hider, 20 shot Lancer mag., 15 in. Provectus rail system, single stage drop-in trigger, ambi Raptor charging handle with Head Down skull engraved milled billet upper and lower receivers, integral trigger guard, flared magwell, HDF stock, Ergo rubber ambi pistol grip, hardcoat anodized finish, includes hard rifle case. Mfg. 2013-2015.

| | $1,575 | $995 | $775 | $575 | $495 | $425 | $395 | *$1,899* |

PREDATOR PACKAGE + NIGHTVISION KIT – 5.56 NATO cal., 16 in. HDP profile barrel with A2 flash hider, two 20 shot Lancer mags., mid-length gas system, HD Provectus 13 in. rail system, single stage drop-in trigger, Luna Gen 2+ Nightvision scope, Luna extended range laser IR, Magpul rail mounted sling adapter, Head Down skull engraved on ambi Raptor charging handle, billet upper and lower receivers, integral trigger guard, flared magwell, HDF stock, Ergo rubber ambi pistol grip, hardcoat anodized finish, includes custom foam hard case. Mfg. 2015-2017.

| | $3,695 | $2,650 | $1,675 | $1,050 | $795 | $725 | $700 | *$4,500* |

PROVECTUS PV9 GEN I BILLET RIFLE – .300 AAC Blackout or 5.56 NATO cal., GIO, 16 in. HDP profile barrel with PVX muzzle device, flat-top Picatinny receiver with integrated 9, 13, or 15 in. Provectus quad rail, billet upper/lower receiver, HDF 6-position buttstock, Ergo rubber ambi pistol grip, 30 shot Lancer mag., integral trigger guard, flared magwell, Type III hardcoat anodized finish. Mfg. 2013-2017.

| | $1,350 | $875 | $650 | $525 | $450 | $385 | $350 | *$1,650* |

Add $85 for 13 in. or $350 for 15 in. Provectus quad rail.
Add $100 for .300 AAC Blackout cal.

PROVECTUS PV10 GEN II BILLET RIFLE – 5.56 NATO cal., 16 in. HDP profile barrel with PVX muzzle device, 30 shot Lancer mag., mid-length gas system, HD Gen II 10 in. rail system, single stage drop-in trigger, Head Down skull engraved on ambi Raptor charging handle, HDF stock, Ergo rubber ambi grip, milled billet upper and lower receivers, integral trigger guard, flared magwell, Type III hardcoat anodized finish. Mfg. 2015-2017.

| | $1,350 | $875 | $650 | $525 | $450 | $385 | $350 | *$1,650* |

PROVECTUS PV13 BILLET RIFLE – 5.56 NATO or .300 AAC Blackout cal., GIO, 16 in. HDP profile barrel, PVX muzzle device, HD Gen II 13 in. Provectus rail system handguard, HDF adj. stock with Ergo rubber ambi pistol grip, 30 shot Lancer mag., nickel boron carrier group, precision milled upper and lower receiver, integral trigger guard, flared magwell, Type III hardcoat anodized matte black finish. Disc. 2017.

| | $1,350 | $875 | $650 | $525 | $450 | $385 | $350 | *$1,650* |

Add $125 for .300 AAC Blackout cal.

PROVECTUS PV15 GEN II BILLET RIFLE – 5.56 NATO or .300 AAC Blackout cal., GIO, 16 in. profile Melonite coated barrel, 15 in. Provectus rail system handguard, HDF adj. stock with Ergo rubber ambi pistol grip, 30 shot Lancer mag., A2 flash hider, Geissele two-stage trigger, nickel boron carrier group, precision milled upper and lower receiver, integral trigger guard, flared magwell, hardcoat anodized matte black finish. Disc. 2017.

| | $1,350 | $875 | $650 | $525 | $450 | $385 | $350 | *$1,650* |

Add $115 for .300 AAC Blackout cal.

TRITON M4 BILLET RIFLE (HDX M4) – 5.56 NATO cal., GIO, 16 in. profile Melonite coated barrel, matte black hardcoat anodized finish, Mil-Spec handguard, 6-position collapsible stock with standard pistol grip, 30 shot mag., A2 flash hider, forged upper and lower receiver, flared magwell. Disc. 2017.

| | $725 | $500 | $435 | $375 | $335 | $315 | $295 | *$849* |

TRITON 7 BILLET RIFLE – 5.56 NATO cal., 15 in. HDP profile barrel with A2 flash hider, 30 shot Lancer mag., carbine length gas system, 7 in. two-piece carbine length quad rail, milled billet upper and lower receivers, flared magwell, integral trigger guard, A2 adj. stock, plastic grip, Type III hardcoat anodized finish. Mfg. 2015-2017.

| | $765 | $515 | $440 | $375 | $335 | $315 | $295 | *$899* |

TRITON 10 GEN II BILLET RIFLE (HDX TAC10) – 5.56 NATO cal., GIO, 16 in. Melonite coated steel barrel, 10 in. free floating rail system handguard, 6-position collapsible stock with standard pistol grip, 30 shot Lancer mag., A2 flash hider, forged upper and lower receiver, flared magwell, vertical bipod grip, two rail covers, Mil-Spec bolt carrier group, hardcoat anodized matte black finish. Disc. 2017.

| | $850 | $550 | $465 | $395 | $350 | $325 | $295 | *$999* |

H 212 HEAD DOWN PRODUCTS, LLC, cont.

MSR	100%	98%	95%	90%	80%	70%	60%	Last MSR

TRITON 12 BILLET RIFLE (HDX TAC12) – 5.56 NATO cal., GIO, 16 in. Melonite coated steel barrel, 12 in. free floating rail system handguard, 6-position collapsible stock with standard pistol grip, two 30 shot mags., A2 flash hider, forged upper and lower receiver, flared magwell, vertical bipod grip, two rail covers, Mil-Spec bolt carrier group, hardcoat anodized matte black finish. Disc. 2017.

	$915	$575	$475	$415	$350	$325	$300	$1,099

TRITON 15 GEN II BILLET RIFLE – 5.56 NATO cal., GIO, 16 in. HDP profile barrel with A2 flash hider, 30 shot Lancer mag., billet upper and lower receivers, 15 in. free floating quad rail, MFT stock, plastic Mil-Spec grip, Type III hardcoat anodized finish. Mfg. 2015-2017.

	$950	$595	$495	$425	$365	$335	$300	$1,149

HECKLER & KOCH

Current manufacturer established in 1949, and located in Oberndorf/Neckar, Germany. Currently imported and distributed beginning mid-2008 by H & K USA, located in Columbus, GA. .22 LR cal. pistols and rifles are currently imported by Walther Arms, located in Fort Smith, AR. Previously imported by Merkel USA, located in Trussville, AL, by Heckler & Koch, Inc. located in Sterling, VA (previously located in Chantilly, VA). During 2004, H & K built a new plant in Columbus, GA, primarily to manufacture guns for American military and law enforcement.

In early 1991, H & K was absorbed by Royal Ordnance, a division of British Aerospace (BAE Systems) located in England. During December 2002, BAE Systems sold Heckler & Koch to a group of European investors. Heckler & Koch, Inc. and HKJS GmbH are wholly owned subsidiaries of Suhler Jag und Sportwaffen Holding GmbH and the sole licensees of Heckler & Koch commercial firearms technology.

RIFLES: SEMI-AUTO

Most of the models listed, being of a tactical design, were disc. in 1989 due to Federal legislation. Sporterized variations mfg. after 1994 with thumbhole stocks were banned in April, 1998.

In 1991, the HK-91, HK-93, and HK-94 were discontinued. Last published retail prices (1991) were $999 for fixed stock models and $1,199 for retractable stock models.

In the early '70s, S.A.C.O. importers located in Virginia sold the Models 41 and 43 which were the predecessors to the Model 91 and 93, respectively. Values for these earlier variations will be higher than values listed.

MR556A1 CARBINE – 5.56 NATO cal., GPO, 10 or 30 shot steel mag., 16 1/2 in. heavy barrel with muzzle brake, free floating rail system handguard with four Mil-Std 1913 Picatinny rails, Picatinny rail machined into top of upper receiver, two-stage trigger, diopter sights, black anodized finish, adj. buttstock with (disc. 2013) or w/o (new 2014) storage compartment, HK pistol grip with optional configurations, 7.6 lbs. Mfg. in the U.S. using American and German made components. New 2009.

MSR $3,295		$2,815	$2,465	$1,995	$1,700	$1,400	$1,200	$1,035

* **MR556A1 Competition** – 5.56 NATO cal., GPO, 16 1/2 in. cold hammer forged barrel with compensator, 10, 20, or 30 shot mag., two-stage trigger, 14 in. lightweight modular rail system, extended magazine release button, upper receiver with charging handle with extended latch, collapsible and locking Magpul CTR stock, no sights, HK grip, 8.8 lbs. New 2014.

MSR $3,199		$2,725	$2,375	$1,925	$1,650	$1,375	$1,150	$995

* **MR556A1-SD** – 5.56 NATO cal., GPO, 16 1/2 in. cold hammer forged barrel, OSS suppressor which comprises two modules - a Back Pressure Regulator (BRM) and a Signature Reduction Module (SRM), 10, 20, or 30 shot mag., two-stage trigger, HK black grip, HK 6-position adj. stock, black finish, 9 1/2 lbs. New 2014.

Please contact the importer directly for pricing and more information on this configuration (see Trademark Index).

MR762A1 CARBINE – 7.62x51mm cal., GPO, 16 1/2 in. barrel, 10 or 20 shot polymer mag., free floating rail system, flip-up front and diopter rear sights, upper and lower accessory rails, adj. buttstock with storage compartment, pistol grip with optional configurations, black anodized finish, 9.84-10.4 lbs. New late 2009.

MSR $3,995		$3,600	$3,150	$2,700	$2,350	$1,950	$1,725	$1,400

* **MR762A1 LRP (Long Rifle Package)** – 7.62x51mm cal., GPO, 16 1/2 in. cold hammer forged barrel, 20 shot mag., two-stage trigger, Ergo SureGrip, collapsible stock with adj. cheekpiece, Blue Force Gear sling and Manta rail covers, tan finish, features a 3-9x40mm Leupold VX-R Patrol rifle scope perched in a set of Leupold rings on a Leupold Pic-rail mount, includes LaRue Tactical BRM-6 bipod, cleaning kit, two mags., and Pelican case, 10.42 lbs. Mfg. 2013-2016.

	$6,250	$5,600	$5,000	$4,500	$4,000	$3,650	$3,250	$6,899

* **MR762A1 LRP II (Long Rifle Package II)** – 7.62x51mm NATO cal., GPO, 16 1/2 in. cold hammer forged barrel with 14.7 in. modular rail system, 10 or 20 shot mag., two-stage trigger, G28 collapsible stock with adj. cheekpiece, buttpad, and LOP, FDE pistol grip with storage, accessory Picatinny rail, integrated quick detachable sling attachment points, 3-9x40mm Leupold VX-R Patrol rifle scope and mount/base, Leupold rings and Pic-rail mount, LaRue/Harris Tactical BRM-S bipod, cleaning kit, and Pelican case, black and tan finish, 13.46 lbs. Mfg. in the USA beginning 2016.

MSR $6,899		$6,250	$5,600	$5,000	$4,500	$4,000	$3,650	$3,250

HERA ARMS 213 H

MSR	100%	98%	95%	90%	80%	70%	60%	Last MSR

HERA ARMS

Current firearms manufacturer located in Triefenstein, Germany. Currently imported by Hera USA located in Draper, UT.

Hera Arms manufactures a complete line of AR-15 style semi-auto rifles in .223 Rem. cal., as well as several styles of conversions for SIG, Glock, Walther, CZ, H&K, and S&W pistols. Hera Arms also manufactures a variety of tactical accessories geared towards military, law enforcement, and sport shooters. Please contact the company directly for more information, including options, U.S. availability, and pricing (see Trademark Index).

HESSE ARMS

Previous manufacturer located in Inver Grove Heights, MN.

Hesse Arms manufactured very limited quantities of semi-auto pistols, bolt action rifles, and semi-auto rifles.

PISTOLS: SEMI-AUTO

HAR-15 – .223 Rem. cal., features carbon/Aramid fiber flat-top upper receiver, 7 1/2 in. barrel, 100% parts interchangeability with AR-15 type firearms. Mfg. 2002 only.

MSR	100%	98%	95%	90%	80%	70%	60%	Last MSR
	$725	$650	$580	$515	$450	$385	$340	$850

RIFLES: SEMI-AUTO, CENTERFIRE

HAR-15A2 SERIES – .223 Rem. cal., AR-15 style action, various configurations, barrel lengths and options. Mfg. 1997-2002.

* ***Standard Rifle/Carbine*** – 16 (carbine) or 20 (rifle) in. heavy match grade barrel, Mil-Spec parts.

	100%	98%	95%	90%	80%	70%	60%	Last MSR
	$675	$500	$425	$375	$335	$315	$295	$779

* ***Bull Gun*** – .223 Rem. cal., 16 in. stainless steel barrel with special front sight base.

	100%	98%	95%	90%	80%	70%	60%	Last MSR
	$695	$500	$425	$375	$335	$315	$295	$825

* ***Dispatcher*** – .223 Rem. cal., 16 in. barrel with full-length handguards, 7.9 lbs. Mfg. 1999-2002.

	100%	98%	95%	90%	80%	70%	60%	Last MSR
	$675	$500	$425	$375	$335	$315	$295	$799

* ***.50 Action Express*** – .50 AE cal., 16 or 20 in. barrel, fixed tube stock, 10 shot mag., 6.9-7.3 lbs. Mfg. 1999-2002.

	100%	98%	95%	90%	80%	70%	60%	Last MSR
	$915	$575	$475	$415	$350	$325	$300	$1,100

* ***X-Match*** – 20 in. heavy barrel with A3 flat-top receiver, free floating aluminum forearm tube, 8.7-9.6 lbs. Mfg. 1999-2002.

	100%	98%	95%	90%	80%	70%	60%	Last MSR
	$665	$500	$415	$375	$335	$315	$295	

* ***National Match*** – features 1/2 minute match sights, CMP legal free floating handguards, match bolt carrier, adj. trigger, individually tested.

	100%	98%	95%	90%	80%	70%	60%	Last MSR
	$915	$575	$475	$415	$350	$325	$300	$1,100

* ***Omega Match*** – top-of-the-line features, including 16 in. stainless steel barrel, hooked style stock with pistol grip, flat-top receiver, capable of 1/4 in. groups.

	100%	98%	95%	90%	80%	70%	60%	Last MSR
	$915	$575	$475	$415	$350	$325	$300	$1,100

* ***High Grade*** – custom built per individual order.

	100%	98%	95%	90%	80%	70%	60%	Last MSR
	$1,150	$750	$550	$465	$415	$375	$350	$1,399

ULTRA RACE – 24 in. stainless barrel, vented free floating handguard, flat-top upper receiver, Palma style rear sight, globe front sight, fully adj. skeleton stock. Mfg. 2001-2002.

	100%	98%	95%	90%	80%	70%	60%	Last MSR
	$1,650	$1,000	$795	$595	$495	$425	$395	$1,999

HIGH STANDARD MANUFACTURING CO.

High Standard is a current trademark of firearms manufactured by Firearms International Inc., established in 1993 and located in Houston, TX.

This company was formed during 1993, utilizing many of the same employees and original material vendors which the original High Standard company used during their period of manufacture (1926-1984). During 2004, Crusader Group Gun Company, Inc. was formed, and this new company includes the assets of High Standard Manufacturing Co, Firearms International Inc., AMT-Auto Mag, Interarms, and Arsenal Line Products.

RIFLES/CARBINES: SEMI-AUTO

HSA-15 – 5.56 NATO, 6x45mm (mfg. 2012-disc.), or .300 AAC Blackout cal., GIO, AR-15 style, A2 configuration, 16 (carbine), or 20 (rifle) in. barrel, A2 flash hider, A2 front sight base with sling swivel, fixed (rifle) or collapsible (carbine) stock, 30 shot mag.

MSR	100%	98%	95%	90%	80%	70%	60%	Last MSR
MSR $785	$675	$500	$425	$375	$335	$315	$295	

H 214 HIGH STANDARD MANUFACTURING CO., cont.

MSR	100%	98%	95%	90%	80%	70%	60%	Last MSR

Add $40 for .300 AAC Blackout cal.

Add $115 for rifle configuration with 20 in. barrel and fixed stock.

Subtract $72 for 6x45mm cal. (mfg. 2012-disc.).

HSA-15 CRUSADER – 5.56 NATO cal., 16 in. M4 barrel with A2 flash hider, aluminum forged upper and lower receivers, 30 shot mag., quad rail in choice of carbine, mid, or rifle length, low profile gas block or Picatinny gas block, M4 style 6-position adj. stock, ambidextrous safety, Ergo pistol grip, ambidextrous single point sling adaptor, black or tan finish. New 2014.

| MSR $1,025 | $865 | $550 | $465 | $395 | $350 | $325 | $300 | |

HSA-15 ENFORCER – 5.56 NATO or .300 AAC Blackout cal., 16 in. M4 style barrel with A2 flash hider, 30 shot mag., aluminum forged upper and lower receivers with hardcoat anodized finish, quad rail in choice of carbine, mid, or rifle length, low profile gas block or Picatinny rail, M4 6-position adj. stock, Ergo pistol grip, front and rear flip-up rail mounted sights, ambidextrous single point sling adaptor, black or tan finish. New 2014.

| MSR $1,000 | $850 | $535 | $450 | $395 | $350 | $325 | $300 | |

Add $50 for .300 AAC Blackout cal.

HSA-15 NATIONAL MATCH – 5.56 NATO cal., AR-15 style, 20 (National Match) or 24 (Long Range Rifle) in. fluted barrel, includes Knight's military two-stage trigger. Mfg. 2006-2012.

| | $1,050 | $650 | $495 | $450 | $395 | $350 | $325 | $1,238 |

Add $12 for Long Range Rifle.

HSA - HUNTER COMBO – 5.56 NATO or .300 AAC Blackout cal., GIO, 16 in. barrel, A2 flash hider, interchangeable uppers, optic ready, low profile gas block, Magpul MOE handguard, Magpul polymer rail, 6-position stock, hard anodized black finish.

| MSR $1,050 | $875 | $550 | $465 | $395 | $350 | $325 | $300 | |

HSA - LONESTAR – 5.56 NATO, GIO, low profile gas block, 16 in. chrome-lined barrel, A2 flash hider, two-stage trigger, Magpul trigger guard, no sights, free floating 15 in. Diamondhead VRS T-556 handguard with Magpul rail attachment, 6-position Magpul stock.

| MSR $1,250 | $1,050 | $650 | $495 | $450 | $395 | $350 | $325 | |

M-4 CARBINE – 5.56 NATO or 9mm Para. cal., 16 in. barrel, fixed A2 (.223 Rem. cal. only, new 2010) or 6-position adj. stock, fixed or adj. sights. Mfg. 2009-disc.

| | $765 | $515 | $440 | $375 | $335 | $315 | $295 | $880 |

Add $35 for adj. sight (disc.).

Add $65 for quad rail with Picatinny gas block.

Add $450 for chrome-lined barrel, free floating quad rails, flip-up sights, flash hider and two-stage match trigger (.223 Rem. cal. only, disc. 2009).

M-4 ENFORCER CARBINE – 5.56 NATO cal., 16 in. barrel with A2 flash hider, SOCOM style 6-position collapsible stock, flip-up battle sights, full-length flat-top receiver, YHM quad rail with smooth sides, Ergo grip, 30 shot mag. Mfg. 2012-2016.

| | $1,795 | $1,050 | $875 | $625 | $550 | $475 | $425 | $2,275 |

HOGAN MANUFACTURING LLC

Current AR-15 style carbines/rifle manufacturer located in Glendale, AZ.

RIFLES: SEMI-AUTO

H-223 DESIGNATED MARKSMAN – .223 Rem. cal., GIO, 18 in. barrel, A1 flash hider muzzle brake, Magpul PMAG, SST, Ergo pistol grip, VLTOR 6-pos. retractable buttstock with Mil-Spec tube, rubber buttpad, billet aluminum charging handle and A3 flat-top upper receiver, aluminum alloy lower receiver with integral oversized trigger guard, aluminum alloy free floating monolithic Tactical or Hunter handguard/rail, black, OD Green, tan, or clear anodize, NP3, or Cerakote finish in Dark Earth or OD Green, includes black plastic hard case with foam liner, 7 lbs. 13 oz. (with Hunter X-Rail) or 8 lbs. 3 oz. (with Tactical X-rail).

| MSR $1,550 | $1,275 | $850 | $600 | $495 | $425 | $375 | $350 | |

Add $200 for Dark Earth or OD Green Cerakote finish.

H-223 HERO MODEL – .223 Rem. cal., AR-15 style, GPO, 16 in. barrel with A2 flash hider, Magpul MOE mid-length plastic handguard, forged aluminum A3 flat-top upper, aluminum alloy lower receiver, M4 retractable buttstock with Mil-Spec tube, A2 pistol grip, black anodized finish.

| MSR $1,399 | $1,250 | $825 | $575 | $475 | $425 | $375 | $350 | |

H-223 SNIPER ELITE – .223 Rem. cal., GIO, 20 in. barrel, A1 flash hider muzzle brake, Magpul PMAG, SST, Ergo pistol grip, VLTOR 6-pos. retractable buttstock with Mil-Spec tube, rubber buttpad, billet aluminum charging handle and A3 flat-top upper receiver, aluminum alloy lower receiver with integral oversized trigger guard, aluminum alloy free floating

HOGAN MANUFACTURING LLC, cont. 215 H

MSR	100%	98%	95%	90%	80%	70%	60%	Last MSR

monolithic Tactical or Hunter handguard/rail, black, OD Green, tan, or clear anodize, NP3, or Cerakote finish in Dark Earth or OD Green, includes black plastic hard case with foam liner, 8 lbs. 5 oz.

MSR $1,600	$1,350	$875	$650	$525	$450	$385	$350	

Add $200 for Dark Earth or OD Green Cerakote finish.

H-223 STANDARD CARBINE – .223 Rem. cal., AR-15 style, GPO, 16 in. button rifled barrel with 5-prong muzzle brake, aluminum alloy free floating monolithic Tactical or Hunter handguards, aluminum forged lower and A3 flat-top upper receiver, Hogan "Gold Standard" trigger system, VLTOR 6-position retractable buttstock with Mil-Spec tube, rubber buttpad, Ergo pistol grip, black or OD Green anodized, Dark Earth or OD Green Cerakote, or NP3 finish, includes hard case with foam liner, one Magpul PMAG, Ergo LowPro rail covers.

MSR $1,490	$1,250	$825	$575	$475	$425	$375	$350	

Add $200 for Dark Earth or OD Green Cerakote finish.

H-308 DESIGNATED MARKSMAN – .308 Win. cal., AR-15 style, GIO, 18 in. button rifled heavy contour barrel with 5-prong muzzle brake, Magpul PMAG, aluminum alloy upper receiver with free floating monolithic Tactical or Hunter handguards, aluminum alloy lower with integral oversized trigger guard, billet aluminum charging handle with oversized grip and locking latch, Hogan "Gold Standard" trigger system, VLTOR 6-position retractable buttstock with Mil-Spec tube, rubber buttpad, Ergo pistol grip, black, ODG, tan, or clear anodized, NP3, or Cerakote finish in Dark Earth or OD Green, includes hard case with foam liner, 9 lbs. 3 oz.-10 lbs. 2 oz.

MSR $1,899	$1,575	$995	$775	$575	$495	$425	$395	

Add $200 for Dark Earth or OD Green Cerakote finish.

H-308 SNIPER ELITE – .308 Rem. cal., AR-15 style, GIO, 20 in. button rifled heavy contour barrel with 5-prong muzzle brake, Magpul PMAG, aluminum alloy upper receiver with free floating monolithic Tactical or Hunter handguards, aluminum alloy lower with integral oversized trigger guard, billet aluminum charging handle with oversized grip and locking latch, Hogan "Gold Standard" trigger system, VLTOR 6-position retractable buttstock with Mil-Spec tube, rubber buttpad, Ergo pistol grip, black, ODG, tan, or clear anodized, NP3, or Cerakote finish in Dark Earth or OD Green, includes hard case with foam liner, 9 lbs. 6 oz.-10 lbs. 5 oz.

MSR $1,949	$1,600	$1,000	$775	$575	$495	$425	$395	

Add $200 for Dark Earth or OD Green Cerakote finish.

H-308 STANDARD CARBINE – .308 Win. cal., AR-15 style, GIO, 16 in. button rifled barrel with 5-prong muzzle brake, aluminum alloy free floating monolithic Tactical or Hunter handguards, aluminum forged lower and A3 flat-top upper receiver, Hogan "Gold Standard" trigger system, VLTOR 6-position retractable buttstock with Mil-Spec tube, rubber buttpad, Ergo pistol grip, black or ODG anodized, Dark Earth or ODG Cerakote, or NP3 finish, includes hard case with foam liner, one Magpul PMAG, Ergo LowPro rail covers.

MSR $1,799	$1,475	$950	$725	$550	$475	$395	$350	

Add $200 for Dark Earth or OD Green Cerakote finish.

HOULDING PRECISION FIREARMS

Previous AR-15 style manufacturer located in Madera, CA until 2015.

In March of 2015, Faxon Firearms acquired Houlding Precision Firearms. All operations were moved to Faxon's corporate facility in Cincinnati, OH. Faxon Firearms will continue the Houlding Precision Firearms brand and assume manufacturing of its products at that location. Please refer to Faxon Firearms for current listings.

RIFLES: SEMI-AUTO

HPF-3 TGR – 5.56 NATO cal., GIO, 16 or 18 in. barrel by Daniel Defense, JP Enterprises tactical compensator or Talon brake, Geissele Super 3-Gun SST, HPF upper and lower receiver, large latch BCM Gunfighter charging handle, Magpul+ grip, Magpul ACS stock. Mfg. 2013 only.

$1,975	$1,150	$925	$650	$575	$495	$425	*$2,403*

HPF-15 MOE – 5.56 NATO cal., GIO, 16 in. M4 barrel with HPF Irish Curse muzzle brake, BTE SST, Magpul MBUS sights, MOE handguard, Magpul MOE 6-position stock, Magpul MOE grip, Cerakote finish, 8.4 lbs. Disc. 2015.

$1,315	$850	$625	$500	$435	$375	$350	*$1,599*

HPF-15 MOE-C – 5.56 NATO cal., GIO, 16 in. M4 profile barrel with Troy Medieval muzzle brake, modular two-piece handguard, pistol grip, integrated oversized trigger guard, flared magwell, receiver height gas block, all Magpul MOE furniture including MOE carbine length handguard, grip, stock, and Magpul MBUS sights, Cerakote ceramic finish, 7 lbs. Disc. 2014.

$1,475	$950	$725	$550	$475	$395	$350	*$1,799*

HPF-15 MOE-M – 5.56 NATO cal., GIO, 16 in. mid-length barrel with Troy muzzle brake, integrated oversized trigger guard, flared magwell, BTE receiver height gas block, all Magpul MOE furniture including MOE mid-length handguard, grip, 6-position stock, and Magpul MBUS sights, Cerakote ceramic finish, 7 lbs. Disc. 2014.

$1,475	$950	$725	$550	$475	$395	$350	*$1,799*

H 216 HOULDING PRECISION FIREARMS, cont.

MSR	100%	98%	95%	90%	80%	70%	60%	Last MSR

HPF-15 MOE-R – 5.56 NATO cal., GIO, 18 in. rifle length barrel with Troy muzzle brake, integrated oversized trigger guard and flared magwell, BTE receiver height gas block, all Magpul MOE furniture including MOE rifle length handguard, grip, 6-pos. stock, and Magpul MBUS sights, Cerakote ceramic finish, 7 lbs. Disc. 2014.

| | $1,475 | $950 | $725 | $550 | $475 | $395 | $350 | $1,799 |

HPF-15 UBR – 5.56 NATO cal., GIO, 16 or 18 in. mid-length match grade barrel with custom muzzle brake, Diamondhead gas block, interchangeable Picatinny rail segments, two-stage Geissele trigger, aluminum upper and lower receivers, polished M4 feed ramps, Troy or JP Enterprises modular handguard, integrated oversized trigger guard and flared magwell, Ergo grip or Magpul+ grip, Magpul ACS or VLTOR collapsible buttstock, Magpul MBUS sights or optic ready, Cerakote finish, 6.14 lbs. Disc. 2015.

| | $1,875 | $1,100 | $895 | $650 | $575 | $495 | $425 | $2,350 |

HPF-15 TGR – 5.56 NATO cal., GIO, 16 or 18 in. mid-length barrel with custom muzzle brake, VLTOR low profile gas block, large or medium latch BCM Gunfighter charging handle, polished M4 feed ramps, 15 in. Troy modular handguard, Magpul BUIS sights or optic ready, billet aluminum upper and lower receiver, integrated oversized trigger guard and flared magwell, Geissele SSA two-stage or duty trigger, Ergo grip or Magpul+ grip, Magpul ACS or VLTOR collapsible stock, 6.14 lbs. Disc. 2015.

| | $1,975 | $1,150 | $925 | $650 | $575 | $495 | $425 | $2,499 |

HOUSTON ARMORY

Previous rifle manufacturer located in Stafford, TX until 2015.

RIFLES

Houston Armory manufactured a line of AR-15 style semi-auto rifles, including the .440 Hash (last MSR was $3,485), .50 Beowulf (last MSR was $3,485), H300IC (last MSR was $3,085), H16IC (last MSR was $3,085), H308IC (last MSR was $4,085), and HASPR16 (last MSR was $2,890). Houston Armory also offered a bolt action rifle (last MSR range was $1,900-$2,900), as well as a complete line of suppressors.

HULDRA ARMS

Previous trademark of AR-15 style semi-auto rifles manufactured by Adams Arms and sold exclusively by Fleet Farm until mid-2016.

RIFLES: SEMI-AUTO

MARK IV CARBINE – 5.45x39mm or 5.56 NATO cal., AR-15 style, GPO, 16 in. M4 contour barrel with A2 flash hider, SST, 6-position tactical buttstock with A2 pistol grip, M4 handguards, forged aluminum upper and lower receivers, 6.2 lbs. Disc. 2016.

| | $800 | $525 | $450 | $385 | $340 | $325 | $295 | $950 |

Add $65 for 5.45x39mm cal.

MARK IV TACTICAL ELITE – 5.56 NATO cal., AR-15 style, GPO, 16 in. Government contour barrel with A2 flash hider, SST, VLTOR IMOD Mil-Spec stock with non-slip removable buttpad, Ergo Ambi pistol grip, free floating extended quad rail forearm with Picatinny rail, forged aluminum upper and lower receivers, includes magazine and soft sided tactical case, 7.2 lbs. Disc. mid-2016.

| | $1,195 | $795 | $550 | $465 | $415 | $375 | $350 | $1,450 |

MARK IV TACTICAL EVO – 5.56 NATO cal., 14 1/2 in. Government contour barrel with permanently affixed elongated flash hider, M4 feed ramps, mid-length gas system, SST, Samson Evolution Series aluminum forearm, Mil-Spec hardcoat anodized finish, 6.8 lbs. Disc. 2014.

| | $1,150 | $750 | $550 | $465 | $415 | $375 | $350 | $1,400 |

X-PRE 1 – 5.56 NATO cal., GPO, 16 in. medium contour fluted stainless steel barrel with Adams Arms compensator, SST, VLTOR IMOD Mil-Spec stock with non-slip removable buttpad, Ergo Ambi grip, monolithic fluted forearm, forged aluminum upper and lower receivers, 7.2 lbs. Disc. 2013.

| | $1,675 | $1,000 | $825 | $625 | $550 | $475 | $425 | $2,000 |

X-PRE 2 – 5.56 NATO cal., GPO, 18 in. Ultra lite match grade barrel with Adams Arms Jet compensator, Mega Arms MKM upper receiver and free float KeyMod, Hipertouch 24 3G trigger, Luth MBA-1 stock, Magpul MOE K-2 grip, approx. 7 1/2 lbs. Mfg. 2015-mid-2016.

| | $1,675 | $1,000 | $825 | $625 | $550 | $475 | $425 | $2,000 |

HUSAN ARMS

Current manufacturer of semi-auto rifles and shotguns located in Konya, Turkey. Shotguns currently imported by Century Arms (Century International Arms, Inc.), located in Delray Beach, FL, and by RAAC, located in Scottsburg, IN.

Husan Arms manufactures a complete line of AR-15 style semi-auto rifles with various stock options and receiver finishes. Currently, these models are not imported into the U.S. Husan also manufactures the MKA 1919 12 ga. AR-15 style shotgun. Please refer to the importers listings for more information.(See Trademark Index).

I SECTION

I.O., INC.

Current manufacturer/importer (I.O., Inc. stands for Inter Ordnance) established in 2008, located in Palm Bay, FL. Previously located in Monroe, NC until mid-2013.

MSR	100%	98%	95%	90%	80%	70%	60%	Last MSR

PISTOLS: SEMI-AUTO

M215 KM-7 – 5.56 NATO cal., 7 1/2 in. barrel, M4 feed ramps, case hardened 8620 steel Nitride coated, M4/AR-15 compatible, 7 in. KeyMod free float rail, Mil-Std 1913 top rail, forged upper receiver, Mil-Spec forward assist, dust cover, and brass deflector, forged I.O Inc. lower receiver, Mil-Spec lower parts kit. New 2018.

MSR $529	$475	$415	$375	$335	$310	$295	$275	

M215 9mm KM-7 – 9mm Para. cal., 8 1/2 in. barrel, accepts Glock mags., last round bolt hold open, forged aluminum upper and lower receivers, 7 in. KeyMod free floating handguard, Mil-Std 1913 top rail, Mil-Spec lower parts kit, Type III hardcoat anodized black finish. New 2018.

MSR $724	$645	$500	$415	$370	$325	$300	$275	

M215 MICRO FL-7 – 5.56x45mm or .300 AAC Blackout cal., 7 in. barrel, 30 shot mag., forged T6 upper and lower receivers, free float handguard, hardcoat anodized finish, 4.3 lbs. Mfg. 2015-2017.

	$675	$600	$525	$450	$375	$325	$275	$750

M215 MICRO QR-7 – 5.56x45mm or .300 AAC Blackout (disc. 2016) cal., 7 in. barrel, 30 shot mag., forged T6 upper and lower receivers, 4 in. (Micro QR-7/4) or full-length free float quad rail, hard anodized finish, 4.3 lbs. Mfg. 2015-2017.

	$675	$550	$475	$425	$375	$325	$275	$750

M215 MICRO QR-10 – 5.56x45mm or .300 AAC Blackout cal., 10 in. barrel, 30 shot mag., T6 upper and lower receivers, full-length quad rail, hard anodized finish, 4.3 lbs. Mfg. 2015-2017.

	$675	$550	$475	$425	$375	$325	$275	$750

M215 ML-7 – 5.56 NATO cal., 7 1/2 in. barrel, M4 feed ramps, case hardened 8620 steel Nitride coated, M4/AR-15 compatible, 7 in. M-LOK free float rail, Mil-Std 1913 top rail, forged upper receiver, Mil-Spec forward assist, dust cover, and brass deflector, forged I.O. Inc. lower receiver, Mil-Spec lower parts kit. New 2018.

MSR $529	$475	$415	$375	$335	$310	$295	$275	

RIFLES: SEMI-AUTO

AR-15A1 – .223 Rem. cal., 16.1 in. barrel, two 30 shot mags., I.O. made lower receiver machined solid aircraft aluminum billets, fixed black polymer stock and forend, pistol grip, carry handle, original Colt Vietnam style upper receiver and bolt assembly. Mfg. 2014-2016.

	$765	$515	$440	$375	$335	$315	$295	$900

CAR-15 – .223 Rem. cal., 16.1 in. barrel with flash hider, two 30 shot mags., I.O. made lower receiver machined out of solid aircraft aluminum billets, matte black finish, adj. 6-position stock, pistol grip, carry handle, original Colt Vietnam style upper receiver and bolt assembly. Mfg. 2014 only.

	$675	$500	$425	$375	$335	$315	$295	$790

M215 A FRAME – 5.56x45mm cal., 16 in. barrel, 30 shot mag., flat-top receiver, Picatinny rail, front sight, round polymer forend, hard anodized finish, 6 lbs. Mfg. 2015-2017.

	$515	$450	$395	$350	$315	$295	$275	$590

M215 KM15 – 5.56x45mm cal., 16 in. M4 profile barrel, 30 shot mag., 6-pos. collapsible buttstock, 15 in. KeyMod free floating handguard, flat-top receiver with Mil-Std 1913 rail, hard anodized black or FDE (disc.) finish, 6 lbs. New late 2016.

MSR $529	$475	$415	$375	$335	$310	$295	$275	

Add $110 for FDE finish (disc. 2017).

M215 9mm KM15 – 9mm Para. cal., 16 in. barrel, accepts Glock mags., 15 in. free float KeyMod handguard, forged aluminum flat-top upper receiver with Mil-Std 1913 rail, forged aluminum lower receiver with last round bolt hold open, Mil-Spec lower parts kit. New 2018.

MSR $650	$550	$475	$400	$350	$315	$295	$275	

M215 LOW PROFILE – 5.56x45mm cal., 16 in. M4 profile barrel, 30 shot mag., 6-pos. adj. buttstock, low profile gas block, forged aluminum upper and lower receiver, Mil-Sted 1913 quad rail handguard, Type III hardcoat anodized black finish, 6 lbs. Mfg. 2015-mid-2018.

	$575	$485	$415	$350	$315	$295	$275	$670

218 I.O., INC., cont.

MSR	100%	98%	95%	90%	80%	70%	60%	Last MSR

M215 ML15 MPDE – 5.56x45mm NATO cal., 16 in. barrel, Magpul trigger guard, collapsible Magpul MOE stock, Magpul pistol grip, ambi safety, forged upper and lower receiver, 15 in. free float M-LOK handguard, Mil-Std 1913 top rail, enhanced charging handle, FDE Teflon coating. New 2018.

| MSR $730 | $645 | $500 | $415 | $370 | $325 | $300 | $275 | |

M215 QR12 – 5.56x45mm cal., 16 in. barrel, 30 shot mag., 6-pos. buttstock, 12 in. quad rail free floating handguard, hard anodized black finish, 6 lbs. Mfg. late 2016-2017.

| | $595 | $485 | $415 | $350 | $315 | $295 | $275 | *$700* |

INDUSTRY ARMAMENT

Current manufacturer located in Mesa, AZ.

Industry Armament manufactures AR-15 style pistols and rifles, as well as competition shotguns for civilian, law enforcement, and military markets.

PISTOLS: SEMI-AUTO

LEGACY MK1 PISTOL – 5.56 NATO or .300 AAC Blackout cal., AR-15 style, pistol length gas system, 7 1/2 or 10 1/2 in. BOSS steel barrel (with Caudle 3 rifling system), flash can muzzle device, extended pistol buffer tube, adj. grip, 9 or 12 (10 1/2 in. barrel only) in. free float rail, upper and lower receivers with Type III hardcoat anodized finish, extended latch charging handle, black finish, 6-6 1/2 lbs. New 2016.

| MSR $1,300 | $1,100 | $995 | $875 | $735 | $650 | $550 | $465 | |

RIFLES: SEMI-AUTO

LEGACY MK1 RIFLE – 5.56 NATO or .300 AAC Blackout cal., AR-15 style, carbine length gas system, 16 in. BOSS steel barrel with Caudle 3 rifling system, Effin-A Mark II compensator, Legacy carbine MKI stock, adj. grip, upper and lower receivers with Type III hardcoat anodized finish, extended latch charging handle, 12 in. free float handguard, black finish, 6.14-7 lbs. New 2016.

| MSR $1,700 | $1,385 | $895 | $675 | $525 | $450 | $385 | $350 | |

LEGACY MK1 .308 – .308 Win./7.62 NATO cal., mid to rifle length gas system, 18 or 20 in. BOSS steel barrel with Caudle 3 system, Effin-A Mark II compensator, Legacy modular stock, adj. grip, DPMS/SR-25 upper and lower receivers with Type III hardcoat anodized finish, 15 1/2 in. free float handguard, extended latch charging handle, nickel boron bolt carrier group, black finish, 7.6 (18 in.) or 9.14 (20 in.) lbs. New 2016.

| MSR $1,950 | $1,600 | $1,000 | $775 | $575 | $495 | $425 | $395 | |

Add $50 for 20 in. barrel.

INTACTO ARMS

Previous manufacturer located in Boise, ID 2008-circa 2017.

PISTOLS: SEMI-AUTO

BATTLE TAC PISTOL – .223 Rem. cal., AR-15 style, 7 or 10 1/2 in. stainless steel match barrel, Magpul flip-up front and rear sight with single or double rail gas block, nickel boron bolt carrier group (new 2016), 6 1/2 or 9 1/2 in. forged or free float handguard, solid billet CNC machined upper and lower, ALG-QMS trigger (new 2016), matte black finish, includes soft carrying case. Disc. 2017.

| | $1,425 | $925 | $700 | $550 | $475 | $395 | $350 | *$1,700* |

RIFLES/CARBINES: SEMI-AUTO

Intacto Arms manufactured a complete line of semi-auto rifles and carbines based on the AR-15 and the AR-10 platforms. A wide variety of options and accessories were available.

BATTLE TAC – .204 Ruger, .22 LR, .223 Rem., .243 Win., .300 AAC Blackout, .300 WSM, 7.62x39mm, or 6.8 SPC cal., 16 in. stainless steel match grade barrel with A2 Predator flash hider, 30 shot PMAG, mid-length low profile gas block, solid billet machined upper and lower, nickel boron bolt carrier group (new 2016), 9 1/2, 12 1/2, or 15 1/2 in. extruded or round free floating handguard, 4 QD sling mount positions and continuous top Picatinny rail, ALG-QMS trigger (new 2016), Magpul CTR adj. stock, Magpul MOE+ grip, matte black or Flat Dark Earth finish, includes tactical soft carrying case.

| | $1,675 | $1,000 | $825 | $625 | $550 | $475 | $425 | *$2,000* |

Add $800 for UBL configuration (Under Barrel Launcher).
Add $100 for any caliber other than .223 Rem.

BATTLE TAC SPECIAL CALIBER – .204 Ruger, .22 LR, .243 Win., .300 AAC Blackout, .300 WSM, 7.62 NATO, or 6.8 SPC cal., customer's choice of caliber, barrel length, and gas system, stainless steel match barrel, Phantom Persuasion flash hider, Magpul 30 shot mag., solid billet upper and lower receiver, nickel boron bolt carrier group, mid-length gas block, ALG QMS trigger, 9 1/2, 12 1/2, or 15 1/2 in. extruded or round free float handguard, Picatinny top rail, Magpul

INTACTO ARMS, cont. 219

MSR	100%	98%	95%	90%	80%	70%	60%	Last MSR

CTR stock, MOE grip, black, FDE, or custom Cerakote finish, includes 34 in. Bulldog 5-pocket tactical soft carrying case. Mfg. 2015-2017.

| | $1,675 | $1,000 | $825 | $625 | $550 | $475 | $425 | $2,000 |

Add $299 for custom Cerakote finish.

CARBON TAC – .308 Win. cal., AR-10 style, 18 1/2 in. National Match chrome moly stainless steel barrel, Doublestar 308 Carlson flash hider, 20 shot PMAG, solid billet CNC machined upper and lower, chrome bolt carrier group, knurled exterior, crenelated muzzle end, Magpul CTR collapsible stock, Precision Reflex 12 1/2 in. carbon fiber triangular free float handguard with rails, matte black finish, includes soft carrying case. Disc. 2017.

| | $2,875 | $1,875 | $1,375 | $795 | $675 | $625 | $575 | $3,500 |

FULL BATTLE RIFLE – .223 Rem. cal., 16.1 in. stainless steel match grade barrel with Phantom Persuasion flash hider, mid-length gas system, 30 shot Magpul PMAG, Magpul MBUS sights, solid billet machined upper and lower receiver, 9 1/2, 12 1/2, or 15 1/2 in. extruded or round free floating handguard, 4 QD sling mount positions and continuous Picatinny top rail, Magpul ACS adj. stock, Magpul ASAP sling mount, Magpul AFG2 forward grip, Magpul MOE+ grip, Geissele two-stage trigger, nickel boron bolt carrier group, BCM Gunfighter charging handle, JP silent buffer system, JP original complete adjustable fire control system (new 2016), matte black, FDE, or custom Cerakote finish, includes tactical soft carrying case. Disc. 2017.

| | $2,050 | $1,250 | $950 | $650 | $575 | $495 | $475 | $2,500 |

Add $299 for custom Cerakote finish.

ICARUS 7 – .223 Rem. cal., 16 in. chrome moly barrel, mid-length F-marked front sight gas system, solid billet machined lower, forged flat-top upper, G.I. Issue standard dual heat shield handguard, matte black finish, includes soft carrying case. Disc. 2017.

| | $765 | $515 | $440 | $375 | $335 | $315 | $295 | $900 |

MANTIS RIFLE – .223 Rem. cal., 18 (new 2016) or 20 in. stainless steel match grade barrel with Phantom Persuasion Tip flash hider, 10 or 30 shot PMAG, mid-length low profile gas block, solid billet machined upper and lower receiver, JP original complete adjustable fire control system (new 2016), nickel boron bolt carrier group (new 2016), 4 QD sling mount positions and continuous top Picatinny rail, 15 1/2 in. extruded or round free floating handguard, BCM Gunfighter large latch charging handle, JP silent buffer system, Magpul PRS or UBR (new 2016) stock, Magpul MOE+ grip, bipod, matte black, FDE, or custom Cerakote finish, includes tactical soft carrying case. Disc. 2017.

| | $2,125 | $1,325 | $995 | $675 | $595 | $525 | $475 | $2,600 |

Add $299 for custom Cerakote finish.

MID TAC – .223 Rem. or .300 AAC Blackout (stainless only) cal., 16 in. black phosphate or stainless steel barrel, 30 shot PMAG, mid-length low profile gas block, ALG-QMS trigger (new 2016), solid billet machined lower, forged flat-top upper, 4 QD sling mount positions and Picatinny top rail, 9 1/2, 12 1/2, or 15 1/2 in. extruded or round free floating handguard, adj. tactical (disc. 2015) or Magpul MOE (new 2016) stock, Magpul MOE grip (new 2016), matte black finish, includes soft carrying case. Disc. 2017.

| | $1,150 | $750 | $550 | $465 | $415 | $375 | $350 | $1,400 |

Add $100 for stainless steel. Add $100 for .300 AAC Blackout cal.

M.O.E. – .223 Rem. cal., 16 in. chrome moly or stainless steel barrel, mid-length F-marked front sight gas system, solid billet machined lower, forged flat-top upper, Magpul MOE handguard, Magpul MOE+ grip, Magpul MOE stock, 30 shot Magpul PMAG, matte black finish, includes soft carrying case. Disc. 2017.

| | $915 | $575 | $475 | $415 | $350 | $325 | $300 | $1,100 |

Add $100 for stainless steel.

INTEGRITY ARMS & SURVIVAL

Current custom AR-15 style rifle manufacturer located in Jefferson, GA. Previously located in Watkinsville, GA.

PISTOLS: SEMI-AUTO

.300 BLK PISTOL – .300 AAC Blackout cal., 12 1/2 in. Melonite treated barrel, Noveske KX5 muzzle device, pistol lengh gas system, Mil-Spec single stage trigger, forged matched set upper and lower receivers, 13 in. slim free float handguard, ambidextrous safety, Ergo grip, SIG arm brace on rear, hardcoat anodized finish. Disc. 2017.

| | $1,050 | $950 | $815 | $715 | $625 | $535 | $450 | $1,250 |

SIDE CHARGING AR PISTOL – 5.56 NATO cal., 10 1/2 in. barrel, Troy Industries Claymore muzzle brake, billet machined lower and non-reciprocating side charging upper receiver, M4 feed ramps, deluxe pistol buffer tube with Tungsten filled heavy buffer, quick detach endplate, ALG Defense QMS trigger group, Dark Earth Hogue rubber grip with beavertail, Troy Industries 11 in. Bravo handguard. Disc. 2017.

| | $1,100 | $995 | $875 | $735 | $650 | $550 | $465 | $1,300 |

RIFLES/CARBINES: SEMI-AUTO

Integrity Arms & Survival manufactures custom AR-15 style rifles in 5.56 NATO, 6.8 SPC, .223 Wylde, or .300 AAC Blackout caliber per customer specifications. **Previously manufactured models include:** Burnt Bronze Battle Rifle (last MSR was $1,350), Civilian Service Carbine

220 INTEGRITY ARMS & SURVIVAL, cont.

MSR	100%	98%	95%	90%	80%	70%	60%	Last MSR

(last MSR was $1,300), Premium Lightweight Wylde Chambered Carbine (last MSR was $1,050), Side Charging Burnt Bronze Carbine (last MSR was $1,500), Special Purpose Rifle (last MSR was $1,590), Foliage Green Premium Carbine (last MSR in 2014 was $1,300), Tungsten Grey Carbine (last MSR in 2014 was $1,350) and Muddy Girl Carbine (last MSR in 2014 was $900).

BATTLE WORN SIDE CHARGING CARBINE – 5.56 NATO cal., mid-length gas system, Melonite treated barrel, billet lower and non-reciprocating side charging upper receiver, 12 in. free floating slim KeyMod handguard, Mil-Spec single stage trigger, VLTOR IMOD Clubfoot stock, Ergo Ambi SureGrip, Battle Worn Cerakote finish. Disc. 2017.

	$1,150	$750	$550	$465	$415	$375	$350	*$1,400*

BASIC M4 CARBINE – 5.56 NATO/.223 Rem. cal., 16 in. barrel (.223 Wylde chamber), M16 type bolt carrier group, forged upper and lower receiver, Mil-Spec single stage trigger, Magpul MOE handguard and stock, hardcoat anodized finish.

MSR $900	$765	$515	$440	$375	$335	$315	$295	

CUSTOM RIFLE BLUE CERAKOTE – 5.56 NATO/.223 Rem. cal., match grade 5R melonite barrel, VG6 Precision Gamma 556 muzzle brake, 30 shot blue Gen2 PMAG, ALG Defense trigger, BCM Gunfighter Mod 0 stock, ambi safety, billet matching set of upper and lower receivers with blue and Tungsten grey Cerakote finish, BCM Gunfighter Mod 3 charging handle, 13 in. SFF handguard, includes Bushnell AR556 with illuminated reticle and bullet drop compensator, American Defense RECON30 one-piece mount, includes soft case. New 2018.

MSR $1,825	$1,525	$975	$750	$575	$495	$425	$375	

SUPERIOR BATTLE CARBINE – 5.56 NATO/.223 Rem. cal., 16 in. lightweight profile barrel, A2 birdcage muzzle brake, Aero Precision all metal flip-up sights, Magpul MOE stock, Ergo textured grips, 13 in. KeyMod handguard, black Nitride BCG, billet charging handle with extended latch, Integrity Peace/War matched upper and lower receiver set, hardcoat anodized black finish, 6 lbs.

MSR range for this model is $1,050-$1,615. Please contact the company directly for options and availability.

ULTRALIGHT FIGHTING CARBINE (UFC) – 5.56 NATO/.223 Rem. cal., 16 in. Melonite treated barrel, mid-length gas system, forged upper and lower receiver, M4 feed ramps, Magpul Gen2 MBUS front and rear sights, rifle length carbon fiber free float handguard, Magpul MOE 6-position collapsible stock, Hogue beavertail soft rubber grip with finger grooves, 5.95 lbs. Disc. 2017.

	$1,050	$650	$495	$450	$395	$350	$325	*$1,250*

INTERARMS ARSENAL

Current trademark of firearms imported and distributed by High Standard Manufacturing Company, located in Houston, TX.

RIFLES: SEMI-AUTO

AR-15 A2 RIFLE – 5.56 NATO cal., AR-15 style, GIO, choice of flat-top (no sights) or A2 configuration, 20 in. barrel with flash hider, choice of black synthetic fixed or collapsible stock, 30 shot mag.

MSR $925	$785	$525	$450	$385	$340	$325	$295	

Add $40 for A2 adj. sights.

INTERCONTINENTAL ARMS INC.

Previous importer located in Los Angeles, CA circa 1970s.

Intercontinental Arms Inc. imported a variety of SA revolvers, an AR-15 type semi-auto rifle, a derringer, a rolling block single shot rifle, and a line of black powder pistol reproductions and replicas. While these firearms were good, utilitarian shooters, they have limited desirability in today's marketplace. The single action revolvers manufactured by Hämmerli are typically priced in the $200-$395 range, the derringer is priced in the $115-$175 range, the AR-15 copy is priced in the $425-$675 range, and the single shot rolling block rifle is priced in the $150-$200 range, depending on original condition.

INVINCIBLE ARMS LLC

Previous AR-15 style rifle, parts, and accessories manufacturer located in Willoughby, OH circa 2013-2016.

PISTOLS: SEMI-AUTO

BLACK FORGE TIER 1 PISTOL – 5.56 NATO cal., AR-15 style, GIO, aluminum flat-top A3 upper receiver, aluminum forged lower receiver, 10 1/2 in. carbine length barrel with Carlson Comps TAC brake, 10 1/2 in. modular rail system with full-length top Picatinny rail, two 3 in. and one 5 in. rail sections, M4 feed ramps, 30 shot detachable mag., Black Forge winter trigger guard, single stage trigger, Magpul Industries or U.S. Palm Battle grip, investment cast fire controls, Carpenter M16 LEO bolt carrier group with Black Forge Niphos coating, hardcoat anodized matte black finish.

Retail pricing was not available for this model.

* ***Black Forge Tier 1 SIG PSB*** – 5.56 NATO cal., similar to Tier 1 pistol, except has fully adj. SIG PSB tactical style stock.

Retail pricing was not available for this model.

RIFLES/CARBINES: SEMI-AUTO

.300 BLACKOUT – .300 AAC Blackout cal., GIO, 16 1/2 in. M4 barrel, Lancer Systems Viper muzzle brake and 30

INVINCIBLE ARMS LLC, cont. 221

MSR	100%	98%	95%	90%	80%	70%	60%	Last MSR

shot mag., KeyMod rail systems w/Picatinny rail sections, front and rear backup iron sights, Fortis REV free float rail system handguard, aluminum flat-top upper receiver with Mil-Spec Picatinny rail, M4 feed ramp, forged aluminum lower w/Invincible Arms logo, low profile gas block, stainless steel gas tube, Mil-Spec buffer tube, Invincible Arms laser engraved charging handle, oversized trigger guard, Hiperfire Hipertouch single stage trigger, Rogers Super-Stoc 6-position telescoping stock, A2 pistol grip, 6.8 lbs. Disc. 2016.

	$1,275	$850	$600	$495	$425	$375	$350	$1,525

.458 SOCOM – .458 SOCOM cal., GIO, 16 1/2 in. heavy barrel, muzzle brake with crush washer, Lancer Systems 30 shot mag., combination KeyMod rail systems w/Picatinny rail sections, front and rear backup iron sights, free floating railed handguard, aluminum flat-top upper receiver with Mil-Spec Picatinny rail, M4 feed ramp, forged aluminum lower w/Invincible Arms logo, low profile gas block, stainless steel gas tube, Mil-Spec buffer tube, Invincible Arms laser engraved charging handle, oversized trigger guard, Hiperfire Hipertouch single stage trigger, Rogers Super-Stoc 6-position telescoping stock, Magpul Gen1 MOE pistol grip, 7.8 lbs. Disc. 2016.

	$1,275	$850	$600	$495	$425	$375	$350	$1,525

5.56 OPTICS READY CARBINE – 5.56 NATO cal., GIO, 16 1/2 in. M4 barrel, A2 flash hider w/crush washer, 30 shot mag., no sights, M4 style dual heat shield handguard, aluminum flat-top upper w/Mil-Spec 1913 Picatinny rail system, M4 feed ramps, low profile gas block, stainless steel gas tube, Mil-Spec buffer tube, Invincible Arms laser engraved charging handle, forged aluminum lower w/Invincible Arms logo, oversized trigger guard, single stage trigger, Invincible Arms 6-position telescoping stock, A2 pistol grip, 6 1/2 lbs. Disc. 2016.

	$695	$500	$425	$375	$335	$315	$295	$821

5.56 PREDATOR RIFLE – 5.56 NATO cal., GIO, 18 in. heavy barrel, Lancer Systems muzzle brake w/crush washer, Lancer Systems 20 shot mag., no sights, Lancer Systems carbon fiber free floating handguard, aluminum flat-top upper w/Mil-Spec 1913 Picatinny rail system, M4 feed ramps, low profile gas block, stainless steel gas tube, Mil-Spec buffer tube, Invincible Arms laser engraved charging handle w/extended latch, aluminum forged lower with IA logo, oversized trigger guard, Hiperfire Hipertouch single stage trigger, Magpul UBR 6-position telescoping stock, Magpul MOE Gen 1 pistol grip, 7.1 lbs. Disc. 2016.

	$2,295	$1,450	$1,075	$675	$595	$525	$475	$2,898

5.56 VARMITER RIFLE – 5.56 NATO cal., GIO, 18 in. heavy barrel, Lancer Systems Viper muzzle brake w/crush washer, Lancer Systems 20 shot mag., no sights, low profile gas block, aluminum flat-top upper with Mil-Spec 1913 Picatinny rail system, M4 feed ramps, Lancer Systems carbon fiber free float handguard, Mil-Spec buffer tube, stainless steel gas tube, IA laser engraved charging handle with extended latch, forged aluminum lower with IA logo, oversized trigger guard, Hiperfire Hipertouch single stage trigger, Magpul UBR 6-position telescoping stock, Magpul MOE Gen 1 pistol grip, 6.9 lbs. Disc. 2016.

	$2,295	$1,450	$1,075	$675	$595	$525	$475	$2,898

5.56 TACTICAL CARBINE – 5.56 NATO cal., GIO, 16 in. M4 barrel, Lancer Systems Viper muzzle brake w/crush washer, Lancer Systems 30 shot mag., combination KeyMod rail system with 1913 Picatinny rail sections, front and rear backup Iron sights, Fortis REV free float handguard, aluminum flat-top upper with Mil-Spec Picatinny rail, M4 feed ramps, low profile gas block, stainless steel gas tube, Mil-Spec buffer tube, IA laser engraved charging handle, forged aluminum lower with IA logo, oversized trigger guard, Hiperfire Hipertouch single stage trigger, Rogers Super-Stoc 6-position telescoping stock, Magpul MOE Gen 1 pistol grip, 7.4 lbs. Disc. 2016.

	$1,275	$850	$600	$495	$425	$375	$350	$1,525

IRON RIDGE ARMS CO.

Current AR-15 style rifle manufacturer located in Longmount, CO.

Iron Ridge Arms Co. manufactures the AR-15 style IRA-X Rifle platform available in three different configurations. Current lead time for individual rifles is approximately six months. Please contact the company directly for more information including customizing, options, pricing, and availability (see Trademark Index).

IVER JOHNSON ARMS, INC. (NEW MFG.)

Current manufacturer established during 2004, located in Rockledge, FL. Dealer and distributor sales.

During 2013, Iver Johnson Arms produced a 1911A1 Carbine/Rifle with Mech-Tech Systems upper and Iver Johnson lower (last MSR $775).

SHOTGUNS: SEMI-AUTO

15 SA – 12 ga., 2 3/4 or 3 in. chamber, AR-15 style, 20 in. barrel, three removable chokes, 5 shot mag., fully adj. rear sight, synthetic stock with rubber buttpad, top and bottom rail, detachable carry handle, black finish, 7 lbs. 12 oz. Mfg. 2016 only.

	$395	$350	$310	$285	$255	$225	$195	$445

MAYBE THE ONLY THING BETTER THAN THIS BOOK IS THE ONLINE SUBSCRIPTION!

Only $19.95/year!

- **Includes monthly updates** keeping you informed of all the new AR-15 makes/models.
- **Features thousands of images** allowing for fast and easy identification.
- **Manufacturer/Model searchable database** allowing you to find the model you need.
- Historical pricing with dynamic interactive graphs keeps you up-to-date on your AR-15 purchases as investments.
- Your own personal online inventory solution - keep track of your collection and track the change in value.
- Includes access to BBP's industry standard Photo Percentage Grading System – why guess a gun's condition when you can be sure?

Visit BlueBookOfGunValues.com
to view sample pages and ordering

Good Information Never Sleeps!

J SECTION

J.B. CUSTOM INC.

Current manufacturer and restorer located in Huntertown, IN. Previously located in Fort Wayne, IN. Consumer direct sales.

J.B. Custom also offers service parts and restoration services for Winchester commemorative lever action rifles and carbines.

RIFLES: SEMI-AUTO

J.B. Custom builds two types of AR-15 style rifles in .223 Rem. cal. - the Target Sniper (MSR$1,195) and the M-4 (MSR $995). Please contact the manufacturer directly for more information including options and availability (see Trademark Index).

JP ENTERPRISES, INC.

Current manufacturer and customizer established in 1978, located in Hugo, MN beginning 2010, previously located in White Bear Lake, MN 2000-2009, Vadnais Heights, MN 1998-2000, and in Shoreview, MN 1995-98. Distributor, dealer, and consumer sales.

JP Enterprises is a distributor for Infinity pistols, and also customizes Remington shotgun Models 11-87, 1100, and 870, the Remington bolt action Model 700 series, Glock pistols, and the Armalite AR-10 series.

JP Enterprises also manufactures a complete line of high quality parts and accessories for AR-15 style rifles, including upper and lower assemblies, sights and optics, machined receivers, barrels/barrel kits, fire control kits, handguards, etc. and gunsmithing services. Please contact the company directly for more information and pricing regarding these parts, accesssories, and services (see Trademark Index).

MSR	100%	98%	95%	90%	80%	70%	60%	Last MSR

PISTOLS: SEMI-AUTO

Level I & Level II custom pistols were manufactured 1995-97 using Springfield Armory slides and frames. Only a few were made and retail prices were $599 (Level I) and $950 (Level II).

GMR-13 – 9mm Para. cal., blowback action, 10 1/2 in. JP Supermatch button rifled barrel with standard profile compensator, JP modular handguard, Phase 5 buffer tube, matte black receiver finish. New 2015.

MSR $1,499	$1,425	$1,250	$1,075	$975	$785	$650	$500	

JP-15 PISTOL – .223 Rem. or 9mm Para. cal., Low Mass Operating System (LMOS), 10 1/2 in. JP Supermatch barrel with black Teflon finish, JP Tactical Recoil Eliminator muzzle or standard profile compensator, JP small frame receiver with matte black finish, Phase 5 Buffer tube, modular or rapid configuration handguard, Hogue pistol grip. New 2015.

MSR $1,699	$1,615	$1,415	$1,210	$1,100	$890	$725	$575	

RIFLES: SEMI-AUTO

The rifles in this section utilize a modified AR-15 style operating system.

BARRACUDA 10/22 – .22 LR cal., features customized Ruger 10/22 action with reworked fire control system, choice of stainless bull or carbon fiber superlight barrel, 3 lb. trigger pull, color laminated "Barracuda" skeletonized stock. Mfg. 1997-2003.

	$1,075	$950	$775	$650	$575	$475	$400	$1,195

A-2 MATCH – .223 Rem. cal., GIO, JP-15 lower receiver with JP fire control system, 20 in. JP Supermatch cryo-treated stainless barrel, standard A2 stock and pistol grip, DCM type free float forend, Mil-Spec A2 upper assembly with Smith National Match rear sight. Mfg. 1995-2003.

	$1,385	$895	$675	$525	$450	$385	$350	$1,695

AR-10T – .243 Win. or .308 Win. cal., GIO, features Armalite receiver system with JP fire control, flat-top receiver, vent. free floating tubular handguard, 24 in. cryo treated stainless barrel, black finish. Mfg. 1998-2004.

	$1,875	$1,100	$895	$650	$575	$495	$425	$2,399

Add $150 for anodized upper assembly in custom color.

Add $350 for laminated wood thumbhole stock.

* AR-10LW – GIO, lightweight variation of the Model AR-10T, includes 16-20 in. cryo-treated stainless barrel, composite fiber tubular handguard, black finish only, 7-8 lbs. Mfg. 1998-2004.

	$1,875	$1,100	$895	$650	$575	$495	$425	$2,399

Add $200 for detachable sights.

CTR-02 COMPETITION TACTICAL RIFLE – .223 Wylde chamber, 5.56 NATO (new 2017), .204 Ruger (mfg. 2012-2015), .22 LR (new 2016), .300 AAC Blackout (new 2016), .223 Rem. (disc. 2016), or 6.5 Grendel (new 2012) cal., GIO, state-of-the-art advanced AR design with many improvements, integral ACOG interface, JP Supermatch polished

J 224 JP ENTERPRISES, INC., cont.

MSR	100%	98%	95%	90%	80%	70%	60%	Last MSR

stainless steel barrel, JP recoil eliminator and fire control system, 10 shot mag., beveled magwell, black synthetic A2 or ACE ARFX buttstock, Hogue pistol grip, rifle or mid-length JP modular handguard system, JP low mass or full mass operating system, black Teflon over hardcoat anodized finish. New 2002.

| MSR $2,499 | $2,350 | $2,050 | $1,750 | $1,600 | $1,300 | $1,050 | $800 | |

Add $599 for presentation grade finish (disc. 2011).

CTR-02 ENGRAVED EDITION RIFLE – .223 Rem. cal., 20 in. JP Supermatch medium contour barrel with polished stainless finish, JP large profile compensator, T6 billet upper and lower receivers with black hardcoat anodizing on aluminum components and Presentation Grade finish with hand engraving, JP MK III 2XL Signature handguard system, JP adj. minimized gas block, Ace ARFX buttstock, Hogue pistol grip, includes polished JP scope mount and accessory pack. New 2015.

| MSR $4,839 | $4,600 | $4,000 | $3,450 | $3,150 | $2,550 | $2,050 | $1,600 | |

CTR-02 MATCH READY RIFLE – .223 Wylde chamber, 18 in. light contour JP Supermatch barrel, 3-port compensator, ACE-ARFX skeletonized stock, Hogue grip, 15 1/2 in. XL MK III signature handguard, LMOS JP enhanced bolt, QD sling swivel, matte black finish.

| MSR $2,739 | $2,225 | $1,395 | $1,050 | $675 | $595 | $525 | $475 | |

GMR-15 RIFLE – 9mm Para. cal., blowback operation, JP Supermatch cryo-treated barrel, JP tactical or competition compensator, flared magwell, JP enhanced reliability fire control package, billet lower and forged upper receiver, Hogue overmolded, Mission First Tactical, Magpul MOE, Magpul CTR, or Magpul ACS-L stock, Hogue pistol grip, JP MK III handguard system, matte black finish, accessory pack includes backpack soft case. New 2017.

| MSR $1,699 | $1,600 | $1,400 | $1,200 | $1,100 | $900 | $700 | $550 | |

GRADE II – .223 Rem. cal., GIO, 18-24 in. cryo-treated stainless barrel, Mil-Spec JP lower receiver with upper assembly finished in a special two-tone color anodizing process, JP fire control, composite skeletonized stock, Harris bipod, choice of multi-color or black receiver and forend, includes hard case. Mfg. 1998-2002.

| | $1,575 | $995 | $775 | $575 | $495 | $425 | $395 | $1,895 |

Add $200 for laminated wood thumbhole stock.

GRADE III (THE EDGE) – .223 Rem. cal., GIO, 18-24 in. barrel (cryo-treated beginning 1998) with recoil eliminator, RND machined match upper/lower receiver system, two-piece free floating forend, standard or laminated thumbhole wood stock, includes Harris bipod, top-of-the-line model, includes hard case. Mfg. 1996-2002.

| | $2,225 | $1,395 | $1,050 | $675 | $595 | $525 | $475 | $2,795 |

Add $250 for laminated thumbhole stock.

JP-15 & VARIATIONS (GRADE I A-3 FLAT-TOP) – .204 Ruger (mfg. 2012-2015), .223 Rem. (disc. 2016), .22 LR, .300 AAC Blackout, or 6.5 Grendel (new 2012) cal., GIO, 18 or 24 in. JP Supermatch cryo-treated stainless barrel, JP Compensator muzzle treatment, 10 shot mag., synthetic modified thumbhole (disc. 2011), synthetic A2 or ACE ARFX buttstock (new 2012), Magpul MOE, or laminated wood thumbhole (disc. 2002) stock, JP vent. two-piece free float forend, Hogue pistol grip, Eagle Arms (disc. 1999), DPMS (disc. 1999) or JP15 lower assembly with JP fire control system, Mil-Spec A3 type upper receiver, gas system and recoil eliminator, black Teflon hardcoat anodized finish. New 1995.

| MSR $1,999 | $1,900 | $1,650 | $1,400 | $1,300 | $1,050 | $850 | $650 | |

Add $400 for NRA Hi-Power version with 24 in. bull barrel and sight package (disc. 2002).

Add $200 for laminated wood thumbhole stock (disc. 2002).

Subtract $300 for Duty Defense rifle (JP-15D), disc.

Subtract $500 for .22 LR cal.

* **JP-15 Gladiator** – .223 Rem. cal., 16 in. Supermatch barrel with black Teflon finish, Tactical compensator with crush washer, Mil-Spec forged upper and lower receivers, 2 and 4 in. full-length top rail, extra long JP Rapid Configuration handguard, Magpul BUIS sights, Magpul CTR stock, Magpul MIAD grips, VTAC sling, matte black hardcoat anodized finish, includes accessory pack. Mfg. 2015-2016.

| | $1,675 | $1,000 | $825 | $625 | $550 | $475 | $425 | $2,049 |

* **JP-15 Grade I IPSC Limited Class** – .223 Rem. cal., similar to Grade I, except has quick detachable match grade iron sights, Versa-pod bipod. Mfg. 1999-2004.

| | $1,475 | $950 | $725 | $550 | $475 | $395 | $350 | $1,795 |

* **JP-15 Grade I Tactical/SOF** – .223 Rem. cal., similar to Grade I, all matte black non-glare finish, 18, 20, or 24 in. Supermatch barrel. Mfg. 1999-2003.

| | $1,315 | $850 | $625 | $500 | $435 | $375 | $350 | $1,595 |

Add $798 for Trijicon ACOG sight with A-3 adapter.

* **JP-15 Hunter Ready Rifle** – .223 Wylde chamber, 18 in. light contour JP Supermatch barrel with black Teflon finish, thread protector, small profile 3-port compensator, Magpul ACS-L buttstock, Magpul MIAD grip, forged upper and lower receiver with matte black finish, 15 1/2 in. XL MKIII RC handguard with FDE Cerakote finish, QS sling swivel, JP flat-top scope mount, Red Rock 2-point sling, JP accessory pack, 6.8 lbs.

| MSR $2,479 | $1,975 | $1,150 | $925 | $650 | $575 | $495 | $425 | |

JP ENTERPRISES, INC., cont. 225

MSR	100%	98%	95%	90%	80%	70%	60%	Last MSR

* **JP-15 Match Ready Rifle** – .223 Wylde chamber, 16 in. light contour Supermatch barrel with polished finish, small profile 3-port compensator, Magpul CTR buttstock, Hogue grip, forged upper and lower receiver, 15 1/2 in. MK III RC handguard, QD sling swivel, matte black finish, 7 lbs.

| MSR $2,189 | $1,725 | $1,050 | $850 | $625 | $550 | $475 | $425 | |

* **JP-15 ORRC** – .223 Rem. cal., 16 or 18 in. JP Supermatch barrel with black Teflon finish, tactical profile JP compensator, extra long JP Rapid Configuration handguard, forged upper and lower receivers, MOE trigger guard, TI-7 (disc.) or A2 fixed stock, Hogue pistol grip, matte black hardcoat anodized finish, includes accessory pack, 6.8-7 lbs. Mfg. 2013-2017.

| | $1,600 | $1,400 | $1,200 | $1,100 | $900 | $700 | $550 | $1,699 |

* **JP-15 Patrol Rifle** – .223 Rem. cal., FMOS (Full Mass Operating System), 16 in. JP Supermatch light contour barrel with black Teflon finish, JP tactical compensator, Magpul MOE trigger guard, TI-7 buttstock, A2 grip, forged upper and lower receiver set, rifle length rapid configuration handguard, matte black finish, 6.7 lbs. New 2016.

| MSR $1,509 | $1,425 | $1,250 | $1,050 | $950 | $800 | $650 | $500 | |

* **JP-15/VTAC Kyle Lamb Signature Rifle** – .223 Rem. cal., GIO, JP FMOS (Full Mass Operating System), 16 in. JP Supermatch barrel, tactical compensator with crush washer, rifle length JP rapid configuration handguard, Mil-Spec forged upper/lower receiver, Magpul CTR buttstock, Hogue pistol grip, black Teflon finish, accessory pack included, 6.4 lbs. Disc. 2016.

| | $1,575 | $995 | $775 | $575 | $495 | $425 | $395 | $1,899 |

JP-22R – .22 LR cal., 18 in. Supermatch light contour stainless steel barrel, A2 or ACE ARFX buttstock, Hogue pistol grip, extra long JP rapid configuration handguard system, matte black finish. New mid-2014.

| MSR $1,499 | $1,400 | $1,200 | $1,050 | $950 | $750 | $600 | $475 | |

Add $150 for polished compensator (Model JP-15/22LR-C).

LRP-07 – .260 Rem., .308 Win., 6.5mm Creedmoor (new 2012), 6mm Creedmoor, or .338 Federal (mfg. 2012-2015) cal., GIO, 22 in. stainless steel cryo-treated barrel, left side charging system (new 2009), tactical compensator, matte black hardcoat anodizing, aluminum components, 10 or 19 shot mag., A2 or ACE ARFX, Tactical TI-7, or Magpul MOE stock, JP modular handguard, JP low mass operating system, Hogue pistol grip, upper accessory rail.

| MSR $3,299 | $3,150 | $2,750 | $2,350 | $2,150 | $1,750 | $1,400 | $1,100 | |

Add $295 for Bench Rest variation with 22 in. barrel.

* **LRP-07H (Hunter)** – .308 Win. cal., LMOS (Low Mass Operating System), 18 in. JP Supermatch cryo-treated barrel with black Teflon finish, JP Competition compensator, 10 shot mag., billet upper and lower receivers, MK III rapid configuration handguard system, JP fire control package, JP adj. gas system, Hogue overmolded buttstock, Hogue grip, matte black hardcoat anodized finish, includes JP 30mm/1 in. flat-top scope mount and Red Rock sling.

| MSR $3,659 | $3,500 | $3,050 | $2,600 | $2,350 | $1,900 | $1,550 | $1,200 | |

* **SASS LRP-07** – .308 Win. cal., similar to LRP-07, except has SASS (Semi-Auto Sniper System) package that includes 20 in. Supermatch barrel, Magpul PRS buttstock, Magpul MIAD grip, scope mount, three 20 shot mags., and soft backpack case. Mfg. 2013-2014.

| | $3,775 | $2,700 | $1,700 | $1,075 | $825 | $750 | $700 | $4,600 |

Add $500 for suppressor.
Add $1,375 for Leupold Mark 4 scope.
Add $1,599 for Bushnell Elite Tactical scope.
Add $2,500 for U.S. Optics SN-3-T-PAL scope.

LRP-07 BILLET BEAUTY SPECIAL EDITION RIFLE – .308 Win. cal., 20 in. JP Supermatch medium contour barrel with custom Cerakote finish, JP large profile compensator, T6 billet upper and lower receivers, JP extra long rapid configuration handguard system, JP adj. minimized gas block, Magpul MOE fixed stock, Magpul MIAD grip, the paint scheme of the Bomber is captured by a special two-tone Cerakote treatment coupled with OD Green Magpul furniture and black accents in the trigger, safety, charging handle slider and mag. release, the stock features a printed homage to the B-17 tail markings, the sides of the magwell have been fitted with plates displaying both the period Army Air Force logo and specially commissioned nose art of the Billet Beauty. Limited mfg. of 25 pieces beginning 2015.

| MSR $4,649 | $4,400 | $3,850 | $3,300 | $3,000 | $2,400 | $2,000 | $1,550 | |

This model pays special tribute to the B-17 bomber, and is in commemoration of American airmen who took to the skies in defense of liberty. It is styled after the iconic aircraft that carried America to victory in WWII.

LRP-07 DESIGNATED MARKSMAN RIFLE – .308 Win. cal., 20 in. medium contour JP Supermatch barrel with black Teflon finish, thread protector, large profile 2-port compensator, Magpul Gen3 PRS stock, Hogue grip, billet upper and lower receiver, 15 1/2 in. XL MK III RC handguard, QD sling swivel, 2 in. modular rail, JP flat-top scope mount, Red Rock 2-point sling, JP accessory pack, matte black finish, 11 lbs.

| MSR $3,919 | $3,200 | $2,150 | $1,525 | $895 | $695 | $650 | $575 | |

J 226 JP ENTERPRISES, INC., cont.

MSR	100%	98%	95%	90%	80%	70%	60%	Last MSR

LRP-07 LONG RANGE COMPETITION RIFLE – 6.5mm Creedmoor cal., 22 in. medium contour JP Supermatch barrel, thread protector, large profile 2-port compensator, Magpul Gen3 PRS stock, Hogue grip, billet upper and lower receiver, 17 1/4 in. XXL MK II Signature handguard, QD sling swivel, 2 in. modular rail, JP flat-top scope mount, Red Rock 2-point sling, JP accessory pack, matte black finish, 11.4 lbs.

MSR $3,959	$3,200	$2,150	$1,525	$895	$695	$650	$575	

LRP-07 MHI CAZADOR SPECIAL EDITION – .308 Win. cal., JP Low Mass Operating System (LMOS), 16 in. JP Supermatch light contour button rifled barrel with silver Thermal Dissipator and black Teflon finish, JP compensator, Magpul ACS adj. stock, Hogue pistol grip, JP adj. minimized gas block, billet upper and lower receiver set with MHI logo and custom distressed Burnt Bronze Cerakote finish over hardcoat anodized black finish on aluminum components, JP XL MK III handguard with custom Cerakote finish, QD sling attachment, 2 and 4 in. modular rail, silver barricade brace, soft case.

MSR $4,499	$3,600	$2,500	$1,650	$1,025	$775	$695	$650	

LRP-07 SUPPRESSOR READY PRECISION PACKAGE – .308 Win. cal., 20 in. medium contour JP Supermatch barrel with black Teflon finish, large profile 2-port compensator, Magpul Gen3 PRS stock with JPPRS-SM QD cup and AP-ABP adj. buttplate, Magpul MIAD grip, billet upper and lower receiver, 15 1/2 in. XL MK III RC handguard, package includes JP flash hider, 34mm flat-top scope mount, four 2 in. modular rails, one 4 in. modular rail, 2-point JP Tactical sling, bipod, monopod, three 20 shot PMAGs, benchrest forearm adapter, matte black finish, 11.8 lbs.

MSR $4,999	$4,250	$3,700	$3,200	$2,900	$2,350	$1,900	$1,500	

NC-22 – .22 LR cal., precision machined Nordic Component upper receiver, 18 in. lightweight stainless steel barrel with JP Compensator, extra long JP modular handguard system, matte black anodized hardcoat finish. Mfg. 2013-2014.

	$1,425	$1,250	$1,075	$975	$785	$650	$500	*$1,499*

PSC-11 – .223 Wylde chamber (new 2017), .204 Ruger (mfg. 2012-2015), .223 Rem. (disc. 2016), .22 LR (new 2016), .300 AAC Blackout (new 2016), 6.5 Grendel (new 2012), or 5.56 NATO (new 2017) cal., GIO, JP adjustable gas system, JP Supermatch polished stainless barrel, JP Compensator, billet upper with left side charging system, MK III handguard system, A2 or ACE ARFX buttstock, Hogue pistol grip, small frame with upper accessory rail, matte black hardcoat anodized finish on aluminum components. New 2011.

MSR $2,599	$2,450	$2,150	$1,850	$1,650	$1,350	$1,100	$850	

PSC-12 – .260 Win. (disc.), .308 Win., 6.5mm Creedmoor (disc.), or 6.5 Grendel (disc.) cal., GIO, large frame, JP Supermatch button rifled barrel with polished stainless finish, JP Compensator, JP adjustable gas system, dual charging upper assembly compatible with DPMS lower receivers, MK III handguard system, A2 or ACE ARFX buttstock, Hogue pistol grip, JP fire control trigger. New 2012.

MSR $3,499	$3,350	$2,950	$2,500	$2,300	$1,850	$1,500	$1,200	

SCR-11 – .223 Wylde chamber, .22 LR (new mid-2014), .204 Ruger (disc. 2015), .300 AAC Blackout (new 2016), .223 Rem. (disc. 2016), 6.5 Grendel, or 5.56 NATO (new 2017) cal., competition side-charging rifle with left side charge system, features JP Supermatch polished stainless barrel with JP compensator, flat-top receiver with Picatinny rail, vent. modular handguard, choice of A2 or ACE ARFX buttstock, Hogue pistol grip, matte black hardcoat anodized finish on aluminum components. New 2011.

MSR $2,299	$2,200	$1,900	$1,600	$1,500	$1,200	$1,000	$750	

Add $400 for .223 Wylde chamber, .300 AAC Blackout (new 2016), or 6.5 Grendel cal.

5.11 ALWAYS BE READY EDITION RIFLES – JP Enterprises has joined forces with 5.11 Tactical to create a series of precision rifles in 5.11 Storm Grey. Three configurations are available and each rifle includes a Cerakote finish upgrade in 5.11 Storm Grey, custom laser markings, and a full tactical rail package. New 2015.

* **JP-15ABR** – .223 Rem. cal., 16 in. medium contour JP Supermatch barrel with black Teflon finish, tactical compensator with crush washer, Mil-Spec forged upper and lower receivers, extra long JP Rapid Configuration handguard, TI-7 buttstock, MOE trigger guard, Hogue pistol grip, 5.11 Storm Grey Cerakote finish, 7.2 lbs. Mfg. 2015-2016.

	$1,975	$1,150	$925	$650	$575	$495	$425	*$2,499*

* **LRP-07 ABR** – .308 Win. cal., 20 in. medium contour barrel with large profile compensator and black Teflon finish, billet aluminum upper and lower receiver with left-side charging system, minimized black JP adj. gas block, extra long JP modular handguard, black Magpul PRS stock, Magpul MIAD black grip, accessories include extra long 14 1/2 in. top rail, 2 and 4 in. modular rails, and JP swivel mount adaptor, 5.11 Storm Grey Cerakote over hardcoat anodized finish with 5.11 logo. New 2015.

MSR $4,539	$4,350	$3,800	$3,250	$2,950	$2,400	$1,950	$1,500	

* **SCR-11 ABR** – .223 Rem. cal., 18 in. JP Supermatch medium contour barrel with small profile compensator and black Teflon finish, T6 upper and lower receivers with left-side charging system on upper receiver, extra long JP modular handguard, flip-up iron sights, 2 in. front sight rail, 2 and 4 in. modular rails, Magpul UBR stock, Hogue pistol grip, Storm Grey Cerakote finish. New 2015.

MSR $3,899	$3,700	$3,250	$2,800	$2,500	$2,050	$1,650	$1,300	

JARD, INC. 227

MSR	100%	98%	95%	90%	80%	70%	60%	Last MSR

JARD, INC.

Current pistol and AR-15 style rifle manufacturer located in Sheldon, IA.

PISTOLS: SEMI-AUTO

J21 – .22 LR cal., blowback operation, 7 in. free floating barrel, upper Picatinny rail, side charging handle, free floating handguard, with or w/o rails and muzzle brake. New 2014.

MSR $715	$625	$540	$470	$400	$350	$310	$295	

Add $47 for rails and muzzle brake.

J23 – .223 Wylde chamber, free floating barrel and handguard, standard AR lower, Picatinny rail upper, side charging handle, includes rails and muzzle brake. New 2014.

MSR $1,009	$850	$725	$650	$585	$515	$450	$395	

RIFLES: SEMI-AUTO

J16 – .223/5.56 NATO cal., GIO, 16 in. barrel, 20 shot mag., folding/telescoping stock, free floating barrel and handguard, flat-top A3 billet aluminum upper receiver, Picatinny rail, side charging handle, JARD sight compensation system, optional quad rail or muzzle brake, black finish.

MSR $1,015	$865	$550	$465	$395	$350	$325	$300	

Add $100 for quad rail kit. Add $75 for muzzle brake.

J17 – .17 HMR or .22 WMR cal., blowback operation, adj. stock, pistol grip, Picatinny rail receiver, detachable magazine, side charging handle, ergonomic safety and magazine release operation, black finish. Disc. 2017.

	$850	$725	$650	$585	$515	$450	$395	*$1,000*

J18 – .243 WSSM, .25 WSSM, or 7mm WSSM cal., GIO, 22 in. barrel, enlarged bolt design, side charging handle, flat-top Picatinny rail, free floating barrel and handguard, QD sling stud standard, 3 shot mag.

MSR $1,181	$995	$625	$495	$450	$395	$350	$325	

J19 – .223/5.56 NATO cal., GIO, standard AR lower, left non-reciprocating charging handle, right fold adj. length stock with adj. cheek pad, Picatinny rail upper, free float barrel and forearm, JARD sight compensation system, brass deflector.

	$1,195	$795	$550	$465	$415	$375	$350	*$1,446*

J19C – .223 Wylde chamber, gas operated, 16 1/8 in. barrel, left charging handle, tactical/competition charging knob, top Picatinny rail, brass deflector, M-LOK compatible slots in forearm, black or tan finish, 5 lbs.

MSR $1,250	$1,050	$650	$495	$450	$395	$350	$325	

J22 – .22 LR cal., blowback operation, 16.2 in. barrel, 26 shot mag., side charging handle, upper Picatinny rail, free floating barrel and handguard, pistol grip, quad rail/muzzle brake is optional, black finish.

MSR $735	$640	$550	$475	$400	$350	$310	$295	

Add $99 for quad rail/muzzle brake.

J48 – .223 Wylde chamber, GIO, 18 5/8 in. barrel, AR mag., right ejection, right side charging, rotating bolt, AR trigger, stock, and grip. New 2014.

MSR $1,125	$935	$575	$475	$415	$350	$325	$300	

J71 – .17 HMR or .17 WSM cal., blowback action, 20 in. button rifled barrel, detachable mag., adj. stock, side charging handle, Picatinny rail receiver.

MSR $1,192	$1,025	$925	$800	$685	$595	$515	$440	

J450 – .450 Bushmaster cal., GIO, 20 in. button rifle threaded barrel, muzzle brake, 7 shot mag., side charging handle, Picatinny rail upper, Mil-Spec AR lower, M-LOK compatible slots, free float barrel and forearm, black finish. New 2018.

MSR $998	$850	$550	$465	$395	$350	$325	$295	

JESSE JAMES FIREARMS UNLIMITED

Current pistol, rifle, and silencer manufacturer/customizer located in Dripping Springs, TX.

RIFLES: SEMI-AUTO

NOMAD AR 10 – .308 Win. cal., GIO, 18 in. steel or Proof Research carbon fiber (disc.) barrel, JJFU needle bearing trigger, milled billet upper and lower receiver, M-LOK system option at the end of handguard.

MSR $5,000	$4,250	$3,750	$3,250	$2,625	$2,200	$1,875	$1,625

NOMAD AR-15 – .223 Rem/5.56 NATO. or .300 AAC Blackout cal., GIO, AR-15 style, 16 or 22 in. chrome-lined match grade barrel w/muzzle brake, two-stage trigger, ACS or Magpul UBR stock, JJFU Skelly grip, billet aluminum upper and lower receivers, Tungsten or Sandman finish.

MSR $3,499	$2,975	$2,600	$2,100	$1,800	$1,500	$1,250	$1,075

J 228 JUGGERNAUT TACTICAL

MSR	100%	98%	95%	90%	80%	70%	60%	Last MSR

JUGGERNAUT TACTICAL

Current AR-15 style gun and accessories manufacturer located in Orange, CA. Dealer and consumer direct sales through FFL.

RIFLES: SEMI-AUTO

JT-10 COMPLETE RIFLE – .308 Win. cal., GIO, 18 in. stainless steel fluted barrel with JT compensator, 10 or 30 shot mag., extended M4 feed ramps, mid-length gas system, billet lower and flat-top upper receivers, 12, 15, or 16 1/2 in. free float KeyMod rail, extended latch charging handle, ALG QMS trigger, 6-pos. receiver extension, carbine buffer, MFT Battlelink Minimalist stock, Hogue pistol grip, includes two rifle carry bag, Mil-Spec phosphate finish in various colors, 6 lbs. New 2015.

| MSR $1,699 | $1,385 | $895 | $675 | $525 | $450 | $385 | $350 | |

JT-15 COMPLETE RIFLE – 5.56 NATO cal., AR-15 style, GIO, 16 or 18 in. stainless steel fluted barrel with JT compensator, 10 or 30 shot mag., extended M4 feed ramps, mid-length gas system, billet lower and flat-top upper receiver, 9, 12, or 15 in. free float KeyMod rail, extended latch charging handle, ALG QMS trigger, no sights, 6-pos. receiver extension, carbine buffer, MFT Battlelink Minimalist stock with JT Hogue pistol grip, Mil-Spec phosphate finish in various colors, approx. 6 lbs. New 2015.

| MSR $1,495 | $1,250 | $825 | $575 | $475 | $425 | $375 | $350 | |

JUST RIGHT CARBINES

Current trademark of carbines established in 2011, and manufactured in Canandaigua, NY. Dealer and distributor sales. Currently distributed by LDB Supply LLC located in Dayton, OH. Previously distributed by American Tactical Imports (ATI), located in Rochester, NY, and by E.M.F., located in Santa Ana, CA.

CARBINES: SEMI-AUTO

M&P TACTICAL – 9mm Para. or .40 S&W cal., straight blowback operation, 17 in. threaded or unthreaded barrel, 15 or 17 shot M&P mag., free floating quad rail or takedown tube, collapsible or fixed stock, pistol grip, black finish. New 2015.

| MSR $824 | $695 | $620 | $550 | $475 | $420 | $365 | $335 | |

MARINE – 9mm Para., .40 S&W, or .45 ACP cal., straight blowback operation, 17 in. stainless steel threaded barrel with birdcage muzzle brake, 13, 15, or 17 shot Glock style mag., telescoping 6-pos. collapsible M4 buttstock, takedown tube forend, AR-15 pistol grip, top Picatinny rail, electroless nickel plated finish, 6 1/2 lbs. New 2015.

| MSR $739 | $650 | $575 | $510 | $440 | $385 | $340 | $325 | |

QUADRAIL – 9mm Para., .40 S&W (disc.), or .45 ACP (mfg. 2011-2016), or .357 SIG (mfg. 2016 only) cal., blowback action, 16 1/4 (disc.) or 17 in. barrel, 13, 15, or 17 shot Glock style mag., collapsible 6-position stock, ambidextrous bolt handle and ejection, flat-top receiver with Picatinny rail, free floating quad rail forend, black, Desert Camo (mfg. 2013-2016), Muddy Girl (mfg. 2013-2016), ReaperZ Green (mfg. 2013-2015), A-TACS Foliage Green (mfg. 2014-2016), Snow Ghost (mfg. 2014-2016), or U.S. Flag (new 2017) finish, approx. 6 1/2 lbs. New 2011.

| MSR $799 | $685 | $615 | $550 | $475 | $420 | $365 | $335 | |

Add $75 for .357 SIG cal. (mfg. 2016 only).

RAIL MODEL – 9mm Para., .40 S&W, or .45 ACP cal., blowback action, 17 in. threaded barrel, 13, 15, or 17 shot Glock or M&P mag., stock and commercial spec buffer tube, telescoping 6-position collapsible M4 style buttstock, M4/AR-15 pistol grip, 13 in. KeyMod handguard, one-piece machined aluminum and hardcoat anodized receiver, black or Kryptek Highlander (new 2017) finish.

| MSR $699 | $615 | $540 | $470 | $400 | $350 | $310 | $295 | |

Add $76 for Kryptek finish (new 2017).

TAKEDOWN – 9mm Para., 10mm (new 2017) .40 S&W, .45 ACP, or .357 SIG (new 2016) cal., blowback operating system, 16 1/4 (disc.) or 17 in. threaded button rifled barrel, 13, 15, or 17 shot Glock or M&P (new 2016) style mag., telescoping 6-pos. collapsible M4 buttstock, takedown tube forend, AR-15 pistol grip, one-piece machined aluminum receiver, top Picatinny rail, commercial spec buffer tube, ambidextrous bolt handle and ejection, black, Kryptek (new 2017), Desert Camo (mfg. 2013-2016), Muddy Girl (mfg. 2013-2016), ReaperZ Green (mfg. 2013-2015), ATACS Foliage Green (mfg. 2014-2016), or Snow Ghost (mfg. 2014-2016) finish, approx. 6 1/2 lbs. New 2011.

| MSR $649 | $575 | $500 | $435 | $365 | $325 | $280 | $265 | |

Add $50 for 10mm cal. (new 2017).
Add $76 for Kryptek finish (new 2017).
Add $95 for Reaper Z Green and 33 shot mag. (mfg. 2013-2015).
Add $100 for tactical package (includes red dot scope, forward folding grip, Tuff1 grip cover and two magazines). Disc.

K SECTION

229 K

KE ARMS

Current manufacturer of complete AR-15 style pistols, rifles, and AR-15 accessories located in Phoenix, AZ.

MSR	100%	98%	95%	90%	80%	70%	60%	Last MSR

PISTOLS: SEMI-AUTO

KE-15 COMMANDO PISTOL – 5.56 NATO cal., SLT-1 or SLT-2 trigger, 9 in. 7 side M-LOK, 9 in. Delta Quad, or 9 in. Delta-S M-LOK rail system, includes SB Tactical pistol stabilizing brace, Mil-Spec BCG, carbine buffer, QD attachment point, includes nylon strap, hardcoat anodized black or Cerakote finish in Elite Concrete, Elite Coyote, or Elite Jungle. New 2018.

| MSR $1,525 | $1,295 | $1,145 | $1,035 | $885 | $765 | $635 | $535 | |

Add $125 for Elite Concrete, Elite Coyote, or Elite Jungle Cerakote finish.

RIFLES: SEMI-AUTO

KE-15 ACTION CARBINE – 5.56 NATO cal., AR-15 style, 16 in. chrome moly vanadium steel mid-length barrel, A2 flash hider, pinned gas block, 30 shot PMAG, SLT-1 trigger, Mission First tactical minimalist stock, X-Tech grip, ambidextrous selector, 15 in. Delta-S M-LOK handguard, KE-15 billet flared magwell lower receiver, bolt carrier group, charging handle, hardcoat black anodized, Elite Coyote, Elite Jungle, or Elite Concrete finish.

| MSR $1,775 | $1,475 | $950 | $725 | $550 | $475 | $395 | $350 | |

Add $125 for Elite Coyote, Elite Jungle, or Elite Concrete finish.

KE-15T – 5.56 NATO cal., 16 in. Ballistic Advantage Modern M4 barrel, collapsible Magpul CTR buttstock, MOE pistol grip, forged aluminum upper and lower receiver, 12 1/2 in. fluted free floating quad rail, M15 bolt carrier group, Picatinny rail, M4 feed ramps, hardcoat anodized black finish, 7 lbs. Disc. 2017.

| | $895 | $575 | $475 | $395 | $350 | $325 | $300 | *$1,069* |

KE-15X – 5.56 NATO cal., 16 in. mid-length barrel, collapsible CTR buttstock, MOE pistol grip, forged aluminum upper and lower receiver, 12 1/2 in. KeyMod rail, low profile gas block, M16 bolt carrier group, Picatinny rail, M4 feed ramps, 7 lbs. Disc. 2017.

| | $1,075 | $675 | $500 | $450 | $400 | $350 | $325 | *$1,300* |

KE ARMS TEAM RIFLE – 5.56 NATO cal., AR-15 style, 17.7 in. mid-length barrel, A2 flash hider, pinned gas block, DMR trigger, ambidextrous selector, 15 in. Delta-S M-LOK, KE-15 billet flared magwell lower receiver, bolt carrier group, charging handle, hardcoat black anodized or FDE finish.

| MSR $1,800 | $1,475 | $950 | $725 | $550 | $475 | $395 | $350 | |

PATROL CARBINE LEVEL 1 – 5.56 NATO cal., 16 in. Hanson profile chrome moly barrel with QPQ corrosion resistant finish, A2 flash hider, extended M4 feed ramp extension, SST, Mil-Spec 6-pos. buttstock, A2 plastic grip, mid-length gas system, pinned gas block, forged flat-top upper and forged aluminum lower receiver, 15 in. KeyMod or M-LOK rail system, enhanced charging handle, M16 BCG, hardcoat anodized black or Cerakote finish in Elite Concrete, Elite Coyote, or Elite Jungle.

| MSR $1,100 | $915 | $575 | $475 | $415 | $350 | $325 | $300 | |

Add $150 for Elite Concrete, Elite Coyote, or Elite Jungle Cerakote finish.

PATROL CARBINE LEVEL 2 – 5.56 NATO cal., 16 in. Hanson profile chrome moly barrel with QPQ corrosion resistant finish, extended M4 feed ramp extension, flash hider, DMR or SLT-1 trigger, Magpul MOE buttstock, Magpul MOE pistol grip, mid-length gas system, pinned gas block, forged aluminum lower and flat-top upper receiver, M16 BCG, enhanced charging handle, 15 in. M-LOK rail system, hardcoat anodized black or Cerakote finish in Elite Concrete, Elite Coyote, or Elite Jungle.

| MSR $1,450 | $1,195 | $795 | $550 | $465 | $415 | $375 | $350 | |

Add $40 for SLT-1 trigger.
Add $150 for Elite Concrete, Elite Coyote, or Elite Jungle Cerakote finish.

KING'S ARSENAL

Current manufacturer established in 2011, located in Abilene, TX.

PISTOLS: SEMI-AUTO

KROWN 15 – .300 Blackout cal., model built to customer specifications.
Please contact the manufacturer directly for options, pricing, and availability.

RIFLES: SEMI-AUTO

Add $265 for 16 in. Noveske stainless barrel.
Add $875 for 16 in. Proof Research carbon fiber wrapped barrel.

K 230 KING'S ARSENAL, cont.

MSR	100%	98%	95%	90%	80%	70%	60%	Last MSR

KROWN 15 BASE MODEL / KROWN 15 KUSTOM – 5.56 NATO, 6.8 SPC, or 6.5 Grendel cal., GIO, 16 in. match med. weight, twist, or straight flute M4 contour barrel, A2 flash hider, ALG trigger, M4 adj. stock, A2 grip, carbine length gas system, 12 in. Samson Evo aluminum handguard with full top rail, aluminum upper and lower receivers, charging handle, Mil-Spec lower parts kit.

| MSR $1,695 | $1,385 | $895 | $675 | $525 | $450 | $385 | $350 | |

This model can be built to customer specifications (Krown 15 Kustom). Please contact the manufacturer directly for additional options and upgrades.

KNIGHT'S ARMAMENT COMPANY

Current manufacturer established in 1983, located in Titusville, FL. Previously located in Vero Beach, FL. Dealer and consumer direct sales.

RIFLES: SEMI-AUTO

Some of the models listed were also available in pre-ban configurations. SR-25 Enhanced Match model has 10 or 20 shot mag. Some of the following models, while discontinued for civilian use, may still be available for military/law enforcement.

STONER SR-15 M-5 RIFLE – .223 Rem. cal., GIO, 20 in. standard weight barrel, flip-up low profile rear sight, two-stage target trigger, 7.6 lbs. Mfg. 1997-2008.

| | $1,525 | $1,350 | $1,150 | $1,050 | $850 | $700 | $550 | $1,837 |

* **Stoner SR-15 M-4 Carbine** – .223 Rem. cal., similar to SR-15 rifle, except has 16 in. barrel, choice of fixed synthetic or non-collapsible buttstock. Mfg. 1997-2005.

| | $1,325 | $1,150 | $1,000 | $900 | $750 | $600 | $475 | $1,575 |

Add $100 for non-collapsible buttstock (SR-15 M-4 K-Carbine, disc. 2001).

* **SR-15 E3 Mod 2 URX 4 Keymod (Stoner SR-15 URX E3 Carbine)** – 5.56 NATO cal., GIO, features 16 in. free floating barrel with URX forearm, E3 type rounded lug improved bolt. New 2004.

| MSR $2,312 | $2,050 | $1,800 | $1,550 | $1,400 | $1,150 | $900 | $700 | |

* **SR-15 E3 Mod 2 URX 4 M-LOK** – 5.56 NATO. cal., GIO, AR-15 style, 16 in. free floating barrel, E3 type rounded lug improved bolt, URX4 M-LOK handguard. New 2016.

| MSR $2,450 | $2,200 | $1,900 | $1,650 | $1,500 | $1,200 | $1,000 | $750 | |

SR-15E IWS LIGHT PRECISION RIFLE – 5.56 NATO cal., 18 in. stainless steel match barrel with custom match chamber, URX (upper receiver extending) free floated barrel system, IWS lower, two-stage match trigger, ambidextrous controls, black furniture, 7.38 lbs.

| | $2,350 | $2,050 | $1,750 | $1,600 | $1,300 | $1,050 | $800 | |

STONER SR-15 MATCH RIFLE – .223 Rem. cal., GIO, flat-top upper receiver with 20 in. match grade stainless steel free floating barrel with RAS forend, two-stage match trigger, 7.9 lbs. Mfg. 1997-2008.

| | $1,800 | $1,550 | $1,350 | $1,200 | $1,000 | $800 | $600 | $1,972 |

SR-15 E3 LPR MOD 2 M-LOK – 5.56 NATO cal., 18 in. match stainless steel barrel with custom match chamber, free floated barrel system, two-stage match trigger, URX4 M-LOK handguard, IWS lower, ambidextrous controls, black furniture, 7.38 lbs. New 2016.

| MSR $2,700 | $2,450 | $2,150 | $1,850 | $1,650 | $1,350 | $1,100 | $850 | |

SR-15 MOD 2 – 5.56 NATO cal., 16 in. hammer forged chrome-lined barrel, mid-length gas system, ambi bolt release, selector, and mag. release, drop-in two-stage trigger, black finish, 6 3/4 lbs. New 2015.

Please contact the manufacturer directly for pricing and availability for this model.

SR-15 E3 LPR MOD 2 KEYMOD (LIGHT PRECISION RIFLE) – 5.56 NATO cal., Mod 2 Gas System, 18 in. match grade stainless steel barrel with a custom match chamber and QDC flash eliminator, adj. micro sights, two-stage match trigger, multi-lug improved E3 bolt, 6-pos. SOPMOD stock, URX 4 handguard with KeyMod mounting points, standard ambidextrous lower receiver, black finish, 7 1/2 lbs. New 2015.

| MSR $2,700 | $2,450 | $2,150 | $1,850 | $1,650 | $1,350 | $1,100 | $850 | |

STONER SR-25 SPORTER – .308 Win. cal., GIO, 20 in. lightweight barrel, AR-15 configuration with carrying handle, 5, 10, or 20 (disc. per C/B 1994) shot detachable mag., less than 2 MOA guaranteed, non-glare finish, 8.8 lbs. Mfg. 1993-97.

| | $2,700 | $2,350 | $2,000 | $1,850 | $1,500 | $1,200 | $950 | $2,995 |

* **Stoner RAS Sporter Carbine (SR-25 Carbine)** – .223 Rem. cal., GIO, 16 in. free floating barrel, grooved non-slip handguard, removable carrying handle, 7 3/4 lbs. Mfg. 1995-2005.

| | $3,150 | $2,750 | $2,350 | $2,150 | $1,750 | $1,400 | $1,100 | $3,495 |

Subtract 15% if w/o RAS.

In 2003, the Rail Adapter System (RAS) became standard on this model.

KNIGHT'S ARMAMENT COMPANY, cont. 231 K

MSR	100%	98%	95%	90%	80%	70%	60%	Last MSR

SR-25 STANDARD MATCH – .308 Win. cal., GIO, free floating 24 in. match barrel, fiberglass stock, includes commercial gun case and 10 shot mag. Disc. 2008.

	$3,500	$3,050	$2,600	$2,400	$1,900	$1,600	$1,200	$3,918

SR-25 RAS MATCH – .308 Win. cal., similar to SR-25 Standard, except has 24 in. free floating match barrel and flat-top receiver, less than 1 MOA guaranteed, RAS became standard 2004, 10 3/4 lbs. Mfg. 1993-2008.

	$3,400	$3,000	$2,550	$2,300	$1,850	$1,550	$1,200	$3,789

Subtract approx. 15% if w/o Rail Adapter System (RAS).

Over 3,000 SR-25s were manufactured.

* SR-25 RAS Match Lightweight – .308 Win. cal., GIO, 20 in. medium contour free floating barrel, 9 1/2 lbs. Mfg. 1995-2004.

	$2,900	$2,550	$2,200	$1,950	$1,600	$1,300	$1,000	$3,244

Add approx. 15% for Rail Adapter System.

SR-25 E2 ACC KEYMOD (ADVANCED COMBAT CARBINE) – 7.62 NATO cal., 16 in. rifled chrome-lined barrel with 5-slot flash hider, ambi controls, carbon cutter bolt carrier, multi-lug improved E2 bolt, drop-in two-stage trigger, URX handguard, two-stage match trigger, black finish, 8.4 lbs. New 2015.

MSR $4,861	$4,350	$3,850	$3,300	$3,000	$2,400	$1,950	$1,550	

SR-25 E2 ACC URX4 M-LOK – 7.62 NATO cal., 16 in. rifled chrome-lined barrel with 5-slot flash hider, ambi controls, carbon cutter bolt carrier, multi-lug improved E2 bolt, drop-in two-stage trigger, URX handguard, black finish, 8.4 lbs. New 2016.

MSR $4,861	$4,350	$3,850	$3,300	$3,000	$2,400	$1,950	$1,550	

SR-25 E2 APC (ADVANCED PRECISION CARBINE) KEYMOD – 7.62 NATO cal., 16 in. barrel with QDC flash suppressor, URX 4 free floating barrel system, drop-in two-stage trigger, ambi bolt release, selector, and mag. release, black furniture, 9.12 lbs. New mid-2014.

MSR $4,861	$4,350	$3,850	$3,300	$3,000	$2,400	$1,950	$1,550	

SR-25 E2 APC M-LOK – 7.62 NATO cal., 16 in. barrel with QDC flash suppressor, URX 4 free floating barrel system, drop-in two-stage trigger, ambi bolt release, selector, and mag. release, black furniture, 9.12 lbs. New 2016.

MSR $4,861	$4,350	$3,850	$3,300	$3,000	$2,400	$1,950	$1,550	

SR-25 E2 APR (ADVANCED PRECISION RIFLE) KEYMOD – 7.62 NATO cal., 20 in. match barrel with QDC flash suppressor, ambi controls, drop-in two-stage trigger, E2 bolt and gas system, URX 4 handguard, black finish, 10 1/2 lbs. New 2015.

MSR $4,861	$4,350	$3,850	$3,300	$3,000	$2,400	$1,950	$1,550	

SR-25 E2 APR M-LOK – 7.62 NATO cal., 20 in. match barrel with QDC flash suppressor, ambi controls, drop-in two-stage trigger, E2 bolt and gas system, URX 4 handguard, black finish, 10 1/2 lbs. New 2016.

MSR $4,861	$4,350	$3,850	$3,300	$3,000	$2,400	$1,950	$1,550	

SR-25 ENHANCED MATCH RIFLE/CARBINE – .308 Win. cal., GIO, 16 or 20 in. barrel, 10 or 20 shot mag., URX rail system, two-stage trigger, ambidextrous mag. release, integrated adj. folding front sight, micro adj. folding rear sight, EM gas block, combat trigger guard, chrome plated multi-lug bolt and bolt carrier, fixed or nine position adj. stock, black anodized finish, flash hider (carbine only), approx. 8 1/2 lbs. Disc. 2013.

	$4,500	$3,950	$3,400	$3,050	$2,500	$2,000	$1,600	$4,994

Add $625 for 16 in. carbine.

SR-25 MK11 MOD O CIVILIAN DELUXE SYSTEM PACKAGE – .308 Win. cal., GIO, consumer variation of the Navy Model Mark Eleven, Mod O, w/o sound suppressor, includes Leupold 3.5-10X scope, 20 in. military grade match barrel, backup sights, cell-foam case and other accessories. Mfg. 2003-2008.

	$7,750	$6,700	$5,750	$5,200	$4,200	$3,450	$2,700	$8,534

SR-25 MK11 MATCH RIFLE – .308 Win. cal., GIO, includes MK11 Mod O features and 20 in. heavy barrel. Mfg. 2004-2008.

	$5,750	$5,050	$4,300	$3,900	$3,150	$2,600	$2,000	$6,325

SR-25 MK11 CARBINE – .308 Win. cal., GIO, includes MK11 Mod O features and 16 in. match grade stainless steel barrel with muzzle brake, URX 4x4 rail forend, 4-position buttstock. Mfg. 2005-2013.

	$6,000	$5,250	$4,500	$4,100	$3,300	$2,700	$2,100	$6,636

SR-25 BR CARBINE – .308 Win. cal., similar to SR-25 MK11 Carbine, except has chrome-lined steel barrel. Mfg. 2005-2008.

	$5,675	$4,950	$4,250	$3,850	$3,100	$2,550	$2,000	$6,307

K 232 KNIGHT'S ARMAMENT COMPANY, cont.

MSR	100%	98%	95%	90%	80%	70%	60%	Last MSR

SR-30 – .300 AAC Blackout cal., 16 in. stainless steel barrel with QDC flash suppressor, URX 3.1 free floating rail system, micro front and rear iron sights, E3 bolt, ambi controls, two-stage trigger, fully adj. SOPMOD stock, black furniture, 6 1/2 lbs. Mfg. mid-2014-2015.

| | $2,375 | $2,100 | $1,800 | $1,600 | $1,300 | $1,050 | $850 | $2,632 |

SR-M110 SASS – 7.62x51mm cal., GIO, 20 in. military match grade barrel, full RAS treatment on barrel, civilian variation of the Army's semi-auto sniper rifle system, includes Leupold long-range tactical scope, 600 meter backup iron sights, system case and other accessories. Mfg. 2006-2009.

| | $13,000 | $11,350 | $9,750 | $8,850 | $7,150 | $5,850 | $4,550 | $14,436 |

"DAVID TUBB" COMPETITION MATCH RIFLE – .260 Rem. or .308 Win. cal., GIO, incorporates refinements by David Tubb, top-of-the-line competition match rifle, including adj. and rotating buttstock pad. Mfg. 1998 only.

| | $5,450 | $4,750 | $4,100 | $3,700 | $3,000 | $2,450 | $1,900 | $5,995 |

STONER SR-50 – .50 BMG cal., GIO, features high strength materials and lightweight design, fully locked breech and two lug rotary breech bolt, horizontal 5 shot box mag., tubular receiver supports a removable barrel, approx. 31 lbs. Limited mfg. 2000, non-commercial sales only.

Last MSR was $6,995.

Extreme rarity factor precludes accurate pricing on this model.

KORSTOG

Current trademark of AR-15 style rifles manufactured by Adams Arms, previously retailed exclusively by Fleet Farm.

Korstog is an ancient Norwegian word meaning "crusade."

RIFLES/CARBINES: SEMI-AUTO

All rifles include a soft sided tactical case.

BRANN – 5.56 NATO cal., carbine length GIO, 16 in. Melonite coated chrome moly valadium steel barrel with M4 contour, high quality aluminum forged upper and lower receivers, aluminum precision machined receiver extension/buffer tube, hardcoat anodized finish, SST, F-marked front sight base and A2 front sight post, 6-position tactical buttstock with carbine USGI forearm, A2 grip, upper receiver adaptable for rear sight or optics, A4 flat-top receiver with M4 feed ramps. New 2013.

| MSR $900 | | $750 | $650 | $550 | $485 | $425 | $350 | $300 |

JAGER – 5.56 NATO cal., rifle length GIO, 20 in. heavy precision fluted stainless steel barrel with Adams Arms Jet compensator, low profile gas block, high quality aluminum upper and lower receivers, hardcoat anodized finish, JP-EZ single stage trigger, no sights, Magpul PRS precision adjustable stock with 15 in. Samson Evolution Series T6 aluminum Mil-zdpec forearm, Ergo Ambi grip, A4 flat-top receiver with M4 feed ramps, steel bolt carrier group, heat-treated gas key, 9.1 lbs. New 2013.

| MSR $1,950 | | $1,650 | $1,450 | $1,375 | $1,095 | $875 | $725 | $625 |

VAR – 5.56 NATO cal., mid-length GIO, 16 in. Melonite coated chrome moly valadium steel barrel with permanently attached flash hider, low profile gas block, high quality aluminum forged upper and lower receivers, machined aluminum Mil-Spec receiver extension/buffer tube, hardcoat anodized finish, JP-EZ single stage trigger, no sights, 6-position VLTOR IMOD collapsible stock with Samson Evolution Series T6 aluminum forearm, Ergo Ambi grip, A4 flat-top receiver with M4 feed ramps, steel bolt carrier group, heat-treated gas key. New 2013.

| MSR $1,450 | | $1,225 | $1,050 | $950 | $800 | $700 | $600 | $500 |

VOLI – 5.56 NATO cal., mid-length GIO, 16 in. Melonite coated chrome moly valadium steel barrel, high quality aluminum upper and lower receivers, hardcoat anodized finish, SST, F-marked front sight base and A2 Magpul front sight post, Magpul MBUS Gen 2 rear sight, 6-position Magpul MOE adjustable collapsible stock, pistol grip, A4 flat-top receiver with M4 feed ramps, steel bolt carrier group, heat treated gas key. New 2013.

| MSR $1,150 | | $950 | $850 | $715 | $685 | $495 | $415 | $350 |

L SECTION

L.A.R. MANUFACTURING, INC.

Previous rifle manufacturer established in 1968, located in West Jordan, UT until 2012. L.A.R. was acquired by the Freedom Group in late 2012 and closed its doors during 2013.

In addition to its .50 cal. bolt action rifles, L.A.R. also made upper receiver assemblies and associated parts/accessories for AR-15 style carbines/rifles.

MSR	100%	98%	95%	90%	80%	70%	60%	Last MSR

RIFLES: SEMI-AUTO

GRIZZLY 15 – .223 Rem. cal., GIO, patterned after the AR-15, available in either A2 or A3 configuration, limited mfg. 2004-2005.

	$675	$500	$425	$375	$335	$315	$295	$795

Add $85 for detachable carry handle.

GRIZZLY A2 SPEC CARBINE – 5.56 NATO cal., AR-15 style, GIO, 16 in. M4 chrome moly threaded barrel with A2 birdcage flash suppressor, 5-position collapsible carbine stock, Grizzly A2 aluminum upper receiver, Mil-Spec forged aluminum LAR Grizzly lower receiver, Mil-Spec or LAR split carbine quad rail handguard, A2 front sight, standard trigger group, A2 Mil-Spec pistol grip. Mfg. 2011-2012.

	$850	$550	$465	$395	$350	$325	$295	$999

GRIZZLY A3 SPEC CARBINE – 5.56 NATO cal., GIO, similar to Grizzly A2 Spec Carbine, except has Grizzly A3 aluminum flat-top upper receiver. Mfg. 2011-2012.

	$850	$550	$465	$395	$350	$325	$295	$979

OPS-4 GRIZZLY H-TACTICAL – 5.56 NATO cal., AR-15 style, GPO, 16 in. M4 chrome moly threaded barrel with A2 birdcage flash suppressor, 5-position collapsible carbine stock, LAR side charged forged aluminum flat-top upper receiver, Mil-Spec forged aluminum LAR Grizzly lower receiver, Mil-Spec or LAR split carbine quad rail handguard, hard anodized aluminum charging handle. Mfg. 2011-2012.

	$935	$575	$475	$415	$350	$325	$300	$1,111

OPS-4 GRIZZLY HUNTER – .223 Rem./5.56 NATO (.223 Wylde chamber) cal., AR-15 style, GIO, 18, 20, or 24 in. bull chrome moly (20 or 24 in.) or stainless steel (18 or 20 in.) barrel, standard A2 black stock, standard trigger or two-stage match trigger group, OPS-4 side charged forged aluminum flat-top upper receiver, Mil-Spec forged aluminum LAR Grizzly lower receiver, LAR free float tube rifle length handguard, LAR aluminum gas block, hard anodized aluminum charging handle. Mfg. 2011-2012.

	$850	$550	$465	$395	$350	$325	$295	$989

OPS-4 GRIZZLY OPERATOR – 5.56 NATO cal., AR-15 style, GIO, 16 in. chrome moly heavy threaded barrel with 5 port muzzle brake and compensator, Magpul CTR collapsible stock, Hogue rubber grip with finger grooves or Magpul MIAD pistol grip, standard trigger group, OPS-4 side charged forged aluminum flat-top upper receiver, Mil-Spec forged aluminum LAR Grizzly lower receiver, LAR mid-length quad rail handguard, LAR aluminum gas block with rail, hard anodized aluminum charging handle. Mfg. 2011-2012.

	$915	$575	$475	$415	$350	$325	$300	$1,099

OPS-4 GRIZZLY PRECISION OPERATOR – .223 Rem./5.56 NATO (.223 Wylde chamber) cal., AR-15 style, GIO, 18 or 20 in. bull stainless steel barrel, Magpul PRS stock, Magpul pistol grip and trigger guard or Magpul MIAD grip, standard trigger or two-stage match trigger group, LAR rifle length free floating quad rail handguard, LAR aluminum low profile gas block, otherwise similar to OPS-4 Grizzly Operator. Mfg. 2011-2012.

	$1,075	$675	$500	$450	$400	$350	$325	$1,299

OPS-4 GRIZZLY SPEC CARBINE – 5.56 NATO cal., AR-15 style, GIO, 16 in. M4 chrome moly threaded barrel with A2 birdcage flash suppressor, standard trigger group, 5-position collapsible carbine stock, OPS-4 side charged forged aluminum flat-top upper receiver, Mil-Spec forged aluminum LAR Grizzly lower receiver, A2 front sight, Mil-Spec or LAR split carbine quad rail handguard, hard anodized aluminum charging handle. Mfg. 2011-2012.

	$825	$535	$450	$385	$340	$325	$295	$959

OPS-4 GRIZZLY SPEC RIFLE – 5.56 NATO cal., AR-15 style, GIO, 20 in. chrome moly heavy threaded barrel with A2 birdcage flash suppressor, standard trigger or two-stage match trigger group, standard A2 black stock, otherwise similar to OPS-4 Grizzly Spec Carbine. Mfg. 2011-2012.

	$850	$550	$465	$395	$350	$325	$295	$999

OPS-4 GRIZZLY STANDARD CARBINE – 5.56 NATO cal., AR-15 style, GIO, 16 in. M4 chrome moly threaded barrel with A2 birdcage flash suppressor, standard trigger group, 5-position collapsible carbine stock, LAR side charged forged aluminum flat-top upper receiver, Mil-Spec forged aluminum LAR Grizzly lower receiver, LAR aluminum gas block with rail, full chrome bolt carrier and gas key, hard anodized aluminum charging handle. Mfg. 2011-2012.

	$850	$550	$465	$395	$350	$325	$295	$999

L 234 L.A.R. MANUFACTURING, INC., cont.

MSR	100%	98%	95%	90%	80%	70%	60%	Last MSR

OPS-4 GRIZZLY STANDARD RIFLE – 5.56 NATO cal., AR-15 style, GIO, 20 in. chrome moly heavy threaded barrel with A2 birdcage flash suppressor, standard trigger or two-stage match trigger group, standard A2 black stock, otherwise similar to OPS-4 Grizzly Standard Carbine. Mfg. 2011-2012.

	$915	$575	$475	$415	$350	$325	$300	$1,099

OPS-22 TERMINATOR – .22 LR cal., GIO, 16 in. carbon steel barrel, free float tube, 30 shot mag., collapsible buttstock. Mfg. 2011-2012.

	$575	$500	$425	$375	$325	$295	$275	$649

LWRC INTERNATIONAL, INC.

Current manufacturer of pistols, rifles, and related AR-15 accessories established during 2006, located in Cambridge, MD. Dealer and distributor sales.

PISTOLS: SEMI-AUTO

IC-PSD (PERSONAL SECURITY DETAIL) (M6IC-PSD) – 5.56 NATO cal., GPO, sub-carbine length gas system, 8 1/2 in. cold hammer forged heavy barrel with black Nitride finish, high efficiency 4-prong flash hider, LWRCI advanced trigger guard, Skirmish sights, pistol buffer tube, Magpul MOE+ grip, 7 in. modular rail, Monoforge upper receiver, ambi charging handle, nickel Teflon coated enhanced fire control group, fully ambidextrous lower receiver, includes 3 LWRCI Rail Skins and Mil-Spec index plate, black anodized or FDE, Olive Drab, Patriot Brown, or Tungsten Grey Cerakote finish, 5.9 lbs. New 2015.

MSR $2,274	$1,925	$1,685	$1,425	$1,225	$1,035	$885	$735	

Add $153 for Patriot Brown, OD Green, FDE, or Tungsten Grey Cerakote finish.

M6A2-PSD (PERSONAL SECURITY DETAIL) – 5.56 NATO cal., GPO, 8 in. ultra compact hammer forged steel barrel, A2 flash hider, 30 shot Magpul PMAG, MIAD pistol grip, shortened recoil system, Troy front sight, folding BUIS rear sight, NiCorr surface treatment, black, FDE, Patriot Brown, or OD Green finish, 5 1/2 lbs. Disc. 2016.

	$1,825	$1,590	$1,325	$1,150	$995	$850	$700	$2,139

Add $153 for FDE, OD Green, or Patriot Brown finish.

SIX8-PDW (PERSONAL DEFENSE WEAPON) – 6.8 SPC cal., 8 1/2 in. barrel, JSG flash hider, Magpul MOE-K grip, one-piece gas block, 7 in. modular rail, LWRCI PDW carrier/buffer/stock system, polymer LWRCI rail panel/hand stop kit, Mil-Spec index plate, black anodized, FDE, OD Green, Patriot Brown, or Tungsten Grey Cerakote finish, 5.9 lbs.

MSR $2,649	$2,250	$1,960	$1,625	$1,400	$1,140	$995	$865	

Add $103 for FDE, OD Green, Patriot Brown, or Tungsten Grey Cerakote finish.

SIX8-PSD – 6.8 SPC II cal., GPO, sub-carbine length gas system, 8 1/2 in. cold hammer forged and NiCorr-treated heavy barrel, A2 birdcage flash hider, 30 shot Magpul mag., enlarged ejection port, enhanced fire control group, Skirmish backup iron sights, LWRCI pistol buffer tube, Magpul MOE+ grip, ambi sling mount, 12 in. user configurable rail system, ambi charging handle, fully ambidextrous lower receiver, includes Picatinny rail section and QD sling mount kit, 3 Rail Skins and foregrip, black anodized or Cerakote finishes in FDE, OD Green, Patriot Brown, or Tungsten Grey, 6 1/4 lbs. New 2015.

MSR $2,192	$1,875	$1,650	$1,400	$1,200	$1,025	$875	$725	

Add $153 for Patriot Brown, OD Green, FDE, or Tungsten Grey Cerakote finish.

RIFLES: SEMI-AUTO

LWRC manufactures a complete line of short-stroke, gas-piston operated AR-15 style, M-16, and M4 semi-auto rifles. These models have a wide variety of sights, accessories, and related hardware available. Please contact the company directly for more information on the available options (see Trademark Index).

C.S.A.S.S. – 7.62 NATO cal., GPO, 16.1 or 20 in. cold hammer forged spiral fluted heavy barrel, Geissele SSA two-stage precision trigger, LWRCI Skirmish BUIS, B5 SOPMOD (16.1 in. model) or Magpul PRS (Precision Rifle/Sniper, 20 in. model) stock, Magpul MOE Plus grip, 12 1/2 in. modular rail system, top side ambidextrous charging handle, nickel Teflon coated bolt carrier group, billet aluminum C.S.A.S.S. upper and lower receivers, black anodized or Cerakote finishes in FDE, Olive Drab, or Patriot Brown, 8 3/4-10 3/4 lbs. New 2016.

This model is available exclusively from a Talo group distributor.

IC-A2 (M6-IC-A2) – 5.56 NATO cal., GPO, carbine length gas system, 16.1 in. cold hammer forged match grade barrel, A2 birdcage flash hider, 30 shot mag., Skirmish backup iron sights, 6-position VLTOR EMOD (disc. 2016), Magpul MOE (disc. 2016), or LWRCI compact (new 2017) stock, H2 buffer, Magpul MIAD (disc. 2016), Magpul MOE+ (new 2017), or LWRCI SnakeSkin pistol grip with sight tool/battery storage (new 2018), H2 buffer, fully ambidextrous lower receiver, ambidextrous sling mount and charging handle, 9 in. quad rail with Picatinny rail sections, three polymer Rail Skins and Mil-Spec index plate, black anodized or FDE, OD Green, Patriot Brown, or Tungsten Grey Cerakote finish, 7.3 lbs.

MSR $2,294	$1,795	$1,050	$875	$625	$550	$475	$425	

Add $153 for FDE, OD Green, Patriot Brown, or Tungsten Grey finish.

LWRC INTERNATIONAL, INC., cont. 235 L

MSR		100%	98%	95%	90%	80%	70%	60%	Last MSR

IC-A5 (M6-IC-A5) – 5.56 NATO cal., GPO, mid-length gas system, 16.1 in. spiral fluted cold hammer forged barrel, A2 birdcage flash hider, LWRCI advanced trigger guard, Skirmish sights, LWRCI adj. compact stock with integrated sling mounting points, Magpul MOE+ grip or LWRCI SnakeSkin pistol grip with sight tool/battery storage (new 2018), full-length top Picatinny rail, ambidextrous charging handle, LWRCI enhanced fire control group, fully ambidextrous lower receiver, dual controls, QD index plate, black anodized or Cerakote finish in FDE, OD Green, Patriot Brown, or Tungsten Grey, 7.3 lbs. New 2015.

| | MSR $2,651 | $2,125 | $1,325 | $995 | $675 | $595 | $525 | $475 | |

Add $153 for Patriot Brown, OD Green, FDE, or Tungsten Grey Cerakote finish.

IC-DI – 5.56 NATO or .300 AAC Blackout cal., GIO, carbine or mid-length gas system, 16.1 in. cold hammer forged spiral fluted heavy barrel, A2 birdcage flash hider, LWRCI advanced trigger guard, LWRCI compact stock w/QD sling, angled ergonomic foregrip, Magpul MOE+ grip or LWRCI SnakeSkin pistol grip with secure storage (new 2018), modular one-piece free float rail, ambidextrous charging handle, Mil-Spec 6-position buffer tube, Monoforge one-piece upper, fully ambidextrous lower receiver, Type III hardcoat anodized black or FDE, Olive Drab, Patriot Brown, or Tungsten Grey Cerakote finish, 6.7 lbs. New late 2015.

| | MSR $1,631 | $1,350 | $875 | $650 | $525 | $450 | $385 | $350 | |

Add $100 for M-LOK handguard (new 2017).

IC-ENHANCED (M6-IC ENHANCED) – 5.56 NATO cal., GPO, 16.1 in. spiral fluted and NiCorr-treated barrel, A2 birdcage flash hider, 30 shot PMAG, enhanced trigger guard, Skirmish backup iron sights, LWRCI adj. compact stock, H2 buffer, Magpul MOE+ grip or LWRCI SnakeSkin pistol grip with sight tool/battery storage (new 2018), adj. two-position gas block with bayonet lug, ambidextrous charging handle and sling mount, 9 in. modular rail, includes Picatinny rail section and QD sling mount, black anodized or FDE, Olive Drab, Patriot Brown, or Tungsten Grey Cerakote finish, 7.3 lbs. New 2014.

| | MSR $2,549 | $2,050 | $1,250 | $950 | $650 | $575 | $495 | $475 | |

Add $153 for FDE, OD Green, or Patriot Brown Cerakote finish.

IC-SPR (M6-IC-SPR) – 5.56 NATO cal., GPO, mid-length gas system, 16.1 in. spiral fluted barrel with high efficiency 4-prong flash hider, 30 shot PMAG, enhanced trigger guard, Skirmish backup iron sights, LWRCI adj. compact stock, QD sling mount, Magpul MIAD (disc. 2016), Magpul MOE+ (new 2017), or LWRCI SnakeSkin pistol grip with sight tool/battery storage (new 2018), LWRCI one-position gas block, ambidextrous charging handle, 12 in. modular rail, includes Picatinny rail section and QD sling mount kit, black anodized or OD Green, FDE, Patriot Brown, or Tungsten Grey Cerakote finish, 7.3 lbs. New 2014.

| | MSR $2,396 | $1,875 | $1,100 | $895 | $650 | $575 | $495 | $425 | |

Add $153 for FDE, OD Green, Patriot Brown, or Tungsten Grey Cerakote finish.

M6-A3 – 5.56 NATO or 6.8 SPC cal., GPO, 16.1 or 18 in. barrel, A2 flash hider, 30 shot mag., VLTOR EMOD adj. stock, Magpul MIAD pistol grip, integrated flip down sight, ARM-R free float rail system, front sight is folding and incorporated in gas block, Olive Drab or black finish, 7.3 lbs.

| | | $1,875 | $1,100 | $895 | $650 | $575 | $495 | $425 | *$2,317* |

M6-A4 – 5.56 NATO or 6.8 SPC cal., GPO, 16 1/2 in. hammer forged steel barrel, 30 shot mag., VLTOR EMOD adj. stock, Magpul MIAD pistol grip, folding rear BUIS sight, folding front sight incorporated in gas block, front handle, quad rail, black finish, 7.4 lbs.

While advertised during 2011, this model has yet to be manufactured.

M6-G – 5.56 NATO or 6.8 SPC cal., GPO, 16.1 in. hammer forged steel barrel, 30 shot mag., Magpul MOE pistol grip stock, folding BUIS front and rear sights, enhanced fire control group, black finish, approx. 7 lbs.

While advertised during 2011, this model has yet to be manufactured.

M6-IC BASIC – 5.56 NATO cal., GPO, 16 in. fluted (first 500) or non-fluted barrel with A2 birdcage flash hider, Monoforge upper receiver, 9 in. M6 modular rail, FDE (initial run of 500 only) or black finish, Magpul MOE pistol grip stock, 7.3 lbs. Mfg. 2013-2014.

| | | $1,875 | $1,100 | $895 | $650 | $575 | $495 | $425 | *$2,349* |

Add $100 for fluted barrel.

M6-SL (STRETCH LIGHTWEIGHT) – 5.56 NATO or 6.8mm SPC cal., GPO, 16.1 in. light contour cold hammer forged barrel, A2 birdcage flash hider, 30 shot mag., enhanced fire control group, fixed A2 front sight, Daniel Defense fixed rear sight, 6-pos. Magpul CTR (disc. 2016) or LWRC adj. compact (new 2017) stock, MOE mid-length handguard and pistol grip, EXO (nickel boron) plated advanced combat bolt, one-piece coated carrier, black anodized or FDE, Patriot Brown or OD Green Cerakote finish, 6.6 lbs. Disc. 2016.

| | | $1,425 | $925 | $700 | $550 | $475 | $395 | $350 | *$1,709* |

Add $153 for FDE, Patriot Brown, or OD Green Cerakote finish.

M6-SPR (SPECIAL PURPOSE RIFLE) – 5.56 NATO or 6.8 SPC cal., GPO, 16.1 in. cold hammer forged fluted barrel, A2 flash hider, 30 shot mag., Magpul ACS stock, Magpul MIAD pistol grip, Skirmish folding BUIS front and rear sights, SPR-MOD rail, Bravo Company Mod4 Gunfighter charging handle, nickel coated bolt carrier and fire control group, black, OD Green, FDE or Patriot Brown finish, 7.3 lbs. Disc. 2014.

| | | $1,975 | $1,150 | $925 | $650 | $575 | $495 | $425 | *$2,479* |

236 LWRC INTERNATIONAL, INC., cont.

MSR	100%	98%	95%	90%	80%	70%	60%	Last MSR

R.E.P.R. (RAPID ENGAGEMENT PRECISION RIFLE) STRAIGHT – 7.62 NATO cal., GPO, 16, 18 (disc.), or 20 in. cold hammer forged heavy straight barrel, A2 birdcage flash hider, Geissele two-stage trigger, 6-position VLTOR EMOD (disc.), Magpul UBR (disc.), B5 SOPMOD (16 in. model) or Magpul PRS (20 in. model) stock, 5, 10, or 20 shot mag., Magpul MIAD pistol (disc.) or Magpul MOE Plus grip, folding BUIS (disc.) or Skirmish backup iron sights, sculpted ARM-R top rail, adj. two-position gas block, ambidextrous bolt release, left side mounted non-reciprocating charging handle, 12 1/2 in. modular rail system, black anodized or Cerakote finishes in Patriot Brown, OD Green, or FDE, 9.3-11 1/4 lbs. Disc. 2016.

| | $2,950 | $1,925 | $1,400 | $825 | $675 | $625 | $575 | $3,672 |

Add $153 for Patriot Brown, OD Green, or FDE Cerakote finish.

Add $204 for 20 in. barrel.

REPR MKII (R.E.P.R. SPIRAL) – 7.62 NATO cal., GPO, rifle length gas system, 16 or 20 in. spiral fluted cold hammer forged or Proof Research carbon fiber (new 2018) barrel, A2 birdcage flash hider (disc. 2017) or LWRCI Ultra Brake 4-port enhanced muzzle brake (new 2018), Geissele SSA-E two-stage trigger, enhanced fire control group, enhanced trigger guard, Skirmish backup iron sights, B5 SOPMOD (16 in. model, disc.), Magpul UBR (16 in. model), or Magpul PRS adj. (20 in. model) stock, Magpul MOE+ grip or LWRCI SnakeSkin pistol grip with sight tool/battery storage (new 2018), Monoforge upper receiver, 11 or 12 1/2 (disc.) in. modular rail system, two-position adj. gas block, side mounted non-reciprocating charging handle, includes Picatinny rail section with QD sling mount kit, black anodized or Cerakote finishes in FDE, Patriot Brown, OD Green, or Tungsten Grey, 9-10.4 lbs. New 2012.

| | $3,350 | $2,300 | $1,575 | $950 | $725 | $675 | $650 | |

Add $103 for Patriot Brown, OD Green, FDE, or Tungsten Grey Cerakote finish.

SIX8-A2 – 6.8 SPC II cal., GPO, 16.1 in. cold hammer forged and NiCorr-treated barrel with LWRCI flash hider, 30 shot PMAG, enlarged ejection port, claw extractor, Mil-Spec trigger, Skirmish backup iron sights, LWRCI adj. compact stock, Magpul MOE+ grip, two-position safety, nickel boron coated bolt carrier group, fully ambidextrous lower receiver, ambi charging handle, 9 in. ARM-R quad rail system, ambi sling mount, black anodized, FDE, Patriot Brown, or OD Green Cerakote finish, 7.3 lbs. New 2013.

| MSR $2,294 | | $1,795 | $1,050 | $875 | $625 | $550 | $475 | $425 |

Add $153 for FDE, Patriot Brown, or OD Green Cerakote finish.

SIX8-A5 – 6.8 SPC II cal., GPO, mid-length gas system, 16.1 in. cold hammer forged spiral fluted and NiCorr-treated barrel, A2 birdcage flash hider, 30 shot PMAG, claw extractor, enhanced fire control group, enhanced trigger guard, Skirmish backup iron sights, Magpul MOE (disc.) or LWRCI adj. compact stock with integrated quick detach points, Magpul MOE+ grip or LWRCI SnakeSkin pistol grip with sight tool/battery storage (new 2018), LWRCI A5 adj. two-position gas block, fully ambidextrous lower receiver, 12 in. user configurable rail system, includes Picatinny rail section and QD sling mount kit, ambi charging handle, black anodized or FDE, Olive Drab, Patriot Brown, or Tungsten Grey Cerakote finish, 7.3 lbs. New 2014.

| MSR $2,651 | | $2,125 | $1,325 | $995 | $675 | $595 | $525 | $475 |

Add $153 for Cerakote finish in Patriot Brown, OD Green, FDE, or Tungsten Grey.

SIX8-SPR – 6.8 SPC II cal., GPO, mid-length gas system, 16.1 in. cold hammer forged heavy barrel with LWRCI flash hider, Magpul 30 shot mag., dual extractor springs, claw extractor, enlarged ejection port, Skirmish sights, LWRCI adj. compact stock with integrated quick-detach points, Magpul MOE+ grip or LWRCI SnakeSkin pistol grip with sight tool/battery storage (new 2018), nickel boron coated bolt carrier group, enhanced fire control group, full-length Picatinny top rail, 12 in. user configurable rail system, ambidextrous charging handle, dual control fully ambidextrous lower receiver, black anodized or Cerakote finishes in FDE, OD Green, Patriot Brown, or Tungsten Grey, 7 .3 lbs. New 2013.

| MSR $2,549 | | $2,050 | $1,250 | $950 | $650 | $575 | $495 | $475 |

Add $153 for FDE, Patriot Brown, OD Green, or Tungsten Grey Cerakote finish.

LANCER SYSTEMS

Current AR-15 style rifle and accessories manufacturer located in Allentown, PA.

RIFLES: SEMI-AUTO

All L15 models ship with three 30 shot mags. and two 20 shot mags.

All L30 models ship with one 20 shot mag. and one 10 shot mag.

Add approx. $40 for Raddlock Device.

L15 COMPETITION – 5.56 NATO cal., .223 Wylde chamber, GIO, 18 in. stainless steel White Oak barrel, Wheaton Arms (disc.) or Lancer Nitrous compensator, extra long free floating handguard, LCS-A1-R Lancer fixed stock, Ergo grip, CMC trigger, 7.7 lbs. New 2013.

| MSR $2,139 | | $1,725 | $1,050 | $850 | $625 | $550 | $475 | $425 |

L15 DMR – 5.56 NATO cal., .223 Wylde chamber, 18 in. White Oak barrel with thread protector, Geissele Hi-Speed National Match two-stage trigger, B5 SOPMOD Bravo stock, Ergo grip, rifle length gas system, 15 in. Lancer LCH5 handguard, 7.3 lbs.

| MSR $2,327 | | $1,875 | $1,100 | $895 | $650 | $575 | $495 | $425 |

LANCER SYSTEMS, cont. 237

MSR	100%	98%	95%	90%	80%	70%	60%	Last MSR

L15 OUTLAW – 5.56 NATO cal., .223 Wylde chamber, 17 in. mid-weight profile Bartlein stainless steel barrel, Lancer Nitrous compensator, Geissele Super Dynamic 3-Gun trigger, LCS-A1-R fixed stock, Ergo grip, rifle length adj. gas block, Raptor charging handle, 15 in. Lancer LCR5 round handguard, 6 3/4 lbs.

	100%	98%	95%	90%	80%	70%	60%	Last MSR
MSR $2,855	$2,295	$1,450	$1,075	$675	$595	$525	$475	

L15 PATROL – 5.56 NATO cal., 16 in. mid-weight CHF chrome-lined barrel, Battle Comp compensator, Mil-Spec trigger, B5 Bravo stock, BCM Gunfighter grip, mid-length gas system, Lancer LCH5 12 in. handguard with 2 in. sight rail, single point sling mount, 6 1/2 lbs.

	100%	98%	95%	90%	80%	70%	60%	Last MSR
MSR $1,894	$1,575	$995	$775	$575	$495	$425	$395	

L15 SHARP SHOOTER – 5.56 NATO cal., GIO, 20 in. heavy profile Krieger barrel, Lancer extra long free float handguard, tactical Magwell lower receiver, EFX-A2 fixed stock, Ergo grip, CMC trigger, 8.9 lbs. Mfg. 2013-2015.

	100%	98%	95%	90%	80%	70%	60%	Last MSR
	$1,725	$1,050	$850	$625	$550	$475	$425	*$2,180*

L15 SPORTER – 5.56 NATO cal., GIO, 16 in. lightweight CHF chrome-lined barrel with A2 flash hider, mid-length gas system, Lancer handguard with 2 in. sight rail, tactical magwell lower receiver, F93 Pro stock, Ergo grip, Mil-Spec trigger, 7.4 lbs. New 2013.

	100%	98%	95%	90%	80%	70%	60%	Last MSR
MSR $1,688	$1,385	$895	$675	$525	$450	$385	$350	

L15 SUPER COMPETITION – 5.56 NATO cal., .223 Wylde chamber, GIO, upgraded version of the L15 Competition featuring 17 in. stainless steel Krieger barrel, Wheaton Arms SS (disc.) or Lancer Nitrous compensator, rifle length gas system, 15 in. Lancer LCH5 octagon handguard, EFX-A2 (disc.) or Lancer LCS-A1-R fixed stock, Ergo grip, CMC trigger, 7 1/2 lbs. New 2013.

	100%	98%	95%	90%	80%	70%	60%	Last MSR
MSR $2,525	$2,050	$1,250	$950	$650	$575	$495	$475	

L30 HEAVY METAL – 7.62 NATO cal., .308 Obermeyer chamber, 18 in. stainless steel White Oak barrel, Lancer Nitrous compensator, Geissele SD3G trigger, Lancer LCS stock, Ergo Tactical Deluxe grip, rifle length adj. gas block, Lancer carbon fiber handguard, 9 1/2 lbs.

	100%	98%	95%	90%	80%	70%	60%	Last MSR
MSR $3,345	$2,700	$1,775	$1,325	$750	$650	$595	$525	

L30 LRT (LONG RANGE TACTICAL) – 7.62 NATO or 6.5mm Creedmoor cal., 24 in. stainless steel Bartlein barrel, Lancer Viper muzzle brake, rifle length adj. gas block, billet aluminum upper with integral carbon fiber handguard and Picatinny rail, oversized mag. release button, ambidextrous bolt release, mission configurable lower receiver, Geissele Hi-Speed National Match trigger, KFS TacMod stock, Ergo Tactical Deluxe grip, 12 1/2 lbs.

	100%	98%	95%	90%	80%	70%	60%	Last MSR
	$3,450	$2,350	$1,600	$975	$725	$675	$650	

L30 MBR (MODERN BATTLE RIFLE) – 7.62 NATO cal., 16 in. black Nitride barrel, Lancer Nitrous compensator, Mil-Spec trigger, B5 SOPMOD stock, Ergo grip, rifle length gas system, Lancer carbon fiber handguard, 9 lbs.

	100%	98%	95%	90%	80%	70%	60%	Last MSR
MSR $2,560	$2,050	$1,250	$950	$650	$575	$495	$475	

LARUE TACTICAL

Current manufacturer established in 1980 and located in Leander, TX.

RIFLES: SEMI-AUTO

LaRue Tactical also offers a complete line of both parts and accessories, including scope mounts, trigger assemblies, and cases.

6.5 GRENDEL FDE RIFLE – 6.5 Grendel cal., 18 in. barrel, LaRue TranQuilo muzzle brake, 5 or 17 shot mag., LaRue MBT-2S trigger, 13 in. handguard, includes LT-104 30mm scope mount, FDE finish, 7 lbs. 13 oz.

	100%	98%	95%	90%	80%	70%	60%	Last MSR
MSR $1,999	$1,650	$1,000	$795	$595	$495	$425	$395	

COSTA SIGNATURE EDITION – 5.56 NATO cal., GIO, 16.1 in. barrel, SureFire muzzle brake, FDE KG GunKote finish, "COSTA LUDUS" logo engraved on left side of receiver, black parts and rail covers, first 500 units are match numbered on the upper and lower. Mfg. 2013-2015.

	100%	98%	95%	90%	80%	70%	60%	Last MSR
	$4,995	$4,500	$4,000	$3,500	$3,000	$2,500	$2,000	*$2,895*

FDE LIMITED EDITION PREDATAR – 7.62 NATO cal., AR-15 style, GIO w/PST (Port Selector Technology), 16 in. heavy barrel, LaRue M308 TranQuilo muzzle brake, 1/10 twist, three 20 round mags., FDE Cerakote finish w/select black parts and GAP rail covers. Approx. 125 mfg. Disc.

Rarity precludes accurate pricing on this model.

OBR (OPTIMIZED BATTLE RIFLE) – 5.56 NATO (new 2011) or .308 Win. cal., AR-15 style, GIO, 16.1, 18, or 20 in. barrel, A2 flash hider, 20 shot box mag., flared magwell, Troy front and optional BUIS rear sight, A2 fixed (20 in. barrel only) or Retract Action Trigger (R.A.T.) stock, A-PEG grip, adj. gas block, detachable side rails, Mil-Std 1913 one-piece upper rail, black anodized finish, approx. 10 lbs.

	100%	98%	95%	90%	80%	70%	60%	Last MSR
5.56 MSR $2,245	$1,795	$1,050	$875	$625	$550	$475	$425	
7.62 MSR $3,370	$2,700	$1,775	$1,325	$750	$650	$595	$525	

A variety of accessories are available on this model for additional cost.

L 238 LARUE TACTICAL, cont.

MSR	100%	98%	95%	90%	80%	70%	60%	Last MSR

PREDATAR – 5.56 NATO or .308 Win./7.62 NATO (new 2013) cal., GIO, 16.1 or 18 in. contoured stainless steel barrel, A2 flash hider, 30 shot mag., 6-position Magpul (disc.) or LaRue R.A.T. stock, A-PEG grip, skeletonized handguard, quad rail forend, charging lever, forward assist, Geissele two-stage trigger, black phosphate finish, approx. 6 1/2 lbs. New mid-2011.

| 5.56 MSR $1,807 | $1,525 | $975 | $750 | $575 | $495 | $425 | $375 |
| 7.62 MSR $2,932 | $2,375 | $1,525 | $1,150 | $700 | $625 | $550 | $475 |

A variety of accessories are available on this model for additional cost.

PREDATOBR – 5.56 NATO, 7.62 NATO, or .260 Rem. cal., GIO, 16.1, 18, 20, or 22 (.260 Rem. only) in. threaded free float barrel, 20 (7.72) or 30 (5.56) shot mag., LaRue MBT trigger, 6-pos. Retract Action Trigger (R.A.T.) stock., adj. gas block, billet aluminum upper and lower receivers, 3 Mil-Std 1913 rail sections. New 2014.

| 5.56 MSR $2,245 | $1,795 | $1,050 | $875 | $625 | $550 | $475 | $425 |
| 7.62 & .260 MSR $3,370 | $2,700 | $1,775 | $1,325 | $750 | $650 | $595 | $525 |

A variety of accessories are available on this model for additional cost.

UDE LIMITED EDITION PREDATOBR – 5.56 NATO cal., AR-15 style, GIO w/PST (Port Selector Technology), 16 in. barrel, LaRue M556 TranQuilo muzzle brake, 1:8 twist, two 30 round mags., black LaRue MBT trigger, UDE LaRue R.A.T. stock and A-PEG pistol grip, UDE GAP rail covers and index clips, UDE finish w/select black part. Approx. 125 mfg. numbered 001-125. Disc.

| | $2,950 | $2,625 | $2,250 | $2,050 | $1,650 | $1,350 | $1,050 |

LAUER CUSTOM WEAPONRY

Current manufacturer of DuraCoat® firearm finishes and custom carbines/rifles located in Chippewa Falls, WI.

RIFLES: SEMI-AUTO

LCW15 BATTLE RIFLE – 5.56 NATO cal., AR-15 style, GIO (available with LCW's MaxGas proprietary high performance gas system), 16 in. barrel, A3 flat-top or A2 carry handle on upper receiver, shorty carbine handguard, A2 buttstock, one 30 shot GI mag., black or Afghan camo finish.
Please contact the manufacturer directly for pricing and availability.

LCW15 TARGET RIFLE – 5.56 NATO cal., GIO (MaxGas proprietary gas system), 24 in. stainless steel bull barrel, matching serial number on upper and lower receiver, A3 flat-top upper receiver, match target trigger, free float aluminum handguard, A2 buttstock, one 20 shot mag., includes hard case and ear plugs.
Please contact the manufacturer directly for pricing and availability.

LCW15 URBAN RESPONDER – 5.56 NATO cal., AR-15 style, GIO, CQB precision carbine, M4 barrel with A2 flash hider, 30 shot mag., TriPower illuminated sight, M6 tactical laser illuminator with remote switch, lightweight 4-rail tactical free float handguard, forward grip, compact skeleton stock, tactical grip with storage compartment, DPMS quick response rear flip-up sight, A.R.M.S. 17 mount, LCW 3-point tactical sling, Urban MirageFlage finish, 7 1/2 lbs.
Please contact the manufacturer directly for pricing and availability.

LAYKE TACTICAL

Current manufacturer of semi-auto pistols and rifles established in 1955, located in Phoenix, AZ.

PISTOLS: SEMI-AUTO

LT9-HD 9mm PISTOL – 9mm Para. cal., 4 or 8 in. barrel, 15 shot Magpul mag., Mil-Spec trigger, Hogue grip, 4 or 7 in. KeyMod handguard, KAK Shockwave (disc.) or SBA3 brace, Type III hardcoat anodized black finish, 5 lbs. 15 oz.

| MSR $999 | $850 | $550 | $465 | $395 | $350 | $325 | $295 |

RIFLES: SEMI-AUTO

LT9-HD RIFLE – 9mm Para. cal., 16 in. barrel, Mil-Spec trigger, Hogue grip, Mission First Minimalist brace, 15 in. KeyMod handguard, Type III hardcoat anodized black finish, 6 lbs. 11 oz.

| MSR $999 | $850 | $550 | $465 | $395 | $350 | $325 | $295 |

LT10-HD TACTICAL – .308 Win. cal., 20 in. Nitride barrel, Magpul STR stock, Hogue grip, Odin Works rail, KAK double extractor Nitride bolt, Type III hardcoat anodized black, black/FDE, black/ODG, black/Forest Green, Forest Green/ODG, Burnt Bronze/black, red/black, blue/black, or purple/black finish, 9 lbs. 8 oz.

| MSR $1,599 | $1,315 | $850 | $625 | $500 | $435 | $375 | $350 |

LT15-HD CARBINE – 5.56 NATO cal., 16 in. Nitride barrel, aluminum construction, Mil-Spec trigger, MFT Minimalist stock, Hogue grip, Magpul MOE handguard, Layke NiB bolt, Type III hardcoat anodized black, black/FDE, black/ODG, black/Forest Green, Forest Green/ODG, Burnt Bronze/black, red/black, blue/black, purple/black, silver/silver, silver/black, or gold/black finish, 7 lbs.

| MSR $999 | $850 | $550 | $465 | $395 | $350 | $325 | $295 |

LAYKE TACTICAL, cont. 239 L

MSR	100%	98%	95%	90%	80%	70%	60%	Last MSR

LT15-HD SPORT – 5.56 NATO cal., 16 in. Nitride barrel, aluminum construction, Mil-Spec trigger, Magpul CTR, SL, or MFT Minimalist stock, Hogue grip, 15 in. ODIN Works KeyMod rail in black or matching, Layke NiB-X bolt, Type III hardcoat anodized black, black/FDE, black/ODG, black/Forest Green, Forest Green/ODG, Burnt Bronze/black, red/black, blue/black, purple/black, silver/silver, silver/black, or gold/black finish, 7 lbs.

	100%	98%	95%	90%	80%	70%	60%	Last MSR
MSR $1,099	$915	$575	$475	$415	$350	$325	$300	

LEGION FIREARMS LLC

Previous firearms/accessories manufacturer and importer located in Temple, TX until 2014.

CARBINES: SEMI-AUTO

LF-10D CARBINE – .308 Win. or 7.62x51 NATO cal., GIO, 16 in. stainless steel barrel, three land polygonal rifling, M4 feed ramps, hex milled fluting, SureFire muzzle brake, micro MOA adj. gas block, aluminum aircraft grade nickel boron coated upper and lower receiver, 12 in. Legion quad-channel concept handguard, ceramic wear resistant coating, Raptor .308 charging handle, ambidextrous bolt release, Phase 5 tactical REVO sling attachment system, BAD lever 90 degree ambi safety selector, Magpul MOE pistol grip, B5 Systems enhanced SOPMOD stock, H3 heavy buffer, steel bolt carrier, single stage trigger, available in Alpha Grey, Burnt Bronze, FDE, OD Green, Sniper Grey, or Black finish. Mfg. 2011-2014.

	100%	98%	95%	90%	80%	70%	60%	Last MSR
	$2,895	$2,525	$2,050	$1,750	$1,450	$1,225	$1,050	$3,390

LF-15D CARBINE – 5.56 NATO cal., GIO, 16 in. stainless steel barrel, three land polygonal rifling, M4 feed ramps, hex milled fluting, aluminum aircraft grade nickel boron coated upper and lower receiver, Wilson Combat handguard, ceramic wear resistant coating, drilled and tapped, ambidextrous bolt release, available in Alpha Grey, Burnt Bronze, Flat Dark Earth, OD Green, Sniper Grey, or Black finish, Noveske QD endplate, single stage trigger, adj. tactical stock, H2 heavy buffer, lightweight billet modular design. Mfg. 2011-2014.

	100%	98%	95%	90%	80%	70%	60%	Last MSR
	$1,875	$1,100	$895	$650	$575	$495	$425	$2,390

LEITNER-WISE DEFENSE, INC.

Current AR-15 style parts/accessories manufacturer located in Alexandria, VA. The company discontinued its semi-auto line of rifles circa 2010.

RIFLES: SEMI-AUTO

M.U.L.E. MOD. 1 (MODULAR URBAN LIGHT ENGAGEMENT CARBINE) – 5.56 NATO cal., GPO, 16 in. steel barrel standard, other lengths optional, op-rod operating system, single stage trigger, Magpul ACS buttstock, MOE pistol grip, black finish, upper and lower rails, 30 shot mag., flared magwell, E sights, includes one mag., manual, and cleaning kit, 7.9 lbs. Disc. circa 2010.

	100%	98%	95%	90%	80%	70%	60%	Last MSR
	$1,385	$895	$675	$525	$450	$385	$350	$1,680

Add $100 for precision trigger.

M.U.L.E. MOD. 2 (MODULAR URBAN LIGHT ENGAGEMENT CARBINE) – .308 Win. cal., GPO, 16 or 20 in. steel barrel, similar to Mod. 1, except has heavier barrel, 8 1/2 lbs. Disc. circa 2010.

	100%	98%	95%	90%	80%	70%	60%	Last MSR
	$1,725	$1,050	$850	$625	$550	$475	$425	$2,100

Add $100 for 20 in. barrel.

LEITNER-WISE RIFLE CO. INC.

Previous manufacturer located in Springfield, VA circa 2006. Previously located in Alexandria, VA 1999-2005.

RIFLES: SEMI-AUTO

LW 15.22 – .22 LR or .22 WMR cal., GIO, patterned after the AR-15, 16 1/2 or 20 in. barrel, forged upper and lower receivers, choice of carry handle or flat-top upper receiver, forward bolt assist, last shot hold open, 10 or 25 shot mag. Mfg. 2000-2005.

	100%	98%	95%	90%	80%	70%	60%	Last MSR
	$550	$495	$450	$400	$350	$300	$275	$850

Add $50 for A2 carrying handle.

LW 15.499 – .499 (12.5x40mm) cal., receiver and action patterned after the AR-15, Mil-Spec standards, 16 1/2 in. steel or stainless steel barrel, flat-top receiver, 5 (disc.), 10, or 14 (new 2006) shot mag., approx. 6 1/2 lbs. Mfg. 2000-2005.

	100%	98%	95%	90%	80%	70%	60%	Last MSR
	$1,350	$1,150	$995	$875	$750	$675	$600	

Add $92 for stainless steel barrel.

LW 6.8/5.56 S.R.T. – 5.56x45mm NATO or 6.8x43mm SPC cal., 16.1 in. barrel, hard chrome-lined bore, gas operated, locking bolt, Troy front and rear sights, forged T7075 aluminum flat-top upper receiver, 6-position collapsible stock, Picatinny rail, removable carry handle, A2 flash hider, LW forged lower receiver, 28 or 30 shot mag., 5.38 lbs. Ltd. mfg. 2006.

	100%	98%	95%	90%	80%	70%	60%	Last MSR
	$2,050	$1,800	$1,600	$1,400	$1,200	$1,000	$850	

Add $100 for 6.8x43mm SPC cal.

240 LES BAER CUSTOM, INC.

MSR	100%	98%	95%	90%	80%	70%	60%	Last MSR

LES BAER CUSTOM, INC.

Current manufacturer and customizer established in 1993, located in LeClaire, IA since 2008. Previously located in Hillsdale, IL until 2008. Dealer sales only.

RIFLES: SEMI-AUTO

CUSTOM ULTIMATE AR MODEL – .204 Ruger (new 2004), .223 Rem., or 6.5 Grendel (mfg. 2007-2009) cal., 18-24 in. stainless steel barrel, Picatinny flat-top rail, individual rifles are custom built with no expense spared, everything made in-house ensuring top quality and tolerances, all models are guaranteed to shoot 1/2-3/4 MOA groups, various configurations include Varmint Model (disc.), Super Varmint Model, Super Match Model (new 2002), M4 Flat-Top Model, Thunder Ranch (disc. 2010), CMP Competion (disc.) and IPSC Action Model. New 2001.

MSR $2,590 $2,350 $2,050 $1,500 $1,000 $750 $650 $550

Add $50 for Super Varmint model in .223 Rem. or $280 in .204 Ruger cal. Add $950 with scope package.

Add $150 for Super Match model in .223 Rem. or $370 in .204 Ruger cal. Add $1,359 with scope package.

Add $300 for IPSC action model or $1,350 with scope package.

Add $349 for Thunder Ranch rifle (disc. 2010). Add $849 for CMP competition rifle (disc.).

Add $245 for Super Varmint model (.204 Ruger cal., disc.) or $210 for 6.5 Grendel cal. with M4 style barrel (disc.).

CUSTOM NRA MATCH RIFLE – .223 Rem. cal., 30 in. bench rest stainless steel barrel, 30 shot mag., forged upper and lower receivers, Picatinny flat-top rail, LBC chromed bolt, extractor, and National Match carrier, Geissele two-stage trigger, free float handguard with locking ring, custom grip with extra material under the trigger guard, Dupont S coating on upper, lower, and small parts, available with or without sights package. Disc. 2017.

    $2,650 $2,300 $1,750 $1,250 $950 $800 $650   *$2,950*

Add $1,040 for sights package.

CUSTOM SPECIAL TACTICAL RIFLE – .223 Rem., 16 in. stainless steel fluted bench rest barrel, two 20 shot mags., Geissele non-adj. two-stage trigger, free float handguard with mounted sling stud, forged upper and lower receivers, Picatinny style flat-top rail, extractor, unique sighting system, includes nylon weather proof sling and lockable front sling swivel, detachable carry handle, Dupont S coating, 7 lbs. 6 oz. New 2011.

MSR $2,720 $2,450 $2,150 $1,625 $1,150 $875 $725 $600

.264 LBC-AR M4 FLATTOP – .264 LBC-AR cal., 16 in. medium weight barrel, two 14 shot mags., 9 in. four-way handguard with locking ring and integral Picatinny rail system, VersaPod installed, free float handguard, fixed stock, Dupont S coating, black finish, includes soft rifle case. New 2010.

MSR $2,790 $2,475 $2,175 $1,635 $1,150 $875 $725 $600

.264 LBC-AR SUPER MATCH – .264 LBC-AR cal., stainless steel barrel, fixed stock, black finish, 14 shot mag., features similar to Super Match Model in .223 cal. New 2010.

MSR $2,840 $2,550 $2,225 $1,685 $1,200 $915 $765 $625

.264 LBC-AR SUPER VARMINT – .264 LBC-AR cal., stainless steel bench rest barrel, two 14 shot mags., fixed stock, black finish, features similar to Super Varmint model in .223 cal. New 2010.

MSR $2,640 $2,400 $2,100 $1,565 $1,075 $825 $685 $575

6x45 ULTIMATE AR – 6x45mm cal., 18-24 in. stainless steel barrel, available in Super Varmint, Super Match, and M4 Flat-top configurations, black finish, fixed stock, similar to Ultimate AR in .223 configuration. New 2010.

MSR $2,640 $2,400 $2,100 $1,565 $1,075 $825 $685 $575

Add $100 for Super Match model.

POLICE SPECIAL – .223 Rem., .264 LBC-AR (disc.), or 6x45mm (disc.) cal., 16 in. precision button rifled steel barrel, 14 or 30 shot mag., removable carry handle with rear sight, Picatinny flat-top upper rail, National Match chromed carrier, flip-up front sight, six position ATI collapsible stock with adj. cheekpiece and grip, Picatinny four-way handguard, A2 flash hider, Timney match trigger group, lockable sling swivel mounted on stud on four-way handguard, includes two mags. Mfg. 2010-2014.

    $1,600 $1,425 $1,050 $750 $575 $485 $395   *$1,790*

.308 LBC ULTIMATE MATCH/SNIPER – .308 Win. cal., 18 or 20 in. stainless steel barrel with precision cut rifling, matte black finish, 20 shot mag., machined upper and lower, no forward assist, Picatinny flat-top rail, steel gas block, free float handguard with lock ring, two-stage trigger group, Dupont S coating on barrel, Harris bipod, fixed or adj. Magpul stock, with or w/o enforcer muzzle brake, available in Match or Sniper (disc.) configuration. New 2011.

MSR $3,640 $3,350 $2,975 $2,350 $1,650 $1,275 $1,000 $800

Add $30 for Match model with PRS Magpul stock.

Add $300 for Sniper model with adj. stock and enforcer muzzle brake (disc.)

.308 ULTIMATE MONOLITH SWAT MODEL – .308 Win. cal., 18 or 24 in. stainless steel barrel with precision cut rifling, matte black finish, 20 shot mag., similar to .308 Ultimate Match/Sniper, except has integrated Mil-Std 1913

LES BAER CUSTOM, INC., cont. 241 L

MSR	100%	98%	95%	90%	80%	70%	60%	Last MSR

Picatinny rail system, Magpul PRS adj. stock, Versa pod and adapter, integral trigger guard is bowed on bottom so shooter can wear gloves. New 2011.

MSR $4,390 $4,100 $3,750 $3,250 $2,595 $1,950 $1,450 $1,000

LEWIS MACHINE & TOOL COMPANY (LMT)

Current tactical rifle and accessories manufacturer established in 1980, and located in Milan, IL.

RIFLES/CARBINES: SEMI-AUTO

LMT manufactures AR-15 style rifles and carbines.

CQB – 5.56 NATO, 6.8 SPC, or .300 AAC Blackout cal., GIO, 16 in. chrome-lined barrel, two-stage trigger, flip-up sights, SOPMOD stock, ergonomic textured grip, built with the MRP (Monolithic Rail Platform), CQB upper with continuous Picatinny rail, and MARS-L lower receiver, low profile gas block and straight gas tube, ambi charging handle, bolt catch, mag. catch, and safety selector, S-A BCG, includes tactical two-point sling and 3 rail panel covers, black or FDE finish is standard, various Cerakote colors also available.

MSR $2,499 $1,975 $1,150 $925 $650 $575 $495 $425

CQB16COP – 5.56 NATO cal., GIO, SST, flip-up sights, SOPMOD stock, ergonomic textured grip, CQB upper receiver has 16 1/4 in. Picatinny rail, MRP (Monolithic Rail Platform), low profile gas block, straight gas tube, includes tactical two-point sling and 3 rail panel covers, Distressed Copper Cerakote finish. Limited mfg. beginning 2018.

MSR $1,999 $1,650 $1,000 $795 $595 $495 $425 $395

CQB MRP DEFENDER MODEL 16 (CQB16 / CQB16 6.8 / CQB16300) – 5.56 NATO, 6.8 SPC (new 2010), or .300 Whisper cal., GIO, 16 in. chrome-lined barrel with A2 birdcage compensator, 25 (6.8 SPC) or 30 (5.56 NATO or .300 Whisper) shot mag., standard trigger, tactical adj. front and rear sights, SOPMOD stock, CQB upper and Defender lower receiver, tactical charging handle assembly, includes sling, heavy duty push button swivels, manual, tactical adj. front and rear sights, torque wrench/driver, and three rail panels, 6.8 lbs. Disc. 2017.

     $1,875 $1,100 $895 $650 $575 $495 $425   *$2,349*

Add $350 for 6.8 SPC cal.

CQBMWS – .308 Win. cal., GIO, 16 or 20 in. chrome-lined standard or lightweight barrel, Magpul 20 shot polymer mag., two-stage trigger, flip-up sights, SOPMOD stock, ergonomic textured grip, ambi mag. catch and safety selector, built with the MWS (Modular Weapon System) platform, CQBMWS upper and 308MWS lower receiver, top Picatinny rail, low profile gas block and straight gas tube, tactical charging handle, includes tactical two-point sling and 3 rail panel covers, black or FDE finish is standard, various Cerakote colors are also available, 9.9 lbs.

MSR $3,529 $2,875 $1,875 $1,375 $795 $675 $625 $575

Add $50 for lightweight barrel.

CQBMWSF – 6.5mm Creedmoor, .243 Win., .260 Rem., 7mm-08 Rem., .308 Win., or .338 Federal cal., GIO, 16 (7.62x51 only), 18 (7.62x51 only), 20, or 24 (6.5mm Creedmoor only) in. stainless steel barrel, Magpul 20 shot polymer mag., two-stage trigger, flip-up sights, SOPMOD stock, ergonomic textured grip, built with the MWS platform, CQBMWS upper and 308 MWS lower receiver, top Picatinny rail, tactical charging handle, low profile gas block and straight tube, ambi mag. catch and safety selector, includes sling and 3 rail panel covers, black or FDE finish is standard, various Cerakote colors also available, 10.23 lbs.

MSR $3,629 $2,950 $1,925 $1,400 $825 $675 $625 $575

Add $50 for lightweight barrel (.308 Win. cal. only).
Subtract $50 for .243 Win., .260 Rem., 7mm-08 Rem., or .338 Federal cal.

CQBODGB – 5.56 NATO cal., GIO, 16 in. heavy barrel with A2 birdcage compensator, 30 shot mag., tactical sights, Defender lower with SOPMOD buttstock, low profile gas block, CQB MRP upper, tactical charging handle, tactical sights, three rail panels, Olive Drab Green finish, 6.8 lbs. Disc. 2016.

     $1,725 $1,050 $850 $625 $550 $475 $425   *$2,100*

CQBPU16 – 5.56 NATO cal., GPO, 16 in. chrome-lined barrel, charging handle, H2 buffer, includes torque wrench and 3 rail panels. Disc. 2013.

     $1,315 $850 $625 $500 $435 $375 $350   *$1,558*

CQBPS (CQB MRP DEFENDER PISTON 16 -CQBPS16 / CQBBPS68) – 5.56 NATO or 6.8 SPC (new 2014) cal., GPO, standard/suppressed option gas block with removable piston rod and spring, 16 in. chrome-lined barrel, 25 (6.8 SPC) or 30 (5.56 NATO) shot mag., ergonomic textured grip, SOPMOD stock, SST, flip-up sights, built with the MRP (Monolithic Rail Platform), CQB upper and Defender (disc.) or MARS-L lower receiver, top Picatinny rail, ambi charging handle, bolt/mag. catch, and safety selector, includes sling and 3 rail panel covers, black or FDE finish is standard, various Cerakote colors are also available, 7.5 lbs. New 2010.

MSR $2,739 $2,225 $1,395 $1,050 $675 $595 $525 $475

L 242 LEWIS MACHINE & TOOL COMPANY (LMT), cont.

MSR	100%	98%	95%	90%	80%	70%	60%	Last MSR

CMP556 – 5.56 NATO cal., GIO, 20 in. ultra cut rifled stainless steel barrel, 30 shot mag., standard flat-top upper receiver, charging handle, Defender lower with fixed rifle length buttstock and standard trigger group, includes sling. Disc. 2017.

	$1,795	$1,050	$875	$625	$550	$475	$425	$2,205

COMPLIANT CQB MRP DEFENDER MODEL 16 (COMPCQB16) – 5.56 NATO cal., GIO, 16 in. chrome-lined target style barrel, tactical charging handle, Defender lower receiver with fixed SOPMOD buttstock and standard trigger group, tactical sights, 10 shot mag., has three rail panels, push button swivel, and includes sling. Disc. 2017.

	$1,795	$1,050	$875	$625	$550	$475	$425	$2,205

COMPLIANT DEFENDER STANDARD MODEL 16 (COMP16) – 5.56 NATO cal., GIO, 16 in. chrome-lined target style barrel, standard flat-top upper receiver, 10 shot mag., tactical charging handle assembly, Defender lower with fixed SOPMOD buttstock, standard trigger group, includes sling, tactical adj. rear sight, and heavy duty push button swivel. Disc. 2017.

	$1,385	$895	$675	$525	$450	$385	$350	$1,685

LM8 – 5.56 NATO, 6.8 SPC, or .300 AAC Blackout cal., GIO, 16 in. chrome-lined barrel, SST, flip-up sights, SOPMOD stock, ergonomic textured grip, built with the MRP (Monolithic Rail Platform), LM8 upper receiver with continuous top Picatinny rail, ambi charging handle, bolt catch, mag. catch, and safety selector, S-A BCG, MARS-L lower, low profile gas block and straight gas tube, includes tactical two-point sling, four rail segments, and 6 segmented grip panels, black or FDE finish is standard, various Cerakote colors are also available.

MSR $2,499	$1,975	$1,150	$925	$650	$575	$495	$425	

LM8MRP / LM8MRPSS – 5.56 NATO cal., GIO, 16 in. chrome-lined or stainless steel barrel, 30 shot mag., tactical charging handle, Defender lower receiver with SOPMOD buttstock and standard trigger group, tactical sights, four rail segments, rubberized grip panels, includes sling. Mfg. 2012-2017.

	$1,975	$1,150	$925	$650	$575	$495	$425	$2,489

Add $100 for 16 in. stainless steel barrel (LM8MRPSS).

LM8MRPSC (SLK8) – 5.56 NATO cal., GIO, 16 or 20 in. ultra match stainless steel barrel, 30 shot mag., two-stage trigger, no sights, four rail segments, six rubberized grip panels, heavy duty push-button swivels, Long Slick upper receiver with SOPMOD 6-position adj. stock, tactical charging handle with Ergo Battle grip, two-position selector safety, Type III hardcoat anodized finish, 7 lbs. 2 oz. Mfg. 2014-2017.

	$2,225	$1,395	$1,050	$675	$595	$525	$475	$2,799

LM8MWSLTFDE – .308 Win. cal., GIO, 16 in. chrome-lined barrel with A2 birdcage compensator, 20 shot mag., two-stage trigger, tactical sights, Defender lower with SOPMOD buttstock, low profile gas block, tactical charging handle, ambi selector and mag. release, four rail segments, slick upper receiver, 5 QD sling swivel attachment points, includes sling, Flat Dark Earth finish, 9.3 lbs. Mfg. 2015-2016.

	$2,775	$1,825	$1,350	$750	$650	$595	$525	$3,456

LM8MWS (LM8MWS SLICK RECEIVER RIFLE) – .308 Win. cal., GIO, 16 or 20 in. chrome-lined barrel, 20 shot mag., Monolithic Rail Platform, LM8MWS upper and Defender (disc. 2017) or 308MWS lower receiver, SOPMOD stock, rubberized grip panels (disc.) or ergonomic textured grip, two-stage trigger, tactical charging handle, top Picatinny rail, low profile gas block and straight gas tube, includes sling, manual, tactical front and rear sights, torque wrench/driver, and four rail panels. New 2010.

MSR $3,529	$2,875	$1,875	$1,375	$795	$675	$625	$575	

Add $50 for lightweight barrel.

LM8MWSF – 6.5mm Creedmoor, .243 Win., .260 Rem., 7mm-08 Rem., .308 Win., or .338 Federal cal., GIO, 16 (.308 Win. only), 18 (.308 Win. only), 20, or 24 (6.5mm Creedmoor only) in. stainless steel barrel with black finish, Magpul 20 shot polymer mag., two-stage trigger, flip-up sights, SOPMOD stock, ergonomic textured grip, built with the MWS platform, LM8MWS upper and 308MWS lower receiver, top Picainny rail, tactical charging handle, low profile gas block and straight tube, ambi mag. catch and safety selector, includes sling and 3 rail panel covers, black or FDE finish is standard, various Cerakote colors also available, 10.14 lbs.

MSR $3,629	$2,950	$1,925	$1,400	$825	$675	$625	$575	

Add $50 for lightweight barrel (.308 Win. cal. only).

Subtract $50 for .243 Win., .260 Rem., 7mm-08 Rem., or .338 Federal cal.

LM8PS – 5.56 NATO or 6.8 SPC cal., GPO, standard/suppressed option gas block with removable piston rod and spring, 16 in. chrome-lined barrel, 25 (6.8 SPC) or 30 (5.56 NATO) shot mag., SST, flip-up sights, SOPMOD stock, ergonomic textured grip, built with the MRP (Monolithic Rail Platform), LM8 upper and MARS-L lower receiver, top Picatinny rail, ambi charging handle, bolt/mag. catch, and safety selector, includes sling, 4 rail segments, and 6 segmented grip panels, black or FDE finish is standard, various Cerakote colors are also available, 7.4 lbs.

MSR $2,739	$2,225	$1,395	$1,050	$675	$595	$525	$475	

LEWIS MACHINE & TOOL COMPANY (LMT), cont. 243 L

MSR	100%	98%	95%	90%	80%	70%	60%	Last MSR

LM308 COMP16 – .308 Win. cal., GIO, 16 in. crowned target barrel, 10 shot mag., tactical charging handle, two-stage match trigger, ambi selector, tactical sights, SOPMOD buttstock, includes 3 rail panels. Mfg. 2012-2017.

	$2,950	$1,925	$1,400	$825	$675	$625	$575	*$3,629*

LM308SS (SHARPSHOOTER WEAPON SYSTEM) – .308 Win. cal., GIO, 16 in. stainless steel barrel with black finish, eight 20 shot Magpul polymer mags., two-stage trigger, flip-up sights, SOPMOD stock, ergonomic textured grip, built with the MWS (Modular Weapon System) platform, CQBMWS upper receiver with continuous top Picatinny rail, 308MWS lower receiver is engraved with "Sharpshooter" logo, low profile gas block and straight gas tube, ambi mag. catch and safety selector, includes bipod, sliding QD mount, tactical two-point sling, 3 rail panel covers, and Pelican hard case, FDE finish. New 2012.

MSR $5,999	$5,050	$4,400	$3,800	$3,450	$2,800	$2,300	$1,750	

LM308SSR – 7.62x51 cal., GIO, 16 in. stainless steel barrel with black finish, Magpul 20 shot polymer mag., two-stage trigger, flip-up sights, SOPMOD stock, ergonomic textured grip, built with MWS (Modular Weapon System), CQBMWS upper receiver with continuous top Picatinny rail, low profile gas block and straight gas tube, 308MWS lower receiver is engraved with "Sharpshooter" logo, ambi mag. catch and safety selector, includes tactical two-point sling and 3 rail panel covers, FDE finish.

MSR $3,999	$3,200	$2,150	$1,525	$895	$695	$650	$575	

LM308MWSE MODULAR WEAPON SYSTEM – .308 Win. cal., GIO, 16 in. chrome-lined barrel, 20 shot mag., two-stage match trigger, SOPMOD buttstock, tactical sights, tactical charging handle, includes 3 rail panels and sling. Mfg. 2012-2017.

	$2,875	$1,875	$1,375	$795	$675	$625	$575	*$3,529*

* LM308MWSF/MWSK Modular Weapon System Stainless – .308 Win. cal., similar to Modular Weapon System (LM308MWSE), except features 16 or 20 in. stainless steel barrel with tactically flat matte blackened finish. Mfg. 2012-2017.

	$3,050	$1,975	$1,425	$850	$675	$625	$575	*$3,739*

LMT 6.5 LONG RANGE – 6.5mm Creedmoor cal., GIO, 24 in. stainless steel barrel, 3-prong flash hider, Magpul 20 shot polymer mag., two-stage trigger, DMR buttstock, ergonomic textured grip, ambi mag. catch and safety selector, MLKMWS upper receiver with 19 1/4 in. Picatinny rail, M-LOK compatible attachment points, low profile gas block, ambi mag. catch and safety selector, black finish, 10.14 lbs. New 2018.

MSR $1,649	$1,350	$875	$650	$525	$450	$385	$350	

MLC – 5.56 NATO, 6.8 SPC, or .300 AAC Blackout cal., GIO, 16 in. chrome-lined barrel, SST, flip-up sights, SOPMOD stock, ergonomic textured grip, built with the MRP (Monolithic Rail Platform), MLC upper and MARS-L lower receiver, top Picatinny rail, M-LOK compatible attachment points, low profile gas block and straight gas tube, ambi charging handle, bolt catch, mag. catch, and safety selector, flip-up sights, includes sling and 3 grip panels, black and FDE finish is standard, various Cerakote colors are also available.

MSR $2,499	$1,975	$1,150	$925	$650	$575	$495	$425	

MLCPS – 5.56 NATO or 6.8 SPC cal., GPO, standard/suppressed option gas block with removable piston rod and spring, 16 in. chrome-lined barrel, 25 (6.8 SPC) or 30 (5.56 NATO) shot mag., SST, flip-up sights, SOPMOD stock, ergonomic textured grip, built with the MRP (Monolithic Rail Platform), MLC upper and MARS-L lower receiver, top Picatinny rail, ambi charging handle, bolt/mag. catch, and safety selector, includes sling, 4 rail segments, and 6 segmented grip panels, black or FDE finish is standard, various Cerakote colors are also available, 7.4 lbs.

MSR $2,739	$2,225	$1,395	$1,050	$675	$595	$525	$475	

MLKMWS – .308 Win. cal., GIO, 16 or 20 in. chrome-lined barrel, 20 shot Magpul polymer mag., flip-up sights, built with the MWS (Modular Weapon System) platform, MLKMWS upper and 308MWS lower receiver, SOPMOD stock, ergonomic textured grip, two-stage trigger, tactical charging handle, top Picatinny rail, low profile gas block and straight gas tube, ambi mag. catch and safety selector, includes sling and four rail panels, black or FDE finish is standard, various Cerakote colors are also available, 9.83 lbs.

MSR $3,529	$2,875	$1,875	$1,375	$795	$675	$625	$575	

MLKMWSF – 6.5mm Creedmoor, .243 Win., .260 Rem., 7mm-08 Rem., .308 Win., or .338 Federal cal., GIO, 16 (.308 Win. only), 18 (.308 Win. only), 20, or 24 (6.5mm Creedmoor only) in. stainless steel barrel with black finish, Magpul 20 shot polymer mag., two-stage trigger, flip-up sights, SOPMOD stock, ergonomic textured grip, built with the MWS platform, MLKMWS upper and 308MWS lower receiver, top Picatinny rail, tactical charging handle, low profile gas block and straight tube, ambi mag. catch and safety selector, includes sling and 3 grip panels, black or FDE finish is standard, various Cerakote colors also available, 10.14 lbs.

MSR $3,629	$2,950	$1,925	$1,400	$825	$675	$625	$575	

Add $50 for lightweight barrel (.308 Win. cal. only).

Subtract $50 for .243 Win., .260 Rem., 7mm-08 Rem., or .338 Federal cal.

244 LEWIS MACHINE & TOOL COMPANY (LMT), cont.

MSR	100%	98%	95%	90%	80%	70%	60%	Last MSR

MLR – 5.56 NATO, 6.8 SPC, or .204 Ruger cal., GIO, 16 (5.56 NATO), 18 (6.8 SPC), or 20 (5.56 or .204 Ruger) in. stainless steel barrel, SST, SOPMOD stock, ergonomic textured grip, built with the MRP (Monolithic Rail Platform), MLR upper and MARS-L lower receiver, top Picatinny rail, M-LOK compatible attachment points, low profile gas block and straight gas tube, ambi bolt catch, mag. catch, and safety selector, includes sling and 3 grip panels, black or FDE finish is standard, various Cerakote colors are also available.

| MSR $2,849 | $2,295 | $1,450 | $1,075 | $675 | $595 | $525 | $475 | |

MRP – 5.56 NATO, 6.8 SPC, or .204 Ruger cal., 20 in. stainless steel barrel, SOPMOD stock, ergonomic textured grip, and safety selector, MRP upper receiver with continuous top Picatinny rail, MARS-L lower receiver, ambi charging handle, bolt catch, mag. catch, and safety selector, S-A BCG, includes tactical two-point sling and 3 rail panel covers, black or FDE finish is standard, various Cerakote colors are also available.

| MSR $2,849 | $2,295 | $1,450 | $1,075 | $675 | $595 | $525 | $475 | |

NEW ZEALAND REFERENCE RIFLE – 5.56 NATO cal., GIO, 16 in. chrome-lined barrel with bayonet lug and SureFire Warcomp flash hider, 30 shot mag., two-stage trigger, enhanced trigger guard, LMT metric flip-up sights, SOPMOD stock, ergonomic textured grip, Monolithic Rail Platform with low profile gas block and straight gas tube, ambi charging handle, QD receiver endplate, CQB upper with 16 1/4 in. Picatinny rail, MARS-L ambi lower receiver, includes tactical two-point sling and 3 rail panel covers, black finish. New 2018.

| MSR $2,699 | $2,125 | $1,325 | $995 | $675 | $595 | $525 | $475 | |

SLK – 5.56 NATO, 6.8 SPC, or .204 Ruger cal., GIO, 16 (5.56 NATO), 18 (6.8 SPC), or 20 (5.56 NATO or .204 Ruger) in. stainless steel barrel, SST, SOPMOD stock, ergonomic textured grip, built with MRP, SLK upper receiver with continuous top Picatinny rail, MARS-L lower receiver, ambi charging handle, bolt catch, mag. catch, and safety selector, SST, low profile gas block and straight gas tube, includes tactical two-point sling, four rail segments, and six segmented grip panels, black or FDE finish is standard.

| MSR $2,849 | $2,295 | $1,450 | $1,075 | $675 | $595 | $525 | $475 | |

SPM16 (DEFENDER STANDARD PATROL MODEL 16) – 5.56 NATO cal., GIO, 16 in. chrome-lined barrel, SST, Defender lower receiver, 6-pos. Generation 2 M4 stock, black finish. New 2010.

| MSR $1,649 | $1,350 | $875 | $650 | $525 | $450 | $385 | $350 | |

STD16 (DEFENDER STANDARD PATROL MODEL 16) – 5.56 NATO cal., GIO, 16 in. chrome-lined barrel, Defender lower receiver, SST, tactical adj. rear sight, SOPMOD buttstock with QD swivel attachment points and storage compartments, black finish, approx. 6 lbs.

| MSR $1,869 | $1,575 | $995 | $775 | $575 | $495 | $425 | $395 | |

VALKYRIE MLK – .224 Valkyrie cal., GIO, 20 in. chrome-lined barrel, 3-prong flash hider, two-stage trigger, SOPMOD stock, ergonomic textured grip, MLK upper receiver with continuous Picatinny rail, remaining 8 sides are M-LOK compatible, ambi charging handle, bolt catch, mag. catch, and safety selector, MARS-L lower receiver, enhanced S-A 6.8 BCG, includes tactical two-point sling and 3 grip panels, black or FDE finish is standard, various Cerakote colors are also available. New 2018.

| MSR $2,499 | $1,975 | $1,150 | $925 | $650 | $575 | $495 | $425 | |

VALKYRIE MRP – .224 Valkyrie cal., GIO, 20 in. chrome-lined barrel, 3-prong flash hider, two-stage trigger, DMR buttstock, ergonomic textured grip, MRP upper receiver with continuous Picatinny rail, ambi charging handle, enhanced BCG, MARS-L lower receiver, low profile gas block and straight gas tube, includes tactical two-point sling and 3 rail panel covers, black or FDE fnish is standard, various Cerakote colors are also available. New 2018.

| MSR $2,499 | $1,975 | $1,150 | $925 | $650 | $575 | $495 | $425 | |

VALKYRIE SLK – .224 Valkyrie cal., GIO, 20 in. chrome-lined barrel, 3-prong flash hider, 25 shot mag., two-stage trigger, SOPMOD stock, ergonomic textured grip, SLK upper with continuous Picatinny rail, MARS-L lower receiver, ambi charging handle, bolt catch, mag. catch, and safety selector, enhanced S-A 6.8 BCG, low profile gas block and straight gas tube, includes tactical two-point sling, 4 rail segments, and 6 segmented grip panels, black or FDE finish is standard, various Cerakote colors are also available. New 2018.

| MSR $2,499 | $1,975 | $1,150 | $925 | $650 | $575 | $495 | $425 | |

LOKI WEAPON SYSTEMS, INC.

Previous manufacturer and distributor circa 2009-2012 and located in Coalgate, OK.

Loki Weapon Systems manufactured AR-15 style tactical rifles and 1911 style pistols. Loki was also the U.S. distributor until 2012 for A.M.S.D., located in Geneva, Switzerland.

PISTOLS: SEMI-AUTO

Loki manufactured custom built 1911 style pistols in .45 ACP cal. Base price began at $1,800 and went up according to options and accessories.

LOKI WEAPON SYSTEMS, INC., cont. 245 L

MSR	100%	98%	95%	90%	80%	70%	60%	Last MSR

RIFLES/CARBINES: SEMI-AUTO

Other calibers were available by request. Loki offered a limited lifetime warranty on all rifles and carbines.

FENRIR – 5.56 NATO, .300 Whisper, .458 SOCOM, 6.5 Grendel, 6.8 SPC, or 6.8 Grendel cal., 16 in. barrel, YHM Phantom flash hider, 40 shot mag., mid-length gas operating system, M4 ramps and extension, machined upper and lower, Fail Zero coated bolt carrier group, 12 in. eight sided forend with full-length Picatinny rail, Ergo F93 eight position stock, hard case, approx. 8 lbs. Mfg. 2009-2011.

	$1,315	$850	$625	$500	$435	$375	$350	$1,575

Subtract $125 for ambidextrous safety selector and 15 in. eight sided forend.

HUNTING RIFLE – .223 Rem./5.56 NATO (.223 Wylde chamber) cal., 20 in. varmint barrel, eight sided forend with three Picatinny rails, single stage trigger, 10 shot mag., fixed stock with Ergo grip, includes hard case. Mfg. mid-2010-2011.

	$1,350	$875	$650	$525	$450	$385	$350	$1,625

LWSF 3G COMPETITION – 5.56 NATO cal., 18 in. double fluted stainless steel barrel, 15 in. vented carbon fiber forend, VLTOR A2 fixed stock, adj. gas block, lightened buffer system and carrier, standard Mil-Spec charging handle, hardcoat anodized Teflon coated black finish, two-stage trigger, integrated CQB Magwell grip with XL magwell and Ergo pistol grip, Nordic Corvette compensator, approx. 6 1/2 lbs. Mfg. 2012.

	$1,525	$975	$750	$575	$495	$425	$375	$1,850

LWSF DMR (DESIGNATED MARKSMAN) – .223 Rem./5.56 NATO (.223 Wylde chamber) cal., 20 in. fluted stainless steel SDMR contoured barrel with Rolling Thunder compensator, standard Mil-Spec charging handle, A2 stock with Magpul MOE grip, hardcoat anodized Teflon coated black finish, multiple Picatinny rails, Loki 14.5 in. handguard, pinned Lo Pro gas block, M4 feed ramps, 7.8 lbs. Mfg. 2012.

	$1,350	$875	$650	$525	$450	$385	$350	$1,645

LWSF MAGPUL MOE – .264 LBC, .300 AAC Blackout, or 5.56 NATO cal., 16.1 in. chrome moly vanadium alloy barrel, A2 birdcage flash hider, Magpul MOE stock with pistol grip, mid-length forend and low profile gas block or YHM flip sight tower gas block, integrated Picatinny rail, oversized trigger guard, hardcoat anodized Teflon coated finish, forward assist and dust cover, polished M4 feed ramps, fail zero full-auto bolt carrier, nickel-boron coated charging handle and fire control group, approx. 6 1/2 lbs. Mfg. 2012 only.

	$1,125	$700	$525	$450	$400	$350	$325	$1,349

LWSF PATROL – .264 LBC, .300 AAC Blackout, or 5.56 NATO cal., 16 (.300 AAC Blackout cal.), 18 (.264 LBC) or 18 in. double fluted stainless steel barrel, mid-length gas block, phantom flash hider, VLTOR EMOD retractable stock with Magpul MOE grip, full-length Picatinny rail, free floating forend, integrated winter trigger guard, creep-adj. polished trigger, M4 feed ramps, forward assist and dust cover, black hardcoat anodized finish, also available with optional tactical comp or Battlecomp, 7 1/2 lbs. Mfg. 2012.

	$1,250	$825	$575	$475	$425	$375	$350	$1,479

LWSF STD – .300 AAC Blackout, 6.5mm Grendel, or 5.56 NATO cal., 16.1 in. chrome moly vanadium alloy barrel, A2 birdcage flash hider, Magpul MOE stock, low profile gas block with rail, black hardcoat anodized finish, mid-length free floating forend, standard M4 pistol grip, oversized trigger guard, integrated CQB Magwell grip with XL magwell, fail zero full-auto rated bolt carrier, polished M4 feed ramps, forward assist and dust cover, optional YHM flip-up sight tower gas block, VLTOR EMOD or Ergo F93 stock, 6.7 lbs. Mfg. 2012 only.

	$1,125	$700	$525	$450	$400	$350	$325	$1,349

LWSF TACTICAL – .300 AAC Blackout or 5.56 NATO cal., 16 in. Nitride treated M4 barrel, 14 1/2 in. modular forend, A2 birdcage flash hider, VLTOR EMOD 6-position retractable stock with Magpul MOE grip, black hardcoat anodized Teflon coated finish, NiB-X coated full-auto rated bolt carrier, integrated winter trigger guard, CQB Magwell grip with XL magwell, creep-adj. polished trigger, optional 9 in. top rail and three 3 in. rails or Troy TRX Extreme handguard, standard Mil-Spec charging handle, forward assist and M4 feed ramps. Mfg. 2012 only.

	$1,275	$850	$600	$495	$425	$375	$350	$1,525

LWS M4 MOE – 5.56 NATO cal., 16 in. Nitride treated barrel, M4 extension, A2 birdcage flash hider, 6-position Magpul MOE stock with pistol grip and trigger guard, standard A2 sight post low profile gas block with integrated rail or YHM gas block with integrated flip-up front sight, Mil-Spec BCG nickel boron bolt carrier, mid-length handguard, black hardcoat anodized Teflon coated finish, forward assist and dust cover, creep-adj. hand stoned trigger, standard Mil-Spec charging handle. Mfg. 2012 only.

	$850	$550	$465	$395	$350	$325	$295	$999

LWS M4 PATROL – .300 AAC Blackout or 5.56 NATO cal., 16 in. Nitride treated barrel, M4 extension, A2 birdcage flash hider, choice of 6-position Magpul MOE stock with pistol grip and trigger guard, EMOD or F93 collapsible stock and Ergo pistol grip, Mil-Spec BCG nickel boron bolt carrier, Loki 12 in. rifle length handguard, black hardcoat anodized Teflon coated finish, forward assist and dust cover, creep-adj. hand stoned trigger, standard Mil-Spec charging handle, optional 12 in. top Picatinny rail and three 3 in. side and bottom rails. Mfg. 2012 only.

	$995	$625	$495	$450	$395	$350	$325	$1,199

L 246 LOKI WEAPON SYSTEMS, INC., cont.

MSR	100%	98%	95%	90%	80%	70%	60%	Last MSR

LWS M4 STD – .300 AAC Blackout or 5.56 NATO cal., 16 in. Nitride treated barrel, M4 extension, 6-position Magpul MOE stock with M4 pistol grip and trigger guard, black, Flat Dark Earth, or OD Green hardcoat anodized Teflon coated finish, M4 flat-top upper, 30 shot PMAG, creep-adj. hand stoned single stage trigger, standard Mil-Spec charging handle, low profile gas block with integrated rail, mid-length handguard, includes case. Mfg. 2012 only.

	$875	$550	$465	$395	$350	$325	$300	$1,049

LWS M4 TACTICAL – .300 AAC Blackout or 5.56 NATO cal., 16 in. Nitride treated M4 barrel, 14 1/2 in. free floating forend, A2 birdcage flash hider, choice of 6-position Magpul MOE, EMOD, or F93 stock with Ergo pistol grip, black hardcoat anodized Teflon coated finish, standard Mil-Spec charging handle, forward assist and dust cover, mid-length gas system, optional 9 in. Picatinny rail, three 3 in. side and bottom rails, hand stoned trigger, XL modular handguard. Mfg. 2012 only.

	$1,025	$625	$495	$450	$395	$350	$325	$1,225

PRECISION SNIPER TACTICAL RIFLE – .223 Rem./5.56 NATO (.223 Wylde chamber) cal., M4 upper and lower, 18 in. fluted stainless steel barrel, three port compensator, eight sided forend with full-length Picatinny rail, ambidextrous safety, two-stage trigger, 30 shot mag., F93 Ergo stock and grip, includes hard case. Disc. 2011.

	$1,475	$950	$725	$550	$475	$395	$350	$1,795

LONE STAR ARMORY

Current manufacturer of custom-built precision firearms established in 2004, located in Fort Worth, TX.

In addition to custom-built firearms, Lone Star Armory offers select accessories and ancillary equipment.

PISTOLS: SEMI-AUTO

TX-15 – Pistol version of the TX15 rifle featuring either the KAK blade brace or the Maxim Defense PDW pistol brace. New 2018.

Please contact the manufacturer directly for pricing, options, and availability.

RIFLES: SEMI-AUTO

TX10 DESIGNATED MARKSMAN HEAVY – .308 Win./7.62 NATO, 6mm Creedmoor, 6.5mm Creedmoor, or .260 Rem. (disc. 2017) cal., GIO, 16, 18, 20, 22, or 24 (disc. 2017) in. stainless steel heavy barrel with Graphite Black Cerakote finish, Dead Air Keymount or SureFire muzzle brake, Geissele SSA-E two-stage trigger, integral trigger guard, Magpul PRS Gen 3 stock, Magpul MOE K2 grip, Radian Talon ambi safety selector, billet aluminum upper and lower receiver, intermediate, rifle, or +2 length gas system, adj. gas block, 15 or 16 in. SLR Ion Lite/Ultra Lite M-LOK handguard, ambi Raptor charging handle, Type III hardcoat anodized black finish.

MSR $3,754		$3,050	$1,975	$1,425	$850	$675	$625	$575

* **TX10 Designated Marksman Heavy Enhanced (Lightweight)** – .308 Win./7.62 NATO, 6mm Creedmoor, or 6.5mm Creedmoor cal., GIO, 16, 18, 20, or 22 in. stainless steel heavy barrel with Graphite Black Cerakote finish, Dead Air Keymount or SureFire muzzle brake, Geissele SSA-E two-stage trigger, integral trigger guard, Magpul PRS Gen 3 stock, Magpul MOE K2 grip, Radian Talon ambi safety selector, lightweight billet receivers, intermediate, rifle, or +2 length gas system, adj. gas block, 15 or 16 in. SLR Ion Lite/Ultra Lite M-LOK handguard, ambi Raptor charging handle, Type III hardcoat anodized black finish.

MSR $3,854		$3,125	$2,100	$1,475	$875	$695	$650	$575

TX10 MULTI-PURPOSE RIFLE – .308 Win./7.62 NATO, 6mm Creedmoor, 6.5mm Creedmoor, or .260 Rem. cal., GIO, 16, 18, 20, 22, or 24 in. stainless steel barrel, Dead Air muzzle brake, Geissele SSA-E trigger, Magpul PRS Gen 3 stock with a rifle buffer and Tac Springs buffer spring, Magpul MOE K2 Grip, 15 or 16 in. SLR Ion Lite/Ultra Lite M-LOK handguard, intermediate, rifle, or +2 length gas system with Melonite treated gas tube and adj. gas block. Disc. 2017.

	$2,700	$1,775	$1,325	$750	$650	$595	$525	$3,380

* **TX10 Multi-Purpose Rifle Enhanced** – .308 Win., 6.5mm Creedmoor, or 6mm Creedmoor cal., GIO, 16, 18, or 20 in. stainless steel barrel with Graphite Black Cerakote finish, Dead Air Keymount or SureFire muzzle brake, Geissele SSA-E two-stage trigger, B5 SOPMOD stock mounted on Mil-Spec 6-pos. receiver extension with a heavy buffer and Tac Springs buffer spring, Magpul MOE K2 grip, Radian Raptor ambi charging handle, Radian Talon 45 ambi safety selector switch, full-length SLR Ion Lite M-LOK handguard, V7 lightweight aluminum EPC and forward assist, billet mag. catch, enhanced bolt catch, mid, intermediate, or rifle length gas system with Inconel gas tube and adj. Superlative gas block, Type III hardcoat anodized black, single Cerakote, or multi-color Cerakote finish. New 2018.

MSR $3,608		$2,950	$1,925	$1,400	$825	$675	$625	$575

Add $360 for single color Cerakote or $475 for multi-color Cerakote finish.

* **TX10 Multi-Purpose Rifle Enhanced (Lightweight)** – .308 Win., 6.5mm Creedmoor, or 6mm Creedmoor cal., GIO, 16, 18, or 20 in. stainless steel barrel with Graphite Black Cerakote finish, Dead Air Keymount or SureFire muzzle brake, lightweight billet receiver set, B5 SOPMOD stock, Magpul MOE K2 grip, Radian Talon 45 ambi safety selector switch, full-length SLR Ion Lite M-LOK handguard, V7 lightweight aluminum EPC and forward assist, billet mag. catch, enhanced bolt catch, mid, intermediate, or rifle length gas system with Inconel gas tube and adj.

LONE STAR ARMORY, cont. 247 L

MSR	100%	98%	95%	90%	80%	70%	60%	Last MSR

Superlative gas block, Type III hardcoat anodized black, single Cerakote, or multi-color Cerakote finish. New 2018.

| MSR $3,708 | $3,050 | $1,975 | $1,425 | $850 | $675 | $625 | $575 | |

Add $360 for single color Cerakote or $475 for multi-color Cerakote finish.

TX10 TRUCK GUN HEAVY ENHANCED – .308 Win., 6mm Creedmoor, or 6.5mm Creedmoor cal., GIO, 16 in. barrel, integral trigger guard, pistol grip, ambidextrous safety, billet aluminum receiver, upper Picatinny rail, Type III hardcoat anodized black finish. New 2018.

| MSR $2,799 | $2,225 | $1,395 | $1,050 | $675 | $595 | $525 | $475 | |

Add $450 for 6mm Creedmoor or 6.5mm Creedmoor cal.

TX15 DESIGNATED MARKSMAN LIGHT STANDARD – 5.56 NATO/.223 Wylde, .264 LBC/6.5 Grendel, or 6.8 SPC II cal., 16 or 18 in. stainless steel barrel, ALG ACT single stage trigger, B5 SOPMOD stock mounted on a Mil-Spec 6-position receiver extension with a heavy buffer and Tac Springs buffer spring, Magpul MOE K2 grip, 15 or 16 in. SLR Ion Lite M-LOK handguard, Bravo Company charging handle, LSA TX16 bolt carrier with a 9310 enhanced bolt assembly, mid, intermediate, or rifle length gas system with a Melonite treated gas tube, adj. gas block, Graphite Black Cerakote finish. Disc. 2017.

| MSR $1,875 | $1,575 | $995 | $775 | $575 | $495 | $425 | $395 | |

* **TX15 Designated Marksman Light Enhanced** – 5.56 NATO/.223 Wylde, .264 LBC/6.5 Grendel, 6.8 SPC II/6.8x43mm, or .224 Valkyrie (new 2018) cal., 16, 18, or 20 in. stainless steel barrel with Graphite Black Cerakote finish, Dead Air Keymount or Surefire muzzle brake, Geissele SSA-E two-stage trigger, Magpul PRS Gen 3 stock with rifle buffer and Tac Springs buffer spring, Magpul MOE K2 grip, Radian Talon ambi safety selector switch, Bravo Company (disc.) or Radian Raptor ambi charging handle, 15 or 16 in. SLR Ion Lite M-LOK handguard, mid, intermediate, or rifle length gas system with Melonite (disc.) or Inconel gas tube, adj. gas block, enhanced bolt assembly, Type III hardcoat anodized black finish.

| MSR $3,204 | $2,625 | $1,725 | $1,300 | $725 | $650 | $595 | $525 | |

TX15 MULTI-PURPOSE CARBINE STANDARD – 5.56 NATO/.223 Wylde, .300 AAC Blackout, .264 LBC/6.5 Grendel, 6.8 SPC II/6.8x43mm, or .224 Valkyrie (new 2018) cal., 16 or 18 in. stainless steel barrel, Mil-Spec A2 flash suppressor, ALG QMS trigger, Magpul MOE stock mounted on a Mil-Spec 6-position receiver extension with a heavy buffer and Tac Springs buffer spring, Magpul MOE grip, Battle Arms enhanced single side safety, mid-length gas system, 13.7 or 15 in. SLR Ion Lite M-LOK handguard, Mil-Spec charging handle.

| MSR $1,526 | $1,275 | $850 | $600 | $495 | $425 | $375 | $350 | |

Add $350 for .300 AAC Blackout, .264 LBC/6.5 Grendel, 6.8 SPC II/6.8x43mm, or .224 Valkyrie (new 2018) cal.

* **TX15 Multi-Purpose Carbine Duty** – 5.56 NATO/.223 Wylde, .300 AAC Blackout, .224 Valkyrie, .264 LBC/6.5 Grendel, or 6.8 SPC II/6.8x43mm cal., 16 in. stainless steel barrel with Graphite Black Cerakote finish, Dead Air Keymount or Surefire muzzle brake, ALG advanced combat trigger, Magpul MOE stock mounted on Mil-Spec 6-pos. receiver extension with a heavy buffer and Tac Springs buffer spring, Magpul MOE grip, BAD enhanced single side safety selector, mid-length gas system, 13.7 or 15 in. SLR Ion Lite M-LOK handguard, VLTOR/BCM Gunfighter charging handle. New 2018.

| MSR $1,760 | $1,475 | $950 | $725 | $550 | $475 | $395 | $350 | |

Add $350 for .300 AAC Blackout, .264 LBC/6.5 Grendel, 6.8 SPC II/6.8x43mm, or .224 Valkyrie cal.

* **TX15 Multi-Purpose Carbine Enhanced** – 5.56 NATO/.223 Wylde, .300 AAC Blackout, .264 LBC/6.5 Grendel, 6.8 SPC II/6.8x43mm, or .224 Valkyrie (new 2018) cal., 16, 18, or 20 in. stainless steel barrel with Graphite Black Cerakote finish, Dead Air Keymount or Surefire muzzle brake, Geissele SSA-E two-stage trigger, B5 SOPMOD stock mounted on a Mil-Spec receiver extension with a heavy buffer and Tac Springs buffer spring, Magpul MOE grip, Radian Talon ambi safety selector switch, mid, intermediate, or rifle length gas system with an Inconel gas tube, adj. Superlative gas block, 13.7, 15, or 16 in. SLR Ion Lite M-LOK handguard, Radian Raptor ambi charging handle, billet mag. catch, enhanced bolt catch, Type III hardcoat anodized black finish.

| MSR $3,035 | $2,450 | $1,595 | $1,200 | $700 | $675 | $575 | $525 | |

Add $273 for .264 LBC/6.5 Grendel cal.

Add $475 for 6.8 SPC II/6.8x43mm, .300 AAC Blackout, or .224 Valkyrie (new 2018) cal.

TX15 TRUCK GUN LIGHT STANDARD – 5.56 NATO or .300 AAC Blackout cal., 16 in. button rifled barrel with Melonite finish, A2 compensator, ALG QMS trigger, Magpul MOE stock mounted on a Mil-Spec 6-pos. receiver extension with a carbine buffer and Tac Springs buffer spring, Magpul MOE grip, mid-length gas system, low profile gas block, ALG EMR V3 rail, 13 or 15 in. M-LOK handguard, M16 BCG, Battle Arms selector and mag. catch, hardcoat anodized black finish.

| MSR $1,338 | $1,125 | $700 | $525 | $450 | $400 | $350 | $325 | |

* **TX15 Truck Gun Light Duty** – 5.56 NATO cal., 16 in. button rifled barrel with Melonite finish, Dead Air Keymount or Surefire flash hider, ALG ACT single stage trigger, Magpul SL-K stock mounted on a Mil-Spec 6-pos. receiver extension with a carbine buffer and Tac Springs buffer spring, Magpul MOE grip, mid-length gas system, low profile gas block, 13 or 15 in. ALG EMR V3 rail, BCM Mod 4 charging handle, ambi selector switch. New 2018.

| MSR $1,521 | $1,275 | $850 | $600 | $495 | $425 | $375 | $350 | |

248 LONE STAR ARMORY, cont.

MSR	100%	98%	95%	90%	80%	70%	60%	Last MSR

* **TX15 Truck Gun Light Enhanced** – .223 Wylde/5.56 NATO, .300 AAC Blackout, .224 Valkyrie (new 2018), 6.8 SPCII/6.8x43mm, or .264 LBC/6.5 Grendel cal., 16 or 18 in. stainless steel button rifled barrel, Dead Air Keymount or Surefire flash hider, Geissele SSA-E two-stage trigger, Magpul SL-K stock mounted on a Mil-Spec 6-pos. receiver extension with a carbine buffer and Tac Springs buffer spring, Magpul MOE grip, mid-length gas system, low profile gas block, ALG EMR V3 rail, 13 or 15 in. M-LOK handguard, Radian Raptor ambi charging handle, TX15 enhanced black Nitride BCG, Graphite Black Cerakote finish.

MSR $2,200	$1,795	$1,050	$875	$625	$550	$475	$425

Add $350 for .300 AAC Blackout, .224 Valkyrie, 6.8 SPC II/6.8x43mm, or .264 LBC/6.5 Grendel cal.

LONE STAR TACTICAL SUPPLY

Previous firearms and current accessories manufacturer located in Tomball, TX.

In addition to manufacturing semi-auto pistols, rifles, and shotguns, Lone Star was also a dealer for Saiga rifles, and offered many shooting accessories.

RIFLES: SEMI-AUTO

BORDER PATROL – .223 Rem./5.56 NATO (.223 Wylde chamber) cal., AR-15 style, GIO, 16 in. chrome moly barrel with A2 flash hider, extended M4 feed ramps, "F" marked A2 front sight base, forged charging handle, laser engraved "T" markings, dry film lube inside upper receiver, ST-T2 Tungsten buffer, Lone Star Tactical logo, bullet pictogram selector markings, 6-position stock, 6-position buffer tube, castle nut, staked latch plate, standard pistol grip, black finish. Mfg. for Lone Star Tactical by Spike's Tactical. Disc.

	$865	$550	$465	$395	$350	$325	$300	$1,025

LUVO PRAGUE LTD.

Current pistol and rifle manufacturer located in Praha 2-Vinohrady, Czech Republic. No current U.S. importation.

RIFLES: SEMI-AUTO

Luvo Prague Ltd. currently manufactures the following AR-15 style rifles: LA-10, LA-11, LA-15, LA-16, LA-110 SASS, CZ Reliable V22, VZ-58V, and VZ-58P. Please contact the manufacturer directly for more information including price, options, and U.S. availability (see Trademark Index).

NOTES

M SECTION

249 M

MG ARMS INCORPORATED

Current manufacturer established in 1980, located in Spring, TX. MG Arms Incorporated was previously named Match Grade Arms & Ammunition. Consumer direct sales.

MSR	100%	98%	95%	90%	80%	70%	60%	Last MSR

RIFLES: SEMI-AUTO

CK-4 – .223 Rem. or .300 Fireball cal., AR-15 style, GIO, 16 or 20 in. barrel with flash hider (16 in. only), 20 or 30 shot mag., MGA 3-piece lower receiver, A3 flat-top upper receiver, 6-position collapsible stock, free floating quad rail handguard, choice of PTFE resin finish, basic, or camo coverage. Mfg. 2011-2015.

	100%	98%	95%	90%	80%	70%	60%	Last MSR
	$1,650	$1,000	$795	$595	$495	$425	$395	*$1,995*

K-YOTE VARMINT SYSTEM – .17 Rem., .204 Ruger, .223 Rem., .243 Win., .260 Rem., 7mm-08 Rem., or .308 Win. cal., AR-15 style, GIO, choice of round fluted or 10-sided match grade fully free floating 20, 24, or 26 in. barrel, custom target trigger, fully adj. stock, 4 rail free floating handguard, machined lower receiver, integral Picatinny scope rail, standard or Zombie Camo finish. New 2009.

MSR $3,695	$2,950	$1,925	$1,400	$825	$675	$625	$575	

TARANIS – 5.56 NATO or .300 AAC Blackout cal., AR-15 style, GIO, 16 in. lightweight match grade tapered barrel with titanium flash hider, 20 or 30 shot mag., custom trigger, CTR 6-position collapsible stock, upper receiver with flat-top Picatinny rail, carbon fiber handguard, skeletonized bolt, PTFE resin, basic, or Tan Zebra camo finish, approx. 4 1/2 lbs. Mfg. 2013-2016.

	100%	98%	95%	90%	80%	70%	60%	Last MSR
	$1,725	$1,050	$850	$625	$550	$475	$425	*$2,195*

TARANIS 2 – 5.56 NATO, .300 AAC Blackout, 6.5 Grendel, 6.8 SPC, .204 Ruger, or .50 Beowulf cal., 16 in. match grade ultra light barrel, Super Eliminator muzzle brake, 20 shot mag., 3 lb. match grade trigger, 6-way ultra light adj. stock, Tacti-Quik safety, carbon fiber handguard, ultra light skeletonized forged receivers, skeletonized bolt and bolt carrier, Picatinny top rail, blue titanium finish, approx. 4 1/2 lbs. New 2017.

MSR $2,295	$1,795	$1,050	$875	$625	$550	$475	$425	

MGI

Current manufacturer located in Old Town, ME. Previously located in Bangor, ME until late 2010.

PISTOLS: SEMI-AUTO

HYDRA VIPERA 5.56 MODULAR PISTOL – 5.56 NATO/.223 Rem. cal., 7 in. barrel, aluminum construction, Mil-Spec internal parts, QCB upper receiver and modular lower, AR-15 mags., black finish. New 2015.

MSR $1,289	$1,075	$965	$825	$715	$625	$535	$450	

HYDRA VIPERA 7.62x39 MODULAR PISTOL – 7.62x39mm cal., 7 in. barrel, aluminum construction, Mil-Spec internal parts, QCB upper receiver and modular lower, AK-47 mags., black finish. New 2015.

MSR $1,289	$1,075	$965	$825	$715	$625	$535	$450	

This model is designed to use standard Warsaw Pact metal magazines and Thermold polymer magazines.

HYDRA VIPERA 9mm SMG-9C MODULAR PISTOL – 9mm SMG-9C cal., 7 1/2 in. barrel, fires 9mm ammo from standard Colt style magazines, aluminum construction, Mil-Spec internal parts, QCB upper receiver and modular lower, black finish. New 2015.

MSR $1,289	$1,075	$965	$825	$715	$625	$535	$450	

HYDRA VIPERA .300 BLACKOUT MODULAR PISTOL – .300 AAC Blackout cal., 7 in. barrel, AR-15 mags., aluminum construction, Mil-Spec internal parts, QCB upper receiver and modular lower, black finish. New 2015.

MSR $1,289	$1,075	$965	$825	$715	$625	$535	$450	

RIFLES: SEMI-AUTO

MARCK 15-001 HYDRA – .223 Rem./5.56 NATO cal., AR-15 style, GIO, 16 in. barrel, A2 front sight base, M4 profile 6-pos. Mil-Spec stock, MGI modular lower receiver with AR magwell, MGI Quick Change Barrel upper receiver (QCB-D), MGI D-Fender D-Ring, MGI modified bolt carrier and firing pin, change barrels in seconds with no tools required and utiliize the correct magazine for the caliber you desire, black or Muddy Girl (disc.) finish, includes hard-sided lockable pistol case.

MSR $1,299	$1,075	$675	$500	$450	$400	$350	$325	

* *Marck 15-AK47-001* – 7.62x39mm cal., GIO, 16 in. barrel, A2 front sight base, modular lower receiver with AK47 magwell, QCB-D upper receiver, MGI D-Fender D-Ring, change barrels in seconds with no tools required and utiliize the correct magazine for the caliber you desire, black or Muddy Girl (disc.) finish, includes hard-sided lockable pistol case.

MSR $1,299	$1,100	$995	$875	$735	$650	$550	$465	

M 250 MGI, cont.

MSR	100%	98%	95%	90%	80%	70%	60%	Last MSR

MARCK 15-003 HYDRA – .223 Rem./5.56 NATO, .330 AAC Blackout, 6.5 Grendel (new 2015), 6.8 SPC (new 2015), .450 Thumper (new 2015), or .458 SOCOM (new 2018) cal., AR-15 style, GIO, complete weapon system, low profile gas block, 16 in. barrel, M4 profile Mil-Spec stock, modular lower receiver with AR magwell, QCB-D upper receiver, MGI D-Fender D-Ring, change barrels in seconds with no tools required and utiliize the correct magazine for the caliber you desire, black or Muddy Girl (disc.) finish, includes hard-sided lockable pistol case.

MSR $1,299	$1,075	$675	$500	$450	$400	$350	$325	

Add $101 for 6.5 Grendel cal. (new 2015).

Add $196 for .450 Thumper cal. (new 2015).

Add $200 for .458 SOCOM cal. (new 2018).

* ***Marck 15-003 Hydra Piston*** – 5.56 NATO cal., similar to Marck 15-003 Hydra, except features GPO. Disc. 2016.

	$1,315	$850	$625	$500	$435	$375	$350	*$1,599*

* ***Marck 15-2545-003 Hydra*** – .25-45 Sharps cal., 16 in. SRC barrel, low profile gas block, MGI modular lower receiver, AR magwell, MGI QCB-D (Quick Change Barrel Upper Receiver), MGI D-Fender D-Ring, M4 profile 6-position Mil-Spec stock, includes hard case. New 2016.

MSR $1,399	$1,150	$750	$550	$465	$415	$375	$350	

* ***Marck 15-50BW Hydra*** – .50 Beowulf cal., muzzle brake, MGI rate and recoil reducing buffer, top Picatinny rail, black finish, includes foam padded case. New 2015.

MSR $1,499	$1,250	$825	$575	$475	$425	$375	$350	

* ***Marck 15-AK47-003-BN*** – 7.62x39mm cal., AK-47 magazine well, 16 in. bull nose barrel, low profile gas block, includes enhanced reliability firing pin and bolt, MGI modular lower receiver with AK-47 magwell, MGI Quick Change Barrel upper receiver, MGI D-Fender D-Ring, M4 profile 6-pos. Mil-Spec stock, includes hard-sided lockable case, black finish.

MSR $1,299	$1,075	$675	$500	$450	$400	$350	$325	

MARCK 15-AR-003-BN MULTI-CALIBER MODULAR HYDRA – 5.56 NATO cal., bull nose barrel, standard M4 profile 6-pos. Mil-Spec stock, low profile gas block, MGI modular lower receiver, AR magwell, Quick Change Barrel Upper receiver, MGI D-Fender D-Ring, standard carbine handuard, also includes the transforming handguard and hard-sided lockable pistol case. New 2018.

MSR $998	$850	$550	$465	$395	$350	$325	$295	

MARCK 15-308 CONFIGURATION (.308 HYDRA) – .308 Win. cal., similar to Marck-15-001/003 Hydra, except offered in .308 configuration, takes a modified M14 magazine, includes a rate recoil reducing buffer and 18 in. barrel. Disc. 2014.

	$1,425	$925	$700	$550	$475	$395	$350	*$1,750*

MARCK 15-SMG-9C – 9mm Para. cal., 16 in. blowback barrel and 9mm blowback bolt, utilizes Colt style 9mm SMG mags., M4 profile 6-pos. Mil-Spec stock, modular lower receiver with a 9mm SMG magwell, QCB-D upper receiver, black finish. New 2015.

MSR $1,299	$1,075	$675	$500	$450	$400	$350	$325	

MARCK 15 AK74-003 – 5.45x39 cal., 16 in. barrel, low profile gas block, MGI modular lower receiver, MGI Quick Change Barrel Upper Receiver (QCB-D), modified bolt carrier and firing pin, MGI D-Fender D-Ring, M4 profile 6-pos. Mil-Spec stock, includes hard-sided lockable case, black finish.

MSR $1,374	$1,135	$725	$525	$465	$415	$375	$350	

MMC ARMORY

Current AR-15 style manufacturer established in 2008, located in Mark, IL.

PISTOLS: SEMI-AUTO

MA15 CQP (CLOSE QUARTER PISTOL) – 5.56 NATO or .300 AAC Blackout cal., black furniture. Disc. 2014.

	$1,750	$1,525	$1,325	$1,200	$975	$795	$700	*$1,950*

RIFLES: SEMI-AUTO

MA15 3GCR (3 GUN COMPETITION READY) – 5.56 NATO cal., GIO, 17 in. barrel with compensator, 30 shot mag., 15 in. Troy Alpha handguard, single stage drop-in velocity trigger, nickel coated bolt carrier group, low profile gas block, ambidextrous charging handle, flat trigger guard, Rogers Super-Stoc and 6-position polished buffer tube, polymer A2 style grip, black furniture, 6.2 lbs. New 2014.

MSR $1,709	$1,425	$925	$700	$550	$475	$395	$350	

MA15 PATROL ELITE – 5.56 NATO or .300 AAC Blackout cal., GIO, 16 in. chrome moly M4 profile Nitride hardened barrel, nickel boron coated carrier group, polished buffer tube, single stage trigger, matte black or Muddy Girl (new 2014) finish, two-piece mid-length handguard with double heat shield, 6-position collapsible polymer stock, A2 style pistol grip, Picatinny gas block, 30 shot mag., A2 dimension compensator, flat Mil-Spec trigger guard, 6.1 lbs.

MSR $1,339	$700	$525	$450	$400	$350	$325		

Add $214 for Muddy Girl finish (new 2014).

MMC ARMORY, cont. 251 M

MSR	100%	98%	95%	90%	80%	70%	60%	Last MSR

MA15 PREDATOR XV – 5.56 NATO or .300 AAC Blackout (new 2015) cal., GIO, 17.1 in. threaded barrel with M4 extension and thread protector, 30 shot mag., enhanced SST, hardcoat anodized receivers with M4 feed ramps and flared magwell, 13 in. Troy Alpha rail, low profile gas block, ambidextrous charging handle, Troy 13 in. Bravo handguard, Rogers Super-Stoc and 6-position polished buffer tube, A2 style pistol grip, black furniture, 6.2 lbs. Mfg. 2014 only.

	$1,315	$850	$625	$500	$435	$375	$350	$1,599

MA15 RECON – 5.56 NATO or .300 AAC Blackout cal., GIO, 16 in. chrome moly M4 profile Nitride hardened barrel, available with flash hider or compensator, 30 shot mag., nickel boron coated carrier group, polished buffer tube, single stage drop-in velocity trigger, matte black finish, 13 in. Troy Bravo quad rail handguard, 6-position Rogers Super-Stoc collapsible polymer stock, A2 style grip, A2 dimension compensator, winter trigger guard, low profile gas block, ambidextrous charging handle, 6.8 lbs.

MSR $1,599	$1,315	$850	$625	$500	$435	$375	$350	

Add $60 for compensator.

MA15 TACTICAL – 5.56 NATO or .300 AAC Blackout cal., GIO, 16 in. chrome moly Nitride hardened barrel with M4 extension, available with flash hider or compensator, nickel boron coated carrier group, polished buffer tube, SST, matte black finish, 13 in. Troy Alpha modular handguard with movable Picatinny rail, 6-position Rogers Super-Stoc collapsible polymer stock, A2 style grip, 30 shot mag., A2 dimension compensator, flat trigger guard, low profile gas block, ambidextrous charging handle, 6.1 lbs.

MSR $1,579	$1,315	$850	$625	$500	$435	$375	$350	

Add $60 for compensator.

MATRIX ARMS

Current AR-15 style pistol/rifle manufacturer located in Claremont, NH.

PISTOLS: SEMI-AUTO

9mm GLOCK AR PISTOL – 9mm Para. cal., 8 1/2 in. steel threaded barrel, A2 flash hider, 32 shot Glock mag., Magpul grip, non-reciprocating side charging upper, 7 in. Matrix handguard, top Picatinny rail, dedicated 9mm Glock lower receiver from forged aluminum alloy, pistol buffer tube, hardcoat anodized finish.

MSR $1,099	$915	$575	$475	$415	$350	$325	$300	

RIFLES: SEMI-AUTO

5.56 REAR CHARGING RIFLE – 5.56 NATO cal., 16 in. chrome moly barrel, A2 flash suppressor, 30 shot PMAG, tactical buttstock, Hogue grip, forged aluminum upper and lower receiver, low profile gas block, Mil-Std rail with laser T markings, top Picatinny rail, 15 in. free floating Matrix handguard, black anodized finish.

MSR $700	$595	$485	$415	$350	$315	$295	$275	

MAUNZ MATCH RIFLES, LLC

Previous manufacturer located in Grand Rapids, OH 2011-2017.

RIFLES: SEMI-AUTO

Maunz Rifles were manufactured in Toledo and Maumee Ohio from the 1960s until 1987 by Karl Maunz for high-end military, law enforcement and competition. Models included the Model 87 Maunz Match Rifle, Model 77 Service Match Rifle, Model 67 Match Grade for practice, Model 67 Sniper Rifle, Model 57 and the Model 47 rifle. All models made on or prior to 2011 were custom order only.

MODEL 97 MATCH/HUNTING RIFLE – chambered for 17 to 45Maunz calibers, modeled after the AR-10 and AR-15, GIO, custom weight barrels, fiberglass stock, custom color stock or classic wood stock with patent pending. Disc. 2017.

	$1,525	$975	$750	$575	$495	$425	$375	$1,850

MODEL 97 SERVICE RIFLE – 5.56 NATO or .223 Rem. cal., modeled after the US M16/AR-15, GIO, black gel coated GI fiberglass stock. Disc. 2017.

	$1,050	$650	$495	$450	$395	$350	$325	$1,250

MODEL 97 TARGET RIFLE – .243 Win. or .308 Win. cal., modeled after the AR-10 and AR-15, custom weight barrels, custom classic wood stock with patent pending. Disc. 2017.

	$1,975	$1,150	$925	$650	$575	$495	$425	$2,400

MODEL M16SA – Service Standard grade rifle modeled after the M16.

Previous MSR on this model was $650.

MAXIM FIREARMS

Current AR-15 style manufacturer located in the U.S.

RIFLES: SEMI-AUTO

MAXIM B7075 – .308 Win., .30-06, or .300 Win. cal., GIO, 16, 18, 20, 24, 26, or 30 in. Lilja, Satern, Black Hole Weaponry, or Lothar Walther barrel finished in Nitro carbonized, stainless steel, or Cerakote, Maxim's compensator, 30

M 252 MAXIM FIREARMS, cont.

MSR	100%	98%	95%	90%	80%	70%	60%	Last MSR

shot mag., nickel boron bolt carrier group, Geissele, POF, or CMMG trigger, Mission First Tactical collapsible stock, Ergo grip, billet Cerakote upper and lower receivers, Maxim Firearms charging handle, 9 1/2, 13 1/2, or 15 1/2 in. MQR forend. **Please contact the company directly for pricing and availability.**

MCDUFFEE ARMS
Previous AR-15 rifle manufacturer located in Westminster, CO 2010-2016.

McDuffee Arms is a family owned and operated business that specialized in AR-15 rifles and receivers. The company continues to work on warranty service work as well as doing custom builds.

RIFLES: SEMI-AUTO

BANSHEE 3G – 3-gun competition rifle, 18 in. stainless steel barrel with stainless steel muzzle brake, power extractor spring, iron sights, 6-pos. adj. stock, ultra slim-line free float handguard, aluminum lower, A3 flat-top upper, Type III hardcoat anodized finish, optional NorGuard coating or nickel boron bolt carrier group, 7.2 lbs. Mfg. 2014-2016.

	100%	98%	95%	90%	80%	70%	60%	Last MSR
	$850	$550	$465	$395	$350	$325	$295	$990

BANSHEE AR-15 CARBINE – 5.56 NATO, .300 AAC Blackout (disc. 2015), or 7.62x39mm cal., 16 in. M4 contour chrome moly barrel, power extractor spring, 6-position adj. stock, railed gas block, free float quad rail handguards, A3 flat-top upper receiver, billet aluminum lower, Type III hardcoat anodized black finish, 6.6 lbs. Disc. 2016.

	100%	98%	95%	90%	80%	70%	60%	Last MSR
	$675	$500	$425	$375	$335	$315	$295	$800

Add $15 for 9 in., $20 for 13 in., or $30 for 15 in. handguard. Add $15 for NorGuard coating or $30 for nickel boron bolt carrier group.

* ***Banshee AR-15 Carbine SS*** – 5.56 NATO, .300 AAC Blackout, 6.8 SPC (disc. 2015), or 7.62x39mm (disc. 2015) cal., similar to Banshee AR-15 Carbine, except features 16 in. M4 contour stainless steel barrel and steel flash suppressor, 6-position adj. stock, 6.6 lbs. Disc. 2016.

	100%	98%	95%	90%	80%	70%	60%	Last MSR
	$725	$500	$435	$375	$335	$315	$295	$850

Add $10 for 9 in., $40 for 13 in., or $45 for 15 in. handguard. Add $15 for NorGuard coating or $30 for nickel boron bolt carrier group.

BANSHEE AR-15 RIFLE – .223 Wylde chamber, railed gas block, 20 in. stainless steel barrel and custom flash suppressor, power extractor spring, 6-position adj. stock, billet aluminum lower, railed gas block, A3 flat-top upper, full-length free float quad rail handguard, Type III hardcoat anodized black finish. Disc. 2016.

	100%	98%	95%	90%	80%	70%	60%	Last MSR
	$865	$550	$465	$395	$350	$325	$300	$1,010

Add $10 for 15 in. handguard. Add $15 for NorGuard coating or $30 for nickel boron bolt carrier group.

MLR-308 BROADSWORD – .308 Win. cal., 20 in. heavy stainless steel barrel with stainless steel muzzle brake, 10 shot Magpul PMAG, integral winter trigger guard, Magpul CTR adj. stock, Ergo grip, billet aluminum lower, nickel boron bolt carrier group, H3 heavy buffer, free float super slim handguard, A3 flat-top upper, railed gas block, Type III hardcoat anodized finish. Mfg. 2014-2016.

	100%	98%	95%	90%	80%	70%	60%	Last MSR
	$1,150	$750	$550	$465	$415	$375	$350	$1,400

Add $25 for nickel boron bolt carrier group or $40 for NorGuard coating.

MIDWEST INDUSTRIES, INC.
Current manufacturer of AR-15 style pistols, rifles, and tactical accessories, located in Waukesha, WI.

PISTOLS: SEMI-AUTO

MI ARP300K/ARP300M – .300 AAC Blackout cal., pistol length gas system with low profile gas block, 10 1/2 in. barrel, 10 shot mag. with HIVIZ follower, forged aluminum upper and lower receiver, M4 feed ramps, pistol buffer tube (for use with or without Sig Sauer SB15 pistol brace), Mil-Std 1913 top rail, five slot M-LOK (ARP300M) or 9 in. KeyMod (ARP300K) rail section, hardcoat anodized finish.

	100%	98%	95%	90%	80%	70%	60%	
MSR $940	$815	$700	$630	$570	$500	$425	$380	

Add $10 for KeyMod rail section (ARP300K). Add $40 for M16 bolt carrier group.

MI ARP223K/ARP223M – 5.56 NATO cal., carbine length gas system with low profile gas block, 10 1/2 in. barrel, 10 shot mag., forged aluminum upper and lower receivers, AR pistol buffer tube (works with or without SIG SB15 pistol brace), Mil-Std top rail, five slot KeyMod (ARP223K) or M-LOK (ARP223M) free float handguard, Type 3 Class 2 hardcoat anodized finish.

	100%	98%	95%	90%	80%	70%	60%	
MSR $915	$775	$685	$615	$550	$485	$415	$370	

Add $10 for KeyMod free float handguard (ARP223K). Add $40 for M16 bolt carrier group.

RIFLES: SEMI-AUTO

MI .308 RIFLE – .308 Win. cal., 16 or 18 in. Criterion stainless steel barrel, 10 shot mag., Magpul buttstock, Magpul grip, forged upper and lower receivers, 12 or 15 (18 in. barrel) in. handguard for M-LOK configuration system, bolt carrier group, Picatinny rail, stainless Nitride finish, 8 1/2-9 1/4 lbs.

	100%	98%	95%	90%	80%	70%	60%	
MSR $1,700	$1,385	$895	$675	$525	$450	$385	$350	

Add $75 for 18 in. barrel with 15 in. handguard.

MIDWEST INDUSTRIES, INC., cont. 253 M

MSR	100%	98%	95%	90%	80%	70%	60%	Last MSR

* MI .308 18 In. Limited Edition Rifle – .308 Win. cal., 16 or 18 in. Criterion stainless steel barrel, two chamber enhanced muzzle brake, 10 shot mag., low profile front and rear sight, Olive Green Magpul buttstock, heavy-duty quick detach endplate, Olive Green Magpul grip, AXTS safety selector, forged upper and lower receivers, 12 or 15 (18 in. barrel) in. handguard for M-LOK configuration system, bolt carrier group, Picatinny rail, AXTS Raptor 308 charging handle, stainless Nitride finish, 9.2. lbs.

MSR $1,899	$1,575	$995	$775	$575	$495	$425	$395	

* MI .308 Rifle 20 In. – .308 Win. cal., 20 in. Criterion stainless steel barrel, 10 shot mag., Magpul PRS buttstock, Magpul MOE grip, forged upper and lower receivers, 15 in. handguard for M-LOK configuration system, bolt carrier group, Picatinny rail, black Nitride finish, 9 1/4 lbs.

MSR $2,050	$1,675	$1,000	$825	$625	$550	$475	$425	

MI 16 IN. HYBRID RIFLE – .223 Wylde chamber, 16 in. Criterion hybrid profile barrel, A2 flash hider, Magpul MOE trigger guard, Magpul CTR buttstock, Magpul MOE grip, forged aluminum upper and lower receivers, MI-SSM 12 in. handguard (M-LOK compatible), M4 feed ramps, M16 bolt carrier group, Mil-Spec buffer tube, Type III Class 2 hardcoat anodized matte black or FDE finish, 6.2. lbs.

MSR $1,185	$995	$625	$495	$450	$395	$350	$325	

Add $40 for M16 bolt carrier group.

MI 16 IN. MID-LENGTH RIFLE – 5.56 NATO cal., mid-length gas system, FN 16 in. chrome-lined barrel, A2 flash hider, Magpul CTR buttstock, Magpul MOE grips, forged aluminum upper and lower receiver, M4 feed ramps, MI-SSM 12 in. handguard (M-LOK compatible), M16 bolt carrier group, Type III Class 2 hardcoat anodized matte black or FDE finish, 6 lbs. 2.9. oz.

MSR $1,185	$995	$625	$495	$450	$395	$350	$325	

Add $40 for M16 bolt carrier group.

* MI 16 In. Mid-Length Lightweight Rifle – .223 Wylde chamber, mid-length gas system, 16 in. Criterion chrome-lined barrel, A2 flash hider, Magpul CTR buttstock, Magpul MOE grip, forged aluminum upper and lower receiver, M4 feed ramps, MI-SSM-LW 12 in. lightweight handguard (M-LOK compatible), M16 bolt carrier group, Type III Class 2 hardcoat anodized matte black or FDE finish, 6 lbs. 2.1 oz.

MSR $1,185	$995	$625	$495	$450	$395	$350	$325	

Add $40 for M16 bolt carrier group.

MI 16 IN. SS 300 AAC RIFLE – .300 AAC Blackout cal., 16 in. Criterion stainless steel barrel, MI muzzle brake, Magpul CTR buttstock, Magpul MOE grip, forged aluminum upper and lower receiver, M4 feed ramps, Mil-Spec diameter buffer tube, M16 bolt carrier group, MI-SSK 12 in. handguard (M-LOK compatible), Type III Class 2 hardcoat anodized matte black or FDE finish.

MSR $1,325	$1,100	$675	$525	$450	$400	$350	$325	

MI 18 IN. KEYMOD RIFLE – .223 Wylde chamber, 18 in. Criterion chrome-lined barrel, A2 flash hider, Magpul CTR buttstock, Magpul MOE grip, forged aluminum upper and lower receiver, M4 feed ramps, MI-SSK 15 in. handguard (M-LOK compatible), Mil-Spec diameter buffer tube, M16 bolt carrier group, BCM charging handle, Type III Class 2 hardcoat anodized matte black or FDE (disc.) finish.

MSR $1,205	$1,025	$625	$495	$450	$395	$350	$325	

Add $40 for M16 bolt carrier group.

MI 20 SQUAD DESIGNATED MARKSMAN – .223 Wylde chamber, Criterion 20 in. stainless steel barrel, MI muzzle brake, CMC 3.5 lb. trigger, Magpul MOE rifle stock, Magpul MOE grip, forged aluminum upper and lower receiver, M4 feed ramps, MI-SSM 15 in. handguard (M-LOK compatible), Mil-Spec diameter buffer tube, Type III Class 2 hardcoat anodized matte black or FDE finish.

MSR $1,500	$1,250	$825	$575	$475	$425	$375	$350	

MI 300H HUNTER – .300 AAC Blackout cal., carbine length gas system with low profile gas block, 16 in. stainless steel Criterion barrel, 10 shot mag. with HIVIZ follower, flared magwell, integrated trigger guard, BCM Gunfighter pistol grip stock, billet aluminum upper and lower receiver, M4 feed ramps, reinforced buffer tube, ambidextrous 45 degree BAD selector, MI-SSK 12 in. KeyMod or M-LOK compatible, Picatinny top rail, BCM Gunfighter Mod 4 charging handle.

MSR $1,549	$1,275	$850	$600	$495	$425	$375	$350	

Add $20 for KeyMod rail section.
Add $40 for bolt carrier group.

MI M4 16 IN. BASIC RIFLE – 5.56 NATO cal., carbine length gas system, 16 in. M4 barrel with A2 flash hider, A2 front sight, USGI M4 buttstock, USGI A2 grip, Mil-Spec charging handle and buffer tube, forged aluminum upper and lower receivers, M4 feed ramps, heat shield handguard, Type III Class 2 hardcoat anodized matte black finish.

MSR $825	$695	$500	$425	$375	$335	$315	$295	

Add $40 for bolt carrier group.

254 MIDWEST INDUSTRIES, INC., cont.

MSR	100%	98%	95%	90%	80%	70%	60%	Last MSR

MI M4 SS12G2 RIFLE – 5.56 NATO cal., carbine length gas system, 16 in. M4 contour barrel, A2 flash hider, M4 buttstock, A2 grip, forged aluminum upper and lower receiver, M4 feed ramps, 12 in. free float handguard, M16 bolt carrier group, Mil-Spec charging handle, Type III Class 2 hardcoat anodized matte black finish.

	100%	98%	95%	90%	80%	70%	60%	
MSR $975	$825	$535	$450	$385	$340	$325	$295	

MI SSK12/SSM12 MINUTE MAN RIFLE – 5.56 NATO cal., mid-length gas system, low profile gas block, 16 in. hammer forged medium contour barrel, 30 shot mag., flared magwell, integrated trigger guard, BCM Gunfighter pistol grip stock, ambidextrous BAD safety selector, BCM Gunfighter Mod 4 charging handle, billet aluminum upper and lower receivers with Type III hardcoat anodized finish, M4 feed ramps, KeyMod (SSK12) or M-LOK (SSM12) 12 in. one-piece free float handguard, Picatinny rail, black or FDE finish on handguard, grip, and stock, 7 lbs.

	100%	98%	95%	90%	80%	70%	60%	
MSR $1,580	$1,315	$850	$625	$500	$435	$375	$350	

Add $20 for KeyMod handguard (SSK12).

MI SENTINEL CONCEPTS CARBINE – .223 Wylde chamber, 16 in. Criterion chrome-lined barrel, two chamber muzzle brake, Magpul 30 shot PMAG, MI SPLP sight package, Magpul SL stock, Magpul K2 grip, AXTS ambidextrous safety, forged aluminum upper and lower receiver, M4 feed ramps, 15 in. M-LOK compatible handguard, M16 bolt carrier group, Type III Class 2 hardcoat anodized matte black finish, Stealth Gray grip and buttstock, 7 lbs.

	100%	98%	95%	90%	80%	70%	60%	
MSR $1,650	$1,350	$875	$650	$525	$450	$385	$350	

MI T12G2 MINUTE MAN RIFLE – 5.56 NATO cal., mid-length gas system, low profile gas block, 16 in. hammer forged medium contour barrel, 30 shot mag., flared magwell, BCM Gunfighter pistol grip stock, integrated trigger guard, ambidextrous BAD safety selector, BCM Gunfighter Mod 4 charging handle, billet aluminum upper and lower receivers with Type III hardcoat anodized finish, M4 feed ramps, 12 in. one-piece free float Gen2 T-Series handguard, Picatinny rail, black or FDE finish on handguard, grip, and stock, 7.1 lbs.

	100%	98%	95%	90%	80%	70%	60%	
MSR $1,600	$1,315	$850	$625	$500	$435	$375	$350	

MI T12G3 MINUTE MAN RIFLE – 5.56 NATO cal., mid-length gas system, 16 in. hammer forged medium contour barrel, 30 shot mag., integrated trigger guard, BCM Gunfighter stock and pistol grip, ambidextrous BAD safety selector, forged aluminum upper and lower receiver, low profile gas block, M4 feed ramps, Type III hardcoat anodized black or FDE finish.

	100%	98%	95%	90%	80%	70%	60%	
MSR $1,600	$1,315	$850	$625	$500	$435	$375	$350	

MI TACTICAL RESPONSE 20TH ANNIVERSARY RIFLE – 5.56 NATO cal., rifle length gas system, 18 in. medium light custom profile barrel, two-chamber muzzle brake, Magpul 30 shot PMAG, MI SPLP sight package, Magpul SLR buttstock, Magpul MOE grip, AXTS ambidextrous safety, forged aluminum upper and lower receivers, M4 feed ramps, 15 in. M-LOK compatible handguard, M16 bolt carrier group, AXTS Raptor charging handle, Mil-Spec buffer tube, Type III Class 2 hardcoat anodized matte black finish, Olive Green or FDE grip and buttstock, 6 1/2 lbs.

	100%	98%	95%	90%	80%	70%	60%	
MSR $1,450	$1,235	$1,100	$985	$835	$725	$615	$515	

MILLER PRECISION ARMS

Previous AR-15 manufacturer located in Columbia Falls, MT until 2017.

RIFLES: SEMI-AUTO

MPA300 GUARDIAN – .300 Win. Mag. cal., 20 in. stainless steel ultra match SPR barrel, Precision Reflex forearm, Magpul PRS stock, Dark Earth Cerakote finish. Disc. 2017.

	100%	98%	95%	90%	80%	70%	60%	Last MSR
	$4,675	$4,100	$3,525	$2,950	$2,500	$2,050	$1,775	$5,399

MPAR 10 – .308 Win. cal., 16-24 in. stainless steel SPR contour barrel, free float aluminum forearm, LMT SOPMOD stock, bead blasted stainless steel finish. Disc. 2017.

	100%	98%	95%	90%	80%	70%	60%	Last MSR
	$1,725	$1,050	$850	$625	$550	$475	$425	$2,199

MPAR 15 – 5.56 NATO cal., 16 in. M4 button rifled chrome moly barrel, Troy Industries forearm, Magpul MOE stock, black anodized finish. Disc. 2017.

	100%	98%	95%	90%	80%	70%	60%	Last MSR
	$1,315	$850	$625	$500	$435	$375	$350	$1,599

MPA 762 – .308 Win. cal., 18 in. stainless steel ultra match SPR contour barrel, Precision Reflex Delta forearm, LMT SOPMOD stock, anodized finish. Disc. 2017.

	100%	98%	95%	90%	80%	70%	60%	Last MSR
	$3,175	$2,775	$2,275	$1,950	$1,625	$1,350	$1,160	$3,750

MILTAC INDUSTRIES, LLC

Previous AR-15 manufacturer located in Boise, ID.

PISTOLS: SEMI-AUTO

AR-15 PISTOL – 5.56 NATO/.223 Rem. or .300 AAC Blackout cal., GIO, 7 1/2 or 10 1/2 in. stainless steel barrel with

MILTAC INDUSTRIES, LLC, cont. 255 M

MSR		100%	98%	95%	90%	80%	70%	60%	Last MSR

KAK Industry "flash can", Sig Sauer SB15 arm brace, Magpul MOE grip, Troy Alpha (disc.) or MT Sierra Tango (new 2015) rail, 30 shot Magpul PMAG, Cerakote finish in black, Burnt Bronze, FDE, OD Green, or Tactical Grey. Mfg. mid-2014-2016.

		$925	$850	$725	$625	$550	$475	$425	$1,099

RIFLES: SEMI-AUTO

ALPHA SERIES – 5.56 NATO cal., GIO, 16 in. M4 chrome-lined barrel with Smith Enterprises Vortex flash hider, two Magpul 30 shot PMAGs, 13 in. modular free float Alpha rail, Geissele Super two-stage trigger, flared magwell, oversized trigger guard, 3D engraving on lower receiver, Troy Industries M4 flip-up iron battle sights, Magpul 6-position collapsible or extended stock, Magpul MIAD grip, includes Crossfire tactical carry case, hardcoat anodized and Cerakote finish in black, FDE, or two-tone, 6 lbs. 12 oz. Disc. 2016.

		$1,875	$1,100	$895	$650	$575	$495	$425	$2,389

BRAVO SERIES – .300 AAC Blackout cal., GIO, 16 in. stainless steel barrel with SP ATC muzzle brake, two Magpul 30 shot PMAGs, 13 in. modular free float Alpha rail, Geissele Super two-stage trigger, flared magwell, oversized trigger guard, 3D engraving on lower receiver, Troy Industries M4 flip-up iron battle sights, Magpul 6-position collapsible or extended stock, Magpul MIAD grip, includes Crossfire tactical carry case, hardcoat anodized and Cerakote finish in black, FDE, or two-tone, 7 lbs. 4 oz. Disc. 2016.

		$1,875	$1,100	$895	$650	$575	$495	$425	$2,389

COMBAT SERIES – 5.56 NATO/.223 Rem. cal., GIO, 16 in. stainless steel barrel with A4 flash hider, 30 shot Magpul PMAG, M4 double heat shield, 6-pos. stock, A2 black plastic grip, hardcoat anodized finish in black, FDE, or two-tone, 6 1/4 lbs. Mfg. mid-2014-2016.

		$995	$625	$495	$450	$395	$350	$325	$1,199

COMPETITION SERIES – 5.56 NATO/.223 Rem. cal., GIO, 18 in. stainless steel match grade 3-Gun threaded barrel, Geissele Match 3-Gun trigger, nickel boron bolt, oversized trigger guard, Cerakote finish. Mfg. mid-2014-2016.

		$2,225	$1,395	$1,050	$675	$595	$525	$475	$2,789

ECHO SERIES – 5.56 NATO cal., GIO, 16 in. M4 chrome-lined barrel with Smith Enterprises Vortex or YHM (new 2014) flash hider, 13 in. modular free float Alpha or Sierra Tango (new 2014) rail, nickel boron bolt carrier group, flared magwell, oversized trigger guard, 3D engraving on lower receiver, no sights, Magpul MOE carbine Mil-Spec stock, Magpul MOE grip, hardcoat anodized and Cerakote finish in black, FDE, or two-tone, 6 lbs. 4 oz. Disc. 2016.

		$1,475	$950	$725	$550	$475	$395	$350	$1,789

SIX SERIES – 6.8 SPC or 6.5 Grendel cal., 16 or 20 in. stainless steel threaded barrel, Geissele two-stage trigger, nickel boron bolt, Cerakote finish. Mfg. mid-2014-2016.

		$2,125	$1,325	$995	$675	$595	$525	$475	$2,639

MITCHELL ARMS, INC.

Previous manufacturer, importer, and distributor located in Fountain Valley, CA.

RIFLES: DISC.

M-16A3 – .22 LR, .22 WMR (disc. 1987), or .32 ACP cal., patterned after Colt's AR-15, GIO. Mfg. 1987-94.

		$450	$395	$350	$300	$275	$250	$225	$266

Add 20% for .22 WMR cal. or .32 ACP (disc. 1988).

MOHAWK ARMORY

Current AR-15 style manufacturer located in Midway, TN.

Mohawk Armory offers a line of AR-15 style semi-auto rifles and pistols. The company is also a Class III dealer and offers many products for law enforcement/military. Please contact the company directly for more information, including pricing and available options (see Trademark Index).

MOSSBERG, O.F. & SONS, INC.

Current manufacturer located in North Haven, CT, 1962-present and New Haven, CT, 1919-1962.

Oscar Mossberg developed an early reputation as a designer and inventor for the Iver Johnson, Marlin-Rockwell, Stevens, and Shattuck Arms companies. In 1915, he began producing a 4-shot, .22 LR cal. palm pistol known as the "Novelty," with revolving firing pin. After producing approx. 600 of these pistols, he sold the patent to C.S. Shattuck, which continued to manufacture guns under the name "Unique." The first 600 had no markings except serial numbers, and were destined for export to South America. Very few of these original "Novelty" pistols survived in this country, and they are extremely rare specimens.

Mossberg acquired Advanced Ordnance Corp. during 1996, a high quality manufacturer utilizing state-of-the-art CNC machinery.

PISTOLS: SEMI-AUTO

At the SHOT Show during 2014, Mossberg unveiled its new Duck Commander Series. Please refer to individual listings.

M 256 MOSSBERG, O.F. & SONS, INC., cont.

MSR	100%	98%	95%	90%	80%	70%	60%	Last MSR

MODEL 715P – .22 LR cal., 6 in. blued barrel with A2 style muzzle brake, 10 (disc. 2015) or 25 shot mag., full-length top Picatinny rail with mounted adj. front/rear sights or 1x30mm red dot sight (715P Red Dot Combo), short vented quad rail forend, pistol grip synthetic stock, black finish, 3-3 1/2 lbs. Mfg. 2014-2017.

| | $275 | $250 | $225 | $200 | $185 | $175 | $165 | *$314* |

Add $44 for 1x30mm red dot sight (715P Red Dot Combo).

MOSSBERG INTERNATIONAL 715P DUCK COMMANDER – .22 LR cal., 6 in. barrel with A2 muzzle brake, 25 shot mag., accessory loader, Picatinny rail mounted red dot sight, adj. front and rear sights, short quad rail forend, pistol grip stock, Realtree Max-5 camo finish, 3 1/2 lbs. Mfg. 2014-2015.

| | $395 | $365 | $330 | $300 | $275 | $250 | $225 | *$447* |

RIFLES: SEMI-AUTO

At the SHOT Show during 2014, Mossberg unveiled its new Duck Commander Series. Please refer to individual listings.

MOSSBERG INTERNATIONAL 715T FLAT TOP DUCK COMMANDER – .22 LR cal., blowback action, 16 1/4 in. blued barrel with A2 style muzzle brake, quad rail forearm, Picatinny rail mounted adj. rifle sights, 25 shot mag., accessory loader, adj. tactical synthetic stock, Realtree Max-5 finish, includes American flag bandana, 5 1/2 lbs. Mfg. 2014-2015.

| | $425 | $375 | $350 | $325 | $300 | $290 | $275 | *$509* |

MODEL 715T TACTICAL CARRY (TACTICAL 22) – .22 LR cal., AR-15 style, blowback action, 18 in. barrel, matte black finish, 10 or 25 shot mag., synthetic fixed or 6-position adj. stock, front post sight, adj. rifle sights, Picatinny quad rail forend, handle mounted top rail, mag. loading assist tool, integrated A2 style carry handle, 5 1/4 lbs. Mfg. 2011-2015.

| | $275 | $250 | $225 | $210 | $200 | $190 | $180 | *$308* |

MODEL 715T FLAT-TOP – .22 LR cal., blowback action, 16 1/4 in. barrel with A2 style muzzle brake, blue barrel finish, 10 or 25 shot mag., flat-top with full-length top rail, removable/adj. sights (disc. 2017) or 30mm red dot sights, fixed (disc. 2017) or adj. synthetic stock, black, Mossy Oak Brush (disc. 2015), Muddy Girl (mfg. 2014-2017), or Muddy Girl Serenity (new 2018) camo finish, 5 1/2-5 3/4 lbs. New 2012.

| MSR $326 | $285 | $250 | $225 | $210 | $200 | $190 | $180 | |

Add $112 for Muddy Girl Serenity camo finish (new 2018).

Add $46 for red dot combo model.

Add $66 for Muddy Girl camo finish (mfg. 2014-2017).

Add $69 for Mossy Oak Brush camo finish (disc. 2015).

Add $10 for removable A2 style Picatinny mounted front and rear sights (disc. 2017).

MMR CARBINE – 5.56 NATO cal., GIO, 16 1/4 in. barrel with A2 style muzzle brake, 10 or 30 shot mag., removable Picatinny mounted adj. front and rear sights, black fixed or synthetic 6-pos. adj. stock, Magpul MOE grip, 13 in. free float forend with M-LOK slots, black anodized finish, 6 3/4 lbs. New 2016.

| MSR $938 | $800 | $525 | $450 | $385 | $340 | $325 | $295 | |

MMR HUNTER – 5.56 NATO cal., GIO, 20 in. carbon steel barrel with black phosphate metal finish, 5 shot mag., SST, anodized aluminum receiver, Picatinny top rail, A2 black synthetic stock, SE-1 pistol grip with battery compartment, checkered aluminum tubular forend, black, Mossy Oak Treestand or Mossy Oak Brush camo finish, no sights, 7 1/2 lbs. Mfg. mid-2011-2015.

| | $875 | $550 | $465 | $395 | $350 | $325 | $300 | *$1,028* |

Add $99 for camo finish.

MMR PRO – 5.56 NATO/.223 Rem. cal., GIO, 18 in. free floating stainless steel barrel, removable suppressor-ready SilencerCo muzzle brake with ASR mount, 30 shot Magpul PMAG, ejection port dust cover, JM Pro drop-in match trigger, black synthetic 6-pos. stock, adj. LOP, interchangeable FLEX pad, 15 in. slim profile forend with M-LOK, Magpul MOE grip and trigger guard, forward assist, full-length top Picatinny rail, AXTS Raptor ambidextrous charging handle, phosphate and hardcoat anodized metal finishes. New 2017.

| MSR $1,393 | $1,150 | $750 | $550 | $465 | $415 | $375 | $350 | |

MMR TACTICAL – 5.56 NATO cal., GIO, 16 1/4 in. carbon steel barrel with black phosphate metal finish, 10 or 30 shot mag., SST, anodized aluminum receiver, black synthetic fixed or 6-position collapsible stock, A2 style muzzle brake, no sights or removable Picatinny rail, Stark SE-1 deluxe pistol grip, quad rail forend, approx. 7-7 1/2 lbs. Mfg. mid-2011-2015.

| | $850 | $550 | $465 | $395 | $350 | $325 | $295 | *$987* |

Add $41 for Picatinny rail.

MMR TACTICAL OPTICS READY – 5.56 NATO/.223 Rem. cal., GIO, 16 in. barrel, removable A2 style muzzle brake, 30 shot Magpul PMAG, JM Pro drop-in match trigger, black synthetic 6-pos. stock with FLEX pad, Magpul MOE grip and trigger guard, 13 in. slim profile forend with M-LOK handguard, full-length top Picatinny rail, phosphate and hardcoat anodized metal finishes, 7 lbs. New 2017.

| MSR $1,253 | $1,065 | $650 | $500 | $450 | $395 | $350 | $325 | |

Add $146 for Vortex StrikeFire II red/green dot sight with cantilever mount.

N SECTION

NEMO ARMS (NEW EVOLUTION MILITARY ORDNANCE)

Current pistol and rifle manufacturer located in Nampa, ID beginning 2016. Previously located in Kalispell, MT. Dealer sales.

MSR	100%	98%	95%	90%	80%	70%	60%	Last MSR

PISTOLS: SEMI-AUTO

BATTLE LIGHT PISTOL – 5.56 NATO or .300 AAC Blackout cal., 8 in. barrel, flash can muzzle device, 30 shot Magpul Gen3 PMAG, Magpul MIAD grip, ambidextrous safety, mag. release, and charging handle, pistol length gas system, 10 1/4 in. M-LOK modular rail, multi-position pistol receiver extension, NEMO billet upper and lower receiver, steel QD mounts, KAK pistol brace, Cerakote Burnt Bronze or Graphite Gray finish, 5.6 lbs. New 2018.

MSR $2,550	$2,150	$1,650	$1,250	$1,000	$850	$700	$650	

RIFLES: SEMI-AUTO

NEMO manufactures many variations of rifles built on the AR-15 style platform. It currently sells weapon systems to the military, law enforcement, special operations, and the civilian marketplace. NEMO also makes tactical bolt action rifles per individual specifications.

BATTLE LIGHT RIFLE – 5.56 NATO cal., GIO, 16 in. stainless steel barrel, NEMO dual chamber compact muzzle brake, Magpul 30 shot Gen3 PMAG, Magpul CTR Mil-Spec carbine stock, Magpul MIAD grip, ambidextrous safety selector, mag. release, and charging handle, pinned low profile gas block, stainless gas tube, NEMO upper and lower receiver, 15 in. M-LOK modular rail, 6-pos. Mil-Spec carbine receiver extension, carbine buffer and spring, Cerakote Burnt Bronze finish, 6.2 lbs. New 2018.

MSR $2,450	$1,975	$1,150	$925	$650	$575	$495	$425	

BATTLE LIGHT SYN-COR – 5.56 NATO cal., GPO, 11 1/2 in. stainless steel barrel with pinned suppressor sleeve (17 in. total barrel length), Magpul 30 shot Gen3 PMAG, Magpul CTR Mil-Spec carbine stock, Magpul MIAD grip, ambidextrous safety selector, mag. release, and charging handle, titanium/stainless hybrid monolithic suppressor core, NEMO upper and lower receiver, 15 in. M-LOK modular rail, 6-pos. Mil-Spec carbine receiver extension, carbine buffer and spring, Cerakote Gray finish, 8 lbs. New 2018.

MSR $3,700	$3,050	$1,975	$1,425	$850	$675	$625	$575	

BATTLE LIGHT VALKYRIE RIFLE – .224 Valkyrie cal., GIO, 20 in. stainless steel barrel, NEMO dual chamber compact muzzle brake, 10 shot PMAG, Magpul CTR Mil-Spec carbine stock, Magpul MIAD grip, ambidextrous safety selector, mag. release, and charging handle, pinned low profile gas block, stainless gas tube, NEMO upper and lower receiver, 15 in. M-LOK modular rail, 6-pos. Mil-Spec carbine receiver extension, carbine buffer and spring, Cerakote Sniper Green finish, 40 in. OAL, 7 lbs. New 2018.

MSR $2,450	$1,975	$1,150	$925	$650	$575	$495	$425	

OMEN ASP (AUXILIARY SNIPER PLATFORM) – .300 Win. Mag. cal., adj. gas block, 16 in. stainless steel barrel, NEMO muzzle brake, includes two 14 shot polymer mags., Geissele SSA-E two-stage trigger, Magpul MOE buttstock, Magpul cheek riser, enhanced pistol grip, billet aluminum receivers with hard anodized finish, nickel boron bolt carrier group with NEMO patented recoil reduction system, steel side charging handle, enhanced Magnum buffer, NEMO integrated free floating handguard with custom finish, two detachable accessory rails, includes custom drag bag, 9.4 lbs. Mfg. mid-2016-2017.

Retail pricing was not available for this model.

OMEN M-210 – .300 Win. Mag. cal., 20 in. stainless steel Bergara barrel, NEMO DC-1 steel dual chamber muzzle brake, 14 shot mag., Magpul MOE fixed rifle stock, Magpul MIAD grip, patented recoil reduction system, 15 in. M-LOK modular rail, NEMO billet upper and lower receivers, Cerakote Armor Black finish, 10.2 lbs. New 2018.

MSR $3,900	$3,350	$2,850	$2,425	$2,000	$1,650	$1,450	$1,200	

OMEN MATCH – 7mm Rem. Mag. or .338 Win. Mag. cal., adj. gas block, 24 in. stainless steel fluted barrel with B1 Tri Lug suppressor ready muzzle brake, two 14 shot mags., Geissele two-stage trigger, Magpul PRS Sniper stock, Hogue overmolded pistol grip, billet aluminum receivers with Custom Tiger Stripe anodized finish, two detachable accessory rails, NiB bolt carrier group, steel side charging handle, NEMO integrated free floating customizable handguard, includes custom drag bag, black finish, 12.6 lbs. Mfg. 2014-2015.

	$5,500	$4,815	$4,125	$3,745	$3,025	$2,475	$1,925	*$6,075*

OMEN/OMEN MATCH 2.0 – .300 Win. Mag. cal., GIO, 22 in. match grade (disc. 2013) or fluted stainless steel (new 2014) barrel with NEMO PC Tornado flash hider (disc. 2013) or NEMO A-10 muzzle brake (new 2014), nickel boron barrel extension and feed ramp, two NEMO 14 shot mags., Geissele two-stage trigger, two detachable handguard accessory rails with built-in QD mounts, NEMO integrated free floating customizable handguard with hard black anodized finish, low profile (disc. 2013) or adj. (new 2014) gas block, NEMO steel side charging handle, Mako adj. SSR-25 sniper stock and Hogue overmolded pistol grip with black finish, Tru-Spec Drag Bag, billet upper and lower receivers with SF Tiger Stripe finish, 10 1/2 lbs. Mfg. 2012-2017.

	$5,500	$4,815	$4,125	$3,740	$3,025	$2,475	$1,925	*$5,699*

Add $151 for Magpul PRS stock (new 2015).

The Omen model was upgraded in 2014 and renamed the Omen Match 2.0.

N 258 NEMO ARMS (NEW EVOLUTION MILITARY ORDNANCE), cont.

MSR	100%	98%	95%	90%	80%	70%	60%	Last MSR

OMEN MATCH 3.0 – .300 Win. Mag. cal., 4-position adj. gas system, 22 in. stainless steel barrel, 14 shot mag. w/ aluminum follower, Geissele SSA-E two-stage trigger, Magpul PRS adj. rifle stock, MIAD pistol grip, ambidextrous safety, suppressor ready, 15 in. M-LOK modular rail, NiB coated receiver, 11.2 lbs.

MSR $5,100	$4,600	$4,025	$3,450	$3,135	$2,550	$2,075	$1,625	

OMEN PRATKA – .300 Win. Mag. cal., GIO, 20 in. ultra lightweight fluted stainless steel barrel with NEMO A-10 muzzle brake, two NEMO 14 shot polymer mags., nickel boron barrel extension and feed ramp, Geissele two-stage trigger, Mission First Tactical Battlelink ultra lightweight Minimalist stock with sling mounts, Hogue overmolded pistol grip, steel side charging handle, NEMO integrated free floated customizable handguard with black anodized finish, two detachable handguard accessory rails with built-in QD mounts, includes carry case, black finish, 9 1/2 lbs. Mfg. 2014-2016.

	$3,600	$3,150	$2,700	$2,450	$1,975	$1,625	$1,265	*$3,999*

OMEN RECON – .300 Win. Mag. cal., 18 in. fluted stainless steel barrel with B1 Tri-Lug suppressor ready muzzle brake, adj. gas block, nickel boron barrel extension, feed ramp, bolt release, and bolt carrier with recoil reduction system, Geissele two-stage trigger, two 14 shot polymer mags., billet aluminum receivers with Custom Tiger Stripe finish, NEMO integrated free float customizable handguard with black finish, two detachable handguard accessory rails with built-in QD mounts, steel side charging handle, Mission First Tactical Battlelink collapsible carbine stock with adj. cheekpiece, Hogue overmolded pistol grip, black finish, includes custom drag bag, 10 lbs. New 2014.

MSR $4,900	$4,550	$3,975	$3,425	$3,095	$2,500	$2,050	$1,595	

OMEN WATCHMAN 2.0 – .300 Win. Mag. cal., adj. gas block, 24 in. carbon fiber barrel with B1 Tri Lug suppressor ready muzzle brake, Picatinny rail on top of aluminum free float integrated customizable handguard and billet aluminum receiver, both with Custom Tiger Stripe anodized finish, Geissele SSA-E two-stage trigger, nickel boron bolt carrier group, steel side charging handle, two 14 shot polymer mags., ambidextrous safety, two detachable accessory rails, Magpul PRS Sniper stock, Hogue overmolded pistol grip, black finish, includes custom drag bag, 12.6 lbs. New 2014.

MSR $6,200	$5,750	$5,050	$4,300	$3,900	$3,150	$2,600	$2,000	

TANGO 2 – 5.56 NATO/.223 Rem. cal., GIO, 16 in. NEMO stainless steel barrel with PC Tornado flash hider, billet upper and lower receivers with SF Tiger Stripe finish, Geissele two-stage trigger, rifle length free float KeyMod handguard with removable rail system in black, low profile gas block, charging handle with tactical latch, Troy micro sights, Mission First Tactical Battlelink collapsible stock with optional cheek riser, Hogue overmolded pistol grip, ambi safety, one PMAG, Timney trigger, black finish, foam lined case, 7 lbs. Disc. 2017.

	$2,375	$1,525	$1,150	$700	$625	$550	$475	*$2,975*

* **Tango 2 Lite** – .223 Wylde chamber, 16 in. barrel, similar configuration to the Tango 2 model, Picatinny rail, FDE finish. 6.2 lbs. Mfg. 2017 only.

Retail pricing was not available for this model.

TANGO 6 – .300 AAC Blackout cal., GIO, 16 in. NEMO stainless steel barrel with NEMO flash hider, low profile gas block, billet aluminum receivers with Custom Tiger Stripe finish, Troy micro sights, two KeyMod Picatinny accessory rails, charging handle with tactical latch, nickel boron bolt carrier assembly, Geissele two-stage trigger, rifle length free float KeyMod handguard, Mission First Tactical Battlelink collapsible stock with optional cheek riser, Hogue overmolded pistol grip, black finish, includes foam lined case, 7 lbs. Disc. 2017.

	$2,375	$1,525	$1,150	$700	$625	$550	$475	*$2,975*

TANGO 8 – .308 Win. cal., 16 in. stainless steel barrel with NEMO flash hider and black nitride finish, low profile gas block, Geissele SSA-E two-stage trigger, NEMO integrated free floated customizable handguard, two detachable handguard accessory rails with built-in QD mounts, Troy micro sights, charging handle with tactical latch, billet aluminum receiver with Custom Tiger Stripe finish, NEMO adj. buttstock assembly with battery storage, Hogue overmolded pistol grip, black finish, includes one Magpul PMAG and foam lined case. Disc. 2017.

	$3,775	$2,700	$1,700	$1,075	$825	$750	$700	*$4,200*

* **Tango 8 MSP** – .308 Win. cal., 16 in. stainless barrel with NEMO muzzle brake, Troy Micro backup iron sights, nickel boron bolt carrier group, low profile gas block, Battle Arms ambi safety selector, BCM Gunfighter charging handle with tactical latch, two detachable handguard accessory rails with built-in QD mounts, rifle length free floated handguard, Geissele two-stage trigger, Magpul PRS buttstock, Hogue overmolded pistol grip, black finish, includes one Magpul PMAG and foam lined case, 8.7 lbs. Disc. 2017.

	$3,925	$2,800	$1,750	$1,150	$875	$775	$700	*$4,825*

* **Tango 8 SASS** – .308 Win. cal., same as Tango 8, except features 20 in. SASS Profile stainless steel barrel, NEMO rifle length integrated free floated customizable handguard, Magpul PRS buttstock, black finish, 10.8 lbs. Disc. 2017.

	$3,775	$2,700	$1,700	$1,075	$825	$750	$700	*$4,675*

Ti ONE TITANIUM RIFLE – .308 Win. cal., AR-15 style, GIO, 16 in. stainless steel HBAR profile barrel, titanium matched receiver set, customizable tube handguard, Troy Tritium micro set backup iron sights, titanium Picatinny handguard rails, low profile gas block, charging handle with tactical latch, 6-pos. buttstock, Hogue grip with battery management system, titanium DRK compensator, Timney trigger, titanium buffer tube, black Nitride finish, 8.65 lbs. Serial No. 1.

Current MSR on this rifle is $95,000.

NEMO ARMS (NEW EVOLUTION MILITARY ORDNANCE), cont. 259 N

MSR	100%	98%	95%	90%	80%	70%	60%	Last MSR

XO CARBON – .308 Win., .260 Rem., or 6.5mm Creedmoor cal., Proof Research 20 or 22 in. carbon fiber wrapped barrel, NEMO dual chamber compact muzzle brake, Magpul 20 shot Gen3 PMAG, Geissele SD-E two-stage trigger, Magpul CTR Mil-Spec carbine stock, Magpul MIAD grip, full ambi-control billet upper and lower receivers, patented recoil reduction system, 15 in. M-LOK modular handguard, Cerakote Tungsten Grey finish, 8.2 lbs. New mid-2016.

| MSR $4,300 | $3,525 | $2,425 | $1,625 | $995 | $725 | $675 | $650 | |

XO STEEL – 6.5mm Creedmoor or .308 Win. cal., 16, 20, or 22 in. Bartlein barrel, NEMO DC-1 6AL-4V titanium dual chamber muzzle device, Magpul 20 shot Gen3 PMAG, Geissele SD-E two-stage trigger, Magpul CTR Mil-Spec carbine stock, Magpul MIAD grip, ambi controls, 15 in. M-LOK modular rail, 7-pos. "Carrier Cradle" anti-tilt receiver extension, multi-function gas block, utilizes the NEMO Arms recoil reduction carrier, billet upper and lower receivers, Cerakote Tungsten Grey finish, 9 1/2 lbs. New mid-2016.

| MSR $3,625 | $2,950 | $1,925 | $1,400 | $825 | $675 | $625 | $575 | |

Add $175 for 20 or 22 in. barrel.

NEWTOWN FIREARMS

Previous manufacturer located in Hangtown, CA until 2017.

CARBINES: SEMI-AUTO

NF-15/GEN 2 TACTICAL – 5.56 NATO cal., AR-15 style, GIO or GPO, 16 in. match grade vanadium steel fluted barrel with flash hider, 10 or 20 shot mag., quad Picatinny rail, black furniture, collapsible stock, sub MOA accuracy guaranteed, 8 lbs. Disc. 2013.

| | $2,375 | $1,525 | $1,150 | $700 | $625 | $550 | $475 | *$2,950* |

NF-15 GEN 3 MATCH – .223 Wylde chamber, GPO, 16 in. McGowen HBAR match stainless steel barrel with black Nitride coating, Gen 3 Mil-Spec T6 heavy mass billet upper and lower receiver set, Timney match trigger, modular free float quad rail, Adams Arms 4-pos. carbine length piston system with Adams Arms piston carrier, Battle Arms ambi safety, billet tactical charging handle, Magpul ACS Mil-Spec stock, Ergo SureGrip pistol grip. Mfg. 2014-2017.

| | $2,295 | $1,450 | $1,075 | $675 | $595 | $525 | $475 | *$2,800* |

GEN-4 NF-15 – .223 Wylde chamber, GIO, 16 in. McGowen HBAR match stainless steel barrel with black Nitride coating and Barnes Precision A2 enhanced flash hider, billet tactical latch charging handle, Battle Arms ambidextrous safety selector, Gen-4 Mil-Spec T6 forged or Gen-4 Mil-Spec T6 billet lower receiver, forged upper receiver, modular free float quad rail, handguard with low heat-sync barrel nut, Barnes Precision gas block or Troy low pro gas block, 6-pos. carbine buffer tube, Magpul CTR stock, Ergo SureGrip pistol grip. Mfg. 2014-2017.

| | $1,250 | $825 | $575 | $475 | $425 | $375 | $350 | *$1,499* |

Add $200 for Gen-4 Mil-Spec T6 billet lower receiver.

GEN-4 NF-15 PISTON – .223 Wylde chamber, S.M.A.A.R.T. Infinitely adj. GPO, 16 in. McGowen HBAR match stainless steel barrel with black Nitride coating and Barnes Precision A2 enhanced flash hider, Gen-4 Mil-Spec T6 forged or Gen-4 Mil-Spec billet lower receiver, forged upper receiver, ACT combat trigger, modular free float quad rail, handguard with low heat-sync barrel nut, 6-pos. carbine buffer tube, billet tactical latch charging handle, Battle Arms ambidextrous safety selector, Magpul CTR stock, Ergo SureGrip pistol grip. Mfg. 2014-2017.

| | $1,675 | $1,000 | $825 | $625 | $550 | $475 | $425 | *$2,099* |

Add $300 for Gen-4 Mil-Spec T6 billet lower receiver.

NOREEN FIREARMS LLC

Current bolt action and AR-15 style rifle manufacturer located in Belgrade, MT.

RIFLES: SEMI-AUTO

BAD NEWS GEN II (BAD NEWS ULTRA LONG RANGE - ULR) – .300 Win. Mag. (disc.), .338 Norma (mfg. 2014-2015), or .338 Lapua cal., GPO, 26 in. barrel, custom muzzle brake, 5 or 10 shot detachable box mag., aluminum receiver, Mil-Spec (disc.) or match (new 2016) trigger, one-piece bolt carrier, Picatinny quad rail on handguard, Magpul PRS adj. stock, matte black finish, 13 lbs.

| MSR $5,996 | $5,250 | $4,675 | $3,925 | $3,475 | $2,800 | $2,295 | $1,775 | |

In 2016, this model's nomenclature changed to Bad News Gen II because it received upgraded receivers, handguard, billet magazines, and a new adj. gas block.

BBN223 – 5.56x45mm cal., GIO, 16 in. barrel with Noreen flash hider, Mil-Spec trigger, Magpul MBUS flip-up sights, 6-position collabsible stock, A2 pistol grip, sling mounts, 6 lbs. New 2016.

| MSR $1,300 | $1,075 | $675 | $500 | $450 | $400 | $350 | $325 | |

BN36 CARBINE ASSASSIN – .30-06 cal., GIO, 16 in. barrel with flash hider, 20 shot mag., Mil-Spec trigger, enlarged trigger guard, collapsible stock, A2 pistol grip, black finish, 7 lbs. Mfg. 2016-2017.

| | $1,425 | $925 | $700 | $550 | $475 | $395 | $350 | *$1,750* |

N 260 NOREEN FIREARMS LLC, cont.

MSR	100%	98%	95%	90%	80%	70%	60%	Last MSR

BN36 CARBINE ASSASSIN-X – .30-06 cal., GIO, 16 in. barrel with flash hider, 20 shot mag., Mil-Spec trigger, Luth-AR stock, Tactical Dynamics pistol grip, black finish, 7 lbs. Mfg. 2016-2017.

	$1,675	$1,000	$825	$625	$550	$475	$425	*$2,050*

Blue Book Publications selected this model as one of its Top 10 Industry Awards from all the new firearms at the 2016 SHOT Show.

BN36X3 CARBINE – .30-06 cal., GIO, side charging, 16 in. barrel with flash hider, 20 shot mag., composite stock, A2 pistol grip, black finish, 7 lbs. New mid-2018.

MSR $1,800	$1,475	$950	$725	$550	$475	$395	$350	

BN36X3 CARBINE X – .30-06 cal., GIO, side charging, 16 in. barrel with flash hider, 20 shot mag., Mil-Spec trigger, Luth-AR stock, Tactical Dynamics pistol grip, black finish, 7 lbs. New mid-2018.

MSR $2,149	$1,725	$1,050	$850	$625	$550	$475	$425	

BN36X3 CARBINE X FEATURELESS – .30-06 cal., GIO, side charging, 16 in. barrel with Noreen muzzle brake, 20 shot mag., match grade trigger, Thordsen barrel, black finish, 7 lbs. New mid-2018.

MSR $2,300	$1,875	$1,100	$895	$650	$575	$495	$425	

BN36X3 LONG RANGE (BN36 LONG RANGE ASSASSIN / BN36 SEMI-AUTO) – .25-06 Rem., .270 Win., .30-06, .300 Win. Mag., or 7mm Rem. Mag. (new 2016) cal., GIO, 22 in. chrome moly barrel, Noreen design muzzle brake, side charging, matte black finish, fixed A2 (disc.) or Luth-AR stock with pistol grip, 5, 10, or 20 shot box mag., Mil-Spec or optional match trigger, 9 lbs. New 2013.

MSR $2,149	$1,725	$1,050	$850	$625	$550	$475	$425	

Add $596 for .300 Win. Mag. or 7mm Rem. Mag. cal.

BN308 – .308 Win. cal., GIO, 16 in. barrel with flash hider, 20 shot mag., Mil-Spec trigger, Luth-AR stock, Tactical Dynamics pistol grip, updated forearm (new 2016) with Picatinny rail, Type III hardcoat anodized black finish, 8 lbs. New 2015.

MSR $2,050	$1,675	$1,000	$825	$625	$550	$475	$425	

NORTHERN COMPETITION

Previous rifle manufacturer located in Racine, WI.

RIFLES: SEMI-AUTO

Northern Competition manufactured a line of AR-15 style rifles in various calibers and configurations. Recent models are described within this section. Previous models included the Predator and Ranch models.

CHEETAH – .22-250, .243 Win., or .308 Win. cal., AR-15 style, GIO, 24 or 26 in. chrome moly barrel, 19 shot Magpul mag., quad rail Picatinny handguard, Magpul PRS stock, NM two-stage trigger, black finish, 12 1/2 lbs. Disc. 2013.

	$1,675	$1,000	$825	$625	$550	$475	$425	*$2,019*

COMPLETE SERVICE RIFLE (NCSR15) – .22-250, .243 Win., or .308 Win. cal., GIO, AR-15 style Classic A2 design, pre or post-ban configuration, 20 in. heavy barrel, A2 style buttstock, two-stage trigger, charging handle, NM float tube assembly, NM front sight housing, NM double pinned minute sights, black finish. Disc. 2017.

	$1,250	$825	$575	$475	$425	$375	$350	*$1,495*

Add $200 for Geissele trigger.

COUGAR – .22-250, .243 Win., or .308 Win. cal., AR-15 style, GIO, 24 or 26 in. chrome moly barrel, single stage trigger, A2 style buttstock, pistol grip, black finish, 12 lbs. Disc. 2013.

	$1,425	$925	$700	$550	$475	$395	$350	*$1,719*

NOSLER, INC.

Current rifle, ammunition, and bullet manufacturer established during 1948 and located in Bend, OR.

Founded in 1948, Nosler, Incorporated is a family owned company. Nosler is most known for revolutionizing the hunting bullet industry with bullets such as the Partition®, Ballistic Tip®, AccuBond®, E-Tip®, and most recently the AccuBond® LR. With the company motto of "Quality First", Nosler manufactures premium component bullets, reloading brass, ammunition, and semi-custom rifles for domestic and international customers making Nosler a comprehensive shooting products company.

Recent company caliber releases include the following: .26 Nosler - 2014, .28 Nosler - 2015, .30 Nosler - 2015, .33 Nosler - 2016, and .22 Nosler - 2017.

RIFLES: SEMI-AUTO

VARMAGEDDON AR – .22 Nosler cal., 18 in. barrel with muzzle and thread protector, Precision Reflex 25 shot mag., Geissele SD-E trigger, MBUS Pro sights, Magpul PRS Gen 3 stock, Magpul MOE grip, STS ambi safety, Picatinny 9-slot rail, NSR 15 in. KeyMod handguard, Super Badass charging handle, quick detach sling swivels, KeyMod quick release swivel mount, KeyMod sling stud, includes NSR polymer accessory pack, soft case, and sling, Flat Dark Earth finish. Built by Noveske Rifleworks beginning 2017.

MSR $2,870	$2,295	$1,450	$1,075	$675	$595	$525	$475	

NOSLER, INC., cont. 261 N

MSR	100%	98%	95%	90%	80%	70%	60%	Last MSR

VARMAGEDDON 5.56 NATO – 5.56 NATO cal., AR-15 style, GIO, 18 in. stainless steel barrel, Geissele SD-E trigger, Magpul PRS stock, adj. LOP and comb, MOE grip, Noveske Gen III upper and lower receiver with Picatinny rail and integrated 13 1/2 in. NSR handguard with KeyMod system, extended feed ramp. Mfg. 2013-2016.

	$2,375	$1,525	$1,150	$700	$625	$550	$475	*$2,995*

Add $900 for package with Leupold Varmageddon scope and CDS turret.

VARMEGEDDON .300 AAC BLACKOUT – .300 AAC Blackout cal., AR-15 style, GIO, 16 in. stainless steel barrel, Geissele SD-E trigger, Magpul STR stock features two storage compartments, adj. LOP, MOE grip, Noveske Gen. III upper and lower receiver with Picatinny rail and integrated 13 1/2 in. NSR handguard with KeyMod system, extended feed ramp. Mfg. 2013-2016.

	$2,375	$1,525	$1,150	$700	$625	$550	$475	*$2,995*

Add $900 for package with Leupold Varmageddon scope and CDS turret.

NOVESKE RIFLEWORKS LLC

Current manufacturer located in Grants Pass, OR. Dealer and distributor sales.

PISTOLS: SEMI-AUTO

GEN III 300 BLK PISTOL – .300 AAC Blackout cal., 8 1/2 in. stainless steel barrel, KX5 flash suppressor, 30 shot mag., ALG Defense ACT trigger, Magpul MBUS Pro folding sights, MIAD pistol grip, low profile gas block pinned to barrel, Gen III billet upper receiver with extended feed ramps, Gen III lower with pistol receiver extension, Noveske marked Geissele Super Badass charging handle, 7 oz. pistol buffer, NSR 9 in. free floating handguard with 1913 top rail, Type III hardcoat anodizing with black Cerakote ceramic coating. New 2018.

MSR $2,095	$1,795	$1,575	$1,325	$1,150	$995	$850	$700	

GEN III DIPLOMAT PISTOL – 5.56 NATO cal., 7 1/2 in. stainless steel barrel, KX5 flash suppressor, 30 shot mag., ALG Defense ACT trigger, Magpul MBUS Pro folding sights, MIAD pistol grip, low profile gas block pinned to barrel, Gen III billet upper receiver with extended feed ramps, Gen III billet lower receiver with pistol receiver extension, staked Noveske QD endplate, Noveske marked Geissele Super Badass charging handle, 7 oz. pistol buffer, NSR 9 in. free floating handguard with 1913 top rail, Type III hardcoat anodizing with black Cerakote ceramic coating. New 2018.

MSR $2,095	$1,795	$1,575	$1,325	$1,150	$995	$850	$700	

RIFLES/CARBINES: SEMI-AUTO

.300 BLK CARBINE LO-PRO/NSR – .300 AAC Blackout cal., GIO, 16 in. stainless steel barrel, Blackout 51T flash suppressor, low profile gas block pinned to barrel, forged Gen. II lower, forged VLTOR MUR upper with anti-rotation interfaced with handguard, Gunfighter charging handle, 11 in. free float handguard with 1913 rails or 13 1/2 in. NSR free floating handguard with 1913 top rail, Mil-Spec receiver extension, black finish, extended feed ramp, H2 buffer, VLTOR IMOD carbine stock, flip-up front and rear sights, approx. 6 lbs. Disc. 2013.

	$1,875	$1,100	$895	$650	$575	$495	$425	*$2,335*

Add $160 for Lo-Pro Model.

BASIC LIGHT RECCE CARBINE – 5.56 NATO or .300 AAC Blackout cal., GIO, 16 in. cold hammer forged barrel, Blackout flash suppressor, 30 shot mag., ALG Defense ACT trigger, fixed front sight gas block, Troy Ind. rear backup iron sight, Magpul CTR stock, Magpul MOE grip, Gen 1 forged lower and flat-top upper receiver with extended feed ramps, Gunfighter (disc.) or Radian Raptor ambi charging handle, mid-length A2 (disc.) or M4 type with double aluminum heat shield handguard, Mil-Spec 6-pos. receiver extension, Type III hardcoat anodized black finish, approx. 6 lbs.

MSR $1,730	$1,425	$925	$700	$550	$475	$395	$350	

GEN I RECCE BASIC SL – 5.56 NATO or .300 AAC Blackout cal., 16 in. cold hammer forged barrel, 30 shot mag., ALG Defense ACT trigger, Magpul enhanced trigger guard, fixed front sight gas block, rear Magpul MBUS Pro folding sights, Magpul SL stock and grip, Gen I forged flat-top upper receiver with extended feed ramps, Gen I forged lower with Mil-Spec 6-pos. receiver extension, Noveske marked Radian Raptor ambi charging handle, Magpul SL mid-length (5.56 NATO) or carbine length (.300 AAC Blackout) handguard, Type III hardcoat anodized black finish. New 2018.

MSR $1,730	$1,425	$925	$700	$550	$475	$395	$350	

GEN III N6 RIFLE – 7.62x51mm cal., 16 in. stainless steel barrel, 25 shot mag., Geissele SSA or SD-C trigger, Magpul MBUS Pro folding sights, Mapgul STR carbine stock, MIAD pistol grip, low profile gas block, Gen III precision machined billet lower and upper receiver w/extended feed ramps, Raptor ambidextrous (disc.) or Geissele Super Badass (new 2018) charging handle, black Nitride (disc.) or black phosphate bolt carrier group, KeyMod or M-LOK NSR 15 in. free floating handguard w/1913 top rail, VLTOR A5 receiver extension. New 2016.

MSR $3,600	$3,050	$2,675	$2,175	$1,875	$1,550	$1,300	$1,125	

GEN III N6 SWITCHBLOCK RIFLE – 7.62x51mm cal., gas block, 16 in. stainless steel barrel, micro Switchblock pinned to barrel, 25 shot mag., Geissele SSA or SD-C trigger, Mapgul STR carbine stock, MIAD pistol grip, machined billet upper and lower receiver w/ extended feed ramps, Raptor ambidextrous charging handle, black Nitride bolt carrier group, KeyMod or M-LOK 15 in. free floating handguard w/1913 top rail, VLTOR A5 receiver extension, hardcoat Type III anodized with black Cerakote ceramic coating. New 2016.

MSR $4,000	$3,600	$3,200	$2,750	$2,325	$1,975	$1,700	$1,500	

N 262 NOVESKE RIFLEWORKS LLC, cont.

MSR	100%	98%	95%	90%	80%	70%	60%	Last MSR

* Gen III N6 Switchblock 6.5 Creedmoor – 6.5mm Creedmoor cal., 20 in. stainless steel barrel, micro Switchblock pinned to barrel, Silencerco Saker Trifecta flash hider, 25 shot mag., Geissele DMR trigger, Magpul MBUS Pro folding sights, Magpul PRS rifle stock, Magpul MIAD pistol grip, STS ambi safety selector, Gen III billet upper receiver with extended feed ramps, Gen III billet lower receiver with ambi controls, Noveske marked Geissele Super Badass charging handle, NSR 15 in. KeyMod free floating handguard with Switchblock cutout and 1913 top rail, Type III hardcoat anodizing with black Cerakote ceramic coating. New 2018.

MSR $4,175	$3,350	$2,300	$1,575	$950	$725	$675	$650	

GEN III NSD – .300 AAC Blackout cal., pistol length gas system, 8 1/2 in. stainless steel barrel with permanently fixed 16 in. Dead Air Sandman TI threaded barrel, 30 shot mag., ALG Defense ACT trigger, Magpul MBUS Pro folding sights, Magpul STR stock, MIAD pistol grip, low profile gas block pinned to barrel, Gen III precision machined billet upper and lower receiver with extended feed ramps, Noveske marked Geissele Super Badass charging handle, NSD-15 in. free floating handguard w/1913 top rail, 6-position receiver extension, Type III hardcoat anodizing with black Cerakote ceramic coating. New 2017.

MSR $3,250	$2,775	$2,425	$1,965	$1,685	$1,385	$1,175	$1,025	

GEN III OMW (ONE MORE WAVE) – .300 AAC Blackout or 5.56 NATO cal., 14 1/2 in. stainless steel (.300 AAC) or cold hammer forged "skinny" (5.56 NATO) barrel w/Silencerco ASR brake pinned to barrel (16 in. OAL), 30 shot mag., Geissele SSA trigger, Magpul MBUS Pro folding sights, Magpul SL stock, Magpul MOE K2 pistol grip, Gen III precision machined billet upper and lower receiver with extended feed ramps, One More Wave engraved on lower receiver in Robins Egg Cerakote finish, Noveske marked Geissele Super Badass charging handle, 13 1/2 in. M-LOK free floating handguard with 1913 top and bottom rail, Mil-Spec 6-position receiver extension, Type III hardcoat anodizing with black Cerekote ceramic coating. New 2016.

MSR $2,350	$1,875	$1,100	$895	$650	$575	$495	$425	

GEN III RIFLE – 5.56 NATO or .300 AAC Blackout cal., 16 or 18 in. stainless steel or cold hammer forged barrel, 30 shot mag., ALG Defense ACT trigger, Noveske Signature backup iron sights by Troy Ind., Magpul STR carbine stock, MIAD pistol grip, low profile gas block, Gen III precision machined billet lower and upper receiver with extended feed ramps, Raptor ambidextrous (disc.) or Geissele Super Badass charging handle, Mil-Spec 6-pos. receiver extension, NSR 13 1/2 or 15 in. KeyMod or M-LOK free floating handguard with top Picatinny rail, Type III hardcoat anodizing with black Cerakote ceramic coating. New mid-2014.

MSR $2,575	$2,050	$1,250	$950	$650	$575	$495	$475	

Add $20 for 18 in. barrel.

* Gen III Rifle 6.5 Grendel – 6.5 Grendel cal., 20 in. barrel with thread protector, 25 shot mag., ALG Defense ACT trigger, Magpul MBUS Pro folding sights, Magpul PRS stock, Magpul MIAD pistol grip, rifle length gas system, low profile gas block pinned to barrel, Gen III precision machined billet lower and upper receiver with extended feed ramps, Noveske marked Geissele Super Badass charging handle, NSR 16.7 in. KeyMod or M-LOK or NHR KeyMod free floating handguard with 1913 top rail, Type III hardcoat anodizing with Cerakote Ceramic coating. New 2018.

MSR $2,650	$2,125	$1,325	$995	$675	$595	$525	$475	

GEN III SWITCHBLOCK RIFLE – 5.56 NATO cal., 16 in. stainless steel or cold hammer forged barrel, Switchblock pinned to barrel, 30 shot mag., ALG Defense ACT trigger, Noveske Signature backup iron sights by Troy Ind. (disc.) or Magpul MBUS Pro folding sights, Magpul STR carbine stock, MIAD pistol grip, mid-length gas system, Gen. III precision machined billet lower and upper receiver, extended feed ramps, Mil-Spec 6-pos. receiver extension, Raptor ambidextrous (disc.) or Geissele Super Badass charging handle, 11 1/2 in. Noveske split rail with 1913 rails, Type III hardcoat anodizing with black Cerakote ceramic finish. New mid-2014.

MSR $2,930	$2,375	$1,525	$1,150	$700	$625	$550	$475	

GEN III VARMAGEDDON .22 NOSLER – .22 Nosler cal., 18 in. barrel with muzzle and thread protector, 25 shot mag., Geissele SD-E trigger, Magpul MBUS Pro folding sights, Magpul PRS stock, Magpul MOE pistol grip, STS ambi safety selector, rifle length gas system, Superlative Arms adj. gas block pinned to barrel, Gen. III billet lower and upper receiver with extended feed ramps, Noveske marked Geissele Super Badass charging handle, NSR 15 in. KeyMod free floating handguard with 1913 top rail, Type III hardcoat anodizing with FDE Cerakote ceramic coating. New 2017.

MSR $2,870	$2,295	$1,450	$1,075	$675	$595	$525	$475	

GEN 4 GHETTO BLASTER – 5.56 NATO cal., GIO, 16 in. cold hammer forged barrel with extended feed ramps, Q Cherry Bomb muzzle brake, 30 shot mag., Geissele SD-E trigger, Magpul MBUS Pro folding sights, Q-PDW style stock, Magpul K2 grip, low profile gas block, Gen 4 precision machined billet upper and lower receiver, ambi controls, 15 in. KeyMod or M-LOK free floating handguard, Geissele Super Badass charging handle, Type III hardcoat anodizing with black Cerakote ceramic coating. Mfg. 2017 only.

	$1,675	$1,000	$825	$625	$550	$475	$425	*$2,070*

GEN 4 N4 PDW – 5.56 NATO cal., 16 in. cold hammer forged barrel, Q Cherry Bomb muzzle brake, 30 shot mag., Geissele SD-E trigger, Magpul MBUS Pro folding sights, Q-PDW style stock, Magpul K2 grip, STS ambi safety selector, low profile gas block pinned to barrel, Gen 4 billet upper receiver with extended feed ramp, Gen 4 billet lower with ambi

NOVESKE RIFLEWORKS LLC, cont. 263

MSR		100%	98%	95%	90%	80%	70%	60%	Last MSR

controls, Noveske marked Geissele Super Badass charging handle, NHR 15 in. KeyMod or M-LOK free floating handuard, Type III hardcoat anodizing with black Cerakote ceramic coating. New 2018.

MSR $2,485		$1,975	$1,150	$925	$650	$575	$495	$425	

INFANTRY RIFLE – 5.56 NATO or .300 Blackout cal., 16 in. barrel, 30 shot mag., ALG Defense ACT trigger, Noveske Signature backup iron sights by Troy Ind., Magpul CTR stock, Magpul MOE grip, low profile gas block, carbine or mid-length gas system, Gen. I flat-top upper receiver with extended feed ramps, MOD 4 Gunfighter charging handle, Gen. I forged lower receiver with 6-pos. receiver extension, Noveske 11 in. quad rail with 1913 rails. Disc. 2017.

		$1,875	$1,100	$895	$650	$575	$495	$425	*$2,365*

LIGHT RECCE CARBINE – 5.56 NATO or .300 AAC Blackout cal., GIO, 16 in. cold hammer forged chrome-lined barrel, Blackout 51T flash suppressor, low profile gas block or Switchblock pinned to barrel, forged Gen. II lower, forged VLTOR upper with anti-rotation interfaced with handguard, Gunfighter charging handle, NSR 13 1/2 in. free float handguard with 1913 top rail or 11 1/2 in. free float handguard with 1913 rails (Switchblock only), ALG combat trigger, Mil-Spec receiver extension, black phosphate finish, approx. 6 lbs. Disc. 2013.

		$1,795	$1,050	$875	$625	$550	$475	$425	*$2,215*

Add $320 for Switchblock.

LIGHT RECCE LO-PRO CARBINE – 5.56 NATO cal., GIO, 16 in. cold hammer forged chrome-lined barrel, Blackout flash supresor, low profile gas block pinned to barrel, forged Gen. II lower, forged VLTOR MUR upper with anti-rotation interfaced with handguard, Gunfighter charging handle, 11 in. free float handguard with 1913 top rail, Mil-Spec receiver extension, black phosphate finish, extended feed ramp, approx. 6 lbs. Disc. 2013.

		$1,875	$1,100	$895	$650	$575	$495	$425	*$2,340*

RECON CARBINE – 5.56 NATO cal., GIO, 16 in. stainless steel barrel, Blackout flash suppressor, optional Switchblock pinned to barrel, low profile gas block, forged Gen II lower, forged VLTOR upper receiver featuring an anti-rotation interface with handguard, Gunfighter charging handle, 11 in. free float handguard with 1913 rails or NSR 13 1/2 in. free float handguard with 1913 top rail, ALG combat trigger, Mil-Spec receiver extension, VLTOR IMOD carbine stock, H buffer, flip-up front and rear sights, extended feed ramps, black finish, approx. 6 lbs. Disc. 2013.

		$1,975	$1,150	$925	$650	$575	$495	$425	*$2,485*

Add $195 for Switchblock.
Subtract $160 for NSR handguard.

THE RIVAL – 5.56 NATO cal., 18 in. stainless steel barrel, Silencerco Saker Trifecta muzzle brake, 30 shot mag., Geissele DMR trigger, Magpul PRS adj. stock, MIAD pistol grip, STS ambi safety, rifle length gas system, Noveske marked Superlative Arms adj. gas block pinned to barrel, Gen III billet lower and upper receiver with extended feed ramps, Geissele Super Badass ambi charging handle, NSR 16.7 in. free floating handguard with 1913 top rail, Type III hardcoat anodizing with Tungsten Cerakote ceramic coating. New 2017.

MSR $2,995		$2,375	$1,525	$1,150	$700	$625	$550	$475	

ROGUE HUNTER 5.56 NATO or .300 AAC Blackout cal., GIO, 16 or 18 in. lightweight stainless steel or cold hammer forged barrel, A2 flash suppressor, 30 shot mag., ALG Defense ACT trigger, Magpul enhanced trigger guard (18 in. bbl. only), VLTOR IMOD (disc.) or Magpul CTR stock, Tango Down (disc.) or Magpul MOE grip, low profile gas block pinned to barrel, Gen 1 forged lower with Mil-Spec 6-pos. receiver extension and flat-top upper receiver with extended feed ramps, Gunfighter (disc.) or Radian Raptor ambidextrous charging handle, NSR 13 1/2 or 15 in. free floating handguard, Type III hardcoat anodized black finish, approx. 6 lbs. 4 oz.

MSR $1,825		$1,525	$975	$750	$575	$495	$425	$375	

Add $20 for 18 in. barrel.

SHOOTING TEAM RIFLE – 5.56 NATO cal., 18 in. stainless steel barrel, 30 shot mag., Gen. III upper receiver with extended feed ramps and anti-rotation interface with handguard, Gen. III lower receiver, Geissele DMR trigger, STS ambidextrous selector, Raptor ambidextrous charging handle, 16.7 in. free floating handguard with Picatinny top rail, Magpul PRS stock, MIAD pistol grip, Cerakote (Tungsten) finish. Mfg. mid-2014-2017.

		$2,450	$1,595	$1,200	$700	$675	$575	$525	*$3,010*

SPR – 5.56 NATO cal., GIO, 18 in. stainless steel barrel, Blackout flash suppressor, flip-up front and rear sights, ALG combat trigger, VLTOR IMOD carbine stock, low profile gas block pinned to barrel, Gen II forged lower, forged VLTOR MUR upper featuring an anti-rotation interface with handguard, Gunfighter charging handle, NSR 13 1/2 in. free float handguard with 1913 top rail, Mil-Spec receiver extension, H buffer, extended feed ramp, black finish, approx. 6 lbs. Disc. 2013.

		$1,875	$1,100	$895	$650	$575	$495	$425	*$2,350*

NUOVA JAGER

Current AR-15 style rifle and parts manufacturer located in Basaluzzo, Italy. No current U.S. importation.

Nuova Jager manufactures high quality AR-15 style rifles in various calibers and configurations. Please contact the factory directly for more information, including pricing and U.S. availability (see Trademark Index).

MAYBE THE ONLY THING BETTER THAN THIS BOOK IS THE ONLINE SUBSCRIPTION!

Only $19.95/year!

- **Includes monthly updates** keeping you informed of all the new AR-15 makes/models.
- **Features thousands of images** allowing for fast and easy identification.
- **Manufacturer/Model searchable database** allowing you to find the model you need.
- Historical pricing with dynamic interactive graphs keeps you up-to-date on your AR-15 purchases as investments.
- Your own personal online inventory solution - keep track of your collection and track the change in value.
- Includes access to BBP's industry standard Photo Percentage Grading System – why guess a gun's condition when you can be sure?

Visit BLUEBOOKOFGUNVALUES.COM to view sample pages and ordering

Good Information Never Sleeps!

O SECTION

265

OBERLAND ARMS

Current manufacturer located in Huglfing, Germany. Previously located in Habach, Germany. No current U.S. importation.

Oberland Arms manufactures a wide variety of high quality rifles, including an OA-15 series based on the AR-15 style carbine/rifle. Oberland Arms also used to manufacture pistols. Many rifle options and configurations are available. Please contact the company directly for more information, including pricing, options, and U.S. availability (see Trademark Index).

OLYMPIC ARMS, INC.

Current manufacturer established in 1976, and while the company announced its closing in Jan. 2017, Olympic Arms, Inc. remains open and is currently selling most of the semi-auto SKU's that it did prior to 2017. Company headquarters is located in Olympia, WA.

Olympic Arms, Inc. was founded by Robert C. Schuetz, and began as Schuetzen Gun Works (SGW) in 1956, manufacturing barrels in Colorado Springs, Colorado. Prior to that Mr. Schuetz had been partnered in business with well known gunsmith P.O. Ackley. In 1975 the company moved to Olympia, Washington, and while its business in rifle barrels and barrel blanks thrived, it also began manufacturing complete custom bolt action rirfles. In 1982, Schuetzen Gun Works began to manufacture AR-15/M16 rifles and components under the trade name of Olympic Arms, Inc., while custom bolt action rifles continued to be produced under the SGW brand. In late 1987, Olympic Arms, Inc. acquired Safari Arms of Phoenix, AZ. As of Jan. 2004, the Safari Arms product name was discontinued, and all 1911 style products were manufactured in the Olympic Arms facility in Olympia, WA. Schuetzen Pistol Works was the in-house custom shop of Olympic Arms. Olympic Arms is one of the few AR-15 manufacturers to make every major component part in-house.

MSR	100%	98%	95%	90%	80%	70%	60%	Last MSR

PISTOLS: SEMI-AUTO

On July 10, 2014, Olympic Arms announced the cancellation of all 1911 pistols, as well as 1911 frames and slides.

K22 – .22 LR cal., SA, 6 1/2 in. button rifled stainless steel barrel, forged flat-top with Picatinny rails, gas block, free floating aluminum tube handguard with knurling, non-chromed bore, A2 flash suppressor, 4.3 lbs. Mfg. 2011-mid-2014.

	100%	98%	95%	90%	80%	70%	60%	Last MSR
	$775	$675	$575	$475	$425	$395	$375	*$896*

K23P SERIES – 5.56 NATO cal., GIO, SA, 6 1/2 in. chrome moly steel button rifled barrel with A2 flash suppressor, forged A2 upper with fully adj. rear sight, post front sight, no bayonet lug, free floating aluminum tube handguard with knurling, carbon recoil buffer in back of frame, with (K23P-FT) or w/o (K23P) flat-top receiver, 5.12 lbs. New 2007.

MSR $876	$725	$650	$580	$515	$450	$385	$340	

Add $65 for optics ready flat-top receiver and gas block (K23P-OR, new 2016).

Add $95 for A3 upper receiver (disc. 2011) or $91 for A3 upper w/Picatinny rail and Firsh handguard (K23P-A3TC, disc. 2011, reintroduced 2016).

K23PGL – 9mm Para. or .40 S&W cal., GIO, AR-15 style, 6 1/2 in. button rifled stainless steel barrel with black oxide finish, A1 style flash suppressor, AR-15 lower that is designed to accept Glock style magazines, forged A2 upper with fully adj. rear sight, elevated adj. post front sight, no bayonet lug, free floating aluminum tube with knurling, padded receiver extension tube, black finish, 5.12 lbs. Limited mfg. 2015 only.

	$925	$850	$725	$625	$550	$475	$425	*$1,091*

* **K23PGL-OR** – 9mm Para. or .40 S&W cal., GIO, AR-15 style, 6 1/2 in. button rifled stainless steel barrel with black oxide finish, A1 style flash suppressor, AR-15 lower that is designed to accept Glock style magazines, forged Picatinny flat-top upper, Picatinny gas block, no sights, free floating aluminum handguard, padded receiver extension tube, black finish, 5.12 lbs. Limited mfg. 2015 only.

	$885	$785	$685	$600	$535	$465	$415	*$1,037*

* **K23P-9, K23P-10, K23P-40, K23P-45** – 9mm Para., 10mm, .40 S&W, or .45 ACP cal., GIO, AR-15 style, 6 1/2 in. button rifled stainless steel barrel with black oxide finish, A1 style flash suppressor, 18 shot AR-15 magazines, forged A2 upper with fully adj. rear sight, elevated adj. post front sight, no bayonet lug, free floating aluminum tube with knurling, padded receiver extension tube, black finish, 5.12 lbs. New 2015.

MSR $941	$775	$685	$615	$550	$485	$415	$365	

Add $45 for OR (optics ready).

K24P – 5.56 NATO, .300 AAC Blackout, or 7.62x39mm cal., GIO, 11 1/2 in. button rifled barrel, choice of A2 fixed sights with carry handle or flat-top (K24P-FT), pistol grip with Fiberite ribbed handguard, extended recoil buffer in back of pistol grip, matte black finish, 6.77 lbs. New 2017.

MSR $896	$735	$665	$585	$515	$450	$385	$340	

266 OLYMPIC ARMS, INC., cont.

MSR	100%	98%	95%	90%	80%	70%	60%	Last MSR

K24P-OR – 5.56 NATO, .300 AAC Blackout, or 7.62x39mm cal., GIO, 11 1/2 in. button rifled barrel, no sights, pistol grip with Fiberite ribbed handguard, Picatinny flat-top with forward top rail on barrel, extended recoil buffer in back of pistol grip, matte black finish, 6.77 lbs. New 2015.

MSR $973	$815	$700	$625	$575	$500	$425	$375	

K24P-9 – 9mm Para., 10mm, .40 S&W, or .45 ACP cal., GIO, 11 1/2 in. button rifled barrel, A2 sights, pistol grip with Fiberite ribbed handguard, extended recoil buffer in back of pistol grip, matte black finish, 6.77 lbs. New 2015.

MSR $928	$775	$685	$615	$550	$485	$415	$365	

K24P-9-OR – 9mm Para., 10mm, .40 S&W, or .45 ACP cal., GIO, 11 1/2 in. button rifled barrel, A2 sights, pistol grip with Fiberite ribbed handguard, Picatinny flat-top w/forward top rail on barrel, extended recoil buffer in back of pistol grip, matte black finish, 6.77 lbs. New 2015.

MSR $974	$815	$700	$625	$575	$500	$425	$375	

OA-93 PISTOL – .223 Rem. (older mfg.), 5.56 NATO, or 7.62x39mm (very limited mfg., disc.) cal., GIO, 6 (most common, disc.), 6 1/2 (new 2005), 9 (disc.), or 14 (disc.) in. button rifled stainless steel threaded barrel with Phantom flash suppressor, forged flat-top upper receiver utilizes integral scope mount base, 30 shot mag., free floating aluminum handguard tube with knurling, without buffer tube stock or charging handle, 4 lbs. 3 oz., approx. 500 mfg. 1993-94 before Crime Bill discontinued production, reintroduced late 2004.

MSR $1,277	$1,065	$965	$835	$725	$625	$535	$450	

Last MSR in 1994 was $2,700.

Add 100% for 7.62x39mm cal.

OA-96 AR PISTOL – .223 Rem. cal., GIO, 6 in. barrel only, similar to OA-93 Pistol, except has pinned (fixed) 30 shot mag. and rear takedown button for rapid reloading, 5 lbs. Mfg. 1996-2000.

	$725	$650	$580	$515	$450	$385	$340	*$860*

OA-98 PISTOL – .223 Rem. cal., GIO, skeletonized, lightweight version of the OA-93/OA-96, 6 1/2 in. non-threaded barrel, 10 shot fixed (disc.) or detachable (new 2006) mag., denoted by perforated appearance, 3 lbs. Mfg. 1998-2003, reintroduced 2005-2007.

	$895	$795	$685	$615	$545	$475	$415	*$1,080*

RIFLES: SEMI-AUTO

As this edition went to press, Olympic Arms currently has inventory on most of its currently manufactured semi-auto carbines/rifles listed in this section. For most up-to-date information on model availability and pricing, please visit www.olyarms.com. MSR's listed below reflect current Olympic Arms pricing.

The PCR (Politically Correct Rifle) variations listed refer to those guns manufactured after the Crime Bill was implemented in September 1994 through 2004. PCR rifles have smooth barrels (no flash suppressor), a 10 shot mag., and fixed stocks. Named models refer to the original, pre-ban model nomenclature.

Olympic Arms also made some models exclusively for distributors. They included the K30R-16-SST (Sports South, LLC), K16-SST (Sports South, LLC), and the PP FT M4 SS (Lew Horton).

COMPETITOR RIFLE – .22 LR cal., Ruger 10/22 action with 20 in. fluted barrel with button rifling, Bell & Carlson thumbhole fiberglass stock, includes bipod, black finish and matte stainless barrel, 6.9 lbs. Mfg. 1996-1999.

	$500	$450	$400	$360	$330	$300	$275	*$575*

ULTRAMATCH/PCR-1 – .223 Rem. cal., GIO, AR-15 action with modifications, 20 or 24 in. match stainless steel barrel, Picatinny flat-top upper receiver, Williams set trigger optional, scope mounts, 10 lbs. 3 oz. Mfg. 1985-disc.

* ***Ultramatch PCR-1*** – disc. 2004.

	$895	$575	$475	$395	$350	$325	$300	*$1,074*

* ***Ultramatch PCR-1P*** – .223 Rem. cal., GIO, premium grade Ultramatch rifle with many shooting enhancements, including Maxhard treated upper and lower receiver, 20 or 24 in. broach cut Ultramatch bull barrel, 1:10 in. or 1:8 in. rate of twist. Mfg. 2001-2004.

	$1,075	$675	$500	$450	$400	$350	$325	*$1,299*

* ***Ultramatch UM-1*** – .223 Rem. cal., GIO, 20 in. stainless Ultramatch barrel with non-chromed bore, gas block, free floating aluminum tube with knurling, approx. 8 1/2 lbs. Disc. 1994, reintroduced late 2004-2012.

	$1,125	$700	$525	$450	$400	$350	$325	

Last MSR in 1994 was $1,515, Last MSR in 2012 was $1,329.

* ***Ultramatch UM-1P*** – .223 Rem. cal., GIO, similar to UM-1 Ultramatch, except has 20 (disc. 2006) or 24 in. Ultramatch bull stainless barrel, premium grade Ultramatch rifle with many shooting enhancements, 9 1/2 lbs. New 2005.

MSR $1,624	$1,350	$875	$650	$525	$450	$385	$350	

OLYMPIC ARMS, INC., cont. 267

MSR	100%	98%	95%	90%	80%	70%	60%	Last MSR

INTERCONTINENTAL – .223 Rem. cal., GIO, synthetic wood-grained thumbhole buttstock and aluminum handguard, 20 in. Ultramatch barrel (free floating). Mfg. 1992-1993.

| | $1,135 | $725 | $525 | $465 | $415 | $375 | $350 | $1,371 |

INTERNATIONAL MATCH – .223 Rem. cal., similar to Ultramatch, except has custom aperture sights. Mfg. 1991-93.

| | $1,050 | $650 | $495 | $450 | $395 | $350 | $325 | $1,240 |

SERVICE MATCH/PCR SERVICE MATCH – .223 Rem. cal., AR-15 action with modifications, GIO, 20 in. SS Ultramatch barrel, carrying handle, standard trigger, choice of A1 or A2 flash suppressor (Service Match only), 8 3/4 lbs.

* **Service Match SM-1** – GIO, 9.7 lbs., disc. 1994, reintroduced late 2004-2012.

| | $1,065 | $650 | $500 | $450 | $395 | $350 | $325 | |

Last MSR in 1994 was $1,200, Last MSR in 2012 was $1,273.

* **Service Match SM-1P Premium Grade** – .223 Rem. cal., GIO, Maxhard upper and lower receiver, 20 in. broach cut Ultramatch super heavy threaded barrel (1 turn in 8 in. is standard), flash suppressor, two-stage CMP trigger, Blak-Tak Armour bolt carrier assembly, Bob Jones NM interchangeable rear sight system, AC4 pneumatic recoil buffer, Turner Saddlery competition sling, GI style pistol grip. Mfg. 2005-2012.

| | $1,425 | $925 | $700 | $550 | $475 | $395 | $350 | $1,728 |

* **Service Match PCR** – disc. late 2004.

| | $895 | $575 | $475 | $395 | $350 | $325 | $300 | $1,062 |

* **Service Match PCR-SMP Premium Grade** – .223 Rem. cal., GIO, 20 in. broach cut Ultramatch super heavy barrel (1 turn in 8 in. is standard), two-stage CMP trigger, Maxhard upper and lower receiver, Blak-Tak Armour bolt carrier assembly, Bob Jones NM interchangeable rear sight system, AC4 pneumatic recoil buffer, Turner Saddlery competition sling, GI style pistol grip. Mfg. 2004 only.

| | $1,350 | $875 | $650 | $525 | $450 | $385 | $350 | $1,613 |

MULTIMATCH ML-1/PCR-2 – .223 Rem. cal., GIO, tactical short range rifle, 16 in. Ultramatch barrel with A2 upper receiver, aluminum collapsible (Multimatch ML-1) or fixed (PCR-2) stock, carrying handle, A2 flash suppressor (Multimatch ML-1 only). Mfg. 1991-2012.

* **Multimatch ML-1** – 7.35 lbs. Disc. 2012.

| | $995 | $625 | $495 | $450 | $395 | $350 | $325 | |

Last MSR in 1994 was $1,200, Last MSR in 2012 was $1,188.

* **Multimatch PCR-2** – disc. late 2004.

| | $825 | $535 | $450 | $385 | $340 | $325 | $295 | $958 |

MULTIMATCH ML-2/PCR-3 – .223 Rem. cal., GIO, Picatinny flat-top upper receiver with stainless steel 16 in. Ultramatch bull (new 2005) barrel, carrying handle (disc.), approx. 7 1/2 lbs. Mfg. 1991-2015.

* **Multimatch ML-2** – .223 Rem. cal., GIO, 16 in. Ultramatch stainless steel bull barrel, crowned muzzle, forged flat-top with Picatinny rails, gas block with Picatinny rails, free floating tubular aluminum handguard with knurling, A2 stock with trapdoor, 7 1/2 lbs. Disc. 1994, reintroduced late 2004.

| MSR $1,253 | $1,065 | $650 | $500 | $450 | $395 | $350 | $325 | |

Last MSR in 1994 was $1,200.

* **Multimatch PCR-3** – disc. late 2004.

| | $825 | $535 | $450 | $385 | $340 | $325 | $295 | $958 |

AR-15 MATCH/PCR-4 – .223 Rem. cal., GIO, patterned after the AR-15 with 20 in. barrel and solid synthetic stock, 8 lbs. 5 oz. Mfg. 1975-2004.

* **PCR-4**

| | $695 | $500 | $425 | $375 | $335 | $315 | $295 | $803 |

* **AR-15 Match**

| | $895 | $575 | $475 | $395 | $350 | $325 | $300 | $1,075 |

CAR-15/PCR-5 – GIO, modified AR-15 with choice of 11 1/2 (disc. 1993) or 16 in. barrel, stow-away pistol grip and collapsible stock (CAR-15 only), 7 lbs. Mfg. 1975-1998, PCR-5 reintroduced 2000-2004.

* **PCR-5** – .223 Rem., 9mm Para. (new 1996), .40 S&W (new 1996), or .45 ACP (new 1996) cal., GIO. Disc. 1998, reintroduced 2000-2004.

| | $665 | $500 | $415 | $375 | $335 | $315 | $295 | $755 |

* **CAR-15** – .223 Rem., 9mm Para., .40 S&W, .45 ACP, or 7.62x39mm cal.

| | $875 | $550 | $465 | $395 | $350 | $325 | $300 | $1,030 |

268 OLYMPIC ARMS, INC., cont.

MSR	100%	98%	95%	90%	80%	70%	60%	Last MSR

CAR-97 – .223 Rem., 9mm Para., 10mm, .40 S&W, or .45 ACP cal., similar to PCR-5, except has 16 in. button rifled barrel, A2 sights, fixed CAR stock, post-ban muzzle brake, approx. 7 lbs. Mfg. 1997-2004.

	$675	$500	$425	$375	$335	$315	$295	$780

Add approx. 10% for 9mm Para., 10mm, .40 S&W, or .45 ACP cal.

* **CAR-97 M4** – .223 Rem. cal., GIO, M4 configuration with contoured barrel, fixed carbine tube stock, factory installed muzzle brake, oversized shortened handguard. Mfg. 2003-2004.

	$725	$500	$435	$375	$335	$315	$295	$839

Add $95 for detachable carrying handle (new 2004).

PCR-6 – 7.62x39mm cal., 16 in. barrel, post-ban only, GIO, A2 stowaway stock, carrying handle, 7 lbs. Mfg. 1995-2002.

	$745	$500	$435	$375	$335	$315	$295	$870

PCR-7 ELIMINATOR – .223 Rem. cal., GIO, similar to PCR-4, except has 16 in. barrel, 7 lbs. 10 oz. Mfg. 1999-2004.

	$725	$500	$435	$375	$335	$315	$295	$844

PCR-8 – .223 Rem. cal., GIO, same configuration as the PCR-1, except has standard 20 in. stainless steel heavy bull barrel with button rifling. Mfg. 2001-2004.

	$725	$500	$435	$375	$335	$315	$295	$834

* **PCR-8 Mag.** – .223 WSSM or .243 WSSM cal., GIO, otherwise similar to PCR-8. Mfg. 2004.

	$895	$575	$475	$395	$350	$325	$300	$1,074

This model was also scheduled to be available in .308 Olympic Mag. and 7mm Olympic Mag. cals.

PCR-9/10/40/45 – 9mm Para., 10mm, .40 S&W, or .45 ACP cal., similar to PCR-5 Carbine except for pistol cal., GIO, A2 upper standard, 16 in. barrel, A2 buttstock, Mil-Spec lower receiver. Mfg. 2001-2004.

	$725	$500	$435	$375	$335	$315	$295	$835

PCR-16 – .223 Rem. cal., GIO, 16 in. match grade bull barrel, two-piece aluminum free floating handguard, Picatinny receiver rail, 7 1/2 lbs. Mfg. 2003-2004.

	$615	$495	$415	$360	$325	$300	$275	$714

PCR-30 – .30 Carbine cal., GIO, forged aluminum receiver with matte black anodizing, parkerized steel parts, A2 adj. rear sight, accepts standard GI M1 .30 Carbine mags., 16 in. barrel with 1:12 in. twist, 7.15 lbs. Mfg. 2004.

	$765	$515	$440	$375	$335	$315	$295	$899

PLINKER – .223 Rem. cal., GIO, similar to PCR-5, except has 16 in. button rifled barrel standard, A1 sights, cast upper/lower receiver, 100% standard Mil-Spec parts, 7 lbs. Mfg. 2001-2004.

	$515	$450	$395	$350	$315	$295	$275	$598

PLINKER PLUS – 5.56 NATO cal., GIO, similar to Plinker, except has 16 (disc. 2009, reintroduced 2011) in. button rifled threaded chrome moly steel barrel with A2 flash suppressor, standard A1 upper, cast upper/lower receiver, 100% standard Mil-Spec parts, A2 stock with trapdoor, 7-8.4 lbs. New 2005.

MSR $727	$645	$500	$415	$370	$325	$300	$275	

* **Plinker Plus Compact** – 5.56 NATO cal., GIO, 16 in. button rifled chrome moly steel barrel with A2 flash suppressor, forged A1 upper with windage only adjustment, elevation adj. front sight post with bayonet lug, Fiberite carbine length handguard, A2 stock with trapdoor, pink handguard and stock, 7.37 lbs. New 2015.

MSR $688	$595	$485	$415	$350	$315	$295	$275	

* **Plinker Plus Flat Top** – 5.56 NATO cal., GIO, similar to Plinker Plus, except has flat-top with Picatinny rails, M4 six point collapsible stock. New 2012.

MSR $714	$615	$495	$415	$360	$325	$300	$275	

* **Plinker Plus 20** – 5.56 NATO cal., GIO, 20 in. button rifled threaded chrome moly steel barrel with A2 flash suppressor, choice of forged A1 upper or flat-top upper with Picatinny rails, adj. post front sight with bayonet lug, 100% standard Mil-Spec parts, A2 stock with trapdoor, 7-8.4 lbs. New 2012.

MSR $740	$645	$500	$415	$370	$325	$300	$275	

FAR-15 – .223 Rem. cal., GIO, featherweight model with A1 contour lightweight button rifled 16 in. barrel, fixed collapsible stock, 9.92 lbs. Mfg. 2001-2004.

	$695	$500	$425	$375	$335	$315	$295	$822

GI-16 – 5.56 NATO cal., GIO, forged aluminum receiver with black matte finish, A1 type upper receiver, parkerized steel parts, A1 adj. rear sights, 16 in. button rifled match grade barrel, M4 collapsible stock, 6.6 lbs. Mfg. 2004, reintroduced 2006-2012.

	$745	$500	$435	$375	$335	$315	$295	$857

OLYMPIC ARMS, INC., cont. 269

MSR	100%	98%	95%	90%	80%	70%	60%	Last MSR

GI-20 – .223 Rem. cal., similar to GI-16, except has 20 in. heavy barrel and A2 lower receiver, 8.4 lbs. Mfg. 2004.

| | $645 | $500 | $415 | $370 | $325 | $300 | $275 | *$749* |

OA-93 CARBINE – .223 Rem. cal., GIO, 16 in. threaded barrel, design based on OA-93 pistol, aluminum side folding stock, flat-top receiver, round aluminum handguard, Vortex flash suppressor, 7 1/2 lbs. Mfg. 1995, civilian sales disc. 1998, reintroduced 2004-2007.

| | $895 | $575 | $475 | $395 | $350 | $325 | $300 | |

Last MSR in 1998 was $1,550.
Last MSR in 2007 was $1,074.

* ***OA-93PT Carbine*** – .223 Rem. cal., GIO, aluminum forged receiver, black matte hard anodized finish, no sights, integral flat-top upper receiver rail system, match grade 16 in. chrome moly steel barrel with removable muzzle brake, push button removable stock, vertical pistol grip, 7.6 lbs. Mfg. 2004 only, reintroduced 2006-2007.

| | $895 | $575 | $475 | $395 | $350 | $325 | $300 | $1,074 |

LTF/LT-MIL4 LIGHTWEIGHT TACTICAL RIFLE – 5.56 NATO cal., GIO, available in LTF (fluted), LT-M4 (new 2011), or LT-MIL4 (disc. 2009) configuration, black matte anodized receiver, Firsh type forearms with Picatinny rails, parkerized steel parts, adj. flip-up sight system, 16 in. non-chromed fluted, M4 stainless steel (new 2011), or MIL4 threaded barrel with flash suppressor, tube style Ace FX buttstock, 6.4 lbs. New 2005.

| MSR $1,240 | $1,050 | $650 | $495 | $450 | $395 | $350 | $325 | |

Subtract $97 for M4 style stainless steel barrel (new 2011).

Subtract approx. 10% if w/o fluted barrel.

LTF PREDATOR – .204 Ruger (new 2012), 5.56 NATO, 7.62 NATO (disc. 2015), or 6.8 SPC (new 2012) cal., GIO, 16 in. button rifled chrome moly barrel with A2 flash suppressor, forged flat-top with Picatinny rails, gas block with Picatinny rail, free floating aluminum tube handguard, Ergo grip, Ace FX skeleton stock, black or 100% camo coverage, 6.44 lbs. New 2011.

| MSR $1,026 | $875 | $550 | $465 | $395 | $350 | $325 | $300 | |

Add $115 for 100% camo coverage.

MPR .308-15 – 7.62 NATO cal., GIO, 16, 18, or 24 in. stainless steel ultra match button rifled barrel w/o sights, 10 shot mag., billet aluminum upper and lower, rifle length Predator aluminum free float handguard (16 in. barrel with knurling), designed to accept all standard AR-15 upper receivers as well as Olympic Arms .308 style lowers, two-position front pivot pin, forward Picatinny rails, A2 buttstock, 9 lbs. New 2015.

| MSR $1,267 | $1,065 | $650 | $500 | $450 | $395 | $350 | $325 | |

Add $291 for 18 in. barrel or $421 for 24 in. barrel.

K3B CARBINE – 5.56 NATO, 6.8 SPC (new 2016), or .300 AAC Blackout (new 2016) cal., GIO, 16 in. match grade chrome moly steel threaded heavy barrel with A2 flash suppressor, adj. A2 rear sight, Fiberite carbine length handguard, A2 (disc.) or M4 collapsible (new 2012) buttstock, adj. front post sight, A3 flat-top receiver became standard 2011, 6 3/4 lbs. New 2005.

| MSR $811 | $695 | $500 | $425 | $375 | $335 | $315 | $295 | |

* ***K3B-FAR Carbine*** – 5.56 NATO cal., GIO, 16 in. FAR button rifled stainless steel barrel with A2 flash suppressor, forged A2 upper with fully adj. rear sight or flat-top upper, post front sight with bayonet lug, Fiberite carbine length handguard, M4 6-pos. collapsible stock, 6 lbs. New 2005.

| MSR $844 | $725 | $500 | $435 | $375 | $335 | $315 | $295 | |

* ***K3B-M4 Carbine*** – 5.56 NATO cal., GIO, 16 in. M4 button rifled stainless steel barrel with A2 flash suppressor, forged A2 upper with fully adj. rear sight or flat-top upper, post front sight with bayonet lug, Fiberite carbine length M4 handguard with heat shield, M4 6-pos. collapsible stock, 6.3 lbs. New 2005.

| MSR $844 | $725 | $500 | $435 | $375 | $335 | $315 | $295 | |

Add $65 for detachable carry handle (K3BM4A3).

* ***K3B-M4-A3-TC Carbine*** – 5.56 NATO cal., GIO, similar to K3B-M4, except is tactical carbine version with Firsh handguard, flat-top upper receiver with Picatinny rail, and detachable carry handle, 6.7 lbs. New 2005.

| MSR $993 | $850 | $550 | $465 | $395 | $350 | $325 | $295 | |

K4B/K4B68 – 5.56 NATO or 6.8 SPC (new 2010) cal., GIO, 20 in. match grade chrome moly steel button rifled threaded barrel with flash suppressor, adj. A2 rear sight, A2 buttstock, adj. front post sight, A2 upper receiver and handguard, 8 1/2 lbs.

| MSR $844 | $725 | $500 | $435 | $375 | $335 | $315 | $295 | |

Subtract $26 for flat-top upper with Picatinny rail (K4B-FT).

K4B-A4 – .223 Rem. cal., GIO, 20 in. barrel with A2 flash suppressor, elevation adj. post front sight, bayonet lug, Firsh rifle length handguard with Picatinny rails, flat-top receiver, 9 lbs. Mfg. 2006-2008.

| | $800 | $525 | $450 | $385 | $340 | $325 | $295 | *$941* |

270 OLYMPIC ARMS, INC., cont.

MSR	100%	98%	95%	90%	80%	70%	60%	Last MSR

K7 ELIMINATOR – 5.56 NATO cal., GIO, 16 in. stainless steel threaded barrel with flash suppressor, adj. A2 rear sight, A2 buttstock, adj. front post sight, 6.8 lbs. New 2005.

| MSR $909 | $785 | $525 | $450 | $385 | $340 | $325 | $295 | |

Add $104 for K7-ORT (Optic Ready Tactical).

K8 – .204 Ruger (new 2012), 6.8 SPC (new 2012) or 5.56 NATO cal., GIO, 20 in stainless steel button rifled bull barrel, A2 buttstock, Picatinny flat-top upper receiver, gas block, free floating aluminum knurled tube, satin bead blast finish on barrel, 8 1/2 lbs. New 2005.

| MSR $909 | $785 | $525 | $450 | $385 | $340 | $325 | $295 | |

This model is marked "Target Match" on mag. well.

* **K8-MAG** – similar to K8, GIO, except available in .223 WSSM, .243 WSSM, .25 WSSM, or .300 OSSM (new 2006) cals., and has 24 in. barrel, 5 shot mag., 9.4 lbs. New 2005.

| MSR $1,364 | $1,135 | $725 | $525 | $465 | $415 | $375 | $350 | |

K9/K10/K40/K45 – 9mm Para. (K9), 10mm Norma (K10), .40 S&W (K40), or .45 ACP (K45) cal., GIO, 16 in. threaded stainless steel barrel with flash suppressor, adj. A2 rear sight, 10 shot converted Uzi (10mm, .40 S&W or .45 ACP cal.) or 32 (9mm Para.) shot converted Sten detachable mag., Fiberite carbine length handguard, M4 6-pos. collapsible buttstock, bayonet lug, 6.7 lbs. Mfg. 2005-early 2017.

| | $865 | $550 | $465 | $395 | $350 | $325 | $300 | $1,006 |

* **K9GL/K40GL** – 9mm Para. or .40 S&W cal., GIO, 16 in. button rifled stainless steel barrel with flash suppressor, forged A2 upper with fully adj. rear sight, adj. post front sight with bayonet lug, lower receiver designed to accept Glock magazines, Fiberite carbine length handguard, M4 6-pos. collapsible stock, does not include magazine, 6.86 lbs. Mfg. 2005-early 2017.

| | $975 | $595 | $495 | $425 | $365 | $335 | $300 | $1,157 |

K16 – 5.56 NATO, 6.8 SPC (new 2012), 7.62x39mm (new 2012), or .300 AAC Blackout (new 2012) cal., GIO, 16 in. button rifled chrome moly bull barrel with crown muzzle, free floating aluminum tube handguard with knurling, forged flat-top upper receiver with Picatinny rails, gas block with Picatinny rails, A2 buttstock with trapdoor, 7 1/2 lbs. New 2005.

| MSR $830 | $725 | $500 | $435 | $375 | $335 | $315 | $295 | |

K22 M4 – .22 LR cal., blowback action, 16 in. stainless steel barrel, A1 flash suppressor, M4 6-point collapsible stock, forged A2 upper, adj. rear sight, adj. post front sight with bayonet lug, Fiberite carbine length handguard with heat shield, 6.6 lbs. Mfg. 2011-2012.

| | $875 | $550 | $465 | $395 | $350 | $325 | $300 | $1,039 |

K22 RIMFIRE TARGET MATCH – .22 LR cal., blowback action, 16 in. stainless steel bull barrel, A2 fixed trapdoor stock, flat-top with Picatinny rails, no sights, free floating aluminum handguard tube with knurling, muzzle crown, 8.6 lbs. Mfg. 2011-2015.

| | $725 | $500 | $435 | $375 | $335 | $315 | $295 | $831 |

K22 SURVIVAL LIGHT – .22 LR cal., blowback action, 16 in. stainless steel featherweight barrel, side folding stock, flat-top with Picatinny rails, gas block, free floating slotted aluminum handguard, A1 flash suppressor, 6 lbs. Mfg. 2011-2012.

| | $725 | $500 | $435 | $375 | $335 | $315 | $295 | $883 |

K30 – .30 Carbine cal., GIO, similar to K16, except has A2 upper receiver, collapsible stock, and threaded barrel with flash suppressor, 6.6 lbs. Mfg. 2005-2006.

| | $785 | $525 | $450 | $385 | $340 | $325 | $295 | $905 |

Add $95 for A3 upper receiver.

K30R – 7.62x39mm cal., GIO, 16 or 20 (new 2016) in. stainless steel barrel, 6-point M4 collapsible stock, A2 flash suppressor, pistol grip, matte black anodized receiver, parkerized steel parts, A2 upper with adj. rear sight, 6 3/4 lbs. New 2007.

| MSR $891 | $765 | $515 | $440 | $375 | $335 | $315 | $295 | |

Add $39 for 20 in. barrel or 16 in. bull barrel with flat-top (K30R16, new 2016).

K68 – 6.8 SPC cal., GIO, 16 or 20 (optional) in. M4 button rifled stainless steel barrel with A2 flash suppressor, A2 upper with adj. rear sight, post front sight with bayonet lug, Fiberite M4 carbine length handguard, 6-position M4 collapsible stock, matte black anodized receiver, parkerized steel parts, pistol grip, 6.62 lbs. New 2017.

| MSR$857 | $745 | $500 | $435 | $375 | $335 | $315 | $295 | |

K74 – 5.45x39mm cal., GIO, 16 in. button rifled stainless steel barrel with A2 flash suppressor, forged A2 upper with adj. rear sight and post front sight with bayonet lug, 6-position M4 collapsible stock, 6 3/4 lbs. New 2009.

| MSR $1,058 | $895 | $575 | $475 | $395 | $350 | $325 | $300 | |

OLYMPIC ARMS, INC., cont. 271

MSR		100%	98%	95%	90%	80%	70%	60%	Last MSR

UMAR (ULTIMATE MAGNUM AR) – .22-250 Rem., .223 WSSM (disc.), .243 WSSM (disc.), .25 WSSM (disc.), or .300 WSSM (disc.) cal., GIO, 24 in. heavy match grade stainless steel bull barrel, black matte anodized aluminum forged receiver, parkerized steel parts, flat-top/gas block with Picatinny rails, sling swivel mount, A2 stock w/trapdoor, Ergo tactical deluxe pistol grip, Predator Firsh free floating handguard, 9.4 lbs. New 2012.

| | MSR $1,559 | $1,315 | $850 | $625 | $500 | $435 | $375 | $350 | |

Add $97 for fluted bull barrel (new 2016).

The upper receiver of this model will not work on standard AR-15 lowers.

GAMESTALKER CAMO – .204 Ruger (mfg. 2011 only), .243 WSSM, .25 WSSM, or .300 OSSM cal., GIO, 22 in. stainless steel barrel, flat-top upper receiver with Picatinny rail, ACE skeleton stock with Ergo SureGrip, 100% camo coverage, approx. 7 1/2 lbs. Mfg. 2010-early 2017.

| | | $1,135 | $725 | $525 | $465 | $415 | $375 | $350 | *$1,364* |

GSG2 (GAMESTOCKER GEN 2) – 5.56 NATO, 6.8 SPC, or 7.62x39mm cal., GIO, 20 in. stainless steel barrel, flat-top upper receiver with Picatinny rail, free floating aluminum handguard, ACE FX skeleton stock with Ergo SureGrip, 100% camo coverage, approx. 7 1/2 lbs. New 2011.

| | MSR $1,234 | $1,050 | $650 | $495 | $450 | $395 | $350 | $325 | |

MPR GAMESTOCKER – .243 Win., .308 Win., .260 Rem., .300 WSM, or 7mm-08 cal., GIO, 22 in. stainless steel bull barrel, Ergo tactical deluxe (Fat Boy) rubberized pistol grip, billet aluminum upper and lower receiver, Picatinny rail, standard slotted aluminum free floating handguard, matte black finish. New 2016.

| | MSR $1,689 | $1,385 | $895 | $675 | $525 | $450 | $385 | $350 | |

OSPREY ARMAMENT

Current M14 type and AR-15 style manufacturer located in Hutto, TX. Previously located in Wilmington, NC.

RIFLES: SEMI-AUTO

Osprey Armament currently manufactures M14 type rifles and previously AR-15 style carbines/rifles, including the most recent X-Series models: Osprey CSASS Rifle (MSR $1,895) and the Osprey MK-12 Rifle (MSR $2,395).

NOTES

MAYBE THE ONLY THING BETTER THAN THIS BOOK IS THE ONLINE SUBSCRIPTION!

Only $19.95/year!

- **Includes monthly updates** keeping you informed of all the new AR-15 makes/models.
- **Features thousands of images** allowing for fast and easy identification.
- **Manufacturer/Model searchable database** allowing you to find the model you need.
- Historical pricing with dynamic interactive graphs keeps you up-to-date on your AR-15 purchases as investments.
- Your own personal online inventory solution - keep track of your collection and track the change in value.
- Includes access to BBP's industry standard Photo Percentage Grading System – why guess a gun's condition when you can be sure?

Visit BlueBookOfGunValues.com
to view sample pages and ordering

Good Information Never Sleeps!

P SECTION

273 P

POF USA
Please refer to the Patriot Ordnance Factory listing in this section.

PALMETTO STATE ARMORY
Current pistol, rifle, and related parts manufacturer with corporate offices located in Columbia, SC.

MSR	100%	98%	95%	90%	80%	70%	60%	Last MSR

PISTOLS: SEMI-AUTO

CLASSIC FREEDOM KEYMOD PISTOL – 5.56 NATO cal., 7 in. A2 style chrome moly barrel with Nitride finish, A2 muzzle device, M4 barrel extension, 30 shot mag., pistol length gas system, M4 style stock, A2 grip, 6 in. KeyMod free float handguard, low profile gas block, forged A3 upper receiver, forward assist, dust cover, aluminum lower with fluted T6 pistol buffer tube, hardcoat anodized black finish. Mfg. 2016-2017.

	100%	98%	95%	90%	80%	70%	60%	Last MSR
	$615	$545	$475	$400	$350	$315	$285	*$700*

PSA CARBINE LENGTH 5.56 NATO M-LOK MOE EPT SHOCKWAVE PISTOL – 5.56 NATO cal., 10 1/2 in. A2 profile chrome moly steel barrel with Nitride finish, M4 barrel extension, A2 flash hider, 30 shot mag., EPT, KAK Industries Shockwave Blade pistol brace, Magpul MOE grip, low profile gas block, carbine length gas system, forged aluminum A3 receivers, lightweight M-LOK 9 in. free float rail, aluminum pistol buffer tube, hardcoat anodized black finish. New 2018.

MSR	100%	98%	95%	90%	80%	70%	60%
MSR $550	$495	$435	$365	$315	$275	$250	$225

RIFLES: SEMI-AUTO

PSA 9mm CLASSIC RIFLE – 9mm Para. cal., 16 in. chrome moly barrel, A2 flash hider, standard AR-15 magwell contains aluminum 9mm magazine adapter that accepts Colt style AR 9mm mags., single stage trigger, F-marked gas sight base, M4 carbine stock, A2 grip, polymer handguard with heat shields, forged aluminum upper and lower receiver, hardcoat anodized black finish. New 2016.

MSR	100%	98%	95%	90%	80%	70%	60%
MSR $750	$650	$575	$510	$440	$385	$340	$325

PSA 9mm GX9 CLASSIC RIFLE – 9mm Para. cal., 16 in. chrome moly barrel, A2 flash hider, Glock style 30 shot mag., single stage trigger, F-marked gas sight base, M4 carbine stock, A2 grip, polymer handguard with heat shields, forged aluminum upper and lower receiver, hardcoat anodized black finish. New 2017.

MSR	100%	98%	95%	90%	80%	70%	60%
MSR $750	$650	$575	$510	$440	$385	$340	$325

PSA CLASSIC A2 RIFLE – 5.56 NATO cal., 20 in. A2 profile barrel with Nitride finish, A2 muzzle device, M4 barrel extension, 30 shot aluminum mag., single stage trigger, F-marked front sight base, A2 style fixed stock, A2 grip, rifle length gas system, forged M4 receiver, polymer handguard with heat shields, Mil-Spec carry handle. New 2017.

MSR	100%	98%	95%	90%	80%	70%	60%
MSR $780	$665	$575	$510	$440	$385	$340	$325

PSA CLASSIC FREEDOM RIFLE – 5.56 NATO cal., AR-15 style, 16 in. M4 barrel with A2 style muzzle, M4 barrel extension, 30 shot mag., carbine length gas system, forged M4 receivers with heat shield, single stage trigger, A2 style grip, carbine length buffer tube, M4 stock, black finish, 6.8 lbs.

MSR	100%	98%	95%	90%	80%	70%	60%
MSR $450	$425	$375	$350	$325	$300	$290	$275

PSA ELITE GX-9 LIMITED EDITION RIFLE – 9mm Para. cal., blowback action, 16 in. lightweight stainless steel barrel, SJC 9mm PCC carbon steel compensator with black oxide finish, 31 shot Glock mags., ODIN Works XGMR-1 extended Glock mag. release, black ATI Tactlite adj. Mil-Spec stock, carbine Mil-Spec buffer tube, black Magpul MOE grip, PSA Slick Side aluminum upper receiver, Lancer Custom 13 3/4 in. carbon fiber handguard with PSA logo engraving, billet aluminum PSA GX-9 9mm lower receiver, Devil Dog Hard Charger tactical charging handle, includes PSA 36 in. single gun case, Tactical Gray, Metallic Black, or Burnt Bronze Cerakote barrel finish, 6.27 lbs. New mid-2017.

MSR	100%	98%	95%	90%	80%	70%	60%
MSR $1,400	$1,200	$1,075	$950	$800	$700	$600	$495

PSA FREEDOM HAMMER M-LOK MOE RIFLE – 5.56 NATO cal., AR-15 style, mid-length gas system, 16 in. A2 style hammer forged barrel with Nitride finish, A2 muzzle device, M4 barrel extension, 30 shot Magpul mag., single stage enhanced precision trigger, Magpul MOE stock, Magpul MOE grip, low profile gas block, forged M4 receivers, 12 in. M-LOK free float handguard, carbine length buffer tube. Mfg. 2017 only.

	100%	98%	95%	90%	80%	70%	60%	Last MSR
	$685	$615	$550	$475	$420	$365	$335	*$800*

PSA FREEDOM HAMMER MOE RIFLE – 5.56 NATO cal., AR-15 style, mid-length gas system, 16 in. A2 style hammer forged barrel with Nitride finish, A2 muzzle device, M4 barrel extension, 30 shot Magpul mag., single stage enhanced precision trigger, F-marked front sight base, Magpul MOE stock, Magpul MOE grip, carbine length buffer tube, forged M4 receivers, Magpul MOE handguard. Mfg. 2017 only.

Retail pricing was not available for this model.

P 274 PALMETTO STATE ARMORY, cont.

MSR	100%	98%	95%	90%	80%	70%	60%	Last MSR

PSA GEN2 PA10 .308 RIFLE – .308 Win. cal., 18 in. chrome moly steel barrel with M4 extension, A2 muzzle device, 20 shot PMAG, front sight post gas block, M4 6-pos. telescoping stock, A2 grip, forged aluminum lower and flat-top upper receiver with feed ramps, forward assist, dust cover, mid-length gas system, polymer handguard, aluminum buffer tube, AR-15 style fire control group, hardcoat anodized black finish, 10.4 lbs. New 2018.

| MSR $630 | $550 | $475 | $400 | $350 | $315 | $295 | $275 | |

* ***PSA Gen2 PA10 Mid-Length .308 Stainless*** – .308 Win. cal., 18 in. stainless steel barrel, M4 barrel extension, A2 muzzle device, 20 shot PMAG, M4 6-pos. telescoping stock, A2 grip, low profile mid-length gas system, forged aluminum lower and flat-top upper receiver, forward assist, dust cover, Nitride treated BCG, 15 in. lightweight M-LOK free float rail, AR-15 style fire control group, hardcoat anodized black finish, 8 lbs. New 2018.

| MSR $730 | $645 | $500 | $415 | $370 | $325 | $300 | $275 | |

PSA KEYMOD RIFLE – 5.56 NATO cal., 20 in. A2 profile barrel with Nitride finish, A2 muzzle device, M4 barrel extension, 30 shot mag., single stage enhanced precision trigger, M4 stock, A2 grip, low profile gas block, forged M4 receivers, 15 in. KeyMod free float handguard, Mil-Spec buffer tube. New 2017.

| MSR $750 | $650 | $500 | $415 | $370 | $325 | $300 | $275 | |

PSA KS47 CLASSIC CARBINE – 7.62x39mm cal., FSB gas block, 16 in. barrel with Nitride finish, A2 muzzle brake, M4 barrel extension, M4 stock, A2 grip, M4 KS Hybrid receiver, PSA classic polymer handguard, carbine length buffer tube, 6 1/2 lbs.

| MSR $900 | $765 | $515 | $440 | $375 | $335 | $315 | $295 | |

PSA KS47 CLASSIC KEYMOD RIFLE – 7.62x39mm cal., mid-length gas system, 16 in. chrome moly medium profile barrel, A2 flash hider, M4 barrel extension, 30 shot Magpul AK mag., low profile gas block, M4 carbine stock, A2 grip, 13 in. KeyMod free float handguard, forged upper and billet aluminum lower receiver, forward assist, dust cover, T6 buffer tube, hardcoat anodized black finish. Mfg. 2016-2017.

| | $850 | $550 | $465 | $395 | $350 | $325 | $295 | $980 |

PSA MID-LENGTH MOE FREEDOM CARBINE – 5.56 NATO cal., GIO, AR-15 style, 16 in. stainless steel barrel with A2 flash hider, M4 barrel extension, 30 shot mag., F-marked gas sight base, forged upper and lower receivers, MOE furniture, hardcoat anodized black finish. Disc. 2016.

| | $595 | $485 | $415 | $350 | $315 | $295 | $275 | $700 |

PSA MID STAINLESS FREEDOM RIFLE – 5.56 NATO cal., GIO, AR-15 style, 16 in. stainless steel barrel with A2 flash hider, M4 barrel extension, F-marked gas sight base, standard handguard, forged upper and lower receivers, buffer tube, 6-pos. M4 carbine stock, A2 style grip, hardcoat anodized black finish. Disc. 2016.

| | $475 | $415 | $375 | $335 | $310 | $295 | $275 | $530 |

PSA MOE FREEDOM KEYMOD RIFLE – 9mm Para. cal., AR-15 style, blowback action, 16 in. A2 style barrel, 32 shot round steel mag., forged aluminum upper and lower receivers, M4 flat-top slick side upper with feed ramp, PSA lightweight Keymod w/QD points free float handguard, T6 aluminum buffer tube, 6-pos. Magpul stock, hardcoat anodized black finish, 6 3/4 lbs. Disc. 2016.

| | $800 | $525 | $450 | $385 | $340 | $325 | $295 | $950 |

PSA M4 CARBINE LIGHTWEIGHT M-LOK CLASSIC RIFLE – 5.56 NATO cal., 16 in. M4 profile chrome moly steel barrel with Nitride finish, M4 barrel extension, A2 flash hider, 30 shot PMAG, Mil-Spec AR-15 fire control group, 6-pos. collapsible PSA classic carbine stock, A2 grip, carbine length gas system, low profile gas block, forged aluminum lower and M4 flat-top upper receiver with feed ramps, forward assist, dust cover, 13 1/2 in. lightweight M-LOK free float handguard/rail, hardcoat anodized black finish, 7 lbs. New 2018.

| MSR $550 | $475 | $415 | $375 | $335 | $310 | $295 | $275 | |

PSA M4 MOE EPT FREEDOM RIFLE – 5.56 NATO cal., 16 in. chrome moly steel barrel, M4 barrel extension, A2 flash hider, single stage EPT (Enhanced Polished Trigger), F-marked gas sight base, Magpul MBUS rear sight, 6-pos. Magpul stock, MOE grip, carbine length gas system, forged aluminum upper and lower receiver with hardcoat anodized black finish, forward assist, dust cover, Magpul MOE FDE carbine length handguard, FDE finish, 6 1/2 lbs. New 2018.

| MSR $500 | $445 | $395 | $365 | $325 | $300 | $290 | $275 | |

PSA M4 MOE RIFLE WITH VORTEX OPTIC – 5.56 NATO cal., GIO, 16 in. chrome moly barrel, A2 flash hider, M4 barrel extension, pinned F-marked front sight post, MOE carbine handguard, forged upper rec., 6-pos. buffer tube, MOE stock, Magpul MOE grip and trigger guard, hardcoat anodized black finish. Disc. 2016.

| | $615 | $540 | $470 | $400 | $350 | $310 | $295 | $700 |

PSA M4 PREMIUM CARBINE – 5.56 NATO cal., carbine gas system, 16 in. M4 profile barrel with black phosphate finish, A2 flash hider, 30 shot D&H mag., aluminum trigger guard, pinned F-marked front sight post, 6-pos. Mil-Spec buffer tube and M4 stock, A2 pistol grip, forged aluminum receivers, carbine handguard, black hardcoat anodized finish. New 2017.

| MSR $750 | $650 | $500 | $415 | $370 | $325 | $300 | $275 | |

PALMETTO STATE ARMORY, cont. 275 P

MSR	100%	98%	95%	90%	80%	70%	60%	Last MSR

PSA PA10 .308 RIFLE – .308 Win. cal., GIO, AR-15 style, 16 in. stainless steel barrel with A2 flash hider, F-marked gas sight base, forged aluminum upper and lower receivers, forward assist and dust cover, buffer tube, 6-pos. M4 stock, single stage trigger, hardcoat anodized finish. Disc. 2016.

	$775	$685	$615	$550	$485	$415	$370	*$900*

PSA PA10 MIAD RIFLE – .308 Win. cal., GIO, AR-15 style, 18 in. stainless steel A2-style barrel, M4 style extension, 20 shot mag., low profile gas block, forged aluminum flat-top upper with feed ramps, forward assist, dust cover, Midwest Industries SSK 15 in. free float handguard, T6 aluminum extended buffer tube, 6-pos. Magpul MOE stock, hardcoat anodized black finish. Disc. 2016.

	$1,025	$925	$800	$685	$595	$515	$440	*$1,200*

PSA PA10 MID-LENGTH MOE/BLACKHAWK RIFLE – .308 Win. cal., GIO, 18 in. stainless steel barrel with A2 flash hider, 20 shot Magpul mag., F-marked front sight base, Magpul MOE handguard, forged upper and lower receivers, Magpul MOE carbine stock, Blackhawk ergonomic grip, hardcoat anodized black finish. Disc. 2016.

	$775	$685	$615	$550	$485	$415	$370	*$900*

PSA 308 STAINLESS KEYMOD CLASSIC RIFLE – .308 Win. cal., mid-length gas system, 18 or 20 in. stainless steel barrel, A2 flash hider, M4 barrel extension, 20 shot Magpul mag., enhanced precision trigger, M4 carbine stock, A2 pistol grip, 13 or 15 in. PSA KeyMod rail, low profile gas block, forged aluminum upper and lower receiver, forward assist, dust cover, T6 buffer tube, hardcoat anodized black finish. New 2016.

MSR $1,100	$925	$850	$725	$625	$550	$475	$425	

Add $100 for 20 in. barrel.

PALMETTO STATE DEFENSE, LLC

Current manufacturer located in Greer, SC.

RIFLES: SEMI-AUTO

Palmetto State Defense manufactures custom AR-15 style rifles in several calibers and configurations. Current models include: Range 15 Special Edition - MSR $2,000, MOE 16 in. Carbine - MSR $1,150, M4 Carbine - MSR $799. Previously manufactured models include: A2.5 20 in. Rifle - last MSR was $1,299, Tactical Match - last MSR was $1,899, .300 BLK - last MSR was $1,199, SRC (Suppressor Ready Carbine) - last MSR was $1,599, Limited Edition Blue, and Straightjacket. Please contact the company directly for more information including options, pricing, and availability (see Trademark Index).

PARA USA, LLC

Previous manufacturer and trademark established in 1985 and discontinued in February of 2015. Previously located in Pineville, NC. Previous company names were Para-Ordnance Mfg. Inc. and Para USA Inc. Para-Ordnance Mfg. Inc was located in Scarborough, Ontario, Canada until June 2009. Previously located in Ft. Lauderdale, FL. Dealer and distributor sales.

Para-Ordnance Mfg. was founded by Ted Szabo and Thanos Polyzos. Szabo was born in Hungary and his family fled the country when the Russians invaded during the Hungarian Revolution of 1956. Polyzos was born in Greece and later emigrated to Canada.

On Jan. 30, 2012, Freedom Group, Inc. purchased the assets of Para USA, Inc. Manufacturing continued in Pineville, NC until the trademark was retired in February 2015.

RIFLES: SEMI-AUTO

TTR SERIES – .223 Rem. cal., tactical design, GIO, 16 1/2 in. chrome-lined barrel, DIGS (delayed impingement gas system) operation, 30 shot mag., flip-up front sight and adj. flip-up rear sight, flat-top receiver with full-length Picatinny rail, black finish, single stage trigger, available in Short Rail with fixed stock (TTR-XASF, mfg. 2009), or 5-position folding stock with Short Rail (TTR-XAS), Long Rail (TTR-XA), and Nylatron (TTR-XN, mfg. 2009) forearm configurations. Mfg. 2009-late 2011.

	$2,050	$1,800	$1,575	$1,350	$1,150	$975	$825	*$2,397*

Add $100 for Nylatron forearm (mfg. 2009).

PATRIOT ORDNANCE FACTORY (POF)

Current manufacturer located in Phoenix, AZ. Previously located in Glendale, AZ.

PISTOLS: SEMI-AUTO

P308 PISTOL – .308 Win. cal., GPO, 12 1/2 in. heavy contour fluted barrel, 3-position gas regulation for normal, suppressed, and single action modes, FMP-A3 muzzle device, Magpul 20 shot PMAG, corrosion resistant operating system, chrome plated Mil-Spec bolt, optional fixed hooded front sight, optional Troy or Diamondhead flip-up sights, hunter/sniper or tactical aircraft aluminum alloy modular railed receiver, nickel and black hardcoat anodized Teflon finish, oversized trigger guard, Magpul MOE pistol grip, PWS enhanced pistol buffer tube, Ergo ladder rail covers, sling, bipod mount, approx. 7 1/2 lbs. Disc. 2014.

	$2,725	$2,375	$1,925	$1,650	$1,375	$1,150	$995	*$3,220*

P 276 PATRIOT ORDNANCE FACTORY (POF), cont.

MSR	100%	98%	95%	90%	80%	70%	60%	Last MSR

P415 EDGE – 5.56 NATO or .300 AAC Blackout cal., 10 1/2 in. barrel, Gen 4 lower receiver, 9 in. M-LOK MRR rail, E2 Extraction Technology, ambidextrous fire controls, black anodized, NP3, Burnt Bronze, or Tungsten finish, 6 1/2 lbs. New 2018.

| MSR $2,000 | $1,700 | $1,500 | $1,250 | $1,100 | $950 | $825 | $675 | |

Add $50 for NP3 coating.

Add $150 for Burnt Bronze or Tungsten finish.

P415 PISTOL – 5.56 NATO cal., GPO, 7 1/4 or 10 1/2 in. heavy contour fluted barrel, 3-position gas regulation for normal, suppressed, and single action modes, FMP-A3 muzzle device, chrome plated Mil-Spec bolt, optional fixed hooded front sight, optional Troy or Diamondhead flip-up sights, hunter/sniper or tactical aircraft aluminum alloy modular railed receiver, nickel and black hardcoat anodized Teflon finish, oversized trigger guard, Magpul MOE pistol grip, PWS enhanced pistol buffer tube, Ergo ladder rail covers, sling, bipod mount, Magpul 30 shot PMAG, approx. 6 1/2 lbs. Disc. 2013.

| | $1,950 | $1,725 | $1,450 | $1,250 | $1,050 | $900 | $750 | $2,320 |

GEN 4 AR PISTOL 415 – .223 Rem./5.56 NATO cal., GPO, 7 1/4 or 10 1/2 in. deep fluted barrel, 6 or 9 in. modular rail, black anodized finish or NP3 coating, 5.7 lbs. Mfg. 2014-2016.

| | $1,795 | $1,575 | $1,325 | $1,150 | $995 | $850 | $700 | $2,130 |

Add $30 for NP3 coating.

GEN 4 AR PISTOL 308 – .308 Win./7.62 NATO cal., GPO, 12 1/2 in. deep fluted barrel, 11 1/2 in. modular rail, black anodized finish or NP3 coating, 7.6 lbs. Mfg. 2014-2016.

| | $2,200 | $1,925 | $1,600 | $1,375 | $1,125 | $975 | $850 | $2,600 |

Add $30 for NP3 coating.

RENEGADE – 5.56 NATO cal., 10 1/2 in. barrel, SB Tactical SBA3 arm brace, Dictator 9-pos. adj. gas block, straight gas tube, forged lower and flat-top upper receiver, 9 in. Renegade rail with M-LOK compatibility, 4 integrated QD slots, E2 Dual Extraction Technology, black or Burnt Bronze finish, 5.8 lbs.

| MSR $1,500 | $1,275 | $1,125 | $1,025 | $875 | $750 | $625 | $525 | |

Add $100 for Burnt Bronze finish.

RENEGADE PLUS – 5.56 NATO or .300 AAC Blackout cal., GIO, 10 1/2 in. Nitride heat-treated barrel, flat match grade trigger, SB Tactical SBA3 arm brace, built on the Gen 4 billet lower receiver, nickel coated Ultimate BCG, fully ambidextrous, Dictator 9-position adj. gas block, straight gas tube, 9 in. M-LOK MRR rail, black or Burnt Bronze finish, 5.8 lbs. New 2018.

| MSR $1,900 | $1,625 | $1,425 | $1,200 | $1,075 | $925 | $795 | $650 | |

Add $100 for Burnt Bronze finish.

REVOLUTION – 7.62 NATO cal., GPO, 12 1/2 in. deep fluted barrel, triple port muzzle brake, Magpul 20 shot mag., single stage match trigger, SB Tactical SBA3 arm brace, 5-pos. adj. gas piston operating system, Gen 4 lower receiver, ambi controls, 11 1/2 in. M-LOK MRR rail, Edge handguard with four built-in QD mounts, E2 Dual Extraction Technology, black anodized finish or NP3 coating, 6.9 lbs. New 2018.

| MSR $2,670 | $2,250 | $1,950 | $1,625 | $1,400 | $1,140 | $995 | $865 | |

Add $30 for NP3 coating.

RIFLES/CARBINES: SEMI-AUTO

Patriot Ordnance Factory manufactures AR-15 style rifles and carbines chambered in 5.56/.223 and 7.62/.308, as well as upper and lower receivers and various parts. The semi-auto carbines and rifles use a unique gas piston operating system that requires no lubrication. A wide variety of options are available for each model. Please contact the company directly for more information, including options and pricing (see Trademark Index).

THE CONSTABLE – 5.56 NATO cal., GIO, 16 in. barrel, A2 flash hider, MFT 30 shot mag., Mil-Spec trigger and furniture, ambi selector switch, carbine length low profile gas block, Mil-Spec upper receiver, 14 1/2 in. M-LOK Renegade free floating rail with four integraded QD sling mounts, Mil-Spec Puritan lower receiver, black anodized finish, 6.14 lbs. New 2018.

| MSR $1,000 | $850 | $550 | $465 | $395 | $350 | $325 | $295 | |

OLDE SCHOOL – .223 Rem./5.56 NATO or .308 Win./7.62 NATO cal., GIO, 16 1/2 in. barrel, E2 Dual Extraction Technology, ambidextrous controls, straight Inconel gas tube, adj. gas system, 11 1/2 in. M-LOK handguard, black anodized or NP3 finish, 8.2 lbs. Mfg. 2015-2016.

| | $2,125 | $1,325 | $995 | $675 | $595 | $525 | $475 | $2,650 |

Add $40 for NP3 coating.

P6.5 EDGE – 6.5mm Creedmoor cal., short stroke, GPO, 16 1/2 or 20 in. Nitride heat-treated barrel, triple port muzzle brake, Magpul 20 shot mag., E2 Dual Extraction Technology, match grade trigger, Luth-AR MBA stock, Mission First Tactical grip, 5-position adj. gas block, ambi controls, 14 1/2 in. M-LOK MRR free floating rail, Gen4 billet lower receiver, black anodized finish, 8.1-9.5 lbs. New 2018.

| MSR $2,400 | $1,975 | $1,150 | $925 | $650 | $575 | $495 | $425 | |

PATRIOT ORDNANCE FACTORY (POF), cont. 277 P

MSR	100%	98%	95%	90%	80%	70%	60%	Last MSR

P15 PURITAN – 5.56 NATO or 7.62 NATO (new 2015) cal., GPO, 16 1/2 in. Nitride heat treated contour barrel with A2 flash hider, 3 shot PMAG, receiver height Picatinny flat-top gas block, ambidextrous safety selector, E2 Dual Extraction Technology, Magpul MOE buttstock, Magpul MOE pistol grip with mid-length polymer handguard, bayonet mount, QD sling mount, nickel boron coated bolt carrier, hardcoat anodized black finish, 6.7 lbs. Mfg. 2014-2016.

| | $1,225 | $825 | $575 | $475 | $425 | $375 | $350 | *$1,470* |

P300 (GEN 4 P300) – .300 Win. Mag. cal., GPO, 18 or 24 in. barrel, oversized triple port muzzle brake, 14 shot mag., Magpul CTR (18 in. model) or Magpul PRS (24 in. model) stock, 14 1/2 in. M-LOK MRR free floating handguard, 9-pos. adj. gas block, Gen4 billet lower receiver, POF-USA Tomahawk ambidextrous charging handle and QD endplate, (18 in. only), ambidextrous bolt release, safety selector, bolt catch, and mag. release, NP3 coating, 9.2-9.8 lbs. New 2016.

| MSR $3,500 | $2,875 | $1,875 | $1,375 | $795 | $675 | $625 | $575 | |

P308 (P308 MID-LENGTH RIFLE) – .308 Win. cal., GPO, 16 1/2 or 20 in. heavy contour fluted barrel, Magpul 20 shot PMAG, 3-position gas regulation for normal, suppressed, and single action modes, FMP-A3 muzzle device, corrosion resistant operating system, chrome plated Mil-Spec bolt, optional fixed hooded front sight, optional Troy or Diamondhead flip-up sights, hunter/sniper or tactical aircraft aluminum alloy modular railed receiver, nickel, black, Olive Drab (new 2013), or Cerakote Burnt Bronze (new 2013) hardcoat anodized Teflon finish, oversized trigger guard, Magpul MOE pistol grip, Magpul CTR 6-position collapsible stock, Ergo ladder rail covers, sling, bipod mount, approx. 9 lbs. Disc. 2014.

| | $2,625 | $1,725 | $1,300 | $725 | $650 | $595 | $525 | *$3,220* |

Add $100 for Olive Drab (new 2013) or Cerakote Burnt Bronze (new 2013) finish.
Add $25 for NP3 nickel/alloy plating.

GEN 4 P308 – .308 Win. cal., GPO, 16 1/2 or 20 in. heavy contour deep fluted barrel, triple port muzzle brake, 20 or 30 shot PMAG, no sights, 3-pos. adj. gas block, E2 extraction technology, ambidextrous fire controls, anti-tilt buffer tube, 11 1/2 or 14 1/2 in. modular free floating rail, drop-in trigger system, Magpul CTR stock with buttpad, nickel boron bolt carrier group, black anodized, NP3 nickel alloy plating, or Cerakote Olive Drab, Burnt Bronze, or Tungsten finish, 8 lbs. 8 oz. Mfg. 2014-2016.

| | $2,225 | $1,395 | $1,050 | $675 | $595 | $525 | $475 | *$2,730* |

Add $30 for NP3 nickel alloy plating.
Add $70 for 14 1/2 in. modular rail.
Add $120 for Cerakote finish in Olive Drab, Tungsten, or Burnt Bronze.

P308 EDGE (GEN 4 P308 EDGE) – 7.62 NATO cal., E2 Extraction Technology, GPO, 16 1/2 or 18 1/2 (SPR Model) in. match grade Nitride heat treated barrel, triple port muzzle brake, Magpul 20 shot mag., Mission First Tactical furniture, ambidextrous fire controls, Gen 4 billet lower receiver, redesigned 14 1/2 in. M-LOK MRR free floating handguard, anti-tilt buffer tube, 5-pos. adj. gas block, nickel coated BCG, black anodized, NP3 coated, Burnt Bronze, or Tungsten Cerakote finish, 8.1-9.5 lbs. New 2017.

| MSR $2,400 | $1,975 | $1,150 | $925 | $650 | $575 | $495 | $425 | |

Add $50 for NP3 coating.
Add $150 for Burnt Bronze or Tungsten Cerakote finish.

P308 EDGE SPR – 7.62 NATO cal., short stroke, GPO, 18 1/2 in. match grade Nitride heat-treated barrel, triple port muzzle brake, Magpul 20 shot mag., E2 Dual Extraction Technology, 4 lb. POF-USA EFP drop-in trigger system, Luth-AR MBA stock, Mission First Tactical grip, ambi safety selector, 5-pos. adj. gas block, 14 1/2 in. M-LOK MRR free floating rail, Gen4 billet lower receiver, black anodized, NP3 coated, or Cerakote finish in Burnt Bronze or Tungsten, 9 1/2 lbs. New 2018.

| MSR $2,400 | $1,975 | $1,150 | $925 | $650 | $575 | $495 | $425 | |

Add $50 for NP3 coating.
Add $150 for Burnt Bronze or Tungsten Cerakote finish.

P308 HUNTING RIFLE – .243 Win or .308 Win. cal., GPO, 20 in. heavy contour fluted barrel, 3-position gas regulation for normal, suppressed, and single action modes, FMP-A3 muzzle device, corrosion resistant operating system, chrome plated Mil-Spec bolt, optional fixed hooded front sight, optional Troy or Diamondhead flip-up sights, hunter/sniper aircraft aluminum alloy modular railed receiver, Olive Drab Cerakote finish, oversized trigger guard, Magpul MOE pistol grip, fixed polymer buttstock, Ergo ladder rail covers, sling, bipod mount, 5 shot stainless steel mag., approx. 9 lbs. Disc. 2013.

| | $2,625 | $1,725 | $1,300 | $725 | $650 | $595 | $525 | *$3,220* |

GEN 4 P415 – .223 Rem. cal., GPO, 16 1/2 or 18 in. deep fluted barrel with triple port muzzle brake, 30 shot PMAG, no sights, 3-pos. adj. gas block, E2 Dual Extraction Technology, ambidextrous fire controls, anti-tilt buffer, 11 1/2 or 14 1/2 in. modular free floating rail, drop-in trigger system, Magpul CTR stock with buttpad, nickel boron bolt carrier group, aluminum billet upper and lower receivers, black anodized, NP3 nickel alloy plating, Olive Drab, or Cerakote finish in Burnt Bronze or Tungsten, 7 lbs. Mfg. 2014-2016.

| | $1,675 | $1,000 | $825 | $625 | $550 | $475 | $425 | *$2,025* |

Add $75 for NP3 nickel alloy plating or Olive Drab finish.
Add $125 for Burnt Bronze or Tungsten Cerakote finish.
Add $105 for 14 1/2 in. modular rail.

P 278 PATRIOT ORDNANCE FACTORY (POF), cont.

MSR	100%	98%	95%	90%	80%	70%	60%	Last MSR

P415 CARBINE – .223 Rem. cal., GPO, 16 in. heavy contour chrome-lined fluted barrel, A3 muzzle device, corrosion resistant operating system, nickel plated A3 flat-top upper receiver and charging handle, M4 feed ramp, nickel and black hardcoat anodized Teflon finish, fixed removable hooded front sight, optional Troy flip-up sight, single stage trigger, oversized trigger guard, Magpul CTR retractable 6-position buttstock, M4 plastic handguard or Predator P-9 tactical rail system, sling/bipod mount, 7-7.4 lbs. Disc. 2011.

	$1,650	$1,000	$795	$595	$495	$425	$395	$1,999

Add $300 for Predator P-9 tactical rail system.

P415 EDGE (GEN 4 P415 EDGE) – 5.56 NATO or .300 AAC Blackout (new 2018) cal., GPO, 16 1/2 in. match grade barrel, triple port muzzle brake, Magpul 20 shot mag., E2 Dual Extraction Technology, Mission First Tactical furniture, ambidextrous safety selector, 5-pos. adj. gas block, redesigned 14 1/2 in. M-LOK MRR free-floating rail, Gen4 billet lower receiver, ambidextrous fire controls, black anodized, NP3 coated, Burnt Bronze, or Tungsten Cerakote finish, 7 lbs. New 2017.

MSR $2,000	$1,675	$1,000	$825	$625	$550	$475	$425	

Add $50 for NP3 coating.

Add $150 for Burnt Bronze or Tungsten Cerakote finish.

P415 HUNTING RIFLE – 5.56 NATO cal., GPO, 18 in. heavy contour fluted barrel, 3-position gas regulation for normal, suppressed, and single action modes, FMP-A3 muzzle device, corrosion resistant operating system, chrome plated Mil-Spec bolt, optional fixed hooded front sight, optional Troy or Diamondhead flip-up sights, hunter/sniper aircraft aluminum alloy modular railed receiver, Olive Drab Cerakote finish, oversized trigger guard, Magpul MOE pistol grip, fixed polymer buttstock, Ergo ladder rail covers, sling, bipod mount, 5 shot stainless steel mag., approx. 8 lbs. Disc. 2013.

	$1,875	$1,100	$895	$650	$575	$495	$425	$2,320

P415 MID-LENGTH RIFLE – 5.56 NATO cal., GPO, 16 1/2 or 18 in. chrome moly vanadium alloy, heavy contour, hand lapped button rifled fluted barrel, 3-position gas regulation for normal, suppressed, and single action modes, FMP-A3 muzzle device, corrosion resistant operating system, chrome plated Mil-Spec bolt, optional fixed hooded front sight, optional Troy or Diamondhead flip-up sights, hunter/sniper or tactical aircraft aluminum alloy modular railed receiver, nickel and black hardcoat anodized Teflon finish, oversized trigger guard, Magpul MOE pistol grip, Magpul CTR 6-position collapsible stock, Ergo ladder rail covers, sling, bipod mount, Magpul 30 shot PMAG, approx. 8 lbs. Mfg. 2012-2014.

	$1,875	$1,100	$895	$650	$575	$495	$425	$2,320

Add $30 for NP3 nickel/alloy plating (new 2014).

P415 RECON CARBINE – .223 Rem. cal., GPO, 16 in. heavy contour chrome-lined fluted barrel, A3 muzzle device, corrosion resistant operating system, nickel plated A3 flat-top upper receiver and charging handle, M4 feed ramp, nickel and black hardcoat anodized Teflon finish, fixed removable hooded front sight, optional Troy flip-up sight, single stage trigger, oversized trigger guard, Magpul PRS or 6-position adj. buttstock, tactical rail handguard, approx. 8 lbs. Disc. 2011.

	$1,650	$1,000	$795	$595	$495	$425	$395	$1,999

P415 SPECIAL PURPOSE RIFLE – .223 Rem. cal., GPO, 18 in. heavy contour chrome-lined fluted barrel, A3 muzzle device, corrosion resistant operating system, nickel plated A3 flat-top upper receiver and charging handle, M4 feed ramp, nickel and black hardcoat anodized Teflon finish, fixed removable hooded front sight, optional Troy flip-up sight, single stage trigger, Magpul PRS or 6-position adj. buttstock, tactical rail handguard, approx. 9 lbs. Disc. 2011.

	$1,650	$1,000	$795	$595	$495	$425	$395	$1,999

RENEGADE – 5.56 NATO or 7.62x39mm (new 2017) cal., GIO, 16 1/2 in. Nitride heat-treated Puritan barrel, A2 flash hider, Mil-Spec trigger, Mission First Tactical magazine, grip, and stock, Dictator 9-position adj. gas block with straight gas tube, E2 Dual Extraction Technology, Mil-Spec upper and lower receiver, 14 1/2 in. M-LOK compatible Renegade rail, 4 integrated QD sling mounts, Type III hardcoat anodized black, NP3 coating (5.56 NATO only, new 2018), or Burnt Bronze Cerakote (5.56 NATO only, new 2018) finish, 6.3 lbs. New 2016.

MSR $1,500	$1,250	$825	$575	$475	$425	$375	$350	

Add $80 for NP3 coating (5.56 NATO only, new 2018).

Add $100 for Burnt Bronze Cerakote finish (5.56 NATO only, new 2018).

RENEGADE+ (GEN 4 RENEGADE+) – 5.56 NATO or .300 AAC Blackout (new 2018) cal., GIO, 16 1/2 in. match grade Nitride heat-treated Puritan barrel, triple port muzzle brake, Mission First Tactical 30 shot mag., 3.5 lb. POF-USA drop-in flat trigger system with KNS anti-walk pins, Mission First Tactical stock and grip, mid-length Dictator 9-position adj. gas block with straight gas tube, E2 Dual Extraction Technology, Mil-Spec upper receiver, 14 1/2 in. M-LOK Renegade free floating rail with five integrated QD sling mounts, Gen4 billet lower receiver, ambi controls, 6-position anti-tilt buffer tube, ambi QD endplate, Ultimate BCG, Type III hardcoat anodized black, NP3 coating (new 2018), or Burnt Bronze (new 2018) finish, 6.3 lbs. New 2016.

MSR $1,900	$1,575	$995	$775	$575	$495	$425	$395	

Add $80 for NP3 coating.

Add $100 for Burnt Bronze finish.

PATRIOT ORDNANCE FACTORY (POF), cont. 279

MSR	100%	98%	95%	90%	80%	70%	60%	Last MSR

RENEGADE+ SPR (GEN 4 RENEGADE+ SPR) – .223 Wylde or .224 Valkyrie (new 2018) cal., GIO, 18 1/2 (.223 Wylde) or 20 (.224 Valkyrie, new 2018) in. match grade Nitride heat-treated Puritan barrel, triple port muzzle brake, MFT 30 shot mag., E2 Dual Extraction Technology, 3.5 lb. POF-USA drop-in flat trigger system with KNS anti-walk pins, oversized integrated trigger guard with grip relief, Luth-AR MBA stock, Mission First Tactical grip, 9-position adj. rifle length Dictator gas block, E2 Dual Extraction Technology, Mil-Spec upper receiver, 14 1/2 in. M-LOK Renegade free floating rail with five integrated QD sling mounts, Gen4 billet lower receiver, ambi controls, roller cam pin, patented heat sink barrel nut, black anodized finish, 7.7 lbs. New 2017.

	100%	98%	95%	90%	80%	70%	60%	
MSR $2,030	$1,675	$1,000	$825	$625	$550	$475	$425	

REVOLUTION (GEN 4 REVOLUTION) – 7.62 NATO cal., GPO, 16 1/2 in. barrel, triple port muzzle brake, single stage match grade trigger, 14 1/2 in. M-LOK MRR handguard, four built-in QD mounts, fully ambidextrous billet receiver set, NP3 coated bolt carrier group, black anodized, NP3 coating, or Burnt Bronze Cerakote (new 2018) finish, 7.3 lbs. New 2017.

	100%	98%	95%	90%	80%	70%	60%	
MSR $2,670	$2,125	$1,325	$995	$675	$595	$525	$475	

Add $30 for NP3 coating.

Add $60 for Burnt Bronze Cerakote finish (new 2018).

GEN 4 SKIRMISH HEAVY – .308 Win. cal., GPO, 16 1/2 in. heavy barrel, 14 1/2 in. modular rail, extended handguard, ambidextrous controls, E2 Dual Extraction Technology, fixed Magpul MOE stock, black anodized or NP3 finish, 8.4 lbs. Mfg. 2015-2017.

	100%	98%	95%	90%	80%	70%	60%	Last MSR
	$2,295	$1,450	$1,075	$675	$595	$525	$475	*$2,820*

Add $40 for NP3 coating.

GEN 4 SKIRMISH LIGHT – 5.56 NATO cal., GPO, 16 1/2 in. barrel, 14 1/2 in. modular rail, extended handguard, ambidextrous controls, E2 Dual Extraction Technology, fixed Magpul MOE stock, black anodized or NP3 finish, 7.4 lbs. Mfg. 2015-2017.

	100%	98%	95%	90%	80%	70%	60%	Last MSR
	$1,795	$1,050	$875	$625	$550	$475	$425	*$2,270*

Add $20 for NP3 coating.

WARHOG HEAVY (GEN 4 WARHOG HEAVY) – 7.62 NATO/.308 Win. cal., GPO, 16 1/2 in. match grade deep fluted heavy barrel with triple port muzzle brake, 20 shot PMAG, E2 Dual Extraction Technology, no sights, adj. Luth-AR MBA stock, Mission First Tactical grip, Gen4 billet lower receiver, 5-pos. adj. gas block, 14 1/2 in. M-LOK MRR free floating handguard, ambidextrous controls, Burnt Bronze Cerakote finish, 9.4 lbs. New 2015.

	100%	98%	95%	90%	80%	70%	60%	
MSR $2,600	$2,125	$1,325	$995	$675	$595	$525	$475	

WARHOG LIGHT (GEN 4 WARHOG LIGHT) – 5.56 NATO cal., GPO, 16 1/2 in. match grade deep fluted barrel with triple port muzzle brake, 30 shot PMAG, E2 Dual Extraction Technology, EFP match trigger, no sights, adj. Luth-AR MBA stock, Mission First Tactical grip, Gen4 billet lower receiver, 5-pos. adj. gas block, 14 1/2 in. M-LOK MRR free floating handguard, ambidextrous controls, Burnt Bronze Cerakote finish, 7.4 lbs. New 2015.

	100%	98%	95%	90%	80%	70%	60%	
MSR $2,350	$1,875	$1,100	$895	$650	$575	$495	$425	

PATRIOT WEAPONRY

Current AR-15 manufacturer located in Waupaca, WI.

PISTOLS: SEMI-AUTO

P-51 – .223 Wylde chamber, mid-length gas system, 7 1/2 or 10 1/2 in. match grade barrel, VG6 Epsilon muzzle brake, Magpul PMAG, billet aluminum upper and lower receivers, Griffin Armament suppressor, titanium bolt carrier, mag. release, and ambi safety selector, modified charging handle, Magpul Pro backup iron sights, KAK buffer tube, SIG SBX arm brace, Magpul K2 pistol grip.

	100%	98%	95%	90%	80%	70%	60%	
MSR $3,438	$2,925	$2,560	$2,195	$1,990	$1,610	$1,315	$1,025	

RIFLES: SEMI-AUTO

B-17 – .260 Rem., .308 Win., or 6.5mm Creedmoor cal., rifle length gas system, 17 in. Proof Research carbon fiber wrapped stainless steel barrel, VS6 Gamma or SilencerCo Saker muzzle brake, adj. gas block, Magpul PMAG, billet aluminum upper and lower receivers, ATC AR gold trigger, Luth-AR stock, ER60 Tactical DLX grip with shelf, Midwest Industries 15 in. free float handguard, titanium bolt carrier, mag. release, ambi safety selector, and grip screws, includes black/FDE/Tactical Gray soft case.

	100%	98%	95%	90%	80%	70%	60%	
MSR $4,195	$3,350	$2,300	$1,575	$950	$725	$675	$650	

P-51 MATCH CHROME – .223 Wylde chamber, mid-length gas system, 16 in. chrome-lined match grade barrel, VG6 Epsilon muzzle brake, Magpul PMAG, billet aluminum upper and lower receivers, lightweight forward assist, Griffin Armament Snatch charging handle, titanium bolt carrier, Magpul Pro backup iron sights, titanium ambidextrous safety selector, Mil-Spec buffer tube, Magpul CTR buttstock, Magpul K2 pistol grip.

	100%	98%	95%	90%	80%	70%	60%	
MSR $3,405	$2,775	$1,825	$1,350	$750	$650	$595	$525	

P 280 PEACE RIVER CLASSICS

MSR	100%	98%	95%	90%	80%	70%	60%	Last MSR

PEACE RIVER CLASSICS

Previous manufacturer located in Bartow, FL until 2001. Peace River Classics was a division of Tim's Guns.

RIFLES: SEMI-AUTO

PEACE RIVER CLASSICS SEMI-AUTO – .223 Rem. or .308 Win. (new 1998, possible prototypes only) cal., available in 3 configurations including the Shadowood, the Glenwood, and the Royale, GIO, hand-built utilizing Armalite action, patterned after the AR-15, match grade parts throughout, special serialization, laminate thumbhole stock. Very limited mfg. 1997-2001.

Last MSR on the .223 Rem. cal. in 2001 was $2,695, or $2,995 for .308 Win. cal.

Due to this model's rarity factor, accurate values are hard to ascertain.

PHASE 5 TACTICAL

Current parts and components manufacturer and previous AR-15 style pistol and rifle manufacturer, located in Roseville, CA.

PISTOL: SEMI-AUTO

AR-15 ATLAS ONE PISTOL - BILLET – 5.56 NATO cal., AR-15 style, 7 1/2 in. barrel with electroless nickel M4 extension, A2 flash hider, integrated Winter Trigger Guard (WTG), Single Point Bungee Sling and A.R.M.S. 71L front and rear flip-up sights, pistol buffer tube, MFT-G27 enhanced pistol grip, matched billet lower and upper receiver set, EN bolt carrier, extended bolt release V2, sling attachment solution, ambidextrous Battle Latch/Charging Handle Assembly (ABL/CHA), Lo-Pro Slope Nose quad rail, 5 lbs. 4 oz. Mfg. 2016-2017.

$1,575	$1,385	$1,185	$1,065	$915	$785	$635		$1,850

AR-15 CQC PISTOL - FORGED – 5.56 NATO cal., AR-15 style, GIO, compact frame, 7 1/2 in. chrome moly barrel, A2 flash hider, Winter Trigger Guard (WTG), pistol buffer tube, forged aluminum receivers, Lo-Pro Slope Nose (LPSN) quad rail, 5 lbs. 4 oz. Mfg. 2016-2017.

$1,050	$950	$815	$715	$625	$535	$450		$1,250

RIFLES: SEMI-AUTO

AR-15 P5T15 – 5.56 NATO cal., GIO, 16 in. chrome-lined, button rifled barrel, winter trigger guard, A.R.M.S. 71L flip-up sights, Mission First Tactical Battlelink 6-pos. utility stock, Mission First Tactical Engaged pistol grip, Phase5 enhanced buffer spring, forged aluminum lower and upper receivers, Lo-Pro Nose Quad Rail, M4 extension/M4 feed ramps, ambidextrious Battle Latch charging handle, 7 lbs. 3 oz. Mfg. late 2015-2017.

$1,475	$950	$725	$550	$475	$395	$350		$1,776

PRECISION FIREARMS LLC

Current rifle manufacturer located in Martinsburg, WV beginning in late 2013. Previously located in Hagerstown, MD. Dealer and consumer sales through FFL.

RIFLES/CARBINES: SEMI-AUTO

AMAZON LIGHT WEIGHT RIFLE – various cals., GIO, lightweight cold hammer forged barrel with muzzle brake, aluminum billet lower and upper receiver, with or w/o sights, carbon figer handguard, BCM Gunfighter Mod 4 or Rainier XCT (disc.) ambi charging handle, Geissele or Timney trigger, Magpul ACS-L stock, PF, Hogue, Magpul, or Ergo grip, matte black finish, 6 1/2 lbs.

MSR $1,700	$1,385	$895	$675	$525	$450	$385	$350

Add $195 for sights.

ARIES T1-B (ARIES T-1) – 5.56 NATO cal., Adams Arms GPO, 16 in. mid-length German-made barrel with Battle Comp compensator, two Magpul mags., aluminum billet upper and lower receiver, M4 feed ramps, Troy folding sights, BAD-ASS ambi safety, Troy ambi bolt release, BCM Mod 4 charging handle, Magpul UBR stock, Hogue pistol grip, Geissele SSA-E trigger, matte black Nitride finish, includes tactical case.

MSR $2,300	$1,875	$1,100	$895	$650	$575	$495	$425

ARION TYPE I – 6.5 Grendel cal., 16 in. fluted barrel with PF LMD muzzle brake, Rainier Compensator, NOX, or AAC flash hider, aluminum billet upper and lower receiver, BAD-ASS ambi safety, BCM Gunfighter charging handle, Geissele two-stage trigger, PF (disc. 2014) or integral (new 2015) trigger guard, nickel boron carrier group, 15 in. Geissele MK 3 (disc. 2014) or Geissele MK8 M-LOK 13 in. handguard with three modular rails, rubberized grip, Magpul UBR stock with battery storage, matte black finish, includes sling and soft tactical case, optional Troy ambi bolt and mag. release.

MSR $2,200	$1,795	$1,050	$875	$625	$550	$475	$425

Add $200 for sights.

EXCALIBUR 3 GUN RIFLE – 5.56 NATO cal., 18 or 20 in. German-made or Lilja match barrel, two Magpul mags., precision machined aluminum billet upper and lower receiver, Magpul ACS- L stock, Magpul MOE or Hogue grip, Lancer

PRECISION FIREARMS LLC, cont. 281 P

MSR	100%	98%	95%	90%	80%	70%	60%	Last MSR

15 in. competition handguard, aluminum trigger guard, Geissele Super 3 Gun trigger, Mil-Spec tube and buffer, sling with QD attachment, BCM Mod 4 charging handle, matte black finish, nickel boron coating, includes tactical case.

MSR $2,200	$1,795	$1,050	$875	$625	$550	$475	$425	

HAVOC SERIES – various cals., German-made barrel with black Nitride coating, precision machined aluminum billet upper and lower receiver, optional Magpul or Troy folding sights, Geissele 13 in. MK3 rail (disc. 2014) or Geissele 13 in. MK8 rail with M-LOK (new 2015), BCM Mod 4 charging handle, Mil-Spec tube and buffer, two Magpul mags., Magpul MOE or PF Hogue grips, Geissele two-stage trigger, aluminum trigger guard, Magpul STR stock, sling and QD attachment, matte black finish, includes case.

MSR $1,800	$1,475	$950	$725	$550	$475	$395	$350	

Add $75 for Magpul or $200 for Troy folding sights.

THE KATANA 3G – .223 Rem./5.56 NATO cal. (.223 Wylde chamber), designed for 3 Gun Competition, stainless steel Lothar Walther barrel, precision machined aluminum billet upper and lower receiver, Samson, VTAC, or ALG handguard, each rifle can be custom crafted per individual needs, includes tactical nylon carry case and 2 magazines. Disc. 2014.

	$1,385	$895	$675	$525	$450	$385	$350	*$1,700*

Add $200 for sights.

THE KATANA II – .223 Wylde chamber, 16 in. free floated stainless steel Lothar Walther barrel with PF NOX flash hider, two 30 shot Troy or Magpul mags., Troy 13 in. VTAC Alpha handguard, Geissele two-stage trigger, mid-length gas system, billet upper and lower receivers, M4 feed ramps, BCM Gunfighter Mod 4 charging handle, Magpul enhanced aluminum trigger guard, Magpul MOE rubberized grip, Magpul ACS-L stock with 6 positions and storage area in the stock, single point mount QD sling, includes soft tactical case.

MSR $1,700	$1,385	$895	$675	$525	$450	$385	$350	

Add $200 for sights.

PRECISION SIDEWINDER AR-X08 RIFLE (PF-X08 LARGE FRAME AR) – .243 Win., .260 Rem., .308 Win., 6.5mm Creedmoor, 6.5x47 Lapua, or 7mm-08 Rem. cal., Bartlein or Lilja barrel, PF muzzle device, Geissele SSA-E trigger, T6 aluminum billet lower and DPMS pattern upper receiver, integral winter trigger guard, forward assist, port cover, shell deflector, Hogue grip, matte black finish, made to customer specifications.

MSR $3,200	$2,625	$1,725	$1,300	$725	$650	$595	$525	

THE STIR (SOFT TARGET INTERDICTION RIFLE) – .204 Ruger, .223 Wylde, or 6.5 Grendel cal., 24 in. Bartlein, Lilja, or Lothar Walther barrel, precision machined aluminum billet upper and lower, upper receiver is heavily walled and matched for fit and finish, lower receiver has tension screw, aluminum or carbon fiber handguard, PF, Hogue, Magpul or Ergo grip, super match carrier, BCM Gunfighter Mod 3, Rainier XCT (disc.), or Armageddon ambi charging handle, Geissele or Timney trigger, Magpul PRS stock, matte black finish, optional barrel fluting, bipod, monopods, Vortex scope, muzzle brakes.

MSR $2,300	$1,875	$1,100	$895	$650	$575	$495	$425	

Add $300 for fully equipped optional model without optics.

THE NIGHTSHADOW – 5.56 NATO cal., lightweight chrome-lined hammer forged barrel with BCM muzzle brake, precision machined upper and lower receivers, BCM KMR 13 in. handguard, BCM Gunfighter Mod 4 charging handle, Geissele two-stage trigger, PF Black Phalanx carrier group, with or w/o sights, Magpul CTR stock, PF rubberized grip, 6 lbs. New 2015.

MSR $1,600	$1,315	$850	$625	$500	$435	$375	$350	

Add $195 for sights.

PRECISION REFLEX, INC.

Current AR-15 manufacturer located in New Bremen, OH.

RIFLES: SEMI-AUTO

Precision Reflex, Inc. manufactures AR-15 style rifles and shooting accessories for commercial, law enforcement, and military use. For more information on the many products they have available, please contact the company directly (see Trademark Index).

3 GUN SHOOTER RIFLE – 5.56 NATO or 6.8 SPC cal., 18 in. stainless steel barrel with threaded muzzle, M4 feed ramps, low profile steel gas block, forged upper and lower receivers, 15 in. black forearm, AR trigger, 6-position carbine stock with recoil pad, A2 pistol grip, flip-up rear sights, Gas Buster charging handle with military latch, 7 1/2 lbs. Mfg. 2014-2017.

	$1,195	$795	$550	$465	$415	$375	$350	*$1,445*

DELUXE RIFLE – 5.56 NATO or 6.8 SPC cal., 16 in. Douglas stainless steel or 16 in. Bergara chrome moly barrel, threaded muzzle, M4 feed ramps, flip-up front and rear sights, AR trigger, intermediate round forearm with natural finish, intermediate length top rail, 6-position carbine stock with recoil pad, A2 pistol grip, Gas Buster charging handle w/military latch, black finish, 7.9 lbs. Mfg. 2014-2017.

	$1,385	$895	$675	$525	$450	$385	$350	*$1,670*

Add $215 for Douglas stainless steel barrel.

P 282 PRECISION REFLEX, INC., cont.

MSR	100%	98%	95%	90%	80%	70%	60%	Last MSR

ENTRY LEVEL RIFLE – 5.56 NATO or 6.8 SPC (disc.) cal., 16 in. stainless steel Douglas or Bergara barrel with black finish, MSTN straight brake, B5 Bravo stock, A2 pistol grip, forged aluminum flat-top upper and lower receiver, low profile gas block, rifle length gas tube, M4 feed ramps, Gas Buster charging handle with big latch, Gen III rifle length carbon fiber free float forearm in black or FDE finish, Mil-Spec 6-pos. buffer tube, black, black/natural, or FDE/black Cerakote finish, 7.2 lbs. New 2014.

MSR $1,357	$1,135	$725	$525	$465	$415	$375	$350	

Add $7 for all black or black/FDE finish with Bergara barrel.

Add $194 for black/FDE finish with Douglas barrel.

ENTRY LEVEL DELTA RIFLE – 5.56 NATO cal., 17 in. Bergara chrome moly barrel, threaded muzzle, AR trigger, 6-pos. carbine stock with recoil pad, A2 pistol grip, M4 feed ramps, forged upper and lower receivers, rifle length Delta forearm in black or FDE finish, Gas Buster charging handle w/military latch, approx. 8 lbs. Mfg. 2014-2017.

	$950	$595	$495	$425	$365	$335	$300	*$1,150*

* **Entry Level Delta Rifle Stainless** – 5.56 NATO or 6.8 SPC cal., 16 in. Bergara stainless steel barrel, threaded muzzle, AR trigger, 6-position carbine stock with recoil pad, A2 pistol grip, Gas Buster charging handle w/military latch, M4 feed ramps, forged upper and lower receivers, rifle length Delta forearm, black or FDE finish, approx. 8 lbs. Mfg. 2014-2017.

	$1,125	$700	$525	$450	$400	$350	$325	*$1,339*

Add $215 for Douglas stainless steel barrel.

MARK 12 MOD O GEN II SPR RIFLE – 5.56 NATO cal., 18 in. Douglas stainless steel 1:7 or 1:8 twist barrel, AE brake and collar, standard trigger, PRI flip-up front gas block front and rear sight, A2 or B5 6-pos. stock, forged aluminum flat-top upper and Mil-Spec forged lower receiver, M4 feed ramps, Gas Buster charging handle with big latch, Gen II rifle length carbon fiber free float forearm, full-length straight top rail, black or FDE finish, 5.2 lbs.

MSR $1,995	$1,650	$1,000	$795	$595	$495	$425	$395	

MARK 12 MOD O GEN III RIFLE – 5.56 NATO cal., 18 in. Douglas stainless steel barrel, 1:7 twist, AE brake and collar, standard trigger group, PRI flip-up front gas block front sight and rear sight, A2 buttstock, forged aluminum flat-top upper and Mil-Spec forged lower receiver, Gas Buster charging handle with big latch, Gen III rifle length carbon fiber free float forearm, full-length top rail with PEQII removable rail section, Mil-Spec buffer and tube, black or FDE Cerakote finish, 5.2 lbs.

MSR $1,956	$1,650	$1,000	$795	$595	$495	$425	$395	

MARK 12 MOD H RIFLE – 5.56 NATO/.223 Rem. cal., 16 in. Douglas stainless steel 1:7 or 1-: twist barrel, AE brake and collar, PRI flip-up rail mounted front sight and rear sight, B5 6-pos. stock, forged aluminum flat-top upper and lower receiver, Mil-Spec buffer and tube, Gen III rifle length carbon fiber free float forearm, Recce top rail, M4 feed ramps, low profile gas block, Gas Buster charging handle with big latch, black or FDE Cerakote finish, 8 lbs. New 2018.

MSR $1,825	$1,525	$975	$750	$575	$495	$425	$375	

MARK 12 MOD O DELTA GEN III RIFLE – 5.56 NATO cal., 18 in. Douglas stainless steel barrel, 1:7 twist, AE brake and collar, PRI flip-up front gas block front sight and rear sight, B5 stock, forged aluminum flat-top receiver, rifle length gas tube, Gas Buster charging handle with big latch, Gen III Delta rifle length carbon fiber free floating forearm with full-length straight top rail, Mil-Spec buffer and tube, black Cerakote finish, 8.7 lbs.

MSR $1,956	$1,650	$1,000	$795	$595	$495	$425	$395	

MARK 12 MOD O SPR RIFLE – 5.56 NATO or 6.8 SPC cal., 18 in. Douglas stainless steel barrel, threaded muzzle, forged upper and lower receivers, flip-up front and rear sights, AR trigger, black rifle length forearm, full-length SPR top rail, 6-position carbine stock with recoil pad, A2 pistol grip, Gas Buster charging handle w/military latch, 8.68 lbs. Mfg. 2014-2017.

	$1,600	$1,000	$775	$575	$495	$425	$395	*$1,931*

* **Mark 12 Mod Delta Rifle** – 5.56 NATO or 6.8 SPC cal., similar to Mark 12 Mod O SPR rifle, except features a full-length SPR Delta top rail, 7.9 lbs. Mfg. 2014-2017.

	$1,600	$1,000	$775	$575	$495	$425	$395	*$1,931*

RK 12 MOD O SPR VARIANT RIFLE – 5.56 NATO or 6.8 SPC cal., 16 in. Bergara stainless steel barrel, ...eaded muzzle, M4 feed ramps, forged upper and lower receivers, AR trigger, 6-position carbine stock with recoil pad, ...istol grip, black finish, intermediate length top rail, flip-up front and rear sights, 7.9 lbs. Mfg. 2014-2017.

	$1,350	$875	$650	$525	$450	$385	$350	*$1,623*

...215 for Douglas stainless steel barrel.

...L OPERATOR RIFLE – 5.56 NATO or 6.8 SPC cal., 16 in. Douglas or Bergara stainless steel barrel, threaded ...MSTN brake, flip-up front and rear sights, B5 Bravo SOPMOD or 6-pos. carbine stock with recoil pad, A2 pistol ... feed ramps, forged flat-top upper and lower receivers, mid-length gas tube, Gen III rifle length carbon fiber ... round forearm with Flat Dark Earth finish with black rails and a Recce length top rail, Gas Buster charging ... military latch, black/FDE finish, 7.9 lbs. New 2014.

...9	$1,350	$875	$650	$525	$450	$385	$350	

...Douglas stainless steel barrel.

MSR	100%	98%	95%	90%	80%	70%	60%	Last MSR

PREDATOR CUSTOM SHOP

Previous custom manufacturer located in Knoxville, TN until 2015.

RIFLES: SEMI-AUTO

Predator Custom Shop manufactured custom AR-15 rifles built to customer specifications. Models included the 5.56 Carnivore and the 5.56 DMR.

PRIMARY WEAPONS SYSTEMS (PWS)

Current manufacturer located in Boise, ID.

Primary Weapons Systems manufactures a series of AR-15 style semi-auto pistols, rifles, and bolt action rifles, as well as SBR models for law enforcement and military.

PISTOLS: SEMI-AUTO

DI-10P MODERN MUSKET – .223 Rem./5.56 NATO (.223 Wylde chamber) cal., AR-15 style, 10 3/4 in. barrel with Sig Sauer SB15 stabilizing brace, matte black hardcoat anodized finish, 6 lbs. Mfg. mid-2014-2015.

| | $1,275 | $1,125 | $1,025 | $875 | $750 | $625 | $525 | $1,500 |

MK1 MOD 1-P – .223 Wylde, .300 AAC Blackout, or 7.62x39mm cal., PWS long stroke piston system, 7 3/4 or 11.85 in. barrel, Triad compensator, PWS MOD 2 enhanced pistol buffer tube, 3-pos. adj. gas block, 5 lb. 11 oz.- 6 lbs. 5 oz. New 2017.

| MSR $1,600 | $1,350 | $1,200 | $1,075 | $950 | $815 | $700 | $575 | |

MK107 SERIES – .223 Rem./5.56 NATO (.223 Wylde chamber), 7.62x39mm (disc. 2012) cal., AR-15 style, GPO, 30 shot mag., 7 1/2 in. Isonite QPQ treated, 1:8 twist button rifled barrel, Mil-Spec upper and lower receiver, ALG Defense QMS trigger, enhanced bolt carrier group, PWS KeyMod rail system, BCM Gunfighter charging handle, Magpul MOE furniture and sights. Disc. 2015.

| | $1,700 | $1,500 | $1,275 | $1,150 | $950 | $775 | $600 | $1,950 |

MK107 MOD 1-M – .223 Wylde chamber, PWS long stroke piston operating system, 7 3/4 in. barrel, Triad556 compensator. New 2018.

| MSR $1,450 | $1,195 | $795 | $550 | $465 | $415 | $375 | $350 | |

MK107 MOD 2 – .223 Wylde or 7.62x39mm (new 2017) cal., PWS long stroke piston system, PicMod technology, 7 3/4 in. barrel, CQB muzzle device, Bravo Company USA PNT (mfg. 2016 only) or ZEV SSR (new 2017) trigger, Maxim CQB pistol EXC, lightweight upper receiver, 5 lbs. 5 oz. Mfg. 2016-2017.

| | $1,775 | $1,525 | $1,275 | $1,125 | $975 | $850 | $685 | $2,050 |

MK107 MOD 2-M – .223 Wylde or 7.62x39mm cal., PWS long stroke piston operating system, 7 3/4 in. barrel, CQB556 or CQB30 compensator, Lancer or ASC 30 shot mag., flared magwell, built-in trigger guard, Talon safety selector, 3-setting adj. gas system, forged upper and lower receivers, PicLok free float handguard, Radian Raptor charging handle, 5 lbs. 10 oz. New 2018.

| MSR $1,850 | $1,525 | $975 | $750 | $575 | $495 | $425 | $375 | |

MK109 SERIES – .300 AAC Blackout cal., GPO, 9 3/4 in. stainless steel, Isonite QPD treated, button rifled barrel, 30 shot polymer mag., Mil-Spec upper and lower receiver, quad rail, available in matte black or FDE finish, enhanced charging handle and bolt carrier group, Micro-slicked Internals, Magpul XT rail panels, Magpul MOE grip, MBUS sights, approx. 5 1/5 lbs. Disc. 2012.

| | $1,525 | $1,300 | $1,100 | $925 | $750 | $675 | $575 | $1,700 |

Add $200 for FDE finish.

MK109 MOD 1-M – .300 AAC Blackout cal., PWS long stroke piston operating system, 9 3/4 in. barrel, Triad 30 compensator, Lancer 30 shot mag., Bravo Company furniture, non-adj. gas system, forged upper and lower receiver, forward assist, M-LOK free float handguard, Radian Raptor charging handle, 5 lbs. 13 oz. New 2018.

| MSR $1,450 | $1,195 | $795 | $550 | $465 | $415 | $375 | $350 | |

MK109 MOD 2-M – .300 AAC Blackout cal., PWS long stroke piston operating system, 9 3/4 in. barrel, Triad 3 compensator, Lancer 30 shot mag., flared magwell, built-in trigger guard, Talon safety selector, non-adj. gas syster forged upper and lower receivers, PicLok free float handguard, Radian Raptor charging handle, pistol storage device lbs. 11 oz. New 2018.

| MSR $1,850 | $1,525 | $975 | $750 | $575 | $495 | $425 | $375 | |

MK110 SERIES – .223 Rem. cal. (.223 Wylde chamber), GPO, similar to MK107 Series, except has 10 3/4 in. ba Mfg. 2014-2015.

| | $1,600 | $1,000 | $775 | $575 | $495 | $425 | $395 | $1,950 |

P 284 PRIMARY WEAPONS SYSTEMS (PWS), cont.

MSR	100%	98%	95%	90%	80%	70%	60%	Last MSR

MK111 MOD 2 – .223 Wylde, .300 AAC Blackout, or 7.62x39mm (new 2017) cal., PWS long stroke piston system, PicMod technology, 11.85 in. barrel, Triad muzzle device, Bravo Company USA PNT (mfg. 2016 only) or ZEV SSR (new 2017) trigger, Maxim CQB pistol EXC, lightweight upper receiver, PWS MOD 2 enhanced pistol buffer tube (new 2017), 6 lbs. Mfg. 2016-2017.

	100%	98%	95%	90%	80%	70%	60%	Last MSR
	$1,675	$1,000	$825	$625	$550	$475	$425	$2,050

MK111 MOD 1-M – .223 Wylde or 7.62x39mm cal., PWS long stroke piston operating system, 11.85 in. barrel, Triad 556 or Triad 30 compensator, ASC or Lancer 30 shot mag., 3-setting adj. gas system, forged upper and lower receivers, forward assist, M-LOK free float handguard, Radian Raptor charging handle, pistol storage device, 6 lbs. 1 oz. New 2018.

MSR $1,450	$1,195	$795	$550	$465	$415	$375	$350	

MK111 MOD 2-M – .223 Wylde or 7.62x39mm cal., PWS long stroke piston operating system, 11.85 in. barrel, Triad 556 or Triad 30 compensator, ASC 30 shot mag., flared magwell, built-in trigger guard, Talon safety selector, 3-setting adj. gas system, forged upper and lower receivers, PicLok free float handguard, pistol mounted solutions pistol storage device, Radian Raptor charging handle, 6 lbs. New 2018.

MSR $1,850	$1,525	$975	$750	$575	$495	$425	$375	

PCC – 9mm Para. cal., blowback gas system, 9 1/2 in. barrel, PCC compensator, accepts Glock mags., free float M-LOK handguard, billet lower receiver, last round hold open feature, black finish. New 2018.

MSR $1,250	$1,050	$650	$495	$450	$395	$350	$325	

RIFLES: SEMI-AUTO

DI-16 MODERN MUSKET – .223 Rem./5.56 NATO (.223 Wylde chamber) cal., 16 in. barrel with removable flash suppressor, adj. tactical stock, pistol grip, quad rail, matte black hardcoat anodized finish, 6 lbs. 12 oz. Mfg. mid-2014-2015.

	100%	98%	95%	90%	80%	70%	60%	Last MSR
	$1,250	$825	$575	$475	$425	$375	$350	$1,500

MK1 SERIES – .223 Rem./5.56 NATO (.223 Wylde chamber) or .300 AAC Blackout cal., GPO, 16 or 18 (new 2014) in. stainless steel Isonite QPD treated button rifled barrel, Triad 30 flash suppressor, 30 shot polymer mag., Mil-Spec upper and lower receiver, quad rail, enhanced bolt carrier group, Micro-slicked Internals, Magpul XT rail panels, Magpul MOE grip, MBUS sights, ALG Defense QMS trigger, PWS KeyMod rail system, BCM Gunfighter charging handle, available in matte black, FDE, or Kryptek camo (new 2014) finish, approx. 7 lbs. Disc. 2014.

	100%	98%	95%	90%	80%	70%	60%	Last MSR
	$1,600	$1,000	$775	$575	$495	$425	$395	$1,950

Add $50 for Kryptek camo finish.

Add $250 for Ranger proof logo.

MK2 SERIES – .308 Win. cal., SR-25 platform, GPO, 16.1 or 20 in. Isonite QPD treated button rifled barrel, 30 shot polymer mag., Mil-Spec upper and lower receiver, quad rail, enhanced bolt carrier group, Micro-slicked Internals, Magpul XT rail panels, Magpul MOE grip, MBUS sights, ALG Defense QMS trigger, PWS KeyMod rail system, BCM Gunfighter charging handle, matte black or FDE finish, 8 lbs. 12 oz. Disc. 2015.

	100%	98%	95%	90%	80%	70%	60%	Last MSR
	$2,125	$1,325	$995	$675	$595	$525	$475	$2,600

MK116 MOD 1-M – .223 Wylde, .300 AAC Blackout, or 7.62x39mm cal., PWS long stroke piston operating system, 16.1 in. barrel, Triad 30 (7.62x39mm or .300 AAC BO) or FSC556 (.223 Wylde) compensator, ASC or Lancer 30 shot mag., Bravo Company furniture, pistol or mid-length piston system, 3-setting adj. or non-adj. (.300 AAC BO only) gas system, forged upper and lower receiver, free float M-LOK handguard, forward assist, Radian Raptor charging handle, 6 lbs. 15 oz. New 2018.

MSR $1,450	$1,195	$795	$550	$465	$415	$375	$350	

116 MOD 1-P – .223 Wylde, .300 AAC Blackout, or 7.62x39mm (new 2017) cal., PWS long stroke piston system, in. barrel, FSC or Triad 30 (7.62x39mm only, new 2017) muzzle device, Bravo Company USA PNT trigger, Bravo pany USA furniture, free float KeyMod handguard, MOD 2 enhanced buffer tube, 6 lbs. 12 oz. Mfg. 2016-2017.

	$1,315	$850	$625	$500	$435	$375	$350	$1,600

6 MOD 2 – .223 Wylde or .300 AAC Blackout cal., PWS long stroke piston system, PicMod technology, 16.1 in. FSC muzzle device, Zev SSR golden trigger, Bravo Company USA furniture, lightweight upper receiver, MOD 2 ed buffer tube, 6 lbs. 8 oz. Mfg. 2016-2017.

	$1,675	$1,000	$825	$625	$550	$475	$425	$2,050

OD 2-M – .223 Wylde chamber, .300 AAC Blackout, or 7.62x39mm cal., PWS long stroke piston operating 5.1 in. barrel, Triad 30 or FSC556 (.223 Wylde only) compensator, flared magwell, built-in trigger guard, hter stock and pistol grip, Talon safety selector, mid-length piston system, 3-setting adj. or non-adj. (.300 t only) gas system, forged upper and lower receiver, PicLok free float handguard, Radian Raptor charging or OD Green (.223 Wylde only) anodized finish, 6 lbs. 11 oz. New 2018.

	$1,525	$975	$750	$575	$495	$425	$375	

PRIMARY WEAPONS SYSTEMS (PWS), cont. 285 P

MSR	100%	98%	95%	90%	80%	70%	60%	Last MSR

MK118 MOD 2 – .223 Wylde chamber, PWS long stroke piston system, PicMod technology, 18 in. barrel, FSC muzzle device, Zev SSR golden trigger, Bravo Company USA furniture, lightweight upper receiver, MOD 2 Enhanced buffer tube, 6 lbs. 11 oz. Mfg. 2016-2017.

	100%	98%	95%	90%	80%	70%	60%	Last MSR
	$1,675	$1,000	$825	$625	$550	$475	$425	*$2,050*

MK118 MOD 2-M – .223 Wylde chamber, PWS long stroke piston operating system, 18 in. barrel, FSC556 compensator, Lancer 30 shot mag., flared magwell, built-in trigger guard, Bravo Company fuirniture, Talon safety selector, mid-length piston system, 3-setting adj. gas system, forged upper and lower receiver, PicLok free float handguard, Radian Raptor charging handle, 7 lbs. 1 oz. New 2018.

MSR $1,850	$1,525	$975	$750	$575	$495	$425	$375	

MK216 MOD 1 – .308 Win. cal., PWS long stroke piston system, 16.1 in. barrel, FSC muzzle device, Geissele ALG QMS trigger, Magpul MOE furniture, free float KeyMod handguard, forward assist, MOD 2 enhanced buffer tube, 8 lbs. 6 oz. Mfg. 2013-2017.

	$1,795	$1,050	$875	$625	$550	$475	$425	*$2,200*

MK216 MOD 1-M – .308 Match cal., PWS long stroke piston operating system, 16 in. barrel, FSC30 compensator, Magpul 20 shot mag., Bravo Company furniture, mid-length piston system, 3-setting adj. gas system, forged upper and lower receiver, free float M-LOK handguard, Radian Raptor charging handle, 8 lbs. 13 oz. New 2018.

MSR $1,975	$1,650	$1,000	$795	$595	$495	$425	$395	

MK220 MOD 1 – .308 Win. or 6.5mm Creedmoor cal., PWS long stroke piston system, 20 in. barrel, PRC muzzle device, Geissele ALG QMS trigger, Magpul MOE furniture, free float KeyMod handguard, forward assist, MOD 2 enhanced buffer tube, 9 lbs. 4 oz. Mfg. 2013-2017.

	$1,795	$1,050	$875	$625	$550	$475	$425	*$2,200*

Add $200 for 6.5mm Creedmoor cal.

MK220 MOD 1-M – .308 Match or 6.5mm Creedmoor cal., PWS long stroke piston operating system, 20 in. barrel, PRC30 compensator, Magpul 20 shot mag., mid-length piston system, 3-setting adj. gas system, forged upper and lower receiver, free float M-LOK handguard, Radian Raptor charging handle, 9 lbs. 3 oz. New 2018.

MSR $1,975	$1,650	$1,000	$795	$595	$495	$425	$395	

PCC – 9mm Para. cal., blowback gas system, 16 in. barrel, PCC compensator, free float M-LOK handguard, billet lower receiver, last round hold open feature, black finish. New 2018.

MSR $1,250	$1,050	$650	$495	$450	$395	$350	$325	

WOODLAND SPORTING RIFLE – .223 Rem./5.56 NATO (.223 Wylde chamber) or .300 AAC Blackout cal., GIO, 16.1 or 18 in. free floating stainless steel Isonite QPQ treated button rifled barrel, 30 shot polymer mag., enhanced charging handle, PWS Mil-Spec upper and lower receiver, enhanced DI carrier, black, olive (disc.) or walnut stock, approx. 7 1/2-8 lbs. Mfg. 2012-2014.

	$1,250	$825	$575	$475	$425	$375	$350	*$1,500*

WRAITH 3GUN COMPETITION RIFLE – .223 Rem./5.56 NATO (.223 Wylde chamber) cal., GIO, 18 in. free floating stainless steel Isonite QPQ treated button rifled barrel, 30 shot polymer mag., enhanced BCM Gunfighter charging handle, PWS Mil-Spec upper and lower receiver, enhanced DI carrier, black olive or walnut stock, Daniel Defense free float handguard, JP Tactical EZ trigger, 7 lbs. 5 oz. Mfg. 2012, reintroduced 2014-2015.

	$2,375	$1,525	$1,150	$700	$625	$550	$475	*$2,900*

This model was also available in an AR-10 platform chambered in .308 Win. cal. with a 20 in. barrel.

PROARMS ARMORY s.r.o.

Current manufacturer located in Czech Republic. No U.S. importation.

RIFLES: SEMI-AUTO

PAR MK3 – 5.56 NATO cal., GPO, 5, 10, 20, or 30 shot mag., 16 3/4 or 18 in. Lothar Walther barrel, four-position adj. gas block, aluminum alloy frame and upper receiver made on CNC, ergonomic beavertail pistol grip, free float handguard with four fixed rails or KeyMod system in four different lengths, telescopic 6-position collapsible stock, folding MBUS sights.

Current retail price is €1,599, including VAT.

PAR MK3 SPARTAN – .223 Rem. or 7.62x39mm cal., GPO, AR-15 style, 16 3/4 in. barrel, A2 muzzle brake, 30 shot mag., folding MBUS, M4 collapsible stock, A2 grip, 4 rail or KeyMod handguard with hex wrench, black finish. New 2016.

Please contact the manufacturer directly for pricing on this model.

P 286 PROFESSIONAL ORDNANCE, INC.

MSR	100%	98%	95%	90%	80%	70%	60%	Last MSR

PROFESSIONAL ORDNANCE, INC.

Previous manufacturer located in Lake Havasu City, AZ 1998-2003. Previously manufactured in Ontario, CA 1996-1997.

During 2003, Bushmaster bought Professional Ordnance and the Carbon 15 trademark. Please refer to the Bushmaster section for recently manufactured Carbon 15 rifles and pistols.

PISTOLS: SEMI-AUTO

CARBON-15 TYPE 20 – .223 Rem. cal., GIO, Stoner type operating system with recoil reducing buffer assembly, carbon fiber upper and lower receiver, hard chromed bolt carrier, 7 1/4 in. unfluted stainless steel barrel with ghost ring sights, 30 shot mag. (supplies were limited), also accepts AR-15 type mags., 40 oz. Mfg. 1999-2000.

	$1,275	$1,125	$1,025	$875	$750	$625	$525	$1,500

CARBON-15 TYPE 21 – .223 Rem cal., GIO, ultra lightweight carbon fiber upper and lower receivers, 7 1/4 in. "Profile" stainless steel barrel, quick detachable muzzle compensator, ghost ring sights, 10 shot mag., also accepts AR-15 type mags., Stoner type operating system, tool steel bolt, extractor and carrier, 40 oz. Mfg. 2001-2003.

	$775	$685	$615	$550	$485	$415	$370	$899

CARBON-15 TYPE 97 – .223 Rem. cal., similar to Carbon 15 Type 20, except has fluted barrel and quick detachable compensator, 46 oz. Mfg. 1996-2003.

	$815	$700	$630	$570	$500	$425	$380	$964

RIFLES: SEMI-AUTO

CARBON-15 TYPE 20 – .223 Rem. cal., GIO, same operating system as the Carbon-15 pistol, 16 in. unfluted stainless steel barrel, carbon fiber buttstock and forearm, includes Mil-Spec optics mounting base, 3.9 lbs. Mfg. 1998-2000.

	$1,275	$850	$600	$495	$425	$375	$350	$1,550

CARBON-15 TYPE 21 – .223 Rem. cal., GIO, ultra lightweight carbon fiber upper and lower receivers, 16 in. "Profile" stainless steel barrel, quick detachable muzzle compensator, Stoner type operating system, tool steel bolt, extractor and carrier, optics mounting base, quick detachable stock, 10 shot mag., also accepts AR-15 type mags., 3.9 lbs. Mfg. 2001-2003.

	$850	$550	$465	$395	$350	$325	$295	$988

CARBON-15 TYPE 97/97S – .223 Rem. cal., GIO, ultra lighweight carbon fiber upper and lower receivers, Stoner type operating system, hard chromed tool steel bolt, extractor and carrier, 16 in. fluted stainless steel barrel, quick detachable muzzle compensator, optics mounting base, quick detachable stock, 30 shot mag., also accepts AR-15 type mags., 3.9 lbs. Mfg. 2001-2003.

	$935	$575	$475	$415	$350	$325	$300	$1,120

Add $165 for Model 97S (includes Picatinny rail and "Scout" extension, double walled heat shield forearm, ambidextrous safety, and multi-point silent carry).

PROOF RESEARCH

Current rifle manufacturer located in Columbia Falls, MT. Consumer sales through FFL dealers.

RIFLES: SEMI-AUTO

MONOLITHIC AR10 – .243 Rem.-.338 RCM cals., GIO, 20 in. carbon fiber wrapped barrel, carbine, mid, or rifle length available, Mega Machine Monolithic upper receiver, Mega Machine lower receiver, Magpul PRS stock is standard, Geissele trigger, Premier 3-15x50LT optics, LaRue Tactical LT 104 mount, anodized Type III black, Cerakote, and custom option finishes available. Disc. 2014.

	$2,775	$1,825	$1,350	$750	$650	$595	$525	$3,417

MONOLITHIC AR15 – .204 Ruger-6.8 SPC cal., GIO, 16 in. carbon fiber wrapped barrel, available in carbine, mid-length, or rifle length, Mega Machine Monolithic upper and matched lower receiver, Magpul ACS stock standard, Geissele trigger, optics are optional and customer defined, LaRue Tactical LT 104 mount, anodized Type II Black, OD Green, and other Cerakote custom finishes available. Disc. 2014.

	$2,550	$1,650	$1,250	$700	$625	$575	$525	$3,113

SOCOM I – .243 Rem.-.338 Win. cals., AR-15 style, GIO, "tactical hunter" rifle, Proof T6 action, 16-28 in. Proof Research carbon fiber wrapped barrel, Proof SOCOM I composite stock with adj. cheekpiece and straight grip, Jewell or Timney trigger, optics are optional and customer defined, Cerakote finish is standard, Flat Dark Earth, OD Green, camo, and other finishes available. Disc. 2014.

	$6,150	$5,375	$4,625	$4,175	$3,375	$2,775	$2,150	$6,850

Q SECTION

287 Q

QUALITY ARMS

Current rifle manufacturer located in Rigby, ID.

MSR	100%	98%	95%	90%	80%	70%	60%	Last MSR

RIFLES: SEMI-AUTO

6.5 GRENDEL – 6.5 Grendel cal., GIO, this rifle will be custom built, but basic specs are as follows: 18, 20, or 24 in. match grade free floated stainless barrel, 10 or 26 shot mag., front and rear Magpul or A.R.M.S. flip-up sights, Magpul ACS 6-pos. collapsible stock, tactical free float rail, nickel plated single stage trigger, hammer, bolt, and carrier, includes black soft tactical case.

MSR $1,595	$1,315	$850	$625	$500	$435	$375	$350	

AMBI GEN 2 SIDE CHARGING – 5.56 NATO cal., 16 in. match grade free floating medium contour stainless barrel, 30 shot Magpul mag., A.R.M.S. flip-up front and rear sights, Midwest Industries Gen 2 forend, forged Mil-Spec lower and custom billet aluminum ambidextrous upper receiver, ambidextrous side charging handle, safety, and mag. release, nickel plated trigger, hammer, bolt, and carrier, includes black soft tactical case. New 2015.

MSR $1,495	$1,250	$825	$575	$475	$425	$375	$350	

BATTLESTORM – 5.56 NATO cal., GIO, 16 in. free floated M4 profile barrel, 30 shot Magpul mag., Battlelink 6-position collapsible stock with storage, ergonomic pistol grip, free float lightweight Spectre length quad rail handguard with ladder rail covers and end cap, low profile gas block, front and rear RTS sights, Primary Arms 1-4x24 optical red dot scope, Battle Blades knife and scabbard, winter trigger guard, nickel plated single stage trigger, hammer, bolt and carrier, includes cleaning kit and black soft tactical case.

MSR $1,895	$1,575	$995	$775	$575	$495	$425	$395	

BIG BORE 50 – .50 cal., 16 or 18 in. barrel, nickel plated trigger, hammer, bolt, and carrier, A.R.M.S. flip-up front and rear sights, Midwest Industries Gen 2 free float forend, Ace skeleton stock, Stark pistol grip with integrated winter trigger guard, side charging billet upper and Mil-Spec lower receivers, includes black soft tactical case. New 2015.

MSR $1,895	$1,575	$995	$775	$575	$495	$425	$395	

DEVASTATOR – 5.56 NATO cal., GIO, 16 in. M4 profile barrel, free float carbine length quad rail handguard with ladder rail covers and end cap, YHM flip-up front sight gas block, rear flip-up sights, single stage trigger, 6-position collapsible stock, 30 shot Mapgul mag., forged upper and lower receivers, includes cleaning kit and black soft tactical case. Disc. 2014.

	$825	$535	$450	$385	$340	$325	$295	*$975*

DOMINATOR – 5.56 NATO cal., GIO, low profile gas block, 18 in. free floated medium profile stainless barrel, 30 shot Magpul mag., single stage nickel plated trigger, hammer, and bolt carrier, front and rear Magpul or A.R.M.S. polymer sights, Magpul ACS 6-position collapsible stock, ergonomic grip, tactical free float rail or YHM custom rail, forged lower receiver, standard M3/M4 forged upper receiver, Primary Arms M3 style red dot scope with cantilever mount, single point sling endplate, includes black soft tactical case. Disc. 2014.

	$1,150	$750	$550	$465	$415	$375	$350	*$1,395*

HUNTER – 6.5 Grendel cal., 18 or 20 in. match grade free floating medium contour stainless barrel, 10 or 26 shot mag., billet side charging upper receiver, Midwest Industries Gen 2 free float rail, nickel plated trigger, hammer, bolt, and carrier, Ace skeleton stock, Cerakote coating in 3-color camo, includes black soft tactical case. New 2015.

MSR $1,895	$1,575	$995	$775	$575	$495	$425	$395	

LIBERATOR – 5.56 NATO cal., GIO, 16 in. free floated M4 profile barrel, 30 shot Magpul mag., nickel plated single stage trigger, hammer, bolt, and carrier, front and rear Magpul or A.R.M.S. flip-up polymer sights, upgraded 6-position collapsible stock, ergonomic pistol grip, free float lightweight Spectre length quad rail handguard with ladder rail covers and end cap, low profile gas block, forged Mil-Spec upper and lower receivers, Primary Arms red dot with cantilever mount, includes black soft tactical case. Disc. 2014.

	$1,075	$675	$500	$450	$400	$350	$325	*$1,295*

LRAR DOMINATOR – 5.56 NATO cal., GIO, 18 in. match grade free floated stainless barrel, 30 shot Magpul mag., ambidextrous upper receiver with fully automatic upward opening ejection port doors, nickel plated single stage trigger, hammer, bolt, and carrier, front and rear Magpul or A.R.M.S. flip-up sight, Magpul ACS 6-position collapsible stock, tactical free float rail, Primary Arms M3 red dot with cantilever mount, includes black soft tactical case. Disc. 2014.

	$1,250	$825	$575	$475	$425	$375	$350	*$1,495*

M4 CARBINE – 5.56 NATO cal., GIO, 16 in. M4 barrel, 30 shot Magpul mag., M4 6-position collapsible stock, A2 grip, forged lower receiver, A3/A4 forged flat-top upper, rear flip-up sight, forged front sight, SST.

MSR $775	$665	$500	$415	$375	$335	$315	$295	

Q 288 QUALITY ARMS, cont.

MSR	100%	98%	95%	90%	80%	70%	60%	Last MSR

ODIN – 5.56 NATO cal., 16 in. M4 profile barrel, 30 shot Magpul mag., ODIN free float forend, Primary Arms red dot with cantilever mount, A.R.M.S. front and rear flip-up sights, Magpul MOE 6-position collapsible stock, Magpul K-Grip, forged upper and lower receivers, includes black soft tactical case. New 2015.
  MSR $1,495 $1,250 $825 $575 $475 $425 $375 $350

THOR – 5.56 NATO cal., 16 in. free floating M4 profile barrel, 30 shot Magpul mag., forged Mil-Spec upper and lower receivers, A.R.M.S. front and rear flip-up sights, Troy Alpha rail, nickel plated trigger, hammer, bolt, and carrier, Magpul STR stock, Magpul K-Grip, includes black soft tactical case. New 2015.
  MSR $1,235 $1,050 $650 $495 $450 $395 $350 $325

QUALITY PARTS CO./BUSHMASTER

Quality Parts Co. was a division of Bushmaster Firearms, Inc. located in Windham, ME that manufactured AR-15 type rifles and various components and accessories for Bushmaster. Please refer to the Bushmaster Firearms International listing in the B section for current model listings and values.

MAYBE THE ONLY THING BETTER THAN THIS BOOK IS THE ONLINE SUBSCRIPTION!

- **Includes monthly updates** keeping you informed of all the new AR-15 makes/models.
- **Features thousands of images** allowing for fast and easy identification.
- **Manufacturer/Model searchable database** allowing you to find the model you need.
- Historical pricing with dynamic interactive graphs keeps you up-to-date on your AR-15 purchases as investments.
- Your own personal online inventory solution - keep track of your collection and track the change in value.
- Includes access to BBP's industry standard Photo Percentage Grading System – why guess a gun's condition when you can be sure?

Only $19.95/year!

Visit *BlueBookOfGunValues.com*

to view sample pages and ordering

Good Information Never Sleeps!

R SECTION

289 R

RAAC

Current importer located in Scottsburg, IN.

Russian American Armory Company is an import company for Molot, located in Russia. Current product/model lines include Vepr. rifles, in addition to a line of bolt action rifles, including the LOS/BAR Series, CM-2 Target rifle, Korshun, and Sobol hunting model. Please check individual heading listings for current information, including U.S. availability and pricing. Please contact the company directly for current offerings (see Trademark Index).

MSR	100%	98%	95%	90%	80%	70%	60%	Last MSR

SHOTGUNS

MKA 1919 – 12 ga., 3 in. chamber, AR-15 style, self-adjusting GIO, 18 1/2 in. barrel with three choke tubes, 5 shot box mag., A2 configuration with carry handle and front sight, Picatinny rail, bolt hold open after last round, fixed or adj. synthetic stock, sling swivels, choice of matte black or 100% camo coverage. Mfg. in Turkey. Disc.

	100%	98%	95%	90%	80%	70%	60%	Last MSR
	$650	$575	$525	$475	$435	$400	$375	$700

Add $100 for 100% camo coverage. Add $500 for flat-top receiver and adj. stock.

R.I.P. TACTICAL

Current AR-15 manufacturer located in Utah.

RIFLES: SEMI-AUTO

R.I.P. Tactical builds custom AR-15 rifles to individual customer specifications. Current models include: RIP-BM (base model), RIP-NT (nickel Teflon coated), RIP-DC (camo), RIP-BA (black anodized), RIP-OD (ceramic coated dark green), and the RIP-SBR (short barreled rifle). Base MSR starts at $1,495. Several options are available for each model. Please contact the company directly for options, delivery time, and an individualized price quotation (see Trademark Index).

RND MANUFACTURING

Current manufacturer established in 1978, and located in Longmont, CO. Previously distributed by Mesa Sportsmen's Association, LLC located in Delta, CO. Dealer or consumer direct sales.

PISTOLS: SEMI-AUTO

RND PISTOL – 5.56 NATO cal., AR-15 style, GIO, round shrouded handguard, 7 1/2 in. barrel with muzzle brake, pistol grip, full-length vent. Picatinny rail, titanium firing pin, 9 1/2 lbs. New 2010.

MSR $2,000			$1,700	$1,500	$1,250	$1,100	$950	$825	$675

RIFLES: SEMI-AUTO

RND EDGE SERIES – .223 Rem. (RND 400), .300 WSM (RND 1000, new 2003), .300 RUM (RND 2100, new 2003), .308 Win. (RND 800, new 2010), .338 LM (RND 2000, new 1999), .375 Super Mag. (RND 2600), .408 CheyTac (RND 2500) or 7.62x39mm (disc.) cal., patterned after the AR-15 style, GIO, 18, 20, 24, or 26 in. barrel, choice of synthetic (Grade I), built to individual custom order, handmade laminated thumbhole (Grade II, disc. 1998), or custom laminated thumbhole stock with fluted barrel (Grade III, disc. 1998), CNC machined, vented aluminum shroud, many options and accessories available, custom order only, approx. 11 1/2-16 lbs. New 1996.

Add $355 for Grade II (disc. 1998) or $605 for Grade III (disc.).

* **RND 400** – .223 Rem. cal., GIO, AR-15 style, 18-26 in. barrel, synthetic A2 style stock, CNC machined upper and lower receivers, integral Picatinny rail, titanium firing pin, free floating handguard, hard black anodized with grey or black finish, 9 1/2 lbs.

MSR $2,295		$1,795	$1,050	$875	$625	$550	$475	$425

* **RND 800** – .308 Win./7.62 NATO cal., GPO, 20-26 in. super match free floating barrel, CNC machined matched upper and lower receivers, left side non-reciprocating charging handle, hard black anodized with black or gray gun coat, integral Picatinny rail, titanium firing pin, modular handguard, adj. stock, 11 lbs. New 2010.

MSR $3,795		$3,225	$2,825	$2,325	$1,975	$1,650	$1,375	$1,175

* **RND 1000** – .300 Win. Mag. cal., GPO, 20-26 in. Super match free floating barrel, CNC machined matched upper and lower receivers, left sided non-reciprocating charging handle, integral Picatinny rail, RND integrated buffer system, modular handguard, fully adj. stock, single feed double stack mag., hard black anodized with black or gray gun coat finish, 11 lbs. New 2003.

MSR $2,295		$2,000	$1,750	$1,300	$1,050	$850	$750	$650

* **RND 2000** – .338 LM cal., GPO, 20-26 in. Super match free floating barrel, CNC machined matched upper and lower receivers, left sided non-reciprocating charging handle, integral Picatinny rail, single feed double stack mag., RND integrated buffer system, modular handguard, fully adj. stock, hard black anodized with black or gray gun coat finish, 14 lbs. New 1999.

MSR $4,795		$4,100	$3,600	$3,100	$2,525	$2,100	$1,800	$1,575

R 290 RND MANUFACTURING, cont.

MSR	100%	98%	95%	90%	80%	70%	60%	Last MSR

* RND 2100 – .300 RUM cal., GPO, otherwise similar to RND 2000. New 2003.

| MSR $4,795 | $4,100 | $3,600 | $3,100 | $2,525 | $2,100 | $1,800 | $1,575 | |

* RND 2500 – .408 CheyTac cal., GPO, similar to RND 2000, except features 26 in. Super match free floating barrel, 18 lbs. New 2004.

| MSR $10,500 | $9,450 | $8,275 | $7,100 | $6,425 | $5,200 | $4,250 | $3,325 | |

* RND 2600 – .375 CheyTac cal., GPO, 20-26 in. Super match free floating barrel, CNC machined matched upper and lower receivers, left sided non-reciprocating charging handle, integral Picatinny rail, single feed double stack mag., RND integrated buffer system, modular handguard, fully adj. stock, hard black anodized with black or gray gun coat finish, 18 lbs.

| MSR $10,500 | $9,450 | $8,275 | $7,100 | $6,425 | $5,200 | $4,250 | $3,325 | |

* RND 3000 – .50 BMG cal., GPO, 26 in. Super match barrel with muzzle brake, double stock mag., fully adj. stock, full-length integrated Picatinny rail, includes optics, scope, and bipod, black or various camo colors, 28 lbs.

| MSR $11,500 | $10,350 | $9,250 | $8,250 | $7,500 | $6,750 | $6,000 | $5,250 | |

* RND 3100 – .416 Rem. Mag. cal., GPO, otherwise similar to RND 3000. Mfg. 2012 only.

| | $10,350 | $9,250 | $8,250 | $7,500 | $6,750 | $6,000 | $5,250 | $11,500 |

RADICAL FIREARMS, LLC

Current manufacturer and retail operation located in Stafford, TX.

Radical Firearms manufactures custom built AR-15s, AR-10s, bolt guns, and silencers in their fully tooled and operational gunsmithing facility.

PISTOLS: SEMI-AUTO

RF 5.56 AR PISTOL WITH FCR RAIL – 5.56 NATO cal., pistol length gas system, 7 1/2 or 10 1/2 in. Melonite treated chrome moly barrel, MFT EPG16V2 grip, M4 feed ramps, 7 or 10 in. FCR rail with full-length top Picatinny rail, Magpul M-LOK slots on sides and bottom of rail, forged Mil-Std lower receiver, pistol buffer assembly, black finish.

| MSR $521 | $450 | $385 | $335 | $285 | $250 | $235 | $215 | |

RF .300 BLACKOUT PISTOL WITH FCR RAIL – .300 AAC Blackout cal., pistol length gas system, 8 1/2 or 10 1/2 in. Melonite treated chrome moly barrel, MFT EPG16V2 grip, low profile gas block, M4 feed ramps, 7 or 10 in. FCR, allows for use of M-LOK accessories and rail attachments, Mil-Std forged lower receiver, pistol buffer assembly with foam piece, black finish.

| MSR $521 | $450 | $385 | $335 | $285 | $250 | $235 | $215 | |

RF .300 BLACKOUT PISTOL WITH FGS RAIL – .300 AAC Blackout cal., pistol length gas system, 8 1/2 or 10 1/2 in. Melonite treated chrome moly barrel, MFT EPG16V2 grip, low profile gas block, M4 feed ramps, 7 or 10 in. FGS (Forward Guard Shield) round rail with top Picatinny rail, allows for use of Magpul MOE or FGSA rail attachments, Mil-Std forged upper and lower receiver, forward assist, shell deflector, dust cover, pistol buffer tube, with or without SIG SB15 arm brace, black finish.

| MSR $521 | $450 | $385 | $335 | $285 | $250 | $235 | $215 | |

Add $95 for SIG SB15 arm brace.

RF .300 BLACKOUT PISTOL WITH FHR RAIL – .300 AAC Blackout cal., 10 1/2 in. Melonite treated chrome moly barrel, pistol length gas system, M4 feed ramps, 9 in. FHR (allows for use of KeyMod accessories and Picatinny rail attachments at the forend of rail), Mil-Std lower receiver, pistol buffer assembly with foam piece, black finish.

| MSR $532 | $465 | $400 | $350 | $300 | $265 | $250 | $225 | |

RF .300 BLACKOUT PISTOL WITH FQR – .300 AAC Blackout cal., pistol length gas system, 8 1/2 or 10 1/2 in. Melonite coated chrome moly barrel, low profile gas block, M4 feed ramps, 7 or 10 in. free float FQR (First-Gen Quad Rail), Picatinny rails on all four sides, Mil-Std forged upper and lower receiver, Mil-Std lower parts kit, pistol buffer assembly, with or without SIG SB15 arm brace, black finish.

| MSR $532 | $465 | $400 | $350 | $300 | $265 | $250 | $225 | |

Add $95 for SIG SB15 arm brace.

RF .458 SOCOM COMPLETE PISTOL WITH MHR – .458 SOCOM cal., GIO, stainless pistol length gas system, 10 1/2 in. HBAR Melonite treated chrome moly barrel, Panzer muzzle brake, MFT grip, low profile micro gas block, 10 in. free float MHR (M-LOK Hybrid Rail), quad Picatinny rails at the forend for mounting, Mil-Std forged upper and lower receiver, black finish.

| MSR $700 | $615 | $545 | $475 | $400 | $350 | $315 | $295 | |

RF 7.62x39 AR PISTOL WITH FQR – 7.62x39mm cal., carbine length gas system, 10 1/2 in. HBAR Melonite treated barrel, extractor booster pre-installed, overmolded grip, 10 in. FQR (First-Gen Quad Rail), forged Mil-Spec lower receiver, pistol length buffer tube with foam sleeve, black finish.

| MSR $532 | $465 | $400 | $350 | $300 | $265 | $250 | $225 | |

RADICAL FIREARMS, LLC, cont. 291 R

MSR	100%	98%	95%	90%	80%	70%	60%	Last MSR

RF 7.62x39 PISTOL WITH FGS AND SB15 – 7.62x39mm cal., pistol or carbine length gas system, 7 1/2 or 10 1/2 in. HBAR Melonite treated chrome moly or stainless steel (10 1/2 in. only) barrel, extractor booster pre-installed, overmolded grip, M4 feed ramps, forged Mil-Spec upper and lower receiver, 7 or 10 in. free float FGS (Forward Guard Shield) round rail, pistol buffer assembly, SIG SB15 tac arm brace, two FGS rail attachments, black finish.

	100%	98%	95%	90%	80%	70%	60%	
MSR $616	$535	$475	$425	$365	$315	$285	$250	

RF COMPLETE PISTOL WITH FHR – 12.7x42mm or .458 SOCOM cal., GIO, stainless pistol or carbine length gas system, 10 1/2 in. HBAR Melonite treated chrome moly barrel, Panzer muzzle brake, MFT EPG16V2 grip, RF .936 gas block (12.7x42) or low profile micro gas block (.458 SOCOM), 9 or 10 in. FHR (Free Float Hybrid Rail), KeyMod (12.7x42 only) or quad Picatinny rails for mounting (.458 SOCOM), Mil-Std forged upper and lower receiver, with or without SIG SB15 arm brace, black finish.

	100%	98%	95%	90%	80%	70%	60%	
MSR $700	$615	$545	$475	$400	$350	$315	$295	

Add $95 for SIG SB15 arm brace.

RF PISTOL WITH FGS RAIL – 5.56 NATO cal., pistol or carbine length gas system, 7 1/2 or 10 1/2 in. Melonite treated chrome moly barrel, with or without SIG SB15 arm brace, M4 feed ramps, 7 or 10 in. FGS rail, Picatinny sections run the full length of the rail, forged Mil-Std lower receiver, pistol buffer assembly with foam piece, Magpul MOE/RF FGS-A attachments on the sides and bottom of rail (7 in. barrel only), black finish.

	100%	98%	95%	90%	80%	70%	60%	
MSR $521	$450	$385	$335	$285	$250	$235	$215	

Add $95 for SIG SB15 arm brace.

RF PISTOL WITH FQR – 5.56 NATO or .300 AAC Blackout cal., pistol length gas system, 7 1/2, 8 1/2, or 10 1/2 in. Melonite treated chrome moly barrel, M4 feed ramps, 7 or 10 in. FQR (First-Gen Quad Rail), full-length top Picatinny sections, forged Mil-Std lower receiver, pistol buffer assembly, with or without SIG SB15 arm brace, black finish.

	100%	98%	95%	90%	80%	70%	60%	
MSR $532	$465	$400	$350	$300	$265	$250	$225	

Add $95 for SIG SB15 arm brace.

RF ROUND RAIL AR PISTOL – 7.62x39mm cal., carbine length gas system, 10 1/2 in. HBAR Melonite treated barrel, overmolded grip, 10 in. FGS round rail, forged Mil-Spec upper and lower receivers, pistol length buffer tube with foam sleeve, black finish.

	100%	98%	95%	90%	80%	70%	60%	
MSR $521	$450	$385	$335	$285	$250	$235	$215	

RIFLES: SEMI-AUTO

RF .300 BLACKOUT – .300 AAC Blackout cal., GIO, 16 in. HBAR Melonite barrel, A2 flash hider, M4 collapsible stock, A2 (disc.) or overmolded grip, low profile micro gas block, stainless pistol length gas tube, 10 in. free float FGS (Forward Guard Shield) rail or 12 in. free float FQR (First-Gen Quad) rail, Picatinny top or quad rails, forged upper and lower receivers.

	100%	98%	95%	90%	80%	70%	60%	
MSR $556	$495	$435	$385	$340	$315	$295	$275	

Add $11 for 12 in. free float FQR rail.

* **RF .300 Blackout w/15 In. Rail** – .300 AAC Blackout cal., GIO, 16 in. Melonite barrel, A2 flash hider, M4 or MFT Minimalist collapsible stock, overmolded or MFT EPG16V2 grip, low profile micro gas block, stainless pistol length gas system, M4 feed ramps, 15 in. free float FHR (First-Gen Hybrid Rail) or 15 in. free float MHR (M-LOK Hybrid Rail), quad Picatinny rails, forged upper and lower receivers, Mil-Spec parts kit.

	100%	98%	95%	90%	80%	70%	60%	
MSR $600	$515	$450	$395	$350	$315	$295	$275	

RF 6.8 SPC – 6.8 SPC II cal., GIO, 16 in. Melonite barrel, A2 flash hider, M4 collapsible stock, overmolded grip, M4 feed ramps, low profile micro gas block, stainless mid-length gas system, 15 in. free float FHR (First-Gen Hybrid Rail), quad Picatinny rails, forged upper and lower receivers. New 2016.

	100%	98%	95%	90%	80%	70%	60%	
MSR $699	$595	$485	$415	$350	$315	$295	$275	

RF 5.56 – 5.56 NATO cal., 16 in. SOCOM barrel, A2 flash hider, MFT Minimalist collapsible stock, MFT EPG16V2 grip, M4 feed ramps, low profile micro gas block, stainless mid-length gas system, 12 or 15 in. free float FCR handguard, M-LOK attachment.

	100%	98%	95%	90%	80%	70%	60%	
MSR $556	$495	$435	$385	$340	$315	$295	$275	

* **RF 5.56 w/15 In. Rail** – 5.56 NATO cal., GIO, 16 in. chrome moly Melonite barrel, A2 flash hider, MFT Minimalist collapsible stock, MFT EPG16V2 grip, M4 feed ramps, low profile micro gas block, stainless carbine length gas system, 15 in. free float FHR (First-Gen Hybrid Rail), FTR (First-Gen Thin Rail), or RPR, KeyMod attachment points along the rail, quad Picatinny rails on the forend, forged uppper and lower receivers, Mil-Spec lower parts kit.

	100%	98%	95%	90%	80%	70%	60%	
MSR $600	$515	$450	$395	$350	$315	$295	$275	

RF 5.56 M4 – 5.56 NATO cal., GIO, 16 in. M4 Melonite barrel, A2 flash hider, M4 feed ramps, M4 collapsible (disc.) or MFT Minimalist stock, Ergo SureGrip (disc.), A2 (disc.), or MFT grip, stainless carbine length gas system, low profile micro gas block, forged upper and lower receivers, Picatinny top rail, 12 in. free float FGS round rail or FQR (First-Gen Quad) rail.

	100%	98%	95%	90%	80%	70%	60%	
MSR $556	$495	$435	$385	$340	$315	$295	$275	

Add $11 for 12 in. FQR rail.

R 292 RADICAL FIREARMS, LLC, cont.

MSR	100%	98%	95%	90%	80%	70%	60%	Last MSR

RF 5.56 SOCOM – 5.56 NATO cal., GIO, 16 in. SOCOM barrel, A2 flash hider, M4 feed ramps, M4 (disc.) or MFT Minimalist collapsible stock, Ergo SureGrip (disc.) or MFT grip, stainless mid-length gas system, low profile micro gas block, forged upper and lower receivers, Picatinny top rail, 12 in. free float FGS round rail or 15 in. free float MHR (M-LOK Hybrid Rail).

| | MSR $556 | $495 | $435 | $385 | $340 | $315 | $295 | $275 | |

Add $44 for 15 in. MHR (M-LOK Hybrid Rail).

RF 7.62x39 – 7.62x39mm cal., GIO, 16 in. HBAR Melonite barrel, A2 flash hider, M4 or A2 collapsible stock, A2 (disc.) or overmolded grip, low profile micro gas block, stainless carbine length gas system, forged upper and lower receiver, Picatinny top rail, 12 in. free float FGS or FQR rail.

| | MSR $556 | $495 | $435 | $385 | $340 | $315 | $295 | $275 | |

Add $11 for A2 collapsible stock and 12 in. FQR rail.

* RF 7.62x39 w/15 In. Rail – 7.62x39mm cal., GIO, 16 in. Melonite barrel, A2 flash hider, M4 collapsible or MFT Minimalist collapsible stock, overmolded or MFG EPG16V2 grip, low profile micro gas block, stainless carbine length gas system, forged upper and lower receiver, 15 in. free float FHR (First-Gen Hybrid Rail) or MHR (M-LOK Hybrid Rail), quad Picatinny rails on the forend, Mil-Spec lower parts kit.

| | MSR $600 | $515 | $450 | $395 | $350 | $315 | $295 | $275 | |

RF .450 BUSHMASTER – .450 Bushmaster cal., GIO, 20 in. HBAR chrome moly barrel, Panzer brake, adaptive tactical collapsible stock, MFT EPG16V2 grip, stainless rifle length gas system, 15 in. free float MHR (M-LOK Hybrid Rail), quad Picatinny rails on the forend, forged upper and lower receivers, Mil-Spec lower parts kit.

| | MSR $830 | $725 | $500 | $435 | $375 | $335 | $315 | $295 | |

RF .458 SOCOM – .458 SOCOM cal., GIO, 16 in. HBAR Melonite barrel, Panzer brake, Luth-AR MBA-2 "Skullaton" stock, Ergo SureGrip, low profile micro gas block, stainless carbine length gas system, 12 in. free float FHR (First-Gen Hybrid Rail), quad Picatinny rails, forged upper and lower receiver. Disc. 2017.

| | | $850 | $550 | $465 | $395 | $350 | $325 | $295 | *$1,000* |

RF 6.5 GRENDEL – 6.5 Grendel cal., 20 or 24 in. stainless steel barrel, stainless Pepper Pot brake, MFT Minimalist collapsible stock, MFT EPG16V2 grip, low profile gas block, rifle length gas system, 15 in. free float FHR (First-Gen Hybrid Rail), RPR with M-LOK attachment points, or MHR (M-LOK Hybrid Rail), Mil-Std forged upper and lower receiver, quad Picatinny rails on forend, KeyMod slots on sides and bottom of rail, M4 feed ramps.

| | MSR $830 | $725 | $500 | $435 | $375 | $335 | $315 | $295 | |

RF .224 VALKYRIE – .224 Valkyrie cal., GIO, 18 or 22 in. stainless steel barrel, A2 flash hider, MFT Minimalist collapsible stock, MFT EPG16V2 grip, M4 feed ramps, low profile micro gas block, stainless carbine gas system, 15 in. free float RPR or MHR (M-LOK Hybrid Rail), M-LOK attachment points along the rail, forged upper and lower receivers, Mil-Spec lower parts kit.

| | MSR $830 | $725 | $500 | $435 | $375 | $335 | $315 | $295 | |

REBEL ARMS CORP.

Current manufacturer of AR-15 pistols and rifles located in East Stroudsburg, PA.

PISTOLS: SEMI-AUTO

RAPTOR PISTOL – 5.56 NATO cal., 10 1/2 in. medium taper barrel, two 30 shot Hexmags, forged aluminum upper and lower receivers, profile gas block, 10 in. KeyMod rail system, standard Mil-Spec charging handle, Nitride bolt carrier group, black Cerakote finish, 5.2 lbs. Disc. 2017.

| | | $1,400 | $1,235 | $1,100 | $975 | $835 | $725 | $585 | *$1,589* |

RAPTOR PISTOL MOD 3 – 5.56 NATO cal., 10 1/2 in. barrel with Nitride finish, SilencerCo ASR 3-port muzzle brake, Magpul PMAG Gen M3, enhanced mag. release, flared magwell, Shockwave blade pistol stabilizer, Magpul MOE grip, Talon ambi safety selector, aluminum upper and lower receivers, 9 in. PicMod with BCM KeyMod rail, full-length Picatinny top rail, Mil-Spec fire control group, enhanced BCG, Mod 2 enhanced buffer tube, Talon ambi safety selector, Raptor-LT ambi charging handle, includes Patriot hard case, hardcoat anodized finish, 7.5 oz. New 2018.

| | MSR $1,800 | $1,525 | $1,350 | $1,175 | $1,050 | $900 | $775 | $625 | |

RAPTOR 300 BLACKOUT – .300 AAC Blackout cal., 8.2 in. medium taper barrel, two 30 shot mags., Mission First Tactical E-VolV enhanced trigger guard, pistol buffer, stabilizing brace, forged aluminum upper and lower receivers, low profile gas block, 7 in. LITE KeyMod rail system, carrying case, black or four color camo Cerakote finish, 5.2 lbs. Disc. 2017.

| | | $1,350 | $1,200 | $1,075 | $950 | $815 | $700 | $575 | *$1,589* |

Add $350 for four color camo Cerakote finish.

REBEL-9 – 9mm Para. cal., Deus Ex Machina 416R stainless match grade barrel, SLR magwell, Deus Ex Machina Gunfighter Trigger, Trijicon Suppressor Height night sights, black grips, Cerakote finish, 1.4 oz. Limited mfg. beginning 2018.

| | MSR $2,400 | $2,050 | $1,795 | $1,500 | $1,300 | $1,075 | $935 | $795 | |

REBEL ARMS CORP., cont. 293 R

MSR	100%	98%	95%	90%	80%	70%	60%	Last MSR

RIFLES: SEMI-AUTO

REBEL RBR-15 MOD 3 – 5.56 NATO cal., 16 in. Nitride barrel, SilencerCo ASR muzzle brake, optics ready, Magpul MOE SL-K stock, Magpul MOE black grip, mid-length gas system, Slim Line gas block, 15 in. PicMod handguard, anodized black or Cerakote finish in Smoke, Burnt Bronze, FDE, Sniper Gray, and OD Green, camo finish in Alpine Eclipse or Alpine Dark, 6 lbs. 2 oz.

	100%	98%	95%	90%	80%	70%	60%	Last MSR
MSR $1,800	$1,475	$950	$725	$550	$475	$395	$350	

Add $150 for Cerakote finish or $300 for camo finish.

REBEL-30 – .308 Win. cal., 16 in. stainless steel barrel, no sights (optics ready), MFT Battlelink Utility stock, MFT Engage grip, 15 in. KeyMod rail, ambidextrous charging handle, low profile gas block, black Nitride bolt carrier group, black anodized finish, 8.4 lbs. Disc. 2017.

	100%	98%	95%	90%	80%	70%	60%	Last MSR
	$2,225	$1,395	$1,050	$675	$595	$525	$475	*$2,700*

* ***Rebel-30 Alpine Arid*** – .308 Win. cal., 16 in. Nitride barrel, SilencerCo ASR muzzle brake, Luth-AR MBA-3 carbine buttstock, MFT Engage grip, 15 in. KeyMod rail, ambi charging handle, low profile gas block, Alpine Arid Cerakote finish, 8.9 lbs.

	100%	98%	95%	90%	80%	70%	60%	Last MSR
MSR $3,050	$2,450	$1,595	$1,200	$700	$675	$575	$525	

RENEGADE MOD II – 5.56 NATO cal., AR-15 style, 16 in. Nitride barrel, aluminum upper and lower receivers, low profile gas block, Nitride bolt carrier group, 10 in. ECO KeyMod handguard, standard Mil-Spec fire control group, black anodized finish, 5 lbs. 6 oz.

	100%	98%	95%	90%	80%	70%	60%	Last MSR
MSR $1,150	$950	$595	$495	$425	$365	$335	$300	

RED X ARMS

Current semi-auto rifle manufacturer located in central MN.

PISTOLS: SEMI-AUTO

RXA 15 .223 WYLDE SLIM M-LOK PISTOL – .223 Wylde chamber, 7 1/2 in. lightweight contour stainless steel barrel, Halestorm muzzle brake, 30 shot PMAG, pistol length gas system, A2 grip, forged aluminum flat-top upper receiver with M4 feed ramps, 7 in. slim design M-LOK handguard, Mil-Spec charging handle, Spike's Tactical forged aluminum lower receiver, RXA diamond fluted pistol buffer assembly, includes soft tactical pistol case with mag. pouches, hardcoat anodized black finish. Disc. 2017.

	100%	98%	95%	90%	80%	70%	60%	Last MSR
	$450	$385	$335	$285	$250	$235	$215	*$499*

RXA MOE PISTOL w/SIG BRACE – 5.56 NATO cal., 7 1/2 in. stainless steel HBAR barrel, stainless steel A2 flash hider, 30 shot PMAG, Magpul MOE grip and trigger guard, forged aluminum A3 flat-top upper and Red X Arms lower, M4 feed ramps, free floating carbine length aluminum quad rail, low profile gas block, pistol length gas tube, aluminum charging handle, KAK Industries buffer tube assembly, SIG brace, ambi endplate sling adapter, includes two ladder rail covers and soft tactical case with mag. pouches, black or FDE finish, 6.2 lbs.

	100%	98%	95%	90%	80%	70%	60%	Last MSR
MSR $860	$725	$650	$575	$515	$450	$385	$345	

RXA SS TACTICAL PISTOL – .223 Wylde chamber, 5.56 NATO, .300 AAC Blackout, or 7.62x39mm cal., 7 1/2 in. stainless steel HBAR barrel, stainless steel A2 flash hider, 30 shot PMAG, A2 pistol grip, M4 feed ramps, low profile gas block, pistol length gas tube, M16 BCG, forged aluminum A3 flat-top upper and Red X Arms lower receiver, Mil-Spec charging handle, free floating carbine length quad rail, straight, spiral, or diamond fluted pistol buffer tube assembly, ambi endplate sling adapter, includes soft tactical rifle case with mag. pouches, hardcoat anodized black finish, approx. 5 lbs.

	100%	98%	95%	90%	80%	70%	60%	Last MSR
MSR $690	$615	$545	$475	$400	$350	$315	$295	

Add $10 for 5.56 NATO, $30 for .300 AAC Blackout, or $40 for 7.62x39mm cal.

RIFLES: SEMI-AUTO

RXA .308 DIAMOND FLUTED HBAR EVO KEYMOD RIFLE – .308 Win. cal., 20 in. HBAR contour stainless steel barrel with Diamond fluting, stainless steel X-treme muzzle brake, 10 shot PMAG, finger grooved flared magwell, built-in winter trigger guard, Magpul ACS buttstock with integral storage compartment, Magpul MOE grip, billet aluminum low profile Gen 1 DPMS A3 flat-top upper and Red X Arms finger groove lower receiver, standard aluminum charging handle, rifle length gas tube, low profile gas block, 15 in. Samson Evolution KeyMod rail system (includes 3 mountable rail sections), includes soft tactical rifle case with mag. pouches, hardcoat anodized black finish, 9.2 lbs.

	100%	98%	95%	90%	80%	70%	60%	Last MSR
MSR $1,565	$1,315	$850	$625	$500	$435	$375	$350	

RXA .308 LIGHTWEIGHT EVO KEYMOD RIFLE – .308 Win. cal., 20 in. lightweight contour stainless steel barrel, stainless steel A2 flash hider, 10 shot PMAG, Magpul ACS buttstock with integral storage compartment, Magpul MOE grip, billet aluminum low profile Gen 1 DPMS A3 flat-top upper and Red X Arms finger groove lower receiver, built-in winter trigger guard, finger grooved flared magwell, standard aluminum charging handle, rifle length gas tube, low profile gas block, 15 in. Samson Evolution KeyMod rail system (includes 3 mountable rail sections), includes soft tactical rifle case with mag. pouches, hardcoat anodized black finish, 8.6 lbs.

	100%	98%	95%	90%	80%	70%	60%	Last MSR
MSR $1,490	$1,250	$825	$575	$475	$425	$375	$350	

R 294 RED X ARMS, cont.

MSR	100%	98%	95%	90%	80%	70%	60%	Last MSR

RXA .308 SPIRAL FLUTED BULL EVO KEYMOD RIFLE – .308 Win. cal., 20 in. stainless steel bull barrel with spiral fluting, target crowned muzzle, 10 shot PMAG, flared magwell, built-in winter trigger guard, Magpul MOE buttstock, Magpul MOE grip, rifle length buffer tube, low profile Gen 1 DPMS A3 flat-top billet aluminum upper and Red X Arms lower receiver, standard aluminum charging handle, rifle length gas system, low profile micro gas block, 15 in. Samson Evolution KeyMod rail system (includes 3 mountable rail sections), includes soft tactical rifle case with mag. pouches, hardcoat anodized matte black finish, 10.3 lbs.

	100%	98%	95%	90%	80%	70%	60%	
MSR $1,470	$1,225	$825	$575	$475	$425	$375	$350	

RXA .308 STRAIGHT FLUTED HBAR MODULAR RIFLE – .308 Win. cal., 16 in. HBAR contoured stainless steel fluted barrel, stainless steel X-Treme muzzle brake, 10 shot PMAG, flared magwell, Magpul MOE 6-pos. buttstock, Magpul MOE grip, carbine length gas tube, low profile micro gas block, low profile Gen 1 DPMS A3 flat-top upper receiver, standard aluminum charging handle, 15 in. ultra thin modular rail system, billet aluminum Red X Arms lower receiver with built-in winter trigger guard, includes soft tactical rifle case with mag. pouches, hardcoat anodized matte black finish, 8.7 lbs.

	100%	98%	95%	90%	80%	70%	60%	
MSR $1,355	$1,135	$725	$525	$465	$415	$375	$350	

RXA .308 STRAIGHT FLUTED HBAR 20 IN. RIFLE – .308 Win. cal., 16 in. HBAR contoured stainless steel fluted barrel, stainless steel X-Treme muzzle brake, 10 shot PMAG, finger grooved flared magwell, Magpul ACS buttstock with integral storage compartment, Magpul MOE grip, rifle length gas tube, low profile gas block, low profile Gen 1 DPMS A3 flat-top upper receiver, standard aluminum charging handle, vented free floating handguard, billet aluminum Red X Arms finger groove lower receiver with built-in winter trigger guard, includes soft tactical rifle case with mag. pouches, hardcoat anodized matte black finish, 10 lbs.

	100%	98%	95%	90%	80%	70%	60%	
MSR $1,375	$1,135	$725	$525	$465	$415	$375	$350	

RXA15 3G RIFLE – 5.56 NATO cal., 18 in. stainless steel heavy barrel with RXA SS tactical Gill muzzle brake, 30 shot PMAG, mid-length gas system with low profile gas block, T6 aluminum lower and upper receiver, 15 in. Samson Evolution rail system, BCM Mod 4 charging handle, Rock River two-stage National Match trigger, Mil-Spec lower parts kit with enhanced trigger guard and MFT G2 grip, Magpul UBR buttstock, hardcoat anodized Class III black finish, includes soft tactical case. Disc. 2017.

	100%	98%	95%	90%	80%	70%	60%	Last MSR
	$1,025	$625	$495	$450	$395	$350	$325	*$1,200*

RXA15 CHROME-LINED M4 RIFLE – 5.56 NATO cal., 16 in. chrome-lined steel M4 barrel, A2 compensator, black 30 shot PMAG, black Magpul MOE grip and trigger guard, black Magpul MOE 6-pos. collapsible stock, carbine length gas system, forged aluminum lower and flat-top upper receiver with Burnt Bronze or Sniper Gray Cerakote finish, M4 feed ramps, 12.37 in. Samson Manufacturing Evolution free floating handguard (includes 3 black mountable rail sections), low profile gas block, Mil-Spec aluminum charging handle, M16 BCG, includes soft tactical rifle case with mag. pouches. Disc. 2017.

	100%	98%	95%	90%	80%	70%	60%	Last MSR
	$675	$500	$425	$375	$335	$315	$295	*$799*

RXA15 M4 MOE – 5.56 NATO cal., 16 in. chrome-lined M4 barrel, A2 compensator, 30 shot PMAG, carbine length gas system, gray Magpul MOE grip and trigger guard, gray Magpul MOE 6-pos. collapsible stock, forged aluminum lower and flat-top upper receiver, M4 feed ramps, gray Magpul MOE carbine length handguard, aluminum top rail gas block, M16 BCG, aluminum charging handle, includes soft tactical rifle case with mag. pouches, hardcoat anodized black finish. Disc. 2017.

	100%	98%	95%	90%	80%	70%	60%	Last MSR
	$515	$450	$395	$350	$315	$295	$275	*$589*

RXA15 MID-LENGTH MOE – 5.56 NATO cal., 16 in. stainless steel SOCOM mid-length barrel with pink Cerakote finish, black Gill muzzle brake, 30 shot PMAG, black Magpul MOE 6-pos. collapsible stock, black Magpul MOE grip and trigger guard, mid-length gas system, M4 feed ramps, forged aluminum lower and flat-top upper receiver with pink Cerakote finish, M4 feed ramps, 9 in. free floating mid-length quad rail handguard, aluminum top rail gas block, M16 BCG, aluminum charging handle, includes soft tactical rifle case with mag. pouches, hardcoat anodized black finish. Disc. 2017.

	100%	98%	95%	90%	80%	70%	60%	Last MSR
	$515	$450	$395	$350	$315	$295	$275	*$599*

RXA 300 BLACKOUT HBAR MOD RIFLE (RXA15 300 BLACKOUT HBAR) – .300 AAC Blackout cal., 16 in. HBAR button rifled barrel, A2 flash hider, 30 shot PMAG, 6-pos. adj. M4 stock, A2 pistol grip, forged aluminum A3 flat-top upper and Red X Arms lower receiver, M4 feed ramps, carbine length gas tube, RXA free floating modular handguard, top rail gas block, M16 bolt carrier group, Mil-Spec charging handle, includes soft tactical rifle case with mag. pouches, matte black hardcoat anodized finish, 6.9 lbs.

	100%	98%	95%	90%	80%	70%	60%	
MSR $725	$615	$495	$415	$360	$325	$300	$275	

RXA 300 BLACKOUT TACTICAL HBAR RIFLE – .300 AAC Blackout cal., 16 in. HBAR button rifled barrel, A2 flash hider, 30 shot PMAG, 6-pos. adj. M4 stock, A2 pistol grip, forged aluminum A3 flat-top upper and Red X Arms lower receiver, M4 feed ramps, standard aluminum charging handle, carbine length gas tube, free floating carbine length quad rail, includes soft tactical rifle case with mag. pouches, hardcoat anodized black finish, 6.9 lbs.

	100%	98%	95%	90%	80%	70%	60%	
MSR $735	$645	$500	$415	$370	$325	$300	$275	

RED X ARMS, cont. 295 R

MSR	100%	98%	95%	90%	80%	70%	60%	Last MSR

RXA HBAR MOD RIFLE (RXA15 STAINLESS HBAR MOD) – 5.56 NATO cal., 16 in. stainless steel HBAR barrel, stainless steel A2 flash hider, 30 shot PMAG, 6-pos. adj. M4 stock, A2 pistol grip, carbine length gas tube, forged aluminum A3 flat-top upper and Red X Arms lower receiver, M4 feed ramps, RXA free floating modular handguard, top rail gas block, M16 bolt carrier group, Mil-Spec charging handle, includes soft tactical rifle case with mag. pouches, matte black hardcoat anodized finish, 6.9 lbs.

MSR $710 $615 $495 $415 $360 $325 $300 $275

RXA M4 AIR LITE KEYMOD SKELETON RIFLE – 5.56 NATO cal., 16 in. M4 contour stainless steel barrel, black straight fluted Halestorm brake, 30 shot PMAG, white skeleton trigger guard and pistol grip, white skeleton buttstock, adj. foam cheek rest, white safety selector and mag. release button, forged aluminum A3 flat-top upper and Red X Arms lower receiver, M4 feed ramps, standard aluminum charging handle, carbine length gas tube, low profile micro gas block, M16 BCG, 15 in. slim KeyMod Air Lite free float handguard, includes soft tactical rifle case, Arctic White Cerakote finish, 6.9 lbs.

MSR $849 $725 $500 $435 $375 $335 $315 $295

RXA MID-LENGTH OCTAGONAL KEYMOD RIFLE – 5.56 NATO cal., 16 in. SOCOM contour chrome moly barrel, straight fluted Halestorm brake, 30 shot PMAG, skeleton trigger guard and pistol grip, red skeleton buttstock, adj. foam cheek rest, red safety selector and mag. release button, mid-length gas tube, low profile micro gas block, forged aluminum A3 flat-top upper and Red X Arms lower receiver, M4 feed ramps, M16 BCG, 16 1/2 in. slim KeyMod octagonal free float handguard, standard aluminum charging handle, octagonal slim line body with shark mouth design, includes soft tactical rifle case with mag. pouches, red anodized finish, 6.9 lbs.

MSR $849 $725 $500 $435 $375 $335 $315 $295

RXA MID-LENGTH SLIM KEYMOD RIFLE – 5.56 NATO cal., 16 in. chrome moly or stainless steel SOCOM barrel, stainless steel Gill brake or A2 flash hider, 30 shot PMAG, Magpul MOE carbine buttstock, Magpul grip and trigger guard, forged aluminum A3 flat-top upper and Red X Arms lower receiver, M4 feed ramps, standard aluminum charging handle, M16 BCG, mid-length gas tube, low profile micro gas block, 15 in. slim design KeyMod handguard, includes soft tactical rifle case with mag. pouches, hardcoat anodized black, FDE, or OD Green finish, 6.1-6.4 lbs.

MSR $825 $695 $500 $425 $375 $335 $315 $295

Add $10 for chrome moly barrel with A2 flash hider.

Add $30 for chrome moly barrel with A2 flash hider with FDE or OD Green finish.

RXA MID-LENGTH SLIM M-LOK RIFLE – 5.56 NATO cal., 16 in. chrome moly or stainless steel SOCOM barrel, stainless steel Gill brake or A2 flash hider, 30 shot PMAG, Magpul MOE carbine buttstock, Magpul grip and trigger guard, forged aluminum A3 flat-top upper and Red X Arms lower receiver, M4 feed ramps, standard aluminum charging handle, M16 BCG, mid-length gas tube, low profile micro gas block, 15 in. slim design M-LOK handguard, includes soft tactical rifle case with mag. pouches, hardcoat anodized black finish, 6.1-6.4 lbs.

MSR $825 $695 $500 $425 $375 $335 $315 $295

Add $10 for chrome moly barrel with A2 flash hider.

RXA MID-LENGTH HONEYCOMB SKELETON RIFLE – 5.56 NATO cal., 16 in. SOCOM contour button rifled barrel, 30 shot PMAG, skeleton buttstock, adj. foam cheek rest, honeycomb skeleton pistol grip, forged aluminum A3 flat-top upper and Red X Arms lower receiver, M4 feed ramps, ambi charging handle, mid-length gas tube, low profile micro gas block, aluminum 15 in. slim KeyMod honeycomb free float handguard, includes soft tactical rifle case with mag. pouches, red, blue, bronze, or gray anodized finish, 6.8 lbs.

MSR $799 $675 $500 $425 $375 $335 $315 $295

RXA TACTICAL BULL RIFLE – 5.56 NATO cal., 20 in. stainless steel bull barrel, target crowned muzzle, 30 shot PMAG, Mil-Spec A2 buttstock, A2 pistol grip, standard aluminum charging handle, hardcoat anodized black finish, M4 feed ramps, forged aluminum A3 flat-top upper and Red X Arms lower receiver, standard aluminum charging handle, rifle length gas tube, top rail gas block, free floating rifle length quad rail, includes soft tactical rifle case with mag. pouches, 10 lbs.

MSR $745 $645 $500 $415 $370 $325 $300 $275

RXA SS M4 MOE RIFLE – 5.56 NATO cal., carbine length gas system, 16 in. stainless steel M4 barrel with stainless steel A2 compensator, 30 shot PMAG, T6 forged aluminum lower and upper receiver, M4 feed ramps, free floating carbine length RXA aluminum quad rail handguard, top rail gas block, M16 bolt carrier group, Mil-Spec aluminum charging handle, Magpul MOE grip and trigger guard, Magpul MOE 6-pos. collapsible stock, black, FDE, or OD Green finish, includes two ladder rail covers and 38 in. soft tactical case with mag. pouches.

MSR $810 $695 $500 $425 $375 $335 $315 $295

X-TREME 16 TACTICAL SS – 5.56 NATO cal., GIO, 16 in. button rifled stainless steel heavy HBAR contour barrel, A2 birdcage muzzle brake, 30 shot Magpul mag., A3 aluminum flat-top upper and lower receiver, forward assist, dust cover, black hardcoat anodized finish, 6-position adj. M4 stock with sling hook, chrome-lined bolt carrier and staked gas key, chrome plated firing pin, aluminum charging handle, two-piece quad rail aluminum handguard, carbine length gas tube, optional sights and bipod. Disc. 2014.

   $615 $495 $415 $360 $325 $300 $275   *$725*

R 296 REMINGTON ARMS COMPANY, INC.

MSR	100%	98%	95%	90%	80%	70%	60%	Last MSR

REMINGTON ARMS COMPANY, INC.

Current manufacturer and trademark established in 1816, with factories currently located in Ilion, NY, Lonoke, AR, Mayfield, KY, and Huntsville, AL.

Founded by Eliphalet Remington II and originally located in Litchfield, Herkimer County, NY circa 1816-1828. Remington established a factory in Ilion, NY next to the Erie Canal in 1828, and together with his sons Philo, Samuel, and Eliphalet III pioneered many improvements in firearms manufacture. Corporate offices were moved to Madison, NC in 1996. DuPont owned a controlling interest in Remington from 1933-1993, when the company was sold to Clayton, Dubilier & Rice, a New York City based finance company. The Mayfield, KY plant opened in 1997. On May 31st, 2007, a controlling interest in the company was sold to Cerberus Capital. Currently, Remington employs 2,500 workers in the U.S., including 1,000 in its Ilion, NY plant alone. Recently, Remington has acquired Harrington & Richardson Firearms (H & R), and Marlin Firearms. The company has moved manufacturing to their Remington plant in Ilion, New York. Remington management has every intention of keeping all three product identities separate.

During 2013, Remington made significant improvements, including the expansion of its ammunition facility, growth of its firearms manufacturing capacity, secured some competitive military and law enforcement contracts, and introduced a series of new products including the Ultimate Defense Handgun Ammunition and Model 783 bolt action rifle.

In February of 2014, Remington announced a major expansion with new manufacturing to occur at the old Chrylser building in Huntsville, AL. The company has indicated that more than 2,000 new jobs will be created in the next 10 years.

RIFLES: SEMI-AUTO - CENTERFIRE

The models have been listed in numerical sequence for quick reference.

Remington also manufactures models R4, R5, R10, R11, and ACR for military and law enforcement only. These models are not covered in this text.

MODEL R-15 – .450 Bushmaster cal., GIO, 18 in. fluted barrel, 4 shot detachable mag., receiver length Picatinny rail, ergonomic pistol grip, fixed stock, Mossy Oak Break-up camo coverage, approx. 7 3/4 lbs. Mfg. 2010-2015.

	100%	98%	95%	90%	80%	70%	60%	Last MSR
	$1,250	$825	$575	$475	$425	$375	$350	$1,499

MODEL R-15 HUNTER – .30 Rem. AR cal., GIO, 22 in. fluted barrel, receiver length Picatinny rail, ergonomic pistol grip, 4 shot detachable mag., 100% Realtree AP HD camo coverage, approx. 7 3/4 lbs. Mfg. 2009-2015.

	100%	98%	95%	90%	80%	70%	60%	Last MSR
	$1,050	$650	$495	$450	$395	$350	$325	$1,229

MODEL R-15 VTR (VARMINT TARGET RIFLE) PREDATOR – .204 Ruger (disc. 2009) or .223 Rem. cal., GIO, 18 (carbine, .204 Ruger disc. 2009) or 22 in. free floating chrome moly fluted barrel, fixed or telestock (Carbine CS) with pistol grip, 5 shot fixed (new 2012, .223 Rem. cal. only) or detachable mag. (compatible with AR-15 style mags.), R-15 marked on magwell, single stage trigger, flat-top receiver with Picatinny rail, no sights, round vent. forearm, 100% Advantage Max-1 HD camo coverage except for barrel, includes lockable hard case, mfg. by Bushmaster in Windham, ME 2008-2011, and in Ilion, NY beginning 2011, 6 3/4 - 7 3/4 lbs. Mfg. 2008-2013.

	100%	98%	95%	90%	80%	70%	60%	Last MSR
	$1,125	$700	$525	$450	$400	$350	$325	$1,327

* ***Model R-15 VTR Stainless*** – .223 Rem. cal., 24 in. stainless triangular VTR barrel, OD Green upper and lower receiver, Advantage Max-1 HD camo finish on fixed stock, pistol grip, and tubed forearm, 7 3/4 lbs. Mfg. 2009-2017.

	100%	98%	95%	90%	80%	70%	60%	Last MSR
	$1,075	$675	$500	$450	$400	$350	$325	$1,299

* ***Model R-15 VTR Thumbhole*** – .223 Rem. cal., similar to VTR Stainless, except has 24 in. fluted barrel, OD Green camo thumbhole stock. Mfg. 2009-2010.

	100%	98%	95%	90%	80%	70%	60%	Last MSR
	$1,225	$825	$575	$475	$425	$375	$350	$1,470

* ***Model R-15 VTR Byron South Signature Edition*** – .223 Rem. cal., GIO, 18 in. barrel, Advantage Max-1 HD camo pistol grip stock. Mfg. mid-2008-2011.

	100%	98%	95%	90%	80%	70%	60%	Last MSR
	$1,525	$975	$750	$575	$495	$425	$375	$1,845

* ***Model R-15 VTR Predator Carbine*** – .223 Rem. cal., GIO, 18 (disc. 2013) or 22 in. free floating button rifled fluted barrel with recessed hunting crown, 5 shot mag., single stage trigger, receiver length Picatinny rail, ergonomic pistol grip, fixed or collapsible (CS, disc. 2013) synthetic stock, Advantage Max-1 HD camo coverage on stock, receiver, and forearm furniture, 6 3/4-7 3/4 lbs. Disc. 2017.

	100%	98%	95%	90%	80%	70%	60%	Last MSR
	$995	$625	$495	$450	$395	$350	$325	$1,199

* ***Model R-15 VTR Predator Magpul MOE*** – .223 Rem. cal., GIO, 16, 18 (disc. 2015), or 22 in. fluted barrel with AAC Blackout muzzle brake, wrap around rubber overmolding on Magpul grip, Magpul trigger guard, Magpul MOE fixed or adj. stock, 5 shot mag., two-stage match trigger, Mossy Oak Brush camo coverage on stock, receiver, and forearm furniture, 6 3/4-7 3/4 lbs. Disc. 2017.

	100%	98%	95%	90%	80%	70%	60%	Last MSR
	$995	$625	$495	$450	$395	$350	$325	$1,199

Add $100 for fixed stock.

REMINGTON ARMS COMPANY, INC., cont. 297 R

MSR	100%	98%	95%	90%	80%	70%	60%	Last MSR

MODEL R-25 – .243 Win., 7mm-08 Rem., or .308 Win. cal., GIO, 20 in. free floating fluted chrome moly barrel, single-stage trigger, ergonomic pistol grip fixed stock with 100% Mossy Oak Treestand camo coverage, front and rear sling swivels, 4 shot fixed (.308 Win. cal. only, new 2012) or detachable mag., R-25 marked on magwell, includes hard case, 7 3/4 lbs. Mfg. 2009-2014.

	$1,385	$895	$675	$525	$450	$385	$350	$1,697

MODEL R-25 GII – .243 Win. (disc. 2015), .260 Rem. (disc. 2015), .308 Win./7.62 NATO, or 7mm-08 Rem. (disc. 2015) cal., GIO, AR-15 style, 20 in. fluted stainless barrel, 4 shot mag., vented carbon fiber free float tube, forged anodized upper and lower receivers, improved extractor, steel feed ramp, dual ejectors, new Remington Hunter stock with SuperCell recoil pad, Hogue rubber pistol grip, single stage trigger, receiver length Picatinny rail, Mossy Oak Infinity camo finish, 7 5/8 lbs. Mfg. 2015-2017.

	$1,385	$895	$675	$525	$450	$385	$350	$1,697

RHINO RIFLES (RHINO ARMS)

Current rifle manufacturer located in St. Louis, MO. Previously located in Washington, MO.

PISTOLS: SEMI-AUTO

MM-47 – 7.62x39mm cal., GPO, 7 1/2 in. medium contour barrel with Rhino Flash Tamer muzzle, Rhino buffer tube, 7 in. Rhino Ultra Light Series carbon fiber handguard, ambi safety, curved trigger, SureGrip. Mfg. 2015-2016.

	$1,875	$1,650	$1,400	$1,200	$1,025	$875	$725	$2,200

RA-4R V2P – 5.56 NATO or .300 AAC Blackout cal., 7 (Ultra Light) or 9 in. light contour barrel with Rhino Flash Tamer muzzle, adj. gas block, 9 or 12 in. M-LOK handguard, beveled magwell, ambi safety, SIG SB15 pistol stabilizing brace, standard charging handle, Rhino curved trigger, SureGrip, black finish. New 2015.

MSR $1,900	$1,625	$1,425	$1,200	$1,075	$925	$795	$650	

Add $50 for .300 AAC Blackout cal.

RA-15 – 5.56 NATO or .300 AAC Blackout cal., 10 1/2 in. light contour barrel with Rhino Flash Tamer muzzle, 9 in. Rhino Ultra Light Series carbon fiber handguard, Rhino buffer tube, curved trigger, SureGrip, black finish. Mfg. 2015-2016.

	$1,450	$1,275	$1,125	$1,000	$850	$735	$595	$1,700

RIFLES: SEMI-AUTO

Rhino Rifles manufactures a complete line of AR-15 style carbines/rifles.

DOUBLE V SERIES II 5.56/.300 BLACKOUT – 5.56 NATO or .300 AAC Blackout (new 2014) cal., GIO, 16 (5.56 NATO cal. only) or 18 (.300 AAC Blackout cal. only) in. chrome moly fluted bull barrel with muzzle brake or non-fluted barrel, 10 or 30 shot Rhino Skin coated mag., Magpul CTR (standard), ACS, PRS, or UBR stock, Ergo grip, machined aluminum receiver, gas block with integrated Picatinny rail, free floating carbon fiber handguard, nickel boron coated precision bolt carrier group, 7.8 (5.56 NATO) or 8.1 lbs. Disc. 2017.

	$1,975	$1,150	$925	$650	$575	$495	$425	$2,405

Add $270 for .300 AAC Blackout cal.
Add $45 for Magpul ACS stock, $155 for Magpul PRS stock, or $165 for Magpul UBR stock.

DOUBLE V SERIES II 308 (RA-5D) – .308 Win. cal., GIO, 18 in. chrome moly heavy fluted bull with muzzle brake or non-fluted barrel, Rhino flash hider, 10 or 20 shot mag., aluminum upper and lower receiver, Magpul UBR, ACS, PRS, or CTR stock, Ergo grip, free float tube, rail gas block, anti-walk retaining pins, 8.8 lbs. Disc. 2017.

	$2,450	$1,595	$1,200	$700	$675	$575	$525	$3,015

Add $45 for Magpul ACS stock, $155 for Magpul PRS stock, or $165 for Magpul UBR stock.

MM-47 MSR – 7.62x39mm cal., GPO, 16 in. medium contour barrel with Rhino Flash Tamer muzzle, carbine length gas block, takes Magpul and surplus AK mags., 15 1/2 in. Rhino Ultra Light handguard, enhanced bolt catch, ambi safety, Mapgul CTR stock, SureGrip, Rhino curved trigger. New 2015.

MSR $2,200	$1,795	$1,050	$875	$625	$550	$475	$425	

RA-4B SERIES – .223 Rem. cal., GIO, 16 or 20 (RA-4BV only) in. chrome moly heavy barrel, A2 flash hider, 10 or 30 shot mag., aluminum lower receiver, flat-top upper, choice of A2 buttstock (RA-4B or RA-4BV) or M4 buttstock (RA-4BG or RA-4BT), anti-walk receiver retaining pins. Disc. 2010.

	$850	$550	$465	$395	$350	$325	$295	$978

Add $44 for RA-4BG model with rail gas block and M4 buttstock.
Add $119 for RA-4BV model with 20 in. barrel, free float tube, and A2 buttstock.
Add $248 for RA-BT model with four rail handguard and M4 buttstock.

RA-4P SERIES – .223 Rem. cal., GIO, 16 or 20 (RA-4PV) in. chrome moly steel barrel, A2 or Rhino flash hider, 10 or 30 shot mag., Magpul CTR or PRS buttstock, Ergo grip, flat-top upper, aluminum lower, anti-walk receiver retaining pins. Disc. 2010.

	$1,050	$650	$495	$450	$395	$350	$325	$1,243

Add $35 for RA-4PG model with four rail gas block, CAR handguard, and CTR buttstock.
Add $185 for RA-4PT model with four rail gas block, four rail handguard, and CTR buttstock.
Add $247 for RA-PV model with four rail gas block, free float tube, and PRS buttstock.

R 298 RHINO RIFLES (RHINO ARMS), cont.

MSR	100%	98%	95%	90%	80%	70%	60%	Last MSR

RA-4R 3GR – 5.56 NATO cal., 16 or 18 in. light contour barrel with 1 in. Rhino muzzle brake, Rhino straight trigger, ARFX stock with carbon fiber sleeve, SureGrip, ambi safety, Raptor extended ambi charging handle, 15 in. carbon fiber M-LOK handguard, extended bolt catch release, beveled magwell, billet aluminum receiver set, adj. gas block, black finish. New 2015.

MSR $2,400	$1,975	$1,150	$925	$650	$575	$495	$425	

RA-4R 50SCR (50 STATE COMPLIANT RIFLE) – 5.56 NATO or .300 AAC Blackout cal., 16 in. heavy barrel, target crown, 10 shot mag., adj. gas block, 13 1/2 in. T.R.I.M. handguard, standard charging handle, full mass bolt carrier, enhanced bolt catch, ambi safety, beveled magwell, Rhino curved trigger, New York stock, SureGrip, black finish. Mfg. 2015-2017.

	$1,795	$1,050	$875	$625	$550	$475	$425	*$2,200*

Add $50 for .300 AAC Blackout cal.

RA-4R ISR (INTEGRALLY SUPPRESSED RIFLE) – .300 AAC Blackout cal., 16.1 in. light contour barrel (7 1/2 in. barrel with titanium mono-core permanently attached brings overall length to 16.1 in.), integral suppressor, Rhino curved trigger, Magpul UBR stock, SureGrip, ambi safety, adj. gas block, billet aluminum receiver set, 12 in. M-LOK handguard, low mass bolt carrier with titanium firing pin, extended bolt catch release, beveled magwell, extended ambi charging handle, black finish. New 2015.

MSR $3,400	$2,775	$1,825	$1,350	$750	$650	$595	$525	

RA-4R PDW (PERSONAL DEFENSE WEAPON) – 5.56 NATO or .300 AAC Blackout cal., compact non-NFA variation rifle, 14 1/2 in. light contour barrel with Rhino Flash Tamer muzzle, adj. gas block, 9 or 12 in. M-LOK handguard, extended charging handle, enhanced bolt catch, ambi safety, beveled magwell, Rhino curved trigger, quick extend PDW stock, SureGrip, black finish. New 2015.

MSR $2,300	$1,875	$1,100	$895	$650	$575	$495	$425	

Add $50 for .300 AAC Blackout cal.

RA-4R V2 – 5.56 NATO or .300 AAC Blackout cal., 16 in. heavy fluted barrel with Rhino muzzle brake, adj. gas block, 13 1/2 in. T.R.I.M. aluminum handguard with modular attachment points, standard charging handle, Rhino curved trigger, Magpul CTR stock, SureGrip, ambi safety, beveled magwell. New 2015.

MSR $2,200	$1,795	$1,050	$875	$625	$550	$475	$425	

Add $50 for .300 AAC Blackout cal.

RA-5R DMR – .260 Rem. (disc. 2017), .308 Win. (disc. 2017), 6mm Creedmoor, or 6.5mm Creedmoor cal., 22 in. heavy fluted barrel with Rhino muzzle brake, two-stage trigger, Magpul PRS stock, SureGrip, ambi safety, rifle length gas block, 17 in. M-LOK handguard, Raptor charging handle, low mass bolt carrier with titanium firing pin, enhanced bolt catch. New 2015.

MSR $3,550	$2,875	$1,875	$1,375	$795	$675	$625	$575	

RA-5R HMR (HEAVY METAL RIFLE) – .308 Win. cal., 16 in. light contour barrel with 1 in. muzzle brake, Rhino straight trigger, ARFX stock with carbon fiber sleeve or Magpul PRS stock, SureGrip, ambi safety, billet aluminum receiver set, adj. gas block, 15 in. carbon fiber M-LOK handguard, Raptor charging handle, low mass bolt carrier with titanium firing pin, extended bolt catch. New 2015.

MSR $3,100	$2,550	$1,650	$1,250	$700	$625	$575	$525	

Add $140 for Magpul PRS stock.

RA-5R HTR (HEAVY TACTICAL RIFLE) – .308 Win. cal., 16 in. pinned medium contour barrel with 1 in. Rhino muzzle brake, Rhino curved trigger, Ace SOCOM stock, SureGrip, ambi safety, mid-length adj. gas block, billet aluminum receiver set, 12 1/2 in. carbon fiber KeyMod handguard, Raptor charging handle, full mass bolt carrier, enhanced bolt catch. New 2015.

MSR $3,100	$2,550	$1,650	$1,250	$700	$625	$575	$525	

RA-5R V2 – .308 Win. cal., 18 in. heavy fluted barrel with Rhino muzzle brake, Rhino curved trigger, Magpul ACS stock, SureGrip, ambi safety, mid-length gas block, billet aluminum receiver set, 13 1/2 in. Rhino Series KeyMod (disc.) or carbon fiber M-LOK handguard, standard charging handle, full mass bolt carrier, enhanced bolt catch, black finish. New 2015.

MSR $2,950	$2,375	$1,525	$1,150	$700	$625	$550	$475	

RA-15 3GR – .223 Wylde chamber, 16 or 18 in. Nordic stainless steel light contour barrel, curved or straight trigger, Magpul CTR or Ace ARFX stock with carbon fiber sleeve, Ergo SureGrip, forged aluminum upper and lower receiver, mid/rifle length adj. gas block, 15 or 17 in. Rhino Ultra Light Series Gen II carbon fiber handguard, standard or extended bolt catch, standard charging handle, 6 lbs. New 2018.

MSR $1,600	$1,315	$850	$625	$500	$435	$375	$350	

Add $50 for 18 in. barrel.

Add $50 for Ace ARFX stock with carbon fiber sleeve.

RHINO RIFLES (RHINO ARMS), cont. 299 R

MSR	100%	98%	95%	90%	80%	70%	60%	Last MSR

RA-15 MSR – 5.56 NATO cal., 16 in. light contour barrel with Rhino Flash Tamer muzzle, Rhino curved trigger, Magpul CTR stock, Ergo SureGrip, carbine length adj. gas block, forged aluminum receiver set, 13 1/2 in. Rhino Ultra-Light carbon fiber handguard, standard charging handle. New 2015.

| MSR $1,700 | $1,385 | $895 | $675 | $525 | $450 | $385 | $350 | |

RISE ARMAMENT

Current AR-15 style carbine/rifle manufacturer located in Broken Arrow, OK.

RIFLES: SEMI-AUTO

C SERIES RA-313C – .223 Wylde chamber, 18 in. stainless steel barrel, RA-701 compensator, includes one mag., RA-535 advanced performance trigger, MBUS, Magpul PRS adj. stock, 15 in. slimline billet aluminum handguard with Picatinny rail system, Striker upper and lower receivers, includes Rise Armament Patriot rifle case, black, black/silver, black/red, red/black, or red/silver finish, 8 lbs. 4 oz. Disc. 2017.

| | $1,650 | $1,000 | $795 | $595 | $495 | $425 | $395 | *$1,983* |

C SERIES RA-315C – .223 Wylde chamber, 16 in. stainless steel fluted barrel, RA-701 compensator, includes one mag., RA-535 advanced performance trigger, MBUS, Magpul PRS adj. stock, 15 in. slimline billet aluminum M-LOK handguard, Ripper billet upper and lower receivers, black, black/silver, black/red, red/black, or red/silver finish, 6 lbs. 12 oz.

| MSR $1,799 | $1,475 | $950 | $725 | $550 | $475 | $395 | $350 | |

C SERIES RA-338 – .223 Wylde chamber, 18 in. stainless steel barrel, RA-701 compensator, includes one mag., RA-535 advanced performance trigger, MBUS, Magpul PRS adj. stock, 15 in. slimline billet aluminum handguard with Picatinny rail system, Ripper upper and lower receivers, includes Rise Armament Patriot rifle case, black, black/silver, black/red, red/black, or red/silver finish, 8 lbs. 4 oz. Disc. 2017.

| | $1,675 | $1,000 | $825 | $625 | $550 | $475 | $425 | *$2,055* |

L SERIES RA-356LR – .223 Wylde chamber, 20 in. stainless steel barrel, RA-701 compensator, includes one mag., RA-535 advanced performance trigger, MBUS, Magpul PRS adj. stock, 13 1/2 in. slimline billet aluminum handguard with Picatinny rail system, Ripper billet upper and lower receivers, includes Rise Armament Patriot rifle case, black, black/silver, foliage green, or FDE finish, 9 lbs. Disc. 2017.

| | $1,650 | $1,000 | $795 | $595 | $495 | $425 | $395 | *$1,993* |

LR SERIES RA-331LR – .223 Wylde chamber, 20 in. stainless steel barrel, RA-701 compensator, includes one mag., RA-535 advanced performance trigger, MBUS, Magpul PRS adj. stock, 13 1/2 in. slimline billet aluminum handguard with Picatinny rail system, Striker billet upper and lower receivers, includes Rise Armament Patriot rifle case, black, black/silver, foliage green, or FDE finish, 9 lbs.

| MSR $1,925 | $1,600 | $1,000 | $775 | $575 | $495 | $425 | $395 | |

LR SERIES 1121XR PRECISION – .308 Win. cal., 20 in. stainless steel barrel, stainless steel RA-701 compensator, RA-53 advanced performance trigger, aluminum billet receivers, 15 in. M-LOK compatible billet aluminum handguard, Picatinny rail upper, Magpul PRS adj. stock, ambidextrous safety selector, black, foliage green, or FDE Cerakote finish, includes hard case and two mags., 9 lbs. 8 oz. New 2018.

| MSR $2,449 | $1,975 | $1,150 | $925 | $650 | $575 | $495 | $425 | |

S SERIES RA-302H – .223 Wylde chamber or .300 AAC Blackout cal., 20 in. stainless steel barrel with black finish, includes one mag., RA-140 super sporting trigger, fixed Magpul MOE rifle stock, 13 1/2 in. slimline billet aluminum handguard with Picatinny rail system, Striker billet upper and lower receivers, black, foliage green, or FDE finish, 8 lbs. 2 oz.

| MSR $1,449 | $1,195 | $795 | $550 | $465 | $415 | $375 | $350 | |

S SERIES RA-303H – .223 Wylde chamber or .300 AAC Blackout cal., 20 in. stainless steel barrel with black finish, includes one mag., RA-140 super sporting trigger, fixed Magpul MOE rifle stock, 13 1/2 in. slimline billet aluminum handguard with Picatinny rail system, Ripper billet upper and lower receivers, black, foliage green, or FDE finish, 8 lbs. 2 oz.

| MSR $1,449 | $1,195 | $795 | $550 | $465 | $415 | $375 | $350 | |

S SERIES RA-302S – .223 Wylde chamber or .300 AAC Blackout cal., 16 in. stainless steel fluted barrel, RA-701 compensator, RA-140 super sporting trigger, Magpul CTR adj. stock, 13 1/2 in. slimline billet aluminum handguard with Picatinny rail system, Striker billet upper and lower receivers, black, foliage green, or FDE finish, 7 lbs. 4 oz. Disc. 2017.

| | $1,195 | $795 | $550 | $465 | $415 | $375 | $350 | *$1,499* |

S SERIES RA-303S – .223 Wylde chamber or .300 AAC Blackout cal., 16 in. stainless steel fluted barrel, RA-701 compensator, includes one mag., RA-140 super sporting trigger, Magpul CTR adj. stock, 13 1/2 in. slimline billet aluminum handguard with Picatinny rail system, Ripper billet upper and lower receivers, black, foliage green, or FDE finish, 7 lbs. 4 oz.

| MSR $1,449 | $1,195 | $795 | $550 | $465 | $415 | $375 | $350 | |

R 300 RISE ARMAMENT, cont.

MSR	100%	98%	95%	90%	80%	70%	60%	Last MSR

T SERIES RA-325T – .223 Wylde chamber or .300 AAC Blackout cal., 16 in. stainless steel fluted barrel, RA-701 compensator, includes one mag., RA-535 advanced performance trigger, MBUS, Magpul UBR adj. stock, 13 1/2 in. slimline billet aluminum handguard with Picatinny rail system, Striker billet upper and lower receivers, includes Rise Armament Patriot rifle case, black, black/red, black/silver, foliage green, or FDE finish, 8 lbs. 2 oz.

| MSR $1,799 | $1,475 | $950 | $725 | $550 | $475 | $395 | $350 | |

T SERIES RA-350T – .223 Wylde chamber or .300 AAC Blackout cal., 16 in. stainless steel fluted barrel, RA-701 compensator, includes one mag., RA-535 advanced performance trigger, MBUS, Magpul UBR adj. stock, 13 1/2 in. slimline billet aluminum handguard with Picatinny rail system, Ripper billet upper and lower receivers, includes Rise Armament Patriot rifle case, black, black/red, black/silver, foliage green, or FDE finish, 8 lbs. 2 oz.

| MSR $1,869 | $1,575 | $995 | $775 | $575 | $495 | $425 | $395 | |

RIVERMAN GUN WORKS

Current rifle manufacturer located in Dalton Gardens, ID. Previously located in Coeur d'Alene, ID.

RIFLES: SEMI-AUTO

RM-15 – 7.62 NATO (disc. 2017), 5.56 NATO, .300 AAC Blackout, or 6.5 Grendel cal., 16 or 20 (new 2018) in. stainless barrel, recessed mag. release, winter trigger guard, billet cut upper and lower receiver, Serpent Series (disc. 2017) or O.A.F. Series KeyMod rail system, hard anodized, Gun Kote (disc. 2017), Hydrographic Dip (disc. 2017), or Cerakote finish, 6.6. lbs.

| MSR $1,600 | $1,315 | $850 | $625 | $500 | $435 | $375 | $350 | |

RM-308 – 7.62 NATO or 6.5mm Creedmoor (new 2018) cal., 18 (disc.) or 20 in. stainless barrel, recessed mag. release, winter trigger guard, Minimalist (disc.) or Bravo stock, Hogue grip, billet cut upper and lower receiver, Serpent Series (disc.) or O.A.F. Series KeyMod or M-LOK rail system, hard anodized, Gun Kote (disc. 2017), Hydrographic Dip (disc. 2017), or Cerakote finish, 8 lbs.

| MSR $2,299 | $1,795 | $1,050 | $875 | $625 | $550 | $475 | $425 | |

ROCK ISLAND ARMORY (CURRENT MFG.)

Current trademark manufactured by Arms Corp. of the Philippines. Currently imported by Armscor Precision International, located in Pahrump, NV.

SHOTGUNS

VR60 SHOTGUN STANDARD – 12 ga., 2 3/4 or 3 in. chamber, semi-auto, AR-15 style, gas operated, 20 in. barrel with F/M/IC choke tubes, 5 shot, bead front sights, enlarged polymer handguard, aluminum alloy upper receiver, removable A2 carry handle, integral Picatinny rail, manual safety, polymer pistol grip stock, red chrome or gray chrome finish. New 2017.

| MSR $489 | $440 | $395 | $360 | $330 | $295 | $265 | $240 | |

Add $10 for gray chrome finish.

VR60 PLUS 1 – 12 ga., 2 3/4 or 3 in. chamber, semi-auto AR-15 style, gas operated, 20 in. barrel with three choke tubes, 5 shot, bead front sight, polymer stock, raised cheekpiece, rubber buttpad, enlarged polymer handguard, aluminum alloy upper receiver, removable A2 carry handle, integral Picatinny rail, black, brown or red finish. New 2017.

| MSR $544 | $460 | $420 | $375 | $335 | $300 | $275 | $250 | |

Add $20 for brown or red finish.

ROCK RIVER ARMS, INC.

Current handgun and rifle manufacturer established in 1996 and located in Colona, IL beginning 2004. Previously located in Cleveland, IL until 2003. Dealer and consumer direct sales.

PISTOLS: SEMI-AUTO

Rock River Arms made a variety of high quality M-1911 based semi-autos through 2011. They specialized in manufacturing their own National Match frames and slides. Previous models included: the Standard Match (disc. 2003, last MSR was $1,150), Ultimate Match Achiever (disc. 2003, last MSR was $2,255), Matchmaster Steel (disc. 2001, last MSR was $2,355), Elite Commando (disc. 2005, last MSR was $1,725), Hi-Cap Basic Limited (disc. 2003, last MSR was $1,895), and the Doug Koenig Signature Series (disc. 2003, last MSR was $5,000, .38 Super cal.). Rock River Arms still offers parts, and reintroduced a 1911 model in 2013. In 2015, Rock River Arms reintroduced several of their renowned steel frame 1911-A1 models.

Add $200 for 1911-A1 Cerakote finish options in Barrett Bronze, Graphite Black, Gunmetal Gray, SOCOM Blue, Magpul Flat Dark Earth, Burnt Bronze (disc.), or Tan (disc.).

LAR-15 A4 – .223 Rem. cal., GPO, 7 or 10 1/2 in. chrome moly barrel with A2 flash hider, single stage trigger, forged LAR-15 lower and A4 upper receivers, Hogue rubber pistol grip, pistol length handguard and TRO free float rail (7 in. barrel only) or R-4 handguard (10 1/2 in. barrel only), matte black finish, 5.2 lbs.

| MSR $1,055 | $885 | $785 | $685 | $600 | $535 | $465 | $415 | |

Add $120 for 7 in. barrel or for gas block sight base.

ROCK RIVER ARMS, INC., cont. 301 R

MSR	100%	98%	95%	90%	80%	70%	60%	Last MSR

LAR-9 A4 – 9mm Para. cal., 7 or 10 1/2 (chrome-lined) in. chrome moly barrel with A2 flash hider, single stage trigger, TRO free float rail and pistol length handguard (7 in. barrel) or R4 handguard (10 1/2 in. barrel), gas block sight base (10 1/2 in. only), RRA LAR-9 lower with integral magwell and forged A4 upper, Hogue rubber grip, includes one mag., 4.8 lbs.

	100%	98%	95%	90%	80%	70%	60%	Last MSR
MSR $1,205	$1,025	$925	$800	$685	$595	$515	$445	

Add $115 for 7 in. barrel.

LAR-40 – .40 S&W cal., GPO, 7 or 10 1/2 in. barrel, forged lower receiver with integral magwell, A2 or A4 upper, single stage trigger, Hogue rubber pistol grip, approx. 5 lbs. Mfg. 2010-2011.

	100%	98%	95%	90%	80%	70%	60%	Last MSR
	$925	$850	$725	$625	$550	$475	$425	*$1,120*

Add $45 for 7 in. barrel and free float tube handguard.

Add $10-$15 for gas block sight base.

PDS PISTOL (PISTON DRIVEN SYSTEM) – .223 Rem. or .300 AAC Blackout (new 2015) cal., GPO, 8 or 9 (new 2013) in. chrome moly barrel, A2 flash hider, single (disc. 2012) or two-stage (new 2013) trigger, ribbed forend, Hogue rubber pistol grip, full-length upper and partial lower Picatinny rails, injection molded ribbed handguard, folding ambidextrous non-reciprocating charging handles, two-position regulator, approx. 5 lbs. New 2010.

	100%	98%	95%	90%	80%	70%	60%
MSR $1,245	$1,050	$950	$815	$715	$625	$535	$450

Add $65 for .300 AAC Blackout cal.

Add $150 for aluminum tri-rail handguard.

RIFLES/CARBINES: SEMI-AUTO

Rock River Arms makes a variety of AR-15 style rifles/carbines in .223 Rem. cal. Previous models included the CAR UTE (disc. 2004, last MSR was $850), Tactical Carbine A2, M4 Entry (disc. 2003, last MSR was $875), and NM A2-DCM Legal (disc. 2005, last MSR was $1,265).

Beginning 2006, Rock River Arms released a series of rifles in 9mm Para. cal. Also during 2006, the company released a series of rifles in .308 Win. cal. A wide variety of options are available for each rifle. Base model assumes black furniture.

LAR-6.8 CAR A2/A4 – 6.8 SPC cal., GIO, forged A2 (disc. 2012) or A4 upper receiver, 16 in. Wilson chrome moly barrel, A2 flash hider, two-stage match trigger, A2 pistol grip, 6-pos. tactical CAR stock, choice of CAR length or mid-length handguard, 7 1/2 lbs.

	100%	98%	95%	90%	80%	70%	60%
MSR $1,055	$895	$575	$475	$395	$350	$325	$300

Add $50 for Operator stock.

LAR-6.8 COYOTE CARBINE – 6.8 SPC cal., GIO, forged A4 upper receiver, 16 in. Wilson chrome moly HBAR barrel, Smith Vortex flash hider, Weaver style light varmint gas block with sight rail, two-stage match trigger, winter trigger guard, Hogue rubber pistol grip, Hogue overmolded free float tube handguard, A2 stock, 7 lbs.

	100%	98%	95%	90%	80%	70%	60%
MSR $1,310	$1,100	$675	$525	$450	$400	$350	$325

LAR-6.8 X-1 RIFLE – 6.8 SPC II cal., GIO, 18 in. fluted stainless steel HBAR barrel, RRA Beast or Hunter muzzle brake, low profile gas block, forged lower and A4 upper receiver, two-stage trigger, winter trigger guard, RRA TRO-XL extended length free float rail, RRA Operator A2 or Operator CAR stock, Hogue rubber pistol grip, Black or Tan finish, includes one 9 in. XL accessory rail and two 2 in. short accessory rails for handguard, 7.9 lbs. New 2014.

	100%	98%	95%	90%	80%	70%	60%
MSR $1,595	$1,315	$850	$625	$500	$435	$375	$350

Add $10 for Operator A2 stock.

Add $50 for RRA Hunter muzzle brake and tan finish.

LAR-8 ELITE OPERATOR – .308 Win. cal., GIO, 16 in. barrel with Smith Vortex flash hider, two-stage match trigger, flip front sight gas block assembly, Operator CAR stock, Hogue rubber grip, advanced half quad free float mid-length handguard with three ladder rail covers, forged A4 upper receiver, forged LAR-8 lower receiver, black finish, 9.1 lbs. New 2010.

	100%	98%	95%	90%	80%	70%	60%
MSR $1,740	$1,425	$925	$700	$550	$475	$395	$350

LAR-8 MID LENGTH A2/A4 – .308 Win. cal., GIO, 16 in. barrel with A2 flash hider, two-stage trigger, gas block with receiver height sight base, 6-pos. tactical CAR stock, Hogue rubber grip, forged A2 (disc. 2012) or A4 upper receiver and forged LAR-8 lower receiver, mid-length handguard, black finish, 8.1 lbs. New 2010.

	100%	98%	95%	90%	80%	70%	60%
MSR $1,335	$1,125	$700	$525	$450	$400	$350	$325

LAR-8M PREDATOR HP – .243 Win. (disc.) or 6.5mm Creedmoor cal., GIO, 20 or 24 (new 2018) in. fluted stainless steel barrel, with or without muzzle brake, two-stage trigger, winter trigger guard, Operator A2 or CAR stock, Hogue rubber grip, forged LAR-8M lower and A4 upper receiver, low profile gas block, RRA LAR-8 DLX free float handguard with three short accessory rails, black finish, 9.2 lbs. New 2017.

	100%	98%	95%	90%	80%	70%	60%
MSR $1,950	$1,600	$1,000	$775	$575	$495	$425	$395

Add $20 for 24 in. barrel (new 2018).

Add $50 for Operator CAR stock and muzzle brake.

R 302 ROCK RIVER ARMS, INC., cont.

MSR	100%	98%	95%	90%	80%	70%	60%	Last MSR

LAR-8 PREDATOR HP – .308 Win./7.62 NATO cal., GIO, 20 in. bead blasted lightweight stainless steel fluted barrel, with or w/o muzzle brake, two-stage trigger, winter trigger guard, Operator A2 or CAR stock, Hogue rubber pistol grip, forged LAR-8 lower and A4 upper receiver, low profile gas block, free float tube handguard (disc.) or LAR-8 DLX free float rifle length handguard with three short accessory rails (new 2017), black finish, 9.2-9.5 lbs. New 2010.

| MSR $1,950 | $1,600 | $1,000 | $775 | $575 | $495 | $425 | $395 | |

Add $50 for Operator CAR stock and muzzle brake.

LAR-8 PREDATOR HP MID LENGTH – .308 Win./7.62 NATO cal., 16 in. fluted stainless steel barrel, with or w/o muzzle brake, two-stage trigger, winter trigger guard, Operator A2 or CAR stock, Hogue rubber grip, low profile gas block, forged LAR-8 lower and A4 upper receiver, LAR-8 DLX free float rail, rifle length handguard with three short accessory rails, black finish, 8.9-9.2 lbs. New 2017.

| MSR $1,900 | $1,575 | $995 | $775 | $575 | $495 | $425 | $395 | |

Add $50 for Operator CAR stock and muzzle brake.

LAR-8 STANDARD A2/A4 – .308 Win./7.62 NATO cal., GIO, 20 in. chrome moly barrel with A2 flash hider, two-stage trigger, gas block sight base, A2 buttstock, Hogue rubber pistol grip, forged LAR-8 lower and A2 (disc. 2012) or A4 upper receiver, A2 handguard, 9 lbs. New 2010.

| MSR $1,370 | $1,135 | $725 | $525 | $465 | $415 | $375 | $350 | |

LAR-8 STANDARD OPERATOR – .308 Win./7.62 NATO cal., GIO, 16 (disc.) or 20 in. barrel, Smith Vortex flash hider, two-stage trigger, flip front sight gas block assembly, Operator A2 stock, Hogue rubber grip, forged LAR-8 lower and forged A4 upper receiver, rifle length advanced half quad free float handguard with three ladder rail covers, black finish, 10.2 lbs. New 2010.

| MSR $1,790 | $1,475 | $950 | $725 | $550 | $475 | $395 | $350 | |

LAR-8 VARMINT A4 – .308 Win./7.62 NATO cal., GIO, 20 or 26 in. cryo treated stainless steel bull barrel, two-stage trigger, Winter trigger guard, A2 buttstock, Hogue rubber pistol grip, forged A4 upper receiver with forward assist and port door, forged LAR-8 lower, varmint gas block with sight rail (disc.) or low profile gas block, rifle length LAR-8 free float tube handguard with one standard and two short TRO accessory rails, black finish, 10.4-11.6 lbs. New 2011.

| MSR $1,655 | $1,385 | $895 | $675 | $525 | $450 | $385 | $350 | |

Add $5 for 26 in. barrel.

LAR-8 X-1 RIFLE – .308 Win./7.62 NATO cal., GIO, 18 in. fluted stainless steel barrel, RRA Beast or Hunter muzzle brake, two-stage trigger, Winter trigger guard, RRA Operator A2 or Operator CAR stock, black or tan Hogue rubber pistol grip, RRA custom low profile gas block, rifle length free float rail with one 8 1/2 in. accessory rail and two 2 in. accessory rails, forged LAR-8 lower and A4 upper with forward assist and port door, black or tan finish, 9 1/2 lbs. New 2014.

| MSR $1,845 | $1,525 | $975 | $750 | $575 | $495 | $425 | $375 | |

Add $50 for RRA Hunter muzzle brake and tan finish.

LAR-9 CAR A2/A4 – 9mm Para. cal., GIO, 16 in. chrome moly heavy barrel, A1 (disc.) or A2 flash hider, single stage trigger, gas block with sight base, six-position tactical CAR stock, A2 (disc.) or Hogue rubber grip, forged LAR-9 lower with integral magwell, forged A2 (disc. 2012) or A4 upper receiver, R4 handguard, black finish, 7.1 lbs.

| MSR $1,180 | $995 | $625 | $495 | $450 | $395 | $350 | $325 | |

Add $50 for Operator stock.

LAR-9 R9 COMPETITION RIFLE – 9mm Para. cal., GIO, 16 in. stainless steel, chain link fluted and cryogenically treated barrel w/mini muzzle brake, two-stage match trigger, Operator CAR stock, Hogue rubber pistol grip, RRA Star safety, forged LAR9 lower with integral magwell and forged A4 upper receiver, mid-length handguard w/upper Picatinny rail (disc. 2017) or lightweight free float M-LOK rail (new 2018), matte black finish, 7.4 lbs. New 2017.

| MSR $1,475 | $1,225 | $825 | $575 | $475 | $425 | $375 | $350 | |

LAR-9 MID-LENGTH A4 – 9mm Para. cal., GIO, 16 in. chrome moly heavy barrel, A2 flash hider, single stage trigger, gas block sight base, 6-pos. tactical CAR stock, Hogue rubber pistol grip, mid-length handguard, forged A4 upper receiver, forged LAR9 lower with integral magwell, black finish, 7.1 lbs.

| MSR $1,180 | $995 | $625 | $495 | $450 | $395 | $350 | $325 | |

Add $50 for Operator stock.

LAR-10 MID-LENGTH A2/A4 – .308 Win. cal., GIO, forged A2 or A4 upper receiver with forward assist and ejection port door, 16 in. Wilson chrome moly barrel, A2 flash hider, A2 front sight or A4 gas block with sight base, two-stage match trigger, mid-length handguard, Hogue rubber pistol grip, 6-position tactical CAR stock, approx. 8 lbs. Disc. 2009.

| | $915 | $575 | $475 | $415 | $350 | $325 | $300 | *$1,100* |

Add $50 for A2 sights.

LAR-10 STANDARD A2/A4 – .308 Win. cal., GIO, forged A2 or A4 upper receiver, with forward assist and ejection port door, 20 in. Wilson chrome moly barrel, A2 flash hider, A2 front sight or A4 gas block sight base, two-stage match trigger, A2 handguard, Hogue rubber pistol grip, A2 buttstock, 9.3 lbs. Disc. 2009.

| | $915 | $575 | $475 | $415 | $350 | $325 | $300 | *$1,100* |

Add $45 for A2 sights.

ROCK RIVER ARMS, INC., cont. 303 R

MSR	100%	98%	95%	90%	80%	70%	60%	Last MSR

LAR-10 VARMINT A4 – .308 Win. cal., GIO, forged A4 upper reciever with forward assist and port door, 26 in. Wilson stainless steel bull barrel, Weaver type sight base gas block, two-stage match trigger, knurled and fluted free floating aluminum tube handguard, Hogue pistol grip, A2 buttstock, 11.6 lbs. Disc. 2010.

	$1,125	$700	$525	$450	$400	$350	$325	$1,350

LAR-15 9.11 COMMEMORATIVE – .5.56 NATO or .223 Rem. cal., GIO, 16 in. lightweight chrome moly barrel, forged A4 upper receiver, low profile gas block, chromed bolt carrier group, RRA tactical muzzle brake, two-stage chrome trigger group, winter trigger guard, Star safety, overmolded pistol grip, Hogue free float tube handguard, non-collapsible or 6-position tactical CAR stock, flat black finish with American flag, and "9*11 Tenth Year Commemoration" engraved on receiver. Limited mfg. mid-2011.

	$995	$850	$725	N/A	N/A	N/A	N/A	$1,011

Add $25 for non-collapsible stock, pinned/welded tactical muzzle brake, and 10 shot mag.

LAR-15 ATH (ADVANCED TACTICAL HUNTER) CARBINE – .223 Wylde chambered for 5.56mm and .223 Rem. cal., GIO, 18 in. heavy match cryo treated stainless steel barrel, muzzle brake, forged A4 upper and LAR-15 lower receiver, two-stage trigger, winter trigger guard, fixed (new 2018) or Operator CAR stock, Ergo SureGrip pistol grip, Star safety, forged A4 upper and LAR-15 lower receiver, low profile gas block, half-quad free float handguard with three ladder rail covers, matte black finish, 7.6 lbs. New 2011.

MSR $1,370	$1,135	$725	$525	$465	$415	$375	$350	

Subtract $25 for fixed stock (new 2018).

LAR -15 BTB CARBINE – 5.56 NATO cal., 16 in. chrome moly HBAR barrel, A2 flash hider, SST, NSP flip-up front and rear sights, NSP2 6-pos. CAR stock, NSP overmolded pistol grip, low profile gas block, forged A4 upper receiver and forged LAR-15 lower receiver, NSP CAR length drop-in rail, includes carrying case and two mags., black or tan finish, 7 lbs. New 2017.

MSR $825	$695	$500	$425	$375	$335	$315	$295	

LAR-15 CAR A2 – 5.56 NATO chambered for 5.56mm and .223 Rem. cal., GIO, 16 in. Wilson chrome moly barrel (disc.) or 16 in. chrome moly HBAR (new 2018), A2 flash hider, two-stage match trigger, A2 front sight base (new 2018), fixed (disc. 2012) or 6-position tactical CAR stock, overmolded A2 pistol grip, forged A2 upper receiver, CAR length handguard, 7 1/2 lbs. Disc. 2012, reintroduced 2018.

MSR $1,035	$875	$550	$465	$395	$350	$325	$300	

Last MSR in 2012 was $960.

LAR-15 CAR A4 – 5.56 NATO chambered for 5.56mm and .223 Rem. cal., 16 in. chrome moly HBAR barrel, A2 flash hider, two-stage trigger, A2 front sight base or gas block with receiver height sight base, 6-pos. tactical CAR stock, overmolded A2 grip, forged A4 upper and forged LAR-15 lower receiver, mid-length CAR handguard, black finish, 7.5 lbs.

MSR $1,035	$875	$550	$465	$395	$350	$325	$300	

Add $145 for left-hand (LAR-15LH Lef-T CAR A4, new 2013).

LAR-15 COYOTE CARBINE – 5.56 NATO chambered for 5.56mm and .223 Rem. cal., GIO, 16 in. chrome moly HBAR barrel with Smith Vortex flash hider, two-stage trigger, winter trigger guard, ACE ARFX skeleton (disc. 2013) or Operator CAR (new 2014) stock, Hogue rubber pistol grip, Star safety, forged LAR-15 lower and A4 upper receiver, Weaver style light varmint gas block with sight rail (disc. 2013) or low profile gas block (new 2014), Hogue overmolded free float tube handguard (disc. 2013) or RRA deluxe extended free float rail (new 2014), 7.2 lbs.

MSR $1,300	$1,075	$675	$500	$450	$400	$350	$325	

Add $145 for left-hand (LAR-15LH, Lef-T, new 2013).

LAR-15 COYOTE RIFLE – .223 Wylde chambered for 5.56mm and .223 Rem. cal., GIO, 20 in. chrome moly HBAR barrel with Smith Vortex flash hider, two-stage match trigger, winter trigger guard, ACE ARFX skeleton (disc. 2013) or RRA Operator A2 (new 2014) stock, Hogue rubber pistol grip, Star safety, forged A4 upper receiver and LAR-15 lower receiver, Weaver style light varmint gas block with sight rail (disc. 2013) or low profile gas block (new 2014), Hogue overmolded free float tube handguard (disc. 2013) or RRA deluxe extended free float rail with three short accessory rails (new 2014), black finish, 8.4 lbs.

MSR $1,355	$1,135	$725	$525	$465	$415	$375	$350	

Add $200 for left-hand (LAR-15LH, Lef-T, new 2013).

LAR-15 DELTA CAR – .223 Rem. cal., GIO, forged upper and lower, 16 in. chrome moly HBAR barrel, A2 flash hider, low profile gas block, two-stage trigger, winter trigger guard, Delta CAR stock, Ergo SureGrip, Delta quad rail CAR two-piece drop-in handguard or mid-length handguard, 7-7.3 lbs. New 2013.

MSR $1,085	$915	$575	$475	$415	$350	$325	$300	

Add $15 for mid-length handguard (Delta Car Mid-Length).

LAR-15 ELITE CAR A4 – 5.56 NATO chambered for 5.56mm and .223 cal., GIO, 16 in. chrome moly barrel with A2 flash hider, two-stage trigger, Star safety, forged receivers, mid-length handguard, 6-pos. tactical CAR stock, Hogue rubber pistol grip, slide mount sling swivel, 7.7 lbs.

MSR $1,065	$895	$575	$475	$395	$350	$325	$300	

Add $40 for chrome-lined barrel.

R 304 ROCK RIVER ARMS, INC., cont.

MSR	100%	98%	95%	90%	80%	70%	60%	Last MSR

LAR-15 ELITE CAR UTE2 – .223 Rem. cal., GIO, 16 in. Wilson chrome moly barrel, A2 flash hider, two-stage match trigger, mid-length handguard, forged Universal Tactical Entry 2 upper receiver, 6-pos. tactical CAR stock, Hogue rubber pistol grip, 7.7 lbs. Disc. 2012.

| | $895 | $575 | $475 | $395 | $350 | $325 | $300 | $1,060 |

LAR-15 ELITE COMP – 5.56 NATO chambered for 5.56mm and .223 Rem. cal., GIO, 16 in. chrome-lined barrel with tactical muzzle brake, forged receivers, flip front sight gas block assembly, two-stage trigger, winter trigger guard, Star safety, A.R.M.S. low profile flip-up rear sight, Magpul CTR (disc.) or Operator CAR stock, Ergo Suregrip pistol grip, free floating half-round, half-quad handguard, 8.4 lbs. Mfg. 2008-2017.

| | $1,275 | $850 | $600 | $495 | $425 | $375 | $350 | $1,515 |

LAR-15 ENTRY TACTICAL – .223 Rem. cal., GIO, 16 in. chrome moly R-4 heavy barrel with A2 flash hider, two-stage trigger, forged lower and A4 upper receiver, Star safety, Hogue rubber pistol grip, R-4 handguard with double heat shields, 6-position tactical CAR stock, 7 1/2 lbs.

| MSR $1,065 | $895 | $575 | $475 | $395 | $350 | $325 | $300 | |

Add $40 for chrome-lined barrel.

LAR-15 FRED EICHLER SERIES PREDATOR – .223 Wylde chambered for 5.56mm and .223 Rem. cal., GIO, 16 in. bead blasted stainless steel cryogenically treated barrel, custom muzzle brake, 20 shot mag., low profile hidden gas block, chrome RRA National Match two-stage trigger with parkerized finish on trigger shoe, winter trigger guard, RRA Fred Eichler Series free floating handguard with full-length Picatinny top rail and 2 1/2 in. rails, tan Hogue rubber grips, Operator A2 or CAR stock, forged A4 upper flat-top, two-tone black/tan finish, includes hard case, 7.6 lbs. New 2012.

| MSR $1,510 | $1,275 | $850 | $600 | $495 | $425 | $375 | $350 | |

Add $10 for Operator A2 stock.

LAR-15 FRED EICHLER SERIES PREDATOR 2 – .223 Wylde chambered for 5.56mm and .223 Rem. cal., GIO, 16 in. fluted stainless steel barrel with directionally tuned and ported muzzle brake, two-stage chrome trigger, winter trigger guard, Operator A2 or CAR buttstock, Hogue rubber pistol grip, Star safety, forged A4 upper, low profile gas block, Fred Eichler Series free float extended length handguard with two rail covers and full top Picatinny rail, receivers and handguard finished in Cerakote Tan, Gunmetal Gray, or ROCKote Ghost Camo (new 2017), 7.6 lbs. New 2015.

| MSR $1,750 | $1,425 | $925 | $700 | $550 | $475 | $395 | $350 | |

Add $10 for Operator A2 stock.
Add $475 for Ghost camo.

LAR-15 FRED EICHLER SERIES LIGHT PREDATOR2L – .223 Wylde chambered for 5.56mm and .223 Rem. cal., 16 in. cryo treated bead blasted lightweight stainless steel barrel with Fred Eichler Series muzzle brake, chrome two-stage trigger, winter trigger guard, Operator CAR stock, Hogue rubber grip, Star safety, low profile gas block, mid-length gas system, BCM Gunfighter charging handle, FES extended carbon fiber free float rail, black or Gunmetal Gray finish, 6.9 lbs. New 2018.

| MSR $1,800 | $1,475 | $950 | $725 | $550 | $475 | $395 | $350 | |

Add $110 for Gunmetal Gray finish.

LAR-15 HUNTER – .223 Rem. cal., GIO, 16 in. chrome moly barrel with RRA tactical muzzle brake, forged A4 upper receiver, low profile gas block, two-stage trigger, winter trigger guard, half-quad free float mid-length handguard with three rail covers, Operator CAR stock, Hogue rubber pistol grip, WYL-Ehide or PRK-Ehide (disc.) anodized camo finish, 7.6 lbs. New 2012.

| | $1,275 | $850 | $600 | $495 | $425 | $375 | $350 | $1,550 |

LAR-15 IRS – 5.56 NATO chambered for 5.56mm and .223 cal., GIO, 16 or 18 (XL model only) in. fluted chrome moly barrel with RRA Helical brake, low profile gas block, forged upper and lower receivers, two-stage trigger, winter trigger guard, IRS CAR, MID, STD, or XL length handguard with integral folding sights, Operator CAR stock, Hogue pistol grip, 7.8-8 lbs. New 2015.

| MSR $1,540 | $1,275 | $850 | $600 | $495 | $425 | $375 | $350 | |

Add $25 for Mid-length handguard (LAR-15 MID).
Add $50 for STD length handguard (LAR-15 STD).
Add $80 for XL length handguard (LAR-15 XL).

LAR-15 LIGHTWEIGHT – 5.56 NATO chambered for 5.56mm and .223 cal., GIO, 16 in. chrome moly lightweight barrel with A2 flash hider, low profile gas block, two-stage trigger, winter trigger guard, forged upper and lower receivers, carbon fiber free float extended handguard in CAR, Mid, STD, or XL lengths, 6-pos. tactical CAR stock, Hogue rubber pistol grips, 5.6-6.1 lbs. New 2015.

| MSR $1,325 | $1,100 | $675 | $525 | $450 | $400 | $350 | $325 | |

Add $25 for mid-length handguard (Lightweight Mid model).
Add $50 for STD length handguard (Lightweight STD model).
Add $75 for XL length handguard (Lightweight XL model).

ROCK RIVER ARMS, INC., cont. 305 R

MSR	100%	98%	95%	90%	80%	70%	60%	Last MSR

LAR-15 LIGHTWEIGHT MOUNTAIN RIFLE – 5.56 NATO chambered for 5.56mm and .223 Rem. cal., GIO, 16 in. chrome moly lightweight barrel with A2 flash hider, lightweight low profile gas block, Star safety, two-stage trigger, winter trigger guard, RRA lightweight aluminum Mountain Rifle handguard, 6-pos. tactical CAR stock, Hogue rubber pistol grip, 6.2 lbs. New 2015.

| MSR $1,150 | $950 | $595 | $495 | $425 | $365 | $335 | $300 | |

LAR-15 MID-LENGTH A2 – 5.56 NATO chambered for 5.56mm and .223 Rem. cal., GIO, 16 in. chrome moly barrel, A2 flash hider, two-stage trigger, A2 buttstock (disc. 2012) or 6-pos. tactical CAR stock (new 2018), overmolded A2 pistol grip, mid-length handguard, forged LAR-15 lower and A2 upper receiver, A2 front sight base (new 2018), black finish, 7 1/2 lbs. Disc. 2012, reintroduced 2018.

| MSR $1,035 | $875 | $550 | $465 | $395 | $350 | $325 | $300 | |

Last MSR in 2012 was $960.

LAR-15 MID-LENGTH A4 – 5.56 NATO chambered for 5.56mm and .223 Rem. cal., GIO, 16 in. chrome moly barrel with A2 flash hider, two-stage trigger, forged LAR-15 lower and forged A4 upper receiver, available with gas block sight base or A2 front sight base, mid-length handguard, 6-pos. tactical CAR stock, overmolded A2 pistol grip, 7.1 lbs.

| MSR $1,035 | $875 | $550 | $465 | $395 | $350 | $325 | $300 | |

LAR-15 NATIONAL MATCH A2 – .223 Wylde chambered for 5.56mm and .223 Rem. cal., GIO, 20 in. heavy match stainless barrel with A2 flash hider, 20 shot mag., two-stage match trigger, match front and rear sights, A2 buttstock, A2 pistol grip, forged LAR-15 lower and forged A2 upper receiver, free float thermo mold handguard, black finish, 9.7 lbs.

| MSR $1,345 | $1,125 | $700 | $525 | $450 | $400 | $350 | $325 | |

LAR-15 NATIONAL MATCH A4 – .223 Wylde chambered for 5.56mm and .223 Rem. cal., GIO, 20 in. heavy match stainless steel cryo treated barrel, A2 flash hider, two-stage match trigger, A2 buttstock, A2 pistol grip, match front and rear sights, chrome bolt carrier group, free float thermo mold handguard with NM barrel sleeve, forged LAR-15 lower and forged A4 upper with detachable NM carry handle, black finish, 9.7 lbs.

| MSR $1,425 | $1,175 | $775 | $550 | $465 | $415 | $375 | $350 | |

LAR-15 NATIONAL MATCH A4 CMP RIFLE – .223 Wylde chambered for 5.56mm and .223 Rem. cal., 16 or 20 in. cryo treated and air gauged heavy match stainless steel barrel, A2 flash hider, 20 shot mag., two-stage match chrome trigger group, gas block with receiver height sight base, Operator CAR stock, A2 pistol grip, forged lower and A4 upper receiver, NM CMP TRO 7 1/4 in. carbine or rifle length free float handguard with three TRO modular rails and NM sling swivel, black finish, 7.3 lbs. New 2016.

| MSR $1,260 | $1,065 | $650 | $500 | $450 | $395 | $350 | $325 | |

LAR-15 NSP CAR – 5.56 NATO chambered for 5.56mm and .223 cal., GIO, 16 in. fluted R4 profile chrome moly barrel with RRA Operator brake, forged upper and lower receivers, gas block with front sight base, RRA NSP flip front and rear sights, NSP two-piece drop-in CAR length rail, two-stage trigger, NSP CAR stock, NSP overmolded pistol grips, black, tan, or pink NSP handguard, stock, grip, sights, and magazine, 7 lbs. New 2015.

| MSR $1,120 | $935 | $575 | $475 | $415 | $350 | $325 | $300 | |

LAR-15 OPERATOR III – 5.56 NATO cal., GIO, similar to Operator Series, except has low profile mid-length gas system, Operator muzzle brake, TRO free float mid-length handguard, Mil-Spec top rail, includes two 30 shot mags. and case, Hogue grip, 8 lbs. Mfg. 2014-2017.

| | $895 | $575 | $475 | $395 | $350 | $325 | $300 | *$1,065* |

LAR-15 OPERATOR SERIES – .223 Rem. cal., GIO, 16 in. chrome moly barrel, tactical muzzle brake, forged LAR-15 lower, forged A4 upper receiver, upper Picatinny rail, Operator CAR stock, matte black finish, two-stage trigger, winter trigger guard, Ergo SureGrip, configurations include the Entry (R-4 handguard and barrel profile), the Tactical (R-4 handguard), and the Elite (half-quad free float handguard with mid-length gas system), designed for left-handed shooters, 7.2-8 lbs. Mfg. 2011-disc.

| | $1,135 | $725 | $525 | $465 | $415 | $375 | $350 | *$1,360* |

Beginning 2013, this model became available in left-hand only (LAR-15LH, Lef-T).

LAR-15 PREDATOR PURSUIT RIFLE/MID-LENGTH – .223 Wylde chamber for 5.56mm and .223 Rem. cal., GIO, 16 (Mid-length model only) or 20 (rifle length model only) in. air gauged heavy match stainless steel barrel, forged A4 upper, low profile gas block, two-stage match trigger, winter trigger guard, Deluxe extended free float rail with rifle or mid-length handguard, A2 buttstock, Hogue rubber pistol grip, 7-7.9 lbs.

| MSR $1,315 | $1,100 | $675 | $525 | $450 | $400 | $350 | $325 | |

Add $35 for rifle length handguard (Predator Pursuit Rifle).

Add $145 for left-hand (LAR-15LH, Lef-T Predator Pursuit, new 2013).

LAR-15 PRO-SERIES ELITE – .223 Rem. cal., GIO, forged A4 upper receiver, chrome-lined 16 in. Wilson chrome moly barrel, RRA tactical muzzle brake, flip front sight and gas block assembly, two-stage match trigger, winter trigger guard, Badger tactical charging handle latch, A.R.M.S. #40L low profile flip-up rear sight, Ergo SureGrip pistol grip,

R 306 ROCK RIVER ARMS, INC., cont.

MSR	100%	98%	95%	90%	80%	70%	60%	Last MSR

6-position tactical CAR stock, MWI front sling adapter, MWI CAR stock endplate adapter loop rear sling mount, Daniel Defense 12.0 FSPM quad rail handguard, SureFire M910A-WH vertical foregrip weaponlight, Aimpoint Comp M2 red dot optical sight and QRP mount with spacer, 9 1/2 lbs. Disc. 2012.

| | $2,225 | $1,395 | $1,050 | $675 | $595 | $525 | $475 | $2,750 |

LAR-15 PRO-SERIES GOVERNMENT – .223 Rem. cal., GIO, 16 in. chrome-lined Wilson chrome moly barrel, A2 flash hider, two-stage match trigger, flip-up rear sight, EOTech 552 Holosight red-dot optical sight, 6-position tactical CAR stock, Hogue rubber pistol grip, forged A4 upper receiver, SureFire M73 quad rail handguard, SureFire M951 WeaponLight system, side mount sling swivel, 8.2 lbs. Disc. 2012.

| | $1,875 | $1,100 | $895 | $650 | $575 | $495 | $425 | $2,375 |

LAR-15 QMC (QUICK MAGAZINE CHANGE) – 5.56 NATO cal., 16 in. barrel with RRA Beast muzzle brake, two-stage trigger, winter trigger guard, Mag-CAR stock with removable spare magazine holder, Hogue rubber pistol grip, RRA Star safety, 14 1/2 in. rifle length free float aluminum rail handguard, forged lower and A4 upper receiver, BCM Gunfighter charging handle, matte black or tan finish, 7.9 lbs. New 2017.

| MSR $1,400 | $1,150 | $750 | $550 | $465 | $415 | $375 | $350 | |

Add $50 for tan finish.

LAR-15 R3 COMPETITION – .223 Wylde chambered for 5.56mm and .223 cal., GIO, 18 in. fluted stainless steel barrel with directionally-tuned and ported muzzle brake, 30 shot mag., low profile gas block, forged LAR-15 lower and forged A4 upper receiver, two-stage match trigger, winter trigger guard, Star safety, RRA TRO-XL free float handguard, RRA adj. Operator A2 or CAR stock, Hogue rubber pistol grips, matte black finish, 7.6 lbs. New 2013.

| MSR $1,355 | $1,135 | $725 | $525 | $465 | $415 | $375 | $350 | |

Add $10 for Operator A2 stock.

LAR-15 RRAGE – 5.56 NATO cal., 16 in. lightweight chrome moly barrel, A2 flash hider, 30 shot polymer mag., single stage trigger, 6-pos. tactical CAR buttstock, A2 pistol grip, CAR length free floated aluminum handguard with MS1913 top rail (M-LOK compatible), CAR length gas system with low profile gas block, forged LAR-15 lower and extruded aluminum A4 upper receiver with port door and no forward assist, black finish, 5.7 lbs. New 2018.

| MSR $760 | $665 | $500 | $415 | $375 | $335 | $315 | $295 | |

LAR-15 STANDARD A2 – .223 Rem. (disc. 2012) or .223 Wylde chambered for 5.56 NATO and .223 Rem. cal., GIO, 20 in. Wilson chrome moly (disc. 2012) or chrome moly HBAR barrel, A2 flash hider, two-stage trigger, A2 buttstock, overmolded A2 grip, A2 handguard, forged LAR-15 lower and A2 upper receiver, A2 front sight base (new 2018), black finish, 8.6 lbs. Disc. 2012, reintroduced 2018.

| MSR $1,085 | $915 | $575 | $475 | $415 | $350 | $325 | $300 | |

Last MSR in 2012 was $980.

LAR-15 STANDARD A4 – .223 Wylde chambered for 5.56mm and .223 Rem. cal., GIO, 20 in. chrome moly HBAR barrel with A2 flash hider, A2 front sight base, forged LAR-15 lower and A4 upper receivers, two-stage trigger, A2 handguard, A2 buttstock, overmolded A2 pistol grip, 8.2 lbs.

| MSR $1,020 | $865 | $550 | $465 | $395 | $350 | $325 | $300 | |

Add $145 for left-hand (LAR-15LH, Lef-T Standard A4, new 2013).

LAR-15 TACTICAL CAR UTE2 – .223 Rem. cal., GIO, forged Universal Tactical Entry 2 upper receiver, 16 in. Wilson chrome moly barrel, A2 flash hider, two-stage match trigger, Hogue rubber pistol grip, R-4 handguard, 6-position tactical CAR stock, 7 1/2 lbs. Disc. 2012.

| | $895 | $575 | $475 | $395 | $350 | $325 | $300 | $1,060 |

LAR-15 TACTICAL CAR A4 – .223 Rem. cal., GIO, 16 in. chrome moly barrel, A2 flash hider, forged A4 upper receiver, two-stage trigger, Hogue rubber pistol grip, R-4 handguard, 6-position tactical CAR stock, 7 1/2 lbs.

| MSR $1,065 | $895 | $575 | $475 | $395 | $350 | $325 | $300 | |

Add $40 for chrome-lined barrel.

Add $115 for left-hand (LAR-15LH, Lef-T, mfg. 2013-2014).

LAR-15 TEXAS RIFLE – .223 Wylde chambered for 5.56mm or .223 Rem. cal., GIO, 16 in. fluted stainless steel barrel with black Cerakote finish, tuned and ported muzzle brake, low profile gas block, two-stage chrome trigger, winter trigger guard, forged A4 upper, Star safety, RRA Texas XL free float handguard with two rail covers, A2 or CAR buttstock, Hogue rubber pistol grip, BCM Gunfighter charging handle, receivers and handguard finished in Cerakote Magpul Flat Dark Earth, Burnt Bronze, or Barrett Bronze, 7.6 lbs. Mfg. 2015-2017.

| | $1,385 | $895 | $675 | $525 | $450 | $385 | $350 | $1,700 |

Add $10 for Operator A2 stock.

LAR-15 VARMINT A4 – .223 Wylde chambered for 5.56mm and .223 Rem. or .308 Win. (mfg. 2010-2011) cal., GIO, 16, 18, 20, or 24 in. Wilson (disc.) air gauged, cryo treated stainless steel bull barrel, two-stage match trigger, winter trigger guard, A2 buttstock, Hogue rubber pistol grip, forged LAR-15 lower and forged A4 upper receiver, Weaver style light varmint gas block with sight rail (disc.) or low profile gas block, knurled and fluted free floating aluminum tube

ROCK RIVER ARMS, INC., cont. 307 **R**

MSR	100%	98%	95%	90%	80%	70%	60%	Last MSR

handguard (disc.) or TRO free float handguard with octagonal top rail and three TRO accessory rails, 7.9-11.6 lbs.

| | MSR $1,265 | $1,065 | $650 | $500 | $450 | $395 | $350 | $325 | |

Add $15 for 18 in., $30 for 20 in., or $40 for 24 in. barrel.

Add $145 for left-hand (LAR-15LH, Lef-T Varmint A4, new 2013).

Add $395 for .308 Win. cal. (mfg. 2010-2011).

LAR-15M VARMINT A4 – .204 Ruger cal., GIO, 20 in. fluted stainless steel bull barrel w/cryogenic treatment, two-stage trigger, winter trigger guard, A2 buttstock, Hogue rubber pistol grip, Star safety, rifle length free floating octagon Picatinny rail, forged lower and A4 upper receiver, matte black finish, 9 lbs. New 2017.

| | MSR $1,400 | $1,150 | $750 | $550 | $465 | $415 | $375 | $350 | |

LAR-15 VARMINT EOP (ELEVATED OPTICAL PLATFORM) – .223 Wylde chambered for 5.56mm or .223 Rem. cal., GIO, 16, 18, 20, or 24 in. Wilson air gauged stainless steel bull barrel, forged EOP upper receiver, low profile gas block, Weaver style light varmint gas block with sight rail, two-stage match trigger, winter trigger guard, knurled and fluted free floating aluminum tube (disc.) or TRO free float handguard, Hogue rubber pistol grip, A2 buttstock, 8.2-10 lbs.

| | MSR $1,300 | $1,075 | $675 | $500 | $450 | $400 | $350 | $325 | |

Add $15 for 18, $30 for 20, or $40 for 24 in. barrel.

LAR-15 X-1 RIFLE – .223 Wylde chambered for 5.56 NATO or .223 cal., GIO, 18 in. fluted stainless steel barrel, RRA Beast or Hunter muzzle brake, forged upper and lower receivers, low profile gas block, two-stage trigger, winter trigger guard, RRA TRO-XL extended length free float rail, Operator A2 or Operator CAR stock, Hogue rubber pistol grip, black or tan finish, includes 9 in. XL accessory rail and two 2 in. short accessory rails, 7.7 lbs. New 2014.

| | MSR $1,495 | $1,250 | $825 | $575 | $475 | $425 | $375 | $350 | |

Add $10 for Operator A2 stock.

Add $50 for RRA Hunter muzzle brake and tan finish.

LAR-40 CAR A2/A4 – .40 S&W cal., GIO, forged A2 (disc. 2011) or A4 upper receiver, 16 in. chrome moly barrel, A2 flash hider, single stage trigger, R-4 handguard, 6-position tactical CAR stock with Hogue pistol grip, approx. 7 lbs. Disc. 2011, reintroduced 2013-2017.

| | | $1,065 | $650 | $500 | $450 | $395 | $350 | $325 | $1,260 |

Add $145 for quad rail.

Add $50 for Operator stock.

LAR-40 MID-LENGTH A2/A4 – .40 S&W cal., GIO, forged A2 (disc. 2011) or A4 (new 2013) upper, 16 in. chrome moly barrel, A2 flash hider, two-stage match trigger, mid-length handguard, Hogue rubber pistol grip, 6-position tactical CAR stock, approx. 7 lbs. Mfg. 2010-2011, reintroduced 2013-2017.

| | | $1,065 | $650 | $500 | $450 | $395 | $350 | $325 | $1,260 |

LAR-47 CAR A4 – 7.62x39mm cal., GIO, 16 in. chrome-lined HBAR barrel with A2 flash hider, gas block front sight base, forged lower and A4 upper, two-stage trigger, CAR handguard, 6-pos. CAR tactical stock, A2 pistol grip, ambidextrous mag. release, 6.4 lbs. New 2013.

| | MSR $1,270 | $1,065 | $650 | $500 | $450 | $395 | $350 | $325 | |

LAR-47 COYOTE CARBINE – 7.62x39mm cal., GIO, 16 in. chrome-lined HBAR barrel with Smith Vortex flash hider, ambi mag. release, two-stage trigger, NSP CAR stock, Hogue rubber pistol grip, forged LAR-47 lower and A4 upper receiver, low profile gas block, deluxe extended free float rifle length handguard with three 2 in. accessory rails, 7.8 lbs. New 2015.

| | MSR $1,740 | $1,425 | $925 | $700 | $550 | $475 | $395 | $350 | |

LAR-47 DELTA CARBINE – 7.62x39mm cal., GIO, 16 in. chrome-lined HBAR barrel with A2 flash hider, ambi mag. release, two-stage trigger, winter trigger guard, gas block front sight base, 6-position Delta CAR stock, Ergo SureGrip, forged lower and A4 upper receiver, two-piece quad rail handguard, 7 3/4 lbs. New 2013.

| | MSR $1,545 | $1,275 | $850 | $600 | $495 | $425 | $375 | $350 | |

LAR-47 TACTICAL COMP – 7.62x39mm cal., GIO, 16 in. chrome-lined HBAR barrel with Operator brake, flip front sight gas block assembly, forged upper and lower receivers, two-stage trigger, ambidextrous mag. release, CAR length free float quad rail, Operator CAR stock, overmolded pistol grips, 7.8 lbs. New 2015.

| | MSR $1,500 | $1,250 | $825 | $575 | $475 | $425 | $375 | $350 | |

LAR-47 X-1 RIFLE – 7.62x39mm cal., GIO, 18 in. fluted stainless steel bull barrel, RRA Beast or Hunter muzzle brake, forged upper and lower receivers, low profile gas block, two-stage trigger, RRA TRO-XL extended length free float rail, Operator A2 or Operator CAR stock, Hogue rubber pistol grip, black or tan finish, includes 9 in. XL accessory rail and two 2 in. short accessory rails for handguard, 8.2 lbs. New 2015.

| | MSR $1,600 | $1,315 | $850 | $625 | $500 | $435 | $375 | $350 | |

Add $10 for Operator A2 stock.

Add $50 for RRA Hunter muzzle brake and tan finish.

R 308 ROCK RIVER ARMS, INC., cont.

MSR	100%	98%	95%	90%	80%	70%	60%	Last MSR

LAR-300 CAR A4 – .300 ACC Blackout cal., GIO, 16 in. chrome moly HBAR barrel with A2 flash hider, forged A4 upper, two-stage trigger, CAR length handguard, 6-pos. tactical CAR stock, overmolded A2 grip, 7.1 lbs. New 2015.

| | MSR $1,070 | $895 | $575 | $475 | $395 | $350 | $325 | $300 | |

LAR-300 COYOTE CARBINE – .300 ACC Blackout cal., GIO, 16 in. chrome moly HBAR barrel with Smith Vortex flash hider, two-stage trigger, winter trigger guard, Operator CAR stock, Hogue rubber pistol grip, low profile gas block, forged A4 upper and LAR-300 lower, deluxe extended CAR handguard with three accessory rails, black finish, 7.2 lbs. New 2015.

| | MSR $1,295 | $1,075 | $675 | $500 | $450 | $400 | $350 | $325 | |

LAR-300 DELTA CAR – .300 ACC Blackout cal., GIO, 16 in. chrome moly barrel with A2 flash hider, low profile gas block, two-stage trigger, winter trigger guard, Delta CAR stock, Ergo SureGrip pistol grip, Delta quad rail CAR length two-piece drop-in handguard, 7 lbs. New 2015.

| | MSR $1,120 | $935 | $575 | $475 | $415 | $350 | $325 | $300 | |

LAR-300 TACTICAL CAR A4 – .300 ACC Blackout cal., GIO, 16 in. chrome moly HBAR barrel with A2 flash hider, A2 front sight base with side mount sling swivel, two-stage trigger, R-4 handguard, 6-pos. tactical CAR stock, Hogue rubber grip, 7 1/2 lbs. New 2015.

| | MSR $1,100 | $915 | $575 | $475 | $415 | $350 | $325 | $300 | |

LAR-300 X-1 RIFLE – .300 ACC Blackout cal., GIO, 18 in. fluted stainless steel HBAR barrel, RRA Beast or Hunter muzzle brake, forged upper and lower receivers, low profile gas block, two-stage trigger, winter trigger guard, RRA TRO-XL extended length free float rail, Operator A2 or Operator CAR stock, Hogue rubber pistol grip, black or tan finish, includes 9 in. XL accessory rail and two 2 in. short accessory rails, 7.9 lbs. New 2015.

| | MSR $1,585 | $1,315 | $850 | $625 | $500 | $435 | $375 | $350 | |

Add $10 for Operator A2 stock.

Add $50 for RRA Hunter muzzle brake and tan finish.

LAR-458 BEAST – .458 SOCOM cal., GIO, 14 1/2 in. chrome moly bull barrel with pinned and welded Beast brake (for 16 in. barrel length), two-stage trigger, Delta 6-pos. CAR stock, Hogue rubber pistol grip, forged LAR-458 lower and A4 upper receiver, low profile gas block, TRO-STD free float handguard, rifle length with one STD and two short accessory rails, black finish, 7.6 lbs. New 2018.

| | MSR $1,390 | $1,150 | $750 | $550 | $465 | $415 | $375 | $350 | |

LAR-458 CAR A4 – .458 SOCOM cal., GIO, 16 in. Wilson chrome moly bull barrel, A2 flash hider, two-stage trigger, Weaver style varmint gas block with sight rail (disc.), A2 buttstock (disc.) or Operator CAR (new 2010) stock, A2 pistol grip, forged A4 upper and LAR-458 lower receiver, low profile gas block, knurled and fluted free floating aluminum tube handguard (disc.) or lightweight free float rail handguard, M-LOK compatible, black finish, 7.6 lbs.

| | MSR $1,145 | $950 | $595 | $495 | $425 | $365 | $335 | $300 | |

LAR-458 MID-LENGTH A4 – .458 SOCOM cal., GIO, forged A4 upper receiver, 16 in. chrome moly bull barrel, A2 flash hider, gas block with sight rail, two-stage match trigger, knurled and fluted free floating aluminum tube handguard, A2 buttstock and pistol grip, 7.8 lbs. Mfg. 2010-2017.

| | | $1,025 | $625 | $495 | $450 | $395 | $350 | $325 | *$1,220* |

Add $290 for Operator model with half quad free float with full length top rail, Vortex flash hider, and CAR stock (new 2010).

LAR-458 TACTICAL CARBINE – .458 SOCOM cal., 16 in. chrome moly bull barrel with Operator muzzle brake, two-stage trigger, winter trigger guard, NSP 6-pos. CAR stock, Hogue rubber pistol grip, forged A4 upper and LAR-458 lower receiver, low profile gas block, deluxe extended free float rail, rifle length with 3 short accessory rails, black finish, 7.8 lbs. New 2015.

| | MSR $1,210 | $1,025 | $625 | $495 | $450 | $395 | $350 | $325 | |

LAR-458 X-1 RIFLE – .458 SOCOM cal., GIO, 18 in. fluted stainless steel bull barrel, RRA Beast or Hunter muzzle brake, low profile gas block, forged RRA LAR-458 lower and A4 upper receiver, two-stage trigger, winter trigger guard, RRA TRO-XL extended length free float rail, RRA Operator A2 or Operator CAR stock, Hogue rubber pistol grip, black or tan finish, includes one 9 in. XL accessory rail and two 2 in. short accessory rails for handguard, 8.7 lbs. New 2014.

| | MSR $1,595 | $1,315 | $850 | $625 | $500 | $435 | $375 | $350 | |

Add $10 for Operator A2 stock.

Add $50 for RRA Hunter muzzle brake and tan finish.

LAR-PDS CARBINE (PISTON DRIVEN SYSTEM) – .223 Rem. cal., GPO, 16 in. chrome moly barrel, A2 flash hider, two-stage trigger, ribbed forend, side folding 6-position tactical stock with receiver extension storage compartment, Hogue rubber pistol grip, full-length upper and partial lower Picatinny rails, injection molded ribbed or tri-rail handguard, folding ambidextrous non-reciprocating charging handles, two-position regulator, black finish, approx. 7.4 lbs. New 2011.

| | MSR $1,595 | $1,315 | $850 | $625 | $500 | $435 | $375 | $350 | |

Add $155 for tri-rail handguard.

ROCK RIVER ARMS, INC., cont. 309 R

MSR	100%	98%	95%	90%	80%	70%	60%	Last MSR

PRO-SERIES TASC – .223 Rem. cal., GIO, chrome-lined 16 in. Wilson chrome-moly barrel with Smith Vortex flash hider, two-stage match trigger, oversize winter trigger guard, A2 rear sight with lockable windage and elevation, Midwest Industries A2 adj. cantilever sight mount, 6-position tactical CAR stock, Hogue rubber pistol grip, graphite fore grip, forged A2 upper receiver, SureFire M85 mid-length quad rail, EOTech 511 Holosight, Midwest Industries A2 adj. cantilever sight mount, 8.7 lbs. Disc. 2009.

	$1,675	$1,000	$825	$625	$550	$475	$425	$2,000

TASC RIFLE – .223 Rem. cal., GIO, 16 in. Wilson chrome moly barrel, A2 flash hider, forged A2 upper receiver with lockable windage and elevation adj. rear sight, two-stage match trigger, Hogue rubber pistol grip, A2 buttstock or 6-position CAR tactical buttstock, choice of R-4 or mid-length handguard, approx. 7 1/2 lbs. Disc. 2009.

	$800	$525	$450	$385	$340	$325	$295	$950

Add $15 for six-position collapsible stock.

ROCKY MOUNTAIN ARMS, INC.

Previous firearms manufacturer located in Longmont, CO 1991-circa 2017.

Rocky Mountain Arms was a quality specialty manufacturer of rifles and pistols. All firearms were finished in a DuPont Teflon-S industrial coating called "Bear Coat".

PISTOLS: SEMI-AUTO

22K PISTOLS – .22 LR cal., AR style pistol, blowback action, 7 in. barrel, choice of matte black or NATO Green Teflon-S finish, will use Colt conversion kit, choice of carrying handle or flat-top upper receiver, 10 or 30 shot mag., includes black nylon case. Mfg. 1993 only.

	$450	$385	$335	$285	$250	$230	$215	$525

Add $50 for flat-top receiver with Weaver style bases.

KOMRADE – 7.62x39mm cal., floating 7 in. barrel, 5 shot mag., includes carrying handle upper receiver with fixed sights, red finish only, 5 lbs. Very limited mfg. was pre-ban 1994 only.

Last MSR was $1,995.

Rarity precludes accurate pricing on this model. Recent sales with case in the $3,500 range.

PATRIOT PISTOL – .223 Rem. cal., AR-15 style, GIO, 7 in. match barrel with integral Max Dynamic muzzle brake, available with either carrying handle upper receiver and fixed sights or flat-top receiver with Weaver style bases, fluted upper receiver became an option in 1994, accepts standard AR-15 mags, 21 in. OAL, 5 lbs. Mfg. 1993-94 (per C/B), reintroduced 2005-2017.

	$2,550	$2,225	$1,825	$1,575	$1,300	$1,100	$950	$3,000

RIFLES: SEMI-AUTO

VARMINTER – .223 Rem. cal. only, AR-15 style, GIO, 20 in. fluted heavy match barrel, flat-top receiver with Weaver style bases, round metal National Match handguard, free float barrel, choice of NATO green or matte black Teflon-S finish, supplied with case and factory test target (sub-MOA accuracy). Mfg. 1993-94.

	$1,975	$1,150	$925	$650	$575	$495	$425	$2,495

PATRIOT MATCH RIFLE – .223 Rem. cal., AR-15 style, GIO, 20 in. bull match barrel, regular or milled upper and lower receivers, two-piece machined aluminum handguard, choice of DuPont Teflon finish in black or NATO green, 1/2 MOA accuracy, hard case. Mfg. 1995-97, reintroduced 2005-2017.

	$2,050	$1,250	$950	$650	$575	$495	$475	$2,500

MAYBE THE ONLY THING BETTER THAN THIS BOOK IS THE ONLINE SUBSCRIPTION!

Only $19.95/year!

- **Includes monthly updates** keeping you informed of all the new AR-15 makes/models.
- **Features thousands of images** allowing for fast and easy identification.
- **Manufacturer/Model searchable database** allowing you to find the model you need.
- Historical pricing with dynamic interactive graphs keeps you up-to-date on your AR-15 purchases as investments.
- Your own personal online inventory solution - keep track of your collection and track the change in value.
- Includes access to BBP's industry standard Photo Percentage Grading System – why guess a gun's condition when you can be sure?

Visit BLUEBOOKOFGUNVALUES.COM
to view sample pages and ordering

Good Information Never Sleeps!

S SECTION

S.W.A.T. FIREARMS
Previous manufacturer of AR-15 style pistols and rifles located in Campbell, TX 1999-2017.

MSR	100%	98%	95%	90%	80%	70%	60%	Last MSR

PISTOLS: SEMI-AUTO

5.56 STANDARD – 5.56 NATO cal., GIO, 10 1/2 in. stainless steel barrel with MB2 muzzle brake/flash hider, low profile steel gas block, 10 1/2 in. slant nose KeyMod handguard. Mfg. 2014-2017.

	$885	$785	$685	$600	$535	$465	$415	$1,050

5.56 STAINLESS – 5.56 NATO cal., GIO, 10 1/2 in. stainless steel barrel with MB2 muzzle brake/flash hider, low profile steel gas block, 10 in. slant nose KeyMod handguard. Mfg. 2014-2017.

	$925	$850	$725	$625	$550	$475	$425	$1,130

.300 BLACKOUT – .300 AAC Blackout cal., GIO, 10 1/2 in. black phosphate barrel with MB2 muzzle brake/flash hider, low profile steel gas block, 10 in. slant nose KeyMod handguard. Mfg. 2014-2017.

	$925	$850	$725	$625	$550	$475	$425	$1,130

7 1/2 IN. PISTOL w/KNURLED TUBE – 5.56 NATO cal., GIO, 7 1/2 in. barrel, knurled tube, top Picatinny rail, black finish. Mfg. 2014-2017.

	$850	$725	$650	$585	$515	$450	$395	$1,020

10 1/2 IN. PISTOL w/CARBINE RAIL – 5.56 NATO cal., GIO, 10 1/2 in. barrel, carbine rail, black finish. Mfg. 2014-2017.

	$850	$725	$650	$585	$515	$450	$395	$1,020

RIFLES: SEMI-AUTO

.300 AAC – .300 AAC Blackout cal., GIO, 16 in. heavy chrome moly barrel (stainless steel barrel upgrade is additional), upper receiver with Picatinny rail, gas block Picatinny rail, collapsible buttstock, pistol grip, 6.7 lbs. Mfg. 2015-2017.

	$895	$575	$475	$395	$350	$325	$300	$1,070

BASE HEAVY (BASE MODERN SPORTING RIFLE) – 5.56 NATO or 7.62 NATO (disc.) cal., GIO, 16 in. heavy chrome moly barrel, free float round knurled handguard or quad rail, flat-top upper with Picatinny rail, gas block Picatinny rail, collapsible buttstock, pistol grip, black finish, 7 lbs. Disc. 2017.

	$765	$515	$440	$375	$335	$315	$295	$880

Add $210 for 7.62 NATO cal. (disc.).

* ***Base Heavy 2*** – 5.56 NATO cal., GIO, 16 in. heavy chrome moly barrel, billet upper and lower receiver, mid-length free floating rail, Ergo textured grip, 39 1/2 in. OAL. Disc. 2017.

	$800	$525	$450	$385	$340	$325	$295	$938

* ***Base Heavy 3*** – 5.56 NATO cal., GIO, 16 in. heavy chrome moly barrel, steel low profile gas block, rifle length free floating rail, billet upper and lower receivers, collapsible buttstock, Disc. 2017.

	$950	$595	$495	$425	$365	$335	$300	$1,150

BASE 20 – 5.56 NATO cal., GIO, 20 in. heavy chrome moly barrel, upper receiver with Picatinny rail, handguard tube, gas block Picatinny rail, fixed stock, pistol grip, black finish, 8.3 lbs. Mfg. 2015-2017.

Retail pricing was not available for this model.

COMPETITOR – 5.56 NATO cal., GIO, 16 in. heavy chrome moly barrel, MB-3 muzzle brake, low profile gas block, flip-up iron sights, extended charging handle, billet upper and lower receiver, Magpul AVG stock, Ergo textured grip, 8.3 lbs. Disc. 2017.

	$1,065	$650	$500	$450	$395	$350	$325	$1,260

DESERT STORM – 5.56 NATO cal., GIO, 16 in. lightweight chrome moly barrel with FH-1 flash hider, rifle length free float quad rail, Magpul MOE stock, Magpul AFG forward grip, Cerakote Magpul FDE finish, 6.97 lbs. Disc. 2017.

	$1,050	$650	$495	$450	$395	$350	$325	$1,229

DRAGON SLAYER – 5.56 NATO cal., GIO, 16 in. barrel with MB-2 muzzle brake, mid-length free floating quad rail, low profile gas block, billet upper and lower receivers, Crimson Cerakote finish, 6.2 lbs. Disc. 2017.

	$975	$595	$495	$425	$365	$335	$300	$1,160

M4 – 5.56 NATO cal., GIO, 16 in. M4 contour barrel with FH-1 flash hider, Ergo grip, carbine length free float quad rail, 7 lbs. Disc. 2015.

	$865	$550	$465	$395	$350	$325	$300	$1,014

S 312 S.W.A.T. FIREARMS, cont.

MSR	100%	98%	95%	90%	80%	70%	60%	Last MSR

PRISON PINK CONVICTION – 5.56 NATO cal., GIO, 16 in. lightweight chrome moly barrel, two-piece quad rail, Prison Pink Cerakote finish, 6.6 lbs. Disc. 2014.

	$1,225	$825	$575	$475	$425	$375	$350	$1,458

TASTANIUM DEVIL – 5.56 NATO cal., GIO, 20 in. heavy barrel with MB-3 muzzle brake, carbine length free float quad rail, Titanium Cerakote finish, 8.3 lbs. Mfg. 2014-2017.

	$995	$625	$495	$450	$395	$350	$325	$1,179

TOP GUN – 5.56 NATO cal., GIO, 16 in. heavy chrome moly barrel with MB-1 muzzle brake (disc.) or FH-1 flash hider, low profile gas block, two-stage trigger, billet upper and lower receivers, YHM quad rail, extended charging handle, Ergo (disc.) or Magpul AFG pistol grip, Magpul CTR stock, ambi-sling mount, 8.3 lbs. Disc. 2017.

	$995	$625	$495	$450	$395	$350	$325	$1,187

SD TACTICAL ARMS

Current rifle manufacturer located in Prescott, AZ and previously in Menomonie, WI.

RIFLES/CARBINES: SEMI-AUTO

SD Tactical Arms manufactures a line of AR style semi-auto carbines and rifles built per individual customer specifications. The company also offers a complete line of tactical gear and accessories, including rails and magazines. Since each rifle is built per custom order, please contact the company directly for pricing, available options, and delivery time (see Trademark Index).

SI DEFENSE, INC.

Previous AR-15 style carbine/rifle manufacturer located in Kalispell, MT until 2015.

RIFLES/CARBINES: SEMI-AUTO

MID-LENGTH CUSTOM – .223 Rem./5.56x45mm cal., internal gas block system, 18 in. stainless steel fluted barrel with SI DRK muzzle brake, flip-up front and rear sights, billet upper and lower receivers, black mid-length handguard, Ace stock, black finish. Disc. 2013.
Retail pricing was not available on this model.

SI-C .223 STANDARD CARBINE – .223 Rem./5.56x45mm cal., internal GIO, 16 in. parkerized barrel with SI DRK muzzle brake, A2 style fixed front sight, flip-up rear sight, billet upper and lower receivers, custom carbine length handguard, available in black, FDE, or ODG finish. Disc. 2014.

	$1,065	$650	$500	$450	$395	$350	$325	

SI-C ATC – 5.56 NATO cal., 16 in. M4 contour, Nitride coated barrel with muzzle brake, 30 shot Magpul mag., 6-position adj. stock, 15 in. floating handguard, Hogue grip, fixed front and adj. rear sight, standard black or Flat Dark Earth finish, 6 1/2 lbs. Mfg. 2014-2015.

	$1,350	$875	$650	$525	$450	$385	$350	$1,650

SI-C M4 CARBINE – 5.56 NATO cal., nickel boron coated bolt carrier group, 16 in. M4 contour, Nitride coated barrel with muzzle brake, 30 shot Magpul mag., Magpul MBUS flip-up rear sight, YHM flip-up front sight, 6-position adj. stock, Magpul MOE handguard, standard black or Flat Dark Earth finish, 7 lbs. Mfg. 2014 only.

	$1,050	$650	$495	$450	$395	$350	$325	

SI-C M406 – 5.56 NATO cal., AR-15 style, 16 in. barrel, carbine length gas system, black Nitride bolt carrier group, folding front and flip rear sights, Magpul CTR stock, 6.4 lbs. Mfg. 2015 only.

	$1,050	$650	$495	$450	$395	$350	$325	$1,250

SI-D .308 AMBI CF BATTLE RIFLE – .308 Win. cal., 18 in. Proof Research match grade carbon fiber barrel, Fortis Red muzzle brake, 20 shot mag., hard black anodized billet upper and lower receiver, ambidextrous controls, quick snap dust cover, forward assist, flared magwell, integrated trigger guard, 15 1/2 in. lightweight free floating KeyMod handguard, CMC trigger, ambi charging handle, Battle Arms Development selector, Mission First tactical stock, 8 1/2 lbs. Mfg. 2015 only.

	$2,775	$1,825	$1,350	$750	$650	$595	$525	$3,499

SI-D .308 AMBI SS BATTLE RIFLE – .308 Win. cal., 16 in. stainless steel black Nitride barrel and SI DRK muzzle brake, 20 shot mag., ambi billet upper and lower receivers, ambidextrous mirrored controls, quick snap dust cover, forward assist, flared magwell, integrated trigger guard, 15 1/2 in. lightweight free floating KeyMod handguard, STD trigger, ambi charging handle, Battle Arms development selector, Mission First Tactical stock, 8 1/2 lbs. Mfg. 2015-2016.

	$2,295	$1,450	$1,075	$675	$595	$525	$475	$2,850

SI-D .308 BATTLE RIFLE – .308 Win./7.62 NATO cal., 16 1/2 in. parkerized barrel with SI DRK muzzle brake, A2 style fixed front sight, carbine length gas system, billet upper and lower receivers, SI Defense carbine handguard, 6-position adj. buttstock, black finish. Disc. 2014.

	$1,475	$950	$725	$550	$475	$395	$350	

SI DEFENSE, INC., cont. 313 S

MSR		100%	98%	95%	90%	80%	70%	60%	Last MSR

SI-D .308 CARBINE (HUNTING/SPORTSMAN) – .308 Win. cal., 16 in. M4 contour barrel with SI Defense DRK compensator, 20 shot Magpul mag., Weaver extra tall scope rings and Nikon 3x9 power scope with BDC reticle, free floating carbine length tube handguard, SI Defense adj. quad rail gas block, adj. 6-position Choate stock, Flat Dark Earth finish, 9.1 lbs. Disc. 2014.

| | | $1,425 | $925 | $700 | $550 | $475 | $395 | $350 | |

SI-D .308 RIFLE – .308 Win. cal., 16 in. stainless steel barrel with black Nitride finish, 20 shot mag., billet upper and lower receiver, flared magwell, forward assist, integrated trigger guard, single stage trigger, rifle length gas system, Magpul MBUS sights, Midwest Industries handguard, Magpul CTR stock, Hogue grip, 8 1/2 lbs. Mfg. 2015 only.

| | | $1,475 | $950 | $725 | $550 | $475 | $395 | $350 | $1,800 |

SI-D .300WM AMBI PETRA RIFLE – .300 WM cal.
While advertised, this model never made it into production.

TREAD – 5.56x45mm cal., 18 in. parkerized barrel with SI Defense DRK muzzle brake, flip-up front and rear sights, billet upper and lower receivers, custom handguard, Ace buttstock, "Don't Tread On Me" engraving, custom Timney skeletonized trigger group, extended charging handle latch, red and white colored lettering. Disc. 2013.
Retail pricing was not available on this model.

SMI ARMS

Previous pistol and rifle manufacturer located in Merriam, KS until 2017.

SMI Arms was a division of Signature Manufacturing. In addition to complete firearms built to order, SMI Arms/Signature Manufacturing also manufactured individual component parts and accessories for the AR-15/AK-47 platform.

PISTOLS: SEMI-AUTO

SMI ENFORCER AR15 PISTOL MOD 1 – 5.56 NATO or .300 AAC Blackout cal., pistol length gas system, 7 1/2 in. match grade M4 carbine barrel, target crown, birdcage flash hider, 30 shot mag., no sights, 7 in. free float ultralight slim KeyMod rail system, billet aluminum upper and lower receiver, flared magwell, pistol buffer tube only, standard Mil-Spec A2 pistol grip in black or FDE, standard Mil-Spec hardcoat anodized trigger guard, 6 lbs. Disc. 2017.

| | | $685 | $615 | $550 | $475 | $425 | $365 | $325 | $799 |

SMI ENFORCER AR15 PISTOL MOD 2 – 5.56 NATO or .300 AAC Blackout cal., pistol length gas system, 7 1/2 in. match grade M4 carbine barrel, target crown, birdcage flash hider, 30 shot Magpul mag., Magpul MBUS 2 front and rear sights, billet aluminum upper and lower receiver, 7 in. free float ultralight slim KeyMod rail system, SMI BETR tactical charging handle, single stage trigger, winter trigger guard, flared magwell, KAK Industries Shockwave blade pistol stabilizer, Magpul MOE grip, Magpul angled forearm grip, hardcoat anodized black or FDE finish, 6 lbs. Disc. 2017.

| | | $1,075 | $675 | $500 | $450 | $400 | $350 | $325 | $1,299 |

RIFLES: SEMI-AUTO

BCR MOD 1 (BAD COMPANY RIFLE) – 5.56 NATO, .300 AAC Blackout, 7.62x30, 6.5 Grendel, or 6.8 SPC II cal., carbine length gas system, 16 in. match grade M4 carbine barrel, target crown, birdcage flash hider, 30 shot mag., billet aluminum upper and lower receiver, flared magwell, no sights, 13 in. free float ultralight slim KeyMod rail system, standard Mil-Spec charging handle and trigger guard, 6-position Mil-Spec buffer tube, Magpul MOE collapsible pistol grip stock, hardcoat anodized finish in black or FDE, 6.7 lbs. Disc. 2017.

| | | $915 | $575 | $475 | $415 | $350 | $325 | $300 | $1,099 |

BCR MOD 2 (BAD COMPANY RIFLE) – 5.56 NATO or .300 AAC Blackout cal., carbine length gas system, 16 in. match grade M4 carbine barrel, target crown, birdcage flash hider, includes two Mil-Spec aluminum 30 shot mags., billet aluminum upper and lower, Magpul MBUS 2 front and rear sights, 15 in. free float ultralight slim KeyMod rail system, 6-position Mil-Spec buffer tube, standard Mil-Spec charging handle, tuned trigger, and trigger guard, Magpul MOE collapsible pistol grip stock, hardcoat anodized finish in black or FDE, 6 1/2 lbs. Disc. 2017.

| | | $995 | $625 | $495 | $450 | $395 | $350 | $325 | $1,199 |

BCR MOD 3 (BAD COMPANY RIFLE) – 5.56 NATO, .300 AAC Blackout, 7.62x30, 6.5 Grendel, or 6.8 SPC II cal., 16 in. match grade M4 carbine barrel, target crown, birdcage flash hider, carbine length gas system, 30 shot mag., Magpul MBUS 2 front and rear sights, 15 in. free float ultralight slim KeyMod rail system, billet aluminum upper and lower receiver, flared magwell, SMI BETR tactical charging handle, 6-position Mil-Spec buffer tube, Magpul MOE collapsible pistol grip stock, BETR tactical winter trigger guard, hardcoat anodized finish in black or FDE, 6 1/2 lbs. Disc. 2017.

| | | $1,050 | $650 | $495 | $450 | $395 | $350 | $325 | $1,249 |

S 314 SMI ARMS, cont.

MSR	100%	98%	95%	90%	80%	70%	60%	Last MSR

BCR MOD 4 (BAD COMPANY RIFLE) – 5.56 NATO or .300 AAC Blackout cal., carbine length gas system, 16 in. match grade M4 carbine barrel, target crown, birdcage flash hider, includes two 30 shot Magpul mags., billet aluminum upper and lower receiver, flared magwell, Magpul MBUS 2 front and rear sights, 15 in. free float ultralight slim KeyMod rail system, SMI BETR tactical charging handle, single stage trigger, and winter trigger guard, 6-position Mil-Spec buffer tube, Magpul MOE collapsible pistol grip stock, hardcoat anodized finish in black or FDE, 6 1/2 lbs. Disc. 2017.

| | $1,150 | $750 | $550 | $465 | $415 | $375 | $350 | *$1,399* |

STR MOD 1 (SPORTING TACTICAL RIFLE) – 5.56 NATO, 7.62x30, 6.5 Grendel, or 6.8 SPC II cal., carbine length gas system, 18 in. match grade barrel, target crown, birdcage flash hider, includes two Magpul 30 shot mags., Magpul MBUS 2 front and rear sights, 13 in. free float P-Mod KeyMod rail system, billet aluminum upper and lower receiver, flared magwell, nickel boron EXO finished bolt carrier group, SMI BETR tactical charging handle, single stage trigger, and winter trigger guard, 6-position Mil-Spec buffer tube, MFT Minimalist collapsible pistol grip stock, hardcoat anodized finish in black or FDE, 6 1/2 lbs. Disc. 2017.

| | $1,315 | $850 | $625 | $500 | $435 | $375 | $350 | *$1,599* |

STR MOD 2 (SPORTING TACTICAL RIFLE) – 5.56 NATO, 7.62x30, 6.5 Grendel, or 6.8 SPC II cal., carbine length gas system, 18 in. match grade barrel, target crown, birdcage flash hider, Magpul MBUS 2 front and rear sights, 15 in. free float P-Mod KeyMod rail system, includes two Magpul 30 shot mags., billet aluminum upper and lower receiver, flared magwell, nickel boron EXO finished bolt carrier group, SMI BETR tactical charging handle, single stage trigger, and winter trigger guard, 6-position Mil-Spec buffer tube, MFT Minimalist collapsible pistol grip stock, hardcoat anodized finish in black or FDE, 6 1/2 lbs. Disc. 2017.

| | $1,350 | $875 | $650 | $525 | $450 | $385 | $350 | *$1,649* |

STR MOD 3 (SPORTING TACTICAL RIFLE) – 5.56 NATO, 7.62x30, 6.5 Grendel, or 6.8 SPC II cal., carbine length gas system, 18 in. match grade barrel, target crown, birdcage flash hider, billet aluminum upper and lower receiver, flared magwell, 6-position Mil-Spec buffer tube, nickel boron EXO bolt carrier group, Magpul MBUS 2 front and rear sights, 17 in. free float P-Mod KeyMod rail system, SMI BETR tactical charging handle, single stage trigger, and winter trigger guard, MFT Minimalist collapsible pistol grip stock, hardcoat anodized finish in black or FDE, includes two Magpul 30 shot mags., 6 1/2 lbs. Disc. 2017.

| | $1,385 | $895 | $675 | $525 | $450 | $385 | $350 | *$1,699* |

STI INTERNATIONAL

Current manufacturer established during 1993, and located in Georgetown, TX. Distributor and dealer sales.

STI International also in steel, stainless steel, aluminum, or titanium - please contact the company directly for pricing and availability (see Trademark Index).

RIFLES/CARBINES: SEMI-AUTO

STI SPORTING/TACTICAL CARBINE – .223 Rem. or 5.56 NATO cal., GIO, 16 in. stainless steel barrel, JP trigger group, STI Valkyrie handguard and gas block, Nordic tactical compensator, black Teflon coating, fixed A2 or collapsible buttstock, optional rails, approx. 7 lbs. Mfg. 2010-2014.

| | $1,225 | $825 | $575 | $475 | $425 | $375 | $350 | *$1,455* |

SABRE DEFENCE INDUSTRIES LLC

Previous manufacturer from 2002-2010, with production headquarters located in Nashville, TN, and sales offices located in Middlesex, U.K. This company was previously known as Ramo Mfg., Inc., which was founded in 1977. Sabre Defence was also the U.S. distributor for Sphinx pistols until 2009.

RIFLES/CARBINES: SEMI-AUTO

Sabre Defence Industries manufactured many variations of the XR15 line of tactical design carbines and rifles for civilians, law enforcement, and military.

LIGHT SABRE – .223 Rem. cal., GIO, 16 in. chrome moly barrel, 30 shot mag., M5 carbine upper, forged front sight, one-piece polymer lower assembly, single stage Mil-Spec trigger, 5.9 lbs. Mfg. 2009-2010.

| | $1,050 | $650 | $495 | $450 | $395 | $350 | $325 | *$1,229* |

XR15A3 A2 NATIONAL MATCH – .223 Rem. cal., GIO, 20 in. stainless steel matte finished HBAR barrel, 30 shot mag., black anodized finish, A3 upper and matched lower, NM handguards, forged front sights, NM rear sight, A2 grip, two-stage trigger, fixed A2 stock, M4 feed ramp, A2 flash hider, includes two mags. Disc. 2009.

| | $1,385 | $895 | $675 | $525 | $450 | $385 | $350 | *$1,699* |

XR15A3 A4 RIFLE – .223 Rem. cal., GIO, 20 in. vanadium Govt. contour barrel, 30 shot mag., black anodized finish, A3 upper and matched lower, A2 round handguard, forged front sight, A2 grip, single stage trigger, fixed A2 stock, M4 feed ramp, A2 flash hider, includes two mags., approx. 7.2 lbs. Disc. 2010.

| | $1,150 | $750 | $550 | $465 | $415 | $375 | $350 | *$1,384* |

Add $34 for chrome-lined barrel.

SABRE DEFENCE INDUSTRIES LLC, cont. 315 S

MSR		100%	98%	95%	90%	80%	70%	60%	Last MSR

XR15A3 COMPETITION EXTREME – .223 Rem. cal., GIO, 16, 18, or 20 in. stainless steel fluted barrel, 30 shot mag., A3 upper and matched lower, black anodized finish, CTR 6-position retractable stock, free float handguard, Ergo grip, match trigger, flip-up sights, mid-length barrel assembly, M4 feed ramp, includes two mags., cleaning kit, and tactical case. Disc. 2010.

| | | $1,725 | $1,050 | $850 | $625 | $550 | $475 | $425 | $2,189 |

XR15A3 COMPETITION SPECIAL – .223 Rem. or 6.5 Grendel cal., GIO, 16 (.223 Rem. cal. only), 18, or 20 in. stainless steel fluted barrel, 30 shot mag., A3 upper and matched lower, black anodized finish, A2 fixed stock, tubular free float handguard, Ergo grip, match trigger, mid-length barrel assembly, M4 feed ramp, includes two mags., cleaning kit, and tactical case. Disc. 2010.

| | | $1,575 | $995 | $775 | $575 | $495 | $425 | $395 | $1,899 |

Add $200 for 6.5 Grendel cal.

XR15A3 COMPETITION DELUXE – .223 Rem. or 6.5 Grendel cal., GIO, 16, 18, or 20 in. stainless or vanadium steel fluted barrel, 25 (6.5 Grendel cal.) or 30 shot mag., A3 upper and matched lower, black anodized finish, five position retractable stock, tactical handguard, Ergo grip, match trigger, flip-up sights, competition Gill-brake, fluted mid-length barrel assembly, M4 feed ramp, includes two mags., cleaning kit, and tactical case. Disc. 2010.

| | | $1,795 | $1,050 | $875 | $625 | $550 | $475 | $425 | $2,299 |

Add $200 for 6.5 Grendel cal.

Add $300 for piston system upgrade (Competition Deluxe Piston, new 2010).

XR15A3 FLAT TOP CARBINE – .223 Rem. cal., GIO, 16 in. vanadium barrel, 30 shot mag., A3 upper and matched lower, black anodized finish, CAR round handguards, flip-up sights, Ergo grip, single stage trigger, 6-position collapsible stock, M4 feed ramp, A2 flash hider, includes two mags. Disc. 2009.

| | | $1,100 | $675 | $525 | $450 | $400 | $350 | $325 | $1,319 |

Add $40 for chrome-lined barrel.

XR15A3 HEAVY BENCH TARGET – .204 Ruger, .223 Rem., or 6.5 Grendel cal., GIO, 24 in. fluted match grade stainless steel heavy barrel, 4 (disc. 2009, 6.5 Grendel only), 10, or 25 (6.5 Grendel) shot mag., black anodized finish, A3 upper and matched lower, tubular free float handguards, flip-up sights, Ergo grip, single stage adj. trigger, fixed A2 stock, sling swivel stud and bipod, includes two mags., cleaning kit, and tactical case, 9.3 lbs. Disc. 2010.

| | | $1,575 | $995 | $775 | $575 | $495 | $425 | $395 | $1,889 |

Add $200 for 6.5 Grendel cal.

XR15A3 M4 CARBINE – .223 Rem., 6.5 Grendel, or 7.62x39mm (disc. 2009) cal., GIO, 16 in. vanadium contoured alloy barrel, 25 (6.5 Grendel cal. only) or 30 shot mag., black anodized finish, A3 upper and matched lower, M4 oval handguard, forged front sight, no rear sight, A2 grip, single stage trigger, 6-position collapsible stock, M4 feed ramp, A2 flash hider, includes two mags., cleaning kit, and tactical case, 6.3 lbs. Disc. 2010.

| | | $1,125 | $700 | $525 | $450 | $400 | $350 | $325 | $1,344 |

Add $100 for 7.62x39mm cal. (disc. 2009).

Add $33 for chrome-lined barrel.

Add $205 for 6.5 Grendel cal.

XR15A3 M4 FLAT TOP – .223 Rem., 6.5 Grendel, or 7.62x39mm (disc. 2009) cal., GIO, 16 in. vanadium contoured barrel, 25 (6.5 Grendel cal. only) or 30 shot mag., A3 upper and matched lower, M4 oval handguard, flip-up sights, black anodized finish, A2 grip, single stage trigger, 6-position collapsible stock, M4 feed ramp, A2 flash hider, includes two mags., cleaning kit, and tactical case, 6.4 lbs. Disc. 2010.

| | | $1,275 | $850 | $600 | $495 | $425 | $375 | $350 | $1,507 |

Add $70 for 7.62x39mm cal. (disc. 2009).

Add $34 for chrome-lined barrel.

Add $193 for 6.5 Grendel cal.

XR15A3 M4 TACTICAL – .223 Rem., 6.5 Grendel, or 7.62x39mm (disc. 2009) cal., GIO, 16 in. vanadium chrome-lined contoured barrel, 25 (6.5 Grendel cal. only) or 30 shot mag., A3 upper and matched lower, multi-rail handguards, flip-up sights, black anodized finish, Ergo grip, single stage trigger, 6-position collapsible stock, M4 feed ramp, A2 flash hider, tactical Gill-brake, includes two mags., cleaning kit, and tactical case, approx. 7 lbs. Disc. 2010.

| | | $1,650 | $1,000 | $795 | $595 | $495 | $425 | $395 | $1,993 |

Add $40 for 7.62x39mm cal. (disc. 2009).

Add $176 for 6.5 Grendel cal.

* M4 Tactical Piston Carbine – .223 Rem. cal., 16 in. chrome moly steel barrel, 30 shot mag., similar to M4 Tactical, except has mid-length GPO, 7 lbs. Mfg. 2010 only.

| | | $1,975 | $1,150 | $925 | $650 | $575 | $495 | $425 | $2,499 |

S 316 SABRE DEFENCE INDUSTRIES LLC, cont.

MSR	100%	98%	95%	90%	80%	70%	60%	Last MSR

XR15A3 M5 CARBINE – .223 Rem., 6.5 Grendel, or 7.62x39mm (disc. 2009) cal., GIO, 16 in. vanadium contoured barrel, 25 (6.5 Grendel cal. only) or 30 shot mag., A3 upper and matched lower, mid-length handguards, black anodized finish, forged front sight, Ergo grip, single stage trigger, 6-position collapsible stock, M4 feed ramp, A2 flash hider, includes two mags., cleaning kit, and tactical case, 6.4 lbs. Disc. 2010.

	$1,125	$700	$525	$450	$400	$350	$325	$1,341

Add $30 for 7.62x39mm cal. (disc. 2009).
Add $33 for chrome-lined barrel.
Add $208 for 6.5 Grendel cal.

XR15A3 M5 FLAT TOP – .223 Rem. or 6.5 Grendel cal., GIO, 16 in. vanadium contoured mid-length barrel, 25 (6.5 Grendel cal. only) or 30 shot mag., black anodized finish, A3 upper and matched lower, flip-up sights, single stage trigger, 6-position collapsible stock, M4 feed ramp, A2 flash hider, mid-length handguard, Ergo grip, includes two mags., cleaning kit, and tactical case, 6 1/2 lbs. Disc. 2010.

	$1,275	$850	$600	$495	$425	$375	$350	$1,504

Add $33 for chrome-lined barrel.
Add $195 for 6.5 Grendel cal.

M5 TACTICAL CARBINE – .223 Rem. or 6.5 Grendel cal., GIO, 16 in. chrome moly chrome-lined barrel, 25 or 30 shot mag., free float quad rail handguards, flip-up front and rear sights, collapsible buttstock, single stage Mil-Spec trigger, ergonomic pistol grip, trigger lock, sling, cleaning kit, and case, approx. 7 lbs. Mfg. 2009-2010.

	$1,725	$1,050	$850	$625	$550	$475	$425	$2,117

Add $235 for 6.5 Grendel cal.

* **M5 Tactical Piston Carbine** – .223 Rem. cal., 16 in. chrome moly steel barrel, 30 shot mag., similar to M5 Tactical, except has mid-length GPO, 7.3 lbs. Mfg. 2010.

	$1,975	$1,150	$925	$650	$575	$495	$425	$2,499

XR15A3 PRECISION MARKSMAN RIFLE – .223 Rem. or 6.5 Grendel cal., GIO, 20 or 24 in. stainless steel barrel, 25 (6.5 Grendel cal.) or 30 shot mag., A3 upper and match lower, rail handguards, Ergo tactical deluxe grip with palm rest, match trigger, fluted mid-length barrel assembly, black anodized finish, M4 feed ramp, Magpul PRS adj. stock, includes Leupold 6.5-20x50 Mark IV scope (standard through 2009), two mags., cleaning kit and tactical case, approx. 10 lbs. Disc. 2010.

	$1,975	$1,150	$925	$650	$575	$495	$425	$2,415

Add $126 for 6.5 Grendel cal.
Add $1,185 for Leupold scope.

XR15A3 SPR – .223 Rem. or 6.5 Grendel cal., GIO, 16, 18, or 20 in. stainless or vanadium steel fluted barrel, 25 (6.5 Grendel cal.) or 30 shot mag., A3 upper and matched lower, black anodized finish, five position retractable stock, tactical handguard, Ergo grip, match trigger, flip-up sights, bipod, fluted mid-length barrel assembly, M4 feed ramp, includes two mags., cleaning kit, and tactical case, 8.7 lbs. Disc. 2010.

	$1,975	$1,150	$925	$650	$575	$495	$425	$2,499

Add $200 for 6.5 Grendel cal.

XR15A3 VARMINT – .223 Rem. cal., GIO, 20 in. fluted match grade stainless steel heavy barrel, 10 shot mag., A3 upper and matched lower, black anodized finish, tubular free float handguards, Ergo grip, match trigger, fixed A2 stock, sling swivel stud, includes two mags., cleaning kit, and tactical case. Disc. 2009.

	$1,425	$925	$700	$550	$475	$395	$350	$1,709

SAVAGE ARMS, INC.

Current manufacturer located in Westfield, MA since 1959, with sales offices located in Suffield, CT. Previously manufactured in Utica, NY - later manufacture was in Chicopee Falls, MA. Dealer and distributor sales.

This company originally started in Utica, NY in 1894. The Model 1895 was initially manufactured by Marlin between 1895-1899. After WWI, the name was again changed to the Savage Arms Corporation. Savage moved to Chicopee Falls, MA circa 1946 (to its Stevens Arms Co. plants). In the mid-1960s the company became The Savage Arms Division of American Hardware Corp., which later became The Emhart Corporation. This division was sold in September 1981, and became Savage Industries, Inc. located in Westfield, MA (since the move in 1960). On November 1, 1989, Savage Arms Inc. acquired the majority of assets of Savage Industries, Inc. On June 24, 2013, ATK acquired Caliber Company, the parent company of Savage Sports Corporation.

Savage Arms, Inc. will offer service and parts on their current line of firearms only (those manufactured after Nov. 1, 1995). Warranty and repair claims for products not acquired by Savage Arms, Inc. will remain the responsibility of Savage Industries, Inc. For information regarding the repair and/or parts of Savage Industries, Inc. firearms, please refer to the Trademark Index in the back of this text. Parts for pre-1989 Savage Industries, Inc. firearms may be obtained by contacting the Numrich Gun Parts Corporation located in West Hurley, NY (listed in Trademark Index).

For Savage Arms, Inc. pre-December 1968 serial number records can be researched from the original company ledgers for

SAVAGE ARMS, INC., cont. 317 S

MSR	100%	98%	95%	90%	80%	70%	60%	Last MSR

rifles, pistols, and shotguns that were serialized. The information will be furnished for Model 1895, 1899, and Model 99 rifles, semi-automatic pistols, and other pre-December 1968 serialized guns. Information on other Savage non-serialized firearms, or post-December 1968 guns. A factory letter authenticating the configuration of a particular specimen may be obtained by contacting Savage (see Trademark Index for listings and address). Please allow 8 weeks for an adequate response.

For more Savage model information, please refer to the Serialization section in the back of this text.

Please refer to the *Blue Book of Modern Black Powder Arms* by John Allen (also online) for more information and prices on Savage's lineup of modern black powder models. For more information and current pricing on both new and used Savage airguns, please refer to the *Blue Book of Airguns* by Dr. Robert Beeman & John Allen (also online).

PISTOLS: SEMI-AUTO

MSR 15 BLACKOUT – .300 AAC Blackout cal., 10 1/2 in. Melonite QPQ coated carbon steel barrel, Savage helical flash hider, detachable box mag., Magpul MBUS flip-up front and rear sights, black synthetic stock, KAK Shockwave brace, Hogue pistol grip, fixed pistol length gas system, aluminum receiver, free float handguard with M-LOK, matte black finish. New mid-2018.

MSR $1,099	$940	$750	$650	$550	$500	$400	$325

RIFLES: SEMI-AUTO, CENTERFIRE, CURRENT/RECENT PRODUCTION

MSR 10 COMPETITION HD – .308 Win. cal., stainless steel barrel with matte black finish, ported muzzle brake, detachable box mag., black synthetic stock, adj. gas block, custom handguard, integral Picatinny rail. New mid-2018.

MSR $3,449	$2,775	$1,825	$1,350	$750	$650	$595	$525

MSR 10 HUNTER – .308 Win., .338 Federal, or 6.5mm Creedmoor cal., GIO, AR-10 design, 16 or 18 in. Melonite QPQ treated medium barrel, muzzle brake, 20 shot mag., Blackhawk Blaze two-stage target trigger, Blackhawk Knox buttstock and pistol grip, adj. LOP, custom forged upper and lower receiver, free float handguard, adj. gas block, 8 lbs. New 2017.

MSR $1,481	$1,250	$825	$575	$475	$425	$375	$350

MSR 10 LONG RANGE – .308 Win., 6mm Creedmoor (new 2018), or 6.5mm Creedmoor cal., compact AR-10 design, 20, 22, or 22 1/2 in. Melonite QPQ treated medium heavy barrel, muzzle brake, 10 shot mag., Blackhawk Blaze two-stage target trigger, adj. gas block, Magpul PRS Gen3 buttstock, pistol grip, custom forged upper and lower receiver, non-reciprocating charging handle, free float M-LOK rail, 9 1/2 lbs. New 2017.

MSR $2,284	$1,795	$1,050	$875	$625	$550	$475	$425

MSR 15 COMPETITION – .223 Rem or .224 Valkyrie cal., stainless steel barrel with matte black finish, ported muzzle brake, detachable box mag., black synthetic stock, adj. gas block, custom handguard, integral Picatinny rail. New mid-2018.

MSR $2,875	$2,295	$1,450	$1,075	$675	$595	$525	$475

MSR 15 PATROL – .223 Rem./5.56 Wylde chamber, 16.13 in. Melonite QPQ treated barrel with 5R rifling, flash hider, 30 shot mag., Mil-Spec trigger, A-frame gas block front sight with Blackhawk rear, Blackhawk furniture, adj. LOP, Mil-Spec upper and lower receiver, mid-length gas system, 6 1/2 lbs. New 2017.

MSR $869	$745	$500	$435	$375	$335	$315	$295

MSR 15 RECON – .223 Rem./5.56 Wylde chamber, 16.13 in. Melonite QPQ treated barrel with 5R rifling, flash hider, 30 shot mag., Blackhawk Blaze trigger, Blackhawk flip-up sights, Blackhawk buttstock and grip, mid-length gas system, free float rail, 7 lbs. New 2017.

MSR $994	$850	$550	$465	$395	$350	$325	$295

MSR 15 RECON LRP – .224 Valkyrie, .22 Nosler, 6.8 SPC, or .223 Rem. cal., 25 in. Melonite QPQ barrel with 5R rifling, muzzle brake, 25 shot mag., two-stage target trigger, Magpul CTR stock, black Hogue pistol grip, custom forged lower, mid-length gas system, adj. gas block, free float M-LOK handguard, 7.42 lbs. New 2018.

MSR $1,249	$1,050	$650	$495	$450	$395	$350	$325

MSR 15 VALKYRIE – .224 Valkyrie cal., adj. mid-length gas system, 18 in. Melonite QPQ heavy barrel, Savage MSR tunable muzzle brake, two-stage target trigger, Hogue pistol grip, custom forged lower, free float M-LOK handguard, adj. gas block, Elite Series FDE Cerakote finish, 7.88 lbs. New 2018.

MSR $1,499	$1,250	$825	$575	$475	$425	$375	$350

SCORPION TACTICAL

Previous AR-15 rifle manufacturer and current AR-15 parts and accessories manufacturer, located in Leander, TX.

S 318 SCORPION TACTICAL, cont.

MSR	100%	98%	95%	90%	80%	70%	60%	Last MSR

RIFLES: SEMI-AUTO

ATS-15 L1 – 5.56 NATO cal., GIO, 16 in. heavy barrel with A2 flash hider, 30 shot mag., SST, fixed front and flip-up adj. rear sights, 6-pos. sliding stock, plastic pistol grip, forged aluminum upper and lower receiver, standard AR charging handle, standard plastic mid-length handguard with heat shield, black finish. Disc. 2014.

	$850	$550	$465	$395	$350	$325	$295	$999

ATS-15 L2 – 5.56 NATO cal., GIO, 16 in. heavy barrel with A2 flash hider, 30 shot PMAG, SST, fixed front and Magpul MBUS rear sights, 6-pos. sliding stock, Ergo grip, forged aluminum upper and lower receivers, standard AR charging handle, mid-length drop-in quad rail, black finish. Disc. 2014.

	$1,050	$650	$495	$450	$395	$350	$325	$1,229

ATS-15 L3 – 5.56 NATO cal., GIO, 16 in. M4 profile barrel with A2 flash hider, 30 shot PMAG, SST, Magpul enhanced aluminum trigger guard, Troy micro flip-up BattleSight sights, Magpul 6-pos. CTR stock, Ergo grip, forged aluminum upper and lower receiver, standard AR charging handle, carbine length free floating quad rail, black finish, 6.9 lbs. Disc. 2014.

	$1,195	$795	$550	$465	$415	$375	$350	$1,449

ATS-15 L5 – 5.56 NATO cal., GIO, 16 in. M4 profile barrel with A2 flash hider, 30 shot PMAG, SST, Magpul enhanced aluminum trigger guard, Magpul Gen2 MBUS front and rear backup sights, Magpul ACS/Adaptable Carbine Storage stock, Ergo grip, forged aluminum upper and lower receivers, standard AR charging handle, 13.8 in. Troy Alpha rail, FDE finish, 6.9 lbs. Disc. 2014.

	$1,795	$1,050	$875	$625	$550	$475	$425	$2,200

SEEKINS PRECISION

Current manufacturer located in Lewiston, ID.

Seekins Precision currently manufactures complete AR-15 style rifles as well as AR-15 parts and accessories.

PISTOLS: SEMI-AUTO

NXP8 – .300 AAC Blackout cal., 8 in. match grade stainless steel barrel, Nest flash hider, SB Tactical PDW pistol brace, ambi safety, 7 in. NOXs rail, DNA charging handle, NX15 upper receiver, SP223 billet lower receiver, adj. gas block. New 2018.

MSR $1,879		$1,575	$1,385	$1,185	$1,065	$915	$785	$635

RIFLES: SEMI-AUTO

3G2 – .223 Wylde chamber, 18 in. match grade stainless steel barrel, ATC muzzle brake, Timney trigger, ProComp 10x stock, MOE Plus grip, ambi controls, adj. gas system, CNC machined billet upper and SP223 billet ambi lower receiver, M4 feed ramp, 15 in. SP3R free float handguard, 8.2 lbs. New 2018.

MSR $1,995		$1,650	$1,000	$795	$595	$495	$425	$395

NXR16 – .223 Wylde chamber, 16 in. button rifled match grade stainless steel barrel with Armor Black coating, NEST flash hider, trigger finger index point and enlarged trigger guard, ACS-L stock, MOE Plus grip, ambi bolt release and selector switch, 15 in. NOXs handguard, skeletonized billet aluminum upper, SP223 lower receiver, adj. gas block, Melonite coated gas tube. New 2018.

MSR $1,659		$1,385	$895	$675	$525	$450	$385	$350

NOXS BILLET – .223 Wylde chamber, 16 in. match grade stainless steel barrel with Armor Black coating, NEST flash hider, QMS trigger, Magpul STR stock, MOE grip, billet aluminum upper and lower receivers, Melonite coated mid-length gas system, 15 in. M-LOK NOXs handguard rail system, adj. gas block, ambidextrous bolt release, M4 feed ramps, Type III Class 2 hardcoat anodized finish, 7.25 lbs.

MSR $1,549		$1,275	$850	$600	$495	$425	$375	$350

SP3G – .223 Rem./5.56 NATO (.223 Wylde chamber) cal., GIO, 18 in. 3G contoured super match barrel, Geissele Super 3-Gun trigger, Magpul UBR stock, Ergo Deluxe tactical pistol grip, 15 in. SP3R rail system, Melonite coated gas tube, bolt carrier, and adj. gas block, BCM Mod 3 charging handle, SP billet lower Gen 2, billet iMRT-3 upper, H buffer, M4 feed ramp, SP Advanced Tactical Compensator. Disc. 2014.

	$2,295	$1,450	$1,075	$675	$595	$525	$475	$2,800

SP10 .308 – .308 Win. cal., 16 (disc. 2017) or 18 in. stainless steel match grade barrel, ATC brake, billet aluminum construction, SST, Timney competition trigger, Magpul STR (disc. 2017) or ProComp 10X (new 2018) stock, adj. gas block, 15 in. SP3R handguard, ambidextrous controls, top Picatinny rail, BCM Mod 3 charging handle, hardcoat anodized matte black finish, 9 lbs. New 2015.

MSR $2,550		$2,050	$1,250	$950	$650	$575	$495	$475

SP10 6.5/.243 – 6.5mm Creedmoor or .243 Win. (disc. 2017) cal., 22 in. stainless steel match grade barrel, ATC brake, billet aluminum construction, CMC (disc.) or Timney trigger, Magpul PRS (disc. 2017) or ProComp 10X

MSR		100%	98%	95%	90%	80%	70%	60%	Last MSR

(new 2018) stock, MOE Plus grip, rifle length gas system, M4 feed ramp, adj. gas block, 15 in. SP3R handguard, ambidextrous controls, top Picatinny rail, hardcoat anodized matte black finish, 10 1/2 lbs. New 2015.

| MSR $2,650 | $2,125 | $1,325 | $995 | $675 | $595 | $525 | $475 | |

SP15 – .223 Wylde or .300 AAC Blackout cal., mid-length gas system, 16 in. match grade stainless steel barrel, Seekins Rook flash hider, Magpul STR stock, Magpul MOE+ grip, ambidextrous safety, BCM MOD 3 charging handle, billet aluminum upper and lower receivers, 15 in. NOXs handguard rail system, adj. gas block and Melonite gas tube, M4 feed ramps, Type III Class 2 hardcoat anodized finish, 6.8 lbs.

| MSR $1,299 | $1,075 | $675 | $500 | $450 | $400 | $350 | $325 | |

SPBRV2 (BATTLEFIELD RIFLE) – .223 Wylde or .300 AAC Blackout cal., 16 in. stainless steel match grade barrel with flash hider, 12 in. SAR quad rail handguard, forged upper and lower receiver, QMS trigger, BCM Mod 3 charging handle, Magpul MOE stock, Ergo grip, Melonite coated gas components, 7.2 lbs. Mfg. 2015-2016.

| | $1,175 | $775 | $550 | $465 | $415 | $375 | $350 | *$1,425* |

SPCBRV1 (COMBAT BILLET RIFLE) – .223 Rem./5.56 NATO (.223 Wylde chamber), or .300 AAC Blackout cal., GIO, 16 in. stainless steel barrel with flash hider, Melonite coated gas tube, bolt carrier and adj. gas block, Magpul MOE stock, Ergo pistol grip, ALG-ACT trigger, BCM Mod 3 charging handle, BAD ambi selector, SP Gen2 billet lower, upper, and 12 in. BAR rail, H buffer, M4 feed ramp. Disc. 2016.

| | $1,525 | $975 | $750 | $575 | $495 | $425 | $375 | *$1,850* |

SPRO3G (PRO SERIES) – .223 Wylde chamber or .300 AAC Blackout cal., 18 in. match grade stainless steel barrel, ATC muzzle brake, CNC machined billet upper and lower receivers, competition style free float 15 in. SP3R handguard, Melonite coated gas tube, bolt carrier group, and adj. gas block, ambidextrous controls, CMC trigger, BCM Mod 3 charging handle, Magpul UBR (disc.) or STR stock, Ergo Deluxe (disc.) or MOE+ grip, 8 1/2 lbs. New 2015.

| MSR $1,995 | $1,650 | $1,000 | $795 | $595 | $495 | $425 | $395 | |

SPROV3 (PRO SERIES) – .223 Wylde or .300 AAC Blackout cal., 16 in. stainless steel match grade barrel, flash hider, ambidextrous controls, CNC machined billet upper and lower receivers, Melonite coated gas components, 15 in. MCSR handguard, ACT trigger, Magpul STR stock, Ergo Deluxe grip, 7 1/2 lbs. Mfg. 2015-2016.

| | $1,650 | $1,000 | $795 | $595 | $495 | $425 | $395 | *$1,995* |

SHARPS MILSPEC

Previous trademark and division of Sharps Rifle Company, located in Chamberlain, SD 2011 only.

RIFLES: SEMI-AUTO

SHARPS 2010 CARBINE – 5.56 NATO cal., AR-15 style, GPO, 16 in. 5 groove rifling barrel with muzzle brake, redesigned charging handle, aluminum free floating handguard with quad Picatinny rails, Magpul ACS buttstock and MIAD pistol grip, supplied with two 30 shot mags. Limited mfg. 2011 only.

| | $2,125 | $1,325 | $995 | $675 | $595 | $525 | $475 | *$2,695* |

SIG SAUER

Current firearms trademark manufactured by SIG Arms AG (Schweizerische Industrie-Gesellschaft) located in Neuhausen, Switzerland. Most models are currently manufactured in the U.S., and some models continue to be imported from Switzerland. SIG Sauer, Inc. was established in 2007, and is located in Newington, NH. Previously imported and distributed from 1985-2006 by Sigarms, Inc. located in Exeter, NH. Previously located in Herndon, VA and Tysons Corner, VA.

In late 2000, SIG Arms AG, the firearms portion of SIG, was purchased by two Germans named Michael Lüke and Thomas Ortmeier (L&O Group), who have a background in textiles. Headquarters for L&O are in Emsdetten, Switzerland. Today the Lüke & Ortmeier group includes independently operational companies such as Blaser Jadgwaffen GmbH, Mauser Jagdwaffen GmbH, John Rigby, J.P. Sauer & Sohn GmbH, SIG-Sauer Inc., SIG-Sauer GmbH and SAN Swiss Arms AG. Please refer to individual listings.

On Oct. 1, 2007, SIG Arms changed its corporate name to SIG Sauer.

PISTOLS: SEMI-AUTO

Beginning 2001, SIG started manufacturing variations which are compliant by state. They include CA (10 shot mag. max only), MA (requires a loaded chamber indicator), and NY (must include empty shell casing) are priced slightly higher than the standard models available for the rest of the states.

The Sigarms Custom Shop, located in Exeter, NH, has recently been established and offers a wide variety of custom shop services, including action enhancement, full servicing, DA/SA conversions, trigger and hammer modifications, barrel replacement, and many refinishing options. Please contact Sigarms Custom Shop directly for more information and current pricing on these services.

During 2005, the Sigarms Custom Shop produced 12 limited editions, including the P229 Rail (January), P245 w/nickel accents and Meprolight night sights (February), P220 .45 ACP Rail (March), P239 Satin Nickel w/Hogue rubber grips (April), GSR 1911 Reverse

S 320 SIG SAUER, cont.

MSR	100%	98%	95%	90%	80%	70%	60%	Last MSR

Two-Tone (May), P229 Satin Nickel Reverse Two-Tone (June), P232 Rainbow Titanium (July), P226 Rail (August), P220 Sport Stock (September), P239 w/extra .357 SIG cal. barrel (October), P228 Two-Tone (November), and the P226 package w/Oakley glasses (December).

Early SIG Sauer pistols can be marked either with the Herndon or Tysons Corner, VA barrel address, and can also be marked "W. Germany" or "Germany". Earlier mfg. had three proofmarks on the bottom front of the slide, with a fourth on the frame in front of the serial number. Early guns with these barrel markings will command a slight premium over prices listed below, if condition is 98%+.

Add $399 for caliber X-Change kit on current models.

SIG M400 ELITE PSB – 5.56 NATO cal., GIO, 11 1/2 in. barrel, 30 shot mag., SIG enhanced trigger, SIG PSB, free float M-LOK handguard, Microlight gas block, black or titanium finish. New 2018.

	100%	98%	95%	90%	80%	70%	60%
MSR $1,303	$1,095	$935	$825	$725	$625	$525	$425

Add $71 for titanum finish.

SIG MCX 9 IN. – 5.56 NATO (mfg. 2015 only), 7.62x39mm (mfg. 2015 only), or .300 ACC Blackout cal., GPO, 9 in. barrel, 30 shot mag., aluminum KeyMod handguard, folding sights (disc. 2016), black or FDE (new 2016) finish, includes SBX stabilizing device and polymer hard case. Mfg. 2015-2017.

100%	98%	95%	90%	80%	70%	60%	Last MSR
$1,850	$1,675	$1,450	$1,250	$1,000	$850	$750	$2,199

Add $136 for FDE finish.
Add $475 for 5.56 NATO conversion kit (disc. 2016).

SIG MCX 11 1/2 IN. – 5.56 NATO cal., 11 1/2 in. barrel, 30 shot aluminum mag., folding sights, aluminum KeyMod handguard, pistol stabilizing brace, black or FDE finish. Mfg. 2016-2017.

100%	98%	95%	90%	80%	70%	60%	Last MSR
$1,850	$1,675	$1,450	$1,250	$1,000	$825	$725	$2,199

Add $136 for FDE finish.

SIG MCX RATTLER PSB – .300 AAC Blackout cal., GPO, 5 in. cold hammer forged barrel, 30 shot aluminum mag., SIG enhanced trigger, telescoping 3-pos. pistol brace, PDW grip, aluminum M-LOK handguard, 5.1 lbs. New 2018.

	100%	98%	95%	90%	80%	70%	60%
MSR $2,719	$2,400	$2,100	$1,800	$1,500	$1,250	$1,000	$850

SIG MCX VIRTUS PSB – 5.56 NATO or .300 AAC Blackout cal., GPO, 9 or 11 1/2 in. interchangeable cold hammer forged barrel, 30 shot polymer mag., Matchlite Duo trigger, 3-pos. collapsible pistol stabilizing brace, polymer grips, ambi controls, aluminum M-LOK free floating handguard, Elite Concrete (Gray) or FDE finish, 7-7.4 lbs. New 2018.

	100%	98%	95%	90%	80%	70%	60%
MSR $2,335	$2,050	$1,750	$1,500	$1,275	$1,050	$975	$800

SIG MPX-P – 9mm Para. cal., AR-15 style pistol, GPO, 8 in. barrel, aluminum handguard, reflex sights, 30 shot mag., with or without pistol stablizing brace. Mfg. 2014-2015.

100%	98%	95%	90%	80%	70%	60%	Last MSR
$1,380	$1,100	$900	$700	$600	$550	$495	$1,576

Add $309 for pistol stabilizing brace (PSB).

SIG MPX – 9mm Para. cal., GPO, 4 1/2 (new 2018) or 8 (disc. 2017) in. barrel, 30 shot mag., folding sights (disc. 2017), no stock, short aluminum KeyMod handguard with handstop, ambidextrous AR-style controls, hardcoat anodized black or FDE (new 2018) finish, 4.6 lbs. New 2016.

	100%	98%	95%	90%	80%	70%	60%
MSR $2,016	$1,700	$1,475	$1,275	$1,150	$900	$750	$650

Add $136 for FDE finish (new 2018).

SIG MPX WITH PISTOL STABILIZING BRACE – 9mm Para. cal., GPO, 4 1/2 (new 2018) or 8 (disc. 2017) in. barrel, 30 shot mag., folding sights (disc. 2017), aluminum KeyMod handguard with handstop, pistol stabilizing brace, black or FDE (new 2017) finish. New 2016.

	100%	98%	95%	90%	80%	70%	60%
MSR $2,162	$1,775	$1,550	$1,325	$1,150	$950	$825	$700

Add $136 for FDE finish (new 2017).

MODEL PM400 – 5.56 NATO cal., pistol equivalent of the M400 carbine/rifle, GIO, 11 1/2 in. barrel, 30 shot mag., flip-up rear sights, Picatinny flat-top upper, integral ambi QD sling, B5 Systems pistol grip, KeyMod handguard, FDE finish, with or w/o pistol stabilizing brace, 7 lbs. Mfg. 2014-2015.

100%	98%	95%	90%	80%	70%	60%	Last MSR
$1,295	$1,150	$995	$900	$750	$600	$475	$1,519

Subtract approx. $125 if without pistol stabilizing brace.

* ***Model PM400 SWAT PSB*** – 5.56 NATO cal., GIO, 11 1/2 in. barrel, 10 shot mag., aluminum handguard, pistol stabilizing brace, flip-up rear sight, integral ambi QD sling mounts, black fnish, 6 lbs. Mfg. 2015-2016.

100%	98%	95%	90%	80%	70%	60%	Last MSR
$1,275	$1,150	$1,000	$900	$750	$600	$475	$1,467

* ***Model PM400 Elite*** – 5.56 NATO (new 2016) or .300 AAC Blackout cal., GIO, 9 in. barrel, 30 shot mag., flip-up front and rear sights, rotating locking bolt, integral ambi QD sling mounts, aluminum KeyMod handguard, pistol stabilizing brace, black finish, 6 lbs. Mfg. 2015-2017.

100%	98%	95%	90%	80%	70%	60%	Last MSR
$1,400	$1,235	$1,100	$975	$830	$720	$585	$1,650

SIG SAUER, cont. 321 S

MSR	100%	98%	95%	90%	80%	70%	60%	Last MSR

MODEL P516 – 5.56 NATO cal., short stroke pushrod GPO with adj. gas valve, 7 or 10 (new 2012) in. barrel with muzzle brake, Magpul MOE grip, flip-up adj. iron sights, 10 or 30 (disc.) shot mag., aluminum quad rail, black finish, with (new 2014) or without pistol stabilizing brace (PSB, became standard 2015). Mfg. 2011-2012, reintroduced 2014-2015.

	$975	$800	$665	$535	$465	$415	$365	$1,199

Subtract approx. $175 if without pistol stabilizing brace (PSB).

MODEL P516G2 – 5.56 NATO cal., 11 1/2 in. barrel, 30 shot mag., aluminum handguard, pistol stabilizing brace, black finish. Mfg. 2017 only.

	$1,750	$1,550	$1,350	$1,150	$975	$825	$675	$1,990

MODEL P522 – .22 LR cal., blowback action, 10.6 in. barrel, aluminum flat-top upper receiver, choice of polymer or quad rail (P522 SWAT) forend, flash suppressor, 10 or 25 shot polymer mag., ambidextrous safety selector, sling attachments, with (new 2014) or without pistol stabilizing brace (PSB, became standard 2015), approx. 6 1/2 lbs. Mfg. 2010 only, reintroduced 2014-2015.

	$525	$450	$400	$360	$315	$290	$260	$628

Subtract approx. $125 if without pistol stabilizing brace (PSB).

Add $71 for P522 SWAT model with quad rail forend (mfg. 2010 only).

Last MSR for P522 SWAT model (disc. 2010) was $643.

MODEL P556 – 5.56 NATO cal., GPO similar to SIG 556 carbine, 10 in. cold hammer forged barrel with A2 type flash suppressor, Picatinny top rail, pistol grip only, ribbed and vented black polymer forearm, black Nitron finish, mini red dot front sight, aluminum alloy two-stage trigger, ambidextrous safety, 30 shot mag. (accepts standard AR-15 style mags.), 6.3 lbs. Mfg. 2009-2010.

	$1,825	$1,650	$1,450	$1,300	$1,200	$1,100	$1,000	$1,876

Add $147 for P556 SWAT model with quad rail forend.

* **Model P556 Lightweight** – 5.56 NATO cal., similar to Model P556, except has lightweight polymer lower unit and forend. Mfg. 2010-2013.

	$1,075	$950	$825	$725	$625	$525	$425	$1,207

Add $133 for quad rail forend (SWAT Model).

MODEL P556xi – 5.56 NATO or 7.62x39mm cal., GPO, 10 in. barrel, polymer handguard, flip-up sights, 30 shot mag., with (became standard 2015) or without pistol stabilizing brace. Mfg. 2014-2016.

	$1,415	$1,250	$1,075	$965	$835	$695	$550	$1,663

Add $131 for 7.62x39mm cal.

Subtract approx. $120 if without pistol stabilizing brace (became standard 2015).

MODEL P556xi SWAT – 5.56 NATO or 7.62x39mm cal., GPO, 10 in. barrel, aluminum handguard, flip-up sights, 30 shot mag., pistol stabilizing brace. Mfg. 2015-2016.

	$1,525	$1,350	$1,175	$1,050	$875	$725	$575	$1,794

Add $141 for 7.62x39mm cal.

MODEL P716 – 7.62 NATO cal., short stroke GPO with 4-position gas valve, 12 in. barrel, 20 shot mag., locking flip-up front and rear sights, integral ambi QD sling mounts, includes pistol stabilizing brace (PSB), 8.6 lbs. Mfg. 2015 only.

	$2,085	$1,800	$1,575	$1,350	$1,100	$950	$825	$2,456

RIFLES: SEMI-AUTO

State compliant rifles on some of the currently manufactured models listed within this section include CA, CO, HA, IL, MA, MD, NJ, and NY. Compliance features will vary from state to state, and typically, these compliant state MSRs are slightly higher than the standard models available from the rest of the states.

SIG M400 – 5.56 NATO cal., GIO, 16 in. barrel, A2 grip, M4 buttstock, 600 meter adj. and removable rear sight, 30 shot mag., includes hard case. Mfg. 2012-2015.

	$1,050	$650	$495	$450	$395	$350	$325	$1,233

Add $93 for aluminum quad rails (disc. 2014).

Add $40 for lightweight steady ready platform (mfg. 2012 only).

* **SIG M400 B5 Series** – 5.56 NATO cal., GIO, 16 in. barrel, 30 shot mag., rear flip-up sights, B5 Systems SOPMOD 6-pos. telescoping stock, pistol grip, KeyMod carbine handguards, Picatinny rail, Gray or Foliage finish, 6.7 lbs. Mfg. 2015 only.

	$1,125	$700	$525	$450	$400	$350	$325	$1,348

* **SIG M400 Carbon Fiber** – 5.56 NATO cal., GIO, 16 in. barrel, carbon fiber forend or choice of SIG or carbon fiber rifle stock, 30 shot Lancer mag. Mfg. 2014-2015.

	$1,725	$1,050	$850	$625	$550	$475	$425	$2,170

Add $172 for carbon fiber forend and carbon fiber rifle stock.

S 322 SIG SAUER, cont.

MSR	100%	98%	95%	90%	80%	70%	60%	Last MSR

* SIG M400 Classic – 5.56 NATO cal., GIO, M4 style polymer handguard, SIG grips, fixed front and rear flip-up sights, 30 shot mag., telestock, black finish. Mfg. 2014-2016.

	$1,050	$650	$495	$450	$395	$350	$325	$1,250

* Sig M400 Elite – 5.56 NATO cal., 16 in. barrel, 30 shot mag., SIG enhanced trigger, with or without red dot sights, 6-pos. telescoping stock, aluminum free floating M-LOK handguard, black or titanium finish. New 2017.

MSR $1,201	$1,025	$625	$495	$450	$395	$350	$325	

Add $135 for titanium finish.

Add $158 for Romeo5 red dot sights.

* SIG M400 Enhanced Carbine – 5.56 NATO cal., GIO, 16 in. barrel, MOE handguard, MOE grip, MOE stock, flip-up rear sights, black, OD Green, or FDE finish, otherwise similar to SIG M400. Mfg. 2012-2014.

	$1,050	$650	$495	$450	$395	$350	$325	$1,234

Add $66 for FDE finish.

* SIG M400 Enhanced Patrol – 5.56 NATO or .300 AAC Blackout cal., GIO, 16 in. barrel, flip-up sights, 30 shot mag., polymer handguard, black, FDE, OD Green (new 2015), or Muddy Girl (disc. 2015) finish. Mfg. 2014-2016.

	$1,195	$795	$550	$465	$415	$375	$350	$1,413

Add $34 for Muddy Girl finish (disc. 2015).

* SIG M400 Hunting – 5.56 NATO cal., GIO, 20 in. barrel, 1:8 twist, MOE handguard and grip, optic ready, black or Mix Pine2 finish, otherwise similar to SIG M400. Mfg. 2012 only.

	$915	$575	$475	$415	$350	$325	$300	$1,099

Add $90 for Mix Pine2 finish.

* SIG M400 Magpul – 5.56 NATO cal., GIO, 20 in. barrel, black finish, Magpul rifle stock, MOE grip and forend. Mfg. 2014-2015.

	$1,075	$675	$500	$450	$400	$350	$325	$1,287

* SIG M400 Predator – 5.56 NATO or .300 AAC Blackout (new 2016) cal., GIO, 18 in. heavy match grade threaded and capped stainless steel barrel, 5 shot mag., Geissele two-stage match trigger, Hogue synthetic rubber grip stock with free float forend, flat-top upper, extended charging handle, no sights, aluminum handguard, black finish, 7.6 lbs. Mfg. 2013-2017.

	$1,315	$850	$625	$500	$435	$375	$350	$1,582

* SIG M400 SWAT – 5.56 NATO cal., GIO, 16 in. barrel, quad rail, SIG grip, M4 style buttstock, rear flip sight, 20 shot mag., black finish. Mfg. 2012 only, reintroduced 2014-2017.

	$1,100	$675	$525	$450	$400	$350	$325	$1,319

* SIG M400 TREAD – 5.56 NATO cal., mid-length gas system, aluminum frame, 16 in. stainless steel barrel, 3-prong flash hider, single stage polished/hardcoat trigger, Magpul SL-K 6-pos. telescoping stock, free floating M-LOK handguard, ambi controls, 7 lbs. New late 2018.

MSR $951	$825	$535	$450	$385	$340	$325	$295	

* SIG M400 Vanish – 5.56 NATO cal., GIO, 20 in. precision Varmint barrel, 30 shot mag., two-stage Matchlite trigger, optic ready, fixed stock, free floating aluminum M-LOK handguard, Microlight gas block, Kuiu Verde 2.0 finish. New 2018.

MSR $1,336	$1,125	$700	$525	$450	$400	$350	$325	

* SIG M400 Varmint – 5.56 NATO cal., GIO, 22 in. heavy stainless steel barrel, 5 shot mag., match trigger. Mfg. 2014 only.

	$1,150	$750	$550	$465	$415	$375	$350	$1,395

* SIG M400 Varminter – 5.56 NATO cal., GIO, 22 in. heavy match grade stainless steel threaded and capped barrel, 5 shot mag., Geissele two-stage match trigger, Hogue rubber grip synthetic stock with free float forend, flat-top upper, extended charging handle, 8.1 lbs. Mfg. 2013-2014.

	$1,150	$750	$550	$465	$415	$375	$350	$1,395

SIG 516 – 5.56 NATO cal., short stroke GPO, 3 or 4 position gas valve, various configurations. New 2011.

* SIG 516 Basic Patrol – 5.56 NATO cal., GPO, polymer handguard and 2 Picatinny rails - one on top of receiver and the other in front of handguard, 16 in. free floating barrel with muzzle brake, Magpul stock and pistol grip, 30 shot mag. Mfg. 2011 only.

	$1,065	$650	$500	$450	$395	$350	$325	$1,252

* SIG 516 Patrol – 5.56 NATO or 7.62x39mm (mfg. 2012 only) cal., GPO, 16 in. cold hammer forged barrel with muzzle brake, Magpul MOE adj. stock and MOE grip (disc.) or B5 Systems Bravo SOPMOD stock, rear charging handle, free floating quad Picatinny rail, 3 position gas valve, 30 shot mag., ladder rail covers (new 2012), PMAG

SIG SAUER, cont. 323

MSR	100%	98%	95%	90%	80%	70%	60%	Last MSR

(new 2012), aluminum KeyMod handguard (new 2016), black, Flat Dark Earth (new 2012) or OD Green (mfg. 2012-2015) finish. New 2011.

| MSR $1,888 | $1,575 | $995 | $775 | $575 | $495 | $425 | $395 | |

Add $136 for Flat Dark Earth finish (new 2012).

* **SIG 516 Carbon Fiber** – 5.56 NATO cal., GPO, 16 in. barrel, flip-up sights, carbon fiber forend, carbon fiber SIG or rifle stock, 30 shot Lancer mag. Mfg. 2014-2015.

| | $1,675 | $1,000 | $825 | $625 | $550 | $475 | $425 | $2,004 |

Add $192 for carbon fiber rifle stock and forend.

* **SIG 516 Precision Marksman** – 5.56 NATO cal., GPO, 18 in. free floating match barrel w/o muzzle brake, 30 shot mag., free floating quad Picatinny rail, two-stage trigger, Magpul PRS stock, MIAD grip. Mfg. 2011-2013.

| | $1,875 | $1,100 | $895 | $650 | $575 | $495 | $425 | $2,399 |

* **SIG 516 SRP (Sight Ready Platform)** – 5.56 NATO cal., GPO, 16 in. barrel, 30 shot mag., aluminum handguard, black or OD Green finish. Mfg. 2015 only.

| | $1,425 | $925 | $700 | $550 | $475 | $395 | $350 | $1,713 |

* **SIG 516 Sport Configuration Model (SCM)** – 5.56 NATO, GPO, fixed stock, A2 pistol grip, 10 shot mag. Mfg. 2011-2012.

| | $1,315 | $850 | $625 | $500 | $435 | $375 | $350 | $1,599 |

SIG 716G2 DMR (DESIGNATED MARKSMAN) – 7.62 NATO or 6.5mm Creedmoor (18 in., new 2018) cal., short stroke pushrod operating system with 4 position gas valve, 16 or 18 (new 2018) in. free floating barrel with enhanced muzzle brake, two-stage match trigger, Magpul PMAG, aluminum KeyMod handguard with Picatinny rail, Magpul UBR stock and MIAD grip, ambi controls, black or Flat Dark Earth (new 2016) furniture, 12.3 lbs. New 2015.

| MSR $3,108 | $2,550 | $1,650 | $1,250 | $700 | $625 | $575 | $525 | |

Add $136 for Flat Dark Earth furniture.

Add $136 for 6.5mm Creedmoor cal. and 18 in. barrel (new 2018).

SIG 716 PATROL – 7.62 NATO cal., GPO, 16 in. barrel, 20 shot mag., Magpul ACS stock and MIAD grip, quad rail, black, Flat Dark Earth, or OD Green (disc. 2015) finish. Mfg. 2011-2016.

| | $1,795 | $1,050 | $875 | $625 | $550 | $475 | $425 | $2,283 |

Add $55 for Flat Dark Earth finish (new 2012).

SIG 716G2 PATROL – 7.62 NATO cal., GPO, 16 in. stainless steel free floating barrel with enhanced muzzle brake, 20 shot mag., 6-pos. telescoping stock, polymer grip, aluminum KeyMod handguard, black or FDE hardcoat anodized finish, 9.5 lbs. New 2017.

| MSR $2,385 | $1,875 | $1,100 | $895 | $650 | $575 | $495 | $425 | |

Add $136 for FDE finish.

SIG 716 PRECISION MARKSMAN – 7.62 NATO cal., short stroke GPO, 18 in. barrel, 20 shot PMAG, four position gas valve, threaded muzzle, upper and lower rails, two-stage Geissele match trigger, MIAD grip, Magpul UBR stock, folding backup iron sights, matte black finish, 11 lbs. Mfg. 2013 only.

| | $2,125 | $1,325 | $995 | $675 | $595 | $525 | $475 | $2,666 |

SINO DEFENSE MANUFACTURING (SDM)

Current manufacturer of carbines/rifles and distributed exclusively by Prima Armi located in Pinerolo, Italy. No current U.S. importation.

SDM manufactures AR-15 style and AK-47 design rifles and carbines. The company also makes a Dragunov and Mauser 98 style carbine, including a sniper variation. Please contact the company directly for more information, including U.S. availability and pricing (see Trademark Index).

SIONICS WEAPON SYSTEMS

Current rifle manufacturer located in Tucson, AZ.

PISTOLS: SEMI-AUTO

PATROL PISTOL III – 5.56 NATO cal., carbine length, GIO, 11 1/2 in. chrome-lined barrel, 30 shot round, Magpul MBUS Pro front and rear sights, Shockwave stock, Magpul ASAP QD endplate, Magpul MOE K2 grip, ambidextrous safety, aluminum upper receiver, Mil-Spec lower receiver, Raptor ambidextrous charging handle, 10.5 M-LOK handguard w/5-slot rail piece.

| MSR $1,440 | $1,225 | $1,070 | $920 | $830 | $675 | $550 | $430 | |

* **Patrol Pistol III-E** – 5.56 NATO cal., GIO, 11 1/2 in. chrome-lined barrel, 30 shot round, Magpul MBUS Pro front sight (optional), Shockwave stock, QD endplate, Magpul MOE K2 grip, single sided safety, forged aluminum upper and lower receiver, Raptor ambidextrous charging handle, 10.5 in. M-LOK handguard w/5-slot rail piece. M16 bolt carrier, black finish.

| MSR $1,099 | $935 | $815 | $700 | $635 | $515 | $420 | $325 | |

S 324 SIONICS WEAPON SYSTEMS, cont.

MSR	100%	98%	95%	90%	80%	70%	60%	Last MSR

RIFLES/CARBINES: SEMI-AUTO, AR-15 STYLE

Sionics Weapon Systems also manufactures NFA items. Current models include Patrol SBR II, and Patrol SBR III. Please contact the company directly for more information and pricing (see Trademark Index).

PATROL LW-ENHANCED – 5.56 NATO cal., GIO, 16 in. lightweight Melonite barrel with A2 flash suppressor, M4 upper and forged aluminum lower receiver, mid-length gas system, VLTOR Gunfighter charging handle, ALG Defense QMS trigger, VLTOR 5-pos. receiver extension, "H" buffer, Midwest Industries SSK 12 in. KeyMod handguard, B5 Systems Bravo stock, Ergo grip, 5 lbs. 9 oz. Disc. 2015.

Retail pricing was not available for this model.

PATROL RIFLE 0 – 5.56 NATO cal., 16 in. medium contour barrel with A2 flash suppressor, forged M4 upper and aluminum lower receiver, mid-length gas system, F-marked front sight base, Magpul MBUS rear sight, VLTOR Gunfighter charging handle, ALG Defense QMS trigger, VLTOR 5-pos. receiver extension, carbine H buffer, Magpul MOE handguard, Ergo grip, VLTOR IMOD stock, 6 lbs. 13 oz. New 2015.

MSR $1,200	$995	$625	$495	$450	$395	$350	$325	

PATROL RIFLE I – 5.56 NATO cal., GIO, 16 in. medium weight chrome-lined barrel, A2 flash suppressor, 9 in. free floating quad rail handguard, forged aluminum lower and upper receivers, M4 feed ramps, mid-length gas system, F-marked front sight base, VLTOR Gunfighter charging handle, ALG Defense QMS trigger, carbine H buffer, VLTOR 5-pos. receiver extension, Ergo grip, VLTOR IMOD stock, 7 lbs.

MSR $1,480	$1,250	$825	$575	$475	$425	$375	$350	

PATROL RIFLE II – 5.56 NATO cal., GIO, 16 in. medium weight chrome-lined barrel, A2 flash suppressor, 30 shot Magpul PMAG, M4 upper receiver, mid-length gas system, VLTOR Gunfighter charging handle, forged aluminum lower, ALG Defense QMS trigger, VLTOR 5-pos. receiver extension, carbine H buffer, 12 in. free floating quad rail handguard, Ergo grip, VLTOR IMOD stock, 7 lbs.

MSR $1,560	$1,315	$850	$625	$500	$435	$375	$350	

PATROL RIFLE II PRO – 5.56 NATO cal., similar to Patrol Rifle II, except has 12 in. free float quad rail handguard and low profile gas block. Disc. 2013.

	$1,385	$895	$675	$525	$450	$385	$350	$1,669

PATROL RIFLE III – 5.56 NATO cal., GIO, 16 in. medium weight chrome-lined barrel with A2 flash suppressor, 30 shot Magpul mag., mid-length gas system, M4 upper receiver, forged aluminum lower, single stage LE (disc.) or ALG Defense QMS trigger, "H" buffer, nickel treated M16 bolt carrier, 12.37 in. free floating "slick side" Samson EVO rail handguard, low profile gas block, VLTOR Gunfighter charging handle, Magpul MOE or VLTOR IMOD stock, Magpul MOE or Ergo grip, 6 lbs. 6 oz.

MSR $1,420	$1,195	$795	$550	$465	$415	$375	$350	

* **Patrol Rifle III XL** – 5.56 NATO cal., similar to Patrol Rifle III, except has 15 in. free floating Samson EVO rail handguard, 6 lbs. 8 oz.

MSR $1,430	$1,195	$795	$550	$465	$415	$375	$350	

* **Patrol Rifle III-E** – 5.56 NATO cal., GIO, 16 in. chrome-lined medium weight barrel, 30 shot mag., aluminum frame, enhanced Mil-Spec trigger, Magpul MBUS Pro Sights (optional), Magpul MOE SL stock, QD endplate, Magpul MOE K2 grip, singled-sided safety, forged upper and lower receiver, 13.5 in. M-LOK handguard, carbine "H" buffer, M16 bolt carrier, black finish.

MSR $1,080	$915	$575	$475	$415	$350	$325	$300	

Add $140 for Magpul MBUS Pro Sights.

PATROL RIFLE MK2 – 5.56 NATO cal., GIO, 16 in. medium contour barrel with A2 flash suppressor, mid-length gas system, forged M4 upper, forged aluminum lower, nickel plated bolt carrier group, VLTOR Gunfighter charging handle, ALG Defense QMS trigger, VLTOR 5-pos. receiver extension, "H" buffer, 13 in. Geissele SMR MK2 rail handguard, VLTOR IMOD stock, Ergo grip, 6 lbs. 13 oz. Disc. 2015.

	$950	$595	$495	$425	$365	$335	$300	$1,150

PATROL SSK-12/SSK-15 – 5.56 NATO cal., GIO, 16 in. barrel with A2 flash suppressor, M4 upper and forged aluminum lower receiver, 30 shot Magpul mag., low profile gas block, ALG Defense QMS trigger, "H" buffer, 12 (SSK-12) or 15 (SSK-15) in. SSK-KeyMod free float handguard rail, Magpul MOE stock, Ergo grip. Disc. 2015.

	$895	$575	$475	$395	$350	$325	$300	$1,070

Add $20 for 15 in. KeyMod rail.

PERIMETER MARKSMAN RIFLE – 5.56 NATO cal., GIO, 18 1/2 in. stainless steel chrome-lined barrel, M4 upper receiver, Magpul MBUS front and rear sight, Sionics muzzle brake, nickel plated bolt carrier and key, heavy extractor spring, forged aluminum lower receiver, single stage LE trigger, 30 shot Magpul mag., standard rifle buffer, ACE skeleton stock, Magpul MOE grip, free floating 15 inch rail EVO handguard, low profile gas block, includes soft case. Disc. 2014.

	$1,425	$925	$700	$550	$475	$395	$350	$1,709

SIONICS WEAPON SYSTEMS, cont. 325 **S**

MSR		100%	98%	95%	90%	80%	70%	60%	Last MSR

SHADES OF GRAY PATROL LIGHTWEIGHT – 5.56 NATO cal., GIO, 16 in. lightweight barrel with A2 flash suppressor, M4 upper, forged aluminum lower, ALG Defense QMS trigger, 6-pos. Mil-Spec receiver extension, "H" buffer, 30 shot Magpul mag., 15 in. SSK-KeyMod free float handguard, low profile gas block, mid-length gas system, Magpul MOE K2 grip in Stealth Gray, Magpul MOE SL stock in Stealth Gray. Mfg. 2015 only.

		100%	98%	95%	90%	80%	70%	60%	Last MSR
		$1,100	$675	$525	$450	$400	$350	$325	*$1,320*

SMITH & WESSON

Current manufacturer located in Springfield, MA, 1857 to date. Partnership with Horace Smith & Daniel B. Wesson 1856-1874. Family owned by Wesson 1874-1965. S&W became a subsidiary of Bangor-Punta from 1965-1983. Between 1983-1987, Smith & Wesson was owned by the Lear Siegler Co. On May 22, 1987, Smith & Wesson was sold to R.L. Tomkins, an English holding company. During 2001, Tomkins sold Smith & Wesson to Saf-T-Hammer, an Arizona-based safety and security company. Smith & Wesson was the primary distributor for most Walther firearms and accessories in the United States from 2002-2012. During 2012, Carl Walther GmbH Sportwaffen and Umarex announced the formation of Walther Arms, Inc. to import, sell, and market all Walther products in the U.S. beginning Jan. 1, 2013.

Smith & Wessons have been classified under the following category names - PISTOLS: LEVER ACTION, ANTIQUE, TIP-UPS, TOP-BREAKS, SINGLE SHOTS, EARLY HAND EJECTORS (Named Models), NUMBERED MODEL REVOLVERS (Modern Hand Ejectors), SEMI-AUTOS, RIFLES, and SHOTGUNS.

Each category is fairly self-explanatory. Among the early revolvers, Tip-ups have barrels that tip up so the cylinder can be removed for loading or unloading, whereas Top-breaks have barrels & cylinders that tip down with automatic ejection.

Hand Ejectors are the modern type revolvers with swing out cylinders. In 1957, S&W began a system of numbering all models they made. Accordingly, the Hand Ejectors have been divided into two sections - the Early Hand Ejectors include the named models introduced prior to 1958. The Numbered Model Revolvers are the models introduced or continued after that date, and are easily identified by the model number stamped on the side of the frame, visible when the cylinder is open. The author wishes to express his thanks to Mr. Sal Raimondi, Jim Supica, Rick Nahas, and Roy Jinks, the S&W Historian, for their updates and valuable contributions.

Factory special orders, such as ivory or pearl grips, special finishes, engraving, and other production rarities will add premiums to the values listed. After 1893, all ivory and pearl grips had the metal S&W logo medallions inserted on top.

FACTORY LETTER OF AUTHENTICITY - S&W charges $50 for a formal letter of authenticity. A form is available for downloading on their website: www.smith-wesson.com for this service. Turnaround time is usually 8-12 weeks.

For more information and current pricing on both new and used Smith & Wesson airguns, please refer to the *Blue Book of Airguns* by Dr. Robert Beeman & John Allen (also online).

Rifles: Performance Center Variations

M&P RIFLE – 5.56 NATO cal., GIO, 10 shot mag., 20 in. stainless steel barrel, synthetic stock with Hogue pistol grip, free floating forend, two-stage match trigger, billet aluminum receiver with Picatinny rail, no sights, hardcoat black or camo anodized finish, includes rifle case, 8 lbs. 2 oz. New 2008.

MSR $1,549		$1,300	$1,075	$925	$825	$725	$625	$525	

Add $40 for camo finish.

Product codes: 178016 (black) or 178015 (camo).

MODEL M&P 15 COMPETITION RIFLE – 5.56 NATO cal., GIO, 18 in. carbon steel barrel, 30 shot mag., alloy frame, two-stage trigger, 6-position adj. VLTOR IMOD stock w/custom free float forend, Hogue pistol grip, manual safety on lower, Armornite black finish, approx 6.4 lbs. New 2017.

MSR $1,579		$1,325	$1,095	$935	$825	$725	$625	$525	

Product Code: 11515

M&P 10 RIFLE – 5.56 NATO (disc. 2017) or 6.5mm Creedmoor (new 2018) cal., GIO, 20 in. barrel, 10 shot mag., alloy frame, Magpul MOE Plus grip, solid fixed stock w/custom free float forend, approx 7 lbs. New 2017.

MSR $2,035		$1,725	$1,550	$1,350	$1,150	$950	$825	$700	

M&P 15-22 PC TB – .22 LR cal., blowback operation, 18 in. fluted barrel, 10 shot detachable mag., fixed (compliant) or 6-position VLTOR adj. buttstock, polymer receiver with modular rail forend, adj. A2 post front sight and adj. dual aperture rear sight, black finish, 5.6 lbs. Mfg. 2011-2015.

		$665	$580	$500	$450	$425	$400	$395	*$789*

Product Codes: 170335 or 170337 (compliant).

M&P 15-22 PC SPORT – .22 LR cal., blowback action, 18 in. fluted threaded barrel, 10 shot mag., two-stage match trigger, Magpul MBUS sights, adj. stock w/Hogue pistol grip and slim handguard, Magpul M-LOK forearm, Picatinny rail, approx. 5.2 lbs. New 2018.

MSR $709		$595	$475	$425	$375	$325	$295	$275	

Product Code: 10205

S 326 SMITH & WESSON, cont.

MSR	100%	98%	95%	90%	80%	70%	60%	Last MSR

M&P 15PC LIMITED EDITION – 5.56 NATO cal., Wylde chambering, GIO, 20 in. barrel, 10 shot mag., skeletonized full-length buttstock, integral Picatinny style rail system, anodized streamlined free floating forend, black rubber pistol grip, swivel stud for sling or bipod attachment, PC marked soft carry case, master trigger lock and manual, marked "M&P 15PC" laser engraved on the right side, no forward assist on upper receiver, black matte finish. Mfg. 2006.

	100%	98%	95%	90%	80%	70%	60%	Last MSR
	$1,675	$1,425	$1,150	$925	$825	$725	$625	$1,999

Product Code: 170293.

Rifles: Semi-Auto

The following is a listing of abbreviations with related feature codes of both centerfire and rimfire semi-auto rifles: Stock: S/6 ADJ - 6 position adj., S/BLK - black synthetic, S/CAM - camo synthetic, S/SF - solid fixed, S/W - wood stock. Pistol Grip: PG - plastic grip, RG - rubber grip, WG - wood grip, NA - no grip. Rear Sight: R/ADJ - adjustable, R/FS - folding sight, R/FSADJ - folding adjustable, NA - no rear sight. Front Sight: F/BB - Black Blade, F/BP - Black Post, F/FO - fiber optic, F/FS - folding sight, F/FSADJ - folding adjustable, F/ GB - Gold Bead, F/WBF - white bead front sight, NA - no front sight. Forend: CFF - custom free float, MR - modular rail, STD - standard, NA - no forend (one piece stock). Receiver Material: AL - alloy, CA - carbon, SS - Stainless steel, POLY - polymer. Action: BA - bolt action, FA - fixed action, SAT - semi-auto.

This database does not take into consideration the state compliant variations of the M&P10 and M&P15 rifles.

M&P10 – .308 Win. cal., GIO, 18 in. barrel, enhanced flash hider, 5, 10, or 20 shot mag., fixed, Magpul MOE fixed (camo only), or 6-pos. CAR stock, pistol grip, ambidextrous controls, chromed gas key, bolt carrier, and firing pin, matte black or Realtree APG camo finish, 7 lbs. 11 oz. New 2013.

MSR $1,619	$1,350	$875	$650	$525	$450	$385	$350	

Add $110 for Realtree APG camo finish.

* **M&P10 Sport Optics Ready** – .308 Win. cal., 16 in. barrel with Armornite finish, flash suppressor, 20 shot mag., optics ready, 6-position telescopic stock, synthetic grip, gas block with Picatinny rail, mid-length handguard, sling swivel, ambi controls, approx. 4.8. lbs.

MSR $1,049	$875	$550	$465	$395	$350	$325	$300	

MODEL M&P15 CENTERFIRE SEMI-AUTO SERIES – .223 Rem./5.56 NATO or 5.45x39mm cal., GIO, AR-15 style design with 16 in. or longer chrome-lined barrel with muzzle brake, 1:9 or 1:7 (new 2017) rate of twist, aluminum upper and lower receiver, 10 or 30 shot mag. (most are Mil-Spec), one-piece fixed position, skeletonized, or 6-position CAR collapsible stock, hardcoat black anodized finish, features detachable carrying handle, A2 post front sight, adj. dual aperture rear sight, thinned handguard, M&P15T features extended Picatinny rail on receiver and barrel, in addition to RAS on both sides and bottom of barrel, supplied with hard carry case, approx. 6 1/2 lbs. New 2006.

The lowest serial number encountered to date is SW00200.

* **Model M&P15 w/Removable Carry Handle** – 5.56 NATO/.223 Rem. cal., GIO, 16 in. carbon steel barrel with Armornite finish, 30 shot PMAG, alloy receiver, adj. A2 post front sight, adj. rear sight, 6-position CAR stock, black polymer grip, removable carry handle, matte black finish, 6.98 lbs.

MSR $1,269	$1,065	$650	$500	$450	$395	$350	$325	

Add $20 for 1:7 rate of twist barrel (new 2017).

Product Codes: 811000, 11511.

* **Model M&P15A** – 5.56 NATO cal., GIO, AR-15 style, 16 in. barrel, 30 shot mag., similar to Model M&P15, except features a receiver Picatinny rail and adj. rear folding battle sight with ribbed handguard, 6 1/2 lbs. Mfg. 2006-2012.

	$1,075	$675	$500	$450	$400	$350	$325	$1,289

Product Code: 811002.

* **Model M&P15T** – 5.56 NATO cal., GIO, AR-15 style, fixed 10 (CA compliant) or detachable 30 shot PMAG, 16 in. barrel with Armornite finish, forged integral trigger guard, folding (disc. 2010) or fixed black post front sight (new 2011), fixed (new 2011) or folding (disc. 2010) adj. rear sight, modular rail (disc. 2010), 10 in. free float quad rail handguard (new 2011), 6-pos. telescopic stock, 6.85 lbs.

MSR $1,159	$975	$595	$495	$425	$365	$335	$300	

Product Codes: 811001 (disc. 2010), 811041 & 811048 (new 2011).

* **Model M&P15T w/M-LOK** – 5.56 NATO/.223 Rem. cal., GIO, 16 in. lightweight contoured barrel with Armornite finish, flash suppressor, 30 shot PMAG, forged integral trigger guard, Magpul MBUS sights, 6-pos. telescopic stock, mid-length gas system, 13 in. M&P slim modular free float handguard with Magpul M-LOK capability, with or w/o Crimson Trace LINQ System, 6.71 lbs. New 2017.

MSR $1,189	$995	$625	$495	$450	$395	$350	$325	

Add $310 for Crimson Trace LINQ System.

Product Codes: 11600, 11777 (Crimson Trace).

SMITH & WESSON, cont. 327 S

MSR	100%	98%	95%	90%	80%	70%	60%	Last MSR

* **Model M&P15FT** – 5.56 NATO cal., GIO, AR-15 style, 16 in. barrel, 10 shot mag. (compliant for CT, MA, MD, NJ, and NY), one-piece pistol grip fixed stock, custom free float forend (new 2012), folding adj. (new 2012) front and rear sights, modular rail (disc. 2011), alloy receiver. Mfg. 2008-2011.

| | $1,425 | $925 | $700 | $550 | $475 | $395 | $350 | |

Last MSR for product code 811004 was $1,709 in 2011.

Product Code: 811004 (disc. 2011), 811048 (new 2012).

* **Model M&P15OR** – 5.56 NATO cal., GIO, 16 in. carbon steel barrel with flat-top Picatinny rail and gas block, 30 shot mag., optics ready alloy receiver, black alloy finish, 6-position adj. stock, no rear sight. New 2008.

| MSR $1,069 | $895 | $575 | $475 | $395 | $350 | $325 | $300 | |

Product Code: 811003.

* **Model M&P15ORC** – 5.56 NATO cal., GIO, AR-15 style, 16 in. barrel, 10 shot mag. (compliant CT, MA, MD, NJ and NY), alloy receiver, optics ready, pistol grip stock, black synthetic grip, Picatinny rail, black alloy finish. Mfg. mid-2008-2017.

| | $875 | $550 | $465 | $395 | $350 | $325 | $300 | $1,039 |

Product Code: 811013.

* **Model M&P15X** – 5.56 NATO/.223 Rem. cal., GIO, AR-15 style, 16 in. barrel, 30 shot PMAG, alloy receiver, adj. A2 post front and Troy rear folding battle sights, 6-position adj. pistol grip stock, Troy carbine length handguard, black alloy finish, 6.35 lbs. Mfg. 2008-2017.

| | $1,150 | $750 | $550 | $465 | $415 | $375 | $350 | $1,379 |

Product Code: 811008.

* **Model M&P15X w/M-LOK** – 5.56 NATO/.223 Rem. cal., GIO, 16 in. barrel with Armornite finish, 30 shot PMAG, forged integral trigger guard, adj. A2 post front and folding Magpul MBUS rear sights, 6-pos. telescopic stock, M&P slim aluminum carbine length Magpul M-LOK handguard, 2 in. M-LOK aluminum Picatinny rail panel, Picatinny top rail, 6.4 lbs. New 2017.

| MSR $1,239 | $1,050 | $650 | $495 | $450 | $395 | $350 | $325 | |

Product Code: 11535.

* **Model M&P15I** – .223 Rem. cal., GIO, AR-15 style, 17 in. barrel, 10 shot mag. (compliant CT, MA, MD, NJ, and NY), black alloy finish, pistol grip stock, adj. rear sight, black post front sight, alloy receiver, 7 lbs. Mfg. mid-2008-2011.

| | $1,065 | $650 | $500 | $450 | $395 | $350 | $325 | $1,259 |

Product Code: 811010.

* **Model M&P15R** – 5.45x39mm cal., GIO, AR-15 style, 16 in. barrel, 30 shot mag., black alloy finish, pistol grip stock, adj. rear and black post front sight, alloy receiver, Picatinny rail, 6 1/2 lbs. Mfg. 2008-2011.

| | $995 | $625 | $495 | $450 | $395 | $350 | $325 | $1,089 |

Product Code: 811011.

MODEL M&P15MOE – 5.56 NATO cal., GIO, AR-15 style, 16 in. barrel, 30 shot mag., black alloy finish, 6-pos. adj. stock, alloy receiver, post front sight, folding rear sight. Mfg. 2010-2011.

| | $1,050 | $650 | $495 | $450 | $395 | $350 | $325 | $1,249 |

Product Codes: 811020 and 811021.

MODEL M&P15 MOE MID – 5.56 NATO cal., GIO, 16 in. barrel, 30 shot mag., alloy receiver, M4 A2 post front sight and Magpul MBUS rear sight, Magpul MOE stock, Magpul MVG (vertical grip), features Magpul hardware, black or Flat Dark Earth finish. Mfg. 2012-2017.

| | $1,065 | $650 | $500 | $450 | $395 | $350 | $325 | $1,259 |

Product Codes: 811053 and 811054.

* **Model M&P15 MOE SL MID** – 5.56 NATO/.223 Rem. cal., GIO, 16 in. barrel with Armornite finish, flash suppressor, 30 shot PMAG, alloy receiver, black post front sight and folding MBUS rear sight, 6-position Mil-Spec stock, Magpul MOE SL grip, mid-length gas system, features Magpul hardware, 2 in. M-LOK polymer Picatinny rail panel, mid-length handguard, black, FDE, or Stealth Gray finish, 6 1/2 lbs. New 2017.

| MSR $1,239 | $1,050 | $650 | $495 | $450 | $395 | $350 | $325 | |

Product Codes: 11512 (black), 11513 (Flat Dark Earth), and 11553 (Stealth Grey).

* **Model M&P15PS** – 5.56 NATO cal., GIO, 16 in. barrel, fixed 10 (CA compliant) or 30 shot mag., black alloy finish, six position adj. stock with standard forend, alloy receiver, solid handguard, Picatinny rail above gas block, no sights, flat-top upper, chrome-lined bore, gas key, and bolt carrier, adj. gas plug with three settings. Mfg. 2010-2013.

| | $1,150 | $750 | $550 | $465 | $415 | $375 | $350 | $1,359 |

Product Code: 811022.

S 328 SMITH & WESSON, cont.

MSR	100%	98%	95%	90%	80%	70%	60%	Last MSR

* **Model M&P15PSX** – 5.56 NATO cal., GIO, 16 in. barrel, 30 shot mag., black alloy finish, 6-pos. adj. stock with standard forend and tactical rail, alloy receiver. Mfg. 2010-2013.

	100%	98%	95%	90%	80%	70%	60%	Last MSR
	$1,250	$825	$575	$475	$425	$375	$350	$1,499

Product Code: 811023.

MODEL M&P15 300 WHISPER – .300 Whisper cal., GIO, 16 in. threaded barrel with or without sound suppressor, 10 shot (camo) or 30 shot PMAG (black), 6-pos. telescopic stock, low recoil and muzzle blast, gas block with integral Picatinny-style rail, black (new 2014) or Realtree APG camo on all surfaces except barrel, 6.11 lbs. New 2012.

MSR $1,119	$935	$575	$475	$415	$350	$325	$300	

Product Code: 811300 (camo) or 811302 (black).

MODEL M&P15-22 SPORT RIMFIRE SEMI-AUTO – .22 LR cal., blowback action, 16 1/2 in. barrel with or w/o threading, 10 or 25 shot mag., A2 post front sight and dual aperture rear sight, fixed or six position CAR adj. stock, quad rail handguard, matte black, Pink Platinum (mfg. 2014 -2015), Black and Tan (mfg. 2014-2015), Purple Platinum (mfg. 2014-2015), Harvest Moon Orange (mfg. 2014-2015), 100% Realtree APG HD (disc. 2015), Kryptek Highlander (new 2016), Muddy Girl (new 2016), or Robins Egg Blue Platinum (new 2018) camo finish, 5 1/2 lbs. New 2009.

MSR $449	$395	$350	$325	$295	$265	$245	$225	

Add 5% for threaded barrel (disc.).

Add $50 for 100% Realtree APG HD camo finish with threaded barrel (mfg. 2011-2015).

Add $50 for Pink Platinum, Black and Tan, Purple Platinum, or Harvest Moon Orange finish (mfg. 2014-2015).

Add $50 for Kryptek Highlander (new 2016), Muddy Girl (new 2016), or Robins Egg Blue Platinum (new 2018) camo finish.

Product Codes: 811030 (Black), 811046 (Camo), 811051 (Pink Platinum), 811059 (Black and Tan), 10041 (Purple Platinum), 10043 (Harvest Moon Orange), 10211 (Kryptek Highlander), or 10212 (Muddy Girl).

During 2015, the model nomenclature was changed from M&P15-22 to M&P15-22 Sport.

* **Model M&P15-22 Sport MOE SL** – .22 LR cal., blowback action, polymer frame, 16 1/2 in. carbon steel barrel with flash hider, 25 shot mag., folding Magpul MBUS front and rear sights, Magpul MOE SL stock, polymer grip, two-pos. safety, black or FDE finish, 5 1/2 lbs. New 2017.

MSR $499	$425	$365	$335	$300	$275	$250	$230	

Product Code: 10210 (FDE), 10213 (black).

* **Model M&P15-22 MOE Rimfire Semi-Auto** – .22 LR cal., similar to Model M&P15-22, except has 16 in. threaded barrel, A1 style compensator, 25 shot detachable mag., folding front and rear sight and skeletonized Magpul MOE stock, flat black or Flat Dark Earth (new 2012) finish, approx. 5 1/2 lbs. Mfg. 2011-2016.

	100%	98%	95%	90%	80%	70%	60%	Last MSR
	$525	$450	$395	$365	$335	$300	$275	$609

Product Codes: 811034 and 811035.

* **Model M&P15-22 PC TB**

Please see listing under Performance Center rifles.

MODEL M&P15 SPORT – 5.56 NATO cal., GIO, 16 in. Melonite treated barrel, A2 flash suppressor, fixed or detachable 10 or 30 shot mag., single stage trigger, hardcoat black anodized upper and lower receiver, polymer handguard, chrome-lined gas key and bolt carrier, adj. A2 post front sight, adj. dual aperture rear sight, 6-position telescoping buttstock. Mfg. 2011-2016.

	100%	98%	95%	90%	80%	70%	60%	Last MSR
	$645	$500	$415	$370	$325	$300	$275	$739

Product Codes: 811036 and 811037 (compliant).

MODEL M&P15 SPORT II – 5.56 NATO cal., GIO, 16 in. threaded or non-threaded barrel w/1:9 twist, 10 or 30 shot mag., Magpul MBUS rear sight, fixed or 6-pos. adj. stock, forged integral trigger guard, forward assist and dust cover, chromed firing pin, Armornite barrel finish. New 2017.

MSR $739	$645	$500	$415	$370	$325	$300	$275	

Product Codes: 10202 (30 shot mag.), 11616 (10 shot mag.), 10203 (fixed stock).

* **Model M&P15 Sport II M-LOK** – 5.56 NATO cal., GIO, 16 in. threaded barrel with Armornite finish, 30 shot mag., forged integral trigger guard, adj. A2 front sight post, folding Magpul MBUS rear sight, 6-pos. adj. stock, black polymer grips, Magpul MOE M-LOK carbine length handguard, 2 in. M-LOK Picatinny-style rail panel, chromed firing pin, forward assist and dust cover, 6.78 lbs. New 2017.

MSR $769	$665	$500	$415	$375	$335	$315	$295	

Product Code: 10305.

* **Model M&P15 Sport II OR** – 5.56 NATO cal., GIO, 16 in. threaded barrel with Armornite finish, 30 shot PMAG, forged integral trigger guard, optics ready, 6-pos. CAR stock, black polymer grips, gas block with integral Picatinny rail, forward assist and dust cover, chromed firing pin, QD sling swivel attachment point, 6 1/2 lbs. New 2017.

MSR $719	$615	$495	$415	$360	$325	$300	$275	

Product Code: 10159.

SMITH & WESSON, cont. 329 S

MSR	100%	98%	95%	90%	80%	70%	60%	Last MSR

MODEL M&P15 TS – 5.56 NATO/.223 Rem. cal., GIO, 14 1/2 in. chrome-lined barrel (16 in. including pinned and welded Smith Vortex flash suppressor), 30 shot PMAG, Magpul MBUS sights, Magpul MOE 6-pos. telescopic stock, Magpul MOE grip, full Troy TRX (disc.) or Troy Alpha Rail free floating handguard, 6 1/2 lbs. New 2011.

MSR $1,569	$1,315	$850	$625	$500	$435	$375	$350	

Product Code: 811024.

MODEL M&P15VTAC – 5.56 NATO cal., GIO, Viking Tactics Model, 16 in. barrel, 30 shot mag., black alloy finish, pistol grip stock, modular rail, alloy receiver. Mfg. mid-2008-2011.

	$1,650	$1,000	$795	$595	$495	$425	$395	*$1,989*

Product Code: 811012.

MODEL M&P15VTAC II – 5.56 NATO/.223 Rem. cal., GIO, 16 in. barrel, flash suppressor, 30 shot PMAG, Geissele Super-V trigger, VLTOR IMOD 6-pos. collapsible stock, mid-length gas system for lower recoil, 13 in. TRX Extreme (disc.) or VTAC/Troy 13 in. BattleRail Apha Rail free float handguard, includes Viking Tactics light mount, tactical sling, and LPSM low profile sling mount, Melonite/hardcoat black anodized finish, 6.28 lbs. New 2012.

MSR $1,949	$1,600	$1,000	$775	$575	$495	$425	$395	

Product Code: 811025.

SOG ARMORY

Previous rifle manufacturer located in Houston, TX until late 2013.

SOG Armory also made a wide variety of components and accessories for both AR-10 and AR-15/M16 carbines and rifles.

RIFLES/CARBINES: SEMI-AUTO

All AR-15 style rifles came standard with one 10 or 30 shot magazine, manual, sling, and hard case.

SOG CRUSADER – .223 Rem. cal., GIO, 16 in. chrome-lined steel barrel, 30 shot mag., Mil-Spec hardcoat anodized upper and lower receiver, enhanced magwell and trigger guard, M16 bolt and carrier, flash hider, Ergo pistol grip, M4 6-position tactical stock, M4 stock pad, charging handle, SOG/Troy four rail handguard, SOG/Troy rear flip-up sight, black, tan, or OD green phosphate finish. Disc. 2013.

	$1,385	$895	$675	$525	$450	$385	$350	*$1,700*

SOG DEFENDER – .223 Rem. cal., GIO, 16 in. chrome-lined steel barrel, 30 shot mag., Mil-Spec hardcoat anodized upper and lower receiver, enhanced magwell and trigger guard, M16 bolt and carrier, flash hider, Ergo pistol grip, M4 6-position tactical stock, M4 stock pad, charging handle, SOG/Troy four rail handguard, detachable carry handle, black, tan, or OD green phosphate finish. Disc. 2013.

	$1,315	$850	$625	$500	$435	$375	$350	*$1,600*

SOG ENFORCER – .223 Rem. cal., 16 in. chrome-lined steel barrel, flash hider, 30 shot mag., Mil-Spec hardcoat anodized upper and lower receiver, black phosphate finish, enhanced magwell and trigger guard, M16 bolt and carrier, Ergo pistol grip, M4 6-position tactical stock, M4 stock pad, charging handle, CAR M4 handguard with double heat shield, SOG/Troy rear flip-up sight. Disc. 2013.

	$1,250	$825	$575	$475	$425	$375	$350	*$1,500*

SOG GUARDIAN – .223 Rem. cal., GIO, 16 in. chrome-lined steel barrel, 30 shot mag., Mil-Spec hardcoat anodized upper and lower, black phosphate finish, enhanced magwell and trigger guard, M16 bolt and carrier, flash hider, Ergo pistol grip, M4 6-position tactical stock, M4 stock pad, charging handle, CAR M4 handguard with double heat shield and detachable carry handle. Disc. 2013.

	$1,150	$750	$550	$465	$415	$375	$350	*$1,400*

SOG OPERATOR – .223 Rem. cal., GIO, 16 in. chrome-lined steel barrel, 30 shot mag., Mil-Spec hardcoat anodized upper and lower receiver, black, tan, or OD green phosphate finish, enhanced magwell, M16 bolt and carrier, flash hider, Ergo pistol grip, 6-position tactical stock, M4 stock pad, charging handle, SOG/Troy four rail handguard, SOG/Troy flip-up sight, Magpul winter trigger guard, Wolf Eye's 260 Lumens tactical light, SOG mount, graphite vertical grip. Disc. 2013.

	$1,875	$1,100	$895	$650	$575	$495	$425	*$2,300*

SOG PREDATOR – .223 Rem. cal., GIO, 20 in. Lothar Walther fully fluted barrel with muzzle brake, SOG Extreme vent. handguard with upper and lower Picatinny rails, SOG sights, low profile gas block, Magpul trigger guard and PRS stock, 8.3 lbs. Mfg. 2011-2013.

	$1,675	$1,000	$825	$625	$550	$475	$425	*$2,000*

SOG WARRIOR – .223 Rem. cal., GIO, 16 in. chrome-lined steel barrel, 30 shot mag., Mil-Spec hardcoat anodized upper and lower receiver, black or tan phosphate finish, enhanced magwell and trigger guard, M16 bolt and carrier, flash hider, Ergo pistol grip, VLTOR EMOD stock, M4 stock pad, charging handle, SOG/Troy Extreme free float handguard with rails, SOG/Troy flip front and rear sights. Disc. 2013.

	$1,475	$950	$725	$550	$475	$395	$350	*$1,800*

S 330 SPECIALIZED DYNAMICS

MSR	100%	98%	95%	90%	80%	70%	60%	Last MSR

SPECIALIZED DYNAMICS
Current custom manufacturer located in Chandler, AZ since 2007.

RIFLES: SEMI-AUTO

CUSTOM RIFLE – rifle manufactured to customer's specifications including choice of caliber, barrel length, handguard, stock, trigger, and accessories, features stainless steel barrel and Specialized Dynamics lower and billet ambi side charger upper receiver. Disc. 2017.

Since each model was built to customer specifications, retail pricing was not available for this model.

LW-HUNTER – .17 Rem., .223 Rem., .204 Ruger, 20 Practical (disc.), 6x45 (disc.), .264 LBC, or 6.8 SPC cal., GIO, stainless steel barrel (choice of length), billet aluminum lower with integrated winter trigger guard, side charge ambi upper receiver, RRA two-stage match trigger, ACE skeleton stock, Ergo Deluxe pistol grip, carbon fiber free float tube, lightweight profile. Disc. 2017.

	$1,315	$850	$625	$500	$435	$375	$350	*$1,599*

LONG RANGE PREDATOR – .243 Win., .260 Rem., 6.5mm Creedmoor, or .308 Win. cal., GIO, stainless steel barrel (choice of length), billet large frame lower and flat-top upper receiver, RRA two-stage match trigger, winter trigger guard, Magpul PRS stock, Ergo Deluxe pistol grip. Disc. 2014.

	$1,725	$1,050	$850	$625	$550	$475	$425	*$2,149*

LRPR (LONG RANGE PRECISION RIFLE) – .243 Win., 6mm Creedmoor, 6.5mm Creedmoor, .260 Rem., .308 Win., or .22-250 cal., large frame, 16-24 in. stainless steel match grade barrel, stainless steel thread protector, Elftmann match adj. trigger, Ergo Deluxe grip, billet ambi safety, low profile adj. gas block, 16 1/2 in. M-LOK handguard, Mil-Spec parts kit, Seekins oversized bolt catch, billet lower and side charging upper receiver, Type III hardcoat anodized finish. New 2018.

MSR $2,499	$1,975	$1,150	$925	$650	$575	$495	$425	

Add $50 for single color KG coating.
Add $325 for multiple color patterns (Kryptek, digital, etc.).

MFR (MULTI-FUNCTION RIFLE) – .17 Rem., .204 Ruger, .22 Nosler, 6.5 Grendel, .223 Rem., 6x45 (disc.), 20 Practical (disc.), .264 LBC, or 6.8 SPC cal., GIO, 16-24 in. stainless steel barrel, billet aluminum upper and lower receivers, 15 in. M-LOK handguard, single stage trigger, winter trigger guard, fixed A1 or 6-pos. stock, Ergo deluxe pistol grip, Type III hardcoat anodized black finish.

MSR $1,399	$1,150	$750	$550	$465	$415	$375	$350	

SPADE – .243 Win., 6mm Creedmoor, 6.5mm Creedmoor, .260 Rem., .308 Win., or .22-250 cal., 16-24 in. match grade stainless steel barrel, thread protector, Elftmann SE trigger, Ergo Deluxe grip, low profile gas block, 16 1/2 in. M-LOK handguard, billet upper and lower receiver, Mil-Spec parts kit, Type III hardcoat anodized finish. New 2018.

MSR $1,799	$1,475	$950	$725	$550	$475	$395	$350	

Add $50 for single color KG coating.
Add $325 for multiple color patterns (Kryptek, digital, etc.).
Add $600 for Proof Research carbon fiber barrel.

VERITAS – .223 Rem., .22 Nosler, Super 6 SD, or 6.5 Grendel cal., 16-24 in. match grade stainless steel barrel, POF 3 port muzzle brake, Elftmann match adj. trigger, Magpul PRS stock, Ergo Deluxe grip, 16 1/2 in. M-LOK handguard, ambi safety selector, billet side charging upper receiver and billet lower, adj. gas block, Mil-Spec parts kit, Type III hardcoat anodized finish. New 2018.

MSR $1,999	$1,650	$1,000	$795	$595	$495	$425	$395	

Add $50 for single color KG coating.
Add $325 for multiple color pattern (Kryptek, digital, etc.).
Add $600 for Proof Research carbon fiber barrel.

SPECIALIZED TACTICAL SYSTEMS
Current OEM parts manufacturer and previous rifle manufacturer located in Ogden, UT. Previously located in Pleasant View, UT.

RIFLES: SEMI-AUTO

TITAN B – 5.56 NATO cal., GPO, 16 in. STS salt bath Nitride stainless barrel, STS SX3 lower receiver, VLTOR upper receiver, Magpul MOE stock, grip, and PMAG, Magpul backup sights, two-stage match trigger, includes STS tactical case, 7 1/2 lbs. Disc. 2017.

	$1,795	$1,050	$875	$625	$550	$475	$425	*$2,299*

SPECIALIZED TACTICAL SYSTEMS, cont. 331 S

MSR	100%	98%	95%	90%	80%	70%	60%	Last MSR

TITAN B DI.L – 5.56 NATO cal., GIO, 16 in. STS salt bath Nitride stainless barrel, STS SX3 lower receiver, Mil-Spec upper, Magpul MOE stock, grip, and PMAG, Magpul backup sights, Mil-Spec trigger, hard anodized with Teflon coating, includes STS tactical case, 6 7/8 lbs. Disc. 2017.

	$1,385	$895	$675	$525	$450	$385	$350	$1,699

ZOMBIE SLAYER – 5.56 NATO cal., GIO, 16 in. STS salt bath Nitride stainless barrel, STS SX3 lower receiver with custom ZOMBIE logo, custom fire control, VLTOR upper receiver, STS "Zombie Muzzle Thumping Device" (ZMTD), Magpul MOE stock, grip, V-grip, and PMAG, Magpul backup sights, two-stage match trigger, Tungsten Grey cerakote finish, includes STS tactical case and "The Zombie Survival Guide" book. Only 50 mfg. 2011-2014.

	$2,050	$1,250	$950	$650	$575	$495	$475	$2,500

This Zombie themed rifle was custom built for the 2011 SHOT Show. The original model was auctioned off and proceeds went to various charities. Only a limited number of these were planned for production.

SPIKE'S TACTICAL LLC

Current AR-15 pistol and rifle manufacturer located in Apopka, FL.

PISTOLS: SEMI-AUTO

.300 BLACKOUT 8.3 – .300 AAC Blackout cal., 8.3 in. premium barrel with black Nitride finish, M4 feed ramp barrel extension, A2 flash hider, jeweled Mil-Spec trigger, black Magpul MBUS front and rear sights, Spike's Pro grip, forged upper and lower receiver, free floating 7 in. SAR3 rail, QD attachment points, billet steel low profile gas block, forged aluminum charging handle, pistol buffer tube, M16 BCG with laser engraved ST Spider logo, includes hard case, Type III Class 2 hardcoat anodized finish, 5 lbs. 2 oz.

MSR $1,040		$885	$785	$685	$600	$535	$465	$415

5.56 CHF 8.1 – 5.56 NATO cal., 8.1 in. cold hammer forged barrel with black Nitride finish, M4 feed ramp barrel extension, A2 flash hider, jeweled Mil-Spec trigger, Spike's Pro grip, black Magpul MBUS front and rear sights, forged upper and lower receiver, pistol tube or Maxim Defense pistol arm brace, free floating 7 or 9 in. SAR3 or 9 in. M-LOK (with pistol brace only) rail, QD attachment points, low profile gas block, forged aluminum charging handle, M16 BCG laser engraved with ST Spider logo, includes hard case, Type III Class 2 hardcoat anodized finish, 5 lbs. 2 oz.-6 lbs. 3 oz.

MSR $1,110		$925	$850	$725	$625	$550	$475	$425

Add $10 for 9 in. SAR3 rail with pistol tube.

Add $535 for Maxim Defense pistol arm brace and 9 in. SAR3 rail.

Add $685 for Maxim Defense pistol arm brace and 9 in. M-LOK rail.

5.56 CHF BILLET 8.1 – 5.56 NATO cal., 8.1 in. cold hammer forged barrel with black Nitride finish, M4 feed ramp barrel extension, black Magpul MBUS front and rear sights, Magpul MOE grip, ambi safety, forged Gen 2 billet lower receiver, free floating 9 in. SAR3 rail, QD attachment points, billet steel low profile gas block, pistol buffer tube, forged aluminum charging handle, M16 BCG with laser engraved ST Spider logo, includes hard case, Type III Class 2 hardcoat anodized finish, 5 lbs. 4 oz.

MSR $1,815		$1,525	$1,350	$1,175	$1,050	$900	$775	$625

KRYPTEK PISTOL – 5.56 NATO or .300 AAC Blackout cal., 8.3 in. premium barrel with black Nitride finish, Barking Spider muzzle brake, two-stage trigger, Spike's Gen 2 billet sights, Maxim Defense pistol brace, Spike's Pro grip, Badass ambi safety, Kryptek Gen 2 forged billet lower with raised Spider logo, M4 feed ramps, 9 in. free floating M-LOK rail, QD attachment points, low profile gas block, pistol gas tube, Radian Raptor charging handle, nickel boron BCG, includes hard case, Kryptek finish in Altitude, Highlander, Neptune, Raid, or Typhon, 6 lbs. 4 oz.

MSR $3,869		$3,275	$2,875	$2,365	$2,000	$1,675	$1,425	$1,200

Add $20 for .300 AAC Blackout cal.

PIPE HITTERS UNION PISTOL – 5.56 NATO cal., 8.1 in. cold hammer forged barrel, M4 feed ramp barrel extension, black Nitride finish, Barking Spider muzzle brake, two-stage trigger, Spike's Gen 2 billet sights, MFT grip, Badass ambi safety, Phase 5 hex pistol tube, 9 in. M-LOK rail, QD attachment points, adj. gas block, pistol length gas tube, Radian Raptor charging handle, forged lower receiver with Pipe Hitter skull logo, nickel boron BCG, includes hard case, Type III Class 2 hardcoat anodized finish, 5 lbs. 2 oz. New 2016.

MSR $2,075		$1,775	$1,525	$1,275	$1,125	$975	$850	$685

SPARTAN PISTOL – 5.56 NATO cal., 8.1 in. cold hammer forged barrel with black Nitride finish, Barking Spider muzzle brake, two-stage trigger, Gen 2 billet sights, Maxim Defense pistol brace, Spike's Pro grip, ambi safety, forged upper and lower receiver with laser engraved Spartan logo, M4 feed ramps, 10 in. M-LOK rail, QD attachment points, adj. gas block, pistol length gas tube, Radian Raptor charging handle, nickel boron BCG, includes hard case, Battle Worn finish, 6 lbs. 7 oz.

MSR $2,695		$2,285	$1,995	$1,650	$1,425	$1,165	$1,000	$875

ST-15 LE PISTOL – 5.56 NATO cal., 8 in. barrel with A2 flash hider, pistol length gas system, 7 in. SAR3, ST-T2 Tungsten buffer, pistol buffer tube, Magpul MBUS front and rear sights, includes hard plastic case. Mfg. late 2014-2017.

	$850	$725	$650	$585	$515	$450	$395	$995

S 332 SPIKE'S TACTICAL LLC, cont.

MSR	100%	98%	95%	90%	80%	70%	60%	Last MSR

RIFLES/CARBINES: SEMI-AUTO

5.56 M4 LE (ST-15 M4 LE CARBINE) – 5.56 NATO cal., GIO, 16 in. M4 profile barrel, A2 flash hider, M4 feed ramped barrel extension, A2 front sight base, Magpul MBUS rear sight, M4 stock, Spike's Pro grip, forged upper and lower receiver with Spider logo, carbine gas tube, 6-pos. Mil-Spec buffer tube, forged aluminum charging handle, M4 double heat shield, Magpul SL, or M-LOK rail/handguard, M16 BCG with laser engraved ST Spider logo, includes hard case, hardcoat anodized black finish, 6 lbs. 5 oz.

| MSR $975 | $825 | $535 | $450 | $385 | $340 | $325 | $295 | |

Add $75 for Magpul SL handguard.

Add $228 for 7 in., $243 for 9 in., $253 for 10 in., $263 for 12 in., or $273 for 13.2 in. M-LOK rail.

* **5.56 M4 LE (ST-15 M4 LE Carbine w/BAR)** – 5.56 NATO cal., similar to 5.56 M4 LE, except has 7, 9, 10, 12, or 13.2 in. BAR2 handguard.

| MSR $1,149 | $950 | $595 | $495 | $425 | $365 | $335 | $300 | |

Add $12 for 10 in., $22 for 12 in., $32 for 13.2 in., or $56 for 7 in. BAR2 handguard/rail.

* **5.56 M4 LE (ST-15 M4 LE Carbine w/SAR)** – 5.56 NATO cal., similar to 5.56 M4 LE, except has free floating one-piece 7, 9, 10, 12, or 13.2 in. SAR3 handguard/rail, 6 lbs. 4 oz.

| MSR $1,203 | $1,025 | $625 | $495 | $450 | $395 | $350 | $325 | |

Add $15 for 9 in., $25 for 10 in., $35 for 12 in., or $45 for 13.2 in. SAR3 handguard/rail.

* **5.56 M4 LE FDE / GREY** – 5.56 NATO cal., GIO, 16 in. M4 profile barrel, A2 flash hider, M4 feed ramped barrel extension, A2 front sight base, Magpul MBUS rear sight, Magpul CTR stock, Magpul MOE grip, Magpul MOE trigger guard, forged upper and lower receiver with Spider logo, carbine gas tube, 6-pos. Mil-Spec buffer tube, forged aluminum charging handle, Magpul MOE handguard, M16 BCG with laser engraved ST Spider logo, includes hard case, FDE or Grey finish, 6 lbs. 8 oz. New 2018.

| MSR $1,175 | $975 | $595 | $495 | $425 | $365 | $335 | $300 | |

5.56 MID-LENGTH LE (ST-15 MID-LENGTH LE CARBINE) – 5.56 NATO cal., GIO, 16 in. mid-length barrel, A2 flash hider, M4 feed ramped barrel extension, A2 front sight base, Magpul MBUS rear sight, Spike's tactical M4 stock, Spike's Pro grip, mid-length gas tube, forged upper and lower receiver with Spider logo, forward assist, forged aluminum charging handle, mid-length, Magpul SL, or M-LOK handguard/rail, QD attachment points, M16 BCG laser engraved with ST Spider logo, 6-pos. Mil-Spec buffer tube, ST-T2 buffer, includes hard case, hardcoat anodized black finish, 6 lbs. 7 oz.

| MSR $975 | $825 | $535 | $450 | $385 | $340 | $325 | $295 | |

Add $75 for Magpul SL handguard/rail.

Add $253 for 9 in., $263 for 10 in., $273 for 12 in., or $283 for 13.2 in. M-LOK handguard/rail.

* **5.56 Mid-Length LE w/BAR2 (ST-15 Mid-Length LE Carbine w/BAR)** – 5.56 NATO cal., similar to Mid-Length LE Carbine, except has 9, 10, 12, or 13.2 in. BAR2 and low profile gas block.

| MSR $1,159 | $975 | $595 | $495 | $425 | $365 | $335 | $300 | |

Add $12 for 10 in., $22 for 12 in., or $32 for 13.2 in. BAR2 handguard/rail.

* **5.56 Mid-Length LE w/SAR (ST-15 Mid-Length LE w/SAR)** – 5.56 NATO cal., similar to Mid-Length LE, except has ST low profile gas block and 9, 10, 12, or 13.2 in. SAR3 rail.

| MSR $1,228 | $1,050 | $650 | $495 | $450 | $395 | $350 | $325 | |

Add $10 for 10 in., $20 for 12 in., or $30 for 13.2 in. SAR3 rail.

* **ST-15 Mid-Length LE Carbine w/Heat Shield** – 5.56 NATO cal., similar to Mid-Length LE Carbine, except has M4 double heat shield handguards. Disc. 2014.

| | $800 | $525 | $450 | $385 | $340 | $325 | $295 | $950 |

5.56 MID-LENGTH CHF – 5.56 NATO cal., GIO, 16 in. mid-length cold hammer forged barrel, A2 flash hider, M4 feed ramp barrel extension, M4 stock, Spike's Pro grip, forged upper and lower receiver with Spider logo, free floating 9, 12, or 13.2 in. BAR2 or SAR3 rail, low profile gas block, 6-pos. Mil-Spec buffer tube, mid-length gas tube, forged aluminum charging handle, M16 BCG laser engraved with ST Spider logo, includes hard case, hardcoat anodized black finish, 6 lbs. 6 oz.

| MSR $1,260 | $1,065 | $650 | $500 | $450 | $395 | $350 | $325 | |

Add $11 for 12 in. BAR2 rail.

Add $58 for 9 in., $78 for 12 in., or $88 for 13.2 in. SAR3 rail.

BLACK ASSASSIN – 5.56 NATO cal., 14 1/2 in. mid-length cold hammer forged barrel with pinned and welded DynaComp (meets 16 in. OAL requirement), M4 feed ramp barrel extension, Spike's Gen 2 billet trigger guard and tactical battle trigger, Magpul MBUS front and rear sights, Magpul CTR stock with extended buttpad, Magpul MOE grip, Battle Arms safety, forged upper and lower receiver, 6-pos. Mil-Spec buffer tube, free floating 12 in. SAR3 rail, QD attachment points, low profile gas block, mid-length gas tube, Radian Raptor charging handle, M16 BCG with laser engraved ST Spider logo, includes hard case, Type III Class 2 hardcoat anodized finish, 6 lbs. 7 oz.

| MSR $1,925 | $1,600 | $1,000 | $775 | $575 | $495 | $425 | $395 | |

SPIKE'S TACTICAL LLC, cont. 333 S

MSR	100%	98%	95%	90%	80%	70%	60%	Last MSR

BLACK ASSASSIN V2 – 5.56 NATO cal., 14 1/2 in. mid-length cold hammer forged barrel with pinned and welded R2 brake (meets 16 in. OAL requirement), M4 feed ramp barrel extension, Spike's Gen 2 billet trigger guard, two-stage trigger, Magpul MBUS front and rear sights, MFT Minimalist stock, Spike's Pro grip, Badass safety, forged upper and lower receiver, 6-pos. Mil-Spec buffer tube, free floating 12 in. M-LOK rail, QD attachment points, low profile gas block, mid-length gas tube, Radian Raptor charging handle, M16 BCG with laser engraved ST Spider logo, includes hard case, Type III Class 2 hardcoat anodized finish, 6 lbs. 3 oz.

MSR $2,100	$1,725	$1,050	$850	$625	$550	$475	$425	

CRUSADER – 5.56 NATO cal., 14 1/2 in. mid-length lightweight barrel with pinned and welded DynaComp 2 (making it 16 in. OAL), M4 feed ramp barrel extension, Spike's tactical battle trigger, built-in trigger guard, Magpul MBUS front and rear sights, Magpul CTR stock with extended buttpad, Spike's Pro grip, ambi safety, 6-pos. Mil-Spec buffer tube, forged upper and lower receiver, Crusader logo and bible verses engraved on lower receiver, free floating 12 in. M-LOK rail, QD attachment points, low profile gas block, mid-length gas tube, forged aluminum charging handle, M16 BCG laser engraved with ST Spider logo, 6 lbs. 2 oz.

MSR $1,580	$1,315	$850	$625	$500	$435	$375	$350	

KRYPTEK RIFLE – 5.56 NATO cal., 16 in. mid-length cold hammer forged barrel, M4 feed ramp barrel extension, R2 brake, two-stage trigger, Spike's Gen 2 billet sights, Leupold LCO red sight, Magpul SL stock, Spike's Pro grip, BAD-ASS ambi safety, free floating 12 in. M-LOK rail, QD attachment points, low profile gas block, mid-length gas tube, Radian Raptor-LT charging handle, nickel boron M16 BCG with laser engraved ST Spider logo, 6-pos. Mil-Spec buffer tube, Kryptek billet upper receiver with integral rail mount, Gen 2 forged billet lower with raised Spider logo, includes hard case, Kryptek finish in Altitude, Highlander, Neptune, Raid, or Typhon, 6 lbs. 12 oz. Limited mfg.

MSR $3,491	$2,775	$1,825	$1,350	$750	$650	$595	$525	

KRYPTEK SPR RIFLE – 5.56 NATO cal., 18 in. cold hammer forged barrel, M4 feed ramp barrel extension, R2 brake, two-stage trigger, Spike's Gen 2 billet sights, Magpul SL stock, Spike's Pro grip, Badass ambi safety, free floating 13.2 in. M-LOK rail, QD attachment points, low profile gas block, rifle length gas tube, Radian Raptor-LT charging handle, nickel boron M16 BCG with laser engraved ST Spider logo, 6-pos. Mil-Spec buffer tube, Kryptek billet upper receiver with integral rail mount, Gen 2 forged billet lower with raised Spider logo, includes hard case, Mark 4 MR-T 2.5-8x36 MI TMR with BSO Myers mount, Kryptek finish in Altitude, Highlander, Neptune, Raid, or Typhon, 6 lbs. 15 oz. Limited mfg.

MSR $3,960	$3,200	$2,150	$1,525	$895	$695	$650	$575	

PIPE HITTERS UNION RIFLE – 5.56 NATO cal., 16 in. cold hammer forged barrel, R2 brake, M4 feed ramp barrel extension, two-stage trigger, billet trigger guard, Spike's Gen 2 billet sights, MFT Battlelink Minimalist stock, MFT grip, Badass ambi safety, forged upper and lower receiver with laser engraved Pipe Hitter logo, free floating 13.2 in. M-LOK rail, QD attachment points, low profile gas block, mid-length gas tube, Radian Raptor charging handle, M16 BCG with laser engraved ST Spider logo, 6-pos. Mil-Spec buffer tube, includes hard case, Type III Class 2 hardcoat anodized finish, 6 lbs. 6 oz.

MSR $2,125	$1,725	$1,050	$850	$625	$550	$475	$425	

PHU JOKER RIFLE – 5.56 NATO cal., 16 in. mid-length cold hammer forged barrel, R2 brake, M4 feed ramp barrel extension, two-stage trigger, Spike's Gen 2 billet sights, MFT Battlelink Minimalist stock, MFT grip, Badass ambi safety, Mil-Spec buffer tube, low profile gas block, mid-length gas tube, forged upper and lower receiver with Pipe Hitter Joker logo free floating 13.2 in. M-LOK rail, QD attachment points, Radian Raptor-LT charging handle, nickel boron BCG with laser engraved ST Spider logo, Battle Worn or Gray Cerakote finish, 6 lbs. 8 oz.

MSR $2,150	$1,725	$1,050	$850	$625	$550	$475	$425	

Add $275 for Battleworn finish.

RETRO BUILD – 5.56 NATO cal., 20 in. A2 profile/HBAR barrel, A2 flash hider, M4 feed ramp barrel extension, A2 front sight base, A2 stock, A2 grip, forged upper and lower receiver with Spider logo, rifle length handguard and gas tube, Mil-Spec charging handle, M16 BCG laser engraved with ST Spider logo, Mil-Spec A2 carry handle, includes hard case, Type III Class 2 hardcoat anodized finish, 9 lbs.

MSR $1,135	$950	$595	$495	$425	$365	$335	$300	

SPARTAN RIFLE – 5.56 NATO cal., 16 in. mid-length cold hammer forged barrel, R2 brake, M4 feed ramp barrel extension, two-stage trigger, Magpul Pro front and rear sights, Magpul MOE SL stock, Spike's Pro grip, ambi safety, Mil-Spec buffer tube, low profile gas block, mid-length gas tube, forged upper and lower receiver with laser engraved Spartan logo, free floating 12 in. M-LOK rail, QD attachment points, Radian Raptor-LT charging handle, nickel boron BCG with laser engraved ST Spider logo, Battle Worn finish.

MSR $2,300	$1,875	$1,100	$895	$650	$575	$495	$425	

SPECIAL PURPOSE RIFLE – 5.56 NATO cal., 18 in. cold hammer forged barrel with black Nitride finish, two-piece suppressor mount, M4 feed ramp barrel extension, Geissele SSA-E trigger, Spike's Gen 2 billet sights, Magpul SL stock, Spike's Pro grip, Mil-Spec buffer tube, low profile gas block, rifle length gas tube, forged upper and lower receiver with Spider logo, free floating 13.2 in. M-LOK rail, QD attachment points, Radian Raptor-LT charging handle, nickel boron M16 BCG with laser engraved ST Spider logo, Type III Class 2 hardcoat anodized finish, 6 lbs. 13 oz.

MSR $2,015	$1,675	$1,000	$825	$625	$550	$475	$425	

S 334 SPIKE'S TACTICAL LLC, cont.

MSR	100%	98%	95%	90%	80%	70%	60%	Last MSR

ULTIMATE ASSASSIN – 5.56 NATO cal., 14 1/2 in. mid-length cold hammer forged barrel with pinned and welded Dynacomp (meets 16 in. OAL requirement), M4 feed ramp barrel extension, Spike's tactical battle trigger, Magpul Pro front and rear sights, Magpul CTR stock with extended buttpad, Magpul MOE grip, Battle Arms safety, free floating 12 in. SAR3 rail, QD attachment points, low profile gas bock, mid-length gas tube, 6-pos. Mil-Spec buffer tube, billet forged upper and lower receiver, Radian Raptor-SD charging handle, nickel boron BCG with laser engraved ST Spider logo, includes hard case, 6 lbs. 10 oz.

MSR $2,430	$1,975	$1,150	$925	$650	$575	$495	$425	

ULTIMATE ASSASSIN V2 – 5.56 NATO cal., 14 1/2 in. mid-length cold hammer forged barrel with pinned and welded R2 brake (meets 16 in. OAL requirement), M4 feed ramp barrel extension, built-in trigger guard, two-stage trigger, Magpul Pro front and rear sights, MFT Minimalist stock, Magpul MOE grip, Battle Arms safety, free floating 12 in. M-LOK rail, QD attachment points, low profile gas bock, mid-length gas tube, 6-pos. Mil-Spec buffer tube, billet forged upper and Gen 2 lower receiver, Radian Raptor-SD charging handle, nickel boron BCG with laser engraved ST Spider logo, includes hard case, Type III Class 2 hardcoat anodized finish, 6 lbs. 6 oz.

MSR $2,620	$2,125	$1,325	$995	$675	$595	$525	$475	

SPIRIT GUN MANUFACTURING COMPANY LLC

Previous manufacturer located in West Palm Beach, FL until 2011.

PISTOLS: SEMI-AUTO

SGM9P – 5.56 NATO cal., GIO, 7 1/2 in. stainless steel barrel with KX3 compensator, 30 shot mag., SGM9 lower with integral three position sling mount and swivel, VLTOR custom CASV handguard, flip-up front sight, VLTOR MUR upper receiver, National Match phosphate and chromed custom bolt carrier, black, green, or tan finish. Limited mfg. Disc. 2011.

	$2,200	$1,950	$1,725	$1,500	$1,300	$1,100	$825	$2,495

RIFLES/CARBINES: SEMI-AUTO

Spirit Gun Manufacturing offered a complete line of AR-15 style rifles and carbines in law enforcement/military and civilian configurations. A variety of options and accessories were available.

SGM-15/SGM-16/SGM-17 – AR-15 style. Disc. 2011.

	$1,975	$1,150	$925	$650	$575	$495	$425	$2,495

SGM-40/SGM-41 – Disc. 2011.

	$1,975	$1,150	$925	$650	$575	$495	$425	$2,495

SGM-A19 – Disc. 2011.

	$2,125	$1,325	$995	$675	$595	$525	$475	$2,695

SGM-A23 – Disc. 2011.

	$2,225	$1,395	$1,050	$675	$595	$525	$475	$2,795

SGM-A24 – Disc. 2011.

	$2,295	$1,450	$1,075	$675	$595	$525	$475	$2,895

SGM-A39 – Disc. 2011.

	$1,975	$1,150	$925	$650	$575	$495	$425	$2,495

SGM-A43 – Disc. 2011.

	$2,125	$1,325	$995	$675	$595	$525	$475	$2,695

SGM-A47 – Disc. 2011.

	$2,225	$1,395	$1,050	$675	$595	$525	$475	$2,795

SGM-A48 – Disc. 2011.

	$2,295	$1,450	$1,075	$675	$595	$525	$475	$2,895

SPRINGFIELD ARMORY (MFG. BY SPRINGFIELD INC.)

Current trademark manufactured by Springfield Inc., located in Geneseo, IL. Springfield Inc. has also imported a variety of models. This company was named Springfield Armory, Geneseo, IL until 1992.

The government owned Springfield Armory closed in 1968, and the "Springfield Armory" trademark was purchased by a private individual in the early 1970's. Initially, the new company manufactured a semi-automatic M14, but when the BATF disapproved the model name, it became the M1A. The company was then sold to the Reese family, and it was moved to Geneseo, IL. Springfield Inc. manufactures commercial pistols and rifles, including reproductions of older military handguns and rifles.

RIFLES: SEMI-AUTO, TACTICAL DESIGN

Many models listed are CA legal, since they do not have a muzzle brake. MSRs are typically the same as those guns available with a muzzle brake. Pricing on CA legal firearms is not included within the scope of this listing - please contact a Springfield dealer directly for this information.

SPRINGFIELD ARMORY (MFG. BY SPRINGFIELD INC.), cont. 335 S

MSR	100%	98%	95%	90%	80%	70%	60%	Last MSR

SAINT – 5.56 NATO cal., GIO, mid-length gas system, 16 in. chrome moly barrel with Melonite coating, 30 shot Magpul PMAG, enhanced nickel boron SST, BCM trigger guard, A2 style front sight and gas block, dual aperture rear sight, 6-pos. stock, rubber buttpad, Bravo Company MOD 0 pistol grip, forged aluminum upper and lower receiver, M4 feed ramps, GI style charging handle, M16 bolt carrier group, carbine "H" style heavy tungsten buffer assembly, BCM PKMR two-piece KeyMod handguard with internal aluminum heat shield, QD and slotted sling attachment points, free float handguard system (new 2017), Type III hardcoat anodized finish, 6 lbs. 11 oz. New 2016.

| MSR $899 | $775 | $685 | $615 | $550 | $485 | $415 | $370 | |

Add $150 for free float handguard (new 2017).

SAINT EDGE – 5.56 NATO cal., adj. gas block, 16 in. CMV Melonite barrel, 30 shot mag., SST, dual aperture sights, adj. flip-up front sight, SOPMOD buttstock, Bravo Company Mod 3 pistol grip, forged aluminum upper and lower receiver, mid-size charging handle, M16 bolt carrier group, full-length M-LOK free floating handguard, includes case, black finish, 6 lbs. 3 oz. New 2017.

| MSR $1,299 | $1,075 | $675 | $500 | $450 | $400 | $350 | $325 | |

STAG ARMS LLC

Current pistol, rifle and accessories manufacturer located in New Britain, CT.

PISTOLS: SEMI-AUTO

MODEL 9 AR PISTOL – 9mm Para. cal., blowback operating system, 5 1/2 in. chrome moly barrel with QPQ corrosion resistant finish, A2 flash hider, 32 shot mag. (utilizes Colt Style Stick and Tavor mags.), single stage AR-15 trigger with Magpul enhanced trigger guard, no sights, 3 in. foam cover on pistol length tube, Magpul MOE grip, 4 in. free float handguard, aluminum upper and lower receiver, 9mm buffer with pistol length extension tube, Mil-Spec charging handle, Type III hardcoat anodized black finish, 21 in. OAL, 4.7 lbs.

| MSR $1,000 | $850 | $725 | $650 | $585 | $515 | $450 | $395 | |

STAG 15 M-LOK PISTOL – 5.56 NATO/.223 Rem. or .300 AAC Blackout cal., GIO, pistol length gas tube with low profile gas block, 7 1/2 or 8 in. chrome moly barrel with QPQ corrosion resistant finish, A2 or .300 AAC Blackout flash hider, 30 shot Magpul PMAG, Mil-Spec single stage trigger with enhanced trigger guard, Shockwave Blade pistol stabilizer, FAB Defense AGR-43 rubberized pistol grip, forged aluminum upper and lower receiver, 7 in. M-LOK free float handguard, Mil-Spec charging handle, heavy buffer with pistol receiver extension tube, right or left-hand configuration, Type III hardcoat anodized black finish, 22 in. OAL, 5.4 lbs. New 2018.

| MSR $850 | $725 | $650 | $575 | $515 | $450 | $385 | $335 | |

Add $50 for left-hand configuration (Stag 15L M-LOK).

STAG 15 VRST S3 PISTOL – 5.56 NATO/.223 Rem. cal., GIO, carbine length gas tube with low profile gas block, 11 1/2 in. chrome-lined barrel, A2 flash hider, 30 shot Magpul PMAG, single stage trigger with enhanced trigger guard, KAK Shockwave 2.0 blade, Magpul MOE pistol grip, forged aluminum receivers, Diamondhead 8 1/4 in. VRST S3 M-LOK handguard, Mil-Spec charging handle, heavy buffer with KAK pistol buffer tube, Type III hardcoat anodized finish, 30.5 in. OAL, 5.9 lbs. New 2018.

| MSR $900 | $775 | $685 | $615 | $550 | $485 | $415 | $375 | |

RIFLES/CARBINES: SEMI-AUTO

All AR-15 style carbines/rifles are available in post-ban configuration for restricted states and include one mag., instruction manual, plastic rifle case, and lifetime warranty.

Add $50 for .300 AAC Blackout cal. upgrade for Model 1, Model 1L, Model 2, Model 2L, Model 2T, Model 2TL, Model 3, Model 3L, Model 3T, Model 3TL, or Model 3TLM (mfg. 2016-2017).

MODEL 1 CARBINE – 5.56 NATO/.223 Rem. cal., GIO, 16 in. chrome-lined barrel, A2 flash hider, 30 shot mag., A3 forged aluminum upper, A2 front post sights/removable carry handle, Picatinny rail under carry handle, standard GI carbine design, polymer handguard, 6-position collapsible stock, A2 plastic grip, available in right or left (Model 1L) hand, Type III hardcoat anodized black finish, 7 lbs. Disc. 2017.

| | $800 | $525 | $450 | $385 | $340 | $325 | $295 | *$949* |

Add $40 for Model 1L.

MODEL 2 CARBINE – 5.56 NATO/.223 Rem. cal., GIO, 16 in. chrome-lined barrel, A2 flash hider, 30 shot mag., A3 forged aluminum upper, standard safety, F-marked A2 front sight post and Midwest Industries ERS flip-up rear sight, tactical top rail, polymer handguard, 6-position collapsible stock, A2 plastic grip, available in right or left (Model 2L) hand, Type III hardcoat anodized black finish, 6 1/2 lbs. Disc. 2017.

| MSR $940 | $800 | $525 | $450 | $385 | $340 | $325 | $295 | |

Add $25 for left-hand (Model 2L).

S 336 STAG ARMS LLC, cont.

MSR	100%	98%	95%	90%	80%	70%	60%	Last MSR

* Model 2T Carbine – 5.56 NATO/.223 Rem. cal., GIO, 16 in. chrome-lined barrel, A2 flash hider, 30 shot mag., A3 forged aluminum upper, ambidextrous (left hand only) or standard safety, free float Picatinny quad rail, F-marked A2 front sight, A.R.M.S. flip-up rear sight, 6-position collapsible stock, A2 plastic pistol grip, available in right or left-hand, Type III hardcoat anodized black finish, approx. 6.8 lbs. Disc. 2017.

	$950	$595	$495	$425	$365	$335	$300	$1,130

Add $25 for left-hand (Model 2T-L).

MODEL 3 CARBINE – 5.56 NATO/.223 Rem. cal., GIO, 16 in. chrome-lined barrel, A2 flash hider, 30 shot mag., A3 forged aluminum upper, standard safety, 6-position collapsible stock, A2 plastic grip, Picatinny railed gas block, available in right or left (Model 3L) hand, Diamondhead drop-in Versa-Base handguard, (V-RS modular rail platform became standard 2011), Type III hardcoat anodized black finish, 6.1 lbs. Disc. 2017.

	$765	$515	$440	$375	$335	$315	$295	$895

Add $25 for left-hand (Model 3L).

MODEL 3G RIFLE – 5.56 NATO/.223 Rem. cal., GIO, 18 in. stainless steel heavy fluted barrel, Stag 3G compensator, 30 shot mag., Geissele Super 3-Gun trigger, Magpul ACS buttstock, MOE pistol grip, 15 in. Samson Evolution free float handguard, accessory rail, right or left-hand action, Type III hardcoat anodized black finish, 7 1/2 lbs. Mfg. 2012-2017.

	$1,225	$825	$575	$475	$425	$375	$350	$1,459

Add $20 for left-hand (Model 3G-L).

MODEL 3T RIFLE – 5.56 NATO cal., GIO, 16 in. chrome-lined barrel with A2 flash hider, 30 shot mag., Diamondhead VRS-T free float handguard, polymer Diamondhead front and rear flip-up sights, 6-position collapsible buttstock, A2 plastic grip, Type III hardcoat anodized black finish, 7.4 lbs. Mfg. 2014-2017.

	$850	$550	$465	$395	$350	$325	$295	$999

Add $20 for Model 3T-L (left-hand).

MODEL 3T-M RIFLE – 5.56 NATO cal., GIO, 16 in. chrome-lined barrel with A2 flash hider, 30 shot mag., Diamondhead VRS-T free float handguard, full-length Picatinnny rail, aluminum Diamondhead front and rear flip-up sights, Magpul ACS 6-pos. buttstock, Magpul MOE grip, 7 1/2 lbs. Mfg. 2014-2017.

	$975	$595	$495	$425	$365	$335	$300	$1,160

Add $20 for left-hand (Model 3TL-M).

MODEL 4 RIFLE – 5.56 NATO/.223 Rem. cal., GIO, 20 in. chrome moly heavy barrel, A2 flash hider, 20 shot mag., A3 forged aluminum upper, Picatinny rail, rifle length polymer handguard, F-marked A2 front sight, removable carry handle, A2 buttstock with trap door for storage, A2 plastic grip, available in right or left (Model 4L) hand, Type III hardcoat anodized black finish, 8 1/2 lbs. Disc. 2017.

	$865	$550	$465	$395	$350	$325	$300	$1,015

Add $50 for left-hand (Model 4L).

MODEL 5 CARBINE – 6.8 SPC cal. with SAAMI SPEC 2 chamber, GIO, 16 in. chrome-lined barrel, A2 flash hider, 25 shot mag., F-marked A2 front sight, polymer handguard, A3 forged aluminum upper, standard or ambidextrous (left-hand only) safety, 6-position collapsible stock, A2 plastic grip, available in right or left (Model 5L) hand, Type III hardcoat anodized black finish, 6.4 lbs. Disc. 2017.

MSR $1,045	$875	$550	$465	$395	$350	$325	$300	

Add $50 for left-hand (Model 5L).

MODEL 6 RIFLE – 5.56 NATO/.223 Rem. cal., GIO, 24 in. stainless steel heavy bull profile barrel with target crown, 10 shot mag., two-stage match trigger, no sights, fixed A2 buttstock, Hogue overmolded pistol grip, standard or ambidextrous (left-hand only) safety, low profile gas block, A3 forged aluminum upper, free floating Hogue handguard, tactical top rail, Type III hardcoat anodized black finish, 10 lbs. Disc. 2017.

	$895	$575	$475	$395	$350	$325	$300	$1,055

Add $40 for left-hand (Model 6L).

MODEL 8 CARBINE – 5.56 NATO/.223 Rem. cal., GPO, 16 in. chrome-lined barrel, A2 flash hider, 30 shot mag., Diamondhead flip-up front and rear sights, 6-position collapsible stock, A2 plastic grip, ambidextrous (left-hand only) or standard safety, A3 forged aluminum upper, polymer handguard, available in right or left (Model 8-L) hand, Type III hardcoat anodized black finish, 6.9 lbs. Mfg. 2011-2017.

	$950	$595	$495	$425	$365	$335	$300	$1,145

Add $30 for left-hand (Model 8L).

* Model 8T Carbine – 5.56 NATO/.223 Rem. cal., GPO, Picatinny gas block with 3 settings, 16 in. chrome-lined Govt. profile barrel, A2 flash hider, 30 shot mag., single stage trigger, matched set of Diamondhead low profile flip-up sights, 6-position collapsible stock, A2 plastic grip, ambidextrous (left-hand only) or standard safety, forged aluminum receiver, Diamondhead VRS-T free floating modular handguard, continuous top rail, Mil-Spec charging handle, Type III hardcoat anodized black finish, 7 1/4 lbs. New 2013.

MSR $950	$800	$525	$450	$385	$340	$325	$295	

Add 10% for Model 8TL (disc. 2016).

STAG ARMS LLC, cont. 337 S

MSR	100%	98%	95%	90%	80%	70%	60%	Last MSR

MODEL 9/9L – 9mm Para. cal., blowback action, 16 in. chrome-lined barrel with A2 flash hider, 32 shot mag., M4 style, Picatinny railed gas block, no rear sight, 6-position collapsible stock, A2 grip, Diamondhead VRS-T 15 in. free float modular handguard, right or left (Model 9L) hand, Type III hardcoat anodized finish, 6.8 lbs. Mfg. mid-2014-2017.

	$850	$725	$650	$585	$515	$450	$395	$990

Add $35 for left-hand action (Model 9L).

MODEL 9T – 9mm Para. cal., GIO, blowback action, 16 in. chrome-lined barrel with A2 flash hider, 32 shot mag., metal Diamondhead premium front and rear sights, right or left (Model 9T-L) hand action, Diamondhead VRS-T 13 1/2 in. free float handguard, 6-position collapsible buttstock, A2 plastic grip, Type III hardcoat anodized black finish, 7.9 lbs. Mfg. 2015-2017.

	$1,060	$950	$815	$715	$625	$535	$450	$1,275

Add $20 for left-hand action (Model 9T-L).

STAG 7 HUNTER – 6.8 SPC cal. with SAAMI SPEC 2 chamber, GIO, 20.8 in. stainless steel heavy profile barrel with target crown, A3 forged aluminum upper, standard or ambidextrous (left-hand only) safety, fixed A2 buttstock, railed gas block front/no rear sights, free float Hogue handguard, tactical top rail, two-stage match trigger, Hogue overmolded pistol grip, available in right or left-hand configuration, Type III hardcoat anodized black finish, 7.8 lbs.

MSR $1,055	$895	$575	$475	$395	$350	$325	$300	

Add $40 for left-hand (Model 7L).

STAG 9 BONES – 9mm Para. cal., blowback operating system, 16 in. chrome-lined heavy profile barrel, A2 flash hider, 32 shot mag., single stage trigger, 6-pos. receiver extension tube, forged aluminum receiver, 9mm bolt carrier with manganese phosphate coating, standard 9mm buffer, Type III hardcoat anodized black finish. New 2018.

MSR $915	$785	$525	$450	$385	$340	$325	$295	

STAG 9 O.R.C. (OPTICS READY CARBINE) – 9mm Para. cal., blowback operating system, 16 in. chrome-lined heavy profile barrel, A2 flash hider, 32 shot mag., single stage trigger with Magpul enhanced trigger guard, 6-pos. stock, Mil-Spec pistol grip, aluminum upper and dedicated 9mm lower receiver, thermoplastic handguard, Mil-Spec charging handle, right or left-hand configuration, Type III hardcoat anodized black finish, 6 1/2 lbs. New 2018.

MSR $1,040	$875	$550	$465	$395	$350	$325	$300	

Add $10 for left-hand configuration (Stag 9L O.R.C.).

STAG 9 TACTICAL – 9mm Para. cal., blowback operating system, 16 in. chrome-lined heavy profile barrel, A2 flash hider, 32 shot mag., single stage trigger with Magpul enhanced trigger guard, Magpul CTR stock, Magpul MOE pistol grip, Stag M-LOK SL 13 1/2 in. handguard, aluminum receiver, Mil-Spec charging handle, standard 9mm buffer, right or left-hand configuration, Type III hardcoat anodized black finish, 6.7 lbs. New 2018.

MSR $1,230	$1,050	$650	$495	$450	$395	$350	$325	

Add $10 for left-hand configuration (Stag 9L Tactical).

STAG 10 BONES – .308 Win./7.62x51 cal., GIO, rifle length gas system, 18 in. chrome-lined barrel, VG6 Gamma 762 muzzle device, 10 shot PMAG, Mil-Spec single stage trigger with Magpul aluminum enhanced trigger guard, no sights, 6-pos. receiver extension tube, Hogue grip, low profile gas block, forged aluminum receiver, QPQ Nitride BCG, standard charging handle, AR10 carbine buffer and spring, 7 1/2 lbs. New 2017.

MSR $1,070	$895	$575	$475	$395	$350	$325	$300	

STAG 10 6.5 CREEDMOOR BONES – 6.5mm Creedmoor cal., GIO, rifle length gas system, 24 in. stainless steel barrel, VG6 Gamma 762 muzzle device, 10 shot PMAG, Stag two-stage trigger with enhanced trigger guard, 6-pos. receiver extension tube, low profile gas block, forged aluminum receiver, carbine buffer, standard charging handle, right or left-hand configuration, Type III hardcoat anodized black finish, 9.8 lbs. New 2017.

MSR $1,270	$1,065	$650	$500	$450	$395	$350	$325	

Add $80 for left-hand configuration (Stag 10L 6.5 Creedmoor Bones).

STAG 10 M-LOK – .308 Win. cal., GIO, 18 in. chrome-lined barrel, VG6 Gamma 762 muzzle device, 10 shot PMAG, Mil-Spec single stage trigger with Magpul aluminum enhanced trigger guard, Magpul ACS stock, Hogue grip, 16 1/2 in. Stag M-LOK handguard, forged aluminum receiver, QPQ Nitride BCG, low profile gas block with rifle length gas tube, AR10 carbine buffer and spring, right or left-hand configuration, Type III hardcoat anodized black finish, 40.5 in. OAL, 8.6 lbs. New 2018.

MSR $1,300	$1,075	$675	$500	$450	$400	$350	$325	

Add $80 for left-hand configuration (Stag 10L M-LOK).

STAG 10 6.5 CREEDMOOR M-LOK – 6.5mm Creedmoor cal., GIO, rifle length gas system, 24 in. stainless steel barrel, VG6 Gamma 762 muzzle device, 10 shot PMAG, Stag two-stage trigger with enhanced trigger guard, Magpul PRS stock, Magpul MOE grip, low profile gas block, forged aluminum receiver, 16 1/2 in. Stag M-LOK handguard, Nitride QPQ BCG, right or left-hand configuration, Type III hardcoat anodized black finish, 11.7 lbs. New 2018.

MSR $1,650	$1,350	$875	$650	$525	$450	$385	$350	

Add $70 for left-hand configuration (Stag 10L 6.5 Creedmoor M-LOK).

S 338 STAG ARMS LLC, cont.

MSR	100%	98%	95%	90%	80%	70%	60%	Last MSR

STAG 10S – 7.62x51 cal., 16 in. chrome-lined barrel, VG6 Gamma 762 muzzle device, no sights, Magpul ACS stock, Hogue grips, Diamondhead VRS-T .308 handguard, .308 BCG, 8.3 lbs. New 2017.
  MSR $1,615 $1,350 $1,200 $1,075 $950 $815 $700 $575

  * Stag 10S .308 TFD – .308 Win./7.62x51 cal., GIO, 16 in. stainless steel barrel with S7 coating, VG6 Gamma 762 muzzle device, 10 shot PMAG, Mil-Spec single stage trigger with enhanced trigger guard, FAB Defense GL-Core stock, FAB Defense AGR43-B pistol grip, low profile gas block with mid-length gas tube, 13 1/2 in. Diamondhead VRS-T 308 handguard, Nitride QPQ BCG, forged aluminum receiver, Type III hardcoat anodized black finish, 8.2 lbs. New 2018.
  MSR $1,200 $995 $625 $495 $450 $395 $350 $325

STAG 10S BONES – .308 Win./7.62x51 cal., GIO, mid-length gas system, 16 in. chrome-lined barrel, VG6 Gamma 762 muzzle device, 10 shot PMAG, Mil-Spec single stage trigger with non-adj. 5-8 lb. trigger pull, 6-pos. receiver extension tube, low profile gas block, forged aluminum receiver, .308 Nitride QPQ BCG, standard charging handle, .308 carbine buffer, Type III hardcoat anodized black finish, 6.4 lbs. New 2018.
  MSR $1,040 $875 $550 $465 $395 $350 $325 $300

STAG 10S 6.5 CREEDMOOR BONES – 6.5mm Creedmoor cal., GIO, rifle length gas system, 22 in. stainless steel barrel, VG6 Gamma 762 muzzle device, 10 shot PMAG, Stag two-stage trigger with enhanced trigger guard, 6-pos. receiver extension tube, low profile gas block, forged aluminum receiver, carbine buffer, standard charging handle, Nitride QPQ BCG, right or left-hand configuration,Type III hardcoat anodized black finish, 9.8 lbs. New 2017.
  MSR $1,270 $1,065 $650 $500 $450 $395 $350 $325
  Add $80 for left-hand configuration (Stag 10SL 6.5 Creedmoor Bones).

STAG 10S M-LOK – .308 Win. cal., GIO, 16 in. chrome-lined barrel, VG6 Gamma 762 muzzle device, 10 shot PMAG, Mil-Spec single stage trigger with Magpul aluminum enhanced trigger guard, Magpul ACS stock, Hogue grip, low profile gas block with mid-length gas tube, forged aluminum receiver, 13 1/2 in. Stag M-LOK handguard, Nitride QPQ BCG, AR10 carbine buffer and spring, right or left-hand configuration, Type III hardcoat anodized black finish, 8.2 lbs. New 2018.
  MSR $1,280 $1,075 $675 $500 $450 $400 $350 $325
  Add $70 for left-hand configuration (Stag 10SL M-LOK).

STAG 10S 6.5 CREEDMOOR M-LOK – 6.5mm Creedmoor cal., GIO, rifle length gas system, 22 in. stainless steel barrel, VG6 Gamma 762 muzzle device, 10 shot PMAG, Stag two-stage trigger with enhanced trigger guard, Magpul PRS stock, Magpul MOE grip, low profile gas block, forged aluminum receiver, 16 1/2 in. Stag M-LOK handguard, Nitride QPQ BCG, right or left-hand configuration, Type III hardcoat anodized black finish, 11.7 lbs. New 2018.
  MSR $1,650 $1,350 $875 $650 $525 $450 $385 $350
  Add $70 for left-hand configuration (Stag 10SL 6.5 Creedmoor M-LOK).

STAG 15 3GUN ELITE – 5.56 NATO/.223 Rem. cal., GIO, rifle length gas system with low profile gas block, 18 in. stainless steel fluted heavy barrel, Stag 3G compensator, 30 shot PMAG, Geissele Super 3-Gun trigger with Magpul aluminum enhanced trigger guard, Magpul ACS stock, Magpul MOE grip, 16 1/2 in. Stag 15 M-LOK SL handguard, Mil-Spec charging handle, H buffer and spring, right or left-hand configuration, Type III hardcoat anodized black finish, 39.5 in. OAL, 7.6 lbs. New 2018.
  MSR $1,050 $875 $550 $465 $395 $350 $325 $300
  Add $30 for left-hand configuration (Stag 15L 3Gun Elite).

STAG 15 BONES – 5.56 NATO/.223 Rem. cal., GIO, carbine length gas system with low profile gas block, 16 in. chrome-lined Govt. profile barrel with A2 flash hider, 30 shot mag., single stage trigger, 6-pos. receiver extension tube, A2 plastic grip, forged aluminum receivers, Mil-Spec charging handle, manganese phosphate coated M16 BCG, right or left-hand configuration, Type III hardcoat anodized black finish, 5.2 lbs. New 2018.
  MSR $540 $475 $415 $375 $335 $310 $295 $275
  Add $30 for left-hand configuration (Stag 15L Bones).

STAG 15 HELICAL – .224 Valkyrie cal., GIO, rifle length gas system with low profile gas block, 22 in. stainless steel helical fluted barrel, VG6 Epsilon muzzle device, 25 shot mag., nickel boron coated two-stage match trigger with Magpul aluminum enhanced trigger guard, XLR Tactical AR buttstock, FAB Defense AGR-43 pistol grip, forged aluminum receivers, Stag 15 16 1/2 in. M-LOK SL handguard, Mil-Spec charging handle, right or left-hand configuration, Type III hardcoat anodized black finish, 40.5 in. OAL, 8.4 lbs. New 2018.
  MSR $1,400 $1,150 $750 $550 $465 $415 $375 $350
  Add $50 for left-hand configuration (Stag 15L Valkyrie Helical).

STAG 15 LEO – 5.56 NATO/.223 Rem. cal., GIO, carbine length gas system with A2 front post, 16 in. chrome-lined Govt. profile barrel, A2 flash hider, 30 shot mag., single stage trigger, F-marked A3 front sight, Mil-Spec 6-pos. buttstock, A2 style plastic grip, forged aluminum receiver, Samson Star-C free floating handguard with Picatinny quad rails, Mil-Spec charging handle, side sling swivel, bayonet lug, right or left-hand configuration, Type III hardcoat anodized black finish, 35.5 in. OAL, 6.8 lbs. New 2018.
  MSR $785 $675 $500 $425 $375 $335 $315 $295
  Add $50 for left-hand configuration (Stag 15L Leo).

STAG ARMS LLC, cont. 339 S

MSR	100%	98%	95%	90%	80%	70%	60%	Last MSR

STAG 15 M4 – 5.56 NATO/.223 Rem. cal., GIO, carbine length gas system with A2 front post, 16 in. chrome-lined Govt. profile barrel, A2 flash hider, 30 shot mag., single stage trigger with Magpul enhanced trigger guard, F-marked A2 front sight and bayonet lug, removable A3 carry handle with integrated rear sight, Mil-Spec 6-pos. stock, A2 style plastic grip, thermoplastic handguard with double heat shield, forged aluminum receiver, Mil-Spec charging handle, right or left-hand configuration, Type III hardcoat anodized black finish, 35.5 in. OAL, 6.75 lbs. New 2018.

MSR $650	$550	$475	$400	$350	$315	$295	$275	

Add $50 for left-hand configuration (Stag 15L M4).

STAG 15 M-LOK LEO – 5.56 NATO/.223 Rem. cal., GIO, carbine length gas system with A2 front post, 16 in. chrome-lined Govt. profile barrel, A2 flash hider, 30 shot mag., single stage trigger, F-marked A2 front sight, side sling swivel, bayonet lug, Mil-Spec 6-pos. stock, A2 style plastic grip, forged aluminum receiver, 7 in. M-LOK handguard, right or left-hand configuration, Type III hardcoat anodized black finish, 35.5 in. OAL, 6.23 lbs. New 2018.

MSR $610	$535	$460	$395	$350	$315	$295	$275	

Add $50 for left-hand configuration (Stag 15L M-LOK Leo).

STAG 15 MX M-LOK – 5.56 NATO/.223 Rem. cal., GIO, carbine length gas system with low profile gas block, 16 in. chrome-lined Govt. profile barrel, A2 flash hider, 30 shot GI mag., Mil-Spec single stage trigger, A2 style plastic grip, forged aluminum receiver, Trinity Force MX M-LOK 15 in. rail, Mil-Spec charging handle, carbine buffer and spring, right or left-hand configuration, Type III hardcoat anodized black finish, 35.5 in. OAL, 6.23 lbs. New 2018.

MSR $600	$515	$450	$395	$350	$315	$295	$275	

Add $30 for left-hand configuration (Stag 15L MX M-LOK).

STAG 15 MINIMALIST – 5.56 NATO/.223 Rem. cal., GIO, carbine length gas system, 16 in. chrome-lined Govt. profile barrel, A2 flash hider, 30 shot Mission First Tactical poly mag., single stage trigger with MFT E-VolV enhanced trigger guard, A2 front sight and MFT polymer flip-up rear sight, MFT Battlelink Minimalist stock, MFT Engage AR-15/M16 pistol grip, forged aluminum receiver, MFT Tekko polymer AR-15 carbine M-LOK rail, Mil-Spec charging handle, carbine buffer and spring, right or left-hand configuration, Type III hardcoat anodized black finish, 35.5 in. OAL, 6.05 lbs. New 2018.

MSR $615	$575	$485	$415	$350	$315	$295	$275	

Add $75 for left-hand configuration (Stag 15L Minimalist).

STAG 15 O.R.C. (OPTICS READY CARBINE) – 5.56 NATO/.223 Rem. cal., GIO, carbine length gas system with railed gas block, 16 in. chrome-lined Govt. profile barrel, A3 flash hider, single stage trigger, Mil-Spec 6-pos. stock, Mil-Spec pistol grip, forged aluminum receiver, thermoplastic handguard, Mil-Spec charging handle, standard carbine buffer and spring, right or left-hand configuration, Type III hardcoat anodized black finish, 35.5 in. OAL, 6 1/2 lbs. New 2018.

MSR $570	$495	$435	$385	$340	$315	$295	$275	

Add $50 for left-hand configuration (Stag 15L O.R.C.).

STAG 15 RETRO – 5.56 NATO/.223 Rem. cal., GIO, rifle length gas system with A2 front post, 20 in. chrome moly heavy profile barrel, A2 flash hider, 20 shot straight mag., single stage trigger with Magpul enhanced trigger guard, F-marked A2 front sight and bayonet lug, removable carry handle with integrated sight, A2 stock with trap door for storage, A2 grip, forged aluminum receivers, thermoplastic handguard with double heat shields, Mil-Spec charging handle, A2 buffer with A2 action spring, right or left-hand configuration, Type III hardcoat anodized black finish, 39.75 in. OAL, 8 1/2 lbs. New 2018.

MSR $675	$575	$485	$415	$350	$315	$295	$275	

Add $30 for left-hand configuration (Stag 15L Retro).

STAG 15 TACTICAL – 5.56 NATO/.223 Rem. cal., GIO, carbine length low profile gas block, 16 in. chrome-lined Govt. profile barrel, A2 flash hider, 30 shot PMAG, single stage trigger with Magpul enhanced trigger guard, Magpul CTR stock, Magpul MOE pistol grip, free floating Stag 15 13 1/2 in. M-LOK SL handguard with QD mounts and top Picatinny rail, Mil-Spec charging handle, right or left-hand configuration, Type III hardcoat anodized black or FDE Cerakote finish, 35.5 in. OAL, 6.3 lbs. New 2018.

MSR $730	$645	$500	$415	$370	$325	$300	$275	

Add $30 for left-hand configuration (Stag 15L).

Add $220 for FDE Cerakote finish.

* ***Stag 15 Tactical Freedom Edition*** – 5.56 NATO/.223 Rem. cal., GIO, carbine length gas system with low profile gas block, 16 in. chrome-lined Govt. profile barrel, A2 flash hider, 30 shot PMAG, single stage trigger with enhanced trigger guard, Magpul CTR stock, Magpul MOE pistol grip, forged aluminum receiver, Mil-Spec charging handle, Stag 15 13 1/2 in. M-LOK SL handguard with QD mounts, features laser engraved symbols on the magwell, upper receiver, dust cover, magazine, and stock, and each model is specially numbered, Type III hardcoat anodized black finish, 35.5 in. OAL, 6.3 lbs. Limited mfg. of 75 beginning 2018.

MSR $1,100	$915	$575	$475	$415	$350	$325	$300	

S 340 STAG ARMS LLC, cont.

MSR	100%	98%	95%	90%	80%	70%	60%	Last MSR

STAG 15 TRINITY – 5.56 NATO/.223 Rem. cal., GIO, carbine length gas system with low profile gas block, 16 in. chrome-lined Govt. profile barrel, A2 flash hider, 30 shot GI mag., Mil-Spec single stage trigger, Trinity Force Cobra stock, Trinity Force DI Slim grip, forged aluminum receivers, Trinity Force 15 in. MX-15 M-LOK rail, Mil-Spec charging handle, right or left-hand configuration, Type III hardcoat anodized black finish, 36.5 in. OAL, 6.63 lbs. New 2018.

MSR $620	$535	$460	$395	$350	$315	$295	$275

Add $40 for left-hand configuration (Stag 15L Trinity).

STAG 15 VALKYRIE – .224 Valkyrie cal., GIO, mid-length gas system with low profile gas block, 18 in. stainless steel fluted heavy barrel, VG6 Epsilon muzzle device, 25 shot mag., nickel boron coated two-stage match trigger with enhanced trigger guard, Magpul PRS stock, Hogue pistol grip, forged aluminum receivers, Mil-Spec charging handle, Stag 16 15 1/2 in. M-LOK SL handguard, right or left-hand configuration, Type III hardcoat anodized black finish, 39 in. OAL, 8.9 lbs. New 2018.

MSR $1,290	$1,075	$675	$500	$450	$400	$350	$325

Add $40 for left-hand configuration (Stag 15L Valkyrie).

STAG 15 VARMINTER – 5.56 NATO/.223 Rem. cal., GIO, rifle length gas system with low profile gas block, 24 in. stainless steel heavy bull barrel with 11 degree target crown, 10 shot mag., two-stage match trigger with Magpul aluminum enhanced trigger guard, Magpul fixed rifle stock, Hogue pistol grip, forged aluminum receivers, Hogue free floating handguard with bipod stud mount, Mil-Spec charging handle, A2 buffer with A2 action spring, right or left-hand configuration, Type III hardcoat anodized black finish, 42.5 in. OAL, 10 lbs. New 2018.

MSR $815	$695	$500	$425	$375	$335	$315	$295

Add $25 for left-hand configuration (Stag 15L Varminter).

STAG 15 FLUTED VARMINTER – 5.56 NATO/.223 Rem. cal., GIO, rifle length gas system with low profile gas block, 19 in. stainless steel fluted heavy barrel, 11 degree target crown, 10 shot PMAG, Stag 2 Stage Trigger, Magpul fixed rifle stock, Hogue pistol grip, forged aluminum upper and lower receiver, Hogue free floating handguard with sling swivel attachment, Mil-Spec charging handle, right or left-hand configuration, Type III hardcoat anodized black finish, 37.25 in. OAL, 7 1/2 lbs. New 2018.

MSR $820	$695	$500	$425	$375	$335	$315	$295

Add $20 for left-hand configuration (Stag 15L Fluted Varminter).

STAG 15 SUPER VARMINTER – 6.8 SPC II cal., GIO, rifle length gas system with low profile gas block, 20.77 in. stainless steel heavy barrel with 11 degree target crown, 10 shot mag., two-stage match trigger with Magpul aluminum enhanced trigger guard, Magpul fixed rifle stock, Hogue pistol grip, forged aluminum receivers, Hogue free floating handguard with bipod stud mount, Mil-Spec charging handle, A2 buffer with A2 action spring, right or left-hand configuration, Type III hardcoat anodized black finish, 39.25 in. OAL, 7.8 lbs. New 2018.

MSR $815	$695	$500	$425	$375	$335	$315	$295

Add $35 for left-hand configuration (Stag 15L Super Varminter).

STAG 15 VRST S3 – 5.56 NATO/.223 Rem. cal., GIO, carbine length gas system with low profile gas block, 16 in. chrome-lined Govt. profile barrel, A2 flash hider, 30 shot PMAG, single stage trigger with enhanced trigger guard, Magpul MOE SL stock, Hogue pistol grip, forged aluminum receivers, Diamondhead VRST Series 3 M-LOK 13 1/2 in. handguard, Mil-Spec charging handle, right or left-hand configuration, Type III hardcoat anodized black finish, 35.5 in. OAL, 6 1/2 lbs. New 2018.

MSR $730	$645	$500	$415	$370	$325	$300	$275

Add $30 for left-hand configuration (Stag 15L VRST S3).

STANDARD MANUFACTURING CO. LLC

Current manufacturer located in New Britain, CT. Previously located in Newington, CT. Dealer and consumer direct sales were through FFL dealer.

RIFLES: SEMI-AUTO

STANDARD MODEL A SPORTING RIFLE (STD-15 SPORTING RIFLE MODEL A) – 5.56 NATO cal., GIO, rail height gas block, right or left-hand action, 16 in. Govt. profile barrel with A2 flash hider, 10 or 30 shot black aluminum mag., stainless steel single stage trigger, Roger's Super-Stoc, standard A2 pistol grip, M4 feed ramps, M-LOK compatible polymer drop-in handguard, A3 upper and aluminum lower receiver with anodized finish, 6-position carbine buffer tube, receiver endplate with ambi single point sling loops, matte black finish, 6 lbs. New late 2016.

MSR $999	$850	$550	$465	$395	$350	$325	$295

Add $50 for left-hand action.

STANDARD MODEL B SPORTING RIFLE (STD-15 SPORTING RIFLE MODEL B) – 5.56 NATO or .300 AAC Blackout (new 2016) cal., GIO, right or left-hand action, extended low profile gas block, 16 in. Govt. profile barrel with Yankee Hill Machine Phantom flash hider, 10 or 30 shot Mission First Tactical polymer mag., stainless steel speed hammer and trigger, front and rear manual flip iron sights, MFT Minimalist adj. stock, MFT EPG16V2 grip, M4 feed ramps, extruded KeyMod 10 in. super light rail, A3 upper and aluminum lower receiver with anodized finish,

STANDARD MANUFACTURING CO. LLC, cont. 341 S

MSR	100%	98%	95%	90%	80%	70%	60%	Last MSR

standard charging handle, Nitride bolt carrier group, 6-position carbine buffer tube, receiver endplate with ambi single point sling loops, black, gold, FDE, tan, or Flat Foliage Green finish, 6.2 lbs. New late 2016.

| MSR $1,199 | $995 | $625 | $495 | $450 | $395 | $350 | $325 | |

Add $50 for left-hand action.

Add $101 for gold finish.

STANDARD MODEL C SPORTING RIFLE (STD-15 SPORTING RIFLE MODEL C) – 5.56 NATO cal., GIO, right or left-hand action, carbine length gas system, 16 in. Govt. profile chrome moly barrel, A2 flash hider, 30 shot black aluminum mag., stainless steel Mil-Spec SST, A2 front sight and detachable carry handle A2 rear sight, 6-pos. M4 adj. or A2 fixed stock, standard A2 grip, ambi safety selector, M4 feed ramps, CAR single heat shield handguard, forged aluminum receiver, 7.5 lbs. New late 2016.

| MSR $899 | $765 | $515 | $440 | $375 | $335 | $315 | $295 | |

Add $50 for left-hand action.

STANDARD MODEL D SPORTING RIFLE (STD-15 SPORTING RIFLE MODEL D) – .223 Wylde chamber, GIO, 18 in. fluted stainless steel heavy barrel, YHM Phantom muzzle brake, SST, MFT Minimalist (disc.) or 6-pos. Magpul STR stock, MFT EPG16v2 grip, ambi safety selector, mid-length gas system, low profile adj. gas block, 13 in. KeyMod super light rail, ambi charging handle with tactical latch, forged aluminum receivers, 7 1/2 lbs.

| MSR $1,449 | $1,250 | $825 | $575 | $475 | $425 | $375 | $350 | |

Add $50 for left-hand action.

STANDARD MODEL E SPORTING RIFLE – 5.56 NATO cal., GIO, 16 in. Govt. profile barrel, A2 flash hider, red/green reflex sight, low profile gas block, carbine length gas system, M4 feed ramps, CAR single heat shield handguard, integral laser, 7 1/2 lbs. New 2018.

| MSR $879 | $765 | $515 | $440 | $375 | $335 | $315 | $295 | |

SHOTGUNS: SEMI-AUTO

SKO – 12 ga., 2 3/4 or 3 in. chamber, gas operating system with AR-style mag. and bolt release, 18 7/8 in. barrel threaded for door breacher and with Tru-Choke thread pattern for screw-in choke system, 5 (standard) and optional 2 and 10 shot mag., adj. stock, polymer AR-style grip, ambidextrous safety, 22 in. Picatinny top rail, 38 in. OAL, 7 lbs. 10 oz. New late 2017.

| MSR $1,000 | $850 | $725 | $650 | $585 | $515 | $450 | $395 | |

STERLING ARMAMENT, LTD.

Previous manufacturer established circa 1900, and located in Dagenham, Essex, England. Previously imported and distributed by Cassi Inc. located in Colorado Springs, CO until 1990.

CARBINES: SEMI-AUTO

AR-180 – please refer to Armalite section for more information and pricing on this model.

STERLING ARSENAL

Current custom firearms manufacturer located in Sterling, VA beginning 2010.

Sterling Arsenal manufactures their own SAR-XV and SAR-30 brands of production and custom AR-15 and AR-30 rifles, respectively. Sterling Arsenal builds custom AK M type rifles and shotguns and converts Saiga and VEPR firearms with U.S. made components. Sterling Arsenal also offers a precision bolt action platform offered as standardized operating system (OS) configurations. Sterling Arsenal also owns Critical Koting, a NIC Certified Cerakote Applicator (Sterling Arsenal brand and line of business), and operates exclusively at Sterling Arsenal's facilities.

PISTOLS: SEMI-AUTO

SAR-XV PREPR AR-15 PISTOL – 9mm Para., 5.56 NATO, or .300 AAC Blackout cal., cold hammer forged chrome-lined barrel, custom forged anodized receivers, SIG arm brace with KAK extended receiver extension, free float quad rail, choice of Magpul AFG or hand stop, black finish. Disc. 2015.

| | $975 | $885 | $765 | $650 | $575 | $495 | $435 | $1,150 |

Add $300 for 9mm Para. cal.

SAR-XV MOD2 AR-15 PISTOL – 5.56 NATO, .300 AAC Blackout, or 9mm Para. (optional upgrade) cal., upgraded variation of the SAR-XV PREPR AR-15 model, 5, 7, 8, or 10 in. QPQ Nitride barrel, custom forged anodized hardened receivers, free float KeyMod rail system, push button quick detach sling mounts, SAR custom tuned trigger, ambidextrous fire controls, Magpul MOE backup flip sights, Magpul grip, AFG or hand stop, pistol receiver extension, black finish. Mfg. 2016-2017.

| | $975 | $885 | $765 | $650 | $575 | $495 | $435 | $1,190 |

S 342 STERLING ARSENAL, cont.

MSR	100%	98%	95%	90%	80%	70%	60%	Last MSR

SAR-XV MOD3 AR-15 PISTOL – 5.56 NATO, .300 AAC Blackout, or 9mm Para. cal., 8 1/2 or 10 1/2 in. QPQ Nitride barrel, SLR muzzle devices, SAR custom tuned trigger, anodized lightweight aluminum backup adj. flip sights, Magpul grip, custom forged anodized hardened receivers, free float M-LOK rail system, push button quick detach sling mounts, ambi fire controls, AFG or hand stop, pistol receiver extension, black finish or custom Cerakote. New 2017.

| MSR $1,390 | $1,150 | $1,035 | $900 | $750 | $685 | $585 | $485 | |

Add $122 for 9mm Para. cal. (8 1/2 in. barrel only).

Add $175 for SAR-PRES (pistol receiver extension buffer system).

Custom Cerakote addition based on level and type of coating application: one-color Cerakote $100; two-color fade pattern $150; multi-color stencil camp patterns (e.g. Digital, Kryptek, or Multi-Cam) $350.

RIFLES: SEMI-AUTO

SAR-30 COMBAT FIELD GRADE RIFLE – .308 Win. cal., 16, 18, or 20 in. cold hammer forged (disc.) or black Nitride (new 2017) barrel, compatible with Magpul mags., free float KeyMod (disc.) or M-LOK (new 2017) handguard, machined and forged lower parts, Mil-Spec single stage trigger, Magpul PRS stock, QD sling mounts, black finish or custom Cerakote. New 2015.

| MSR $1,850 | $1,525 | $975 | $750 | $575 | $495 | $425 | $375 | |

SAR-30 PRECISION MATCH COMPETITION RIFLE – .308 Win. or 6.5mm Creedmoor cal., 18, 20, or 22 in. JP Enterprise medium contour barrel, PWS muzzle brake (disc.), SLR flash hider (new 2017), or silencer mount, compatible with Magpul mags., free float KeyMod (disc.), SAR HexSphere (disc.), or M-LOK (new 2017) handguard, machined and forged lower parts, SAR custom tuned match trigger and ambidextrous fire controls, Magpul PRS stock, QD sling mounts, Cerakote finish. New 2015.

| MSR $2,650 | $2,125 | $1,325 | $995 | $675 | $595 | $525 | $475 | |

SAR-XV COMBAT MATCH (GLADIUS V4) – 5.56 NATO, 6.8 SPC, .300 AAC Blackout (new 2014), or .458 SOCOM cal., 16 or 18 in. stainless steel barrel with phantom flash suppressor, mid-length gas ported, low profile DI gas block, front and rear alloy flip BUIS sights, custom forged billet upper and lower receivers, SAR HexSphere modular free float handguard, choice of Magpul CTR or STR stock, K2 pistol grip, black finish. Mfg. late 2014-mid-2015.

| | $1,600 | $1,000 | $775 | $575 | $495 | $425 | $395 | *$1,950* |

SAR-XV PREPR (PRACTICAL READY EVERDAY PATROL RIFLE) – 5.56 NATO or .300 AAC Blackout cal., 16 in. cold hammer forged chrome-lined barrel, F-marked front sight gas block and rear Magpul flip sight, custom forged anodized receivers, two-piece quad rail, machined and forged lower parts, Mil-Spec buffer tube, MFT Minimalist stock and grip, black finish. Disc. 2015.

| | $725 | $500 | $435 | $375 | $335 | $315 | $295 | *$850* |

SAR-XV MOD2 – 5.56 NATO, .300 AAC Blackout, 6.8 SPC, or .458 SOCOM cal., upgraded variation of Sar-XV PREPR model, mid-length ported 16 in. QPQ Nitride barrel, A2 flash hider, free float 15 in. extended KeyMod rail system, Magpul MOE backup flip sights, push button quick detach sling mounts, SAR custom tuned trigger, ambidextrous fire controls, forged anodized hardened receivers, low profile DI gas block, Mil-Spec pattern 6-position extension buffer assembly, Magpul stock and grip, black finish. Mfg. 2016-2017.

| | $1,050 | $650 | $495 | $450 | $395 | $350 | $325 | *$1,250* |

SAR-XV MOD2 MATCH – 5.56 NATO cal., mid-length ported 16 in. stainless steel barrel, PWS muzzle brake, low profile gas block, Magpul Pro Steel backup flip sights, push button quick detach sling mounts, forged anodized hardened receivers, free float 15 in. extended KeyMod rail system, JP match tuned trigger, ambidextrous fire controls, Mil-Spec pattern 6-position extension H-Series buffer assembly, Magpul stock and grip, grey finish. Mfg. 2016-2017.

| | $1,350 | $875 | $650 | $525 | $450 | $385 | $350 | *$1,650* |

SPATHA INTERMEDIATE LONG RANGE SPR – 5.56 NATO, 6.8 SPC, or .458 SOCOM cal., GPO, 18 in. stainless steel barrel with phantom flash suppressor, billet upper receiver side charger model, single stage short travel adj. trigger, front and rear alloy flip BUIS sights, SAR HexSphere modular free float handguard, alternative enhanced stock, K2 pistol grip, black finish. Mfg. late 2014-2016.

| | $1,600 | $1,000 | $775 | $575 | $495 | $425 | $395 | *$1,950* |

SAR-XV MOD3 AR-15 RIFLE – 5.56 NATO cal., mid-length 16 in. ported stainless steel barrel, SLR Hybrid comp/ flash hider, Magpul PMAG, alloy adj. flip-up sights, SAR-Custom Shop tuned trigger, Magpul SL stock, K grip, forged 7075-T6 anodized R70c hardened receivers with variable tension adjustment, low profile stainless steel Nitride DI gas block, 15 in. extruded anodized M-LOK rail system, QD sling mounts, ambi fire controls, extended changing latch, Mil-Spec 6-pos. receiver buffer extension, 7 lbs. New 2017.

| MSR $1,450 | $1,195 | $795 | $550 | $465 | $415 | $375 | $350 | |

Add $60 for adj. gas block.

STONER RIFLE

Please refer to the Knight's Armament Company listing in the K section.

STURM, RUGER & CO., INC. 343 **S**

MSR	100%	98%	95%	90%	80%	70%	60%	Last MSR

STURM, RUGER & CO., INC.

Current manufacturer with production facilities located in Newport, NH, Prescott, AZ, and Mayodan, NC. Previously manufactured in Southport, CT 1949-1991 (corporate and administrative offices remain at this location). A second factory was opened in Newport, NH in 1963, and still produces single action revolvers, rifles and shotguns. During September 2013, Ruger purchased a 220,000 square foot facility in Mayodan, NC. New production began in late fall of 2013.

In January of 1949, partners William B. Ruger and Alexander Sturm began manufacturing .22 pistols in a leased 4,400 square foot wooden structure on Station St. in Southport, CT. By 1956 they acquired an additional 2,300 square feet that is today affectionately known as the Red Barn. By January of 1959 they completely moved into a newly finished building on Lacey Place, not too far from Station St. The company continued to expand its product line and in 1967 began producing long guns in a factory building located in Newport, NH. By 1988 Ruger set up another facility in Prescott, AZ to make the P-series center-fire pistols. In July 1991 they completely suspended production at Southport. The corporate offices remain there to this day. Then, in 2013 Ruger opened a third large factory in Mayodan, NC. Over time production of the extensive variety of products was divided up and dispersed among these facilities.

Red Barn on Station St. 1949-1959 pistols & revolvers

Lacey Place 1959-1991 pistols, revolvers & rifles

Pinetree Casting Newport, NH 1963 - current investment castings

Newport, NH 1967 - current shotguns, rifles, and since 1992 revolvers

Prescott, AZ 1988 - current all centerfire pistols and since 1992 rimfire pistols

Mayodan, NC 2013 - current modern rifles. In 2015 an additional line was also made up for producing SR22 pistols.

From 2004-2007 the Ruger Studio of Art & Decoration offered factory engraving on any current Ruger model. The engraving could range from presentation inscriptions to bas-relief and extensive gold in-laid masterpieces. Prices could range from a few hundred dollars to $40,000 or more.

Ruger emerged as America's largest small arms maker, and offers a complete line of firearms for sportsmen, law enforcement and military. Over a 68 year span, from five separate factories Ruger has shipped over 29 million firearms.

Alex Sturm passed away in November 1951. Bill Ruger carried on until July 6, 2002 when he too passed away at his home in Prescott, AZ. Ruger, America's greatest 20th century arms inventor, is buried on his estate Corbin Park at Croydon, NH.

RIFLES: SEMI-AUTO, CENTERFIRE

Beginning 2013, all Mini-14 models and variations include a drilled and tapped receiver.

AR-556 – 5.56 NATO cal., GIO, 16.1 in. cold hammer forged chrome moly barrel with M4 feed ramp cuts, 10 or 30 shot Magpul PMAG, single stage trigger, enlarged trigger guard, Ruger Rapid Deploy folding rear sight, milled F-height gas block with post front sight, black synthetic 6-pos. collapsible, Magpul MOE synthetic collapsible (new 2018), or fixed (new 2016) stock, ergonomic pistol grip, forged aluminum upper and lower receivers, forward assist, dust cover, brass deflector, 6 1/2 lbs. New 2015.

MSR $799	$675	$500	$425	$375	$335	$315	$295

Add $50 for Magpul MOE synthetic collapsible stock (new 2018).

* ***AR-556 With Monsterman Grip*** – 5.56 NATO cal., 16.1 in. barrel with factory installed thread protector, 10 shot mag., fixed A2 stock, MonsterMan grip, 7 1/2 lbs. New 2018.

MSR $849	$725	$500	$435	$375	$335	$315	$295

AR-556 MPR (MULTI-PURPOSE RIFLE) – 5.56 NATO cal., 18 in. threaded barrel, muzzle brake, 30 shot Magpul PMAG, no sights, Ruger Elite 452 AR-Trigger, rifle length gas system, forged aluminum flat-top upper with forward assist, dust cover, and brass deflector, lower receiver with Mil-Spec buffer tube, free floating 15 in. handguard with Magpul M-LOK accessory attachment slots, Magpul MOE grip, Magpul MOE SL collapsible buttstock, Type III hardcoat anodized black finish, 6.8 lbs. New late 2017.

MSR $899	$765	$515	$440	$375	$335	$315	$295

SR-556/SR-556 CARBINE – 5.56 NATO or 6.8 SPC (mfg. mid-2010-2011) cal., GPO, 10, 25 (6.8 SPC only, disc. 2011), or 30 shot mag., 16.1 in. barrel with flash suppressor or target crown, matte black finish, four position chrome plated gas regulator, quad rail handguard, with or without Troy folding sights, fixed (556SC) or 6-position telescoping M4 style buttstock, Hogue monogrip pistol grip with finger grooves, upper receiver has integrated Picatinny rail, chrome plated bolt, bolt carrier, and extractor, includes rail covers, soft sided carry case and three magazines, 7.4 (Carbine) or 7.9 lbs. Mfg. mid-2009-2015.

	$1,675	$1,000	$825	$625	$550	$475	$425	$2,049

* ***SR-556E*** – 5.56 NATO cal., GPO (two-stage with regulator), 10 (SR-556ESC) or 30 shot mag., 16.1 in. cold hammer forged barrel with flash suppressor, Ruger Rapid Deploy folding sights (new 2013), A2 style pistol grip, 6-position telescoping M4 style buttstock, vented aluminum handguard with full-length Picatinny rail, upper receiver has integrated Picatinny rail, 7.35 lbs. Mfg. mid-2011-2014.

	$1,135	$725	$525	$465	$415	$375	$350	$1,375

S 344 STURM, RUGER & CO., INC., cont.

MSR	100%	98%	95%	90%	80%	70%	60%	Last MSR

SR-556 TAKEDOWN – 5.56 NATO cal., GPO, 16.1 in. takedown threaded barrel with flash suppressor, three 30 shot Magpul PMAGs, Elite 452 AR trigger, folding iron sights, black synthetic collapsible stock, Magpul MOE grip, Mil-Spec buffer tube, KeyMod handguard (new 2016, for reduced overall weight), includes ballistic nylon case, three rail covers, and a lock, manganese phosphate/hardcoat anodized finish, 7.1 lbs. New mid-2015.

MSR $2,199	$1,725	$1,050	$850	$625	$550	$475	$425	

SR-556VT – 5.56 NATO cal., GPO, 5 shot mag., 20 in. hammer forged stainless steel barrel, round, lightweight adaptable vented handguard with Picatinny rail on top, fixed A2-style buttstock, Magpul MOE grip, two-stage trigger, charging handle with tactical latch, 8 1/2 lbs. Mfg. 2013-2014.

	$1,650	$1,000	$795	$595	$495	$425	$395	*$1,995*

Ruger has issued a recall on this model because the disconnector in the two-stage trigger system was not properly heat-treated by a vendor and can wear prematurely. This can result in an unsafe condition in which the rifle delays firing or doubles. No incidents have been reported, but this is an important safety issue. Please contact Ruger customer service at 603.865.2442 or at recall@Ruger.com to determine if your gun is part of the recall.

SR-762 CARBINE – 7.62 NATO cal., two-stage piston driven, AR-15 style, 16.1 in. heavy contour chrome-lined cold hammer forged barrel, includes three 20 shot Magpul PMAGs, folding backup iron sights, 6-pos. adj. M4-style stock, Hogue monogrip, lightweight adj. adapatable handguard, full-length top Picatinny rail and two side rails, one-piece bolt carrier, four position gas regulator, sight adjustment tool, includes soft side carry case, matte black finish, 8.6 lbs. New late 2013.

MSR $2,349	$1,875	$1,100	$895	$650	$575	$495	$425	

SUN DEVIL MANUFACTURING LLC

Current rifle and billet aluminum parts and accessories manufacturer located in Mesa, AZ.

RIFLES: SEMI-AUTO

DOUBLE DEVIL TWIN AR – 5.56 NATO cal., 16 in. chrome moly barrels, Sun Devil Mfg. dual function brakes/compensators, monolithic billet heavy wall twin side by side upper receivers, BAD lever compatible, free floated modular handguards with integral top Picatinny rails, billet bipod mount, black finish. New 2016.

Please contact the manufacturer directly for pricing and availability for this model.

SUPERIOR ARMS

Current manufacturer located in Wapello, IA since 2004.

PISTOLS: SEMI-AUTO

Superior Arms manufactured complete AR-style semi-auto pistols with either an A4 flat-top or A2 carry handle and 10 1/2 or 11 1/2 inch barrels.

RIFLES: SEMI-AUTO

S-15 CARBINE – .223 Rem. cal., GIO, 16 in. chrome moly barrel with A2 flash hider, 6-pos. telescoping stock, A2 pistol grip, A4 flat-top receiver with integral rail, M4 handguard, bayonet lug, front sling swivel.

MSR $995	$850	$550	$465	$395	$350	$325	$295

S-15 H-BAR RIFLE – .223 Rem. cal., GIO, 20 in. chrome moly barrel, A2 flash hider, A4 flat-top receiver with integral rail, A2 buttstock, bayonet lug, A2 pistol grip, front sling swivel.

MSR $1,075	$895	$575	$475	$395	$350	$325	$300

S-15 M4 CARBINE – .223 Rem. cal., GIO, 16 in. chrome moly barrel, A2 flash hider, A4 flat-top receiver with integral rail, M4 handguard, 6-position telescoping stock, A2 pistol grip, front sling swivel.

MSR $995	$850	$550	$465	$395	$350	$325	$295

S-15 MID-LENGTH CARBINE – .223 Rem. cal., GIO, 16 in. chrome moly barrel with A2 flash hider, 6-pos. telescoping stock, A2 pistol grip, A4 flat-top receiver with integral rail, mid-length handguard, bayonet lug, front sling swivel.

MSR $1,010	$865	$550	$465	$395	$350	$325	$300

S-15 VARMINT RIFLE – .223 Rem. cal., GIO, 20 in. stainless steel bull contour barrel, A2 buttstock, A2 pistol grip, A4 flat-top receiver with integral rail, Picatinny rail gas block, aluminum free floating handguard with sling swivel stud, bayonet lug.

MSR $1,095	$915	$575	$475	$415	$350	$325	$300

T SECTION

TNW FIREARMS, INC.

Current firearms manufacturer located in Vernonia, OR. Consumer direct sales.

MSR	100%	98%	95%	90%	80%	70%	60%	Last MSR

PISTOLS: SEMI-AUTO

ASP (AERO SURVIVAL PISTOL) – .45 ACP, 9mm Para., .40 S&W, 10mm, or .357 SIG cal., compact, aircraft aluminum construction, no optics, hard black anodized, pink/black or green/black finish. New 2014.

MSR $799	$700	$615	$550	$475	$420	$265	$335	

Add $500 for the ASP (Aero Survival Pistol) multi-caliber package that allows the user to convert to any of the three available calibers they choose. Package includes: ASP pistol with flip-up sights, two additional bolt heads, mags., and barrels, one extra trigger housing, and one TNW specially designed backpack.

SDI – .223 Rem. cal., billet aluminum receivers, newly designed buffer system with rear sling attachment, black anodized finish. Mfg. 2014-2016.

	$850	$725	$685	$600	$535	$465	$415	*$995*

RIFLES: SEMI-AUTO

SGP-QCB – .223 Wylde chamber, GPO, 16 or 20 in. quick change barrel, 30 shot mag., black anodized finish, 7.62 lbs. New 2013.

MSR $1,495	$1,250	$825	$575	$475	$425	$375	$350	

SDI – 5.56 NATO cal., GIO, AR-15 style, 16.2 in. barrel, stock has quad rails, billet upper and lower receiver, black finish, 7.45 lbs. New 2014.

MSR $995	$850	$550	$465	$395	$350	$325	$295	

TR IMPORTS

Current importer located in Fort Worth, TX. Previously located in Keller, TX.

SHOTGUNS

Silver Eagle shotguns are manufactured in five plants in Central Turkey.

Current **O/U models include** the Silver Eagle 103DE ($999 MSR), Silver Eagle 103FE ($1,153 MSR), Silver Eagle Light Super ($584 MSR), and Silver Eagle Custom Grade (MSR $2,586). **SxS models include** the Silver Eagle Custom Grade (MSR $2,586), 200A ($999 MSR), and 200ACE ($1,153 MSR). **Semi-Auto models include** the Sporter Series ($459-$559 MSR), SE12 Tactical ($499 MSR), SE122 ($529-$539 MSR), SE122TAC ($599 MSR), SE122TACB ($659 MSR), SE202 Series ($529 MSR), Kinetic12 Series ($441-$519 MSR), and the M13 Tactical ($489 MSR). **Slide Action models include** XP 12 ga. Marine (chrome/synthetic) and Standard (black/walnut) - $334-$486 MSR. **Single Shot models include:** Stalker Youth Slug, Stalker Youth Field, Stalker Full Size Slug, and Stalker Full-Size Field. All in .410 and 12 ga. (MSR $199). **Previously imported O/U models** included the Silver Eagle Fieldmaster ($999 last MSR), Silver Eagle Fieldmaster Deluxe ($1,153 last MSR), Model 101B Competition Trap, Model 101SE Competiton Skeet, Model 101BE Competition Trap, Skeet, Sporting Clays, Model 103C Patagonian, Model 103DE Rangemaster, Model 103FE Rangemaster Deluxe, Model 104A Sharptail, Kofs Cavalry ($759 last MSR), and the Model 105A Eagle Ultra-Light. **Previously imported Custom Grade Models** included: SGR Series SGR1-SGR20 and the Custom Grade ($1,852 last MSR). **Previously imported SxS models** included: Model 200A Grouse (last MSR was $994-$1,173), Model 200AC Ptarmigan (last MSR was $1,050-$1,297), Model 201A Hungarian, and the Model 202B Chukar. **Previously imported semi-auto models** included: Waltter Series (MSR $489), Express 12 ga. (MSR $334-$486), SE121 ($449 last MSR), Model 901GB Excellence, Model 601GM Canadian, Model 701GB Widgeon, Model SE12B Silver Eagle and the Model SE12 Silver Eagle Combo. Please contact the company directly for more information including current options and availability (see the Trademark Index).

TACTICAL ARMS MANUFACTURER, INC.

Previous manufacturer located in Huntersville, NC until circa 2016.

RIFLES: SEMI-AUTO

Tactical Arms Manufacturer, Inc. manufactured AR-15 M4 or M16 style rifles in various calibers and configurations. Base prices started at $1,195.

TACTICAL ARMS OF TEXAS

Current AR-15 rifle manufacturer and customizer established in 2011, located in Stafford, TX. Dealer sales.

RIFLES: SEMI-AUTO

STANDARD RIFLE – 5.56 NATO or .300 AAC Blackout cal., carbine (5.56 NATO) or pistol (.300 AAC Blackout) gas system, 16 in. heavy barrel, birdcage hider, flip-up BUIS, collapsible stock, Mil-Spec LPK pistol grip and stock, 9 3/4 in. quad rail, forged upper and lower receivers, black Cerakote finish, 6 lbs. 13 oz.

MSR $875	$745	$500	$435	$375	$335	$315	$295	

T 346 TACTICAL ARMS OF TEXAS, cont.

MSR	100%	98%	95%	90%	80%	70%	60%	Last MSR

STANDARD BATTLE RIFLE – 5.56 NATO or .300 AAC Blackout cal., carbine (5.56) or pistol (.300) gas system, 16 in. barrel, birdcage hider, flip-up BUIS, Magpul MOE pistol grip and stock, 12 1/2 in. ODIN KeyMod, forged upper and lower receiver, Mil-Spec LPK, black or FDE Cerakote finish, 6 lbs. 13.6 oz.

MSR $1,150	$950	$595	$495	$425	$365	$335	$300	

TACTICAL BATTLE RIFLE – 5.56 NATO or .300 AAC Blackout cal., carbine (5.56) or pistol (.300) gas system, 16 in. honeycomb fluted barrel, Magpul MBUS sights, collapsible stock, Magpul MOE pistol grip and stock, 12 in. Fortis Knight rail, billet upper and lower receiver, XTC 2.0 compensator, black, FDE, Urban Warganics, Woodland Warganics, or Desert Warganics Cerakote finish.

MSR $1,450	$1,195	$795	$550	$465	$415	$375	$350	

TACTICAL ARMZ

Previous rifle and suppressor manufacturer located in Springfield, MO until early 2018.

RIFLES: SEMI-AUTO

TA-15 HAVOC – 5.56 NATO cal., 16 in. chrome moly barrel with YHM Phantom muzzle brake, YHM low profile gas block, SST, modified Battle stock, Ergo rubber pistol grip, 12 1/2 in. Tactical Armz quad rail, Magpul MBUS flip-up sights, billet milled upper and lower receiver, enhanced magwell, nickel boron bolt carrier group, Cerakote Tungsten ceramic finish, includes PMAG M3 maglevel magazine w/MagGrips, hard flight case, 9 lbs. Disc. early 2018.

	$1,650	$1,000	$795	$595	$495	$425	$395	*$1,999*

TA-15 LANCER – 5.56 NATO cal., 16 in. chrome moly barrel with YHM Phantom flash hider, YHM low profile gas block, black Nitride bolt carrier group, SST, reinforced CQB buttstock, A2 pistol grip, Magpul MBUS flip-up sights, 12 1/2 in. quad rail handguard, Cerakote Armor black ceramic finish, 7.2 lbs. Disc. early 2018.

	$995	$625	$495	$450	$395	$350	$325	*$1,199*

TA-15 RONIN – 5.56 NATO cal., 16 in. chrome moly barrel with YHM Phantom flash hider, billet milled lower and forged and milled upper receiver, nickel boron bolt carrier group, YHM low profile gas block, SST, modified Battle stock with Hogue rubber pistol grip, Magpul MBUS flip-up sights, 12 1/2 in. Tactical Armz slim rail handguard, Cerakote Armor black finish, includes PMAG M3 magazine w/MagGrips, hard case, 7 lbs. Disc. early 2018.

	$1,250	$825	$575	$475	$425	$375	$350	*$1,499*

TACTICAL EDGE ARMS

Current AR-15 style pistol and rifle manufacturer located in Clarksville, TN.

PISTOLS: SEMI-AUTO

HEATHEN PISTOL – 5.56 NATO cal., 12 1/2 in. chrome moly barrel with Nitride finish, Lantac Dragon muzzle brake, WARFIGHTER advanced combat trigger, integrated enhanced trigger guard, Magpul MBUIS flip-up sights, SB Tactical pistol brace, Magpul+ grip, ambi safety selector, mid-length gas system, billet aluminum upper and lower receivers, MRS11-M-LOK rail, advanced angled handstop. New 2018.

MSR $2,100	$1,795	$1,575	$1,325	$1,150	$995	$850	$700	

WARFIGHTER 10 PISTOL – 5.56 NATO or .300 AAC Blackout (new 2018) cal., pistol (.300 AAC Blackout) or carbine (5.56 NATO) length gas system, 10 1/2 in. M4 profile barrel, Lantac Dragon muzzle brake, single stage Dynamic Combat trigger, WARFIGHTER billet trigger guard, ambidextrous safety selector, M4 feed ramps, DLC bolt carrier group, aluminum WRS10 or WRS10KM rail (WARFIGHTER Rail System), QD endplate, KAK Industries Blade brace, includes hard case, Type III hardcoat anodized black finish.

MSR $1,650	$1,400	$1,235	$1,100	$975	$835	$725	$585	

WARFIGHTER LIMITED EDITION BILLET MK18 PISTOL – 5.56 NATO cal., 10 1/2 in. M4 profile barrel with Nitride finish, Geissele two-stage trigger, Magpul MBUIS, SB Tactical pistol brace, Magpul+ grip, ambi safety, carbine length gas system, M4 feed ramps, WRS10 rail, four QD sling mounts, DLC BCG, Type III hardcoat anodized black finish. Limited mfg. beginning 2018.

MSR $1,880	$1,575	$1,385	$1,185	$1,065	$915	$785	$635	

RIFLES: SEMI-AUTO

WARFIGHTER – 5.56 NATO cal., carbine length gas system, 16 in. M4 profile barrel with Lantac Dragon muzzle brake, single stage Dynamic Combat trigger, Mission First Tactical Battlelink Minimalist stock, QD endplate, ambi safety selector, M4 feed ramps, aluminum WRS12 rail, four QD sling mounts, DLC bolt carrier group, Type III hardcoat black anodized, Burnt Bronze, Camo, FDE, or Sniper Grey Cerakote finish.

MSR $1,850	$1,525	$975	$750	$575	$495	$425	$375	

Add $150 for Burnt Bronze, FDE, or Sniper Grey Cerakote finish.

Add $325 for Camo Cerakote finish.

TACTICAL EDGE ARMS, cont. 347

MSR	100%	98%	95%	90%	80%	70%	60%	Last MSR

WARFIGHTER 300BLK – .300 AAC Blackout cal., carbine length gas system, 16 in. M4 barrel with Lantac Dragon muzzle brake, target crown, Dynamic Combat single stage trigger, Mission First Tactical Battlelink Utility stock, aluminum WRS12 rail, four QD sling mounts, DLC bolt carrier group, Mil-Spec 6-position extension with QD latch plate, Type III hardcoat anodized black, Burnt Bronze, Camo, FDE, or Sniper Grey Cerakote finish.

MSR $1,680	$1,385	$895	$675	$525	$450	$385	$350	

Add $150 for Burnt Bronze, FDE, or Sniper Grey Cerakote finish.
Add $325 for Camo Cerakote finish.

WARFIGHTER 3GUN – 5.56 NATO cal., mid-length gas system, 16 in. M4 barrel with Lantac Dragon muzzle brake, target crown, single stage TiN Dynamic Combat trigger, Mission First Tactical Battlelink Minimalist stock, MOD2 billet aluminum upper and lower receiver (new 2016), aluminum WRS12KM rail (WARFIGHTER Rail System KeyMod), DLC bolt carrier group, Mil-Spec 6-position extension with QD latch plate, Type III hardcoat anodized black, Burnt Bronze, Camo, FDE, or Sniper Grey Cerakote finish.

MSR $1,780	$1,475	$950	$725	$550	$475	$395	$350	

Add $150 for Burnt Bronze, FDE, or Sniper Grey Cerakote finish.
Add $325 for Camo Cerakote finish.
Add $100 for MOD2 billet aluminum upper and lower receiver (new 2016).

WARFIGHTER GRUNT – 5.56 NATO cal., carbine length gas system, 16 in. M4 profile barrel with A2 flash hider, T.E.A. Mil-Spec single stage trigger, Mission First Tactical Battlelink Minimalist stock, M4 feed ramps, aluminum WRS12 rail, four QD sling mounts, DLC bolt carrier group, Mil-Spec 6-position lower receiver extension with QD latch plate, Type III hardcoat anodized black, Burnt Bronze, Camo, FDE, or Sniper Grey Cerakote finish.

MSR $1,550	$1,275	$850	$600	$495	$425	$375	$350	

Add $150 for Burnt Bronze, FDE, or Sniper Grey Cerakote finish.
Add $325 for Camo Cerakote finish.

WARFIGHTER LIMITED EDITION – 5.56 NATO cal., carbine length gas system, 16 in. M4 barrel with Nitride treatment, A2 flash hider, target crown, Magpul MBUIS sights, Magpul MOE SL Mil-Spec carbine stock, Magpul MOE SL carbine length handguard, Mil-Spec 6-position lower receiver extension with QD latch plate, DLC bolt carrier group, includes hard case, FDE Cerakote finish. Limited mfg. beginning 2016.

MSR $1,400	$1,150	$750	$550	$465	$415	$375	$350	

WARFIGHTER MOE SL – 5.56 NATO cal., carbine length gas system, 16 in. M4 barrel, A2 flash hider, target crown, T.E.A. Mil-Spec single stage trigger, Magpul MOE SL Mil-Spec carbine stock, Magpul MOE SL carbine length handguard, Mil-Spec 6-position lower receiver extension with QD latch plate, includes hard case, black, FDE, OD Green, or grey finish.

MSR $1,300	$1,100	$675	$525	$450	$400	$350	$325	

WARFIGHTER OWR – 5.56 NATO cal., carbine length gas system, 17.3 in. M4 barrel with A2 flash hider, target crown, Geissele SSA two-stage trigger, Mission First Tactical Battlelink Utility stock, aluminum WRS14 rail, four QD sling mounts, DLC bolt carrier group, Mil-Spec 6-position extension with QD latch plate, Type III hardcoat anodized black, Burnt Bronze, Camo, FDE, or Sniper Grey Cerakote finish.

MSR $1,880	$1,575	$995	$775	$575	$495	$425	$395	

Add $150 for Burnt Bronze, FDE, or Sniper Grey Cerakote finish.
Add $325 for Camo Cerakote finish.

WARFIGHTER SOE EDITION – 5.56 NATO cal., mid-length gas system, 16 in. chrome moly barrel with Lantac Dragon muzzle brake, Mission First Tactical Battlelink Minimalist stock, ambidextrous safety with Assisted Short Throw Technology, WRS12-KM (WARFIGHTER Rail System), one-piece billet machined, Mil-Spec 6-pos. extension with QD latch plate, Mil-Spec 1913 Picatinny rail, includes hard case, custom Toxic Green or SOE Red Cerakote finish. Disc. 2017.

	$1,875	$1,100	$895	$650	$575	$495	$425	*$2,300*

WARFIGHTER10 .308 – .308 Win. cal., mid-length gas system, 18 in. M4 barrel, Lantac Dragon muzzle brake, target crown, Geissele SSA two-stage trigger, Mission First Tactical Battlelink Utility stock, billet aluminum upper and lower receivers, aluminum WRS10 12 in. rail, four QD sling mounts, steel bolt carrier group, Mil-Spec 6-position extension with QD latch plate, Type III hardcoat anodized black, Burnt Bronze, Camo, FDE, or Sniper Grey Cerakote finish.

MSR $2,700	$2,225	$1,395	$1,050	$675	$595	$525	$475	

WARFIGHTER10 WARHAMMER – .308 Win. cal., mid-length gas system, 14 1/2 in. M4 barrel with Lantac Dragon muzzle brake (pinned and welded to make 16 in. barrel), target crown, Geissele SSA two-stage trigger, Magpul PRS precision stock, billet aluminum upper and lower receivers, aluminum WRS10 14 in. rail, four QD sling mounts, steel bolt carrier group, Mil-Spec 6-position extension with QD latch plate, Harris bipod with American Defense QD bipod mount, Type III hardcoat anodized black, Burnt Bronze, Camo, FDE, or Sniper Grey Cerakote finish.

MSR $2,700	$2,225	$1,395	$1,050	$675	$595	$525	$475	

Add $150 for Burnt Bronze, FDE, or Sniper Grey Cerakote finish.
Add $325 for Camo Cerakote finish.

T 348 TACTICAL RIFLES

MSR	100%	98%	95%	90%	80%	70%	60%	Last MSR

TACTICAL RIFLES

Current rifle manufacturer located in Zephyrhills, FL. Previously located in Dade City, FL until 2010.

RIFLES: SEMI-AUTO

Previous models included the Dow Custom AR 10 (disc. 2004, last MSR was $2,695).

Hydrographics or custom painted finishes are available on all rifles - POR.

DOW FAL 15 – .223 Rem. or 6.8 SPC cal., patterned after AR-15, GIO, medium weight match grade stainless steel barrel, matte black receiver finish, flat-top Picatinny upper, match grade trigger, hand rubbed oil finished wood stock. Disc. 2013. **This model was POR.**

TACTICAL AR-15 – .223 Rem. cal., AR-15 style, GIO, Krieger heavy match grade free floating barrel with birdcage flash hider, two-stage match trigger, Mil-Spec handguard, black, green, or sand colored stock.

MSR $2,395	$1,875	$1,100	$895	$650	$575	$495	$425	

Add $95 for titanium or chrome match bolt carrier.

Add $115 for Vortex style tempered steel flash suppressor.

Add $185 for Picatinny machined forend.

TACTICAL M4C – 5.56 NATO, .233 Rem. cal., or .223 Wylde chamber, AR-15 style, GIO, 16 1/2 in. heavy match grade barrel, A2 birdcage compensator, 20 shot mag., National Match Grade trigger, Standard M4 sights, collapsible stock, gas block, full-length free float Picatinny rail system, Extreme Environment finish in black or green, fully adj. Magpul stock available, 7 1/2 lbs.

MSR $2,285	$1,795	$1,050	$875	$625	$550	$475	$425	

Add $95 for titanium or chrome match bolt carrier.

Add $115 for Vortex style tempered steel flash suppressor.

Add $50 for Harris bipod adapter stud with push button release swivel.

Add $179 for PRI folding front sight.

Add $139 for ARMS low profile folding Picatinny rail mounted rear sight.

TACTICAL SPG – .264 LBC, 6.5 CSS, 6.5 Grendel (new 2013), or .308 Win. (disc.) cal., AR-15 style, GIO, 20 in. Kreiger stainless match grade barrel with Surefire muzzle brake, 17 shot mag., two-stage trigger, Magpul PRS fully adj. stock, ergonomic pistol grip, billet upper and lower receiver, free float full-length Picatinny forend, zero headspace match grade black Nitride coated bolt carrier group, Extreme Environmental black finish, optional Mil-Spec flip-up front and rear sights, 10 1/2 lbs.

MSR $3,695	$2,950	$1,925	$1,400	$825	$675	$625	$575	

Add $154 for flip-up foresight with integral gas block.

Add $129 for flip-up rear sight assembly.

TACTICAL SVR (SPECIAL VARMINT RIFLE) – .204 Ruger or .223 Rem. cal., AR-15 style, 24 in. full profile heavy match grade stainless steel barrel with target crown plain muzzle, free float forend, 20 shot mag., flat-top Picatinny rail, A2 style fixed or Magpul adj. stock, ergonomic custom grip, adj. trigger, black or green finish is standard, custom camo finishes are optional, 10 1/2 lbs.

MSR $3,195	$2,550	$1,650	$1,250	$700	$625	$575	$525	

Add $95 for titanium or chrome match bolt carrier.

Add $185 for Picatinny machined forend.

Add $249 for Magpul adj. stock.

TACTICAL SOLUTIONS, INC.

Current rifle and components manufacturer located in Boise, ID. Dealer sales.

PISTOLS: SEMI-AUTO

KESTREL .22 LR AR PISTOL – .22 LR cal., 9 in. barrel with Linear compensator, 25 shot Black Dog mag., ALG Defense QMS trigger, Magpul MOE K2+ grip, 7 in. Samson KeyMod or M-LOK handguard, Mil-Spec lower receiver, pistol length buffer tube, 3.9 lbs. New 2015.

MSR $995	$850	$725	$650	$585	$515	$450	$395	

RIFLES: SEMI-AUTO

Tactical Solutions makes a Pac-Lite barrel assembly for the Ruger Mark and .22/.45 Series pistol frame and conversion units for both pistols and AR-15 style rifles. Please contact the manufacturer directly for additional information, availability, and current pricing (see Trademark Index).

AR-22 LT – .22 LR cal., 16 1/2 in. threaded barrel, 12 in. XG Pro KeyMod or M-LOK forend, TacSol lower receiver, ALG Defense QMS trigger, Magpul MOE SL carbine stock, Magpul MOE K2+ grip, 5 lbs. New 2015.

MSR $1,025	$860	$650	$550	$475	$425	$375	$325	

TACTICAL SOLUTIONS, INC., cont. 349

MSR	100%	98%	95%	90%	80%	70%	60%	Last MSR

AR-22 M4 – .22 LR cal., 16.1 in. threaded barrel, 25 shot Black Dog mag., TacSol lower receiver, ALG Defense QMS trigger, two-piece polymer carbine handguard, Magpul MOE SL carbine stock, Magpul K2+ grip, 6 lbs. New 2015.

MSR $895	$775	$525	$450	$400	$375	$325	$295	

AR-22 SBX – .22 LR cal., 16.6 in. barrel, 9 in. XG Pro KeyMod or M-LOK forend, TacSol lower receiver, ALG Defense QMS trigger, Magpul MOE SL carbine stock, Magpul K2+ grip, 4.8 lbs. New 2015.

MSR $1,025	$860	$650	$550	$475	$425	$375	$325	

TSAR-223 – .223 Rem. cal., 16.1 in. barrel (12 in. barrel w/SB-X style shroud fixed to make legal length), 10 shot mag., ALG Defense QMS trigger, Magpul MOE SL carbine stock, Magpul MOE K2+grip, Mil-Spec lower, two-piece aluminum handguard, Tacsol XG Pro forend in choice of KeyMod or M-LOK, 6.55 lbs. New 2017.

MSR $1,395	$1,150	$750	$550	$465	$415	$375	$350	

TSAR-300 – .300 AAC Blackout cal., 16.1 in. barrel with inert suppressor, 10 shot mag., Mil-Spec lower, Tacsol XG Pro forend in choice of KeyMod or M-LOK, two-piece aluminum handguard, ALG Defense QMS trigger, Hogue 6-position stock, Hogue pistol grip, 5 1/2 lbs. New 2015.

MSR $1,395	$1,150	$750	$550	$465	$415	$375	$350	

TACTICAL SUPPLY

Current manufacturer located in Yakima, WA.

In addition to customized rifles, Tactical Supply offers a customized semi-auto pistol based on the Smith & Wesson M&P platform, as well as a wide variety of tactical gear, accessories, ammo, and professional gunsmithing services.

RIFLES: SEMI-AUTO

Values reflect base rifle price only without options. Please contact the company directly for the wide variety of rifle options, including optics and accessories (see Trademark Index).

TS-ASSAULT – 5.56 NATO, .300 AAC Blackout, or .458 SOCOM cal., customer choice of 16 in. select, premium, or match grade barrel, forged billet machined upper and lower receiver, nickel boron or chrome bolt carrier group, Timney competition trigger, Noveske 60° ambidextrous safety, Magpul furniture, 10 to 15 in. quad rail design handguard or top rail with removable pic blocks, black, FDE, or OD green Cerakote finish.

MSR $1,500	$1,250	$825	$575	$475	$425	$375	$350	

TS-CADDY – 5.56 NATO, .300 AAC Blackout, or .458 SOCOM cal., customer choice of 16 in. select, premium, or match grade barrel, precision billet machined upper and lower receiver, nickel boron or chrome bolt carrier group, Timney competition trigger, Noveske 60° ambidextrous safety, Magpul furniture, Raptor ambi charging handle, 10 to 15 in. quad rail design handguard or top rail with removable pic blocks, customer choice of over 80 Cerakote colors.

MSR $2,500	$2,050	$1,250	$950	$650	$575	$495	$475	

TACTICAL WEAPONS SOLUTIONS

Previous manufacturer located in Apopka, FL until 2015.

Tactical Weapons Solutions manufactured and sold a variety of fine quality AR-15 rifles as well as AR-15 pistols and survival supplies.

PISTOLS: SEMI-AUTO

MODEL P01 – 5.56 NATO cal., GIO, chrome moly steel barrel with A2 flash hider, forged upper and lower receivers, extended feed ramps, aluminum pistol length handguard, pistol buffer tube, forged "F" front sight base with bayonet lug, ambidextrous rear sling mount, 6.6 lbs. Disc. 2015.

	$950	$825	$725	$650	$525	$425	$350	$1,050

* Model P02 – 5.56 NATO cal., GIO, similar to Model P01, except features pistol length quad rail. Disc. 2015.

	$975	$850	$750	$675	$550	$450	$350	$1,100

MODEL P03 – 5.56 NATO cal., GIO, chrome moly steel barrel, CQB compensator, forged upper and lower receiver, extended feed ramps, carbine length quad rail, pistol buffer tube, forged "F" front sight base with bayonet lug, ambidextrous rear sling mount, 7 lbs. Disc. 2015.

	$1,195	$1,050	$900	$815	$650	$550	$425	$1,330

MODEL P04 – 5.56 NATO cal., GIO, 7 1/2 in. chrome moly barrel with CQB compensator, forged lower and forged M4 upper receivers, Magpul MBUS front and rear flip-up sights, extended feed ramps, carbine length quad rail, pistol buffer tube, ambidextrous sling mount, extractor upgrade with Viton O-Ring, black finish, 7 lbs. Disc. 2015.

	$1,250	$1,095	$950	$850	$700	$575	$450	$1,400

T 350 TACTICAL WEAPONS SOLUTIONS, cont.

MSR	100%	98%	95%	90%	80%	70%	60%	Last MSR

RISK TAKERS STANDARD CQB – 5.56 NATO cal., GIO, 7 1/2 in. chrome moly barrel with CQB compensator, forged lower and forged M4 upper receiver, Magpul MBUS front and rear flip-up sights, extended feed ramps, carbine length quad rail, pistol buffer tube, ambidextrous sling mount, extractor upgrade with Viton O-Ring, black finish, includes Risk Takers logos, 7 lbs. Disc. 2015.

	$1,075	$950	$800	$725	$595	$485	$375	$1,202

* **Risk Takers CQB** – 5.56 NATO cal., similar to Risk Takers Standard CQB, except includes Troy Medieval flash hider, Ergo Super tactical grip, NiB-X trigger, hammer, disconnect, FDE finish. Disc. 2015.

	$1,425	$1,250	$1,075	$975	$785	$650	$525	$1,604

RIFLES: SEMI-AUTO

MODEL 01 – 5.56 NATO cal., GIO, chrome moly steel barrel with A2 flash hider, forged upper and lower receiver, extended feed ramps, two-piece handguard with Delta assembly, 6-position adj. stock, receiver extension tube, forged "F" front sight base with bayonet lug, ambidextrous rear sling mount, extractor upgrade with Viton O-Ring, 6 1/2 lbs. Disc. 2015.

	$765	$515	$440	$375	$335	$315	$295	$880

Subtract $80 for El-Model 01 without extractor upgrade with Viton O-Ring.

* **Model 02** – 5.56 NATO cal., GIO, similar to Model 01, except features two-piece quad rail, 6.8 lbs. Disc. 2015.

	$765	$515	$440	$375	$335	$315	$295	$900

* **Model 03** – 5.56 NATO cal., GIO, similar to Model 01, except features free floating quad rail, low profile or single rail gas block, 6.7 lbs. Disc. 2015.

	$850	$550	$465	$395	$350	$325	$295	$1,000

MODEL 4 ALPHA – 5.56 NATO cal., GIO, 16 in. chrome moly barrel with flash hider, extended feed ramps, forged lower and forged M4 upper receivers, extractor upgrade w/Viton O-Ring, free float quad rail, rec. extension tube, ambidextrous rear sling mount, nickel boron trigger, hammer, and disconnector, upgraded front and rear sights, 6-pos. adj. stock, pistol grip, black finish, 6 1/2 lbs.

	$1,175	$775	$550	$465	$415	$375	$350	$1,425

MODEL 5 ELITE – 5.56 NATO cal., GIO, 16 in. chrome moly barrel with flash hider, nickel boron barrel extension, upgraded hammer pins, upgraded trigger, upgraded front and rear sights, 6-pos. adj. stock, pistol grip, BCM Gunfighter charging handle, extended feed ramps, forged lower and forged M4 upper receivers, extractor upgrade w/Viton O-Ring, free float quad rail, rec. extension tube, ambidextrous rear sling mount, black finish. Disc. 2015.

	$1,475	$950	$725	$550	$475	$395	$350	$1,800

MODEL 06 MOE – 5.56 NATO cal., chrome moly barrel with A2 flash hider, forged lower and forged M4 upper receivers, extended feed ramps, forged front sight base w/bayonet lug, ambidextrous rear sling mount, Magpul MOE handguard, buttstock, and pistol grip, Magpul MBUS rear flip-up sight, black finish, 6.4 lbs. Disc. 2015.

	$800	$525	$450	$385	$340	$325	$295	$950

MODEL 7 LOADED – 5.56 NATO cal., GIO, chrome moly barrel with A2 flash hider, extended feed ramps, forged lower and forged M4 upper receiver, two-piece quad rail with Delta assembly, 6-position adj. stock, receiver extension tube, ambidextrous rear sling mount, forged front sight base with bayonet lug, black finish, extractor upgrade with Viton O-Ring, includes 5mW green laser, 90 Lumen tactical flashlight, 6x32 scope, 5-position foldable foregrip, and tactical bipod, 6 1/2 lbs. Disc. 2015.

	$1,065	$650	$500	$450	$395	$350	$325	$1,251

MODEL 08/MODEL 09/MODEL 10/MODEL 11 – 5.56 NATO cal., GIO, chrome moly barrel with A2 flash hider, extended feed ramps, forged lower and forged M4 upper receiver, two-piece quad rail with Delta assembly, 6-position adj. stock, receiver extension tube, ambidextrous rear sling mount, forged front sight base with bayonet lug, extractor upgrade with Viton O-Ring, Cerakote FDE (Model 08), OD Green (Model 09), Pink (Model 10), or MultiCam camo (Model 11) finish, 6.8 lbs. Disc. 2015.

	$850	$550	$465	$395	$350	$325	$295	$990

MODEL 12/MODEL 14/MODEL 16/MODEL 18 – 5.56 NATO cal., GIO, chrome moly barrel with A2 flash hider, extended feed ramps, forged lower and forged M4 upper receiver, two-piece quad rail with Delta assembly, 6-position adj. stock, receiver extension tube, ambidextrous rear sling mount, forged front sight base with bayonet lug, extractor upgrade with Viton O-Ring, free floating quad rail, low profile or single rail gas block, Cerakote MultiCam (Model 12), Digital ACU (Model 14), Digital Desert (Model 16), or Reaper (Model 18) finish, 6.7 lbs. Disc. 2015.

	$935	$575	$475	$415	$350	$325	$300	$1,120

MODEL 13/MODEL 15/MODEL 17/MODEL 19/MODEL 20 – 5.56 NATO cal., GIO, chrome moly barrel with A2 flash hider, extended feed ramps, forged lower and forged M4 upper receiver, two-piece quad rail with Delta assembly, 6-position adj. stock, receiver extension tube, ambidextrous rear sling mount, forged front sight base with bayonet lug, extractor upgrade with Viton O-Ring, Digital ACU (Model 13), Desert Digital (Model 15), Reaper (Model 17), Muddy Girl (Model 19), or MultiCam Pink (Model 20) finish, 6.8 lbs. Disc. 2015.

	$850	$550	$465	$395	$350	$325	$295	$990

TACTICAL WEAPONS SOLUTIONS, cont. 351 T

MSR	100%	98%	95%	90%	80%	70%	60%	Last MSR

.308 INTIMIDATOR – .308 Win. cal., GIO, 16 in. chrome moly steel barrel, fixed stock, pistol grip, oversized trigger guard, DPMS style upper receiver, black finish. Disc. 2015.

	100%	98%	95%	90%	80%	70%	60%	Last MSR
	$1,875	$1,100	$895	$650	$575	$495	$425	$2,350

TALON ORDNANCE

Previous AR-15 style rifle manufacturer located in Richland, MS.

RIFLES: SEMI-AUTO

Talon Ordnance manufactured a prototype TM4 that is select fire for military and law enforcement use.

TM4-A1 – 5.56 NATO cal., GIO, 16 in. barrel with removable flash hider, 30 shot stainless steel mag. with anti-tilt follower and chrome/silicon spring, hardcoat anodized black finish, includes custom hard case, 7 1/2 lbs.

While this model was prototyped in 2015 with a projected MSR of $2,795, it never made it to production.

TM4-A1SE SPECIAL EDITION – 5.56 NATO cal., GIO, 16 in. barrel with removable flash hider, 30 shot stainless steel mag. with anti-tilt follower and chrome/silicon spring, black or OD Green Cerakote finish on upper and lower receivers, charging handle, and forearm, includes custom hard case, 7 1/2 lbs. New 2015.

While this model was prototyped in 2015 with a projected MSR of $3,195, it never made it to production.

TAURUS INTERNATIONAL MFG., INC.

Currently manufactured by Taurus Forjas S.A., located in Porto Alegre, Brazil and in Miami, FL (certain models). Currently, handguns made in Brazil are imported by Taurus International Mfg., Inc. located in Miami, FL since 1982. Beginning 2007, Taurus Tactical, a separate entity, was created for law enforcement/military sales and service. Distributor sales only.

During late 2012, Taurus Holdings purchased an exclusive global distribution agreement with Diamondback Firearms, LLC. Taurus assumed all sales and marketing efforts of the Diamondback branded products from its Miami office.

All Taurus products are known for their innovative design, quality construction, and proven value, and are backed by a lifetime repair policy.

Taurus order number nomenclature is as follows: the first digit followed by a dash refers to type (1 = pistol, 2 = revolvers, 3 = longuns, 4 = Magazines/Accessories, 5 = grips, and 10 = scope mount bases), the next 2 or 3 digits refer to model number, the next digit refers to type of hammer (0 = exposed, 1 = concealed), the next digit refers to barrel length (w/o fractions), the last digit refers to finish (1 = blue, 9 = stainless), and the suffix at the end refers to special features (T = total titanium, H = case hardened, M = matte finish, PLY = polymer, UL = Ultra-Lite, C = ported (compensation), G = gold accent, PRL = mother-of-pearl grips, R = rosewood grips, NS = night sights, MG = magnesium, and FO = fiber optic). Hence, 2-454089M refers to a Model 454 Raging Bull revolver in .454 Casull cal. with an exposed hammer and a 8 3/8 in. barrel in matte stainless finish.

RIFLES: SEMI-AUTO

T4SA – 5.56 NATO or .223 Rem. cal., GIO, 16 in. Melonite chrome moly M4 profile barrel, Magpul 30 shot PMAG, AR/M4 Gen M2 window, oversized Magpul trigger guard, 6-pos. Magpul CTR buttstock with QDs and sling mounts, friction lock, Magpul MOE black grip with storage, carbine length low profile gas system, forged aluminum lower and A3 flat-top upper receiver with T-Markings, aluminum KeyMod, 1913 top rail with four integrated quick disconnect points, aluminum M-LOK, or 1913 top rail handguard, Mil-Spec buffer tube, matte black, Cerakote Elite Sand, or Jungle finish, 6 1/2 lbs. New 2017.

MSR $1,199							
	$1,025	$925	$800	$685	$595	$515	$440

TEMPLAR CUSTOM ARMS

Current custom pistol and AR-15 rifle/shotgun manufacturer located in Windham, OH since 2010.

Templar Custom Arms specializes in combative pistols and AR-15 platform rifles/shotguns built to customer specifications. Please contact the company directly for more information including pricing, options, and availability (see Trademark Index).

TEMPLAR CUSTOM, LLC (TEMPLAR CONSULTING)

Previous AR-15 rifle and component manufacturer located in Apex, NC 2008-2017.

RIFLES: SEMI-AUTO

MCWS (MULTI-CALIBER WEAPONS SYSTEM) – .223 Rem./5.56 NATO (.223 Wylde chamber), 6.5 Grendel, and .50 Beowulf cal., GIO, 16 in. stainless steel button rifled barrel (.50 Beowulf), 16 in. chrome moly steel button rifled barrel (5.56 NATO), and 16 in. stainless steel button rifled barrel (6.5 Grendel), all quick change barrels with stainless WCI muzzle brakes, forged lower and matched upper receiver, Magpul ACS stock, Ergo ambi grip, Geissele SSA trigger, PRI low pro witness sights, Templar Fastrail system includes 14 in. handguard, swivel sling stud, one case hardened black oxide barrel tool and allen wrench, multi-caliber cleaning kit, choice of hard or soft case, Desert Snake Duracoat finish. Disc. 2017.

	100%	98%	95%	90%	80%	70%	60%	Last MSR
	$2,295	$1,450	$1,075	$675	$595	$525	$475	$2,899

Add $450 for cut rifle barrel upgrade.
Add $400 for MCWS 3 caliber kit.

352 TEMPLAR CUSTOM, LLC (TEMPLAR CONSULTING), cont.

MSR	100%	98%	95%	90%	80%	70%	60%	Last MSR

TEMPLAR CUSTOM SPR (SPECIAL PURPOSE RIFLE) – .223 Rem./5.56 NATO (.223 Wylde chamber) cal., GIO, 16 in. chrome moly steel medium contour barrel with A2 flash hider, forged upper and lower receiver, steel bolt carrier, 12 1/2 in. Templar FastRail, Magpul ACS or MOE stock, Ergo Ambi grip, A2 front sight assembly, other options available on this model. Disc. 2017.

	$1,975	$1,150	$925	$650	$575	$495	$425	$2,449

Add $550 for single point cut rifle stainless steel barrel.

TEMPLAR CUSTOM STANDARD RIFLE – .223 Rem./5.56 NATO (.223 Wylde chamber) cal., GIO, 16 in. chrome moly steel medium contour barrel with A2 flash hider, forged lower and upper receiver, steel bolt carrier, 12 1/2 in. Templar FastRail, Magpul ACS or MOE stock, Ergo Ambi grip, A2 front sight assembly. Disc. 2017.

	$1,975	$1,150	$925	$650	$575	$495	$425	$2,249

TEMPLAR TACTICAL ARMS LLC

Previous AR-15 manufacturer located in Bozeman, MT 2008-2014.

RIFLES: SEMI-AUTO

TTA MARK 12 RIFLE – 5.56 NATO/.223 Rem. cal., GIO, 18 in. SPR profile match barrel, billet upper and lower receivers, carbon fiber full floating forend with Picatinny rails on bottom and both sides, full-length Swan Sleeve Picatinny rail, front and rear flip-up iron sights, Magpul MOE or Magpul ACS buttstock. Disc. 2014.
Base MSR was $2,150-$2,450.

TTA 15 TACTICAL – 5.56 NATO/.223 Rem. or 6.8 SPC cal., GIO, 16 in. match grade barrel, billet upper and lower receivers, front and rear flip-up sights, choice of 10 or 12 in. Daniel Defense full floating rail, collapsible stock, custom models feature single stage trigger, Magpul grip, and Magpul ACS stock. Disc. 2014.
Base MSR was $1,700-$2,000.

TEXAS BLACK RIFLE COMPANY

Current semi-auto pistol and rifle manufacturer located in Shiner, TX.

CARBINES: SEMI-AUTO

MODEL 1836 – 5.56 NATO or .300 AAC Blackout cal., AR-15 style, 16 in. chrome-lined barrel, TBRC lower and upper receiver with Delta long horn logo, Magpul MOE front and rear sights, 11.4 in. ARS KeyMod lightweight rail, M16 bolt carrier group, CMC Flat Bow trigger, Magpul ACS-L Mil-Spec side storage adjustable stock, MOE trigger guard and grip, Type III hardcoat anodized Mil-Spec finish, commemorates Texas Year of Independence in 1836, 6.6 lbs. New 2014.

MSR $1,559		$1,315	$850	$625	$500	$435	$375	$350

* **Model 1836L** – 5.56 NATO or .300 AAC Blackout cal., 16 in. barrel, TBRC lower and upper receiver with Delta long horn logo, CMC flat bow trigger, 13.2 in. Keymod rail, Magpul MOE front and rear sights, MOE trigger guard and grip, Magpul ACS-L stock, hardcoat anodized black finish, 6.65 lbs. New 2015.

MSR $1,569		$1,315	$850	$625	$500	$435	$375	$350

* **Model 1836XL** – 5.56 NATO or .300 AAC Blackout cal., 16 in. barrel, TBRC lower and upper receiver with Delta long horn logo, CMC flat bow trigger, 15 in. KeyMod rail, Magpul MOE front and rear sights, MOE trigger guard and grip, Magpul ACS-L stock, hardcoat anodized black finish, 6.7 lbs. New 2015.

MSR $1,589		$1,315	$850	$625	$500	$435	$375	$350

MODEL 1836 MOE – 5.56 NATO cal., 16 in. barrel, Magpul MBUS rear sight, front sight gas block, Magpul MOE handguard, Magpul CTR stock, hardcoat anodized black finish, 9.75 lbs. New 2015.

MSR $995		$850	$550	$465	$395	$350	$325	$295

PISTOLS: SEMI-AUTO

MODEL 1836P – 5.56 NATO cal., AR-15 style, 7 1/2 in. barrel, TBRC upper and lower receiver with Delta long horn logo, CMC flat bow trigger, 7.2 in. ARS lightweight KeyMod rail, Magpul MOE sights, MOE trigger guard and grip, M16 bolt carrier group, hardcoat anodized black finish, commemorates Texas Year of Independence in 1836, 5 lbs. New 2015.

MSR $1,559		$1,310	$1,150	$1,040	$875	$750	$625	$525

MODEL 1836PX – 5.56 NATO cal., 10 1/2 in. barrel, TBRC upper and lower receiver with skull Delta logo, CMC flat bow trigger, ARS 9.6 in. KeyMod lightweight rail, Magpul MOE sights, MOE trigger guard and grip, hardcoat anodized black finish, 5 3/4 lbs. New 2015.

MSR $1,569		$1,320	$1,150	$1,040	$875	$750	$625	$525

MODEL 1836 .300 BLACKOUT – .300 AAC Blackout cal., 8 in. barrel, TBRC upper and lower receiver with skull Delta logo, 7.2 in. ARS lightweight KeyMod rail, CMC flat bow trigger, Magpul MOE sights, MOE trigger guard and grip, hardcoat anodized black finish, 8 1/2 lbs. New 2015.

MSR $1,559		$1,310	$1,150	$1,040	$875	$750	$625	$525

MSR		100%	98%	95%	90%	80%	70%	60%	Last MSR

TEXAS CUSTOM GUNS

Previous AR-15 style custom rifle manufacturer located in Alvin, TX 2009-2017.

RIFLES: SEMI-AUTO

TCG-15 – 5.56 NATO cal., AR-15 style, vanadium alloy Mil-Spec steel barrel, chrome bore and chamber, parkerized finish, threaded muzzle, Mil-Spec trigger, Magpul CTR buttstock, Magpul MOE pistol grip, CNC machined aluminum alloy upper and lower receiver, nickel boron coated parts, M4 extension, free float Mil-Std 1913 rails, Type III hardcoat anodized black finish. Disc. 2017.

		100%	98%	95%	90%	80%	70%	60%	Last MSR
		$1,425	$925	$700	$550	$475	$395	$350	$1,750

THOR

Current trademark established during 2001 and manufactured by Thor Global Defense Group, located in Van Buren, AR. Distributed by Knesek Guns, located in Van Buren, AR.

RIFLES: SEMI-AUTO

THOR TR-15 – 5.56 NATO cal., GPO, 16.1, 18 (DMR Model, disc.), or 20 in. barrel with or w/o PA flash hider, muzzle brake, 30 shot mag., flat-top upper receiver, F marked front sight post, collapsible Mil-Spec stock, detachable carry handle, plastic M4 handguard, variety of Cerakote custom finishes available, optional THOR rail system.

	MSR $1,350	$1,125	$700	$525	$450	$400	$350	$325	

Add $250 for THOR rail system.
Add $1,100 for 20 in. barrel.
Add $760 for 18 in. barrel (disc.).

* **Thor TR-15 CQB Carbine** – 5.56 NATO cal., GPO, 16 in. barrel with Noveske KX3 flash suppressor, 30 shot Magpul PMAG, Troy rear flip-up sights, VLTOR EMOD stock, Knight's Armament rear sling swivel mount, Magpul MIAD grip, flat-top upper receiver, Daniel Defense Omega X12 OFSP quad rail, detachable carry handle, Ergo ribbed rail covers, Thor rail system, KNS Precision anti-walk pins, FDE Cerakote finish. New 2014.

	MSR $2,350	$1,875	$1,100	$895	$650	$575	$495	$425	

THOR TR-16 SERIES – 5.56 NATO cal., AR-15 style, 16 or 18 in. barrel with permanently attached muzzle brake, unified top rail modular forearm. New 2013.

	MSR $2,750	$2,225	$1,395	$1,050	$675	$595	$525	$475	

Add $45 for DMR model with 18 in. barrel.

* **Limited Edition Steven Seagal TR-16** – 5.56 NATO cal., 16 in. barrel, black finish, Steven Seagal signature. Mfg. 2013-disc.

		$2,125	$1,325	$995	$675	$595	$525	$475	$2,699

THOR TR-17 SERIES – 7.62x51mm/.308 Win. cal., Mil-Spec configuration, 16 (disc.) or 18 in. barrel with permanently attached muzzle brake, 20 shot mag., THOR stock, THOR grip, anti-walk firing tri-pins, quad rail forearm, black finish. New 2013.

	MSR $11,800	$10,500	$9,200	$7,900	$7,150	$5,800	$4,700	$3,700	

Add $6,650 for TR-17 System package (includes scope, rings, suppressor, bipod, cleaning kit and hard case.) Disc.

* **Limited Edition Steven Seagal TR-17** – 7.62x51mm cal., 16 in. barrel with permanently attached muzzle brake, Steven Seagal signature. Mfg. 2013-2017.

		$2,125	$1,325	$995	$675	$595	$525	$475	$2,699

TRACKINGPOINT

Current bolt action rifle manufacturer established late 2011 and located in Pflugerville, TX. Previously located in Austin, TX.

RIFLES: SEMI-AUTO

AR 300WM – .300 Win. Mag. cal., GIO, long range precision guided firearm features TrackingPoint Networked optics, 16 in. S2W profile chrome moly vanadium steel cold hammer forged barrel with Daniel Defense flash suppressor, 30 shot Magpul PMAG, Mil-Spec lower receiver with enhanced flared magwell and rear receiver QD swivel attachment point, upper receiver with indexing marks and M4 feed ramps, 12 in. Daniel Defense modular float rail, Daniel Defense low profile gas block, TrackingPoint AR Series buttstock, includes integrated Network tracking scope, TriggerLink (electronic connection between tracking optic and guided trigger), HUD (Heads Up Display - the digital display that shows the field of view and more), Tag-and-Shoot (tag button), includes cleaning kit, three batteries and chargers, 15.6 lbs. Mfg. late 2014-2016.

Last MSR was $18,995.

The networked tracking scope streams video to Android and iOS smart phones and tablets. Wind speed is the only data you'll manually input to the scope, using a toggle button.

T 354 TRACKINGPOINT, cont.

MSR	100%	98%	95%	90%	80%	70%	60%	Last MSR

AR 556 – 5.56 NATO cal., similar to AR 300WM, except features mid-length gas system, 12 lbs. Mfg. late 2014-2016.
Last MSR was $7,495.

AR 762 – 7.62 NATO cal., 16 in. S2W profile barrel with flash suppressor, low profile gas block, carbine gas system, lower receiver with multiple QD swivel attachment points, upper receiver with indexing marks, two 20 shot PMAGs, Picatinny rail with rail segments, TrackingPoint AR Series buttstock, includes integrated Network tracking scope, guided trigger, and Tag-and-Shoot (tag button), cleaning kit, three batteries, and chargers, 14.6 lbs. Mfg. late 2014-2016.
Last MSR was $14,995.

The networked tracking scope streams video to Android and iOS smart phones and tablets. Wind speed is the only data you'll manually input to the scope, using a toggle button.

Mi4 – .300 AAC Blackout cal., 16 in. light contour barrel, 10 shot mag., 3 1/2 hour operating time, lock range of 400 yards, 10 MPH target velocity, 2x-14x zoom, includes 3 dual lithium-ion batteries, battery charger, 6-9 in. pivot bipod, shuttered eye guard, Gen 2 night vision kit, 11.4 lbs. New 2018.
Current MSR on this model is $6,995.

Mi4S – .300 AAC Blackout cal., lock range of 300+ yards, 20 MPH target velocity, 2x-14x zoom, 3 1/2 hour operating time, includes 3 dual lithium-ion batteries, battery charger, shuttered eye guard, 11.4 lbs. New 2018.
Current MSR on this model is $12,995.

Mi6 – 5.56 NATO cal., 16 in. chrome-lined barrel, A2 birdcage flash hider, 10 shot mag., Stag 15 tactical upper, 13 1/2 in. free float M-LOK handguard, lock range of 600 yards, 15 MPH target velocity, 2x-14x zoom, 3 1/2 hour operating time, includes 3-dual lithium-ion batteries, battery charger, shuttered eye guard, 6-9 in. pivot bipod, 12 lbs. New 2018.
Current MSR on this model is $9,995.

Mi8 – 7.62 NATO cal., 18 in. barrel, 10 shot mag., lock range of 800 yards, 20 MPH target velocity, 3x-21x zoom, 3 1/2 hour operating time, includes 3 dual lithium-ion batteries, battery charger, 6 in. Harris-S model bipod upgraded with DLOC-S and SARG knobs, shuttered eye guard, 14.6 lbs. New 2018.
Current MSR on this model is $15,995.

Mi13 – .300 Win. Mag. cal., lock range of 1,200 yards, 20 MPH target velocity, 3x-21x zoom, 3 1/2 hour operating time, includes dual lithium-ion batteries, battery charger, 14.6 lbs. New 2018.
Current MSR on this model is $12,995.

M300FE – 5.56 NATO cal., 16 in. barrel, 10 shot mag., full fire control with guided trigger, 300 yard lock range, 10 MPH target velocity, primary iron sights, night mode for Gen2, Gen3, and thermal attachments, RapidLok target acquisition, includes battery charger, breech guide rod, and dual lithium-ion batteries, black finish, 12 lbs. Disc. 2017.
Last MSR on this model was $5,995.

M400 XHDR – .300 AAC Blackout cal., AR platform, precision guided system features 16 in. light contour barrel, 10 shot mag., 400 yard lock range, 10 MPH target velocity, RapidLok target acquisition, records voice and audio, includes Gen2 night vision upgrade with rail-mounted IR illuminator, three dual lithium-ion batteries, battery charger, pivot bipod, eye guard, cleaning link took, breech rod guide, hard case, black finish, 11.4 lbs. Mfg. 2017 only.
Last MSR on this model was $6,995.

SA300 – .300 Win. Mag. cal., 22 in. barrel, 15.6 lbs. Mfg. 2015-2017.

Last MSR on this model was $18,995.

TRISTAR ARMS INC.

Current importer established in 1994, and located in N. Kansas City, MO. Distributor and dealer sales.

In 2015, the company name changed from TriStar Sporting Arms, Ltd. to TriStar Arms Inc.

SHOTGUNS: SEMI-AUTO

Shim kits and fiber optic sights became standard on all hunting models beginning 2011.

KRX TACTICAL – 12 ga., 2 3/4 or 3 in. chamber, detachable 5 shot mag., 20 in. barrel, front sight, fixed pistol grip stock, removable carry handle, full-length upper and partial lower Picatinny rails, black or FDE or forearm (new 2018) finish 7.4 lbs. New 2016.

MSR $594	$495	$425	$385	$340	$300	$260	$230

Add $30 for FDE finish (new 2018).

TROJAN FIREARMS

Current manufacturer of AR-15 style rifles and accessories located in Phoenix, AZ.

RIFLES: SEMI-AUTO

1776 (MPV2 "1776 EDITION") – 5.56 NATO/.223 Rem. cal., GIO, 20 in. barrel, Grater Gen 2 tunable muzzle brake, enhanced flared magwell, custom engraving, rifle length gas system, fully adj. drop-in trigger group, black Nitride and

TROJAN FIREARMS, cont. 355 T

MSR	100%	98%	95%	90%	80%	70%	60%	Last MSR

nickel boron M16 BCG, Gen 2 (disc.) or Gen 3 ambi charging handle, free float KeyMod handguard, enhanced buttstock with extended cheek riser. Limited mfg. with only 10 being produced.

| MSR $1,776 | $1,475 | $950 | $725 | $550 | $475 | $395 | $350 | |

TFA-15 (MPV2) – 5.56 NATO/.223 Rem. cal., GIO, various barrel options available, standard coating is black Nitride, Gen 2 adj. muzzle brake (new 2018), Magpul mag., enhanced flared lower magwell, fully adj. drop-in trigger group, enhanced black Nitride and nickel boron M16 BCG, Gen 2 (disc. 2017) or Gen 3 (new 2018) ambi charging handle, billet aluminum upper and lower receivers, free float KeyMod handguard, two-piece low profile gas block, Magpul CTR 6-pos. stock, Graphite Black, Burnt Bronze (new 2018), Desert Tan (new 2018), ODG (disc. 2017), or Sniper Grey (new 2018) Cerakote finish.

| MSR $1,450 | $1,195 | $795 | $550 | $465 | $415 | $375 | $350 | |

Add $100 for Burnt Bronze Cerakote finish.

In 2018, the model name changed from MPV2 to TFA-15.

TFA-HELEN (ULV1) – .223 Rem./5.56 NATO cal., GIO, mid-length gas system, stainless steel Wylde chambered Hanson barrel, Magpul mag., enhanced flared magwell, SST, free float KeyMod Gen III handguard, Gen III ambi charging handle, PVD coated bolt carrier group, adj. gas block, Minimalist stock, Blue Titanium, Satin Mag (disc. 2017), Sniper Grey (new 2018), or Burnt Bronze (new 2018) Cerakote finish, 5 lbs. 11 oz.

| MSR $1,669 | $1,385 | $895 | $675 | $525 | $450 | $385 | $350 | |

Add $100 for Sniper Grey or Burnt Bronze Cerakote finish (new 2018).
Add $100 for the Featherweight package upgrade.

In 2018, the model name changed from ULV1 to TFA-HELEN.

TFA-300 (BPV2) – .300 AAC Blackout cal., GIO, various barrel options with black Nitride coating, pistol length gas system, A2 birdcage flash hider, Magpul mag., Grade A parts and components, fully adj. drop-in trigger group, enhanced black Nitride and nickel boron M16 BCG, Gen 2 ambi charging handle, upgraded extractor spring, billet aluminum upper and lower receivers, free float KeyMod handguard system, two-piece low profile gas block, Magpul CTR 6-pos. stock, Graphite Black (new 2018) or Sniper Grey (new 2018) Cerakote finish.

| MSR $1,450 | $1,195 | $795 | $550 | $465 | $415 | $375 | $350 | |

In 2018, the model name changed from BPV2 to TFA-300.

TFA-NOS – .22 Nosler cal., GIO, 18 in. barrel, Grater Gen II muzzle brake, SST, enhanced buttstock, mid-length gas sytem, carbine buffer system, 14 in. Gen II KeyMod handguard, two-piece gas block, Gen III ambi charging handle, FDE or Burnt Bronze Cerakote finish. New 2018.

| MSR $1,850 | $1,525 | $975 | $750 | $575 | $495 | $425 | $375 | |

TFA-PCC9G (PRO9V1-G) – 9mm Para. cal., blowback action, 16 in. lightweight contour barrel with Nitride finish, Grater Gen 2 tunable (disc. 2017) or PCC9 Gen 1 (new 2018) muzzle brake, Glock mag. compatibility, enhanced flared lower magwell, fully adj. drop-in trigger group, free float KeyMod handguard, Gen II (disc. 2017) or Gen III (new 2018) ambi charging handle, billet aluminum upper and lower receivers, black, Trojan Red, or Metallic Blue hardcoat anodized finish.

| MSR $1,450 | $1,195 | $795 | $550 | $465 | $415 | $375 | $350 | |

In 2018, the model name changed from PRO9V1-G to TFA-PCC9G.

TFA-PCC9M (PRO9V1-M) – 9mm Para. cal., blowback action, 16 in. lightweight contour barrel with Nitride finish, Grater Gen 2 tunable (disc. 2017) or PCC9 Gen 1 (new 2018) muzzle brake, MBX/STI mag. compatibility, enhanced flared magwell, 15 in. free float KeyMod handguard, fully adj. drop-in trigger group, Gen II (disc. 2017) or Gen III (new 2018) ambi charging handle, billet aluminum upper and lower receiver, Metallic Blue (disc. 2017), Graphite Black (new 2018), Trojan Red (new 2018), or Trojan Blue (new 2018) Cerakote finish.

| MSR $1,549 | $1,275 | $850 | $600 | $495 | $425 | $375 | $350 | |

In 2018, the model name changed from PRO9V1-M to TFA-PCC9M.

TROMIX CORPORATION

Previous firearms manufacturer established in 1999, located in Inola, OK. Previously located in Broken Arrow, OK.

Tromix currently offers conversions for Saiga shotguns, as well as accessories and modifications. Please contact the company directly for its current services and conversion pricing (see Trademark Index).

RIFLES: SEMI-AUTO

Tromix manufactured AR-15 style rifles until 2008. Tromix lower receivers bear no caliber designation. Serialization was TR-0001-0405.

The models listed were also available with many custom options.

TR-15 SLEDGEHAMMER – .44 Rem. Mag. (disc. 2001), .440 Cor-Bon Mag., .458 SOCOM, .475 Tremor, or .50 AE cal., GIO, 16 3/4 in. barrel, other lengths and weights available by custom order. Mfg. 1999-2006.

| | $1,125 | $700 | $525 | $450 | $400 | $350 | $325 | *$1,350* |

356 TROMIX CORPORATION, cont.

MSR	100%	98%	95%	90%	80%	70%	60%	Last MSR

TR-15 TACKHAMMER – various cals., GIO, 24 in. bull barrel, other lengths and weights were available by custom order. Mfg. 1999-2006.

| | $1,125 | $700 | $525 | $450 | $400 | $350 | $325 | $1,350 |

TROY DEFENSE

Current AR-15 style rifle and pistol manufacturer located in West Springfield, MA.

Troy Defense, created in 2011, is the firearms division of Troy Industries. Troy is well-known for its high quality accessories, including sights and rails. Troy Defense offers a complete line of AR-15 style rifles for military and law enforcement, as well as some models for the civilian marketplace. A wide variety of options and accessories are available.

RIFLES/CARBINES: SEMI-AUTO

.308 RIFLE – 7.62 NATO cal., 16 in. barrel with Medieval flash suppressor, 20 shot mag., includes one polymer magazine, Troy rear folding BattleSight and Troy M4 folding BattleSight, Troy BattleAx stock, BattleAx Control grip, 15 in. Troy Alpha 308 BattleRail, ambidextrous charging handle, black finish, 8 1/2 lbs.

| MSR $1,499 | $1,250 | $825 | $575 | $475 | $425 | $375 | $350 |

AGF 5.56 CARBINE – 5.56 NATO cal., GIO, 16 in. barrel with Troy Medieval flash suppressor, 10 or 30 shot mag., forged lower and M4A4 flat-top upper receiver, M4 feed ramps, Mil-Spec trigger, 6-pos. telescoping Troy BattleAx CQB stock, BattleAx control grip, manual safety, 13 in. Alpha rail with integrated front M4 folding sight, black or FDE finish, 6 1/2 lbs.

| MSR $854 | $745 | $500 | $435 | $375 | $335 | $315 | $295 |

AGF 5.56 CARBINE OPTICS READY – 5.56 NATO cal., GIO, 16 in. barrel, Medieval flash suppressor, 30 shot mag., Mil-Spec bolt and carrier with upgraded extractor, Troy BattleAx 6-pos. buttstock (fixed or folded), BattleAx control grip, forged lower receiver, M4A4 flat-top forged upper, M4 feed ramps, Troy 13 in. Alpha rail, black finish, 6 1/2 lbs. New 2017.

| MSR $769 | $665 | $500 | $415 | $375 | $335 | $315 | $295 |

A3-LW – 5.56 NATO cal., 16 in. barrel, A2 flash suppressor, enhanced trigger guard, M4 style 6-pos. stock with Troy markings, BattleAx control grip, forged lower receiver, M4A4 flat-top forged upper receiver, M4 feed ramps, 13 in. TRX2 BattleRail, black hardcoat anodized finish, 6 lbs. New 2017.

| MSR $849 | $725 | $500 | $435 | $375 | $335 | $315 | $295 |

ALPHA CARBINE – 5.56 NATO cal., AR-15 style, GIO, 16 in. barrel with pinned Medieval flash suppressor, 30 shot mag., Troy rear folding BattleSight, PDW (disc. 2016) or Tomahawk standard (new 2017) stock, Squid grips, 13 in. Alpha rail with built-in flip-up BattleSight, Proctor sling, M4 feed ramps, black finish, 6 3/4 lbs. New 2015.

| MSR $1,249 | $1,050 | $650 | $495 | $450 | $395 | $350 | $325 |

CONQUEROR 3-GUN RIFLE – 5.56 NATO cal., AR-15 style, 18 in. fluted match grade barrel, suppressor mount pronged flash hider, Geissele Super 3 gun trigger, enhanced trigger guard, offset folding BattleSights, Troy BattleAx CQB stock, 15 in. Alpha Revolution M-LOK carbon fiber BattleRail, ambidextrous charging handle and safety selector, M4 feed ramps, forged M4 flat-top upper and billet lower receiver, black or tan finish. New 2015.

| MSR $1,499 | $1,250 | $825 | $575 | $475 | $425 | $375 | $350 |

Add $200 for tan finish.

CQB-SPC A3 CARBINE – 5.56 NATO cal., 16 in. barrel, A2 flash suppressor, no sights, forged lower receiver, M4A4 flat-top forged upper, M4 feed ramps, enhanced trigger guard, BattleAx control grip, M4 style 6-pos. stock with Troy markings, black hardcoat anodized finish. New 2015.

| MSR $799 | $675 | $500 | $425 | $375 | $335 | $315 | $295 |

CQB-SPC A4 CARBINE – 5.56 NATO cal., AR-15 style, 16 in. barrel, Troy Medieval muzzle brake, Troy front and rear folding BattleSights, BattleAx CQB stock and grip, 13 in. TRX2 KeyMod BattleRail, black finish, 6 lbs.

| MSR $999 | $850 | $550 | $465 | $395 | $350 | $325 | $295 |

DELTA CARBINE – 5.56 NATO cal., GIO, 16 in. barrel with A2 flash suppressor, 30 shot mag., enhanced trigger guard, A2 front fixed and rear fixed BattleSights, M4 6-pos. stock with Troy markings, Troy BattleAx control grip, manual safety, M4 flat-top upper receiver, M4 feed ramps, black finish, 6 lbs.

| MSR $1,099 | $915 | $575 | $475 | $415 | $350 | $325 | $300 |

GAU-5/A/A – 5.56 NATO cal., 12 1/2 in. barrel with 4 1/2 in. permanently attached flash suppressor, 30 shot mag., A1 front sight, A1 drum rear, coated aluminum buttstock, original US Govt. issue A2 pistol grip, carbine handguard with single heat shield, M4 feed ramps, forged Slick-Side upper receiver w/no forward assist, 4 1/2 in. Moderator with "Grenade Ring" permanently attached, black finish, includes small arms sling. Limited mfg. beginning 2016.

| MSR $1,199 | $995 | $625 | $495 | $450 | $395 | $350 | $325 |

This firearm replicates the weapon used by the Son Tay Raiders in the largest rescue attempt of American POWs. Portions of the proceeds for this model will go directly to the National League of POW/MIA families.

TROY DEFENSE, cont. 357

MSR	100%	98%	95%	90%	80%	70%	60%	Last MSR

GUU-5P – 5.56 NATO cal., 14.7 in. lightweight steel chrome-lined barrel, A2 flash suppressor (pinned and welded to make 16 in. OAL), Mil-Spec trigger, A-frame gas block with front peep, A1 drum rear sight, M4-style 6-pos. stock, carbine handguard with single heat shield, black finish, 5.5 lbs. New 2017.

| MSR $999 | $850 | $550 | $465 | $395 | $350 | $325 | $295 | |

M5 9mm RIFLE – 9mm Para. cal., blowback action, 16 in. barrel, Troy Medieval flash suppressor, 30 shot mag., designed for Glock magazines, enhanced trigger guard, Troy front and rear folding BattleSights, Troy Airborne stock (new 2017), 13 in. M-LOK BattleRail, Troy SOCC ambidextrous safety selector (new 2017), forged flat-top upper and lower receiver, forward assist, M4 feed ramps, includes a built-in shell deflector, black finish. New 2016.

| MSR $1,299 | $1,100 | $995 | $875 | $735 | $650 | $550 | $465 | |

M10A1 CSASS RIFLE – 7.62 NATO cal., AR-15 style, 16 in. heavy fluted barrel with 3-prong flash suppressor, ambidextrous mag. release, one polymer mag., nickel boron bolt carrier group, Geissele G2S trigger, Troy 45 Degree Offset folding BattleSights, Troy BattleAx stock, ambidextrous safety selector and charging handle, Troy 15 in. M-LOK 308 BattleRail, ambi charging handle and safety selector, IC sling with two QD swivels, includes Atlas bipod, tan finish, 9 lbs.

| MSR $2,499 | $1,975 | $1,150 | $925 | $650 | $575 | $495 | $425 | |

M10A1 GOVERNMENT CARBINE – 7.62 NATO cal., 16 in. heavy fluted match grade barrel, 3-prong flash hider with suppressor mount, includes one 20 shot polymer mag., rear folding and front folding M4 BattleSights, ambi charging handle, ambi safety selector, Geissele G2S trigger, Troy Alpha rail, Squid grips, BattleAx CQB stock, black finish, 8 3/4 lbs.

| MSR $2,399 | $1,875 | $1,100 | $895 | $650 | $575 | $495 | $425 | |

MK-12 MOD 1 COMMEMORATIVE EDITION – 5.56 NATO cal., 18 in. stainless steel barrel, 12th Model muzzle brake with suppressor mount and thread protector, A2 buttstock, Ergo grip, polymer rail covers and forward grip, forged upper receiver w/round forward assist, aluminum handguard, crane style gas block, Harris bipod w/mount, 2-point sling, Troy sling swivel mount, Troy 2-piece scope mount, black finish, 9.4 lbs. Limited mfg. beginning 2017.

| MSR $2,599 | $2,200 | $1,925 | $1,600 | $1,375 | $1,125 | $975 | $850 | |

OPPRESSED XM177E2 – 5.56 NATO cal., 12 1/2 in. steel chrome-lined barrel with welded flash suppressor, A1 front and A1 drum rear sight, coated aluminum buttstock, original US Govt. issue A1 pistol grip, forged upper receiver with tear drop forward assist, carbine handguard with single heat shield, 4 1/2 in. Moderator with "Grenade Ring" permanently attached, M4 feed ramps, gray finish. Limited mfg. beginning 2017.

| MSR $1,199 | $995 | $625 | $495 | $450 | $395 | $350 | $325 | |

PROCTOR CARBINE – 5.56 NATO cal., GIO, 16 in. match grade barrrel, 30 shot mag., enhanced trigger guard, match grade CMC trigger, rear folding and front folding M4 Tritium BattleSights, Troy BattleAx CQB buttstock, BattleAx control grip, manual safety, M4A4 flat-top upper receiver, M4 feed ramps, 13 in. enhanced Troy Alpha rail, includes Proctor sling, 3 Troy BattleMags, and BattleSight adjustment tool, hardcoat anodized black or tan finish, 6 lbs.

| MSR $1,749 | $1,425 | $925 | $700 | $550 | $475 | $395 | $350 | |

Add $150 for Tan finish.

SDMR – 5.56 NATO cal., AR-15 style, 16 in. match grade barrel, Troy suppressor mount pronged flash hider, 30 shot mag., Geissele trigger, nickel boron bolt carrier group, BattleAx control grip, 15 in. SDMR rail, Troy rear folding BattleSight and Troy front folding M4 Tritium BattleSight, SDMR BattleRail, BattleAx stock, black finish, includes Troy IC sling and two QD swivels, and two Troy BattleMags, 7 lbs.

| MSR $1,299 | $1,075 | $675 | $500 | $450 | $400 | $350 | $325 | |

SGM LAMB CARBINE – 5.56 NATO cal., 16 in. barrel, Medieval flash suppressor, 30 shot mag., Geissele G2S trigger, enhanced trigger guard, M4 front, DOA rear folding BattleSights, Troy BattleAx stock, BattleAx control grip, 15 in. Troy/VTAC M-LOK BattleRail, sling, and sling mount, two QD swivels, 3 VTAC quick attach rail sections, M4 feed ramps, M4 flat-top upper receiver, black finish, 6 lbs.

| MSR $1,599 | $1,315 | $850 | $625 | $500 | $435 | $375 | $350 | |

Add $150 for Tan finish.

SOFD-D M16A2 CARBINE COMMEMORATIVE EDITION – 5.56 NATO cal., 14.9 in. steel chrome-lined barrel with A2 flash hider (16 in. OAL), A2 square front post, A1 windage wheel w/A2 peep, 6-pos. adj. buttstock, original US Govt. issue pistol grip, carbine handguard with single heat shield, large forward assist, M4 feed ramps, 2-point adj. sling, scope mounting bracket and 2 1/2 in. rail section, gray finish, 6.1 lbs. Limited mfg. beginning 2017.

| MSR $1,299 | $1,100 | $995 | $875 | $735 | $650 | $550 | $465 | |

This model is manufactured to commemorate the Battle of Mogadishu, Oct. 3, 1993-Oct. 4, 1993.

VTAC 308 CARBINE – .308 Win. cal., 16 in. fluted match grade barrel, 3-prong flash hider with suppressor mount, 13 in. Troy M-LOK BattleRail, Geissele Super V trigger, Troy 45 Degree Offset folding BattleSights, black or tan finish. New 2015.

| MSR $1,899 | $1,575 | $995 | $775 | $575 | $495 | $425 | $395 | |

Add $100 for Tan finish.

T 358 TROY DEFENSE, cont.

MSR	100%	98%	95%	90%	80%	70%	60%	Last MSR

XM177E2 – 5.56 NATO cal., 12 1/2 in. barrel with 4 1/2 in. permanently attached flash suppressor, 30 shot mag., A1 front sight, A1 drum rear, carbine handguard with single heat shield, includes small arms sling, black finish. Limited mfg. beginning 2016.

| MSR $1,199 | $995 | $625 | $495 | $450 | $395 | $350 | $325 | |

Proceeds of each XM177E2 sold will go to support the charitable efforts of The Special Forces Association and the Special Operations Association.

TURNBULL RESTORATION CO., INC.

Current firearms restoration and manufacturing company established in 1990 and located in Bloomfield, NY, specializes in the faithful and accurate restorations of period firearms from initial polishing to final finishing. These finishes include period correct bone charcoal color case hardening, charcoal bluing, rust bluing, and Nitre bluing.

Turnbull Restoration Co., Inc. (previous company name was Doug Turnbull Restoration), specializes in the restoration of Colt 1911s, early Colt semi-auto pistols, Colt SAAs, USFA SAAs, shotguns from makers A.H. Fox, L.C. Smith, Parker Brothers and lever action rifles from Winchester, Browning and Marlin just to name a few. Restoration services include upgrades and antique finishes that replicate natural aging and patina.

RIFLES

Turnbull Restoration also announced the introduction of its Big Bore Classics line during late 2003, utilizing either new or original Winchester and Browning Model 1886 receivers. Chambering includes: .45-70, .45-90, .450 Alaskan (new 2005), .50-110 (.50 Express), and .50 Alaskan. Many metal options and wood choices are available - please contact the company directly for more information on these custom rifles.

Turnbull Restoration introduced its own .475 Turnbull proprietary rifle cartridge during 2007. This caliber can be used in the company's modified Winchester Model 1886 or Model 71.

Turnbull Restoration introduced another proprietary rifle cartridge during 2008. The .470 Turnbull is designed specifically for use in the Marlin 1895 action, and can be used in the company's modified Marlin 1895 rifles.

During 2009, Turnbull Restoration introduced the .475 Turnbull, designed for the Winchester Model 1886.

TAR-10 SEMI-AUTO – .308 Win. cal., scaled down AR-15 style, 16 1/2 in. fluted chrome moly barrel with screw on muzzle brake, carbine gas system, color case hardened steel lower and flat-top upper with high Picatinny rail, MOE trigger guard, premium American walnut forend, pistol grip, 4 or 10 shot mag., includes lockable hard case, approx. 13 lbs. 35 mfg. mid-2012-2013.

| | $4,250 | $3,715 | $3,185 | $2,885 | $2,335 | $1,910 | $1,485 | *$4,995* |

TAR-10 SEMI-AUTO HUNTING HERITAGE TRUST 2013 SHOT SHOW AUCTION GUN – .308 Win. cal., based on original AR-10, 20 in. stainless barrel with screw on JP Enterprises muzzle brake, carbine gas system, color case hardened steel lower and flat-top upper with high Picatinny rail, engraved by Adams and Adams, 50 in. gold wire used in engraving, MOE trigger guard, custom exhibition grade American walnut forend, pistol grip and stock, 4 and 10 shot mag., ser. no. 1, includes display case, approx. 13 lbs.

This model was auctioned off at the 2013 SHOT Show for over $134,000.

TAR-15 SEMI-AUTO – .223 cal., AR-15 style, 16 1/2 in. fluted chrome moly barrel with screw on muzzle brake, carbine gas system, color case hardened steel lower and flat-top upper with Picatinny rail, oversized built in trigger guard, premium American walnut stock and forend, pistol grip, 4 or 10 shot mag., includes lockable hard case, approx. 9 lbs. New mid-2013.

| MSR $2,750 | $2,325 | $2,035 | $1,750 | $1,575 | $1,275 | $1,050 | $815 | |

TAR-40 SEMI-AUTO – .308 Win. cal., scaled down AR-10 style, 16 1/2 in. fluted chrome moly barrel with screw on muzzle brake, carbine gas system, color case hardened steel lower and flat-top upper with high Picatinny rail, MOE trigger guard, premium American walnut forend, pistol grip, 4 or 10 shot mag., includes lockable hard case, approx. 12 lbs. New mid-2013. Only 100 available.

| MSR $4,995 | $4,250 | $3,715 | $3,185 | $2,885 | $2,335 | $1,910 | $1,485 | |

U SECTION

359 U

USA TACTICAL FIREARMS

Current manufacturer located in Statesville, NC.

USA Tactical Firearms currently manufactures rifles, parts, and components for the AR-15 market. They also offer training classes. Please contact the company directly for more information on all their products and services (see Trademark Index).

PISTOLS: SEMI-AUTO

USA Tactical Firearms currently manufactures the USATF AR-15 Pistol. Please contact the manufacturer directly for more information including pricing and availability.

MSR	100%	98%	95%	90%	80%	70%	60%	Last MSR

RIFLES: SEMI-AUTO

MODEL USA-15 PACKAGE A – .223 Rem./5.56 NATO cal., GIO, 16 in. M4 barrel, pinned and welded muzzle brake, multi-caliber lower receiver, flat-top upper receiver with removable carry handle, A2 front sight, single stage trigger, carbine length Picatinny handguard with covers, standard 6-position stock with buttpad, Sniper pistol grip, 10 shot mag., includes black hard case.

MSR $1,499	$1,250	$825	$575	$475	$425	$375	$350

* Model USA-15 Package B – .223 Rem./5.56 NATO cal., similar to Package A, except features 16 in. HBAR barrel.

MSR $1,649	$1,350	$875	$650	$525	$450	$385	$350

* Model USA-15 Package C – .223 Rem./5.56 NATO cal., similar to Package A, except features single rail gas block with flip-up front sight.

MSR $1,539	$1,275	$850	$600	$495	$425	$375	$350

MODEL USA-15 PACKAGE D – 7.62x39mm cal., GIO, 16 in. HBAR barrel, pinned and welded muzzle brake, flat-top upper receiver with removable carry handle, A2 front sight, single stage trigger, carbine length Picatinny handguard with covers, standard 6-position stock with buttpad, Sniper pistol grip, 10 shot mag., includes black hard case.

MSR $1,688	$1,385	$895	$675	$525	$450	$385	$350

ULTIMATE ARMS (USELTON ARMS INC)

Current manufacturer located in Franklin, TN. Previously located in Madison, TN. Company name was changed during 2015.

RIFLES: SEMI-AUTO

BLACK WIDOW A3 MODEL – 5.56 NATO/.223 Rem. cal., GPO, 16 in. barrel with door jammer flash suppressor, round counter mag., adj. sight, Magpul CTR 6-position stock, quad rail with front grip, FDE finish. Disc. 2017.

	$2,625	$1,725	$1,300	$725	$650	$595	$525	$3,200

* Black Widow A4 Model – 7.62 NATO/.308 Win. cal., 18 in. barrel with door jammer flash suppressor, otherwise similar to Black Widow A3 model. Disc. 2017.

	$2,125	$1,325	$995	$675	$595	$525	$475	$2,600

M4-AR LITE BLACK WIDOW – 5.56 NATO cal., 16 in. barrel, 30 shot mag., front and rear adj. sight, 6-pos. stock, quad rail with front grip, magnesium blend upper and lower receivers, approx. 5 lbs. New 2018.

MSR $2,300	$1,875	$1,100	$895	$650	$575	$495	$425

UTAS

Current shotgun manufacturer located in Antalya, Turkey. The UTS-15 is currently manufactured by UTAS-USA, located in Des Plaines, IL.

SHOTGUNS: SEMI-AUTO

XTR-12 – 12 ga., 3 in. chamber, gas operated with rotating bolt, 18.7 (disc. 2016) or 20 (new 2017) in. barrel with muzzle, two 5 or 10 (new 2018) shot mags., sights are optional, 5-position telescopic stock, integrated quad Picatinny rail, 8-position sling attachment housing, standard Cerakote black or optional Burnt Bronze, Flat Dark Earth, OD Green, or Tungsten finish, approx. 8 lbs. New 2015.

MSR $1,099	$995	$875	$800	$725	$625	$550	$475

Add $69 for 10 shot mag. (new 2018).

Add $100 for optional finishes.

Add $138 for front and rear sights.

MAYBE THE ONLY THING BETTER THAN THIS BOOK IS THE ONLINE SUBSCRIPTION!

Only $19.95/year!

- **Includes monthly updates** keeping you informed of all the new AR-15 makes/models.
- **Features thousands of images** allowing for fast and easy identification.
- **Manufacturer/Model searchable database** allowing you to find the model you need.
- Historical pricing with dynamic interactive graphs keeps you up-to-date on your AR-15 purchases as investments.
- Your own personal online inventory solution - keep track of your collection and track the change in value.
- Includes access to BBP's industry standard Photo Percentage Grading System – why guess a gun's condition when you can be sure?

Visit BLUEBOOKOFGUNVALUES.COM to view sample pages and ordering

Good Information Never Sleeps!

V SECTION

361 V

VM HY-TECH LLC

Previous rifle manufacturer located in Phoenix, AZ.

MSR	100%	98%	95%	90%	80%	70%	60%	Last MSR

RIFLES

VM15 – .223 Rem. or 9mm Para. cal., AR-15 style, semi-auto, 16, 20, or 24 in. fluted and ported Wilson barrel, unique side charging on left side of receiver operated by folding lever which does not limit mounting/placement of optics, aluminum free floating handguard, forged lower receiver, A2 style buttstock with pistol grip, black finish. Mfg. 2002-2009.

	$745	$500	$435	$375	$335	$315	$295	$865

Add $34 for side charging loading (new 2005).

VALOR ARMS

Curent rifle manufacturer established in 1997, located in Akron, OH.

CARBINES: SEMI-AUTO

OVR-16 – various cals. including 5.56 NATO and 6.5 Grendel, AR-15 style, GIO, 16.1 in. barrel, 30 shot mag., black Valorite coated stainless steel, single stage match trigger, six or eight (includes ambi-sling adapter) position adj. stock, rifle length forearm, free floating quad rail standard, flat-top receiver with Picatinny rail continuing into quad rail, ergonomic soft rubber grip with battery storage, with or w/o sight package, approx. 8 lbs.

MSR $2,350		$1,875	$1,100	$895	$650	$575	$495	$425

Add $200 for iron sight package.
Add $300 for .264 LBC-AR cal.
Add $700 for Designated Marksmen Rifle (DMR).

VICTOR ARMS CORPORATION

Previous manufacturer located in Houston, TX.

Victor Arms Corporation manufactured limited quantities of a .22 LR upper unit for the AR-15. The V22 and its .22 LR cal. magazine replaced the standard .223 upper assembly/magazine. Additionally, a complete protoype gun was also manufactured.

VIGILANT ARMS

Current AR-15 manufacturer located in Jacksonville, FL.

Vigilant Arms manufactures high quality AR-15 pistols and rifles built to customer specifications. Please contact the company directly for more information including pricing and availability (see Trademark Index).

VIKING ARMAMENT, INC.

Current rifle/carbine manufacturer located in Grand Junction, CO.

Viking Armament also offers a full range of modern gunsmithing services and in-house Cerakote finishing. Please contact the company directly for more information (see Trademark Index).

RIFLES: SEMI-AUTO

CRUCIBLE AR-15/M4 RIFLE – 5.56 NATO/.223 Rem., 6.5 Grendel, 12.7x42, or .458 SOCOM cal. GIO, AR-15/M4 style, 16 1/2 in. SOCOM Nitride barrel, includes one Hexmag magazine, Magpul sights, Ergo grip, includes Nitride BCG, Mil-Spec fire control group, QD single point bungee sling, extended charging handle, and soft side rifle case, black anodized finish with black or FDE hardware.

MSR $1,695		$1,385	$895	$675	$525	$450	$385	$350

Add $300 for 6.5 Grendel, 12.7x42, or .458 SOCOM cal.

GUNGINR AR-15/M4 RIFLE – 5.56 NATO cal., 16 1/2 in. Nitride barrel, 30 shot mag., Magpul MOE buttstock, Magpul MOE grip, slim-line free float handguard, hardcoat black anodized finish.

MSR $995		$850	$550	$465	$395	$350	$325	$295

TYR AR 10 PRECISION RIFLE – 6.5mm Creedmoor cal., GIO, OSS flash hider, one Magpul mag., Ergo grip, NiB-X BCG, 45 degree offset sight mounts, multi-point padded bungee sling, extended charging handle, Atlas bipod, black anodized or FDE Cerakote finish, includes soft sided rifle case. Disc. 2017.

	$2,050	$1,250	$950	$650	$575	$495	$475	$2,595

V 362 VIKING ARMAMENT, INC., cont.

MSR	100%	98%	95%	90%	80%	70%	60%	Last MSR

ULFBERHT AR-15/M4 RIFLE – 5.56 NATO/.223 Rem. cal., GIO, AR-15/M4 style, 16 1/2 in. SOCOM Nitride barrel, OSS flash hider, Hexmag magazine, Magpul sights, Ergo grip, NiB-X BCG, ambidextrous 45 degree selector, QD single point bungee sling, extended charging handle, includes soft sided rifle case, black anodized or FDE Cerakote finish with black or FDE hardware. Disc. 2017.

	$1,575	$995	$775	$575	$495	$425	$395	$1,895

ULLR AR-15 PRECISION RIFLE – .223 Wylde, .458 SOCOM, .375 SOCOM, 12.7x42, or 6.5 Grendel cal., GIO, AR-15 style, 18 in. stainless steel heavy barrel with Viking muzzle brake, one Magpul 10 shot mag., Ergo grip, 16 in. handguard, Nitride BCG, ambidextrous 45 degree selector, multi-point bungee sling, black anodized or Kryptek Cerakote finish with black or FDE hardware, includes soft sided rifle case.

MSR $1,995	$1,650	$1,000	$795	$595	$495	$425	$395	

Add $300 for .458 SOCOM, .375 SOCOM, 12.7x42, or 6.5 Grendel cal.

ULLR II RIFLE – .223 Wylde, .458 SOCOM, .375 SOCOM, 12.7x42mm, or 6.5 Grendel cal., 18 in. stainless steel heavy barrel with muzzle brake, 10 shot Magpul mag., billet matched receiver set, Viking side charging handle, Nitride BCG, ambi selector, SLR Rifleworks 16 in. ION ultralight handguard, Ergo grip, black anodized, Kryptek camo in Nomad or Highlander, or Yeti Cerakote finish. New 2018.

MSR $2,495	$1,975	$1,150	$925	$650	$575	$495	$425	

Add $200 for .458 SOCOM, .375 SOCOM, 12.7x42, or 6.5 Grendel cal.

VLTOR WEAPON SYSTEMS

Current manufacturer of AR-15 style rifles, receivers, parts, and related accessories located in Tucson, AZ.

CARBINES: SEMI-AUTO

PRAETORIAN – 5.56 NATO cal., Noveske stainless steel barrel, VC-A2 flash hider, VLTOR VIS extended mid-length monolithic upper with forward assist and KeyMod system, VLTOR 7-position A5 receiver extension with VLTOR A5H2 5.3oz buffer with rifle spring, Geissele SSA trigger, Diamondhead front and rear sights, five piece Picatinny rail section, VLTOR/BCM Mod 4 Gunfighter charging handle, VLTOR low profile gas block with Nitride surface finish, VLTOR IMOD stock, TangoDown pistol grip, VLTOR lower receiver with oversized mag. release and side saddle sling plate, black finish. New 2015.

MSR $2,400	$1,975	$1,150	$925	$650	$575	$495	$425	

TS3 CARBINE – 5.56 NATO cal., AR-15 style, GIO, 16 1/4 in. barrel with muzzle brake, flat-top VLTOR receiver with full-length Picatinny rail, 30 shot mag., Geissele high speed National Match trigger, flip-up combat sights, collapsible stock, quad rail, black finish, approx. 7 1/2 lbs. Mfg. 2011-2013.

	$1,975	$1,150	$925	$650	$575	$495	$425	$2,495

XVI DEFENDER – 5.56 NATO cal., GIO, 16 in. M4 barrel with A1 flash hider, extended mid-length handguard with KeyMod system, low profile gas block, flip-up front and Diamondhead rear sights, BCM Mod 4 Gunfighter charging handle, lower receiver with oversized mag. release and side saddle sling plate, upper receiver with forward assist, 5-pos. receiver extension with carbine spring and buffer, standard trigger, VLTOR IMOD stock, TangoDown pistol grip, black, Foliage Green, or FDE finish, includes a rifle bag, two mags., and one 2 in. Picatinny rail section. New 2014.

MSR $1,560	$1,315	$850	$625	$500	$435	$375	$350	

XVI WARRIOR – 5.56 NATO cal., GIO, 16 in. chrome-lined Noveske barrel with VC-A2 flash hider, low profile gas block, lower receiver with oversized mag. release and side saddle sling plate, VLTOR VIS rifle length monolithic upper with forward assist and KeyMod system, 7-pos. A5 receiver extension with VLTOR A5H2 5.3 oz. buffer with rifle spring, Diamondhead sights, BCM Mod 4 Gunfighter charging handle, Geissele DMR trigger, VLTOR EMOD stock, TangoDown pistol grip, black finish, includes rifle bag, two mags., and one 2 in. Picatinny rail section, 7 1/4 lbs. New 2014.

MSR $2,360	$1,875	$1,100	$895	$650	$575	$495	$425	

PISTOLS: SEMI-AUTO

VWS-IX DEFENDER AR PISTOL – 5.56 NATO cal., 9 in. barrel with VC-AKSU22 flash hider, VLTOR MUR-1A upper receiver with forward assist, lower receiver with oversized mag. release and side saddle sling plate, VLTOR CASV handguard in mid-length with KeyMod system, Diamondhead rear sight and VLTOR CAS-FS front sight, low profile gas block, VLTOR/Bravo Company Mod 4 Gunfighter charging handle, A5 system receiver extension and spring/buffer kit, TangoDown pistol grip, black, FDE, or Foliage Green finish. Mfg. 2015-2016.

	$1,225	$1,085	$965	$815	$715	$600	$500	$1,440

VWS-IX WARRIOR AR PISTOL – 5.56 NATO cal., 9 in. barrel with VC-AKSU22 flash hider, VLTOR VIS mid-length monolithic upper with forward assist and KeyMod system, Picatinny rail, Diamondhead front and rear sights, low profile gas block, BCM Mod 4 Gunfighter charging handle, VLTOR A5 system pistol receiver extension and spring/buffer kit, TangoDown pistol grip, black finish. Mfg. 2015-2016.

	$1,350	$1,200	$1,075	$950	$815	$700	$575	$1,600

VLTOR WEAPON SYSTEMS, cont. 363

MSR	100%	98%	95%	90%	80%	70%	60%	Last MSR

VWS-VII WARRIOR AR PISTOL – 5.56 NATO cal., 7 in. barrel with VC-AKSU22 flash hider, VLTOR VIS carbine length monolithic upper with forward assist and KeyMod system, Picatinny rail, Diamondhead front and rear sights, low profile gas block, BCM Mod 4 Gunfighter charging handle, VLTOR A5 system pistol receiver extension and spring/buffer kit, TangoDown pistol grip, black finish. Mfg. 2015-2016.

	$1,350	$1,200	$1,075	$950	$815	$700	$575	$1,600

VWS-XII DEFENDER AR PISTOL – 5.56 NATO cal., 12 1/2 in. barrel with VC-A1 flash hider, VLTOR MUR-1A upper receiver with forward assist, VLTOR CASV handguard in extended mid-length with KeyMod system, Picatinny rail, Diamondhead rear and VLTOR CAS-FS front sights, low profile gas block, BCM Mod 4 Gunfighter charging handle, A5 system pistol receiver extension and spring/buffer kit, TangoDown pistol grip, black, Foliage Green, or FDE finish. Mfg. 2015-2016.

	$1,225	$1,085	$965	$815	$715	$600	$500	$1,440

VWS-XII WARRIOR AR PISTOL – 5.56 NATO cal., 12 1/2 in. barrel with VC-A1 flash hider, VLTOR VIS extended mid-length monolithic upper receiver with forward assist and KeyMod system, Picatinny rail, Diamondhead front and rear sights, low profile gas block, BCM Mod 4 Gunfighter charging handle, A5 system pistol receiver extension and spring/buffer kit, TangoDown pistol grip, black finish. Mfg. 2015-2017.

	$1,350	$1,200	$1,075	$950	$815	$700	$575	$1,600

VULCAN ARMAMENT, INC.

Previous rifle manufacturer located in Inver Grove Heights, MN, 1991-circa 2013. Previously located in South St. Paul, MN.

Vulcan Armament specialized in tactical style firearms and offered a complete line of parts and accessories.

RIFLES/CARBINES: SEMI-AUTO

Vulcan Armament made a wide variety of AR-15 style semi-auto carbines and rifles, including configurations for military and law enforcement.

All rifles included sling, manual, cleaning kit, Vulcan knife, and hard case.

Add $20-$25 for removable carry handle.

V15 9MM CARBINE SERIES – 9mm Para. cal., GIO, 16 in. chrome moly vanadium steel barrel with threaded muzzle, A2 front sight bases with bayonet lug, all parts manganese phosphate finished, M4 contour, M4 length handguard, full heat shield, A2 upper receiver or A3 flat-top receiver, carry handle, adj. sights, Picatinny rail, black hardcoat anodized finish, forward assist, hinged ejection port cover, 6-position adj. buttstock, removable flash hider, accepts Sten magazines, 6 1/2 lbs. Disc. 2012.

	$745	$500	$435	$375	$335	$315	$295	$860

V15 DISPATCHER SERIES – .223 Rem. cal., GIO, 16 in. chrome moly vanadium steel barrel with threaded muzzle, gas block mounted under the handguard, A2 flash hider, A2 front sight bases, bayonet lug, fixed A2 stock, A2 or A3 flat-top upper receiver, black hardcoat anodized finish, 6 1/2 lbs.

	$850	$550	$465	$395	$350	$325	$295	$999

V15 M4 CARBINE SERIES – .223 Rem. cal., GIO, 16 in. chrome moly vanadium steel button rifled barrel with threaded muzzle, A2 flash hider, A2 front sight bases, bayonet lug, A2 or A3 flat-top upper reciever, M4 length handguard with full heat shields, 6-position M4 buttstock, black hardcoat anodized finish, 6.4 lbs.

	$850	$550	$465	$395	$350	$325	$295	$999

V15 POLYMER SERIES – .223 Rem. cal., GIO, 16 or 20 in. chrome moly vanadium steel button rifled HBAR barrel with threaded muzzle, all parts manganese phosphate finished, A2 flash hider, A2 sight bases, bayonet lug, 6-position M4 buttstock, Picatinny rail, A2 or A3 polymer receiver, forward assist, hinged ejection port cover. Disc. 2012.

	$595	$485	$415	$350	$315	$295	$275	$700

V15 TARGET RIFLE – .223 Rem. cal., GIO, 20 in. chrome moly vanadium steel threaded button rifled heavy barrel, A2 flash hider, all parts manganese phosphate finished, rifle length handguard, full heat shield, A2 or A3 flat-top upper receiver, Picatinny rail, hardcoat anodized black finish, fixed A2 buttstock, removable flash hider, aluminum spacer, trap door buttplate.

	$850	$550	$465	$395	$350	$325	$295	$999

V15 VARMINATOR SERIES – .223 Rem. cal., GIO, 16 (new 2013), 20 or 24 in. stainless steel bull barrel, full-length aluminum handguard, aluminum gas block, four Picatinny rails, forged A3 upper receiver, forward assist, hinged ejection port cover, fixed A2 buttstock, aluminum spacer, trap door buttplate, hardcoat anodized finish, 9-9.2 lbs.

	$850	$550	$465	$395	$350	$325	$295	$999

V15 200 SERIES – 7.62x39mm cal., GIO, 16 in. chrome moly vanadium steel threaded barrel, A2 flash hider, hinged ejection port, A2 front sight bases, 6-position buttstock, forged A2 or A3 flat-top upper receiver, forward assist, bayonet lug, M4 length handguard, full heat shields, all parts manganese phosphate finished, 6.4 lbs.

	$915	$575	$475	$415	$350	$325	$300	$1,100

MSR	100%	98%	95%	90%	80%	70%	60%	Last MSR

* **V15 200 Piston Series** – .223 Rem. cal., similar to V15 200 Series, except has proprietary short stroke GPO.
    $1,050 $650 $495 $450 $395 $350 $325   *$1,250*

V15 202 MODULAR CARBINE – .223 Rem. cal., GIO, 16 in. chrome moly vanadium steel threaded barrel, A2 flash hider, hinged ejection port cover, 6-position buttstock, low profile aircraft aluminum gas block, A3 flat-top upper receiver, four Picatinny rails, forward assist, modular handguard, black hardcoat anodized finish, all parts manganese phosphate finished, 6 1/2 lbs.
    $785 $525 $450 $385 $340 $325 $295   *$925*

V18 SERIES – .223 Rem. cal., short stroke GPO, 16 1/2 or 20 in. chrome-lined barrel, copy of the AR-180, machined gas block, front sight base, Picatinny rail, A2 flash hider, FAL style handguard, ambidextrous charging handle, carbon fiber lower, AR pistol grip, polymer FAL stock, rubber buttpad, aluminum recoil plate, last round hold open, 6.8 lbs.
    $765 $515 $440 $375 $335 $315 $295   *$889*

V73 SERIES – 7.62x39mm, .223 Rem., or .308 Win. cal., GIO, copy of Israeli Galil, 100% part interchangeability, including mags. and accessories, machined monobloc receiver, skeletonized black tactical stock, available in AR, ARM, SAR, and Micro configurations. Disc. 2012.
    $1,275 $850 $600 $495 $425 $375 $350   *$1,550*

Add $300 for .308 Win. cal.
Add $100 for ARM model with top carry handle.
Add $449 for SAR or Micro configuration.

MAYBE THE ONLY THING BETTER THAN THIS BOOK IS THE ONLINE SUBSCRIPTION!

- **Includes monthly updates** keeping you informed of all the new AR-15 makes/models.
- **Features thousands of images** allowing for fast and easy identification.
- **Manufacturer/Model searchable database** allowing you to find the model you need.
- **Historical pricing with dynamic interactive graphs** keeps you up-to-date on your AR-15 purchases as investments.
- **Your own personal online inventory solution** - keep track of your collection and track the change in value.
- **Includes access to BBP's industry standard Photo Percentage Grading System** – why guess a gun's condition when you can be sure?

Only $19.95/year!

Visit BLUEBOOKOFGUNVALUES.COM
to view sample pages and ordering

Good Information Never Sleeps!

W SECTION

365 W

WMD GUNS

Current manufacturer of pistols, AR-15 style rifle/carbines, and proprietary coating (NiB-X) located in Stuart, FL.

MSR	100%	98%	95%	90%	80%	70%	60%	Last MSR

PISTOLS: SEMI-AUTO

BEAST AR-15 PISTOL – 5.56 NATO cal., 10 1/2 in. chrome moly match grade barrel, optics ready, black pistol grip, pistol buffer, forged aluminum upper and lower receiver, 9 in. free floating handguard, Picatinny rail. New 2016.

MSR $1,235	$1,050	$950	$815	$715	$625	$535	$450

RIFLES/CARBINES: SEMI-AUTO

THE BEAST – 5.56 NATO cal., GIO, 16 in. match grade Government or M4 profile barrel, stainless steel compensator, carbine gas system, low profile gas block, billet aluminum upper and lower receivers, M4 feed ramps, free float rail system with adj. optic ready Picatinny rails, aluminum handguard, black pistol grip, NiB-X coated barrel, receivers, fire control group, gas block, and charging handle, triangular 5-pos. ergonomic buttstock, rubber buttplate, with or w/out color accent kit (new 2018), color bolt carrier group (new 2018), or color charging handle (new 2018), includes Drago tactical bag.

MSR $1,450	$1,195	$795	$550	$465	$415	$375	$350

Add $5 for charging handle or bolt carrier group (various colors available, new 2018).

Add $60 for color accent kit (various colors available, new 2018).

* ***The Dirty Beast*** – similar to The Beast, except has Flat Dark Earth topcoat finish.

MSR $1,450	$1,195	$795	$550	$465	$415	$375	$350

* ***The Forged Beast (Lightweight)*** – 5.56 NATO cal., AR-15 style, carbine gas system, 16 in. lightweight chrome moly match grade barrel, rubber-like buttplate, pistol grip, forged Mil-Spec aluminum receiver, M4 feed ramps, NiB-X nickel boron finish, 5.8 lbs. New 2016.

MSR $1,620	$1,350	$875	$650	$525	$450	$385	$350

* ***The Range/Duty Ready Patrol Rifle*** – 5.56 NATO cal., GIO, carbine gas system, 16 in. chrome moly barrel, Magpul BUIS polymer folding front and rear sights, Magpul MOE rubber-like buttstock, Magpul MOE pistol grip, fire control grip, carbine buffer, 6.8 lbs. New 2016.

MSR $1,150	$950	$595	$495	$425	$365	$335	$300

* ***The Special Purpose Rifle*** – 5.56 NATO cal., AR-15 style, 18 in. stainless steel barrel, optic-ready sights, fixed modular buttstock w/adj. cheekpiece, black pistol grip, Picatinny rail, forged upper and lower aluminum receiver, low profile gas block, free floating cylindrical handguard, M4 feed ramps, M16 bolt-carrier group. New 2016.

MSR $1,620	$1,350	$875	$650	$525	$450	$385	$350

BIG BEAST .308 Win./7.62 NATO cal., AR-10 rifle, GIO, 18 or 20 in. free floating barrel, Melonite bore, barrel extension, Magpul 20 shot mag., adj. (18 in. barrel) or fixed (20 in. barrel) stock, carbine length gas system, low profile gas block, billet aluminum upper and lower receivers, all exterior surfaces and key internal components are permanently coated in the NiB-X process, includes WMD/Drago tactical rifle case, black or FDE finish, 8 lbs. New 2016.

MSR $2,359	$1,875	$1,100	$895	$650	$575	$495	$425

Add $140 for 20 in. barrel with fixed stock.

* ***Big Beast 6.5 Creedmoor*** – 6.5mm Creedmoor cal., AR-15 style, 20 in. mid-heavy or 22 in. heavy stainless steel and NiB-X coated match grade barrel, 10 shot Magpul mag., fixed modular buttstock assembly with adj. cheek rest and LOP, Hipertouch 24-E trigger/fire control group, adj. gas block, free float low profile KeyMod handguard, aluminum NiB-X billet upper and lower receivers, includes 42 in. Drago rifle case, 9.1 lbs. New 2018.

MSR $2,559	$2,050	$1,250	$950	$650	$575	$495	$475

SURVIVOR SERIES THE BEAST – 5.56 NATO cal., GIO, 16 in. barrel, two 30 shot mags., triangular 5-pos. ergonomic buttstock, free float rail system with adj. optic ready Picatinny rails, NiB-X coating on all parts, similar to The Beast model except has Battle Worn/Distressed finish giving it the look of being well used and battle tested. New 2018.

MSR $1,650	$1,350	$875	$650	$525	$450	$385	$350

SURVIVOR SERIES LIGHTWEIGHT BEAST – 5.56 NATO/.223 Rem. cal., 16 in. lightweight barrel, two NiB-X 30 shot mags., Distressed/Battle Worn finish, includes WMD Guns tactical bag, 5.8 lbs. New 2018.

MSR $1,820	$1,525	$975	$750	$575	$495	$425	$375

SURVIVOR SERIES BIG BEAST – .308 Win. cal., AR-10, Nitride and NiB-X coated 20 in. match grade barrel, 10 shot Magpul mag., NiB-X coated BCG and Hipertouch EDT2 trigger/fire control group, fixed FDE modular buttstock assembly with adj. cheek rest, NiB-X coated free float low profile KeyMod handguard, aluminum NiB-X billet upper and lower receivers, Battle Worn/Distressed finish, includes 42 in. Drago rifle case, 8 lbs. New 2018.

MSR $2,559	$2,050	$1,250	$950	$650	$575	$495	$475

MSR	100%	98%	95%	90%	80%	70%	60%	Last MSR

WAR SPORT

Previous AR-15 style pistol and rifle manufacturer located in Robbins, NC until 2017. War Sport also manufactured a line of parts and accessories including upper build kits, barrels, muzzle devices, and related small parts.

PISTOLS: SEMI-AUTO

LVOA-SP – .223 Wylde chamber, AR-15 style, 11 3/4 in. barrel, WS Top Hat compensator, CMC 3 1/2 lb. flat trigger, MBUS Pro sights, Magpul XTM foregrip, SIG SB-15 brace, ambi fire controls, mag. release, and charging handle, black, Foliage, FDE, or Wolf Grey finish, ships in a hard shell case, 6 3/4 lbs. Disc. 2017.

| | $2,515 | $2,185 | $1,800 | $1,550 | $1,275 | $1,075 | $935 | *$2,950* |

RIFLES: SEMI-AUTO

GPR-C – .223 Rem./5.56 NATO, .223 Wylde chamber, 6.8 SPC (new 2017), .300 AAC Blackout (new 2017), or .22 Nosler (new 2017) cal., AR-15 style, 16 or 18 (new 2017) in. barrel, War Sport muzzle brake (new 2017), Geissele SSA trigger, MBUS Pro sights, B5 SOPMOD stock, ambi fire controls, mag. release, and charging handle, black, Foliage, FDE, or Wolf Grey finish, 6 1/2 lbs. Mfg. 2016-2017.

| | $2,125 | $1,325 | $995 | $675 | $595 | $525 | $475 | *$2,650* |

GPR-HC – .308 Win. or 6.5mm Creedmoor cal., AR-10 style, 18, 20, or 22 in. stainless or carbon steel barrel, muzzle brake, enhanced two-stage trigger, billet upper and lower receivers, black, Foliage, FDE, or Wolf Grey finish. Mfg. 2017 only.

Retail pricing was not available for this model.

LVOA-HC308 – .308 Win./7.62 NATO cal., 16 in. barrel, black, Foliage, FDE, or Wolf Grey finish, 8.6 lbs. Mfg. 2017 only.

| | $2,775 | $1,825 | $1,350 | $750 | $650 | $595 | $525 | *$3,400* |

WARRIOR ARMS LLC

Current AR-15 style pistol and rifle manufacturer established during 2011, located in Valparaiso, IN.

PISTOLS: SEMI-AUTO

WAR-15 SS PISTOL – 5.56 NATO cal., 10 1/2 in. stainless steel barrel, A2 flash hider, 30 shot mag., single-stage trigger, MOE pistol grip and trigger guard, forged aluminum upper and lower receiver, Picatinny rail, carbine length handguard, padded pistol buffer tube, includes gun lock and chamber safety tool in chamber, hardcoat anodized black finish, 5 lbs.

| MSR $750 | | $650 | $575 | $510 | $440 | $385 | $340 | $325 | |

RIFLES/CARBINES: SEMI-AUTO

WAR-15 DEFENDER RIFLE – 5.56 NATO cal., 16 in. chrome moly vanadium SB Nitride barrel, Smith Vortex flash hider, 30 shot mag., SST, Magpul MOE stock w/Mil-Spec buffer tube, Magpul MOE grip and trigger guard, forged aluminum upper and lower receiver, right-hand ejection, 9 1/2, 12, or 15 in. KeyMod rail system, includes gun lock and chamber safety tool in chamber, black hardcoat anodized finish, 7 lbs.

| MSR $1,050 | | $875 | $550 | $465 | $395 | $350 | $325 | $300 | |

WAR-15 M4 CARBINE – 5.56 NATO cal., 16 in. chrome moly vanadium Nitride barrel, A2 flash hider, 30 shot mag., M4 buttstock w/Mil-Spec buffer tube, forged aluminum upper and lower receiver, right-hand ejection, Magpul trigger guard, M16 bolt carrier group, M4 feed ramp, 12 or 15 in. M-LOK rail includes gun lock and owners manual, hardcoat anodized black finish, 6.3 lbs.

| MSR $700 | | $595 | $485 | $415 | $350 | $315 | $295 | $275 | |

WILKINSON TACTICAL

Current AR-15 style shotgun manufacturer located in Laramie, WY.

RIFLES: SEMI-AUTO

CR-12 RIFLE – 6mm Creedmoor, 6.5mm Creedmoor, or .308 Win. cal., GIO, 18 in. barrel, Fail Zero double set high precision trigger, HiViz custom tactical sighting system, M4 type adj. stock, tactical sling ring, full ambi controls, free floating M-LOK or KeyMod handguard, nickel boron plated internal components, black anodized finish. New 2018.

| MSR $2,495 | | $1,975 | $1,150 | $925 | $650 | $575 | $495 | $425 | |

SHOTGUNS: SEMI-AUTO

CR-12 – 12 ga., 2 3/4 or 3 in. chamber, GIO, 18 in. ported barrel, 5 shot mag., Fail Zero double set high precision trigger, HiViz custom tactical sighting system, M4 type adj. stock, tactical sling ring, full ambi controls, free floating M-LOK or KeyMod handguard, nickel boron plated internal components, black anodized finish. New 2016.

| MSR $2,495 | | $2,125 | $1,875 | $1,550 | $1,325 | $1,100 | $950 | $825 | |

MSR	100%	98%	95%	90%	80%	70%	60%	Last MSR

WILSON COMBAT

Current firearms manufacturer, customizer, and supplier of custom firearms parts and accessories established in 1978, and located in Berryville, AR.

PISTOLS: SEMI-AUTO

Prices reflect .45 ACP cal. base model w/o upgrades. A wide variety of options are available - contact the company directly for pricing. Add $325 for the WCR-22 pistol suppressor (new 2016).

AR9 – 9mm Para. cal., 8 or 11.3 in. barrel, threaded muzzle with QComp flash hider, Wilson Combat two-stage TTU (Tactical Trigger Unit), standard AR furniture, BCM pistol grip, billet aluminum flat-top upper and lower receiver, Wilson Combat T.R.I.M. rail, Shockwave Blade pistol firearm support, Armor-Tuff finish, 5-6 lbs. New 2016.

| MSR $1,995 | $1,700 | $1,500 | $1,250 | $1,100 | $950 | $825 | $675 |

ARP TACTICAL – 5.56x45/.223 Rem. cal., carbine length gas system with low profile gas block, 11.3 in. ARP Tactical match grade barrel, threaded muzzle with Accu-Tac flash hider, Wilson Combat tactical trigger guard, single stage TTU (Tactical Trigger Unit), BCM pistol grip, forged flat-top upper and lower receiver, 10.4 in. Wilson Combat T.R.I.M. rail, Shockwave Blade pistol forearm support, Armor-Tuff finish, 6 lbs. New 2016.

| MSR $2,250 | $1,915 | $1,685 | $1,425 | $1,225 | $1,035 | $885 | $735 |

RIFLES: SEMI-AUTO

All rifles come standard with nylon tactical case.

A variety of accessories are available for additional cost - please contact the company directly for more information on available options (see Trademark Index).

Add $325 for WCR-22 rimfire rifle suppressor (new 2016).

.308 SUPER SNIPER – .308 Win. cal., GIO, 20 in. button rifled stainless steel fluted or non-fluted barrel, billet AR machined aluminum upper and lower receivers, 12 or 14 in. free floating T.R.I.M. rail, customer's choice of tactical trigger unit and Armor-Tuff finish colors, 9.2 lbs. New 2015.

| MSR $3,095 | $2,450 | $1,595 | $1,200 | $700 | $675 | $575 | $525 |

Add $50 for fluted barrel.

AR9 CARBINE – 9mm Para. cal., closed bolt blowback, 16 in. fluted or non-fluted barrel, QComp flash hider, T.R.I.M. rail, two-stage tactical trigger, BCM Starburst Gunfighter grip, Wilson/Rogers Super-Stoc, billet aluminum flat-top upper and lower receiver, standard AR furniture/sight compatibility, hard anodized black finish, 6 lbs. New 2017.

| MSR $1,995 | $1,650 | $1,000 | $795 | $595 | $495 | $425 | $395 |

Add $100 for fluted barrel.

M4 TACTICAL CARBINE – .223 Rem. cal., GIO, 16 1/4 in. fluted match grade barrel with muzzle brake, 20 shot mag., aluminum flat-top upper and lower receiver, quad rail free float aluminum handguard, single stage trigger, Ergo pistol grip, 6-position collapsible stock, black, green, tan or gray anodized finish, 6.9 lbs. Disc. 2011.

| | $1,675 | $1,000 | $825 | $625 | $550 | $475 | $425 | *$2,000* |

PAUL HOWE TACTICAL CARBINE – 5.56 NATO cal., 14.7 in. stainless steel fluted barrel with permanently attached Accu-Tac flash hider (meets the 16 in. barrel requirement), two-stage TTU, Daniel Defense fixed front sight tower, CSAT rear aperture flip-up sight, BCM Starburst Gunfighter grip, 10.4 in. T.R.I.M. rail, Armor-Tuff camo finish, 6 1/4 lbs. New 2018.

| MSR $2,600 | $2,125 | $1,325 | $995 | $675 | $595 | $525 | $475 |

SPR (SPECIAL PURPOSE RIFLE) – 5.56 NATO cal., GIO, 18 in. stainless steel match grade barrel with Accu-Tac flash hider, low profile gas block, forged flat-top upper and lower receiver, quad rail free float aluminum handguard (disc.) or T.R.I.M. rail, 20 shot mag., single stage trigger, Ergo (disc.) or Bravo pistol grip, A2 fixed (disc.) or Wilson/Rogers Super-Stoc buttstock, black, green, tan or gray anodized finish, 6.9 lbs.

| MSR $2,450 | $1,975 | $1,150 | $925 | $650 | $575 | $495 | $425 |

SS-15 SUPER SNIPER RIFLE – .223 Rem./5.56 NATO (.223 Wylde chamber, new 2012) cal., GIO, 18 in. fluted heavy match grade stainless steel barrel with muzzle brake, aluminum flat-top upper and lower receiver, aluminum free float handguard, black, green, tan, federal brown, green base camo, or gray anodized finish, 20 shot mag., single stage trigger, Ergo pistol grip, fixed A2 stock, 8.7 lbs.

| | $1,795 | $1,050 | $875 | $625 | $550 | $475 | $425 | *$2,225* |

Add $400 for green base camo.

RANGER – 5.56 NATO, 6.8 SPC, .300 AAC Blackout, .243 Win., 6.5mm Creedmoor, .308 Win., or .358 Win. cal., GIO, 16 in. Ranger match grade fluted or non-fluted barrel, threaded muzzle with QComp, Rogers/Wilson Super-Stoc, black BCM Starburst Gunfighter grip, M2 Tactical Trigger Unit, SLR Rifleworks adj. gas block, 10 in. M-LOK rail with three Falcon/ Ergo rail covers, lightweight billet lower and flat-top upper receiver, hard anodized black or green finish, 8 lbs. New 2017.

| MSR $2,350 | $1,875 | $1,100 | $895 | $650 | $575 | $495 | $425 |

Add $745 for AR-10 platform.

W 368 WILSON COMBAT, cont.

MSR	100%	98%	95%	90%	80%	70%	60%	Last MSR

RECON TACTICAL .458 SOCOM – .458 SOCOM cal., GIO, 16 or 18 in. match grade stainless steel fluted barrel, threaded muzzle with QComp muzzle brake, single stage TTU, Rogers/Wilson Super-Stoc, mid-length gas system with adj. gas block, billet lower and flat-top upper receivers, M-LOK rail, NP3 coated BCG, Armor-Tuff finish over hardcoat anodized black or green finish, 7 lbs. New 2018.

MSR $2,655	$2,125	$1,325	$995	$675	$595	$525	$475	

Add $200 for green finish.

RECON TACTICAL 5.56 NATO / .224 VALKYRIE – 5.56 NATO or .224 Valkyrie (new 2018) cal., 16 in. medium weight stainless steel match grade barrel, threaded muzzle with QComp flash hider, BCM Starburst Gunfighter grip, tactical trigger guard, Rogers/Wilson Super-Stoc, single stage TTU, T.R.I.M. rail, mid-length gas system with low profile gas block, billet lower and flat-top upper receiver, NP3 coated BCG, black, FDE (disc.), gray (disc.) or green finish, 7 lbs.

MSR $2,250	$1,795	$1,050	$875	$625	$550	$475	$425	

RECON TACTICAL 6.5mm CREEDMOOR – 6.5mm Creedmoor cal., 16, 18, or 20 in. match grade stainless steel fluted or non-fluted barrel, threaded muzzle with QComp flash hider, single stage TTU, Rogers/Wilson Super-Stoc, rifle length gas system with low profile gas block, billet lower and flat-top upper receiver, 14 in. T.R.I.M. rail, NP3 coated BCG, Armor-Tuff finish over hardcoat anodized finish, 7.85 lbs. New 2018.

MSR $2,995	$2,375	$1,525	$1,150	$700	$625	$550	$475	

Add $50 for fluted barrel.

RECON TACTICAL 6.8 SPC II / 6.5 Grendel – 6.8 SPC II or 6.5 Grendel (new 2018) cal., GIO, 16, 18, or 20 in. match grade stainless steel barrel, threaded muzzle with Accu-Tac (6.8 SPC II) or QComp (6.5 Grendel) flash hider, tactical trigger guard, single stage TTU, Rogers/Wilson Super-Stoc, Bravo Company pistol grip, billet upper and lower receivers, mid-length gas system with low profile gas block, T.R.I.M. (6.8 SPC) or M-LOK (6.5 Grendel) rail, Armor-Tuff finish over black, green, or camo hardcoat anodized finish, 7 lbs.

MSR $2,550	$2,050	$1,250	$950	$650	$575	$495	$475	

Add $50 for 18 in. fluted barrel.

Add $125 for camo finish.

RECON TACTICAL .300 AAC BLACKOUT / .204 RUGER – .300 AAC Blackout or .204 Ruger (new 2018) cal., GIO, 16 or 18 in. stainless steel match grade barrel, QComp muzzle brake, Rogers/Wilson Super-Stoc, Bravo Company pistol grip, carbine or mid (18 in. barrel) length gas system with low profile gas block, forged upper and lower receivers, T.R.I.M. or M-LOK rail, single stage TTU, tactical trigger guard, NP3 coated BCG, Armor-Tuff finish over hard anodized finish, 7 lbs.

MSR $2,550	$2,050	$1,250	$950	$650	$575	$495	$475	

Add $50 for 18 in. barrel.

RECON TACTICAL .308 WIN. / .338 FEDERAL / 7mm-08 REM. / 6mm CREEDMOOR – .308 Win., .338 Federal (16. in. barrel only), 6mm Creedmoor (new 2018, 16 in. only), or 7mm-08 Rem. (new 2018, 16 in. only) cal., GIO, 16, 18, or 20 in. match grade stainless steel barrel, threaded muzzle with Accu-Tac or QComp flash hider, billet lower and flat-top upper receiver, mid-length gas system with low profile gas block, T.R.I.M. or M-LOK (7mm-08 Rem. or 6mm Creedmoor only) rail, single stage Tactical Trigger Unit, Rogers/Wilson Super-Stoc, NP3 coated BCG, Armor-Tuff finish applied over hardcoat anodized black finish, 7.85-8 lbs.

MSR $2,995	$2,375	$1,525	$1,150	$700	$625	$550	$475	

Add $210 for .338 Federal cal.

RECON TACTICAL 7.62x40 WT – 7.62x40 WT cal., GIO, 20 in. match grade stainless steel barrel, threaded muzzle with Accu-Tac flash hider, tactical trigger guard, single stage TTU, Rogers/Wilson Super-Stoc, black Ergo grip, mid-length gas system with low profile gas block, forged lower and flat-top upper receivers, T.R.I.M. rail, Armor-Tuff finish over hardcoat anodized black finish, 7 lbs.

MSR $2,550	$2,050	$1,250	$950	$650	$575	$495	$475	

SUPER SNIPER – .260 Rem., 6mm Creedmoor, 6.5mm Creedmoor, 6.5 Grendel, .224 Valkyrie, or .223 Wylde chamber (compatible with .223/5.56) cal., rifle length gas system, 20, 22 (6.5mm Creedmoor only), or 24 (6.5mm Creedmoor only) in. stainless match grade barrel, single stage TTU, Rogers Super-Stoc buttstock, Wilson Combat/BCM Starburst Gunfighter grip, low profile gas block, 13.8 or 14 (6.5 Creedmoor) in. T.R.I.M. rail, billet lower and flat-top upper receiver, NP3 coated BCG, Armor-Tuff finish over hard anodized finish, 8 lbs. 11 oz.-10 lbs. 2 oz. New 2018.

MSR $2,225	$1,795	$1,050	$875	$625	$550	$475	$425	

Add $920 for 6.5mm Creedmoor cal.

TACTICAL HUNTER – .22 Nosler (new 2018), .204 Ruger, .308 Win., 7mm-08 Rem., 6.8 SPC (new 2018), 6.5 Grendel (new 2018), .338 Federal, 6.5mm Creedmoor, 6mm Creedmoor, .260 Rem., or .458 SOCOM (new 2018) cal., GIO, 18 or 20 in. threaded match grade fluted or non-fluted barrel, threaded muzzle with thread protector, 14.6 in. Wilson Combat M-LOK rail, billet lower and flat-top upper receiver, rifle-length gas system with SLR Rifleworks adj. gas block, Rogers/Wilson Super-Stoc, Tactical Trigger Unit, BCM charging handle, standard buffer, black Starburst Gunfighter grip, black or green hardcoat anodized finish. New 2017.

MSR $3,145	$2,675	$2,300	$1,900	$1,625	$1,325	$1,115	$965	

Add $50 for fluted barrel.

WILSON COMBAT, cont. 369

MSR	100%	98%	95%	90%	80%	70%	60%	Last MSR

* Tactical Hunter .458 HAM'R – .458 HAM'R cal., 18 in. fluted match grade barrel, threaded muzzle with thread protector, 7 or 9 shot mag., Rogers/Wilson Super-Stoc, Wilson Combat/BCM Starburst Gunfighter grip, mid-length gas system with SLR Rifleworks adj. gas block, billet lower and flat-top upper receiver, 13.8 in. M-LOK rail with three Falcon/Ergo rail covers, custom length buffer, NP3 coated BCG, Armor-Tuff finish applied over hard anodized finish, green/black finish is standard, additional color/camo options available, 7 lbs. 11 oz. New 2018.

	100%	98%	95%	90%	80%	70%	60%	
MSR $2,905	$2,375	$1,525	$1,150	$700	$625	$550	$475	

TACTICAL LIGHTWEIGHT – 5.56 NATO, 6.8 SPC II, or 7.62x40 WT cal., GIO, 16.2, 18 (7.62x40 WT cal. only), or 20 (7.62x40 WT cal. only) in. match grade barrel, low profile gas block, Picatinny rail, Ergo pistol grip, tactical trigger guard, two-stage trigger, black Armor-Tuff finish, 20 shot mag., adj. black synthetic Rogers/Wilson Super-Stoc buttstock. Mfg. 2012-2016.

	100%	98%	95%	90%	80%	70%	60%	Last MSR
	$1,795	$1,050	$875	$625	$550	$475	$425	$2,250

UT-15 URBAN TACTICAL CARBINE – .223 Rem. cal., GIO, 16 1/4 in. fluted match grade barrel with muzzle brake, aluminum flat-top upper and lower receiver, quad rail free float aluminum handguard, black, green, tan or gray anodized finish, 20 shot mag., single stage trigger, Ergo pistol grip, 6-position collapsible stock, 6.9 lbs. Disc. 2011.

	100%	98%	95%	90%	80%	70%	60%	Last MSR
	$1,675	$1,000	$825	$625	$550	$475	$425	$2,025

ULTIMATE HUNTER – .204 Ruger (new 2018), .308 Win., .338 Federal, .358 Win., 6.8 SPC (new 2018), 6.5mm Creedmoor, or .458 SOCOM (new 2018) cal., GIO, 18, 20, or 22 in. fluted button rifled, stainless steel match grade barrel, crowned muzzle, Smoke Composite carbon fiber closed shoulder buttstock with Limbsaver pad, black Mission First Tactical pistol grip, lightweight billet lower and flat-top upper receiver, Wilson/SLR click-adjustable gas block, Tactical Trigger Unit, BCM charging handle, 14.6 in. Wilson Combat M-LOK rail, green or black finish, 7 lbs. 5 oz. New 2017.

	100%	98%	95%	90%	80%	70%	60%	
MSR $3,345	$2,825	$2,400	$1,950	$1,650	$1,325	$1,115	$965	

* Ultimate Hunter .458 HAM'R – .458 HAM'R cal., 18 in. fluted match grade barrel, crowned muzzle, 7 or 9 shot mag., Tactical Trigger Unit, Smoke Composite carbon fiber closed shoulder buttstock with Limbsaver pad, MFT black pistol grip, mid-length gas system with SLR Rifleworks adj. gas block, billet lower and lightweight flat-top upper receiver, 13.8 in. M-LOK rail with three Falcon/Ergo rail covers, NP3 coated BCG, custom length buffer, Armor-Tuff Finish applied over hard anodized green/black (standard) finish, other colors/camo is optional, 7 lbs. 4 oz. New 2018.

	100%	98%	95%	90%	80%	70%	60%	
MSR $3,055	$2,450	$1,595	$1,200	$700	$675	$575	$525	

ULTRALIGHT HUNTER – .204 Ruger (new 2018), 6.8 SPC (new 2018), .458 SOCOM (new 2018), .308 Win., .338 Federal, or .358 Win. cal., GIO, 16.2 in. Ultralight Hunter match grade barrel, crowned muzzle, Tactical Trigger Unit, Smoke Composite carbon fiber closed shoulder buttstock with Limbsaver pad, black Mission First Tactical pistol grip, intermediate-length gas system with SLR Rifleworks adj. gas block, BCM charging handle, standard buffer, lightweight billet lower and flat-top upper receiver, 12.6 in. M-LOK rail, black or green hardcoat anodized finish, 7 lbs. New 2017.

	100%	98%	95%	90%	80%	70%	60%	
MSR $3,295	$2,775	$2,350	$1,925	$1,625	$1,300	$1,100	$950	

ULTRALIGHT RANGER – 5.56 NATO, 6.8 SPC, .300 AAC Blackout, .243 Win., 6.5mm Creedmoor, .308 Win., or .358 Win. cal., GIO, 16 in. Ranger match grade fluted or non fluted barrel, threaded muzzle with QComp, Smoke Composite carbon fiber closed shoulder buttstock, M2 Tactical Trigger Unit, black Mission First Tactical pistol grip, 10 in. M-LOK rail with three Falcon/Ergo rail covers, lightweight billet upper and lower receiver, SLR Rifleworks adj. gas block, hard anodized black or green finish, 7 lbs. 6 oz. New 2017.

	100%	98%	95%	90%	80%	70%	60%	
MSR $2,450	$1,975	$1,150	$925	$650	$575	$495	$425	

Add $745 for AR-10 platform model.

URBAN SUPER SNIPER – 6.8 SPC cal. or .223 Wylde chambered, GIO, 18 in. stainless steel Urban Super Sniper match grade barrel, M4 feed ramps, mid-length gas system with low profile gas block, Rogers Super-Stoc buttstock, single stage Tactical Trigger Unit, 10.4 in. T.R.I.M. rail, BCM Starburst Gunfighter grip, billet lower and flat-top upper receiver, Armor-Tuff finish, 7 lbs. 5 oz.

	100%	98%	95%	90%	80%	70%	60%	
MSR $2,225	$1,795	$1,050	$875	$625	$550	$475	$425	

WINDHAM WEAPONRY

Current manufacturer of AR-15 style pistols, rifles, receivers, parts, barrels, and related accessories established in 2011, located in Windham, ME. Windham Weaponry is located in the former Bushmaster Manufacturing plant in Windham, ME.

PISTOLS: SEMI-AUTO

.223/5.56mm AR PISTOL – .223 Rem./5.56 NATO cal., 11 1/2 in. heavy chrome moly barrel with A2 flash suppressor, 30 shot mag., forged aluminum flat-top upper receiver with aluminum trigger guard, steel bolt, no sights, AR pistol rec. tube with foam sleeve and W.W. engraved logo, 10 in. Midwest Industries stainless steel KeyMod free float forend with 2 in. rail segment, A2 black plastic grip, hardcoat anodized black finish, 5.65 lbs. New 2014.

	100%	98%	95%	90%	80%	70%	60%	
MSR $1,264	$1,050	$950	$815	$715	$625	$535	$450	

W370 WINDHAM WEAPONRY, cont.

MSR	100%	98%	95%	90%	80%	70%	60%	Last MSR

.300 BLACKOUT AR PISTOL – .300 AAC Blackout cal., GIO, 9 in. medium profile barrel, A2 flash suppressor, 30 shot mag., Magpul Enhanced trigger guard, Hogue overmolded pistol grip, flat-top upper with Mil-Std 1913 rail, AR pistol type rec. tube with WW laser engraved logo, QD endplate, QD sling swivel, 7 1/4 in. carbine free float vented forend, black finish, 4.85 lbs. New 2016.

| MSR $1,160 | $975 | $885 | $765 | $655 | $575 | $495 | $435 | |

RIFLES/CARBINES: SEMI-AUTO

Windham Weaponry also makes several variations of the SBR (Short Barreled Rifle) for military/law enforcement. All Windham rifles and carbines carry a lifetime transferable warranty.

20 INCH GOVERNMENT RIFLE – .223 Rem./5.56 NATO cal., GIO, 20 in. Government A2 profile chrome moly barrel, A2 flash suppressor, 30 shot mag., forged aluminum flat-top upper with A4 detachable carry handle, M4 feed ramps, rifle length fiberglass handguard with aluminum heat shield, machined aluminum trigger guard, A4 dual aperture rear sight and adj. front sight base, A2 solid stock with trapdoor storage compartment, A2 black plastic pistol grip with finger groove and checkering, hardcoat anodized black finish, 7.7 lbs. New 2014.

| MSR $1,192 | $995 | $625 | $495 | $450 | $395 | $350 | $325 | |

.300 BLACKOUT – .300 AAC Blackout cal., GIO, 16 in. medium profile chrome-lined barrel with Diamondhead "T" brake, 30 shot mag., flat-top upper receiver with Magpul enhanced trigger guard, no sights, 13 1/2 in. Diamondhead VRS-T free float forend, two Q.D. sling swivels, Hogue 6-positon telescoping buttstock, Q.D. socket endplate, Hogue overmolded beavertail pistol grip, hardcoat anodized black finish, 6.9 lbs.

| MSR $1,680 | $1,385 | $895 | $675 | $525 | $450 | $385 | $350 | |

.300 BLACKOUT SRC – .300 AAC Blackout cal., GIO, 16 in. medium profile barrel with Diamondhead "T" brake, A2 flash suppressor, 30 shot mag., forged aluminum flat-top upper receiver, 6-pos. telescoping buttstock with Windham Weaponry logo, A2 black plastic grips, no rear sights, Mil-Std 1913 rail gas block, QD socket endplate, M4 double heat shield handguard, includes hard plastic gun case with black web sling, hardcoat black anodized finish.

| MSR $1,056 | $895 | $575 | $475 | $395 | $350 | $325 | $300 | |

.308 HUNTER – .308 Win. cal., GIO, 18 in. fluted chrome-lined barrel with A2 flash suppressor, 5 shot mag., forged aluminum flat-top upper receiver with Picatinny rail, electroless nickel plating (new 2016) or hardcoat Coyote Brown anodized finish, integral trigger guard, no sights, laminated wood stock and forend with Nutmeg or Pepper (new 2016) finish, Hogue overmolded beavertail pistol grip, includes black web sling, QD sling swivel, and hard plastic gun case, 7.6 lbs. New 2015.

| MSR $1,587 | $1,315 | $850 | $625 | $500 | $435 | $375 | $350 | |

.308 SRC – .308 Win. cal., GIO, AR-15 style, 16 1/2 in. medium profile chrome-lined barrel, 20 shot Magpul PMAG, collapsible buttstock, Hogue overmolded beavertail pistol grip, matte black finish, 7.55 lbs.

| MSR $1,413 | $1,175 | $775 | $550 | $465 | $415 | $375 | $350 | |

.308 SRC TIMBERTEC CAMO – .308 Win. or 7.62x51mm cal., GIO, 16 1/2 in. chrome-lined barrel with A2 flash suppressor, 20 shot Magpul PMAG, mid-length shielded handguards, no sights, forged aluminum flat-top upper receiver with Picatinny rail, integral trigger guard, 6-pos. telescoping buttstock with Stark Grip pistol grip, TimberTec camo finish, includes black web sling and hard plastic case, 7 1/2 lbs. New 2015.

| MSR $1,533 | $1,275 | $850 | $600 | $495 | $425 | $375 | $350 | |

.308 WITH FREE FLOAT FOREND – .308 Win. or 7.62x51mm. cal., GIO, 16 1/2 in. medium profile or 18 in. fluted barrel, A2 flash suppressor, 20 shot Magpul PMAG, integral trigger guard, no sights, 6-pos. telescoping buttstock with Windham Weaponry logo, Hogue overmolded beavertail pistol grip, forged aluminum lower and flat-top upper receivers, 15 in. Midwest Industries KeyMod free float forend, includes hard plastic case, black web sling, QD sling swivel, and operators manual, hardcoat anodized black finish, 8.05 lbs. New 2017.

| MSR $1,645 | $1,350 | $875 | $650 | $525 | $450 | $385 | $350 | |

Add $63 for 18 in. barrel.

.308 WITH MAGPUL ACCESSORIES – .308 Win. cal., GIO, 20 in. fluted barrel, A2 flash suppressor, 5 shot mag., integral trigger guard, Magpul MOE fixed buttstock, Hogue overmolded pistol grip, forged aluminum flat-top upper receiver, Magpul MOE M-LOK handguard, Mil-Std 1913 gas block rail, includes hard plastic gun case with black web sling, QD sling swivel, hardcoat anodized black finish, 9.05 lbs. New 2017.

| MSR $1,668 | $1,385 | $895 | $675 | $525 | $450 | $385 | $350 | |

.450 THUMPER – .450 Bushmaster cal., GIO, 16 in. chrome-lined barrel, A2 flash hider, 5 shot mag., no sights, Luth-AR buttstock w/adj. buttplate and cheek rest, free float forend, Hogue overmolded beavertail pistol grip, manual safety w/indicator markings on both sides of receiver, flat-top upper receiver w/laser engraved caliber, includes hard plastic case, black web sling, and operators manual, black finish, 7.2 lbs. New 2017.

| MSR $1,413 | $1,175 | $775 | $550 | $465 | $415 | $375 | $350 | |

WINDHAM WEAPONRY, cont. 371

MSR	100%	98%	95%	90%	80%	70%	60%	Last MSR

CARBON FIBER SRC – .223 Rem. cal., GIO, 16 in. M4 profile chrome moly barrel, A2 flash suppressor, 30 shot mag., M4A4 flat-top upper receiver with molded Picatinny rail, molded carbon fiber composite receiver, matte black finish, steel bolt, 6-position telescoping buttstock with A2 pistol grip, M4 double heat shield handguards, integral molded carbon fiber trigger guard, no sights, manual safety, includes black sling and hard plastic case, 5.6 lbs.

| MSR $846 | $725 | $500 | $435 | $375 | $335 | $315 | $295 | |

CDI CARBINE – .223 Rem. cal., GIO, 16 in. M4 chrome-lined barrel with Vortex flash suppressor, 30 shot mag., forged aluminum lower and M4A4 flat-top upper receiver, steel bolt, Magpul MOE 6-position telescoping buttstock with pistol grip, Diamondhead free float forend, Magpul AFG angled foregrip, Magpul MOE pistol grip, machined aluminum trigger guard, Diamondhead flip-up front and rear sights, manual safety, includes black sling and hard plastic case, hardcoat anodized black finish, 7 lbs.

| MSR $1,680 | $1,385 | $895 | $675 | $525 | $450 | $385 | $350 | |

DISSIPATOR M4 – .223 Rem./5.56 NATO cal., GIO, 16 in. M4 profile chrome moly standard or heavy barrel, A2 flash suppressor, 30 shot mag., aluminum trigger guard, A4 dual aperture rear sight, adj. front sight post in A2 standard base at rifle length position, 6-position telescoping buttstock with Windham Weaponry logo, rifle length heat shielded handguards, A2 black plastic pistol grip, manual safety, forged aluminum flat-top upper with A4 detachable carry handle, black web sling, hardcoat black anodized finish, 7.2 lbs. New 2015.

| MSR $1,192 | $995 | $625 | $495 | $450 | $395 | $350 | $325 | |

HBC CARBINE – .223 Rem. cal., GIO, 16 in. heavy profile chrome-lined barrel with A2 flash suppressor, 30 shot mag., M4A4 flat-top upper receiver with detachable carry handle, aluminum forged lower receiver, steel bolt, 6-position telescoping buttstock with A2 pistol grip, M4 double heat shield handguards, machined aluminum trigger guard, adj. dual aperture rear sight, adj. square post front sight, manual safety, includes black sling and hard plastic case, hardcoat anodized black finish, 7 1/2 lbs.

| MSR $1,096 | $915 | $575 | $475 | $415 | $350 | $325 | $300 | |

7.62x39mm SRC – 7.62x39mm cal., GIO, 16 in. chrome moly barrel, A2 flash suppressor, aluminum trigger guard, 6-position telescoping buttstock with Windham Weaponry logo, M4 double heat shield handguards, A2 black plastic pistol grip, manual safety, forged aluminum flat-top upper, Mil-Std 1913 railed gas block, black web sling, hardcoat anodized black finish, 6.15 lbs.

| MSR $1,056 | $895 | $575 | $475 | $395 | $350 | $325 | $300 | |

MODEL R16SFST-308 – .308 Win. cal., GIO, 16 1/2 in. medium profile chrome moly barrel with A2 flash suppressor, 20 shot Magpul PMAG, forged aluminum flat-top upper with integral trigger guard, 15 in. Midwest Industries KeyMod handguard, 6-position telescoping buttstock with Windham Weaponry logo, Hogue overmolded grips, no sights, hardcoat anodized black finish, 8 lbs. Mfg. 2014-2015.

| | $1,350 | $875 | $650 | $525 | $450 | $385 | $350 | *$1,645* |

MODEL R18FSFSM-308 – .308 Win. cal., GIO, 18 in. fluted chrome-lined barrel with A2 flash suppressor, 20 shot Magpul PMAG, forged aluminum flat-top upper receiver with integral trigger guard, no sights, 15 in. Midwest Industries KeyMod handguard, Magpul MOE fixed buttstock, Hogue overmolded grip, hardcoat anodized black finish, 8.45 lbs. New 2014.

| MSR $1,733 | $1,425 | $925 | $700 | $550 | $475 | $395 | $350 | |

MODEL R18FSFST-308 – .308 Win. cal., GIO, 16 1/2 in. non-fluted or 18 in. fluted chrome moly barrel with A2 flash suppressor, 20 shot Magpul PMAG, forged aluminum flat-top upper with integral trigger guard, 15 in. Midwest Industries KeyMod handguard, 6-position telescoping buttstock with Windham Weaponry logo, Hogue overmolded beavertail pistol grip, no sights, hardcoat anodized black finish, 8 lbs. New 2014.

| MSR $1,708 | $1,425 | $925 | $700 | $550 | $475 | $395 | $350 | |

Subtract $63 for 16 1/2 in. non-fluted barrel.

MPC CARBINE – .223 Rem. cal., GIO, 16 in. M4 chrome-lined barrel, A2 flash suppressor, 30 shot mag., forged aluminum lower and M4A4 flat-top upper receiver with detachable carry handle, steel bolt, 6-position telescoping buttstock with A2 pistol grip, M4 double heat shield handguards, machined aluminum trigger guard, adj. dual aperture rear sight, adj. square post front sight, manual safety, includes black sling and hard plastic case, hardcoat anodized black finish, 6.9 lbs.

| MSR $1,086 | $915 | $575 | $475 | $415 | $350 | $325 | $300 | |

* ***MPC-RF Carbine*** – .223 Rem. cal., similar to MPC Carbine, except does not have carry handle, includes Diamondhead rear flip-up sight. New mid-2013.

| MSR $1,086 | $915 | $575 | $475 | $415 | $350 | $325 | $300 | |

Add $162 for Mission First Tactical quad rail handguard (MPC-RF MFT Model).

W 372 WINDHAM WEAPONRY, cont.

MSR	100%	98%	95%	90%	80%	70%	60%	Last MSR

SRC CARBINE – .223 Rem./5.56 NATO cal., GIO, 16 in. M4 chrome-lined barrel with A2 flash suppressor, 30 shot mag., forged aluminum lower and M4A4 flat-top upper receiver w/Picatinny rail, steel bolt, 6-position telescoping buttstock with Windham Weaponry logo, A2 pistol grip, M4 double heat shield handguards, machined aluminum trigger guard, no sights, manual safety, includes black sling and hard plastic case, hardcoat anodized black finish, 6.3 lbs.

MSR $1,040	$875	$550	$465	$395	$350	$325	$300	

* **SRC Camouflage** – .223 Rem./5.56 NATO cal., GIO, 16 in. M4 chrome-lined barrel with A2 flash suppressor, 30 shot mag., machined aluminum trigger guard, no sights, 6-position telescoping buttstock, A2 pistol grip, manual safety, M4 feed ramps, forged aluminum flat-top upper receiver w/Picatinny rail, M4 double heat shield handguards, includes black sling and hard plastic case, Muddy Girl, True Timber Snowfall (disc.), King's Snow (new 2015), TimberTec, or Desert Digital (mfg. 2015 only) hydrographic camo finish, 6.3 lbs. New 2014.

MSR $1,160	$975	$595	$495	$425	$365	$335	$300	

* **SRC .308 Carbine** – .308 Win. cal., GIO, 16 1/2 in. medium profile chrome-lined barrel with A2 flash suppressor, 20 shot Magpul PMAG, M4A4 flat-top upper receiver, aluminum forged lower receiver, steel bolt, mid-length tapered heat shield handguards, 6-position telescoping buttstock, Hogue overmolded beavertail pistol grip, integral trigger guard, includes black web sling, QD sling swivel, and hard plastic case, hardcoat anodized black finish, 7 1/2 lbs. Mfg. 2014-2015.

	$1,175	$775	$550	$465	$415	$375	$350	$1,413

VEX-SS STANDARD ("VARMINT EXTERMINATOR") – .223 Rem. cal., GIO, 20 in. matte finished fluted stainless steel barrel, 5 shot mag., forged aluminum flat-top upper receiver with 1913 rail and optics riser blocks, aluminum free floating forend with sling swivel, machined aluminum trigger guard, no sights, manual safety, Hogue overmolded rubber pistol grip, skeleton stock with sling swivel, hardcoat anodized black finish, includes black sling and hard plastic case, 8.2 lbs.

MSR $1,295	$1,075	$675	$500	$450	$400	$350	$325	

* **VEX-SS Camo Series** – .223 Rem. cal., GIO, 20 in. matte finished fluted stainless steel barrel, 5 shot mag., forged aluminum flat-top upper receiver, steel bolt, solid A2 stock with sling swivel, free floating tubular forend, aluminum trigger guard, no sights, Snow Camo or True Timber (new 2015) hydrographic printed camo pattern on forend, receiver, pistol grip, and stock, 8.2 lbs.

MSR $1,470	$1,225	$825	$575	$475	$425	$375	$350	

* **VES-SS Wood Stocked Series** – .223 Rem. cal., GIO, 20 in. matte finished fluted stainless steel barrel, 5 shot mag., forged aluminum flat-top upper receiver with 1913 rail and optics riser blocks, receiver finish in electroless nickel (Pepper model), Olive Drab (Forest Camo model), or Coyote Brown (Nutmeg model), knurled vented aluminum free floating forend with sling swivel, machined aluminum trigger guard, no sights, manual safety, hardwood laminated stock with Pepper, Forest Camo, or Nutmeg finish, Hogue rubber pistol grip, includes black sling and hard plastic case, 8.35 lbs. New 2014.

MSR $1,480	$1,225	$825	$575	$475	$425	$375	$350	

WAY OF THE GUN PERFORMANCE CARBINE – .223 Rem./5.56 NATO cal., GIO, 16 in. medium profile chrome-lined barrel with BCM compensator, 30 shot mag., Midwest Industries 15 in. free float KeyMod railed handguard, no sights, Magpul MOE telescoping buttstock, BCM Gunfighter Mod 2 pistol grip, charging handle, CMC trigger, includes hard plastic case, Frank Proctor's Way of the Gun DVD, and a black Way of the Gun sling. New 2015.

MSR $1,795	$1,475	$950	$725	$550	$475	$395	$350	

WYOMING ARMS LLC

Current manufacturer of AR-15 style carbines/rifles and pistols located in Cody, WY.

PISTOLS: SEMI-AUTO

WY-15 SERIES 5500 PISTOL – 5.56 NATO cal., GIO, 12 in. stainless steel match grade barrel, BCM Gunfighter Mod O compensator, Geissele trigger, pistol buffer with Shockwave pistol stabilizing brace, 10 in. SLR lightweight forend, Magpul MOE+ pistol grip, ambi safety selector and bolt catch/release, forged upper and lower receivers, BCM Gunfighter Mod 4 charging handle, includes custom soft gun case. New 2017.

MSR $2,599	$2,200	$1,925	$1,600	$1,375	$1,125	$975	$850	

RIFLES/CARBINES: SEMI-AUTO

WY-15 SERIES 4400 – 5.56 NATO cal., GIO, stainless steel match grade barrel with threaded muzzle, forged upper and lower receiver, Geissele two-stage trigger, Magpul MOE stock, quad rail system surrounding barrel, Picatinny rail on top of receiver.

MSR $1,999	$1,650	$1,000	$795	$595	$495	$425	$395	

WYOMING ARMS LLC, cont. 373

MSR	100%	98%	95%	90%	80%	70%	60%	Last MSR

WY-15 SERIES 5500 – 5.56 WYO, .220 WYO, .240 WYO, 6.5 Grendel, or .300 AAC Blackout cal., GIO, 16, 18, or 20 in. match grade barrel, BCM Gunfighter Mod O compensator, 10, 20, or 30 shot mag., fixed or adj. buttstock, Magpul MOE pistol grip, forged upper and lower receivers, SLR ION M-LOK or Geissele SMR forend, ambi safety selector, includes custom soft gun case, black, matte sand, or FDE finish. New 2016.

MSR $2,599 $2,050 $1,250 $950 $650 $575 $495 $475

   * **WY-15 Series 5500 LWT** – 5.56 NATO cal., GIO, 16 in. lightweight stainless steel match grade barrel, 10, 20, or 30 shot mag., titanium construction, Geissele high speed trigger w/ceramic coating, lightweight 10 in. forend, Magpul MOE pistol grip, ambidextrous safety and bolt catch/release, forged upper and lower receiver, VLTOR A-5 carbine buffer system w/Magpul CTR stock, soft gun carrying case, optional optics package, 6 lbs. 3 oz.

MSR $2,599 $2,050 $1,250 $950 $650 $575 $495 $475

WY-15 SERIES 6600 – 5.56 NATO/.223 Rem. (disc.) 5.56 WYO, .220 WYO, .240 WYO, 6.5 Grendel, or .300 AAC Blackout cal., GIO, 16, 18, or 20 in. stainless steel hand lapped match grade fluted barrel, threaded muzzle, titanium barrel nut and mid weight barrel profile, 10, 20, or 30 (5.56 WYO) or 10, 15, or 25 shot mag., Geissele Hi Speed trigger, Magpul MOE stock, Magpul MOE+ grip, ambi safety selector, billet upper with redesigned case deflector, billet lower with integral trigger guard and flared magwell, mid or rifle (on 18 or 20 in. barrel depending on cal.) length gas system, Geissele MK1 13 in. super modular rail, BCM Gunfighter Mod 4 charging handle and Mod 0 compensator, Wyoming Arms H4 rifle buffer, black finish with matte sand or gun metal gray receiver finish.

MSR $3,199 $2,550 $1,650 $1,250 $700 $625 $575 $525

WY-15 SERIES 6600LWT – 5.56 WYO cal., GIO, 16 in. stainless steel hand lapped match grade fluted barrel, threaded muzzle with BCM Gunfighter Mod 0 compensator timed to barrel, titanium barrel nut, and lightweight barrel profile, 10, 20, or 30 shot mag., Geissele Hi Speed trigger, Magpul MOE or optional VLTOR A-5 carbine buffer system with Magpul CTR stock, Magpul MOE+ grip, ambi safety selector, billet upper with redesigned case deflector, billet lower with integral trigger guard and flared magwell, mid-length gas system, 10 in. SLR ION M-LOK rail, BCM Gunfighter Mod 4 charging handle, Wyoming Arms H4 rifle buffer, black finish with matte sand, green, or gun metal gray receiver finish.

MSR $3,199 $2,550 $1,650 $1,250 $700 $625 $575 $525

WY-12 SERIES 6612 – 7.62 NATO, 6mm Creedmoor (new 2018), or 6.5mm Creedmoor cal., GIO, 18 or 20 in. stainless steel match grade fluted barrel, BCM Gunfighter Mod1 compensator, Geissele trigger, Magpul MOE pistol grip stock, ambidextrous safety selector, 12 in. Midwest Industries lightweight forend, DPMS Gen2 forged upper and lower receivers and bolt carrier group, includes custom soft gun case, black or matte sand finish. New 2016.

MSR $3,299 $2,625 $1,725 $1,300 $725 $650 $595 $525

MAYBE THE ONLY THING BETTER THAN THIS BOOK IS THE ONLINE SUBSCRIPTION!

Only $19.95/year!

- **Includes monthly updates** keeping you informed of all the new AR-15 makes/models.
- **Features thousands of images** allowing for fast and easy identification.
- **Manufacturer/Model searchable database** allowing you to find the model you need.
- **Historical pricing with dynamic interactive graphs** keeps you up-to-date on your AR-15 purchases as investments.
- Your own personal online inventory solution - keep track of your collection and track the change in value.
- Includes access to BBP's industry standard Photo Percentage Grading System – why guess a gun's condition when you can be sure?

Visit BLUEBOOKOFGUNVALUES.COM
to view sample pages and ordering

Good Information Never Sleeps!

X-Y-Z SECTIONS

XN ARMS INDUSTRY AND TRADE CO.

Current tactical semi-auto shotgun manufacturer located in Istanbul, Turkey. Currently imported by EAA Corp, located in Rockledge, FL.

MSR	100%	98%	95%	90%	80%	70%	60%	Last MSR

SHOTGUNS: SEMI-AUTO

EKSEN MKE 1919 – 12 ga. only, 2 3/4 or 3 in. chamber, gas operated, AR-15 style, 19.7 in. barrel, 3 chokes, two 5 shot detachable mags., ribbed handguard with A2 front post sight, detachable carrying handle, integral Picatinny rail, black finish or 100% "BONZ" camo coverage, 6 1/2 lbs.

| MSR $699 | $625 | $550 | $495 | $475 | $450 | $425 | $395 | |

XTREME MACHINING

Current rifle manufacturer located in Drifting, PA. Previously located in Grassflat, PA. Previously distributed until 2012 by American Tactical Imports, located in Rochester, NY.

PISTOLS: SEMI-AUTO

XM15 – 5.56 NATO cal., GIO, 7 1/2 in. barrel with birdcage flash hider, 30 shot mag., Xtreme Machining enhanced charging handle and 7 in. free float handguard system with low profile gas block, pistol buffer tube, black finish. Mfg. 2015-2017.

| | $550 | $480 | $400 | $340 | $300 | $265 | $250 | $640 |

RIFLES: SEMI-AUTO

STANDARD M4 – 5.56 NATO cal., 16 in. M4 profile barrel with birdcage flash hider and manganese phosphate coating, 30 shot mag., standard M4 handguard with Picatinny gas block, Xtreme Machining enhanced charging handle, 6-position stock, black finish. Mfg. 2015-2017.

| | $535 | $460 | $395 | $350 | $315 | $295 | $275 | $610 |

XM15 CARBINE WITH QUAD RAIL – 5.56 NATO cal., 16 in. M4 profile barrel with birdcage flash hider and manganese phosphate coating, 30 shot mag., Xtreme Machining enhanced charging handle and 12 in. free float handguard system with low profile gas block, 6-position stock, black finish. Mfg. 2015-2017.

| | $615 | $495 | $415 | $360 | $325 | $300 | $275 | $719 |

YANKEE HILL MACHINE CO., INC. (YHM)

Current manufacturer of AR-15 style rifles, receivers, parts, suppressors, and related accessories established in 1951, located in Florence, MA. Consumer direct and dealer sales.

PISTOLS: SEMI-AUTO

YHM-9 9mm PISTOL – 9mm Para. cal., gas blowback system, 5 1/2 in. threaded barrel with Phantom 5C2 flash hider, 30 (disc.) or 32 shot mag., forged upper and lower receivers, extended top Picatinny rail, EZ Pull takedown pins, mini KeyMod handguard, standard pistol grip, 9mm pistol buttstock assembly, caliber marked dust cover. New 2015.

| MSR $1,339 | $1,125 | $1,010 | $875 | $735 | $650 | $550 | $465 | |

5.56mm PISTOL – 5.56mm cal., GIO, 10 1/2 in. threaded and fluted barrel with Phantom 5C2 flash hider, 30 shot mag., forged upper and lower receivers, KR7 series mid-length handguard, extended top Picatinny rail, KeyMod mounting system, pistol buttstock assembly, caliber marked dust cover, EZ Pull takedown pins, standard pistol grip, black finish. Mfg. 2015-2017.

| | $1,025 | $925 | $800 | $685 | $595 | $515 | $440 | $1,205 |

.300 BLK PISTOL – .300 AAC Blackout cal., GIO, 9.1 in. barrel with YHM Phantom flash hider, 30 shot mag., KR7 Series carbine length handguard, extended top Picatinny rail, KeyMod mounting system, EZ Pull takedown pins, black finish. Mfg. 2016-2017.

| | $1,025 | $925 | $800 | $685 | $595 | $515 | $440 | $1,205 |

RIFLES/CARBINES: SEMI-AUTO

YHM manufactures a complete line of AR-15 style tactical rifles and carbines, as well as upper receivers and a wide variety of accessories. Please contact the company directly for more information about available options and dealer listings (see Trademark Index).

BLACK DIAMOND CARBINE – 5.56 NATO, 7.62x39mm (mfg. 2011-2013), .300 AAC Blackout (new 2014), or 6.8 SPC (new 2010) cal., GIO, 16 in. chrome moly vanadium steel threaded barrel, Diamond fluting, Phantom flash hider, 30 shot mag., aluminum lower and flat-top upper receiver, Mil-Spec bolt carrier assembly, forward assist, carbine length Diamond handguard, free floating continuous top Picatinny rail, flip-up tower front and rear sights, 6-position adj. carbine stock, standard A2 grip, black anodized finish, 6.7 lbs.

| MSR $1,517 | $1,275 | $850 | $600 | $495 | $425 | $375 | $350 | |

Add $84 for 6.8 SPC cal.

Y 376 YANKEE HILL MACHINE CO., INC. (YHM), cont.

MSR	100%	98%	95%	90%	80%	70%	60%	Last MSR

BLACK DIAMOND SPECTER CARBINE – 5.56 NATO, 7.62x39mm (mfg. 2011-2013), .300 AAC Blackout (new 2014), or 6.8 SPC (new 2010) cal., GIO, similar to Black Diamond Carbine, except features Specter length Diamond handguard, 6.9 lbs.

| MSR $1,544 | $1,275 | $850 | $600 | $495 | $425 | $375 | $350 | |

Add $83 for 6.8 SPC cal.

BLACK DIAMOND SPECTER XL CARBINE – 5.56 NATO, 7.62x39mm (mfg. 2011-2013), .300 AAC Blackout (new 2014), or 6.8 SPC (new 2010) cal., GIO, similar to Black Diamond Specter Carbine, except has Specter XL length Diamond handguard, approx. 7 lbs.

| MSR $1,573 | $1,315 | $850 | $625 | $500 | $435 | $375 | $350 | |

Add $54 for 6.8 SPC cal.

BLACK DIAMOND RIFLE – 5.56 NATO, 7.62x39mm (mfg. 2011-2013), or 6.8 SPC cal., GIO, 20 in. chrome moly vanadium steel barrel, 30 shot mag., black anodized finish, aluminum lower and flat-top upper receiver, Mil-Spec bolt carrier assembly, forward assist, rifle length Diamond handguard, Picatinny rail risers, A2 fixed stock, A2 pistol grip, single rail gas block, two mini-risers, 8 lbs. Disc. 2015.

| | $1,195 | $795 | $550 | $465 | $415 | $375 | $350 | *$1,445* |

BURNT BRONZE SPECTER XL BILLET CARBINE – 5.56 NATO, 6.8 SPC, or .300 AAC Blackout cal., 16 in. steel fluted barrel with YHM Slant compensator/muzzle brake, two-stage trigger, rifle length SLR-Slant handguard, billet aluminum lower and flat-top upper with M4 feed ramps, low profile gas block, Q.D.S. hooded front and rear sight, tactical charging handle latch, adj. Magpul CTR buttstock, Magpul MOE grip, Burnt Bronze Cerakote finish, includes 25 shot round metal mag. (6.8 SPC only), or two Magpul Gen 2 mags., a front sight adjustment tool, and hard plastic case, 7.76 lbs. Mfg. 2014-2015.

| | $1,875 | $1,100 | $895 | $650 | $575 | $495 | $425 | *$2,395* |

Subtract $100 for Specter-length handguard (Burnt Bronze Specter Billet Carbine).

CUSTOMIZABLE CARBINE – 5.56 NATO, 7.62x39mm (new 2011), or 6.8 SPC (new 2010) cal., GIO, 16 in. chrome moly vanadium steel barrel, black anodized finish, aluminum lower and flat-top upper receiver, Mil-Spec bolt carrier assembly, forward assist, Phantom flash hider, carbine length customizable handguard, adj. carbine stock, flip-up front tower sight and flip-up rear sight, 6.3 lbs. Disc. 2013.

| | $1,225 | $825 | $575 | $475 | $425 | $375 | $350 | *$1,472* |

CUSTOMIZABLE RIFLE – 5.56 NATO, 7.62x39mm (new 2011), or 6.8 SPC (new 2011) cal., GIO, 20 in. chrome moly vanadium steel barrel, black anodized finish, aluminum lower and flat-top upper receiver, Mil-Spec bolt carrier assembly, forward assist, rifle length customizable handguard, 12 in. Co-Witness rail, fixed A2 stock, single rail gas block, two mini-risers, 8 lbs. Disc. 2013.

| | $1,195 | $795 | $550 | $465 | $415 | $375 | $350 | *$1,445* |

DESERT ENFORCER – 5.56 NATO, 6.8 SPC (new 2016) or .300 AAC Blackout (new 2016) cal., GIO, 16 in. threaded barrel with 6 grooves and Diamond fluting, YHM Annihilator flash hider, EZ Pull takedown pins, forged aluminum lower and flat-top A3 upper, Gen. 2 PMAG, TJ Competition Series rifle length handguard with top Picatinny rail, Quick Deploy Sights, Magpul 6-pos. adj. stock, Magpul MOE pistol grip, FDE finish with contrast of black parts, 7.1 lbs. Mfg. 2014-2016.

| | $1,675 | $1,000 | $825 | $625 | $550 | $475 | $425 | *$2,050* |

* **Tank Tough Desert Enforcer (OD Green SLR Specter Smooth Carbine)** – 5.56 NATO cal., GIO, carbine length gas system, 16 in. threaded barrel with 5C2 flash hider/compensator, Gen 2 black PMAG, Tactical Q.D.S. sight system, adj. TI-7 carbine stock, Ergo grips, mid-length SLR smooth handguard, EZ Pull takedown pins, OD Green Cerakote finish with contrast of black parts. Mfg. mid-2013-2017.

| | $1,600 | $1,000 | $775 | $575 | $495 | $425 | $395 | *$1,950* |

ENTRY LEVEL CARBINE – 5.56 NATO, 7.62x39mm (mfg. 2011-2013), .300 AAC Blackout (new 2014), or 6.8 SPC (new 2010) cal., GIO, 16 in. chrome moly vanadium steel threaded barrel with YHM Phantom flash hider, 30 shot mag., 6-pos. adj. carbine stock, A2 pistol grip, aluminum lower and flat-top upper receiver, Mil-Spec bolt carrier assembly, forward assist, carbine length handguard, single rail gas block, black anodized finish, 6.4 lbs. Disc. 2014.

| | $1,075 | $675 | $500 | $450 | $400 | $350 | $325 | *$1,284* |

ENTRY LEVEL RIFLE – 5.56 NATO, 7.62x39mm (mfg. 2011-2013), or 6.8 SPC (new 2011) cal., GIO, 20 in. chrome moly vanadium steel non-fluted barrel, 30 shot mag., black anodized finish, aluminum lower and flat-top upper receiver, Mil-Spec bolt carrier assembly, forward assist, rifle length tube handguard, fixed A2 stock, A2 pistol grip, single rail gas block, two mini-risers, 8 lbs. Disc. 2015.

| | $1,100 | $675 | $525 | $450 | $400 | $350 | $325 | *$1,311* |

HUNT READY CARBINE – 5.56 NATO, 7.62x39mm (disc. 2013), .300 AAC Blackout (new 2014), or 6.8 SPC cal., GIO, low profile gas block, 16 in. steel threaded and fluted barrel with YHM-28-5C2 flash hider, 5 shot mag., vented round customizable forearm, adj. carbine buttstock, standard pistol grip, forged aluminum flat-top upper and lower receiver, two 3 in. modular rails, bolt carrier assembly, forward assist, includes Bushnell Banner 3-9x40mm camo scope with Circle-X reticule, Grovetec deluxe padded camo sling, matte black (disc.), 100% Realtree AP (disc. 2016), or Kryptek Highlander (new 2017) camo finish. New 2012.

| MSR $1,579 | $1,315 | $850 | $625 | $500 | $435 | $375 | $350 | |

Add $54 for 6.8 SPC cal.

YANKEE HILL MACHINE CO., INC. (YHM), cont. 377

MSR	100%	98%	95%	90%	80%	70%	60%	Last MSR

HUNT READY RIFLE – 5.56 NATO, 7.62x39mm (disc. 2013), or 6.8 SPC cal., GIO, 20 in. free floating steel barrel, diamond fluting, forged aluminum flat-top upper and lower receiver, low profile gas block, 5 shot mag., A2 Trapdoor buttstock, vented round customizable forearm, rifle length M-LOK handguard, bolt carrier assembly, forward assist, matte black (disc.), 100% Realtree AP (disc. 2016), or Kryptek Highlander (new 2017) camo finish, includes Bushnell Banner 3-9x40mm camo scope with Circle-X reticule, Grovetec deluxe padded camo sling. New 2012.

MSR $1,611	$1,350	$875	$650	$525	$450	$385	$350	

Add $43 for 6.8 SPC cal.

KR7 SERIES CARBINE – 5.56 NATO, 6.8 SPC, or .300 AAC Blackout cal., GIO, 16 in. steel threaded barrel with YHM Phantom 5C2 flash suppressor, 30 shot mag., KR7 mid-length KeyMod handguard, forged aluminum lower and flat-top upper with M4 feed ramps, low profile gas block, 6-pos. adj. commercial carbine stock, matte black finish, includes hard plastic case, 6.3 lbs. New 2015.

MSR $1,324	$1,100	$675	$525	$450	$400	$350	$325	

Add $56 for 6.8 SPC cal.

* **KR7 9mm** – 9mm Para. cal., GIO, 16 in. barrel, 32 shot mag., stainless steel hammer and trigger pins, KR7 Series mid-length handguard, dedicated 9mm lower, buffer, and bolt, matte black finish. Mfg. 2016-2017.

	$1,195	$795	$550	$465	$415	$375	$350	$1,443

LIGHTWEIGHT CARBINE – 5.56 NATO, 7.62x39mm (new 2011), or 6.8 SPC (new 2010) cal., GIO, 16 in. chrome moly vanadium steel barrel with Phantom flash hider, flip-up tower front sight, flip-up rear sight, adj. carbine stock, forearm endcap, aluminum lower and flat-top upper receiver, Mil-Spec bolt carrier assembly, forward assist, carbine length lightweight handguard, black anodized finish, 6.7 lbs. Disc. 2013.

	$1,195	$795	$550	$465	$415	$375	$350	$1,445

LIGHTWEIGHT RIFLE – 5.56 NATO, 7.62x39mm (new 2011), or 6.8 SPC (new 2011) cal., GIO, 20 in. chrome moly vanadium steel barrel, aluminum lower and flat-top upper receiver, Mil-Spec bolt carrier assembly, forward assist, rifle length lightweight handguard, fixed A2 stock, single rail gas block, two mini-risers, black anodized finish, 8 lbs. Disc. 2013.

	$1,195	$795	$550	$465	$415	$375	$350	$1,445

MODEL 57 BILLET CARBINE – 5.56 NATO, 6.8 SPC, or .300 AAC Blackout cal., GIO, 16 in. threaded barrel with fluting, YHM Slant Comp/Brake, two 30 shot Gen. 2 black PMAGs, oversized magwell, two-stage trigger, Quick Deploy Sight System, Magpul CTR 6-pos. buttstock, Magpul MOE pistol grip, mid-length top rail aluminum handguard (SLR Slant Series), EZ Pull takedown pins, aluminum flat-top A3 upper receiver, tactical charging handle, includes three KeyMod handguard covers (new 2015), matte black or Burnt Bronze (Limited Edition, new 2016) finish. New 2014.

MSR $2,261	$1,795	$1,050	$875	$625	$550	$475	$425	

Add $74 for 6.8 SPC cal.

MODEL 57 SPECTER XL BILLET CARBINE – 5.56 NATO, 6.8 SPC, or .300 AAC Blackout cal., GIO, 16 in. fluted steel barrel, YHM Slant brake, two Gen2 windowless PMAGs, two-stage Geissele trigger, Q.D.S. Sight System, adj. Magpul CTR buttstock, Magpul MOE pistol grip, forward assist, rifle length SLR Slant handguard, billet aluminum lower and flat-top upper receiver, M4 feed ramps, tactical charging handle latch, 7.45 lbs.

MSR $2,365	$1,875	$1,100	$895	$650	$575	$495	$425	

Add $71 for 6.8 SPC cal.

S.L.K. SPECTER CARBINE – 5.56 NATO, 6.8 SPC, or .300 AAC Blackout cal., 16 in. steel Diamond fluted and threaded barrel, YHM Phantom 5C2 flash hider/compensator, SLK KeyMod mid-length handguard, forged aluminum lower and flat-top upper with M4 feed ramps, low profile gas block, Q.D.S. flip front and rear sights, EZ Pull Pin set, adj. commercial carbine stock, includes hard plastic case, 6.3 lbs. Mfg. 2014-2016.

	$1,385	$895	$675	$525	$450	$385	$350	$1,700

Add $25 for rifle length handguard (S.L.K. Specter XL).

S.L.R. SMOOTH SPECTER – 5.56 NATO, 6.8 SPC, or .300 AAC Blackout cal., GIO, 16 in. threaded barrel with Diamond fluting, Phantom flash hider, Quick Deploy Sight System, mid-length free floating handguard with continuous top Picatinny rail, EZ Pull takedown pins, 30 shot mag., forged aluminum lower and flat-top A3 upper receiver, 6-pos. adj. carbine stock, A2 pistol grip, matte black finish. Disc. 2015.

	$1,385	$895	$675	$525	$450	$385	$350	$1,700

* **SLR Quad Specter** – 5.56 NATO, 6.8 SPC, or .300 AAC Blackout cal., GIO, similar to SLR Smooth Specter, except has mid-length quad rail handguard, 7.3 lbs. Disc. 2015.

	$1,385	$895	$675	$525	$450	$385	$350	$1,700

S.L.R. SPECTER SMOOTH CARBINE – 5.56 NATO cal., GIO, 16 in. threaded barrel with Diamond fluting and Melonite QPQ finish, YHM 5C2 flash hider/compensator, 30 shot mag., tactical Q.D.S. (Quick Deploy Sight system), adj. TI-7 carbine stock, Ergo grip, forged aluminum YHM lower and flat-top upper receiver with M4 feed ramps, mid-length S.L.R. Smooth handguard with continous top Picatinny rail, EZ Pull takedown pins, OD Green Cerakote finish, 6.9 lbs.

MSR $1,950	$1,700	$1,495	$1,275	$1,150	$935	$765	$595	

Y 378 YANKEE HILL MACHINE CO., INC. (YHM), cont.

MSR	100%	98%	95%	90%	80%	70%	60%	Last MSR

S.L.R. SMOOTH SPECTER XL – 5.56 NATO, 6.8 SPC, or .300 AAC Blackout cal., GIO, 16 in. threaded barrel with rifling grooves and Diamond fluting, Phantom flash hider, 30 shot mag., aluminum rifle length free floating customizable handguard with continuous top Picatinny rail, Quick Deploy Sight System, EZ Pull takedown pins, forged aluminum lower and flat-top A3 upper receiver, 6-pos. adj. carbine stock, A2 pistol grip, matte black finish, 7.1 lbs. Disc. 2015.

	$1,425	$925	$700	$550	$475	$395	$350	$1,725

* **SLR Quad Specter XL** – 5.56 NATO, 6.8 SPC, or .300 AAC Blackout cal., GIO, similar to SLR Specter XL, except features mid-length quad rail handguard, 7.4 lbs. Disc. 2015.

	$1,425	$925	$700	$550	$475	$395	$350	$1,725

SMOOTH CARBINE – 5.56 NATO, 7.62x39mm (mfg. 2011-2013), .300 AAC Blackout (new 2014), or 6.8 SPC (new 2010) cal., GIO, 16 in. chrome moly vanadium steel threaded barrel, Diamond fluting, Phantom flash hider, 30 shot mag., oversized magwell, aluminum lower and flat-top upper receiver, Mil-Spec bolt carrier assembly, forward assist, carbine length smooth handguard, 6-position adj. carbine stock, A2 pistol grip, flip-up front tower sight and flip-up rear sight, black anodized finish, 6.8 lbs. Disc. 2016.

	$1,225	$825	$575	$475	$425	$375	$350	$1,472

SMOOTH RIFLE – 5.56 NATO, 7.62x39mm (new 2011), or 6.8 SPC (new 2011) cal., GIO, 20 in. chrome moly vanadium steel barrel, black anodized finish, aluminum lower and flat-top upper receiver, Mil-Spec bolt carrier assembly, forward assist, rifle length smooth handguard, fixed A2 stock, single rail gas block, forearm end cap, two mini-risers, 8 lbs. Disc. 2014.

	$1,195	$795	$550	$465	$415	$375	$350	$1,445

SPECTER LIGHTWEIGHT CARBINE – 5.56 NATO, 7.62x39mm (new 2011), or 6.8 SPC (new 2010) cal., GIO, 16 in. chrome moly vanadium steel barrel, Phantom flash hider, aluminum lower and flat-top upper receiver, Mil-Spec bolt carrier assembly, forward assist, Specter length lightweight handguard, adj. carbine stock, forearm end cap, flip-up front and rear sights, low profile gas block, black anodized finish, 6.9 lbs. Disc. 2013.

	$1,250	$825	$575	$475	$425	$375	$350	$1,498

SPECTER XL LIGHTWEIGHT CARBINE – 5.56 NATO, 7.62x39mm (new 2011), or 6.8 SPC (new 2010) cal., GIO, similar to Specter Lightweight Carbine, except has XL length lightweight handguard, 7.1 lbs. Disc. 2013.

	$1,275	$850	$600	$495	$425	$375	$350	$1,525

SPORTSMAN SCOUT CARBINE – 5.56 NATO, 7.62x39mm, or 6.8 SPC cal., GIO, 16 in. free floating steel barrel with Phantom 5C2 flash hider, Diamond fluting, aluminum lower and flat-top upper receiver with Picatinny rail, 100% Realtree AP camo coverage, forward assist, low profile gas block, M4 telescoping buttstock, includes two 3 in. modular rails, Specter length customizable handguard, forearm end cap. Mfg. 2011-2013.

	$1,150	$750	$550	$465	$415	$375	$350	$1,391

SPORTSMAN SERIES RIFLE – 5.56 NATO, 7.62x39mm, or 6.8 SPC cal., GIO, 20 in. free floating steel barrel, Diamond fluting, aluminum lower and flat-top upper receiver with Picatinny rail, 100% Realtree AP camo coverage, forward assist, low profile gas block, A2 trapdoor buttstock, includes two 3 in. modular rails, rifle length customizable handguard, forearm endcap. Mfg. 2011-2013.

	$1,195	$795	$550	$465	$415	$375	$350	$1,445

TODD JARRETT COMPETITION SERIES CARBINE – 5.56 NATO or 6.8 SPC cal., GIO, 16 in. chrome-lined threaded barrel, fluted with YHM's signature "Diamond Flute" and Phantom 5C2 flash hider, 30 shot mag., free floating forearm, available with carbine, rifle, or mid-length handguard, ergonomic pistol grip, padded ACE stock, Q.D.S. flip-up front and rear sights, EZ Pull takedown pins, forged aluminum lower and flat-top "T" marked upper with Picatinny rail, low profile gas block, forearm end cap, matte black finish. Mfg. mid-2013-2015.

	$1,675	$1,000	$825	$625	$550	$475	$425	$2,007

Z-M WEAPONS

Previous rifle manufacturer and pistol components maker located in Richmond, VT. Previously located in Bernardston, MA.

RIFLES: SEMI-AUTO

LR 300 & VARIATIONS – .223 Rem. cal., modified GIO using AR-15 style action, 16 1/4 in. barrel, pivoting skeletal metal stock, flat-top receiver, aluminum or Nylatron handguard, matte finish, 7.2 lbs. Mfg. 1997-disc.

	$1,795	$1,050	$875	$625	$550	$475	$425	$2,208

Add $23 for Nylatron handguard.

ZOMBIE DEFENSE

Previous custom manufacturer located in Henrico, VA 2009-2016.

RIFLES: SEMI-AUTO

Zombie Defense built custom rifles on the AR-15 platform to the customer's specifications using their own unique custom lower receivers. Models with base MSRs included: Entry Level Z4 - last MSR was $775, Z4 .300 Blackout - last MSR was $850, Z4 6.8 SPC - last MSR was $850, and Z4 18 in. SPR - last MSR was $950.

AR-15 CURRENT MANUFACTURERS/TRADEMARK INDEX

Without question, this is the most complete listing of current domestic and international AR-15 manufacturers/trademarks ever compiled. Twenty years ago, there were fewer than 30, and as this 1st edition went to press, there are almost 250! It simply proves that AR-15s have become an industry onto themselves.

Remember, this invaluable section is also available online at no charge and is updated monthly. Please visit BlueBookofGunValues.com under CONTENT INFORMATION and click on Trademark Index. There you will find complete listings with address, phone/fax numbers, and email addresses.

If parts are needed for older, discontinued AR-15 makes and models, it is recommended you contact either Numrich Gun Parts Corp. located in West Hurley, NY (www.e-gunparts.com), or Jack First, Inc. located in Rapid City, SD (www.jackfirstgun.com) for domestic availability and prices. For current manufacturers, it is recommended that you contact an authorized warranty repair center or stocking gun shop, unless a company/trademark has an additional service/parts listing.

If you should require additional assistance in "tracking" any of the current companies listed in this publication (or perhaps, current companies that are not listed), please contact us and we will try to help you regarding these specific requests. We hope you appreciate this service – no one else in the industry has anything like it.

2 VETS ARMS CO., LLC
www.2vetsarms.com

2A ARMAMENT LLC
www.2a-arms.com

5TC (5 TOES CUSTOM)
www.5toescustom.com

A06 ARMS
www.a06arms.com

AR 57 LLC
www.57center.com

ACCURATE TOOL & MFG. CO.
www.accuratearmory.com

ADAMS ARMS
www.adamsarms.net

ADCOR DEFENSE
www.adcordefense.com

ADEQ FIREARMS COMPANY
www.adeqfirearms.com

ADVANCED ARMAMENT CORP.
www.advanced-armament.com

AERO PRECISION USA
www.aeroprecisionusa.com

AKLYS DEFENSE LLC
www.aklysdefense.com

AKSA ARMS
www.aksaarms.com

ALAN & WILLIAM ARMS, INC.
www.alanandwilliamarms.com

ALASKA MAGNUM AR'S
www.alaskamagnumars.com

ALBERTA TACTICAL RIFLE SUPPLY
www.albertatacticalrifle.com

ALEXANDER ARMS LLC
www.alexanderarms.com

ALEX PRO FIREARMS
www.apfarmory.com

AMBUSH FIREARMS
www.danieldefense.com

AMERICAN DEFENSE MFG. LLC
www.adm-mfg.com

AMERICAN PRECISION ARMS
www.americanprecisionarms.com

AMERICAN SPIRIT ARMS
www.americanspiritarms.com

AMERICAN TACTICAL INC. (AMERICAN TACTICAL IMPORTS - ATI)
www.americantactical.us

AM-TAC PRECISION
www.am-tac.com

ANDERSON MANUFACTURING
www.andersonmanufacturing.com

ANGSTADT ARMS
www.angstadtarms.com

ARCHER MANUFACTURING
Phone No.: 512-962-2849

ARIZONA ARMORY
www.azarmory.net

ARMALITE, INC.
www.armalite.com

ARMS LLC
www.customfirearmsllc.com

THE ARMS ROOM (ARMS ROOM LLC)
www.armsroom.com

ARMS TECH LTD.
www.armstechltd.com

ARMSCOR
www.armscor.com

ASTRA ARMS S.A.
www.astra-arms.ch

AXELSON TACTICAL
www.axelsonusa.com

AZTEK ARMS
www.aztekarms.com

BCI DEFENSE LLC
www.bcidefense.com

BNTI ARMS
www.bntiarms.com

BARNES PRECISION MACHINE, INC.
www.barnesprecision.com

BARRETT FIREARMS MANUFACTURING, INC.
www.barrett.net

BATTLE ARMS DEVELOPMENT, INC. (B.A.D., INC.)
www.battlearmsdevelopment.com

BATTLE RIFLE COMPANY
www.battleriflecompany.com

BAZOOKA BROTHERS MFG.
www.bazookabrothers.com

BLACK CREEK PRECISION
www.blackcreekprecision.com

BLACK DAWN ARMORY (BLACK DAWN INDUSTRIES)
www.blackdawnguns.com

BLACKHEART FIREARMS (BLACKHEART INTERNATIONAL LLC)
www.blackheartarms.com

BLACK RAIN ORDNANCE, INC.
www.blackrainordnance.com

BRAVO COMPANY MFG., INC.
www.bravocompanyusa.com

BUSHMASTER FIREARMS INTERNATIONAL
www.bushmaster.com

CMMG, INC.
www.cmmginc.com

CARACAL
www.caracalusa.com

CENTURY ARMS (CENTURY INTERNATIONAL ARMS, INC.)
www.centuryarms.com

CHATTAHOOCHEE GUN WORKS, LLC
www.c-gw.com

CHRISTENSEN ARMS
www.christensenarms.com

CHRISTIAN ARMORY WORKS
www.christianarmoryworks.com

CIMARRON F.A. CO.
www.cimarron-firearms.com

COLT'S MANUFACTURING COMPANY, LLC
www.coltsmfg.com
AR-15 Rifles, .22 LR cal. only - please refer to Umarex USA listing.
www.colt.com

CONTROLLED CHAOS ARMS
www.controlledchaosarms.com

CORE RIFLE SYSTEMS
www.core15.com

CORONADO ARMS
www.coronadoarms.com

D&L SPORTS, INC.
www.dlsports.com

380 AR-15 CURRENT MANUFACTURERS/TRADEMARK INDEX, cont.

D.A.R. GmbH (DYNAMICS ARMS RESEARCH)
www.dar-germany.com

DPMS FIREARMS (LLC)
www.dpmsinc.com

DRD TACTICAL
www.drdtactical.com

DSA INC.
www.dsarms.com

DANIEL DEFENSE
www.danieldefense.com

DEL-TON INCORPORATED
www.del-ton.com

DESERT ORDNANCE
www.desertord.com

DEVIL DOG ARMS LLC
www.devildogarms.com

DEZ TACTICAL ARMS, INC.
www.deztacticalarms.com

DIAMONDBACK FIREARMS
Marketing/Sales- Please refer to TAURUS
INTERNATIONAL listing
www.diamondbackfirearms.com

DLASK ARMS CORP.
www.dlaskarms.com

DOUBLE D ARMORY, LTD
www.ddarmory.com

DOUBLESTAR CORP.
www.star15.com

E.M.F. CO., INC.
www.emf-company.com

EDWARD ARMS COMPANY
www.edwardarms.com

EVOLUTION USA
www.evo-rifles.com

F-1 FIREARMS
www.f-1firearms.com

FN AMERICA LLC (FNH USA)
www.fnamerica.com

FALKOR DEFENSE
www.falkordefense.com

FAXON FIREARMS
www.faxonfirearms.com

FIREBIRD PRECISION
www.firebirdprecision.com

FLINT RIVER ARMORY LLC
www.flintriverarmory.com

FORT DISCOVERY, INC.
www.fortdiscoveryusa.com

FOSTECH MFG.
www.fostech.us

FRANKLIN ARMORY
www.franklinarmory.com

FULTON ARMORY
www.fulton-armory.com

G2 PRECISION, LLC
www.g2precision.com

GA PRECISION
www.gaprecision.net

G.A.R. ARMS
www.gar-arms.com

GWACS ARMORY
www.gwacsarmory.com

GILBOA
www.gilboa-rifle.com or
www.silver-shadow.com

GREY GHOST PRECISION
www.greyghostprecision.com

HM DEFENSE & TECHNOLOGY
www.hmdefense.com

HAHN TACTICAL
www.hahntactical.com

HAILEY ORDNANCE CO.
www.haileyord.com

HARDENED ARMS
www.hardenedarms.com

HATCHER GUN COMPANY
www.hatchergun.com

HEAD DOWN PRODUCTS, LLC
www.hdfirearms.com

HECKLER & KOCH
www.heckler-koch.com

HERA ARMS
www.hera-arms.com

HIGH STANDARD MANUFACTURING CO.
www.highstandard.com

HOGAN MANUFACTURING LLC
www.hoganguns.com

HULDRA ARMS
www.huldraarms.com

HUSAN ARMS
www.husan.com.tr

I.O., INC.
www.ioinc.us

INDUSTRY ARMAMENT
www.industryarmament.com

INTACTO ARMS
www.intactoarms.com

INTEGRITY ARMS & SURVIVAL
www.customar15.net

INVINCIBLE ARMS LLC
www.invinciblearms.com

IRON RIDGE ARMS CO.
www.ironridgeguns.com

IVER JOHNSON ARMS, INC. (NEW MFG.)
www.iverjohnsonarms.com

JP ENTERPRISES, INC.
www.jprifles.com

JARD, INC.
www.jardinc.com

JESSE JAMES FIREARMS UNLIMITED
www.jjfu.com

JUGGERNAUT TACTICAL
www.jtactical.com

JUST RIGHT CARBINES
www.justrightcarbines.com

KE ARMS
www.kearms.com

KING'S ARSENAL
www.kingsarsenal.com

KNIGHT'S ARMAMENT COMPANY
www.knightarmco.com

L.A.R. MANUFACTURING, INC.
www.largrizzly.com

LWRC INTERNATIONAL, INC.
www.lwrci.com

LANCER SYSTEMS
www.lancer-systems.com

LARUE TACTICAL
www.larue.com

LAUER CUSTOM WEAPONRY
www.lauerweaponry.com

LAYKE TACTICAL
www. layketactical.com

LEITNER-WISE DEFENSE, INC.
www.leitner-wise.com

LES BAER CUSTOM, INC.
www.lesbaer.com

LEWIS MACHINE & TOOL COMPANY (LMT)
www.lmtdefense.com

LONE STAR ARMORY
www.lonestarmory.us

LUVO PRAGUE LTD.
www.luvo.cz

MG ARMS INCORPORATED
www.mgarmsinc.com

MGI
www.mgimilitary.com

MMC ARMORY
www.mmcarmory.com

MATRIX ARMS
www.matrix-arms.com

MAUNZ MATCH RIFLES, LLC
www.maunzmatchrifles.com

MAXIM FIREARMS
www.maximfirearms.com

MCDUFFEE ARMS
www.mcduffeearms.com

MIDWEST INDUSTRIES, INC.
www.midwestindustriesinc.com

MOHAWK ARMORY
www.mohawkarmory.com

MOSSBERG, O.F. & SONS, INC.
www.mossberg.com

NEMO ARMS (NEW EVOLUTION MILITARY ORDNANCE)
www.nemoarms.com

NOREEN FIREARMS LLC
www.onlylongrange.com

NOSLER, INC.
www.nosler.com

NOVESKE RIFLEWORKS LLC
www.noveske.com

NUOVA JAGER
www.nuovajager.it

OBERLAND ARMS
www.oberlandarms.com

OLYMPIC ARMS, INC.
www.olyarms.com

OSPREY ARMAMENT
www.ospreyarmament.com

PALMETTO STATE ARMORY
www.palmettostatearmory.com

AR-15 CURRENT MANUFACTURERS/TRADEMARK INDEX, cont. 381

PALMETTO STATE DEFENSE, LLC
www.psdmfg.com

PATRIOT ORDNANCE FACTORY (POF)
www.pof-usa.com

PATRIOT WEAPONRY
www.patriotweaponry.us

PHASE 5 TACTICAL
www.phase5wsi.com

PRECISION FIREARMS LLC
www.pfirearms.com, www.precisionfirearms.com
www.pf15.com

PRECISION REFLEX, INC.
www.precisionreflex.com

PRIMARY WEAPONS SYSTEMS (PWS)
www.primaryweapons.com

PROARMS ARMORY s.r.o.
www.proarms-armory.com

PROOF RESEARCH
www.proofresearch.com

QUALITY ARMS
www.qualityarmsidaho.com

QUALITY PARTS CO./BUSHMASTER
Please refer to Bushmaster Firearms, Inc. listing

RAAC
www.raacfirearms.com

R.I.P. TACTICAL
www.rip-tactical.com

RND MANUFACTURING
www.rndrifles.com

RADICAL FIREARMS, LLC
www.radicalfirearms.com

REBEL ARMS CORP.
www.rebelarms.com

RED X ARMS
www.redxarms.com

REMINGTON ARMS COMPANY, INC.
www.remington.com

RHINO RIFLES (RHINO ARMS)
www.rhinorifles.com

RIVERMAN GUN WORKS
www.rivermangunworks.com

ROCK RIVER ARMS, INC.
www.rockriverarms.com

ROCKY MOUNTAIN ARMS, INC.
www.rockymountainarms.us

S.W.A.T. FIREARMS
www.swatfirearms.com

SD TACTICAL ARMS
www.sdtacticalarms.com

STI INTERNATIONAL
www.stiguns.com

SAVAGE ARMS, INC.
www.savagearms.com

SEEKINS PRECISION
www.seekinsprecision.com

SIG SAUER
www.sigsauer.com

SIONICS WEAPON SYSTEMS
www.sionicsweaponsystems.com

SMITH & WESSON
www.smith-wesson.com

SPECIALIZED DYNAMICS
www.specializeddynamics.com

SPECIALIZED TACTICAL SYSTEMS
www.specializedtctical.com

SPIKE'S TACTICAL LLC
www.spikestactical.com

SPRINGFIELD ARMORY (MFG. BY SPRINGFIELD INC.)
www.springfield-armory.com

STAG ARMS LLC
www.stagarms.com

STANDARD MANUFACTURING CO. LLC
www.stdgun.com

STERLING ARSENAL
www.sterlingarsenal.com

STURM, RUGER & CO., INC.
www.ruger.com
www.ruger-firearms.com

SUN DEVIL MANUFACTURING LLC
www.sundevilmfg.com

SUPERIOR ARMS
www.superiorarms.com

TNW FIREARMS, INC.
www.tnwfirearms.com

TR IMPORTS
www.trimports.com

TACTICAL ARMS OF TEXAS
www.tacticalarmsoftexas.com

TACTICAL ARMZ
www.tacticalarmz.com

TACTICAL EDGE ARMS
www.tactical-edgearms.com

TACTICAL RIFLES
www.tacticalrifles.net

TACTICAL SOLUTIONS, INC.
www.tacticalsol.com

TACTICAL SUPPLY
www.tacticalsupply.com

TACTICAL WEAPONS SOLUTIONS
www.twsarms.com

TALON ORDNANCE
www.talonordnance.com

TAURUS INTERNATIONAL MFG., INC.
www.taurususa.com

TEMPLAR CUSTOM ARMS
www.templarcustomarms.com

TEXAS BLACK RIFLE COMPANY
www.tbrci.com

TEXAS CUSTOM GUNS
www.texascustomguns.net

THOR
www.thorgdg.com

TRACKINGPOINT
www.tracking-point.com

TRISTAR ARMS INC.
www.tristararms.com

TROY DEFENSE
www.troyind.com

TURNBULL RESTORATION CO., INC.
www.turnbullrestoration.com

USA TACTICAL FIREARMS
www.usatf.us

ULTIMATE ARMS (USELTON ARMS INC)
www.uaarms.com

UMAREX USA
www.umarexusa.com

UTAS
www.utasturk.com, www.utas-usa.com

VALOR ARMS
www.valorarms.us

VIGILANT ARMS
www.vigilantarms.us

VIKING ARMAMENT, INC.
www.vikingarmament.com

VLTOR WEAPON SYSTEMS
www.vltor.com

WMD GUNS
www.wmdguns.com

WAR SPORT
www.warsport.com

WARRIOR ARMS LLC
www.warrior-arms.com

WILSON COMBAT
www.wilsoncombat.com

WINDHAM WEAPONRY
www.windhamweaponry.com

WYOMING ARMS LLC
www.wyomingarms.com

XN ARMS INDUSTRY AND TRADE CO.
www.mkaarms.com

XTREME MACHINING
www.xtrememachining.biz

YANKEE HILL MACHINE CO., INC. (YHM)
www.yhm.net

INDEX

TITLE PAGE 1

PUBLISHER'S NOTE, COPYRIGHT 2

TABLE OF CONTENTS 3

GENERAL INFORMATION 4

MEET THE STAFF 5

ACKNOWLEDGEMENTS, CREDITS,
ABOUT THE COVER 6

FOREWORD BY S.P. FJESTAD 7

AMERICA'S RIFLE - THE AR-15 &
VARIATIONS - ITS TURBULENT
HISTORY & UNPREDICTABLE
FUTURE BY S.P. FJESTAD 8-13

HOW TO USE THIS BOOK 14-15

ANATOMY OF AN AR-15 RIFLE/
CARBINE.............................16

ANATOMY OF AN AR-15 PISTOL &
SHOTGUN 17

AR-15 TERMINOLOGY PICTURED &
DESCRIBED 18-28

AR-15 GAS OPERATING SYSTEMS &
COMPONENTS......................18-19

AR-15 HANDGUARD STYLES &
MOUNTING PLATFORMS.................20

AR-15 POPULAR ACCESSORY
MOUNTING OPTIONS 20-21

AR-15 MUZZLE DEVICES.................22

AR-15 STOCKS, BRACES & BUFFER
TUBES 23-24

AR-15 TRIGGERS 25

AR-15 SIGHTS & OPTICS 26-28

AR-15 PARTS DIAGRAMS............ 29-31

GLOSSARY 32-43

ABBREVIATIONS 44-45

AR-15 CALIBERS AND DANGEROUS
COMBINATIONS 46

AR-15 GRADING CRITERIA 47

PPGS CONVERSION GUIDELINES/NRA
CONDITION STANDARDS 48

NRA MEMBERSHIP 148

A-Z SECTIONS 49-378

#

2 VETS ARMS CO., LLC 49

2A ARMAMENT LLC 49

5TC (5 TOES CUSTOM) 50

A

A06 ARMS..............................50

AR 57 LLC..............................51

ACCURATE TOOL & MFG. CO. 51

ADAMS ARMS.........................52

ADCOR DEFENSE 54

ADEQ FIREARMS COMPANY 55

ADVANCED ARMAMENT CORP. 56

AERO PRECISION USA 56

AKLYS DEFENSE LLC 57

AKSA ARMS 58

ALAN & WILLIAM ARMS, INC. 58

ALASKA MAGNUM AR'S 58

ALBERTA TACTICAL RIFLE SUPPLY 58

ALEXANDER ARMS LLC 58

ALEX PRO FIREARMS 61

ALPHA FOXTROT 64

AMBUSH FIREARMS 64

AMERICAN DEFENSE MFG. LLC..........64

AMERICAN PRECISION ARMS 66

AMERICAN SPIRIT ARMS 66

AMERICAN SPIRIT ARMS CORP..........68

AMERICAN TACTICAL INC. (AMERICAN
TACTICAL IMPORTS - ATI) 69

AM-TAC PRECISION 71

ANATOLIA MANUFACTURING
COMPANY LLC 71

ANDERSON MANUFACTURING 72

ANGSTADT ARMS 74

ARCHER MANUFACTURING 75

ARIZONA ARMORY 76

ARMALITE.............................76

ARMALITE, INC. 77

ARMS LLC 82

THE ARMS ROOM
(ARMS ROOM LLC) 82

ARMS TECH LTD. 82

ARMSCOR 83

ASTRA ARMS S.A. 83

AUSTRALIAN AUTOMATIC
ARMS PTY. LTD. 83

AXELSON TACTICAL 83

AZTEK ARMS 86

B

BCI DEFENSE LLC......................87

BNTI ARMS 88

BARNES PRECISION MACHINE, INC. ..88

BARRETT FIREARMS
MANUFACTURING, INC. 89

BATTLE ARMS DEVELOPMENT, INC.
(B.A.D., INC.) 90

BATTLE RIFLE COMPANY 90

BAZOOKA BROTHERS MFG. 93

BLACK CREEK PRECISION 93

BLACK DAWN ARMORY
(BLACK DAWN INDUSTRIES)..........93

BLACK FORGE LLC.....................96

BLACKHEART FIREARMS (BLACKHEART
INTERNATIONAL LLC) 97

BLACK RAIN ORDNANCE, INC. 99

BLACK RIFLE COMPANY LLC............ 101

BLACK WEAPONS ARMORY 102

BOHICA 102

BRAVO COMPANY MFG., INC. 102

BUSHMASTER FIREARMS
INTERNATIONAL 106

C

C3 DEFENSE, INC. 113

CMMG, INC. 113

CARACAL 119

CAVALRY ARMS CORPORATION 120

CENTURY ARMS (CENTURY
INTERNATIONAL ARMS, INC.) 120

CHARLES DALY: 1976-2010 121

CHATTAHOOCHEE GUN WORKS, LLC .. 122

CHRISTENSEN ARMS.................. 123

CHRISTIAN ARMORY WORKS 124

CIMARRON F.A. CO. 124

CIVILIAN FORCE ARMS 124

COBALT KINETICS 129

COBB MANUFACTURING, INC. 131

COLT'S MANUFACTURING
COMPANY, LLC 131

CONTROLLED CHAOS ARMS 142

CORE RIFLE SYSTEMS 142

CORONADO ARMS 147

CRUSADER WEAPONRY 147

D

D&L SPORTS, INC. 149

D.A.R. GmbH
(DYNAMICS ARMS RESEARCH) 149

DPMS FIREARMS (LLC) 149

DRD TACTICAL 155

DSA INC. 156

DANE ARMORY LLC 159

DANIEL DEFENSE.................... 159

DARK STORM
INDUSTRIES, LLC (DSI) 162

DEL-TON INCORPORATED.............. 166

DESERT ORDNANCE 170

DEVIL DOG ARMS LLC 170

INDEX, CONT.

DEVIL DOG ARMS INC. 170
DEZ TACTICAL ARMS, INC. 172
DIAMONDBACK FIREARMS 174
DLASK ARMS CORP. 177
DOUBLE D ARMORY, LTD 178
DOUBLESTAR CORP. 178

E

E.M.F. CO., INC. 183
EAGLE ARMS, INC. 183
EDWARD ARMS COMPANY 185
EVOLUTION USA 185

F

F-1 FIREARMS 187
FN AMERICA LLC (FNH USA) 189
FALKOR DEFENSE 191
FAXON FIREARMS 192
FIGHTLITE INDUSTRIES (ARES
    DEFENSE SYSTEMS INC.) 192
FIREBIRD PRECISION 193
FLINT RIVER ARMORY LLC 193
FORT DISCOVERY, INC. 193
FOSTECH MFG. 194
FRANKLIN ARMORY 194
FULTON ARMORY 198

G

G2 PRECISION, LLC 201
GA PRECISION 201
G.A.R. ARMS 201
GWACS ARMORY 203
GILBOA 203
GREY GHOST PRECISION 204
GUN ROOM CO., LLC 204

H

HM DEFENSE & TECHNOLOGY 205
HAHN TACTICAL 206
HAILEY ORDNANCE CO. 206
HARDENED ARMS 206
HATCHER GUN COMPANY 209
HEAD DOWN PRODUCTS, LLC 210
HECKLER & KOCH 212
HERA ARMS 213
HESSE ARMS 213
HIGH STANDARD
    MANUFACTURING CO. 213
HOGAN MANUFACTURING LLC 214

HOULDING PRECISION FIREARMS ... 215
HOUSTON ARMORY 216
HULDRA ARMS 216
HUSAN ARMS 216

I

I.O., INC. 217
INDUSTRY ARMAMENT 218
INTACTO ARMS 218
INTEGRITY ARMS & SURVIVAL 219
INTERARMS ARSENAL 220
INTERCONTINENTAL ARMS INC. 220
INVINCIBLE ARMS LLC 220
IRON RIDGE ARMS CO. 221
IVER JOHNSON
    ARMS, INC. (NEW MFG.) 221

J

J.B. CUSTOM INC. 223
JP ENTERPRISES, INC. 223
JARD, INC. 227
JESSE JAMES
    FIREARMS UNLIMITED 227
JUGGERNAUT TACTICAL..................... 228
JUST RIGHT CARBINES 228

K

KE ARMS 229
KING'S ARSENAL 229
KNIGHT'S ARMAMENT COMPANY 230
KORSTOG 232

L

L.A.R. MANUFACTURING, INC. 233
LWRC INTERNATIONAL, INC. 234
LANCER SYSTEMS 236
LARUE TACTICAL 237
LAUER CUSTOM WEAPONRY 238
LAYKE TACTICAL 238
LEGION FIREARMS LLC 239
LEITNER-WISE DEFENSE, INC. 239
LEITNER-WISE RIFLE CO. INC. 239
LES BAER CUSTOM, INC. 240
LEWIS MACHINE &
    TOOL COMPANY (LMT) 241
LOKI WEAPON SYSTEMS, INC. 244
LONE STAR ARMORY 246
LONE STAR TACTICAL SUPPLY 248
LUVO PRAGUE LTD. 248

M

MG ARMS INCORPORATED 249
MGI 249
MMC ARMORY 250
MATRIX ARMS 251
MAUNZ MATCH RIFLES, LLC 251
MAXIM FIREARMS 251
MCDUFFEE ARMS 252
MIDWEST INDUSTRIES, INC. 252
MILLER PRECISION ARMS.................. 254
MILTAC INDUSTRIES, LLC 254
MITCHELL ARMS, INC. 255
MOHAWK ARMORY 255
MOSSBERG, O.F. & SONS, INC. 255

N

NEMO ARMS (NEW EVOLUTION
    MILITARY ORDNANCE) 257
NEWTOWN FIREARMS 259
NOREEN FIREARMS LLC 259
NORTHERN COMPETITION 260
NOSLER, INC. 260
NOVESKE RIFLEWORKS LLC 261
NUOVA JAGER 263

O

OBERLAND ARMS................................ 265
OLYMPIC ARMS, INC. 265
OSPREY ARMAMENT............................ 271

P

POF USA 273
PALMETTO STATE ARMORY 273
PALMETTO STATE DEFENSE, LLC 275
PARA USA, LLC 275
PATRIOT ORDNANCE
    FACTORY (POF) 275
PATRIOT WEAPONRY........................... 279
PEACE RIVER CLASSICS...................... 280
PHASE 5 TACTICAL 280
PRECISION FIREARMS LLC 280
PRECISION REFLEX, INC. 281
PREDATOR CUSTOM SHOP 283
PRIMARY WEAPONS
    SYSTEMS (PWS) 283
PROARMS ARMORY s.r.o. 285
PROFESSIONAL ORDNANCE, INC. 286
PROOF RESEARCH............................... 286

INDEX, CONT.

Q

QUALITY ARMS 287

QUALITY PARTS CO./BUSHMASTER . 288

R

RAAC 289

R.I.P. TACTICAL 289

RND MANUFACTURING 289

RADICAL FIREARMS, LLC 290

REBEL ARMS CORP. 292

RED X ARMS 293

REMINGTON ARMS COMPANY, INC. . 296

RHINO RIFLES (RHINO ARMS) 297

RISE ARMAMENT 299

RIVERMAN GUN WORKS 300

ROCK ISLAND ARMORY (CURRENT MFG.) 300

ROCK RIVER ARMS, INC. 300

ROCKY MOUNTAIN ARMS, INC. 309

S

S.W.A.T. FIREARMS 311

SD TACTICAL ARMS 312

SI DEFENSE, INC. 312

SMI ARMS 313

STI INTERNATIONAL 314

SABRE DEFENCE INDUSTRIES LLC ... 314

SAVAGE ARMS, INC. 316

SCORPION TACTICAL 317

SEEKINS PRECISION 318

SHARPS MILSPEC 319

SIG SAUER 319

SINO DEFENSE MANUFACTURING (SDM) 323

SIONICS WEAPON SYSTEMS 323

SMITH & WESSON 325

SOG ARMORY 329

SPECIALIZED DYNAMICS 330

SPECIALIZED TACTICAL SYSTEMS ... 330

SPIKE'S TACTICAL LLC 331

SPIRIT GUN MANUFACTURING COMPANY LLC 334

SPRINGFIELD ARMORY (MFG. BY SPRINGFIELD INC.) 334

STAG ARMS LLC 335

STANDARD MANUFACTURING CO. LLC 340

STERLING ARMAMENT, LTD. 341

STERLING ARSENAL 341

STONER RIFLE 342

STURM, RUGER & CO., INC. 343

SUN DEVIL MANUFACTURING LLC 344

SUPERIOR ARMS 344

T

TNW FIREARMS, INC. 345

TR IMPORTS 345

TACTICAL ARMS MANUFACTURER, INC. 345

TACTICAL ARMS OF TEXAS 345

TACTICAL ARMZ 346

TACTICAL EDGE ARMS 346

TACTICAL RIFLES 348

TACTICAL SOLUTIONS, INC. 348

TACTICAL SUPPLY 349

TACTICAL WEAPONS SOLUTIONS ... 349

TALON ORDNANCE 351

TAURUS INTERNATIONAL MFG., INC. 351

TEMPLAR CUSTOM ARMS 351

TEMPLAR CUSTOM, LLC (TEMPLAR CONSULTING) 351

TEMPLAR TACTICAL ARMS LLC 352

TEXAS BLACK RIFLE COMPANY 352

TEXAS CUSTOM GUNS 353

THOR 353

TRACKINGPOINT 353

TRISTAR ARMS INC. 354

TROJAN FIREARMS 354

TROMIX CORPORATION 355

TROY DEFENSE 356

TURNBULL RESTORATION CO., INC. .. 358

U

USA TACTICAL FIREARMS 359

ULTIMATE ARMS (USELTON ARMS INC) 359

UTAS 359

V

VM HY-TECH LLC 361

VALOR ARMS 361

VICTOR ARMS CORPORATION 361

VIGILANT ARMS 361

VIKING ARMAMENT, INC. 361

VLTOR WEAPON SYSTEMS 362

VULCAN ARMAMENT, INC. 363

W

WMD GUNS 365

WAR SPORT 366

WARRIOR ARMS LLC 366

WILKINSON TACTICAL 366

WILSON COMBAT 367

WINDHAM WEAPONRY 369

WYOMING ARMS LLC 372

X

XN ARMS INDUSTRY AND TRADE CO. 375

XTREME MACHINING 375

Y

YANKEE HILL MACHINE CO., INC. (YHM) 375

Z

Z-M WEAPONS 378

ZOMBIE DEFENSE 378

AR-15 CURRENT MANUFACTURERS/ TRADEMARK INDEX 379-381

INDEX 382-384